Coin World
● THE WEEKLY NEWSPAPER OF THE ENTIRE NUMISMATIC FIELD ●

ALMANAC

A HANDBOOK FOR COIN COLLECTORS

Compiled by the staff of Coin World

Edited by
P. Bradley Reed

SIXTH EDITION
1990

Published by Amos Press Inc., P.O. Box 150, Sidney, Ohio 45365.

WORLD ALMANAC
AN IMPRINT OF PHAROS BOOKS • A SCRIPPS HOWARD COMPANY
NEW YORK

ALMANAC

Publisher: Ann Marie Aldrich

**Project Editor
P. Bradley Reed**

Cover design: Bea H. Jackson

**The Coin World Almanac
Copyright © 1990 by Amos Press Inc.**

Pharos Books ISBN (Hardcover) 0-88687-462-9

Pharos Books ISBN (Paperback) 0-88687-460-2

Amos Press ISBN (Hardcover) 0-944945-08-2

Amos Press ISBN (Paperback) 0-944945-07-4

Printed in the United States of America

WORLD ALMANAC
AN IMPRINT OF PHAROS BOOKS • A SCRIPPS HOWARD COMPANY
NEW YORK

Contents

Review of the News, 1987-1990   1

News happenings, 1987 1
News happenings, 1988 10
News happenings, 1989 18
News happenings, 1990 25
Obituaries 29

Numismatics and Washington   33

Senate 33
House of Representatives 33
Senate Committee on Banking, Housing and Urban Affairs 34
House Committee on Banking, Finance and Urban Affairs 35
Effective letters to Washington 35
Federal Trade Commission 36
Federal Bureau of Investigation 38
General Services Administration 41
National Archives and Records Administration 42
Government Printing Office 44
Commission of Fine Arts 46

Numismatics and the Law   47

United States Code, Title 31 48
Other legal and legislative issues 60
Treasury regulations 70
Executive orders 91
United States Code, Title 18 95
Key American coinage laws, resolutions 103
Recent numismatic bills 105
Freedom of Information Act 115
Coin laws since 1965 120
Extracts of texts of laws 125
Government marketing of commemorative coins 146
Tax Act changes of 1986 146
Numismatic sections of the U.S. Code 147
Sales tax and numismatic items 151
Regulations by governmental agencies 153
Treasury, Secret Service advisory policies 157
Government regulatory activity 160
Recent Federal Register Activity 162

The Treasury   165

History of the Treasury Department 165
Secretaries of the Treasury 169
Treasurers of the United States 171
Treasury officials 172
Department of the Treasury seal 172
Function of the Treasury Department 173

The United States Mint   179

Mint officials 180
Present Mint institutions 181
Former Mint Institutions 191
Directors of the United States Mint 196
Mint Superintendents 197
Chief Engravers 201
Services offered by the Mint 213
Medals produced by the Mint 213
History of presidential medals 215
Descriptions of presidential medals 219
Seigniorage 221
The Assay Commission 223
Medals produced by the U.S. Mint, FY89 214

Bureau of Engraving and Printing   225

How paper money is printed 229
Tours of the BEP 233
Products sold by the BEP 233
BEP officials 234

The Federal Reserve   237

History of the Federal Reserve System 237
Functions of the Federal Reserve 244
Federal Reserve Bank Branches and Offices 246
Board of Governors 247

U.S. Paper Money   249

Pre-federal paper money 249
Large-sized paper money catalog 250
U.S. postage and fractional currency 262
United States small-sized paper money 264
Features of current U.S. paper money 269
Portraits on U.S. paper money 272
Military payment certificates 281
Signatures on U.S. paper money 283
Signers of U.S. paper money 290

U.S. Coins 301

Coins in use in America before 1793 301
History of U.S. coinage 303
Pioneer gold coins 312
U.S.-Philippine coinage 314
Current U.S. coins 317
History of Mint marks 323
Dates, edge designs, mottoes, symbols 326
Issue dates, designers, original engravers, models 331
How coins are made 337
Specifications of U.S. coins 339
Regular issue U.S. coins 343
Proof coinage 360
Branch Mint Proofs 363
Proof set mintages 368
Uncirculated sets 369
Bicentennial sets 371
Varieties of Anthony dollars, Eisenhower dollars and Kennedy half
    dollars 372

Commemoratives 375

Commemoratives to 1954 375
Commemoratives since 1982 376
Commemorative coin statistics 379

Errors 385

Error coins 386
Altered and damaged coins 391
Paper money errors 394
Altered and damaged notes 397
Counterfeit coins 399
Collectors' Clearinghouse 402

A Numismatic Chronology 403

United States 403
Canada 405
Mexico 406
Central America 407
South America 409
Caribbean Islands 411
Europe 413
British Colonies 422
India, Southeast Asia 423
Near East, Africa 426
The Orient 428
Pacific Region 429

World Coins 433

World coin collecting 433
Canadian numismatics 436
Mexico 438
World coinage report, 1988 440
Coinage Mints active since 1987 441
Foreign coin production in the U.S. 442
World monetary units 444
A primer of ancient coins 448
Bank notes and other paper money 452

Precious Metals 455

Gold history 455
Gold chronology 466
Silver history 477
Silver chronology 494
Silver and gold coinage, 1988 504
Platinum and palladium 505

Bullion Coins 509

Gold and silver bullion coins 514
American Arts Gold Medallions 516

Grading 517

Grading coins and paper money 517
Grading U.S. coins 527
Grading ancient and foreign coins 530
Grading U.S. paper money 532

Coins as Investments 533

Rarities 559

How a coin becomes rare 559
Famous collections 561
Pedigrees 567
High prices of rare coins 571

Potpourri 587

Ordering coins 587
Auctions — how to participate 589
Exonumia 601
Storage and preservation 607
Weights and measures 610
Copyright 612

Museums 615

History of the national collection.. 615
American Numismatic Society.. 621
American Numismatic Association 624
United States.. 625
World 632

Organizations 639

American Numismatic Society.. 639
American Numismatic Association 644
Fédération Internationale de la Médaille 659
Professional Numismatists Guild 660
Numismatic Literary Guild.. 663
Industry Council for Tangible Assets.................................... 664
Coin and Bullion Dealer Accreditation Program 665
National, regional coin associations 667
State numismatic associations 668
Syngraphic organizations... 670
Treasure hunting clubs... 670
American Israel Numismatic Association............................. 671
American-based world numismatic organizations............... 671
Canadian Numismatic Association... 672
Canadian coin associations 674
World coin organizations.. 676
World coin dealer organizations... 686
International Association of Professional Numismatists 687

Books and Periodicals 689

U.S. coins.. 690
U.S. paper money 695
Modern world coins.. 695
Ancient coins.. 701
Medieval coins.. 703
World paper money 704
Investing.. 705
Common book references 706
Commercial numismatic publications..................................... 707

Numismatic Terms 709

Index 717

Review of the News, 1987-1990

News happenings, 1987

Date refers to Coin World issue in which the news item was published.

JANUARY 7

The American Numismatic Society will kick off a $4 million fund-raising campaign Jan. 8 to combat a financial situation that ANS officials say threatens its resources and the society's ability to reach out and affect the world at large.

Surcharges generated by sales of the 1986 Statue of Liberty coinage surpassed the surcharges raised by the former surcharge record holder, the Olympic coin program, during the week of Dec. 19, in half the time and with less than half the number of coin varieties available.

The dramatic story of the adoption of the U.S. Constitution is captured on the 1987 Bicentennial of the Constitution medal by Marcel Jovine commissioned by the United States Capitol Historical Society.

JANUARY 14

The United States Mint will not produce business strike versions of 1986-dated American Eagle gold and silver coins in 1987, having met year-end production targets.

1986 in the rare coin market appears to be the year of retracement as values of rare coins tended to move lower from the highs posted in 1985, according to *Coin World* Index charts.

The Royal Canadian Mint's 1987 commemorative silver dollar will honor the exploration of Canada's Cumberland Sound and Davis Strait by British explorer John Davis.

JANUARY 21

The American Numismatic Society bestowed its two most prestigious honors, recognizing excellence in medallic design and numismatic scholarship, to Finnish medalist Kauko Rasanen and Belgian scholar Paul Naster at its 128th annual meeting Jan. 28 at ANS headquarters in New York City.

The mysterious disappearance of a pair of master dies for Canada's new smaller Voyageur aureate-nickel dollar has forced the Canadian Parliament to approve a new reverse design depicting a common loon, selected from a Royal Canadian Mint bank of coinage designs obtained in past design competitions.

The potential damage from the manipulation of the numismatic market has long been cited as a reason for keeping secret the list of coins used in compiling the influential Salomon Brothers survey of the annual price performance of rare coins; however, a version of the list was published in *The Investor's Guide to United States Coins* by Neil S. Berman with Hans M.F. Schulman.

JANUARY 28

A-Mark Precious Metals Inc. will likely be granted an American Eagle gold coin distributorship because of an out-of-court settlement in the company's lawsuit against the United States Mint over its rejection as a gold bullion coin distributor.

The American Numismatic Society launched its $4 million development campaign Jan. 8 with an announcement that more than 50 percent of the goal has been received in the form of pledges.

The first issue of *World Coins* debuts, a magazine-style feature-oriented monthly supplement focusing on numismatic of the world. "A Guided Tour of Gold Coins of the World" by William S. Snyder.

FEBRUARY 4

The U.S. Mint Office of Marketing is in place, headed by recently appointed Associate Director for Marketing Daniel P. Cahill.

On Feb. 25, New York entrepreneur Bernard Rome will hold his first televised rare coin auction, establishing the format for regularly scheduled monthly auctions thereafter.

FEBRUARY 11

The 125th anniversary year of the Bureau of Engraving and Printing was ushered in Jan. 29 with a formal ceremony attended by high-ranking officials from the Department of the Treasury, the United States Postal Service and the Federal Reserve System.

"Currency Worth Noting" is the theme of the April 19-25 National Coin Week 1987, in recognition of the 125th Anniversary of the Bureau of Engraving and Printing.

FEBRUARY 18

The United States Treasury Department is inviting a limited number of American artists to submit designs for two U.S. coins to be issued in 1987 which will commemorate the Bicentennial of the drafting of the U.S. Constitution.

The United States Mint offered the American Eagle gold bullion coins two days in a row during the third week of sales in 1987, taking orders for a total of 241,000 gold coins.

The education of the public and working with the media regarding fraudulent advertising were the subjects of a hearing Feb. 5 before the Commodities Futures Trading Commission in Washington, D.C.

FEBRUARY 25

Four hundred years of North Carolina are commemorated in *Coin World's*

special issue marking the American Numismatic Association's Midwinter convention in Charlotte.

United States Mint officials expect to have designs for the 1987 Constitution coins in hand by the first of March and be ready by mid-June to begin striking the commemorative gold and silver coins.

American Numismatic Association President Florence Schook has named ANA Governor David L. Ganz to head a six-member task force charged with developing "a comprehensive program for the self-regulation of the coin industry by the participants in the industry."

The Dec. 1 postmark was not the final determining factor in the final cut-off of orders for the Proof 1986 American Eagle bullion coins, according to a five-page reply from the U.S. Mint to Rep. Frank Annunzio, D-Ill.

World Coins — "Collecting World Paper Money" by John G. Humphris

MARCH 4

Approximately 6,500 coins making up the American portion of the Norweb collection, one of the most important numismatic collections ever gathered in the United States, will be offered at public auction in a series of three sales beginning in October in New York City.

Coin World takes an inside look at the operations of the Professional Coin Grading Service.

A court-ordered special counsel has closed the doors of New England Rare Coin Galleries in Boston and fired all but a dozen employees as the result of a court order to liquidate the assets of the rare coin firm.

MARCH 11

The American Numismatic Association Board of Governors Feb. 26 approved a change in the way the ANA Certification Service grades coins to make the service more marketable in the face of declining revenues.

Heritage Numismatic Auctions Inc. has been selected to auction nearly $1 million worth of coins and currency confiscated three years ago by the Federal Deposit

Insurance Corporation as the result of a California bank failure.

The American Numismatic Association, the largest coin collector organization in the United States, has formally declared advocacy for changing all designs on the five circulating denominations of United States coins — the cent, 5 cents, dime, quarter dollar and half dollar.

MARCH 18

Self-regulation of the rare coin industry appears to be the prime focus of efforts to seek a blueprint for good business conduct individually launched by at least two of the most active organizations in numismatics, the ANA and Industry Council for Tangible Assets.

Steve Ivy, co-chairman of the board of Heritage Capital Corp., Dallas, presents a plan for self-regulation of the numismatic industry.

Diane Wolf, member of the Commission of Fine Arts, makes seeking new designs for U.S. coinage her "full-time crusade."

MARCH 25

Great Britain will enter the gold bullion coins market in 1987 with the release of the Britannia, a legal tender coin containing an ounce of fine gold, to be followed by three smaller pieces.

United States Mint and Treasury officials attempted to reassure Congress that the American Eagle gold bullion coin program will not be pulled out of the US. Bullion Depository at West Point.

Budget reductions for the fiscal year ending 1988 have resulted in a reorganization at American Numismatic Association headquarters and a staff reduction resulting in the layoff of several ANA staff members in the past 30 days, according to ANA Executive Director Ruthann Brettell.

World Coins — "A Beginner's Guide to Ancient Coins" by Richard Giedroyc

APRIL 1

A nine-question survey sent by the House Banking Subcommittee on Consumer Affairs and Coinage to 25 eligible distributors of the American Eagle

gold bullion coins has created feelings of uncertainty among some distributors which could change the initial high-flying course of the coins into a fatal plummet.

A 1787 Brasher doubloon, purchased for $430,000 in 1979 by Chicago dealer Walter Perschke, is now on a cross-country tour as a numismatic window dressing for the most important documents in democracy — the Magna Carta, the Declaration of Independence, the Articles of Confederation and the Bill of Rights.

APRIL 8

From 1976 to 1986 the United States Mint deposited $224,064,000 into the general fund of the Treasury form the sale of numismatic items. More than half of that figure, $167,339,000, was raised between fiscal years 1982-1986.

In response to heavy demand for intermediate grading of commemorative gold coinage, commemorative half dollars and U.S. gold coinage of the period 1807-1908, the American Numismatic Association Certification Service now has the necessary representative coins to add the Mint State 62 and MS-64 grades to all six gold denominations and MS-64 for all commemoratives, both silver and gold.

Excessive delays in processing orders for its products have caused the Bureau of Engraving and Printing to adopt a series of changes to its order-fulfillment system.

APRIL 15

A bold eagle and a representation of one of the most revered documents in United States history, the Constitution, will be featured on the obverses of the 1987 Bicentennial of the Constitution commemorative coins.

For the first time in marketing commemorative coins, the United States Mint is considering limiting the number of coins it will make available in its pre-issue discount, direct mail offering to customers on its mailing list.

APRIL 22

The American Numismatic Association 1988 Midwinter Convention will be held in Little Rock, Ark., as planned, after city and state officials granted the ANA certain exemptions to severe restrictive regulations concerning dealer purchases of numismatic items.

"Roads to Liberty:Magna Carta to the Constitution," a traveling exhibit sponsored by the Commission on the Bicentennial of the United States Constitution, the U.S. Constitution Council of the Thirteen Original States Inc. and American Express Co., began its six-month journey March 11 in Washington, D.C.

APRIL 29

The American Numismatic Association's 11-point Mint State grading system has been standardized in written for for the first time, in the third edition of the *Official ANA Grading Standards for United States Coins*, just off the printing presses.

The Walt Disney Co. will start circulating its own paper money soon.

Allegations that the United States Mint has sold millions of underweight American Eagle gold bullion fractional coins has been strongly refuted by Mint Director Donna Pope.

World Coins — "British Tokens and the Industrial Revolution" by Richard G. Doty

MAY 6

In an effort to take a leadership role in the self-regulation of the coin and precious metals industry, the Industry Council for Tangible Assets is proposing a national certification program.

Like the legendary phoenix which rises from its own ashes, the silver price levitated from $5.50 per troy ounce March 13 to $8.90 when the market closed April 23.

A U.S. District Court has decided order forms issued by the United States Mint for the Statue of Liberty/Ellis Island commemorative coins were solicitations of offers, not contracts as alleged in a lawsuit filed by a Georgia couple against the Mint.

MAY 13

The U.S. Mint is adamant that the American Eagle bullion coins will not be offered to the public like numismatic coins, U.S. Mint Director Donna Pope told members of the Gold Institute April 22.

With an April 25 ground-breaking ceremony the Bureau of Engraving and Printing has moved one step closer to the realization of a western currency-production facility in Fort Worth, Texas.

If a U.S. District Court judge approves a settlement submitted by the Federal Trade Commission and the principal officers of Rare Coin Galleries of America Inc., a Massachusetts rare coin firm, and its two subsidiaries, those principal officers will be permanently prohibited from selling rare coins to the public and from grading rare coins for sale to the public.

MAY 20

Coin World sponsors a petition drive to provide the American public with an opportunity to call upon government officials in both the executive and legislative branches to bring about issuance of new designs for all circulating coins in the United States.

Canada begins striking its new small-sized aureate-nickel dollar coin with loon reverse at ceremonies at the Royal Canadian Mint's Winnipeg facility May 7.

MAY 27

Rep. John Hiler, R-Ind., ranking minority member of the House Banking Subcommittee on Consumer Affairs and Coinage, does not expect Congress to make any changes in the distribution plan of the American Eagle bullion coins.

What appears to be a plague of production errors has some collectors and dealers criticizing the newly-published third edition of the *Official ANA Grading Standards for United States Coins*, while American Numismatic Association officials, in conceding there are problems, say they are trying to determine just to what extent.

JUNE 3

Nora Hussey, Superintendent of the Denver Mint, notifies U.S. Mint officials of her intention to retire effective with the appointment of a replacement by President Reagan.

The San Francisco Assay Office celebrates its 50th anniversary May 15 with a reservation-only open house and rare tour.

World Coins — Israel: Coins of the Old-New Land" by David T. Alexander.

JUNE 10

Don MacKay-Coghill, the architect of the marketing plan that launched the South African Krugerrand as a world-renowned gold bullion coin, unwraps plans for introducing the new Australian Nugget gold bullion coins.

Tentative prices for the gold and silver Constitution Bicentennial commemorative coins have been released by the U.S. Mint, with pre-issue orders given the deepest discount possible because those customers will probably have to wait as long as six months before receiving their coins.

JUNE 17

The American Numismatic Association Certification Service to begin adjectival grading of world coins July 1.

A new organization of foreign coin dealers — the International Numismatic Trade Organization — is in the process forming.

JUNE 24

After six years of development and $31 million of government expense, the Treasury Department announces that it may be another two years before it begins production of Federal Reserve notes incorporating security thread and microprinting anti-counterfeiting devices.

United States coins rank sixth in Salomon Brothers survey of investment vehicles.

World Coins — "Byzantine Coins" by David R. Cervin

JULY 1

James A. Baker III, U.S. Secretary of the Treasury, is scheduled to strike the first of the Bicentennial of the Constitution coins July 1 in Philadelphia with other federal officials and dignitaries expected to be in attendance.

The historic town of Schuylerville, N.Y., will mark the 199th anniversary of its founding July 26 with the presentation to national, state and local officials of plaques containing the five medals struck to commemorate the Bicentennial of the Battle of Saratoga a decade earlier.

Industry Council for Tangible Assets representatives battled a firestorm of protests and fielded a barrage of questions June 6 regarding ICTA's newly proposed program to certify coin dealers.

JULY 8

Legislation calling for the minting of 1 million gold coins and 10 million silver coins in 1988 to commemorate the participation of American athletes in the 1988 Winter and Summer Olympic Games was introduced June 23, barely a week before the U.S. Mint launched its latest commemorative coin program.

U.S. Mint mailing list customers interested in ordering Bicentennial of the Constitution coins at pre-issue prices should send in their orders immediately, according to Mint Director Donna Pope.

JULY 15

The spirit of a 200-year-old document was captured in gold and silver with the push of a button during ceremonial first strikes of the Bicentennial of the Constitution commemorative coins July 1 in Philadelphia.

Works of approximately 1,000 medallic artists will be on exhibit in Colorado Springs, Colo., Sept. 11-15 as part of the 50th Anniversary Congress and Exposition of the Federation Internationale de la Medaille.

JULY 22

Destined to replace Canada's current large-sized $1 coin in 1987 and its paper dollar by 1989, the 100 million Loon dollars which have been struck seem to have won a place in the hearts of Canadians, said Royal Canadian Mint Director of Communications Murray Church.

The introduction of America's small-sized dollar coin eight years ago was such a monumental debacle that the Susan B. Anthony dollar has the dubious distinction of lending its name to the coining of a new word in the American vocabulary:

"anthonize."

JULY 29

A "Buy American" amendment to the 1988 United States Mint appropriations bill was introduced in the House of Representatives July 15, sparking criticism from Mint officials, who say that if the amendment is passed the cost of producing coins will increase and will require them to violate several international trade agreements.

A circulating commemorative coin honoring the Bicentennial of the Bill of Rights in 1991 is being recommended by members of the Commission on the Bicentennial of the United States Constitution.

The Uncirculated version of the 1987-P Constitution silver dollar will go on sale Aug. 26-30 at the United States Mint's booth in Atlanta during the American Numismatic Association's 96th Anniversary Convention.

World Coins — "The Art of the Medal" by Cory Gillilland.

AUGUST 5

The U.S. Mint's $46.5 million appropriation has been deleted from the House Appropriations Committee's 1988 Treasury appropriations bill at the last-minute request of Rep. Frank Annunzio, D-Ill.

Beginning in this issue, Coin World Trends covers 34 percent more values for U.S. coins and is presented in a new format.

Pre-issue discount orders for the Bicentennial of the Constitution coins continued to climb as of July 20, with three options already exceeding final sales figures for similar options in the Statue of Liberty program.

AUGUST 12

The Industry Council for Tangible Assets is in the final stages of fine tuning its comprehensive plan for self-regulation of the rare coin industry and expects to launch it by the end of August.

U.S. Commissioner of Fine Arts Diane Wolf says the campaign to change the designs of America's circulating coins

"looks very encouraging."

The American Numismatic Association's new ANA professional membership category has been selected as the primary topic for discussion at a round table just prior to the opening of the 96th Anniversary Convention in Atlanta.

AUGUST 19

Scientists at Battelle Memorial Institute of Columbus, Ohio, believe that current technology can be harnessed to objectively grade rare coins.

A new world record price for a single coin — $10 million — is estimated for a Mogul gold coin of the 17th century previously known only to a few specialists.

Acrobatics and politics were flying high Aug. 5 when the House Banking Subcommittee on Consumer Affairs and Coinage held a hearing on legislation calling for the minting of commemorative coins to support the training of American athletes participating in the 1988 Olympic Games.

Robert J. Leuver, director of the Bureau of Engraving and Printing, is actively being pursued to become the executive head of the 30,000-member American Numismatic Association based in Colorado Springs, Colo.

AUGUST 26

The American Numismatic Association's 96th Anniversary Convention Aug. 26-30 in Atlanta and the Bureau of Engraving and Printing's 125th Anniversary combine in a special Coin World issue.

Five collectors and one dealer have been elected to the American Numismatic Association Board of Governors, including two former employees of what is the world's largest coin collector organization.

A bill authorizing 1988 Olympic coinage passed the full House by voice vote Aug. 7 and has been referred to the Senate Banking Committee where it is pending due to the congressional recess, which ends Sept. 9.

The first Britannia, Britain's new gold

bullion coin, was struck Aug. 12 at the British Royal Mint's Llantrisant, Wales, facility, approximately two months before its October release.

World Coins — "A Numismatic Tribute: Porfirio Diaz, President of Mexico 1877-1880, 1884-1911" by Miguel L. Muñoz.

SEPTEMBER 2

Internationally renowned medalist and sculptor Mico Kaufman has created a limited edition commemorative medal for participants in the 50th Anniversary Congress and Exposition of the Federation Internationale de la Medaille, which will be held at the American Numismatic Association in Colorado Springs, Colo., Sept. 11-15.

Edward Gans was to be the guest of honor at a party to mark his 100th birthday Aug. 30 at the University of California, Berkeley, to which he recently bequeathed his collection of more than 5,000 seals from ancient civilizations throughout the world.

SEPTEMBER 9

The governing board of the American Numismatic Association, faced with a projected operating deficit of just under $125,000 for its fiscal year ending March 31, 1988, has approved a number of measures — including a $5 dues increase — which organizational leaders hope will reverse the flow of red ink.

The nine-coin Proof set presented to the King of Siam in 1836 by the United States, called "The most desirable numismatic item in the world" and containing the finest known 1804 dollar, will go on the auction block Oct. 14 with a reserve bid of $2 million.

Edward C. Rochette and the late Virginia Culver were named winners of the Farran Zerbe Memorial Award, the highest honor awarded an American Numismatic Association member, at the 96th Anniversary Convention banquet in Atlanta Aug. 29.

SEPTEMBER 16

Ingrid Smith, a Canadian coin dealer, voluntarily turned over to U.S. Mint officials at the American Numismatic Association convention in Atlanta a reverse working die for the 1986 Ellis Island commemorative silver dollar that is one of 44 dies that have been missing for 16 months.

The American Numismatic Association Board of Governors voted Aug. 30 to suspend implementation of its Professional Membership program pending the results of a survey of the association's 32,000 members to determine if it is "needed or wanted."

SEPTEMBER 23

Legislation was expected to be introduced in Congress in late September calling for a dollar coin and the gradual phase-out of the $1 Federal Reserve note.

The West Point Bullion Depository is not equipped to produce all gold coins issued by the U.S. Mint, report Mint officials, who say they are going to have to make some serious decisions if the Mint hopes to continue its present production schedule for the American Eagle bullion coins, Bicentennial of the Constitution coins and the proposed 1988 Olympic coins.

Jack Robinson believes numismatics has evolved to the point that a "true market" can exist and he intends to prove it with an electronic public auction of PCGS graded coins during the Sept. 24-27 Long Beach (Calif.) Numismatic and Philatelic Expo.

SEPTEMBER 30

Medallic artists from 25 countries and individuals who study and collect their creations on five continents gathered in Colorado Springs, Colo., in mid-September for what Federation Internationale de la Medaille officials are calling one of the most outstanding congresses in FIDEM's 50-year history.

The fifth edition of the Coin World Almanac, now available, will for the first time be marketed to bookstores, schools and libraries, newsstands and book clubs, as well as the numismatic community.

American Numismatic Association Certification Service Director Rick

Montgomery, 25, has tendered his resignation from that post and will be assuming the position Oct. 1 of grader/authenticator with the Professional Coin Grading Service of Newport Beach, Calif.

World Coins — "The Solemn Procession: Coinage of the Papal Mints" by Thomas F. Fitzgerald.

OCTOBER 7

The redesign of circulating coinage is gaining momentum on Capitol Hill with the introduction of a bill Sept. 21 calling on the Secretary of the Treasury to modernize the portraits of the presidents now on the obverses and to eliminate the requirement of an eagle on the reverse of the dollar, half dollar and quarter dollar coins.

Sales of the 1987 $5 gold half eagle commemorating the Bicentennial of the Constitution are nearing the 800,000 mark, almost 80 percent of its maximum allowable mintage.

The personal collection of medals and related material belonging to famed medalist Victor D. Brenner has been donated to the American Numismatic Society in New York, according to Dr. Alan Stahl, ANS curator of medals.

OCTOBER 14

The topic of redesigning the nation's circulating coinage has captured the imagination of more than 20 House legislators in the week that followed the introduction of legislation calling for such changes.

A dollar coin is an idea whose time has come, according to members of Congress who met Sept. 29 to rally support for legislation calling for a dollar coin and the gradual phase-out of the estimated 3.8 billion $1 Federal Reserve notes currently in circulation.

President Reagan has nominated Denver native Cynthia Jeanne Grassby Baker, 41, to succeed Nora Walsh Hussey as superintendent of the Denver Mint.

OCTOBER 21

A new allegorical representation of an "elegant and enlivened Britannia" as "a woman of the times" was unveiled in London Oct. 13 by officials of the British Royal Mint, on Britain's new Britannia gold bullion coins.

The sale of a unique 1872 Liberty Head U.S. gold pattern set was made public at the Long Beach (Calif.) Numismatic and Philatelic Expo in September.

The United States Mint has characterized an unofficial Coinage Subcommittee staff report addressing the Mint's distribution of the American Eagle gold bullion coins as being "based on a totally incorrect premise that bullion and numismatic coins are identical and should be marketed similarly."

OCTOBER 28

At least a dozen world record prices for Colonial and United States coins were set Oct. 12-13 during the Norweb collection auction in New York City.

Legislation authorizing the striking of gold and silver coins to commemorate the participation of American athletes in the 1988 Olympic Games has been approved by Congress and sent on to President Reagan for his signature.

World Coins — "Collecting World Crowns" by William S. Snyder.

NOVEMBER 4

U.S. Mint Director Donna Pope reflects on the American Eagle gold bullion coin program on its one-year anniversary Oct. 20.

"Coins and Medals — Twenty Centuries of French Art" is the title of an exhibition which opened to the public Oct. 21 at the International Monetary Fund Visitors' Center in Washington, D.C.

NOVEMBER 11

Gold and silver coins commemorating the participation of American athletes in the 1988 Olympic Games were authorized Oct. 28 when President Ronald Reagan signed into law a bill passed by Congress.

Paper money and gold coins which have spent the last 75 years on the ocean floor aboard the Titanic provided surprises for numismatic experts Yasha Beresiner and Sabine Bourgey and millions of television viewers around the world.

NOVEMBER 18

A request to the Treasury Department to study the feasibility of a dollar coin has left supporters of the coin on hold but not without hope.

Two privately-made obverse dies depicting an 1879 Morgan dollar are scheduled for a Nov. 18 auction appearance in London, although U.S. Secret Service officials are in contact with British officials to determine whether the dies and a two-headed "Morgan dollar" offered as part of the same lot violate British laws.

Legislation which would authorize the striking of gold, silver and copper-nickel clad coinage to commemorate the Bicentennial of the U.S. Congress will have to wait for consideration in the Senate until the U.S. Mint evaluates the legislation.

NOVEMBER 25

Despite floor bids of $8 million and $2.8 million, two gold medieval coins of Mogul India did not sell when bidders failed to meet the consignor's reserve at a public auction conducted by Habsburg, Feldman S.A. Nov. 9 in Geneva, Switzerland.

An ancient Athenian decadrachm (ca. 465 B.C.) which lay buried for more than 2,000 and discovered in an ancient coin hoard in Turkey about three years ago sold for $600,000 to an anonymous Beverly Hills businessman Nov. 5 in a private sale arranged by the Beverly Hills, Calif., firms of Numismatic Fine Arts Inc. and Superior Stamp and Coin Co.

All paper used in printing U.S. paper money, securities and passports would have to be manufactured in the United States by American companies if the provisions of a House of Representatives joint resolution (H.J.R. 395), a rider on an appropriations bill, become law.

World Coins — "Numismatics of Spanish Colonial Mexico" by Don Bailey.

DECEMBER 2

A private study by Numismatic News Editor David C. Harper claiming profits for the federal government of $2.3 billion over a six-year period if changes are made to the designs of circulating U.S. coinage has left doubts in the minds of some federal officials.

Two privately-made copy dies depicting the obverse of an 1879 Morgan dollar and a medallic piece struck from them were sold to a London-area coin dealer for $7,980 at a Nov. 18 auction by Glendining's.

Despite a snowstorm which complicated travel for many of the attendees, the American Bank Note Co. successfully completed the destruction of the master plates used to produce ABNCo.'s 1987 "Archive Series" of intaglio vignette sheets.

DECEMBER 9

The complete mintage of 10,000 four-coin gold bullion Britannia Proof sets was sold out within an month of issue, according to British Royal Mint officials.

Sales of the American Eagle bullion silver dollars more than triple the original estimates predicted by U.S. Mint officials during its first year.

The glitter is not off gold as an investment despite the thundering crash of the stock market in October, according to some experts in the precious metals market.

Legislative update tracks the progress of 21 numismatically related bills through Congress.

DECEMBER 16

Legislation introduced Nov. 18 calls for the striking of a commemorative silver dollar coin honoring the 100th anniversary of the birth of Dwight D. Eisenhower in 1990.

The U.S. Treasury will sponsor a limited, invitational, compensated competition to gather designs for the U.S. 1988 Olympic commemorative coins.

During a Senate Committee on Banking, Housing and Urban Affairs mark-up session Dec. 2, members voted to delete several sections of the 1988 U.S. Mint Appropriation bill which would have required the Mint to purchase only gold and silver mined and refined in the United

States and to establish cash rooms at all Mint facilities; and approved the nomination of Cynthia Grassby Baker for Superintendent of the Denver Mint.

DECEMBER 23

The American Numismatic Society in New York City received an early holiday gift from the United States government Dec. 15 in the form of a $300,000 Challenge Grant from the National Endowment for the Humanities in Washington, D.C.

The American Numismatic Association's 1988 Midwinter Convention in Little Rock, Ark., will likely be its last, following an ANA Board of Governors vote Dec. 5 eliminating the annual Midwinter conventions.

The American Numismatic Association Board of Governors voted Dec. 5 to overturn a controversial August decision that required dealers seeking bourse tables

at the annual summer convention to remit full payment in November, months before dealers would learn whether they were to be awarded tables.

DECEMBER 30

The United States Mint began an education program in conjunction with the Bicentennial of the Constitution commemorative coin program with an information packet titled to be sent to about 77,000 schools.

After spending nearly half a century assembling the largest collection of United States paper money in existence, Aubrey and Adeline Bebee of Omaha, Neb., are giving the 500-piece collection with an estimated value of $2 million to the American Numismatic Association museum in Colorado Springs Colo.

World Coins — "A Numismatic Illustration of the Bible" by Robert D. Leonard Jr.

News happenings, 1988

Date refers to Coin World issue in which the news item was published.

JANUARY 6

With the first issue of 1988, *Coin World* introduces a new design for its editorial product and a new format for its advertising pages.

United States Treasurer Katherine D. Ortega invites 10 American artists and the U.S. Mint staff sculptor-engravers to participate in a compensated competition for designs for the 1988 Olympic commemorative coins.

JANUARY 13

John Cook, an American medalist, is the recipient of the American Numismatic Society's J. Sanford Saltus Medal Award for medallic design. Parmeshwari Gupta, an Indian scholar, is the ANS's choice for the Archer M. Huntington Medal Award for numismatic scholarship.

John F.W. Rogers, assistant secretary for management in the Treasury Department, resigns his position in late December to take a job with a Washington, D.C., commercial real estate developer.

JANUARY 20

The U.S. Department of the Treasury and the Federal Reserve announces plans to upgrade counterfeiting deterrents in United States paper money.

Final sales of 1986 Proof sets and Uncirculated Mint sets are the lowest since the advent of copper-nickel clad coinage in 1965, but there appears to be a turn-around for sales of the 1987-dated sets.

JANUARY 27

The United States coin market registers a 1987 gain of 2.21 percent over December 1986 levels, according to *Coin World's* Trends Index values. *Coin World* keeps track of 16,576 values of U.S. coins in Mint State and circulated grades for its U.S. Trends Index.

The 250th anniversary of the first industrial refinery in Canada, the Quebec-based Saint Maurice Ironworks, will be the theme of Canada's 1988 commemorative silver dollar, the 23rd commemorative in the series, which started in 1935.

World Coins — "O Canada: Wampum to Tokens, Beavers to Loons" by James E. Charlton.

FEBRUARY 3

For the first time in history, the Secretary of the Treasury will have the benefit of the recommendations of the Commission of Fine Arts when he selects the designs for the gold and silver commemorative coins which will be produced later this year honoring America's participation in the 1988 Olympic Games.

The tragedy of the *Challenger* space shuttle explosion moves space enthusiast Leo Vogel of Danbury, Conn., so much that he initiates a fund-raising campaign to build a monument dedicated to the seven astronauts lost in the disaster, and to the three astronauts who died in a January 1967 flash fire during pre-testing of their Apollo spacecraft. To launch the drive, a medal is being released in several different varieties.

A Professional Coin Grading Service proposal outlined in a letter testing the potential market for the grading of foreign coins is receiving strong opposition from an organization of world coin dealers.

FEBRUARY 10

The designs of two U.S. Mint sculptor-engravers and two artists outside the Mint have been selected for the 1988 Olympic gold and silver commemorative coins.

Ruthann Brettell, executive director of the American Numismatic Association, believes the ANA Certification Service, which grades coins for a fee, should turn back the clock to June 1986 and use only the five Mint State grades in use at that time plus the MS-64 grade.

A proposed Federal Trade Commission consumer alert brochure concerning rare coins, presented to the American Numismatic Association in December and since slightly modified in a Jan. 22 draft, has attracted a variety of comments, including a revised draft offered by a member of the ANA Board of Governors.

FEBRUARY 17

The American Numismatic Association Board of Governors votes to jointly issue a revised draft of the Federal Trade Commission's proposed consumer alert brochure concerning rare coins, pending minor changes.

U.S. Treasury officials confirm that the ceremonial first strike of the Uncirculated 1988-D Olympic commemorative dollar will take place at the Denver Mint May 3. Cynthia Grassby Baker assumes her duties as Denver Mint Superintendent following a Jan. 28 swearing-in ceremony.

The United States Mint will replace a number of damaged Proof 1987-S American Eagle bullion silver dollars, which received gouges and other marks while being handled by an encapsulating machine at the San Francisco Assay Office.

A change on accounting procedures at the United States Mint explains the apparent discrepancy in mintage figures for 1987 Kennedy half dollars.

FEBRUARY 24

New York state entrepreneur Henry Merton stakes claim to the "first totally objective coin grading and identification system using computer technology."

The International Numismatic Trade Organization and the Professional Coin Grading Service hold separate meetings to discuss widely different views concerning the issue of world coin grading at the Long Beach (Calif.) Numismatic and Philatelic Exposition Feb. 4-7.

The United States Mint sets pre-issue discount prices for the 1988 Olympic coins but customer orders must be postmarked by May 15 to receive the discounts.

World Coins — "Pursuing Excellence: Collecting Coins and Medals of the Olympics" by Richard Giedroyc.

MARCH 2

The five interlocking rings symbolizing the Olympics will not appear on the gold $5 half eagle or silver dollar Olympic commemorative coins, Deputy Mint Director Eugene Essner told the

Commission of Fine Arts Feb. 18.

Associate memberships will be offered beginning March 2 to individual collector-investors and coin firms by the American Numismatic Exchange Inc., giving members of the public their first access to ANE's electronic network for the "sight unseen" purchase and sales of coins graded by the Professional Coin Grading Service.

MARCH 9

The Senate Committee on Banking, Housing and Urban Affairs will conduct a hearing April 22 concerning coin redesign legislation.

A copper trial piece of the 1794 Flowing Hair half dollar is donated to the Smithsonian Institution's National Numismatic Collections by Norman and Harvey G. Stack.

MARCH 16

The U.S. Treasury decides to reinstate the Olympic rings on the 1988 Olympic commemorative coins after several behind-the-scenes meetings between the Treasury Department, the United States Olympic Committee, the Commission of Fine Arts and the staff of Rep. Frank Annunzio, D-Ill.

The Soviet Union is preparing to sell czarist and modern coin issues through the Soviet export-import firm EMAC Trading Ltd. in Vancouver, British Columbia, to the numismatic market in the United States.

MARCH 23

The San Francisco Assay Office and West Point Bullion Depository are a presidential signature away from gaining Mint status, after House passage of the 1988 Mint authorization bill.

The Board of Governors of the American Numismatic Association approves the final draft of the Federal Trade Commission's "Consumer Alert on Investing in Rare Coins," which ANA is co-sponsoring.

MARCH 30

Numismatic Guaranty Corporation of America is developing a quarterly index for rare U.S. coins.

Panamanian commemorative coins and U.S. paper money are being used to pay partial wages to Panamanian government workers as the cash shortage continues there due to economic pressures recently imposed on the Noriega government by the United States.

World Coins — "From Rus to Revolution: Russian Coins Through a Thousand Years" by Robert W. Julian.

APRIL 6

Bureau of Engraving and Printing Director Robert J. Leuver resigns his government post to become executive director of the American Numismatic Association.

The International Olympic Committee taps Robert Huot, vice president of marketing of the Royal Canadian Mint, to fill the newly created IOC post of director of coin programs.

An extremely rare 1776 New Hampshire copper becomes part of the American Numismatic Society's collection Feb. 11 as the result of a bequest by the late Herbert M. Oechsner.

The Industry Council for Tangible Assets March 22 launches the Coin and Bullion Dealer Accreditation Program.

APRIL 13

President Ronald Reagan March 31 signs legislation into law authorizing Mint status for both the San Francisco Assay Office and West Point Bullion Depository.

Five notables in numismatics will testify about their ideas concerning the redesign of all U.S. circulating coinage when the Senate Committee on Banking, Housing and Urban Affairs convenes April 22 for a hearing on pending redesign legislation.

APRIL 20

New American Numismatic Association Executive Director Robert J. Leuver faces budgetary problems and a host of other challenges as he assumes his job, not the least of which is earning the ANA enough money in excess of its currently approved budget to pay his own salary.

Abandoned, forgotten, and now in a

rapidly advancing state of decay, the old hydraulic-powered Mint in Segovia, Spain, beckons to be saved from ruin.

APRIL 27

Saying "you can't legislate good taste or beauty," Curtis Prins, staff director for the House Banking Subcommittee on Consumer Affairs and Coinage, said subcommittee chairman Frank Annunzio, D-Ill., has been taking a "bad rap" from supporters of legislation calling for the redesign of all U.S. circulating coinage.

To follow up on it s 1987 medal, which commemorated the Bicentennial of the U.S. Constitution, the United States Capitol Historical Society's 1988 medal recognizes the ratification of the Constitution.

Discussion are in the final stages between the U.S. Treasury and the American Numismatic Association to arrange an exhibition of the design sketches submitted for the 1988 U.S. Olympic commemorative coins during the ANA's 97th Anniversary Convention in Cincinnati.

World Coins — "Down Under: Australian Coins by the Pouchful" by William S. Snyder.

MAY 4

Redesign of United State circulating coinage clears a major hurdle April 22 as Mint Director Donna Pope tells members of the Senate Committee on Banking, Housing and Urban Affairs that the "Treasury find generally nothing objectionable" to legislation calling for design changes.

The plummeting sales of the American Eagle gold bullion coins during the first three months of 1988 are being attributed by some U.S. bullion dealers to "sufficient inventories" and not necessarily due to a lack of interest in the American coin.

MAY 11

Canada's greatest numismatic rarity, the 1911 pattern silver dollar, sets a new world's record price for a modern world coins at $353,430 in U.S. funds.

Kagin's Numismatic Investment Corp., which owns the San Francisco Old Mint's display of possibly the finest overall collection of pioneer gold pieces, asks the U.S. Bankruptcy Court for permission to auction the collection.

MAY 18

Treasury officials, hobbyists and Olympic representatives gather at the Denver Mint May 2 to participate in a first-strike ceremony for the 1988-D Olympic silver dollar.

The first independent program of self-regulation for the rare coin industry — the Coin and Bullion Dealer Accreditation Program — initially accredits 19 coin and bullion dealers.

MAY 25

After four weeks of intensive meetings with officials in Segovia and Madrid, Spain, American numismatist Glenn Murray receives firm commitments for sponsorship of the Segovia Mint project.

The second in a series of the collectible Disney Dollars, featuring new illustrations on the backs of the $1 and $5 bills, are available.

World Coins — "Pomp and Circumstance — Heraldry on Coins" by Richard Giedroyc.

JUNE 1

A gentlemanly truce in the fiercely competitive battle for the high-stakes bullion coin marketplace appears to prevail during the May 15-19 XV Mint Directors' Conference in Washington, D.C.

An exhibition titled "From Shang to Republic: China's Money," arranged by George Hebert of the National Numismatic Collection staff at the Smithsonian Institution, was on display May 18 at the Willard Hotel in Washington, D.C., during a reception for Mint Directors hosted by MTB Banking Corp.

JUNE 8

Two major pieces of numismatic legislation, one calling for the redesign of U.S. coins and a second seeking commemoratives honoring the Bicentennial of Congress, are sent to the full Senate following a May 24 Senate

Committee on Banking, Housing and Urban Affairs mark-up session.

Walter Breen's comprehensive numismatic reference book, *Walter Breen's Complete Encyclopedia of U.S. and Colonial Coins*, is off the press after years of research.

Risking what it considers an enormous loss of potential income from grading fees, Numismatic Guaranty Corporation of America in Parsippany, N.J., expand the list of coins the company will not grade.

JUNE 15

Representations used to depict the obverse and reverse of the 1988 Olympic $5 gold coin in the U.S. Mint's print media advertising campaign and promotional brochures are not the actual design and Elizabeth Jones, the creator of the coin design, is hopping mad about the Madison Avenue sleight of hand.

After nine years in development, Gold Standard Corp. of Kansas City, Mo., is releasing GOLD STANDARD® certificates redeemable for its interchangeable gold bullion pieces.

The United States Secret Service is investigating the disappearance in January of 24 obverse dies for the 1988 American Eagle 1-ounce bullion coins.

JUNE 22

Rare coins ave been moving up over the short term and continue to hold the tops spot over the long term, according to the latest annual report on the performance of financial and tangible assets prepared by the Salomon Brothers Inc.

"The serious collector is alive" is the reaction of one of the bidders at Superior Galleries' June 5-7 auction of the H.W. Blevins Estate and the George Bodway collections held in Beverly Hills, Calif.

Legislation to mint a series of three commemorative coins to mark the golden anniversary of the completion of the Mount Rushmore National Memorial in 1991 is introduced in the Senate May 24 by Sen. Larry Pressler, R-S.D.

JUNE 29

In a surprise move June 15, the U.S. Senate votes 96-0 in favor of H.R. 3251, a bill calling for the striking of commemorative coins for the Bicentennial of the U.S. Congress, and adds five amendments from the Senate floor incorporating pending legislation calling for the redesign of circulation coinage, a commemorative palladium coin and a commemorative Dwight D. Eisenhower silver dollar.

Fierce bidding wars and prices approaching records from early in the decade characterize the June 13-15 sale of the Everson and Faught collection by Bowers and Merena Inc. at the St. Moritz on-the-Park Hotel in New York.

World Coins — "Vive La Revolution! Numismatics of the French Revolution" by David T. Alexander.

JULY 6

A hoard of decadrachms follows a trail of intrigue and controversy on its way to the rare coin market.

Legislation authorizing commemorative coins for the Bicentennial of the U.S. Congress sails out of the House of Representatives after an eight-day overhaul which saw three coinage amendments left on the dock.

JULY 13

The Federal Trade Commission would be authorized to prosecute those firms or individuals who misrepresent or defraud consumers in the sale of numismatic items if the Coin Fraud Prevention Act introduced June 21 in the House of Representatives is approved.

Supporters of dollar coin legislation will have to wait another month to find out what the U.S. Treasury Department has to say about the feasibility of dollar coin proposals now pending in both the House and Senate.

JULY 20

In a last-minute effort to get all U.S. coins and most bullion coins eligible for inclusion in Individual Retirement Accounts, the membership of the Industry Council for Tangible Assets is asked to contribute $127,000 to beef up lobbying pressure on Capitol Hill.

Cincinnati's bicentennial provides the

backdrop for the American Numismatic Association's 97th Anniversary Convention July 20-24.

JULY 27

All denominations of the 1988 American Eagle bullion coins will be available later this year in a Proof version for the first time.

H.R. 3251, which calls for $5 gold half eagle, silver dollar and clad half dollar commemorative coins to mark the 200th anniversary of Congress, was approved by the Senate July 12, by the House July 13 and sent to the White House for approval later that same day, but because of an amendment offered by Sen. William Proxmire, D-Wis., all provisions relating to the coins will be repealed the day after the date of enactment, if and when the president signs the bill into law.

American Eagle bullion coins are aboard "The American Train in Japan," which departed Tokyo Station July 4, and will be available for direct purchase by the Japanese public.

World Coins — "Beyond Cash: A Numismatic Survey of Korea" by Joseph E. Boling.

AUGUST 3

American Numismatic Association President Stephen R. Taylor opened the first public session of the ANA Board of Governors July 19 in Cincinnati with the declaration that the ANA is "well under way" toward achieving the three primary goals he set upon taking the reins of leadership just one year ago.

Auction '88 — held in Cincinnati July 16-17 — yields prices which have many dealers very excited about the future of the rare coin market.

The Farran Zerbe Memorial Award, the American Numismatic Association's highest honor, is awarded to Aubrey and Adeline Bebee of Omaha, Neb., during ceremonies at the ANA's 97th Anniversary Convention in Cincinnati July 23.

AUGUST 10

A reducing diet designed to slim down the diameter and production limit as well as specify the destination of surcharges for a proposed $5 palladium commemorative coin makes the legislation attractive enough to gain the approval of the Senate Banking, Housing and Urban Affairs Committee July 27.

The five-session Heritage auction in conjunction with the American Numismatic Association's 97th Anniversary Convention July 20-24 in Cincinnati was active, entertaining large crowds of approximately 250 per session and realizing strong bids leading to prices indicative of the current bull market.

An investigation is continuing into what Professional Coin Grading Service officials describe as a "small quantity of illicit PCGS-graded coins" which have been identified in the wholesale marketplace.

AUGUST 17

A Washington source says Secretary of the Treasury James A. Baker III will order a change in at least one design of a currently circulating U.S. coin before leaving his cabinet post Aug. 17.

Space exploration is the theme of the gold, silver and bronze national medals scheduled to be struck by the U.S Mint in late September. Proceeds from the sale of the medals will benefit the activities of the Young Astronaut Council's more than 550,000 students in 22,000 chapters.

The estates of two well-known numismatists, Philip M. Mann Jr. and Glenn B. Smedley, will cross the auction block in New York City Sept. 13 and 14.

McDonald's brings poultry and Latin American coins together for its Chicken McNuggets Fiesta numismatic program.

AUGUST 24

A late-night session in the Senate on Aug. 11 results in the taking of a "hostage" in the form of the Jesse Owens gold medal bill and the failure to pass several coinage bills before Congress left for its annual August recess.

A request by the United States Treasury Department for more time to study the feasibility of a new $1 coin means a decision on the matter will be at least two more years in coming.

Helen Broadfield, 19-year-old president of Vend-A-Coin, places vending machines dispensing collectible coins in Illinois and Florida.

AUGUST 31

Royal Canadian Mint officials, citing the country's criminal codes, label as counterfeit a 1981 coin struck from the muled dies of a $100 gold coin and 50-cent coins, which was seized by the Royal Canadian Mounted Police June 17.

Speculation about whether Secretary of the Treasury James A. Baker III would change designs of U.S. circulating coinage appeared to end Aug. 17 when Baker officially resigned without the Treasury Department acknowledging any decision to redesign coins.

World Coins — "The Grandeur that was Rome" by David Vagi.

SEPTEMBER 7

Kagin's Numismatic Investment Corp. is given bankruptcy court approval to sell the Clifford-Kagin Pioneer Gold Collection housed at the San Francisco Old Mint Museum, for $2.3 million to Tangible Investments of America Inc.

The U.S. Treasury Department appoints Peter H. Daly to be the 22nd Director of the Bureau of Engraving and Printing.

SEPTEMBER 14

More than 16,000 numismatic lots are scheduled to cross the block in six public auctions during the next 35 days. In volume alone, September 1988 represents a greater than 5,500-lot increase over September's total.

American Numismatic Exchange Inc. will coordinate comprehensive independent evaluations, on a periodic basis, of Professional Coin Grading Service internal and external security controls relating to PCGS coins by hiring an as-yet-to-be-determined internationally recognized security specialist firm, according to ANE President John Schneider.

SEPTEMBER 21

Scholars from three continents will convene in New York City Oct. 29-30 to present research papers regarding the coinage of the colonial Viceroyalty of El Peru and its successor states at the American Numismatic Society's fifth annual Coinage of the Americas Conference.

In an effort to gauge public support for his stand against coinage redesigns, Rep. Frank Annunzio, D-Ill., has sent a two-question survey to the more than 500,000 residents within the 11th Congressional District he represents.

SEPTEMBER 28

Issuance of a United States commemorative silver dollar in 1990 honoring the centennial of the birth of President Dwight David Eisenhower appears to be a certainty Sept. 16 as authorizing legislation moves swiftly through both houses of Congress.

Numismatic eyes will be focused on the auction block in New York City Nov. 14-15, when the third and final portion of the Norweb Collection, highlighted by the finest known 1870-S Seated Liberty dollar and 1861 Coronet, Paquet Reverse double eagle, will be sold by Auctions by Bowers and Merena Inc.

World Coins — "A Living Collection: Numismatic Holdings of the British Royal Mint" by Graham Dyer.

OCTOBER 5

The American Numismatic Association Certification Service will introduce its new coin encapsulation option, "slab," in January, two months later than originally scheduled, because the holders are not available to meet the original November target date.

Like a prism offering different views from different angles, the designs for the U.S. Olympic coins submitted by 16 American artists run the conceptual spectrum of the Olympic Games.

OCTOBER 12

The Professional Numismatists Guild Inc. and the American Numismatic Association have singed an agreement whereby PNG member dealers will serve as "verifiers" for the new encapsulated coin service to be offered beginning in

January by the ANA Certification Service.

Congressionally mandated sales of U.S. Treasury silver reserves will begin in 1989 in an effort to cut back on the nearly 40 million ounces held by the Treasury.

OCTOBER 19

Legislation calling for three United States commemorative coins marking the Bicentennial of the U.S. Congress in 1989 is passed by the House of Representatives Oct. 3 and is sent to the Senate for consideration.

President Ronald Reagan signs legislation Oct. 3 authorizing the issuance of a United States commemorative silver dollar in 1990 honoring the centennial of the birth of President Dwight David Eisenhower.

OCTOBER 26

The Federal Trade Commission intends to amend the Hobby Protection Act to permit use of smaller markings of the word "COPY" to accommodate miniature imitations of coins.

A commemorative medal is issued to honor Commodore Uriah Phillips Levy, a 19th century patriot, the Jewish American Hall of Fame's honoree for 1988.

The last of the original holdings from the Redfield Hoard of silver dollars were purchased Oct. 3 by Blanchard and Company of Jefferson, La., from A-Mark Precious Metals Inc. of Santa Monica, Calif.

World Coins — "The Philippines — A Multi-Cultured Numismatic Mosaic" by David T. Alexander.

NOVEMBER 2

Legislation commemorating the Bicentennial of Congress with three denominations of coins was approved by voice vote in the Senate Oct. 20 and sent to the White House for President Reagan's signature.

The famed Byron Reed collection, a multi-million dollar collection of rare coins, medals, paper money, books, manuscripts and autographs formed in the mid-19th century by the Omaha, Neb., pioneer realtor and business leader, will be placed on permanent exhibit at the Western Heritage Museum, Omaha's history museum, beginning in March.

NOVEMBER 9

"Rome at War as Seen Through Coins," a traveling exhibition offering a numismatic perspective of ancient Rome at war, opens with a reception Oct. 21 in the Hall of Money and Medals at the Smithsonian Institution's National Museum of American History in Washington, D.C., and a colloquium Oct. 22 at the museum.

Becoming the first diver ever to win back-to-back gold medals in springboard and platform diving in successive Summer Olympic Games, Greg Louganis can add another to his growing list of achievements: having his likeness portrayed on a legal tender coin.

NOVEMBER 16

Hundreds of people, including French government officials, artists, museum curators and journalists, crowded into the Paris Mint's courtyard and chambers awaiting the inauguration of the Musee de la Monnaie Oct. 27.

A comprehensive survey of the production of coinage in the Spanish viceroyalty of El Peru was presented by 13 speakers at the American Numismatic Society in New York Oct. 29-30.

NOVEMBER 23

The 25th anniversary of the assassination of President John F. Kennedy prompts a look at the events surrounding the creation of the Kennedy half dollar.

The American Numismatic Association Board of Governors votes Nov. 5 to designate 4 percent of ANA Certification Service revenues to provide sufficient financial support in the event that ANACS finds it necessary to remove from the market improper authentication or grade decisions involving any ANACS product or any counterfeit or altered ANACS holders.

NOVEMBER 30

Collectors ignored reports of a generally lackluster market and shattered numerous price records as they battled each other for the remaining U.S. rarities in the third and final offering of U.S. coins from the Norweb collection.

The art of medallic sculpture in its infinite variety took the spotlight Nov. 12 in an exhibition sponsored by the American Medallic Sculpture Association at the Janus Gallery in Santa Fe, N.M., Nov. 12-14.

President Reagan Nov. 17 signs into law legislation authorizing three denominations of coins to commemorate the Bicentennial of Congress.

World Coins — "The Mexican Revolution: A Numismatic Remembrance" by Miguel L. Muñoz.

DECEMBER 7

United States Olympic team members will be visiting department stores across the country Dec. 1-18 to promote the sale of the 1988 U.S. Olympic coins and say thank you to the American public for its support of the program.

MTB Banking Corp. — which paid $600,000 plus 10 percent buyer's fee at the Norweb sale for a Mint State 67 1861 Coronet, Paquet Reverse double eagle, the finer of two known — was willing to set a world record, if need be, to obtain the coin MTB considers to have "awesome potential."

DECEMBER 14

The United States Mint's policies for bulk purchases of American Eagle bullion coins and for buying gold for the bullion coin program are "consistent" and "appropriate," according to audit reports by the Office of the Inspector General in the U.S. Treasury Department.

A ceremonial currency signing Nov. 30 at the Bureau of Engraving and Printing officially inaugurates the Series 1988 U.S. Federal Reserve notes, bearing the signatures of Treasury Secretary Nicholas F. Brady and U.S. Treasurer Katherine D. Ortega.

DECEMBER 21

James C. Benfield, executive director of the Dollar Coalition, a Washington, D.C., based lobbying group, predicts that the 101st Congress will consider legislation calling for a gold-colored dollar coin.

Veteran Rep. Henry B. Gonzalez, D-Texas, Dec. 6 is selected chairman of the House Banking, Housing and Urban Affairs Committee.

DECEMBER 28

Perestroika comes to numismatics as the Soviet Union announces plans to market precious metals coinage within its own borders.

World Coins — "A Numismatic Orientation to China" by R.C. Bell.

News happenings, 1989

Date refers to Coin World issue in which the news item was published.

JANUARY 4

Coin World introduces a new book — *The 1989 Coin World Guide to U.S. Coins, Prices & Value Trends* — which presents for the first time in book form "price performance graphs" tracking more than 16,000 United States coin values.

Curtis Prins, longtime staff director of the House Banking Subcommittee on Consumer Affairs and Coinage, and a guiding force in the issuance of modern U.S. Mint products, for more than a decade, will be departing the subcommittee with the start of the new Congress in early January.

JANUARY 11

The Young Astronaut Council is selectively offering 6-ounce and 12-ounce gold and silver versions of its America in Space medals as part of test marketing research.

A three-year tradition continues Feb. 3 with the issuance of 1989 Disney Dollars at Disneyland in Anaheim, Calif., and at Walt Disney World in Lake Buena Vista, Fla.

JANUARY 18

Eleven private artists and seven artists on the sculptor-engraver staff of the United States Mint indicate to Mint authorities that they will compete in the compensated design competition for designs for the 1989 Bicentennial of Congress commemorative coins.

The year 1989 may have a silver lining if legislative proposals for a special silver Proof set and a silver commemorative for the centennial of statehood of six western states gain speedy acceptance.

An undetermined amount of coins — speculated to be valued at millions of dollars — is missing from a Chicago Federal Reserve independent depository, according to a recent audit.

JANUARY 25

Legislation is expected to be introduced in Congress this year to allow the United States Mint to run its special coinage programs more like a private sector business venture and less like a temporary government coinage program.

The International Numismatic Society Authentication Bureau will introduce its encapsulated coin holder, commonly called a "slab," at the 14th Annual INS Convention Jan. 27-29 in Wilmington, Del., according to INSAB Director Charles Hoskins.

The opening of the Byron Reed Collection exhibit at its new permanent home in Omaha, Neb., has been postponed until April 9.

FEBRUARY 1

The 101st Congress takes the first step toward the redesign of all U.S. circulating coinage Jan. 19 when Reps. Henry B. Gonzalez, D-Texas, Charles B. Rangel, D-N.Y., and Lindy Boggs, D-La., introduce the 1989 Coinage Redesign Act, H.R. 505.

The American Numismatic Society receives a belated Christmas present Jan. 11 of a $500,000 grant from the Arcana Foundation, completing the $1 million needed to support the Margaret Thompson Chair in Greek Numismatics.

Brita Malmer of Sweden is the recipient of the 1988 Archer M. Huntington Medal Award for outstanding numismatic research and Jirí Harcuba is the recipient of the 1988 J. Sanford Saltus Medal award for distinguished achievement in the field of the medal from the American Numismatic Society.

FEBRUARY 8

The 500th anniversary of the British sovereign gold coin is the occasion for a new design.

Legislation seeking three commemorative coins honoring the 50th anniversary of Mount Rushmore National Park in 1991 is introduced Jan. 25 in the Senate.

FEBRUARY 15

Rep. Richard Lehman, D-Calif., is the new chairman of the House Banking Subcommittee on Consumer Affairs and Coinage.

Michael J. Brown, special assistant to U.S. Mint Director Donna Pope, is leaving the post he has held since 1981 to become director of public relations for the Gold and Silver Institutes in Washington, D.C.

FEBRUARY 22

Artisans, politicians and students alike gather Feb. 2 to welcome home Elizabeth Jones, Chief Sculptor-Engraver of the United States Mint, to the place where she started her career, the School of the Medal Art in Rome, Italy.

American Numismatic Association officials, anxious to cash in on the market for encapsulated coins, introduce the "ANACS Cache" Feb. 2 during the Long Beach Numismatic and Philatelic Exposition.

MARCH 1

A computerized network to aid law enforcement agencies in tracking stolen coins is now in operation at the FBI Laboratory in Washington, D.C.

Pikes Peak provides the backdrop for the American Numismatic Association's 11th Midwinter Convention March 3-5 at the Broadmoor Hotel complex in Colorado Springs, Colo.

MARCH 8

The U.S. Capitol Building and symbols

of freedom and legislative authority resident in and on the Capitol are expected to be the dominant design elements of the three commemorative coins which will be issued this year celebrating the Bicentennial of Congress.

Legislation calling for a new circulating United States dollar coin and an end to the regular production of the $1 Federal Reserve notes was introduced Feb. 22 in the U.S. House of Representatives.

MARCH 15

Members of Congress and cable television viewers March 2 were treated to the first public glimpse of designs approved for the three coins which are to be issued in 1989 to commemorate the Bicentennial of Congress.

The new Heisei era in Japan that began with the coronation of the new emperor is reflected in the dating on Japanese coins released in February by the Osaka Mint in Kita Ward, Osaka.

MARCH 22

U.S. Mint Director Donna Pope in testimony before the Senate Appropriations Subcommittee on Treasury, Postal Service and General Government on March 7, asked congressional support for the creation of a Public Enterprise Fund which would "enable the Mint to be more responsive to changes in the public's demand for numismatic and bullion coins and would permit the Mint to operate existing programs in a more business-like fashion."

The Board of Governors of the American Numismatic Association gave the nod to a $4.7 million budget, approved a new logo and reaffirmed the concept of a Midwinter convention during its business meetings March 1-2 during the ANA's 11th Midwinter Convention in Colorado Springs, Colo.

MARCH 29

Controversy rages whether a hoard of ancient Greek coins from the Black Sea region are genuine after a Michigan State University researcher concludes they are, contradicting an earlier conclusion reached at the British Museum.

Three United States Proof error coins have been removed from an Auctions by Bowers and Merena Inc. auction at the request of the United States Mint, in order for Mint technicians to examine and determine whether the coins were illegally removed from a Mint facility.

APRIL 5

A U.S. 90 percent silver Proof set may be available for collectors at the price of the bullion plus minting expenses if legislation introduced March 17 is approved by Congress and signed into law.

The final official figures for sales of Proof gold and silver 1988 American Eagle bullion coins show sales of 1-ounce Proof 1988 gold American Eagles totaled one-fifth of the 1-ounce Proof 1986 gold American Eagles sold when the program began.

APRIL 12

Three United States Proof error coins which were to be offered in a March rare coin auction have been seized by the United States Mint and will be turned over to the U.S. Secret Service for an investigation after the Mint technicians determined them to be illegitimate error coins and thus U.S. Mint property.

Historic preservation organizations and agencies support the need for a new visitors' entrance on the east side of the Denver Mint but consider the current proposed architectural scheme as "unsympathetic" and having an "adverse impact" on the original structure.

APRIL 19

Plaster models by sculptor Marcel Jovine of the 1989 United States Capitol Historical Society medal commemorating the Bicentennial of the U.S. Congress are unveiled April 4 at a reception held before the Washington, D.C., premier of the society's videotape documentary about the Capitol building.

Reactions among error coin dealers and collectors to the seizure of three United States Proof error coins from a U.S. auction firm by the U.S. Mint in late March range from complete agreement with the Mint's action to skeptical questioning.

APRIL 26

Capitol Hill may become a branch of the United States Mint for a few hours June 14 if Congress passes special legislation to move coining presses to the ground of the U.S. Capitol.

If confirmed by the Senate, President George Bush's intended nominee for Treasurer of the United States — Catalina Vasquez Villalpando — will have the longest name ever to appear on U.S. paper money while serving in the federal post.

MAY 3

Shearson Lehman Hutton begins offering "certified" coins — those graded and encapsulated by third-party grading services — to approximately 3 million customers through 11,000 Shearson brokers nationwide.

California heart surgeon and coin collector Dr. Juan Suros — who was to be among several persons honored April 15 by the American Numismatic Society in New York for their contributions to the society — is arrested by New York City police a few hours before the awards banquet and charged with the theft of 13 rare coins valued at more than $100,000 from the society sometime in the previous two days.

MAY 10

A "numismatic university" was the setting for students of numismatics who gathered in Washington, D.C., April 19-21 for the American Coins and Currency program sponsored by the Smithsonian National Associates Lecture and Seminar Program, part of the institution's membership organization.

More than five dozen coins allegedly stolen from the American Numismatic Society in New York City in the past year by one of its members have been recovered and returned safely to the society's vaults.

MAY 17

The Clifford-Kagin pioneer gold collection is sold intact for $3.1 million to an anonymous collector/investor from Rhode Island; the new owner plans to keep the collection on display indefinitely at the San Francisco Old Mint, where it has been housed since 1974.

A recent agreement of cooperation signed between Project Segovia '92 and the United States committee of the International Council on Monuments and Sites results in tax-deductible status for contributions to help sponsor the American Numismatic Association's participation in the restoration of the historic Segovia Mint in Spain.

MAY 24

Attorneys for the Young Astronaut Council and the United States Mint are reviewing a letter to be sent to customers who have purchased the YAC medals offering them the opportunity to return the medals and get their money back if they are not satisfied with their purchase.

The U.S. Senate approves a joint resolution May 10 to allow the first-strike ceremony for the Bicentennial of Congress commemoratives to be held June 14 on the grounds of the U.S. Capitol. If approved by the House, the resolution would set a precedent by allowing official U.S. legal tender coins to be struck outside of a U.S. Mint facility.

MAY 31

Legislation is introduced in the U.S. House of Representatives May 4 to require large non-resident mail-order firms, including coin dealers, to collect state and local taxes on goods sent into another state.

The American Numismatic Association's 98th Anniversary Convention will be commemorated in an official ANA medal designed by John Mercanti, a sculptor-engraver at the United States Mint in Philadelphia.

JUNE 7

The doors of the 151-year-old New Orleans Mint could close permanently if proposed budget cuts become reality in Louisiana during the fiscal year beginning July 1. The Mint is operated as a tourist site by the Louisiana State Museum.

The Professional Coin Grading Service

of Newport Beach, Calif., restructures its coin certification fees effective May 19 due to increased volume.

JUNE 14

An error 1989 Washington quarter which is missing its Mint mark has received wide national exposure.

The Annual Report of the Director of the Mint for Fiscal Year 1987 shows increased revenues and an upturn in the demand for cents.

JUNE 21

The 1989 Washington quarter dollars without a Mint mark, currently receiving so much national media attention as potentially very valuable finds, are worth a maximum of $3, according to the board of the Combined Organizations of Numismatic Error Collectors of America.

Katherine Davalos Ortega, Treasurer of the United States, will spend her last day in that post June 30, according to Ortega's press secretary.

JUNE 28

With the Statue of Freedom looking down from her perch high atop the dome of the U.S. Capitol, the first strikes of the Proof versions of the 1989 gold half eagle and silver dollar commemorating the Bicentennial of the U.S. Congress are struck June 14 on coining presses set up in the east front parking lot of the Capitol grounds.

Rare coins surged in value, returning an average of 30 percent for the year ending June 1, according to the annual Salomon Brothers survey of tangible assets.

JULY 5

Stack's offers the King of Siam Proof set, which contains a specimen of the 1804 dollar, for private sale.

Indiana coin dealer Leon Hendrickson is set to sell his specimen of the 1804 dollar.

JULY 12

A new portrait of Queen Elizabeth II to be used on all Canadian coins beginning in 1990 is unveiled at a special striking ceremony June 26 at the Royal Canadian Mint facility in Winnipeg.

The House Banking Subcommittee on Consumer Affairs and Coinage sets July 12 as the date for a hearing on H.R. 505, which calls for the redesign of all circulating U.S. coinage.

JULY 19

A new auction record is set for a world coin June 20 as an Umayyad Islamic gold dinar was bid to $301,704 at the Spink & Son Numismatics Ltd. Zürich auction in Zürich, Switzerland.

Rep. Frank Annunzio, D-Ill., introduces legislation calling for coins commemorating the 500th anniversary of Christopher Columbus' discovery of the Americas.

JULY 26

A world's record price for a United States coin is set when $900,000 was bid for the Dexter specimen of the 1804 Draped Bust dollar July 7 during Auction '89.

Controversy erupts at a House Banking Subcommittee on Consumer Affairs and Coinage hearing concerning legislation to redesign circulating U.S. coinage.

AUGUST 2

The Federal Trade Commission says a July settlement of a complaint involving two Texas coin firms and two of its principals "should provide guidance to the coin industry as to how the FTC Act is applied to the wholesaling and certification of rare coins."

Two members of the Senate Foreign Relations Committee have responded to a call for a ban on the importation of the Chinese Panda coins.

The Secret Service makes its largest seizure of counterfeit United States Federal Reserve notes produced on a color laser photocopier July 11 in Phoenix, Ariz.

AUGUST 9

Legislation calling for the striking of $5 palladium and silver dollar coins commemorating the statehood centennial of six states and the minting of U.S. Proof sets with 90 percent silver coins passes in the United States Senate July 18.

Numismatic treasures hidden from view for decades, including selections from the

George H. Clapp collection of large cents, will be placed on public exhibition at the Carnegie Museum of Natural History in Pittsburgh Aug. 8- Oct. 18.

AUGUST 16

The King of Siam set has been sold for a price "substantially in excess of $2 million" by Stack's of New York City. The price now stands as the largest sum paid for a Proof set of U.S. coins.

Congress should establish a public enterprise revolving fund, subject to the appropriations process, to finance the United States Mint's numismatic program operations, according to a recommendation in a review of Mint operations by the General Accounting Office.

Legislation calling for a ban on importing the Chinese Panda gold bullion coins seems less likely after a New Hampshire senator indicated he would not support such a ban although his office had sent a letter to a coin dealer constituent saying that he would consider that option.

AUGUST 23

Dealers at future American Numismatic Association conventions will not have an opportunity to offer customers non-numismatic materials, after the ANA Board of Governors voted to withdraw a motion which would have permitted a change in ANA policy.

Harry X Boosel of Chicago receives the American Numismatic Association's highest honor, the Farran Zerbe Memorial Award, during ceremonies at the ANA's 98th Anniversary Convention in Pittsburgh Aug. 12.

AUGUST 30

An altered 1989 Washington quarter dollar with Mint mark removed to look like an error coin appears on the market.

Except for one, the entire Engraving Division at the Philadelphia Mint has endorsed the retention of Elizabeth Jones as Chief Sculptor-Engraver of the United States Mint. The lone holdout is John Mercanti, who has officially applied for the position held by Jones since 1981.

SEPTEMBER 6

As final selection of designs nears for the fourth commemorative coinage program using a limited, invitational design competition, details of how the United States Mint goes about choosing designs are made public.

The King of Siam set, which sold in early August for more than $2 million, is graded by the Numismatic Guaranty Corporation of America Inc. and the nine coins will soon be encapsulated by the coin grading firm.

SEPTEMBER 13

New circulating coins being phased in by South Africa over a three-year period replace larger, heavier coins now in circulation; the 2-rand note will be replaced by a coin.

About 2.5 million unsold South Korean coins of the 1988 XXIV Olympiad coin program will be melted by the Bank of Korea.

SEPTEMBER 20

A single United States coin, an 1852/1 Augustus Humbert $20 pioneer gold piece, sells for a reported $1.35 million in private transaction, breaking all previous records.

The U.S. Mint contributes $675.7 million to the General Fund of the Treasury in Fiscal Year 1988, $200 million less than FY87, according to the Annual Report of the Director of the Mint released Sept. 5.

SEPTEMBER 27

United States numismatic history could be revolutionized as a result of the discovery of thousands of U.S. and pioneer gold coins, part of a 77,000-ounce golden treasure just discovered aboard a paddle-wheel steamer sunk off the South Carolina coast in 1857.

Patriotic colors and music compliment the theme of "Financing Freedom for 200 Years" as U.S. Treasury officials and employees launch the Bicentennial of the Treasury celebration Sept. 11.

OCTOBER 4

Legislation seeking the redesign of all

circulation United States coinage, three commemorative coins to honor the 50th anniversary of the Mount Rushmore National Memorial and Fiscal Year 1990 appropriations for the U.S. Mint moves through the first session of the 101st Congress.

The Commission of Fine Arts gives its approval of designs for the 1990 Dwight D. Eisenhower commemorative silver dollar.

OCTOBER 11

Designs for the 1990 Dwight D. Eisenhower commemorative silver dollar are made public the week of Sept. 25 after having undergone a slight lettering style modification.

Introduction of new legislation that would authorize the Secretary of the Treasury to select one currently circulating U.S. coin for redesign and mandate the U.S. Mint to provide new designs for the remaining four circulating coins and then come back to Congress for permission to implement them is delayed indefinitely due to scheduling conflicts.

OCTOBER 18

Seven witnesses testifying before the House Banking Subcommittee on Consumer Affairs and Coinage Oct. 5 voice strong support for issuance of coins to commemorate the statehood centennials of six western states and the return of silver to two of the three circulating coins in a special silver Proof set.

Final but still unofficial pre-issue sales totals for 1989 Congress half eagle, silver dollar and clad half dollar coins ordered during the discount period ending July 17 show the Uncirculated half eagles with the lowest mintage so far of the three coins offered.

OCTOBER 25

It may be a year before the first gold coins recovered from the wreck of the *SS Central America* become available to collectors, but one numismatist who has seen some of the salvaged coins believes the rare coin market will be changed.

Young people get weekly encouragement to collect coins and paper

money on "Street Cents," a new television series which began Oct. 7 on Canadian Broadcasting Corporation television in Ottawa with technical and financial support from the Royal Canadian Mint.

NOVEMBER 1

Coinage production at the San Francisco Mint is halted for more than 24 hours following the Oct. 17 earthquake, but both the 1937 and 1874 facilities survive the temblor unscathed.

An amendment to the Senate's Omnibus Drug Act included provisions for the formulation of a task force to review the feasibility of printing U.S. paper money with a serial number traceable by an optical scanning device of the type used in grocery stores.

NOVEMBER 8

In an effort to evaluate printing quality, the Bureau of Engraving and Printing prints 500,000 paper money test sheets with the new anti-counterfeiting security features expected to be implemented in the early 1990s.

An employee of the Professional Coin Grading Service in Newport Beach, Calif., has been arrested and charged with the theft of an estimate $200,000 in coins submitted to the firm for grading and encapsulation.

NOVEMBER 15

The chairman of the House Subcommittee on Consumer Affairs and Coinage, Rep. Richard Lehman, D-Calif., requests that the United States General Accounting Office conduct a study concerning proposed legislation calling for a $1 coin and the phase-out of the $1 Federal Reserve note and also the phase-out of the 1-cent coin.

Minnie Mouse is the featured portrait on the new $10 denomination note in the Disney Dollars series issued by Disneyland and Walt Disney World.

NOVEMBER 22

The discovery that the 1861 Coronet, Paquet Reverse double eagle is a *piece de caprice* and not a survivor of the abortive Jan. 2-5, 1861, production run is among the revelations during the American

Numismatic Society's 1989 Coinage of the Americas Conference.

Commemorative coins honoring the 50th anniversary of the Mount Rushmore National Memorial are a step closer to reality after the Senate approves the legislation Nov. 3.

U.S. Rep. James A. Hayes, D-La., says he plans to form a non-profit organization to raise funds for expanding the display capabilities for the National Numismatic Collection at the Smithsonian Institution in time for the Bicentennial of the U.S. Mint in 1992.

NOVEMBER 29

The House Banking Subcommittee on Consumer Affairs and Coinage Nov. 16 amends H.R. 1553 by deleting provisions in the Statehood Centennial Commemorative Coin Act of 1989 which had originally called for the minting of up to 350,000 commemorative palladium coins with a new $5 denomination for a non-gold coin.

Gold coins and bars recovered from the wreck site of the *SS Central America* may go on public display for the first time in the spring, but will probably not be offered for sale until 1991.

DECEMBER 6

The nation's retail consumers may get a free lesson in mathematics, and the cent may become extinct in daily commerce, if H.R. 3761, "The Price Rounding Act of 1989," calling for the rounding of final cash transactions up or down to the nearest 5 cents gains congressional approval.

Catalina Vasquez Villalpando is confirmed as the 39th Treasurer of the United States by the full Senate Nov. 18.

DECEMBER 13

The recent conclusion that the 1861 Coronet, Paquet Reverse double eagle is an unofficially struck *piece de caprice* is taking heat from the current owner of one of the two coins, who disagrees with the revelation announced during the Nov. 4-5 Coinage of the Americas Conference.

The American Numismatic Exchange and the Numismatic Guaranty Corporation of America confirm an agreement signed Nov. 27 to allow NGC coins to trade on the Numismatic Quote System sight-unseen.

DECEMBER 20

One of the world's most complete Canadian coin collections compiled by U.S. numismatist Jean Bullen is now on display at the visitors' gallery of the Royal Canadian Mint offices in Ottawa.

A set of obverse and reverse galvanoes of the Eisenhower dollar dated 1970 is donated to the American Numismatic Association Money Museum, but the origin of the galvanoes is unclear.

DECEMBER 27

Collectors of United States paper money will have something new to collect sometime in the spring of 1990 — Federal Reserve Notes bearing the signature of the new Treasurer of the United States, Catalina Vasquez Villalpando, who was sworn into office Dec. 11.

News happenings, 1990

Date refers to Coin World issue in which the news item was published.

JANUARY 3

The Bureau of Engraving and Printing contracts with a United States firm to purchase a web intaglio press which would be the first of its kind used to produce Federal Reserve notes.

David J. Ryder is appointed Deputy Treasurer of the United States Dec. 13 by Treasury Secretary Nicholas F. Brady; Ryder succeeds Emily Ford Cooksey, who resigned Dec. 22.

JANUARY 10

Circulating United States coinage in 1990 will contain design enhancements to improve the images on the individual finished coins.

Order forms for the Proof and Uncirculated versions of the 1990 Eisenhower silver dollar are sent out beginning the first week in January to persons on the United States Mint's mailing list.

JANUARY 17

The Republic of Turkey files a civil lawsuit in the U.S. District Court of Massachusetts seeking to take possession of ancient coins known as the "Decadrachm Hoard" or the "Elmali Hoard," coins it alleges smugglers removed from Turkey in 1984.

Unknown quantities of Federal Reserve notes printed from "problem" ink have entered circulation and are exhibiting abnormal flaking of the black ink on the face side of $1 and $5 notes.

JANUARY 24

Reactions vary among collectors, coin dealers and museum curators concerning possible ramifications from a civil lawsuit filed in late December in the U.S. District Court of Massachusetts by the Republic of Turkey seeking possession of ancient coins allegedly smuggled out of that country in 1984.

Sen. Steve Symms, R-Idaho, makes an inquiry to the U.S. Senate's legislative council inquiring about the possibility of lifting the ban on importation of Soviet gold coins.

JANUARY 31

At least five record auction prices for U.S. dimes — including a choice Proof 1894-S Barber dime at $250,000 — are established during the first session of a public auction by Stack's of New York Jan. 16.

The wreck of the *SS Central America* yields its first discovery piece, a small gold ingot bearing the name Blake & Co.

FEBRUARY 7

The 300th anniversary of Henry Kelsey's exploration of the Canadian prairies is commemorated on the 25th annual commemorative silver dollar for 1990 unveiled Jan. 26 by the Royal Canadian Mint in Ottawa.

The American Numismatic Association will use the April 16-21 National Coin Week to promote the regular use of numismatics in classrooms throughout the United States, rather than sending traditional packets of buttons and information to participating coin clubs.

FEBRUARY 14

Rare coins and other collectibles would continue to be excluded from preferential treatment if President Bush's budget proposal passes unchanged by both houses of Congress.

Gold sales are down and silver sales up, according to Canadian bullion Maple Leaf coin sales figures for 1989.

FEBRUARY 21

Professional Coin Grading Service graders as of March 1 will no longer be allowed to deal in coins.

The Nelson Bunker Hunt collection of ancient coins and Greek vases and the William Herbert Hunt collection of ancient bronze artifacts and Byzantine coinage will be sold beginning June 19 in New York by Sotheby's as part of each brother's bankruptcy proceedings.

The Wall Street investment firm Merrill Lynch, Pierce Fenner & Smith files registration papers Feb. 8 with the Securities and Exchange Commission for formation of a $50 million publicly-offered limited partnership in rare United States and foreign coins, with the option to push the ceiling to $75 million.

FEBRUARY 28

The fabled King of Siam Proof set — regarded by many one of the rarest and most historical sets of coins ever struck by the United States Mint — is consigned to be auctioned May 28 by Superior Galleries.

Continental Investment Group Inc., trading adviser to the owners of the King of Siam Proof set and the 1872 Liberty Head U.S. gold pattern set, confirm Feb. 8 that both sets were recently graded and encapsulated by the Professional Coin Grading Service; the sets had previously been graded and encapsulated by the Numismatic Guaranty Corporation of America.

MARCH 7

The United States of America formally accepts its satellite Bureau of Engraving and Printing facility in ceremonies at Fort Worth, Texas, Feb. 16; notes will be distinguished by a micro-printed "FW" on the face near the check number.

Canada's 1990 $100 commemorative gold coin shows living women on both sides and an inscription in the Inuktitut language, both for the first time on a Canadian coin.

MARCH 14

Caution is in the air as testimony for six numismatic bills is heard Feb. 28 by the House Banking Subcommittee on Consumer Affairs and Coinage; Director of the Mint Donna Pope gives decisive testimony, warning that the bills are too much, too soon.

The James A. Stack Sr. specimen of the 1894-S Barber dime is acquired by a group of five investors along with a 1901-S Barber quarter dollar in a cash transaction approaching $500,000.

Japanese medalist Keiichi Uryu receives the American Numismatic Association's 1990 J. Sanford Saltus Medal award.

MARCH 21

The Federal Trade Commission is likely to continue to take an active interest in numismatics and can be expected to pursue an aggressive litigation policy in cases involving misrepresentation of value, investment potential and grading, predicts Phoebe Morse, director of the FTC's regional office in Boston.

The American Numismatic Association Board of Governors, in a closed-door executive session March 1, approve a $5.4 million operating budget for Fiscal Year 1990/91.

MARCH 28

Designs of the 1992 XVI Albertville and Savoie Winter Olympic Games coin series are revealed at a special unveiling and tour of the Olympic sites March 6-8 in France.

The effort to unite the leading numismatic organizations in the pooling of resources and creation of a comprehensive, independent entity to deal with dealer accreditation and resolve consumer complaints appears to be dead in the water, as both the Professional Numismatists Guild and the American Numismatic Association rebuff overtures to join with the Coin and Bullion Dealer Accreditation Program.

APRIL 4

A 152-year tradition in die production is coming to an end as the United States Mint plans to eliminate the practice of placing Mint marks on each individual working die by hand over the next several years, and has already done so for 1990 cents and 5-cent coins. Mint marks will be added at the master die stage.

Robert J. Leuver, former Director of the Bureau of Engraving and Printing, was the subject of two investigations by the U.S. government dealing with buying practices and fraternization with suppliers while he headed the BEP.

The American Numismatic Association explores many options, including the possibility of selling its grading service, says ANA president Kenneth L. Hallenbeck.

APRIL 11

A bill calling for a 1993 commemorative coin program honoring America's involvement in World War II is introduced March 22 by Rep. Marcy Kaptur, D-Ohio.

A national gold medal honoring Olympic track star Jesse Owens is presented to Owens' widow, Ruth, by President Bush in White House ceremonies March 28.

APRIL 18

The House Banking Subcommittee on Consumer Affairs and Coinage unanimously approves legislation April 4 authorizing a commemorative coin program to mark the 50th anniversary of the United Services Organization in 1991 but not before it agreed to a substitute amendment to reduce the number of coins, mintage and length of the program.

Patrick Magnus Bruun will receive the

Archer M. Huntington Medal Award of the American Numismatic Society.

APRIL 25

The *Coin World Comprehensive Catalog & Encyclopedia of United States Coins* is off the press.

The Industry Council for Tangible Assets lobbying effort to repeal or revise the status of Internal Revenue Service reporting regulations for coin sale transactions under Treasury Regulation 6045 receives a donation approved by the American Numismatic Association Board of Governors.

The third of four planned sales of 625,000 troy ounces each of silver from the Strategic and Critical Minerals Stockpile during Fiscal Year 1990 is scheduled for May 1 by the Department of Defense, Defense Logistics Agency.

MAY 2

Although the General Accounting Office calculates the U.S. Mint could save $2.4 million by mailing the Mint's pre-issue offerings Third Class, the Mint says such an approach would be penny wise and pound foolish.

The threat of counterfeit U.S. paper money and the awarding of sole-source contracts to suppliers by the Bureau of Engraving and Printing are hot topics at an April 18 appropriations hearing.

A report about the sale of American Numismatic Association Certification Service is "nothing more than talk," according to ANACS Director Leonard Albrecht.

MAY 9

A last-minute, walk-in consignment of a pedigreed six-piece presentation set of Proof Trade dollar patterns in the original holder is a highlight of Superior Galleries' May 27-29 "Boys Town" auction.

The New Jersey Numismatic Society seeks support from other numismatic organizations to lobby Congress to authorize a Proof coin set commemorating the Bicentennial of the United States Mint in 1992.

MAY 16

At least nine entities are in various stages of research and development into computer-assisted coin grading and others are looking into the concept, along with the possible integration of lasers and optical scanners.

MAY 23

U.S. Mint Director Donna Pope says that mintages of 1990 Proof gold and silver American Eagle bullion coins will be limited.

The United States Senate, which has passed legislation for the redesign of circulating coinage four times before, is being tempted once again — this time with an amendment to a Senate bill that calls for a medal to honor the 100th anniversary of Yosemite National Park.

United States trade negotiators will seek legislative removal of the import ban on Soviet gold coins after the signing of a new trade pact with the Soviet Union.

MAY 30

The Professional Coin Grading Service of Newport Beach, Calif., unveils its computer-assisted grading breakthrough in a demonstration May 16.

A Mount Rushmore commemorative coin program is within striking distance of becoming law and a bill for a commemorative coin program for the 50th anniversary of the United Services Organization has jumped a major hurdle.

The advisory committee overseeing the American Numismatic Association Certification Service unanimously approves a resolution "strongly opposing the sale of ANACS."

JUNE 6

The idea of replacing the $1 Federal Reserve note with a dollar coin, which can be traced back to the 1920s, resurfaces in Washington in the for of legislation before Congress and an investigation recently completed by the General Accounting Office.

The full Senate for the fifth time since 1988 passes legislation authorizing the redesign of U.S. circulating coinage during a May 23 voice vote, as an amendment to a bill seeking medals commemorating Yosemite National Park.

CompuGrade, a New Orleans-based numismatic research and development company, expects to be able to provide computer grading and encapsulation of Mint State Morgan dollars, and possibly two other coin series, by the last quarter of 1990.

JUNE 13

Auction price records fall during the three-day, seven-session Superior Galleries May 27-29 auction as the sale tops $19.6 million, a record for a single numismatic auction.

Iraj Sayah and Terry Brand join to purchase the King of Siam Proof set for $2.9 million.

Though Congress is faced with legislation that would stop the minting of the cent and half dollar, a spokesman for the General Accounting Office says an investigation he conducted found "no compelling reason" to eliminate them.

JUNE 20

The American Numismatic Association agrees to sell the ANA Certification Service to Amos Press Inc. in Sidney, Ohio, for $1.5 million and as much as $3 million in royalties over the next five years.

Olympic athletes may be the beneficiaries of the coin collector's pocket if a new commemorative coin bill calling for a $5 gold coin and a silver dollar for the 1992 Olympic Games wins the favor of Congress.

Salomon Brothers Inc.'s portfolio of rare coins drops one position to fourth place in the company's annual survey of investments released June 4.

JUNE 27

Although technical topics related to more efficient and economical production of circulation coins dominates the formal sessions of the 16th Mint Directors' Conference June 3-6, concern for maintaining and expanding markets for numismatic and bullion products seems ever-present in informal discussions.

The federal and state court systems are honored as the "dual guardians of the rights of all citizens under the law" on the 1990 commemorative medal designed by Marcel Jovine and issued by the United States Capitol Historical Society in Washington, D.C.

Obituaries

1987 Obituaries
Date refers to Coin World issue in which the news item was published.

JANUARY 14

Dr. J. Hewitt Judd, 87, author of *United States Pattern, Experimental and Trial Pieces*.

MARCH 25

Clement F. Bailey, 66, numismatic journalist.

APRIL 8

Esther Lasure Gaver, 62, former president of Collectors Research.

APRIL 29

Lee F. Hewitt, founder of *Numismatic Scrapbook* magazine.

MAY 6

Virgil Hancock, 84, past president and four-term governor of the American Numismatic Association.

JULY 29

Morris Bram, 78, president of the American Israel Numismatic Association.

AUGUST 19

Arthur Sipe, 83, prominent Pennsylvania numismatist and past president of the American Numismatic Association.

AUGUST 26

Dr. James O. Sloss, 73, a nationally-known numismatist.

SEPTEMBER 23

Edwin O. Neuce, 65, former Coin World news editor and former editor of Linn's Stamp News.

SEPTEMBER 30

Joseph Hugo Serrano, 74, Coin World cartoonist.

NOVEMBER 18

Alfred Charley, 57, internationally acclaimed sculptor and medalist.

DECEMBER 23

Christopher E. Blunt, 83, numismatic scholar and British banker.

1988 Obituaries

Date refers to Coin World issue in which the news item was published.

JANUARY 20

Glenn Smedley, 85, officer and staff member of the American Numismatic Association; Dec. 31 in Colorado Springs, Colo.

JANUARY 27

Paul Marvin, 79, pioneer in the numismatic error field and co-author of *The Design Cud* (1979), the definitive volume concerning the subject; Dec. 31 in Van Wert, Ohio.

FEBRUARY 10

Leon "Lee" Grossman, 68, numismatist and author; Jan. 22 in San Antonio, Texas.

MARCH 16

Adelbert P. "Del" Bertschy, 91, Wisconsin numismatist; Feb. 22 in Milwaukee.

Robert L. Wilson, 57, Oklahoma coin dealer; Feb. 23 in Enid, Okla.

MARCH 30

Freeman Lee Craig Sr., 68, collector and researcher; March 4 in San Antonio, Texas.

APRIL 6

F. Morton Reed, 75, numismatic author, illustrator and collector; March 19 in Wooster, Ohio.

APRIL 13

Herbert J. Erlanger, 82, numismatist; Feb. 29 in New York City.

W. Laird Townsend, 77, Colorado collector; March 2 in Fort Collins, Colo.

APRIL 20

Elliott L. Goldberg, 59, New England numismatist; March 31 in Dedham, Mass.

JULY 6

James Norman Schultz, 95, coin dealer and longest continuous member of the American Numismatic Association; June 16 in Salt Lake City.

Byron F. Johnson, 57, former American Numismatic Association governor; June 14 in Seattle.

JULY 13

C.P. Wogoman, 74, president of the Long Beach Coin Club; May 27 in Long Beach, Calif.

AUGUST 3

Edmund Ware May, 83, founding member of the Orders & Medals Society of Northern California; May 29 in San Mateo, Calif.

AUGUST 24

Morton J. Zerder, 66, professional numismatist, writer, speaker and American Israel Numismatic Association stalwart; July 1.

SEPTEMBER 7

Walter Alcott, 50, California dealer in physical documents and Americana; Aug. 1 in California.

SEPTEMBER 21

Leonor K. Sullivan, 86, former chairman of the Subcommittee on Consumer Affairs of the House Banking and Currency Committee; Aug. 31 in St. Louis.

Donald H. DeLue, 90, medallic artist and sculptor; Aug. 26 in Red Bank, N.J.

SEPTEMBER 28

Alan H. Bible, 78, Nevada senator who led the fight to ban coin collecting to prevent a national shortage of pocket change; Sept. 12 in Auburn, Calif.

OCTOBER 5

Louis Irwin, 68, coin and stamp dealer; Aug. 16 in Lyndhurst, Ohio.

NOVEMBER 9

Henrietta Spitz Kagin, 71, wife of Arthur M. Kagin; Oct. 19 in Rochester, Minn.

NOVEMBER 23

Richard S. Yeoman, 84, numismatist and author known as "Mr. Red Book"; Nov. 9 in Tucson, Ariz.

Herbert M. Bergen, 91, former American Numismatic Association president; Nov. 1 in Fullerton, Calif.

DECEMBER 7

Edward M. Meister, 74, 52-year member of the American Numismatic Association; Oct. 18 in Bergenfield, N.J.

DECEMBER 21

Leonard Overcash Jr., 47, secretary-treasurer of the Love Token Society; Nov. 4 in Chicago.

Samuel Fisher, 80, Los Angeles coin dealer; Nov. 21 in Los Angeles.

DECEMBER 28

Barbara Hyde, 73, medallic sculptor and numismatist; Dec. 10 in Rochester, Minn.

1989 Obituaries

Date refers to Coin World issue in which the news item was published.

JANUARY 4

Paul Snedaker, 80, numismatist and founding member of the San Francisco Coin Club; Dec. 9 in San Francisco.

Abram Belskie, 81, award-winning medalist and sculptor; Nov. 17 in Westwood, N.J.

FEBRUARY 8

Salvador Dali, 84, surrealist painter, illustrator, sculptor and designer of a number of art medals; Jan. 23 in Figueras, Spain.

FEBRUARY 22

Lena Bram, 78, widow of American Israel Numismatic Association founder Morris Bram; Jan. 21 in Tamarac, Fla.

MARCH 1

Richard P. Breaden, 79, librarian of the American Numismatic Society from 1948-66; Oct. 20 in Smithfield, N.C.

APRIL 12

Melvin Owen Warns, 86, national bank note collector and founding member of the Society of Paper Money Collectors; Feb. 25 in Milwaukee.

Eldridge Jones, 76, former treasurer and governor of the American Numismatic Association; March 25 in Tacoma Park, Md.

MAY 3

William H. Brett, 95, Director of the United States Mint during the Eisenhower administration; April 10 in Palm Desert, Calif.

MAY 10

Nancy M. Waggoner, former curator of Greek coins for the American Numismatic Society; April 10 in Rye, N.Y.

MAY 24

Janice Martin, 68, Florida coin dealer; April 23 in Fort Lauderdale, Fla.

JUNE 7

Gilvin "Corky" Ayers, 74, president of the Numismatic Association of Southern California; May 20 in Pomona, Calif.

JUNE 21

William C. Henderson, 73, former treasurer of the American Numismatic Association; June 5 in Colorado Springs, Colo.

JULY 5

Calme L. Lazard, 83, Louisiana coin dealer; June 1 in New Orleans.

AUGUST 2

Glenn E. Jackson, 83, paper money collector, researcher and writer; July 14 in Watertown, Conn.

AUGUST 9

Miguel L. Muñoz, 80, world-renowned numismatist, researcher and scholar; July 6 in Mexico City.

SEPTEMBER 13

William F. Swagler, 67, vice president of the Baltimore Coin Club; Aug. 20 in Fullerton, Md.

OCTOBER 4

Matthew H. Rothert Sr., 85, prime mover in adding "In God We Trust" to U.S. paper money; Sept. 18 in Camden, Ark.

NOVEMBER 8

Martin R. Brown, 78, co-author of *A Guide to the Grading of United States Coins*; Oct. 21 in Oklahoma City, Okla.

NOVEMBER 22

Robert Eugene "Gene" Medlar Jr., 43, Texas coin dealer; Nov. 3 in San Antonio.

1990 Obituaries

Date refers to Coin World issue in which the news item was published.

JANUARY 24

Benjamin Odesser, 78, charter member No. 9 of the Token and Medal Society; Jan. 10 in Skokie, Ill.

FEBRUARY 28

Cüneyt Olcer, president of the Turkish Numismatic Society; Feb. 2.

MARCH 7

Charles M. Wormser, 78, former president of the New Netherlands Coin Company; Feb. 10 in Hamden, Conn.

MARCH 28

Hans M.F. Schulman, 76, numismatist, coin dealer and *Coin World* contributor; March 8 in New York City.

Harry Strayer, 62, Florida numismatist and coin dealer; March 9 in Palm Coast, Fla.

APRIL 11

Nathan Bromberg, 71, West Coast numismatist; March 17 in Whittier, Calif.

Joseph A. Clarke, 74, 1987 recipient of the American Numismatic Association's Medal of Merit; March 22.

APRIL 18

Joseph F. Person, 69, Florida coin dealer; March 15 in St. Petersburg, Fla.

JUNE 13

Roger S. Cohen Jr., 63, half cent specialist; May 26 in Bethesda, Md.

Numismatics and Washington

2

Senate

Phone numbers
(All numbers Area Code 202)

Information, Capitol Switchboard (office telephone and room numbers)........... 224-3121
Senate Information 224-2115
Senate Locator Office (individual's phone number).. 224-3207
Bill Clerk (for bill status try Office of Legislation first)....................................224-2120
Cloakroom — Democratic (tape of floor action and scheduling information) 224-8541
Cloakroom — Democratic (Assistant Secretary for the Majority) 224-4691
Cloakroom — Republican (tape of floor action and scheduling information) 224-8601
Cloakroom — Republican (Assistant Secretary for the Minority)......................224-6391
Daily Digest (chamber action, committee meetings as in back of *Record*)........ 224-2658
Document Room (copies of bills, reports, public laws, calendars, etc.) 224-7860
Document Room (recorded requests)..224-1356
Enrolling Clerk (whether bill has been signed, sent to the White House)........... 224-6250
Executive Clerk (status of treaties and nominations).. 224-4341
Legislative Information (bill status — first place to call) 224-2971
Librarian (legislative history, general reference) 224-7106
National Association of Manufacturers (tape of legislative activity).................. 626-3900
Periodical Press Gallery.. 224-0265
Press Gallery 224-0241
Radio-Television Gallery 224-6421
Secretary of the Senate (calendars, membership rosters, etc.)............................ 224-2115

Senate office buildings

Senate Dirksen Office Building, Constitution Ave. between 1st St. and 2nd St., NE, Washington, D.C. 20510

Senate Hart Office Building, 2nd St. and Constitution Ave., NE, Washington, D.C. 20510

Senate Russell OB, Constitution Ave., between Delaware Ave. and 1st St., NE. Washington, D.C. 20510

Immigration and Naturalization Building, 119 D St., NE, Washington, D.C. 20510

Plaza Hotel (offices), 331 1st St., NE, Washington, D.C. 20510

190 D. St, NE, Washington, D.C. 20510

400 North Capitol St., NW, Washington, D.C. 20510

House of Representatives

Phone numbers
(All numbers Area Code 202)

Information, Capitol Switchboard (office telephone and room numbers).......... 224-3121
Personnel Locator in the House Finance Office (individual's phone number)... 225-6515
Bill Clerk (for bill status try Office of Legislation first) 225-4470
Cloakroom — Democratic (updated tape of current House floor action)........... 225-7400
Cloakroom — Democratic (legislative program, upcoming floor schedule)...... 225-1600
Cloakroom — Democratic (manager) 225-7330
Cloakroom — Democratic (messages) 225-0466
Cloakroom — Republican (updated tape of current House floor action)........... 225-7430
Cloakroom — Republican (legislative program, upcoming floor schedule)...... 225-2020
Cloakroom — Republican (manager)..225-7350
Daily Digest (chamber action, committee meetings as in back of *Record*)........ 225-2868
Enrolling Clerk (Whether bill has been signed, sent to the White House)......... 225-5848
House Document Room (copies of bills, reports, public laws, calendars, etc.).. 225-3456
House Librarian (legislative history) 225-0462
House Press Gallery 225-3945
National Association of Manufacturers (tape of legislative activity)................. 626-3900
Office of Legislative Information (bill status - first place to call)...................... 225-1772
Periodical Press Gallery.. 225-2941
Radio-Television Gallery 225-5214

House office buildings

Cannon House Office Building, Independence Ave. between C St. and 1st St., SE, Washington, D.C. 20515
Longworth House Office Building, Independence Ave. between C St. and South Capitol St., SE, Washington, D.C. 20515
Rayburn House Office Building, Independence Ave. between South Capitol St. and 1st St., SW, Washington, D.C. 20515
Annex 1, 300 New Jersey Ave., SE, Washington, D.C. 20515
Annex 2, 2nd St. and D St., SW, Washington, D.C. 20515
Annex 3, New Jersey Ave. and E St., SE, Washington, D.C. 20515

Senate Committee on Banking, Housing and Urban Affairs

Bills introduced to the Senate concerning coinage and other numismatic subjects are referred to the Senate Committee on Banking, Housing and Urban Affairs.

Consisting of 21 Senators, the committee is referred all proposed legislation, messages, petitions, memorials and other matters related to the following subjects:

1) Banks, banking and financial institutions. 2) Control of prices of commodities, rents and services. 3) Deposit insurance. 4) Economic stabilization and defense production. 5) Export and foreign trade promotion. 6) Export controls. 7) Federal monetary policy, including Federal Reserve System. 8) Financial aid to commerce and industry. 9) Issuance and redemption of notes. 10) Money and credit, including currency and coinage. 11) Nursing home construction. 12) Public and private housing (including veterans' housing). 13) Renegotiation of government contracts. 14) Urban development and urban mass transit.

Chairman .... Sen. Donald W. Riegle, D-Mich.
Ranking minority member .... Sen. Jake Garn, R-Utah

534 Senate Dirksen Office Building .... (202) 224-7391
Staff Director .... Kevin C. Gottlieb .... (202) 224-7391
Minority Staff Director .... W. Lamar Smith .... (202) 224-1575

House Committee on Banking, Finance and Urban Affairs

Bills introduced to the House concerning coinage and other numismatic subjects are referred to the House Committee on Banking, Finance and Urban Affairs, specifically to the Subcommittee on Consumer Affairs and Coinage.

The 50-member committee's scope includes: 1) Banks and banking, including deposit insurance and federal monetary policy. 2) Money and credit, including currency and the issuance of notes and redemption thereof; gold and silver, including the coinage thereof; valuation and revaluation of the dollar. 3) Urban development. 4) Public and private housing. 5) Economic stabilization, defense production, renegotiation, and control of the price of commodities, rents and services. 6) International finance. 7) Financial aid to commerce and industry (other than transportation). 8) International financial and monetary organizations.

The Chairman and Ranking Minority Member are ex officio members of all subcommittees.

Chairman .... Rep. Henry B. Gonzalez, D-Texas
Ranking minority member .... Rep. Chalmers P. Wylie, R-Ohio

Majority Staff
2129 Rayburn House Office Building .... (202) 225-4247
Clerk and Staff Director .... Kelsay R. Meek .... (202) 225-7057

Minority Staff
B-301C Rayburn House Office Building .... (202) 225-7502
Staff Director and General Counsel ...... Anthony F. Cole .... (202) 225-7502

Subcommittee on Consumer Affairs and Coinage
Chairman .... Rep. Richard Lehman, D-Calif.
Ranking minority member .... Rep. John P. Hiler, R-Ind.
Staff Director .... Scott H. Nishioki 604 Annex 1   (202) 225-8872
Source: Congressional Staff Directory

Effective letters to Washington

Because senators and representatives rely in large part on the opinions of their constituents for direction in voting on legislation, it is important to make your voice heard in Congress.

There are several ways to inform your elected representatives. One way is to visit personally, but in session he is likely to have a tight schedule, and it is difficult for most people to travel to Washington, D.C. You can also place a telephone call, and the information numbers for both House and Senate are included in this chapter for that reason, but it can be extremely difficult to catch him free in his office in session. Personal visits and phone calls are possible when the congressman is home during recess, but then issues are not timely.

The most effective voice you can have in Congress, therefore, is by way of a well-written personal letter. Some letters are more effective than others in influencing your senator or representative's vote, however. Following are some tips on how to write an effective letter to your elected representatives to maximize your influence on his voting.

• Know your congressman's full name and spell it correctly. Guessed-at or incorrect spelling sends a signal that you are not well-informed and your letter will carry little weight. Proper forms of address are included for both the House and Senate.

• Identify yourself at the head of the letter by name, mailing address, and phone number if you wish. This will help your congressman if he should wish to communicate with you on the issue in the future.

• Use plain stationery or personal letterhead. Use business or organization letterhead only if you officially represent its opinion.

• Be concise. Keep the letter to one typed, double-spaced page if possible. Don't hesitate to go longer than that if necessary, but the shorter the letter, the more likely your congressman will pay close attention to it.

• If you can't type the letter, use clear handwriting on ruled paper and double-space it. Use ball-point pens rather than felt tips or pencils, as these tend to smudge. Neatness counts.

• Identify the measure or bill by number when possible. Also include the name of the bill and be specific as to its content or subject. A letter concerning a measure the congressman cannot identify is useless.

• State your position or opinion clearly and at the beginning of the letter. Don't waste time with personal chit-chat; get to the point. Stating your case first will get the congressman's attention and help him classify your vote as for or against the measure.

• Having gotten to the point, stay there. If you have comments on more than one issue, separate letters will be more effective. By no means include impertinent facts or opinions on non-related matters. If you want to comment on coin legislation, don't bring up aid to foreign countries.

• Include any reasons why you hold a certain stance on an issue. Knowing why you think the way you do is as important to the congressman as knowing what side of the issue you are on. Again, keep to the issue at hand. Include a brief statement on how an issue would affect the congressman's constituency. He listens to voters in his home district.

• Be polite and sincere. Anger, sarcasm and flattery will subtract from the weight your voice carries.

• Finally, sign your name in your own handwriting, and follow that with your city and state. Use your voice in Congress to your best advantage.

Federal Trade Commission

Pennsylvania Ave. at 6th St. NW, Washington, D.C. 20580.

Phone (Public Affairs)	**(202) 326-2180**
Chairman	Janet D. Steiger
Commissioner	Terry Calvani
Commissioner	Mary Azcuenaga
Commissioner	Andrew J. Strenio Jr.
Commissioner	Deborah K. Owen
Secretary	Donald S. Clark
General Counsel	James Spears
Executive Director	Robert S. Walton III
Acting Director, Office of Public Affairs	Marvin Lieberman
Bureau of Consumer Protection Director	Barry J. Cutler

The Federal Trade Commission was organized as an independent administrative agency in 1951, pursuant to the Federal Trade Commission Act of 1914.

The basic objective of the Commission is the maintenance of strongly competitive enterprise as the keystone of the American economic system. Although the duties of the Commission are many and varied under law, the foundation of public policy underlying all these duties is essentially the same: to prevent the free enterprise system from being stifled, substantially lessened or fettered by monopoly or restraints on trade, or corrupted by unfair or deceptive trade practices.

The FTC has in recent years taken an active role in policing the rare coin business, especially as it relates to telemarketing and coin grading.

The Commission is charged with keeping competition both free and fair. Part of the FTC's responsibility is the enforcement of the Hobby Protection Act (See Chapter 3 for details).

This basic purpose finds its primary expression in the Federal Trade Commission Act, cited above, and the Clayton Act, both passed in 1914 and both successively amended in the years that have followed. The Federal Trade Commission Act lays down a general prohibition against the use in commerce of "unfair methods of competition" and "unfair or deceptive acts or practices." The Clayton Act outlaws specific practices recognized as instruments of monopoly.

As an administrative agency, acting quasi-judicially and quasi-legislatively, the Commission was established to deal with trade practices on a continuing and corrective basis. It has no authority to punish; its function is to prevent, through cease-and-desist orders and other means, those practices condemned by the law of federal trade regulation; however, court-ordered civil penalties up to $10,000 may be obtained for each violation of a commission order.

Sources of information

PUBLICATIONS

A copy of the "Federal Trade Commission — List of Publications," which lists publications of interest to the general public, is available free upon application to the Division of Legal and Public Records, Federal Trade Commission, Washington, D.C. 20580.

CONSUMER PROTECTION, RESTRAINT OF TRADE INFORMATION, AND COMPLAINTS

For information about consumer protection, restraint of trade questions, or to register a complaint, should contact the nearest Federal Trade Commission office.

FEDERAL TRADE COMMISSION REGIONAL OFFICES

Telephone and Address Listings

ATLANTA, Room 1000, 1718 Peachtree St. NW., Atlanta, Ga. 30367. Phone (404) 347-4836. Serves Alabama, Florida, Georgia, Mississippi, North Carolina, South Carolina, Tennessee, Virginia.

BOSTON, Room 1184, 10 Causeway St., Boston, Mass. 02222. Phone (617) 565-7240. Serves Connecticut, Maine, Massachusetts, New Hampshire, Rhode Island, Vermont.

CHICAGO, Suite 1437, 55 E. Monroe St., Chicago, Ill. 60603. Phone (312) 353-4423. Serves Illinois, Indiana, Iowa, Kentucky, Minnesota, Missouri, Wisconsin.

CLEVELAND, 520 A, 668 Euclid Ave., Cleveland, Ohio 44144. Phone (216) 522-4210. Serves Michigan, western New York, Ohio, Pennsylvania, West Virginia, Delaware, Maryland.

DALLAS, Suite 500, 100 North Central Expressway, Dallas, Texas 75247. Phone (214) 767-5503. Serves Arkansas, Louisiana, New Mexico, Oklahoma, Texas.

DENVER, Room 2900, 1405 Curtis St., Denver, Colo. 80202. Phone (303) 844-2271. Serves Colorado, Kansas, Montana, Nebraska, North Dakota, South Dakota, Utah, Wyoming.

LOS ANGELES, 11000 Wilshire Blvd., Los Angeles, Calif. 90024. Phone (213) 209-7890. Serves Arizona, southern California.

NEW YORK, Room 2243, Federal Building, 26 Federal Plaza, New York, N.Y. 10278. Phone (212) 264-1207. Serves New Jersey, eastern New York.

SAN FRANCISCO, Suite 570, 901 Market St., San Francisco, Calif. 94103. Phone (415) 995-5220. Serves northern California, Hawaii, Nevada.

SEATTLE, Room 2806, Federal Building, 915 Second Ave., Seattle, Wash. 98174. Phone (206) 442-4656. Serves Alaska, Idaho, Oregon, Washington.

For further information, contact the Director, Office of Public Affairs, Federal Trade Commission, Pennsylvania Avenue at Sixth Street NW., Washington, D.C. 20580. Phone (202) 326-2183.

Federal Bureau of Investigation
Ninth St. and Pennsylvania Ave. NW, Washington, D.C. 20535
Phone (202) 324-3444

Director...William S. Sessions

The Federal Bureau of Investigation (FBI) is a division of the Department of Justice, headed by the Attorney General.

The FBI is charged with investigating all violations of federal laws with the exception of those which have been assigned by legislative enactment or otherwise to some other federal agency.

The FBI's jurisdiction includes a wide range of responsibilities in the criminal, civil, and security fields. Among these are major numismatic thefts, extortion, bank robbery, and interstate transportation of stolen property. Cooperative services of the FBI for other duly authorized law enforcement agencies include fingerprint identification, laboratory services, police training and the National Crime Information Center.

In early 1989, the FBI launched a computerized network to aid law enforcement agencies in tracking stolen coins. Based at the FBI Laboratory in Washington, D.C., the National Stolen Coin File was established with the expertise of the American Numismatic Association and greatly improves the recovery possibilities of stolen coins. Only law enforcement agencies may access the file.

For more information about the system or for copies of the filing form, local law enforcement agencies may write to: Director, Federal Bureau of Investigation, Laboratory Division, ATTN: National Stolen Coin File, 10th and Pennsylvania Ave. NW, Washington, D.C. 20535, or call (202) 324-4434.

Field Divisions — Federal Bureau of Investigation

Division	Address	Office Phone
Alabama		
Birmingham, Ala. 35203.........	Room 1400, 2121 Building....................	(205) 252-7705
Mobile, Ala. 36602	One St. Louis Centre............................	(205) 438-3674
Alaska		
Anchorage, Alaska 99513	222 W. 7th Ave.	(907) 276-4441
Arizona		
Phoenix, Ariz. 85012...............	201 E. Indianola	(602) 279-5511
Arkansas		
Little Rock, Ark. 72211	10825 Financial Parkway......................	(501) 221-9100

California
Los Angeles, Calif. 90024	11000 Wilshire Blvd.	(213) 477-6565
Sacramento, Calif. 95825	2800 Cottage Way	(916) 481-9110
San Diego, Calif. 92188	880 Front St.	(619) 231-1122
San Francisco, Calif. 94102	450 Golden Gate Ave.	(415) 553-7400

Colorado
Denver, Colo. 80202	Federal Office Bldg.	(303) 629-7171

Connecticut
New Haven, Conn. 06510	150 Court St.	(203) 777-6311

District of Columbia
Washington, D.C. 20535	1900 Half St. SW	(202) 324-3000

Florida
Jacksonville, Fla. 32211	7820 Arlington Expressway	(904) 721-1211
Miami, Fla. 33169	16320 NW Second Ave.	(305) 944-9101
Tampa, Fla. 33602	Room 610, 500 Zack St., Federal Office Bldg.	(813) 228-7661

Georgia
Atlanta, Ga. 30303	77 Forsyth St. SW	(404) 521-3900
Savannah, Ga. 31405	5401 Paulsen St.	(912) 354-9911

Hawaii
Honolulu, Hawaii 96850	Kalanianaole Federal Office Bldg.	(808) 521-1411

Illinois
Chicago, Ill. 60604	Everett McKinley Dirksen Federal Office Bldg.	(312) 431-1333
Springfield, Ill. 62702	535 W. Jefferson St.	(217) 522-9675

Indiana
Indianapolis, Ind. 46204	575 N. Pennsylvania St.	(317) 639-3301

Kentucky
Louisville, Ky. 40202	600 Federal Pl.	(502) 583-3941

Louisiana
New Orleans, La. 70112	1250 Poydras St.	(504) 522-4671

Maryland
Baltimore, Md. 21207	7142 Ambassador Rd.	(301) 265-8080

Massachusetts
Boston, Mass. 02203	John F. Kennedy Federal Office Bldg...	(617) 742-5533

Michigan
Detroit, Mich. 48226	Patrick V. McNamara Federal Office Bldg.	(313) 965-2323

Minnesota
Minneapolis, Minn. 55401	392 Federal Bldg.	(612) 339-7861

Mississippi
Jackson, Miss. 39269	100 W. Capitol St.	(601) 948-5000

Missouri
Kansas City, Mo. 64106	300 U.S. Courthouse Bldg.	(816) 221-6100
St. Louis, Mo. 63103	1520 Market St.	(314) 241-5357

Montana
Butte, Mont. 59702 .... U.S. Courthouse and Federal Bldg. .... (406) 782-2304

Nebraska
Omaha, Neb. 68102 .... 215 N. 17th St. .... (402) 348-1210

Nevada
Las Vegas, Nev. 89104 .... 700 East Charlston Blvd. .... (702) 385-1281

New Jersey
Newark, N.J. 07102 .... Gateway 1, Market St. .... (201) 622-5613

New Mexico
Albuquerque, N. M. 87102 ..... 301 Grand Ave. NE................................ (505) 247-1555

New York
Albany, N.Y. 12201-1219 .... 502 U.S. Post Office and Courthouse .... (518) 465-7551
Buffalo, N.Y. 14202................ 111 W. Huron St. .... (716) 856-7800
New York, N.Y. 10278 .... 26 Federal Plaza .... (212) 553-2700

North Carolina
Charlotte, N.C. 28217 .... 6010 Kenley Lane. .... (704) 529-1030

Ohio
Cincinnati, Ohio 45202 .... Federal Building, 550 Main St. .... (513) 421-4310
Cleveland, Ohio 44199............ 1240 E. 9th St.. (216) 522-1400

Oklahoma
Oklahoma City, Okla. 73118 .. 50 Penn Pl. .... (405) 842-7471

Oregon
Portland, Ore. 97201 .... Crown Plaza Bldg., 1500 SW First Ave. (503) 224-4181

Pennsylvania
Philadelphia, Pa. 19106.......... 600 Arch St. .... (215) 629-0800
Pittsburgh, Pa. 15222 .... 1000 Liberty Ave. .... (412) 471-2000

Puerto Rico
San Juan, P.R. 00918............... Room 526, U.S. Courthouse and Federal
Office Bldg., Hato Rey, P.R................... (809) 754-6000

South Carolina
Columbia, S.C. 29201 .... 1835 Assembly St. .... (803) 254-3011

Tennessee
Knoxville, Tenn. 37901........... 710 Locust St. .... (615) 544-0715
Memphis, Tenn. 38103............ 167 N. Main St. .... (901) 525-7373

Texas
Dallas, Texas 75202 .... 1801 N. Lamar .... (214) 720-2200
El Paso, Texas 79901 .... 700 E. San Antonio Ave. .... (915) 533-7451
Houston, Texas 77002 .... 2500 East T.C. Jester............................... (713) 224-1511
San Antonio, Texas 78205 ...... 615 E. Houston.. (512) 225-6741

Utah
Salt Lake City, Utah 84138..... 125 S. State St. .... (801) 355-7521

Virginia
Norfolk, Va. 23510 .... 200 Granby Mall...................................... (804) 623-3111
Quantico, Va. 22135................ FBI Academy .... (703) 640-6131
Richmond, Va. 23220 .... 200 W. Grace St....................................... (804) 644-2631

Washington
Seattle, Wash. 98174 .... Room 710, 915 Second Ave., Federal
Office Bldg. .... (206) 622-0460
Wisconsin
Milwaukee, Wis. 53202 .... 517 E. Wisconsin Ave. .... (414) 276-4684

General Services Administration
General Services Bldg., 18th and F streets NW, Washington, D.C. 20405
Phone (202) 566-0705

Administrator of General Services .... Richard G. Austin

The General Services Administration (GSA) establishes policy and provides an economical and efficient system for the management of the government's property and records, including construction and operation of buildings, procurement and distribution of supplies, utilization and disposal of property, transportation, traffic, and communications management, stockpiling of strategic materials, and the management of the government-wide resources program.

Numismatically, the GSA is best known for its sales of precious metals. Beginning in April 1968, and continuing through November 1970, the GSA sold silver on the market of varying fineness and amounts.

The same law authorizing the Eisenhower dollar, signed Dec. 31, 1970, authorized the GSA to sell the 2.9 million silver dollars in the vaults of the Treasury. The Carson City specimens went on sale on a bid basis beginning Oct. 31, 1972, and continued through Oct. 31, 1973. In 1980, the GSA administered a sale of nearly 1 million Carson City silver dollars. On Oct. 14, 1981, the GSA began weekly sales of 1.25 million troy ounces of silver from the National Defense Strategic and Critical Materials Stockpile in the form of 1,000-ounce bars, with expected total disposal of 46.5 million ounces (see SILVER CHRONOLOGY, Chapter 13).

In Fiscal Year 1990, four sales of 625,000 troy ounces each, or 2.5 million ounces of stockpile silver, were planned. Another 2.5 million ounces was to be offered in Fiscal Year 1991. The sales consist of silver of various finenesses held at San Francisco and West Point, in bars weighing between 450 and 1,100 ounces each. Minimum bids are for at least 6,000 ounces.

Some members of Congress, especially from states with heavy silver mining industry, oppose the "dumping" of stockpile silver. They contend that such a flood dampens the market for new silver. As an alternative, they prefer "slow-release" programs by mandating the use of stockpile silver in coinage programs. Congress has mandated the use of stockpile silver in such coins as the George Washington commemorative, issued in 1982 and the silver dollar coin issued to mark the 1984 Olympic Games in Los Angeles.

Then in 1986, the Ellis Island silver dollar was issued to mark the 100th anniversary of the Statue of Liberty. Authorizing legislation allowed for 10 million of the coins to be issued. Included in that legislation was authorization for a 1-ounce silver bullion dollar coin to be issued later that year.

Both coins were mandated to use stockpile silver but while the Ellis Island coin was released for a limited time the bullion coin, later named the American Eagle, has an unlimited mintage. Through early 1990, about 30 million ounces of silver had been sold through the American Eagle bullion program. The open-ended program could provide an even larger decrease in the stockpile.

GSA consists of operating services and supporting staff offices, with functions carried out at three levels of organization: the central office, regional offices, and field activities. Operations are administered largely by the regional and field offices.

The General Services Administration was established by Section 101 of the Federal Property and Administrative Services Act of 1949, effective July 1, 1949. The act consolidated and transferred to the agency a variety of real and personal property and related functions formerly assigned to various agencies.

Subsequent laws and executive orders assigned other related functions and programs.

For further information concerning the General Services Administration, contact the Director of Information, General Services Administration, Washington, D.C. 20405. Phone (202) 566-1231.

National Archives and Records Administration

Constitution between 7th and 9th streets NW, Washington, D.C. 20408

Information ....(202) 501-5525
Recorded events and lectures..(202) 501-5000
Archivist of the United States .... Don W. Wilson
Deputy Archivist of the United States .... Claudine J. Weiher

The Declaration of Independence, the Constitution, and the Bill of Rights, as well as other exhibits depicting the history of the nation, are on display for visitors to the National Archives Building.

Functions and activities

ARCHIVAL PROGRAM

The National Archives and Records Administration, performs a variety of functions relating to the preservation, use, and disposition of the records of the U.S. Government. In the National Archives Building and regional branches, NARA preserves and makes available for further government use and for private research the nation's records of enduring value, both textual and audiovisual.

Among its other activities are the administration of a regional network of storage-type facilities for non-archival records, operation of the Presidential library system and a government records management program, and publication of legislative, regulatory, and other widely used materials.

In addition to furnishing information about the nature and extent of the records in the custody of the Archivist and the conditions under which they may be used, NARA also supplies data from the records themselves. Persons who come to the National Archives Building and the Archives branches in the regional records centers to use the records are assisted in every way possible. Insofar as personnel are available, guides, inventories, lists, and indexes are prepared and they are made available. A trained reference staff is ready to aid researchers in finding and using the material desired. NARA is equipped to provide photographs, photostats, or microfilm copies of documents to investigators.

RECORDS MANAGEMENT

NARA maintains liaison with federal agencies to improve the management and the quality of records created by the government; to facilitate prompt and orderly disposition of inactive records; and to improve the usefulness of those that may be offered to the Archivist for preservation.

Upon request, advice and technical assistance is given on organizing records management programs and establishing schedules and procedures for the retirement of records no longer needed currently. Evaluations of the record creation, maintenance, and disposition practices of federal agencies are made and agencies may request guidance and assistance in their paperwork problems.

FEDERAL RECORDS CENTERS

Federal Records Centers are maintained to store and service noncurrent records of federal agencies and historically valuable regional records of the National Archives of the United States. Federal Records Centers also provide reimbursable microfilming service for federal agencies.

PUBLISHING LAWS AND PRESIDENTIAL DOCUMENTS

Federal legislation consists of both the acts of Congress and "regulations" which government agencies have issued under authority delegated by the Congress. Acts of Congress are published immediately upon issuance in slip law form and are cumulated and published for each session of Congress in the "United States Statutes at Large."

All current Presidential proclamations and Executive orders and regulations of government agencies having general applicability and legal effect are published in the Federal Register which appears five times a week. At least annually, all regulations in force are published in codified form in the Code of Federal Regulations.

Presidential speeches, news conferences, messages, and other materials made public by the White House are published currently in the "Weekly Compilation of Presidential Documents" and annually in the "Public Papers of the Presidents." Further information on federal agencies is provided in the annual United States Government Manual.

PRESIDENTIAL LIBRARIES

The libraries preserve, describe, and render reference service on Presidential papers and collections, prepare documentary and descriptive publications and exhibit historic documents and museum items.

For general information on Presidential libraries, contact: John T. Fawcett, Assistant Archivist for Presidential Libraries, Room 104, 7th and Pennsylvania Ave., NW, Washington, D.C. 20408

Herbert Hoover Library, Parkside Drive, Box 488, West Branch, Iowa 52358. Phone (319) 643-5301. Director: Richard N. Smith.

Franklin D. Roosevelt Library, 259 Albany Post Road, Hyde Park, N.Y. 12538. Phone (914) 229-8835. Director: Dr. William R. Emerson.

Harry S. Truman Library, Independence, Mo. 64050. Phone (816) 833-1400. Director: Dr. Benedict K. Zorbrist.

Dwight D. Eisenhower Library, Abilene, Kan. 67410. Phone (913) 263-4751. Director: Dr. John E. Wickman.

John F. Kennedy Library, Columbia Point, Boston, Mass. 02125. Phone (617) 929-4500. Acting Director: Charles U. Daly.

Lyndon Baines Johnson Library, 2313 Red River St., Austin, Tex. 78705. Phone (512) 482-5137. Director: Harry J. Middleton.

Gerald R. Ford Library, 1000 Beal Avenue, Ann Arbor, Mich. 48109. Phone (313) 668-2218. Director: Frank H. Mackaman.

Gerald R. Ford Museum, 303 Pearl St., NW, Grand Rapids, Mich. 49504. Phone (616) 456-2675.

Nixon Presidential Materials Staff, Office of Presidential Libraries, National Archives, Washington D.C. 20408. Phone (703) 756-6498. Director: James J. Hastings.

Jimmy Carter Library, One Copenhill Ave., Atlanta, Ga. 30307. Phone (404) 331-3942. Director: Dr. Donald B. Schewe.

Reagan Presidential Materials Staff, 9055 Exposition Drive, Los Angeles, Calif 90034. Clarence L. Henley.

Sources of information

READING ROOMS

Archives and other historical material for research purposes are available at the National Archives Building, Constitution between 7th and 9th streets NW, Washington, D.C.; at the Presidential Libraries; and the national and regional Federal Records Centers.

AUDIO-VISUAL

The National Audiovisual Center has motion pictures, film strips, slide sets, and video and audio tapes available to schools, educational, civic, and community groups on a sale, rental, or free distribution basis, depending on the particular film. The subject matter includes vocational training, educational, documentary, and military films, made for and by government agencies. Requests for additional information should be directed to the National Audiovisual Center, 8750 Edgeworth Drive, Capitol Heights, Md. Phone (301) 763-1872.

PUBLICATIONS

The National Archives has many publications of interest to the public. For a list, write the Office of the Director, Publications Division, National Archives and records Administration, Constitution between 7th and 9th streets NW, Washington, D.C. 20408.

Government Printing Office

N. Capitol and H streets NW, Washington, D.C. 20401, Phone (202) 783-3238
Public Printer... Joseph E. Jenifer

The Government Printing Office (GPO) began operations in accordance with Congressional Joint Resolution 25 of June 23, 1860. The activities of the Government Printing Office are outlined and defined in the Act of Oct. 22, 1968, as amended.

The congressional Joint Committee on Printing acts as the board of directors of the Government Printing Office. The Public Printer is required by law to be a practical printer versed in the art of bookbinding and is appointed by the President with the advice and consent of the Senate.

The Government Printing Office executes orders for printing and binding placed by Congress and the departments and establishments of the federal government. It furnishes blank paper, inks, and similar supplies to all governmental activities on order. It prepares catalogs and distributes and sells government publications.

The Annual Report of the Director of the Mint, and other Mint and Treasury Department publications are available from the GPO.

GPO invites bids from commercial suppliers on a wide variety of printing and binding services, awards and administers contracts, and maintains liaison between ordering agencies and contractors.

Printing and binding processes used are electronic photocomposition; linotype, monotype and hand composition; letterpress printing and photopolymer platemaking; offset photography, stripping, platemaking, and press; and manual and machine bookbinding.

GPO sells through mail orders and government bookstores nearly 20,000 different publications which originated in various government agencies, and administers the depository library program through which selected government publications are made available in libraries throughout the country.

Sources of information

CONTRACTS

Printing and binding enterprises should direct inquiries to the Manager, Printing Procurement Department, Government Printing Office, Washington, D.C. 20401, or contact the GPO Regional Printing Procurement Office in the following cities: Atlanta, Boston, Chicago, Columbus, Dallas, Denver, Hampton, Va., Los Angeles, New York, Philadelphia, St. Louis, San Francisco, Seattle, or Washington, D.C.

Suppliers of paper and kindred products; printing and binding equipment, related parts, and supplies; purchasers of scrap, or surplus printing and binding equipment, waste, and salvage materials; and freight carriers should contact the Director of Materials Management, Government Printing Office, Washington, D.C. 20401.

A booklet, "How to Do Business with the Government Printing Office, A Guide for Contractors" is available on request from any of the offices above.

EMPLOYMENT

Office of Personnel Management registers are used in filling administrative, technical and clerical positions. College recruitment is directed toward filling positions in printing management and general administration. Inquiries should be directed to Government Printing Office, Chief, Employment Branch, Washington, D.C. 20401. Phone (202) 275-2476.

PUBLICATIONS

Orders and inquiries concerning publications for sale by the Government Printing Office should be directed to the Assistant Public Printer (Superintendent of Documents), Government Printing Office, Washington, D.C. 20402. Phone (202) 783-3238.

The "GPO Sales Publications Reference File (PRF)" provides author, title and subject access to government publications available for sale through the Superintendent of Documents. Issued in bimonthly microfiche editions, it is available as a subscription from the Superintendent of Documents.

The "Monthly Catalog of U.S. Government Publications" is the most comprehensive listing of government publications issued by federal departments and agencies. It is available as a subscription from the Superintendent of Documents.

Remittance for all publications ordered from the Superintendent of Documents must be received in advance of shipment by check or money order payable to the Superintendent of Documents. Orders may also be charged to MasterCard or VISA accounts.

A list of depository libraries is available from the Assistant Public Printer (Superintendent of Documents).

Popular government publications may be purchased at the GPO bookstores listed below.

Government Printing Office bookstores

Washington, D.C.:
Main Bookstore, 710 N. Capitol St.
Retail Sales Branch, 8660 Cherry Lane, Laurel, Md.
Farragut West, 1510 H Street NW

Atlanta, Ga.:
Room 100, Federal Bldg., Box 56445, 275 Peachtree St. NE, 30343. Phone (404) 221-6947

Birmingham, Ala.:
O'Neil Building, 2021 3rd Ave N., 35203. Phone (205) 254-1056

Boston, Mass.:
Room 179, T.P. O'Neill Jr. Federal Building, 10 Causeway St., 02222. Phone (617) 565-6680

Chicago, Ill.:
Room 1365, Everett McKinley Dirksen Building, 219 S. Dearborn St., 60604. Phone (312) 353-5133

Cleveland, Ohio:
Anthony J. Celebrezze Federal Building, 1240 E. Ninth St., 44199. Phone (216) 522-4922

Columbus, Ohio:
Room 207, Federal Office Bldg., 200 N. High St., 42315. Phone (614) 469-6956

Dallas, Tex.:
Room IC46, Federal Bldg.-U.S. Courthouse, 1100 Commerce St., 75242. Phone (214) 767-0076

Denver, Colo.:
Room 117, Federal Bldg., 1961 Stout St., 80294. Phone (303) 844-3964

Detroit, Mich.:
Suite 160, Federal Bldg., 477 Michigan Ave., 48226. Phone (313) 226-7816

Houston, Texas:
Texas Crude Building, 801 Travis St., 77002. Phone (713) 653-3100

Jacksonville, Fla.:
Room 158, Federal Bldg., 400 W. Bay St., 32202. Phone (904) 791-3801

Kansas City, Mo.:
Room 120, Bannister Mall, 5600 E. Bannister Road, 64137. Phone (816) 765-2256

Los Angeles, Calif.:
ARCO Plaza, C Level, 505 S. Flower St., 90071. Phone (213) 688-5841

Milwaukee, Wis.:
Room 190, Federal Bldg., 517 E. Wisconsin Ave., 53202. Phone (414) 291-1304

New York, N.Y.:
Room 110, Federal Building, 26 Federal Plaza, 10278. Phone (212) 264-3825

Philadelphia, Pa.:
Robert Morris Building, 100 North 17th St., 19103. Phone (215) 597-0677

Pittsburgh, Pa.:
Room 118, Federal Office Bldg., 1000 Liberty Ave., 15222. Phone (412) 644-2721

Portland, Ore.:
1305 SW First Ave., 97201. Phone (503) 221-6217

Pueblo, Colo.:
P.O. Box 4007, 81003. Phone (719) 544-3142

San Francisco, Calif.:
Room 1023, Federal Office Bldg., 450 Golden Gate Ave., 94102. Phone (415) 556-0643

Seattle, Wash.
Room 194, Federal Building, 915 Second Ave., 98174. Phone (206) 422-4270.

Commission of Fine Arts
Suite 312, 441 F St. NW, Washington, D.C. 20006
Phone (202) 504-2200

Chairman..J. Carter Brown
Secretary (Administrative Officer)...Charles H. Atherton
Commissioners...Neil Porterfield
....Joan Abrahamson
.... Robert Peck
.... George Hartman
....Adele Chatfield-Taylor
.... (vacant)

The Commission of Fine Arts was established by Congress May 17, 1910, to meet the need for a permanent advisory body on government matters pertaining to the arts, and to guide the architectural development of Washington, D.C.

Commissioners are appointed by the president to four-year terms.

In recent years, that scope has been broadened to include advisory powers for coin designs. Diane Wolf, commissioner during the Reagan administration, took on the redesign of circulating United States coinage as a "personal crusade," and while she is no longer on the commission, that interest has been maintained.

Occasionally, as with the Eisenhower commemorative silver dollar of 1990, Congress may mandate that designs be reviewed by the commission prior to their being rendered into coins.

Past commissioners include coin designers James E. Fraser (1915-20) and Adolph Weinman (1929-33).

Numismatics and the Law

3

Edited by David L. Ganz

David L. Ganz, a special correspondent and columnist for *Coin World* since 1974, is an attorney admitted to practice in New York, New Jersey and Washington, D.C. He has developed a specialty in coinage law and its subsidiary aspects. He is in private practice as managing partner of Ganz, Hollinger & Towe, P.C., 1394 Third Avenue, New York, N.Y. 10021, (212) 517-5500.

Ganz has served as legislative counsel since 1978 to the American Numismatic Association. Since 1985, Ganz has served as an elected governor of the ANA. He has been general counsel to the Professional Numismatists Guild, Inc., since 1981. The research assistance of Paul Walsh and Rebecca Megna, doctor of law candidates at St. John's University Law School, and clerks for Ganz, Hollinger & Towe, Professional Corporation, is acknowledged with thanks. The continued assistance of Barbara Parrotto, executive assistant at Ganz & Sivin P.A., in maintaining files over the last three years to prepare for this edition, and in the preparation of this manuscript, is also deeply appreciated.

Introduction

Numismatics and the law is a fairly broad field. When the first edition of *Coin World Almanac* was published in 1975, this chapter largely consisted of a listing of recent numismatic laws and bills, statutory authority for coinage, the advisory policies of the Treasury Department, and a listing of the contents of Title 18 of the Criminal Code (counterfeiting) Title 31 (governing coinage and gold) and a listing of laws authorizing medals.

Changes in the following edition, published in 1977, the number of features began to crop up with my editorship of this chapter. Many new laws were passed, of course, and by the time that the 1984 *Almanac* was published, there was considerable information concerning the amendment to all of Title 31 (now enacted as positive law) and increased government regulation in the coin field.

By 1987, Congress had enacted a number of bills that had an intense impact on the coin field, regulatory agency activity was heightened in ways that affected all collectors, investors and dealers, and the chapter was considerably expanded.

This sixth edition in 1990 includes a considerable amount of new information, much of which is elsewhere unavailable in convenient, compiled form. Much of it is derived from queries that my firm has had from individuals, and other lawyers, seeking numismatic information for a variety of reasons that range from scholarship to lawsuits.

Potential users of the chapter concerning numismatics and the law should be aware that certain legal shorthands are utilized as a space saver. Abbreviations will be explained the first time that they are used in order to avoid confusion. A more complete explanation can be found in various legal style publications available in most public libraries.

It is impossible, within the scope of a chapter, to cover everything that ought to be found in "Numismatics and the Law". It would be ideal to be able to list, for example, every bill introduced in Congress in the last 25 years that relates to coins. The problem is that in each Congress, more than 25,000 bills are introduced in the House of Representatives alone. Perhaps as many as 200-300 relate to coins, medals, gold, silver, or other assorted topics in which researchers might have an interest in. The Senate has a comparable number.

By contrast, perhaps a half dozen to a dozen bills each year that have a direct impact on the coinage field go on to hearings or some type of staff report. These have been noted and annotated because of their important historical use.

So have the hearings themselves, which provide a serial or chronicle of what has transpired in the field of coinage law over the decades.

All of the material contained in this chapter is designed for desk top analysis, and a quick answer. It is not designed for in-depth research; however, it will usually lead the reader to a source where a more encyclopedic view can be found through a list of bibliographic sources, where appropriate, so that interested researchers can locate more definitive and additional information.

Most of the resources referred to are available in larger public libraries, at colleges or universities with federal depositories for government documents or in larger law libraries. The library of the American Numismatic Association also contains a comprehensive collection of coinage law materials.

United States Code, Title 31

The coinage laws of the United States, for many years, were uncodified. The Coinage Act of 1873 was the first attempt to codify existing law, and in many instances (for example, the elimination of the 2-cent piece, and the demonetization of the Trade dollar) changed existing law extensively. The Revised Statutes of 1874-1878 actually constituted the first serious revision and codification of the minting and coinage laws, and for a century that followed, these were the official versions that were referred to. Elsewhere, a correlation table notes what became of the various sections of the Revised Statutes as pertains to contemporary numismatics.

Interestingly enough, some of the sections in the revised statute, and indeed in the laws of today, actually date back to the United States' founding when, for example, Congress first debated the designs that ought to be on the coinage of the United States.

Back in March 1792, the House of Representatives debated the possible use of the portrait of the president appearing on the coinage "with an inscription which shall express the initial or first letter of his Christian or first name, and his surname at length, and the year of coinage; and upon the reverse...the figure or representation of an eagle with the inscription "United States of America...." [3 Annals of Congress 1348 (1792)].

What emerged as Sec. 10 of the original Mint Act was an "impression emblematic of liberty with an inscription of the word Liberty and the year of coinage." On the reverse, of course, precious metal coinage was required to bear the figure of an eagle in addition to the imprimatur of national origin.

This ultimately became Sec. 18 of the Coinage Act of 1873, Sec. 3517 of the revised statutes, and later, in uncodified form, was known as 31 USC 324. It is today found in 31 USC 5112.

The relevance of this section, in 1990, can be seen in the continuing calls that have been made for changing and revamping the designs that appear on U.S. coinage, governed by this section and another section which permits the Secretary of the Treasury to change the design or die of a coin only once every 25 years. This came from the Coinage Act of Sept. 26, 1890, not found in the Revised Statutes, and later located in 31 USC 276 [today 31 USC 5112(d)(2)].

These are the very sections that will have to be considered by the Secretary of the Treasury, or if he declines to exercise his mandate, by Congress, in making any design alterations.

Starting in the 97th session of Congress, a proposal was advanced to revise, codify and enact without substantive change certain general and permanent laws relative to money and finance as Title 31 of the United States Code. The bill, H.R. 6128, in its final form, and H.R. 4774 in its earlier version, was reported on as H.R. Rep. No. 97-651, and ultimately became Public Law 97-258, approved by President Ronald Reagan on Sept. 13, 1982.

Section 4(a) of Public Law 97-258, 96 Stat. 1067, provided that "sections 1-3 of this Act [encompassing all of the money and finance and coinage laws] restate, without substantive change, laws enacted before April 16, 1982, that were replaced by those sections. Those sections may not be construed as making a substantive change in the laws replaced. Laws enacted after April 16, 1982, that are inconsistent with this Act supersede this Act to the extent of the inconsistency." To the extent that there are any outstanding order, rules of regulations that precede the codification in terms of time, Sec. 4(c) of the Act provides that they shall remain "in effect under the corresponding provision enacted by this Act until repealed, amended, or superseded."

For this reason, earlier editions of the *Coin World Almanac* which list, verbatim, the text of the earlier Title 31 have considerable value in researching the current state of coinage law. When in doubt, the actual Statutes at Large, published as part of each Congress, are controlling.

Unlike earlier versions of the United States Code, Title 31 is now considered to be positive law. That means that each section, as stated, is the law itself, rather than an interpretation of it.

Excerpts from United States Code, Title 31

Following are some important excerpts from U.S. Code, Title 31, "Money and Finance," as applicable to numismatics. Sections not dealing with numismatics have been omitted.

Sec. 301. Department of the Treasury

(a) The Department of the Treasury is an executive department of the United States government at the seat of the government.

(b) The head of the department is the Secretary of the Treasury. The Secretary is appointed by the president, by and with the advice and consent of the Senate.. . .

. . .(c) The department shall have a seal.

Sec. 302. Treasury of the United States

The United States government has a Treasury of the United States. The Treasury is in the Department of the Treasury.

Sec. 303. Bureau of Engraving and Printing

(a) The Bureau of Engraving and Printing is a bureau in the Department of the Treasury.

(b) The head of the Bureau is the Director of the Bureau of Engraving and Printing appointed by the Secretary of the Treasury. The Director

(1) shall carry out duties and powers prescribed by the Secretary; and

(2) reports directly to the Secretary.

Sec. 304. Bureau of the Mint

(a) The Bureau of the Mint is a bureau in the Department of the Treasury.

(b)(1) The head of the Bureau is the Director of the Mint. The Director is appointed by the president, by and with the advice and consent of the Senate. The term of the Director is five years. The president may remove the Director from office. On removal, the president shall send a message to the Senate giving the reasons for removal.

(2) The Director shall carry out duties and powers prescribed by the Secretary of the Treasury.

Sec. 307. Office of the Comptroller of the Currency

The Office of the Comptroller of the Currency, established under Section 324 of the Revised Statues (12 U.S.C. 1), is an office in the Department of the Treasury.

Sec. 308. United States Customs Service

The United States Customs Service, established under Section 1 of the Act of March 3, 1927 (19 U.S.C. 2071), is a service in the Department of the Treasury.

Sec. 309. Office of Thrift Supervision omitted.

Sec. 310. Continuing in office

When the term of an office of the Department of the Treasury ends, the officer may continue to serve until a successor is appointed and qualified.

Administrative

Sec. 321. General authority of the Secretary

(a) The Secretary of the Treasury shall issue warrants for money drawn on the Treasury consistent with appropriations;

mint coins, engrave and print currency and security documents, and refine and assay bullion, and may strike medals;. . .

b) The Secretary may

(1) prescribe regulations to carry out the duties and powers of the Secretary;

(2) delegate duties and powers of the Secretary to another officer or employee of the Department of the Treasury; . . .

Sec. 331. Reports

The Secretary of the Treasury shall submit to Congress each year an annual report.

The Secretary shall report to either House of Congress in person or in writing, as required, on matters referred to the Secretary by that House of Congress.

Sec. 3301. General duties of the Secretary of the Treasury

(a) The Secretary of the Treasury shall

(1) receive and keep public money;

(2) take receipts for money paid out by the Secretary;

(3) give receipts for money deposited in the Treasury;

(4) endorse warrants for receipts for money deposited in the Treasury;

(5) submit the accounts of the Secretary to the Comptroller General every three months, or more often if required by the Comptroller General; and

(6) submit to inspection at any time by the Comptroller General of money in the possession of the Secretary.

Sec. 3327. General authority to issue checks and other drafts

The Secretary of the Treasury may issue a check or other draft on public money in the Treasury to pay an obligation of the United States government. When the Secretary decides it is convenient to a public creditor and in the public interest, the Secretary may designate a depositary to issue a check or other draft on public money held by the depositary to pay an obligation of the government. As directed by the Secretary, each depositary shall report to the Secretary on public money paid and received by the depositary.

Monetary system

Sec. 5101. Decimal system

United States money is expressed in dollars, dimes or tenths, cents or hundredths, and mills or thousandths. A dime is a tenth of a dollar, a cent is a hundredth of a dollar, and a mill is a thousandth of a dollar.

Sec. 5102. Standard weight

The standard troy pound of the National Institute of Standards and Technology of the Department of Commerce shall be the standard used to ensure that the weight of the United States coins conforms to specifications in Section 5112 of this title.

Sec. 5103. Legal tender

United States coins and currency (including Federal reserve notes and circulating notes of Federal reserve banks and national banks) are legal tender for all debts, public charges, taxes, and dues. Foreign gold or silver coins are not legal tender for debts.

General Authority

Sec. 5111. Minting and issuing coins, medals, and numismatic items

(a) The Secretary of the Treasury

(1) shall mint and issue coins described in Section 5112 of this title in amounts the Secretary decides are necessary to meet the needs of the United States;

(2) may prepare national medal dies and strike national and other medals if it does not interfere with regular minting operations but may not prepare private medal dies;

(3) may prepare and distribute numismatic items; and

(4) may mint coins for a foreign country if the minting does not interfere with regular minting operations, and shall prescribe a charge for minting the foreign coins equal to the cost of the minting (including labor, materials, and the use of machinery).

(b) The Department of the Treasury has a coinage metal fund and a coinage profit fund. The Secretary may use the coinage metal fund to buy metal to mint coins. The Secretary shall credit the coinage profit fund with the amount by which the nominal value of the coins minted from the metal exceeds the cost of the metal. The Secretary shall charge the coinage profit fund with waste incurred in minting coins and the cost of distributing the coins. The Secretary shall deposit in the Treasury as miscellaneous receipts excess amounts in the coinage profit fund.

(c) Procurements relating to coin production.

(1) In general. The Secretary may make contracts, on conditions the Secretary decides are appropriate and are in the public interest, to acquire articles, materials, supplies, and services (including equipment, manufacturing facilities, patents, patent rights, technical knowledge, and assistance) necessary to produce the coins referred to in this title.

(2) Domestic control of coinage.

(A) Subject to subparagraph (b), in order to protect the national security through domestic control of the coinage

process, the Secretary shall acquire only such articles, materials, supplies, and services (including equipment, manufacturing facilities, patents, patent rights, technical knowledge, and assistance) for the production of coins as have been produced or manufactured in the United States unless the Secretary determines it to be inconsistent with the public interest, or the cost to be unreasonable, and publishes in the Federal Register a written finding stating the basis for the determination.

(B) Subparagraph (A) shall apply only in the case of a bid or offer from a supplier the principal place of business of which is in a foreign country which does not accord to United States companies the same competitive opportunities for procurements in connection with the production of coins as it accords to domestic companies.

(3) Determination.

(A) In general. Any determination of the Secretary referred to in paragraph (2) shall not be reviewable in any administrative proceeding or court of the United States.

(B) Other rights unaffected. This paragraph does not alter or annul any right of review that arises under any provision of any law or regulation of the United States other than paragraph (2).

(4) Nothing in paragraph (2) of this subsection in any way affects the procurement by the Secretary of gold and silver for the production of coins by the United States Mint.

(d)(1) The Secretary may prohibit or limit the exportation, melting, or treatment of United States coins when the Secretary decides the prohibition or limitation is necessary to protect the coinage of the United States.

(2) A person knowingly violating an order or license issued or regulation prescribed under paragraph (1) of this subsection, shall be fined not more than $10,000, imprisoned not more than five years, or both.

(3) Coins exported, melted, or treated in violation of an order or license issued or regulation prescribed, and metal resulting

from the melting or treatment, shall be forfeited to the United States government.
. . .

Sec. 5112. Denominations, specifications, and design of coins

(a) The Secretary of the Treasury may mint and issue only the following coins:

(1) a dollar coin that is 1.043 inches in diameter and weighs 8.1 grams.

(2) a half dollar coin that is 1.205 inches in diameter and weighs 11.34 grams.

(3) a quarter dollar coin is 0.955 inch in diameter and weighs 5.67 grams.

(4) a dime that is 0.705 inch in diameter and weighs 2.268 grams.

(5) a 5-cent coin that is 0.835 inch in diameter and weighs 5 grams.

(6) except as provided under subsection (c) of this section, a 1-cent coin that is 0.75 inch in diameter and weighs 3.11 grams.

(7) A fifty dollar gold coin that is 32.7 millimeters in diameter, weighs 33.931 grams, and contains one troy ounce of fine gold.

(8) A twenty-five dollar gold coin that is 27.0 millimeters in diameter, weighs 16.9666 grams, and contains one-half troy ounce of fine gold.

(9) A ten dollar gold coin that is 22.0 millimeters in diameter, weighs 8.483 grams, and contains one-fourth troy ounce of fine gold.

(10) A five dollar gold coin that is 16.5 millimeters in diameter, weighs 3.393 grams, and contains one-tenth troy ounce of fine gold.

(b) The dollar, half dollar, quarter dollar, and dime coins are clad coins with three layers of metal. The two identical outer layers are an alloy of 75 percent copper and 25

percent nickel. The inner layer is copper. The outer layers are metallurgically bonded to the inner layer and weight at least 30 percent of the weight of the coin. The 5-cent coin is an alloy of 75 percent copper and 25 percent nickel. In minting 5-cent coins, the Secretary shall use bars that vary not more than 2.5 percent from the percent of nickel

required. Except as provided under subsection (c) of this section, the 1-cent coin is an alloy of 95 percent copper and 5 percent zinc. The specifications for alloys are by weight.

(c) The Secretary may prescribe the weight and the composition of copper and zinc in the alloy of the 1-cent coin that the Secretary decides are appropriate when the Secretary decides that a different weight and alloy of copper and zinc are necessary to ensure an adequate supply of 1-cent coins to meet the needs of the United States.

(d)(1) United States coins have the inscription IN GOD WE TRUST. The obverse side of each coin has the inscription LIBERTY. The reverse side of each coin has the inscriptions UNITED STATES OF AMERICA and E PLURIBUS UNUM and a designation of the value of the coin. The design on the reverse side of the dollar, half dollar, and quarter dollar is an eagle. The eagle on the reverse side of the dollar is the symbolic eagle of Apollo 11 landing on the moon. The obverse side of the dollar has the likeness of Susan B. Anthony. The coins have an inscription of the year of minting or issuance. However, to prevent or alleviate a shortage of a denomination, the Secretary may inscribe coins of the denomination with the year that was last inscribed on coins of the denomination.

(2) The Secretary shall prepare the devices, models, hubs, and dies for coins, emblems, devices, inscriptions, and designs authorized under this chapter. The Secretary may adopt and prepare new designs or models of emblems or devices that are authorized in the same way as when new coins or devices are authorized. The Secretary may change the design or die of a coin only once within 25 years of the first adoption of the design, model, hub, or die for that coin. The Secretary may procure services under Section 3109 of Title 5 in carrying out this paragraph.

(e) Notwithstanding any other provision of law, the Secretary shall mint and issue, in quantities sufficient to meet public demand, coins which:

(1) are 40.6 millimeters in diameter and weigh 31.103 grams;

(2) contain .999 fine silver;

(3) have a design

(A) symbolic of Liberty on the obverse side; and

(B) of an eagle on the reverse side;

(4) have inscriptions of the year of minting or issuance, and the words "Liberty", "In God We Trust", "United States of America", "1 Oz. Fine Silver", "E Pluribus Unum", and "One Dollar"; and

(5) have reeded edges.

(f) Silver coins.

(1) Sale price. The Secretary shall sell the coins minted under subsection (e) to the public at a price equal to the market value of the bullion at the time of sale, plus the cost of minting, marketing, and distributing such coins (including labor, materials, dies, use of machinery, and promotional and overhead expenses).

(2) Bulk sales. The Secretary shall make bulk sales of the coins minted under subsection (e) at a reasonable discount.

(3) Numismatic items. For purposes of section 5132(a)(1) of this title, all coins minted under subsection (e) shall be considered to be numismatic items.".

(g) For purposes of section 5132(a)(1) of this title, all coins minted under subsection (e) of this section shall be considered to be numismatic items.

(h) The coins issued under this title shall be legal tender as provided in section 5103 of title 31, United States Code.

(i) (1) Notwithstanding section 5111(a)(1) of this title, the Secretary shall mint and issue the gold coins described in paragraphs (7), (8), (9), and (10) of subsection (a) of this section, in quantities sufficient to meet public demand, and such gold coins shall

(A) have a design determined by the Secretary, except that the fifty dollar gold coin shall have

(i) on the obverse side, a design symbolic of Liberty; and

(ii) on the reverse side, a design representing a family of eagles, with the male carrying an olive branch and flying above a nest containing a female eagle and hatchlings;

(B) have inscriptions of the denomination, the weight of the fine gold content, the year of minting of issuance, and the words "Liberty", "In God We Trust", "United States of America", and "E Pluribus Unum"; and

(C) have reeded edges.

(2) (A) The Secretary shall sell the coins minted under this subsection to the public at a price equal to the market value of the bullion at the time of sale, plus the cost of minting, marketing, and distributing such coins (including labor, materials, dies, use of machinery, and promotional and overhead expenses).

(B) The Secretary shall make bulk sales of the coins minted under this subsection at a reasonable discount.

(3) For purposes of section 5132(a)(1) of this title, all coins minted under this subsection shall be considered to be numismatic items.

Sec. 5113. Tolerances and testing of coins

(a) The Secretary of the Treasury may prescribe reasonable manufacturing tolerances for specifications in Section 5112 of this title (except for specifications that are limits) for the dollar, half dollar, quarter dollar, and dime coins. The weights of the 5-cent coin

may vary not more than 0.194 gram. The weight of the 1-cent coin may vary not more than 0.13 gram. Any gold coin issued under section 5112 of this title shall contain the full weight of gold stated on the coin.

(b) The Secretary shall keep a record of the kind, number, and weight of each group of coins minted and test a number of the coins separately to determine if the coins conform to the weight specified in Section 5112(a) of this title. If the coins tested do not conform, the Secretary

(1) shall weigh each coin of the group separately and deface the coins that do not conform and cast them into bars for reminting; or

(2) may remelt the group of coins.

Sec. 5114. Engraving and printing currency and security documents

(a) The Secretary of the Treasury shall engrave and print United States currency and bonds of the United States government and currency and bonds of United States territories and possessions from intaglio plates on plate printing presses the Secretary selects. However, other security documents and checks may be printed by any process the Secretary selects. Engraving and printing shall be carried out within the Department of the Treasury if the Secretary decides the engraving and printing can be carried out as cheaply, perfectly, and safety as outside the department.

(b) United States currency has the inscription "In God We Trust" in a place the Secretary decides is appropriate. Only the portrait of a deceased individual may appear on United States currency and securities. The name of the individual shall be inscribed below the portrait.

(c) The Secretary may make a contract for a period of not more than four years to manufacture distinctive paper for United States currency and securities. To promote competition among manufacturers of the distinctive paper, the Secretary may split the award for the manufacture of the paper between the two bidders with the lowest prices a pound. When the Secretary decides that is necessary to operate more than one mill to manufacture distinctive paper, the Secretary may

(1) employ individuals temporarily at rates of pay equivalent to the rates of pay of regular employees; and

(2) charge the pay of the temporary employees to the appropriation available for manufacturing distinctive paper.

Sec. 5115. United States currency notes

(a) The Secretary of the Treasury may issue United States currency notes. The notes

(1) are payable to bearer; and

(2) shall be in a form and in denominations of at least $1 that the Secretary prescribes.

Sec. 5116. Buying and selling gold and silver

(a)(1) With the approval of the president, the Secretary of the Treasury may

(A) buy and sell gold in the way, in amounts, at rates, and on conditions the Secretary considers most advantageous to the public interest; and

(B) buy the gold with any direct obligations of the United States government or United States coins and currency authorized by law, or with amounts in the Treasury not otherwise appropriated.

(2) Amounts received from the purchase of gold are an asset of the general fund of the Treasury. Amounts received from the sale of gold shall be deposited by the Secretary in the general fund of the Treasury and shall be used for the sole purpose of reducing the national debt.

(3) The Secretary shall acquire gold for the coins issued under section 5112(i) of this title by purchase of gold mined from natural deposits in the United States, or in a territory or possession of the United States, within one year after the month in which the ore from which it is derived was mined. The Secretary shall pay not more than the average world price for the gold. In the absence of available supplies of such gold at the average world price, the Secretary may use gold from reserves held by the United States to mint the coins issued under section 5112(i) of this title. The Secretary shall issue such regulations as may be necessary to carry out this paragraph.

(b)(1) The Secretary may buy silver mined from natural deposits in the United States, or in a territory or possession of the United States, that is brought to a United States mint or assay office within one year after the month in which the ore from which it is derived was mined. The Secretary may use the coinage metal fund under section 5111(b) of this title to buy silver under this subsection.

(2) The Secretary may sell or use Government silver to mint coins, except silver transferred to stockpiles established under the Strategic and Critical Materials

Stock Piling Act (50 U.S.C. 98 et seq.). The Secretary shall obtain the silver for the coins authorized under section 5112(e) of this title by purchase from stockpiles established under the Strategic and Critical Materials Stock Piling Act (50 U.S.C. 98 et seq.). The Secretary shall sell silver under conditions the Secretary considers appropriate for at least $1.292929292 a fine troy ounce.

Sec. 5117. Transferring gold and gold certificates

(A) All right, title, and interest, and every claim of the Board of Governors of the Federal Reserve System, a Federal Reserve Bank, and a Federal Reserve agent, in and to gold is transferred to and vests in the United States government to be held in the Treasury. Payment for the transferred gold is made by crediting equivalent amounts in dollars in accounts established in the Treasury under the 15th paragraph of Section 16 of the Federal Reserve Act (12 U.S.C. 467). Gold not in the possession of the government shall be held in custody for the government and delivered on the order of the Secretary of the Treasury. The Board of Governors, Federal Reserve Banks, and Federal Reserve agents shall give instructions and take action necessary to ensure that the gold is so held and delivered.

(b) The Secretary shall issue gold certificates against gold transferred under subsection (a) of this section. The Secretary may issue gold certificates against other gold held in the Treasury. The Secretary may prescribe the form and denominations of the certificates. The amount of outstanding certificates may be not more than the value (for the purpose of issuing those certificates, of 42 and two-ninths dollars a fine troy ounce) of the gold held against gold certificates. The Secretary shall hold gold in the Treasury equal to the required dollar amount as security for gold certificates issued after January 29, 1934.

(c) With the approval of the president, the Secretary may prescribe regulations the Secretary considers necessary to carry out this section.

Sec. 5118. Gold clauses and consent to sue

(a) In this section

(1) "gold clause" means a provision in or related to an obligation alleging to give the obligee a right to require payment in

(A) gold;

(B) a particular United States coin or currency; or

(C) United States money measured in gold or a particular United States coin or currency.

(2) "public debt obligation" means a domestic obligation issued or guaranteed by the United States government to repay money or interest.

(b) The United States Government may not pay out any gold coin. A person lawfully holding United States coins and currency may present the coins and currency to the Secretary of the Treasury for exchange (dollar for dollar) for other United States coins and currency (other than gold and silver coins) that may be lawfully held. The Secretary shall make the exchange under regulations prescribed by the Secretary.

(c)(1) The government withdraws its consent given to anyone to assert against the government, its agencies, or its officers, employees, or agents, a claim

(A) on a gold clause public debt obligation or interest on the obligation;

(B) for United States coins or currency; or

(C) arising out of the surrender, requisition, seizure, or acquisition of United States coins or currency, gold, or silver involving the effect or validity of a change in the metallic content of the dollar or in a regulation about the value of money.

(2) Paragraph (1) of this subsection does not apply to a proceeding in which no claim is made for payment or credit in an amount greater than the face or nominal value in dollars of public debt obligations or United States coins or currency involved in the proceeding.

(3) Except when consent is not

withdrawn under this subsection, an amount appropriated for payment on public debt obligations and for United States coins and currency may be expended only dollar for dollar.

(d)(1) In this subsection, "obligation" means any obligation (except United States currency) payable in United States money.

(2) An obligation issued containing a gold clause or governed by a gold clause is discharged on payment (dollar for dollar) in United States coin or currency that is legal tender at the time of payment. This paragraph does not apply to an obligation issued after October 27, 1977.

Sec. 5119. Redemption and cancellation of currency

(a) Except to the extent authorized in regulations the Secretary of the Treasury prescribes with the approval of the president, the Secretary may not redeem United States currency (including Federal Reserve notes and circulating notes of Federal Reserve Banks and national banks) in gold. However, the Secretary shall redeem gold certificates owned by the Federal Reserve Banks at times and in amounts the Secretary decides are necessary to maintain the equal purchasing power of each kind of United States currency. When redemption in gold is authorized, the redemption may be made only in gold bullion bearing the stamp of a United States Mint or assay office in an amount equal at the time of redemption to the currency presented for redemption.

(b)(1) Except as provided in subsection (c)(1) of this section, the following are public debts bearing no interest:

(A) gold certificates issued before January 30, 1934.

(B) silver certificates.

(C) notes issued under the Act of July 14, 1890 (ch. 708, 26 Stat. 289).

(D) Federal Reserve notes for which payment was made under Section 4 of the Old Series Currency Adjustment Act.

(E) United States currency notes, including those issued under Section 1 of the Act of February 25, 1862 (ch. 33, 12

Stat. 345), the Act of July 11, 1862 (ch. 142, 12 Stat. 532), the resolution of January 17, 1863 (P.R. 9; 12 Stat. 822), Section 2 of the Act of March 3, 1863 (ch. 73, 12 Stat. 710), or Section 5115 of this title.

(2) The Secretary shall redeem from the general fund of the Treasury and cancel and destroy currency referred to in paragraph (1) of this subsection when the currency is presented to the Secretary.

(c)(1) The Secretary may determine the amount of the following United States currency that will not be presented for redemption because the currency has been destroyed or irretrievably lost:

(A) circulating notes of Federal Reserve Banks and national banks issued before July 1, 1929, for which the United States government has assumed liability.

(B) outstanding currency referred to in subsection (b)(1) of this section.

(2) When the Secretary makes a determination under this subsection, the Secretary shall
reduce the amount of that currency outstanding by the amount the Secretary determines will not be redeemed and credit the appropriate receipt account.

(d) To provide a historical collection of United States currency, the Secretary may withhold from cancellation and destruction and transfer to a special account one piece of each design, issue, or series of each denomination of each kind of currency (including circulating notes of Federal Reserve Banks and national banks) after redemption. The Secretary may make appropriate entries in Treasury accounts because of the transfers.

Sec. 5120. Obsolete, mutilated, and worn coins and currency

(a)(1) The Secretary of the Treasury shall melt obsolete and worn United States coins withdrawn from circulation. The Secretary may use the metal from melting the coins for reminting or may sell the metal. The Secretary shall account for the following in the coinage metal fund under Section 5111(b) of this title:

(A) obsolete and worn coins and the

metal from melting the coins.

(B) proceeds from the sale of the metal.

(C) losses incurred in the sale of the metal.

(D) losses incurred because of the difference between the face value of the coins melted and the coins minted from the metal.

(2) The Secretary shall reimburse the coinage metal fund for losses under paragraph (1)(C) and (D) of this subsection out of amounts in the coinage profit fund under Section 5111(b) of this title.

(b) The Secretary shall

(1) cancel and destroy (by a secure process) obsolete, mutilated, and worn United States currency withdrawn from circulation; and

(2) dispose of the residue of the currency and notes.

(c) The Comptroller General shall audit the cancellation and destruction of United States currency and the accounting of the cancellation and destruction. Records the Comptroller General considers necessary to make an effective audit easier shall be made available to the Comptroller General.

Sec. 5121. Refining, assaying, and valuation of bullion

(a) The Secretary of the Treasury shall

(1) melt and refine bullion;

(2) as required, assay coins, metal, and bullion;

(3) cast gold and silver bullion deposits into bars; and

(4) cast alloys into bars for minting coins.

(b) A person owning gold or silver bullion may deposit the bullion with the Secretary to be cast into fine, standard fineness, or unrefined bars weighing at least 5 troy ounces. When practicable, the Secretary shall weigh the bullion in front of the depositor. The Secretary shall give the depositor a receipt for the bullion stating the description and weight of the bullion. When the Secretary has to melt the bullion or remove base metals before the value of the bullion can be determined,

the weight is the weight after the melting or removal of the metals. The Secretary may refuse a deposit of gold bullion if the deposit is less than $100 in value or the bullion is so base that it is unsuitable for the operations of the Bureau of the Mint.

(c) When the gold and silver are combined in bullion that is deposited and either the gold or silver is so little that it cannot be separated economically, the Secretary may not pay the depositor for the gold or silver that cannot be separated.

(d)(1) Under conditions prescribed by the Secretary, a person may exchange unrefined bullion for fine bars when

(A) gold and silver are combined in the bullion in proportions that cannot be economically refined; or

(B) necessary supplies of acids cannot be procured at reasonable rates.

(2) The charge for refining in an exchange under this subsection may be not more than the charge imposed in an exchange of unrefined bullion for refined bullion.

(3) The Secretary shall prepare bars for payment of deposits. The Secretary shall stamp each bar with a designation of the weight and fineness of the bar and a symbol the Secretary considers suitable to prevent fraudulent imitation of the bar.

Sec. 5122. Payment to depositors

(a) The Secretary of the Treasury shall determine the fineness, weight, and value of each deposit and bar under Section 5121 of this title. The value and the amount of charges under subsection (b) of this section shall be based on the fineness and weight of the bullion. The Secretary shall give the depositor a statement of the charges and the net amount of the deposit to be paid in money or bars of the same species of bullion as that deposited.

(b) The Secretary shall impose a charge equal to the average cost of material, labor, waste, and use of machinery of a United States Mint or assay office for

(1) melting and refining bullion;

(2) using copper as an alloy when bullion deposited is above standard;

(3) separating gold and silver combined

in the bullion; and

(4) preparing bars.

(c) The Secretary shall pay to the depositor or to a person designated by the depositor money or bars equivalent to the bullion deposited as soon as practicable after the value of the deposit is determined. If demanded, the Secretary shall pay depositors in the order in which the bullion is deposited with the Secretary. However, when there is an unavoidable delay in determining the value of a deposit, the Secretary shall pay depositors in the denominations requested by the depositors. After the depositor is paid, the bullion is the property of the United States government.

(d) To allow the Secretary to pay depositors with as little delay as possible, the Secretary shall keep in the Mints and assay offices, when possible, money and bullion the Secretary decides are convenient and necessary.

Sec. 5131. Organization

(a) The Bureau of the Mint has

(1) a United States Mint at Philadelphia, Pennsylvania.

(2) a United States Mint at Denver, Colorado.

(3) a United States Mint at West Point, New York.

(4) a United States Mint at San Francisco, Calif.

(b) The Secretary of the Treasury shall carry out duties and powers related to refining and assaying bullion, minting coins, striking medals, and numismatic items at the Mints. However, until the Secretary decides that the Mints are adequate for minting and striking an ample supply of coins and medals, the Secretary may use any facility of the Bureau to Mint coins and strike medals and to store coins and medals.

(c) Each Mint has a superintendent and an assayer appointed by the President, by and with the advice and consent of the Senate. The Mint at Philadelphia has an engraver appointed by the president, by and with the advice and consent of the Senate.

(d) Laws on Mints, officers and employees of Mints, and punishment of offenses related to Mints and minting coins apply to assay offices, as applicable.

(e) The Secretary shall operate, maintain, and have custody of, the Mint at Philadelphia. However, the administrator of General Services shall make repairs and improvements to the Mint.

Section 5132, Administrative

(a) (1) Except as provided in this chapter, the Secretary of the Treasury shall deposit in the Treasury as miscellaneous receipts amounts the Secretary receives from the operations of the Bureau of the Mint. However, amounts from numismatic items shall be reimbursed to the current appropriation used to pay the cost of preparing and selling the items. The Secretary shall annually sell to the public, directly and by mail, sets of uncirculated and proof coins minted under paragraphs (1) through (6) of section 5112(a) of this title, and shall solicit such sales through the use of the customer list of the Bureau of the Mint. The Secretary may not use amounts the Secretary receives from profits on minting coins or from charges on gold or silver bullion under section 5122 of this title to pay officers and employees.

(2) Not more than $46,511,000 may be appropriated to the Secretary for the fiscal year ending September 30, 1988, to pay costs of the mints. Not more than $965,000 of amounts appropriated pursuant to the preceding sentence shall remain available until expended for research and development.

(3) Of amounts appropriated pursuant to Paragraph (2), not more than $75,000 may be expended for the purpose of hosting the International Mint Directors' Conference in the United States in 1988, including reception, representation, and transportation expenses.

(4) Notwithstanding sections 3302 and 9701 of this title, the Director of the Mint may

(A) collect from participants at the International Mint Directors' Conference reasonable amounts imposed as fees and other assessments in connection with such conference;

(B) hold and administer the amounts referred to in subparagraph (A); and

(C) spend on behalf of the United States the amounts referred to in subparagraph (A) to pay expenses incurred in connection with such conference, including reception, representation, and transportation expenses.

(b) To the extent the Secretary decides is necessary, the Secretary may use amounts received from depositors for refining bullion and the proceeds from the sale of byproducts (including spent acids from surplus bullion recovered in refining processes) to pay the costs of refining the bullion (including labor, material, waste and loss on the sale of sweeps). The Secretary may not use amounts appropriated for the mints and assay offices to pay those costs.

(c) The Secretary shall make an annual report at the end of each fiscal year on the operation of the Bureau.

Section 5133. Settlement of accounts

(a) The Secretary of the Treasury shall

(1) charge the superintendent of each mint with the amount in weight of standard metal of bullion the superintendent receives from the Secretary;

(2) credit each superintendent with the amount in weight of coins. clippings, and other bullion the superintendent returns to the Secretary; and

(3) charge separately to each superintendent, who shall account for, copper to be used in the alloy of gold and silver bullion.

(b) Settlement of accounts.

(1) In general. At least once each year, the Secretary of the Treasury shall settle the accounts of the superintendents of the mints.

(2) Procedure. At any settlement under this subsection, the superintendent shall

(A) return to the Secretary any coin, clipping, or other bullion in the possession of the superintendent; and

(B) present the Secretary with a statement of bullion received and returned since the last settlement (including any bullion returned for settlement).

(3) Audit. The Secretary shall

(A) audit the accounts of each superintendent; and,

(B) allow each superintendent the waste of precious metals, that the Secretary decides is necessary

(i) for refining and minting (within the limitations which the Secretary shall prescribe); and

(ii) for casting fine gold and silver bars (within the limit prescribed for refining), except that any waste allowance under this clause may not apply to deposit operations.

(c) After settlement, the Secretary shall compare the amount of gold and silver bullion and coins on hand with the total liabilities of the mints. The Secretary also shall make a statement of the ordinary expense account.

(d) The Secretary shall procure for each mint a series of standard weights corresponding to the standard troy pound of the National Institute of Standards and Technology of the Department of Commerce. The series shall include a one pound weight and multiples and subdivisions of one pound from .01 grain to 25 pounds. At least once a year, the Secretary shall test the weights normally used in transactions at the mint and assay offices against the standard weights.

Section 5141. Operation of the Bureau of Engraving and Printing

(a) The Secretary of the Treasury shall prepare and submit to the President an annual business-type budget for the Bureau of Engraving and Printing.....

Section 5142. Bureau of Engraving and Printing Fund

(a) The Department of the Treasury has a Bureau of Engraving and Printing Fund. Amounts

(1) in the Fund are available to operate the Bureau of Engraving and Printing;

(2) in the Fund remain available until expended; and

(3) may be appropriated to the Fund.

(b) The Fund consists of

(1) property and physical assets (except building and land) acquired by the Bureau;

(2) all amounts received by the Bureau;

Section 5144. Providing impressions of portraits and vignettes

The Secretary of the Treasury may provide impressions from an engraved portrait or vignette in the possession of the Bureau of Engraving and Printing. An impression shall be provided

(1) at the request of

(A) a member of Congress;

(B) a head of an agency;

(C) an art association; or

(D) a library; and

(2) for a charge and under conditions the Secretary decides are necessary to protect the public interest.

Other legal and legislative issues

Banning of the Krugerrand

The South African Krugerrand was the world's best selling gold bullion coin until anti-apartheid movements in the mid-1980s took some of the glitter off the coin. Some 40 million pieces have been produced, and nearly half of them were imported into the United States. Difficulties with the racial apartheid policies of South Africa caused political consternation, and the Krugerrand became an important symbol that opponents of apartheid sought to ban, in order to use an economic weapon against the South African government.

As Congress moved towards a legislative ban on the Krugerrand, which some claimed might be illegal under the Articles of Agreement of the International Monetary Fund which govern foreign exchange, including legal tender pieces such as the Krugerrand, or under the General Agreement on Tariffs and Trade (GATT), which prohibits any discriminatory tariff, President Ronald Reagan took the matter out of the hands of Congress by issuing Executive Order 12535 on Oct. 1, 1985 (50 Fed. Reg. 40325), which effectively banned future importation of the coin.

The text of the regulation is as follows:

"By the authority vested in me as President by the Constitution and laws of the United States of America, including the International Emergency Economic Powers Act (50 U.S.C. 1701 et seq.) in order to take steps additional to those set forth in Executive Order No. 12532 of Sept. 9, 1985, to deal with the unusual and extraordinary threat to the foreign policy and economy of the United States referred to in that Order, and in view of the continuing nature of that emergency, the recommendations made by the United Nations Security Council in Resolution No. 569 of July 26, 1985, and the completion of consultations by the Secretary of State and the United States Trade Representative directed by Section 5(a) of Executive Order No. 12532, it is hereby ordered that the importation into the United States of South African Krugerrands is prohibited effective 12:01 a.m. Eastern Daylight Time Oct. 11, 1985. The Secretary of the Treasury is authorized to promulgate such rules and regulations as may be necessary to carry out this prohibition.

/s/ Ronald Reagan THE WHITE HOUSE, Oct. 1, 1985"

Regulations covering this are found in Volume 31 of the Code of Federal Regulations commencing at Sec. 545.101 et seq. Only the pertinent portions of these regulations dealing with Krugerrands are listed; the act governs all transactions with South Africa:

Sec. 545.201 Prohibition on the importation of Krugerrands.

Except as authorized under this part, the importation into the United States of South African Krugerrands is prohibited.

Sec. 545.204 Evasions.

Any transaction for the purpose of, or which has the effect of, evading any of the prohibitions in this part is prohibited.

Sec. 545.301 Krugerrands.

The term "Krugerrands" includes Krugerrands of all denominations and sizes, and Krugerrands that have been modified, as by addition of a clasp or loop, into items that can be worn as jewelry.

Sec. 545.403 Krugerrand jewelry.

Section 545.201 prohibits the importation into the United States of Krugerrands that have been modified, as by the addition of a clasp or loop, into items that can be worn as jewelry. For example, importation of a necklace consisting of a Krugerrand mounted on a chain would be prohibited. Section 545.201 does not prohibit the reimportation into the United States of Krugerrand jewelry which was originally imported into the United States prior to October 11, 1985.

Sec. 545.701 Penalties.

(a) A civil penalty of not to exceed $10,000 may be imposed on any person who violates any license, order, or regulation issued under this title. (b) Whoever willfully violates any license, order, or regulation issued under this title shall, upon conviction, be fined not more than $50,000, or, if a natural person, may be imprisoned for not more than ten years, or both. . . .

Sec. 545.801 Licensing.

(b) Transactions prohibited under subpart B [including Krugerrand importation] may be effected only under specific license. (1) The specific licensing activities of the Office of Foreign Assets Control are performed by its Washington Office and by the Foreign Assets Control Division of the Federal Reserve Bank of New York. (2) Applications for specific licenses. Applications for specific licenses to engage in any transaction prohibited under this part are to be filed in duplicate with the Federal Reserve Bank of New York, Foreign Assets Control Division, 33 Liberty Street, New York, NY 10045. . . .

Soviet Gold Banning

For a variety of political reasons, gold coinage of the Soviet Union was banned in 1986 (Public Law 99-631, 100 Stat. 3518, approved Nov. 7, 1986) partially in reaction to the Krugerrand ban during the same period, and partially for reasons of partisan politics. Diverse political interests teamed up to accomplish this. In 1990, with *glastnost* reality, there was considerable pressure for the ban to be lifted. The text of the law involved is found below.

22 USC 5100. Prohibition on the importation of Soviet gold coins

(a) Persons subject to prohibition No person, including a bank, may import into the United States any gold coin minted in the Union of Soviet Socialist Republics or offered for sale by the Government of the Union of Soviet Socialist Republics. (b) Violations; fine: amount Any individual who violates this section or any regulations issued to carry out this section shall be fined not more than five times the value of the gold coins involved.

Collectibles in retirement accounts

Utilizing a collection of numismatic material for long-term investment is a significant economic and emotional issue to many individuals. Use of numismatic acumen to help plan a "rare coin retirement" still remains a widely used method that many people use.

Until passage of the Economic Recovery Act of 1981, self-directed pension plans and individual retirement accounts (IRAs) were permitted to purchase coins as part of retirement planning.

The reason that this made economic sense was that coins, in the long run, have a good track record of substantially increasing in value. From the Salomon Brothers survey of a selected portfolio of collectibles to nearly every other objective view of the marketplace, coins are a significant tangible asset from which an individual can reap substantial financial rewards.

Section 314-b of the Economic Recovery Act of 1981 (now section 408(m) of the Internal Revenue Code), placed severe restrictions on the ability of using coins in this vehicle. Persons who placed coins in an individual retirement account, or in the self-directed retirement plans such as a Keogh Plan were considered having made a "distribution"; this meant that income tax would have to be paid, and, additionally, that the plans could not further be used for a five-year period of time. In effect, there was an economic bar.

It should be noted that the original section, and the present law, do not prohibit a trustee of a pension plan who believes that it is prudent to invest in rare coins to do so. The "prudent person" rule applies. For details concerning this little-explored aspect, one should consult with his own accountant or legal counsel.

While in general collectors are no longer able to place most coins in an individual retirement account, Congress did make a modification of the law to give a specific allowance to coins produced under the Gold Bullion Coin Act of 1985 (Public Law 99-185), and the Liberty Coin Act (Pub. L. 99-61, Title II). "State coins" are also now permitted because of an addition to the tax laws, though it is unclear whether this covers only modern bullion issues, or those coins of the states issued prior to creation of federal coinage by the Mint Act of April 2, 1792.

The primary exception applies only to U.S. 1-ounce, half-ounce, quarter-ounce and tenth-ounce American Eagle gold bullion coins, and the new American Eagle 1-ounce silver coin, each of which was first produced by the Treasury Department in October 1986. A number of banks and some dealers have created individual retirement account programs involving these pieces. One may use existing funds in an IRA account to purchase them (a "rollover"), or may place 1986 or 1987 contributions, and subsequent years as well if eligible. State coins apparently were intended to include South Dakota, Texas and California state bullion issues; however, the statute was poorly drafted. The word "coin" is used, when none of these items is a legal tender; and, as

mentioned earlier, it is unclear from the clear verbiage as to whether or not it also refers to real coin of an earlier era prior to the 19th century.

Section 408(m) Investment in collectibles treated as distributions

(1) In general. The acquisition by an individual retirement account or by an individually-directed account under a plan described in section 401(a) [26 USC Sec.

401(a)] of any collectible shall be treated (for purposes of this section and section 402 [26 USC Sec. 402]) as a distribution from such account in an amount equal to the cost to such account of such collectible.

(2) Collectible defined. For purposes of this subsection, the term "collectible" means—

(A) any work of art,

(B) any rug or antique,

(C) any metal or gem,

(D) any stamp or coin,

(E) any alcoholic beverage, or

(F) any other tangible personal property specified by the Secretary for purposes of this subsection.

(3) Exception for certain coins. In the case of an individual retirement account, paragraph (2) shall not apply to

(A) any gold coin described in paragraph (7), (8), (9), or (10) of section 5112(a) of title 31,

(b) any silver coin described in section 5112(e) of title 31, or

(c) any coin issued under the laws of any State.

On Jan. 23, 1984, some three years after passage of the original legislation, the Treasury Department issued a proposed regulation Sec. 1.408-1 governing investment in collectibles. The regulation does not reflect amendments made to the Internal Revenue Code to allow, for example, gold American Eagles and silver American Eagles or state "coins" to be placed in an IRA.

The regulation appears below:

Sec. 1.408-1. Investment in collectibles.

(a) In general. The acquisition by an individual retirement account or by an individually-directed account under a plan described in Section (401(a) of any collectible shall be treated (for purposes of Section 402 and 408) as a distribution from such account in an amount equal to the cost to such account of such collectible.

(b) Collectible defined. For purposes of this section, the term "collectible" means—

(1) Any work or art,

(2) Any rug or antique,

(3) Any metal or gem,

(4) Any stamp or coin,

(5) Any alcoholic beverage,

(6) Any musical instrument,

(7) Any historical objects (documents, clothes, etc.), or

(8) Any other tangible personal property which the Commissioner determines is a "collectible" for purposes of this section.

(c) Individually-directed account. For purposes of this section, the term "individually-directed account" means an account under a plan that provides for individual accounts and that has the effect of permitting a plan participant to invest or control the manner in which the account will be invested.

(d) Acquisition. For purposes of this section, the term acquisition includes purchase, exchange, contribution, or any method by which an individual retirement account or individually-directed account may directly or indirectly acquire a collectible.

(e) Cost. For purposes of this section, cost means fair market value.

(f) Premature withdrawal penalty. The 10 percent described in Sections 72(m)(5) and 408(f)(1) shall apply in the case of a deemed distribution from an individual retirement account described in paragraph (a) of this section.

(g) Amounts subsequently distributed. When a collectible is actually distributed from an individual retirement account or an individually-directed account, any amounts included in gross income because of this section shall not be included in gross income at the term when the collectible is actually distributed.

(h) Effective date. This section applies to property acquired after December 31, 1981, in taxable years ending after such date.

The IRS issued a notice offering guidance with respect to certain provisions of the Economic Recovery Tax Act of 1981 on qualified retirement plans, Keogh plans, individual retirement accounts and simplified employee pensions. Some, in part, relate to collectibles, and an extract appears below in the form issued by IRS in Notice 82-13, 1982-1 Cumulative Bulletin 360. III. Miscellaneous

A. Investments in Collectibles

1. For taxable years ending after December 31, 1981, the acquisition of a "collectible" by an individually-directed account under a plan described in section 401(a), or by an individual described in section 401(a), or by an individual retirement account (whether or not individually-directed), is treated as a distribution from the plan or account.

2. Questions and Answers

III-1. Q. What is a collectible?

A. The term "collectible" includes: (a) any work of art; (b) any rug or antique; (c) any metal or gem; (d) any stamp or coin; (e) any alcoholic beverage; or (f) any other tangible personal property that may be specified by the Secretary of the Treasury for this purpose.

III-2. Q. What is an individually-directed account?

A. The term "individually-directed account" means in account under a qualified plan that provides for individual accounts and that has the effect of permitting a participant or beneficiary to direct the manner in which his or her account will be invested.

III-3. Q. What is the effect of the new requirement on collectibles that were acquired on or before December 31, 1981?

A. Since the new provision is not applicable to collectibles that were acquired on or before December 31, 1981, the retention of a collectible acquired prior to January 1, 1982, by an IRA or an individually-directed account is not treated as a distribution.

III-4. Q. If an owner-employee who has not attained age 59/4 directs the investment in a "collectible" by his or her individual-directed account, is the owner-employee liable for the penalties on premature distributions?

A. Yes. An investment in a collectible by an individually-directed account is treated as a distribution from the plan and is subject to the premature distribution penalty if the participant is not age 59/4 or disabled. A similar conclusion would apply in the case of an IRA.

III-5. Q. Is the acquisition of a collectible by a plan treated as a distribution to the plan participant if the participant has the authority to direct that assets in the participant's account will be invested in collectibles but has no authority to direct that a specific investment be acquired?

A. Yes. An account is "individually directed" for purposes of this provision even if the participant's control over the assets in the participant's account is limited to the authority to determine that such assets will be used to acquire a class of collectibles even if it does not permit the participant to identify specific investments within that class.

"Brokers" and reporting sales

Just as section 314-b of the Economic Recovery Act of 1981 had a profound impact on the manner in which collectibles could be utilized in pension accounts, a little-noted provision contained in the Tax Equity and Fiscal Responsibility Act (TEFRA) passed by Congress has affected the privacy of investors and collectors, and also on the manner in which they can buy and sell coins.

The substances of the provision added a new section to the Internal Revenue Code (Section 6045) and required that regulations be written to encompass brokerage transactions, and the prices paid by brokers for tendered commodities. While there is substantial dispute about the position taken by the Internal Revenue Service in the regulations (the Industry Council for Tangible Assets and its counsel believe that the IRS is mistaken in its position that all coin and bullion sales are intended to be, and are covered a view shared by the Senate Appropriations Committee, but not the Senate Finance Committee) it does seem clear that there is an intent with respect to certain commodities such as 33-ounce gold contracts, 1,000-ounce silver bars, and some silver coins there is a requirement that a dealer buying such commodities must issue a "1099" tax form to the seller (Senate Report 98-562).

The IRS issued one set of regulations, but as a result of the embroiling dispute, withdrew them and planned to substitute a new set. A final version had not been released (though was planned) when the 5th edition of the Almanac was contemplated in the spring of 1987; by the summer of 1990, they also had yet to be issued, and some serious penalties (of $50,000) had been imposed for failure to file. ICTA expects to have the regulations finalized before the end of 1990.

This is clearly a case where (because of the confusion) there is a genuine, factual dispute that may not be resolved in the absence of litigation; however, the IRS points out that the fact that there is a dispute in some quarters does not obviate the alleged requirement that the filing take place.

The best bet in a case like this is that one should consult with his accountant, tax professional, or attorney for a formalized opinion based upon available facts as to whether or not the pertinent provisions apply to you.

It is useful to remember that the text of the regulation is very specific as to who it perceived as covered; only sales by individuals must be reported. Sales by corporations, even if owned by a single shareholder, are not reportable.

Public Law 99-514 amended section 6045(b) of the Internal Revenue Code [the text below is for returns due after Dec. 31, 1986] in order to make clear that the requirement to supply a copy of the information return to the taxpayer is

737eztgg fg5g

triggered where there is an obligation to file (instead of the actual filing of) an information return with the IRS.

For convenience, the text of Internal Revenue Code Section 6045 and Treasury Regulation 1.6045-1, accompany this section.

Text of 6045 and Reg. follow:

Sec. 6045. Returns of brokers.

(a) General rule. Every person doing business as a broker shall, when required by the Secretary, make a return, in accordance with such regulations as the Secretary may prescribe, showing the name and address of each customer, with such details regarding gross proceeds and such other information as the Secretary may by forms or regulations require with respect to such business.

(b) Statements To Be Furnished To Customers. Every person required to make a return under subsection (a) shall furnish to each customer whose name is required to be set forth in such return a written statement showing-

(1) the name and address of the person required to make such return, and

(2) the information required to be shown on such return with respect to such customer. The written statement required under the preceding sentence shall be furnished to the customer on or before January 31 of the year following the calendar year for which the return under subsection (a) was required to be made.

(c) Definitions. For purposes of this section

(1) Broker. The term "broker" includes

(A) a dealer,

(B) a barter exchange, and

(C) any other person who (for a consideration) regularly acts as a middleman with respect to property or services.

(2) Customer. The term "customer" means any person for whom the broker has transacted any business.

(3) Barter exchange. The term "barter exchange" means any organization of members providing property or services who jointly contract to trade or barter such property or services.

(4) Person. The term "person" includes any governmental unit and any agency or instrumentality thereof.***

Sec. 1.6045-1 (Proposed Treasury Regulation, published 11/15/82.)
Returns of information of brokers and barter exchanges.

(a) Meaning of terms. The following definitions apply for purposes of this section:

(1) the term "brokerage transaction" means

(i) A transfer of property;

(ii) A redemption of securities;

(iii) A retirement of indebtedness; or

(iv) A closing transaction.

(2) The term "broker" means a person who, in the ordinary course of a trade or business, stands ready to effect brokerage transactions in securities, commodities or forward contracts for others.

(3) The term "customer" means, with respect to a broker, a person for whom a sale is executed by the broker acting as

(i) An agent in such sale for such person; or

(ii) A principal in such sale.

(4) The term "security" means

(i) A share of stock in a corporation (foreign or domestic);

(ii) An interest in a trust;

(iii) An interest in a partnership;

(iv) A debt obligation;

(v) An interest in or right to purchase any of the foregoing . . .

(vi) An interest in a security described in paragraph (a)(4)(i) or (iv) . . .

(6) The term "commodity" means

(i) Any type of personal property or an interest therein (other than securities as defined in paragraph (a)(4) of this section) the trading of regulated futures contracts in which has been approved by the Commodity Futures Trading Commission;

(ii) Lead, palm oil, rapeseed, tea, tin, or an interest in any of the foregoing; or

(iii) Any other personal property or an interest therein that is of a type the Secretary determines is to be treated as a "commodity" under this section, from and after the date specified in a notice of such determination published in the Federal Register.

Proposed revision

(5)(i) Except as otherwise provided in paragraph (a)(5)(ii) of this section, the term "commodity" means

(A) Any form or quality of personal property that is deliverable (whether or not subject to price adjustment for form or quality) in satisfaction of a regulated futures contract that has been approved for trading by the Commodity Futures Trading Commission (whether or not the regulated futures contract is actually traded);

(B) Any form or quality of lead, palm oil, rapeseed, tea, or tin;

(C) Any form or quality of personal property that the Secretary determines is to be treated as a "commodity" under this section, from and after the date specified in a rule-related notice of such determination published in the Federal Register;

(D) Any form or quality of personal property a form or quality of which is described in paragraph (a)(5)(i) (A) of this section; or

(E) Any interest in personal property that is described in paragraph (a)(t)(i)(A), (B), (C), or (D) of this section.

(ii) The term "commodity" does not include

(A) A security as defined in paragraph (a)(3) of this section;

(B) A regulated futures contract as defined in paragraph (A)(6) of this section;

(C) A forward contract as defined in paragraph (a)(7) of this section;

(D) A form of tangible personal property, or an interest therein, gross proceeds from

the sale of which exceed by more than 15 percent the value on the date of sale of the underlying personal property determined, at the election of the broker, by either exact valuation or approximate valuation (as defined in paragraph (a)(5)(ii) of this section); or

(E) A form of quality of tangible personal property or an interest therein if

no single type of tangible personal property described in paragraph (a)(t)(i) of this section comprises at least 30 percent of the weight or volume of the underlying personal property and the gross proceeds from the sale of such property are less than three thousand dollars ($3,000).

(iii) For purposes of paragraph (a)(5)(ii)(D) of this section

(A) The term "exact valuation" means to determine the value of the underlying personal property

(1) By separately determining the value of each type of tangible personal property described in paragraph (a)(5)(i) of this section of which the underlying personal property is composed at the price at which each such type of tangible personal property is bought and sold in the ordinary course of the buyer's business, or a similarly situated business if such price cannot be determined for the buyer's business; and

(2) Aggregating all such separately determined values; and

(B) The term "approximate valuation" means to determine the value of the underlying personal property

(1) Solely with reference to its weight or volume;

(2) As if such weight or volume were composed entirely of a single type of tangible personal property described in paragraph (a)(5)(i) of this section identical in kind and quality to the most valuable type of tangible personal property described in paragraph (a)(5)(i) of this section that comprises at least 30 percent of such weight or described in paragraph (a)(5)(i) of this section comprises at least 30 percent of such weight or volume, the most valuable type of tangible personal property described in paragraph (a)(5)(i) of this section that comprises any portion of the underlying personal property);

(3) At the price at which the tangible personal property treated as composing the entire weight or volume is bought and sold in the ordinary course of the buyer's business, or a similarly situated business if such price cannot be determined for the buyer's business.

(iv) For purposes of paragraph (a)(5)(ii)(E) and (iii) of this section, "type of tangible personal property" means any tangible personal property described in paragraph (a)(5)(i)(A), (B), or (C) of this section and any other tangible personal property that cannot be commercially reduced into two or more elements.

(7) The term "regulated futures contract" means a regulated futures contract within the meaning of section 1256(b).

(8) The term "forward contract" means

(i) A regulated futures contract;

(ii) A contract that requires delivery of a commodity; or

(iii) A contract that requires delivery of personal property or an interest therein that is of a type the Secretary determines is to be treated as a "forward contract" under this section, from and after the date specified in a notice of such determination published in the Federal Register.

(9) . . .

(10) The term "sale" means all dispositions of securities, commodities and forward contracts for cash, and includes redemptions of securities, retirements of indebtedness, closing transactions . . .

(11) The term "effect" means, with respect to a sale, to act as

(i) An agent in such sale for a party thereto; or

(ii) A principal in such sale.

Acting as an agent or principal with respect to the grant or purchase of an opinion, the entry into a contract that requires delivery of personal property or an interest therein, or the entry into a short sale, is not of itself effecting a sale. A broker that has on its books a forward contract under which delivery is made effects such delivery.

(b) Examples. The following examples illustrate the definitions in paragraph (a) of this section:

Example (1). The following persons generally are brokers within the meaning of paragraph (a)(2) of this section:

(i) A mutual fund or an underwriter of the mutual fund that stands ready to redeem shares in such a mutual fund.

(ii) A borrower that regularly issues and retires its own short-term or demand notes.

(iii) A clearing organization.

Example (2). The following persons are not brokers within the meaning of paragraph (a)(2) of this section in the absence of additional facts that indicate the person is a broker:

(i) A stock transfer agent for a corporation, which agent daily records transfers of stock in transactions to which such corporation and the agent are not parties and which agent receives an amount of compensation for its activities with respect to such transfers that indicates the agent is only providing recordkeeping.

(ii) A person, such as a stock exchange, that merely provides facilities in which others effect brokerage transactions and that does not clear such transactions.

(iii) An escrow agent or nominee if such agency is not pursuant to the ordinary course of a trade or business.

(iv) An escrow agent who is not otherwise a broker and who effects no brokerage transactions other than such transactions as are incidental to the purpose of the escrow (such as sales to collect on collateral).

(v) A corporation that issues and retires long-term debt on an irregular basis.

Example (3). A, B, and C belong to a carpool in which they commute to and from work. Every third day, each member of the carpool provides transportation for the other two members. Because the carpool arrangement provides solely for the informal exchange of similar services on a noncommercial basis, it is not a barter exchange within the meaning of paragraph (a)(5) of this section . . .

Example (9). If the gross proceeds from the sale of a gold coin (such as a Krugerrand, Maple Leaf, 50-peso coin, or 100-crown coin) do not exceed by more than 15 percent the bullion value of the gold in the coin, the coin is a commodity under paragraph (a)(5)(i)(D) of this section and is not excluded by paragraph (a)(5)(ii)(D) of this section.

Example (10). U.S. silver dimes, quarters, and half dollars minted before

1965 are personal property deliverable in satisfaction of a regulated futures contract approved by the Commodity Futures Trading Commission. The coins are a commodity under paragraph (a)(5)(i)(A) of this section. If, however, the gross proceeds from the sale of an individual coin exceed by more than 15 percent the bullion value of the silver in the coin, the coin is not a commodity under paragraph (a)(5)(ii)(D) of this section. If the gross proceeds from the sale of coins as a unit do not exceed by more than 15 percent the bullion value of the silver in the entire unit, all the coins in the unit are a commodity under paragraph (a)(5)(i)(A) of this section notwithstanding the possibility that the gross proceeds from the sale of one or more individual coins in the unit might exceed by more than 15 percent the bullion value of the silver in such individual coins.

Example (11). If the gross proceeds from the sale of a U.S. silver dollar minted before 1970 do not exceed by more than 15 percent the bullion value of the silver in the coin, the coin is a commodity under paragraph (a)(5)(i)(D) of this section and not excluded by paragraph (a)(5)(ii)(D) of this section.

Example (12). Customer E sells to jewelry store S, a broker, a gold necklace. The gross proceeds from the sale of the necklace do not exceed by more than 15 percent of the value of the gold as bullion. Consequently, the gold necklace is a commodity under paragraph (a)(5)(i)(D) of this section and not excluded under paragraph (a)(5)(ii)(D) of this section.

Example (13). Customer F sells to jewelry store T, a broker, a diamond ring. The diamond ring (composed of a gold band and gem) weighs 0.5 troy ounces. The gold in the ring comprises more than 30 percent of the total weight of the ring, and the gross proceeds from the sale of the diamond ring exceed by more than 15 percent the value of 0.5 troy ounces of gold as bullion. Consequently, the diamond ring is not a commodity under paragraph (a)(5)(i)(D) of this section because of its exclusion under paragraph

(a)(5)(ii)(D) of this section.

Example (14). Customer G sells to smelter U, a broker, a gold and silver goblet. More than 30 percent of the weight or volume of the goblet is gold. Assume that the broker chooses to use the "approximate valuation" method described in paragraph (a)(5)(iii)(B) of this section and that the goblet weighs 10 troy ounces. If the gross proceeds from the sale of the goblet do not exceed by more than 15 percent the value of 10 troy ounces of gold as bullion, the goblet is a commodity under paragraph (a)(5)(i)(D) of this section and not excluded under paragraph (a)(5)(ii)(D) of this section.

Example (15). V, a jeweler, generally purchases inventory (that is a commodity under paragraph (a)(5) of this section) from wholesalers and purchases inventory from the general public only when sufficient inventory cannot be secured from wholesalers. V does not accept offers for sale, but seeks out sellers when inventory is needed. Since V does not stand ready to effect sales to be made by others, V is not a broker.

Example (16). W, a coin dealer, regularly advertises that it will buy gold items for bullion value. Since W stands ready to effect sales to be made by others, W is a broker.

Example (17). X, a coin dealer, regularly buys gold items when they are offered for sale and this is known to sellers of such items. Since X stands ready to effect sales to be made by others, X is a broker whether or not it advertises.

(c) Reporting by brokers (1) Requirement of reporting. Any broker shall, except as otherwise provided, report in the manner prescribed in this section.

(2) Sales required to be reported. Except as provided in paragraphs (c)(3) and (g) of this section, a broker shall return of information with respect to each sale of securities, commodities, or forward contracts that the broker effects for a person who is a customer of the broker in such sale.

(3) Exceptions(i) Sales for exempt recipients. No return of information is

required with respect to a sale effected for a customer who is an exempt recipient described in section 3452(c)(2)(A) through (I) and (K)(i) and (ii) (relating to exemptions from withholding) [by U.S. and foreign corporations editor's note] as determined under Section 35.3452(c)-1 insofar as it relates to persons described in section 3452(c)(2)(A) through (1) and (K)(i) and (ii) . . .

(vii) Foreign currency. No return of information is required with respect to a sale of foreign currency unless

(A) Such sale is pursuant to a regulated futures contract or forward contract that requires or permits delivery of foreign currency; or

(B) Such foreign currency is a form or quality of or interest in gold or silver (not) described in paragraph (a)(5)(ii)(D) of this section . . .

(d)(2) Transactional reporting. As to each sale with respect to which a broker is required to make a return of information under this section, the broker shall show on Form 1099 the name, address, and taxpayer identification number of the customer for whom the sale was effected, the property sold, the Committee on Uniform Security Identification Procedures number of the security sold (if known), the gross proceeds of the sale, the date on which the sale occurred, and such other information as may be required by Form 1099, in the form, manner, and number of copies required by Form 1099 . . .

(4) Sale date(i) In general. Except as otherwise provided . . . a sale is considered to occur for purposes of this section on the date the customer becomes entitled to the gross proceeds therefrom . . .

(k) Use of magnetic media(1) In general. Except as otherwise provided by paragraph (k)(2) of this section, a broker who effects sales for 250 or more customers during a calendar year or a barter exchange who has 250 or more members or clients during a calendar year,

in lieu of filing Forms 1099 for such year, shall submit returns of information required by this section on magnetic media authorized by the Commissioner and shall follow the appropriate revenue procedures for such magnetic media filing in lieu of following Form 1099.

(2) Exceptions. (i) The Commissioner may authorize the submission of returns of information on other media if undue hardship is shown on an application filed with the appropriate Internal Revenue Service Center.

(ii) In the case of a person who is a broker or barter exchange on July 1, 1983, an application to file returns of information on Form 1099 must be filed on or before (INSERT 30 DAYS AFTER PUBLICATION OF THIS DOCUMENT IN THE FEDERAL REGISTER). In the case of a person who becomes a broker or barter exchange after July 1, 1983, such application must be filed by the later of (INSERT 30 DAYS AFTER PUBLICATION OF THIS DOCUMENT IN THE FEDERAL REGISTER) or the end of the second month following the month in which such person becomes a broker or barter exchange.

(3) When permitted. Any broker or barter exchange required to submit a return of information under this section not required to do so on magnetic media may make such returns on magnetic media upon consent thereto from the Commissioner under Sec. 1.9101-1.

(l) Reporting on options transactions. (Reserved.)

(m) Reporting on bond discounts. (Reserved.)

(n) Additional reporting by stock transfer agents. (Reserved.)

(o) Effective date. This section applies to calendar year 1983 and all succeeding calendar years, and, as to 1983, only to transactions occurring on or after July 1, 1983.

(p) (Reserved.)

Treasury regulations

Regulations are a key way in which the government operates. Below appears the current regulations of the manner in which the Mint operates, and performs a number of its functions. In years past, Treasury regulations contained in Title 31 of the Code of Federal Regulations included the Office of Domestic Gold and Silver Operations, now defunct. Part 56 of the Code of Federal Regulations is its vestige. Part 90 relates to the table of charges and regulations for processing bullion. Part 91 relates to the Mint. A subsequent part relating to the Bureau of Engraving and Printing is with substantive matters only; the on-sight regulation is virtually identical to that of the Bureau of the Mint, except for the change in name.

PART 56 Domestic gold and silver operations sale of silver

Sec. 56.1 Conditions upon which silver will be sold.

The General Services Administration, as agent for the Treasury Department, will conduct periodic sales of silver as agreed upon between GSA and the Treasury Department. Sales will be under competitive bidding procedures established by agreement between GSA the Treasury Department. Details of the bidding and selling procedures are obtainable by telephone or by writing to General Services Administration, Property Management and Disposal Service, Industry Materials Division, Metals Project, Washington, D.C. 20405.

Sec. 56.2 Sales price.

Sales of silver will be at prices offered through the competitive bidding procedures referred to in Sec. 56.1, and accepted by the GSA.

Note: Subject to the provisions of Pub. Law 90-29, approved June 24, 1967, silver certificates will continue to be exchangeable for silver on demand until June 24, 1968, as specified in the first paragraph of the notice appearing at 29 FR 3819, March 27, 1964.

PART 90 (1976) Table of Charges and Regulations of the Mints and Assay Offices of the United States for Processing Silver and Assaying Bullion Metals, and Ores.

Source: 35 Fed. Reg. 19177 (12/18/70). The information below is for historical purposes only and is no longer in effect. It nonetheless is useful to note the standards of the Mint.

Sec. 90.1 Application and general regulations.

(a) Scope. This part prescribes policies, regulations, and charges of the U.S. Mints and Assay Offices governing the acceptance and treatment of silver deposited for purchase, under provisions of the Newly Mined Domestic Silver Regulations of 1965, the regulations of the Office of Domestic Gold and Silver Operations (Parts 81 and 93 of this chapter, respectively) and Title 31 of the United States Code.

(b) Assaying, melting, parting and refining and other related services. The charges for the various operations on bullion deposited, for the preparation of bullion deposited, for the preparation of bars, and for the assay of samples of bullion and ores are fixed from time to time by the Director of the Mint, with the concurrence of the Secretary of the Treasury, so as to equal but not exceed in their judgment the actual average costs. The U.S. Mints and Assay Offices shall impose appropriate charges for services performed under this regulations.

(c) Metals not returned to depositors. Metals other than silver contained in bullion accepted will not be returned to the depositor, nor will credit or payment be given for them.

Sec. 90.2 Silver bullion which may be accepted.

The U.S. Mints and Assay Offices will

accept for purchase, silver which meets the requisites set forth in Parts 81 and 93 of this chapter, and the general regulations in this part.

Sec. 90.3. Requisites for acceptable bullion as to fineness.

(a) Silver governed by the regulations in Parts 81 and 93 of this chapter must contain at least 600 parts of silver in 1,000 to be eligible for deposit under the regulation in this part.

(b) In addition to this requisite as to fineness, deposits in this category must also be accompanied by duly executed affidavits as evidence that such silver is eligible. Forms for this purpose are prescribed in Part 93 of this chapter.

Sec. 90.4 Return or rejection of silver deposited.

(a) Unsatisfactory silver bullion. Any silver bullion that fails to meet the necessary requisites set forth in parts 81 and 93 of this chapter, and this part, or that is unsuitable for Mint operations, shall not be accepted, but shall be returned according to provisions of paragraph (b) of this section.

(b) Return of bullion. Subject to payment in cash to the government for charges incurred, bullion may be returned to the depositor at any time before settlement is made or payment is tendered therefore, and thereafter at the option of the Superintendent of the Mint or the officer in charge of the Assay Office handling the bullion.

Sec. 90.5 Charges for treating and processing silver.

(a) Melting charges. A melting charge of $5 shall be imposed for the first 1,000 gross troy ounces of each deposit of bullion. An additional melting charge of 50 cents shall be imposed for each additional 100 gross troy ounces or fraction thereof. These rates shall be applied to the after-melting gross weight of the deposit.

(b) Excess melting loss charge. When there is a melting loss in excess of 15 percent of the before-melting weight of a deposit of bullion, an additional melting charge of $3 shall be imposed for the first 100 gross troy ounces. An additional melting charge of $1 shall be imposed in this case for each additional 100 gross troy ounces or fraction thereof. These additional rates shall be applied to the before-melting gross weight of the deposit.

(c) Abnormal treatment charges. At the discretion of the Superintendent of the Mint or the officer in charge of the Assay Office, deposits of bullion which require abnormal treatment shall be subjected to additional charges equal to the extra cost, including remelting and retreatment if necessary. When charges for abnormal treatment are assessed, a charge will not be made for an excess melting loss.

(d) Parting and refining charge (rate per gross troy ounce to the nearest hundredth) — Silver Bullion.

Silver content:	Charge (cents)
600 to 850 thousandths	12
850-1/2 to 995-3/4 thousandths	6

Sec. 90.6 Charges for special assays and assays of ores and fine gold certification.

(A) Bullion Special Assays. Gold or silver bullion samples for special assay will be accepted at the U.S. Assay Office in N.Y. and at the U.S. Mint in Denver. Charges will be in accordance with the following table of charges.

Charges per assay

	Gold or silver bullion (under 800 base metal)	Plated or filled goods and white gold
Gold	$11	$12
Silver	11	12
Gold and silver (same sample)	19	23
Additional charge when the sample contains any of the platinum group metals	5	5

(B) Assay of ores. Assays of ore samples will be made at the U.S. Mint in Denver. The charge for each metal determined will be:

Charge

Gold.. $5
Silver 5
Gold and silver (same sample).............. 8
Lead.. 8
Zinc 8
Copper...7

Sec. 90.7 Transactions not subject to various treating and processing charges.

(a) Deposits exempt from melting charges.

(1) Uncurrent U.S. Coin.

(2) Silver bullion of at least .999 thousandths fineness when a satisfactory assay can be obtained without melting.

(b) Deposits exempt from parting and refining charges. Deposits of domestic mutilated or uncurrent silver coin received in accordance with Part 100 of this chapter, are not subject to charges for parting and refining, except as provided in Sec. 90.5

Sec. 90.8 Settlement for transactions conducted.

(A) Advance settlement. When the approximate fineness of bullion containing 5,000 or more ounces of silver may be readily determined, settlement of 90 percent of the value may be made at the discretion of the Superintendent or officer in charge. If the fineness is closely determined by assay, and the bullion is awaiting remelting and reassay for exact determination, settlement of 98 percent of the value may be made. Other advances may be authorized by the Secretary of the Treasury. In any case of an advance the depositor may give a written guarantee that the value of the deposit is at least equal to the amount advanced.

(b) Statement of charges. The detailed memorandum of the weight of bullion after melting, the report of the Assayer as to fineness, the value of the bullion deposited and the amount of the charges shall be given to the depositor.

(c) Payment for silver bullion deposits. Payment for silver bullion is made, in so far as practicable, in the order in which the deposits are received, by check drawn in favor of the depositor or to such other person as he may designate. In no case is a check in payment of a deposit drawn in favor of any officer or employee of the institution where the deposit is made, and in no case may any person employed in the institution act as agent for the depositor. Checks may be sent by ordinary mail at the risk of the payee or by registered mail at his request and expense.

PART 91 Regulations governing conduct in or on the Bureau of the Mint buildings and grounds

Authorized by 31 USC Sec. 301 by delegation of the Administrator of General Services, 35 Federal Register 14426, and Treasury Department No. 177-25 (Revision No. 2), 38 Federal Register 21947. The source of this is 34 Federal Register 503, Jan. 14, 1969, unless otherwise noted.

In the case of Sec. 91.1 and 91.2, as well as the section concerning hallucinogens and drugs, the source is Federal Register of September 11, 1973, 38 Federal Register 24897.

Sec. 91.1 Authority.

The regulations in this part governing conduct in and on the Bureau of the Mint buildings and grounds located as follows: U.S. Mint, Colfax, and Delaware Streets, Denver, Colo.; U.S. Bullion Depository, Fort Knox, Ky.; U.S. Assay Office, 32 Old Slip New York, N.Y.; U.S. Mint, 5th and Arch Streets, Philadelphia, Penn.; U.S. Assay Office, 155 Hermann Street, and the Old U.S. Mint Building, 88 Fifth Street, San Francisco, Calif.; and U.S. Bullion Depository, West Point, New York; are promulgated pursuant to the authority vested in the Secretary of the Treasury . . .

Sec. 91.2 Applicability.

The regulations in this part apply to the buildings and grounds of the Bureau of the Mint located as follows: U.S. Mint, Colfax and Delaware Streets, Denver, Colo.; U.S. Bullion Depository, Fort Knox, Ky.; U.S. Assay Office, 32 Old Slip, New York, New York; U.S. Mint, Fifth and Arch Streets, Philadelphia, Penn.; U.S. Assay Office, 155 Hermann Street, and the Old U.S. Mint Building, 88 Fifth Street, San

Francisco, Calif.; and U.S. Bullion Depository, West Point, N.Y.; and to all persons entering in or on such property. Unless otherwise stated herein, the Bureau of the Mint buildings and grounds shall be referred to in these regulations as the "property".

Sec. 91.3 Recording presence.

Except as otherwise ordered, the property shall be closed to the public during other than normal working hours. The property shall also be closed to the public when, in the opinion of the senior supervising official of any Bureau of the Mint establishment covered by these regulations, or his delegate, an emergency situation exists, and at such other times as may be necessary for the orderly conduct of the Government's business. Admission to the property during periods when such property is closed to the public will be limited to authorized individuals who will be required to sign the register and/or display identification documents when requested by the guard.

Sec. 91.4 Preservation of property.

It shall be unlawful for any person without proper authority to willfully destroy, damage, deface, or remove property or any part thereof or any furnishings therein.

Sec. 91.5 Compliance with signs and directions.

Persons in and on the property shall comply with the instructions of uniformed Bureau of the Mint guards (U.S. Special Policemen), other authorized officials, and official signs of a prohibitory or directory nature.

Sec. 91.6 Nuisances.

The use of loud, abusive, or profane language, unwarranted loitering, unauthorized assembly, the creation of any hazard to persons or things, improper disposal of rubbish, spitting, prurient prying, the commission of any obscene or indecent act, or any other

disorderly conduct on the property is prohibited. The throwing of any articles of any kind in, upon, or from the property and climbing upon any part thereof, is

prohibited. The entry, without specific permission, upon any part of the property to which the public does not customarily have access, is prohibited.

Sec. 91.7 Gambling.

(a) Participating in games for money or other property, the operation of gambling devices, the conduct of a lottery or pool, the selling or purchasing of numbers tickets, or any other gambling in or on the property, is prohibited.

(b) Possession in or on the property of any numbers slip or ticket, record, notation, receipt, or other writing of a type ordinarily used in any illegal form of gambling such as a tip sheet or dream book, unless explained to the satisfaction of the head of the bureau or his delegate, shall be prima facie evidence that there is participation in an illegal form of gambling in or on such property.

Sec. 91.8 Alcoholic beverages, narcotics, hallucinogenic and dangerous drugs.

Entering or being on the property, or operating a motor vehicle thereon by a person under the influence of alcoholic beverages, narcotics, hallucinogenic or dangerous drugs is prohibited. The use of any narcotic, hallucinogenic or dangerous drug in or on the property is prohibited. The use of alcoholic beverages in or on the property is prohibited except on occasions and on property upon which the Director of the Mint has for appropriate official uses granted an exemption permit in writing.

Sec. 91.9 Soliciting, vending, debt collection, and distribution of handbills.

The unauthorized soliciting of alms and contributions, the commercial soliciting and vending of all kinds, the display or distribution of commercial advertising, or the collecting of private debts, in or on the property, is prohibited. This rule does not apply to Bureau of the Mint concessions or notices posted by authorized employees on the bulletin boards. Distribution of material such as pamphlets, handbills, and flyers is prohibited without prior approval from the Director of the Mint, or the delegate of the Director.

Sec. 91.10 Photographs.

The taking of photographs on the property is prohibited, without the written permission of the Director of the Mint.

Sec. 91.11 Dogs and other animals.

Dogs and other animals, except seeing-eye dogs, shall not be brought upon the property for other than official purposes.

Sec. 91.12 Vehicular and pedestrian traffic.

(a) Drivers of all vehicles in or on the property shall drive in a careful and safe manner at all times and shall comply with the signals and directions of guards and all posted traffic signs.

(b) The blocking of entrances, driveways, walks, loading platforms, or fire hydrants in or on the property is prohibited.

(c) Parking in or on the property is not allowed without a permit or specific authority. Parking without authority, parking in authorized locations or in locations reserved for other persons or continuously in excess of eight hours without permission, or contrary to the direction of a uniformed Bureau of the Mint guard, or of posted signs, is prohibited.

(d) This paragraph may be supplemented from time to time with the approval of the Director of the Mint, or the delegate of the Director, by the issuance and posting of such specific traffic directives as may be required and when so issued and posted such directives shall have the same force and effect as if made a part hereof.

Sec. 91.13 Weapons and explosives.

No person while on the property shall carry firearms, other dangerous or deadly weapons, or explosives, either openly or concealed, except for official purposes.

Sec. 91.14 Penalties and other law.

Whoever shall be found guilty of violating any of the regulations in this part while on the property is subject to a fine of not more than $50, or imprisonment of not more than 30 days or both (see 40 U.S.C. 318c. Nothing contained in the regulations in this part shall be construed to abrogate any other Federal laws or regulations or those of any state or municipality applicable to the property referred to in Sec. 91.2 and governed by the regulations in this part.

Part 92 Bureau of the Mint operations and procedures

Authority: U.S.C. 301.

Source: 47 FR 56353, Dec. 16, 1982, unless otherwise noted.

Sec. 92.1 Manufacture of medals.

With the approval of the Director of the Mint, dies for medals of a national character designated by Congress may be executed at the Philadelphia Mint, and struck in such field office of the Mints and Assay Offices as the Director shall designate.

Sec. 92.2 Sale of "list" medals.

Medals on the regular Mint list, when available, are sold to the public at a charge sufficient to cover their cost, and to include mailing cost when mailed. Copies of the list of medals available for sale and their selling prices may be obtained from the Director of the Mint, Washington, D.C.

Sec. 92.3 Manufacture and sale of "proof" coins.

"Proof" coins, i.e., coins prepared from blanks specially polished and struck, are made as authorized by the Director of the Mint and are sold at a price sufficient to cover their face value plus the additional expense of their manufacture and sale. Their manufacture

and issuance are contingent upon the demands of regular operations. Information concerning availability and price may be obtained from the Director of the Mint, Treasury Department, Washington, D.C. 20220.

Sec. 92.4 Uncirculated Mint Sets.

Uncirculated Mint Sets, i.e., specially packaged coin sets containing one coin of each denomination struck at the Mints at Philadelphia and Denver, and the Assay Office at San Francisco, will be made as authorized by the Director of the Mint and will be sold at a price sufficient to cover their face value plus the additional expense of their processing and sale. Their manufacture and issuance are contingent upon demands of regular operations. Information concerning availability and price may be obtained from the Director of the Mint, Treasury Department, Washington, D.C. 20220.

Sec. 92.5 Procedure governing availability of Bureau of the Mint records.

(a) Regulations of the Office of the Secretary adopted. The regulations on the Disclosure of Records of the Office of the Secretary and other bureaus and offices of the Department issued under 5 U.S.C. 301 and 552 and published as Part 1 of this title, 32 FR No. 127, July 1, 1967, except for Sec. 1.7 of this title entitled "Appeal," shall govern the availability of Bureau of the Mint records.

(b) Determination of availability. The Director of the Mint delegates authority to the following Mint officials to determine, in accordance with Part 1 of this title, which of the records or information requested is available, subject to the appeal provided in Sec. 92.6: The Deputy Director of the Mint, Division Heads in the Office of the Director, and the Superintendent or Officer in Charge of the field office where the record is located.

(c) Requests for identifiable records. A written request for an identifiable record shall be addressed to the Director of the Mint, Washington, D.C. 20220. A request presented in person shall be made in the public reading room of the Treasury Department, 15th Street and Pennsylvania Avenue, NW, Washington, D.C., or in such other office designated by the Director of the Mint.

Sec. 92.6 Appeal

Any person denied access to records requested under Sec. 92.5 may file an appeal to the Director of the Mint within 30 days after notification of such denial. The appeal shall provide the name and address of the appellant, the identification of the record denied, and the date of the original request and its denial.

31 CFR Part 94 (1976)

Information concerning regulations prohibiting the exportation of 1-cent pieces, as well as their melting, has expired. It is reprinted for historical significance, since it is possible that higher metal prices for this or other coins may create a situation wherein it could be utilized again.

It is interesting to note in the course of this that there have been criminal prosecutions, and convictions, for violation of this section. The penalties, as stated, are quite substantial.

Sec. 94.1 Prohibition.

Except as specifically authorized by the Secretary of the Treasury (or any person, agency, or instrumentality designated by him) or as provided in this part, no 1-cent coin of the United States may be melted, treated, or exported from the United States or any place subject to the jurisdiction thereof. This prohibition shall not apply to any department or agency of the United States.

Sec. 94.2 Exceptions.

The prohibition contained in Sec. 94.1 against exporting 1-cent coin of the United States shall not apply to the following:

(a) Exports of 1-cent coins having an aggregate face amount value not exceeding $5 in any one shipment, to be legitimately used as coins or for numismatic purposes. This paragraph does not authorize export for the purpose of the sale or resale of coins for melting or treating by any person;

(b) 1-cent coin of the United States having an aggregate face amount value not exceeding $1 carried in the personal effects of any individual departing from a place subject to the jurisdiction of the United States.

Sec. 94.3 Definitions.

(a) "Person" means an individual, partnership, association, corporation, or other organization.

(b) "Treat" means to melt, smelt, refine, or otherwise treat by heating or by a chemical or electrical process.

(a) Any person who melts, treats or exports 1-cent coin of the United States in violation of Sec. 94.1 shall be subject to the penalties provided in section 105 of the Coinage Act of 1965, which provides:

Sec. 94.4 Penalties.

(1) Whenever in the judgment of the Secretary such action is necessary to protect the coinage of the United States, he is authorized under such rules and regulations as he may prescribe to prohibit, curtail, or regulate the exportation, melting, or treating of any coin of the United States.

(2) Whoever knowingly violates any order, rule, regulation, or license issued pursuant to paragraph (a) of this section shall be fined not more than $10,000, or imprisoned not more than five years, or both.

(b) Any coins exported, melted, or treated (or any metal resulting from such melting or treating) in violation of any provision of this part or of the provisions of any authorization, license, ruling, regulation, order, direction, or instruction issued by or pursuant to the direction or authorization of the Secretary of the Treasury pursuant to this part shall be forfeited to the United States as provided in section 106 of the Coinage Act of 1965.

(c) Attention is also directed to 18 U.S.C. 1001 which provides:

Whoever, in any matter within the jurisdiction of any department or agency of the United States knowingly and willfully falsifies, conceals or covers up by any trick, scheme, or device a material fact, or makes any false, fictitious or fraudulent statements or representations, or makes or uses any false writing or document knowing the same to contain any false, fictitious, or fraudulent statement or entry, shall be fined not more than $10,000 or imprisoned not more than five years, or both.

Part 100 Exchange of paper currency and coin

Authority: Sec. 1, 49 Stat. 938; 31

U.S.C. 773a.

Source: 47 FR 32044, July 23, 1982, unless otherwise noted.

Section 100.2 Scope of regulations; transactions effected through Federal Reserve Banks and branches; distribution of coin and currencies.

The regulations in this part govern the exchange of the coin and paper currency of the United States (including national bank notes and Federal Reserve Bank notes and Federal Reserve Bank notes in process of retirement and Federal Reserve notes). Under authorization in the act approved May 29, 1920, 41 Stat. 655 (31 U.S.C. 476), the Secretary of the Treasury transferred to the Federal Reserve Banks and branches the duties and functions performed by the former Assistant Treasurers of the United States in connection with the exchange of paper currency and coin of the United States. Except for the duties in this respect to be performed by the Treasurer of the United States and the director of the Mint, as may be indicated from time to time by the Secretary of the Treasury, exchanges of the paper currency and coin of the United States and the distribution and replacement thereof will, so far as practicable, be effected through the Federal Reserve Banks and branches. The Federal Reserve Banks and branches are authorized to distribute available supplies of coin and currency to depository institutions, as that term is defined in Section 103 of the Monetary Control Act of 1980 (Pub. L. 96-221). As authorized by Section 107 of the Act, transportation of coin and currency and coin wrapping services will be provided according to a schedule of fees established by the Board of Governors of the Federal Reserve system. Inquiries by depository institutions regarding distribution and related services should be addressed to the Federal Reserve Bank of the district where the institution is located.

Subpart A In general

Sec. 100.3 Lawfully held coin and currencies in general.

The official agencies of the Department of the Treasury will continue to exchange lawfully held coins and currencies of the United States, dollar for dollar, for other coins and currencies which may be lawfully acquired and are legal tender for public and private debts. Paper currency of the United States which has been falsely altered and coins altered to render them for use as other denominations will not be redeemed since such currency and coins are subject to forfeiture under title 18, United States Code, section 492. Persons receiving such currency and coins should notify immediately the nearest local office of the U.S. Secret Service of the Department of the Treasury, and hold the same pending advice from the Service.

Sec. 100.4 Gold coin and gold certificates in general.

Gold coins, and gold certificates of the type issued before Jan. 30, 1934, are exchangeable, as provided in this part, into other currency or coin which may be lawfully issued.

Subpart B Exchange of mutilated paper currency

Sec. 100.5 Mutilated paper currency.

(a) Lawfully held paper currency of the United States which has been mutilated will be exchanged at face amount if clearly more than one-half of the original whole note remains. Fragments of such mutilated currency which are not clearly more than one-half of the original whole note will be exchanged at face value only if the Commissioner, Bureau of Government Financial Operations, Department of the Treasury, is satisfied that the missing portions have been totally destroyed. The Commissioner's judgment shall be based on such evidence of total destruction as is necessary and shall be final.

Definitions

(1) Mutilated currency is currency which has been damaged to the extent that (i) one-half or less of the original note remains or (ii) its condition is such that its value is questionable and the currency must be forwarded to the Treasury Department for examination by trained experts before any exchange is made.

(2) Unfit currency is currency which is unfit for further circulation because of its physical condition such as torn, dirty, limp, worn or defaced. Unfit currency should not be forwarded to the Treasury, but may be exchanged at commercial banks.

Sec. 100.6 Destroyed paper currency.

No relief will be granted on account of lawfully held paper currency of the United States which has been totally destroyed.

Section 100.7 Treasury's liability.

(a) Payment will be made to lawful holders of mutilated currency at full value when: (a)(1) Clearly more than 50% of a note identifiable as United States currency is present; or

(a)(2) Fifty percent or less of a note identifiable as United States currency is present and the method of mutilation and supporting evidence demonstrate to the satisfaction of the Treasury that the missing portions have been totally destroyed. â (b) No payments will be made when:

(b)(1) Fragments and remnants presented are not identifiable as United States currency; or

(b)(2) Fragments and remnants presented which represent 50% or less of a note are identifiable as United States currency but the method of destruction and supporting evidence do not satisfy the Treasury that the missing portion has been totally destroyed.

(c) All cases will be handled under proper procedures to safeguard the funds and interests of the claimant. In some cases, the amount repaid will be less than the amount claimed. In other cases, the amount repaid may be greater. The amount paid will be determined by an examination made by trained mutilated currency examiners and governed by the above criteria.

(d) The Commissioner of the Bureau of Government Financial Operations shall have final authority with respect to settlements for mutilated currency claims.

Sec. 100.8 Packaging of mutilated currency.

Mutilated currency examiners are normally able to determine the value of mutilated currency when it has been carefully packed and boxed as described below:

(a) Regardless of the condition of the currency, do not disturb the fragments more than is absolutely necessary.

(b) If the currency is brittle or inclined to fall apart, pack it carefully in cotton and box it as found, without disturbing the fragments, if possible.

(c) If the money was in a purse, box, or other container when mutilated, it should be left therein, if possible, in order to prevent further deterioration of the fragments or from their being lost.

(d) If it is absolutely necessary to remove the fragments from the container, send the container with the currency and any other contents found, except as noted in (h) below.

(e) If the money was flat when mutilated, do not roll or fold.

(f) If the money was in a roll when mutilated, do not attempt to unroll or straighten.

(g) If coin or any other metal is mixed with the currency, remove carefully. Do not send coin or other metal in the same package with mutilated paper currency, as the metal will break up the currency. Coin should be forwarded as provided in Section 100.12 (c) and (d).

(h) Any fused or melted coin should be sent to: Superintendent, United States Mint, P.O. Box 400, Philadelphia, Pa. 19105.

Sec. 100.9 Where mutilated currency should be transmitted.

Mutilated currency shipments must be addressed as follows: Department of the Treasury, Bureau of Government Financial Operations, Room 132, Treasury Annex No. 1, DCS/BEPA, Washington, D.C. 20226.

Subpart C Exchange of Coin

Sec. 100.10 Exchange of uncurrent coins.

(a) Definition. Uncurrent coins are whole U.S. coins which are merely worn or reduced in weight by natural abrasion yet are readily and clearly recognizable as to genuineness and denomination and which are machine countable.

(b) Redemption basis. Uncurrent coins will be redeemed at face value.

(c) Criteria for acceptance. Uncurrent coins, forwarded for redemption at face value, must be shipped at the expense and risk of the owner. Shipments of subsidiary or minor coins for redemption at face value should be sorted by denomination into packages in sums of multiples of $20. Not more than $1,000 in any silver or clad coin, $200 in 5-cent pieces, or $50 in 1-cent pieces should be shipped in one bag or package.

(d) Redemption sites. Uncurrent coins will be redeemed only at the Federal Reserve banks and branches listed in Sec. 100.17.

Sec. 100.11 Exchange of bent and partial coins.

(a) Definitions.

(1) Bent coins are U.S. coins which are bent or deformed so as to preclude normal machine counting but which are readily and clearly identifiable as to genuineness and denomination.

(2) Partial coins are U.S. coins which are not whole; partial coins must be readily and clearly identifiable as to genuineness and denomination.

(b) Redemption basis. Bent and partial coins shall be redeemed on the basis of their weight and denomination category rates, (which is the weight equivalent of face value) provided such coins are presented separately by denomination category in lots of at least one pound for each category. Bent and partial coins not presented separately by denomination category will be redeemed as mixed coins. Denomination categories and rates are 1.

Cents, * $1.4585 per pound 2. 5-cent pieces, * $4.5359 per pound 3. Dimes, Quarters, Halves, and Eisenhower Dollars * $20.00 per pound and 4. Anthony Dollars * $56.00 per pound. Copper plated zinc cents shall be redeemed at the face value equivalent of copper 1-cent coins.

(c) Redemption Site. Bent and partial coins will be redeemed only at the United States Mint, P.O. Box 400, Philadelphia, Pa. 19105. Coins are shipped at sender's risk and expense.

Sec. 100.12 Exchange of fused and mixed coins.

(a) Definitions.

(1) Fused coins are U.S. coins which are melted to the extent that they are bonded together and the majority of which are readily and clearly identifiable as U.S. coins.

(2) Mixed coins are U.S. coins of several alloy categories which are presented together, but are readily and clearly identifiable as U.S. coins.

(b) Redemption basis.

(1) Fused and mixed coins shall be redeemed at the lesser of:

(i) The inventory value of the copper and nickel as priced in the Philadelphia Mint, Coinage Metal Account at the end of the preceding calendar quarter or;

(ii) $1.5327 per pound of contained copper, which is the face value equivalent of a pound of copper in the copper 1-cent coin plus $18.1442 per pound of contained nickel which is the face value equivalent of a pound of nickel in the 5-cent coin.

(2) The redemption rate (discussed in subparagraph (1) (a)) will take effect on the 15th day of each new calendar quarter.

(c) Criteria for acceptance.

(1) A minimum of two pounds of fused and mixed coins is required for redemption.

(2) Fused and mixed coins containing lead, solder, or other substance which will render them unsuitable for coinage metal will not be accepted.

(d) Redemption site. Fused and mixed coins will be redeemed only at the United States Mint, P.O. Box 400, Philadelphia, Pa. 19105. Coins are shipped at sender's risk and expense.

Sec. 100.13 Criminal penalties.

Criminal penalties connected with the defacement or mutilation of U.S. coins are provided in the United States Code, Title 18, Section 331.

Subpart D Other information

Sec. 100.16 Exchange of paper and coin to be handled through Federal Reserve banks and branches.

Other than as provided in this document all transactions including the exchange of paper currency and coin shall be handled through the Federal Reserve banks and branches.

Sec. 100.17 Location of Federal Reserve banks and branches.

[See Federal Reserve chapter for banks and branches]

Sec. 100.18 Counterfeit notes to be marked; "redemption" of notes wrongfully so marked.

The act of June 30, 1876 (19 Stat. 4; 31 U.S.C. 424), provides that all U.S. Officers charged with the receipt or disbursement of public moneys, and all officers of national banks, shall stamp or write in plain letters the word "counterfeit," "altered," or "worthless" upon all fraudulent notes issued in the form of, and intended to circulate as money, which shall be presented at their places of business; and if such officers shall wrongfully stamp any genuine note of the United States, or of the national bank, they shall, upon presentation, "redeem" such notes at the face amount thereof.

Sec. 100.19 Disposition of counterfeit notes and coins.

All counterfeit notes and coin found in remittances are canceled and delivered to the U.S. Secret Service of the Department of the Treasury or to the nearest local office of that service, a receipt for the same being forwarded to the sender. Communications with respect thereto should be addressed to the Director, U.S. Secret Service, Department of the Treasury, Washington, D.C. 20223.

Sec. 100.20 Disposition of counterfeit notes and coins.

All counterfeit notes and coins found in remittance are canceled and delivered to the U.S. Secret Service of the Treasury Department or to the nearest local office of that Service, a receipt for the same being forwarded to the sender. Communications with respect thereto should be addressed to the Director, U.S Secret Service, Treasury Department, Washington, D.C. 20226.

Part 101 Mitigation of Forfeiture of Counterfeit Gold Coins

Authority: 18 U.S.C. 492.

Sec. 101. 1 Purpose and scope

The purpose of this part is to establish a policy whereby certain purchasers or holders of gold coins who have forfeited them to the United States because they were counterfeit may, in the discretion of the Secretary of the Treasury, recover the gold bullion from the coins. This part sets forth the procedures to be followed in implementing this policy.

Sec. 101.2 Petition for mitigation.

(a) Who may file. Any person may petition the Secretary of the Treasury for return of the gold bullion of counterfeit gold coins forfeited to the United States if:

(1) The petitioner innocently purchased or received the coins and held them without the knowledge that they were counterfeit, and,

(2) The petitioner voluntarily submitted the coin to the Treasury Department for a determination of whether they were legitimate or counterfeit; and,

(3) The coins were determined to be counterfeit and were seized by the Treasury Department and forfeited to the United States.

(b) To whom addressed. Petitions for mitigation of the forfeiture of counterfeit gold coins should be addressed to the Assistant Secretary, Enforcement, Operations, Tariff Affairs, Department of Treasury, 15th and Pennsylvania Avenue, N.W., Washington, D.C. 20220.

(c) Form. The petition need not be in any particular form, but must be under oath, and set forth at least the following:

(1) The full name and address of the petitioner;

(2) A description of the coin or coins involved;

(3) The name and address of the person from whom the coins were received or purchased by the petitioner;

(4) The date and place where they were voluntarily submitted for examination;

(5) Any other circumstances relied upon by the petitioner to justify the mitigation;

(6) A statement that the petitioner purchased or received and held the coins without the knowledge that they were counterfeit.

Sec. 101.3 Petitions reviewed by Assistant Secretary, Enforcement, Operations, Tariff Affairs.

(a) The Assistant Secretary will receive and review all petitions for mitigation of the forfeiture of counterfeit gold coins. He shall conduct such further investigation, and may request such further information from the petitioner as he deems necessary. Petitions will be approved if the Assistant Secretary determines that:

(1) The gold coins have not been previously disposed of by normal procedures;

(2) The petitioner was an innocent purchaser or holder of the gold coins and is not under investigation in connection with the coins at the time of submission or thereafter;

(3) The coins are not needed and will not be needed in the future in any investigation or as evidence in legal proceedings; and

(4) Mitigation of the forfeiture is in the best interest of the government.

Sec. 101.4 Extraction of gold bullion from the counterfeit coins.

If the petition is approved, the Assistant Secretary shall then forward the gold coins to the Bureau of the Mint where if economically feasible, the gold bullion will be extracted from the counterfeit coins. The Bureau of the Mint will then return the bullion to the Assistant Secretary.

Sec. 101.5 Payment of smelting costs.

The petitioner shall be required to pay all reasonable costs incurred in extracting the bullion from the counterfeit coins, as shall be determined by the Assistant Secretary. Payment must be made prior to the return of the gold bullion to the petitioner.

Sec. 101.6 Return of the bullion.

After receiving the gold bullion from the Bureau of the Mint, the Assistant Secretary shall notify the petitioner that his petition has been approved and that payment of the smelting costs in an amount set forth in such notice must be made prior to the return of the bullion.

Sec. 101.7 Exceptions.

The provisions of this part shall not apply where the cost of smelting the gold coins exceeds the value of the gold bullion to be returned.

Sec. 101.8 Discretion of the Secretary.

The Secretary of the Treasury retains complete discretion to deny any claim of any petitioner when the Secretary believes it is not in the best interest of the government to return the bullion to the petitioner or when the Secretary is not convinced that the petitioner was an innocent purchaser or holder without knowledge that the gold coins were counterfeit.

(FR Doc. 77-566 Filed 1-5-77;)

31 CFR Part 601 Distinctive Paper For United States Currency and Other Securities.

Source: Department Circular 394, Feb. 1, 1928, unless otherwise noted.
Redesignated at 39 FR 17839, May 21, 1974.

Sec. 601.1 Notice to the public.

Notice is hereby given that the Secretary of the Treasury, by authority of law, has adopted a new distinctive paper for use in printing United States currency and other securities.

Sec. 601.2 Description of paper.

The paper is cream-white bank-note paper which closely resembles in general appearance the paper now in use, and which must conform to specifications prescribed by the Secretary of the Treasury, in which currency paper and bond paper may be differentiated. The distinctive feature, identical for all paper used for the production of paper currency and public debt issues of the United States, shall consist of small segments of fiber, either natural or synthetic, colored red and blue, incorporated in the body of the paper while in process of manufacture and evenly distributed throughout.

Sec. 601.3 Use of paper.

The new distinctive paper shall be used for printing currency of the reduced size, including United States notes, gold certificates, silver certificates, Federal Reserve notes, and national bank notes. The use of the present distinctive paper adopted on July 30, 1891, the distinctive feature of which consists of localized red and blue silk fiber incorporated in the body of the paper while in the process of manufacture so placed as to form perpendicular stripes, will be continued for any printing of currency of the present size hereafter required.

Sec. 601.4 Use of paper; interest-bearing securities of the United States.

After the issue of the reduced size currency, the new distinctive paper shall thereafter be used for the printing of interest-bearing securities of the United States, and for any other printing where the use of distinctive paper is indicated: Provided, however, That any then existing stocks of blank paper containing the present distinctive feature may be utilized.

Sec. 601.5 Penalty for unauthorized control or possession.

The Secretary of the Treasury hereby gives notice that the new distinctive paper, together with any other distinctive paper, heretofore adopted for the printing of paper currency or other obligations or securities of the United States is and will be subject to the provisions of section 474 of Public Law 722, 80th Congress, which provides, in part as follows:

Whoever has or retains in his control or

possession, after a distinctive paper has been adopted by the Secretary of the Treasury for the obligations and other securities of the United States, any similar paper adapted to the making of any such obligation or other security, except under the authority of the Secretary of the Treasury or some other proper officer of the United States, shall be fined not more than $5,000, or imprisoned not more than 15 years, or both.

Sec. 601.6 Modifications of Department Circular No. 121.

The provisions of Department Circular No. 121, dated July 30, 1891, are modified accordingly.*

Footnote:

*Department Circular No. 121, July 30, 1891, provided for a new distinctive paper for all obligations except checks and drafts, the distinctive feature of which consisted of localized red and blue silk fiber incorporated in the body of the paper while in process of manufacture so placed as to form perpendicular stripes on either side of the center portrait or vignette.

Department of the Treasury Use of Metal Tokens

On Sept. 2, 1983, the Mint notified the public that it was proposing to change its policy that opposed the use of metal tokens provided that certain criteria was met. 48 Federal Register 40054. Public comment was invited and, for the most part, comments were received that were aimed at preventing the unlawful use of tokens in vending machines and other coin operated devices. On June 21, 1984, the Mint published revised token restrictions which generally adopted the increased restrictions, but invited additional comments. 49 Fed. Reg. 25556. Those proposed revisions are found on Pages 128 and 129 of the fourth edition of the *Coin World Almanac*. Effective July 15, 1985, final regulations were issued by the Mint. The policy reflected is intended as advice and guidance for token manufacturers and users as well as the general public. It

represents the views of the Treasury Department concerning measures which should minimize the possibility of violating the counterfeiting provisions of Title 18 of the United States Code. It does not prescribe mandatory specifications concerning the size, composition or any other requirements of the metal token. These matters, however, may be the subject of state or local regulation. What it does state is that the Treasury Department does not object to tokens which meet the restrictions set forth in the notice. It should be noted that prosecution of violations of the counterfeiting statutes is vested in the Justice Department which assesses each claimed violation based upon the facts presented.

Restrictions on the diameter of metal tokens is the most essential means of minimizing the possibility that tokens will be unlawfully used to slug vending and other gaming machines, according to the Treasury Department. 50 Fed. Reg. 28680 (July 15, 1985). The Treasury Department determine that restrictions on minimum weight and thickness on tokens are not necessary in view of the restrictions imposed on token diameters.

Below follow the conditions for departmental approval:

Conditions for Department Approval

The Department does not oppose the production or use of tokens which meet the following conditions:

1: Tokens should be clearly identified with the name and location of the establishment from which they originate on at least one side. Alternatively, tokens should contain an identifying mark or logo which clearly indicates the identity of the manufacturer.

2. Tokens should not be within the following diameter ranges (inches):

0.680 — 0.775
0.810 — 0.860
0.910 — 0.980
1.018 — 1.068
1.180 — 1.230
1.475 — 1.525

3. Tokens shall not be manufactured

from a three-layered material consisting of a copper-nickel alloy clad on both sides of a pure core, nor from a copper-based material except if the total of zinc, nickel, aluminum, magnesium and other alloying materials is a least 20 percent of the token's weight. In addition, tokens shall not be manufactured from material which possesses sufficient magnetic properties so as to be accepted by a coin mechanism.

4. Establishments using these tokens shall prominently and conspicuously post signs on their premises notifying patrons that federal law prohibits the use of such tokens outside the premises for any monetary purpose whatever.

5. The issuing establishment shall not accept tokens as payment for any goods or services offered by such establishment with the exception of the specific use for which the tokens were designed.

6. The design on the token shall not resemble any current or past foreign or U.S. coinage.

The Department of Treasury believes that the observance of these restrictions will minimize the possibility of a violation of the counterfeiting statutes. The prosecution of violations of these statutes is vested with the Department of Justice which must evaluate any claimed violation on the particular facts presented.

Katherine D. Ortega, Treasurer of the United States

Cash Transactions

Internal Revenue Code Sec. 6050I acts as a supplement to a prior existing record-keeping transaction for financial institutions found in 31 CFR Part 103.

Essentially, Sec. 6050-I provides that any person engaged in a trade or business who receives $10,000 or more in cash in one transaction or two or more related transactions is required to file a return with the Secretary of the Treasury.

Below follows the text of the law, after which the regulations (with examples involving auction firms, and coin dealers) may be found. Following that is 31 CFR Part 103 which relates to financial institutions (coin dealers were found not to

be financial institutions, informally, a number of years ago but they are covered under 6050I). It should be noted that penalties for failure to report a transaction are quite severe. For example, assume a transaction involving $10,001 takes place. Assume that, innocently, and without any type of improper intent, a report is not properly filed. Internal Revenue Service takes the position that this is the same as failure to withhold income for an employee. This leaves the employer (or in this case, the recipient) liable for a penalty of 25 percent. It also leaves the person liable for an additional penalty of 5 percent per month (up to a total of 25 percent), plus statutory interest. Thus, on a relatively modest transaction, a draconian penalty comes into play.

For further details, consult with your lawyer, or your certified public accountant.

The version appearing below includes the latest set of amendments, including Public Law 99-514, applying to returns due after Dec. 31, 1986 (i.e., in calendar year 1987 and beyond). As is also true under Sec. 6045, the bill clarifies the provisions relating to furnishing a written statement to the taxpayer of the number of substantive information reporting provisions. The obligation will be triggered, under the new provision, when there is an obligation to file (instead of the actual filing) of the return. To see the Committee Reports on this underlying provision, created by Public Law 98-369, see 1984-3 Cumulative Bulletin at 241. Text of Internal Revenue Law Sec. 6050-I. Returns relating to cash received in trade or business.

(a) Cash receipts of more than $10,000. Any person

(1) who is engaged in a trade or business, and

(2) who, in the course of such trade or business, receives more than $10,000 in cash in 1 transaction (or 2 or more related transactions), shall make the return described in subsection (b) with respect to such transaction (or related transactions) at such time as the Secretary may by

regulations prescribe.

(b) Form and manner of returns. A return is described in this subsection if such return

(1) is in such form as the Secretary may prescribe,

(2) contains

(A) the name, address, and [taxpayer identification number] of the person from whom the cash was received,

(B) the amount of cash received,

(C) the date and nature of the transaction, and

(D) such other information as the Secretary may prescribe.

(c) Exceptions.

(1) Cash received by financial institutions. Subsection (a) shall not apply to

(A) cash received in a transaction reported under title 31, United States Code [31 USCS Sec. 101 et seq.], if the Secretary determines that reporting under this section would duplicate the reporting to the Treasury under title 31, United States Code [31 USCS Sec. 101 et seq.], or

(B) cash received by any financial institution (as defined in subparagraphs (A), (B), (C), (D), (E), (F), (G), (J), (K), (R), and (S) of section 5312(a)(2) of title 31, United States Code [31 USCS Sec. 5312(a)(2)(A)-(G), (J), (K), (R), (S)]).

(2) Transactions occurring outside the United States. Except to the extent provided in regulations prescribed by the Secretary, subsection (a) shall not apply to any transaction if the entire transaction occurs outside the United States.

(d) Cash includes foreign currency. For purposes of this section, the term "cash" includes foreign currency.

(e) Statements to be furnished to persons with respect to whom information is required.

Every person required to make a return under subsection (a) shall furnish to each person whose name is required to be set forth in such return a written statement showing

(1) the name and address of the person required to

make such return, and

(2) the aggregate amount of cash described in subsection (a) received by the person required to make such return. The written statement required under the preceding sentence shall be furnished to the person on or before January 31 of the year following the calendar year for which the return under subsection (a) was required to be made.

Regulations Sec. 1.6050 I-1. Returns relating to cash in excess of $10,000 received in a trade or business.

(a) Reporting requirement

(1) In general. Any person (as defined in section 7701(a)(1)) who, in the course of a trade or business in which such person is engaged, receives cash in excess of $10,000 in 1 transaction (or 2 or more related transactions) shall, except as otherwise provided, make a return of information with respect to the receipt of cash.

(2) Cash received for the account of another. Cash in excess of $10,000 received by a person for the account of another must be reported under this section. Thus, for example, a person who collected delinquent accounts receivable for an automobile dealer must report with respect to the receipt of cash in excess of $10,000 from the collection of a particular account even though the proceeds of the collection are credited to the account of the automobile dealer (i.e., where the rights to the proceeds from the account are retained by the automobile dealer and the collection is made on a fee-for-service basis).

(3) Cash received by agents (i) General rule. Except as provided in paragraph (a)(3)(ii) of this section, a person who in the course of a trade or business acts as an agent (or in some other similar capacity) and receives cash in excess of $10,000 from a principal must report the receipt of cash under this section.

(ii) Exception. An agent who receives cash from a principal and uses all of the cash within 15 days in a cash transaction (the "second cash transaction") which is reportable under section 6050I or section

5312 of Title 31 of the United States Code and the regulations thereunder (31 CFR Part 103), and who discloses the name, address, and taxpayer identification number of the principal to the recipient in the second cash transaction need not report the initial receipt of cash under this section. An agent will be deemed to have met the disclosure requirements of this paragraph (a)(3)(ii) if the agent discloses only the name of the principal and the agent knows that the recipient has the principal's address and taxpayer identification number. ...

(b) Multiple payments. The receipt of cash deposits or cash installment payments (or other similar payments or prepayments) relating to a single transaction (or two or more related transactions) are reported under this section in different manners depending on the dollar amounts of the initial and subsequent payments. Reporting of multiple payments is effected as follows:

(1) Initial and subsequent payments in excess of $10,000. If the initial payment exceeds $10,000 and any subsequent payment exceeds $10,000, the recipient must report each payment that exceeds $10,000. These payments must be reported separately (or if the payments are made less than 15 days apart, the recipient may (if it so elects) make a single report with respect to such payments).

(2) Initial payment only in excess of $10,000. If the initial payment exceeds $10,000 but no subsequent payment exceeds $10,000, the recipient must report with respect to the initial $10,000 payment (within 15 days of receipt of the initial payment), but need not report with respect to any subsequent payment.

(3) Initial payment of $10,000 or less. If the initial payment does not exceed $10,000, the recipient must aggregate the initial payment and subsequent payments made within one year of the initial payment until such aggregate amount exceeds $10,000, and report with respect to the aggregate amount within 15 days after receipt of the payment that causes the aggregate amount to exceed $10,000. Any

subsequent payment which by itself exceeds $10,000 must be separately reported.

(c) Meaning of terms. The following definitions apply for purposes of this section

(1) The term "cash" means the coin and currency of the United States or of any other country, which circulate in and are customarily used and accepted as money in the country in which issued. Cash includes United States notes and Federal Reserve notes, but does not include bank checks, travelers checks, bank drafts, wire transfers or other negotiable or monetary instruments not customarily accepted as money.

(2) The term "trade or business" has the same meaning as under section 162 of the Internal Revenue Code of 1954.

(3)(i) The term "transaction" means the underlying event precipitating the payer's transfer of cash to the recipient. ...

(ii) The term "related transactions" means any transaction conducted between a payer (or its agent) and a recipient of cash in a 24-hour period. Additionally, transactions conducted between a payer (or its agent) and a cash recipient during a period of more than 24 hours are related if the recipient knows or has reason to know that each transaction is one of a series of connected transactions.

(iii) The following examples illustrate the definition of paragraphs (c)(3)(i) and (ii).

Example (1). A person has a tacit agreement with a gold dealer to purchase $36,000 in gold bullion. The $36,000 purchase represents a single transaction under paragraph (c)(3)(i) of this section and the reporting requirements of this section cannot be avoided by recasting the single sales transaction into 4 separate $9,000 sales transactions. ...

Example (4). K, an individual, attends a one day auction and purchases for cash two items, at a cost of $9,240 and $1,732.50 respectively (tax and buyer's premium included). Because the transactions are related transactions as defined in paragraph (c)(3)(ii) of this section, the auction house is required to report the aggregate amount of cash received from the related sales ($10,972.50), even though the auction house accounts separately on its books for each item sold and presents the purchaser with separate bills for each item purchased.

Example (5). F, a coin dealer, sells for cash $9,000 worth of gold coins to an individual on three successive days. Under paragraph (c)(3)(ii) of this section the three $9,000 transactions are related transactions aggregating $27,000 if F knows, or has reason to know, that each transaction is one of a series of connected transactions.

(4)(i) The term "recipient" means the person receiving the cash. Except as provided in paragraph (c)(4)(ii) of this section, each store, division, branch, department, headquarters, or office ("branch") (regardless of physical location) comprising a portion of a person's trade or business shall for purposes of this section be deemed a separate recipient.

(ii) A branch that receives cash payments will not be deemed a separate recipient if the branch (or a central unit linking such branch with other branches) would in the ordinary course of business have reason to know the identity of payers making cash payments to other branches of such person. ...

(e) Time, manner, and form of reporting (1) Time of reporting. The reports required by paragraph (a) of this section must be filed with the Internal Revenue Service by the 15th day after the date the cash is received. If a person elects to report as one payment several independently reportable payments received within a 15-day period (as described in paragraph (b)(1) of this section), the report must be filed with the Internal Revenue Service by the 15th day after the date the initial payment is received.

(2) Form of reporting. A report required by paragraph (a) of this section must be made on Form 8300. A return of information made in compliance with this paragraph must contain the name, address, and taxpayer identification number of the person from whom the cash was received; the name, address, and taxpayer identification number of the person on whose behalf the transaction was conducted (if the recipient knows or has reason to know that the person from whom the cash was received conducted the transaction as an agent for another person); the amount of cash received; the date and nature of the transaction; and any other information required by Form 8300. Form 8300 can be obtained from any Internal Revenue Service Forms Distribution Center.

(3) Manner of reporting (i) Where to file. A person making a return of information under this section must file Form 8300 by mailing it to the address shown in the instructions to the form.

(ii) Verification. A person making a return of information under this section must verify the identity of the person from whom the reportable cash is received. Verification of the identity of a person who purports to be an alien must be made by examination of such person's passport, alien identification card, or other official document evidencing nationality or residence. Verification of the identity of any other person may be made by examination of a document normally acceptable as a means of identification when cashing or accepting checks (for example, a driver's license or a credit card). In addition, a return will be considered incomplete if the person required to make a return knows (or has reason to know) that an agent is conducting the transaction for a principal, and the return does not identify both the principal and the agent.

(iii) Retention of returns. A person required to make an information return under this section must keep a copy of each return filed for five years from the date of filing.

(f) Requirement of furnishing statements (1) In general. Any person required to make an information return under this section must furnish a single, annual, written statement to each person whose name is set forth in a return ("identified person") filed with the Internal Revenue Service.

(2) Form of statement. The statement required by the preceding paragraph need not follow any particular format, but it must contain the following information:

(i) The name and address of the person making the return;

(ii) The aggregate amount of reportable cash received by the person who made the information return required by this section during the calendar year in all cash transactions relating to the identified person; and

(iii) A legend stating that the information contained in the statement is being reported to the Internal Revenue Service.

(3) When statement is to be furnished. Statements required under this paragraph (f) must be furnished to an identified person on or before January 31 of the year following the calendar year in which the cash is received. Part 103

The following are the financial record-keeping and reporting requirements of currency and foreign transactions, which mostly apply to banks. However the underlying regulations, here, form the basis for the reporting requirements under 6050I.

Part 103

Following are extracts from part 103 relating to the financial recordkeeping requirements imposed on transactions of $10,000 and more. The authority for most of these records is Pub. L. 91-508, Title I, 84 Stat. 1114 (12 U.S.C. 1730d, 1829b and 1951-1959); and the Currency and Foreign Transactions Reporting Act, Pub. L. 91-508, Title II, 84 Stat. 1118, as amended (31 U.S.C. 5311-5326). Various regulations have been published over the years and can be found in the following general sources: 37 FR 6912, Apr. 5, 1972; 50 FR 27824, July 8, 1985; 50 FR 42692, Oct. 22, 1985; 51 FR 45109, Dec. 17, 1986; 52 FR 11441, 11442, April 8, 1987; 52 FR 23978, June 26, 1987; 52 FR 35545, Sept. 22, 1987, and finally 54 FR 3027, Jan. 23, 1989. The actual regulations take over 100 printed pages, but are highly relevant to all businessmen as well as consumers.

Section 103.21 Determination by the Secretary.

The Secretary hereby determines that the reports required by this subpart have a high degree of usefulness in criminal, tax, or regulatory investigations or proceedings.

Section 103.22 Reports of currency transactions.

(a)(1) Each financial institution other than a casino or the Postal Service shall file a report of each deposit, withdrawal, exchange of currency or other payment or transfer, by, through, or to such financial institution which involves a transaction in currency of more than $10,000. Multiple currency transactions shall be treated as a single transaction if the financial institution has knowledge that they are by or on behalf of any person and result in either cash in or cash out totalling more than $10,000 during any one business day.
* * *

(a)(3) The Postal Service shall file a report of each cash purchase of postal money orders in excess of $10,000. Multiple cash purchases totaling more than $10,000 shall be treated as a single transaction if the Postal Service has knowledge that they are by or on behalf of any person during any one day.

(a)(4) A financial institution includes all of its domestic branch offices for the purpose of this paragraph's reporting requirements.

(b) Except as otherwise directed in writing by the Assistant Secretary (Enforcement) or the Commissioner of Internal Revenue: (b)(1) This section shall not require reports:* * *

(b)(1)(iii) By nonbank financial institutions of transactions with commercial banks (however, commercial banks must report such transactions with nonbank financial institutions).

(b)(2) A bank may exempt from the

reporting requirement of paragraph (a) of this section the following:

(b)(2)(i) Deposits or withdrawals of currency from an existing account by an established depositor who is a United States resident and operates a retail type of business in the United States. For the purpose of this subsection, a retail type of business is a business primarily engaged in providing goods to ultimate consumers and for which the business is paid in substantial portions by currency, except that dealerships which buy or sell motor vehicles, vessels, or aircraft are not included and their transactions may not be exempted from the reporting requirements of this section.

(b)(2)(ii) Deposits or withdrawals of currency from an existing account by an established depositor who is a United States resident and operates a sports arena, race track, amusement park, bar, restaurant, hotel, check cashing service licensed by state or local governments, vending machine company, theater, regularly scheduled passenger carrier or any public utility.

(b)(2)(iii) Deposits or withdrawals, exchanges of currency or other payments and transfers by local or state governments, or the United States or any of its agencies or instrumentalities.

(b)(2)(iv) Withdrawals for payroll purposes from an existing account by an established depositor who is a United States resident and operates a firm that regularly withdraws more than $10,000 in order to pay its employees in currency.

(c) In each instance the transactions exempted under paragraph (b) of this section must be in amounts which the bank may reasonably conclude do not exceed amounts commensurate with the customary conduct of the lawful, domestic business of that customer, or in the case of transactions with a local or state government or the United States or any of its agencies or instrumentalities, in amounts which are customary and commensurate with the authorized activities of the agency or instrumentality. This section does not permit a bank to exempt its transactions with nonbank financial institutions (except for check cashing services licensed by state or local governments and the United States Postal Service) nor will additional exemption authority by granted for such transaction (except transactions by other check cashers).

(d) After October 27, 1986, a bank may not place any customer on its exempt list without first preparing a written statement, signed by the customer, describing the customary conduct of the lawful domestic business of that customer and a detailed statement of reasons why such person is qualified for an exemption. The statement shall include the name, address, nature of business, taxpayer identification number, and account number of the customer being exempted. The signature, including the title and position of the person signing, will attest to the accuracy of the information concerning the name, address, nature of business, and tax identification number of the customer. * * *

Section 103.23 Reports of transportation of currency or monetary instruments.

(a) Each person who physically transports, mails, or ships, or causes to be physically transported, mailed, or shipped, or attempts to physically transport, mail or ship, or attempts to cause to be physically transported, mailed or shipped, currency or other monetary instruments in an aggregate amount exceeding $10,000 at one time from the United States to any place outside the United States, or into the United States from any place outside the United States, shall make a report thereof. A person is deemed to have caused such transportation, mailing or shipping when he aids, abets, counsels, commands, procures, or requests it to be done by a financial institution or any other person.

(b) Each person who receives in the U.S. currency or other monetary instruments in an aggregate amount exceeding $10,000 at one time which have been transported, mailed, or shipped to such person from any place outside the

United States with respect to which a report has not been filed under paragraph (a) of this section, whether or not required to be filed thereunder, shall make a report thereof, stating the amount, the date of receipt, the form of monetary instruments, and the person from whom received. * * *

(d) A transfer of funds through normal banking procedures which does not involve the physical transportation of currency or monetary instruments is not required to be reported by this section. This section does not require that more than one report be filed covering a particular transportation, mailing or shipping of currency or other monetary instruments with respect to which a complete and truthful report has been filed by a person. * * *

Section 103.24 Reports of foreign financial accounts.

Each person subject to the jurisdiction of the United States (except a foreign subsidiary of a U.S. person) having a financial interest in, or signature or other authority over, a bank, securities or other financial account in a foreign country shall report such relationship to the Commissioner of the Internal Revenue for each year in which such relationship exists* * *

Section 103.26 Reports of certain domestic coin and currency transactions.

(a) If the Secretary of the Treasury finds, upon the Secretary's own initiative or at the request of an appropriate Federal or State law enforcement official, that reasonable grounds exist for concluding that additional recordkeeping and/or reporting requirements are necessary to carry out the purposes of this Part and to prevent persons from evading the reporting/recordkeeping requirements of this Part, the Secretary may issue an order requiring any domestic financial institution or group of domestic financial institutions in a geographic area and any other person participating in the type of transaction to file a report in the manner and to the extent specified in such order. The order shall contain such information as the Secretary may describe concerning any transaction in which such financial institution is involved for the payment, receipt, or transfer of United States coins or currency (or such other monetary instruments as the Secretary may describe in such order) the total amounts or denominations of which are equal to or greater than an amount which the Secretary may prescribe.

(b) An order issued under paragraph (a) of this section shall be directed to the Chief Executive Officer of the financial institution and shall designate one or more of the following categories of information to be reported: Each deposit, withdrawal, exchange of currency or other payment or transfer, by, through or to such financial institution specified in the order, which involves all or any class of transactions in currency and/or monetary instruments equal to or exceeding an amount to be specified in the order.

(c) In issuing an order under paragraph (a) of this section, the Secretary will prescribe:

(c)(1) The dollar amount of transactions subject to the reporting requirement in the order;

(c)(2) The type of transaction or transactions subject to or exempt from a reporting requirement in the order;

(c)(3) The appropriate form for reporting the transactions required in the order;* * *

Section 103.27 Filing of reports.

(a)(1) A report required by s 103.22(a) shall be filed by the financial institution within 15 days following the day on which the reportable transaction occurred.

(a)(2) A report required by s 103.22(g) shall be filed by the bank within 15 days after receiving a request for the report.

(a)(3) A copy of each report filed pursuant to s103.22 shall be retained by the financial institution for a period of five years from the date of the report. * * *

Section 103.28 Identification required.

Before concluding any transaction with

respect to which a report is required under s 103.22, a financial institution shall verify and record the name and address of the individual presenting a transaction, as well as record the identity, account number, and the social security or taxpayer identification number, if any, of any person or entity on whose behalf such transaction is to be effected. * * *

Section 103.37 Additional records to be made and retained by currency dealers or exchangers.

(a)(1) After July 7, 1987, each currency dealer or exchanger shall secure and maintain a record of the taxpayer identification number of each person for whom a transaction account is opened or a line of credit is extended within 30 days after such account is opened or credit line extended. Where a person is a non-resident alien, the currency dealer or exchanger shall also record the person's passport number or a description of some other government document used to verify his identity.* * *

Section 103.41 Dollars as including foreign currency.

Wherever in this part an amount is stated in dollars, it shall be deemed to mean also the equivalent amount in any foreign currency.

Section 103.42 Photographic or other reproductions of Government obligations.

Nothing herein contained shall require or authorize the microfilming or other reproduction of (a) Currency or other obligation or security of the United States as defined in 18 U.S.C. 8, or (b) Any obligation or other security of any foreign government, the reproduction of which is prohibited by law.

Section 103.47 Civil penalty.

(a) For any willful violation, committed on or before October 12, 1984, of any reporting requirement for financial institutions under this Part or of any recordkeeping requirements of section 103.22, the Secretary may assess upon any domestic financial institution, and upon any partner, director, officer, or employee

thereof who willfully participates in the violation, a civil penalty not to exceed $1,000. (b) For any willful violation committed after October 12, 1984 and before October 28, 1986, of any reporting requirement for financial institutions under this part or of the recordkeeping requirements of s 103.32, the Secretary may assess upon any domestic financial institution, and upon any partner, director, officer, or employee thereof who willfully participates in the violation, a civil penalty not to exceed $10,000. * * *

Section 103.48 Forfeiture of currency or monetary instruments.

Any currency or other monetary instruments which are in the process of any transportation with respect to which a report is required under section 103.23 are subject to seizure and forfeiture to the United States if such report has not been filed as required in section 103.25, or contains material omissions or misstatements. The Secretary may, in his sole discretion, remit or mitigate any such forfeiture in whole or in part upon such terms and conditions as he deems reasonable.

Section 103.50 Enforcement authority with respect to transportation of currency or monetary instruments.

(a) If a customs officer has reasonable cause to believe that there is a monetary instrument being transported without the filing of the report required by sections 103.23 and 103.25 of this chapter, he may stop and search, without a search warrant, a vehicle, vessel, aircraft, or other conveyance, envelope or other container, or person entering or departing from the United States with respect to which or whom the officer reasonably believes is transporting such instrument.* * *

Part 406 - Seizure and Forfeiture of Gold for Violations of Gold Reserve Act of 1934 and Gold Regulations

Authority: R.S. 161, as amended, sec. 4, 48 Stat. 340; 5 USC 301, 31 USC 443. Source: 33 FR 4258, March 7, 1968, unless otherwise noted.

Sec. 406.1 Secret Service officers authorized to make seizures of gold.

All agents of the U.S. Secret Service, in addition to officers of the customs, are hereby authorized and designated to seize any gold which may be subject to forfeiture for violations of the Gold Reserve Act of 1934 (31 USC 440-445) and the Gold Regulations.

Sec. 406.2 Custody of seized gold valued not in excess of $2,500.

Any gold, the value of which does not exceed $2,500, seized by officers of the Secret Service pursuant to the Gold Reserve Act of 1934 and the Gold Regulations, if not needed as evidence or for further investigation by the Secret Service, shall be placed forthwith by the seizing officer in the custody of the district director of customs for the customs district in which such seizure is made. Such gold shall be accompanied by a report from the Secret Service showing the basis of the seizure and a citation to each of the statutes and sections of the Gold Regulations violated.

Sec. 406.3 Forfeiture of gold valued not in excess of $2,500.

The district director of customs receiving custody of gold seized by the Secret Service, shall, if no petition is filed for the remission of mitigation of the forfeiture incurred, institute summary forfeiture proceedings in the judicial district in which such seizure is made under the appropriate provisions of the law and Customs Regulations applicable to the forfeiture of merchandise imported contrary to law.

Sec. 406.4 Duties of customs officers.

The appropriate officials of the Bureau of Customs are hereby authorized and designated as the officers who shall perform such administrative duties in connection with the summary forfeiture of gold seized by the Secret Service, the sale or other disposition of such gold, and the remission of mitigation of the forfeiture of such gold, as may be necessary of proper by virtue of the provisions of the Gold Reserve Act of 1934 and the Gold Regulations, and by virtue of the provisions of the customs laws which the said Gold Reserve Act makes applicable in connection with the seizures and forfeitures incurred or alleged to have been incurred under the said act and regulations. In the performance of said administrative duties the appropriate officials of the Bureau of Customs shall be governed by the procedures established by the Customs Regulations insofar as such procedures are applicable and not inconsistent with the provisions of the Gold Reserve Act of 1934 and the Gold Regulations.

Sec. 406.5 Forfeiture of gold valued in excess of $2,500.

When the value of the gold seized by the Secret Service exceeds $2,500, the seizing officer shall furnish a report, approved by the principal local officer, to the U.S. attorney, and shall include in such report a statement of all the facts and circumstances of the case, together with the names of the witnesses and a citation to each of the statutes and sections of the Gold Regulations believed to have been violated and on which reliance may be had for forfeiture.

Executive orders

Executive Orders Relating to Coins (March 4, 1921, to date)

The Executive Order is a prerogative of the president which, when constitutionally permitted, has the full force of law. For example, the president has the authority to proclaim "National Coin Week," either of his own volition (as President Nixon did in 1974) or at the request of Congress (as President Reagan did in 1983). Below follows a brief listing of the use of Executive Orders in the coin field from the Harding administration (March 4, 1921) to the present.

The use has been sparing, and foreign

financial transaction in foreign exchange, credit, coin and currency restrictions with respect to occupied countries during World War II have been omitted.

The largest single use relates to gold and silver, and is simply presented for historic interest. The abbreviations used in the Congressional Information Service Index to Presidential Executive Orders and Proclamations includes: PR, for Presidential Proclamation, and EO, for Executive Order. No designation means it was an administrative order.

The fact that the annual Assay Commission has its membership designated by an Executive Order in 1926 does not mean that it was subsequently followed. Subsequent years, typically, had their recipient's name listed in the official Presidential Documents.

Annual Assay Commission, 1926-
Membership designation
1926-08-9

Coin Week, Natl, proclamation
1974-PR-4286; 1983-PR-5027

Commission of Fine Arts functions expansion
1921-EO-3524

Emergency preparedness, economic functions assignment to Treas. Dept. Sec.
1969-EO-11490

Gold Coin, bullion, and currency transactions, restrictions estab.
1933-EO-6260

Holding abroad by persons subject to U.S. jurisdiction, prohibition with exception for licensed coin collectors
1962-EO-11037

Revision
1934-EO-6556; 1960-EO-10896; 1961-EO-10905

Revocation
1974-EO-11825

Gold dollar weight, established
1934-PR-2072

Silver and silver coins importation and transportation regulations revision
1935-24-1

Silver coinage suspension until Dec. 31, 1937, previously extracted silver minting authorization
1937-24-1

Silver coinage suspension until Dec. 31, 1938, previously extracted silver minting authorization
1938-24-2

Silver mined from U.S. natural deposits, coinage mints receipt and addition to U.S. monetary stocks regs extension
1938-PR-2317

Regulations implementation
1933-PR-2067

Regulations partial revocation
1938-PR-2282

Regulations revision
1934-PR-2092; 1935-PR-2124; 1935-PR-2125

Regulations revision and extension
1937-PR-2268; 1939-PR-2342

Silver purchase for U.S. mints, delivery requirement and procedure established
1934-EO-6814

Revision
1934-EO-6895-A

Revocation
1938-EO-7877

Silver withdrawal from monetary use, suspension of free silver sales and use in coinage
1961-21-20

Gold ownership

It is 55 years, now, since Americans were prohibited from private gold ownership. The right was not restored until Dec. 31, 1974.

It is easy, with a dozen years of retrospect, and hindsight, to reflect on how ridiculous it seems that Americans were prohibited from owning gold. What follows now are extracts from the Order of the Acting Secretary of the Treasury, Henry Morgenthau Jr., requiring the delivery of gold coin bullion and gold certificates to the Treasurer of the United States, followed by Executive Order 6260, relating to the hoarding, export and earmarking of gold coin, bullion, or currency, issued by President Franklin Delano Roosevelt Aug. 28, 1933. Those form the substantive basis for gold prohibition regulations.

Gold coin turn-in order of the Secretary of the Treasury

Requiring the Delivery of Gold Coin, Gold Bullion, and Gold Certificates to the Treasurer of the United States

WHEREAS Section 11 of the Federal Reserve Act of December 23, 1913, as amended . . . provides . . .

"Whenever in the judgment of the Secretary of the Treasury such action is necessary to protect the currency system of the United States, the Secretary of the Treasury, in his discretion, may require any or all individuals, partnerships, association and corporations to pay and deliver to the Treasurer of the United States any or all gold coin, gold bullion, and gold certificates owned by such individuals, partnerships, associations and corporations. Upon receipt of such gold coin, gold bullion or gold certificates, the Secretary of the Treasury shall pay therefor an equivalent amount of any other form of coin or currency coined or issued under the laws of the United States. . . .

WHEREAS in my judgment such action is necessary to protect the currency system of the United States;

NOW, THEREFORE, I, HENRY MORGENTHAU, JR., ACTING SECRETARY of the TREASURY, do hereby require every person subject to the jurisdiction of the United States forthwith to pay and deliver to the Treasurer of the United States all gold coin, gold bullion, and gold certificates situated in the United States, owned by such person, except as follows:

A. Gold bullion owned by a person now holding such gold under a license heretofore granted by or under authority of the Secretary of the Treasury, pursuant to the Executive Order of August 23, 1933, Relating to the Hoarding, Export, and Earmarking of Gold Coin, Bullion, or Currency and to Transactions in Foreign Exchange;

B. Gold coin having a recognized special value to collectors or rare and unusual coin (but not including quarter eagles, otherwise known as $2.50 pieces);

C. Unmelted scrap gold and gold sweepings in an amount not exceeding in the aggregate $100 belonging to any one person; . . .

D. Gold coin, gold bullion, and gold certificates owned by a Federal reserve bank or the Reconstruction Finance Corporation; and

E. Gold bullion and foreign gold coin now situated in the Philippine Islands, American Samoa, Guam, Hawaii, Panama Canal Zone, Puerto Rico, or the Virgin Islands of the United States, owned by a person not domiciled or doing business in the continental United States.

Section 2. Delivery. The gold coin, gold bullion, and gold certificates herein required to be paid and delivered to the Treasurer of the United States shall be delivered by placing the same forthwith in the custody of a Federal reserve bank or branch or a bank member of the Federal Reserve System for the account of the United States. . . .

Section 3. Payment and Reimbursement of Costs. Upon receipt of the confirmation signed and delivered as required under Section 2, the Secretary of the Treasury will pay for the gold coin, gold bullion, and gold certificates placed in custody for the account of the United States in accordance with Section 2, and equivalent amount of any form of coin or currency coined or issued under the laws of the United States designated by the Secretary of the Treasury. . . .

Section 4. Definitions. As used in this Order, the term "person" means any individual, partnership, association, or corporation; the term "United States" means the United States and any place subject to the jurisdiction thereof; the term "continental United States" means the States of the United States, the District of Columbia, and the Territory of Alaska; the term "gold coin" means any coin containing gold, including foreign gold coin; and the term "gold bullion" means any gold which has been put through a process of smelting or refining that is in such form that its value depends upon the gold content and not upon the form, but does not include gold coin or metals containing less than five troy ounces of fine gold per short ton.

Section 5. Any individual, partnership, association, or corporation failing to comply with any requirement hereof or of any rules or regulations issued by the Secretary of the Treasury hereunder shall be subject to the penalty provided in Section 11(n) of the Federal Reserve Act, as amended.

This order may be modified or revoked at any time.

H. Morgenthau, Jr., Acting Secretary of the Treasury.
APPROVED: Franklin D. Roosevelt
THE WHITE HOUSE
December 28, 1933

Executive Order [No. 6260] August 28, 1933

Relating to the Hoarding, Export, and Earmarking of Gold Coin, Bullion, or Currency and to Transactions in Foreign Exchange:

By virtue of the authority vested in me by section 5(b) of the act of October 6, 1917, as amended by section 2 of the act of March 9, 1933, entitled "An act to provide relief in the existing national emergency in banking and for other purposes," I, FRANKLIN D. ROOSEVELT, PRESIDENT of the UNITED STATES OF AMERICA, do declare that a period of national emergency exists, and by virtue of said authority and of all other authority vested in me, do hereby prescribe the following provisions for the investigation and regulation of the hoarding, earmarking, and export of gold coin, gold bullion, and gold certificates by any person within the United States or any place subject to the jurisdiction thereof; and for the investigation and regulation of transactions in foreign exchange and transfers of credit and the export and withdrawal of currency

from the United States or any place subject to the jurisdiction thereof by any person within the United States or any place subject to the jurisdiction thereof. . . .

Section 3. Returns. Within 15 days from the date of this order every person in possession of and every person owning gold coin, gold bullion, or gold certificates shall make under oath and file as hereinafter provided a return to the Secretary of the Treasury containing true and complete information relative thereto, including the name and address of the person making the return; the kind and amount of such coin, bullion, or certificates held and the location thereof; if held for another, the capacity in which held and the person for whom held, together with the post-office address of such person; and the nature of the transaction requiring the holding of such coin, bullion, or certificates and a statement explaining why such transaction cannot be carried out by the use of currency other than gold certificates; provided that no returns are required to be filed with respect to —

(a) Gold coin, gold bullion, and gold certificates in an amount not exceeding in the aggregate $100 belonging to any one person; (b) Gold coin having a recognized special value to collectors of rare and unusual coin; (c) Gold coin, gold bullion, and gold certificates acquired or held under a license heretofore granted by or under authority of the Secretary of the Treasury; and (d) Gold coin, gold bullion, and gold certificates owned by Federal Reserve banks. . . .

Section 4. Acquisition of gold coin and gold bullion. No person other than a Federal Reserve bank shall after the date of this order acquire in the United States any gold coin, gold bullion, or gold certificates except under license therefor issued pursuant to this Executive order. . . .

The Secretary of the Treasury, subject to such further regulations as he may prescribe, shall issue licenses authorizing the acquisition of —

(a) Gold coin or gold bullion which the Secretary is satisfied is required for a necessary and lawful transaction for which currency other than gold certificates cannot be used, by an applicant who establishes that since March 9, 1933, he has surrendered an equal amount of gold coin, gold bullion, or gold certificates to a banking institution in the continental United States or to the Treasurer of the United States; (b) Gold coin or gold bullion which the Secretary is satisfied is required by an applicant who holds a license to export such an amount of gold coin or gold bullion issued under subdivisions (c) or (d) of section 66 hereof, and (c) Gold bullion which the Secretary, or such agency as he may designate, is satisfied is required for legitimate and customary use in industry, profession, or art by an applicant regularly engaged in such industry, profession, or art, or in the business of furnishing gold therefor. Licenses issued pursuant to this section shall authorize the holder to acquire gold coin and gold bullion only from the sources specified by the Secretary of the Treasury in regulations issued hereunder.

Section 5. Holding of gold coin, gold bullion, and gold certificates. After 30 days from the date of this order no person shall hold in his possession or retain any interest, legal or equitable in any gold coin, gold bullion, or gold certificates situated in the United States. . . .

Section 9. The Secretary of the Treasury is hereby authorized and empowered to issue such regulations as he may deem necessary to carry out the purposes of this order. Such regulations may provide for the detention in the United States of any gold coin, gold bullion, or gold certificates sought to be transported beyond the limits of the continental United States, pending an investigation to determine if such coin, bullion, or certificates are held or are to be acquired in violation of the provisions of this Executive order. Licenses and permits granted in accordance with the provisions of this order and the regulations prescribed hereunder, may be issued through such officers or agencies as the Secretary may designate.

Section 10. Whoever willfully violates any provision of this Executive order or of any license, order, rule, or regulation issued or prescribed hereunder, shall, upon conviction, be fined not more than $10,000, or, if a natural person, may be imprisoned for not more than 10 years, or both; and any officer, director, or agent of any corporation who knowingly participates in such violation may be punished by a like fine, imprisonment, or both.

Section 11. The Executive orders of April 5, 1933, forbidding the hoarding of gold coin, gold bullion, and gold certificates, and April 20, 1933, relating to foreign exchange and the earmarking and export of gold coin or bullion or currency, respectively, are hereby revoked. . . .

FRANKLIN D. ROOSEVELT.
THE WHITE HOUSE,
August 28, 1933.

United States Code, Title 18

Title 18 of the United States Code governs "crimes and criminal procedure," and several sections relate to currency mutilation, debasement of coinage, counterfeiting and other criminal offenses. What follows are extracts of Title 18. Title 18 has been enacted as positive law. This means that unlike many other sections of the United States Code, which merely evidence what the law is, Title 18 is itself the law of the land. The same is applicable to Title 31.

One recent development is worth noting. The Supreme Court recently had occasion to analyze Sec. 504, concerning illustrations utilizing numismatic themes. See the notation (footnote) following Sec. 504 for an analysis of this.

The title has been clarified for use by the layman and to make it easily readable. Sections not dealing with numismatics have been omitted.

Presidential seal

A section of Title 18 not outlined below gives the president authority to change regulations governing the seals of the president and vice president.

On May 28, 1976, President Ford, by authority of this section of the Title, amended subsection (b) of section 1 of Executive Order No. 11649 to read that the presidential and vice presidential seals may be used "in encyclopedias, dictionaries, books, journals, pamphlets, periodicals, or magazines incident to a description or history of seals, coats of arms, heraldry or the Presidency or Vice Presidency."

Chapter 17 coins and currency

Sec. 331. Mutilation, diminution, and falsification of coins

Whoever fraudulently alters, defaces, mutilates, impairs, diminishes, falsifies, scales, or lightens any of the coins coined at the Mints of the United States, or any foreign coins which are by law made current or are in actual use or circulation as money within the United States; or

Whoever fraudulently possesses, passes, utters, publishes, or sells, or attempts to pass, utter, publish, or sell, or brings into the United States, any such coin, knowing the same to be altered, defaced, mutilated, impaired, diminished, falsified, scaled, or lightened

Shall be fined not more than $2,000 or imprisoned not more than five years, or both.

Sec. 332. Debasement of coins; alteration of official scales, or embezzlement of metals

If any of the gold or silver coins struck or coined at any of the Mints of the United States shall be debased, or made worse as to the proportion of fine gold or fine silver therein contained, or shall be of less weight or value than the same ought to be, pursuant to law, or if any of the scales or weights used at any of the Mints or assay offices of the United States shall be defaced, altered, increased, or diminished through the fault or connivance of any officer or person employed at the said Mints or assay offices, with a fraudulent intent; or if any such officer or person shall embezzle any of the metals at any time committed to his charge for the purpose of being coined, or any of the coins struck or coined at the said Mints, or any medals, coins, or other moneys of said Mints or assay offices at any time committed to his charge, or of which he may have assumed the charge, every such officer or person who commits any of the said offenses shall be fined not more than $10,000 or imprisoned not more than 10 years, or both.

Sec. 333. Mutilation of national bank obligations

Whoever mutilates, cuts, defaces, disfigures, or perforates, or unites or cements together, or does any other thing to any bank bill, draft, note, or other evidence of debt issued by any national banking association, or Federal Reserve bank, or the Federal Reserve System, with intent to render such bank bill, draft, note, or other evidence of debt unfit to be reissued, shall be fined not more than $100 or imprisoned not more than six months, or both.

Sec. 334. Issuance of Federal Reserve or national bank notes

Whoever, being a Federal Reserve Agent, or an agent or employee of such Federal Reserve Agent, or of the Board of Governors of the Federal Reserve System, issues or puts in circulation any Federal Reserve notes, without complying with or in violation of the provisions of law regulating the issuance and circulation of such Federal Reserve notes; or

Whoever, being an officer acting under the provisions of Chapter 2 of Title 12, countersigns or delivers to any national banking association, or to any other company or person, any circulating notes contemplated by that chapter except in strict accordance with its provisions,

Shall be fined not more than $5,000 or imprisoned not more than five years, or both.

Sec. 335. Circulation of obligations of

expired corporations

Whoever, being a director, officer, or agent of a corporation created by Act of Congress, the charter of which has expired, or trustee thereof, or an agent of such trustee, or a person having in his possession or under his control the property of such corporation for the purpose of paying or redeeming its notes and obligations, knowingly issues, reissues, or utters as money, or in any other way knowingly puts in circulation any bill, note, check, draft, or other security purporting to have been made by any such corporation, or by any officer thereof, or purporting to have been made under authority derived therefrom, shall be fined not more than $10,000 or imprisoned not more than five years, or both.

Sec. 336. Issuance of circulating obligations of less than $1

Whoever makes, issues, circulates, or pays out any note, check, memorandum, token, or other obligation for a less sum than $1, intended to circulate as money or to be received or used in lieu of lawful money of the United States, shall be fined not more than $500 or imprisoned not more than six months, or both.

Sec. 337. Coins as security for loans

Whoever lends or borrows money or credit upon the security of such coins of the United States as the Secretary of the Treasury may from time to time designate by proclamation published in the Federal Register, during any period designated in such a proclamation, shall be fined not more than $10,000 or imprisoned not more than one year, or both.

Chapter 25 counterfeiting and forgery

Sec. 471. Obligations or securities of United States

Whoever, with intent to defraud, falsely makes, forges, counterfeits, or alters any obligation or other security of the United States, shall be fined not more than $5,000 or imprisoned not more than 15 years, or both.

Sec. 472. Uttering counterfeit

obligations or securities

Whoever, with intent to defraud, passes, utters, publishes, or sells, or attempts to pass, utter, publish, or sell, or with like intent brings into the United States or keeps in possession or conceals any falsely made, forged, counterfeited, or altered obligation or other security of the United States, shall be fined not more than $5,000 or imprisoned not more than 15 years, or both.

Sec. 473. Dealing in counterfeit obligations or securities

Whoever buys, sells, exchanges, transfers, receives, or delivers any false, forged, counterfeited, or altered obligation or other security of the United States, with the intent that the same be passed, published, or used as true and genuine, shall be fined not more than $5,000 or imprisoned not more than 10 years, or both.

Sec. 474. Plates or stones for counterfeiting obligations or securities

Whoever, having control, custody, or possession of any plate, stone, or other thing, or any part thereof, from which has been printed, or which may be prepared by direction of the Secretary of the Treasury for the purpose of printing, any obligation or other security of the United States, uses such plate, stone, or other thing, or any part thereof, or knowingly suffers the same to be used for the purpose of printing any such or similar obligation or other security, or any part thereof, except as may be printed for the use of the United States by order of the proper officer thereof; or

Whoever makes or executes any plate, stone, or other thing in the likeness of any plate designated for the printing of such obligation or other security; or

Whoever sells any such plate, stone, or other thing, or brings into the United States any such plate, stone, or other thing, except under the direction of the Secretary of the Treasury or other proper officer, or with any other intent, in either case, than that such plate, stone, or other thing be used for the printing of the obligations or other securities of the United States; or

Whoever has in his control, custody, or possession any plate, stone, or other thing in any manner made after or in the similitude of any plate, stone, or other thing, from which any such obligation or other security has been printed, with intent to use such plate, stone, or other thing, or to suffer the same to be used in forging or counterfeiting any such obligation or other security, or any part thereof; or

Whoever has in his possession or custody, except under authority from the Secretary of the Treasury or other proper officer, any obligation or other security made or executed, in whole or in part, after the similitude of any obligation or other security issued under the authority of the United States, with intent to sell or otherwise use the same; or

Whoever prints, photographs, or in any other manner makes or executes any engraving, photograph, print, or impression in the likeness of any such obligation or other security, or any part thereof, or sells any such engraving, photograph, print, or impression, except to the United States, or brings into the United States, any such engraving, photograph, print, or impression, except by direction of some proper officer of the United States; or

Whoever has or retains in his control or possession, after a distinctive paper has been adopted by the Secretary of the Treasury or some other proper officer of the United States,

Shall be fined not more than $5,000 or imprisoned not more than 15 years, or both.

Sec. 475. Imitating obligations or securities; advertisements

Whoever designs, engraves, prints, makes, or executes, or utters, issues, distributes, circulates, or uses any business or professional card, notice, placard, circular, handbill, or advertisement in the likeness or similitude of any obligation or security of the United States issued under or authorized by any Act of Congress or writes, prints, or otherwise impresses upon or attaches to any such instrument,

obligation, or security, or any coin of the United States, any business or professional card, notice, or advertisement, or any notice or advertisement whatever, shall be fined not more than $500.

Sec. 476. Taking impressions of tools used for obligations or securities

Whoever, without authority from the United States, takes, procures, or makes an impression, stamp, or imprint of, from or by the use of any tool, implement, instrument, or thing used or fitted or intended to be used in printing, stamping, or impressing, or in making other tools, implements, instruments, or things to be used or fitted or intended to be used in printing, stamping, or impressing any obligation or other security of the United States, shall be fined not more than $5,000 or imprisoned not more than 10 years, or both.

Sec. 477. Possessing or selling impressions of tools used for obligations or securities

Whoever, with intent to defraud, possesses, keeps, safeguards, or controls, without authority from the United States, any imprint, stamp, or impression, taken or made upon any substance or material whatsoever, of any tool, implement, instrument or thing, used, fitted or intended to be used, for any of the purposes mentioned in Section 476 of this title; or

Whoever, with intent to defraud, sells, gives, or delivers any such imprint, stamp, or impression to any other person shall be fined not more than $5,000 or imprisoned not more than 10 years, or both.

Sec. 478. Foreign obligations or securities

Whoever, within the United States, with intent to defraud, falsely makes, alters, forges, or counterfeits any bond, certificate, obligation, or other security of any foreign government, purporting to be or in imitation of any such security issued under the authority of such foreign government, or any Treasury note, bill, or promise to pay, lawfully issued by such foreign government and intended to circulate as money, shall be fined not more than $5,000 or imprisoned not more than five years, or both.

Sec. 479. Uttering counterfeit foreign obligations or securities

Whoever, within the United States, knowingly and with intent to defraud, utters, passes, or puts off, in payment or negotiation, any false, forged, or counterfeited bond, certificate, obligation, security, Treasury note, bill, or promise to pay, mentioned in Section 478 of this title, whether or not the same was made, altered, forged, or counterfeited within the United States, shall be fined not more than $3,000 or imprisoned not more than three years, or both.

Sec. 480. Possessing counterfeit foreign obligations or securities

Whoever, within the United States, knowingly and with intent to defraud, possesses or delivers any false, forged, or counterfeit bond, certificate, obligation, security, Treasury note, bill, promise to pay, bank note, or bill issued by a bank or corporation of any foreign country, shall be fined not more than $1,000 or imprisoned not more than one year, or both.

Sec. 481. Plates or stones for counterfeiting foreign obligations or securities

Whoever, within the United States except by lawful authority, controls, holds, or possesses any plate, stone, or other thing, or any part thereof, from which has been printed or may be printed any counterfeit note, bond, obligation, or other security, in whole or in part, or any foreign government, bank, or corporation, or uses such plate, stone, or other thing, or knowingly permits or suffers the same to be used in counterfeiting such foreign obligations, or any part thereof; or

Whoever, except by lawful authority, makes or engraves any plate, stone, or other thing in the likeness or similitude of any plate, stone, or other thing designated for the printing of the genuine issues of the obligations of any foreign government, bank, or corporation; or

Whoever, except by lawful authority, prints, photographs, or makes, executes, or sells any engraving, photograph, print, or impression in the likeness of any genuine note, bond, obligation, or other security, or any part thereof, of any foreign government, bank, or corporation; or

Whoever brings into the United States any counterfeit plate, stone, or other thing, engraving, photograph, print, or other impressions of the notes, bonds, obligations, or other securities of any foreign government, bank, or corporation shall be fined not more than $5,000 or imprisoned not more than five years, or both.

Sec. 482. Foreign bank notes

Whoever, within the United States, with intent to defraud, falsely makes, alters, forges, or counterfeits any bank note or bill issued by a bank or corporation of any foreign country, and intended by the law or usage of such foreign country to circulate as money, such bank or corporation being authorized by the laws of such country, shall be fined not more than $2,000 or imprisoned not more than two years, or both.

Sec. 483. Uttering counterfeit foreign bank notes

Whoever, within the United States, utters, passes, puts off, or tenders in payment, with intent to defraud, any such false, forged, altered, or counterfeited bank note or bill, mentioned in Section 482 of this title, knowing the same to be so false, forged, altered, and counterfeited, whether or not the same was made, forged, altered, or counterfeited within the United States, shall be fined not more than $1,000 or imprisoned not more than one year, or both.

Sec. 484. Connecting parts of different notes

Whoever so places or connects together different parts of two or more notes, bills, or other genuine instruments issued under the authority of the United States, or by any foreign government, or corporation, as to produce one instrument, with intent to defraud, shall be guilty of forgery in the same manner as if the parts to put together were falsely made or forged, and shall be fined not more than $1,000 or imprisoned not more than five years, or both.

Sec. 485. Coins or bars

Whoever falsely makes, forges, or counterfeits any coin or bar in resemblance or similitude of any coin of a denomination higher than 5 cents or any gold or silver bar coined or stamped at any Mint or assay office of the United States, or in resemblance or similitude of any foreign gold or silver coin current in the United States or in actual use and circulation as money within the United States; or

Whoever passes, utters, publishes, sells, possesses, or brings into the United States any false, forged, or counterfeit coin or bar, knowing the same to be false, forged, or counterfeit, with intent to defraud any body politic or corporate, or any person, or attempts the commission of any offense described in this paragraph, shall be fined not more than $5,000 or imprisoned not more than 15 years, or both.

Sec. 486. Uttering coins of gold, silver or other metal

Whoever, except as authorized by law, makes or utters or passes, or attempts to utter or pass, any coins of gold or silver or other metal, or alloys of metals, intended for use as current money, whether in the resemblance of coins of the United States or of foreign countries, or of original design, shall be fined not more than $3,000 or imprisoned not more than five years, or both.

Sec. 487. Making or possessing counterfeit dies for coins

Whoever, without lawful authority, makes any die, hub, or mold, or any part thereof, either of steel or plaster, or any other substance, in likeness or similitude, as to the design or the inscription thereon, of any die, hub, or mold designated for the coining or making of any of the genuine gold, silver, nickel, bronze, copper, or other coins coined at the Mints of the United States; or

Whoever, without lawful authority, possesses any such die, hub, or mold, or any part thereof, or permits the same to be used for or in aid of the counterfeiting of any such coins of the United States, shall be fined not more than $5,000 or imprisoned not more than 15 years, or both.

Sec. 488. Making or possessing counterfeit dies for foreign coins

Whoever, within the United States, without lawful authority, makes any die, hub, or mold, or any part thereof, either of steel or of plaster, or of any other substance, in the likeness or similitude, as to the design or the inscription thereon, of any die, hub, or mold designated for the coining of the genuine coin of any foreign government; or

Whoever, without lawful authority, possesses any such die, hub, or mold, or any part thereof, or conceals, or knowingly suffers the same to be used for the counterfeiting of any foreign coin, shall be fined not more than $5,000 or imprisoned not more than five years, or both.

Sec. 489. Making or possessing likeness of coins

Whoever, within the United States, makes or brings therein from any foreign country, or possesses with intent to sell, give away, or in any other manner uses the same, except under authority of the Secretary of the Treasury or other proper officer of the United States, any token, disk, or device in the likeness or similitude as to design, color, or the inscription thereon of any of the coins of the United States or of any foreign country issued as money, either under the authority of the United States or under the authority of any foreign government shall be fined not more than $100.

Sec. 490. Minor coins

Whoever falsely makes, forges, or counterfeits any coin in the resemblance or similitude of any of the one-cent and 5-cent coins minted at the Mints of the United States; or

Whoever passes, utters, publishes, or sells, or brings into the United States, or possesses any such false, forged, or counterfeited coin, with intent to defraud any person, shall be fined not more than $1,000 or imprisoned not more than three years, or both.

Sec. 491. Tokens or paper used as money

(a) Whoever, being 18 years of age or over, not lawfully authorized, makes, issues, or passes any coin, card, token, or device in metal, or its compounds, intended to be used as money, or whoever, being 18 years of age or over, with intent to defraud, makes, utters, inserts, or uses any card, token, slug, disk, device, paper, or other thing similar in size and shape to any of the lawful coins or other currency of the United States or any coin or other currency not legal tender in the United States, to procure anything of value, or the use or enjoyment of any property or service from any automatic merchandise vending machine, postage-stamp machine, turnstile, fare box, coinbox telephone, parking meter or other lawful receptacle, depository, or contrivance designed to receive or to be operated by lawful coins or other currency of the United States, shall be fined not more than $1,000, or imprisoned not more than one year, or both.

(b) Whoever manufactures, sells, offers, or advertises for sale, or exposes or keeps with intent to furnish or sell any token, slug, disk, device, paper, or other thing similar in size and shape to any of the lawful coins or other currency of the United States, or any token, disk, paper, or other device issued or authorized in connection with rationing or food and fiber distribution by any agency of the United States, with knowledge or reason to believe that such tokens, slugs, disks, devices, papers, or other things are intended to be used unlawfully or fraudulently to procure anything of value, or the use or enjoyment of any property or service from any automatic merchandise vending machine, postage-stamp machine, turnstile, fare box, coinbox telephone, parking meter, or other lawful receptacle, depository, or contrivance designed to receive or to be operated by lawful coins or other currency of the United States shall be fined not more than $1,000 or imprisoned not more than one year, or both.

Nothing contained in this section shall create immunity from criminal prosecution under the laws of any state, Commonwealth of Puerto Rico, territory, possession, or the District of Columbia.

(c) "Knowledge or reason to believe," within the meaning of paragraph (b) of this section, may be shown by proof that any law enforcement officer has, prior to the commission of the offense with which the defendant is charged, informed the defendant that tokens, slugs, disks, or other devices of the kind manufactured, sold, offered, or advertised for sale by him or exposed or kept with intent to furnish or sell, are being used unlawfully or fraudulently to operate certain specified automatic merchandise vending machines, postage-stamp machines, turnstiles, fare boxes, coin-box telephones, parking meters, or other receptacles, depositories, or contrivances, designed to receive or to be operated by lawful coins of the United States.

Sec. 492. Forfeiture of counterfeit paraphernalia

All counterfeits of any coins or obligations or other securities of the United States or of any foreign government, or any articles, devices, and other things made, possessed, or used in violation of this chapter or of this title, or any material or apparatus used or fitted or intended to be used, in the making of such counterfeits, articles, devices or things, found in the possession of any person without authority from the Secretary of the Treasury or other proper officer, shall be forfeited to the United States.

Whoever, having the custody or control of any such counterfeits, material, apparatus, articles, devices, or other things, fails or refuses to surrender possession thereof upon request by any authorized agent of the Treasury Department, or other proper officer, shall be fined not more than $100 or imprisoned not more than one year, or both.

Whenever, except as hereinafter in this section provided, any person interested in any article, device, or other thing, or material or apparatus seized under this section files with the Secretary of the Treasury, before the disposition thereof, a petition for the remission or mitigation of such forfeiture, the Secretary of the Treasury, if he finds that such forfeiture was incurred without willful negligence or without any intention on the part of the petitioner to violate the law, or finds the existence of such mitigating circumstances as to justify the remission or the mitigation of such forfeiture, may remit or mitigate the same upon such terms and conditions as he deems reasonable and just.

If the seizure involves offenses other than offenses against the coinage, currency, obligations or securities of the United States or any foreign government, the petition for the remission or mitigation of forfeiture shall be referred to the Attorney General, who may remit or mitigate the forfeiture upon such terms as he deems reasonable and just.

Sec. 504. Printing and filming of United States and foreign obligations and securities*

Notwithstanding any other provision of this chapter, the following are permitted:

(1) the printing, publishing, or importation, or the making or importation of the necessary plates for such printing or publishing, of illustrations of

(A) postage stamps of the United States,

(B) revenue stamps of the United States,

(C) any other obligation or other security of the United States, and

(D) postage stamps, revenue stamps, notes, bonds, and any other obligation or other security of any foreign government, bank, or corporation, for philatelic, numismatic, educational, historical, or newsworthy purposes in articles, books, journals, newspapers, or albums (but not for advertising purposes, except illustrations of stamps and paper money in philatelic or numismatic advertising of

legitimate numismatists and dealers in stamps or publishers of or dealers in philatelic or numismatic articles, books, journals, newspapers, or albums). Illustrations permitted by the foregoing provisions of this section shall be made in accordance with the following conditions

(i) all illustrations shall be in black and white, except that illustrations of postage stamps issued by the United States or by any foreign government, and stamps issued under the Migratory Hunting Stamp Act of 1934 may be in color;

(ii) all illustrations (including illustrations of uncanceled postage stamps in color) shall be of a size less than three-fourths or more than one and one-half, in linear dimension, of each part of any matter so illustrated which is covered by subparagraph (A), (B), (C), or (D) of this paragraph, except that black and white illustrations of postage and revenue stamps issued by the United States or by any foreign government and colored illustrations of canceled postage stamps issued by the United States may be in the exact linear dimension in which the stamps were issued; and

(iii) the negatives and plates used in making the illustrations shall be destroyed after their final use in accordance with this section.

(2) the making or importation, but not for advertising purposes except philatelic advertising, of motion-picture films, microfilms, or slides, for projection upon a screen or for use in telecasting, of postage and revenue stamps and other obligations and securities of the United States, and postage and revenue stamps, notes, bonds, and other obligations or securities of any foreign government, bank, or corporation. No prints or other reproductions shall be made from such films or slides, except for the purposes of paragraph (1), without the permission of the Secretary of the Treasury.

For the purposes of this section the term "postage stamp" includes postage meter stamps.

*The Supreme Court of the United States offered a definitive interpretation of the meaning of this section of the law in Regan v. Time Inc., 468 US 641 (1984). The court held that subsection D, which purports to regulate the use in a newsworthy article, or for a newsworthy purpose, was unconstitutional. Despite the declaration, no change was made in the law or regulation.

Key American coinage laws, resolutions

Following is a list of key coinage laws and resolutions laws, American coinage acted on by Congress from the Joint Resolution which authorized creation of a Mint in March 1791, through the present day. The list is incomplete in that it does not include every enacted bill pertaining to coinage, but insofar as today's laws are derived from historical precedent, the listings may be of use to collectors and researchers.

To further assist in this, a brief annotation offering explanation of the general tenor of the legislation follows each law. The manner that the law is listed is as follows: The date of passage (either approved by the president, or date a veto was overridden by the Senate and House), followed by the chapter in the session laws or, if after 1959, the Public Law number. This is then followed by a number signifying in which volume of the Statutes at Large the complete text of the law is found.

In addition to containing public laws and resolutions acted on by Congress, some key executive orders and proclamations are also listed inasmuch as they relate to the coinage field.

Following the date of passage of an Act, reference is made to the Statutes at Large (Stat.) in which the law appears. The number preceding "Stat." is the volume; the number following is the page.

The abbreviation "ch." stands for the chapter of the session law in which the act passed.

Where a resolution or proclamation or other relevant citation is appropriate, it is likewise noted.

In 1983 Title 31 of the United States Code (which contained many of these older laws) was revised and cleansed of obsolete statutes, while those remaining were codified into

more contemporary language. The precise text of each of these laws that resulted appears elsewhere under the heading "United States Code, Title 31." The codified Title 31, rather than the original text of the law, is now enacted as positive law (though there remains a provision calling for the original to prevail in case of doubt). The laws referred to below, the dates of passage, and prior citations appear as a matter of historical record.

It is useful to remember that the legal effect of government on numismatics is not limited to laws. In 1974, for example, President Nixon proclaimed "National Coin Week," Presidential Proclamation No. 4286 (April 19, 1974), page 14,183 (Federal Register), just as President Reagan did a decade later (Proclamation No. 5027, 48 Fed. Reg. 9837). The "Hobby Protection Act," passed by Congress, became effective with the passage of regulations by the Federal Trade Commission (16 CFR part 304). The information following is a short list of those legislative pieces which are of recurring usefulness.

J. Res. No. 3, March 3, 1791, 1 Stat. 225	Joint Resolution to authorize a Mint for the United States.
April 2, 1792, ch. 16, 1 Stat. 246.	Original Mint Act.
May 8, 1792, ch. 39, 1 Stat. 283.	Authorization for purchase of copper for cents and half cents.
Jan. 14, 1793, ch. 2, 1 Stat. 299.	Changes weight of copper cent and half cent.
Feb. 9, 1793, ch. 5, 1 Stat. 300.	Legal status of foreign coins in U.S.
March 3, 1795, ch. 47, 1 Stat. 439.	Permits president to reduce weight of copper coinage and allows seigniorage.
Feb. 1, 1798, ch. 11, 1 Stat. 539.	Legal status of foreign coins in U.S.
May 14, 1800, ch. 70, 2 Stat. 86.	Extension of Mint location at Philadelphia for two years.
March 3, 1801, ch. 21, 2 Stat. 111.	Further extension of Mint location at Philadelphia.

April 10, 1806, ch. 22, 2 Stat. 374.	Legal status of foreign coins in U.S.
March 3, 1819, ch. 97, 3 Stat. 525.	Continues in force legal tender values of foreign coin in U.S.
May 19, 1828, ch. 67, 4 Stat. 277.	Continuation of Mint at Philadelphia until otherwise provided by law.
June 28, 1834, ch. 96, 4 Stat. 700.	Reduces weight of foreign gold coins (revaluation of the dollar).
March 3, 1835, ch. 39, 4 Stat. 774.	Authorizes establishment of branch Mints.
Jan. 18, 1837, ch. 3, 5 Stat. 136.	Coinage Act of 1837, codification repealing all prior inconsistent laws.
April 22, 1864, ch. 64, 13 Stat. 54.	Two-cent piece created.
Feb. 12, 1873, ch. 131, 17 Stat. 424.	Coinage Act of 1873 (codification).
Jan. 29, 1874, ch. 19, 18 Stat. 6, 31 U.S.C. Sec. 5111(a)(4).	Permits U.S. Mint to strike coins for foreign governments.
June 20, 1874, ch. 320, 18 Stat. 97.	Re-establishes New Orleans as a branch Mint.
Jan. 14, 1875, ch. 15, 18 Stat. 296.	Resumption of specie payment authorized.
March 3, 1875, ch. 143, 18 Stat. 478.	Creation of 20-cent piece.
April 17, 1876, ch. 63, 19 Stat. 33.	Use of silver coin to redeem fractional currency permitted.
Feb. 28, 1878, ch. 20, 20 Stat. 25.	Bland-Allison Act.
May 2, 1878, ch. 79, 20 Stat. 47.	Prohibits further coining of 20-cent piece.
June 9, 1879, ch. 12, 21 Stat. 8, now part of 31 U.S.C. Sec. 5103.	Limits legal tender status of silver coins.
March 3, 1887, ch. 396, 24 Stat. 634.	Trade dollar eliminated.
July 14, 1890, ch. 708, 26 Stat. 289.	Silver purchase act, discontinuance of dollar coinage.
Sept. 26, 1890, ch. 944, 26 Stat. 484, 31 U.S.C. Sec. 5112.	Prohibits design changes more often than once in 25 years.
Sept. 26, 1890, ch. 945, 26 Stat. 485.	Discontinues $3 and $1 gold coins, nickel 3-cent piece.
Nov. 1, 1893, ch. 8, 28 Stat. 4 (formerly 31 USC 311)	Bimetallism.
June 4, 1897, ch. 2, 30 Stat. 27.	Recoinage of uncurrent gold and silver coin authorized by appropriation.
March 14, 1900, ch. 41, 31 Stat. 45.	Gold Standard Act of 1900.
Aug. 23, 1912, ch. 350, 37 Stat. 384.	Redefines duties of superintendents of the Mints and New York Assay Office.
Aug. 28, 1933, EO 6260.	Recall of all gold coins.
Jan. 30, 1934, ch. 6, 48 Stat. 337.	Gold Reserve Act of 1934, effectively ending gold coinage.
Dec. 18, 1942, ch. 767, 56 Stat. 1064.	War Powers Act of 1942 (authorizes compositional change in cent and creation of a 3-cent piece).
Sept. 5, 1962, Pub. L. 87-643, 76 Stat. 440.	Compositional change eliminating tin.
Aug. 20, 1963, Pub. L. 88-102, 77 Stat. 129.	Permits appropriations for new Philadelphia Mint; subsequently, Denver Mint.
Dec. 30, 1963, Pub. L. 88-256, 77 Stat. 843.	Authorizes Kennedy half dollar.
Sept. 3, 1964, Pub. L. 88-580, 78 Stat. 908, repealed by Pub. L. 89-81, Title II Sec. 204(b).	Authorizes "date freeze" on coinage.
July 23, 1965, Pub. L. 89-81, 79 Stat. 254, 31 U.S.C.	Coinage Act of 1965; clad coinage composition; Joint Commission on the Coinage.
Dec. 31, 1970, Pub. L. 91-607, Title II, 84 Stat. 1769.	One Bank Holding Company Act of 1970, creation of Eisenhower dollar, elimination of silver in half dollar.
Feb. 15, 1972, Pub. L. 92-228, 86 Stat. 37.	Bicentennial medallic commemoration authorized.
Oct. 18, 1973, Pub. L. 93-127, 87 Stat. 456, 31 U.S.C.	Bicentennial coinage legislation (creates new reverse for quarter, half dollar and dollar, authorizes dual-date obverse, and silver-clad collector coins)
Nov. 29, 1973, Pub. L. 93-167, 87 Stat. 686, 15 U.S.C. Sec. 2101 et seq.	Hobby Protection Act.
Dec. 11, 1973, Pub. L. 93-179, 87 Stat. 704.	Bicentennial medal program curtailed.
Oct. 11, 1974, Pub. L. 93-441.	Authorizes compositional change in 1-cent coin under certain prescribed circumstances, by either lowering the copper content or alternatively permitting a new composition other than copper-zinc.
Dec. 26, 1974, Pub. L. 93-541.	Amends Bicentennial legislation to permit simultaneous production of Bicentennial coinage and other dates during calendar year 1975 and gives Mint additional time to produce the whole 45 million silver-clad commemorative collector issues.
Oct. 10, 1978, Pub. L. 95-447, 92 Stat. 1072.	Approved Susan B. Anthony dollar.

Nov. 10, 1978, Pub. L. 95-630, 92 Stat. 3679.	American Arts Gold Medallion Act.
March 14, 1980, Pub. L. 96-209. Title II, 94 Stat. 98.	Abolition of Assay Commission.
Dec. 23, 1981, Pub. L. 97-104, 95 Stat. 1491 (formerly 31 U.S.C. 399).	George Washington commemorative coin authorized.
July 22, 1982, Pub. L. 97-220, 96 Stat. 222.	Olympic commemorative coin legislation.
Sept. 13, 1982, Pub. L. 97-258, 96 Stat. 877.	Revision of Title 31, U.S. Code (codification).
Nov. 14, 1983, Pub. L. 98-151, 97 Stat. 979.	Section 123 directs annual sale of Uncirculated and Proof sets.
July 9, 1985, Pub. L. 99-61, Title 1, 99 Stat. 113 (31 USC Sec. 5112 note).	Statue of Liberty-Ellis Island Commemorative Coin Act.
July 9, 1985, Pub. L. 99-61, Title 2, 99 Stat. 113 (31 USC Sec. 5112)	Liberty Coin Act-Silver Dollar Liberty Coin
Pub. L. 99-185	Gold Bullion Coin Act of 1985
Pub. L. 99-188, Dec. 17, 1985, 99 Stat. 1177 (31 USC Sec. 5112)	Gold Bullion Coin Act of 1985 and Silver Bullion Coin.
Oct. 29, 1986, Pub. L. 99-582, 100 Stat. 3315 (31 USC Sec. 5112 note)	Bicentennial of Constitution commemorative coins.
Nov. 7, 1986, Pub. L. 99-631, 100 Stat. 3518	Ban importation of Soviet gold coins, 22 USC sec 5100.
Oct. 28, 1987, Pub. L. 100-141, 101 Stat. 832	Olympic Commemorative Coin Act of 1988
Aug. 1, 1988, Pub. L. 100-378, 102 Stat. 887	Bicentennial of U.S. Congress Commemorative Coin Act.
Oct 3, 1988, Pub. L. 100-467, 102 Stat. 2275	Dwight D. Eisenhower Commemorative Coin Act of 1988.
Nov. 11, 1988, Pub. L. 100-647, 26 USC sec. 408(m)(3)	Sec. 6057. Prohibition on collectibles not to include State coins.
Nov. 17, 1988, Pub. L. 100-673, 102 Stat. 3992.	Sec'y of Treasury authorized to mint coins in commemoration of the Bicentennial of the U.S. Congress.
Nov. 17, 1988, Pub. L. 100-674, 102 Stat. 49.	Congressional Award Act Amendments of 1988-Gold Medal Awards ceremony in District of Columbia.
Nov. 18, 1989, Pub. L. 100-696, 102 Stat. .	Surcharges on commemorative coin uses.
Jun. 9, 1989, Pub. L. 101-36, 103 Stat. 69.	First strike ceremony for the Bicentennial of the Congress Commemorative Coin at U.S. Capitol. S.J. Res. No. 128
Mar. 30, 1990, Pub. L. 101-260, 104 Stat. 122	Provides for striking of medals in commemoration of the bicentennial of the U.S. Coast Guard.

Recent numismatic bills

Numerous numismatically related pieces of legislation have been introduced in the House and the Senate. From 1963, onward, the vast majority of these related to the proposed issuance of national medals by the United States Mint. National Mint medals emerged as a major alternative to commemorative coins nearly half a century ago. Following 1963 hearings by the subcommittee on Consumer Affairs (which then had jurisdiction over coinage matters), it became clear that the Mint would continue to oppose commemorative coinage issues, but would accept national medals as an alternative.

The present requirements for national medal status are multifold; dies for the medals must be of national character (not further defined), they must be produced at the Philadelphia Mint, may be executed by the Chief Sculptor-Engraver provided the work does not interfere with regular coinage, and no private medal dies may be prepared at the Mint or any machinery used for that purpose. Despite these requirements, Congress has always had the power to alter them, which it did in 1973 by allowing the San Francisco Assay Office to strike a national Mint medal commemorating the Centennial of the San Francisco Cable Car. Likewise, the Centennial of Colorado Statehood was authorized to be struck as a national medal at the Denver Mint. There were even bills passed which would have allowed a bill to be designated a national medal if it were struck by a private mint, however that option has never been availed to.

Under current standards, a national Mint medal (like a commemorative coin bill) will not be considered in the House of Representatives in the absence of 218 co-sponsors, one vote more than a simple majority of the membership of the House of Representatives. This is purely a procedural decision on the part of the chairman, and staff, of the House Subcommittee on Consumer Affairs and Coinage of the House Banking Committee, initiated under Rep. Frank Annunzio (D-Ill.) and staff director Curtis Prins, was continued by Rep. Richard Lehman (D-Calif.), chairman of the House Banking Subcommittee on Consumer Affairs and Coinage.

The mere fact that 218 Representatives support a measure (a simple majority in the House) does not necessarily mean that the bill's passage is assured in the House, or the Senate. The American Coinage Redesign Act, designed to modernize circulating coin designs is a case in point. Introduced as H.R. 3314 in the House and as S. 1776 in the Senate during the 100th Congress, its principal architect was Diane Wolf, a federal Commissioner of Fine Arts. Though she was successful in obtaining nearly unanimous Senate support, and well over half the House, the bill was never even reported out of subcommittee (chaired by Rep. Annunzio) no less considered by the full committee. Even if it had, the odds seem strong that a Rule would never have been approved to bring it to the floor of the House in its present form. This brings to the forefront the issue of how a bill becomes law, something increasing relevant in the numismatic field where commemorative coin and medal bills seem to be enacted into law with alacrity.

What follows is a brief description of the legislative history of some of the bills introduced over the past 15 years in the House and Senate that relate to coin collectors in several ways: legislation affecting the Mint, the Bureau of Engraving and Printing, and the Department of the Treasury (other than ordinary annual appropriations), together with proposals for commemorative coinages, national medals, alteration of coin designs or compositions, and topics that are of general concern to collectors such as counterfeits, metal stockpiles, and sale of government numismatic properties. National and other medals authorized by Congress up to 1971 are categorized separately in the section "Public laws authorizing medals."

Congress meets for a two-year period commencing in early January in odd-numbered years. (Elections take place in even-numbered years, with presidential elections every other term, such as 1988). Each meeting of Congress is divided into two sessions (usually one for each year, though in earlier times a "lame duck" third session was known to take place). During each two-year period, more than 20,000 bills are introduced in the House, with 435 members, and a slightly lesser number in the Senate, with 100 members (two per state). Few bills are actually enacted into law, usually no more than 700 per Congressional session.

Typically, when a coin-related bill is introduced in the House, it is referred to the House Committee on Banking, Finance and Urban Affairs, and then to a subcommittee, usually the Subcommittee on Consumer Affairs and Coinage.

Historically, the parent committee was known as the House Committee on Banking, Housing and Urban Affairs (presently under the chairmanship of Rep. Henry Gonzalez, D-Tex., earlier under the chairmanships of Rep. Fernand St. Germain, D-R.I., and Rep. Henry Reuss, D-Wis.); before that it was the House Committee on Banking and Currency (whose chairman was Rep. Wright Patman, D-Texas, from 1963-74).

Numismatic matters were handled first by a numbered subcommittee (later named the Subcommittee on Consumer Affairs), chaired by Rep. Leonor K. Sullivan, D-Mo., whose key aide was Charles B. ("Chuck") Holstein, until 1974. In 1975, the name of the committee handling these matters became the Subcommittee on

Historic Preservation and Coinage, chaired by Rep. Robert G. Stephens Jr., D-Ga., whose staff director, Jackson O'Neal Lamb, also served the successor, Rep. Walter E. Fauntroy, D-D.C., in the following Congress. Starting in 1979, Rep. Frank Annunzio, D-Ill., has headed the Subcommittee on Consumer Affairs and Coinage with Curtis Prins as staff director. In 1988, Rep. Annunzio became chairman of the House Administration Committee and relinquished his chairmanship of the House coinage subcommittee to move to another Banking subcommittee which, as second ranking member of the committee, he was entitled to do; he was replaced as chairman by Rep. Richard Lehman, D-Calif.; Curtis Prins followed the former chairman. The staffer handling coinage matters presently is John Ryan.

In the Senate, Sen. William Proxmire, D-Wis., was the chairman of the Senate Committee on Banking, Finance and Urban Affairs, with Marian Mayer as his chief of staff for numismatics until Republicans gained control of the Senate in 1980. Earlier, an ad hoc subcommittee on Minting and Coinage, chaired by Sen. William Hathaway, D-Maine, handled coinage legislation that came up with the assistance of Edward Sokol. Then, in 1981, Sen. Jake Garn, R-Utah, became committee chairman and Linda Zemke became the key staff person in charge of numismatic matters. In 1987, the Democrats regained control of the Senate. Proxmire became chairman; Garn assumed the role of ranking minority member. A major staff shakeup took place. Sharon Bauman has served as the professional staff member on Senate Banking for several years and is herself a collector.

While the popular perception remains that members of Congress handle most matters including the drafting of legislation and the follow-up that brings it to a vote, and, if successful, the law books, the more knowledgeable are well aware that it is the staff aide who closely governs the position taken by a political leader. Typically, it is the aide (and not the lawmaker) who prepares the draft of a bill,

writes the introductory remarks reprinted in the Congressional Record that are made when the bill is introduced, records questions that are to be asked (and answered) at hearings, and often advances the theory behind a particular piece of legislation.

Thus, Marian Mayer of the Proxmire staff was singularly responsible for advancing the idea of utilizing the Susan B. Anthony portrait on the new smaller-sized dollar as a concept to advance women's rights, and Curtis Prins of the Annunzio office pushed hard for the contemporary Olympic commemorative coin program that contemplated the first gold coin in half a century.

In the listing that follows, bills of interest that have become law since 1965 are listed with their legislative history. (This includes all of the medal bills since 1971.)

Since the passage of the Bland-Allison Act of 1878 (which created the Morgan dollar) over the veto of President Hayes, no numismatic-related bill has been passed over the veto of an incumbent president. (Some commemorative coin bills were vetoed between 1928 and 1960; all were sustained by Congress. In 1973, when debate over a gold bicentennial coin took place in the Senate, Senator John Tower, R-Texas, advised that President Nixon would veto the bill because of the then-problem with issuing gold coinage. Hence, no mention is made of the chief executive who signed the bill into law.

Bills introduced on numismatic subjects that have not passed, or received some affirmative action, are not listed simply by reason of space.

With one exception all appropriations and authorizations are ignored in the chronology because they are annual events. The exception is a bill that refers to authorization and appropriations, and which was added to the U.S. Code as 31 USC 5132(a) (1) in November 1983 requiring Uncirculated (Mint) sets to be produced by the Mint.

Also left out for reasons of space are the intricacies of how various measures became law, itself a fascinating story. In the 25 years that this writer has examined and reviewed Congress, several numismatic measures have become law after intricate battles of major newsworthiness. Still others have become reality for political usefulness of the sponsor, or the advancement of the nation as a whole.

A good introduction to one of the bills, in about 100 printed pages in length, affords an understanding as to why each cannot be so annotated. It is found in "Tribute to 200 Years of Freedom: The Story of How the U.S. Got Its Bicentennial Coinage," which appeared in the American Numismatic Association's monthly journal, *The Numismatist*, from March to June of 1975. A book reprinting the story, with the documents, is entitled *14 Bits* and is available from the ANA Library. On more recent legislation, the index to the Wall Street Journal (and that publication itself) for the year 1982 will afford interesting coverage from a different perspective of the move to create Olympic commemorative coinage.

Finally, the texts of several laws that are deemed of continuing significance to serious collectors are provided for easy reference and use. All are available in the Statutes at

Large, which can be found in many public libraries, nearly all law libraries as well as federal government document centers around the country.

For those interested in serious research on how a particular coin bill became law, there are several starting points. First, there are indices to the committee hearings held on Capitol Hill, and the texts of the hearings themselves. Next are speeches and comments found in the Congressional Record, and, earlier (prior to 1873) The Congressional Globe as well as the Annals of Congress, a virtual register of debates constituting a privately published summary. There may be presidential messages and other documents (usually referred to on the engrossed copy of the bill found in the Statutes at Large, together with the dates of House and Senate passage) and unofficial documents available in the national archives. Each forms a part of a history of contemporary American coinage law.

Below, grouped by categories, are bills that have been introduced and considered by Congress since 1981. Most fall into the status of those bills referred to in the introduction -- legislative proposals that were never enacted and that never even were considered in the hearing process. They are noted for historical accuracy only. When a bill went further (i.e., hearings were held) it is noted. Where no committee is cited, it is the House Banking Committee (Subcommittee on Consumer Affairs and Coinage) or the Senate Banking Committee (full committee) that held the hearings. Those bills which were enacted into law have their fuller history printed elsewhere and are cited to public law number.

Susan B. Anthony dollar legislative history

Following is a complete legislative history of the Susan B. Anthony dollar.

5/12/75 Contract for study of coinage awarded by U.S. Mint to Research Triangle Institute.

9/15/76 RTI recommends small-sized dollar in completed study as Frank Gasparro works on experimental Liberty design.

12/31/76 Treasury Secretary William Simon's "State of the Coinage" report recommends 26.5mm diameter dollar coin.

4/7/77 Treasury Secretary Blumenthal concurs with Simon recommendation.

4/17/78 Carter administration's recommendation to Congress.

5/1/78 H.R. 12444 introduced by Rep. Walter E. Fauntroy for administration.

5/3/78 S. 3036 introduced by Sen. William Proxmire for administration (same as H.R. 12444).

5/15/78 H.R. 12728 introduced by Reps. Mary Rose Oakar and Patricia Schroeder calling for Susan B. Anthony portrait.

5/17/78 Hearings on H.R. 12444 before Subcomm. on Historic Preservation and Coinage.

5/22/78 H.R. 12819 introduced by Rep. William Frenzel, for Susan B. Anthony portrait.

5/25/78 H.R. 12872 introduced by Rep. James A.S. Leach for Anthony and Harriet Tubman portrait.

5/31/78 Rep. Mary Rose Oakar introduced H.R. 12904 for Anthony coin (same as HR 12819) with multiple co-sponsors.

June, 1978 Frank Gasparro, chief engraver, starts Anthony design.

6/14/78 H.R. 13134 introduced by Rep. Oakar in house (same as prior Susan B. Anthony bills, but with additional co-sponsors).

7/11/78 H.R. 13415 introduced by Rep. Oakar, same as prior bills with additional co-sponsors.

7/17/78 S. 3036 hearings before Senate Banking Committee.

7/18/78 H.R. 13520 introduced by Rep. Oakar. Same as prior bills with additional cosponsors.

7/20/78 H.R. 13558 introduced by Rep. Oakar. Additional co-sponsors.

7/21/78 H.R. 13570 introduced by Rep. Oakar. Additional co-sponsors.

7/25/78: H.R. 12728 from House subcommittee to full Banking committee.

8/16/78 S. 3036 passed by voice vote.

9/7/78 S. 3036 referred to House Banking Committee.

9/18/78 H.R. 12728 approved by House Banking unit 38 to 1.

9/18/78 House Banking unit recommends passage (Rept. 95-1576).

5/16/78 House passages H.R. 12728 by 368 to 38 vote; vacates and passes S. 3036; Fine Arts Commission approves Gasparro design.

9/29/78 S. 3036 delivered to the president.

10/10/78 Public Law 95-447 signed.

George Washington commemorative coinage legislative history

The first commemorative coin issue since 1954 marked the 250th anniversary of the birth of George Washington. Struck in 90 percent silver, with a maximum mintage of 10 million pieces, and offered for sale by the Mint in 1982 and 1983, the coin's issuance was remarkably uncontroversial — despite the prior opposition of the Treasury Department over a half century to any commemorative issues, a policy which successfully ended all commemorative coin issues in 1954.

At the hearings before the House coinage subcommittee, the Treasury Department came out in favor of the issue, making it a foregone conclusion that the coins would be issued.

3/16/81 H.R. 2524 introduced by Rep. Barnard.

4/7/81 H.R. 3133 introduced by Rep. Annunzio and Barnard.

5/7/81 H.R. 3483 introduced by Rep. Annunzio and Barnard with Treasury modifications (10 million maximum mintage); use of earmarked silver from Ike dollar program; hearings before House coinage subcommittee.

5/18/81 S. 1228 introduced by Sen. McClure (similar to H.R. 3483).

5/19/81 H.R. 3483 Passes House on voice vote (unanimous) (H. Rept. 97-3484).

11/20/81 H.R. 3493 reported by Senate Banking Committee to full Senate (Sen. Rept. 97-277).

12/9/81 Senate approved by unanimous consent.

12/13/81 Signed into Public Law 97-104 by President Reagan.

11/6/83 S. 1822 introduced by Sens. McClure and Symms (90 percent silver $10 coin). No further action.

Olympic commemorative coinage legislative history

In modern times, the Olympic commemorative coinage program initiated 1983-84 constitutes the most ambitious American commemorative coinage program ever conceived. A total of 50 million silver coins and 2 million gold coins were authorized.

Final sales of the Olympic coinage confirmed that this was the most impressive showing to that time: 573,364 gold coins were sold, and 4,472,110 silver dollars were sold. Total surcharges exceeded $73.3 million; total sales were in excess of $308 million.

It is no secret that the Olympic program was also one of the most controversial in modern times, with private interests competing with the U.S. Mint for the right to market the program that initially began as a 29-coin program and eventually was enacted as a three-coin issue (two silver dollars, one gold coin) that, with Mint marks and Proof and Uncirculated versions, became a 13-coin issue.

Some of the controversy spilled over into the daily press as well as the hobby journals. The Wall Street Journal index will list fully those articles concerning the Olympic program that were covered there, including at least one Page One story that offers analysis of the behind-the-scenes machinations.

5/20/81 S. 1230 introduced in Senate by Cranston. Original proposal calling for 29 coins.

6/11/81 H.R. 6069 introduced by Rep. Annunzio. Single $1 coin.

6/17/81. H.R. 3958 introduced in House by Rep. Patterson. Parallels S. 1230.

9/23/81 Rep. Annunzio attacks S. 1230 & H.R. 3958 in Congressional Record.

10/15/81 Senate Banking Committee meets and marks up S. 1230 in modified form (25 coins).

10/30/81 Senate Report 97-264 issued on S. 1230.

12/9/81 S. 1230 passes Senate unanimously (Rept. 97-264).

3/23/82 H.R. 5933 introduced. Calls for one copper-nickel $1 coin; 12 silver coins; four gold coins. (17 coins).

3/29/82 Senate passes H.R. 5708 (17-coin proposal).

4/1/82 H.R. 6058 introduced by Rep. St Germain (same as Senate bill, with private marketer).

4/5/82 H.R. 6069 introduced by Rep. Annunzio (one coin proposal).

4/6/82 Hearings before House coinage subcommittee.

4/21/82 Hearings before House coinage subcommittee.

4/26/82 H.R. 6158 introduced by Rep. Annunzio (three coin bill); Wall Street Journal article appears.

4/29/82 Hearings before House coinage subcommittee.

5/11/82 Hearings before House coinage subcommittee.

5/12/82 Hearings before House coinage subcommittee.

5/13/82 House Coinage subcommittee reports bill to full committee; H.R. 6058 substituted for S. 1230. (Replaced by H.R. 6158, Annunzio version).

5/13/82 House Banking Committee substitutes St Germain bill for Annunzio version by 32 to 7 vote.

5/20/82 H. Res. 470 is considered for debate on Olympic coin proposals. House votes down St Germain bill 302-84 and approves Annunzio version, H.R. 6158. (Rept. 97-554).

6/10/82 Senate Hearing on S. 1230 as amended.

7/1/82 Senate concurs with House amendments.

7/22/82 President Reagan signed Public Law 97-220 into law.

Statue of Liberty-Ellis Island commemorative coinage and Liberty Coin Act of 1985 legislative history

The 100th anniversary of the dedication of the Statue of Liberty was celebrated in 1986 with three U.S. commemorative coins: a gold $5 half eagle honoring the Statue of Liberty, a silver dollar honoring the Ellis Island immigration facility and a copper-nickel half dollar commemorating the accomplishments of immigrants to the United States. All three coins were offered in Proof and Uncirculated versions.

By the time sales had ended Dec. 31, 1986, sales of the Statue of Liberty commemorative coins had raised a record $83.1 million in surcharges.

1/3/85 H.R. 47 introduced in House by Rep. Annunzio.

1/3/85 H.R. 47 referred to House Banking Committee.

2/20/85 Hearings held before House Banking Subcommittee on Consumer Affairs and Coinage.

3/5/85 H.R. 47 discharged by House Banking Committee, with amendments adopted by voice vote.

3/6/85 Referred to the Senate Banking Committee.

3/6/85 Reported without amendments by the Senate Banking Committee.

6/21/85 Passed by the Senate, voice vote, with amendments authorizing a silver bullion dollar.

6/24/85 House agreed to the Senate amendment.

7/2/85 Sent to the president.

7/9/85 Signed into Public Law 99-61 by President Reagan.

Gold Bullion Coin Act of 1985 legislative history

As noted earlier, numerous bills calling for one or more gold bullion coins were introduced in Congress after Americans regained the right to own gold coins in December 1974. None were successful until 1985, when the Gold Bullion Coin Act of 1985 passed through both houses of Congress and was signed into law by President Reagan.

The act authorized four gold coins: a $50 coin containing 1 ounce of .999 fine gold; a $25 half-ounce coin; a $10 quarter-ounce coin; and a $5 tenth-ounce coin.

The reverse design for the 1-ounce coin was specified by the legislation to ensure use of a design by Dallas sculptor Miley Busiek, showing a family of American eagles. The design was used on the reverses of all four designs.

9/12/85 S. 1639 introduced in Senate by Sen. J. James Exon.

11/13/85 S. 1639 reported with amendments.

11/14/85 Passed by the Senate.

11/20/85 Rejected by the House by unanimous consent.

12/2/85 Passed in House under suspension.

12/5/85 Sent to the president.

12/17/85 Signed into Public Law 99-185 by President Reagan.

Constitution Bicentennial commemorative coin legislative history

The 200th anniversary of the framing of the United States Constitution in 1987 is latest national event to be commemorated by U.S. coinage. Two coins were authorized: a gold $5 half eagle and a silver dollar. A provision in the legislation calling for national medals was dropped before a vote in the full House.

After the legislation became law, Treasury officials announced a limited competition for the designs, and designs by two non-Mint employees were selected.

9/23/85 H.R. 3415 introduced in House by Rep. Annunzio.

9/23/85 Referred to House Banking Committee.

10/1/85 House Banking Committee discharged H.R. 3415, and voted on amendments.

10/10/85 H.R. 3415 passed by the House.

10/16/85 Passed by Senate, voice vote.

10/16/85 Senate amendments adopted in House by voice vote.

10/29/85 Signed into Public Law 99-582 by President Reagan.

Other legislative histories

Young Astronauts

S. 1952 (A bill to provide for the striking of medals to commemorate the young astronaut program.)

Sponsor: GARN (R-UT)

Introduced: DECEMBER 16, 1985
Comm.S:
Senate Comm. on Banking, Housing, &
  Urban Affairs.......................Passed (100)
03/13/86 Ordered Rept.
03/26/86 Report Filed (No Written Report)
House Comm. on Banking, Finance &
  Urban Affairs..................DISCHARGED
Floor(s):
Senate 03/27/86 Voice Vote .... Passed
House 04/28/86 Voice Vote .... Passed
Senate 04/30/86 Presented to the President
Senate 05/12/86 became Pub. Law
  (P.L.99-295)

Shcharansky gold medals

S. 2308 (A bill to authorize the president
of the united states to award
congressional gold medals to Anatoly &
Avital Shcharansky in recognition of
their dedication to human rights, & to
authorize the Secretary of the Treasury to
sell bronze duplicates of those medals.)
Sponsor: LAUTENBERG·(D-NJ)
Introduced: APRIL 15, 1986
Comm.(S):
Senate Comm. on Banking, Housing, &
  Urban Affairs.......................Passed (100)
05/08/86 Ordered Rept.
05/08/86 Report Filed (No Written Report)
Floor(s):
Senate 05/08/86 Voice Vote .... Passed
House 05/12/86 REPLACES H.R.4186
House 05/12/86 Voice Vote .... Passed
Senate 05/12/86 Presented to the President
Senate 05/13/86 became Pub. Law
  (P.L.99-298)

Aaron Copland gold medal

S. 2462 (A bill to provide for the awarding
of a Special gold medal to Aaron
Copland.)
Sponsor: KENNEDY (D-MA)
Introduced: MAY 15, 1986
Comm.(S):
Senate Comm. on Banking, Housing, &
  Urban Affairs Passed (100)
08/13/86 Ordered Reported
08/13/86 Report Filed (No Written Report)
House Comm. on Banking, Finance &
  Urban Affairs ....DISCHARGED
Floor(s):

Senate 08/15/86 Voice Vote .... Passed
House 09/09/86 Voice Vote .... Passed
Senate 09/23/86 became Pub. Law
  (P.L.99-418)

Constitution Bicentennial

H.R. 3415 (a bill to authorize the minting
of coins & the striking of medals in
commemoration of the Bicentennial of
the U.S. Constitution.)
Sponsor: ANNUNZIO (D-IL)
Introduced: SEPTEMBER 23, 1985
Comm.(S): House Comm. on Banking,
  Finance, & Urban
  Affairs ....DISCHARGED
Floor(s):
House 10/01/86 Voice Vote .... Passed
Senate 10/16/86 Voice Vote
  (Amended) ....Passed
House 10/29/86 became Pub. Law
  (P.L.99-582)

1988 Olympic commemorative

H.R. 2741 (a bill to authorize the minting
of commemorative coins to support the
training of American athletes
participating in the 1988 Olympic
Games.)
Sponsor: ANNUNZIO (D-IL)
Introduced: JUNE 23, 1987
Comm.(S):
House Comm. on Banking, Finance, &
  Urban Affairs ....DISCHARGED
Senate Comm. on Banking, Housing &
  Urban Affairs ....Passed (100)
09/30/87 Ordered Reported (REPLACES
  S.1587)
10/07/87 Report Filed (S.Rept.100-197)
Floor(s):
House 08/06/87 Voice Vote............. Passed
Senate 10/13/87 Voice Vote .... Passed
House 10/28/87 became Pub. Law
  (P.L.100-141)

Mary Lasker gold medal

H.R. 390 (A bill to provide that a special
gold medal be presented to Mary Lasker
for her humanitarian contributions in the
areas of medical research & education,
urban beautification, & the fine arts.)
Sponsor: PEPPER (D-FL)
Introduced: JANUARY 6, 1987
Comm.(S):

House Comm. on Banking, Finance, &
Urban Affairs ....Passed (100)
Senate Comm. on Banking, Housing &
Urban Affairs Passed (100)
12/02/87 Ordered Reported
12/16/87 Report Filed (No Written Report)
Floor(s):
House 09/29/87 Voice Vote .... Passed
Senate 12/17/87 Voice Vote .... Passed
House 12/24/87 became Pub. Law
(P.L.100-210)

Merchant Marine medal

H.R. 1430 (A bill to authorize decorations,
medals, & other recognition for service
in the United States Merchant Marine, &
for other purposes.)
Sponsor: BIAGGI (D-NY)
Introduced: MARCH 5, 1987
Comm.(S):
House Comm. on Merchant Marine &
Fisheries .... Passed (100)
02/24/88 Ordered Reported
03/04/88 Report Filed (H.Rept.100-510)
Senate Comm. on Commerce, Science &
Transportation ....Passed (100)
Floor(s):
House 03/08/88 Voice Vote .... Passed
Senate 05/13/88 Voice Vote .... Passed
House 05/30/88 became Pub. Law (P.L.
NO. 100-324)

Jesse Owens gold medal

H.R. 1270 (A bill to award a congressional
gold medal to Mrs. Jesse Owens.)
Sponsor: STOKES (D-OH)
Introduced: FEBRUARY 25, 1987
Comm.(S):
House Comm. on Banking, Finance, &
Urban Affairs ....Passed (100)
Senate Comm......................... Passed (100)
Floor(s):
House 08/08/88 Voice Vote .... Passed
Senate 09/08/88 Voice Vote (Unanimous
Consent) .... Passed
House 09/20/88 became Pub. Law (P.L.
NO. 100-437)

Andrew Wyeth gold medal

H.R. 593 (A bill to request the President to
award a gold medal on behalf of
Congress to Andrew Wyeth, & to
provide for the production of bronze

duplicates of such medal for sale to the
public.)
Sponsor: SCHULZE (R-PA)
Introduced: JANUARY 8, 1987
Comm.(S):
House Comm. on Banking, Finance, &
Urban Affair ....Passed (100)
Senate Comm. ....Passed (100)
Floor(s):
House 08/08/88 Voice Vote .... Passed
Senate 10/21/88 Voice Vote .... Passed
Became Public Law 100-639 (11/9/88)

Harry Chapin gold medal

H.R. 1207 (A bill to award a special gold
medal to the family of Harry Chapin.)
Sponsor: DORGAN (D-ND)
Introduced: FEBRUARY 21, 1985
Comm.(S):
House Comm. on Banking, Finance, &
Urban Affairs. .... DISCHARGED
Senate Comm. on Banking, Housing &
Urban Affairs. ....Passed (100)
05/08/86 Ordered Rept.
05/08/86 Report Filed (No Written Report)
Floor(s):
House 05/05/86 Voice Vote .... Passed
Senate 05/08/86 Voice Vote .... Passed
House 05/12/86 Presented to the President
House 05/20/86 became Pub. Law
(P.L.99-311)

Congressional Bicentennial

H.R. 3251 (a bill to require the Secretary
of the Treasury to mint coins in
commemoration of the bicentennial of
the U.S. Congress.)
Sponsor: FASCELL (D-FL)
Introduced: SEPTEMBER 10, 1987
Comm.(S):
House Comm. on Banking, Finance, &
Urban Affairs ....Passed (100)
Senate Comm. on Banking, Housing &
Urban Affairs ....Passed (100)
Ordered Reported 05/24/88 (Amended)
Report Filed 06/10/88 (S.Rept. 100-383)
Floor(s):
House 09/29/87 Voice Vote .... Passed
Senate 06/15/88 Record Vote (Vote No.
2186: 96-0) ....Passed

Eisenhower commemorative

S. 2789 (A bill to require the Secretary of

the Treasury to mint and issue $1 coins in commemoration of the 100th anniversary of the birth of Dwight David Eisenhower).

Sponsor: DOLE (R-KS)
Introduced: SEPTEMBER 14, 1988
Comm.(S):
House Comm.............................. No action
Floor(s):
Senate 09/14/88 Voice Vote............ Passed
House 09/16/88 Voice Vote............ Passed
Senate 10/03/88 became Pub. Law (No. 100-467)
House 08/01/88 became Pub. Law (P.L. 100-378)

Congressional Bicentennial

H.R. 5280 (A bill to require the Secretary of the Treasury to mint COINS in commemoration of the Bicentennial of the U.S. Congress).

Sponsor: FASCELL (D-FL)
Introduced: SEPTEMBER 13, 1988
Comm.(S):
House Comm. on Banking, Finance, & Urban Affairs .... Passed (100)
Senate Comm......................... Passed (100)
Floor(s):
House 10/04/88 Record Vote (Vote No. 2394: 411-8) .... Passed
Senate 10/07/88 Voice Vote............ Passed
PUB. L. 100-673 (11/17/88)

National Coin Week

National Coin Week has been sponsored by the American Numismatic Association since Julius Guttag conceived it in 1924. It was proclaimed nationally by President Nixon (Proc. No. 4286) in 1974, on its 50th anniversary. In 1983, President Reagan declared National Coin Week acting pursuant to the request of Public Law 97-239, asking that the president proclaim April 17-24, 1983, as National Coin Week. Below is the National Coin Week Proclamation as it appeared in the Federal Register on March 8, 1983.

Proclamations

National Coin Week 1983

(No. 5027, 48 Fed. Reg. 9837)

National Coin Week, 1983.

By the president of the United States of America,
A Proclamation.

Since the beginning of history, coins have played an important role in the story of civilization. They reflect the economic development of their country of origin, as well as the scientific advancement and artistic values of the people who produce and use them. Today, millions of Americans collect coins for both pleasure and profit. To help foster the public's interest in coin collecting, the United States Mint annually offers Proof sets of the current year's coinage. In 1982, the United States Mint struck a commemorative silver half dollar, marking the 250th anniversary of the birth of George Washington. In 1983-1984, the first commemorative Olympic coinage ever issued by our country will be introduced in gold and silver. Recognizing that coin collecting has educational and cultural value, promotes greater understanding of our history and heritage, and is enjoyed by millions of Americans, the Congress, pursuant to House Joint Resolution 516 (Public Law 97-239), has authorized and requested the president to issue a proclamation designating the week beginning April 17, 1983, as "National Coin Week." NOW, THEREFORE, I, RONALD REAGAN, president of the United States of American, do hereby proclaim the week beginning April 17, 1983, as "National Coin Week" and call upon the people of the United States to observe this week with appropriate ceremonies and activities. IN WITNESS WHEREOF, I have hereunto set my hand this 7th day of March, in the year of our Lord nineteen hundred and eighty-three, and of the Independence of the United States of America the two hundred and seventh.

Ronald Reagan

Freedom of Information Act

Collectors can avail themselves of privileges under the Freedom of Information Act, Public Law 93-502, passed by the 93rd Congress (H. R. 12471 Nov. 21, 1974, over a presidential veto.)

Known as 5 U.S.C. 552, the act requires agencies to maintain and make available for public inspection and copying, current indexes providing identifying information for the public as to any matter issued, adopted or promulgated after July 4, 1967, and required to be made available or published. There are certain exceptions.

The agency involved will answer inquiries as to the availability of records under the Freedom of Information Act.

The Freedom of Information Act (FOIA) is a boon to researchers and scholars, as well as collectors. Material that has yet to reach the National Archives is accessible under the FOIA. All administrative agencies of the government are liable (except for certain specific exceptions) to comply, and must furnish the information requested. There may be charges for the information requested, designed to reflect its actual cost, and (usually) it must be requested with specificity. A number of detailed books on the FOIA are available in many libraries. It is worth noting that some state governments have similar acts.

Each agency is required to separately state and publish in the Federal Register the procedures it will follow. It is required to make a determination within 10 days of receipt (Saturdays, Sundays and public holidays excepted) whether or not they will reply, and, if an appeal is taken, determine that within 20 days. If an agency improperly withholds documents, it is possible for attorney's fees and other litigation costs to be assessed against the government.

There are several types of documents which are specifically exempt from disclosure. First, those pertaining to national defense or foreign policy; second, those relating solely to internal personnel rules and practices; third, those exempted from disclosure by statute; fourth, trade secrets and commercial and financial nature obtained in a confidential or privileged manner; fifth, inter-agency or intra-agency memorandums which would not be available in litigation against the agency; sixth, personnel and medical files which would create an unwarranted invasion of personal privacy; seventh, investigatory records compiled for law enforcement purposes; eighth, regulatory reports concerning financial institutions; ninth, geological or geophysical information including maps concerning wells.

Below appears significant and relevant extracts from the Freedom of Information Act regulations of the Department of the Treasury, which covers the Bureau of the Mint, the Bureau of Engraving and Printing, the Customs Service, and a number of other agencies.

Sec. 1.1 Purpose and scope of regulations.

The regulations in this subpart are issued to implement the public information provisions of section 552 of Title 5, United States Code, as amended. These regulations apply to all constituent units of the Department of the Treasury. . . .

The constituent units of the Department of the Treasury for the purposes of this part are:

(a) The Office of the Secretary of the Treasury, which includes the offices of:

(1) The Secretary, including immediate staff;

(2) The Deputy Secretary, including immediate staff;

(3) The Under Secretary for Monetary Affairs, including immediate staff;

(4) The Under Secretary, including immediate staff;

(5) The General Counsel and also the Legal Division, . . .

Sec. 1.2 Information made available.

(a) General. Section 552 of Title 5 of

the United States Code provides for access to information and records developed or maintained by Federal agencies. Generally, such section divides agency information into three major categories and provides methods by which each category is to be made available to the public. The three major categories, for which the disclosure requirements of the constituent units of the Department of the Treasury are set forth in this subpart, are as follows:

(1) Information required to be published in the Federal Register (see Sec. 1.3 below);

(2) Information required to be made available for public inspection and copying or, in the alternative, to be published and offered for sale (see Sec. 1.4 below); and

(3) Information required to be made available to any member of the public upon specific request (see Sec. 1.5 below). The provisions of section 552 are intended to assure the right of the public to information. Section 552 is not authority to withhold information from Congress.

(b) Subject only to the exemptions set forth in Sec. 1.2(c) the public generally or any member thereof shall be afforded access to information or records in the possession of any constituent unit of the Department of the Treasury. Such access shall be governed by the regulations in this subpart A and any regulations of a constituent unit implementing or supplementing them.

(c) Exemptions — (1) In general. Under 5 U.S.C. 552(b), the disclosure requirements of section 552(a) do not apply to certain matters which are: [a list of statutory criteria follows]. . .

(3) Segregable portions of records. Any reasonably segregable portion of a record shall be provided to any person, after deletion of the portions which are exempt under 5 U.S.C. 552(b) (see paragraph (c)(1) of this section). The term "reasonably segregable portion" as used in this paragraph means any portion of the record which is not exempt from disclosure by 5 U.S.C. 552 (b) and which

after deletion of the exempt material still conveys meaningful and nonmisleading information. . . .

Sec. 1.4 Public inspection and copying.

(a) In general. Subject to the application of the exemptions described in Sec. 1.2(c) each constituent unit of the Department of the Treasury is hereby required in conformance with 5 U.S.C. 552(a)(2), to make available for public inspection and copying or, in the alternative, to promptly publish and offer for sale the following information with respect to such constituent unit:

(1) Final opinions, including concurring and dissenting opinions, and orders, if such opinions and orders are made in the adjudication of cases;

(2) Those statements of policy and interpretations which have been adopted by the constituent unit but are not published in the Federal Register; and

(3) Its administrative staff manuals and instructions to staff that affect a member of the public.

(b) Indexes. Each constituent unit of the Department of the Treasury is hereby also required, in conformance with 5 U.S.C. 552(a)(2), to maintain and make available for public inspection and copying current indexes identifying any matter described in paragraphs (a)(1) through (3) of this section which is issued, adopted, or promulgated after July 4, 1967, and which is required to be made available for public inspection or published. In addition, each constituent unit shall promptly publish, quarterly or more frequently, and distribute (by sale of otherwise) copies of each index or supplements thereto unless the head of such unit (or his delegate) determines by order published in the Federal Register that the publication would be unnecessary and impracticable, in which case the constituent unit shall nonetheless provide copies of such index on request at a cost not to exceed the direct cost of duplication. . . .

(3) Public reading rooms. Each constituent unit of the Department of the Treasury shall make available for

inspection and copying, in a reading room or otherwise, the matters described in paragraphs (a) (1) through (3) of this section which are required by such paragraph (a) to be made available for public inspection or published in the current indexes such matters. Facilities shall be provided whereby a person may inspect the material and obtain copies of that which is shelved. Fees shall not be charged for access to materials, but fees are to be charged in accordance with Sec. 1.6 for copies of material provided to the person. (See the appendices to this subpart for the location of established reading rooms of constituent units of the Department of the Treasury.)

Sec. 1.5 Specific requests for other records.

(a) In general. Except with respect to the records made available . . . above, but subject to the application of the exemptions . . . each constituent unit of the Department of the Treasury, shall, in conformance with 5 U.S.C. 552 (a) (3), upon any request, which is for reasonably described records and conforms in every respect with the rules and procedures of this Subpart A, . . . make the requested records promptly available to any person. . . .

(c) Form of request. In order to be subject to the provisions of this section, a request for records shall:

(1) Be made in writing and signed by the person making the request,

(2) State that it is made pursuant to the Freedom of Information Act, 5 U.S.C. 552 or these regulations,

(3) Be addressed to the office or officer of the constituent unit to which the subject matter of the request is of paramount concern, unless the requester is unable to ascertain the appropriate unit, in which event, the request shall be addressed as specified in Appendix A hereto for the Office of the Secretary (See the appendices to this subpart for the office or officer to which requests shall be addressed for each constituent unit),

(4) Reasonably describe the records in accordance with paragraph (d) of this section,

(5) Set forth the address where the person making the request desires to be notified of the determination as to whether the request will be granted,

(6) State whether the requester wishes to inspect the records or desires to have a copy made and furnished without first inspecting them, and

(7) State the firm agreement of the requester to pay the fees for search and duplication ultimately determined in accordance with Sec. 1.6 hereof, or request that such fees be reduced or waived and state the justification for such request (see Sec. 1.6(d) below). Where the initial request, rather than stating a firm agreement to pay the fees ultimately determined in accordance with Sec. 1.6, places an upper limit on the amount the requester agrees to pay, which upper limit is deemed likely to be lower than the fees estimated to ultimately be due, or where the requester asks for an estimate of the fees to be charged, the requester shall be promptly advised of the estimate of fees due and asked to agree to pay such amount. . . .

(g) Initial determination (1) In general. Initial determinations as to whether to grant requests for records will be made by the officers designated in the appendices to this part. Those determinations will be made and notification thereof mailed within 10 days (excepting Saturdays, Sundays, and legal public holidays) after the date of receipt of the request, . . .

(3) Denial of request. If it is determined that the request for records should be denied (whether in whole or in part or subject to conditions or exceptions), the person making the request will be so notified by mail. . . .

(h) Administrative appeal. At any time within 35 days after the date of the notification described in paragraph (g) of this section or the date of the letter transmitting the last records released, whichever is later, the requester may submit an administrative appeal to the official specified in the appropriate appendix to this subpart whose title and address should also have been included in the initial determination to deny access to the records. The appeal shall:

(1) Be made in writing and signed by the requester,

(2) Be addressed to and mailed or hand delivered, within 35 days of the date of the initial determination, to the office or officer specified in the appropriate appendix to this subpart and also in the initial determination. (See the appendices to this subpart for the address to which appeals made by mail should be addressed.),

(3) Reasonably describe, in accordance with paragraph (d) of this section, the records requested from the denial of access to which an appeal is being taken,

(4) Specify the date of the initial request and date of the letter denying the initial request, and

(5) Petition such official to grant the request for records and state any arguments in support thereof. . . .

Sec. 1.6 Fees for services.

(a) In general. (1) This fee schedule is applicable uniformly to all constituent units of the Department of the Treasury and supersedes fees schedules heretofore published by any constituent unit of the Department. . . .

(e) Avoidance of unexpected fees. In order to protect the requester from unexpected fees, all requests for records shall state the agreement of the requester to pay the fees determined in accordance with paragraph (g) of this section or state the amount which the requester has set as an acceptable upper limit he is willing to pay to cover the costs of processing the request. When the fees for processing the request are estimated by the constituent unit of the Department of the Treasury to exceed that limit, or when the requester has failed to state a limit and the costs are estimated to exceed $50 and the relevant constituent unit has not then determined to waive or reduce the fees, a notice shall be sent to the requester. This notice shall:

(1) Inform the requester of the estimated costs;

(2) Extend an offer to the requester to confer with personnel of the relevant constituent unit of the Department of the Treasury in an attempt to reformulate the request in a manner which will reduce the fees and still meet the needs of the requester; and

(3) Inform the requester that the running of the time period, within which the relevant constituent unit of the Department of the Treasury is obliged to make a determination on the request, has been tolled pending a reformulation of the request or the receipt of advance payment or an agreement from the requester to bear the estimated costs.

(f) Form of payment

(1) Payment shall be made by check or money order payable to the order of the Treasury of the United States or that relevant constituent unit of the Department of the Treasury.

(2) When the estimated costs exceed $50, the requester may be required to enter into a contract for the payment of actual costs determined in accordance with paragraph (g) of this section, which contract may provide for prepayment of the estimated costs in whole or in part.

(3) The Department of the Treasury reserves the right to request prepayment before releasing documents. If fees for previous requests have not been paid, documents will not be released without prepayment.

(g) Amounts to be charged for specified services. The fees for services performed by the relevant constituent unit of the Department of the Treasury shall be imposed and collected as set forth in this paragraph. . . .

(1) Copying records. (i) $.15 per copy of each page, up to 8-1/2" X 14", made by photocopy or similar process.

(ii) Photographs, films, and other materials-actual cost of reproduction.

(iii) Records may be released to a private contractor for copying and the requester will be charged the actual cost of duplication charged by the private contractor.

(2) Search services. (i) Searches other

than for computerized records — $10.00 for each hour or fraction thereof for time spent by each clerical, professional, and supervisor in finding the records and information within the scope of the request, and for transportation of personnel and records necessary to the search at actual cost.

(ii) Searches for computerized records — Actual direct cost of the search. The fee for computer printouts will be actual cost. . . .

Appendix A-Office of the Secretary

1. In general. This appendix applies to the Office of the Secretary as defined in 31 CFR 1.1(a). It identifies the location of the public reading room at which Office of the Secretary documents are available for public inspection and copying, the officers designated to make the initial and appellate determinations with respect to requests, the officer designated to receive service of process and the addresses for delivery of requests, appeals and service of process.

2. Public reading room. The public reading room for the Office of the Secretary is maintained at the following location: Library, Room 5030, Main Treasury Building, 1500 Pennsylvania Avenue NW, Washington, D.C. 20220.

3. Requests for records. Initial determinations under 31 CFR 1.5 (g) as to whether to grant requests for records for the Office of the Secretary will be made by the head of the organizational unit having immediate custody of the records. . . .

Appendix H-Bureau of the Mint

1. In General. This appendix applies to the Bureau of the Mint. It identifies the location of the public reading room at which documents of the Bureau of the Mint are available for public inspection and copying, the titles of officers designated to make the initial and appellate determinations with respect to requests, the officer designation to receive service of process and the addresses for delivery of requests, appeals and service of process.

2. Public reading rooms. No room has been set aside for this purpose. The Bureau of the Mint will provide a room on an ad hoc basis when necessary.

3. Requests for records. Initial determinations under 31 CFR 1.5 (g) as to whether to grant requests for records of the Bureau of the Mint will be made by the Assistant Director for Public Services, Bureau of the Mint. Requests made by mail should be addressed to: Chief, Information Systems and Documentation Branch, Bureau of the Mint, Department of the Treasury, Room 912, Warner Building Washington, D.C. 20220.

Requests may be delivered personally to Information Systems and Documentation Branch of the Bureau of the Mint, Room 912, Warner Building located at 501 13th Street NW, Washington, D.C.

4. Administrative appeal of initial determination to deny records. Appellate determinations under 31 CFR 1.5(h) with respect to records of the Bureau of the Mint will be made by the Director of the Mint. Appeals made by mail should be addressed to: Director of the Mint, Department of the Treasury, Washington, D.C. 20220.

Requests may be delivered personally to the office of the Director of the Mint in Room 2064, Main Treasury Building, 1500 Pennsylvania Avenue NW, Washington, D.C.

5. Delivery of process. Service of process will be received by the Director of the Mint and shall be delivered to such officer at the following location: Director of the Mint, Judiciary Square Building, 633 Third Street NW, Washington, D.C. 20220.

Similar regulations are applicable for the Bureau of Engraving and Printing (also no public reading room) and other agencies.

Coin laws since 1965

The following are coin-related laws that have passed Congress since 1965 which may be of interest to collectors. (Medal legislation increases commencing in 1971 because some of the significant Bicentennial and other medals, precursors to debate over the future of national medals, and ultimately, a return to commemorative coinage, became more numerous then. Prior medal issues are listed separately.) The citations given show the public law number and page reference to the Statutes at Large (Stat.), which is available in many libraries. Where codification in the United States Code has taken place, it is also noted. When the U.S. Code was revised in 1982, some provisions were deleted as obsolete (the most obvious of which related to Bicentennial coin issues, last produced in 1976). The listings are necessarily duplicative at least in part of the section listing "significant" laws. Appended are hearings and legislative developments of potential interest to researchers, identified by the number preceding each law.

Pub. L. 89-81 July 23, 1965 79 Stat. 254	Authorized clad coinage; silver-clad half dollars.	The Coinage Act of 1965, Hearings on Coin Shortage, House Subcom. of Comm. on Government Operations, 6/30/64; 7/1-2/64 On silver dollars: Appropriations Committee, 5/24/65 Hearing on H.R. 8746 (Banking Comm) 6/4-7 and 8/65 Hearing on S. 2671 (4/1-2/64) Sixth Rept. of Comm. on Gov't Operations (Rept. 194) 3/22/65 House debate: 7/13-14/65 (H. Rept. #509); Senate debate: 6/23-24; 7/15/65 (Sen. Rept. #317)
Pub. L. 90-29, Sec. 5 June 24, 1967 81 Stat. 77	Restores Mint marks to coinage.	Hearings (S. 1008) Senate Financial Institutions Subcomm. 3/67
Pub. L. 91-607, Title II Dec. 31, 1970 84 Stat. 1768	Authorizes Eisenhower dollar; ends silver in half dollar; directs transfer of Carson City silver dollars to General Services Administration.	Eisenhower dollar (Hearing on Coinage Act of 1969, H.R. 13252), 10/1 and 3/69; "CC" dollars: Hearing on H.R. 13150, 7/26-28/66
Pub. L. 92-228 Feb. 15, 1972 86 Stat. 37	Authorizes Bicentennial medal production by Mint for American Revolution Bicentennial Commission.	Hearing on H.R. 7987, 6/29/71
Pub. L. 92-266 March 30, 1972 86 Stat. 116	Medals for Transpo '72.	
Pub. L. 92-268 March 31, 1972 86 Stat. 116	Set value of gold at $38 an ounce.	
Pub. L. 92-384 Aug. 14, 1972 86 Stat. 539	Medal for 175th anniversary of frigate Constitution.	
Pub. L. 92-463 Oct. 6, 1972 86 Stat. 770	Federal Advisory Committee Act of 1972; effectively abolished Assay Commission as of Jan. 4, 1975. See Pub. L. 96-209 below.	
Pub. L. 93-33 May 14, 1973 87 Stat. 71	Roberto Clemente national medal.	
Pub. L. 93-110 Sept. 21, 1973 87 Stat. 352	Set gold value at $42.22 an ounce. Legalizes private gold ownership when Treasury Secretary determines it to be in national interest (see Pub. L. 93-373).	Private gold ownership, Hearing (S. 929) 2/27/73; Hearing (S. 359, 395, 413, 741), 5/1-2/73
Pub. L. 93-114 Oct. 1, 1973 87 Stat. 417	San Francisco cable car national medal.	Hearing on H.R. 2353 and 7358, 5/2-3/73

Pub. L. 93-132 Oct. 19, 1973 87 Stat. 461	Jim Thorpe national medal.	Hearing on H.R. 5760, 5/2-3/73
Pub. L. 93-127 Oct. 18, 1973 87 Stat. 455	Creates America's Bicentennial coinage.	Hearing on H.R. 5244, 5/2-3/73 Hearing on S. 422 and others, 6/6/73 Debate: (H. Rept. 93-391) 9/12; 10/4/73; (S. Rept. 93-144) 7/11; 10/4/73; Conference Rept. (H. Rept. 93-521)
Pub. L. 93-167 Nov. 29, 1973 87 Stat. 686	Hobby Protection Act (text and regulations appear elsewhere in this section). Debate: House (H. Rept. 93-159) 5/16/73 Senate: (S. Rept. 93-345) 7/31 - 8/1-2; 11/16/82	Hearing (H.R. 4678) before Comm. on Interstate and Foreign Commerce, 2/28/73 (Serial 93-3)
Pub. L. 93-177 Dec. 11, 1973 87 Stat. 704	Repeals portion of Pub. L. 92-228.	
Pub. L. 93-179 Dec. 11, 1973 87 Stat. 697	American Revolution Bicentennial Administration created as successor to Bicentennial Commission.	
Pub. L. 93-221 Dec. 23, 1973 87 Stat. 913	International Environmental Exposition national medal.	Hearing on H.R. 5760, 5/2-3/73
Pub. L. 93-227 Dec. 29, 1973 87 Stat. 944	National medal for Colorado statehood centennial.	Hearing on H.R. 4738, 5/2-3/73
Pub. L. 93-309 June 8, 1974 88 Stat. 234	National medal for J. Edgar Hoover, FBI director.	Hearing on H.R. 1817, 5/2-3/73
Pub. L. 93-373 Aug. 14, 1974 88 Stat. 445	Legalizes private gold ownership Dec. 31, 1974.	
Pub. L. 93-441 Oct. 11, 1974 88 Stat. 1262	Authorizes transfer of 10 percent of Ike dollar sales to Eisenhower College; authorizes date changes for Bicentennial coins; allows compositional change in cent to zinc-copper until 1977.	Eisenhower college receipts, Hearing on H.R. 1020 and 7322, 5/2-3/73; 1 cent composition change: Hearing on H.R. 11841 3/27/74; Hearing on "The Proposed Change in the Penny" (House Serial #97-4) 3/31/81
Pub. L. 93-541 Dec. 26, 1974 88 Stat. 1739	Amends Bicentennial coinage legislation to allow for simultaneous striking of Bicentennial and regular-dated (1974) coins.	No hearings. Debate: (S. Rept. 93-1303) 12/11/74; House 12/13/74
Pub. L. 93-554 Dec. 17, 1974 88 Stat. 1771	Releases funds to Eisenhower College from Pub. L. 93-441.	
Pub. L. 93-617 Jan. 2, 1975 88 Stat. 1978	Jim Thorpe national medal; San Francisco cable car national medal (adds time to produce).	
Pub. L. 94-117 Oct. 17, 1975 89 Stat. 602	Medallic commemoration of Army and Navy bicentennial.	
Pub. L. 94-179 Oct. 17, 1975 89 Stat. 1029	Medal for Gen. "Chuck" Yeager.	Hearing on H.R. 8051 and others, 9/23/75
Pub. L. 94-257 April 1, 1976 90 Stat. 302	Commemorates bicentennial of John Carroll (of Maryland) signing Declaration of Independence.	Hearing on H.R. 3427, 9/23/75
Pub. L. 94-564 Oct. 19, 1976 90 Stat. 2661	Bretton Woods Agreements Act regarding value of gold/dollar.	
Pub. L. 95-9 March 8, 1977 91 Stat. 18	Gold medal for Marian Anderson.	
Pub. L. 95-229 Feb. 14, 1979 92 Stat. 26	Capitol Historical Society medal legislation.	Hearing on H.J. Res. 386, 6/29/77; Senate hearing on H.J. Res. 386, 11/28/77

Pub. L. 95-438 Oct. 10, 1978 92 Stat. 1068	Gold medal for Gen. Ira C. Eaker	Hearing (numerous bills) 4/26/78
Pub. L. 95-447 Oct. 10, 1978 92 Stat. 1072	Authorizes Susan B. Anthony dollar design.	Hearings (S. 3036) 7/17/78; Hearings (H.R. 12444), 5/17 and 31/78 House Oversight hearings Serial 96-30, 9/25-26/79 Debate: House (H. Rept. 95-1576) 9/26/78; Senate (S. Rept.95-1576) 8/22/78. Presidential statement in Weekly Compilation of Presidential Documents, 10/10/78.
Pub. L. 95-560 Nov. 1, 1978 92 Stat. 2142	Gold medal for Robert F. Kennedy.	Hearing (numerous bills) 4/26/78
Pub. L. 95-630 Nov. 10, 1978 92 Stat. 3679	American Arts Gold Medallion Act.	Hearings (S. 2843) 8/25/78
Pub. L. 96-2 March 7, 1979 93 Stat. 4	Carson City silver dollar sale (final disposal).	(H.R. 9937), Hearings 4/3/78 Also see Hearing (Serial 96-67) 8/19/80 and follow-up: Committee Print 96-23 (12/80) reporting on sale.
Pub. L. 96-15 May 26, 1979 93 Stat. 32	John Wayne gold medal.	Hearings (H.R. 3767) 5/21/79. Senate Rept. 96-110. Debate: Senate 5/3/79; House 5/23/79
Pub. L. 96-20 June 13, 1979 93 Stat. 45	Ben Abruzzo, Maxie Anderson, Larry Newman (transatlantic balloon trip) gold medal.	See Senate Rept. 96-108. Debate: Senate 5/3 and 6/5/79; House 6/4/79
Pub. L. 96-21 June 13, 1979 93 Stat. 46	Hubert H. Humphrey gold medal.	See Senate Rept. 96-109
Pub. L. 96-138 Dec. 12, 1979 93 Stat. 1063	National medal for U.S. Red Cross.	
Pub. L. 96-201 March 6, 1980 94 Stat. 79	National medal for Canadian ambassador Kenneth Taylor (Iranian hostage situation).	
Pub. L. 96-209 March 14, 1980 94 Stat. 98	Abolishes position of Assay Commissioner.	
Pub. L. 96-211 March 17, 1980 94 Stat. 101	Gold medal for Simon Wiesenthal.	
Pub. L. 96-306 July 8, 1980 94 Stat. 937	Gold plated medals to U.S. Olympic team because of nonparticipation in Olympic Games (U.S. boycott of Moscow Games).	
Pub. L. 97-104 Dec. 23, 1981 95 Stat. 1491	George Washington commemorative half dollar.	(H.R. 3133) 5/7/81
Pub. L. 97-158 March 22, 1982 96 Stat. 18	Gold medal to Her Majesty Queen Beatrix (Netherlands) in commemoration of 200 years of friendship with the Netherlands.	(H.J. Res. 348) 2/26/82
Pub. L. 97-201 June 23, 1982 96 Stat. 126	Gold medal for Adm. Hyman G. Rickover.	Adm. Rickover medal (H.R. 5432) 3/9/82
Pub. L. 97-220 July 22, 1982 96 Stat. 222	Olympic coin legislation.	Olympic coinage. Hearings, S. 1230 (7/14/81); (House) 4/6, 21 and 29/82; 5/11-12/82; Oversight hearings on Olympic coin designs: House serial #97-98, 12/1/82; Hearings (S. 1230) 6/10/82 Senate debate: 12/9/81 (Rept. 97-264); House debate: 5/20/82 (Rept. 97-554)
Pub. L. 97-239 Aug. 20, 1982 96 Stat. 271	National Coin Week request proposal.	No hearings held. President did proclaim as requested (3/7/83).
Pub. L. 97-246 Aug. 26, 1982 96 Stat. 315	Gold medals for Fred Waring, Joe Louis, Louis L'Amour.	(H.R. 4647) 7/22/81

Pub. L. 97-258 Sept. 13, 1982 96 Stat. 877	Codifies Title 31 of the United States Code into positive law (repealing all inconsistent laws).	
Pub. L. 98-94 Sept. 24, 1983 97 Stat. 614	Contains a section providing for striking of bronze medal honoring missing Vietnam veterans.	Defense Authorization Act (contains bronze medals for Missing In Action). Numerous hearings on bill (not related to numismatics).
Pub. L. 98-136 Oct. 24, 1983 97 Stat. 863	Medal for Louisiana World Exposition.	(H.R. 3321) 9/20/83
Pub. L. 98-151 Nov. 14, 1983 97 Stat. 979	Directs Treasury Secretary to produce Mint (Uncirculated coin) sets.	See Senate rept. 98-131 (5/18/83)
Pub. L. 98-159 Nov. 18, 1983 97 Stat. 992	Gold medal for Rep. Leo Ryan (murdered in Jonestown, Guyana).	
Pub. L. 98-172 Nov. 29, 1983 97 Stat. 1119	Gold medal for Danny Thomas.	
Pub. L. 98-278 May 5, 1984 98 Stat. 173	Gold medals for Harry S Truman, Lady Bird Johnson, Elie Wiesel.	Hearings on H.R. 3614 and H.J. Res. 394 (3/6/84) Serial No. 98-74
Pub. L. 98-285 May 17, 1984 98 Stat. 186	Gold medal for Roy Wilkins.	Hearing on H.R. 3240 (3/6/84) Serial No. 98-74
Pub. L. 98-306 May 31, 1984 98 Stat. 223	National Medal of the Arts.	
Pub. L. 98-566 Oct. 30, 1984 98 Stat. 2923	Vietnam Veterans National Medal Act.	
Pub. L. 98-599 Oct. 30, 1984 98 Stat. 3144	Missing in Action Medal Act.	
Pub. L. 99-61, Title I July 9, 1985 99 Stat. 113	Statue of Liberty commemorative coin.	
Pub. L. 99-61, Title II July 9, 1985 99 Stat. 115	Liberty Coin Act (silver bullion coin).	
Pub. L. 99-86 Aug. 9, 1985 99 Stat. 288	George & Ira Gershwin medal.	
Pub. L. 99-185 Dec. 17, 1985 99 Stat. 1177 (31 USC Sec. 5712)	Gold Bullion Coin Act of 1985.	See Staff Report on Distribution of American Eagle Gold Coins, Comm. Print 100-4 (House Banking Comm., 1987)
Pub. L. 99-295 May 12, 1986 100 Stat. 427	Young Astronaut Program Medal Act.	Hearing on H.R. 2578 before Subcomm. on Consumer Affairs & Coinage of House Comm. Banking, Finance & Urban Affairs, Serial 99-70 (Apr. 22, 1986).
Pub. L. 99-298 May 13, 1986 100 Stat. 432	Natan (Anatoly) Shcharansky Gold Medal.	
Pub. L. 99-311 May 20, 1986 100 Stat. 464	Harry Chapin Gold Medal.	
Pub. L. 99-418 Sept. 23, 1986 100 Stat. 952	Aaron Copland Medal Act.	
Pub. L. 99-514 Oct. 11, 1986 Sec. 1144, (26 USC 408(m))	Tax Reform Act of 1986 (Bullion coins with IRAs).	
Pub. L. 99-582 Oct. 29, 1986 100 Stat. 3315	Bicentennial of Constitution commemorative coin.	
Pub. L. 99-631 Nov. 7, 1986 100 Stat. 3518	Ban importation of Soviet gold coins, 22 USC sec 5100.	See Cong Record 9/19/83, p H7007-8

Pub. L. 100-141 Oct. 28, 1987 101 Stat. 832	Olympic Commemorative Coin Act of 1988	1988 Olympic Commemoratives, Hearing on H.R. 2741 before House Banking Subcomm. on Consumer Affairs & Coinage, Aug. 4, 1987.; 133 Cong. Record S 14181, 14271, H8671 (Oct. 13-4, 1987); S Rept. 100-197.
Pub. L. 100-210 Dec. 24, 1987 101 Stat. 1441	Gold medal to Mary Lasker (medical research); Young Astronaut program extended to 12/31/88	Report filed 12/16/87 (not written)
Pub. L. 100-269 Mar. 28, 1988 102 Stat. 43	Congress directs Dep't of Defense to issue medal to former prisoners of war. J. Res. No. 253.	
Pub. L. 100-274 Mar. 31, 1988 102 Stat. 48 (31 USC Sec. 5132(a))	Appropriations for Bureau of Mint.	Hearing on H.R. 2631 before House Banking Consumer Affairs & Coinage Subcommittee, July 15, 1987
Pub. L. 100-324 May 30, 1988 102 Stat. 576.	Act authorizing decorations and medals for recognition of service in the U.S. Merchant Marine.	H. Rept. 100-510
Pub. L. 100-378 Aug. 1, 1988 102 Stat. 887	Bicentennial of U.S. Congress Commemorative Coin Act.	See 135 Cong. Record S 6575; 135 Cong. Record E642 (March 2, 1989) S Rept 100-383.
Pub. L. 100-404 Aug. 19, 1988 102 Stat. 1014	Appropriations to carry out National Science Foundation Act to establish National Medal of Science.	
Pub. L. 100-437 Sep. 20, 1988 102 Stat. 1717	Congressional medal awarded to Mrs. Jesse Owens. Young Astronaut program extended to 12/31/89	Hearings on H.R. 1270 before House Banking Consumer Affairs & Coinage Subcommittee, Serial 100-78 (July 12, 1988)
Pub. L. 100-463 Oct. 1, 1988	Presidential Medal of Freedom awarded posthumously to Charles E. Thorton, Lee Shapiro, and Jim Lindelhof for their brave efforts in Afghan struggle.	
Pub. L. 100-467 Oct 3, 1988 102 Stat. 2275	Dwight D. Eisenhower Commemorative Coin Act of 1988.	Hearing on S. 2789 & H.R. 3654 before House Banking Consumer Affairs & Coinage Subcommittee, Sept. 14, 1988; 134 Cong. Record S 12510 (Sept. 14, 1988).
Pub. L. 100-639 Nov. 9, 1988 102 Stat. 3331	Congressional gold medal to Andrew Wyeth	Hearings on H.R. 593 before House Banking Consumer Affairs & Coinage Subcommittee, Serial 100-78 (July 12, 1988)
Pub. L. 100-647 Nov. 11, 1988 26 USC sec. 408(m)(3)	Sec. 6057. Prohibition on collectibles not to include State coins.	Extensive history on tax law. Colloquy in Congressional Record between Symms & McClure of some note. See House Conf. Rept 1104, vol 2, pp 158-59.
Pub. L. 100-673 Nov. 17, 1988 102 Stat. 3992	Sec'y of Treasury authorized to mint coins in commemoration of the Bicentennial of the U.S. Congress.	Hearing on H.R. 3251 before House Banking Consumer Affairs & Coinage Subcommittee, Sept. 15, 1987; 134 Cong Record H9462, Oct. 4, 1988; 134 Cong Record H 9304 (Oct. 3 1988).
Pub. L. 100-674 Nov. 17, 1988 102 Stat. 49	Congressional Award Act Amendments of 1988 - Gold Medal Awards ceremony in District of Columbia	
Pub. L. 100-696 Nov. 18, 1989	Surcharges on commemorative coin uses	
Pub. L. 101-13 Apr. 13, 1989 103 Stat. 36	National Former Prisoners of War Recognition Day designated (Medal given to former prisoners of war).	
Pub. L. 101-36 Jun. 9, 1989 103 Stat. 69.	First strike ceremony for the Bicentennial of the Congress Commemorative Coin. S.J. Res. No. 128	See 135 Cong Record E1983, June 5, 1989; 135 Cong. Record H2064, May 23, 1989. 135 Cong Record S5129, May 10, 1989.
Pub. L. 101-144 Nov. 9, 1989 103 Stat. 839.	Appropriations bill; National Medal of Science and other purposes.	Mint Budget Authorization Hearing on H.R. 2931 before Subcomm. on Consumer Affairs & Coinage of House Banking Comm., Serial 101-46 (Aug. 1, 1989)

Pub. L. 101-189 Nov. 28, 1989 103 Stat. 1350	Sec. 516 Eligibility for Prisoner of War Medal
Pub. L. 101-260 Mar. 30, 1990 104 Stat. 122	Provides for striking of medals in commemoration of the bicentennial of the U.S. Coast Guard.
Pub. L. 101-266 Apr. 5, 1990 104 Stat. 129	Congress directed Dep't of Defense to issue medal to former prisoners of war.

Extracts of texts of laws

Following are the edited texts of major numismatic laws passed since 1955. To the extent that numismatic portions are included as separate sections, or as titles to laws which do not relate to the subject matter of Coin World Almanac, they have been omitted. Other sections have been edited for convenience. A complete version may be found in The Statutes at Large, available in most public libraries, as well as in government document centers at universities and law schools. Some of the legislative reports may conveniently be found in U.S. Code Congressional & Administrative News, a legal publication also found in many libraries.

All laws begin with the identical language: "Be it enacted by the Senate and House of Representatives of the United States of American in Congress assembled," after which the text of the law appears.

Sometimes, the legislation has what is call a "short title," meaning an official version or abbreviation. For example, for coins produced to honor the 200th anniversary of the American Constitution, the short title is called the "Bicentennial of the Constitution Coins Act," which might be the official version, but inevitably will be parochialized into the Constitution Bicentennial Coin Act, or something similar.

Some laws are printed elsewhere in this chapter. For example, the law concerning prohibition on Soviet gold coin importation, and that concerning placement of state "coins" in individual retirement accounts, appears in a more logical sequence near the section discussing importation bans and tax laws, respectively.

First Strike Ceremony at the Capitol

Public Law 101-36, June 9, 1989, 103 Stat. 69 (S.J. Res. 128)(31 USC sec. 5112 note).

Sec. 1 First Strike Ceremony at the United States Capitol for the Bicentennial of the Congress Commemorative Coin.

(a) On June 14, 1989, or at any date that the President pro tempore of the Senate and the Speaker of the House of Representatives jointly designate, a first strike ceremony may be conducted at the United States Capitol and on the Capitol Grounds to strike coins authorized by the Bicentennial of the United States Congress Commemorative Coin Act (Public Law 100-673).

(b) All activities of and preparations for the ceremony authorized by subsection (a),

including the striking and distribution of coins, shall be jointly coordinated with the Commissions on the Bicentennial of the United States Senate and the United States House of Representatives and the Secretary of the Treasury.

(c) Notwithstanding the Bicentennial of the United States Congress Commemorative Coin Act or any other provision of law, the United States Mint may strike coins authorized by the United States Congress Commemorative Coin Act in Washington, District of Columbia, during first strike ceremonies conducted as authorized by subsection (a). Such coins shall bear the mint mark of the mint facility which is designated to strike the

coins.

Sec. 2. Responsibility of Congressional Officers & Physical Preparations.

(a) Under the direction of the President pro tempore of the Senate and the Speaker of the House, the Secretary of the Senate, the Clerk of the House, the Architect of the Capitol and the Capitol Police Board shall take any action necessary to carry out section 1.

(b) The Architect of the Capitol may prescribe conditions for physical preparations for the ceremony authorized in section 1.

Eisenhower commemorative coin
Public Law 100-467, Oct. 3, 1988

Sec. 1. Short Title. This Act may be cited as the "Dwight David Eisenhower Commemorative Coin Act of 1988."

Sec. 2. DWIGHT DAVID EISENHOWER COMMEMORATIVE COINS.

(a) Authorization. Subject to subsection (b), the Secretary of the Treasury (hereinafter in this Act referred to as the "Secretary") shall mint and issue one-dollar coins in commemoration of the one hundredth anniversary of the birth of Dwight David Eisenhower.

(b) Limitation on the number of coins. The Secretary may not mint more than four million of the coins referred to in subsection (a).

(c) Specifications and design of coins. Each coin referred to in subsection (a) shall

(1) weigh 26.73 grams;

(2) have a diameter of 1.500 inches;

(3) contain 90 percent silver and 10 percent copper;

(4) designate the value of such coin;

(5) have an inscription of

(A) the year "1990"; and

(B) the words "Liberty", "In God We Trust", "United States of America", and "E Pluribus Unum";

(6) have the likeness of Dwight David Eisenhower on the obverse side of such coin; and

(7) have an illustration of the home of Dwight David Eisenhower located in the Gettysburg National Historic Site on the reverse side of such coin.

(d) Numismatic items. For purposes of section 5132(a)(1) of title 31, United States Code, the coins referred to in subsection (a) shall be considered to be numismatic items.

(e) Legal tender. The coins referred to in subsection (a) shall be legal tender as provided in section 5103 of Title 31, United States Code.

Sec. 3 Sources of bullion.

The Secretary shall obtain silver for the coins referred to in section 1(a) only from stockpiles established under the Strategic and Critical Materials Stock Piling Act (50 U.S.C. 98 et seq.).

Sec. 4 Minting and issuance of coins.

(a) Uncirculated and proof qualities. The Secretary may mint and issue the coins referred to in section 1(a) in uncirculated and proof qualities.

(b) Use of the United States Mint. The Secretary may not use more than 1 facility of the United States Mint to strike each such quality of the coins referred to in section 1(a).

(c) Commencement of authority to sell coins. The Secretary may begin selling the coins referred to in section 1(a) on January 1, 1990.

(d) Termination of authority to mint coins. The Secretary may not mint the coins referred to in section 1(a) after December 31, 1990.

Sec. 5 Sale of Coins.

(a) In general. Subject to subsections (b) and (c), and notwithstanding any other provision of law, the Secretary shall sell the coins referred to in section 1(a) at a price equal to

(1) the face value of such coins; and

(2) the cost of designing, minting, dies, use of machinery, and overhead expenses.

(b) Bulk sales. The Secretary shall make any bulk sales of the coins referred to in section 1(a) at a reasonable discount to reflect the lower costs of such sales.

(c) Prepaid orders. Before January 1, 1990, the Secretary shall accept prepaid orders for the coins referred to in section 1(a). The Secretary shall make sales with respect to such prepaid orders at a reasonable discount to reflect the benefit to the Federal Government of prepayment.

(d) Surcharges. The Secretary shall include a surcharge of $7 per coin on all sales of the coins referred to in section 1(a).

Sec. 6 Financial assurances.

(a) No net cost to the government. The Secretary shall take such actions as may be necessary to ensure that the minting and issuance of the coins referred to in section 1(a) shall result in no net costs to the Federal Government.

(b) Payment for the coins. The Secretary may not sell a coin referred to in section 1(a) unless the Secretary has received

(1) full payment for such coin;

(2) security satisfactory to the Secretary to indemnify the Federal Government for full payment; or

(3) a guarantee of full payment satisfactory to the Secretary from a depository institution whose deposits are insured by the Federal Deposit Insurance Corporation, the Federal Savings and Loan Insurance Corporation, or the National Credit Union Administration Board.

Sec. 7. Procurement of goods and services.

(a) In general. Except as provided in subsection (b), no provision of law governing procurement or public contracts shall be applicable to the procurement of goods or services necessary for carrying out the provisions of this Act.

(b) Equal employment opportunity. Subsection (a) shall not apply with respect to any law relating to equal employment opportunity.

Sec. 8 Reduction of Federal debt.

The Secretary shall deposit in the general fund of the Treasury for the purpose of reducing the Federal debt an amount equal to the amount of all surcharges that are received by the Secretary from the sale of the coins referred to in section 1(a)

United States Congress Commemorative Coin Act
Public Law 100-378, August 1, 1988, 102 Stat. 887

Sec. 1. Short Title. This Act may be cited as the Bicentennial of the United States Congress Commemorative Coin Act.

Sec. 2. Specifications of coins.

(a)Five Dollar Gold Coins.

(1) The Secretary of the Treasury (hereinafter in this Act referred to as the "Secretary") shall mint and issue not more than 1,000,000 five dollar coins each of which shall--

(A) weigh 8.359 grams;

(B) have a diameter of 0.850 inches; and

(C) be composed of 90 percent gold and 10 percent alloy.

(2) The design of the five dollar coins shall, in accordance with section 4, be emblematic of the bicentennial of the United States Congress. Each five dollar coin there shall bear a designation of the value of the coin, an inscription of the year "1989", and inscriptions of the words "Liberty", "In God We Trust", "United States of America", and "E Pluribus Unum".

(b)One dollar silver coins

(1) The Secretary shall mint and issue not more than 10,000,000 one dollar coins each of which shall

(A) weigh 26.73 grams,

(B) have a diameter of 1.500 inches, and

(C) shall contain 90 percent silver and 10 percent copper.

(2) Design. The design of such dollar coins shall, in accordance with section 4, be emblematic of the bicentennial of the United States Congress. Each one dollar coin shall bear a designation of the value of the coin, an inscription of the year

"1989", and inscriptions of the words "Liberty", "In God We Trust", "United States of America", and "E Pluribus Unum".

(c) Half dollar clad coins.

(1) Issuance. The Secretary shall issue not more than 10,000,000 half dollar coins each of which shall

(A) weight 11.34 grams

(B) have a diameter of 1.205 inches, and

(C) be minted with the specifications for half dollar coins contained in section 5112(b) of title 31, United States Code.

(2) Design. The design of such half dollar coins shall, in accordance with section 4, be emblematic of the bicentennial of the United States Congress. Each one dollar coin shall bear a designation of the value of the coin, an inscription of the year "1989", and inscriptions of the words "Liberty", "In God We Trust", "United States of America", and "E Pluribus Unum".

(d) The coins minted under this Act shall be legal tender as provided in section 5103 of title 31, United States Code.

(e) For purposes of section 5132(a)(1) of title 31, United States Code, all coins minted under this title shall be considered to be numismatic items.

Sec. 3. Sources of Bullion

(a) The Secretary shall obtain gold for the coins minted under this title pursuant to the authority of the Secretary under existing law.

(b) The Secretary shall obtain silver for the coins minted under this title only from stockpiles established under the Strategic and Critical Minerals Stock Piling Act (50 USC 98 et seq.).

Sec. 4 Design of Coins.

The director of the Mint shall submit the proposed designs of the coins to be minted under this Act to the Commission of Fine Arts for comments. After receiving the comments on the design from such Commission, the Director of the Mint shall submit the proposed designs together with such comments to the Secretary. After receiving the proposed design and the comments, the Secretary shall select the design of the coins to be minted under this Act.

Sec. 5 Issuance of Coins

(a) Five dollar coins. The five dollar coins authorized under this title may be issued in uncirculated and proof qualities and shall be struck at the United States Mint at West Point.

(b) One dollar and half dollar coins. The one dollar and half dollar coins may be issued in uncirculated and proof qualities, except that not more than one facility of the United States Mint may be used to strike any particular combination of denomination and quality.

(c) Commencement of Issuance. The Secretary may issue the coins minted under this title beginning January 1, 1989.

(d) No coins shall be minted under this title after June 30, 1990.

Sec. 6. Sale of Coins.

(a) In General. Notwithstanding any other provision of law, the coins issued under this title shall be sold by the Secretary at a price equal to the face value, plus the cost of designing and issuing such coins (including labor, materials, dies, use of machinery, and overhead expenses).

(b) Bulk Sales. The Secretary shall make bulk sales at a reasonable discount to reflect the lower costs of such sales.

(c) Prepaid Orders. The Secretary shall accept prepaid orders for the coins prior to the issuance of such coins. Sales under this subsection shall be at a reasonable discount to reflect the benefit of prepayment.

(d) Surcharges. All sales shall include a surcharge of $35 per coin for the five dollar coins, $7 per coin for the one dollar coins, and $1 per coin for the half dollar coins.

Sec 7. Financial Assurances

(a) No net cost to the Government. The Secretary shall take all actions necessary to ensure that the minting and issuing of the coins authorized under this Act will not result in any net cost to the United States Government.

(b) Payment for coins. No coin shall be issued under this title unless the Secretary has received

(1) full payment for the coin;

(2) security satisfactory to the Secretary to indemnify the United States for full payment; or

(3) a guarantee of full payment satisfactory to the Secretary from a depository institution whose deposits are insured by the Federal Deposit Insurance Corporation, the Federal Savings and Loan Insurance Corporation, or the National Credit Union Administration Board.

Sec. 8 Reduction of National Debt

An amount equal to the amount of all surcharges which are received by the Secretary from the sale of coins issued under this title shall be deposited in the general fund of the Treasury and shall be used for the sole purpose of reducing the national debt.

Sec. 9 General Waiver of Procurement

Regulations

(a) In General. Except as provided in section (b), no provision of law governing procurement or public contracts shall be applicable to the procurement of goods or services necessary for carrying out the provisions of this title.

(b) Equal Employment Opportunity. Subsection (a) shall not relieve any person entering into a contract under the authority of this title from complying with any law relating to equal employment opportunity.

Sec. 10. [amendments not related]

Sec. 11 Sunset.

All provisions of this Act other than section 10 shall be repealed on the day after enactment of this Act and no person shall be liable for not complying with such provisions (other than section 10) while they are in effect.

1988 Olympic Commemoratives
Public Law 100-141, Oct. 28, 1987, 101 Stat. 833 (31 USC sec. 5112 note)

Sec. 1 Short title. This Act may be cited as the "1988 Olympic Commemorative Coin Act."

Sec. 2 Coin Specifications.

(a)Five Dollar Gold Coins.

(1) The Secretary of the Treasury (hereinafter in this Act referred to as the "Secretary") shall mint and issue not more than 1,000,000 five dollar coins each of which shall weigh 8.359 grams, have a diameter of 0.850 inches, and shall contain 90 percent gold and 10 percent alloy.

(2) The design of such five dollar coins shall be emblematic of the participation of American athletes in the 1988 Olympic Games. On each such coin, there shall be a designation of the value of the coin, an inscription of the year "1988", and inscriptions of the words "Liberty", "In God We Trust", "United States of America", and "E Pluribus Unum".

(b)One dollar silver coins

(1) The Secretary shall mint and issue not more than 10,000,000 one dollar coins each of which shall weigh 26.73 grams, have a diameter of 1.500 inches, and shall contain 90 percent silver and 10 percent copper.

(2) Design. The design of such five dollar coins shall be emblematic of the participation of American athletes in the 1988 Olympic Games. On each such coin, there shall be a designation of the value of the coin, an inscription of the year "1988", and inscriptions of the words "Liberty", "In God We Trust", "United States of America", and "E Pluribus Unum".

(c) The coins minted under this Act shall be legal tender as provided in section 5103 of title 31, United States Code.

Sec. 3. Sources of Bullion

(a) The Secretary shall obtain silver for the coins minted under this title only from stockpiles established under the Strategic and Critical Minerals Stock Piling Act (50 USC 98 et seq.).

(b) The Secretary shall obtain gold for the coins minted under this title pursuant to the authority of the Secretary under existing law.

Sec. 4 Selection of design

The design for each coin authorized by this Act shall be selected by the Secretary after consultation with the United States

Olympic Committee and the Commission on Fine Arts.

Sec. 5. Sale of Coins.

(a) Sale price. Notwithstanding any other provision of law, the coins issued under this title shall be sold by the Secretary at a price equal to the face value, plus the cost of designing and issuing such coins (including labor, materials, dies, use of machinery, and overhead expenses).

(b) Bulk Sales. The Secretary shall make bulk sales at a reasonable discount to reflect the lower costs of such sales.

(c) Prepaid Orders. The Secretary shall accept prepaid orders for the coins prior to the issuance of such coins. Sales under this subsection shall be at a reasonable discount

to reflect the benefit of prepayment.

(d) Surcharges. All sales shall include a surcharge of $35 per coin for the five dollar coins and $7 per coin for the one dollar coins.

Sec. 6 Issuance of Coins

(a) Gold coins. The five dollar coins authorized under this title shall be issued in uncirculated and proof qualities and shall be struck at the United States Bullion Depository at West Point.

(b) Silver coins. The one dollar coins authorized under this Act may be issued in uncirculated and proof qualities, except that not more than one facility of the United States Mint may be used to strike each such quality.

(c) Sunset provision. No coins shall be minted under this Act after June 30, 1989.

Sec. 7 General Waiver of Procurement Regulations

No provision of law governing procurement or public contracts shall be applicable to the procurement of goods or services necessary for carrying out the provisions of this title. Nothing in this section shall relieve any person entering into a contract under the authority of this title from complying with any law relating to equal employment opportunity.

Sec. 8 Distribution of Surcharges.

All surcharges which are received by the Secretary from the sale of coins issued under this Act shall be promptly paid by the Secretary to the United States Olympic Committee. Such amounts shall be used by the United States Olympic Committee solely to train United States Olympic athletes, to support local or community amateur athletic programs, and to erect facilities for the training of such athletes.

Sec. 9. Audits.

The Comptroller General shall have the right to examine such books, records, documents and other data of the United States Olympic Committee as may be related to the expenditure of amounts paid under section 8.

Sec. 10. Coinage profit fund.

Notwithstanding any other provision of law

(1) all amounts received from the sale of coins issued under this Act shall be deposited in the coinage profit fund;

(2) the Secretary shall pay the amounts authorized under this Act from the coinage profit fund; and

(3) The Secretary shall charge the coinage profit fund with all expenditures under this Act.

Sec 11. Financial Assurances

(a) No net cost to the Government. The Secretary shall take all actions necessary to ensure that the minting and issuing of the coins authorized under this Act will not

result in any net cost to the United States Government.

(b) Payment for coins. No coin shall be issued under this title unless the Secretary has received

(1) full payment for the coin;

(2) security satisfactory to the Secretary to indemnify the United States for full payment; or

(3) a guarantee of full payment satisfactory to the Secretary from a depository institution whose deposits are insured by the Federal Deposit Insurance Corporation, the Federal Savings and Loan Insurance Corporation, or the National Credit Union Administration Board.

Constitution Bicentennial

Public Law 99-582, 99th Congress, approved Oct. 29, 1986.

SHORT TITLE

Section 1. This Act may be cited as the "Bicentennial of the Constitution Coins Act".

Definitions Sec. 2. For purposes of this Act-

(1) the term "Commission" means the Commission on the Bicentennial of the United States Constitution; and

(2) the term "Secretary" means the Secretary of the Treasury.

Title I-Bicentennial of the United States Constitution Commemorative Coins

COIN SPECIFICATIONS

Sec. 101. (a)(1) The Secretary shall issue not more than 1,000,000 five dollar coins which shall weigh 8.359 grams, have a diameter of 0.850 inches, and shall contain 90 percent gold and 10 percent alloy.

(2) The design of such five dollar coins shall be emblematic of the bicentennial of the United States Constitution. On each such five dollar coin there shall be a designation of the value of the coin, an inscription of the year "1987", and inscriptions of the words "Liberty", "In God We Trust", "United States of America", and "E Pluribus Unum".

(b)(1) The Secretary shall issue not more than 10,000,000 one dollar coins which shall weigh 26.73 grams, have a diameter of 1.500 inches, and shall contain 90 percent silver and 10 percent copper.

(2) The design of such dollar coins shall be emblematic of the bicentennial of the United States Constitution. On each such dollar coin there shall be a designation of the value of the coin, an inscription of the year "1987", and inscriptions of the words "Liberty", "In God We Trust", "United States of America", and "E Pluribus Unum".

(c) The coins issued under this title shall be legal tender as provided in section 5103 of title 31, United States Code.

(d) For purposes of section 5132(a)(1) of title 31, United States Code, all coins minted under this title shall be considered to be numismatic items.

SOURCES OF BULLION

Sec. 102. (a) The Secretary shall obtain gold for the coins minted under this title pursuant to the authority of the Secretary under existing law.

(b) The Secretary shall obtain silver for the coins minted under this title only from stockpiles established under the Strategic and Critical Minerals Stock Piling Act (50 USC 98 et seq.).

DESIGN OF THE COIN

Sec. 103. The design for each coin authorized by this title shall be selected by the Secretary after consultation with the Commission and the Commission of Fine Arts.

SALE OF THE COINS

Sec. 104. (a) Notwithstanding any other provision of law, the coins issued under this title shall be sold by the Secretary at a price equal to the face value, plus the cost of designing and issuing such coins (including labor, materials, dies, use of machinery, and overhead expenses).

(b) The Secretary shall make bulk sales at a reasonable discount to reflect the lower costs of such sales.

(c) The Secretary shall accept prepaid orders for the coins prior to the issuance of such coins. Sales under this subsection shall be at a reasonable discount to reflect the benefit of prepayment.

(d) All sales shall include a surcharge of $35 per coin for the five dollar coins and $7 per coin for the one dollar coins.

ISSUANCE OF COINS

Sec. 105. (a) The gold coins authorized under this title shall be issued in uncirculated and proof qualities and shall be struck at the United States Bullion Depository at West Point.

(b) The silver coins authorized under this title may be issued in uncirculated and proof qualities, except that not more than one facility of the United States Mint may be used to strike each such quality.

(c) The Secretary may issue the coins minted under this title beginning January 1, 1987.

(d) No coins shall be minted under this title after June 30, 1988.

FINANCIAL ASSURANCES

Sec. 106. (a) The Secretary shall take all actions necessary to ensure that the issuance of the coins authorized by this title shall result in no net cost to the United States Government.

(b) No coin shall be issued under this title unless the Secretary has received —

(1) full payment therefor;

(2) security satisfactory to the Secretary to indemnify the United States for full payment; or

(3) a guarantee of full payment satisfactory to the Secretary from a depository institution whose deposits are insured by the Federal Deposit Insurance Corporation, the Federal Savings and Loan Insurance Corporation, or the National Credit Union Administration Board.

NATIONAL DEBT REDUCTION

Sec. 107. An amount equal to the amount of all surcharges which are received by the Secretary from the sale of coins issued under this title shall be deposited in the general fund of the Treasury and shall be used for the sole purpose of reducing the national debt.

PROCUREMENT OF GOODS AND SERVICES

Sec. 108. No provision of law governing procurement or public contracts shall be applicable to the procurement of goods or services necessary for carrying out the provisions of this title. Nothing in this section shall relieve any person entering into a contract under the authority of this title from complying with any law relating to equal employment opportunity.

Gold Bullion Coins
Public Law 99-185, 99th Congress, approved December 17, 1985.

SHORT TITLE

Section 1. This Act may be cited as the "Gold Bullion Coin Act of 1985".

MINTING GOLD BULLION COINS

Sec. 2. (a) Section 5112(a) of title 31, United States Code, is amended by adding at the end thereof the following new paragraphs:

"(7) A fifty dollar gold coin that is 32.7 millimeters in diameter, weighs 33.931 grams, and contains one troy ounce of five gold.

"(8) A twenty-five dollar gold coin that is 27.0 millimeters in diameter, weighs 16.966 grams, and contains one-half troy ounce of fine gold.

"(9) A ten dollar gold coin that is 22.0 millimeters in diameter, weighs 8.483 grams, and contains one-fourth troy ounce of fine gold.

"(10) A five dollar gold coin that is 16.5 millimeters in diameter, weighs 3.393 grams, and contains one-tenth troy ounce of fine gold."

(b) Section 5112 of title 31, United States Code, is amended by adding at the end thereof the following new subsection:

"(i)(1) Notwithstanding section 5111(a)(1) of this title, the Secretary shall mint and issue the gold coins described in paragraphs (7) (8), (9), and (10) of subsection (a) of this section, in quantities sufficient to meet public demand, and such gold coins shall —

"(A) have a design determined by the Secretary, except that the fifty dollar gold coin shall have —

"(i) on the obverse side, a design symbolic of Liberty; and

"(ii) on the reverse side, a design representing a family of eagles, with the male carrying an olive branch and flying above a nest containing a female eagle and hatchlings;

"(B) have inscriptions of the denomination, the weight of the fine gold content, the year of minting or issuance, and the words "Liberty', "In God We Trust', "United States of America', and "E Pluribus Unum'; and

"(C) have reeded edges.

"(2)(A) The Secretary shall sell the

coins minted under this subsection to the public at a price equal to the market value of the bullion at the time of sale, plus the cost of minting, marketing, and distributing such coins (including labor, materials, dies, use of machinery, and promotional and overhead expenses).

"(B) The Secretary shall make bulk sales of the coins minted under this subsection at a reasonable discount.

"(3) For purposes of section 5132(a)(1) of this title, all coins minted under this subsection shall be considered to be numismatic items."

(c) Section 5116(a) of title 31, United States Code, is amended by adding at the end thereof the following:

"(3) The Secretary shall acquire gold for the coins issued under section 5112(i) of this title by purchase of gold mined from natural deposits in the United States, or in a territory or possession of the United States, within one year after the month in which the ore from which it is derived was mined. The Secretary shall pay not more than the average world price for the gold. In the absence of available supplies of such gold at the average world price, the Secretary may use gold from reserves held by the United States to mint the coins issued under section 5112(i) of this title. The Secretary shall issue such regulations as may be necessary to carry out this paragraph."

(d) Section 5118(b) of title 31, United States Code, is amended —

(1) in the first sentence, by striking out "or deliver"; and

(2) in the second sentence, by inserting "(other than gold and silver coins)" before "that may be lawfully held".

(e) The third sentence of section 5132(a)(1) of title 31, United States Code, is amended by striking out "minted under section 5112(a) of this title" and inserting in lieu thereof "minted under paragraphs (1) through (6) of section 5112(a) of this title".

(f) Notwithstanding any other provision of law, an amount equal to the amount by which the proceeds from the sale of the coins issued under section 5112(i) of title 31, United States Code, exceed the sum of —

(1) the cost of minting, marketing, and distributing such coins, and

(2) the value of gold certificates (not exceeding forty-two and two-ninths dollars a fine troy ounce) retired from the use of gold contained in such coins, shall be deposited in the general fund of the Treasury and shall be used for the sole purpose of reducing the national debt.

(g) The Secretary shall take all action necessary to ensure that the issuance of the coins minted under section 5112(i) of title 31, United States Code, shall result in no net cost to the United States Government.

EFFECTIVE DATE

Sec. 3. This Act shall take effect on October 1, 1985, except that no coins may be issued or sold under section 5112(i) of title 31, United States Code, before October 1, 1986.

Public Law 99-514 (approved October 22, 1986) authorizes these coins to be placed in an individual retirement account under Sec. 408(m) of the Internal Revenue Code.

The same applies to the silver issues of the Statue of Liberty-Ellis Island coin program.

Statue of Liberty-Ellis Island Commemorative Coins
Public Law 99-61, 99th Congress, approved July 9, 1985.

SHORT TITLE

Sec. 101. This Act may be cited as the "Statue of Liberty-Ellis Island Commemorative Coin Act".

COIN SPECIFICATIONS

Sec. 102. (a)(1) The Secretary of the Treasury (hereafter in this title referred to as the "Secretary") shall issue not more than 500,000 five dollar coins which shall weigh 8.359 grams, have a diameter of 0.850 inches, and shall contain 90 percent gold and 10 percent alloy.

(2) The design of such five dollar coins

shall be emblematic of the centennial of the

Statue of Liberty. On each such five dollar coin there shall be a designation of the value of the coin, an inscription of the year "1986", and inscriptions of the words "Liberty", "In God We Trust", "United States of America", and "E Pluribus Unum".

(b)(1) The Secretary shall issue not more than ten million one dollar coins which shall weigh 26.73 grams, have a diameter of 1.500 inches, and shall contain 90 percent silver and 10 percent copper.

(2) The design of such dollar coins shall be emblematic of the use of Ellis Island as a gateway for immigrants to America. On each such dollar coin there shall be a designation of the value of the coin, an inscription of the year "1986", and inscriptions of the words "Liberty", "In God We Trust", "United States of America', and "E Pluribus Unum".

(c)(1) The Secretary shall issue not more than twenty-five million half dollar coins which shall weigh 11.34 grams, have a diameter of 1.205 inches, and shall be minted to the specifications for half dollar coins contained in section 5112(b) of title 31, United States Code.

(2) The design of such half dollar coins shall be emblematic of the contributions of immigrants to America. On each such half dollar coin there shall be a designation of the value of the coin, an inscription of the year "1986", and inscriptions of the words "Liberty", "In God We Trust", "United States of America", and "E Pluribus Unum".

(d) The coins issued under this title shall be legal tender as provided in section 5103 of title 31, United States Code.

SOURCES OF BULLION

Sec. 103. (a) The Secretary shall obtain silver for the coins minted under this title only from stockpiles established under the Strategic and Critical Materials Stock Piling Act (50 USC 98 et seq.).

DESIGN OF THE COINS

Sec. 104. The design for each coin authorized by this title shall be selected by the Secretary after consultation with the Chairman of the Statue of Liberty-Ellis Island Foundation, Inc. and the Chairman of the Commission of Fine Arts.

SALE OF THE COINS

Sec. 105. (a) Notwithstanding any other provision of law, the coins issued under this title shall be sold by the Secretary at a price equal to the face value, plus the cost of designing and issuing such coins (including labor, materials, dies, use of machinery, and overhead expenses).

(b) The Secretary shall make bulk sales at a reasonable discount to reflect the lower costs of such sales.

(c) The Secretary shall accept prepaid orders for the coins prior to the issuance of such coins. Sales under this subsection shall be at a reasonable discount to reflect the benefit of prepayment.

(d) All sales shall include a surcharge of $35 per coin for the five dollar coins, $7 per coin for the one dollar coins, and $2 per coin for the half dollar coins.

ISSUANCE OF THE COINS

Sec. 106. (a) The gold coins authorized by this title shall be issued in uncirculated and proof qualities and shall be struck at no more than one facility of the United States Mint.

(b) The one dollar and half dollar coins authorized under this title may be issued in uncirculated and proof qualities, except that not more than one facility of the United States Mint may be used to strike any particular combination of denomination and quality.

(c) Notwithstanding any other provision of law, the Secretary may issue the coins minted under this title beginning October 1, 1985.

(d) No coins shall be minted under this title after December 31, 1986.

GENERAL WAIVER OF PROCUREMENT REGULATIONS

Sec. 107. No provision of law governing procurement or public contracts shall be applicable to the procurement of goods or services necessary for carrying out the provisions of this title. Nothing in this section shall relieve any person entering into a contract under the authority of this title from complying with any law relating to equal employment opportunity.

DISTRIBUTION OF SURCHARGE

Sec. 108. All surcharges which are received by the Secretary from the sale of coins issued under this title shall be promptly paid by the Secretary to the Statue of Liberty-Ellis Island Foundation, Inc. (hereinafter in this title referred to as the "Foundation"). Such amounts shall be used to restore and renovate the Statue of Liberty and the facilities used for immigration at Ellis Island and to establish an endowment in an amount deemed sufficient by the Foundation, in consultation with the Secretary of the Interior, to ensure the continued upkeep and maintenance of these monuments.

AUDITS

Sec. 109. The Comptroller General shall have the right to examine such books, records, documents, and other data of the Foundation as may be related to the expenditure of amounts paid, and the management and expenditures of the endowment established, under section 108.

COINAGE PROFIT FUND

Sec. 110. Notwithstanding any other provision of law —

(1) all amounts received from the sale of coins issued under this title shall be deposited in the coinage profit fund;

(2) the Secretary shall pay the amounts authorized under this title from the coinage profit fund; and

(3) the Secretary shall charge the coinage profit fund with all expenditures under this title

FINANCIAL ASSURANCES

Sec. 111. (a) The Secretary shall take all actions necessary to ensure that the issuance of the coins authorized by this title shall result in no net cost to the United States Government.

(b) No coin shall be issued under this title unless the Secretary has received —

(1) full payment therefor;

(2) security satisfactory to the Secretary to indemnify the United States for full payment; or

(3) a guarantee of full payment satisfactory to the Secretary from a depository institution whose deposits are insured by the Federal Deposit Insurance Corporation, the Federal Savings and Loan Insurance Corporation, or the National Credit Union Administration Board.

Title II-Liberty Coins

SHORT TITLE

Sec. 201. This title may be cited as the "Liberty Coin Act".

MINTING OF SILVER COINS

Sec. 202. Section 5112 of title 31, United States Code, is amended to striking out subsections (e) and (f) and inserting in lieu thereof the following new subsections:

"(e) Notwithstanding any other provision of law, the Secretary shall mint and issue, in quantities sufficient to meet public demand, coins which —

"(1) are 40.6 millimeters in diameter and weigh 31.103 grams;

"(2) contain .999 fine silver;

"(3) have a design —

"(A) symbolic of Liberty on the obverse side; and

"(B) of an eagle on the reverse side;

"(4) have inscriptions of the year of minting or issuance, and the words 'Liberty', 'In God We Trust', 'United States of America', '1 Oz. Fine Silver', 'E Pluribus Unum', and 'One Dollar'; and

"(5) have reeded edges.

"(f) The Secretary shall sell the coins minted under subsection (e) to the public at a price equal to the market value of the bullion at the time of sale, plus the cost of minting, marketing, and distributing such coins (including labor, materials, dies, use of machinery, and overhead expenses).

"(g) For purposes of section 5132(a)(1) of this title, all coins minted under subsection (e) of this section shall be considered to be numismatic items.

"(h) The coins issued under this title shall be legal tender as provided in section 5103 of title 31, United States Code."

PURCHASE OF SILVER

Sec. 203. Section 5116(b) of title 31, United States Code, is amended-

(1) in the first sentence of paragraph (1), by striking out "The Secretary shall" and inserting in lieu thereof "The Secretary may";

(2) by striking out the second sentence of paragraph (1); and

(3) by inserting after the first sentence of paragraph (2) the following new sentence: "The Secretary shall obtain the silver for the coins authorized under section 5112(e) of this title by purchase from stockpiles established under the Strategic and Critical Materials Stock Piling Act (50 USC 98 et seq.)."

CONFORMING AMENDMENT

Sec. 204. The third sentence of section 5132(a)(1) of title 31, United States Code, is amended by inserting "minted under section 5112(a) of this title" after "proof coins".

EFFECTIVE DATE

Sec. 205. This title shall take effect on October 1, 1985, except that no coins may be issued or sold under subsection (e) of section 5112 of title 31, United States Code, before September 1, 1986, or before the date on which all coins minted under title I of this Act have been sold, whichever is earlier.

Olympic Coins (1984)

Public Law 97-220, 97th Congress, approved July 22, 1982.

SHORT TITLE

Section 1. This Act may be cited as the "Olympic Commemorative Coin Act".

COIN SPECIFICATIONS

Sec. 2. (a)(1) Notwithstanding any other provision of law, the Secretary of the Treasury (hereinafter in this Act referred to as the "Secretary") shall issue not more than 50 million $1 coins which shall weigh 26.73 grams, have a diameter of 1.50 inches, and shall contain 90 per centum silver and 10 per centum copper.

(2) The Secretary shall determine the design of such $1 coins. Such design shall be emblematic of the 1984 Summer Olympic Games which are to be held in Los Angeles, Calif. On each such $1 coin there shall be a designation of the value of the coin, an inscription of the year of issue, and inscriptions of the words LIBERTY, IN GOD WE TRUST, UNITED STATES OF AMERICA, and E PLURIBUS UNUM.

(3) The coins shall be issued in two separate designs, one in 1983 and one in 1984.

(b)(1) Notwithstanding any other provision of law, the Secretary shall issue not more than two million $10 coins which shall weigh 16.718 grams, have a diameter of 1.06 inches, and shall contain 90 per centum gold and 10 per centum copper.

(2) The Secretary shall determine the design of such $10 coin. Such design shall be emblematic of the 1984 Summer Olympic Games which are to be held in Los Angeles, Calif. On each such $10 coin there shall be a designation of the value of the coin, an inscription of the year 1984, and inscriptions of the words LIBERTY, IN GOD WE TRUST, UNITED STATES OF AMERICA, and E PLURIBUS UNUM.

(c) The coins issued under this section shall be issued in Uncirculated and Proof qualities.

(d) All coins issued under this section shall be legal tender as provided in Section 102 of the Coinage Act of 1965.

(e)(1) The Secretary shall obtain gold for the coins minted under this Act pursuant to the authority of the Secretary under existing law.

(2) The Secretary shall obtain silver for the coins minted under this Act from stocks of silver held by the Secretary of the Treasury or from any other federally owned stocks of silver.

SALES WITHIN THE UNITED STATES

Sec. 3. (a) Notwithstanding any other provision of the law, the coins issued under this Act shall be sold within the United States (including United States military and diplomatic establishments outside the United States) by the Secretary under such regulations as he may prescribe and at a price equal to face value, plus the cost of issuing such coins (including labor, materials, dies, use of machinery, and overhead expenses).

(b) The Secretary shall make bulk sales at a reasonable discount to reflect the lower costs of such sales.

(c) The Secretary shall accept prepaid orders for the coins prior to the issuance of such coins. Sales under this subsection shall be at a reasonable discount to reflect the benefit of prepayment.

(d) All sales shall include a surcharge, established by the Secretary, of not less than $10 per coin for $1 coins and not less than $50 per coin for $10 coins.

INTERNATIONAL SALES

Sec. 4. (a) The Secretary shall assign the rights to market the coins outside the United States (excluding United States military and diplomatic establishments outside the United States) to a marketing organization selected under Section 5.

(b) The marketing organization assigned the rights under this section shall pay a price determined under Sections 3 (b) and (d).

SELECTION OF INTERNATIONAL MARKETERS

Sec. 5. (a) As soon as possible after the effective date of this Act, a committee consisting of the Secretary of the Treasury, the executive director of the United States Olympic Committee, and the president of the Los Angeles Olympic Organizing Committee, shall solicit, in accordance with procedures specified by the Secretary of the Treasury, proposals from marketing organizations to carry out a marketing agreement. Such procedures shall include the publication of evaluation criteria that will serve as a basis for selecting one or more marketing organizations. Such criteria shall include —

(1) the financial resources and coin marketing experience of the marketing organization;

(2) the estimated proceeds from the sale or other disposition of the coins; and

(3) the commitment of the marketing

organization to purchase a certain minimum number of such coins or to pay the surcharge on such coins; and

(4) the terms and conditions for the marketing of the coins, including —

(A) proper and equitable distribution of the coins, and

(B) accurate and otherwise appropriate advertising materials to be used in promoting the coins.

(b) Within 45 days after the effective date of this Act, the committee shall consider all proposals received from marketing organizations under subsection (a) and select by majority vote one or more marketing organizations which offer the terms for marketing of the coins most favorable in accordance with the published evaluation criteria. Any marketing organization selected shall be acceptable to the Secretary of the Treasury.

DISTRIBUTION OF PROCEEDS

Sec. 6. (a) Fifty per centum of the amount of all surcharges which are received by the Secretary from the sale of coins issued under this Act shall be promptly paid by the Secretary to the United States Olympic Committee. Such amounts shall be used to train United States Olympic athletes, to support local or community amateur athletic programs, and to erect facilities for the training of such athletes.

(b) Fifty per centum of the amount of all surcharges which are received by the Secretary from the sale of coins under this Act shall be promptly paid by the Secretary of the Los Angeles Olympic Organization Committee. Such amounts shall be used to stage and promote the 1984 Los Angeles Olympic games.

(c) Amounts received by the Secretary from advance sale of coins to be issued under this Act shall be paid to the United States Olympic Committee and the Los Angeles Olympic Organization Committee under subsections (a) and (b), provided that any amounts paid to the Committees shall not exceed an amount equivalent to the surcharges received by the Secretary from the advance sale of coins.

(d)(1) On March 31, 1985, the Los Angeles Olympic Organization Committee shall remit to the United States Olympic Committee all amounts remaining from the disposition of the coins under this Act. In no event may such amount be less than that portion of the unobligated funds of the committee on that date represented by the ratio of the total amount of income received by the committee from the disposition of the coins minted under this Act to the total amount of income received by the committee from all sources.

(2) After March 31, 1985, all amounts received by the committee from the disposition of coins minted under this Act shall be remitted within 10 days to the United States Olympic Committee.

(3) All amounts received by the United States Olympic Committee under this subsection shall be used solely for the purposes described in subsection (a).

IMPLEMENTATION AGREEMENT

Sec. 7. (a) The Secretary of the Treasury shall enter into an agreement with the marketing organization selected under Section 5 which shall provide for the implementation of that section and which shall include an agreement on —

(1) the price and schedule of payments for the coins;

(2) the schedule and other provisions for the delivery of the coins; and

(3) the proportions of Proof and Uncirculated coins.

(b) The agreement between the Secretary of the Treasury and the committee shall ensure that the issuance of coins under this section shall result in no net cost to the United States government.

(c) The agreement between the Secretary of the Treasury and the marketing organization shall direct that the marketing organization shall not use any words, perform any act, or make any statement, written or oral, which would imply or indicate, or tend to imply or indicate, that any portion of the coins' sale price to the public constitutes a tax-deductible contribution.

(d) To the extent possible, the agreement between the Secretary of the Treasury and the marketing organization shall be concluded within 60 days of the date of the selection of the marketing organization.

(e) The Secretary may terminate the implementation agreement and cease minting and the delivery of the coins issued under this section if the Secretary of the Treasury finds that such termination is in the best interests of the United States. Reasons for such termination may include actions which are inconsistent with the terms of the implementation agreement or advertising materials that are inappropriate for advertising the sale of United States coinage or otherwise not in keeping with the dignity of the United States coinage.

(f) If the Secretary of the Treasury exercises his authority under subsection (e), the amount of any proceeds guaranteed to the Los Angeles Olympic Organization Committee and the United States Olympic Committee by a marketing organization under a marketing agreement shall not be reduced.

COINAGE PROFIT FUND

Sec. 8. Notwithstanding any other provision of law —

(1) all amounts received from the sale of coins issued under this Act shall be deposited in the coinage profit fund;

(2) the Secretary shall pay the amounts authorized under Section 6 from the coinage profit fund; and

(3) the Secretary shall charge the coinage profit fund with all expenditures under this Act.

AUDITS

Sec. 9. The Comptroller General of the United States shall have the right to examine such books, records, documents, and other data of the United States Olympic Committee and the Los Angeles Olympic Organization Committee as may be related to the expenditure of amounts paid under Section 6.

FINANCIAL ASSURANCES

Sec. 10. (a) The Secretary shall take all actions necessary to ensure that the issuance of the coins authorized by this

Act shall result in no net cost to the United States Government.

(b) No coin shall be issued under this Act unless the Secretary has received full payment therefor.

(c) The Secretary shall certify, in reports required to be filed under Section 11 of this Act, that he is in compliance with this section.

REPORTS TO CONGRESS

Sec. 11. Not later than 45 days after the last day of each calendar quarter, the Secretary shall transmit a report to the Congress regarding the activities carried out under this Act during such calender quarter. No such report shall be required with respect to any calendar quarter beginning after December 31, 1985.

Bank Holding Company Act amendments

Public Law 91-607 (31 U.S.C. 391), 91st Congress, H.R. 6778, approved Dec. 31, 1970.

TITLE II PROVISIONS RELATING TO COINAGE

Sec. 201. Section 101 of the Coinage Act of 1965 (31 U.S.C. 391) is amended to read as follows:

"Sec. 101. (a). The Secretary may mint and issue coins of the denominations set forth in subsection (c) in such quantities as he determines to be necessary to meet national needs.

"(b). Any coin minted under authority of subsection (a) shall be a clad coin. The cladding shall be an alloy of 75 per centum copper and 25 per centum nickel, and shall weigh not less than 30 per centum of the weight of the whole coin. The core shall be copper.

"(c). (1) The dollar shall be 1.500 inches in diameter and weigh 22.68 grams.

"(2) The half dollar shall be 1.205 inches in diameter and weigh 11.34 grams.

"(3) The quarter dollar shall be 0.955 inch in diameter and weigh 5.67 grams.

"(4) The dime shall be 0.705 inch in diameter and weigh 2.268 grams.

"(d). Notwithstanding the foregoing, the Secretary is authorized to mint and issue not more than 150 million $1 pieces which shall have

"(1) a diameter of 1.500 inches;

"(2) a cladding of an alloy of 800 parts of silver and 200 parts of copper; and

"(3) a core of an alloy of silver and copper such that the whole coin weighs 24.592 grams and contains 9.837 grams of silver and 14.755 grams of copper."

Sec. 202. For the purposes of this title, the Administrator of General Services shall transfer to the Secretary of the Treasury 25.5 million fine troy ounces of silver now held in the national stockpile established pursuant to the Strategic and Critical Materials Stock Piling Act (50 U.S.C. 98-98h) which is excess to strategic needs. Such transfer shall be made at the value of $1.292929292 for each fine troy ounce of silver so transferred. Such silver shall be used exclusively to coin $1 pieces authorized in section 101(d) of the Coinage Act of 1965, as amended by this Act.

Sec. 203. The dollars initially minted under authority of section 101 of the Coinage Act of 1965 shall bear the likeness of the late President of the United States Dwight David Eisenhower, and on the other side thereof a design which is emblematic of the symbolic eagle of Apollo 11 landing on the moon.

Sec. 204. Half dollars, as authorized under section 101(a) (1) of the Coinage Act of 1965, as in effect prior to the enactment of this Act may, in the discretion of the Secretary of the Treasury, continue to be minted until January 1, 1971.

Sec. 205. (a) The Secretary of the Treasury is authorized to transfer, as an accountable advance and at their face value, the approximately three million silver dollars now held in the Treasury to the administrator of General Services. The administrator is authorized to offer these coins to the public in the manner recommended by the Joint Commission on the Coinage at its meeting on May 12, 1969. The administrator shall repay the accountable advance in the amount of that face value out of the proceeds of and at the time of the public sale of the silver dollars. Any proceeds received as a result of the public sale in excess of the face value of these coins shall be covered into the Treasury as miscellaneous receipts.

(b) There are authorized to be appropriated, to remain available until expended, such amounts as may be necessary to carry out the purposes of this section.

Sec. 206. The last sentence of section 3517 of the Revised Statutes, as amended (31 U.S.C. 324), is amended by striking the following: "except that coins produced under authority of sections 101(a) (1), 101(a) (2), and 101(a) (3) of the Coinage Act of 1965 shall not be dated earlier than 1965".

Sec. 207. Section 4 of the Act of June 24, 1967 (Public Law 90-29; 31 U.S.C. 405a-1 note), is amended by adding at the end thereof the following new sentence: "Out of the proceeds of and at the time of any sale of silver transferred pursuant to this Act, the Treasury Department shall be paid $1.292929292 for each fine troy ounce."

Sec. 208. Section 3513 of the Revised Statutes (31 U.S.C. 316) and the first section of the Act of February 28, 1878 (20 Stat. 25; 31 U.S.C. 316,458) are repealed.

Sec. 209. Coins produced under the authority of section 101(d) of the Coinage Act of 1965, as amended by this Act, shall bear such date as the Secretary of the Treasury determines.

Approved December 31, 1970.

Silver certificates

Public Law 90-29, 90th Congress, S. 1352, approved June 24, 1967.

An Act To authorize adjustments in the amount of outstanding silver certificates, and for other purposes.

Be it enacted by the Senate and House of Representatives of the United States of America in Congress assembled, that the Secretary of the Treasury is authorized to determine from time to

time the amount of silver certificates (not exceeding $200,000,000 in aggregate face value), issued after June 30, 1929, which in his judgment have been destroyed or irretrievably lost, or are held in collections, and will never be presented for redemption. In the case of each determination he shall credit the appropriate receipt account with an equivalent amount, and shall reduce accordingly the amount of silver certificates outstanding on the books of the Treasury.

Sec. 2. Silver certificates shall be exchangeable for silver bullion for one year following the enactment of this Act. Thereafter they shall no longer be redeemable in silver but shall be redeemable from any moneys in the general fund of the Treasury not otherwise appropriated.

Sec. 3. Effective upon the expiration of one year after the date of enactment of this Act, section 2 of the Act of June 4, 1963, as amended (31 U.S.C. 405a-1), is amended to read as follows:

"Sec. 2. The Secretary of the Treasury is authorized to use for coinage, or to sell on such terms and conditions as he may deem appropriate, any silver of the United States (other than silver transferred to the stockpiles established pursuant to the Strategic and Critical Materials Stock Piling Act) at a price not less than the monetary value of $1.292929292 per fine troy ounce."

Sec. 4. From and after the date of enactment of this Act, and until transferred to the stockpiles established pursuant to the Strategic and Critical Materials Stock Piling Act in accordance with this Act, the Secretary of the Treasury shall hold as a reserve for purposes of the common defense not less than 165 million fine troy ounces of silver. Upon the expiration of one year after the date of enactment of this Act, the Secretary of the Treasury shall transfer not less than 165 million fine troy ounces of silver to the stockpiles established pursuant to the Strategic and Critical Materials Stock Piling Act. For the purposes of that Act, the silver shall be deemed to have been transferred pursuant to that Act.

Sec. 5. The last sentence of section 3517 of the Revised Statutes (31 U.S.C. 324) is repealed.

Legislative history

House Report No. 261 accompanying H.R. 7476 (Committee on Banking and Currency).

Senate Report No. 232 (Committee on Banking and Currency).

Congressional Record, Vol. 113 (1967): June 1: Considered in Senate. June 5: Considered and passed Senate. June 12: Considered and passed House, in lieu of H.R. 7476.

Coinage Act of 1965

Public Law 89-81, 89th Congress, S. 2080, approved July 23, 1965.

An Act To provide for the coinage of the United States.

Be it enacted by the Senate and House of Representatives of the United States of America in Congress assembled, That this Act may be cited as the "Coinage Act of 1965".

TITLE I AUTHORIZATION OF ADDITIONAL COINAGE

Sec. 101. (a) The Secretary may coin and issue pursuant to this section half dollars or 50-cent pieces, quarter dollars or 25-cent pieces, and dimes or 10-cent pieces in such quantities as he may determine to be necessary to meet the needs of the public. Any coin minted under authority of this section shall be a clad coin the weight of whose cladding is not less than 30 per centum of the weight of the entire coin, and which meets the following additional specifications:

(1) The half dollar shall have

(A) a diameter of 1.205 inches;

(B) a cladding of an alloy of 800 parts of silver and 200 parts of copper; and

(C) a core of an alloy of silver and copper such that the whole coin weighs 11.5 grams and contains 4.6 grams of silver and 6.9 grams of copper.

(2) The quarter dollar shall have

(A) a diameter of 0.955 inch;

(B) a cladding of an alloy of 75 per centum copper and 25 per centum nickel; and

(C) a core of copper such that the weight of the whole coin is 5.67 grams.

(3) The dime shall have

(A) a diameter of 0.705 inch;

(B) a cladding of an alloy of 75 per centum copper and 25 per centum nickel; and

(C) a core of copper such that the weight of the whole coin is 2.268 grams.

(b) Half dollars, quarter dollars, and dimes may be minted from 900 fine coin silver only until such date as the Secretary of the Treasury determines that adequate supplies of the coins authorized by this Act are available, and in no event later than five years after the date of enactment of this Act.

(c) No standard silver dollars may be minted during the five-year period which begins on the date of enactment of this Act.

Sec. 102. All coins and currencies of the United States (including Federal Reserve notes and circulating notes of Federal Reserve banks and national banking associations), regardless of when coined or issued, shall be legal tender for all debts, public and private, public charges, taxes, duties, and dues.

Sec. 103. (a) In order to acquire equipment, manufacturing facilities, patents, patent rights, technical knowledge and assistance, metallic strip, and other materials necessary to produce rapidly an adequate supply of the coins authorized by Section 101 of this Act, the Secretary may enter into contracts upon such terms and conditions as he may deem appropriate and in the public interest.

(b) During such period as he may deem necessary, but in no event later than five years after the date of enactment of this Act, the Secretary may exercise the authority conferred by subsection (a) of this section without regard to any other provisions of law governing procurement or public contracts.

Sec. 104. The Secretary shall purchase at a price of $1.29 per fine troy ounce any silver mined after the date of enactment of this Act from natural deposits in the United States or any place subject to the jurisdiction thereof and tendered to a United States Mint or assay office within one year after the month in which the ore from which it is derived was mined.

Sec. 105. (a) Whenever in the judgment of the Secretary such action is necessary to protect the coinage of the United States, he is authorized under such rules and regulations as he may prescribe to prohibit, curtail, or regulate the exportation, melting, or treating of any coin of the United States.

(b) Whoever knowingly violates any order, rule, regulation, or license issued pursuant to subsection (a) of this section shall be fined not more than $10,000, or imprisoned not more than five years, or both.

Sec. 106. (a) There shall be forfeited to the United States any coins exported, melted, or treated in violation of any order, rule, regulation, or license issued under Section 105(a), and any metal resulting from such melting or treating.

(b) The powers of the Secretary and his delegates, and the judicial and other remedies available to the United States, for the enforcement of forfeitures of property subject to forfeiture pursuant to subsection (a) of this section shall be the same as those provided in part II of subchapter C of Chapter 75 of the Internal Revenue Code of 1954 for the enforcement of forfeitures of property subject to forfeiture under any provision of such Code.

Sec. 107. The Secretary may issue such rules and regulations as he may deem necessary to carry out the provisions of this Act.

Sec. 108. For the purposes of this title

(1) The term "Secretary" means the Secretary of the Treasury.

(2) The term "clad coin" means a coin composed of three layers of metal, the two outer layers being of identical composition and metallurgically bonded to an inner layer.

(3) The term "cladding" means the outer layers of a clad coin.

(4) The term "core" means the inner layer of a clad coin.

(5) A specification given otherwise than as a limit shall be maintained within such reasonable manufacturing tolerances as the Secretary may specify.

(6) Specifications given for an alloy are by weight.

TITLE II AMENDMENTS TO EXISTING LAW

Sec. 201. The first sentence of Section 3558 of the Revised Statutes (31 U.S.C. 283) is amended to read: "The business of the United States assay office in San Francisco shall be in all respects similar to that of the assay office of New York except that until the Secretary of the Treasury determines that the Mints of the United States are adequate for the production of ample supplies of coins, its facilities may be used for the production of coins."

Sec. 202. Section 4 of the Act of August 20, 1963 (Public Law 88-102; 31 U.S.C. 294), is amended by changing "$30,000,000" to read "$45,000,000".

Sec. 203. (a) Section 3 of the Act of December 18, 1942 (56 Stat. 1065; 31 U.S.C. 317c), is amended by striking "minor" each place it appears.

(b) Section 9 of the Act of March 14, 1900 (31 Stat. 48; 31 U.S.C. 320), is repealed.

Sec. 204. (a) Section 3517 of the Revised Statutes (31 U.S.C. 324) is amended to read:

"Sec. 3517. Upon one side of all coins of the United States there shall be an impression emblematic of liberty, with an inscription of the word "Liberty', and upon the reverse side shall be the figure or representation of an eagle, with the inscriptions "United States of America' and "E Pluribus Unum' and a designation of the value of the coin; but on the dime, 5-, and 1-cent piece, the figure of the eagle shall be omitted. The motto "In God we trust' shall be inscribed on all coins. Any coins minted after the enactment of the

Coinage Act of 1965 from 900 fine coin silver shall be inscribed with the year 1964. All other coins shall be inscribed with the year of the coinage or issuance unless the Secretary of the Treasury, in order to prevent or alleviate a shortage of coins of any denomination, directs that coins of that denomination continue to be inscribed with the last preceding year inscribed on coins of that denomination, except that coins produced under authority of Sections 101(a) (1), 101(a) (2), and 101(a) (3) of the Coinage Act of 1965 shall not be dated earlier than 1965. No Mint mark may be inscribed on any coins during the five-year period beginning on the date of enactment of the Coinage Act of 1965, except that coins struck at the Denver Mint as authorized by law prior to such date may continue to be inscribed with that Mint mark."

(b) The Act of September 3, 1964 (Public Law 88-580; 31 U.S.C. 324 note), is repealed.

Sec. 205. The first sentence of Section 3526 of the Revised Statutes (31 U.S.C. 335) is amended to read: "In order to procure bullion for coinage or to carry out the purposes of Section 104 of the Coinage Act of 1965, the Secretary of the Treasury may purchase silver bullion with the bullion fund."

Sec. 206. (a) Section 3528 of the Revised Statutes (31 U.S.C. 340) is amended to read:

"Sec. 3528. The Secretary of the Treasury may use the coinage metal fund for the purchase of metal for coinage. The gain arising from the coinage of metals purchased out of such fund into coin of a nominal value exceeding the cost of such metals shall be credited to the coinage profit fund. The coinage profit fund shall be charged with the wastage incurred in such coinage, with the cost of distributing such coins, and with such sums as shall from time to time be transferred therefrom to the general fund of the Treasury."

(b) The effect of the amendment made by subsection (a) of this section shall be to redesignate the minor coinage metal fund established under Section 3528 of the Revised Statutes as the coinage metal fund, and not to authorize the creation of a new fund.

Sec. 207. The second sentence of Section 3542 of the Revised Statutes (31 U.S.C. 355) is amended by changing ", in the case of the superintendent of melting and refining department, one-thousandth of the whole amount of gold, and one and one-half thousandths of the whole amount of silver delivered to him since the last annual settlement, and in the case of the superintendent of coining department, one-thousandth of the whole amount of silver, and one-half thousandth of the whole amount of gold that has been delivered to him by the superintendent" to read "such limitations as the Secretary shall establish".

Sec. 208. Section 3550 of the Revised Statutes (31 U.S.C. 366) is repealed.

Sec. 209. The second sentence of Section 2 of the Act of June 4, 1963 (Public Law 88-36; 31 U.S.C. 405a-1), is amended to read: "The Secretary of the Treasury is authorized to use for coinage, or to sell on such terms and conditions as he may deem appropriate, at a price not less than the monetary value of $1.292929292 per fine troy ounce, any silver of the United States in excess of that required to be held as reserves against outstanding silver certificates."

Sec. 210. The last sentence of Section 43(b) (1) of the Act of May 12, 1933 (Public Law 10, 73d Congress; 31 U.S.C. 462), is repealed.

Sec. 211. (a) Section 485 of Title 18 of the United States Code is amended to read: (see reprinted statute section).

Sec. 212. (a) Chapter 17 of Title 18 of the United States Code is amended by adding at the end:

"Sec. 337. Coins as security for loans.

"Whoever lends or borrows money or credit upon the security of such coins of the United States as the Secretary of the Treasury may from time to time designate by proclamation published in the Federal Register, during any period designated in such a proclamation, shall be fined not more than $10,000 or imprisoned not more than one year, or both."

(b) The table of sections at the beginning of such chapter is amended by adding at the end:

"337. Coins as security for loans."

(c) The amendments made by this section shall apply only with respect to loans made, renewed, or increased on or after the 31st day after the date of enactment of this Act.

TITLE III JOINT COMMISSION ON THE COINAGE

Sec. 301. The president is hereby authorized to establish a Joint Commission on the Coinage to be composed of the Secretary of the Treasury as chairman; the Secretary of Commerce; the Director of the Bureau of the Budget; the Director of the Mint; the chairman and ranking minority member of the Senate Banking and Currency Committee, and four members of the Senate, not members of such committee, to be appointed by the president of the Senate; the chairman and ranking minority member of the House Banking and Currency Committee, and four members of the House of Representatives, not members of such committee, to be appointed by the Speaker; and eight public members to be appointed by the president, none of whom shall be associated or identified with or representative of any industry, group, business, or association directly interested as such in the composition, characteristics, or production of the coinage of the United States.

Sec. 302. No public official or member of Congress serving as a member of the Joint Commission shall continue to serve as such after he has ceased to hold the office by virtue of which he became a member of the Joint Commission. Any

vacancy on the Joint Commission shall be filled by the choosing of a successor member in the same manner as his predecessor.

Sec. 303. The Joint Commission shall study the progress made in the implementation of the coinage program established by this Act, and shall review from time to time such matters as the needs of the economy for coins, the standards for the coinage, technological developments in metallurgy and coin-selector devices, the availability of various metals, renewed minting of the silver dollar, the time when and circumstances under which the United States should cease to maintain the price of silver, and other considerations relevant to the maintenance of an adequate and stable coinage system. It shall, from time to time, give its advice and recommendations with respect to these matters to the president, the Secretary of the Treasury, and the Congress.

Sec. 304. There are authorized to be appropriated to remain available until expended, such amounts as may be necessary to carry out the purposes of this title.

Legislative history

House Report No. 509 accompanying H.R. 8926 (Committee on Banking and Currency).

Senate Report No. 317 (Committee on Banking and Currency).

Congressional Record, Vol. 111 (1965): June 23: Considered in Senate. June 24: Considered and passed Senate. July 13: H.R. 8926 considered in House. July 14: Considered and passed House, amended, in lieu of H.R. 8926. July 15: Senate concurred in House amendments.

(Commission phased out Jan. 5, 1975).

1964 date freeze

Public Law 88-580, 88th Congress, S. 2950, approved Sept. 3, 1964.

An Act To authorize the Mint to inscribe the figure 1964 on all coins minted until adequate supplies of coins are available.

Be it enacted by the Senate and House of Representatives of the United States of

America in Congress assembled, That, notwithstanding section 3517 of the Revised Statutes (31 U.S.C. 324), all coins minted from the date of enactment of this Act until July 1 or January 1, whichever date first occurs after the date on which the

Secretary of the Treasury determines that adequate supplies of coins are available, shall be inscribed with the figure "1964" in lieu of the year of the coinage.

Sec. 2. The requirement of section 3550 of the Revised Statutes (31 U.S.C. 366) that the obverse working dies at each Mint shall be destroyed at the end of each calendar year shall not be applicable during the period provided for in section 1 of this Act.

Legislative history

House Report No. 1644 accompanying H.R. 11893 (Committee on Banking and Currency).

Senate Report No. 1237 (Committee on Banking and Currency).

Congressional Record, Vol. 110 (1964): July 24: Considered and passed Senate. Aug. 20: Considered and passed House, amended, in lieu of H.R. 11893. Aug. 21: Senate agreed to House amendments.

Kennedy half dollar
Public Law 88-256, 88th Congress, H.R. 9413, approved Dec. 30, 1963.

An Act To provide for the coinage of 50-cent pieces bearing the likeness of John Fitzgerald Kennedy.

Be it enacted by the Senate and House of Representatives of the United States of America in Congress assembled, that in lieu of the coinage of the 50-cent piece known as the Franklin half dollar, there shall be coined a silver 50-cent piece which shall bear on one side the likeness of the late president of the United States John Fitzgerald Kennedy, and on the other side an appropriate design to be prescribed by the Secretary of the Treasury.

Legislative history

House Report No. 1038 (Committee on Banking and Currency).

Congressional Record, Vol. 109 (1963): Dec. 17: Considered and passed House. Dec. 18: Considered and passed Senate.

Tin eliminated from 1-cent piece
Public Law 87-643, 87th Congress, H.R. 11310, approved Sept. 5, 1962.

An Act To amend section 3515 of the Revised Statutes to eliminate tin in the alloy of the 1-cent piece.

Be it enacted by the Senate and House of Representatives of the United States of America in Congress assembled, That the third sentence of section 3515 of the Revised Statutes, as amended (31 U.S.C. 317) is amended to read as follows: "The alloy of the 1-cent piece shall be 95 per centum of copper and 5 per centum of zinc."

Sec. 2. The first and second sentences of section 3552 of the Revised Statutes, as amended (31 U.S.C. 369), are amended by striking out "medals and proof coins" and inserting "medals, proof coins, and uncirculated coins" in lieu thereof.

"In God We Trust"
Public Law 84-140, 84th Congress, H.R. 619, July 11, 1955.

An Act To provide that all United States currency shall bear the inscription IN GOD WE TRUST.

Be it enacted by the Senate and House of Representatives of the United States of America in Congress assembled, that at such time as new dies for the printing of currency are adopted in connection with the current program of the Treasury Department to increase the capacity of presses utilized by the Bureau of Engraving and Printing, the dies shall bear, at such place or places thereon as the Secretary of the Treasury may determine to be appropriate, the inscription IN GOD WE TRUST, and thereafter this inscription shall appear on all United States currency and coins.

Government marketing of commemorative coins

One of the most interesting aspects in recent times has been the marketing by the government of commemorative coins. The Treasury has managed to go to non-traditional sources, including the banking community. One of the reasons that the banking community has been a non-traditional source has been the fact that, at least among bank examiners, acquisition of coins for purposes of disposition to the public was frowned upon. A 1981 directive prohibited national banks from buying or selling coins except in very narrow circumstances. Banking circular 58 (revised) supplement 1, dated Dec. 28, 1983, concerned the sale of commemorative coins. Its contents appear below.

To: Chief Executive Officer of All National Banks, Deputy Comptrollers/Regional Administrators, and Examining Personnel. Purpose: This banking circular provides general guidelines for national banks which are considering purchasing and reselling or acting as agent in the sale of commemorative coins minted by the Bureau of the Mint for the U.S. Department of the Treasury. Policy BC-58 (REV) dated 11-3-81 states that national bank are prohibited from buying or selling coins the value of which is not based on metallic content. The Circular makes it clear that banks may not speculate by purchasing coins, such as rare coins, the value of which is based upon such factors as rarity, age, condition, a mistake in the minting or other intangible factors. Commemorative coins are minted by the Bureau of the Mint for the U.S.

Department of the Treasury. The coins commemorate events such as George Washington's birthday, the Olympic Games and other events of national importance. The fixed price of such coins is based upon the cost of the metal, production, distribution and, in the case of the Olympic coins, a surcharge earmarked for contribution to the U.S. Olympic Committee. National banks may take such commemorative coins on a consignment basis and act as selling agent for the Department of the Treasury. National banks may also choose to purchase an inventory of commemorative coins for resale to their customers. Prudence and care should be exercised by Boards of Directors in formulating policies and procedures when purchasing commemorative coins. Dollar limits on coin inventories should be consistent with safe and sound banking practices. Accounting Commemorative coins purchased by a national bank should be recorded as Other Assets. The bank's books should reflect the lower of cost or market value with adjustments made monthly. This is consistent with the accounting treatment stated in BC-58 (Rev). Originating Office, Chief National Bank Examiner's Office, Commercial Examinations Division (202) 447-1165.

In the 1990s, the government's use of commemorative coinage seems destined to increase. Nearly all of the commemorative coinage bills now introduced — and passed — allow for circumstances under which consignment agreements with major financial institutions, or other vendors, is permissible.

Tax Act changes of 1986

One effect of the 1986 Tax Act was to add a customs duties surcharge to all imported items, including gold and silver coinage and medals. Its effect on collectors is minimal but it has had impact on pricing by sellers and importers. There was some talk in 1990 of the elimination of the customs users surcharges.

Numismatic sections of the U.S. Code

The following are selected other sections of law involving numismatics which may be of interest to readers.

18 USCS Sec. 3056. Powers, authorities, and duties of United States Secret Service.

(a) Under the direction of the Secretary of the Treasury, the United States Secret Service is authorized to protect the following persons:

(1) The President, the Vice President...(b) Under the direction of the Secretary of the Treasury, the Secret Service is authorized to detect and arrest any person who violates...(2) Funds expended from appropriations available to the Secret Service for the purchase of counterfeits and subsequently recovered shall be reimbursed to the appropriations available to the Secret Service at the time of the reimbursement...

41 USCS Sec. 24. Contracts for transportation of moneys, bullion, coin, and securities.

Whenever it is practicable contracts for the transportation of moneys, bullion, coin, notes, bonds, and other securities of the United States, and paper shall be let to the lowest responsible bidder therefor, after notice to all parties having means of transportation.

50 USCS Sec. 5. Suspension of provisions relating to ally of enemy; regulation of transactions in foreign exchange of gold or silver, property transfers, vested interests, enforcement and penalties.

(b)(1) During the time of war, the President may, through any agency that he may designate, and under such rules and regulations as he may prescribe, by means of instructions. licenses, or otherwise-

(A) investigate, regulate, or prohibit, any transactions in foreign exchange, transfers of credit or payments between, by, through, or to any banking institution, and the importing, exporting, hoarding, melting, or earmarking of gold or silver coin or bullion, currency or securities, and...

Sec. 2461 Congressional Space Medal of Honor; appropriations. The President may award, and present in the name of Congress, a medal of appropriate design, which shall be known as the Congressional Space Medal of Honor, to any astronaut who in the performance of his duties has distinguished himself by exceptionally meritorious efforts and contributions to the welfare of the Nation and of mankind.

46 USCS Sec. 3249. Merchant Marine distinguished service and meritorious service medals; award; restriction.

(a) The Secretary of Transportation is authorized,...to provide and award: A merchant marine distinguished service medal to any person serving in the United States merchant marine who distinguished himself by outstanding act, conduct, or valor beyond the line of duty, and a merchant marine meritorious service medal to any person serving in the United States merchant marine for meritorious act, conduct, or service in line of duty,...

(b) No more than one distinguished service medal or meritorious service medal shall be awarded to any one person,...

46 USCS Sec. 249-249c. Officers and crews of vessels. [Repealed]

46 USCS Appx. Sec. 249a. Distinctive service ribbon bar; issuance; cost; replacements.

The Secretary of Transportation is authorized to provide and issue, under such rules and regulations as he may from time to time prescribe, a distinctive service ribbon bar to each master, officer, or member of the crew of any United States ship who serves or has served after June 30, 1950, in any time of war, or national emergency proclaimed by the President or by Congress,...Such bars shall be provided at cost by the Secretary or at reasonable prices by private persons when authorized for manufacture and sale by the Secretary...

46 USCS Appx. Sec 249b. Ship citation; issuance; award of plaque; citation ribbon bar.

The Secretary of Transportation is authorized to issue[,,] a citation as public evidence of deserved honor and distinction to any United States ship or to any foreign ship which participates in outstanding or gallant action in marine disasters or other emergencies for the purpose of saving life or property. The Secretary of Transportation may award a plaque to a ship so cited, and a replica of such plaque may be preserved, under such rules and regulations as the Secretary may prescribe, as a permanent historic record. The Secretary of Transportation may also award an appropriate citation ribbon bar to the master or each person serving on board such ship...

46 USCS Appx. Sec. 249c. Regulations governing manufacture, sale, possession, or display of decorations; penalties.

The manufacture, sale, possession, or display of any insignia, decoration, medal, device, or rosette thereof,...is prohibited, except as authorized by this Act...Whoever violates any provision of this section shall be punished by a fine

not exceeding $250 or by imprisonment not exceeding six months, or both.

42 USCS Sec. 1921. Establishment of medals for bravery; rules and regulations, conditions governing awards.

The Department of Justice...is hereby, authorized and directed to promulgate rules and regulations establishing a medal;...that an award shall be made to any child residing in the United States, who is eighteen years old or under, who has exhibited exceptional courage, extraordinary decision, presence of mind, and unusual swiftness of action, regardless of his or her own personal safety, in an effort to save or successfully saving the life or lives of any person or persons whose life or lives were in actual imminent danger.

42 USCS Sec. 1922. Establishment of medals for character and service;

condition governing awards.

The Department of Justice shall also honor by an appropriate medal such American boy or girl citizens, eighteen years old or under, who, in the opinion of the said Department of Justice, shall have achieved outstanding or unusual recognition for character and service during any given year.

42 USCS Sec. 1923. Names of medals; presentation.

The medal to be awarded for bravery or valor...shall be known as the Young American Medal for Bravery, while the medal for outstanding character and service...shall be known as the Young American Medal for Service, and such medals shall be presented personally by the President of the United States...

42 USCS Sec. 1924. Certificate of commendation accompanying awards; limitation on number of yearly awards.

Accompanying such medals herein designated there shall be an appropriate certificate of commendation presented to the recipient or recipients stating (a) the circumstances under which the act of bravery was performed, and (b) citing the outstanding recognition for character and service:...

42 USCS Sec. 1925. Report to Congress.

It shall be the duty of the Department of Justice to make a report to the Congress at the end of each fiscal year and to furnish the Congress with a list of the names of all those upon whom the President shall have conferred either of such medals.

46 USCS Appx. Sec. 181. Liability of masters as carriers.

If any shipper of platina, gold, gold dust, silver, bullion, or other precious metals, coins, jewelry, bills of any bank of public body, diamonds, or other precious stones, or any gold or silver in a manufactured or unmanufactured state, watches, clocks, or timepieces of any description, trinkets, orders, notes, or securities for payment of money, stamps,....shall lade the same as freight or baggage, on any vessel, without at the time of such lading giving to the master, clerk, agent, or owner of such vessel receiving the same written notice of the true character and value thereof, and having the same entered on the bill of lading therefor, the master and owner of such vessel shall not be liable as carriers thereof in any form or manner; nor shall any such master or owner be liable for any such goods beyond the value and according to the character thereof so notified and entered.

49 USCS Sec. 1201. Awards for acts of heroism involving railroads or motor vehicles.

The President of the United States be, and he is hereby, authorized to cause to be prepared bronze medals of honor, with suitable emblematic devices, which shall be bestowed upon any persons who shall hereafter, by extreme daring, endanger their own lives in saving, or endeavoring to save, lives from any wreck, disaster, or grave accident, or in preventing or endeavoring to prevent such wreck, disaster, or grave accident, upon any railroad within the United States engaged in interstate commerce or involving any motor vehicle on the public highways, roads, or streets of the United States:...

49 USCS Sec. 1202. Rosettes and ribbons; replacement.

The President of the United States be, and he is hereby, authorized to issue to any person to whom a medal of honor may be awarded under the provisions of this Act [49 USCS Sections 1201 et seq.] a rosette or knot, to be worn in lieu of the medal, and a ribbon to be worn with the medal; said rosette or knot and ribbon to be each of a pattern to be prescribed by the President of the United States:...

18 USCS Sec. 1956. Laundering of monetary instruments.

(a)(1) Whoever, knowing that the property involved in a financial transaction represents the proceeds of some form of unlawful activity, conducts or attempts to conduct such a financial transaction which in fact involves the proceeds of specified unlawful activity-...shall be sentenced to a fine of not more than $500,000 or twice the value of the property involved in the transaction, whichever is greater, or imprisonment for not more than twenty years, or both.

(2) Whoever transports, transmits, or transfers, or attempts to transport, transmit, or transfer a monetary instrument or funds from a place in the United States to or through a place outside the United States or to a place in the United States from or through a place outside the United States-...shall be sentenced to a fine of $500,000 or twice the value of the monetary instrument or funds involved in the transportation, whichever is greater, or imprisonment for not more than twenty years, or both.

(3) the term "transaction" includes a purchase, sale, loan, pledge, gift, transfer, delivery, or other disposition, and with respect to a financial institution includes a deposit, withdrawal, transfer between accounts, exchange of currency, loan, extension of credit, purchase or sale of any stock, bond, certificate of deposit, or other monetary instrument, or any other payment, transfer, or delivery by, through, or to a financial institution, by whatever means effected;

(4) the term "financial transaction" means a transaction involving the movement of funds by wire or other means or involving one or more monetary instruments, which in any way of degree affects interstate or foreign commerce, or a transaction involving the use of a financial institution which is engaged in, or the activities of which affect, interstate or foreign commerce in any way or degree.

(5) the term "monetary instruments" means coin or currency of the United States or of any other country, travelers' checks, personal checks, bank checks, money orders, investment securities in bearer form or otherwise in such form that title thereto passes upon delivery, and negotiable instruments in bearer form or otherwise in such form that title thereto passes upon delivery;...

(f) There is extraterritorial jurisdiction over the conduct prohibited by this section if-

(1) the conduct is by a United States

citizen or, in the case of a non-United States citizen, the conduct occurs in part in the United States; and

(2) the transaction or series of related transactions involves funds or monetary instruments of a value exceeding $10,000.

46 USCS Appx. Sec. 2001. Authorization of decorations, medals, and other recognition for merchant marine service.

The Secretary of Transportation may award decorations and medals of appropriate design (including ribbons, ribbon bars, emblems, rosettes, miniature facsimiles, plaques, citations, or other suitable devices or insignia) for individual acts or service in the United States merchant marine.

46 USCS Appx. Sec. 2002. Distinguished Service Medal, Meritorious Service Medal, decorations or medals for war or national emergency, or conspicuous gallantry, etc.

The Secretary of Transportation may award-

(1) a Merchant Marine Distinguished Service Medal...

(2) a Merchant Marine Meritorious Service Medal...

(3) a decoration or medal to an individual for service in time of war or national emergency...

(4) a decoration or medal to an individual for other acts or service of conspicuous gallantry, intrepidity, and extraordinary heroism under conditions of danger to life and property...

46 USCS Sec. 2003. Gallant Ship Award and citation.

The Secretary of Transportation may issue a Gallant Ship Award and a citation to a United States vessel or to a foreign-flag vessel participating in outstanding or gallant action in marine disasters or other emergencies for the purpose of saving life or property at sea....

46 USCS Sec. 2004. Individual not to receive more than one of any type of decoration; acceptance by personal representative; replacements.

(a) The Secretary of Transportation may not award more than one of any type of decoration or medal to an individual. For each succeeding act or service justifying the same decoration or medal, a suitable device may be awarded to be worn with the decoration or medal....

46 USCS Sec. 2005. Authorization for flag and grave marker for deceased merchant marine member.

Except as authorized under another law, the Secretary of Transportation may issue at no cost a flag of the United States and a grave marker to the family or personal representative of a deceased individual, who served in the United States merchant marine...

46 USCS Sec. 2006. Certificate of recognition for service of certain other individuals.

(a) The Maritime Administrator may issue a special certificate in recognition of service to an individual, or the personal representative of an individual, whose service in the United States merchant marine has been determined to be active duty...

46 USCS Sec. 2007. Exclusiveness of right to decoration or medal; civil penalty for violation.

Except as authorized by this Act, a person may not manufacture, sell, possess, or display a decoration or medal provided for in this Act. A person violating this section is liable to the United States Government for a civil penalty of $2,000.

46 USCS Sec. 98. Conveyance of bullion, coin, notes, or bonds for United States.

All vessels belonging to citizens of the United States, and bound from any port in the United States to any other port therein, or to any foreign port,....shall, before clearance, receive on board all such bullion, coin, United States notes and bonds and other securities, as the Government of the United States...shall offer, and shall securely convey and promptly deliver the same to the proper authorities or consignees, on arriving at the port of destination; and shall receive for such service such reasonable compensation as may be allowed to other carriers in the ordinary transactions of business.

42 USCS Sec. 1880. National Medal of Science.

There is hereby established a National Medal of Science (hereafter referred to as the "medal"), which shall be of such design and materials and bear such inscriptions as the President, on the basis of recommendations submitted by the National Science Foundation, may prescribe,...

42 USCS Sec. 1881. Award of National Medal of Science.

(a) Recommendations. The President shall from time to time award the medal,...to individuals who in his judgment are deserving of special recognition by reason of their outstanding contributions to knowledge in the physical, biological, mathematical, engineering, behavioral or social sciences....

42 USCS Sec. 213. Military benefits...

(b) The President may prescribe the conditions under which commissioned officers of the Service may be awarded military ribbons, medals, and decorations.

50 USCS Appx. Sec. 14. False manifest; refusal of clearance; reports of gold or silver coin in cargoes for export.

During the present war, whenever there is a reasonable cause to believe that the manifest or the additional statements under oath...are false or that any vessel, domestic or foreign, is about to carry out of the United States any property to or for the account or benefit of an enemy,...the collector of customs for the district in which such vessel is located is hereby authorized and empowered,...to forbid the departure of such vessel from the port, and it shall thereupon be unlawful for such vessel to depart.

The collector of customs shall, during the present war, in each case report to the President the amount of gold or silver coin or bullion or other moneys of the United States contained in any cargo intended for export....

18 USCS Sec. 704. Military medals or decorations.

Whoever knowingly wears, manufactures, or sells any decoration or medal authorized by Congress for the armed forces of the United States, or any of the service medals or badges awarded to the members of such forces, or the ribbon, button, or rosette of any such badge, decoration or medal, or any colorable imitation thereof, except when authorized under regulations made pursuant to law, shall be fined not more than $250 or imprisoned not more than six months, or both.

18 USCS Sec. 705. Badge or medal of veterans' organizations.

Whoever knowingly manufactures, reproduces, sells or purchases for resale,...any article of merchandise manufactured or sold, any badge, medal, emblem, or other insignia...of any veterans' organization incorporated by enactment of Congress...except when authorized under rules and regulations prescribed by any such organization, shall be fined not more than $250 or imprisoned not more than six months, or both.

Sales tax and numismatic items

Perhaps no more emotional issue has recently surfaced among collectors than the right of various states to impose sales tax on coin and bullion purchases. There are several states, of course, that have no sales tax at all (Alaska, Delaware, Montana, New Hampshire and Oregon), and others who have (by statute or regulation or court fight) altered the use of sales tax collection on numismatic sales.

Sometimes the dispute centers around precious metal coinage such as the South African Krugerrand, the Canadian Maple Leaf, and other coins bought as much for their bullion value as a brick of gold would be. (In most states, even with sales taxes, purchases of commodities such as gold and silver — in futures contracts, or on "paper" without physical delivery — are not taxed on acquisition.)

Purchases of what is frequently termed monetized bullion are permitted in several other states.

In some other locales, for example Florida, sales of Krugerrands are not subject to sales tax because they have been judicially declared to be coin of the realm the same as a Kennedy half dollar sold for 50 cents.

When collectors buy by mail from a dealer in another state, whether or not that state has sales tax or not, there is no obligation for the selling merchant to collect the tax and remit it to the state where the buyer resides. The purchaser is, however, under an obligation to pay what is called a compensating use tax on the purchase. Until recently, as New York State officials once acknowledged, the compensating use tax had been on the books for more than a dozen years and there were no forms available, anywhere in the state, to allow someone to do so except in the case of the purchase of an automobile.

That, however, is in the process of changing. States in the Great Lakes region recently signed an agreement to collect use taxes by out-of-state purchasers. New York and New Jersey have a voluntary compact. The individual states began notifying merchants in early 1987 that they would be required to collect use taxes in addition to sales taxes.

Because sales taxes are usually considered to be trust funds, and subject a collector to personal liability, it is suggested that questions regarding them be referred to competent tax counsel.

In the late 1980s and early 1990s, the Industry Council for Tangible Assets (ICTA) was among those leading the fight to repeal sales taxes. They were successful in Maryland, Ohio and (for bullion) in New York.

The following table is supplied by the Industry Council for Tangible Assets.

State Sales Tax Reference Guide
May 1990

This table is designed as a quick reference guide only. Please consult the individual state statutes for exact interpretation of state sales tax laws. ICTA is not liable for any decisions based on the information contained herein.

State	Tax Rate	Collector coins	Bullion coins	Bullion
Alabama	4%	yes	yes	yes
Alaska	0%	—	—	—
Arizona	5%	exempt	exempt	exempt (except bullion for use in jewelry and works of art)
Arkansas	4%	yes	yes	yes
California	5%	exempt (sales of $1,000+)	exempt (sales of $1,000+)	exempt (sales of $1,000+)
Colorado	3%	exempt	exempt	exempt
Connecticut	8%	yes	exempt (sales of $1,000+)	exempt (sales of $1,000+)
Delaware	0%	—	—	—
District of Columbia	6%	yes	yes	yes
Florida	6%	exempt (legal tender only, excludes coins of antiquity)	exempt (legal tender only, excludes coins of antiquity)	yes
Georgia	4%	yes	yes	yes
Hawaii	4%	yes	yes	yes
Idaho	5%	exempt (excluding bullion for use in jewelry and works of art)	exempt (excluding bullion for use in jewelry and works of art)	exempt (excluding bullion for use in jewelry and works of art)
Illinois	6.25%	exempt	exempt	exempt
Indiana	5%	yes	yes	yes

State	Tax			
Iowa	4%	yes	yes	yes
Kansas	4.25%	yes	yes	yes
Kentucky	6%	yes	yes	yes
Louisiana	4%	exempt (sales of $1,000+)	exempt (sales of $1,000+)	yes
Maine	5%	yes	yes	yes
Maryland	5%	exempt (sales of $1,000+; effective 7/1/90)	exempt (sales of $1,000+; effective 7/1/90)	exempt (sales of $1,000+; effective 7/1/90)
Massachusetts	5%	exempt (sales of $1,000+)	exempt (sales of $1,000+)	exempt (sales of $1,000+)
Michigan	4%	yes	yes	yes
Minnesota	6%	yes	yes	yes
Mississippi	6%	yes	yes	yes
Missouri	4.225%	yes	yes	yes
Montana	0%	—	—	—
Nebraska	5%	yes	yes	yes
Nevada	5.75%	yes	yes	yes
New Jersey	6%	yes	yes	yes
New Hampshire	0%	—	—	—
New Mexico	5%	yes	yes	yes
New York	4%	yes	exempt (sales of $1,000+)	exempt (sales of $1,000+)
North Carolina	3%	yes	yes	yes
North Dakota	5%	exempt	exempt	yes
Ohio	5%	exempt	exempt	exempt
Oklahoma	4.5%	yes	yes	yes
Oregon	0%	—	—	—
Pennsylvania	6%	yes	yes	yes
Rhode Island	6%	exempt	exempt	exempt
South Carolina	5%	yes	yes	yes
South Dakota	4%	yes	yes	yes
Tennessee	5.5%	yes	yes	yes
Texas	6%	exempt (sales of $1,000+)	exempt (sales of $1,000+)	exempt (sales of $1,000+)
Utah	5%	exempt	exempt	exempt
Vermont	4%	yes	yes	yes
Virginia	3.5%	yes	yes	yes
Washington	6.5%	exempt	exempt	exempt
West Virginia	6%	yes	yes	yes
Wisconsin	5%	yes	yes	yes
Wyoming	3%	yes	yes	yes

State sales tax categories

No state sales tax	Full exemption	Full exemption — $1,000+	Partial exemption
Alaska Delaware Montana New Hampshire Oregon	Arizona Colorado Idaho Illinois Ohio Rhode Island Utah Washington	California Louisiana Maryland Massachusetts Texas	Connecticut ($1,000 bullion/bullion coins) Florida (coins/bullion coins) New York ($1,000 bullion/bullion coins) North Dakota (coins/bullion coins)

Source: Industry Council for Tangible Assets

Regulations by governmental agencies

In order for various laws and procedures to be effected and have public impact, governmental agencies must frequently write rules and regulations to explain the impact, and state how a particular course of action or conduct is to be carried out.

As a means of internal government, comparable rules are required within each government agency or bureau.

Rules written by each of the governmental agencies must first be published in the Federal Register, a daily government publication. When the tentative plans are approved, they are annually compiled into a many volumed set known as the Code of Federal Regulations, usually abbreviated CFR. In the CFR are all the necessary requirements for operating entities such as the United States Mint and the Bureau of Engraving and Printing, as well as actions that the U.S. Customs Service can take against attempted importation of counterfeit coins.

Often, it is the governmental interpretation of a statute in the CFR that is the dominant factor in enforcement, rather than the law itself. This is true, for example, in the case of the Hobby Protection Act, whose regulations promulgated by the Federal Trade Commission are the keystone of its effectiveness.

Below are reprinted in edited form selected sections from the CFR that pertain to numismatics. The volume of the CFR that the material appears in precedes the Code, while the section follows it. The year of publication of the volume appears in parentheses following this. Thus, 16 CFR sec. 304.1(d) would refer to Volume 16 of the Code of Federal Regulations at Section 304.1 (d), which was printed by the government in 1977.

United States Customs Service

Counterfeit Coins, Obligations and Other Securities; Illustrations or Reproduction of Coins or Stamps

19 CFR Sec. 12.48 Importation prohibited; exception to prohibition of importation; procedure.

(a) In accordance with Chapter 25, Title 18, United States Code, any token, disk, or device in the likeness or similitude of any coin of the United States or of a foreign country; counterfeits of coins in circulation in the United States; counterfeited, forged, or altered obligations or other securities of the United States(31) or of any foreign government; or plates, dies, or other apparatus which may be used in making any of the foregoing, when brought into the United States, shall be seized, and

delivered to the nearest representative of the United States Secret Service, together with a report of the facts, for appropriate disposition.

(b) In accordance with Section 504 of Title 18, United States Code, the printing, publishing, or importation or the making or importation of the necessary plates for such printing or publishing for philatelic, numismatic, educational, historical, or newsworthy purposes in articles, books, journals, newspapers, or albums (but not for advertising purposes, except illustrations of stamps and paper money in philatelic or numismatic advertising of legitimate numismatists and dealers in stamps or publishers of or dealers in philatelic or numismatic articles, books, journals, newspapers, or albums) of black and white illustrations of canceled and uncanceled United States postage stamps shall be permitted.

(c) The importation (but not for advertising purposes except philatelic advertising) of motion-picture films, microfilms, or slides, for projection upon a screen or for use in telecasting, of postage and revenue stamps and other obligations and securities of the United States and postage and revenue stamps, notes, bonds, and other obligations or securities of any foreign government, bank or corporation shall be permitted.

(d) Printed matter of the character described in Section 504, Title 18, United States Code(32), containing reproductions of postage or revenue stamps, executed in accordance with any exception stated in Section 504, or colored reproductions of canceled foreign postage stamps may be admitted to entry. Printed matter containing illustrations or reproductions not executed in accordance with such exceptions shall be treated as prohibited importations. If no application for exportation or assent to forfeiture and destruction is received by the district director within 30 days from the date of notification to the importer that the articles are prohibited, the articles shall be reported to the United States attorney for forfeiture.

It should be noted that the Supreme Court has declared the plenary statutory section under which this has been enacted, unconstitutional. The regulation, likewise, should follow. No change, however, has been made.

Footnotes

(31)The term "obligation or other security of the United States' includes all bonds, certificates of indebtedness, national bank currency, Federal Reserve notes, Federal Reserve Bank notes, coupons, United States notes, Treasury notes, gold certificates, silver certificates, fractional notes, certificates of deposits, bills, checks, or drafts for money, drawn by or upon authorized officers of the United States, stamps and other representatives of value, of whatever denomination, issued under any act of Congress, and canceled United States stamps. (18 U.S.C. 8.)

(32)Notwithstanding any other provision of this chapter, the following are permitted:

(1) The printing, publishing, or importation, or the making or importation of the necessary plates for such printing or publishing, or illustrations of:

(A) Postage stamps of the United States,

(B) Revenue stamps of the United States,

(C) Any other obligation or other security of the United States, and

(D) Postage stamps, revenue stamps, notes, bonds, and any other obligation or other security of any foreign government, bank, or corporation, for philatelic, numismatic, educational, historical, or newsworthy purposes in articles, books, journals, newspapers, or albums (but not for advertising purposes, except illustrations of stamps and paper money in philatelic or numismatic advertising of legitimate numismatists and dealers in stamps or publishers of or dealers in philatelic or numismatic articles, books, journals, newspapers, or albums). Illustrations permitted by the foregoing provisions of this section shall be made in accordance with the following conditions

(i) All illustrations shall be in black and white, except that illustrations of postage stamps issued by the United States or by any foreign government may be in color;

(ii) All illustrations (including illustrations of uncanceled postage stamps in color) shall be of a size less than three-fourths or more than one and one-half, in linear dimension, of each part of any matter so illustrated which is covered by subparagraph (A), (B), (C), or (D) of this paragraph, except that black and white illustrations of postage and revenue stamps issued by the United States or by any foreign government and colored illustrations of canceled postage stamps issued in the United States may be in the exact linear dimension in which the stamps were issued; and

(iii) The negatives and plates used in making the illustrations shall be destroyed after their final use in accordance with this section.

(2) The making or importation, but not for advertising purposes except philatelic advertising, of motion-picture films, microfilms, or slides, for projection upon a screen or for use in telecasting, of postage and revenue stamps and other obligations and securities of the United States, and postage and revenue stamps, notes, bonds, and other obligations or securities of any foreign government, bank, or corporation. No prints or other reproductions shall be made from such films or slides, except for the purposes of paragraph (1), without the permission of the Secretary of the Treasury.

For the purposes of this section the term "postage stamp" includes "postage meter stamps." (18 U.S.C. 504).

Coins across borders

A U.S. Customs Service advisory, issued Oct. 13, 1976, in response to the American Numismatic Association inquiry concerning the transport of coins to Canada and back into the United States, suggests consultation with a Customs pamphlet, "Know Before You Go," which contains general information of interest to all U.S. residents who travel to a foreign country. Restraints on gold coins were lifted on Dec. 31, 1974.

Dealers may wish to take the coins they plan to carry to Canada to the Customs office nearest them, and register them on Customs Form 4455, certificate of registration. A copy of the form will be given to the dealers to present to U.S. Customs on their return from Canada. This will facilitate the identification of the coins on their return to the United States.

With regard to coins which dealers purchase in Canada, the Customs Service has ruled that metal coins issued or specifically authorized by the government whose coinage it is, including official restrikes or exact copies authorized by the government concerned, are classifiable under the provision for metal coins in item 653.22, Tariff Schedules of the United States (TSUS), and are free of duty.

The Customs Service has also had occasion to issue a ruling with respect to certain unofficial reproductions of various gold coins manufactured by a foreign private Mint. In brief, these unofficial reproductions are generally under the provision for articles of precious metal, of gold, including rolled gold, in item 656.10, TSUS, and dutiable at the rate of 20 percent ad valorem.

Also, these gold pieces would be subject to the marking requirements of the Hobby Protection Act as imitation numismatic items, and must be marked "Copy" if imported into the United States, pursuant to regulations issued by the Federal Trade Commission.

Finally, if the unofficial gold pieces were manufactured in a country other than the country of issuance as shown on the faces of the pieces, they would be required to be marked "Made in (name of country)" pursuant to 19 U.S.C. 1304 and Section 134.47 of the Customs Regulations.

All coins imported into the United States for non-monetary purposes (for example, for resale or numismatic purposes) are considered merchandise subject to Customs entry requirements, even though they are free of duty.

Therefore, if the coins are part of a dealer's personal hand-carried baggage, they should be reported on the back side of Customs Declaration Form 6059-B as articles acquired while abroad. The District Director of the port of entry has the discretion to require a formal Customs entry to be made if he feels that the particular importation could be handled more properly by such an entry procedure.

In any event, the value which should be declared for the coins should be the actual numismatic value of the coins in the place where they were purchased. Ordinarily, this would mean that the importer would declare as value the price which he actually paid for the coins and this does of course include an equivalent valuation of foreign currency.

An individual collector who took his collection to Canada solely for viewing could return his collection to the United States free of duty, pursuant to item 813.10, Tariff Schedules of the United States, which exempts from duty personal and household effects taken abroad by a person who is a returning resident of the United States. For a dealer who is in the business of buying and selling these reproductions or commemorative medals, however, these items would not be considered his personal effects and, accordingly, this exemption would not be applicable.

A dealer could bring back his unofficial reproductions or medals free of duty as tools of trade or samples for taking orders under Section 10.68 of the Customs Regulations if he took the articles to Canada for the sole purpose of viewing and taking orders. Unless such merchandise is imported under carnet, the dealer must register it on Customs Form 4455 at the time of exportation and file an appropriate entry or declaration at the time of return.

If the dealer is taking such merchandise out for sale or if he sells some of the merchandise, he is liable for the duty on the returning items. If not all the medals or reproductions listed on CF 4455 are returned, there will be a presumption that the missing medals were sold and the returning ones will be dutiable, unless the dealer can show Customs that the missing medals were not sold.

With regard to medals, Customs has held that they are classifiable as articles of metal depending on the metal they are composed of, under one of the items 656.10, 656.15, or 657.35 TSUS. Item 656.10 TSUS, applies to articles of gold (20 percent ad valorem), item 656.15 TSUS, applies to articles of silver (10.5 percent ad valorem), and item 657.35 TSUS applies to articles of bronze (0.6 cents/lb. plus 7.5 percent ad valorem). Some medals could, in fact be jewelry, if designed as objects of personal adornment, i.e., if the medal has a loop for attaching with a neck chain or ribbon.

For further information regarding procedures for taking rare coins into Canada and returning them, collectors and dealers can write to Customs and Excise, Connaught Building, Sussex Drive, Ottawa, Ontario, Canada KIA-OL5, for information and guidance.

For those importing and exporting coins, there are currency control requirements both in the exporting country and the importing country that must be taken into consideration. In the case of the United States, where items are still a legal tender they must be reported if on your person and in an amount exceeding $5,000. (No duty is charged, but the sum must be reported; not to do so is a serious violation of the law.) In the case of exporting countries, there is also the added requirement (particularly true in the case of ancient coins) that the national patrimony not be unduly disturbed in a manner violative of the UNESCO convention regulating removal of antiquities.

It is also useful to remember that reproductions of coins must also be in accordance with the marking requirements of the Hobby Protection Act to be eligible for importation into the United States.

Treasury, Secret Service advisory policies

Following is a guide to Treasury and Secret Service advisory policies frequently requested by Coin World readers. These policies are interpretations the Treasury has made of various parts of the U.S. Code dealing with numismatics.

Coin jewelry

Most coin jewelry, including cut-out coinage and engraved coinage, is legal, according to the present interpretation of Sec. 331, Title 18, United States Code, which prohibits fraudulent mutilation of coins.

Coin jewelry is not prohibited by this section in the absence of fraud and treating of the coins used to produce these novelties. Manufacture and sale of two-headed and two-tailed coins are also legal according to the Secret Service.

This opinion is advisory only, and is not binding upon the Department of Justice or any U.S. attorney, however, according to the Secret Service.

The official Treasury Department statement pertaining to coin jewelry is:

"Section 331, Title 18, U.S. Code, prohibits the fraudulent alteration and mutilation of United States and foreign coins, but does not prohibit said defacement if done without fraudulent intent, or if the mutilated coins are not used fraudulently.

"The Bureau of the Mint feels that it is unfortunate that laws at this time do not specifically prohibit this undesirable and reprehensible practice.

"The Mint also has very strong feelings about disfigurement of United States coins or their use other than as a means of exchange. If the practice cannot otherwise be prevented, the Mint would strongly support legislation prohibiting this use of coins.

"Coins so withdrawn from circulation must be replaced and when practiced on a wholesale scale by many firms, an unnecessary cost and burden is imposed upon the Mint."

Coin replicas

Sec. 489, Title 18, United States Code, prohibits making, importing, possessing with intent to sell, give away or use in any manner, any token, disk or device in the likeness or similitude as to design, color or inscription of any of the coins of the United States, or of any foreign country.

This section is directed at devices which, although not strictly counterfeit coins, may be mistaken for genuine coins by unwary persons, because they approximate genuine coins in size, color, design and inscription.

However, items made to sell, give away or use in any manner, which are substantially larger and heavier than any coin of the United States, or any coin of a foreign country, and which do not bear any indication of value and therefore do not purport to be money, do not violate Sec. 489.

The policy of the Treasury regarding substantially enlarged replicas of coins is that any coin reproduction must be more than twice the size of a United States dollar coin, the largest United States coin. Consequently, all reproductions must be more than three inches in diameter. Thickness of the item is not material, according to the Treasury.

The manufacture of a raised impression of a coin is considered to be in violation of Sec. 489, if the impression is removable; approximately the size of a genuine coin; and is sufficiently in likeness of a genuine coin to be capable of being passed off as such.

Gold-plated coins

Since the gold regulations were amended April 19, 1971, it has been legal to obtain, hold, transport, import or export any gold-plated coins.

These restrictions were imposed to prevent the diversion of coins to decorative uses during the coin shortage of the 1960s. Since all coins are now in ample supply, such restrictions became unnecessary, according to the Treasury

Department.

Paper money reproductions

According to Title 18, U.S. Code, Section 504, and other sections of the U.S. Code, printed illustrations of paper money, checks, bonds and other obligations and securities of the United States and foreign governments are permissible for numismatic, educational, historical and newsworthy purposes, and for numismatic or philatelic advertising but not for general advertising purposes.

Illustrations must be in black and white and must be less than three-fourths or more than one and one-half times the size of the genuine instrument. No individual facsimiles of such obligations are permitted, and no illustrations of paper money, checks or bonds may be in color.

Several years ago, Time Inc. challenged the regulations, and for a time succeeded in having them declared unconstitutional. In mid-1984, however, the U.S. Supreme Court, in a major decision interpreting the statute, declared that the regulations were valid insofar as they prohibited color reproduction of paper currency and required illustrations to be black and white, and of a particular size.

To meet these regulations, paper money art reproduction must be at least these measurements:

Fractional Currency

Actual size: sizes vary; smallest note is the 3-cent third issue note, measuring 39mm by 64mm; largest note in width is the 50-cent third issue, measuring 46mm by 133mm; deepest note is the Crawford 50-cent fifth issue note at 52mm by 108mm.

Unless exact note size is known so as to comply with legal requirements, illustrations should be at least 2-1/4x3-3/4 in. (58.5 x 96mm) or smaller than 1-1/8 by 1-7/8 in. (29.25 x 48mm).

Small Size Paper Money

(Including Federal Reserve notes, silver certificates, etc.)
Actual size: 6-1/8 x 2-5/8 in. or 156 x 67mm

Over 1-1/2: 9-1/4 x 4 in. or 235 x 102mm

Under 3/4: 4 19/32 x 1 31/32 in. or 117 x 50mm

Large Size Paper Money

Actual size: 7-1/2 x 3-1/8 in. or 191 x 79mm

Over 1-1/2: 1122 x 4-3/4 in. or 286 x 121mm

Under 3/4: 5-5/8 x 2 7/32 in. or 143 x 56mm

To be permissible, an illustration must be accompanied by numismatic, educational, historical or newsworthy information relating directly to the item that is illustrated, according to the Treasury.

Insofar as this purports to allow the government to examine newspapers for the "educational" content of their illustrations, the Supreme Court ruling declares that this is indeed unconstitutional. But the bulk of the requirement remains.

Motion-picture films, microfilms and slides of paper money, checks, bonds and other obligations and securities of the United States and foreign governments are permitted in black and white or in color for projection upon a screen or for use in telecasting. They may not be used for advertising purposes, except philatelic or numismatic advertising.

However, Treasury regulations permit the illustration of United States bonds in connection with a campaign to sell of such bonds.

The plates and negatives, including glossy prints, of any United States or foreign obligations produced for any of these purposes must be destroyed after their final use for the purpose for which they were made.

Notes issued by the various states are not obligations or securities of the United States, and it is probable that most of them do not resemble such obligations or securities.

In some cases, however, it has been found that certain features appearing on such notes, such as the numerals and lettering, bear a close resemblance to the corresponding features of genuine currency of the United States. In such cases, the reproduction of such features would constitute a technical violation of the U.S.Code.

Defacing paper money

Sec. 333 of Title 18 of the U.S. Code prohibits, among other things, mutilating, cutting, defacing, disfiguring, or perforating or uniting or cementing together any National Bank or Federal Reserve note with intent to render such currency unfit to be reissued.

Instances such as dollar bills embedded in jewelry, or portraits of popular persons superimposed on Federal Reserve notes as souvenirs do not usually constitute intent to render the currency unfit to be reissued, and so are not prohibited.

Stamp reproduction

Printed illustrations of canceled and uncanceled United States postage stamps are permissible for articles, books, journals, newspapers or albums for philatelic, educational, historical and newsworthy purposes.

Black and white illustrations may be of any size. Colored illustrations of canceled United States postage stamps may be of any size. However, illustrations in color of uncanceled United States postage stamps must be less than three-fourths or more than one and one-half times and size of the genuine stamp.

Printed illustrations of canceled foreign stamps in black and white or color are permissible in any size and for any purpose.

Black and white and color illustrations of uncanceled foreign postage stamps are permitted for philatelic, educational, historical and newsworthy purposes. Black and white illustrations may be of any size, but color illustrations must be more than one and one-half times the size of the genuine stamp, or less than three-fourths times its size.

Motion-picture films and slides of postage stamps are permissible in black and white or in color for projection upon a screen or for use in telecasting. They are not permissible for advertising purposes except for philatelic advertising.

Black and white illustrations of canceled and uncanceled United States and foreign postage stamps, as well as colored illustrations of canceled postage stamps are permissible in any size, for philatelic advertising. Uncanceled colored illustrations of United States and foreign postage stamps are permitted for philatelic advertising, but must meet the three-fourths or one and one-half size restrictions.

Canceled U.S. and foreign postage stamps must bear an official cancellation mark, i.e., the stamps must have been used for postage.

Regulations for printed illustrations of United States and foreign revenue stamps are the same as for postage stamps, except that colored illustrations of United States revenue stamps are not permitted.

Coin reproductions

Photographs or printed illustrations, motion-picture films or slides of United States and foreign coins may be used for any purpose including advertising.

With few exceptions, existing law generally prohibits the manufacture, sale or use of any token, disk or device in the likeness or similitude of any coins which are issued as money.

Scrip

Congress has enacted legislation to prevent scrip certificates from circulating as or in lieu of lawful money. Sec. 336 of Title 18 of the U.S. Code prohibits the making, issuing, circulating, or payment out of any obligation of less than a dollar "intended to circulate as money or to be received or used in lieu of lawful money of the United States."

After analyzing the statute and the cases interpreting it the Treasury has ruled that scrip redeemable only in merchandise and not in coin or currency, that is not negotiable and that is redeemable only at the particular store location where issued would not be in violation of the statute.

The Treasury is still examining the question of whether scrip that is redeemable at more than one store under single ownership or franchise would violate the statute.

Government regulatory activity

During the past several years, the Federal Trade Commission has brought a number of cases against individuals, and firms, alleging that numismatic items sold were overgraded, or overpriced.

Until recently, the *Riverside Coin Co.* case, a 1977 postal service decision, and *U.S. v Kail*, an 8th Circuit Court of Appeals case, were the leading authorities on the issue of grading.

This has been superceded, or at least supplemented, by *FTC v Security Rare Coin*, decided by the U.S. District Court for the District of Minnesota in September, 1989.

One important extract from the case is reprinted below in which the Court dealt with the issue of grading, its uniformity, and the setting up of standards in the field. Quoted in almost its entirety from numbered paragraph 27 of the Court's

opinion to numbered paragraph 36, there has been minor editing (omitting mention of exhibits). Any significant changes are marked with an ellipsis. While not definitive, it is a view point that is difficult to ignore.

"27. There are a number of grading services. Today, the most accepted grading service is the Professional Coin Grading Service (PCGS), an independent grading service established in early 1986 and based in California. Before PCGS gained acceptance, the American Numismatic Association Certification Service (ANACS) was the most widely used service and was widely recognized during 1985 and 1986, even though some dealers raised questions about its reliability.

28. It is not uncommon for dealers to send certified coins back to PCGS for regrading, and it is not uncommon for such

returned coins to receive a different grade.

29. The grading of coins is an art, not a science, and always involves a certain amount of subjectivity. In addition, grading standards have changed over the years.

30. The Official ANA Grading Standards for United States Coins (3d ed. 1987) ("ANA Book") is published and endorsed by the American Numismatic Association. It states: Interpretations of grades within the uncirculated category MS-60 to MS-70 are apt to vary from person to person. Further, such interpretations could change over a period of time, as it has not been possible to define these grades photographically or verbally on a precise, consistent basis.

31. The ANA Book also states: The term "overgrading" refers to describing a coin as a grade higher than it actually is. The ANA Board of Governors has recognized that grading differences of less than four points on the 1-70 scale can be reasonable differences between people. Thus, an MS-65 graded coin could reasonably be interpreted to be an MS-63 by some or an MS-63 uncirculated coin might reasonably be called MS-65. An MS-60 coin would be overgraded if it were termed MS-67 or even MS-64.

32. "The Statement of the American Numismatic Association With Respect to Change in Interpretations of Grading Standards" ("ANA Statement") states: Grading is an art and not an exact science. More precisely, grading is a matter of opinion. Differences of opinion may occur among graders as to a particular coin, and any grader could conceivably change his interpretations of the grading standards over the years. . . . The grading standards as enumerated in the (ANA) book were and are not precise, with the descriptions lending themselves to different interpretations.

33. As a matter of policy, the ANA Board of Governors does not intervene in grading disputes involving three points or less on the numerical scale.

34. That experts can differ in assigning grades was illustrated by two FTC experts* * * who graded the same 31 U.S. gold and silver coins and disagreed as to 19 of them, in five cases by more than two points. One coin, a $ 20 gold piece * * * was assigned four different grades by five FTC experts, ranging from AU-58 to a "very nice" MS-63. Another gold piece * * * was graded MS-63 by one expert and MS-60 by another.

35. Grading standards tightened during the applicable time period. It is not possible to define precisely when changes in grading standards occurred, since the changes were gradual, and were recognized by different dealers at different times. The weight of the evidence indicates that the tightening of grading standards, while largely complete in 1985, continued into 1986. The Court also finds that the changes in grading standards primarily affected the higher grades (grade MS-64 and higher) but also affected grade MS-63. The ANA Book indicates that: [I]n 1985 and 1986 commercial interpretations of such grades as MS-63, MS-65, and MS-67 tightened considerably . . . . Interpretations of the grading standards can and have changed over the years and may continue to do so in the future.

36. The ANA Statement indicates that: The marketplace -- composed of collectors and dealers -- has tightened its interpretation in recent years and ANACS has reflected those changes. Accordingly, the ANA Grading Service, endeavoring to keep in step with current market interpretations (rather than create interpretations of its own), has in recent times graded coins more conservatively than in the past, in many instances. Hence, it may be the situation that a coin which was graded MS-65 by the Grading Service in 1981 and 1982, for example, may, if regraded in 1985 or 1986, merit the current interpretation of MS-63 or less. Similarly, dealers and others in the commercial sector have found that coins that they graded MS-65 several years ago may merit MS-63 or lower interpretations today.... Because of its imprecise nature, which admits a great deal of subjectivity and opinion, it may be the case that the

interpretation of grading standards will continue to change in the future, as indeed they have done over a long period of past years."

Selected Legal Articles of Interest

GANZ, David L. "Toward A Revision Of The Minting And Coinage Law Of The United States", *26 Cleveland State Law Review* 175-257 (1977).

——., "Probative Value Of 'Currency Dating' For Income In Respect Of A Decedent", 51 *New York State Bar Journal* 487-495 (1978).

——., "Value of Coin Collection", 5 *Proof of Facts* 3rd 577-604 (1989).

GILBERG, David L., "Precious Metals Trading — The Last Frontier of Unregulated Investment", 41 *Wash. & Lee L. Rev.* 943-991 (1984).

Recent Federal Register Activity

The Federal Register is a rich source for information concerning the inner workings of government. Below appear a relatively recent change in the Hobby Protection Act regulations, and one pertaining to the Fine Arts Commission and its coinage role.

Rules and Regulations

Federal Trade Commission

16 CFR Part 304

Hobby Protection Act; Imitation Numismatic Items Tuesday, October 4, 1988 (53 Fed. Reg. 38942)

ACTION: Final amendment.

SUMMARY: The Federal Trade Commission, pursuant to the Hobby Protection Act (15 U.S.C. 2101 et seq.), has amended section 304.6 of the Rules and Regulations under the Hobby Protection Act (16 CFR Part 304). The rule currently requires that the word "Copy" be marked on imitation numismatic items in dimensions no less than 2 millimeters high and 6 millimeters wide. The amendment permits use of a smaller marking to accommodate coins that are issued as miniature imitations.

EFFECTIVE DATE: The amendment will be effective on November 3, 1988. For further information contact:Lewis Franke, Attorney, Federal Trade Commission, Washington, DC 20580, (202) 326-3009.

Supplementary information: The Hobby Protection Act requires that all imitation numismatic items sold in, or imported into, the United States shall be marked with the word "Copy" in a manner to be determined by the Federal Trade Commission. In 1975, the Commission promulgated rules requiring the word "Copy" to be marked on either the obverse or the reverse surface of the item. The words must have a vertical dimension of not less than two millimeters and a horizontal dimension of not less than six millimeters.

The concept of requiring the word "Copy" to be a minimum size rather than to vary with the size of the coin or words on a coin was selected because it minimized the burden of compliance for industry.

After the rules were promulgated, miniature imitation numismatic items became more popular in the market. Marking some of these miniature imitations has posed a hardship since many are as small as or smaller than the minimum size required for the word "Copy." When an item covered by the rules is of such a small size that it is impossible to conform with the minimum size requirement, the manufacturer must request the Commission to issue a variance.

On May 23, 1983, the Commission published a notice in the Federal Register proposing to amend the rules and providing notice to the public of the opportunity to comment.

Based on the comments received, the Commission has determined that the amendment is warranted and is in the public interest. The amendment to the rule permits manufacturers of miniature numismatic items to mark the word "Copy" in smaller dimensions than those required under the present rule. For example, a coin having a diameter of only six millimeters could have the word "Copy" in a horizontal dimension of no less than one-half the diameter or three millimeters. The vertical dimension would be required to be no less than one-sixth of the diameter or one millimeter. The amendment will facilitate compliance with the rule and thus should result in the lessening of deception.

By allowing a relative size for the word "Copy", the amendment will encourage manufacturers and importers to increase the number of imitation miniatures which are properly marked. As a result, more consumers will be put on notice that such coins are imitations and not originals. The current rule, with its absolute minimum size requirement and use of a variance request procedure, may impede entry into the market for imitation miniature numismatic items.

Manufacturers and importers may forego the opportunity to sell imitation miniatures because of the costs and physical difficulties of compliance with the rule. The amendment will eliminate this barrier and should promote competition and allow the increased availability of imitation miniature numismatic items. Finally, the amendment will eliminate the potential costs, in both time and resources, to industry and the Commission necessitated by individual variance applications for miniature numismatic items. List of Subjects in 16 CFR Part 304 Hobbies, Labeling, Trade practices.

Accordingly, Chapter I of 16 CFR Part 304 is amended as follows: PART 304-- [AMENDED]

1. The authority citation for Part 304 continues to read as follows: Authority: 15 U.S.C. 2101 et seq.

2. Section 304.1 is amended by adding paragraph (k) to read as follows: section 304.1 Terms defined. * * * * * (k) "Diameter of a reproduction" means the length of the longest possible straight line connecting two points on the perimeter of the reproduction.

3. Section 304.6 is amended by revising paragraphs (b)(3) and (b)(4) to read as follows: section 304.6 Marking requirements for imitation numismatic items. * * * * *

(b) * * * (3) An imitation numismatic item of incusable material shall be incused with the word "COPY" in sans-serif letters having a vertical dimension of not less than two millimeters (2.0 mm) or not less than one-sixth of the diameter of the reproduction, and a minimum depth of three-tenths of one millimeter (0.3 mm) or to one-half (1/2) the thickness of the reproduction, whichever is the lesser. The minimum total horizontal dimension of the word "COPY" shall be six millimeters (6.0 mm) or not less than one-half of the diameter of the reproduction.

(4) An imitation numismatic item composed of nonincusable material shall be imprinted with the word "COPY" in sans-serif letters having a vertical dimension of not less than two millimeters (2.0 mm) or not less than one-sixth of the diameter of the reproduction. The minimum total horizontal dimension of the word "COPY" shall be six millimeters (6.0 mm) or not less than one-half of the diameter of the reproduction. By direction of the Commission. Donald S. Clark, Secretary. [FR Doc. 88-22790 Filed 10-3-88; 8:45 am]

NOTICES: DEPARTMENT OF THE TREASURY

Committee on Coinage, Medal and Currency Design

Thursday, February 19, 1987

The Department of the Treasury has decided not to proceed with the establishment of the Advisory Committee on Coinage, Medal and Currency Design, which notice was published in the Federal Register January 8, 1987, Volume 52 No. 5. Instead, the Department will rely to a greater extent on the advice and counsel of the Commission of Fine Arts to guarantee the quality of future designs. Dated:

February 12, 1987.
  John F. W. Rogers, Assistant Secretary of the Treasury (Management). [FR Doc. 87-3540 Filed 2-18-87.;

The Treasury

4

History of the Treasury Department

Even before the signing of the Declaration of Independence, the Continental Congress provided by resolution on Feb. 17, 1776, "that a committee of five be appointed for superintending the Treasury." During the first session of the Constitutional Congress, a law "to establish the Treasury Department" was enacted on Sept. 2, 1789. This was only six months after the Constitution became the basic law of the land on March 4, 1789.

For several years Philadelphia was the temporary capital of the nation. When plans to move the seat of government to Washington were made, they included recommendations for a Treasury building. This building, located on the east side of the site of the present building, was completed in 1799 and occupied in 1800 by the 69 employees of Treasury, seven employees (total employment) of the State Department, and some personnel of the Navy Department.

This first building was partially destroyed by fire in 1801. Repaired, it continued to house Treasury personnel until 1814, when a fire set by the British as a spectacle for an invading army destroyed the building.

Following withdrawal of the British forces, prompt authority was granted for a new Treasury building. Once again the Treasury fell victim to a fire when the second structure and most of its contents were destroyed in the early morning of March 31, 1833. A searching investigation authorized by President Jackson led to the arrest of two brothers who were charged with setting the fire to destroy certain papers which would prove fraudulent conduct by persons engaged as Treasury agents. One brother was finally acquitted after four trials because of the statute of limitations, while the other was sentenced to 10 years in prison.

Apparently the next three years left the department without a home of its own, but on July 4, 1836, Congress authorized the construction of a "fireproof building of such dimensions as may be required for the present and future accommodations" of the Treasury Department. Perhaps the building when completed in 1842 was an imposing structure at the time, but it fell far short of providing accommodations for the future. Having cost less than $700,000, the building, which is now only a part of the east wing, contained 150 rooms.

It was necessary in a few years to enlarge the building, and Congress in March of 1855 granted authority to extend the building. Construction of what is now the south wing was begun in July 1855 and completed in September 1861. The Civil War more or less interrupted further construction, but by 1864 the west wing had been carried up to the line of the present north facade.

The department continued to grow, and the government building housing the Department of State was removed from the north area of the site to make room for the north wing which was completed in 1869.

On its way up

Thus, after more than a third of a century, the Treasury building became the structure originally intended. But one of the results of its expansion was the violation of the original plan for the city — to leave unobstructed the view from the White House to the Capitol. The building as it is today is estimated to have cost approximately $8 million.

Because early planning had the entire official city facing the canal which at one time ran through downtown Washington where the mall is now located, the south entrances of both the White House and the Treasury building are the historical front entrances of the buildings. However, as the city grew, the north entrance of the White House became its front entrance; and many people think of the 15th Street entrance to the Treasury as its main entrance, perhaps because it is the easiest to enter since the other three have long flights of stone steps.

The stone used in the south, west and north wings was quarried on Dix Island, near Rockland, Maine, and transported in sailing vessels. The facades are adorned by monolithic columns of the Ionic order, each 36 feet tall, each costing $5,000 and weighing 30 tons. There are 34 of these pillars on the 15th Street side of the building, 30 of them forming a colonnade 341 feet long. This colonnade has for many years provided viewing space for inaugural parades and other state functions. There are 18 columns on the west side and 10 each on the north and south sides.

A statue of Alexander Hamilton, first Secretary of the Treasury, is located on the south patio of the building, while a statue of Albert Gallatin, fourth Secretary of the Treasury, who served as Secretary for the longest period of time, 1801 to 1814, is located on the north patio. The grounds of the building — rose gardens at the north and south ends, and grass, magnolia trees and other plants gracing the west side — add much to the beauty of the building.

The interior, although it has been altered many times, reminds one that this is an old building. The deeply worn stone steps leading to all floors show the many years they were used before elevators were installed. Until 1959, even the elevators were nearly collector's items, one having been installed in 1898. Since 1959, all elevators have been replaced by automatic, self-operating cars. There are still signs of the early heating devices in the form of fireplaces, some of which can still be used. The building was originally lighted by oil lamps, and the sanitary accommodations were just as primitive.

Offices for 10 percent

The Treasury building is used primarily for executive offices, the Secretary of the Treasury occupying a suite on the third floor. Despite its size, the building can today accommodate only about 10 percent of all Treasury personnel located in Washington, D.C. More than 20 other buildings house Treasury employees, and it is necessary to rent additional space to meet all needs.

In the basement there are 15 vaults ranging in size from 10-by-16-feet to 50-by-90-feet. Stored therein are currency, coins, bonds and securities. At one time most of the nation's gold and silver bullion was also stored in the vaults, but there are no longer any bulk quantities of bullion located in the Main Treasury building. The vaults are securely protected by combination and time locks and by an electrical protection system which alerts the captain of the guard, the U.S. Secret Service and local police headquarters to any attempt to tamper with the locks or otherwise violate the security of the system. Partially because of these vaults, the building is protected by the Treasury Security Force, supervised by the Secret Service. The basement also houses a pistol range used by the Secret Service and other enforcement personnel to maintain marksmanship. The rest of the basement area is used for maintenance equipment and personnel, store rooms, etc.

The large Cash Room at the north end of the building was often used for special occasions such as the March 4, 1869, inaugural ball for President Grant's first inauguration. However, it was used daily as a check cashing facility and operated well into the early 1970s. Treasury officials then determined the cost of clerical and security personnel could no longer be justified and the room was closed June 30, 1976.

After a brief period of renovation the room was reopened for special events such as the presentation by Treasury officials of a $24 million check to the Statue of Liberty/Ellis Island renovation fund.

In early 1987, the Cash Room was closed for a total floor-to-ceiling renovation. The reopening of the Cash Room headlined the Treasury's 200th birthday celebration in September 1989.

Beginning with that celebration, public tours of historical areas of the building became an ongoing activity, offered on alternate Saturday mornings. (Call (202) 343-9136 for recorded tour information. Reservations are required by the Wednesday preceding the Saturday tour. Tours last about an hour.)

Among the many interesting architectural features of the main Treasury building are the unique stairways that appear somehow to be suspended in mid-air. Actually the steps are cut-worked granite and marble blocks cantilevered from structural walls, partially supported by the arch action of the steps.

The fifth floor, which was formerly the attic, was renovated for office space in 1910. It is also interesting to note that the name of the building was not made a permanent part of the structure until 1958, more than 100 years after the Treasury was built.

Treasury souvenirs

The Treasury no longer maintains an exhibit hall but information about the Treasury as well as the Mint and other Washington D.C. area attractions is available at the Washington Tourist Information Center, 1400 Pennsylvania Ave. NW, (202) 566-5221.

Top officials

In addition to the Secretary of the Treasury and his top staff, the Main Treasury Building houses the top officials of the Office of the Treasurer of the United States, and the Office of the Assistant Secretary for International Affairs. Other important activities of the department, such as the United States Mint, Internal Revenue Service, Engraving and Printing, Customs, the Savings Bonds Division, the U.S. Secret Service, Bureau of the Public Debt, Comptroller of the Currency, and the Bureau of Accounts, are housed in nearby buildings.

Among the activities which once were a part of the Treasury Department and are now parts of other organizations are the Postal Service, until 1829; the General Land Office (now the Interior Department); some of the activities which later were assigned to the Departments of Commerce and Labor in 1903; some of the major functions now assigned to the General Accounting Office; the Public Health Service of the Department of Health, Education, and Welfare; the Public Buildings Service (formerly the Supervising Architect) and the Federal Supply Service (formerly the Procurement Division) of the General Services Administration; the Bureau of the Budget; the United States Coast Guard (now a part of the Department of Transportation); and the Bureau of Narcotics (now the Bureau of Narcotics and Dangerous Drugs of the Department of Justice).

Location for history

In this building were developed the ideas for organizations such as the International Monetary Fund and the International Bank for Reconstruction and Development, and more recently the Inter-American Development Bank and the Asian Development Bank. Also in this building plans were made for the lend-lease program of World War II, and for expediting the building of the United States Air Corps as it was in World War II. The Treasury Department building has been the locale of a number of interesting events, one of the earliest involving President Jackson who, during the laying of the cornerstone, placed therein a satin-lined case containing a golden lock of the hair of the infant daughter of his confidential adviser and secretary, who was Mrs. Jackson's nephew. This girl, Mary Emily Donelson, was later employed in the Treasury. Today the location of that cornerstone is inaccessible because of the extension of the outer limits of the building.

President Andrew Johnson used one of the Treasury offices on the present third floor as his office immediately following the assassination of President Lincoln, to allow Mrs. Lincoln to move from the White House unhurried. A picture of a Cabinet meeting held in that room testifies to this unusual arrangement.

During World War II a tunnel connected the White House to the Treasury. There was in the basement a furnished shelter area for the President of the United States in case he was unable to avoid enemy attack any other way. During this period the basement of the Treasury would also have served as a refuge for the entire Cabinet, had that been necessary.

As recently as the early 1940s, some of the offices contained important historical documents — the Louisiana Purchase, one of George Washington's travel account books, files containing notes from President Lincoln. These have been turned over to the National Archives and other organizations for preservation.

The First Baptist Church of Washington, D.C., held its first meeting in the building, and in recent years has held commemorative meetings on the south steps. These steps were used during World War II for massive bond rallies in which entertainment celebrities participated to sell war bonds to finance the nation's war effort. They have also been used for inaugurating community chest and other drives.

Treasury Historical Association

To help preserve the Treasury building itself, an organization called the Treasury Historical Association was formed Dec. 13, 1973.

Although the Treasury Historical Association was chartered as an "in-house" organization, with memberships open to present and former Treasury employees, members of the public interested in the maintenance and preservation of this important Federal landmark are invited to join the association also.

Treasury Historical Association chairman is Dr. Charles E. Walker. Applications for membership should be mailed to: Treasury Historical Association, 1500 Pennsylvania Ave. N.W., Washington, D.C. 20220.

Membership categories include:

General, $10, and supporting, $50. These members shall receive a membership card, publications issued by the association periodically, and are eligible for historic tours and to attend quarterly and annual meetings. All members have voting rights.

Patron, $100; members will be listed in the annual report of the association and will receive an engraved certificate.

Sustaining, $250; members will be listed in the annual report of the association and will receive an engraved certificate.

Life sponsor, $500; members will receive membership for life, will be listed in the annual report as those making a regular contribution to the activities of the association, and will receive an engraved certificate.

Life donor, $1,000 or more; members will receive membership for life, will be listed in the annual report as those making a regular contribution to the activities of the association, and will receive an engraved certificate. The names of life donors will be inscribed on a plaque on display in the Treasury Building.

Time capsule

Early in 1976 as part of the Treasury Department's celebration of the Bicentennial, Secretary of the Treasury

William E. Simon approved the establishment of a Time Capsule to be dedicated in a ceremony on Sept. 8, 1976, and to be opened by the Secretary of the Treasury in the tricentennial year. The capsule will serve as a symbol to Americans living in the 21st century of 20th century Americans' faith in the nation's future.

Treasury officials were asked to prepare messages to be read by their counterparts in 2076 for inclusion in the capsule. These messages addressed the key issues facing each office or bureau so that future generations of Americans may have a clearer perspective on the times in which we are living. A message from President Gerald R. Ford is included in the contents of the capsule, along with various Bicentennial medals, a $2 bill signed by U.S. Treasurer Francine I. Neff and Secretary Simon, and other contemporary memorabilia. The container itself remained unsealed until the end of the year so that other mementos of the Bicentennial celebration could be included.

The capsule, which measures 40 inches in height, 36 inches at the base, and 30 inches at the top, was designed by the Department's Graphics Branch and was to stand on display in the Main Treasury Building for 100 years. Its four sides are made of reinforced concrete three inches thick. The Treasury seal and the numerals "2076" will be displayed on one side of the container. An airtight inner chamber preserves the contents of the capsule.

"America's greatest resource is the vibrant heritage of a free people. May we have the wisdom and the vision to nourish this birthright forever." — William E. Simon

These words, inscribed on the capsule's dedication plaque, form the keystone of Secretary Simon's message to his counterpart in 2076 and serve as a message of hope and confidence to Americans celebrating the 300th anniversary of the United States.

Secretaries of the Treasury

President	Secretaries	Term
Washington	Alexander Hamilton, New York	Sept. 11, 1789 - Jan. 31, 1795
	Oliver Wolcott, Connecticut	Feb. 3, 1795 - Mar. 3, 1797
Adams, John	Oliver Wolcott, Connecticut	Mar. 4, 1797 - Dec. 31, 1800
	Samuel Dexter, Massachusetts	Jan. 1, 1801 - Mar. 3, 1801
Jefferson	Samuel Dexter, Massachusetts	Mar. 4, 1801 - May 13, 1801
	Albert Gallatin, Pennsylvania	May 14, 1801 - Mar. 3, 1809
Madison	Albert Gallatin, Pennsylvania	Mar. 4, 1809 - Feb. 8, 1814
	George W. Campbell, Tennessee	Feb. 9, 1814 - Oct. 5, 1814
	Alexander J. Dallas, Pennsylvania	Oct. 6, 1814 - Oct. 21, 1816
	William H. Crawford, Georgia	Oct. 22, 1816 - Mar. 3, 1817
Monroe	William H. Crawford, Georgia	Mar. 4, 1817 - Mar. 6, 1825
Adams, J.Q.	Richard Rush, Pennsylvania	Mar. 7, 1825 - Mar. 5, 1829
Jackson	Samuel D. Ingham, Pennsylvania	Mar. 6, 1829 - June 20, 1831
	Louis McLane, Delaware	Aug. 8, 1831 - May 28, 1833
	William J. Duane, Pennsylvania	May 29, 1833 - Sept. 22, 1833
	Roger B. Taney, Maryland	Sept. 23, 1833 - June 25, 1834
	Levi Woodbury, New Hampshire	July 1, 1834 - Mar. 3, 1837
Van Buren	Levi Woodbury, New Hampshire	Mar. 4, 1837 - Mar. 3, 1841
Harrison, W.H.	Thomas Ewing, Ohio	Mar. 6, 1841 - Apr. 4, 1841
Tyler	Thomas Ewing, Ohio	Apr. 5, 1841 - Sept. 11, 1841
	Walter Forward, Pennsylvania	Sept. 13, 1841 - Mar. 1, 1843
	John C. Spencer, New York	Mar. 8, 1843 - May 2, 1844
	George M. Bibb, Kentucky	July 4, 1844 - Mar. 4, 1845

President	Secretaries	Term
Polk	George M. Bibb, Kentucky	Mar. 5, 1845 - Mar. 7, 1845
	Robert J. Walker, Mississippi	Mar. 8, 1845 - Mar. 5, 1849
Taylor	Wm. M. Meredith, Pennsylvania	Mar. 8, 1849 - July 9, 1850
Fillmore	Wm. M. Meredith, Pennsylvania	July 10, 1850 - July 22, 1850
	Thomas Corwin, Ohio	July 23, 1850 - Mar. 6, 1853
Pierce	James Guthrie, Kentucky	Mar. 7, 1853 - Mar. 6, 1857
Buchanan	Howell Cobb, Georgia	Mar. 7, 1857 - Dec. 8, 1860
	Philip F. Thomas, Maryland	Dec. 12, 1860 - Jan. 14, 1861
	John A. Dix, New York	Jan. 15, 1861 - Mar. 6, 1861
Lincoln	Salmon P. Chase, Ohio	Mar. 7, 1861 - June 30, 1864
	Wm. P. Fessenden, Maine	July 5, 1864 - Mar. 3, 1865
	Hugh McCulloch, Indiana	Mar. 9, 1865 - Apr. 15, 1865
Johnson, A.	Hugh McCulloch, Indiana	Apr. 16, 1865 - Mar. 3, 1869
Grant	Geo. S. Boutwell, Massachusetts	Mar. 12, 1869 - Mar. 16, 1873
	Wm. A. Richardson, Massachusetts	Mar. 17, 1873 - June 3, 1874
	Benjamin H. Bristow, Kentucky	June 4, 1874 - June 20, 1876
	Lot M. Morrill, Maine	June 7, 1876 - Mar. 3, 1877
Hayes	Lot M. Morrill, Maine	Mar. 4, 1877 - Mar. 9, 1877
	John Sherman, Ohio	Mar. 10, 1877 - Mar. 3, 1881
Garfield	William Windom, Minnesota	Mar. 8, 1881 - Sept. 19, 1881
Arthur	William Windom, Minnesota	Sept. 20, 1881 - Nov. 13, 1881
	Charles J. Folger, New York	Nov. 14, 1881 - Sept. 4, 1884
	Walter Q. Gresham, Indiana	Sept. 25, 1884 - Oct. 30, 1884
	Hugh McCulloch, Indiana	Oct. 31, 1884 - Mar. 3, 1885
Cleveland	Hugh McCulloch, Indiana	Mar. 4, 1885 - Mar. 7, 1885
	Daniel Manning, New York	Mar. 8, 1885 - Mar. 31, 1887
	Charles S. Fairchild, New York	Apr. 1, 1887 - Mar. 3, 1889
Harrison, B.	Charles S. Fairchild, New York	Mar. 4, 1889 - Mar. 6, 1889
	William Windom, Minnesota	Mar. 7, 1889 - Jan. 29, 1891
	Charles Foster, Ohio	Feb. 25, 1891 - Mar. 3, 1893
Cleveland	Charles Foster, Ohio	Mar. 4, 1893 - Mar. 6, 1893
	John G. Carlisle, Kentucky	Mar. 7, 1893 - Mar. 3, 1897
McKinley	John G. Carlisle, Kentucky	Mar. 4, 1897 - Mar. 5, 1897
	Lyman J. Gage, Illinois	Mar. 6, 1897 - Sept. 14, 1901
Roosevelt, T.	Lyman J. Gage, Illinois	Sept. 15, 1901 - Jan. 31, 1902
	L.M. Shaw, Iowa	Feb. 1, 1902 - Mar. 3, 1907
	G.B. Cortelyou, New York	Mar. 4, 1907 - Mar. 7, 1909
Taft	Franklin MacVeagh, Illinois	Mar. 8, 1909 - Mar. 5, 1913
Wilson	W.G. McAdoo, New York	Mar. 6, 1913 - Dec. 15, 1918
	Carter Glass, Virginia	Dec. 16, 1918 - Feb. 1, 1920
	David F. Houston, Missouri	Feb. 2, 1920 - Mar. 3, 1921
Harding	Andrew W. Mellon, Pennsylvania	Mar. 4, 1921 - Aug. 2, 1923
Coolidge	Andrew W. Mellon, Pennsylvania	Aug. 3, 1923 - Mar. 3, 1929
Hoover	Andrew W. Mellon, Pennsylvania	Mar. 4, 1929 - Feb. 12, 1932
	Ogden L. Mills, New York	Feb. 13, 1932 - Mar. 4, 1933
Roosevelt, F.D.	William H. Woodin, New York	Mar. 5, 1933 - Dec. 31, 1933
	Henry Morgenthau, Jr., New York	Jan. 1, 1934 - Apr. 12, 1945
Truman	Henry Morgenthau, Jr., New York	Apr. 13, 1945 - July 22, 1945
	Fred M. Vinson, Kentucky	July 23, 1945 - June 23, 1946
	John W. Snyder, Missouri	June 25, 1946 - Jan. 20, 1953
Eisenhower	George M. Humphrey, Ohio	Jan. 21, 1953 - July 29, 1957

President	Secretaries	Term
	Robert B. Anderson, Connecticut.........	July 29, 1957 - Jan. 20, 1961
Kennedy.............	Douglas Dillon, New Jersey..................	Jan. 21, 1961 - Nov. 22, 1963
Johnson, L.B.	Douglas Dillon, New Jersey..................	Nov. 23, 1963 - Apr. 1, 1965
	Henry H. Fowler, Virginia....................	Apr. 1, 1965 - Dec. 20, 1968
	Joseph W. Barr, Indiana........................	Dec. 21, 1968 - Jan. 20, 1969
Nixon	David M. Kennedy, Utah......................	Jan. 22, 1969 - Feb. 10, 1971
	John B. Connally, Texas.......................	Feb. 11, 1971 - June 12, 1972
	George P. Shultz, Illinois.....................	June 12, 1971 - May 7, 1974
	William E. Simon, New Jersey.............	May 8, 1974 - Aug. 9, 1974
Ford...................	William E. Simon, New Jersey	Aug. 10, 1974 - Jan. 20, 1977
Carter	W. Michael Blumenthal, Michigan.......	Jan. 23, 1977 - Aug. 4, 1979
	G. William Miller, Rhode Island..........	Aug. 7, 1979 - Jan. 20, 1981
Reagan..............	Donald T. Regan, Massachusetts..........	Jan. 22, 1981 - Feb. 2, 1985
	James A. Baker III, Texas	Feb. 3, 1985 - Aug. 17, 1988
	Nicholas F. Brady, New Jersey	Sept. 14, 1988 - Jan. 20, 1989
Bush	Nicholas F. Brady, New Jersey	Jan. 20, 1989 -

Treasurers of the United States

Treasurer	Term
Michael Hillegas, Pennsylvania......................................	July 29, 1775 - Sept. 11, 1789
Samuel Meredith, Pennsylvania	Sept. 11, 1789 - Oct. 31, 1801
Thomas T. Tucker, South Carolina	Dec. 1, 1801 - May 2, 1828
William Clark, Pennsylvania...	June 4, 1828 - May 31, 1829
John Campbell, Virginia..	May 26, 1829 - July 20, 1839
William Selden, Virginia..	July 22, 1839 - Nov. 23, 1850
John Sloan, Ohio...	Nov. 27, 1850 - April 6, 1852
Samuel Casey, Kentucky..	April 4, 1853 - Dec. 22, 1859
William C. Price, Missouri	Feb. 28, 1860 - Mar. 21, 1861
F.E. Spinner, New York...	Mar. 16, 1861 - June 30, 1875
John C. New, Indiana...	June 30, 1875 - July 1, 1876
A.U. Wyman, Wisconsin..	July 1, 1876 - June 30, 1877
James Gilfillan, Connecticut	July 1, 1877 - Mar. 31, 1883
A.U. Wyman, Wisconsin..	April 1, 1883 - April 30, 1885
Conrad N. Jordan, New York...	May 1, 1885 - May 23, 1887
James W. Hyatt, Connecticut..	May 24, 1887 - May 10, 1889
J.N. Huston, Indiana..	May 11, 1889 - April 24, 1891
Enos H. Nebecker, Indiana..	April 25, 1891 - May 31, 1893
D.N. Morgan, Connecticut...	June 1, 1893 - June 30, 1897
Ellis H. Roberts, New York..	July 1, 1897 - June 30, 1905
Charles H. Treat, New York...	July 1, 1905 - Oct. 30, 1909
Lee McClung, Tennessee..	Nov. 1, 1909 - Nov. 21, 1912
Carmi A. Thompson, Ohio...	Nov. 22, 1912 - Mar. 31, 1913
John Burke, North Dakota...	April 1, 1913 - Jan. 5, 1921
Frank White, North Dakota	May 2, 1921 - May 1, 1928
H.T. Tate, Tennessee	May 31, 1928 - Jan. 17, 1929
W.O. Woods, Kansas...	Jan. 18, 1929 - May 31, 1933
W.A. Julian, Ohio...	June 1, 1933 - May 29, 1949
Georgia Neese Clark, Kansas	June 21, 1949 - Jan. 27, 1953
Ivy Baker Priest, Utah...	Jan. 28, 1953 - Jan. 29, 1961

Elizabeth Rudel Smith, California.................................... Jan. 30, 1961 - April 13, 1962
Kathryn O'Hay Granahan, Pennsylvania......................... Jan. 3, 1963 - Nov. 20, 1966
Dorothy Andrews Elston Kabis, Delaware..................... May 8, 1969 - July 3, 1971
Romana Acosta Banuelos, California.............................. Dec. 17, 1971 - Feb. 15, 1974
Francine Irving Neff, New Mexico................................. June 21, 1974 - Jan. 19, 1977
Azie Taylor Morton, Texas... Sept. 12, 1977 - Jan. 20, 1981
Angela Buchanan, Maryland.. Jan. 21, 1981 - July 1, 1983
Katherine Davalos Ortega, New Mexico .... Sept. 23, 1983 - June 30, 1989
Catalina Vasquez Villalpando, Texas............................. Dec. 11, 1989 -

Treasury officials
15th Street and Pennsylvania Avenue NW, Washington, D.C. 20220.
Phone (202) 566-2000

Secretary of the Treasury .... Nicholas F. Brady
Executive Assistant.. Jean Schneebeli
Deputy Secretary of the Treasury.................... John E. Robson
Treasurer of the United States......................... Catalina Vasquez Villalpando
Director, United States Mint .... Donna Pope.
Director, Bureau of Engraving and Printing .... Peter H. Daly
Comptroller of the Currency .... Robert L. Clark
General Counsel.. Edith E. Holiday
Fiscal Assistant Secretary............................... Gerald Murphy.
Undersecretary for Finance.............................. Robert R. Glauber
Under Secretary for International Affairs .... David C. Mulford.
Assistant Secretary (Management) .... David M. Nummy
Assistant Secretary (Domestic Finance) .... David W. Mullins Jr.
Assistant Secretary (Economic Policy)............................ Sidney Jones
Assistant Secretary (Enforcement).................... Salvatore R. Martoche
Assistant Secretary (Legislative Affairs) .... Bryce L. Harlow
Assistant Secretary (Public Affairs and Public Liaison)... John Roger Bolton
Assistant Secretary (Tax Policy)........................ Kenneth W. Giddeon
Director, Bureau of Alcohol, Tobacco and Firearms........ Stephen E. Higgins.
Commissioner, U.S. Customs Service .... Kim Bleck
Commissioner, Internal Revenue Service .... Fred T. Goldberg Jr.
Commissioner, Bureau of the Public Debt........................ Richard L. Gregg.
Director, U.S. Secret Service .... John R. Simpson.
Inspector General .... Alexandra B. Keith
Director, U.S. Savings Bonds Division............................ Catalina Vasquez Villalpando

Department of the Treasury seal

The seal of the Treasury Department is older than the United States government. The Continental Congress in 1778 appointed a committee of finance, or board of treasury, and John Witherspoon, Gouverneur Morris and Richard Henry Lee were authorized to design a Treasury seal. The earliest example of the seal is found on papers dated 1782. When the U.S. government was established in 1789, the Continental seal was continued in use.

In 1849 the Treasury needed to replace its badly worn seal and ordered Edward Stabler to make a facsimile. Apparently Stabler carried out his orders with reservations, for his seal showed differences from the original; but they are so minute that a casual observer would not notice them.

The seal of the Department of the

Treasury is overprinted on the face of each note printed in the U.S.

On Jan. 29, 1968, a revision of the official seal was approved. The new seal has an inscription, in English, reading "The Department of the Treasury." This inscription replaces the earlier Latin legend "Thesaur. Amer. Septent. Sigil.," an abbreviation said to represent "Thesauri Americae Septentrionalis Sigillum," translated as "The Seal of the Treasury of North America." The new seal bears the date 1789, recording the year of the department's creation.

The arms on the seal depict balance scales, representing the scales of justice; a key, the emblem of official authority; and a chevron with 13 stars for the original states. The revised design of the seal appears on $100 United States notes, beginning with Series 1966, and on Federal Reserve notes, beginning with Series 1969.

On United States notes, the Treasury seal, along with the serial numbers, is overprinted in red; on Federal Reserve notes, these features are overprinted in green.

Function of the Treasury Department

The Department of the Treasury performs four basic functions: formulating and recommending financial, tax and fiscal policies; serving as a financial agent for the U.S. government; law enforcement; and manufacturing coins and currency.

Office of the Secretary

As a major policy adviser to the President, the Secretary has primary responsibility for formulating and recommending domestic and international financial, economic and tax policy; participating in the formulation of broad fiscal policies that have general significance for the economy; and managing the public debt. The Secretary also oversees the activities of the department in carrying out its major law enforcement responsibility; in serving as the financial agent for the U.S. government; and in manufacturing coins, currency and other products for customer agencies.

Office of the Comptroller of the Currency

The Office of the Comptroller of the Currency was created by act of Congress approved Feb. 25, 1863, as an integral part of the national banking system.

The Comptroller, as the administrator of national banks, is responsible for the execution of laws relating to national banks and promulgates rules and regulations governing the operations of approximately 4,550 national and District of Columbia banks. Approval of the Comptroller is required for the organization of new national banks, conversion of state-chartered banks into national banks, consolidations or mergers of banks where the surviving institution is a national bank, and the establishment of branches by national banks.

The Office of the Comptroller exercises general supervision over the operations of national banks, including trust activities and overseas operations. Each bank is examined periodically through a nationwide staff of approximately 2,100 bank examiners under the immediate supervision of six deputy comptrollers and six regional administrators. These examinations operate in the public interest by assisting the Comptroller in appraising the financial condition of the banks, the soundness of their operations, the quality of their management, and their compliance with laws, rules and regulations.

For further information, contact the Communications Division, Office of the Comptroller of the Currency, Department of the Treasury, 490 L'Enfant Plaza East SW, Washington, D.C. 20219. Phone (202) 447-1810.

U.S. Customs Service
1301 Constitution Ave. NW
Washington, D.C. 20229

Phone, (202) 566-8195

The U.S. Customs Service was created by the act of March 3, 1927. Authority for the collection of customs revenue was established by the second, third, and fifth acts of the first Congress in 1789.

Customs engages in activities for the collection and protection of the revenue; the prevention of fraud and smuggling; and the processing and regulation of people, carriers, cargo and mail into and out of the United States; and performs a variety of functions for other government agencies in safeguarding agriculture, business, health, security and related consumer interests.

Customs is active in suppressing the traffic in illegal narcotics (in conjunction with the Drug Enforcement Administration and in cooperation with foreign governments); in enforcing munitions control in cargo theft prevention; in enforcing regulations affecting articles in international trade where parallel regulations control domestic articles (such as copyright, trademark, and patent restrictions regulated domestically by the Patent Office or the Copyright Office; and special marking provisions for wool, fur and textile products, controlled domestically by the Federal Trade Commission); and in enforcing regulations related to dumping.

The Bureau of Customs enforces certain environmental protection programs for other agencies, such as enforcing the prohibition on discharge of refuse and oil into or upon coastal navigable waters of the United States (for the U.S. Coast Guard) as outlined in the Oil Pollution Act; enforcing laws and regulations regarding wild animals and birds of the endangered species and those injurious to community health, plant and animal life, as well as other agriculture and plant quarantine regulations concerning animal, poultry, animal byproducts; and insuring that imported vehicles and equipment conform to safety and emission standards required under the National Traffic and Motor Vehicle Safety Act of 1966 and the Clean Air Act.

Headquarters for the Customs Service is located in Washington, D.C., under the supervision of the Commissioner of Customs who is appointed by the Secretary of the Treasury. The Service is decentralized and most of its personnel are stationed throughout the country and overseas, where its operational functions are performed.

The 50 states, plus the Virgin Islands and Puerto Rico, are divided into seven Customs Regions. Contained within these regions are 46 subordinate district offices under which there are approximately 300 ports of entry.

For further information, contact the Public Affairs Office, U.S. Customs Service, Department of the Treasury, 1301 Constitution Avenue NW, Washington, D.C. 20229. Phone, (202) 566-5286.

United States Mint
633 Third St. NW
Washington, D.C. 20220
Phone, (202) 376-0560

The Mint of the United States was established by act of Congress April 2, 1792. The Bureau of the Mint was established by act of Congress February 12, 1873. Mint Director Donna Pope changed the name of the agency to the U.S. Mint on Jan. 25, 1984.

The functions of the Mint are the production of coins, both domestic and foreign; the manufacture and sale of medals of a national character; the manufacture and sale of Proof and Uncirculated coin sets and other numismatic items; and the custody, processing and movement of bullion. The Mint disburses gold and silver for authorized purposes; directs the distribution of coins from the Mints to the Federal Reserve Banks and branches; and compiles and analyzes general data of worldwide scope relative to gold, silver and coins.

For further information, contact the United States Mint, Department of the Treasury, 633 Third St. NW, Washington, D.C. 20220. Phone, (202) 376-0560.

United States Secret Service
1800 G Street NW
Washington, D.C. 20223
Phone, (202) 535-5708

The responsibilities and jurisdiction of the United States Secret Service are prescribed by law in Title 18, United States Code, Section 3056.

Subject to the direction of the Secretary of the Treasury, the United States Secret Service is authorized to protect the person of the president of the United States, the members of his immediate family, the president-elect, the vice president or other officer next in the order of succession to the Office of President, the immediate family of the vice president, the vice president-elect, major presidential and vice presidential candidates, former presidents and their wives during his lifetime, widows of former presidents until their death or remarriage, and minor children of a former president until they reach age 16, and visiting heads of a foreign state or foreign government.

The Secret Service is also authorized to detect and arrest any person committing any offense against the laws of the United States relating to coins, currency, and other obligations, and securities of the United States and of foreign governments; detect and arrest any person violating any of the provisions of sections 508, 509, and 871 of Title 18 of the United States Code; execute warrants issued under the authority of the United States; carry firearms; and perform such other functions and duties as are authorized by law.

The Director of the Secret Service is charged with the supervision of the Executive Protective Service and the Treasury Security Force.

For further information, contact any District Office or Office of Public Affairs, United States Secret Service, Department of the Treasury, 1800 G Street NW, Washington, D.C. 20223. Phone, (202) 535-5708.

Bureau of Engraving and Printing
14th and C streets SW
Washington, D.C. 20228
Phone (202) 447-0193

The Bureau operates on basic authorities conferred by the acts of July 11, 1862, March 3, 1877, June 4, 1897, and additional authorities contained in past appropriations made to the Bureau for work to be undertaken, which are still in force. A working capital fund of $3,250,000 was established in accordance with the provisions of Section 2 of the Act of Aug. 4, 1950, which placed the Bureau on a completely reimbursable basis. The Bureau is headed by a Director who is appointed by the Secretary of the Treasury.

The Bureau of Engraving and Printing designs, engraves and prints all major items of financial character issued by the U.S. government. It produces paper currency; Treasury bonds, bills, notes, and certificates; postage, revenue and certain customs stamps. Operations are conducted in Washington, D.C., and a satellite plant in Fort Worth, Texas.

For further information, contact the Public Affairs Section, Bureau of Engraving and Printing, Department of the Treasury, Room 602-11A, 14th and C streets SW, Washington, D.C. 20228. Phone (202) 447-0193.

Fiscal Services
The Fiscal Service of the Treasury Department was created by Reorganization Plan III, effective June 30, 1940 (5 U.S.C. Appendix).

BUREAU OF GOVERNMENT FINANCIAL OPERATIONS
The Bureau of Government Financial Operations has responsibility for a variety of fiscal activities of a government-wide scope.

CENTRAL ACCOUNTING AND REPORTING
The Bureau maintains a system of central accounting and reporting, disclosing the monetary assets and

liabilities of the United States Treasury and providing for the integration of Treasury cash and funding operations with the financial operations of disbursing and collecting officers and of Federal program agencies. Periodic reports are prepared to show budget results, other financial operations, and the financial status of the government.

CENTRAL DISBURSING AND CHECK CLAIMS

Disbursing service is provided for most civilian agencies of the government, including the issuance of monthly payments to beneficiaries under major federal benefit programs and the issuance of U.S. Savings Bonds under the Federal Payroll Savings Plan. Through the Department of State, foreign disbursing service is provided for agencies other than the Department of Defense. The Bureau adjudicates and settles claims against the United States on Treasury checks that are lost in the mails, or which bear forged endorsements, and issues new checks to authorized payees.

FEDERAL TAX DEPOSITS

The Bureau provides technical support, including the issuance of federal tax deposit forms, for the system of tax payments by business organizations through authorized commercial banks and the Federal Reserve System.

CASH MANAGEMENT

The Bureau supervises the government-wide letter-of-credit system for financing federal grant-in-aid programs; monitors all cash held outside the Treasury, including foreign currency balances resulting from federal programs; and supervises the government's depository system.

MUTILATED CURRENCY

The Bureau handles claims from the public for the redemption of partially destroyed U.S. currency, determines its value and authorizes payment to claimants.

SURETY BONDING

The Bureau administers functions relating to the qualification of surety companies as acceptable sureties on bonds

running in favor of the United States, including the examination of financial statements and the determination of underwriting limitations for such companies.

MISCELLANEOUS FINANCIAL ACTIVITIES

The Bureau makes payment to holders of claims awards under international claims programs, judgments rendered by certain United States courts and private relief acts passed by the Congress; supervises the liquidation of terminated agencies; bills and collects amounts due from foreign governments under lend-lease, surplus property agreements and other Treasury loans; and audits the procedures of Federal Reserve Banks in verifying and destroying U.S. currency which is unfit for circulation.

For further information, contact the Comptroller's Office, Bureau of Government Financial Operations, Department of the Treasury, 490 L'Enfant Plaza East SW, Washington, D.C. 20219.

Office of the Treasurer

The Office of the Treasurer of the United States was originally created by the act of Sept. 2, 1789, for the purpose of receiving, holding and paying out the public moneys for the federal government. However, most of the responsibilities of the office were transferred to the Bureau of Government Financial Operations with its creation Feb. 1, 1974.

The Treasurer is responsible for reviewing and endorsing U.S. currency and represents the Secretary of the Treasury and Undersecretary for Monetary Affairs as a major spokesman in communicating and coordinating departmental programs and policies.

During the Reagan administration, the office of Treasurer was upgraded to include the responsibilities of direct oversight of the United States Mint, the Bureau of Engraving and Printing and the United States Savings Bond program, and serving on the Treasury Secretary's senior staff.

As National Director of the U.S.

Savings Bond Division, the Treasurer supervises a bureau-level organization of the Department of the Treasury whose primary mission is to promote the sale of U.S. savings bonds. Among other duties, the Treasurer consults with the Secretary and Undersecretary on the role of the savings bonds program in Treasury's debt management policies.

For further information, contact the Office of the Treasurer, Department of the Treasury, 15th St. and Pennsylvania Ave. NW, Washington, D.C. 20220. Phone (202) 566-2843.

The United States Mint

5

United States Mint

The Act of April 2, 1792, provided for gold, silver and copper coinage, and also created the first United States Mint in the city of Philadelphia, which was then the nation's capital. President Washington placed the operation under the supervision of the secretary of state where it remained until 1799, when the Mint became an independent agency reporting directly to the president. Subsequent legislation set up branch Mints, Assay Offices, and fixed public depository functions upon such establishments. The Coinage Act of 1873 put all Mint and Assay Office activities under the newly-organized Bureau of the Mint in the Department of the Treasury.

The Director of the Mint is appointed by the president, with the advice and consent of the Senate. The Director is responsible for coinage production and the distribution of coins to and among the Federal Reserve Banks and Branches, which in turn release them, as required, to commercial banks.

In addition, the Mint maintains physical custody of Treasury stocks of gold and silver and moves, places into storage and releases these metals from custody for such purposes as authorized. It also manufactures coinage dies.

On a reimbursable basis, the Mint manufactures and sells medals of a national character, produces Proof and Uncirculated coin sets for sale to collectors, and strikes commemorative coinage for sale to the public.

The Director administers the Philadelphia, Denver, San Francisco and West Point Mints, and the gold bullion depository in Fort Knox, Ky.

The Mint also maintains the restored Old San Francisco Mint, which houses the Mint Museum. Mint service activities are administered by the Director of the Mint and staff from Mint headquarters in Washington, D.C.

A customer service center is located in suburban Washington, D.C., in Lanham, Md.

The United States Mint Director makes annual reports to the Secretary of the Treasury concerning Mint operations for the fiscal year. The report includes estimates of domestic and foreign production of gold and silver, as well as monetary statistics pertaining to the United States and most of the countries of the world.

The main offices of the Mint are located in Washington, D.C., in the Judiciary Square Building. The Mint moved its offices from the Warner Building in 1985. The Mint and its Washington officials, named later in this chapter, may be contacted by writing:

United States Mint, Department of the Treasury, 633 Third St. NW, Washington, D.C. 20220.

Questions concerning the purchase of collector coins sold by the Mint should be directed to U.S. Mint Customer Service, 10001 Aerospace Road, Lanham, Md. 20706; telephone (301) 436-7400.

For general information, address the request to Office of Public Services.

Mint officials

Office of the Director

Director.. Donna Pope
Assistant to the Director and Press Secretary .... David L. Karmol
Special Assistant .... Jon B. Rawlson
Deputy Director.. Eugene H. Essner
Counsel to the Mint... Kenneth B. Gubin
Security Officer .... William F. Daddio

Office of Marketing

Associate Director... David Pickens
Assistant Director... John J. Papa
Assistant Director for Marketing Operations........................ Kevin M. Cullinane
Assistant Director for Sales Operations .... Francis B. Frere

Office of Operations

Associate Director... Andrew Cosgarea Jr.
Chief, Federal Reserve Liaison... Francis R. DeLeo
Chief, Engineering Division.. Leon Butzky
Assistant Director (Technology).. George E. Hunter
Chief, Assay Control Division .... Jerome A. Yellin
Chief, Quality Control Division.. Yancey Clark

Office of Policy and Management

Assistant Director (Management Services) .... Judith L. Wagner
Assistant Director (Procurement)... Joseph N. Hoback

Mint facilities

Philadelphia Mint
Fifth St. at Independence Mall
Philadelphia, Pa. 19106
John T. Martino, Superintendent

Denver Mint
Colfax and Delaware Streets
Denver, Colo. 80204
Barbara McTurk, Superintendent

San Francisco Mint
155 Hermann St.
San Francisco, Calif. 94102
Carol Mayer Marshall, Superintendent

United States Bullion Depository
Fort Knox, Ky. 40121
James Curtis, Officer in Charge

West Point Mint
West Point, N.Y. 10996
Clifford M. Barber, Superintendent

Old Mint
88 Fifth St.
San Francisco, Calif. 94103
Thomas H. Miller, Officer in Charge

Customer Service Center
10001 Aerospace Road
Lanham, Md. 20706

Mint Director's report

The latest Annual Report of the Director of the Mint, giving complete Mint statistics and a report of Mint activities for fiscal year which ended Sept. 30, 1989, 48 pages, is available from the Superintendent of Documents, U.S. Government Printing Office, Washington, D.C. 20402.

Beginning with fiscal year 1981, the Mint has released greatly abbreviated reports from those issued prior to 1981.

Present Mint institutions

Philadelphia Mint

The Act passed on April 2, 1792, established the United States Mint. As a result, a plot of ground was purchased in Philadelphia, located on the east side of Seventh Street, below Arch Street. This was the first public building to be erected by the government of the fledgling United States. For 40 years the federal government continued to use the building on Seventh Street as the national Mint.

Guards are essential to the Mint's elaborate security system. In the past, as now, security precautions were very important. In 1793, the sum of $3 was paid for a watchdog to protect the Mint. The first dog, named Nero, was a savage one which accompanied the watchman on his hourly rounds. The watchman, armed with a dirk and pistol, in making his rounds would ring a bell at regular intervals in order that the populace of Philadelphia might know that the Mint was still safe. Food for the dog was considered an essential expense of the Mint, the same as hay and other food was considered essential for the horses which provided power for operating the Mint machinery in those days.

On the Fourth of July, 1829, construction began for a new Mint on the northwest corner of Chestnut and Juniper streets, at a cost of $291,000. For more than 70 years this building was used as the Philadelphia Mint.

The third Mint building on Spring Garden Street between 16th and 17th streets, built in 1900, covered a ground area of 58,000 square feet. The exterior of the building was of Maine granite and faced a street on each of the four sides. The main entrance was on Spring Garden Street.

The front portion of the building rose three stories above the basement and terraces. The rear portion was one story lower than the front, but owing to the slope of the ground the basement was almost entirely above ground, which gave three clear stories to this portion also.

The lobby, reached by the Spring Garden Street entrance, was finished with strongly-veined Italian marble walls and vaulted mosaic ceilings. The panels were formed by mosaics illustrating the ancient methods and processes of coinage. These mosaics formed one of the most beautiful and expressive features in the building. The ceilings were covered with a solid mosaic of gold — each unit being a piece of glass backed with gold.

These beautiful mosaics make a link between the third Philadelphia Mint and its replacement, dedicated Aug. 14, 1969. The third Mint served the nation for more than 65 years, but the growth of the country made demands which could no longer be handled by the then-outmoded facilities.

After the completion of the fourth Philadelphia Mint, the mosaics were painstakingly removed and re-installed in the new facility. There they are a prime attraction for the Mint's thousands of visitors.

Groundbreaking ceremonies held Sept. 17, 1965, launched construction of the fourth Philadelphia Mint, nearly three times the size of the Spring Garden Street plant. On Aug. 14, 1969, another milestone in Mint history was marked by the official opening of an impressive modern building with a pink granite facade and bronze-tinted glass, covering more than five acres of ground, approximately three city blocks. The main entrance plaza and lobby, facing Fifth Street at Independence Mall, overlooks the original site.

Offices, production divisions and public areas occupy more than 500,000 square feet of space and are planned to afford the maximum in efficiency of operation and comfortable working conditions.

The new Mint was designed for an annual production capability of 2 billion coins on a five-day, 40-hour week, or a total capacity of about 8 billion coins per year on a 24-hour day, seven-day week basis. Facilities originally included melting, casting, rolling and annealing facilities, plus cladding lines to produce clad strip for composite coins, in addition to the coining areas. However, the Mint began shutting cladding operations down during fiscal year 1982, and officially shut down the facilities in fiscal 1983, relying instead totally on private sector strip producers.

The entire operation can be viewed from a glass-enclosed elevated gallery designed to accommodate 2,500 visitors an hour.

The numismatic room on the mezzanine ordinarily contains Mint relics, historic coins and medals.

A sales counter is maintained where Mint medals, coin sets and certain Mint publications may be purchased.

Denver Mint

Gold was first discovered in 1858 in what is now the state of Colorado, on the Platte River, near the city of Denver. For some years mining in Colorado was chiefly from placer claims, which were deposits formed by water currents in river beds. Lode gold was found, however, near present Central City, Colo., on May 6, 1859, and other discoveries followed.

When the California Gold Rush of '49 lost its impetus with the declining production of mines in California, miners turned their attention to Denver City where, within a few years, a small village of cottonwood log cabins began to emerge. This town became an "outfitting" point for miners. Recognizing a need for a circulating medium, much as necessity is the mother of invention, several firms in Colorado organized themselves as private Mints. They melted "raw" gold in the form of dust and nuggets, all of which contained an appreciable amount of silver, and formed it into what are now known as Pikes Peak coins. These were much like some of the gold coins struck privately in California some years previously.

Congress, in January 1862, received a proposal from the Treasury Department that a branch Mint be established at Denver, Colo., for gold coinage. As indicative of the need, they were informed that in the two preceding years the private Mint of Clark, Gruber and Co. had turned out gold coins to the extent of $120,000. The government bought the Clark-Gruber plant in the fall of 1862, for the sum of $25,000.

In the early days of Denver, when Indian raids were anticipated, the Mint building was used as a place of refuge for women and children, it being the town's most substantial structure. "The hostility of the Indian tribes along the routes . . ." was one of the reasons given by the Director of the Mint for the Denver plant not being able to assume its position as a branch Mint.

Not to achieve its destiny as a Mint until some years later, the Denver plant opened its doors in September 1863 as an Assay Office. Its activities were restricted to melting and stamping bullion brought in by miners without refining. Under the regulations which were prescribed, the plant was to accomplish this task "within a day or an hour" after it was received. The bars were to be stamped as to the "fineness" (amount of gold and silver contained) and weight. Also stamped on the bars was a device bearing the American eagle and around it the words "U.S. Branch Mint, Denver."

By 1867 the miners had exhausted, to a large extent, the rich beds of placer gold appearing in the streams, and the Assay Office at Denver had little business while miners turned their attention to "lode" mining, uncovering underground veins of ores having a high percentage of gold and silver. It was found, however, that to crush and pulverize these ores and to extract the precious metals required complicated apparatus and skilled labor, as well as rail transportation, all of which were lacking to a large extent.

Heartbroken as they were to see the Union Pacific Railroad pass them to the north, a group of Colorado citizens banded together. Through their enterprise a rail line was built in 1870 which connected Denver with Cheyenne, Wyo., tying them in with the economic life of the nation, from coast to coast.

In the late 19th century Colorado felt the effect of an acceleration in silver mining because of government purchasing programs. When they were terminated, the abrupt reduction in silver output was offset by the rise of the great gold camp at Cripple Creek, Colo.

The Clark-Gruber plant which the government had used continuously began to deteriorate and in 1877 was reported as being so dilapidated as to be considered unsafe.

Hopes for a branch Mint status were again kindled when on Feb. 20, 1895, Congress provided for the establishment of a Mint at Denver for the coinage of gold and silver. A $500,000 appropriation provided that until it could become a Mint in accordance with law it would have to operate as an Assay Office.

On April 22, 1896, a site was purchased at a cost of about $60,000. In the meantime, the deposit activity at the Denver Mint stepped up considerably. The sources of the deposits were principally the mines of Arizona, New Mexico, Colorado and Utah. In 1895 the aggregate value of gold and silver deposited annually was in excess of $5.6 million.

Plans for the new Mint developed slowly, but surely. Moving day took place on Sept. 1, 1904, when the Mint transferred its operations from the historic Clark-Gruber building at 16th and Market streets to the handsome Renaissance structure at West Colfax and Evans streets.

Coinage organization was effected by the naming of officials for the superintendency and various departments on Oct. 15, 1904. Earlier it had been the practice for Denver to send its bullion deposits to Philadelphia for parting and refining. Bullion shipments to Philadelphia ceased Dec. 31, 1904.

The new structure, viewed from the street, provided two stories above ground. Actually it had five floors. It was 175 feet long and 100 feet wide.

The stone facing of the building is Colorado granite, up to and including the water table. The Arkins granite between the water table and the cornice was procured in Maine. Tennessee marble forms the window trimmings, and the marble used in the interior finish was obtained in Vermont.

The decorations of the main corridor on the first floor, the mezzanine floor, and the second floor were completed in 1909 under the direction of John Gibson, a member of an old Philadelphia firm. This firm also furnished the three mural paintings in the area above the cornice inside the main vestibule. They are the work of an Italian named Vincent Adriente who worked under the supervision of the celebrated mural artist Edwin Howland Blashfield, of New York City. The paintings are purely symbolic and typify Commerce, Mining and Manufacturing.

The Great Seal of the United States, in the form of a large metal casting, was placed in the center of the vestibule floor. In the summer of 1961 this seal had worn so smooth it was considered unsafe and was replaced by a mosaic replica.

The new Mint was equipped with all the latest methods and machinery, the coinage apparatus having been built at Philadelphia where a large part of the machinery used by the Mints was made.

In its first year of operation the coining room turned out gold coin valued at $23.8 million, and subsidiary coin, halves, quarters and dimes, amounting to $3.2 million.

By Act of Congress, the Mint has had authority since 1874 to strike coins for friendly foreign governments. In 1906 the Denver Mint started its first production of foreign coinage — 4.8 million 5-peso gold pieces for the government of Mexico.

The Mint Act of 1873, which codified all existing Mint laws, had restricted the manufacture of 5-cent pieces and cents to the Mint at Philadelphia. At the time that act was passed few if any of these coins were in use in the West, although by legislation in 1906 Congress gave recognition to the fact that they were then in circulation all over the country. The Secretary of the Treasury was then authorized to direct the coinage of 5-cent pieces and cents at any of the Mints. Minor coinage started at the Denver Mint in 1911, the production of cents that year amounting to 12.6 million pieces.

It had always been the practice in the United States to conduct refineries in connection with coinage operations, thus enabling the facilities to receive crude bullion. The installation of a refinery at the Denver Mint in 1906 was itself as momentous as its commencement of coinage. In its first six months of operations the new Denver refinery turned out refined gold and silver valued at $32 million. Operating through the years, it contributed substantially to the total output of refined gold and silver of the Mint.

In 1937 an addition was made to the Denver Mint, covering an area of approximately 6,000 square feet and consisting of a basement and two stories. The old building was remodeled and 10 coining presses, with back-up equipment, were installed.

In October 1945, ground was broken for a three-story addition, 161 feet long by 96 feet wide. The cost of this addition was more than $1.5 million. The new wing was built to house modern "brass mill" melting and rolling equipment. The rolling system and equipment, designed by one of the foremost rolling mill engineering firms in the nation, was engineered to process a bronze coinage ingot weighing 420 pounds.

Out of consideration for an interested public, a visitor's balcony was constructed in each of the first two floors, suspended under the 24-foot ceilings, from which spectators may look down on money-making operations.

As coinage demands grew in the late 1960s and into 1970, Mint Director Mary Brooks began to explore the possibility of building a new Denver Mint. Although present Mint facilities were keeping up with the public's demand for coins, she believed by 1980 those facilities would be outdated.

After a series of congressional hearings and conferences, Congress voted July 3, 1971, to allocate $1.5 million to purchase a site for a new Denver Mint. The Bureau of the Mint went shopping for land.

Two sites were chosen, the South Platte River basin and the Clayton Trust property in the Park Hill section of Denver. The first site was abandoned when the Burlington Northern Railroad stuck to its plans to install mainline tracks adjacent to the area.

Brooks announced on July 16, 1974, the new Mint would be built on the Park Hill site. Construction was set to begin in the fall of 1975 or early 1976 with a completion date around 1980.

The new Mint was to be designed to produce 10.7 billion coins annually and possibly up to 16 billion.

A House bill to provide funds for the new Denver Mint was introduced March 26, 1975. It passed the House Sept. 19, 1975, and went to the Senate Public Works Committee Sept. 22, 1975.

In an unusual procedure, Assistant Secretary of the Treasury David Macdonald and Frank H. MacDonald, Deputy Director of the Mint, testified at an executive session of the Public Works Committee. Witnesses are not normally called into an executive session.

If passed, the bill would have authorized an increase of $60 million in the amount of money that could be appropriated to the Treasury Department for the construction of Mint facilities. The bill would have raised the total authorized by Congress since 1963 for Mint construction to $105 million.

On Feb. 27, 1976, Mint and Treasury officials testified in support of the Denver Mint legislation before the Senate Banking, Housing and Urban Affairs committee.

At one point, Mint officials considered the purchase of an empty tire manufacturing plant in Littleton, Colo., as a potential site for the Denver Mint. However, the plant was sold in March 1976 to a tire firm.

Rep. William Armstrong, R-Colo., said moving the Mint to suburban Littleton would save the Bureau of the Mint about

$20 million. Rep. Pat Schroeder, D-Colo., opposed the Littleton move, advocated the continued use of the present Mint downtown in Denver, and expansion of the Philadelphia Mint.

At this point, Sen. William Proxmire, D-Wis., chairman of the Senate Banking committee, directed a General Accounting Office examination of all Bureau of the Mint facilities to determine total-picture needs.

The GAO came out against the construction of a new branch Mint in Denver, primarily because of the 1-cent coin's then-dubious future in the U.S. coinage lineup.

The GAO report criticized Treasury Department estimates of future coinage demands. The proposed phase-out of the cent, which accounts for more than 70 percent of the production of the nation's Mints, diminishes the need for construction of a new coinage facility at this time, the GAO report said.

The report proposed several alternatives, including upgrading current production capacity and modifying production strategies to meet the short-term needs.

The report concluded with the recommendation that the Treasury Secretary require the Bureau of the Mint to make a comprehensive study of the various options for increasing production within its present facilities.

On March 7 during budgetary hearings before the House Appropriations Subcommittee, Acting Mint Director Frank H. MacDonald told representatives the Bureau management was "totally in disagreement with" the GAO report regarding the Denver Mint.

He characterized the report as being full of things that "seem like cheap shots like how we can put coinage presses in the restrooms."

Mint officials abandoned their plans for a new Denver Mint in the Nixon administration and sold the Park Hill site to an Alaskan firm six years later on Jan. 19, 1984, for $3,351,356.05.

Expansion of the present Denver facility was approved, and construction began in late May 1984. Mint Director Donna Pope reported that the expansion would be done in two phases. Phase one would comprise construction of an expanded south dock for all material deliveries and coin shipments, roadway approaches and departures from the south dock, and a two-story building addition on the west side to provide for storage and processing of coinage materials on the ground floor, and secured storage in the basement for coins. The second phase included the relocation and installation of production equipment, support facilities for increased coin production and utilities systems.

Improvement of the facilities continued under flamboyant Superintendent Cynthia Grassby Baker. While the Mint's technology staff worked to install high-speed coinage presses and automated material handling systems, Baker directed the refurbishing of the building's historical decor. Some controversy erupted in 1989 when plans for a new visitors' entrance drew fire from architectural critics who claimed the addition did not fit with the building's classic style.

San Francisco Mint and Assay Office

The discovery of gold at Coloma (Sutter's Mill) by John Marshall, in 1848, was the world-echoing event which contributed to the recommendation by President Millard Fillmore in 1850 that a branch Mint be established in California. Gold being mined in the hills had grown from a trickle to a deluge too heavy for facilities at the distant Philadelphia Mint to handle and much time was consumed in transporting the precious metal on its hazardous journey. The coinage situation in the West was in a chaotic state. Many different kinds circulated — French louis d'ors, Dutch guilders, Indian rupees, Mexican reales, English shillings, as well as American pieces — but even so, there was a scarcity; and gold dust, while acceptable, was not a convenient medium of exchange. To remedy the difficulty, private Mints sprang up which converted the gold into coins, but this was not the solution to the problem.

The United States Mint at San Francisco, Calif., was authorized by the Act of Congress approved July 3, 1852, and the coins produced there gradually replaced the miscellaneous assortment in circulation. The Mint commenced receiving deposits on April 3, 1854. Supply of materials retarded and diminished the coinage operations during that year. However, $4,084,207, all in gold pieces, was coined between April and December 1854.

Operations were conducted in a small building on Commercial Street, just 60 feet square. The Director remarked: "It is almost impossible to conceive how so much work can be well done, and so much business transacted safely, in so small a space. The entrance to the business office is up a steep pair of stairs and through a dark hall rendered unwholesome by the fumes of acids, and uncomfortable by the noise of machinery and the heat of the engine. The apartments of the different officers and the desks of the clerks are cramped and inconvenient, and the vaults depend for their safety chiefly upon the presence of well-tried watchmen."

About 10 years later, the suggestion was made that there be purchased "a suitable site upon which should be speedily erected a mint building creditable to the Government, and commensurate with the wants of the great mineral districts of the Pacific Coast." It was not until 1872-73, however, that the building was completed and the work of fitting up the necessary machinery, fixtures and apparatus was begun. The new Mint at Fifth and Mission was occupied in the summer of 1874, and was one of the best-appointed Mints in the world.

The work of the San Francisco Mint was interrupted by the great earthquake of April 18, 1906. The structure and its contents were saved from the fire by intelligent and courageous work on the part of the superintendent and employees, but as the fuel used for its melting, annealing and assaying operations was city

gas, the destruction of the gas works made a discontinuance of operations necessary. Moreover, the Mint, by reason of the destruction of the subtreasury and all of the banks of the city, became the only financial institution able to do business in the city and the agency through which all remittances to and from the city, and disbursements within the city were made. The Mint became the depository and treasury for the relief fund, and its superintendent, Frank A. Leach, had many new and very important responsibilities suddenly thrust upon him, all of which were borne with fidelity and ability.

The steadily increasing coinage demands of the nation following the Depression made mandatory the enlargement of minting facilities, and in the summer of 1937, San Francisco personnel made another move, this time into an imposing three-story marble edifice some distance from the principal business district where the 1874 building was located. The approximately 33,000 square feet of space in the 1937 structure housed the most modern facilities of the day and new equipment to replace worn and obsolete machinery.

The newest San Francisco Mint went into operation in 1937, striking U.S. coins of all denominations, plus coins for the Philippine Islands in 1944 and 1945, as World War II came to a close. In most years, the San Francisco mintages of U.S. coins lagged behind those of Philadelphia and Denver, although for some denominations, San Francisco totals were slightly higher than Denver mintages during a few years.

Meanwhile, in the decade following the end of World War II, the Philadelphia and Denver Mints were being improved. It was the belief that these expanded facilities would be adequate to meet the nation's coin demand for some time to come. Therefore, in March 1955, coinage operations at San Francisco were discontinued. The equipment was removed and most of the building was remodeled for occupancy by other agencies of the government. Only a small area was retained by the Mint for the conduct of assay functions, including receipts of gold and silver deposits.

A profound change in the classification of the 1937 Mint structure came in the mid-1960s when it once again became an operating minting facility. During the fall of 1963, it became apparent that a coin shortage was building up, and by July 1964, emergency measures had been adopted to relieve the situation. One of these measures was the utilization of space in the 1937 San Francisco Mint building (called the San Francisco Assay Office since approval of a law July 11, 1962, until it regained Mint status March 31, 1988). The Treasury reacquired and once again adapted the space to the making of coins. However, despite its rebirth as a minting facility, the Bureau of the Mint continued to call the 1937 facility an Assay Office.

With the additional equipment secured from the Department of Defense, San Francisco began producing 1-cent and 5-cent coin blanks and took on annealing and upsetting operations also, thus lessening the load at the Denver Mint and allowing it more leeway for the other manufacturing functions. The finished blanks were then shipped to Denver for the final stamping process. This enabled the making of many more coins at Denver than would ordinarily have been possible.

Reactivation of coining operations at San Francisco was authorized by the Coinage Act of 1965, approved by President Johnson July 23, and on Sept. 1 the presses began turning out the first coins struck there since coinage was discontinued 10 years before.

In 1968, the San Francisco Assay Office assumed production of all Proof coinage; not until 1983 and 1984 with the Olympic coinage program were U.S. Proof coins intended for public purchase struck at another Mint facility. From 1968 to 1974, only some of the business-strike coinage bore the San Francisco Mint mark. Since 1974, only the Anthony dollars of 1979-1981 struck in San Francisco have borne the S Mint mark, except for Proof coinage. The San Francisco Mint specializes in the production of Proof coins, as well as the Uncirculated and Proof versions of the silver American Eagle bullion coin. It also finishes Proof dies prior to coinage.

Old San Francisco Mint

After it was abandoned by the Mint in 1937, the 1874 Mint building, which came to be lovingly known as the "Granite Lady," spent decades in limbo, serving various government organizations. In 1968, however, the federal government vacated the nearly century-old building and declared it surplus to government needs.

Various groups fought over the empty and deteriorating building, some wanting to demolish it, and others wanting to restore and preserve it. In the spring of 1972, President Nixon intervened to save the 1874 Mint structure at Fifth and Mission streets from its then uncertain fate. He announced the transfer of the building from the General Services Administration to the Department of the Treasury's Bureau of the Mint for restoration and continued use by the government and the enjoyment of the public.

A year later, in April 1973, the Mint's Special Coins and Medals and Computer employees were able to move their operations into the rooms in the rear of the building, newly renovated and equipped to speed the processing of mail orders received from the public for the special coins and medals produced by the Mint.

On June 16, 1973, the Old San Francisco Mint was officially re-opened as a public museum and working Mint facility under Mint Director Mary Brooks. The museum rooms are authentically restored to their original 1874 appearance and are open to the public. Exhibits of historical and educational significance will continue to be developed for display.

Produced as a Bicentennial project by the Bureau of the Mint was a film titled "The Granite Lady," which tells the story of the Old San Francisco Mint. With Mercedes McCambridge as narrator, the film features two child actors and some of the 200 Mint employees in contemporary costumes.

Following a preview on National Educational Television, the award-winning film is screened daily for visitors to the Mint.

On Nov. 7, 1976, a VIP reception hosted by Mint Director Mary Brooks celebrated the completion of the restoration of the Old San Francisco Mint. Brooks told the several hundred reception guests that the sale of the millions of U.S. coins and national medals financed the $4.5 million restoration of the century-old edifice.

Jan. 28, 1977, was another "red letter" day in the illustrious history of the Old Mint. Ceremonies at the Mint that day were held to commemorate official recognition of the Fifth and Mission streets' structure as "California Registered Historical Landmark No. 875."

A plaque unveiled that day is inscribed with the following thumbnail sketch of the role played by the Old Mint in the growth of San Francisco from a tiny mission to a great metropolis:

"The Old Mint (1869), San Francisco's second, is California's only such Greek Revival structure. Due to unsurpassed productivity, it became a subtreasury in 1874. Intact after the 1906 disaster, it served as a clearing house-bank, thus aiding in the city's reconstruction. Closed in 1937: Restored 1972-76 by Mint Director Mary Brooks."

Although the Old San Francisco Mint, its current official designation, continues to serve the United States Mint, some of its duties have been transferred to other facilities. Among the changes were the transfer of the Mint Data Center and consolidation of the Old San Francisco Mint with the San Francisco Mint

As this almanac was going to press in late June 1990, the Clifford-Kagin pioneer gold collection which had been on display at the Old Mint, was being removed from display over a dispute as to insurance liability..

Fort Knox Gold Bullion Depository

A large amount of the monetary gold stocks of the United States is stored in the vault of the Fort Knox Bullion Depository. The balance of the government's holdings is stored at the Denver Mint and the West Point Mint, with only small quantities stored at the Philadelphia Mint and the San Francisco Mint.

The Depository was completed in December 1936 at a cost of $560,000. It is located approximately 30 miles southwest of Louisville, Ky., on a site which formerly was a part of the Fort Knox military reservation. The first gold was moved to the Depository by railroad in January 1937. That series of shipments was completed in June 1937.

The two-story basement and attic building is constructed of granite, steel and concrete; exterior dimensions measure 105 by 121 feet. Its height is 42 feet above the first floor level. Construction was under supervision of the Procurement Division of the Treasury Department, now the Public Buildings Administration of the General Services Administration. Upon completion, the Depository was placed under the jurisdiction of the Director of the Mint.

Within the building is a two-level steel and concrete vault, divided into compartments. The vault door weighs more than 20 tons. No one person is entrusted with the combination. Various members of the Depository staff must separately dial combinations known only to them. The vault casing is constructed of steel plates, steel I-beams and steel cylinders laced with hoop bands and encased in concrete. The vault roof is of similar construction and is independent of the depository roof.

Between the corridor encircling the vault and the outer wall of the building is space utilized for offices, storerooms and the like.

The outer wall of the depository is of granite, lined with concrete. Included in the materials used in construction were

16,500 cubic feet of granite, 4,200 cubic yards of concrete, 750 tons of reinforcing steel and 670 tons of structural steel.

Over the marble entrance at the front of the building is the inscription "United States Depository" with the seal of the Treasury Department in gold. Offices of the Officer in Charge and the Captain of the Guard open upon the entrance lobby. At the rear of the building is another entrance for the reception of bullion and supplies.

At each corner of the structure, on the outside, but connected with it, are four guard boxes. Sentry boxes, similar to the guard boxes at the corners of the Depository, are located at the entrance gate. A driveway encircles the building and a steel fence marks the boundaries of the site.

The building is equipped with the latest and most modern protective devices. The nearby Army Post gives additional protection. The Depository is equipped with its own emergency power plant, water system and other facilities. In the basement is a pistol range for the guards.

The gold in the Depository is in the form of standard Mint bars of almost pure gold, or coin gold bars resulting from the melting of gold coins. These bars are slightly smaller than an ordinary building brick. The approximate dimensions are 7 x 3-5/8 x 1-3/4 inches. The fine gold bars contain approximately 400 troy ounces of gold. The avoirdupois weight is about 27.5 pounds. They are stored without wrappings in the vault compartments. When they are handled, great care is exercised to avoid abrasion of the soft metal.

While all of the physical gold stock is stored in the various institutions of the United States Mint, it is not, as sometimes supposed, "kept out of circulation." Most of it is made part of the money stream through the medium of gold certificates or gold certificate credits, which are issued only to the Federal Reserve Banks. The Federal Reserve Banks may obtain gold by redemption of the certificates when necessary for the settlement of international balances.

The guard force, under the supervision of the Officer in Charge, is made up of men selected from various government agencies, or recruited from Civil Service Registers.

Ordinarily, no visitors are allowed inside the Fort Knox Depository. Franklin D. Roosevelt visited there in 1943, the one and only time a gold vault was opened for inspection for anyone other than authorized personnel until Sept. 23, 1974.

On that date, a seven-man congressional inspection team and nearly 100 reporters toured the Depository for the first public check of the nation's gold hoard.

Rep. Philip M. Crane, R-Ill., started things off when he discussed a rumor with Treasury Secretary William Simon in mid-1974 that gold was missing from the vault.

To dispel any doubts that the gold was really there, Mint Director Mary Brooks conducted the Fort Knox inspection. A special audit followed the tour, conducted by the General Accounting Office and the Treasury. Provision has since been made by Congress for continuing audits by the Bureau of the Mint.

Secretary of the Treasury W. Michael Blumenthal paid his first visit to the Depository in July 1977, accompanied by Undersecretary of the Treasury Bette B. Anderson. This was the first visit to Fort Knox by a Secretary of the Treasury since John W. Snyder paid a call in 1947.

Director of the Mint Donna Pope paid a visit to the Depository in the summer of 1981. In June of 1985, James M. Curtis was appointed Officer in Charge of the Depository, replacing Eugene Kimbler as acting officer in charge. Curtis, formerly a Staff Inspector with the New York Police Department, retired from the NYPD after 23 years of service to take the Mint position.

West Point Bullion Depository, West Point Mint

Formerly the West Point Silver Bullion Depository, in New York, the facility serves as a fourth Mint of the United States, in addition to its status as the main storehouse of the nation's silver and the holder of one-quarter of the nation's gold supply.

The depository was completed at a cost of about $500,000 and occupied in 1938. It is a rectangular, windowless, one-story concrete building, 170 x 256 feet, situated on a four-acre tract of land formerly a part of the West Point Military Reservation. The building is within 500 feet of the Storm King Highway, near West Point's "Old North Gate."

Offices and guard rooms are on the first floor and mezzanine, at the front of the building, with entrance through a vestibule. Light and air for this section are obtained through skylights. The remainder of the structure is under a solid composition roof. A vertical-lift steel door in the center of the front affords passage for bullion trucks. With this door closed, complete isolation is provided for loading operations. To the rear of the loading platform are rolling steel doors and checking rooms through which the storage vault is reached. A series of vault compartments is guarded by a master vault door and an emergency door. The master vault door is equipped with a time lock, and is of drill-proof and flame-proof metal.

A nine-foot steel fence surrounds the building, with a steel gate controlled by guards that regulates the entrance and departure of persons and vehicles. The outside walls are of reinforced concrete. An inside corridor connects the four turrets or watchtowers at the corners, where sentries may observe the terrain in all directions. The depository's outside walls may be placed under floodlight.

Gold from the New York Assay Office began to arrive at the Depository Nov. 8, 1981, with the last shipment from the NYAO arriving Aug. 12, 1982. During that time, 25 convoys using 133 tractor-trailers transferred 193,782 gold bars weighing from 5 ounces to 125 pounds each. The total gross weight transferred was about 2,318 tons. Law enforcement officials cooperating in the move included U.S. Secret Service special agents, New York and New Jersey state police, and local law enforcement agencies. The U.S. Army assisted in security on arrival at the Depository.

Permission to use the Depository facilities to coin money was granted in the law providing for the Bicentennial coinage, signed Oct. 18, 1973. The section reads:

"Until the Secretary of the Treasury determines that the Mints of the United States are adequate for the production of ample supplies of coins and medals, any facility of the Bureau of the Mint may be used for the manufacture and storage of medals and coins."

Mint Director Mary Brooks announced in mid-1974 that some of the older Mint presses were being installed at West Point to produce coins and medals.

Twenty dual coin presses, some retired from the Philadelphia Mint, were installed. Ten began operations in November 1974, and the others began operations in early 1975.

Following the end of the Bicentennial program, the West Point facility continued to produce cents on its coin presses. In late 1976, it began test striking quarters. In 1975 and again in May 1977 it also produced bronze 1-centesimo coins for Panama.

At first, no West Point-struck coins bore Mint marks. That changed on Sept. 13, 1983, when the ceremonial first 1984 Olympic $10 gold eagles were struck, each bearing a W Mint mark. The Proof and Uncirculated versions of the Statue of Liberty gold half eagles, which were struck at West Point in 1986, also bear a W Mint mark.

All of the American Arts Gold Medallions were also struck at West Point. Gold commemorative coins and American Eagle gold bullion coins are also struck at West Point.

Public Law 100-274, approved March 31, 1988, gave official Mint status to the West Point coining facility, along with the San Francisco Mint.

Former Mint institutions

Charlotte, North Carolina

The discovery of gold in the southern Appalachian Mountains and the unearthing of large quantities of the precious metal presented a major problem for prospectors in that then-inaccessible region of the nation, in the 1820s.

Miners, once they had recovered the gold, were faced with a long trip to the Philadelphia Mint to have their finds smelted and struck into gold coins. The infant industry soon sought relief from Washington, D.C.

When the demands for a local Mint were not met by the federal government, a German immigrant named Christian Bechtler established a private Mint at Rutherfordton, N.C., in 1831. Seeing a potentially large supply of gold being diverted away from government control inspired Congress to authorize the Charlotte Mint in 1835.

The building and equipment were budgeted at $50,000, but the costs overran this figure and the opponents of a branch Mint tried to use this to stop the construction. The Mint opened on July 27, 1837, for the assaying and processing of gold, but no coins were struck until the following year.

Like the Dahlonega Mint in Georgia, the Charlotte facility struck only gold coins. Its production was limited to half eagles, quarter eagles and dollars, with a more even distribution of the three than at Dahlonega.

Production was halted for a year and a half, until 1846, after a fire damaged the building on the night of July 27, 1844. The fire has been attributed to a burglar who was either careless or malicious.

The branch Mints were considered by the Philadelphia Mint to be poor stepsisters, and they consequently received the worst equipment. Worn-out presses received repairs when they should have received a decent burial, and rusted reverse dies unfit for duty in Philadelphia

were Mint-marked and shipped south. One redeeming feature of this practice is that it is hard to convincingly alter a Philadelphia coin to one from a scarcer Mint, because the resulting fake will be literally too good to be true.

During the 1850s production at the Charlotte Mint became increasingly irregular, as the local gold supplies dried up and were not replaced by California bullion. Half eagles were the only denomination consistently struck during this decade.

Throughout the entire period of Federal control the Charlotte Mint struck a total of $5,059,188 worth of gold coin. This compares with $4,084,773 worth of gold coin struck in San Francisco in 1854 alone, and $18,008,300 struck there the following year.

The Mint struck 5,992 half eagles in 1861 before it was seized by the Confederate forces on April 20, and 887 pieces afterward. A quantity of bullion remained uncoined, either because of technical difficulties or because the bullion value of the gold was greater than the face value of the coins that could have been made from it.

It is a tribute to the dedication of bureaucrats everywhere that somebody in the then Confederate Mint in October 1861 sent to Philadelphia 12 half eagles that had been struck under the Federal government in early 1861 and had been set aside for assay purposes. Millions of dollars' worth of Federal property had been seized by the Confederacy, and yet somebody was more concerned with the integrity of the Charlotte Mint than the Confederate Treasury.

Throughout the remainder of the Civil War the building was used for office space by the Confederate armed forces. After the war it was occupied for a while by officials of the Union army, and eventually it was restored to the status of an Assay Office.

In 1935, one century after the

authorization of the Mint, it was decided to tear the building down to make room for a new post office building. A local citizens' group purchased the materials and reconstructed the building on a new site, where it now serves as an art museum.

Dahlonega, Georgia

The Dahlonega Mint was opened in 1838 to accommodate the gold miners of northern Georgia, and to help the Charlotte Mint compete with the private Bechtler Mint doing business in North Carolina.

The area of northern Georgia had been a part of the Cherokee nation, but it was obtained in 1830 in exchange for lands in Oklahoma. The name of the town is taken from the Indian word Tah-lon-e-ka, which means "yellow metal."

Gold had been known in small quantities in this area for many years by the Indians and the white men, but the first large strike did not occur until the 1820s. The exact year is uncertain, but there are many colorful tales describing the first major find.

The most popular story is that a running deer kicked up a nugget which was spotted by the pursuing hunter. History does not record the name of the hunter or the fate of the deer.

Throughout its existence the Dahlonega Mint struck gold coins exclusively. The most common denomination produced was the half eagle, with only token coinages of quarter eagles and dollars.

In 1854, the Mint produced its only issue of $3 pieces. Presumably this denomination was less popular in the South than it was in the North, as the New Orleans Mint also struck it in just this first year, and the Charlotte Mint never did. Only 1,120 pieces were struck at Dahlonega.

Although all Dahlonega gold coins bear the name of the United States of America, this legend did not always apply. In 1861 the Confederate States of America confiscated all Federal property within its boundaries, including the three branch Mints in the South. The Dahlonega Mint was placed under the management of the governor of Georgia.

Unlike the New Orleans Mint, there was little bullion on hand at the Dahlonega and Charlotte Mints at the commencement of hostilities. The Dahlonega Mint is thought to have contained $13,345 worth of uncoined gold when it was seized on April 8, 1861, but the official records were never recovered after the Civil War.

The small quantity of 1861-D dollars in existence must have been struck under either Confederate or Georgian authority, as the U.S. Mint Report lists no dollars for this date and Mint. It is thought that a number of half eagles may also have been produced, and poorly struck pieces are often attributed to this alleged striking. As the Mint did produce half eagles under Federal auspices in this year, and as it had never been known for its fine workmanship, it is impossible to state with certainty who produced any particular piece.

The small amount of bullion remaining on hand was not struck into coins for a number of reasons, mainly because of technical problems and the lack of die-making facilities. Late in the war the Mint served as a temporary repository for the Confederate Treasury, before the city was overrun.

The Dahlonega and Charlotte Mints were considered by many to have been redundant ever since the opening of the San Francisco Mint, and there were proposals to close them even before the Civil War. The Dahlonega Mint never reopened after the war, and its building was donated to the state of Georgia for educational purposes.

The structure was reopened as the main building of North Georgia College in 1873, but it was destroyed by fire in 1878. Price Memorial Hall was built on its foundation the following year and occupied in 1880. It stands today as the administration building for the college, and houses a complete set of Dahlonega Mint gold coins, assembled by H.A. Alexander, an Atlanta lawyer.

The "golden heritage" of the area is attested to by a large plaque, erected in connection with "Project Golden Steeple," through which Price Memorial Hall's steeple was leafed with native gold donated for the purpose.

Carson City, Nevada

The bill to establish a branch Mint in Nevada was passed on March 3, 1863. It was urged in the Senate that the heavy tax of transportation cost upon producers in Nevada, the wonderful increase of gold and silver bullion and the necessity of keeping it in the United States through coinage, were to be considered sufficient inducements for Congress to order the establishment of a Mint.

Hugh McCulloch, U.S. Secretary of the Treasury, on Dec. 27, 1865, authorized a committee of three Nevada citizens to select and approve a location for a Mint in Carson City. The committee included Abe Curry (founder of Carson City), F. Rice and John Mills. Curry facilitated the work of the commissioners by donating an entire city block as the Mint site.

On July 18, 1866, the three commissioners received authority to proceed with the construction of the Mint. On Sept. 18, 1866, the cornerstone was dedicated and laid by the Grand Masonic Lodge of Nevada.

The Director's Report for 1866 carried the following item: ". . . This building is in rapid process of erection. It is of good size, sixty by ninety feet, of two stories, built of a good quality of sandstone, and is exceedingly well arranged. It is located upon a large and handsome lot of ground, entirely disconnected from other buildings. . . .

"As the mines of Nevada are almost entirely silver, and as the exportation of silver is almost wholly in bars, there being very little demand for silver coin, it will be inexpedient to introduce machinery for coinage into this institution at present. . . ."

All of 1868 and most of 1869 were spent installing machinery and fixtures and it was not until December of 1869 that the fitting of the branch Mint at Carson City for business as a Mint was completed. On Jan. 8, 1870, it was opened for the receipt of bullion.

On Nov. 6, 1885, it was directed that the Mint be closed, except for the receipt of bullion for "parting and refining" and local purchases of silver for the standard dollar coinage. The Mint remained closed to the receipt of deposits until Oct. 1, 1886. Under the usual provision for the Mint at Carson City in the legislative appropriation act for the year, it was reopened for deposits as an Assay Office, with an acid refinery.

The coinage department of the Mint was reopened July 1, 1889, but owing to the dilapidated condition in which the building and machinery were found, after four years of idleness, repairs and betterments of the building and overhauling and repairing of the machinery were necessary. Consequently, coinage of gold and silver was not commenced until Oct. 1, 1889.

Coinage operations continued until 1893 when, by direction of the Secretary of the Treasury, they were suspended, effective June 1, and the force employed in the coiner's department dispensed with.

Upon suspension of coinage operations, the presses and other machinery used in the coining department were painted and leaded under the supervision of Charles Colburn, the retiring coiner, to prevent corrosion.

From July 1 to Nov. 14, 1898, the Mint was open to the receipt of gold and silver deposits. Following this came the order of the Secretary of the Treasury reducing the Mint to an Assay Office, to take effect July 1, 1899, as authorized by an Act of Congress approved Feb. 24, 1899.

A steadily decreasing volume of work resulted in the final closing of the Carson City Mint. No appropriation having been provided for its maintenance, operations ceased June 30, 1933. The property then passed out of the custody of the Mint Service but remained under government control until legislation approved May 22, 1939, authorized the sale of the property. It is now owned by the state of Nevada and a museum is operated on the premises.

Contained in the museum is the original Carson City dollar press. The old press was used to strike the official Nevada 1976 Bicentennial medals.

The state Bicentennial commission paid approximately $29,000 to get the press into operation once again. It was built originally in the Virginia and Truckee Railroad shops in Carson City.

The press is to be continued for automated use as a revenue source.

The museum, in addition to housing the Carson City dollar press, also possesses the original 1876 Nevada U.S. Centennial medal die. This was used to strike the state Bicentennial medal.

New Orleans, Louisiana

The Act of Congress approved March 3, 1835, established a branch Mint at New Orleans, and for that purpose the mayor and city council offered to deed to the United States government a portion of ground bounded by Esplanade, Barracks Street and Bayou Road, which was surrounded by a moat, and formerly known as old Fort St. Charles.

"On the 19th of June 1835 the municipal authorities of the city of New Orleans conveyed to the United States, . . . a certain piece . . . of land situated in the City of New Orleans, known as "Jackson Square,' immediately fronting the river Mississippi, for the express purpose of erecting thereon a branch of the Mint of the United States . . ."

By this liberal and patriotic act, the United States became possessed of one of the most valuable squares of ground in the city, without any cost to the government. The value of this donation has been estimated at a little less than $500,000.

In consideration for deeding this ground it was agreed that a building should be erected thereon for minting purposes, and should it happen in the future that this Mint cease to operate, the title of the property would revert back to the city.

The Mint building was erected under the supervision of William Strickland, the architect who drew the plans. The cornerstone of the original building, an edifice 280 feet long and three stories high, was laid in September 1835. Due to

sickness and other delays, the work was not completed until 1838; operations commenced March 8, 1838. It is presumed since legislation authorizing Mints at Charlotte, N.C., and Dahlonega, Ga., for the coinage of gold was passed at the same time, that the New Orleans Mint was meant to handle, along with the other two, the influx of metal from recently opened mines in the Southern region. The first coinage consisted of dimes, in the sum of $40,242.00; this was the total coinage for 1838.

The Mint suspended operations in 1839, from July 1 until Nov. 30, because of an outbreak of yellow fever, which is said to have been one of the worst scourges the city has ever known.

At the beginning, the machinery used for minting purposes was run by hand, and it was not until 1845 that the first steam boiler and steam press were used in New Orleans. Coinage operations continued until Jan. 31, 1861, when the Mint was taken over by the state of Louisiana and all operations were carried on by it with the same officers who functioned under the United States. On March 31, it was again taken over, this time by the Confederate States of America, in whose custody it continued until it was closed on May 31 of that year. According to old records, there was in the vaults at that time more than $200,000 in bullion, which was coined by the Confederate forces, and a good portion of the machinery was later taken from the Mint by the Confederates and transferred to various gun factories in the state.

Acting under orders of Secretary of the Treasury Salmon P. Chase, Dr. M.F. Bonzano, Melter and Refiner at New Orleans, returned to that city from the North, whence he had gone during the war, and took possession of the Mint and its property following recapture of the city May 1, 1862.

During the war much of the machinery had been damaged and otherwise rendered ineffective by disuse and other causes incident to the war. Extensive repairs, besides additional machinery, were required before coinage operations could be resumed. In 1874, John Jay Knox, then Deputy Comptroller of the Currency, said that it was not probable that coinage would ever again be necessary in New Orleans and that the Mint at Philadelphia had sufficient capacity for all coinage requirements. However, after a period of inactivity, the New Orleans Mint reopened its doors Oct. 23, 1876, as an Assay Office.

Because the provisions of the original land grant were not being followed, and no coins were being manufactured, the United States marshal, a Mr. Packard, proposed on July 28, 1876, that the Mint be seized for the state of Louisiana, on the grounds that it was not being used as a Mint. No action was taken, however, for the Mint continued in the capacity of an Assay Office until 1879, when coinage operations were resumed.

In connection with the reopening of the New Orleans Mint, the Annual Report of the Director of the Mint for 1878 contains the following:

"The Act of Congress making appropriation for the Mint at New Orleans provided that no expenditure of money should be made for that Mint until the city should release all title and claim and all conditions of forfeiture to the lands or premises upon which the Mint is located, and negotiations looking to that effect were entered into with the city authorities, which resulted in the square of ground being deeded in fee-simple to the government."

In the early days, the officers were housed in the Mint, and an old record book contains an entry to the effect that "Dr. Bonzano moved his residence from the Mint to his plantation . . ." In 1884, all persons still maintaining living quarters in the building were informed by the Director that they must move out by Aug. 1 of that year.

Coinage operations continued uninterrupted from 1879 to 1909, at which time they were discontinued because it was felt that facilities at the more modern Denver and San Francisco Mints were adequate to handle the demand. From 1909 to 1919, the building was used exclusively as an Assay Office. The Veterans Bureau was granted permission to occupy a portion of the space, remaining for one year, during 1919. Beginning in 1922, the Veterans Bureau Dispensary was housed in the Mint and continued there for a number of years. The building was vacated June 30, 1931, and the Assay Office activities transferred to space in the customhouse, where operations were continued until June 30, 1942, when they ceased for good.

In 1966, the federal government presented the Mint building to Louisiana with the understanding that the state would provide face-lifting funds and renovation work would be completed in 10 years.

The Louisiana legislature faced a deadline in 1976 on the proposed appropriation of $3.5 million to the state's museum board for the restoration of the New Orleans Mint.

In 1976, the state was given four more years of grace by the federal government in which to renovate the Old Mint.

Meanwhile, in April 1976 a numismatic exhibit sponsored by the Orleans Token and Medal Society was installed in the Old Mint which was opened to the public on an extended basis by the New Orleans Bicentennial Commission.

A set of "O" Mint coins represented the first of several exhibits planned by OTAMS on both concurrent and alternating bases.

State plans to renovate the New Orleans Mint, however, came to a temporary halt on May 27, 1976, because of a Louisiana state supreme court ruling that tidelands revenues received from the federal government could not be used at this time. The Louisiana state museum board had counted on this funding to develop the Mint restoration.

Exactly one year later on May 27, 1977, Gov. Edwin W. Edwards of Louisiana told state legislators he agreed to support amendments to bond bills to provide the full $3.5 million necessary to restore the Old Mint in New Orleans.

Plans for the restoration called for

leasing part of the space in the Mint for private business, such as curio shops and restaurants, developing an area for media presentations for tourists, plus creating an auditorium and museum library on the third floor of the building.

The capital outlay bill, which included funds for the Mint restoration, was signed into law July 14 by Gov. Edwards. The bill was divided into cash and bond portions and included other construction projects besides the Mint restoration.

The restoration process began in 1977, with the majority of the work being done in 1979. The interior and exterior of the building were restored to their mid-1850s appearance, and a new roof was erected.

The third floor of the Mint houses the Louisiana Historical Center, including the museum's 40,000-volume library concerning the history of Louisiana. Also on the third floor is the Amistad Research Center, a 2-million volume library about minorities in the United States.

Louisiana state budget cuts in 1989 threatened to close the doors of the museum.

Former Assay Offices

U.S. Assay Office, St. Louis, Mo., authorized by the Act of Feb. 1, 1881; opened July 1, 1881; closed June 30, 1911.

U.S. Assay Office, Helena, Mont., authorized by the Act of May 12, 1874; commenced operations Jan. 15, 1877; closed June 30, 1933.

U.S. Assay Office, Salt Lake City, Utah, authorized by the Act of May 30, 1908; opened Feb. 1, 1909; closed June 30, 1933.

U.S. Assay Office, Deadwood, S.D., established by the Acts of June 11, 1896, and Feb. 19, 1897; opened April 20, 1898; closed June 30, 1927.

U.S. Assay Office, Boise, Idaho, established by the Act of Feb. 19, 1869, first deposits received in March of 1872; closed June 30, 1933.

U.S. Assay Office, Seattle, Wash., authorized by the Act of May 21, 1898; closed March 31, 1955.

U.S. Assay Office, New York, N.Y., authorized by Act of March 3, 1853; commenced operation Oct. 10, 1854; closed Dec. 30, 1982.

Source: United States Mint

Directors of the U.S. Mint, 1792-1987

The Director of the Mint is appointed by the President of the United States, by and with the advice and consent of the Senate. The length of the term of office was not fixed by law from 1792 to 1873. The Act of February 12, 1873, fixed the term of the Director at five years. However, there is no restriction on the reappointment of Directors.

Director	Term of service
David Rittenhouse, Pennsylvania	April 1792-June 1795
Henry William de Saussure, South Carolina	July 1795-October 1795
Elias Boudinot, New Jersey	October 1795-July 1805
Robert Patterson, Pennsylvania	January 1806-July 1824
Samuel Moore, Pennsylvania	July 1824-July 1835
Robert Maskell Patterson, Pennsylvania	July 1835-July 1851
George N. Eckert, Pennsylvania	July 1851-April 1853
Thomas M. Pettit, Pennsylvania	April 1853-May 1853
James Ross Snowden, Pennsylvania	June 1853-April 1861
James Pollock, Pennsylvania	May 1861-September 1866
William Millward, Pennsylvania	October 1866-April 1867
Henry Richard Linderman, Pennsylvania	April 1867-April 1869
James Pollock, Pennsylvania	May 1869-March 1873
Henry Richard Linderman, Pennsylvania	April 1873-December 1878

Horatio C. Burchard, Illinois .... February 1879-June 1885
James P. Kimball, Pennsylvania.................................... July 1885-October 1889
Edward O. Leech, District of Columbia......................... October 1889-May 1893
Robert E. Preston, District of Columbia......................... November 1893-Feb. 1898
George E. Roberts, Iowa.. February 1898-July 1907
Frank A. Leach, California.. September 1907-Nov. 1909
A. Piatt Andrew, Massachusetts..................................... November 1909-June 1910
George E. Roberts, Iowa.. July 1910-November 1914
Robert W. Wooley, Virginia... March 1915-July 1916
F.J.H. von Engelken, Florida..September 1916-Feb. 1917
Raymond T. Baker, Nevada .... March 1917-March 1922
F.E. Scobey, Ohio.. March 1922-September 1923
Robert J. Grant, Colorado... November 1923-May 1933
Nellie Tayloe Ross, Wyoming.. May 1933-April 1953
William H. Brett, Ohio.. July 1954-January 1961
Eva Adams, Nevada.. October 1961-August 1969
Mary Brooks, Idaho... September 1969-February 1977
Stella Hackel Sims, Vermont.. November 1977-April 1981
Donna Pope, Ohio .... July 1981-present

Mint Superintendents

It was 80 years from the time David Rittenhouse took over as first director of the U.S. Mint until future directors were given an "assistant" via the office of the superintendent.

The Coinage Act of 1873 put all Mint and assay office activities under the newly-organized Bureau of the Mint in the Department of the Treasury and the director's headquarters were moved to the Treasury Building in Washington, D.C. The top officer at Philadelphia was thereafter designated as superintendent.

Philadelphia

Superintendents, their term of service, and the name of the Mint director(s) at the time of their service, include:

Superintendent	Mint Director(s)	Term
James Pollock	Henry R. Linderman	1873-1879
Col. A. Loudon Snowden	Horatio C. Burchard	1879-1885
Daniel M. Fox	James P. Kimball	1885-1889
Col. O.C. Bosbyshell	Edward O. Leech, Robert E. Preston	1889-1894
Dr. Eugene Townsend	Robert E. Preston	1894-1895
Maj. Herman Kretz	Robert E. Preston	1895-1898
Henry Boyer	George E. Roberts	1898-1902
John H. Landis	George E. Roberts, Frank A. Leach, A. Piatt Andrews, George E. Roberts	1902-1914
Adam M. Joyce	R.W. Woolley, F.J.H. von Engelken, Raymond T. Baker	1914-1921
Freas Styer	Raymond Baker, F.E. Scobey, R.S. Grant, Nellie T. Ross	1921-1934
A. Raymond Raff	Nellie Tayloe Ross	1934-1935
Edward H. Dressel	Nellie Tayloe Ross	1935-1953
Rae V. Biester	William H. Brett	1953-1961
Michael H. Sura	Eva Adams	1961-1969
Nicholas G. Theodore	Eva Adams, Mary Brooks, Stella Hackel	1969-1977
Shallie M. Bey Jr.	Stella Hackel Sims	1978-1981

Anthony H. Murray Jr. .... Donna Pope...................................... 1981- July 29, 1988
John T. Martino..................... Donna Pope.................................... Oct. 16, 1989 -present

Denver
Superintendent	Term
Frank M. Downer	Oct. 15, 1904-Aug. 29, 1913
Thomas Annear	Aug. 29, 1913-July 1, 1921
Robert J. Grant	July 1, 1921-Nov. 12, 1923
Frank E. Shepard	Nov. 25, 1923-June 30, 1933
Mark A. Skinner	June 16, 1933-Dec. 1, 1942
Moses E. Smith	April 1, 1943-April 5, 1952
Gladys P. Morelock	Aug. 1, 1952-Feb. 8, 1953
Alma K. Schneider	Feb. 9, 1953-May 18, 1961
Fern V. Miller	May 19, 1961-July 31, 1967
Marian N. Rossmiller	Aug. 1, 1967-March 20, 1969
Betty Higby	March 21, 1969-March 18, 1978
Evelyn Davidson	March 20, 1978-Aug. 14, 1981
Nora Hussey	Aug. 9, 1981- July 31, 1987
Cynthia Grassby Baker	Jan. 28, 1988 - May 5, 1989
Barbara McTurk	Oct. 27, 1989 - present

San Francisco
Superintendent	Term
L. A. Birdsall	June 30, 1853-June 29, 1855
P.G. Lott	June 30, 1855-June 29, 1857
C.H. Hempstead	June 30, 1857-June 29,1861
R.J. Stevens	June 30, 1861-June 29, 1863
R.B. Swain	June 30, 1863-July 31, 1869
A.H. La Grange	Aug. 1, 1869-Dec. 31, 1877
H.L. Dodge	Jan. 1, 1878-June 30, 1882
E.F. Burton	July 1, 1882-July 31, 1885
I. Lawton	Aug. 1, 1885-July 31, 1889
W.H. Diamond	Aug. 1, 1889-July 31, 1893
J. Daggett	Aug. 1, 1893-July 31, 1897
F.A. Leach	Aug. 1, 1897-Sept. 18, 1907
E. Sweeney	Sept. 19, 1907-Aug. 17, 1912
F.A. Leach	Aug. 23, 1912-Aug. 15, 1913
T. W. Shanahan	Aug. 16, 1913-June 30, 1921
M. J. Kelly	July 1, 1921-June 30, 1933
P. J. Haggerty	July 1, 1933-Dec. 31, 1944
N. H. Callaghan	June 1, 1945-Nov. 4, 1947
G. B. Gillin	July 1, 1948-Nov. 30, 1951
J. P. McEnery	June 1, 1952-Nov. 5, 1952
R. P. Buell	July 1, 1953-June 30, 1955
A. C. Carmichael	July 1, 1955-July 31, 1958

OFFICER IN CHARGE, U.S. ASSAY OFFICE
J. R. Carr	Aug. 1, 1958-Oct. 1968
John F. Brekle	Oct. 1968-June 30, 1972
Bland T. Brockenborough	Aug. 20, 1972-Nov. 15, 1980
Thomas H. Miller	Nov. 30, 1980-March 31, 1988

SUPERINTENDENT, U.S. MINT
Carol Mayer Marshall	March 27, 1990 -present

West Point

Superintendent	Term
Clifford M. Barber	March 31, 1988 - present*

*As this almanac was going to press in late June 1990, the White House had announced intention to nominate Bert W. Corneby as West Point Mint Superintendent.

Charlotte

Superintendent	Term
John Hill Wheeler	Jan. 19, 1837 - July 1841
Burgess Sidney Gaither	July 1841-1844
Greene Washington Caldwell	1844-1846
William Julius Alexander	1846-1849
James Walker Osborne	1849-1853
Greene Washington Caldwell	1853-April 20, 1861*

OFFICER IN CHARGE, U.S. ASSAY OFFICE

Isaac W. Jones	1867-1869
Calvin Josiah Cowles	1869-1885
Robert P. Waring	1885-1889
Stuart Warren Cramer	1889-1893
W.E. Ardrey	1893-1897
W.S. Clanton	1897-1903
D. Kirby Pope	1903-1908
William S. Pearson	1908-1911
Frank Parker Drane	1911-1913

The Charlotte Assay Office was closed June 30, 1913.

*On April 20, 1861, the Charlotte Mint was seized by Confederate forces, who continued coining operations until May 20, 1861. The Mint was officially closed May 31, 1861. An Assay Office was authorized by an Act of the Confederate Congress approved Aug. 24, 1861, and Dr. J.H. Gibbon received appointment as Assayer. In May 1862, the facility was turned over to the Confederate Navy Department. Following the war, it was reopened as a U. S. Assay Office March 19, 1867.

Carson City

Superintendent	Term
Abraham Curry	Jan. 1870-Sept. 1870
H.F. Rice	Sept. 1870-May 1873
Frank D. Hetrich	May 1873-Aug. 1875
James Crawford	Sept. 1875-March 8, 1885
Theodore R. Hofer	(temporary superintendent)
William Garrard	March 18, 1885-June 30, 1889
Samuel Coleman Wright	July 1, 1889-Aug. 1, 1892
Theodore R. Hofer	Aug. 6, 1892-May 20, 1894
Jewett W. Adams	May 20, 1894-Sept. 1898
Roswell K. Colcord	Sept. 1898-July 1, 1899

The Carson City Mint became an Assay Office effective July 1, 1899.

Dahlonega

Superintendent	Term
Joseph J. Singleton	Jan., 1837-April, 1841
Paul Rossignol	April, 1841-May, 1843
James F. Cooper	May, 1843-Sept., 1849

Anderson W. Redding.. Sept., 1849-June, 1853
Julius M. Patton.. June, 1853-Sept., 1860
George Kellogg.. Oct. 1860-?

Coiner
David H. Mason... March, 1837-Aug., 1848
John D. Field, Jr. .... Sept., 1848-Nov., 1849
Robert H. Moore.. Nov., 1849-May, 1853
John D. Field, Jr. .... May, 1853-?

Assayer
Joseph W. Farnum.. Feb., 1837-May, 1843
Isaac L. Todd... May, 1843-Dec. 1850
M.F. Stephenson... Dec., 1850-May, 1853
Isaac L. Todd.. May, 1853-?

The Dahlonega Mint was seized by Confederate forces April 8, 1861; continued in operation until May 14, 1861; and officially closed May 31, 1861. An Act of the Confederate Congress, approved Aug. 24, 1861, authorized the opening of an Assay Office and Lewis W. Quillian was appointed Assayer.

New Orleans

Superintendent	Term
David Bradford	1837-1839
Joseph M. Kennedy	Oct. 18, 1839-Sept. 1850
Robert M. McAlpine	1850-May 13, 1853
Charles Bienvenu	1853-Dec. 31, 1857
Logan McNight	Jan. 1, 1858-May 8, 1858
John H. Alpuente (acting)	May 8, 1858-May 25, 1858
Howard Millspaugh (acting)	May 25, 1858-July 9, 1858
William A. Elmore	July 9, 1858-Jan. 30, 1861*
M.F. Bonzano (Assayer in Charge)	1874-1875
M.F. Bonzano (Custodian)	1875-1876
M.F. Bonzano (Assayer in Charge and Superintendent)	1876-1877
M.F. Bonzano (Assayer in Charge)	1877-1878
Michael Hahn	1878-Dec. 28, 1878
Henry S. Foote	Dec. 28, 1878-May 19, 1880
Martin V. Davis	June 11, 1880-1882
A.W. Smyth	Aug. 15, 1882-June 24, 1885
Gabriel Montegut	June 24, 1885-1893
Overton Cade	1893-1898
Charles W. Boothby	1898-99(?)-1902
Hugh S. Sithon	1902-1911
William M. Lynch	1911-1914
Leonard Magruder	1914-1932
Cecil Grey	1932-1933
Hugh T. Rippeto	1933-1941
Charles M. Miller	April 21, 1941-June 30, 1942

The New Orleans Mint closed June 30, 1942.

*The State of Louisiana took possession of the Mint Jan. 31, 1861, and carried on all the operations with the same officers as under the U.S. until March 31. The Confederate States of America took possession April 1 and continued with the same officers and men. Operations were suspended May 14, 1861, and the facility was closed May 31, 1861. An Assay Office was established by an Act of the Confederate Congress approved Jan. 27,

1862. The facility reverted to federal control following the recapture of the city May 1, 1862, and M.F. Bonzano, under orders of Secretary of the Treasury Salmon P. Chase, dated May 16, 1862, returned to New Orleans and took possession of the Mint and its property.

Chief Engravers

President George Washington, as fitting for the first president of the United States, had the honor in August 1793 of appointing the man who was to become the first Engraver of the United States Mint — Joseph Wright.

Although Wright (1756—1793), a native of Bordentown, N.J., and a portrait painter, never lived to see his appointment become official, Coin World and many numismatic scholars count him as the first Engraver because he was the first to serve in that capacity. However, because his appointment was never official, the Mint considers his successor the first Engraver, or as the title is known today, Chief Sculptor—Engraver.

Wright was first appointed as a draughtsman and later became the first designer and die—sinker at the newly—formed Mint. He made the dies of a medal honoring George Washington, the bust on the obverse of which was considered to be the best medallic profile likeness of Washington. Wright also made the medal honoring Maj. Henry Lee which was authorized by Congress Sept. 24, 1779. The medal was for the Battle of Paulus Hook.

Wright is also believed to have designed the Liberty Cap cent struck on the thick cent planchets between 1793—95, and to have engraved the 1793 Liberty Cap cent.

However, before Wright's official appointment as engraver of the Mint could take place, he died of yellow fever in September 1793. On Nov. 6, 1793, Thomas Jefferson reportedly wrote a letter suggesting that David Rittenhouse, the first Director of the U.S. Mint, recommend an engraver to replace Wright.

Robert Scot

At the time of Wright's death, Henry Voight (also spelled Voigt), acting Chief Coiner and Superintendent, filled in for a few months before a replacement was found. He continued to make the dies used by the Mint until the appointment of Robert Scot. Voight held the office of Chief Coiner until his death in February 1814. Voight is credited with the nation's first coins and the production of the Washington half dismes and silver-center cents of 1792.

According to the Mint's records, it is believed that Rittenhouse recommended Scot to be the first official Chief Engraver. On Nov. 23, 1793, Scot received a letter from Jefferson advising him of his appointment and enclosing his commission signed by Washington.

There is very little known of Scot, except that he was sometimes confused with the Scottish bank note engraver of the same name. What is known comes from Foster Wild Rice's book, Antecedents of the American Bank Note Company of 1858, which states Scot, born in England, came to Philadelphia about 1783 and engraved for Dodson's edition of Ree's Encyclopedia from 1794 to 1803.

The length of Scot's term as Chief Engraver varies depending on which source is checked. In Frank Stewart's book, First United States Mint, Scot reportedly served until Nov. 1, 1823, and Leonard Forrer, in his Biographical Dictionary of Medalists, says Scot served until January 1824. However, it is believed that Scot died in November 1823.

William Kneass

The third man to become Chief Engraver, William Kneass (1781—1840), was appointed to the position Jan. 28, 1824, with a salary of $2,000 a year. Little is known about Kneass's early life or training, except he was born in Lancaster, Pa. He became famous as an engraver in

Philadelphia in 1815 with studios located on Fourth Street near Chestnut. His studio was well known as a rendezvous for many prominent Philadelphians. Most researchers say a friend, Adam Eckfeldt, the Chief Coiner at that time, was most responsible for his appointment. Kneass had been chiefly a plate engraver for bookwork before his appointment as Chief Engraver.

During his term as Chief Engraver there were some notable changes in coinage, as in 1834 and 1838 for gold, and 1836, 1838 and 1840 for silver, although some of this work was done by Christian Gobrecht, an Assistant Engraver at the Mint. He is also credited with a pattern half dollar dated 1838.

Christian Gobrecht

Kneass died in office Aug. 27, 1840. His successor was his assistant, Christian Gobrecht, who, although he was Chief Engraver for only three years and eight months, left behind many mementos of his work. Gobrecht designed pattern coins and regular-issue coins. He is probably best known for his designing of the famous silver dollars of 1836, 1838 and 1839, generally called Gobrecht dollars, although his work in medallic art is also famous.

Gobrecht was born in Hanover, Pa., in 1785 and exhibited mechanical ability and a talent for drawing and design at an early age, according to a December 1911 article in The Numismatist. He began his working years as an apprentice to a clockmaker. After spending several years in the trade he turned to engraving.

Gobrecht began small, cutting headlines for newspapers and punches for type founders. He later became a writer and seal engraver. In 1811, Gobrecht moved to Philadelphia where he continued to supply portrait plates for publishers while becoming established as an engraver and diesinker for medals.

In 1816 he began working for Murray, Draper, Fairman and Co., bank note engravers. Within 10 years he had furnished designs and models of dies to the U.S. Mint in Philadelphia. Among his better known dies and medals at this time were the Franklin Institute medal of 1825 based on a design by Thomas Sully; a portrait medal of Charles Wilson Peale; a portrait medal of Charles Carroll of Carrollton; the seal of St. Peter's Church, Philadelphia; and award medals for the New England Society for the Promotion of Manufactures and the Massachusetts Charitable Merchants Association and the Seal of Pennsylvania Hospital.

In 1836, Gobrecht was appointed draughtsman and diesinker to the U.S. Mint and Kneass' assistant. After Kneass' death, Gobrecht held the position of Chief Engraver until his death July 23, 1844. Coins he designed include the famous dollars of 1836, 1838 and 1839 and several varieties of half dollars of that period. His obverse design of one of the dollars, with stars around a seated figure of Liberty, was retained as the regular device in 1840 (although a new reverse was selected) and was used on the dollar until 1873 when the denomination was abandoned briefly.

When the first 1836 silver dollars were struck, Gobrecht's name appeared in the field between the base and the date. Because he received much criticism for doing this, his name was removed, but later in the year it was added on the base by the order of Mint Director Robert Patterson.

Gobrecht's obverse design was continued on the half dollar, quarter dollar, dime and half dime. The first three designs being used until 1892, when the new Barber designs were adopted. Gobrecht also produced six varieties of large cents.

James Barton Longacre

James Barton Longacre succeeded Gobrecht as Chief Engraver Sept. 6, 1844. He was born in Delaware County, Pa., in 1794 and as a young man he was an apprentice in a bookstore in Philadelphia. He later studied under George Murray of Philadelphia who taught him engraving. While serving his apprenticeship, Longacre did some high—class plate work before he became free of his apprenticeship in 1834. His earliest known work is in the S.F. Bradford Encyclopedia.

There are no records of Longacre ever serving as an Assistant Engraver at the U.S. Mint. He was hired specifically as the Chief Engraver. Among the coins designed by Longacre are the Flying Eagle cent, Indian Head cent, the 2-cent coin, both 3-cent coins, Shield 5-cent coin, all three gold dollars, the $3 gold coin and the Coronet double eagle. In 1867, Longacre completely remodeled the coinage of the Republic of Chile.

Two of Longacre's coins were known to have caused some controversy, the Coronet double eagle and the Flying Eagle cent, but the criticism was minor and ignored by Longacre. But when the design and execution of the designs were criticized, he reportedly became upset, according to various Mint scholars' research.

Although Longacre spent 25 years as Chief Engraver, he only designed two medals, the reverse of the medal awarded to Capt. Ingrahm, the obverse of which was done by P.F. Cross, one of his assistants. Longacre also designed the 1860 Assay Commission medal.

In 1928 Longacre's work was represented in the exhibition of the 100 notable American engravers held in the New York Public Library. Longacre's hiring of William Barber in 1865 as an Assistant Engraver paved the way for the first of two Barbers to occupy the position of Chief Engraver. But that did not come until after Longacre's death Jan. 1, 1879.

William Barber

William Barber (1807—1879) was appointed Chief Engraver shortly after James B. Longacre's death and served in that post until his death Aug. 31, 1879. Although he is one of the most well-known Mint Engravers who did much original work on pattern coins, he only designed two coins for circulation — the 20-cent coin and the Trade dollar.

Barber produced more than 40 public and private medals. Among his most famous works are medals honoring David Rittenhouse, Jean Louis Rodolphe Agassiz and Cyrus Field. Other medal works include medals of James Pollock, Joseph Pancoast, Dr. Henry Linderman, the Centennial medals of 1876 and the Valley Forge medal of 1877.

He also designed several Assay Commission medals, the most famous of which was his 1868 piece showing Liberty using her torch to destroy the implements of the recent Civil War. His Assay Commission medal of 1876 commemorates the 100th anniversary of America's Independence with a bust of Washington on the reverse.

Two of Barber's assistants at the time would later become Chief Engravers — Charles E. Barber and George T. Morgan. His son, Charles was appointed to the position in 1880 upon the death of his father.

Charles E. Barber

Charles E. Barber (1840—1917) served as an assistant for 10 years before being appointed to the top engraver post. Among his designs, known as the Liberty Head or Barber design, were the half dollar which was struck from 1892 until 1915; the quarter struck from 1892 until 1916; and the dime obverse struck from 1892 until 1916. He also designed the Liberty Head 5-cent coin struck from 1883 until 1913. He also designed the 1915-S Panama-Pacific Exposition gold $2.50 piece.

Charles Barber is also credited with the Flowing Hair Stella $4 pattern obverse, as well as the obverse of the Columbian Exposition half dollar with a bust of Columbus, issued in 1892 and 1893 (the reverse was done by George Morgan).

In 1905, the U.S. government sent him to study the Mints of Europe and as the result of his travels the medal department of the U.S. Mint improved, according to historical records. His work is visible in all the principal medals executed after 1869. His best work is seen in the medals of Presidents Garfield and Arthur; Indian Peace, Army and Marksmanship medals; and the Great Seal of the United States.

Other medals include the Metis

shipwreck and John Horn medals; a medal for the International Medical Congress at Washington in 1887; the International Exhibition, Chicago, 1893; and President Cleveland medals. Reports conflict on whether Charles or his father did the Assay Commission medal of 1879, honoring H.R. Linderman, a Director of the Mint and Joseph Henry, the first director of the Smithsonian Institution.

Charles Barber continued his service until his death Feb. 18, 1917. At that time, his assistant, George T. Morgan, was appointed to the position.

George T. Morgan

George T. Morgan (1845—1925) was 31 years old when he was appointed as an Assistant Engraver and worked at the Mint until his death 48 years later. Little is known about his early life except he was born in Birmingham, England, and attended the Birmingham Art School before he won a national scholarship to the South Kensington Art School. He studied at South Kensington for two years and later studied under Wyon of the Royal Mint in London for four years.

Probably his most famous work while employed by the U.S. Mint was the Morgan dollar (called the ""Bland" dollar when it was first struck) of 1878 to 1904 and 1921.

The Morgan dollar was the first U.S. coin to bear an engraver's initial (large M) on the obverse and reverse. The dollar was authorized by the Bland-Allison Act of Feb. 28, 1878, which provided for a minimum monthly silver coinage of 2 million and established this coin weighing 412.5 grains troy as legal tender.

The name Bland dollar is taken from the name of Rep. Richard Bland of Missouri, one of the authors of the act responsible for the minting of the Morgan dollar.

In addition to his well-known dollar, Morgan designed the reverse of the 1892 Columbian Exposition half dollar, the obverse of the 1918 Lincoln-Illinois Centennial half dollar, the reverse of the 1916 and 1917 McKinley Memorial gold dollar and collaborated with Charles Barber to design the 1915-S Panama-Pacific Exposition quarter eagle. He also designed the obverse of the Coiled Hair Stella patterns.

He was also known for his portraits of the Mint's presidential series of medals. He designed presidential medals honoring Rutherford B. Hayes, Woodrow Wilson and Warren G. Harding. Collaborating with Charles Barber, he designed medals depicting Abraham Lincoln, Martin Van Buren, James Garfield, Chester Arthur, Benjamin Harrison, William McKinley, Theodore Roosevelt and William Taft. His portraits of Presidents Hayes, Cleveland and Harrison appeared on the obverse of the Assay Commission medals of 1880, 1886 and 1893.

In addition to his work at the U.S. Mint, Morgan also designed a medal of David Roberts for the Art Union Co. of London; Thomas Carlyle on his 80th birthday; Railway Exhibition at Chicago in 1883 (in conjunction with Barber); and Henry Bessemer, 1879 (a specimen in gold was presented to King Edward VII in 1906).

Morgan also designed medals honoring Secretaries of the Treasury Alexander Hamilton, Daniel Manning, George Cortelyou, Franklin MacVeagh, William McAdoo and Carter Glass. Medals done by Morgan and Barber honoring Treasury Secretaries include William Windom, John G. Carlisle, Lyman J. Gage and Leslie Shaw. He also designed four Directors of the Mint medals and collaborated with Barber to design four others.

Morgan was also a life member of the Philadelphia Academy of the Fine Arts and a member of the famous Philadelphia Sketch Club.

John Ray Sinnock

When George T. Morgan died in 1925, John R. Sinnock was appointed Chief Engraver by President Calvin Coolidge. Sinnock had served as Assistant Engraver and medalist in 1917 before he resigned two years later.

Sinnock, born in Raton, N.M., in 1888 attended the Pennsylvania Museum Art School in Philadelphia. There he won the

A.W. Mifflin scholarship for advanced study and traveled in Europe.

When he returned from Europe, he served as an instructor at the Pennsylvania Museum Art School for eight years and also taught art classes at Western Reserve University in Cleveland.

His appointment as Assistant Engraver came when he was 29 but it would be eight years before he would assume the Chief Engraver's duties. He worked at that job until his death May 14, 1947, at the age of 59 after an illness of several months' duration.

In his 22 years as Chief Engraver, Sinnock left behind many works including his best known, the redesigned Purple Heart in 1931. But probably the best known of his coin designs, and the only one still being minted today, is the Roosevelt dime, placed into circulation in 1946.

According to an interview with Sinnock shortly after the release of the coin, he said the obverse portrait of Roosevelt is a composite of two studies, sculptured in relief, which he made from life in 1933-1934. He also consulted photographs of Roosevelt taken shortly before his death.

One of the best known stories that circulated about the dime was the mild uproar created because of the designer's initials, "JS," at the trunk of Roosevelt's neck. Some of the public mistook the initials for those of Joseph Stalin, the Soviet Union's leader.

Sinnock was also the designer of the Franklin half dollar, which didn't appear in circulation until after his death. The Franklin half was struck from 1948 until 1963. Sinnock's initials, JRS, appear under Franklin's shoulder.

In 1926 Sinnock designed two commemorative coins for the Philadelphia Sesquicentennial celebration — the gold quarter eagle and silver half dollar. The half dollar is known as the Sesquicentennial of American Independence commemorative half; the dies were in very low relief. The $2.50 gold piece and commemorative half dollar were to help raise funds for financing the International Fair held in Philadelphia in 1926.

Sinnock also designed the reverse of the 1918 Lincoln-Illinois Centennial half dollar, while he was an assistant at the Mint. The obverse was done by George T. Morgan, who was then Chief Engraver. Sinnock also designed the Cuban 1-peso coin of 1934, the 1 lempira for Honduras in 1931 and a $1 pattern piece for China in 1929 which was never adopted by the Chinese. A medal design by Sinnock, "Vanguard of the Nation," was purchased by the French government.

Among the most notable and nationally award-winning medals Sinnock designed were the special congressional gold medals honoring Thomas A. Edison; the Yangtze medal for Naval and Marine Corps personnel serving in 1926-27 and in the Shanghai-Yangtze area in 1930-32; and the Ellsworth-Admundsen-Nobile medal commemorating the flight over the North Pole of the dirigible Norge in 1929.

Sinnock designed four medals for the Mint's presidential series including those depicting Calvin Coolidge in 1926; Herbert Hoover in 1929; Franklin D. Roosevelt in 1935; and the obverse of the Harry S Truman medal in 1945. He also designed Secretaries of the Treasury medals for Andrew Mellon in 1931; Ogden L. Mills in 1932; William Woodin in 1933; Henry Morgenthau Jr. in 1938; Fred Vinson; and John W. Snyder.

Sinnock also designed medals for two under secretaries of the Treasury and four assistant secretaries of the Treasury. Sinnock designed two medals honoring Directors of the Mint, Robert J. Grant in 1931 and the obverse of the Nellie Taylor Ross medal in 1933.

Sinnock is also credited with a special congressional silver medal to honor members of the party with Adm. Perry in his 1909 expedition to the North Pole, and the 1945 Navy Department medal. He also designed Assay Commission medals in 1926, 1927, the obverse of 1928, 1929, 1930, 1931, 1932, 1933, 1934, 1935, 1937 and 1938.

He was a member of the National

Sculpture Society, the Philadelphia Sketch Club, the American Federation of Arts, the Philadelphia Art Alliance and American Artists Professional League and an honorary member of the Philadelphia Water Color Club.

Gilroy Roberts

Gilroy Roberts was appointed as Chief Engraver July 22, 1948, but he was no stranger to the U.S. Mint. By the time he received the appointment he had worked both at the Philadelphia Mint and the Bureau of Engraving and Printing in Washington, D.C.

Roberts, who was born in Philadelphia March 5, 1905, was appointed by President Harry S. Truman to head the Mint's engraving division in 1948. Roberts, whose father originally wanted him to be a musician, took his inherited artistic talents into medallic art.

He grew up in an artistic world. His father was a sculptor and Roberts' earliest sculpturing experience was with modeling clay, then wood carving and stone sculpturing. In 1934 and 1935, Roberts attended evening art classes at Frankfort High in Philadelphia, where he studied under Paul Remy. In his spare time, he modeled and carved small sculptures for commission and for exhibit in national exhibitions.

In 1936, Roberts took and passed a competitive Civil Service examination for the position of Assistant Sculptor-Engraver at the U.S. Mint. He was hired June 3, 1936, as Sinnock's understudy and continued in that job until Jan. 6, 1938, when he became an Engraver in the Bureau of Engraving and Printing in Washington.

While serving at the BEP, Roberts became proficient in the art of note and stamp engraving. He did the portraits on a number of official revenue stamps and postage stamps, including the 3-cent Ralph Waldo Emerson stamp and the 3-cent Charles W. Elliot stamp, the 1-cent Stephen Collins Foster stamp and the 1-cent Eli Whitney stamp in the Famous American series.

During his time in Washington, Roberts studied under Eugene Weis and Heinz Warneke at the Corcoran Art School from 1939 until 1943. He returned to the Mint May 1, 1944, as an assistant to Sinnock, where he continued the study of bas-relief with Sinnock.

Roberts' best known work is the obverse of the John F. Kennedy half dollar. Upon completion of the half dollar, Roberts placed his stylized initials, GR, on the truncated bust of the coin. When the coin was released, rumors flew around that the initials were really a hammer and sickle — a symbol of the Soviet Union — marking the spot where the late president was shot.

The Treasury Department continuously denied the rumor and eventually issued a press release, which included an enlargement of the coin showing Roberts' initials, not a hammer and sickle.

Other coins designed by Roberts include the Denmark 5 kroner in 1944; El Salvador, 50 and 25 centavos, obverse in 1953; Cuba, 1 peso, obverse in 1953; 50-, 25-, 5- and 1-centavo coins in 1953; Haiti, 10- and 5-centime coins, obverse in 1958; and the Liberian $1, 50-, 25-, 10-, 5- and 1-cent obverses in 1959.

United States Mint list medals: presidential series, Harry S Truman reverse; portraits of Dwight D. Eisenhower, first and second terms; John F. Kennedy; and Lyndon B. Johnson. Secretary of the Treasury series: portraits of G.M. Humphrey and Douglas Dillon. Director of the Mint series: portraits of William H. Brett and Eva Adams.

Roberts also designed several congressional medals including: Irving Berlin, 1954; Dr. Jonas Salk, 1955; Sir Winston Churchill, obverse, 1955; a medal of Ulysses S. Grant and Robert E. Lee honoring the surviving veterans of the Civil War, 1956; and Adm. Hyman George Rickover, reverse, 1958. Other medals include: annual Assay Commission series of many years, both obverse and reverse; Perry Navy, reverse, 1945; Director of the Mint marksman, 1948; Department of the Interior award, obverse,

1948; Atomic Energy Commission medals: Enrico Fermi, 1956; Ernest Orlando Lawrence, 1960; Citation medal, 1960.

Some of his private commissions include: American Numismatic Society medal of Louis C. West; Medallic Art Co. of New York, medals of William T. Louth, Julius Lauth, Frances Trees; Helen Keller Foundation portrait of Helen Keller; Drexel Institute medal of founder Anthony Drexel; memorial tablet of Charles T. Bach; Patriots Memorial, Valley Forge, Pa.; a series of state seals; Institute for Advanced Study, Princeton, N.J. medal of Albert Einstein; Metropolitan Life Insurance Co. portrait of F.W. Eckers; Scripps Howard Newspaper Alliance medal of Ernie Pyle.

Also included in Roberts' portfolio: a portrait of Bobby Jones for the American Golf Association; Life Golf Tournament portrait of Ben Hogan; Yeshiva University, New York City, portrait of Albert Einstein; Radio Corporation of America medal of Gen. David Sarnoff; Woods Hole Oceanographic Institute portrait of Henry Bigelow; American Medical Association portrait of Dr. Hektoen; Montana Centennial Medal of three governors of Montana, Babcock, Toole and Edgerton; National Commemorative Society, "In God We Trust" medal and others.

His exhibitions have included the Pennsylvania Academy of Fine Arts, Philadelphia in 1930, 1934, 1945, 1946; Corcoran Gallery of Art, Washington, D.C.; National Sculpture Society in New York; Paris, France and Italy, 1961; The Hague, Netherlands, 1963.

He has also lectured about U.S. coins at the American Numismatic Society in New York in 1961 and the Exchange Club in Philadelphia in 1962. Among his awards are the National Sculpture Society Bas-Relief exhibition, 1951, honorable mention. International exhibition coins and medals in Madrid, Spain, 1951, gold medal and citation.

Roberts resigned his position as Chief Engraver at the age of 59 Oct. 8, 1964, when he became the first Chief Engraver in the history of the Mint who did not die in office. He had served as Chief Engraver for 16 years and had spent a total of 28 years working for the government, 26 years at the Mint and two years at the BEP.

Roberts resigned from the Mint under the advice of his physician, but he did not resign from the world of minting, however. He accepted a position as chairman of the board of General Numismatics Corp., forerunner of the Franklin Mint. He later became chairman of the board emeritus and a director of the Franklin Mint.

In this capacity, Roberts was given the opportunity to travel and he personally "shopped" for the intricate machinery being installed in the Franklin Mint. His travels took him to the Orient, among other places.

Roberts is married to the former Lillian Pancoast and they have one son. When he is not designing medals or sculpture, he is interested in astronomy, telescope making and boating. In 1960, Roberts presented a lecture about Maksutov telescopes at the Astronomical League Convention at Haverford College at Haverford, Pa.

Roberts also designed dozens of medals including the following for commemorative societies while he was with the Franklin Mint: Abba Eban, Martin Luther King, Malcom X, Mahalia Jackson, Geoffrey Chaucer, Miraculous medal, Cardinal Spellman, Saint Peter, Abraham, Eisenhower, Three Astronauts, First Step on the Moon, Joan of Arc and Sarah Bernhardt.

He also designed special medallic greeting cards from 1965-1968 as well as the Robert F. Kennedy Memorial medal and the Richard Nixon and Spiro Agnew Inauguration medal in 1973. Other medallic series include the U.S. president's series for the White House Historical Association, the Franklin Mint's "Roberts' Birds" series of 50 silver medals, Pandora's Box, baby announcement medals for boys and girls, 12 signs of the Zodiac (also made into jewelry). Also, he designed the Franklin Mint's Bicentennial medals with portraits of 30 great Americans 1976, a John F. Kennedy Inaugural 25th Anniversary medal in 1986 and the Encyclopaedia Britannica Award in 1986 struck by Medallic Art Co.

Large plaques designed by Roberts include: Benjamin Franklin, Franklin Mint official emblem; John F. Kennedy Memorial, wild geese, horses, 12 signs of the zodiac, self-portrait for Pennsylvania Association of Numismatists Award.

He also designed plates including a Liberty Tree etched in glass, Nixon and Agnew in silver and 12 signs of the Zodiac in silver as well as three-dimensional sculptures, a large sundial at the Franklin Mint museum, a Great American Eagle and four bird groups in pewter.

Frank Gasparro

Gilroy Roberts' successor, Frank Gasparro, was sworn in Feb. 23, 1965. He was born in Philadelphia Aug. 26, 1909, and showed his artistic talent at a young age. He attended classes at the Samuel Fleisher Art Memorial school in Philadelphia while still in grade school. At the age of 15, he began taking private lessons from Guiseppe Donato, a former foreman to the sculptor Rodin. Donato took Gasparro under his wing and when Gasparro would visit Donato's studio, the master would show him the fine points of the art.

Gasparro continued to study under Donato until 1929, even after his graduation from South Philadelphia High School. He enrolled at the Pennsylvania Academy of Fine Arts in Philadelphia in 1928, where he studied under sculptors and medalists Charles Grafly, Walker Hancock and Albert Laessle until 1931.

Gasparro launched his professional career in 1932, at the age of 23, as a freelance sculptor working primarily in statuary art and commercial plaster models. He continued in that field until 1937 when he joined the staff of the Federal Art Administration, which was a part of the Works Progress Administration

under the Roosevelt administration during the Great Depression.

Under the FAA, each artist was given a salary and allowed to work on any project; all the artists' work became the property of the government. He did sculptures at this time which were placed in wading pools in playgrounds in the Philadelphia area, where some can still be seen.

He returned to freelance sculpturing in 1941 and then became a junior engraver in 1942 at the U.S. Mint. On Feb. 11, 1965, Gasparro was appointed to the Chief Engraver's position by President Lyndon B. Johnson.

During his tenure, Gasparro supervised the production of some 30,000 dies a year for all U.S. coinage and medals produced at the Philadelphia Mint. His work at the Mint included portraiture, low and high relief medals and insignia designing. He is probably best known to coin collectors for his reverse of the Kennedy half dollar, 1964; his design and execution of the reverse of the Lincoln Memorial cent in 1959; his Eisenhower/Apollo 11 dollar introduced in 1971; and the Susan B. Anthony dollar.

He also designed the Philadelphia Medal of Honor in 1955. In 1964, he won the emblem contest sponsored by the Treasury Safety Council. Foreign coins also occupied his design capabilities including 1943 Guatemala Revenue 25 centavos, among others.

Gasparro also designed annual Assay Commission medals in 1949, 1950, 1951, 1952 and 1965. He also designed the Eisenhower reverse in 1954 and the Kennedy reverse for the presidential medals series of the Mint.

Other designs and models prepared by Gasparro at the U.S. Mint include: Federal Security Agency medal and Federal Security Agency Service Award emblem in 1951; Provost Marshal General badge, 1951; Coast Guard Commendation medal, 1952; White House Cap Device insignia, 1953; Secretary of the Treasury medal, 1953; Department of Commerce medal and emblem, 1952; Central Intelligence medal, 1953; Central Intelligence star,

1953; Central Intelligence Distinguished medal, 1955; Treasury department Secret Service Guard Cap and Breast Badge, 1954; U.S. Secretary of the Treasury, Robert B. Anderson; Dr. Thomas A. Dooley III congressional medal.

Also included among his works are: the 1-5/16 inch and the 2.25-inch Pony Express medals, 1960; U.S. Secretary of the Treasury medal George M. Humphrey and one for Douglas Dillon. Private commissions include the Stroud Jordan medal, 1953.

Exhibitions include: Victory medal of World War II in plaster, private collection, at the Pennsylvania Academy of the Fine Arts in 1950. His work has also been exhibited at the Philadelphia Museum of Arts. His medallion works and his sculptures in the round have also been placed on display. He has five medals on permanent exhibition at the Smithsonian Institution. His work has been shown in foreign exhibits at the Paris Mint, 1949-50 annual Assay Commission medals, 1949; International Medallic Exposition, 1951; and at the Rome International Medallic Exhibition he showed a 1953 Coast Guard Commendation medal and the reverse of the 1949 annual Assay Commission medal.

He has also been an instructor in sculpture at the Fleisher Art Memorial in Philadelphia and he was honored by the Italian government in 1973 with the decoration of Cavaliere Ufficiale.

In 1968 Gasparro was named the Outstanding Numismatic Sculptor of the Year by the American Numismatic Association and in 1969 he designed the medal for the ANA's convention. He is also credited with the Jimmy Carter medal in the Mint's presidential series as well as a congressional medal honoring Marian Anderson.

He is a member of the Society of Medalists, the French Society of the Medal and Pennsylvania Academy of the Fine Arts Fellowship board of directors.

Gasparro is married to the former Julia Johnston and he and his wife have a daughter. After his retirement as Chief Engraver Jan. 16, 1981, Gasparro continued his artistic work including a George Washington 250th anniversary commemorative medal in 1982 and President's Day Celebration medal in 1983 for Design-Pak Inc.

He also has designed a number of medals for Bowers and Merena Galleries including Virgil Brand medal in 1983, the Salute to the Olympics medal in 1984, the President Ronald Reagan medal in 1984, the Walter Mondale medal in 1984, the Frank Gasparro medal in 1985, the Abraham Lincoln medal in 1986 and the Jefferson Davis medal in 1986.

Gasparro continued to work on additional medals, the following from Unicover Corp.: St. Francis di Assisi commemorative in 1981, Jacques Cartier in 1984, Rose Bowl in 1984, space shuttle-NASA in 1983, Babe Ruth in 1983, Migratory Bird Stamp medal in 1984, Brandenburg Gate-Berlin Anniversary in 1986, President Ronald Reagan in 1984 and Walter Mondale in 1984.

In 1986, Gasparro was the designer of the American Numismatic Association medal and then he did several medal series for Paramount International Coin Co. including an 11-medal series for the Statue of Liberty Centennial, 1985-1986, and an 11-medal series to commemorate the United States Constitution in 1987.

Elizabeth Jones

U.S. Mint Chief Engraver Elizabeth A.B. Jones has Italy to thank for many of the high points in her life. In part her appointment as Chief Engraver in 1981 can be traced back to her studies in Rome when she switched from oil painting to sculpture. That change lead her to medallic art and a wide range of artistic endeavors.

Before moving to Italy, Jones graduated from Vassar College with a bachelor's degree in the History of Art in 1957. She then studied at the Art Students League in New York City until 1962. She spent the next two years studying at the Scuolo dell'Arte della Medaglia inside the Italian Mint.

It was there, under the guidance of the

Italian Mint's paper money engraver, Jones and other students learned how to engrave in steel. She also learned how to sculpture medals, medallic art and low relief.

While still a student, she was invited to exhibit her work in the Federation Internationale de la Medaille. Shortly thereafter, her services as a translator were called upon when fellow American U.S. Mint Director Eva Adams visited the Italian Mint.

"I really hadn't been noticed by Americans until then. She asked me right then and there if I would come back and work in Philadelphia," Jones said, recalling her first meeting with the woman who was to become a good friend. "I said I had only been here two or three years and I really want to stay. When Mr. Gasparro retired, she was on the phone to me in Washington, D.C., where I was visiting during the Christmas holidays, and told me to apply for the position."

Jones was nominated by President Ronald Reagan July 13, 1981, confirmed by the Senate Sept. 28 and sworn in Oct. 27. She is the first woman named Chief Sculptor-Engraver of the United States.

It was less than six months after her nomination was confirmed that she was faced with her first major project — designing the first U.S. commemorative coin issued since 1954 to honor the 250th anniversary of the birth of George Washington.

"As soon as I heard about the possibility of my doing the Washington half dollar coin, I decided instantaneously I was going to put him on a horse," she said. "He was such a famous horseman and general, often portrayed in paintings on his horse in battles, and he is also portrayed in innumerable outdoor equestrian monuments throughout the country."

In her mind, she envisioned a move away from the standard profile-type of design which Jones said is so prominent in all other medals, paintings and coins, to a younger-looking Washington astride a horse.

She had already decided on the image she wanted when, in the course of her research, she visited the portrait gallery of the Second Bank of the United States and came across an oval painting by Rembrandt Peale which depicts Washington astride a horse.

"I really was shocked. It was almost like a vision because that's just what I had in mind of doing," she said.

In order to carry out her design image, Jones said she often worked weekends but admits now she was nervous and she overdrew.

"When you work too long at something, you don't see it anymore," she said, recalling her first drawings for the Washington commemorative. That may have made it all the worse for her when, after turning the sketch over to U.S. Mint Director Donna Pope for her approval, Jones was invited to a function at the Union League Club in Philadelphia.

While there, inspiration arrived in the form of a floor-to-ceiling portrait by Thomas Sully of Washington on horseback.

"I was so inspired. I wanted to stop the original design and I asked Mrs. Pope, "Please don't let it be published,' because I wanted to make changes but she said it was too late," Jones said. "I was sick. But I knew in my mind what I was going to do anyway with the coin. And as it turns out, the coin came out far better than the original design."

That's just a small part of the extensive research Jones does when looking for different versions of a subject's face or clothing.

It was a different kind of atmosphere when it came time to submit designs for the 1984 Los Angeles Olympic Games. Jones said when she and her staff of sculptor/engravers, which she affectionately refers to as "my guys," were approached to design the commemorative 1983 $1 silver Olympic coin. The initial designs were an attempt to move away from traditional themes.

"We did not do the discus thrower on purpose, because it had been done and re-done over and over again. But at a certain point, after [Treasury] Secretary [Donald] Regan had seen everything, he still wasn't satisfied and he said he wanted some drawings using the discus thrower," she recalled.

Jones and the other engravers submitted the discus thrower designs, which she said presented a challenge to provide a fresh, different and modern look to the "discobolus," so she employed the technique of a multiple image to convey motion. The design apparently caught the Treasury Secretary's eye.

But even then Regan was still not pleased, Jones recalled, because her design displayed only the Olympic rings, without the stars, for the sake of simplicity and clarity of design.

"He insisted that the stars be placed with the Olympic rings as he said it was the official logo of the Los Angeles Olympic Games," she said. "That was a terrible job because the stars had to be much bigger than they should have been because of the reduction process. To me it just fouled up the whole coin because it complicated and overloaded the design."

But that disappointment faded and two years later, Jones again felt the exhilaration of designing a successful and popular coin — the Statue of Liberty gold $5 commemorative coin. She said because the dimensions of the coin were so small, 21.59 millimeters, the design needed to be as simple and direct as possible.

"You simply have to have a bold concept when you do such a tiny coin," she said. "I didn't want to cut the Statue in half, I had seen that on some medals and I think that's a very graceless design on a small coin."

She saw the view she had in mind in a photograph used in a mail-order advertisement. Although part of Liberty's face was in the shadows, Jones used her knowledge of the structural elements of the face to reconstruct what she needed. That was just one of the times photographs, her own or someone else's, played a major part in the design process and her work in general.

"If you look at a group of different photographs of the Statue, from some angles her nose looks very Roman, in another photographs her forehead is very pronounced. She changes in many photographs, in some her face looks oval, some her chin is very square and her face is very full," Jones observed. "One photograph is never enough. When I did portraits of people, I would do the photographs myself. I would take four of five rolls of 36 frames each. I would take them from all angles, on different days and in different lights."

That interest in photography began years ago and her tastes run towards cityscapes and landscapes but she is also attracted to bold combinations of color. But that hobby, like the many different art forms she practiced before becoming Chief Engraver, have been set aside for now.

"Designing coins is much more difficult than designing medals. You have much more freedom in designing medals, in every aspect," she said. "I did seven different pieces for the Franklin Mint so I was used to working in low relief. But they did not have the criteria of incredible precision that we have because they would tell me it couldn't be higher than "such and such.' Well, that was child's play compared to making a coin in the U.S. Mint. They didn't have the problem of making thousands of dies. I imagine they could afford to throw away the die after 800 strikes where we have to get 8,000 strikes or more for the 'penny,' for example. The design has to be compatible with long die life."

In addition to honing her administrative skills, the job has provided Jones with a variety of new challenges and opportunities to learn.

"This is such a unique experience here. It's been fascinating and I certainly enjoyed it immensely," she said. "I've learned so much, especially technically. You can't know everything before you get inside a Mint. It's very tough work inside here. We have very tough schedules, very tight deadlines. I just hope I've contributed something artistically to the U.S. Mint."

In addition to contributing to her professional success, Rome also holds special personal memories — she was married to Ludwig Glaeser there April 26, 1986.

As a tribute to her artistic successes, the Scuolo dell'Arte della Medaglia in Rome hosted a retrospective exhibition of her work in September 1987. It was the first in a series of alumni retrospective exhibits planned by the school. Elvira Clain-Stefanelli, Executive Director of the Smithsonian's National Numismatic Collection, wrote the preface for the exhibition catalog.

In addition, Jones has participated in numerous one-person shows and group exhibitions. Before her appointment as Chief Engraver, she completed several commemorative medals including those depicting Picasso and Wolfgang Amadeus Mozart for the Stefano Johnson Mint in Milano, Italy; Pablo Casals, International Numismatic Agency in New York City; the University of Pennsylvania Art Museum (Lucy Wharton Drexel Award — gold medal); the Johns Hopkins University; Creighton University; silver medal of Cardinal Spellman for the American Episcopate; Salute to Israel (25th anniversary); Gloria Steinem for the Food and Agricultural series of CERES medals honoring outstanding women of the world; the Holy Year Jubileum for the Medallic Art Co.; medal for Israel's 30th anniversary for the Judaic Heritage Society; annual prize medals for St. Stephen's School, Rome; Dubai Sheraton Hotel, United Arab Emirates, including the portrait of H.E. Sheikh Rashid; Pope Paul II, for Premier Giulio Andreotti — medal cast in solid gold as gift of Italian Government; Nobel Prize Laureates, Stockholm, 1979; anniversary medal, Judaic Heritage Society in 1980.

She was awarded an honorary diploma from the Academia Brasileiro das Belas Artes in Rio de Janeiro in 1967; the Outstanding Sculptor of the Year from the American Numismatic Association in 1972; and the Louis Bennett Award from the National Sculpture Society in 1978.

Her commissioned work for the Franklin Mint includes medallic portraits of Albert Schweitzer, Susan B. Anthony, Charles Dickens, Richard Wright, Walter Reed and Gen. Campbell. She has also completed dozens of commissioned oil paintings and several pieces of commissioned jewelry.

Jones is a member of both national and international numismatic and medallic associations including American Numismatic Association, American Medallic Sculpture Association, American Numismatic Society, Federation Internationale de la Medaille and the National Sculpture Society. Since 1981 she has been a member of the advisory committee of the National Museum of Women in the Arts in Washington, D.C., which was formally inaugurated in April 1987.

As this almanac was going to press in June 1990, Jones reported that she would be leaving office in August 1990. She is the first Chief Engraver to be removed from office. Traditionally, presidential appointees tender their resignations at a change of administration; and traditionally for the position of Chief Engraver, that resignation is rejected. However, Jones' resignation was being accepted, more than a year and a half after it was tendered. No word of her successor was forthcoming at press time.

Jones — the first female Chief Engraver — will have the added distinction of being the first Chief Engraver to leave office neither as a result of death nor retirement.

Services offered by the Mint

The United States Mint offers several collector's items and services to collectors and interested non-collectors. Among these are Proof sets, Uncirculated Mint sets, souvenir Mint sets, bronze duplicates of national medals and Mint tours. Since 1982, the Mint has offered a variety of commemorative coins and since 1986, gold and silver bullion coins (through wholesalers).

Annual offerings comprise Proof sets and sets of Uncirculated coinage (after the Mint did not produce Uncirculated sets in 1982 and 1983, Congress passed a law requiring yearly sales). National medals are struck when supplies run low to fill orders. Souvenir sets — each offering the coins of a single Mint — are offered as well.

Persons on the Mint's customer mailing list will receive order forms for all Mint products offered by mail as well as a catalog each fall. The catalog of Mint products was first issued in late 1985 and was an immediate success. To be placed on the Mint's mailing list, interested persons may write to United States Mint, Customer Services, 10001 Aerospace Road, Lanham, Md. 20706. The Mint's customer service telephone number is (301) 436-7400.

Some items, like the souvenir Mint sets, are offered at over-the-counter locations only, and not through the mail. The Mint also produces special souvenir sets of coins or medals for selected numismatic conventions, including the annual American Numismatic Association show; these, too, are not offered through the mail.

The Mint in 1983 experimented with sales of Proof sets at over-the-counter locations to attract more non-collectors to the hobby of coin collecting. Mint officials have continued to offer Proof sets at its over-the-counter outlets since then.

Mint tours

Philadelphia Mint, (215) 597-2529; Monday through Friday, 9 a.m. to 4:30 p.m. January, February and March. Monday through Saturday April and October, November and December. Monday through Sunday May through September.

San Francisco Old Mint, (415) 454-0788); Monday through Friday, 10 a.m. to 3 p.m.

Denver Mint, (303) 327-5588; Monday through Friday, 8:30 a.m. to 3 p.m. September through May and 8 a.m. to 3 p.m. May through September. Tours are available Wednesdays year-round from 9:30 a.m. to 3 p.m.

Admission is free. Hours are subject to change without notice. Call for information.

The San Francisco Mint, the Fort Knox Gold Bullion Depository, and the West Point Mint are closed to the public.

Medals produced by the U.S. Mint

Medals produced for sale to the public by the Mint normally are produced in bronze (90 percent copper, 10 percent zinc). They are often referred to as "list medals" because they are listed in Mint sales brochures. The brochures contain photographs and descriptions of products offered (medals, easels, presentation cases, and display albums) and pricing for both mail order and over-the-counter sales.

Large medals may be up to 3 inches in diameter and require multiple strikes of the press to bring up the relief. These medals are hand-finished and individually packaged. Each large medal comes with a plastic display easel. Smaller medals, such as the 1-1/2-inch and 1-5/16-inch "miniature" sizes are produced on presses similar to those used for the manufacture of coins. Generally, only one strike is required for the smaller medals. Though not hand-finished like the larger medals, the miniature medals are laquered to protect their surfaces from tarnish. The smaller medals are packaged by machine.

For a free copy of the current list of medals for sale to the public, write

Customer Service Center
United States Mint
10001 Aerospace Road
Lanham, Md. 20706
(301) 436-7400.
The full line of Mint coins, medals and other items are for sale at the following sales centers:

Philadelphia Mint
5th and Arch Streets
Philadelphia, Pa. 19106

San Francisco Old Mint Museum
88 Fifth Street
San Francisco, Calif. 94103

Denver Mint
320 W. Colfax Avenue
Denver, Colo. 80204

Medals produced by the U.S. Mint, FY89

The following table shows the number of medals produced during Fiscal Year 1989. The figures are useful in comparing what medals are most popular; however, the Mint may have backlogged stocks of some medals in any given year.

Presidential

No.	Subject	Philadelphia	Denver
101	George Washington	487	
102	John Adams	136	
104	James Madison	72	
106	John Quincy Adams	1	
107	Andrew Jackson	94	
111	James K. Polk	63	
114	Franklin Pierce	88	
116	Abraham Lincoln	416	
117	Andrew Johnson	16	
118	Ulysses S. Grant	128	
135	John F. Kennedy	870	
142	Ronald Reagan	3,042	
	Total presidential	**5,413**	

Army

No.	Subject	Phila	Denver
402	General Horatio Gates	71	
403	General Daniel Morgan	58	
429	200th Anniversary of the Army	1	
	Total Army	**130**	

Navy

No.	Subject	Phila	Denver
506	Captain Stephen Decatur	47	
510	Captain Oliver Perry	135	
525	Rescue of San Francisco	48	
535	200th Ann. of the Marine Corps	112	
	Total Navy	**342**	

Miscellaneous (3")

No.	Subject	Phila	Denver
648	Benjamin Franklin	753	
662	Brig. General Charles Yeager	266	
664	Lt. Gen. Ira C. Eaker	45	
666	John Wayne	613	
686	Vietnam Veterans National Medal	2	
687	Lady Bird Johnson	736	
689	George and Ira Gershwin	1,046	
691	Natan (Anatoly) and Avital Shcharansky	845	
693	Harry Chapin	1,368	
697	Mary Lasker	190	
707	Treasury Building	198	
	Total Miscellaneous (3")	**6,062**	

Miscellaneous (2-7/16" and 2-3/4")

No.	Subject	Phila	Denver
636	Great Seal Centennial	167	
645	Charles A. Lindbergh	261	
	Total Miscellaneous	**428**	

Miscellaneous (1-1/2")

No.	Subject	Phila	Denver
681	Harry S. Truman	4,090	
685	Vietnam Veterans National Medal	8,489	
688	Lady Bird Johnson	3,010	
690	George and Ira Gershwin	7,965	
692	Natan (Anatoly) and Avital Shcharansky	2,582	
694	Harry Chapin	12,724	
698	Mary Lasker	2,778	
720	Bicentennial of the Treasury	520	
	Total Miscellaneous (1-1/2")	**42,158**	

Miniature Presidential (1-5/16")

No.	Subject	Phila	Denver
801	George Washington	55,092	
802	John Adams	6,770	
803	Thomas Jefferson	60,032	
804	James Madison	12,350	
805	James Monroe	13,710	
806	John Quincy Adams	11,860	
807	Andrew Jackson	21,305	
808	Martin Van Buren	10,695	
809	William Henry Harrison	2,614	490
810	John Tyler	7,142	
811	James K. Polk	9,211	
812	Zachary Taylor	6,544	
813	Millard Fillmore	15,886	
814	Franklin Pierce	11,008	
815	James Buchanan	18,173	

816	Abraham Lincoln	81,016
817	Andrew Johnson	10,477
818	Ulysses S. Grant	15,623
819	Rutherford B. Hayes	3,911
820	James A. Garfield	3,927
821	Chester A. Arthur	6,000
822	Grover Cleveland	4,492
824	William McKinley	4,017
825	Theodore Roosevelt	41,202
826	William Howard Taft	3,900
827	Woodrow Wilson	5,890
828	Warren G. Harding	4,622
829	Calvin Coolidge	3,500
830	Herbert Hoover	11,713
831	Franklin D. Roosevelt	9,376
832	Harry S. Truman	9,056
833	Dwight D. Eisenhower (1st term)	20,980
835	John F. Kennedy	42,169	1,181
837	Lyndon B. Johnson (2nd term)	8,646
838	Richard M. Nixon (1st term)	8,455

839	Richard M. Nixon (2nd term)		674
841	Jimmy Carter	5,065	
842	Ronald Reagan	29,765	6,324
	Total Miniature Presidential 596,194		**8,669**

Miniature Miscellaneous (1-5/16")

No.	Subject	Phila	Denver
667	John Wayne	9,826	
678	MIA in Southeast Asia	9,000	
703	Denver Mint		5,050
706	The White House	16,368	
710	U.S. Bullion Dep., Fort Knox	2,034	
713	Treasury Building	6,583	
750	New Orleans Mint	3,055	
944	Bureau of Engraving	5,000	
	Total Miniature Misc.	**51,866**	**5,050**
	Total, all series	**702,593**	**13,719**

Source: U.S. Mint

History of the United States presidential medal series

Many of the medals which are now included in the U.S. Mint's presidential series were made originally for presentation to American Indian chiefs and warriors. The Spanish, the French and the British had presented medals to the Indians, and the British especially had produced large and magnificent silver medals, each bearing the likeness of the reigning monarch on one side and his coat of arms on the other. The British medals were solid silver, impressed in clear relief, and were given to the Indian chiefs as marks of friendship and special recognition. They were highly prized by the Indians.

When the United States replaced the British in dealing with the Indians, the new government found that it was necessary to continue the practice of presenting medals if it hoped to have peaceful relations with the tribes and influence with the chiefs. The federal government, then, began the production of Indian peace medals, which became a settled and extremely important part of American Indian policy.

As early as 1787, Henry Knox, the secretary of war under the Articles of Confederation, urged Congress to comply with the request of the Indians for "medals, gorgets, wrist and arm bands with the arms of the United States impressed or engraved thereon." Congress was pressed for funds, but Knox noted that the Indians would turn in their British medals, which could be melted down to produce new ones. Thomas Jefferson, as secretary of state, outlined the policy behind the distribution of medals to the Indians; he spoke of it as "an ancient custom from time immemorial." The medals, he said, "are considered as complimentary things, as marks of friendship to those who come to see us, or who do us good offices, conciliatory of their good will toward us, and not designed to produce a contrary disposition towards others. They confer no power, and seem to have taken their origin in the European practice, of giving medals or other marks of friendship to the negotiators of treaties and other diplomatic characters, or visitors of distinction."

Firm hold

Whatever the origin, the practice took firm hold in the United States. Medals were given to Indian chiefs on important occasions, such as the signing of a treaty, a visit of important Indians to the national capital, or a tour of the Indian country by some federal official. Lewis and Clark, on their famous exploratory expedition to the Pacific Coast in 1804-06, carried along a large supply of medals, which they handed out with impressive ceremonies to important chiefs along the way. Indian agents on the frontier distributed the medals to their charges, in recognition of friendship and peace with the United States. These Indian agents or treaty negotiators used their own discretion in making the presentations, but they were guided by fixed norms. In 1829, in fact, Lewis Cass, governor of Michigan Territory, and William Clark, superintendent of Indian Affairs at St. Louis, drew up a series of regulations for the governing of the Indian Department, including rules for the presentation of medals. What these two experienced Indian agents set down in their proposed regulations represented the practice that they had observed on the frontier:

"In the distribution of medals and flags, the following rules will be observed:

"1. They will be given to influential persons only.

"2. The largest medals will be given to the principal village chiefs, those of the second size will be given to the principal war chiefs, and those of the third size to the less distinguished chiefs and warriors.

"3. They will be presented with proper formalities, and with an appropriate speech, so as to produce a proper impression upon the Indians.

"4. It is not intended that chiefs should be appointed by an officer of the department, but that they should confer these badges of authority upon such as are selected or recognized by the tribe, and as are worthy of them, in the manner heretofore practiced.

"5. Whenever a foreign medal is worn, it will be replaced by an American medal, if the Agent should consider the person entitled to a medal."

The Indians expected to receive medals, and it was impossible to conduct Indian affairs without the use of them. Thomas L. McKenney, head of the Office of Indian Affairs, in 1829 wrote to the secretary of war about the policy of distributing medals. "So important is its continuance esteemed to be," he said, "that without medals, any plan of operations among the Indians, be it what it may, is essentially enfeebled. This comes of the high value which the Indians set upon these tokens of Friendship. They are, besides this indication of the Government Friendship, badges of power to them, and trophies of renown. They will not consent to part from this ancient right, as they esteem it; and according to the value they set upon medals is the importance to the Government in having them to bestow."

The U.S. government took great pains to produce medals of real artistic merit for the Indians. This cultural concern is surprising in a young nation trying to establish itself in a troubled world. Yet the medals which were made in the early years of the nation's existence are collector's items, not only because of the history associated with them, but also because of their artistic value. And this was a conscious policy. About one of the medals, McKenney wrote: "I am certainly anxious that these medals should be as perfect in their resemblance of the original, as the artist can make them. They are intended, not for the Indians, only, but for posterity."

The medals given to the Indians were supposed to bear the likeness of the president currently in office, and the medals can be traced administration by administration.

Washington medals

The Washington medals were unique. The government presented a number of medals to Indian chiefs during Washington's term of office, but it did not mass-produce the medals — undoubtedly because it did not command the technical means to do so. Instead, each medal was a separate production, hand engraved on oval plates of silver, the large ones roughly 4 by 6 inches in size. On one side was engraved the figure of Washington with that of an Indian in the peaceful gesture of throwing away his tomahawk. On the reverse was an eagle bearing the crest of the United States on its breast, with an olive branch in its right talon, a sheaf of arrows in its left. The plate was bound with a silver band and provided with a loop at the top by which it could be hung around the neck of the chief. The most famous of these Washington Indian medals was the one presented to the Seneca chief, Red Jacket, in 1792. The medal of Washington in today's presidential series, however, was designed to match later Indian medals and was not made until early in the 20th century.

No medals for Indians were made while John Adams was president. Medals distributed to the chiefs during his term of office were the so-called Seasons medals, which had been produced in England during Washington's second administration. They showed scenes of a farmer sowing grain, women spinning and weaving, and domestic cattle, which were supposed to incite in the Indians a desire for white civilization. Later, a John Adams medal similar in design to other Indian peace medals was struck in order to make the presidential series complete.

The production of Indian peace medals began to be regularized during the administration of President Thomas Jefferson. The pattern for the medals was more or less established, although the methods of manufacture were still not quite set. Medals in three sizes were ordered — large (4 inches in diameter), medium (3 inches), and small (2 inches). The medals were struck from dies cut by a special engraver who worked directly in the steel of the die, cutting out the features that would appear in relief on the finished medal. On the obverse was a bust of Jefferson in profile, with a legend which read: TH. JEFFERSON PRESIDENT OF THE U.S. A.D. 1801. On the reverse were two hands clasped, one with a cuff showing three stripes and three buttons, the other wearing a bracelet engraved with spread eagle. A crossed peace pipe and tomahawk and the words PEACE AND FRIENDSHIP completed the design.

One feature of the Jefferson medals distinguished them from later medals. They were hollow shells rather than solid medals. Possibly because there was no press in the country at the time powerful enough to strike the medals from solid discs of silver, two thin plates were used. The obverse and reverse of the medals were struck separately, then fastened together with a silver band to form a hollow medal. It was a satisfactory expedient as far as the appearance of the medal was concerned, but the Indians compared them unfavorably with the heavy medals they were accustomed to receiving from the British. The Jefferson medal issued today by the Mint in the presidential series is a solid medal which follows the 3-inch design of the original medals.

New design

When James Madison succeeded Jefferson in 1809, new medals had to be designed and struck. The task of ordering the medals fell to John Mason, who held the office of superintendent of Indian Trade. He turned to a friend in Philadelphia, John Vaughan, to engage an artist and to oversee the production of the medals at the Mint. Mason insisted that the hollow medals be replaced by solid ones and the Mint undertook to strike such medals. The Madison medals, like the Jefferson ones, came in three sizes, although the diameters — 3, 2.5, and 2 inches — differed from those of the Jefferson medals. They were solid silver, and at the suggestion of Vaughan, the reverse had a slightly changed design.

Vaughan objected to having both the wrists encuffed as they appeared on the Jefferson medals. This, he said, did not indicate the diversity of the races who were joined in the handclasp of friendship. He had the artist leave one of the arms bare, and this new design was used repeatedly until completely new designs were substituted for the reverse of the medals in the 1850s and later. Mason asked that the lettering on both sides of the medal be "so arranged that a small hole may be made through the medal exactly over the head of the President (so as to suspend it erect when worn by the Chiefs) without interfering with the letters." But for some unaccountable reason this wise advice was never heeded.

When it was time to have medals struck for President James Monroe, both the man directing the work and the artist-engraver were new. Thomas L. McKenney had replaced John Mason as superintendent of Indian Trade, and Moritz Furst was engaged in place of John Reich, who had engraved the Madison medals. The general form of the medals, nevertheless, followed the set formula. Furst prepared satisfactory likenesses of Monroe on the three sizes of the medals, and the dies of the previous reverse were used again.

Furst was also engaged to make the medals of Presidents John Quincy Adams, Andrew Jackson and Martin Van Buren. These medals, like those that followed, were ordered by the head of the Indian Office (the commissioner of Indian Affairs, after that office was created in 1832), who was the official responsible for the distribution of the medals to the chiefs. It was the custom to order 100 of each of the three sizes, although from time to time not all the medals were given out during the administration they represented. Rather than give the Indian chiefs medals of a previous administration, with the portrait of a president who was no longer in office, medals left over at the end of a president's tenure were regularly melted down to help provide the silver needed for the new medals.

As the series of medals progressed, they began to be considered as "presidential medals," quite apart from their original purpose as Indian peace medals. Franklin Peale, who became Chief Coiner at the Mint in 1839, believed that the Mint should be the depository of dies of all national medals, and he urged that medals missing from the presidential series (for example, one for John Adams) be supplied. He was supported by Robert M. Patterson, Director of the Mint, who in 1841 suggested making a medal of President William Henry Harrison, whose term had been too short to permit making Indian medals bearing his portrait. Nothing came of the proposals at the time, however.

Technical advance

When it came time to prepare medals for President John Tyler, technical advances had taken some of the difficulties out of medal making. The invention in France of a "portrait lathe," a mechanical means of cutting dies, did away with the need for the special engraver. A medallion of the president could now be modeled in wax, with full possibilities for making corrections until a suitable likeness was obtained. From this, by use of an intermediate plaster cast, a casting in fine iron was made of the medallion. With the use of the steam-powered lathe, reduced facsimiles were turned out in steel, and the lettering was then stamped in.

The new machine at the Mint was used for making the dies of the President John Tyler Indian peace medal from a medallion modeled by Ferdinand Pettrich, the President James K. Polk medal from a model made by the artist John Gadsby Chapman, and the President Zachary Taylor medal from a medallion sculptured by Henry Kirke Brown. The portrait lathe was adjusted to make the various sizes of the dies from the same model, so that all three sizes of these medals are identical and do not show the variations that occurred in the earlier medals, when the dies were cut individually by hand.

The next medals were again made from dies cut by engravers, who signed contracts with the commissioner of Indian Affairs to engrave the dies and strike the medals for presentation to the Indians. The two young New York artists who were engaged were Salathiel Ellis and Joseph Willson. Ellis engraved the dies for the portraits of Presidents Millard Fillmore, Franklin Pierce, James Buchanan and Abraham Lincoln, while Willson made the reverses for the medals. The old peace and friendship design which had been used for so many years on the reverse of the medals was now laid aside, and scenes depicting the adoption of civilization were used instead. One such design was used on the reverse of the Fillmore and Pierce medals, another on the Buchanan and Lincoln

Indian peace medals. For these medals only the large and medium size were made; the small size was discontinued.

Copies of the medals designed for presentation to the Indians from Jefferson to Buchanan are issued by the Mint in bronze as part of the presidential series, uniformly now in the 3-inch size, although in past times the smaller sizes as well were reproduced. With President Buchanan, however, the presidential series begins to diverge from the Indian peace medal series. The Buchanan medal uses the reverse from the Fillmore and Pierce medals, instead of the one designed for it by Willson, and the Lincoln medal in the Mint presidential series is an inaugural medal, not the one designed for presentation to the Indian chiefs.

Paquet designs

The Indian peace medal for President Andrew Johnson's administration was engraved by Anthony Paquet. He had begun to make the medal for presentation to Indians during Lincoln's second administration and changed the obverse to show the bust of Johnson after Lincoln's assassination. The reverse was a completely new design, one suggested by the commissioner of Indian Affairs to show the change from Indian culture to white civilization. This medal became part of the presidential series.

Although the presidential series for presidents following Andrew Johnson are not those made for the Indians, special peace medals continued to be produced for each administration up to and including that of President Benjamin Harrison. That for President Ulysses S. Grant was made by Paquet and was struck in only one size, 2.5 inches in diameter. Those for Presidents Rutherford B. Hayes, James A. Garfield, Chester A. Arthur and Grover Cleveland were oval medals measuring 3 by 2.25 inches and on the reverse showed an Indian and a white man in a rural scene. They were designed by the engravers in the Mint, Charles E. Barber and George T. Morgan. For Benjamin Harrison, both an oval and a round Indian peace medal were made. Only small numbers of these later medals were struck in silver, for the Indian tribes were no longer treated as sovereign nations, and the importance of the chiefs in dealings with the U.S. government had declined. Bronze copies of all these Indian medals are available in the Mint's miscellaneous series.

Many persons today who collect these medals do not realize that the medals are relics of U.S. policy toward Indians and that the early medals were designed and produced exclusively to provide suitable symbols of peace and friendship for the Indian chiefs. But in a sense, Thomas L. McKenney's prophecy has come true. These medals were indeed designed "not for the Indians only, but for posterity."

Source: U.S. Mint

Description of presidential medals

George Washington, 1789
Obv. GEORGE WASHINGTON PRESIDENT OF THE UNITED STATES. Nude bust to right; below, 1789. By DuVivier.
Rev. PEACE : AND : FRIENDSHIP. Pipe of peace and tomahawk, in saltire, above two clasped hands.

John Adams, 1797.
Obv. JOHN ADAMS PRESIDENT OF THE U.S. Bust to right; below, A.D. 1797.
Rev. Similar to Washington medal.

Thomas Jefferson, 1801
Obv. TH. JEFFERSON PRESIDENT OF THE U.S., A.D. 1801. Bust to left.
Rev. Similar to Washington medal. By Reich.

James Madison, 1809.
Obv. JAMES MADISON PRESIDENT OF THE U.S., A.D. 1809. Bust to left.
Rev. Similar to Washington medal. By Reich.

James Monroe, 1817.
Obv. JAMES MONROE PRESIDENT OF THE U.S., A.D. 1817. Bust to right.
Rev. Similar to Washington medal. By Furst.

John Quincy Adams, 1825
Obv. JOHN QUINCY ADAMS PRESIDENT OF THE UNITED STATES. Draped bust to right; below, 1825.
Rev. Similar to Washington medal. By Furst.

Andrew Jackson, 1829.
Obv. ANDREW JACKSON PRESIDENT OF THE UNITED STATES. Bust to right; below, 1829.
Rev. Similar to Washington medal. By Furst.

Martin Van Buren, 1837
Obv. MARTIN VAN BUREN PRESIDENT OF THE UNITED

STATES. Bust to right; below, A.D. 1837.
Rev. Similar to Washington medal. By Furst.

William Henry Harrison, 1841
Obv. WILLIAM H. HARRISON. Facing bust.
Rev. INAUGURATED : PRESIDENT : OF THE : UNITED
STATES : MARCH 4, 1841. : DIED : APRIL 4, 1841,
within a laurel wreath. By Morgan.

John Tyler, 1841.
Obv. JOHN TYLER PRESIDENT OF THE UNITED STATES.
Draped bust to left; below, 1841.
Rev. Similar to Washington medal.

James K. Polk, 1845
Obv. JAMES K. POLK PRESIDENT OF THE UNITED STATES.
Draped bust to left; below, 1845.
Rev. Similar to Washington medal.

Zachary Taylor, 1849.
Obv. ZACHARY TAYLOR PRESIDENT OF THE UNITED
STATES. Draped bust to left; below, 1849.
Rev. Similar to Washington medal.

Millard Fillmore, 1850
Obv. MILLARD FILLMORE PRESIDENT OF THE UNITED
STATES. Nude bust to right; below, 1850; beneath
truncation of bust, S. Ellis.
Rev. A white man and an Indian, standing before a
flag, in an agricultural scene; above, LABOR
VIRTUE HONOR. By Ellis and Willson.

Franklin Pierce, 1853
Obv. FRANKLIN PIERCE, PRESIDENT OF THE UNITED
STATES. Nude bust to left; below, 1853.
Rev. Similar to Fillmore medal.

James Buchanan, 1857
Obv. JAMES BUCHANAN, PRESIDENT OF THE UNITED
STATES. Bust to right; below, 1857.
Rev. Similar to Fillmore medal. By Ellis and Willson.

Abraham Lincoln, 1862
Obv. ABRAHAM LINCOLN, PRESIDENT OF THE UNITED
STATES. Bust to right; below, 1862.
Rev. In center, scenes of white civilization, with Indian
behind plow, church and other buildings in
background. Top, around, Indian preparing to
scalp second man; below, at left, quiver with
arrows, and at right, long bow and peace pipe.
Bust below, center.

Andrew Johnson, 1865.
Obv. ANDREW JOHNSON PRESIDENT OF THE UNITED
STATES. Nude bust to right; below, 1865; beneath
bust, PAQUET F.
Rev. A female figure, Columbia, in long chiton and
flowing robe, grasping the hand of an Indian
chief before a tomb surmounted with a bust of
Washington; below, PAQUET.

Ulysses S. Grant, 1869.
Obv. ULYSSES S. GRANT. Nude bust to right; beneath,
W. & C. BARBER F.
Rev. PRESIDENT OF THE UNITED STATES. Within a laurel
wreath, INAUGURATED : FIRST TERM : MARCH 4.
1869 : — + — : SECOND TERM : MARCH 4. 1873;
beneath, two small branches of oak, in saltire. W.
& C. BARBER.

Rutherford B. Hayes, 1877
Obv. RUTHERFORD B. HAYES. Nude bust to left.
Rev. Similar to Grant medal, but within the wreath
reading INAUGURATED : MARCH 5 : 1877; outside
wreath, PRESIDENT OF THE UNITED STATES. By
Morgan.

James A. Garfield, 1881.
Obv. JAMES A. GARFIELD. Nude bust to left. By C.E.
Barber.
Rev. Similar to Lincoln medal, but within the wreath

reading INAUGURATED : PRESIDENT : OF THE :
UNITED STATES : MARCH 4, 1881 : — + — :
ASSASSINATED : JULY 2, 1881 : DIED : SEPT. 19,
1881. By Morgan.

Chester A. Arthur, 1881
Obv. CHESTER A. ARTHUR. Nude bust to right.
Rev. Similar to Grant medal, but within the wreath
reading INAUGURATED : SEPTEMBER 20 : 1881. By
C.E. Barber.

Grover Cleveland, 1885 and 1893
Obv. GROVER CLEVELAND. Bust to right.
Rev. Within a laurel wreath, INAUGURATED :
PRESIDENT : OF THE : UNITED STATES : MARCH 4 :
1885. By C.E. Barber.

Benjamin Harrison, 1889
Obv. BENJAMIN HARRISON. Bust to left.
Rev. Similar to Cleveland medal, but inside wreath,
INAUGURATED : PRESIDENT : OF THE : UNITED
STATES : MARCH 4 : 1889. By C.E. Barber.

William McKinley, 1901.
Obv. WILLIAM McKINLEY. Bust to left.
Rev. INAUGURATED : PRESIDENT OF THE : UNITED
STATES : MARCH 4, 1897. : SECOND TERM :
MARCH 4, 1901 : ASSASSINATED : SEPT. 6, 1901 :
DIED SEPT. 14, 1901 : To left Columbia standing,
weeping; below palm branch and oak wreath.
By Barber & Morgan.

Theodore Roosevelt, 1901.
Obv. THEODORE ROOSEVELT. Bust to left.
Rev. INAUGURATED : PRESIDENT : OF THE : UNITED
STATES : SEPT. 14, 1901 : SECOND TERM : MARCH
4, 1905. To left, Columbia standing, her right hand
resting upon an altar, on which is a cinerary urn,
in her extended left, a scroll; above NATIONAL
CAPITOL. By Barber and Morgan.

William H. Taft, 1909.
Obv. WILLIAM H. TAFT. Bust to right.
Rev. INAUGURATED : PRESIDENT OF THE : UNITED
STATES : MARCH 4, 1909. Sibyl seated in front of
National Capitol. By Barber and Morgan.

Woodrow Wilson
Obv. Portrait bust to left; around border, left
WOODROW; right WILSON.
Rev. An eagle with wings spread standing on oak
and laurel branches; in background the Capitol
building in Washington; across lower field,
INAUGURATED : PRESIDENT OF THE : UNITED STATES
: MAR. 4 1913 : SECOND TERM : MAR. 5 1917. By
George T. Morgan.

Warren G. Harding
Obv. Portrait bust to left; around left border, WARREN
G.; around right border HARDING.
Rev. Female figure draped in mourning facing right,
holding laurel branch; column on left; upper
field, an eagle within a wreath; INAUGURATED :
PRESIDENT OF THE : UNITED STATES : MAR. 4 1921;
a horizontal band of leaves; below, DIED : AUG. 2
: 1923; at bottom a laurel wreath, flowers and
palm branches; on exergue a patterned band.
By George T. Morgan.

Calvin Coolidge
Obv. Portrait bust to right; around border, CALVIN
COOLIDGE, PRESIDENT OF THE UNITED STATES.
Rev. Seated draped female figure of Liberty, holding
fasces, facing left; in left field INAUG : URATED
and U.S. shield with eagle; upper right field, AUG.
3 1923 : AND : MAR. 4 1925; lower right field, a
cornucopia; in exergue, 1928 around edge, a
border of 48 leaves, one for each state in the
Union. By John R. Sinnock.

Herbert Hoover:
Obv. Portrait of President Hoover to right, above PRESIDENT OF THE UNITED STATES. In background MCMXXIX HERBERT HOOVER.
Rev. Standing figure of Columbia facing front and holding a fasces in either arm; in background INAUGURATED MARCH 4 1929, ENGINEER SCHOLAR STATESMAN HUMANIST. By John R. Sinnock.

Franklin D. Roosevelt
Obv. Portrait of President Roosevelt facing right.
Rev. A seated figure, draped, with head bowed, represents the sorrowing nation and all the human race. Her right hand is extended in the act of dropping a wreath upon waters upon which a ship symbolizing the spirit of the late president sails into the distant mists of the horizon, and in her left hand is the palm branch of mourning. The inscription at the top, FOR COUNTRY AND HUMANITY, is intended to indicate his labors for the benefit of the oppressed of all mankind. In the left field are the dates of inauguration; in the right background are rows of crosses signifying that he also was a war casualty. Below this is the date of death. In the lower left field is a stump of an olive tree from which new leaves are sprouting, representing the dawn of a new era of peace; in the exergue, IN MEMORIAM. By John R. Sinnock.

Harry S Truman
Obv. Portrait of President Truman to left; around border PRESIDENT OF THE UNITED STATES; in the background HARRY S TRUMAN.
Rev. In center view of the White House; above, the seal of the president; below, inscription INAUGURATED APRIL 12 1945 JANUARY 20 1949. By Sinnock and Gilroy Roberts.

Dwight D. Eisenhower
Obv. Portrait of President Eisenhower to left; around border DWIGHT D. EISENHOWER.
Rev. Standing draped female figure of Freedom, which stands on the Capitol dome; background to left, pioneers on the prairie schooner and oxen; to right, ploughman; above, 13 stars; around border INAUGURATED PRESIDENT JAN. 20, 1953; lower background, UNITED STATES OF AMERICA. By Gilroy Roberts and Frank Gasparro.

Dwight D. Eisenhower
Obv. Portrait of President Eisenhower to left; around border DWIGHT D. EISENHOWER.
Rev. Center figure is reproduced from statue of Freedom above the Capitol dome; directly below, the shield of the United States, with 13 stars representing original 13 States. Upper left of center is the atomic symbol; the kneeling figure on the upper left represents Agriculture: the figure on the upper right, Industry; lower left, Science, Research; lower right, Commerce, Transportation. Above around border the inscription ATOMS FOR PEACE. Below is the inscription: INAUGURATED PRESIDENT OF THE UNITED STATES, SECOND TERM, JANUARY 20, 1957. By Gilroy Roberts and von Hebel.

John F. Kennedy
Obv. Portrait of President Kennedy to left: Around border JOHN F. KENNEDY.
Rev. seal of the president of the United States, above INAUGURATED PRESIDENT; below a portion of President Kennedy's Inaugural Address, his name and the date JANUARY 20, 1961. On either side, a lighted torch denoting enlightenment. By Gilroy Roberts and Frank Gasparro.

Lyndon B. Johnson
Obv. Portrait of President Johnson to left: around border LYNDON B. JOHNSON.
Rev. seal of the president of the United States, below NOVEMBER 22, 1963; encircling seal PRESIDENT OF THE UNITED STATES; below seal a portion of his address before the joint session of Congress on Nov. 27, 1963. By Gilroy Roberts and Frank Gasparro.

Richard M. Nixon
Obv. Portrait of President Nixon to right: above and around border PRESIDENT OF THE UNITED STATES; to left of bust RICHARD MILHOUS NIXON.
Rev. seal of the president of the United States within a wreath of 50 stars; below the date of inauguration and a statement from his August 1968 speech accepting the nomination for president. By Frank Gasparro.

Richard M. Nixon
second term medal: same Obv.
Rev. seal of the president of the United States within a wreath of 50 stars; above PEACE; below date JANUARY 20, 1973, and an excerpt from a speech on world peace. By Frank Gasparro.

Gerald R. Ford
Obv. Portrait of President Ford to right: Above and around border GERALD R. FORD.
Reverse dominated by the presidential seal, surrounded by the date of the Ford inauguration, AUGUST 9, 1974, and the legend, "I WILL BE PRESIDENT OF ALL THE PEOPLE." By Frank Gasparro and Matthew Peloso.

Jimmy Carter
Obv. Three-quarters bust of President Carter facing left. Above PRESIDENT OF THE UNITED STATES, at right JIMMY CARTER.
Rev. Presidential seal; eagle with olive branch and arrows, surrounded by 50 stars. INAUGURATED : JANUARY 20, 1977 : "THE AMERICAN DREAM : ENDURES . . . WE MUST : ONCE AGAIN HAVE FAITH : IN OUR COUNTRY . . . : JIMMY CARTER. By Frank Gasparro.

Ronald Reagan
Obv. President Reagan facing right, E.A.B. JONES below. RONALD REAGAN above; PRESIDENT OF THE UNITED STATES below.
Rev. View of Half Dome in Yosemite National Park. Above, "LET US RENEW OUR FAITH AND OUR HOPE. WE HAVE EVERY RIGHT TO DREAM HEROIC DREAMS." By Elizabeth Jones.

George Bush
Designs pending at press time; no official information available.

Source: U.S. Mint

Seigniorage

Seigniorage is the difference between the monetary value of coins and their cost, including the manufacturing expense. The seigniorage on coins, arising from the exercise of the government's monetary powers, differs from receipts coming from the public, since there is no corresponding payment on the part of another party. Therefore, seigniorage is excluded from receipts and treated, like borrowing, as a means of financing a budget deficit, or as a supplementary amount to be applied (to reduce debt or to increase the cash in the treasury) in the years of a budget surplus.

In a historical sense, seigniorage is a charge imposed by the agency that is legally entrusted with the power to produce coins for circulation as money. The term is borrowed from the French word "seigneurage," which literally means "the right of the lord."

Indeed, the delegation of the right (or privilege) to the sovereign is a tradition that can be traced back to Roman times. In the Middle Ages, the prerogative was exercised by the governing nobles of each state — the feudal lords and kings — and it was mainly the abuse of the prerogative that caused the most famous cases of currency debasements.

In fact, up to the reign of Charles VII, the seigniorage obtained by reducing the amount of gold or silver in coins or by raising the charge for manufacturing coins was considered an important source of revenue for the French crown. It was not until 1803 that France passed laws to limit the seigniorage charge that could be imposed by the state.

The question of seigniorage in the U.S. goes back to the first Secretary of the Treasury, Alexander Hamilton, whose views on seigniorage were generally unfavorable. Hamilton apparently preferred to have the metallic value of coins equal to their monetary value, as he believed counterfeiters would be induced to duplicate coins if the monetary value of coins exceeded the metallic value.

Thus, when Congress adopted Hamilton's coinage recommendations in 1792, the seigniorage charge was limited to one half of 1 percent of the value of bullion presented to the Mint for immediate coinage. If the person presenting bullion had to wait for delivery of the coins, there was to be no seigniorage charge at all. In practice, however, seigniorage did not actually disappear. Increased coin production after 1795 resulted in lower minting costs and the weight of some of the minor coins was reduced.

In 1800, the U.S. Mint showed a net profit of about $5,000 on coinage, and in the years that followed, a small margin of seigniorage was usually realized.

During fiscal years 1934-1964, total silver seigniorage in the U.S. amounted to $1,916.2 million. Of this total, $1,172.9 million originated from the revaluation of silver bullion behind silver certificates and $743.3 million was from the production of silver coins. The seigniorage from revaluation of silver bullion was the result of increases in the price of silver during 1934-1964 and a law in May 1933 that permitted the Treasury to hold silver in either bullion (bar) form or coins as reserve backing for the Treasury's silver certificates in circulation. Before May 1933, the law allowed only silver dollars as reserve backing for silver certificates.

The price of silver in the New York market increased from an average price of 45 cents per troy ounce in 1933 to $1.293 in 1964; as a result, the dollar value of silver bars was required as reserve for the same amount of certificates, with the difference representing the amount of seigniorage.

The nature and composition of seigniorage after fiscal year 1964 reflect the results of changes in the law regarding coinage, as well as increases in coin production. During fiscal years 1964-1967, the U.S. Treasury received a total of $1,665.1 million of seigniorage. Unlike the 1934-1964 period, nearly all the seigniorage in the latter period resulted from coin production, with a relatively small amount due to revaluation. The difference between the two periods largely reflects that in recent years the market price of silver has been as high as the monetary value of silver; consequently, no revaluation of seigniorage could be realized.

A huge jump in coin seigniorage occurred in fiscal year 1966, an increase of $530 million over fiscal year 1965. The major reason for the sharp increase reflects the enactment of the Coinage Act of 1965, which, by altering the metallic composition of half dollars, quarters and dimes, drastically reduced the cost of metals used in producing coins. The bulk ($546 million) of seigniorage was the result of coining clad quarters and clad dimes.

Coinage seigniorage is the difference between the cost of the metals that go into coin — alloy costs — and the monetary value of the coin. Not all seigniorage thus derived can be considered as net profit to the government, because in addition to the cost of the metal, coin manufacturing also involves the cost of production.

In 1966, for example, the cost to the government for producing 8.7 billion coins amounted to $11.1 million. This figure, however, does not include production and security costs, nor capital investment outlays for plants and equipment. All these costs are associated with coin production, and when taken into account, indicate that the seigniorage that goes into the general fund of the government does not represent net profit.

Seigniorage in Fiscal Year 1988 totaled $467 million, and in FY89 it jumped to $594 million.

The Assay Commission

The Assay Commission was one of the oldest institutions in the annals of American history until public participation was eliminated during the Carter administration. The original provision for this body was made in the Act of April 2, 1792, Section 18, which established the Mint and provided for a national coinage.

The duty of the Commission was to test the weight and fineness of the coins reserved by the operating Mints during the preceding calendar year, in order to assure that they conformed to their respective legal standards. During each calendar year, coins were selected at random from each Mint's coinage and shipped quarterly to the Philadelphia Mint, where they were preserved for delivery with the selected Philadelphia coins, to the Commission when it met the following February.

If it appeared by such examination and test that these coins did not differ from the standard fineness and weight by a greater quantity than is allowed by law, the trial was considered and reported as satisfactory. If, however, any greater deviation from the legal standard or weight appeared, this fact was certified to the president of the United States; and if, on a view of the circumstances of the case, he so decided, the officers implicated in the error were thenceforward disqualified from holding their respective offices.

Those pyx coins not used for the assay test were returned to Mint stocks for circulation. They were not mutilated or marked in any manner to distinguish them from other coins. The pieces upon which assay tests were made were returned to the Mint for melting.

The Assay Commission was established by the founding fathers to serve as an impartial check upon the nation's coinage, additional to that routinely performed by Mint employees.

The Commission met in one-day session at the Mint in Philadelphia, on the second Wednesday in February, as required by law.

There were three ex officio members of the Commission: A judge of the United States District Court for the Eastern District of Pennsylvania; the Comptroller of the Currency; and the Assayer of the United States Assay Office at New York. The membership always included a representative of the National Bureau of Standards. The weights used by the Commission were sent to the National Bureau of Standards to be calibrated before the Assay Commission meeting to assure that they conformed to the standard troy weight measure used in the Mints. The standards representative delivered them.

While there was no statutory limit to the number who could serve, both a ceiling on appropriated funds for expenses to cover the meeting, and that the membership must be divided into three small committees assigned to the task of counting, weighing and assaying coin samples, dictated the size. Owing to the smallness of the Commission, and the honor which attaches to service, it had been customary to make very few repeat appointments in the final years.

First authorized to serve on the commission in 1837, public members had been appointed by the president continuously at least since 1874, according to available records.

Although outgoing Director of the Mint Mary Brooks had submitted 117 names to the White House, a list from which about 25 members would by tradition have been named to the 1977 Assay Commission, the Carter administration declined to name any public members to the historic body. It is believed about 34 public members would have been nominated.

Thirty-one of the original 50 1977 Assay Commission medals produced were distributed to participants, key Treasury and Mint officials and staff and to the Smithsonian Institution Division of Numismatics and the Bureau of the Mint archives. The remaining 19 were melted.

However, following public outcry over distribution of the medals, the Mint struck pewter duplicates of the medal for sale to collectors. The only distinguishing marks on the original medals are the names of the persons receiving them engraved on the edges.

The failure of the Carter Administration to name public members to the 1977 Commission sent shock waves through the numismatic fraternity, which had a natural predilection for the mission of the Assay Commission and had enjoyed notable recognition among commissioners in years past.

Hobby representation on this select body was not of recent origin, however. Numismatists had a natural inclination towards the tradition and mission of the Assay Commission and had readily accepted appointment to the group as a signal honor, despite being obliged to pay their own expenses. The Mint expended $2,500 annually for the event.

Among the scores of hobby notables accepting this appointment early in this century were James E. Fraser, designer of the Indian Head 5-cent piece (1921), and former American Numismatic Association presidents Waldo C. Moore (1912), H.O. Granberg (1916 and 1917), J.M. Henderson (1911, 1916, 1920 and 1921) and Judson Brenner (1912, 1913, 1921, 1922, 1926 and 1928).

The last meeting of the statutory members of the Assay Commission came in 1980. No meetings were held during the Reagan administration and with the closing of the New York Assay Office, the statutory member's position has been eliminated.

Bureau of Engraving and Printing 6

The Bureau of Engraving and Printing

The Bureau of Engraving and Printing, which came into existence Aug. 29, 1862, is an indirect consequence of the Civil War, and primarily the result of the self-confidence, courage, ingenuity and patriotism of one man — Spencer Morton Clark. It also is the result of the foresight of Salmon P. Chase (President Lincoln's first Secretary of the Treasury), his confidence in Clark's ability, and his recognition of Clark's accomplishments.

President Lincoln called Congress into extra session on July 4, 1861, following the firing on Fort Sumter. At the time the nation was on the edge of bankruptcy and hardly in condition to finance a war. During the special session of Congress, Secretary Chase recommended that Congress set up a system of taxation and one of floating loans. His scheme for borrowing included the issuance of non-interest-bearing notes which would circulate as money.

Although there was some doubt that the government had the constitutional authority to issue paper money, Congress adopted Chase's plan in the Act of July 17, 1861, and as a result the first U.S. government-issued paper money came into being. The first notes, popularly known as "demand notes" because of certain provisions of their issuance, were produced by the American Bank Note Co. and the National Bank Note Co., both of New York, under contract with the government.

One of the provisions of the new law specified that the authorized securities should be signed by the First or Second Comptroller, or the Register of the Treasury, and countersigned by such other officers of the Treasury as the Secretary of the Treasury cared to designate. It was soon evident that if the designated officers were to perform duties other than signing currency, the law would have to be revised.

Signatures

On Aug. 5, 19 days after enactment of the original law, President Lincoln signed a bill to change the signature requirements. Under the new law, the notes were to be signed by the Treasurer of the United States and the Register of the Treasury. The new legislation also provided that the Secretary could designate other personnel to sign the notes for these officers. A force of 70 clerks was assigned to sign these early notes — with their own names.

With such a variety of signatures on notes, security was poor. Spencer Clark, the chief clerk of the Bureau of Construction in the department, who at the time was acting engineer in charge of the Bureau, suggested to Secretary Chase that the notes be imprinted with the facsimile signatures of the required officers. Also, he suggested that the notes be imprinted with a copy of the Treasury seal as additional evidence of lawful issue.

The Secretary approved Clark's proposal and Congress approved the act on Feb. 25, 1862. Clark was then directed to procure the necessary machinery for the imprinting. A variation of the seal designed by Clark is still used on U.S. securities.

Clark described the original seal design as having for its interior a facsimile of the seal adopted by the Treasury Department for its documents on a ground of geometric lathe work, the exterior being composed of 34 similar points. "These points," Clark said, "were designed to be typical of the 34 states, and to simulate the appearance of the seals ordinarily affixed to public documents."

Clark was loyal to the government and gave no recognition to the rebellion then going on and included a point in his design for each of the 11 states then in secession. He further said of his seal: "It was difficult of execution, and it was believed that counterfeiters could not readily make a successful imitation of it. So far [1864] the belief has seemed well founded, for it has not, that I am aware of, been successfully imitated."

Clark told Secretary Chase that it would be both proper and economical to print the signatures by "a peculiar process and with peculiar ink." Two presses were secured for overprinting the signatures, an operation that began in March of 1862. Early records do not explain how long this practice continued.

Automation

Notes printed by the two New York bank note companies were delivered to the Treasury for final processing and issuing. The notes were printed in sheets of four subjects and in the beginning were trimmed and separated manually by the use of shears. Approximately 70 women were employed, at a salary of $50 per month, for the trimming and separating operations.

Because of the expense and tediousness of this method, Clark gained authority to construct two machines on a trial basis, one for trimming and one for separating. The trials of Clark's machines were reported to Secretary Chase as failures and Chase gave orders to have them removed.

However, Clark asked the Secretary to personally check the machines, an inspection which revealed to Chase that actually the machines were quite effective. He rescinded his order to have them removed and directed Clark to submit plans for performing the work on machines operated by steam.

A steam engine and boilers were secured, along with necessary auxiliary equipment, and set up in the southwest room of the south wing of the basement in the main Treasury building. Presses for sealing, trimming and separating also were installed. On Aug. 29, 1862, Clark commenced with one male assistant and four female operators. Chase, in a diary entry dated Sept. 13, 1862, said: "Visited Mr. Clark's sealing and trimming machines for the ones and twos and found them a perfect success."

Secretary Chase was so pleased with Clark's machines that he asked him to investigate further possibilities relating to the printing of securities. Clark's investigations determined that the government was paying enormous prices to the bank note companies for printing notes. He told Secretary Chase that he could produce the work in the department for "a comparatively small outlay, at a great saving of cost in the issues."

Chase had introduced in Congress a proposal based on Clark's report, asking for authority to engrave and print notes at the Treasury in Washington. This authority was given by the Act of July 11, 1862, and in August, little more than a month after passage of the act, Clark reported to Chase that the first engraver (James Duthie) had been hired and was progressing satisfactorily. Date of the first printing in the department is in question. A congressional report of 1864 states that printing of some public moneys was begun in the autumn of 1862, but Clark reported to Secretary Chase on Dec. 13, 1862, "no printers are yet employed." One account says plate printing in the Treasury did not begin until January 1863.

Clark had great executive talent and was very careful in his selection of skilled artists and tradesmen for the department. He submitted a list of American engravers of known reputation. Two of those named, Joseph P. Ourdan and John F.E. Prud'homme, became full-time employees in the department. Other well-known engravers, working on a piece basis, included Charles Burt, Louis Delnoce, Alfred Sealey and Archibald McLees. Joseph James P. Ourdan, father of Joseph P. Ourdan, also came to work for the department. He had been instructed in the art of engraving by his son.

The Bureau's first engraver, James Duthie, was a skilled etcher, and served as Superintendent of Engraving until 1865. Another early craftsman was Elisha Hobart, trained as an engraver, but later a transferrer. Hobart is remembered for his engraving of Sargent's painting "Landing of the Pilgrims," on which he worked for two years.

Clark also hired George W. Casilear as an engraver, but soon afterward he was made Custodian of Dies and Rolls. Later, he became Superintendent of Engraving and served in that capacity, except during President Cleveland's first administration, until October 1893.

Still another early engraver was Henry Gugler, hired in January 1863. A native of Germany, Gugler had been in the United States only about 10 months when hired by Clark. Gugler later founded the lithographic firm of H. Gugler and Son, Milwaukee, Wis., which is now the Gugler Lithographic Co.

Fractional currency

One of the first products produced by the Bureau was fractional currency, issued in place of coins during and for some 10 years after the Civil War. In all, there were five issues of postage and fractional currency. The second and third were printed at the department. The greater part of the fourth issue was produced by a private bank note firm but were sealed by the plate printers at the Bureau. There were three different 50-cent notes in the fourth issue and the faces of two of these were printed at the Bureau. Faces of the fifth issue were done at the Bureau and the work on the reverses was done by a private firm.

The third issue of 5-cent fractional currency bore a portrait of Clark and was the subject of much controversy (see Chap. 9, "Portraits on U.S. Paper Money"). The controversy reached Congress and resulted in the law that remains in effect today that the portrait of a living person shall not be used on a security of the U.S. (31 U.S.C. 413).

The first paper money produced at the Treasury establishment, other than fractional notes, were the compound interest notes of 1863 and 1864 and the 5 percent Treasury notes of 1863.

By 1864, the Bureau had grown to a point where it employed 237 men and 288 women. In November 1864, Clark reported equipment in use as 15 transfer machines, 72 hydraulic and 96 hand presses, 14 sealing presses, six ink mills and 22 numbering machines.

It is not known for certain when the title "Bureau of Engraving and Printing" began. Early records show such names for the Bureau as "Small Note Department," "Small Note Bureau," "Small Note Room," "Note Bureau," "National Note Bureau," and "First Division of the National Currency Bureau."

Formal recognition

The first reference on record of the use of the name "Bureau of Engraving and Printing" is found in a copy of an order of July 31, 1868, placed with John R. Hoole and Sons, New York City, for an ornamental strip with that wording, for use in printing a form needed by the Bureau. The first legislative recognition of the agency is found in the Act of March 3, 1869, which prohibited any work from being done "in the engraving and printing bureau for private parties."

Additional organizational recognition is found in the Act of July 11, 1896, which provides "That all business of the Bureau of Engraving and Printing shall be under the immediate control of the director of the Bureau, subject to the direction of the

Secretary of the Treasury, and the director of said Bureau shall report to and be responsible directly to the Secretary of the Treasury."

The extent to which steam presses were being used in those early days of the Bureau is recounted in the Bureau's annual report for the fiscal year 1888, which reads: "The steam presses are now printing much more than one-third of the work at the Bureau, with a great economy of rooms, labor and expense. The cost of the printing done by them is less than $80,000. To print the same work by hand would cost $180,000."

The use of distinctively marked paper in printing paper money, limited by law to this single purpose, was early recognized as one of the prime deterrents to counterfeiting.

In 1862, Secretary Chase authorized Clark to make "investigations and experiments in reference to the manufacture of a distinctive paper in the [Treasury] building." Early suppliers of such distinctive paper were Stuart Gwynn of Boston, Mass.; J. M. Wilcox and Co., Philadelphia, Pa.; and the Crane Paper Co. of Dalton, Mass. Crane, the latest firm contracted with, still supplies the Bureau with distinctive paper, which will soon include an embedded plastic security thread.

Although Spencer Clark made a formal recommendation for separate facilities for the printing and processing of currency a scant three years after beginning operations, it was a good many years before the Bureau had its own building. Land for this purpose was purchased on June 26, 1878, from William W. Corcoran, Washington historical figure best known as the founder of the world-famous Corcoran Gallery of Art.

A contract for the excavation for the project was awarded the following month, and the structure, designed in Romanesque style by James G. Hill, Supervising Architect of the Treasury, was completed in record time at a cost of $300,000. It was ready for occupancy on July 1, 1880. The Bureau remained in this building until 1914 when the present Bureau headquarters was built. An annex to the Bureau was completed in 1938.

The Bureau today

The Bureau of Engraving and Printing is the world's largest securities manufacturing establishment. It employs more than 2,000 people and operates 24 hours a day. The Bureau designs, engraves, and prints United States paper currency; Treasury bonds and notes; United States postage, customs and revenue stamps; and miscellaneous engraved items for approximately 75 departments and independent agencies of the Federal government, and its insular possessions. White House invitations, commissions, diplomas, certificates, identification cards and liquor strip stamps are some of the approximately 800 miscellaneous products printed by the Bureau.

Operations of the century-old Bureau of Engraving and Printing are housed in two specially constructed buildings with a combined floor space of approximately 25 acres. The Bureau will add 288,000 square feet of additional floor space when a $15 million western currency-producing facility is completed near Fort Worth, Texas. The Fort Worth plant is expected to be producing notes as early as Fall 1990. Notes will be distinguishable by a small "FW" near the face check number.

Ground was broken for the Fort Worth printing plant on April 25, 1987; the plant is to produce 25 percent of the annual U.S. currency supply and will serve the Kansas City, Dallas and San Francisco Federal Reserve banks.

On Aug. 4, 1950, Public Law 656 was passed by the 81st Congress, which authorized the working capital fund method of financing the operations of the Bureau, placing all operations on a completely reimbursable basis and providing for business-type accounting and budgeting procedures. The effective date of the law was July 1, 1951, and on that date the Bureau's accounting and budgeting procedures were operating fully under the new system.

The principal product of the Bureau is United States paper currency. A face value of more than $78 billion is printed annually, averaging approximately 25 million notes a day.

All of the currency notes printed are Federal Reserve notes, which are issued in denominations of $1, $2, $5, $10, $20, $50, and $100. They are primarily used to replace worn or mutilated currency taken out of circulation. The Bureau has printed $100 United States notes as recently as the early first Nixon administration (by Act of Congress dated May 3, 1878, the value of United States notes outstanding must be maintained at $346,681,016).

Federal Reserve notes and United States notes are the only classes that can now be printed; printing of Federal Reserve Bank notes, national bank notes, gold certificates, and most recently, silver certificates, has been discontinued. Some notes from each of these classes are still in public circulation.

The Department of the Treasury announced on July 14, 1969, that currency in denominations of $500, $1,000, $5,000, and $10,000 would no longer be produced because of the lack of demand.

The largest denomination of currency ever printed was the $100,000 gold certificate of 1934, which featured the portrait of President Wilson. This note was designed for official transactions only, and none of these notes ever circulated outside Federal Reserve Banks.

The $2 Federal Reserve note was issued on April 13, 1976, as the latest permanent addition to the denominations of United States currency.

Beginning in 1966, a collection of 306,275 of the BEP's "certified proofs," proofs which were produced for nearly every instrument printed by that agency, was transferred in 1984 to the Smithsonian Institution's Division of Numismatics.

The transfer began when the BEP ran out of room to store the proofs, which represent all the major note types of the United States, plus such other items as Cuban silver certificates and Philippine Treasury certificates, printed for former U.S. possessions, bonds, stocks, revenue items, checks and other instruments.

The proofs are inked impressions pulled from new printing plates and submitted to BEP officials for examination and approval.

How paper money is printed

To assure the best protection against counterfeiting, all United States paper money, as well as nearly all postage stamps and other evidences of a financial character issued by the United States government, are printed by the "line engraved," or intaglio process, from engraved plates.

Intaglio-printed documents are the most difficult to produce and to counterfeit. Other processes lack the fidelity of fine lines and the distinctive three-dimensional effect of raised line on paper inherent in intaglio printing. An outstanding element of protection is the portrait. The use of portraits in security designs takes full advantage of the characteristics of intaglio printing since even a slight alteration in breadth, spacing, or depth of line on the part of a counterfeiter will cause a perceptible facial change. The portraits used in the designs of securities are those of persons of historical importance. By law, no portrait of a living person may be used.

In the intaglio process, the individual features of a chosen design are hand-tooled by highly skilled engravers who engrave in varying depths into steel with delicate steel-cutting instruments called gravers. With infinite care, each feature, such as the portrait, the vignette, the numerals, the lettering, the script, and the scroll work is hand-engraved by a different master craftsman expertly trained in his own particular skill.

The Bureau prints all paper money by the intaglio process on high-speed sheet-fed Giori presses. Each press has four 32-note printing plates and is capable of printing 9,000 sheets per hour. Each sheet is forced, under extremely high pressure, into the fine engraved lines of a plate to pick up the ink. The backs of the notes are printed with green ink on one day, and the faces are printed with black ink at least 24 hours later.

The use of a specially formulated fast-drying non-offset ink, developed in the Bureau's laboratories, has eliminated the former time-consuming need for tissuing or interleaving between sheets. The inks and distinctive paper used by the Bureau in the manufacture of currency are produced under specifications designed to deter counterfeiting and to assure a high-quality product.

Other counterfeiting deterrents are in the experimental stage. The distinctive paper (75 percent cotton and 25 percent linen) used to produce the paper money of the United States has red and blue fibers embedded in it. A security thread, a strip of clear polyester, will be embedded in the paper. The thread will include microprinting of the letters USA and the denomination of the note. Another security feature will be micro-engraved UNITED STATES OF AMERICA around the portrait. The micro-printing is designed to foil counterfeiting by high-quality photocopiers.

COPE Pak

In June 1985, the Bureau began using a system called COPE Pak to streamline the printing, overprinting and cutting operations, as well as the parceling and shrink wrapping phases of the currency making process.

COPE Pak is an acronym for "Currency Overprinting, Processing and Packaging Equipment." Before the acquisition of the COPE Pak equipment, the overprinting, note examining and packaging operations took place in three separate areas of the Bureau.

COPE Pak machines reduce the number of times employees must handle the money.

The printing process for the COPE Pak machinery begins in the same way as with the previously-used COPE machines.

Currency is still printed in 32-subject sheet form, first the back, then 24 or more hours later, the face. The sheets are then trimmed, split into two 16-subject sheets and examined by human inspectors in the mechanical examining process.

The 16-subject sheets are then delivered to the COPE Pak machines for overprinting, examining, counting and packaging. They are fed into the equipment in two 10,000-sheet stacks.

Blowers separate the sheets and suction feet pick up one sheet at a time. Grippers then pull the sheets along the feedboard into the printing cylinders. "Two-sheet detectors," actuated by the excessive thickness of the combined sheets, tell the system to shut down when more than one sheet is picked up by the suction heads.

At the printing cylinders the black Federal Reserve Bank seals and FRB letters, plus the green Treasury seals and serial numbers are applied to the face of the note.

Sheets are then collated into stacks of 100. When a stack of 100 sheets accumulates, it is cut lengthwise and widthwise and the stacks of individual notes are fed into a paper bander.

With the paper banding process, the similarity between COPE and COPE Pak ends.

With the COPE Pak system, after the notes have been banded, they pass into a note examining station, where an examiner randomly samples and inspects the stacks for quality and accountability purposes.

Once the notes are inspected, they travel to a rotating carousel with 32 compartments, corresponding to each plate position number on the 32-subject printing plates.

When 10 packages of 100 notes are collated in the carousel, they pass to another paper bander. From this bander 1,000-note packages are automatically sent on to counting stations where the contents are counted twice to ensure 100 percent accountability for all the notes processed.

Upon being counted, the packages get shrink-wrapped and labeled. A label placed on the end of the package identifies the package by denomination, bank and beginning and ending serial numbers.

Finally, the shrink-wrapped 1,000-note packages are collated in groups of four in a collating drum and delivered to another shrink-wrapping apparatus, making a finished "brick" of 4,000 notes, ready for shipment to the 12 Federal Reserve Banks.

COPE Pak combines into a single streamlined continuum the operations of overprinting (serial numbers, Treasury seals, Federal Reserve seals and bank numbers), inspection, counting, banding and shrink-wrapping, all with automatic mechanical transfer of work from station to station.

If a mechanical problem should occur in the system, a malfunction indicator provides a digital readout, telling the operator which part is malfunctioning. More than 700 functions can be monitored by this device.

Despite the potential complications of combining operations, BEP officials say the COPE Pak machines can overprint more notes per shift than the COPE equipment, which only overprinted and banded the 100-note bundles.

The net increase in production of notes per shift by the COPE Pak equipment is approximately 10 percent. COPE Paks have been known to turn out as many as 41,500 notes in a nine-hour day.

Besides increased productivity and reduced costs, there has been improvement in the quality of the product itself, BEP officials say.

All currency is now counted four times, double overwrapped for greater protection, bar-coded to facilitate accountability and inventory control and is separable into four packages of 1,000 notes to admit easier breakdown and transfer of currency from Federal Reserve District Banks to other, smaller institutions.

COPE Pak machines are the result of a combined manufacturing effort by factories in several West German cities and one English factory. The headquarters

of this combination is in Switzerland, where the U.S. government has a contract for the machines with DeLaRue Giori of Lausanne.

Koenig and Bauer of Wurzburg makes the numerota (the serial numbering system); Zeiser of Emmingen produces the numbering boxes and computer controls; Bielomatic of Nueffen is responsible for the processing lines; Herma of Stuttgart makes the labeling equipment; and Kalfass, also of Stuttgart, makes the overwrapping apparatus. The English company Vacuumatic, in Harwich, manufactures the counting equipment.

The parts are collected and assembled by Koenig and Bauer in its Wurzburg facility.

A further step in the direction of advancing the technological level of the BEP was taken when the Bureau awarded a $10.2 million contract to the Hamilton Tool Co. of Hamilton, Ohio, for the construction of a web-fed press for printing U.S. currency.

The press will be able to perform simultaneous intaglio face and back printing on the continuous roll of currency paper and adds the overprinting during a single pass through the machine.

As of June 1990, a prototype web press had been constructed and was in the testing phase. Once a satisfactory simulated production run is completed, the press will be dismantled and shipped to the BEP's Washington facility.

BEP officials estimate that one web press could do the same work as four "I8" sheet-fed presses, a rate of almost half a million notes per hour.

In the event a finished note is found to be imperfect after it has been overprinted, it is replaced with a "star" note. In design, star notes are exactly like the notes they replace, but they carry an independent series of serial numbers. The star appears in place of the prefix letter before the serial number on United States notes and after the serial number in place of the suffix letter on Federal Reserve notes. The serial number of the imperfect note which was replaced is not used again in the same numbering sequence.

The life of a $1 note is about 18 months. Higher denominations remain in circulation longer since they are not used in transactions as frequently as the $1 note. The average $5 bill lasts two years; a $10 bill lasts three years; a $20 bill lasts five years; a $50 lasts nine years; and a $100 bill lasts about 23 years. The size of a currency note is approximately 2.61 inches x 6.14 inches and the thickness is .0043 inch. There are 233 new notes to an inch-high stack (not compressed) and 490 equal a pound. A million notes weigh approximately a ton and occupy approximately 42 cubic feet of space (with moderate pressure).

Distribution

After paper money is printed, the Bureau of Engraving and Printing ships the currency to the 12 Federal Reserve Banks and their 26 branches. These agencies, in turn, distribute the money to the commercial banking system throughout the country.

Member banks of the Federal Reserve System carry their reserve accounts with the Federal Reserve Bank of their district. When member banks need additional currency, they authorize the Federal Reserve Bank to charge their reserve account and ship the currency. The Federal Reserve Banks will ship such currency as is required. Usually, nonmember banks procure their currency through a correspondent member bank located in the same city with the Federal Reserve Bank, or by arrangement whereby the currency is shipped directly to the nonmember bank with the reserve account of the correspondent bank charged for the shipment.

To obtain Federal Reserve notes, a Federal Reserve Bank applies to the Federal Reserve agent, a representative of the board of governors of the Federal Reserve System, who is located at the reserve bank and who maintains a stock of unissued notes. In applying for notes, a Federal Reserve Bank must pledge with the agent the required collateral equal to the face value of the notes. This collateral must consist of the following assets, alone or in any combination: 1) gold certificates, 2) Special Drawing Rights certificates, 3) United States government securities, and 4) "eligible paper" as described by statute.

United States government securities are acquired by the Federal Reserve Banks in open market operations. Eligible paper consists of short-term notes, drafts, bills of exchange, or acceptances discounted or purchased by the Reserve banks.

Exchange of mutilated paper currency

Lawfully held paper currency of the United States which has been mutilated will be exchanged at its face amount if clearly more than one-half of the original whole note remains.

Fragments of mutilated currency which are not clearly more than one-half of the original whole note will be exchanged at face value only if the Bureau of Government Financial Operations is satisfied that the missing portions have been totally destroyed. This judgment is based on such evidence of total destruction as is deemed necessary and is final.

No relief will be granted an account of paper currency of the United States which has been totally destroyed.

The public should address all correspondence regarding mutilated currency to the Department of the Treasury, Bureau of Engraving and Printing, OCS/BEPA, Room 344, P.O. Box 37048, Washington, D.C. 20013. Return receipt requested when sending mutilated currency; this address accepts only mutilated paper money and not coins.

Destruction of unfit currency

When paper currency becomes worn and no longer fit for general use, it is withdrawn from circulation, destroyed, and replaced by new notes. The worn out notes are destroyed by incineration or shredding at Federal Reserve banks and branches throughout the country, under procedures prescribed by the Department of the Treasury. The destruction process is not complete until the notes have been reduced to an unidentifiable residue so that no recovery of the notes and of the distinctive paper on which they are imprinted is possible. About 98 percent of the currency is shredded and 2 percent is incinerated.

Before they are destroyed, the currency is verified as to genuineness, kind, value, and number of pieces. One-dollar bills make up the bulk of the currency which is retired because of unfitness.

Silver certificates, United States notes and Federal Reserve notes in all denominations below $500 that are no longer fit for use are verified and destroyed at Federal Reserve Banks and branches throughout the country, under procedures prescribed by the Department of the Treasury.

Federal Reserve notes in denominations of $500 and above are canceled with distinctive perforations and cut in half lengthwise. The lower halves are shipped to the Department of the Treasury in Washington, D.C., where they are verified and destroyed. The upper halves are retained by the Federal Reserve Banks and destroyed after the banks are notified by the Treasury that the lower halves have been verified.

Tours of the BEP

The Bureau of Engraving and Printing is charged with the responsibility for the production of major items of a financial character issued by the United States, the two most prominent of which are the government's paper money and postage stamps. A tour facility is available for the public to view the various operations in the manufacture of currency notes.

Location: The Bureau is located in Washington, D.C., at 14th and C streets S.W., just south of the Washington Monument and in the vicinity of the Smithsonian complex.

Tour admission and hours: The tour facility is open Monday through Friday (except legal holidays), 9 a.m. to 2 p.m. Admission is free and the tour takes approximately 25 minutes.

24-hour information: Current information can be obtained by dialing (202) 447-9709.

At the end of the tour, visitors can browse in the newly-remodeled Visitors' Center, which is situated at the 15th Street entrance to the Bureau.

The Visitors' Center offers exhibits aimed at all audiences, from small children to the handicapped to senior citizens and includes items of interest to both numismatists and philatelists.

At the center, visitors can use interactive exhibits which test their knowledge of the placement of special features on U.S. paper money or practice examining for defective currency. They may try their hand at distinguishing between real and counterfeit currency or they may test their knowledge with a paper money trivia game.

BEP products such as sheets of uncut currency and bags of shredded money are also obtainable at the center.

The Bureau is included on the Tourmobile "Washington Mall" Tour. Service operates continually during the day among 11 of Washington's landmarks. There is a Tourmobile stop across the street from the Bureau on 15th Street.

Products sold by the BEP

Sheets of U.S. paper money
The Bureau offers uncut sheets and partial sheets of U.S. $1 and $2 Federal Reserve notes in two series: 1976 $2 FRNs and 1985 $1 FRNs. The sheets are available in three sizes: full 32-note sheets ($1 only), half sheets of 16 notes each and four-note partial sheets.

Prices for over-the-counter sales are

$7.50 for $1 four-note sheets and $12 for four $2 notes; $21.50 for 16-note $1 half sheets and $38.50 for 16-note $2 half sheets; and $40.50 for 32-note $1 sheets.

Mail orders are priced at $10.25 for four-note $1 sheets and $14.75 for $2 four-note sheets; $28 for 16-note $1 half sheets and $45 for $2 half sheets; and $47 for 32-note $1 sheets.

Money orders, bank-type cashier's checks and certified checks only are accepted for mail orders; no personal checks will be accepted. Orders should be sent to Bureau of Engraving and Printing, Uncut Currency/Souvenir Card Sales Program, 14th and C streets, S.W., Washington, D.C. 20228.

Customs regulations and prohibitive mailing costs prevent the Bureau from accepting orders for sheets of currency from customers outside the United States.

Souvenir cards

Beginning in 1969, the BEP has engraved and manufactured in honor of special events souvenir cards containing engraved reproductions of various United States paper currency issues. The cards measure 8.5 by 10.5 inches except the 1969 American Numismatic Association card, which measures 6 by 9 inches.

Souvenir cards of the Bureau of Engraving and Printing are available in unlimited quantity for 90 days after issue, unless stocks are depleted sooner. Plate proofs are available for 30 days after issue.

Spider press plate prints

Beginning with the 1984 Florida United Numismatists Convention in Tampa, Fla.,

the Bureau began issuing plate prints produced on an operational 19th century spider press. The press was purchased by the Bureau between 1890 and 1904 for currency production, and was also used by the Flatbed Printing Division for specialized printing until the late 1930s or early 1940s. It features a single-plate hand roller and a long radial handle. The iron bed on which the plate is mounted moves between two steel rollers, the top covered with felt.

The Bureau began taking the spider press to numismatic conventions with the FUN '84 show, demonstrating its use by printing examples of plate prints. However, all plate prints sold at the conventions are produced before the convention since the paper is dampened before printing and takes several days to dry.

Engraved and lithographed printings

The BEP also produces for sale to the public engraved and lithographed printings of presidential portraits, building vignettes, government seals, and miscellaneous printings. Bureau products, unless otherwise indicated, are black-ink engravings produced from intaglio plates in a manner similar to currency and postage stamp reproductions.

Write to the BEP, Office of Public Affairs, 14th and C streets S.W., Washington, D.C. 20228, for product availability.

BEP officials
14th and C streets SW, Washington, D.C. 20228, Phone (202) 447-0193

Director..Peter H. Daly
Deputy Director..Michael F. Hill
Assistant Director (Administration)..............................L. Paul Blackmer Jr.
Assistant Director (Operations).....................................Carl V. D'Allesandro
Assistant Director (Research and Engineering)..............Milton J. Seidel
Executive Assistant to the Director................................Ira Polikoff
Chief, Office of Counterfeit Deterrence ....Thomas Ferguson
Public Sales Manager...Christiane K. Carter

Bureau Directors

Director	Term
Spencer Morton Clark	Aug. 22, 1862 - Nov. 17, 1868
George B. McCartee	March 18, 1869 - Feb. 19, 1876
Henry C. Jewell	Feb. 21, 1876 - April 30, 1877
Edward McPherson	May 1, 1877 - Sept. 30, 1878
O.H. Irish	Oct. 1, 1878 - Jan. 27, 1883
Truman N. Burrill	March 30, 1883 - May 31, 1885
Edward O. Graves	June 1, 1885 - June 30, 1889
William M. Meredith	July 1, 1889 - June 30, 1893
Claude M. Johnson	July 1, 1893 - May 10, 1900
William M. Meredith	Nov. 23, 1900 - June 30, 1906
Thomas J. Sullivan	July 1, 1906 - May 4, 1908
Joseph E. Ralph	May 11, 1908 - Oct. 31, 1917
James L. Wilmeth	Dec. 10, 1917 - March 31, 1922
Louis A. Hill	April 1, 1922 - Feb. 14, 1924
Wallace W. Kirby	June 16, 1924 - Dec. 15, 1924
Alvin W. Hall	Dec. 22, 1924 - Dec. 15, 1954
Henry J. Holtzclaw	Dec. 16, 1954 - Oct. 8, 1967
James A. Conlon	Oct. 9, 1967 - July 1, 1977
Seymour Berry	June 30, 1978 - April 6, 1979
Harry R. Clements	July 15, 1979 - Jan. 3, 1983
Robert J. Leuver	Feb. 22, 1983 - April 1, 1988
Peter H. Daly	August 26, 1988 - date

The Federal Reserve

7

History of the Federal Reserve System

A National Monetary Conference, appointed by Congress in 1908, sought to remedy money crises involving banks in the United States. Senator Nelson W. Aldrich was chairman.

A recognized depression had occurred in 1907, similar to previous crises in 1837, 1857, 1871 and 1894. The National Monetary Conference was to seek a solution to mitigating or eliminating these recurring dips in the economy.

The result of their efforts was reflected in the Federal Reserve Act, signed Dec. 23, 1913, by President Woodrow Wilson. The basic purpose of the new organization was "to give the country an elastic currency, to provide facilities for discounting commercial paper and to improve supervision of banking."

Founders of the Federal Reserve System believed that the amount of currency and credit would be balanced if issued against real bills, that is, short-term, self-liquidating paper based on commercial, industrial and agricultural transactions. Excessive changes in the domestic price level, they believed, could also be held in check if rules of the international gold standard were faithfully observed.

The founders also believed that if the money and credit system were based on real bills and gold, it would work more or less automatically; there would be no need to "manage" money. Finally, policies could be adapted closely to local conditions, and control by either politicians or Wall Street could be avoided if power were decentralized by regions.

The first decade

As the new Federal Reserve System felt its way, the act was amended from time to time primarily in the interest of greater operating efficiency: procedure for electing directors simplified, larger denomination Federal Reserve notes provided, trust powers of national banks broadened, etc.

Amendments were also passed to strengthen the financial structure of the Federal Reserve Banks. Member bank reserves were concentrated in the Federal Reserve Banks, gold was mobilized and provision was made to build up the surplus of Federal Reserve Banks. Some of these measures and the experience gained from a few years of operations enabled the Federal Reserve System to undertake successfully its job of helping to finance World War I.

After the war came inflation and sharp recession. Farmers were particularly hard hit, and changes in the act give a hint of the repercussions on the Federal Reserve System. The number of appointed members of the Federal Reserve Board was increased from five to six, and agricultural interests were given representation on the board. Not long after, the act was amended further to facilitate agricultural financing.

Although action was taken to strengthen the Federal Reserve System generally during the first decade, no major new tool of credit control was added. In 1920, it is true, the Federal Reserve Banks were given authority to impose graduated discount rates on banks which borrowed excessively, but this provision was repealed in 1923. As early as 1916 the board recommended that it be given power to raise reserve requirements in emergencies; this authority was not obtained until 17 years later.

Two early changes which, at first glance, seem only technical, really marked a departure from the strict real-bills principle. In 1916, Federal Reserve Banks were authorized to make direct advances to member banks on their promissory notes secured by government securities or eligible paper. The change was made primarily in the interest of operating efficiency, but it actually broke the direct link, so important to founders of the Federal Reserve System, between self-liquidating transactions and the flow of credit.

The next year the relation between real bills and Federal Reserve notes was officially changed. The original act provided that notes must be collateraled by an equivalent amount of eligible paper. Whenever a Federal Reserve Bank had to issue notes it would get them from the Federal Reserve Agent, depositing eligible paper as collateral. In practice, however, the bank could then cancel its liability for the notes by depositing gold with the Federal Reserve Agent and taking back the eligible paper. The close relationship between real bills and Federal Reserve notes was actually broken because, in essence, notes were collateraled by gold in addition to eligible paper. In 1917, an amendment to the act turned practice into law by permitting the use of gold as collateral for notes.

The "new era"

After the first decade came a period of legislative quiet — the age of "new era" complacency. Confidence in monetary policy as a solution to the economic troubles of the country rose to an all-time peak.

For several years after its organization, the Federal Reserve Board included in its annual reports a section describing legislation passed during the year and another section detailing legislation which it recommended for action. Proposed legislation in one year was likely to be reported as actual legislation the next. Congress acted promptly on most of these recommendations during the early years of the Federal Reserve System, particularly during World War I.

In the 1920s the situation was quite different. The section on proposed legislation did not appear in the annual reports for a number of years. No amendments were proposed or enacted for the years 1924-26 and only minor changes were made in most other years. Only one of the proposed changes was enacted in 1928, none in 1929.

The board's list of recommended legislation in 1929 included items like these: permit officers of mutual savings banks to be Class B or C directors of Federal Reserve Banks, clarify the section of the act which describes procedures for counting ballots in elections of Federal Reserve Bank directors, make it a federal offense to rob a Federal Reserve Bank or member bank, etc.

All this time, pressures were building up within the economy which were to show that the '20s were not so calm as this legislative status quo might suggest.

Depression and emergency

The early '30s were as hectic as the '20s were placid. Within five years the act was amended 23 times, and most of the action was confined to two years — 1933 and 1935.

Business activity was already well on its way downward in 1930. During that year a few minor changes were made in the act along lines recommended in the Board's annual report for the year before. No amendments were made in 1931.

It was not until 1932 that the act was changed materially. In that year and the one following, the Depression hit the banking system hard. Banks were caught by three developments: (1) panicky withdrawals of currency, (2) conversion of deposits and currency into gold, and (3) declining values on which bank assets were based. The result was a severe liquidity crisis in 1932 and a banking crisis in 1933.

In this atmosphere of emergency, reluctant permission was given to temporary deviations from some of the principles on which the original act was based. The Glass-Steagall Act, passed early in 1932, reduced further the relationship between real bills and Federal Reserve notes. Collateral requirements, first altered in 1917, were relaxed once again, this time because they stood in the way of an easy-money policy. The Federal Reserve wanted to meet the public's demand for liquidity and also to buy more government securities to help stimulate the economy. But the Federal Reserve System was hamstrung by collateral requirements. Federal Reserve Banks were required to hold 100 percent collateral, in the form of eligible paper and gold, against their notes. They also had to hold gold reserves equal to 40 percent of their note liabilities and 35 percent of their deposit liabilities. Any gold used as collateral against notes could also be used as reserve against notes, but not as reserve against deposits. With the amount of commercial paper shrinking with commerce, and gold disappearing into private hoards, there just was not enough to permit the necessary expansion of the money supply.

In order to break this logjam, Congress authorized Federal Reserve Banks to use government securities, in addition to eligible paper and gold, as collateral for Federal Reserve notes. The grant of authority was temporary, but after a number of extensions, it was finally made permanent in 1945.

The year 1932 also saw a further break in the link between real bills and credit. The public was seeking greater liquidity and safety by drawing out currency and converting to gold; the banks, in turn, sought liquidity by calling loans and selling assets on an already depressed market. A vicious spiral developed, feeding upon itself and making banks weaker and weaker. Banks could not get enough funds from Federal Reserve Banks to break out of this spiral because they did not have enough eligible paper to discount.

So the Glass-Steagall Act provided that Federal Reserve Banks could make loans to member banks on notes "secured to the satisfaction of such Federal Reserve Banks." But these loans were to be made only "in exceptional and exigent circumstances," the discount rate was to be at least 1 percent higher than the regular rate, and the authority was granted only for about a year. The real-bills principle was dying, but it was dying hard. After two extensions, a significant break with the real-bills principle came with the Banking Act of 1935 which removed most of the conditions, reduced the interest rate differential to 0.5 percent, and made this provision a permanent part of the act.

1933 crisis

The year 1933 was even more hectic. On March 9, five days after the new administration took office and in the midst of the banking holiday, the Emergency Banking Act of 1933 passed through the complete legislative process in a single day. E. A. Goldenweiser relates that a draft of the law was prepared by the General Counsel of the Federal Reserve Board in one night. Among its many provisions, the Emergency Banking Act amended the Federal Reserve Act in several respects. In an effort to make currency more readily available, Congress broadened the powers of the Federal Reserve Banks to issue Federal Reserve bank notes. In order to facilitate access to Federal Reserve Bank credit, it liberalized the 1932 provision authorizing loans to member banks on paper previously considered ineligible, and gave the Federal Reserve Banks power to make advances to individuals, partnerships and corporations on notes secured by government obligations.

Shortly after this, Congress passed the so-called Thomas Inflation Amendment. This law contained several measures affecting the Federal Reserve — especially provision for direct purchases of government securities from the Treasury — but actually amended the Federal Reserve Act, as such, in only one major respect. Curiously, this particular provision was anti-inflationary, not inflationary; it provided that the Federal Reserve Board could change reserve requirements if "an emergency existed by reason of credit expansion."

Up to this point, action was essentially of an emergency nature. The Banking Act of 1933, however, (passed, incidentally, just about when the depression hit bottom) undertook to get at some of the basic causes of the situation.

In the first place, it struck at speculative excesses to which banks had contributed. Banks were required to divorce themselves from security affiliates and to correct certain other undesirable practices which had developed during the 1920s. Behind some of these measures was increasing doubt about the real-bills principle as a means of channeling credit into "productive" uses. Thus one provision required the Reserve Banks to keep informed as to the uses which banks were making of Federal Reserve credit so as to avoid "undue use . . . for the speculative carrying of or trading in securities, real estate or commodities, or for any other purposes inconsistent with the maintenance of sound credit conditions."

Meanwhile the idea of regional autonomy was also being reassessed. Ten years earlier Federal Reserve Banks had discovered that their open-market operations, undertaken initially to bolster earnings, had noticeable effects on the money market. So in order to coordinate their activities, they set up an informal committee. The Banking Act of 1933 gave statutory basis to this committee and authorized the Federal Reserve Board to prescribe regulations for its conduct. No member of the board was a member of the committee, however, and any Reserve Bank could still decline to go along with the committee's policies.

In the case of dealings with foreign central banks, the change was more abrupt. Most of the negotiations on foreign matters had been carried on by the Federal Reserve Bank of New York, which handled the financial operations involved. The Banking Act of 1933 changed that by providing that "no officer or other representative of any Federal Reserve Bank shall conduct negotiations of any kind with the officers or representatives of any foreign bank or banker without first obtaining the permission of the Federal Reserve Board."

Among the many provisions of the Banking Act designed to strengthen the banking system perhaps the most outstanding was deposit insurance. Although this measure related only indirectly to the Federal Reserve, Congress included it in the Federal Reserve Act. It remained there after a major revision in 1935 and was not removed until 1950 when it became the subject of a separate law.

In 1934 the government called in all gold. Actually, most of the rules of the gold standard as a guide for monetary policy had not been honored for years, but no indication of this can be seen in the Federal Reserve Act. Even in 1934 about the only hint that something had happened was the substitution of the words "gold certificates" for the word "gold" wherever it occurred. If we were to judge by the act alone, gold would seem to occupy today essentially the same position it did in 1913.

During the same year, however, two other developments reflected a widening concept of the Federal Reserve System's responsibilities. One was the grant of authority for Federal Reserve Banks to make working capital loans to existing industrial and commercial businesses unable to get credit through usual channels. This marked a further departure from the traditional idea that the Federal Reserve Banks should be simply bankers' banks. The other development had nothing to do with the Federal Reserve Act itself, but because it introduced a new principle of credit control it deserves special mention. It was a provision of the Securities Exchange Act which authorized the Federal Reserve Board to prescribe margins for stock purchases and sales. This was the first of the selective credit regulations and the permanent tool of policy.

Major revision

By 1935, business was on its way up again. Compared with 1933, unemployment was down by two million and industrial production was up 25 percent. All the time the economy was recovering from depression, ideas were fermenting. The result was the most comprehensive reappraisal and revision of the Federal Reserve Act in all its history.

The Banking Act of 1935 contained many important provisions which need not be discussed in detail; it clarified many sections of the act and generally strengthened the banking system. As had been mentioned, it marked a significant break with the real-bills doctrine. It also marked a further departure from the principle of regional decentralization. The organization of the Federal Reserve System as we know it dates from 1935.

The Federal Reserve Board became the Board of Governors of the Federal Reserve System. Congress provided terms of four years for the chairmanship and vice-chairmanship (both officials being eligible for reappointment), lengthened terms of board members from 12 to 14 years, and removed the Secretary of the Treasury and the Comptroller of the Currency (who had been serving as ex-officio members) from the board.

The internal structure of the Federal Reserve Banks was reorganized. Executive responsibilities, which had been divided between the chairman of the board of directors and non-statutory governor, were consolidated in the newly created position of president, and the chairmanship became a non-salaried position. The president and first vice president were to be appointed by the board of directors for five-year terms, subject to approval of the Board of Governors.

The makeup of the Federal Open Market Committee was changed even more drastically. The Banking Act of 1933 had set up a committee of 12 men, one from each Federal Reserve Bank. The Banking Act of 1935 reduced representation of the Federal Reserve Banks to five men and included all seven members of the Board of Governors.

Changes in powers went in the same direction as changes in organization. Decisions of the Open Market Committee were made binding on all Federal Reserve Banks. The Board of Governors was given power to change reserve requirements, within limits, without the necessity of declaring an emergency or securing approval of the President. Federal Reserve Banks were required to establish their discount rates every 14 days, or more often if deemed necessary by the board; this meant that the rate would come up for formal review and determination more frequently.

After 1935

The repairs of the early 1930s put the Federal Reserve Act in good working order. It has, in fact, weathered war and inflation, prosperity and recession without another major overhaul. But this is not to say that Federal Reserve operations have been standing still. For the most part, the Federal Reserve System has been able to adapt and up-date its techniques within the existing framework of the Act.

The recession of 1937-1938 passed with no noticeable repercussions on the act. Then came Munich, Poland, Dunkirk and Pearl Harbor. Congress made several changes to facilitate war financing. It gave the Federal Reserve power to buy limited amounts of securities direct from the Treasury and exempted war-loan accounts from reserve requirements, a temporary war-time measure. To ease reserve positions, Congress reduced the gold certificate backing required against Federal Reserve notes and deposits to 25 percent. Without changing the act, the President gave the Federal Reserve selective controls over consumer credit.

The purpose was to fight inflation and help divert resources to military production. This executive order expired in 1947.

After the war the Federal Reserve continued the war-time policy of supporting the government securities market. The Board of Governors, concerned with the inability of the Federal Reserve System to restrain inflation and support securities prices at the same time, suggested additional powers — either new kinds of reserve requirements or an across-the-board increase in ordinary reserve requirements. Congress granted the board authority to raise requirements above regular limits in 1948. The provision was temporary, however, and expired about a year later.

When fighting broke out in Korea, the Federal Reserve System was given selective controls over consumer and real estate credit. As in World War II, selective controls were instituted by executive order without changing the act. The board requested controls on a permanent, stand-by basis but Congress did not comply.

In 1951 the Federal Reserve again sharpened its tools without legislative action. It negotiated an accord with the Treasury which ended the bond support program. This left the Federal Reserve System free to pursue a vigorous, contra-cyclical policy with its existing monetary instruments.

Legislative changes in the act since 1953, as in the preceding 18 years, have been relatively minor. More effective regulation of bank holding companies was added and certain sections regarding real estate loans by national banks were changed. In 1954 Federal Reserve Banks were permitted to pay out notes of other Reserve Banks, thus eliminating another vestige of the old idea of regional autonomy. In 1958 authority for Reserve Banks to make commercial and industrial loans under Section 13b of the Federal Reserve Act was terminated by the Small Business Investment Act, effective August 21, 1959. And in 1959 Congress passed legislation affecting reserve requirements. Vault cash may be counted as legal reserves; the central reserve city classification has terminated; and the board was given broader authority in reclassifying banks for reserve purposes.

In the year 1958, a new problem emerged to confront the Federal Reserve System, one that had lain dormant for many years. That problem was a persistent deficit in the United States balance of payments. The United States was spending more abroad for imports, investments, military and economic aid than it received for exports of goods and services and for other transactions. One result was a substantial outflow of gold.

The Federal Reserve System reacted to this new problem on several fronts, mostly within the framework of the existing Act. In 1961, the so-called "bills only" policy of the Federal Open Market Committee was discontinued. Under "bills only," Federal Reserve System purchases and sales of securities had been confined primarily to short maturities, but the Open Market Committee now authorized operations throughout the maturity structure. The Committee hoped thereby "to encourage bank credit and monetary expansion while avoiding direct downward pressures on short-term interest rates and thus moderate outflows of short-term capital attracted by higher interest rates abroad."

In 1962, the Federal Open Market Committee authorized open market transactions in foreign currencies to "moderate and offset short-term pressures on the dollar in the foreign exchange markets." One technique devised by the Federal Reserve System to gain foreign funds to implement these transactions was the "swaps" arrangements first negotiated in August 1962 with several foreign central banks and with the Bank for International Settlements. In essence, the "swaps" provide us with reciprocal "lines of credit" which may be drawn upon when foreign currencies are needed to provide temporary relief from international flows of funds which might affect adversely U.S. balance-of-payments and gold position.

Congress also, for balance-of-payments

reasons, amended the Federal Reserve Act in 1962 "to exempt for three years deposits of foreign governments and certain foreign institutions from regulation by the Board of Governors as to rates of interest that member banks may pay on time deposits."

Finally, in a 1963 measure unrelated to the balance of payments, the Federal Reserve Act was amended to authorize Federal Reserve System issuance of $1 and $2 Federal Reserve notes. This legislation was aimed at eliminating Treasury silver certificates of those denominations and thus making "monetary silver available for coinage."

Since 1963, several changes have been made in the way the international and domestic money system operates. In 1965, Congress passed legislation to repeal the remaining requirement for 25 percent gold backing of commercial banks' deposits at Federal Reserve banks, freeing about $5 billion of the country's gold stock for additional sale to dollar-holding foreign governments and for future growth of the domestic money supply.

That same year the Coinage Act of 1965 was passed, eliminating silver in United States coins. Despite these measures, the gold and silver draining out of Treasury coffers continued at a steady, debilitating rate.

In 1967, then, President Johnson signed a bill authorizing the eventual end of the redemption of silver certificates with silver bullion, setting a June 24, 1968, deadline for their redemption. Reserve requirements for Federal Reserve notes, United States notes and Treasury notes of 1890 were removed by Congress in March 1968.

Congress from time to time has introduced legislation to curb the power of the Federal Reserve System. The latest of these attempts was a bill, strongly opposed by the Federal Reserve System, recommended by the House Banking and Currency committee in October 1973, calling for an outside audit of the Federal Reserve System every three years. So far the idea has not been enacted into law.

In 1974, the System joined with the Treasury in putting into effect regulations prohibiting the export, melting or treating of the 1-cent piece to help offset the cent shortage.

With the International Banking Act of 1978, the Federal Reserve Board gained the authority to impose reserve requirements and interest rate ceilings on branches and agencies of foreign banks in the United States. The act also gave the board the authority to grant loans to foreign banks in the United States and to limit interstate banking activities.

Under the Depository Institutions Deregulation and Monetary Control Act of 1980, Federal Reserve Banks receive and hold on deposit the reserve or clearing account deposits of depository institutions. In addition, the act requires the Fed to open its discount window to any nonmember depository institution that maintains transaction accounts or nonpersonal time deposits, on the same basis as to banks that are members of the Federal Reserve System.

The Federal Reserve adopted a new operating procedure Oct. 6, 1979, that changed the emphasis from tight control on interest rates to better short-run control of the money supply (i.e., to lower inflation) at the expense of short-term volatility in interest rates. The money supply is now controlled by adjustments to the federal funds rate, which influences banks to buy or sell assets, thus changing the money supply. If the federal funds rate is higher than rates for other assets, banks tend to sell more assets and place the funds into the federal funds market, decreasing the money supply. Conversely, a lower federal funds rate causes an increase in the money supply — inflation.

The strength wielded by the Federal Reserve, and its chairman, plus its relative freedom to control the money supply and interest rates without congressional curbs, has given it considerable power over the economy.

Function of the Federal Reserve System

The Federal Reserve System as it operates today consists of the Board of Governors in Washington; the 12 Federal Reserve Banks, their 25 branches and other facilities situated throughout the United States; the Federal Open Market Committee; the Federal Advisory Council; the Consumer Advisory Council; the Thrift Institutions Advisory Council; and the member commercial banks, which include all national banks in the United States and any state-chartered banks that have voluntarily joined the Federal Reserve System. Some of these functions are outlined below.

Board of Governors

Broad supervisory powers are vested in the Board of Governors, which has its offices in Washington. The board is composed of seven members appointed by the President by and with the advice and consent of the Senate. The chairman of the Board of Governors is by executive order a member of the National Advisory Council on International Monetary and Financial Policies.

The board determines general monetary, credit and operating policies for the Federal Reserve System as a whole and formulates the rules and regulations necessary to carry out the purposes of the Federal Reserve Act. The board's principal duties consist of exerting an influence over credit conditions and supervising the Federal Reserve Banks and member banks.

POWER TO INFLUENCE CREDIT CONDITIONS

The Board is given the power, within statutory limitations, to fix the requirements concerning reserves to be maintained by member banks against deposits and the power to determine the maximum rate of interest that may be paid by member banks on their time and savings deposits. Another important instrument of credit control is found in open market operations. The members of the Board of Governors are also members of the Federal Open Market Committee. The Board of Governors reviews and determines the discount rates charged by the Federal Reserve Banks on their discounts and advances. For the purpose of preventing excessive use of credit for the purchase or carrying of securities, the board is authorized to regulate the amount of credit that may be initially extended and subsequently maintained on any security (with certain exceptions).

Pursuant to the provisions of the Defense Production Act of 1950 and Executive Order 10480 of Aug. 14, 1953, the board prescribes regulations under which the Federal Reserve Banks act as fiscal agents of certain government departments and agencies in guaranteeing loans made by banks and other private financing institutions to finance contracts for the procurement of materials or services which the guaranteeing agencies consider necessary for the national defense.

SUPERVISION OF FEDERAL RESERVE BANKS

The board is authorized to make examinations of the Federal Reserve Banks, to require statements and reports from such banks, to supervise the issue and retirement of Federal Reserve notes, to require the establishment or discontinuance of branches of Federal Reserve Banks, and to exercise supervision over all relationships and transactions of those banks with foreign banks. The Board of Governors reviews and follows the examination and supervisory activities of the Federal Reserve Banks with a view to furthering coordination of policies and practices.

SUPERVISION OF MEMBER BANKS

The board has jurisdiction over the admission of state banks and trust companies to membership in the Federal Reserve System, the termination of membership of such banks, the establishment of branches by such banks, and the approval of bank mergers and consolidations where the resulting institution will be a state member bank. It receives copies of condition reports submitted by them to the Federal Reserve Banks. It has power to examine all member banks and the affiliates of member banks and to require condition reports from them. It has authority to require periodic and other public disclosure of information with respect to an equity security of a member state bank that is held by 500 or more persons.

It establishes minimum standards with respect to installation, maintenance and operation of security devices and procedures by member state banks. It has authority to issue cease and desist orders in connection with violations of law or unsafe or unsound banking practices by member state banks and to remove directors or officers of such banks in certain circumstances, and it may, in its discretion, suspend member banks from the use of the credit facilities of the Federal Reserve System for making undue use of bank credit for speculative purposes or for any other purpose inconsistent with the maintenance of sound credit conditions.

The board may grant authority to member banks to establish branches in foreign countries or dependencies or insular possessions of the United States, to invest in the stocks of banks or corporations engaged in international or foreign banking, or to invest in foreign banks. It also charters, regulates, and supervises certain corporations that engage in foreign or international banking and financial activities.

The board is authorized to issue general regulations permitting interlocking relationships in certain circumstances between member banks and organizations dealing in securities or between member banks and other banks.

OTHER FUNCTIONS

Under the Bank Holding Company Act of 1956 the board is required to pass upon certain acquisitions of bank stock or assets by bank holding companies and to make determinations relating to engagement in non-banking activities and to the acquisition and retention of non-bank stock by bank holding companies. Under the Change in Bank Control Act of 1978, the board is required to review other bank acquisitions. Under the Truth in Lending Act, the board is required to prescribe regulations to assure a meaningful disclosure by lenders of credit terms so that consumers will be able to compare more readily the various credit terms available and avoid the uninformed use of credit, and with respect to issuance of credit cards and liabilities for their unauthorized use.

Under the International Banking Act of 1978, the board has the authority to impose reserve requirements and interest rate ceilings on branches and agencies of foreign banks in the United States, to grant loans to them, to provide them access to Federal Reserve services, and to limit their interstate banking activities. The board also is the rule-making authority for the Equal Credit Opportunity Act, the Home Mortgage Disclosure Act, the Fair Credit Billing Act, and certain provisions of the Federal Trade Commission Act as they apply to banks.

EXPENSES

To meet its expenses and pay the salaries of its members and its employees, the board makes semiannual assessments upon the Federal Reserve Banks in proportion to their capital stock and surplus.

CURRENCY ISSUE

An important function of the Federal Reserve System is to ensure that the economy has enough currency and coin to meet the public's demand. Currency and coin are put into or retired from circulation by the Federal Reserve Banks, which use depository institutions as the channel of distribution. The Federal Reserve Banks issue Federal Reserve notes, which constitute the bulk of money in circulation. These notes are obligations of the United States and are a prior lien upon the assets of the issuing Federal Reserve Bank. They are issued against a pledge by the Reserve Bank with the Federal Reserve agent of collateral security consisting of gold certificates, paper discounted or purchased by the bank, and direct obligations of the United States.

OTHER POWERS

The Federal Reserve Banks are empowered to act as clearinghouses and as collecting agents for depository institutions in the collection of checks and other instruments. They are also authorized to act as depositories and fiscal agents of the United States and to exercise other banking functions specified in the Federal Reserve Act. They perform a number of important functions in connection with the issue and redemption of United States government securities.

Sources of information

READING ROOM

A reading room where persons may inspect records that are available to the public is located in Room B-1122 at the board's headquarters, 20th and C streets NW., Washington, D.C. Information regarding the availability of records may be obtained by calling 202-452-3684.

FILMS

The board has available for public use a variety of 16mm sound films relating to money, credit and the Federal Reserve, and a filmstrip for consumers explaining the basic provisions of the Truth in Lending Act. For further information call 202-452-3244.

PUBLICATIONS

Among publications issued by the board are *The Federal Reserve System — Purposes and Functions*, and these short pamphlets suitable for classroom use: "What Truth in Lending Means to You," "U.S. Currency," "If You Borrow To Buy Stock," "Fair Credit Billing," "Alice in Debitland," "If You Use A Credit Card," "Consumer Handbook," "Consumer Handbook on Adjustable Rate Mortgages," "Consumer Handbook to Credit Protection Laws," "Federal Reserve Glossary," "Guide to Federal Reserve Regulations," "How to File A Consumer Credit Complaint," "Instructional Materials of the Federal Reserve System," and several pamphlets describing the Equal Credit Opportunity Act. Multiple copies of these pamphlets are available free of charge. Information regarding publications may be obtained by writing Publication Services, Mail Stop 138, Board of Governors of the Federal Reserve System, Washington, D.C. 20551. Phone 202-452-3244.

Federal Reserve Bank Branches and Offices

1 Boston*

2 New York*
  Buffalo

3 Philadelphia*

4 Cleveland*
  Cincinnati
  Pittsburgh

5 Richmond*
  Baltimore
  Charlotte (Culpepper Communications and Records Center)

6 Atlanta*
  Birmingham

  Jacksonville
  Miami
  Nashville
  New Orleans

7 Chicago*
  Detroit

8 St. Louis
  Little Rock
  Louisville
  Memphis

9 Minneapolis
  Helena

10 Kansas City
  Denver

Oklahoma City
Omaha

11 Dallas
El Paso
Houston
San Antonio

12 San Francisco
Los Angeles
Portland
Salt Lake City
Seattle

* Additional offices of these banks are located at Lewiston, Maine 04240; Windsor Locks, Conn. 06096; Cranford, N.J. 07016; Jericho, N.Y. 11753; Utica at Oriskany, N.Y. 13424; Columbus, Ohio 43216; Columbia, S.C. 29210; Charleston, W.V. 25311; Des Moines, Iowa 50306; Indianapolis, Ind. 46204; and Milwaukee, Wis. 53202.

Board of Governors

Chairman .... Alan Greenspan
Vice Chairman .... (Vacant)*
Member .... Martha R. Seger
Member .... Wayne D. Angell
Member .... Edward W. Kelley Jr.
Member .... John P. LaWare
Member .... David W. Mullins Jr.

* Manuel H. Johnson tendered his resignation in June 1990 to be effective Aug. 3, 1990.

U.S. Paper Money

8

Pre-federal paper money

When paper money was issued in America, it became the first authorized paper money to be issued by a government in the western world.

American paper money was produced in a number of different phases before the Bureau of Engraving and Printing effectively took over sole production in 1862.

Colonial currency

The Massachusetts Bay Colony financed a military expedition to Canada in 1690 by issuing bills of credit. Other military campaigns were financed by other colonies in a similar way.

Revolutionary War state issues

The states also issued money during the American Revolution to cover their governmental and military expenditures.

Some of these notes carried messages freighted with propaganda, like the Maryland issue of July 25, 1775, which depicted George III trampling on the Magna Carta while setting fire to an American city, and American Liberty trampling on slavery while backed by a large army.

Continental Currency

Beginning in the middle of 1775, the Continental Congress issued paper money with which to purchase war supplies from foreign countries. The Congress asked the states to redeem the currency, but most states were preoccupied with the need to support their own military activities;

consequently, taxes were neglected.

The English forbade the circulation of the money in areas they occupied and attempted to undermine public confidence in it in other areas, often counterfeiting the money.

By 1780, economic circumstances had combined to reduce Continental Currency to one-fortieth of its original face value and the Continental Congress ceased printing it.

1812 interest-bearing notes

When the War of 1812 began, the U.S. government once again found itself being forced to borrow money. In 1812, Congress began issuing Treasury Notes to cover short-term loans.

Five series of these notes were authorized for issue during the war, between 1812 and 1815, in denominations ranging from $3 to $1,000.

The notes were not legal tender, but were receivable for all public dues and payable to public creditors. All notes under $100 were payable to the bearer on demand. The $5 notes did not bear interest.

Obsolete notes

Between 1800 and 1865, during periods when the need for a medium of exchange exceeded the amounts of available specie, numerous banks and companies began printing their own paper currency. Although states were Constitutionally forbidden to issue their own money, a large number of state-chartered banks circumvented this problem by issuing bank notes as private entities, which were not expressly restrained by the Constitution.

Although commonly called "broken-bank notes," not all banks which issued this currency failed. Some of the issuers successfully liquidated and others converted into national banks.

The tremendous demand for currency created by the Civil War eventually exceeded the production capacities of the private banking system and the governments of both the north and south began to print national currency. The end of currency production in the private sector was hastened by steep taxes levied by the federal government on private emissions.

Before the private banking era was over, bank notes had been produced by such diverse concerns as railroads, insurance companies, mining companies and pharmacies.

Large-sized paper money catalog

Early federal issues

In 1862 the United States government issued its first legal tender paper money although government obligations were issued periodically between 1812 and 1861 in the form of interest-bearing Treasury notes. These bore interest at 5 or 6 percent and were payable after two years.

The demand notes were authorized by Congressional Acts of July 17 and Aug. 5, 1861. They were soon nicknamed "greenbacks," a term that became so popular it was passed on through the years and is heard even today, most often when paper money specialists, or syngraphists, get together.

The demand notes bear the signatures of various employees of the Treasury Department who signed their own names, as well as the words "For The" for the Register of the Treasury and Treasurer of the United States. Demand notes do not carry the Treasury Seal nor the actual names of the Register and Treasurer, and are unique in that respect.

With this beginning, the United States soon settled down and began production of paper money as it is known today, that is, with series year, signatures of the Treasury officials, and so on.

Notes issued until 1928 were large-sized notes, commonly called "horse blankets," sometimes known as "saddle blankets."

Interest-bearing Treasury notes

The constitutionality of the Treasury notes issued between 1812 and 1861 was an ever-present topic in Congress. Most interest-bearing notes bore interest at 5 or 6 percent and were payable after two years. A few 60-day notes, in denominations of $50 through $5,000, were issued. With few exceptions all of the 121,000-plus notes that were issued have been redeemed and are unavailable to collectors.

Demand notes of 1861

Demand notes of 1861, authorized by the July 17 and Aug. 5, 1861, Acts of Congress, were issued in three denominations: $5, $10 and $20. Each note bears the first authorization date, July 17, and also the date of issue, Aug. 10. These notes were not originally legal tender but were later specified as such. The major portion of the face designs are identical to the legal tender notes of the same denominations.

The demand notes were made payable, on demand, by the Assistant Treasurer of the United States at Boston, New York, Philadelphia, St. Louis and Cincinnati. The $5 note features a portrait of Alexander Hamilton at right and a statue of Columbia at left. Lincoln is portrayed at left on the $10 note with a woman representing Art at right. The $20 note features Liberty.

Legal tender notes

Legal tender notes consisted of five

issues. The first issue of March 10, 1862, was produced in $5, $10, $20, $50, $100, $500 and $1,000 denominations. Issue two was confined to $1 and $2 notes, although the face design does indicate that a $3 denomination was planned, but not released. The third issue, dated March 10, 1863, was printed in the same denominations as the first issue, but changes were made in the back design.

The fourth issue consisted of series 1869, 1875, 1878, 1880, 1907, 1917 and 1923, with all except the 1869 notes carrying the designation "United States note." The 1869 series was designated as "Treasury note." Also, with the 1869 series, the U.S. introduced paper with silk threads as a deterrent to counterfeiting.

Denominations in the fourth issue are as follows:

1869 series, $1, $2, $5, $10, $20, $50, $100, $500, and $1,000.

1874 series, $1, $2, $50, and $500.

1875 series, $1, $2, $5, $10, $20, $50, $100, and $500.

1878 series, $1, $2, $5, $10, $20, $50, $100, $500, $1,000, $5,000 and $10,000.

1880 series, $1, $2, $5, $10, $20, $50, $100, $500 and $1,000.

1907 series, $5.

1917 series, $1, and $2.

1923 series, $1, and $10.

The fifth issue was limited to the $10 denomination.

Face designs on the first and third issues are:

$5, Alexander Hamilton on lower right, with Washington Capitol statue of Columbia on left side.

$10, Vignette of Lincoln, upper right, allegorical female representing Art, on left.

$20, Liberty with shield and sword.

$50, Alexander Hamilton. Different pose than on $5 note.

$100, American eagle. This was the first note to feature the American eagle.

$500, Albert Gallatin, Secretary of the Treasury 1801-1813.

$1,000, Robert Morris, a signer of the Declaration of Independence, and

Superintendent of Finance 1781-1784.

Face designs on second issue:

$1, Vignette of Salmon P. Chase, Secretary of the Treasury, 1861-1864.

$2, Capitol building and Thomas Jefferson.

The obligation on the first, second and third issues states "United States will pay the Bearer . . . Dollars at the Treasury of New York."

Back designs of the first, second and third issues are:

First and third issues, denominations $5 to $1,000, feature lathe-work design with two types of inscriptions, commonly called obligations.

Type one states: "This note is Legal Tender for all debts public and private, except on duties on Imports and Interest on Public Debt, and is exchangeable for U.S. Six percent Twenty Years Bonds, redeemable at the pleasure of the U. States after Five Years."

Type two states: "This note is a Legal Tender for all debts public and private, except duties on Imports and Interest on the Public Debt, and is receivable in payment for all Loans made to the United States."

The type two inscription (obligation) appears in the center of lathe-work design on the $1 and $2 notes of the second issue.

Face designs on the fourth issue are:

$1, 1869 to 1917, head of Washington facing left, and Columbus sighting land.

$1, 1923, head of Washington facing right.

$2, Capitol building and vignette of Thomas Jefferson.

$5, "Pioneer Family" and bust of Andrew Jackson.

$10, 1869 to 1880, Daniel Webster, and presentation of Indian Princess, representing introduction of Old World to the New. Popular name of this note is "Jackass Note," so-called because the eagle on face design, when note is inverted, appears to be a jackass.

$10, 1923, Andrew Jackson.

$20, Alexander Hamilton and figure of Victory with shield and sword.

$50, 1869, Henry Clay, and female

holding statue of Mercury.

$50, 1874 to 1880, Benjamin Franklin, with figure of Liberty.

$100, Abraham Lincoln, with allegorical figure of Architecture.

$500, 1869, John Quincy Adams.

$500, 1874 to 1880, Major General Joseph K. Mansfield.

$1,000, Dewitt Clinton, governor of New York.

$5,000, James Madison.

$10,000, Andrew Jackson.

The major portion of the face designs in the fourth issue remained the same. The obligation states "United States will pay the Bearer . . . Dollars." The words "At the Treasury in New York" which appeared on the first three issues were removed and the single word "Washington" substituted on the 1869 series, and "Washington, D.C." on later issues. Stars following serial numbers on the 1869 series do not indicate replacement notes.

Back designs of the fourth issue differ from previous issues in that the words "and is receivable in payment for all Loans made to the United States" have been removed from the Type Two clause. Throughout the fourth issue, except on Series 1923 $1 and $10 notes, the warning against counterfeiting, which first appeared on the 1869 series, is used.

Series 1923 $1 has plain back, unlike the ornate lathe-work of earlier issues.

Series 1923 $10 notes have lathe-work design.

Face design of the fifth issue, consisting of a $10 note, features a bison in center, with portraits of Lewis and Clark on sides.

Back design of the fifth issue shows Columbus standing between two pillars and two scrolls which carry the inscription found on the fourth issue.

Compound interest Treasury notes

The Congressional Acts of March 3, 1863, and June 30, 1864, authorized $10, $20, $50, $100, $500 and $1,000 compound interest Treasury notes. They bear the following inscription: "Three years after date the United States will pay

the bearer . . . dollars with interest at the rate of six percent compounded semi-annually" on the face. The back has "By Act of Congress, this note is legal tender for . . . dollars but bears interest at six percent only at maturity as follows [table of interest]. This sum . . . will be paid the holder for principal and interest at maturity of note three years from date."

These notes were issued to raise money to finance the Civil War.

Interest-bearing notes

The interest-bearing notes were the successors to the Treasury notes which were issued between 1812 and 1861 and were issued for the same purpose as the compound interest Treasury notes, to raise money to finance the Civil War.

One- and two-year notes bearing interest at 5 percent were authorized by the Act of March 3, 1863. Three-year notes bearing 7.3 percent interest were authorized by the Acts of July 17, 1861, June 30, 1864, and March 3, 1865, and were issued at three different times. These three-year notes had five attached coupons which were detached and redeemed at six-month intervals.

The one-year notes were issued in denominations of $10 to $5,000, the two-year notes in denominations of $50 to $1,000 and the three-year notes ranged from $50 to $5,000. All are extremely rare due to immediate redemption on the expiration date.

Currency certificates of deposit

The Secretary of the Treasury was authorized to issue currency certificates of deposit by the Act of June 8, 1872. Denominations of the notes were $5,000 and $10,000. The $5,000 notes were payable on demand in U.S. notes at the place of deposit and were also accepted in settlement of clearinghouse balances at the locations where deposits were made. The $10,000 notes were receivable on deposit without interest from national banking houses but were not to be included in the legal reserves.

Authorization of these large

denomination certificates was repealed March 14, 1900.

Silver certificates

The large-sized silver certificates were authorized by Acts of Congress dated Feb. 28, 1878, and Aug. 4, 1886. There were five issues from series 1878 to series 1923.

The first issue, Series 1878 and 1880, consisted of $10, $20, $50, $100, $500 and $1,000 denominations. The front side states that "There have been deposited with the Treasurer of the United States at Washington, D.C. payable at his office to the bearer on demand . . . Silver Dollars." "Certificate of Deposit" is inscribed on the notes. All certificates of the 1878 series and one of the notes in the 1880 series are countersigned by Assistant Treasurers of the United States at New York and bear the signatures of G.W. Scofield and James Gilfillan.

Face designs of the first issue feature the following:

$10, Robert Morris, signer of the Declaration of Independence, and U.S. senator.

$20, Stephen Decatur, naval commander.

$50, Edward Everett, governor of Massachusetts, U.S. senator and secretary of state under President Fillmore.

$100, James Monroe, fifth president.

$500, Charles Sumner, U.S. senator and leader in the abolition of slavery.

$1,000, William L. Marcy, governor of New York, secretary of war under President Polk and secretary of state under President Pierce.

The Treasury seal on countersigned certificates of 1878 has the key in red seal pointing to the right instead of to the left. This error was corrected on the 1880 series.

The face design of Series 1878-1880 silver certificates has the word SILVER in large letters appearing on black scroll work. The inscription says "This Certificate is Receivable for Customs, Taxes, and all Public Dues and When So Received May be Reissued."

The second issue of silver certificates consists of Series 1886, 1891 and 1908. The 1886 series was printed in denominations of $1, $2, $5, $10 and $20. The 1891 series includes these, but added denominations of $50, $100 and $1,000. Only the $10 note was issued in Series 1908. On the front of Series 1886, 1891 and 1908 appears the wording "This certifies that there have been deposited in the Treasury of the United States . . . Silver Dollars payable to the Bearer on Demand."

Face designs of the second issue are:

$1, Series 1886 and 1891, Martha Washington.

$2, Series 1886, General Winfield Scott Hancock.

$2, Series 1891, William Windom, twice Secretary of the Treasury.

$5, Series 1886 and 1891, Ulysses S. Grant.

$10, Series 1886 and 1908, Thomas A. Hendricks, U.S. vice president.

$20, Series 1886 and 1891, Daniel Manning, Secretary of the Treasury.

$50, Series 1891, Edward Everett.

$100, Series 1891, James Monroe.

$1,000, Series 1891, William L. Marcy.

Back design of the 1886 series features green overall lathe-work. Large numbers denoting the denomination also are used. The certification is identical to that on the 1878 and 1880 series. The back design of the $5 note is unique, featuring five silver dollars with the obverse of one dated 1886.

The back design of Series 1891 and 1908 features a more open lathe-work presentation. Large numbers, and on some denominations, Roman numerals, indicate the denomination. The certification remains the same as on previous series.

The third issue of silver certificates, Series 1896, is one of the most popular and deemed by collectors as the most beautiful series ever produced by the United States. Titled the "Educational Series," the notes were designed or redesigned by Thomas F. Morris, designer and chief of the Engraving Division of the Bureau of Engraving and Printing from Nov. 1, 1893, to June 30, 1897. Other designers of this famed series were Will H.

Low, $1; Edwin H. Blashfield, $2; and Walter Shirlaw, $5. Known engravers of the series were Charles Schlecht and George F.C. Smillie.

Claude M. Johnson, who was chief of the Bureau, is credited with advocating the printing of more artistic and representative designs in paper money, and the original plan was to have educational designs on all silver certificate denominations from $1 to $1,000 but only the $1, $2 and $5 were released. The $10 was designed but never released, and records do not indicate that higher denominations were ever designed.

The fronts of these educational notes are as follows:

$1, History Instructing Youth, with the background featuring the Washington Monument and the Capitol building. The U.S. Constitution is shown in an open book, and the names of 23 great Americans are featured in the border design.

$2, Steam and Electricity, represented by two youthful figures being presented to Commerce and Manufacture, represented by two mature female figures. Another mature female figure, Science, is making the presentation.

$5, Electricity, represented by a winged female, is depicted as a controlling factor in world history.

The obligation to redeem the notes in silver dollars is carried on the front of all three notes.

The backs of the Educational notes feature portraits of George and Martha Washington on the $1; inventors Samuel Morse and Robert Fulton on the $2; and Gens. Ulysses Grant and Philip Sheridan on the $5.

The fourth issue, Series 1899, was released in three denominations, $1, $2 and $5. The front design of the $1 features the American eagle with portraits of Lincoln and Grant. The $2 note portrays Washington between figures representing Mechanics and Agriculture, and the $5 note features Ta-to-ka-in-yna-ka, Running Antelope, a Sioux Indian.

There is an interesting story behind the printing of the $5 note. Running Antelope was a member of the Oncpapa or Hunkpapa Sioux tribe. The portrait used on the note came from a photograph taken in 1872 for the Bureau of Ethnology; however, Running Antelope wore a headdress with three feathers which projected too high for a good image on the note. To correct the problem, an employee of the Bureau of Engraving and Printing posed wearing a warbonnet belonging to another tribe, and the headdress was cut out and superimposed on the photograph of Running Antelope; George F.C. Smillie engraved the design in November of 1899. The headdress, ironically, belonged to the Pawnee tribe, rivals of the tribe of Running Antelope.

Back designs for the fourth issue were modified from those of earlier issues. The denomination is indicated by large numerals, with the Roman numeral "V" in the center design of the $5 note. The notes carry the same inscription on the backs as do earlier issues.

The fifth issue of silver certificates, Series 1923, consists of two denominations, $1 and $5. Washington is portrayed on the $1 and Lincoln on the $5. On the latter note, Lincoln is shown in the center of a circular design and as a result this note is sometimes called the "porthole" note.

Certification on the fifth issue is the same as on previous issues. However, the inscription, previously part of the back design, was moved to the front at left of the seal. The back of the $1 note in the fifth issue features the words "United States of America" prominently in the center. The $5 note shows the front of the Great Seal of the United States and the words "United States of America."

Refunding certificates

The U.S. government authorized refunding certificates, on Feb. 26, 1879, to reduce the circulation of the "fiat" greenbacks when specie payments were resumed. The more notes that were converted to non-legal tender obligations, the less cold, hard, cash that the Treasury had to pay out on its paper obligations. The face design of the notes, issued in $10 denomination only, bears the portrait of Benjamin Franklin (most probably based on the painting by James Barton Longacre).

The 4 percent annual interest was to accumulate indefinitely. However, by 1907 the $10 note was worth $21.30 so Congress passed a law that allowed the government to stop payment on July 1 of that year.

Treasury or coin notes

The Legal Tender Act of July 14, 1890, authorized Series 1890 and 1891 coin notes in denominations of $1 to $1,000. The Treasury Department used these notes to purchase silver bullion. It was left to the Secretary of the Treasury to decide if gold or silver would be paid out when the notes were redeemed. The redemption of the notes almost bankrupted the Treasury by 1893 and caused a major panic.

National bank notes

The national bank notes were authorized by the National Currency Act of Feb. 25, 1863, and National Banking Act of June 3, 1864, and were issued by chartered banks from 1863 to 1928.

During the Civil War coins of gold and silver were hoarded and practically disappeared from circulation. The unsecured legal tender notes commonly known as "greenbacks" were not popular and not readily accepted by skeptical persons having no confidence in the government's promise to pay.

Although Secretary of the Treasury Chase recommended a national bank currency secured by government bonds in his financial report of December 1861, the National Currency Act was not passed until February 1863. Spencer M. Clark, Chief of Construction of the Treasury Department, as early as April 1862 conceived the plan to have the national banks issue their own currency. The plan was endorsed by then Secretary of the Treasury Salmon P. Chase, who directed Clark to invite artists and engravers to submit proposals and designs.

Clark had previously suggested that historic pictures be used as back designs for the "greenbacks" of 1862 claiming that these designs offered greater protection against counterfeiting. His proposed designs were not adopted for the legal tender notes, but were adopted for the national bank notes issued under Secretary of the Treasury W.P. Fessenden. Clark suggested that these designs cover the entire back of the notes, but while the designs were adopted the size of each was reduced to allow space for denomination and legends.

National banks qualifying under terms of the Act were granted 20-year charters which were renewable for 20-year periods. Banks so chartered were permitted to issue national bank notes not to exceed 90 percent of the total of the U.S. government bonds deposited with the Treasurer of the United States.

Early issues will be found with the imprints of the American Bank Note Co., Continental Bank Note Co. and National Bank Note Co. These companies supplied the paper and delivered the printed notes to the Treasury. The Treasury number and Treasury seal were then imprinted by the Bureau.

The History of the Bureau of Engraving and Printing supplies this information: "National bank notes were printed exclusively by private contractors until September 1875. Thereafter this type of currency was partially printed by the Bureau of Engraving and Printing. Beginning in October 1877, the Bureau executed all work in connection with the printing of national currency."

Some notes will be found bearing the imprint of one of the three bank note companies in the design, and in very small type in the margin of the note, the notation: "Printed at the Bureau of Engraving and Printing."

The dates appearing on national bank notes do not always indicate the date the charter was granted, nor the date the notes were issued. Nor do these dates denote the term of office of the Treasury officials whose signatures appear on the notes. Plates with the names of the U.S. Treasurer and Register of the Treasury were frequently used after the officials left office. The date appearing on the note is usually later than the granting of the charter. Some banks organized late in the First Charter period continued to issue Series 1875 notes until February 1902.

At the close of 1928, 13,269 banks had been chartered but many did not issue bank notes. Notes issued by banks in small communities were usually scarcer than those of large city banks. This thinking has at times been upset when a small-town bank released a stock of notes held in their reserve funds.

In addition to the engraved signatures of the two Treasury officials, national bank notes have the signatures of two bank officers, usually the president and cashier. Early issues did not carry the plate number on face or back.

The First Charter notes of $1 and $2 denominations were usually printed in sheets of three $1 notes and one $2 note. Check letters on notes so printed are A, B, and C, on the $1 notes and A on the $2 note. Known exceptions to "three ones and a two" are:

The Westchester County National Bank, Peekskill, N.Y., Charter #1422; The Merchants National Bank, Bangor, Maine, Charter #1437; The City National Bank, Manchester, N.H., Charter #1530. The above three banks were supplied with sheets of two $1 notes, check letters A and B, and two $2 notes, check letters A and B.

The other known exception is the First National Bank of Philadelphia, with sheets of four $1 and sheets of four $2 notes.

The word "National" appears in the title of all chartered banks with the exception of The Bank of North America, Philadelphia, Pa., which was allowed to retain the title it used as a state bank.

To assist in sorting notes presented for redemption, a large letter was printed with the charter numbers on national bank notes for a period of about 25 years, approximately 1901-1925. These regional letters indicated the geographical area or region in which the issuing bank was located, and may be found on Second and Third Charter notes. Six letters were used as follows: E - Eastern Region, M - Middle States Region, N - New England Region, P - Pacific Region (including Alaska and Hawaii), S - Southern Region and W - Western Region.

Bank charter numbers were overprinted on Series 1875 and all later series, and may also be found on some notes of the Original Series. The exact position varies on the face of the notes. These numbers on the first issue are in red with the exception of a very few banks which were supplied with notes bearing black charter numbers.

Known "Black Charters" are the $5 notes of the following banks: Merchants National Bank, Minneapolis, Minn., charter 1830; First National Bank, Central City, Colorado Territory, charter 2129; First National Bank, Red Oak, Iowa, charter 2130; National Bank, Green Lane, Pa., charter 2131; Kellogg National Bank, Green Bay, Wis., charter 2132; First National Bank, Boyertown, Pa., charter 2137; National Bank, Rochester, N.H., charter 2138; and The National Bank, Pontiac, Ill., charter 2141.

The first charter period covered the years 1862-1882.

The first issue of national bank notes is known as the "Original Series." This was followed by Series 1875. These two series comprise the issue of First Charter notes, and were issued in denominations of $1 to $1,000. Very few banks issued First Charter notes in denominations higher than $100.

The obligation of the issuing bank to pay appears on the face of the notes and reads: "This note is secured by Bonds of the United States, deposited with the United States Treasurer at Washington. The . . . [Bank] . . . will pay the Bearer on Demand . . . Dollars."

Face designs of the First Charter notes are as follows:

$1, "Concordia." Two maidens clasping hands before an altar of earlier times, which bears the coat of arms of the

United States. The design represents the new Union brought about with the aid of Heaven, and the eventual return to peace. Vignette designed by T. A. Liebler, and engraved by Charles Burt.

$2, "America Seated" depicted by a maiden unfurling the American flag. The bank serial number is at upper right, and the Treasury number is at lower left in a vertical position. This design is best known as the "Lazy 2" because of the large numeral "2" which re clines on its side and carries the certification that bonds have been deposited with the Treasurer of the United States in Washington. The design is very popular. Similar large numeral designs were previously used on obsolete currency.

$5, "Columbus Sighting Land" showing the discoverer with some of his crew on the deck of the caravel. The scene at lower right depicts Columbus introducing America, represented by an Indian princess, to the Old World, Africa, Asia and Europe. Continental Bank Note Co. designer Fenton produced the design for engraving by Charles Burt.

$10, "Franklin and the Lightning" is the historical scene at left, representing Benjamin Franklin's experimentation with electrical energy and his assistant seated near him with a Leyden jar placed nearby. The year is marked by the figures "1752" in the corner. Eagle in flight bearing Liberty is shown at right, symbolizing "America Grasping the Lightning." Engraving by Alfred Jones.

$20, "Battle of Lexington 1775" depicted by Colonists in action and nurses attending the wounded. At right a symbolic design of "Loyalty," a procession for the defense and preservation of the Union, is led by Columbia with flag. The design is by Felix O.C. Darley.

$50, "Washington Crossing the Delaware" before his victorious battle at Princeton is the vignette at left. "A Prayer for Victory" is depicted at right. Engraved by Alfred Jones.

$100, Powell's painting "The Battle of Lake Erie" was the inspiration for the vignette at left, which shows Commodore Perry leaving his burning ship The Lawrence. At right, Columbia is seated with a fasces, a bundle of rods with a projecting ax handle. Inscribed are the words "The Union" and to the right "Maintain It." Engraved by Louis Delnoce.

$500, Civilization appears on the left. At right is a nautical scene titled "Arrival of the Sirius, 1838."

$1,000, General Scott entering Mexico City, is shown at left. At right the Capitol Building, Washington, D.C. The painting is by John Trumbull. The engraving by Alfred Jones. This note is believed to be nonexistent.

Tableau scenes are illustrated on the back designs of the notes of the First Charter period. The original murals decorated the rotunda of the Capitol Building in Washington and were the work of early American artists.

The coat of arms of the state of issue appears in the oval at left, with the exception of notes issued by banks in Arizona, New Mexico, Oklahoma and the state of Washington, on which the American eagle is shown in oval at right. A rather lengthy inscription qualifying the acceptance of the note, and the warning against counterfeiting "punishable by $1000 fine, or fifteen years' imprisonment at hard labor, or both" is also part of the back design.

The border designs are green with center illustrations in black on the reverses:

$1, "Landing of the Pilgrims" in center of back design depicts one of the memorable events in United States history. It is framed by the legend. Engraved by Charles Burt.

$2, Sir Walter Raleigh, with a long-stemmed smoking pipe, demonstrates the use of tobacco brought from America. Engraved by Louis Delnoce.

$5, "The Landing of Columbus" from the well-known mural by John Vanderlyn.

$10, "DeSoto Discovering the Mississippi 1541." The mural by W.H. Powell shows a group of natives, soldiers and monks. A crucifix is being erected on the spot. Engraved by Girsch.

$20, "The Baptism of Pocahontas" at Jamestown, Va. The scene shows Pocahontas kneeling, with John Smith and spectators, some of whom express interest and surprise. The painting is by John G. Chapman.

$50, "Embarkation of the Pilgrims," a reproduction of Robert W. Wier's mural, which depicts the Pilgrims before departing for America, kneeling to ask the Divine blessing. Engraved by W.W. Rice.

$100, "The Signing of the Declaration of Independence" July 4, 1776. One of John Trumbull's masterpieces, showing Washington, Jefferson, Franklin and a dignified group assembled for the acceptance and signing of the historic document. Engraved by Girsch.

$500, "The Surrender of Burgoyne." Another mural by artist John Trumbull vividly portraying the surrender of the general to General Gates of the American Army, at Saratoga, N.Y., Oct. 17, 1777. Engraved by Girsch.

$1,000, "Washington Resigning His Commission" Dec. 23, 1783, at Annapolis, Md. John Trumbull's mural shows the commander-in-chief presenting his resignation to the Congress. Engraved by Girsch and Delnoce.

The Second Charter Period spans Series 1882 Brown Backs; Series 1882-1908; and Series 1882 with denomination spelled out on back of note.

First Issue: Series 1882. The well-known and very popular Brown Backs.

Second Issue: Series 1882-1908 emergency issue. Whereas banks had previously been required to deposit United States government bonds with the Treasurer, by Act of Congress, May 30, 1908, they were permitted to deposit other types of securities, thus enabling the banks to place a larger number of notes into circulation.

Third Issue: Series 1882. Denomination spelled out on back. Scarcest of the three series of 1882 nationals. Not all banks issued this series.

Face designs of the first, second and third issues are as follows:

The face designs of the three Second Charter issues are the same as the First Charter issues, with the exception of the $5 notes. The bank obligation to pay is also the same.

The face design of the $5 denomination of all three issues of 1882 is distinctly different from the higher denominations of this series, or the $5 First Charter notes. A portrait of James A. Garfield, 20th president, is in oval at left, possibly used to immortalize the statesman following his assassination in 1881, the same year in which he assumed office. The design is by Geo. W. Casilear, engraved by Alonzo C. Hatch.

Back Designs of the first issue — 1882 Brown Backs — are as follows:

"Brown Backs" is the well-known description of the First Series of Second Charter notes. The state seals are in ovals at left in the back design, as on the First Charter notes, and the American eagle is again shown in oval at right.

The striking change in the "Brown Backs" is in the center design, which prominently features the Bank Charter Number in large numerals against a green background, surrounded by brown lathework design.

The legend appears in the top margin and the rather lengthy counterfeiting warning, extends across bottom of back design.

Green Back designs of the second issue, 1882-1908 series are as follows:

The back design of the Emergency Series, 1882-1908, shows various persons and designs in the small oval at left, instead of the state seals as used on the Brown Backs and First Charter notes. Various subjects are shown in the oval at right. Featured are the following:

$5, Washington at left; Capitol Building, Washington, D.C., at right.

$10, William P. Fessenden at left; right,

Mechanics represented by seated workmen.

$20, American eagle, two different poses, left and right ovals.

$50, eagle with shield, left and right.

$100, eagle with flag at left, and with shield at right.

Green Back designs of the third issue, "Denomination Back," are as follows:

The center designs spell out in large letters the denomination of the notes. Vignettes in small ovals at left and right, remain the same as the Second Issue, also legend at top and the counterfeiting warning at bottom.

The Third Charter period started in 1902. The First Issue was Series 1902, Red Seals and Numbers.

Notes of this issue are scarce, having been issued by comparatively few of all chartered banks. Red Seals were printed with only three signature combinations of Treasury officials.

Second Issue: 1902-1908, blue seals, Emergency Series. Dates on back.

Authorized under Act of May 30, 1908, as were the Series 1882-1908 Second Charter notes. First issued in 1908 and with two exceptions discontinued in 1916. Fifty dollar and $100 denominations were issued through 1925.

Third Issue: 1902 Blue Seals. No dates on back.

First issued in 1916 and most common of the three issues of Third Charter notes. There were 15 signature combinations, the scarcest being the Jones-Woods signatures. Edward E. Jones assumed the office of Register, and Walter O. Woods the office of Treasurer in 1929, the same year in which large-sized notes were discontinued.

Face designs of the Third Charter notes are as follows:

The Treasury seal is at right on all denominations in the three issues. Prominent statesmen are featured in oval, at left.

$5, Benjamin Harrison, 23rd president of the United States.

$10, William McKinley, 25th president, assassinated in Buffalo, 1901.

$20, Hugh McCulloch, Secretary of Treasury, 1865-1869 and 1884-1885.

$5, John Sherman, Secretary of the Treasury 1877-1881; Secretary of State 1897-1898.

$100, John J. Knox, Comptroller of Currency 1872-1884, later, president of the National Bank of the Republic, New York City.

Ostrander Smith designed all of the above. The $20 note was engraved by Charles Burt, all others by Geo. F.C. Smillie.

Back designs of the Third Charter notes are as follows:

Back designs of the three issues of Third Charter notes feature:

$5, Landing of the Pilgrims.

$10, Female figure, with ships in background.

$20, Columbia and Capitol at Washington.

$50, Allegorical scene. Train and female figure at right. Railroad worker reclining at left.

$100, American eagle on shield, with two male figures.

The back design of all denominations bear a rather lengthy inscription: "This note is receivable at par in all parts of the United States in payment of all taxes and excises and all other dues to the United States except duties on imports and also for all salaries and other debts and demands owing by the United States to individuals, corporations and associations within the United States except interest on public debt."

Gold certificates

Acts of March 3, 1863, July 12, 1882, March 14, 1900, and Dec. 24, 1919, authorized the issuance of gold certificates.

First, Second and Third Issues may be considered to be non-collectible, having been used principally in transactions between banks. Some of these issues were uniface. In the First Issue, denominations ranged from $20 to $10,000, in later issues $100 to $10,000. The $20 and $100 certificates of these issues are extremely rare. The higher denominations have not been discovered. Dates of issue were filled in with pen and ink on these three issues.

Fourth Issue of Series 1882 is as follows:

$20 to $10,000 denomination. As with the first three issues, denominations higher than $100 are extremely rare, practically unknown.

The obligation to pay in gold is on the face of the note. It reads: "This certifies that there have been deposited in the Treasury of the United States . . . Dollars in Gold Coin, payable to the Bearer on Demand." This issue is indicated as "Department Series" on the face of the certificates.

Face designs of Series 1882 are as follows:

$20, James A. Garfield, 20th president. Assassinated six months after his inauguration in 1881. Portrait at right.

$50, Silas Wright, U.S. senator 1833-1844; New York governor 1845-1846. Portrait at left.

$100, Thomas H. Benton, U.S. senator for more than 30 years, left.

$500, Abraham Lincoln, portrait at left.

$1,000, Alexander Hamilton, at right.

$5,000, James Madison, at left.

$10,000, Andrew Jackson, at left.

Some notes of the 1882 series, bearing Bruce-Gilfillan signatures and a brown seal, were countersigned by Thomas C. Acton, Assistant Treasurer, and were payable in New York. Notes so countersigned are rare.

Back designs of Series 1882 are as follows:

The American eagle in various poses is featured on the back design of all denominations of this series. There is no legend or inscription. Large Roman numerals "C" "D" and "M" in the back design, indicate the $100, $500 and $1,000 denominations. "United States" without "of America" is used on all back designs of this series.

Fifth Issue of Series 1888 is as follows:

Two denominations only: $5,000 James Madison, portrait at left. Back design: "5000" and eagle. $10,000 Andrew Jackson, portrait at left, Back design:

"10000" and eagle with flag.

Sixth Issue of Series 1900 is as follows:

$10,000 only. Andrew Jackson, as on Series 1888. Back design same as 1888.

Seventh Issue of Series 1905, 1906 and 1907 is as follows:

$10, Series 1907. Michael Hillegas, center, U.S. Treasurer 1775-1789. Large "X" Roman equivalent of "10" at left.

$20, Series 1905, George Washington. The blending of gold, red, black and white, has caused this note to be known as the "technicolor" note.

$20, Series 1906, George Washington. Gold and black design with Roman numeral "XX."

The back design of gold for this series, carries no inscription, simply the designation "Gold Certificate," the denomination and the seal.

Eighth Issue of Series 1907 is as follows:

$1,000, Alexander Hamilton. One denomination.

Ninth Issue of Series 1913 is as follows:

$50, Series 1913. Portrait of Grant. Issued with two signature combinations, both of which were offered in the Grinnell sale, in 1945. Series 1913 and Series 1922, were the only two issues of the $50 denomination.

Last Issue of Series 1922 is as follows:

$10 to $1,000 denominations. All bear signature combination Speelman-White.

A legend was added to the face of the notes: "This certificate is a Legal Tender in the amount thereof, in payment of all debts and dues public and private. Acts of March 14, 1900, as amended, and December 24, 1919."

$10, Michael Hillegas, first U.S. Treasurer.

$20, George Washington

$50, Ulysses Grant

$100, Thomas H. Benton

$500, Abraham Lincoln

$1,000, Alexander Hamilton

The back designs in gold feature the seal, the denomination and the words "United States of America." There is no legend or inscription.

National gold bank notes

The national gold bank notes are gold-tinted and are extremely rare. Ten national gold banks were authorized by Congress to assuage the burden of handling the gold produced by the California Gold Rush. Nine of the banks were in California and one was in Boston. It is generally believed that the Kidder National Gold Bank of Boston did not circulate gold notes, though proof impressions do exist.

Authorized denominations were $5 to $5,000, redeemable in gold. Since the gold banks were also national banks, it was necessary for them to deposit U.S. bonds as security with the U.S. Treasurer. The obligation on these notes is similar to the national bank notes except that the gold bank notes were payable in gold coin.

Federal Reserve Bank notes

The large-sized Federal Reserve Bank notes were authorized by the Federal Reserve Acts of Dec. 23, 1913, and April 23, 1918. They were issued in two series in denominations of $1 to $50 and are often confused with national bank notes because they have the inscription "National Currency" across the top. They have blue seals and blue serial numbers.

The first issue, Series 1913, consisted only of $5, $10 and $20 notes issued by the Federal Reserve Banks of Atlanta, Chicago, Kansas City, Dallas and San Francisco. Only $5 notes were issued by the San Francisco Federal Reserve Bank.

The obligation to pay the bearer is similar to that on the first charter national bank notes, differing only slightly in wording but not in meaning.

The second issue, Series 1918, consisted of $1, $2, $5, $10, $20 and $50 notes issued by all 12 Federal Reserve Banks (though all banks did not necessarily issue all denominations).

The obligation to pay the bearer differs completely from the first issue, reading "Secured by United States Bonds or Certificates of Indebtedness or one-year gold notes."

Although Federal Reserve Bank notes are a rather recent issue, all are quite scarce. Treasury Department records show that only slightly more than $2 million is outstanding from a total issue of nearly $762 million.

Federal Reserve notes Series 1914 and 1918

Federal Reserve Act, Dec. 23, 1913.

Series 1914, Red Seals, $5 to $100, scarce. Signatures: John Burke, Treasurer of the United States; Wm. G. McAdoo, Secretary of the Treasury.

Series 1914, Blue Seals, $5 to $100.

Series 1918, Blue Seals, $500 to $10,000.

Blue Seal signatures: John Burke-Wm. G. McAdoo; John Burke-Carter Glass; John Burke-D.F. Houston; Frank White-A.W. Mellon.

There are three types of notes with White-Mellon signatures. Type one: District numeral and letter, rather large, lower left and upper right. Most common of the three types. Type two: Smaller numerals and letters of the various districts. Type three: Larger numerals and letters, slightly to the left and higher. Seals closer to center of note. Scarcest of the three types.

Unlike the Federal Reserve Bank notes, the obligation to pay is by the United States and reads: "The United States of America will pay the Bearer on Demand .. . Dollars."

Face designs of Series 1914 are as follows:

Portraits of presidents featured on Federal Reserve Bank notes, are repeated on Federal Reserve notes on denominations $5 to $50, but are shown in center oval of the face design. Seal with numeral and letter of issuing bank is at left, and seal of the Treasury is at right. $100 Series 1914, Portrait of Benjamin Franklin, American statesman.

Face designs of Series 1918 all with Blue Seals are as follows:

$500, John Marshall, secretary of state and Chief Justice of the United States.

$1,000, Alexander Hamilton, first

Secretary of the Treasury.

$5,000, James Madison, fourth president of the United States.

$10,000, Salmon P. Chase, Secretary of Treasury under Lincoln.

Back Designs of Series 1914 and 1918, Red and Blue seals are as follows:

Series 1914, $5 to $50 same as back design of the Federal Reserve Bank notes. The back design of the $100 note features five allegorical figures.

Back Designs of Series 1918 Blue Seals are as follows:

Series 1918, $500, De Soto discovering the Mississippi, as on the $10 First Charter, national bank note.

Series 1918, $1,000, American eagle with flag.

Series 1918, $5,000, Washington resigning his commission, as on the $1,000 First Charter note.

Series 1918, $10,000, Embarkation of the Pilgrims, as on the $50 First Charter note.

The lengthy inscription in the lower border of the back design differs from that on the Federal Reserve Bank notes. It stipulates that the note is payable in gold, and reads:

"This note is receivable by all national and member banks and the Federal Reserve Banks, and for all taxes, customs and other public dues. It is redeemable in gold on demand at the Treasury Department of the United States in the city of Washington, District of Columbia, or in gold or lawful money at any Federal Reserve Bank."

U.S. postage and fractional currency

In 1862 the need for small coins to make change became acute. Following the suspension of specie payments by the large Northeastern banks and the federal Treasury late the previous year, coinage became widely hoarded and commanded premium values as compared to the government greenbacks. The result of this hoarding was extreme difficulty in making change for ordinary business transactions.

Private attempts to remedy the small change shortage were ingenious but proved futile. Neither municipal, corporate nor private scrip could completely replace the withdrawn subsidiary silver coinage on a nationwide scale and local expedients such as John Gault's encased postage were little more than temporary measures.

To relieve the citizenry of the "worthless paper trash" which was circulating, F.E. Spinner, Treasurer of the United States, convinced Congress of the necessity for a federal, fractional currency. He proposed that the U.S. issue these small notes in values less than $1 and in sufficient quantities to meet the demand for small change. Congress responded with the Act of July 17, 1862, which monetized the postage and other stamps of the United States.

The immediate effect of the law was a run on the U.S. post offices to secure stamps for change. By Aug. 21, however, the first notes of the belated postage currency issue reached circulation. Privately printed, these notes bore the imprints of the contemporary 5- and 10-cent postage stamps. Jefferson appears on the 5- and 25-cent issues and Washington on the 10- and 50-cent notes. Both perforate and imperforate varieties exist.

The reverse obligation on these notes states, "Exchangeable for United States Notes by any Assistant Treasurer or designated U.S. Depositary in sums not less than five dollars. Receivable in payment of all dues to the U. [sic] States less than five Dollars."

Because of the prevalence of counterfeiting, the designs of the successive fractional note issues were changed frequently. The fractional currency, which succeeded the makeshift (and some students contend illegal) postage currency, was issued in four series under authorization of the Act of March 3, 1863, which also provided that the Treasury Department print its own notes.

The so-called "Second Issue" (first issue under the latter act) consists of four notes in the same denominations as the earlier issue, but all bearing a bust of Washington in a bronze oval frame on obverse.

The reverse obligation was altered to read, "Exchangeable for United States Notes by the Assistant Treasurers and designated depositaries of the U.S. in sums not less than three dollars. Receivable in payment of all dues to the United States less than five dollars except customs." As with the postage currency, these notes were also receivable for U.S. postage stamps.

The third general issue added a 3-cent denomination, and each denomination has a different design. Washington appears on the 3-cent note; Spencer M. Clark, on the 5-cent issue; Washington, on the 10-cent bill; William Pitt Fessenden, on the 25-cent note; and either a seated figure of Justice or F.E. Spinner on the 50-cent issue. The Spinner note also exists with two distinct reverse varieties. The proposed 15-cent Grant-Sherman essay

also exists in the form of uniface specimens.

The fourth general issue includes only 10-, 15-, 25- and 50-cent denominations. The 10-cent note bears a bust of Liberty; Columbia appears on the 15-cent issue; Washington, on the 25-cent bill; and Lincoln, Edwin Stanton or Samuel Dexter appear on the 50-cent bill.

The short fifth issue is confined to three notes: William Meredith, on the 10-cent note; Robert Walker, on the 25-cent bill; and William Crawford, on the 50-cent issue.

The small notes continued to circulate until the Resumption Act of Jan. 14, 1875, provided for their retirement by subsidiary silver coinage. In all, nearly $370 million worth of these small bills were issued, but most have long since been redeemed or destroyed. It is estimated that less than $5,000 face value remains available to collectors.

Fractional note statistics

The summary tabulation below shows the extent and value of the five fractional note issues:

First Issue
Aug. 21, 1862 to May 27, 1863

	Number	Value
5 cent	44,857,780	$2,242,889.00
10 cent	41,153,780	4,115,378.00
25 cent	20,902,784	5,225,696.00
50 cent	17,273,344	8,631,672.00
Totals	124,187,688	$20,215,635.00

Second Issue
Oct. 10, 1863 to Feb. 23, 1867

	Number	Value
5 cent	55,896,522	$2,794,826.10
10 cent	61,760,843	6,176,084.30
25 cent	30,593,365	7,648,341.25
50 cent	13,090,464	6,545,232.00
Totals	161,341,194	$23,164,483.65

Third Issue
Dec. 5, 1864 to Aug. 16, 1869

	Number	Value
3 Cent	20,064,130	$601,923.90
5 Cent	13,140,055	657,002.75
10 Cent	169,761,345	16,976,134.50
15 Cent (Specimen)	9,016	1,352.40
25 Cent	124,572,755	31,143,188.75
50 Cent	73,470,853	36,735,426.50
Totals	401,018,154	$86,115,028.80

Fourth Issue
July 14, 1869 to Feb. 16, 1875

	Number	Value
10 Cent	349,409,600	$34,940,960.00
15 Cent	35,361,440	5,304,216.00
25 Cent	235,689,024	58,922,256.00
50 Cent	154,799,200	77,399,600.00
Totals	154,799,200	$77,399,600.00

Fifth Issue
Feb. 26, 1874 to Feb. 15, 1876

	Number	Value
10 Cent	199,899,000	$19,989,900.00
25 Cent	144,368,000	36,092,000.00
50 Cent	13,160,000	6,580,000.00
Totals	357,427,000	$62,661,990.00

Summary of all issues

	Number	Value
3 Cent	20,064,130	$601,923.90
5 Cent	113,894,357	5,694,717.85
10 Cent	821,984,568	82,198,456.80
15 Cent (Specimen)	9,016	1,352.40
15 Cent	35,361,440	5,304,216.00
25 Cent	556,125,928	139,031,482.00
50 Cent	271,783,861	135,891,930.50
Totals	1,819,223,300	$368,724,079.45

United States small-sized paper money

The current small-sized notes were first issued in mid-1929, though some carry the series year designation of 1928. Issues in the small-sized category comprise United States notes, silver certificates, national bank notes, Federal Reserve Bank notes, Federal Reserve notes, and gold certificates.

United States notes

The $1 United States note was issued only in Series 1928. It features a portrait of Washington on the front and is the only small-sized $1 note to feature a red seal. The inscription is printed over the seal and states: "This note is legal tender at its face value for all debts public and private except duties on imports and interest on the public debt." The note also advises that "The United States of America will pay to the bearer on demand One Dollar." On the back on the $1 note a large "ONE" appears with smaller letters stating "ONE DOLLAR" over the larger "ONE."

The $2 note, featuring a portrait of Jefferson on the front and his home, Monticello, on the back, was first printed in the Series 1928 and was discontinued in 1966. Final series year for the $2 United States note was 1963A. Jefferson and Monticello remained on the $2 issues from the beginning to the end, but there were some changes in the inscription and the Treasury seal was relocated starting with the 1953 series. On this and later issues the seal is on the right, while on earlier issues it was on the left.

The first inscription says, "This note is legal tender at its face value for all debts public and private except duties on imports and interest on the public debt." Beginning with the 1953 series the inscription reads, "This note is a legal tender at its face value for all debts public and private," and on the 1963 and 1963A series the inscription advises, "This note is legal tender for all debts public and private." The motto "In God We Trust" was added to the $2 note beginning with the 1963 series, and with

this same series the wording "Will pay to the bearer on demand" was removed.

The $5 note went through the same inscription and seal changes as did the $2 note. It features Lincoln on the front and the Lincoln Memorial on the back. The motto was added with the 1963 (final) series. The last delivery of $5 United States notes was in late 1967.

Benjamin Franklin is featured on the front of the $100 United States note, and the back features Independence Hall. First issued in Series 1966 (the only note to have that series year) it is the first note to use the newly redesigned Treasury seal. All United States notes have red seals and serial numbers.

Silver certificates

The small-sized silver certificates were issued in denominations of $1, $5 and $10 and were discontinued in 1963. The early issues stated that the notes were redeemable in silver dollars on demand — a clause later changed to "In silver payable to the bearer on demand." After the change it was possible to exchange silver certificates for silver bullion.

However, on June 24, 1967, President Johnson signed into law a bill which spelled the end of silver certificate redemption. The Treasury Department announced it would redeem the certificates until June 24, 1968, and one of the wildest "silver rushes" in American history was under way. Collectors, dealers and speculators bought all the silver certificates they could get their hands on, paying premium prices, then exchanging them for silver bullion to be sold back on the silver market.

Redemptions were made at the U.S. Assay Offices in San Francisco, Calif., and in New York, N.Y. During the final days of redemption, long lines of certificate holders lined the sidewalks around the assay offices to trade notes for silver before the deadline.

For small transactions, the assay offices

issued small envelopes each valued at $1, containing .77-plus ounces of fine silver in the form of crystals or pellets. For larger transactions plastic bags of silver granules or bars of silver were used. The standard bar varied in weight from 1,000 to 1,100 ounces at $1.292929292 per fine troy ounce, raised to the next highest dollar. The exchanges had to be made in person because the assay offices were instructed not to exchange silver by mail.

It was possible, however, for the individual having large holdings of silver certificates to arrange with certain banks to perform the redemption, as a goodwill gesture. Not all banks, though, were willing to perform this service. The banks that did cooperate would contact a bank in New York City or San Francisco and arrange for that bank to send an agent to purchase the silver. The purchasing agent in either of the two cities would ship the silver direct to the home bank's customer.

Although this mad rush to redeem silver certificates did deplete the numismatic stock somewhat, it also served to introduce additional persons to the hobby of numismatics, due to the great amount of publicity that newspapers gave the modern-day silver rush. Silver certificates, like other issues that have been discontinued, remain legal tender.

The $1 silver certificate portrays Washington on the front side. On the 1928 to 1928E series the Treasury seal is on the left and a large "ONE" is on the right. The back side is similar to the 1928 $1 United States note.

On the 1934 series silver certificate the Treasury seal changes from the left to right side and a large number "1" appears where the seal was on the left. A third design, for Series 1935-1957, reduces the size of the number "1" and the Treasury seal. On the second two designs, the reverse side features the Great Seal of the United States and a large "ONE." The motto "In God We Trust" was added to the reverse of some 1935G notes, and all of 1935H, 1957, 1957A and 1957B notes.

The $5 silver certificate portrays Lincoln on the front and the Lincoln Memorial on the back. The figure "5" and the Treasury seal, left and right sides respectively, are larger on the 1934 through 1934D series than they are on following series, 1953 through 1953C.

Alexander Hamilton is featured on the front of the $10 silver certificate, with the U.S. Treasury building on the back. On the first series, 1933, to the left of Hamilton is the Treasury seal and to the right "TEN" appears. The seal was placed upon the "TEN" for series 1934 through 1934D, and was replaced on the left by "10." On later series $10 notes, the seal and "10" are reduced in size from the previous issues.

The first $10 silver certificates stated "Ten Dollars payable in silver coin to the bearer on demand." This was changed for the 1934 through 1953B series and these notes read "Ten Dollars in silver payable to the bearer on demand."

The inscription on 1933 series $10 silver certificates says: "This certificate issued pursuant to sections of the Act of May 12, 1933, and is legal tender at its face value for all debts public and private." Later issues simply said, "This certificate is legal tender for all debts public and private."

All silver certificates have blue seals and serial numbers, with certain exceptions. Special notes were printed for use during North African and European invasions of World War II and these notes have blue serial numbers and yellow seals. These latter notes were printed as follows: $1, 1935A; $5, 1934 and 1934A; and $10, 1934 and 1934A. Special $1 silver certificates were printed, and overprinted with "HAWAII," for use in Hawaii and other islands during World War II. The "HAWAII" notes have brown seals and serial numbers.

A special printing (experimental) of the $1 notes was included in the series year 1935A. The United States was testing the quality of currency paper and used two types of paper for the experimental issue. Some of the notes are marked with a large "R" in the lower right side, and others with a large "S" in the lower right. Like the regular certificates, these notes have blue seals and numbers.

Small-sized national bank notes

Small-sized national bank notes were all of Series 1929, but were issued through 1935. Issued by hundreds of banks throughout the nation, all carry the signatures of the issuing bank's president and cashier, along with the signatures of the Register of the Treasury and the United States Treasurer. Designs are similar to designs on other small-sized notes of the same denomination. They were issued in denominations of $5, $10, $20, $50 and $100. All state "National Currency" at the top center of each note, and all have brown seals and brown serial numbers.

There are two types of the 1929 series national bank notes. Type one features the issuing bank's charter number in black at each end of the face of the note. These notes were numbered in sheets of six notes with identical numbers on each but different prefix letters: A, B, C, D, E and F from top to bottom.

The serial numbers ended with a suffix letter: A for the first 999,999 sheets, B for the second 999,999 sheets, and so on.

In 1933, a new method of numbering national bank notes was approved, effective on July 1. The sheets still contained six notes each but the numbers ran consecutively from one to six on the first sheet, seven through 12 on the second sheet, and so on, with prefix letters A and without a suffix letter. The bank charter number preceded the serial number in the upper right corner and followed the serial number in the lower left corner of the notes.

After the numbering sequence reached 999,999 the prefix letter changed to B. This sequence continued with one exception _ the letter O was never used.

The notes carried the issuing bank's name, city and state as well as the bold, black, charter number on both types. Also featured on both types were words stating that the notes were secured by United States bonds deposited with the Treasurer of the United States of America.

Records do not reveal the number of national bank notes issued by type and denomination to the issuing banks, nor do the records of outstanding notes give reliable information about the number of unredeemed notes. National bank notes have one thing in common with all other discontinued notes _ they remain legal tender of the United States.

Federal Reserve Bank notes

Only one series of small-sized Federal Reserve Bank notes was issued, Series 1929. They are often confused with Federal Reserve notes and are often mistaken for national bank notes.

The confusion arises in part from design similarities and in part from the fact that plates for national bank notes were used to print the Federal Reserve Bank notes. To further complicate matters, they are inscribed "National Currency" across the top.

They were authorized by Act of Congress March 9, 1933, to permit the Federal Reserve Banks to issue currency equal to 100 percent of the face value of U.S. bonds, or 90 percent of the value of commercial paper, used as collateral.

The obligation to pay the bearer is the same as it is on the national bank notes, but the words, "or by like deposit of other securities," have been added below the United States of America at the top of the notes.

Series 1929 FRBNs were printed in denominations of $5, $10, $20, $50 and $100. They have brown seals and brown serial numbers. Although they carry the series year of 1929, the first notes were not delivered until March 11, 1933, and the last of the notes was delivered on Dec. 21 of that same year.

Federal Reserve notes

Federal Reserve notes are authorized by the Act of Congress of Dec. 23, 1917. These notes are issued by the Federal Reserve Banks. They were authorized in denominations of $5, $10, $20, $50, $100, $500, $1,000, $5,000 and $10,000. However, the printing of Federal Reserve notes in denominations of $500 and higher was discontinued by action of the board of governors of the Federal Reserve System on June 26, 1946.

Federal Reserve notes are obligations of the United States and were secured by the deposit with Federal Reserve agents of an equivalent amount of collateral, consisting of gold certificates or gold certificate credits with the Treasurer of the United States; such discounted or purchased paper as is eligible under the terms of the Federal Reserve Act as amended; and direct obligations of the United States.

Until 1968, Federal Reserve Banks were required to maintain a reserve in gold certificates or gold certificate credits equal to at least 25 percent of these notes in actual circulation, including in this reserve the redemption fund (equal to not less than 5 percent of the notes outstanding less the amount of gold certificates held by the Federal Reserve agent as collateral) which was deposited with the Treasurer of the United States and any gold certificates or gold certificate credits held as collateral for Federal Reserve notes. This requirement was abolished in 1968.

Federal Reserve notes have always been printed at the Bureau of Engraving and Printing — although this is not required by law — the Federal Reserve Act merely stating that the Comptroller of the Currency, under the direction of the Secretary of the Treasury, shall have the plates engraved and the notes printed. The entire expense of engraving and printing the notes is paid by the Federal Reserve Banks, and is credited to the Bureau's revolving fund.

The number to be ordered is determined by the board of governors of the Federal Reserve System, but the printing order is issued by the Comptroller of the Currency. As the volume of Federal Reserve currency fluctuates, it is necessary to keep a large stock on hand before issue. This reserve stock is kept in the vaults of the Bureau until it is shipped to the several banks.

The storage of these notes is not, strictly speaking, a Bureau activity. The law requires that the stock be kept in the Treasury, subtreasury, or a Mint until delivered to the banks.

The packages of completed notes are delivered by the Currency Processing Division of the Bureau to the Federal Reserve vault in the main Bureau building and remains under the control of the Bureau until shipment is made to Federal Reserve banks. See Chapter 6 (Bureau of Engraving and Printing) for how paper money is printed.

Bicentennial $2 notes

Federal Reserve note denominations increased by one April 13, 1976, when the Series 1976 $2 note was issued in commemoration of the American Independence Bicentennial. Treasury Secretary William Simon announced Nov. 3, 1975, that the note would be reissued bearing Thomas Jefferson's portrait as on the $2 United States note, but with a reverse depicting a scene from John Trumbull's "Signing of the Declaration of Independence." The April 13 release date was Jefferson's birthday.

Treasury officials hoped public acceptance of the $2 bill would alleviate demand for the $1 bill, thus relieving pressure on the Bureau of Engraving and Printing. The $1 bill represents the bulk of the work of the BEP. However, the $2 note never became popular in most areas of the United States, and today most of the $2 FRNs rest in bank vaults.

The release of the note did trigger a new collector's item — the postally canceled note. U.S. Postal Service officials agreed to permit collectors to attach stamps to the bills which were then postally canceled on April 13 as a first day issue, and later on other commemorative dates. Collectors today continue to issue and collect postally canceled notes.

Small-sized currency series

Since July 10, 1929, the date the small-sized currency was first put into circulation, the Bureau of Engraving and Printing has printed and delivered the following series of notes:

$1 silver certificates: Series 1928, 1928A, 1928B, 1928C, 1928D, 1928E, 1934, 1935, 1935A, 1935B, 1935C, 1935D, 1935E, 1935F, 1935G, 1935H, 1957, 1957A and 1957B.

$5 silver certificates: Series 1934, 1934A, 1934B, 1934C, 1934D, 1953, 1953A, 1953B and (printed but not released) 1953C.

$10 silver certificates: Series 1933, 1933A, 1934, 1934A, 1934B, 1934C, 1934D, 1953, 1953A and 1953B.

$1 United States notes: Series 1928.

$2 United States notes: Series 1928, 1928A, 1928B, 1928C, 1928D, 1928E, 1928F, 1928G, 1953, 1953A, 1953B, 1953C, 1963 and 1963A.

$5 United States notes: Series 1928, 1928A, 1928B, 1928C, 1928D, 1928E, 1928F, 1953, 1953A, 1953B, 1953C and 1963.

$10 and $20 United States notes: Series 1928 (reported but unverified).

$100 United States notes: Series 1966 and 1966A.

$1 Federal Reserve notes: Series 1963, 1963A, 1963B, 1969, 1969A, 1969B, 1969C, 1969D, 1974, 1977, 1977A, 1981, 1981A,1985, 1988, and 1988A.

$2 Federal Reserve notes: 1976.

$5 Federal Reserve notes: Series 1928, 1928A, 1928B, 1928C, 1928D, 1934, 1934A, 1934B, 1934C, 1934D, 1950, 1950A, 1950B, 1950C, 1950D, 1950E, 1963, 1963A, 1969, 1969A, 1969B, 1969C, 1974, 1977, 1977A, 1981, 1981A,1985, 1988 and 1988A.

$10 Federal Reserve notes: Series 1928, 1928A, 1928B, 1928C, 1934, 1934A, 1934B, 1934C, 1934D, 1950, 1950A, 1950B, 1950C, 1950D, 1950E, 1963, 1963A, 1969, 1969A, 1969B, 1969C, 1974, 1977, 1977A, 1981, 1981A,1985, 1988 and 1988A.

$20 Federal Reserve notes: Series 1928, 1928A, 1928B, 1928C, 1934, 1934A, 1934B, 1934C, 1934D, 1950, 1950A, 1950B, 1950C, 1950D, 1950E, 1963, 1963A, 1969, 1969A, 1969B, 1969C, 1974, 1977, 1981, 1981A,1985, 1988 and 1988A.

$50 and $100 Federal Reserve notes: Series 1928, 1928A, 1934, 1934A, 1934B, 1934C, 1934D, 1950, 1950A, 1950B, 1950C, 1950D, 1950E, 1963A, 1969, 1969A, 1969B, 1969C, 1974, 1977 and 1981, 1981A,1985 and 1988 (1988A anticipated but not reported at press time).

$500 Federal Reserve notes: Series 1928, 1934, 1934A, 1934B and 1934C.

$1,000 Federal Reserve notes: Series 1928, 1934, 1934A and 1934C.

$5,000 and $10,000 Federal Reserve notes: Series 1928, 1934, 1934A and 1934B.

$5, $10, $20, $50 and $100 Federal Reserve Bank notes: Series 1929.

$5, $10, $20, $50 and $100 national bank notes: Series 1929.

$10 and $20 gold certificates: Series 1928 and (printed but not released) 1928A.

$50, $500 and $5,000 gold certificates: Series 1928.

$100, $1,000 and $10,000 gold certificates: Series 1928 and (printed but not released) 1934.

$100,000 gold certificates: Series 1934.

Barr notes

Barr notes are those signed by Secretary of the Treasury Joseph W. Barr, who served from Dec. 21, 1968, to Jan. 20, 1969. Appointed to fill out the unexpired term of Henry H. Fowler, Barr was replaced by Nixon appointee David M. Kennedy.

Born in Vincennes, Ind., Barr had been Undersecretary of the Treasury since April 1965. A former U.S. representative from Indiana, he joined the Treasury Department in 1961 as an assistant to the Secretary.

Barr, while serving as Treasury Secretary, was also governor for the United States on the International Monetary Fund, the International Bank for Reconstruction and Development, the Inter-American Development Fund, and the Asian Development Bank.

Following his short term as Treasury Secretary, Barr was a director of the American Society Corporation. After resigning that post, he joined the Franklin

National Bank of New York to serve as chairman and chief executive officer.

Because Barr served such a short term as Secretary of the Treasury, one month, some felt those notes signed by Barr were issued in limited numbers and would soon become rare.

However, production of Barr notes did not stop on Jan. 20, 1969, when he resigned. It wasn't until June 4, 1969, that notes bearing the signature of Barr's successor, David Kennedy, came off the presses.

Barr notes are not considered rare by informed paper money collectors. The following chart shows how many Barr notes were delivered to the Federal Reserve Banks.

Barr note statistics

Federal Reserve District	Regular Notes	Star Notes
New York	123,040,000	3,680,000
Richmond	93,600,000	3,200,000
Chicago	91,040,000	2,400,000
Kansas City	44,800,000	None Printed
San Francisco	106,400,000	3,040,000
Total notes printed	458,880,000	12,320,000
Less spoilage*	27,532,800	547,200
Estimated total notes released	431,347,200	11,612,800

*Based on past reports, spoilage is estimated at 6 percent for regular notes and 4.5 percent for star notes.

Official serial number range

	Regular notes		Star notes	
New York	B57 600 001G	B80 640 000H	B48 800 001★	B52 480 000★
Richmond	E32 000 001F	E25 600 000G	E41 600 001★	E44 800 000★
Chicago	G84 480 001H	G75 520 000I	G52 640 001★	G55 040 000★
Kansas City	J19 200 001C	J64 000 000C	None printed	
San Francisco	L76 800 001F	L83 200 000G	L43 040 001★	L46 080 000★

The first delivery of notes bearing Joseph Barr's signature took place on Jan. 16, 1969 (Richmond District), and the last delivery was Nov. 12, 1969 (New York District).

Features of current U.S. paper money

Plate position numbers

The small capital letter and number which appear in the upper left-hand corner just below the denomination numeral on the face of a bill comprise what is referred to as the plate position number. This item designates the position of the note on the 32-subject face plate from which a particular bill was printed.

Each modern 32-note sheet is split into four quadrants, with two vertical rows of four notes each. The upper left quadrant is No. 1, the lower left, No. 2; the upper right is No. 3, and the lower right, No. 4. Within the quadrant, the left four notes, from top to bottom, are A, B, C, D; the right row is E, F, G, H. Thus, a note with position number B3 would be in the upper right quadrant, left row, second note from top. An H1 note would be from the upper left quadrant, right row, fourth note from top.

Plate serial numbers

The small number in the lower right-hand corner relates to the face plate from which a note was printed. This is referred to as the plate serial number. This number is assigned in sequential order at the time the plate is manufactured. It can be used to determine the number of the press plate from which a particular note was printed. The letter preceding the plate serial number is always the same as the letter in the upper left-hand corner.

Series date

The series date on the face of each bill signifies the year in which the design of the note was adopted. The series does not change each calendar year; usually only when the basic design has a major revision. The capital letter following the series year indicates that a minor change was authorized in a particular series. Minor revisions usually occur when a new Secretary of the Treasury or Treasurer of the United States is appointed, and a corresponding change is made in the signature of one or both of these officials.

Size of currency

Currency of the present size was first issued in July 1929, replacing the old, large (7.50 by 3.125 inches) notes. The present size of a U.S. bill is 6.14 inches by 2.61 inches, and the thickness is .0043 inch. New notes stack 233 to an inch, not compressed, and weigh 490 notes to a pound. A million notes will weigh approximately 2,000 pounds and occupy approximately 42 cubic feet of space, with moderate pressure.

Serial numbers on small-sized currency

The two numbers, with prefix and suffix letters or "stars," in the upper right-hand and lower left-hand corners of all small-sized currency are referred to as serial numbers. The letters in the Federal Reserve Bank seal and the prefix letter of the serial numbers are always identical on Federal Reserve notes.

Serial numbers are designed to foil counterfeiters and to accommodate the large volume of notes printed by the Bureau of Engraving and Printing. No two notes of a class, denomination and series have the same serial number, except for error notes. Each serial number has eight digits and an alphabetical prefix and suffix letter.

When a new series of Federal Reserve notes is initiated, a new number sequence generally begins (although serial numbers continued from Series 1977 to 1977A). The first of the sequence is 00 000 001A, with a prefix letter indicating the Federal Reserve district issuing the note. The second is 00 000 002A, the hundredth is 00 000 100A, the thousandth 00 001 000A, until the number 99 920 000A is reached, at which point the suffix letter

changes to B and the numbering system starts over. The letter O is never used as a suffix letter because it could be confused with the digit 0.

Serial numbers do not advance sequentially from note to note on an individual sheet, but from sheet to sheet. On a sheet, the numbers advance 100,000 digits from note to note, since sheets are overprinted in 100,000-sheet runs.

On United States notes and silver certificates, the first note is numbered A 00 000 001A, continuing in numerical sequence with the prefix and suffix letters remaining the same. When the number A 99 999 999A is reached, the suffix letter A is retained and the prefix letter changes alphabetically until 25 blocks of 99 999 999 are printed, each with a different prefix letter of the alphabet from A to Z, omitting O.

Federal Reserve symbols

On the face of every Federal Reserve note, the black seal to left of the portrait identifies the particular Federal Reserve Bank which issued the bill. There are 12 Federal Reserve Banks (see Chapter 7), each identifiable by a letter and a number, with the letter corresponding to the number, as follows:

1	A	Boston
2	B	New York
3	C	Philadelphia
4	D	Cleveland
5	E	Richmond
6	F	Atlanta
7	G	Chicago
8	H	St. Louis
9	I	Minneapolis
10	J	Kansas City
11	K	Dallas
12	L	San Francisco

The Federal Reserve Bank number, which appears four times, is repeated in the upper and lower and the left and right sections of the bill for identification purposes. These numbers are particularly helpful in cases involving claims made by the public for redemption of burned or mutilated notes, when only portions of the notes remain.

The Great Seal of the United States

Both the obverse and the reverse of the Great Seal of the United States are reproduced on the backs of $1 bills. The Great Seal was adopted in 1782. Its obverse depicts an American eagle breasted by a shield with the national colors. The eagle holds in his right talon an olive branch of 13 leaves and 13 berries, symbolic of peace.

In his left talon he holds 13 arrows signifying the original Colonies' fight for liberty. A ribbon flying from the beak of the eagle is inscribed with the Latin motto, "E Pluribus Unum," which is translated "One out of many," in reference to the unity of the 13 Colonies as one government.

Over the eagle's head is a constellation of 13 five-pointed stars surrounded by a wreath of clouds.

The reverse of the seal depicts a pyramid, with the Roman numerals "MDCCLXXVI" on its base — 1776, the year of the Declaration of Independence. The pyramid represents permanence and strength. Its unfinished condition symbolizes that there was still work to be done to form a more perfect government and signifies the expectation that new states would be admitted to the Union.

The eye in the triangular glory represents an all-seeing Deity. The words "Annuit coeptis," translated as "He (God) has favored our undertakings," refer to the many interpositions the founding fathers saw of divine providence in the forming of the government. "Novus Ordo Seclorum," translated as "A new order of the ages," signifies a new American era.

"In God We Trust"

In October 1957, $1 silver certificates bearing the motto, "In God We Trust," were first placed in circulation.

The suggestion to include the motto on U.S. paper currency was presented to the Secretary of the Treasury George W. Humphrey in November of 1953 by Matthew H. Rothert of Camden, Ark. Like the Baptist preacher who wrote to the Secretary of the Treasury in 1861 suggesting mention of the Deity on U.S. coins. Rothert also directed his inquiry to the Secretary of the Treasury. He followed through with letters to several senators and representatives and to his personal friend, Thomas Weeks, Secretary of Commerce.

Rothert's idea came to him while he was attending church on Sunday morning in Chicago. As the collection plate was passed, it occurred to him that only the coins in the plate had this motto. He then thought that since U.S. paper money has a much wider circulation abroad than U.S. coins, a message about the country's faith in God could be easily carried throughout the world if it were on United States paper currency.

The 84th Congress passed Public Law 140 and it was signed into law by President Dwight D. Eisenhower on July 11, 1955. The law provided, "At such times as new dies for the printing of currency are adopted in connection with the current program of the Treasury Department to increase the capacity of the presses utilized by the Bureau of Engraving and Printing, the dies shall bear, at such place or places as the Secretary of the Treasury may determine to be appropriate, the inscription 'In God We Trust,' and thereafter this inscription shall appear on all United States currency and coins."

The $ sign

The origin of the $ sign has been variously accounted for, with perhaps the most widely accepted explanation being that it is the result of evolution, independently in different places, of the Mexican or Spanish "P's" for pesos, or piastres, or pieces of eight. The theory, derived from a study of old manuscripts, is that the "S" gradually came to be written over the "P," developing a close equivalent to the $ mark, which eventually evolved. It was widely used before the adoption of the United States dollar in 1785.

Portraits on United States paper money

Listed by denomination

Denom.	Type of Note	Series	Portrait
3¢	Fractional Currency	3rd issue	George Washington
5¢	Postage Currency	1st issue	Thomas Jefferson
	Fractional Currency	2nd issue	George Washington
	Fractional Currency	3rd issue	Spencer M. Clark
10¢	Postage Currency	1st issue	George Washington
	Fractional Currency	2nd issue	George Washington
	Fractional Currency	3rd issue	George Washington
	Fractional Currency	5th issue	William M. Meredith
25¢	Postage Currency	1st issue	Thomas Jefferson
	Fractional Currency	2nd issue	George Washington
	Fractional Currency	3rd issue	William P. Fessenden
	Fractional Currency	4th issue	George Washington
	Fractional Currency	5th issue	Robert J. Walker
50¢	Postage Currency	1st issue	George Washington
	Fractional Currency	2nd issue	George Washington
	Fractional Currency	3rd issue	Gen. F. E. Spinner
	Fractional Currency	4th issue	Abraham Lincoln; E. M. Stanton; or Samuel Dexter
	Fractional Currency	5th issue	William H. Crawford
$1	Federal Reserve Note	1963 to date	George Washington
	Federal Reserve Bank Note	1918	George Washington
	United States Note	1862	Salmon P. Chase
	United States Note	1869-1928	George Washington
	Silver Certificate	1886-1891	Martha Washington
	Silver Certificate	1899	Lincoln & Grant
	Silver Certificate	1923-1957B	George Washington
	Treasury or Coin Note	1890-1891	Edwin M. Stanton
$2	Federal Reserve Bank Note	1918	Thomas Jefferson
	Federal Reserve Note	1976	Thomas Jefferson
	United States Note	1862	Alexander Hamilton
	United States Note	1869-1963A	Thomas Jefferson
	Silver Certificate	1886	General Hancock
	Silver Certificate	1891	William Windom
	Silver Certificate	1899	George Washington
	Treasury or Coin Note	1890-1891	Gen. James McPherson
$5	Demand Note	1861	Alexander Hamilton
	Federal Reserve Note	1914 to date	Abraham Lincoln
	Federal Reserve Bank Note	1915-1929	Abraham Lincoln
	United States Note	1869-1907	Andrew Jackson
	United States Note	1928-1963A	Abraham Lincoln
	National Bank Note	1882	James Garfield
	National Bank Note	1902	Benjamin Harrison
	National Bank Note	1929	Abraham Lincoln
	Silver Certificate	1886	Ulysses S. Grant
	Silver Certificate	1899	Running Antelope
	Silver Certificate	1923-1953C	Abraham Lincoln
	Treasury or Coin Note	1890-1891	Gen. George Thomas
$10	Demand Note	1861	Abraham Lincoln
	Compound Interest Treasury Note	1863-1864	Salmon P. Chase
	Interest Bearing Note, 3 year	1863	Salmon P. Chase
	Federal Reserve Note	1914	Andrew Jackson
	Federal Reserve Note	1928 to date	Alexander Hamilton
	Federal Reserve Bank Note	1915-1918	Andrew Jackson
	Federal Reserve Bank Note	1929	Alexander Hamilton
	Gold Certificate	1907-1922	Michael Hillegas
	Gold Certificate	1928	Alexander Hamilton
	United States Note	1862-1863	Abraham Lincoln
	United States Note	1869-1880	Daniel Webster
	United States Note	1901	Lewis & Clark
	United States Note	1923	Andrew Jackson
	National Bank Note	1902	William McKinley
	National Bank Note	1929	Alexander Hamilton
	Refunding Certificate	1879	Benjamin Franklin
	Silver Certificate	1878-1880	Robert Morris
	Silver Certificate	1886-1908	Thomas A. Hendricks

	Silver Certificate	1933-1953B	Alexander Hamilton
	Treasury or Coin Note	1890-1891	General Sheridan
$20	Compound Interest Treasury Note	1863-1864	Abraham Lincoln
	Federal Reserve Note	1914	Grover Cleveland
	Federal Reserve Note	1928 to date	Andrew Jackson
	Federal Reserve Bank Note	1915-1918	Grover Cleveland
	Federal Reserve Bank Note	1929	Andrew Jackson
	Gold Certificate	1882	James Garfield
	Gold Certificate	1905-1922	George Washington
	Gold Certificate	1928	Andrew Jackson
	Interest Bearing Note, 1 year	1863	Abraham Lincoln
	United States Note	1869-1880	Alexander Hamilton
	National Bank Note	1902	Hugh McCulloch
	National Bank Note	1929	Andrew Jackson
	Silver Certificate	1878-1880	Stephen Decatur
	Silver Certificate	1886-1891	Daniel Manning
	Treasury or Coin Note	1890-1891	John Marshall
$50	Compound Interest Treasury Note	1863-1864	Alexander Hamilton
	Federal Reserve Note	1914 to date	Ulysses S. Grant
	Federal Reserve Bank Note	1918-1929	Ulysses S. Grant
	Gold Certificate	1882	Silas Wright
	Gold Certificate	1913-1928	Ulysses S. Grant
	Interest Bearing Note, 1 year	1863	Alexander Hamilton
	United States Note	1862-1863	Alexander Hamilton
	United States Note	1869	Henry Clay
	United States Note	1874-1880	Benjamin Franklin
	National Bank Note	1902	John Sherman
	National Bank Note	1929	Ulysses S. Grant
	Silver Certificate	1878-1891	Edward Everett
	Treasury or Coin Note	1890-1891	William H. Seward
$100	Compound Interest Treasury Note	1863-1864	George Washington
	Federal Reserve Note	1914 to date	Benjamin Franklin
	Federal Reserve Bank Note	1929	Benjamin Franklin
	Gold Certificate	1875-1882	Thomas H. Benton
	Gold Certificate	1928-1934	Benjamin Franklin
	Interest Bearing Note, 1 year	1863	George Washington
	Interest Bearing Note, 3 year	1864	General Scott
	United States Note	1869-1880	Abraham Lincoln
	National Bank Note	1902	John J. Knox
	National Bank Note	1929	Benjamin Franklin
	Silver Certificate	1878-1891	James Monroe
	Treasury or Coin Note	1890-1891	Commodore Farragut
$500	Federal Reserve Note	1914	John Marshall
	Federal Reserve Note	1928-1934	William McKinley
	Gold Certificate	1875-1922	Abraham Lincoln
	Gold Certificate	1928	William McKinley
	Interest Bearing Note, 3 year	1864	Alexander Hamilton
	United States Note	1862-1863	Albert Gallatin
	United States Note	1869	John Quincy Adams
	United States Note	1874-1880	Maj. Gen. Mansfield
	Silver Certificate	1878-1880	Charles Sumner
$1,000	Federal Reserve Note	1918	Alexander Hamilton
	Federal Reserve Note	1928-1934A	Grover Cleveland
	Gold Certificate	1875-1922	Alexander Hamilton
	Gold Certificate	1928-1934	Grover Cleveland
	Interest Bearing Note, 3 year	1863	Salmon P. Chase
	United States Note	1862-1863	Robert Morris
	United States Note	1869-1880	DeWitt Clinton
	Silver Certificate	1878-1891	William L. Marcy
	Treasury or Coin Note	1890-1891	Gen. George Meade
$5,000	Federal Reserve Note	1918-1934	James Madison
	Gold Certificate	1882-1928	James Madison
	United States Note	1878	James Madison
$10,000	Federal Reserve Note	1918-1934	Salmon P. Chase
	Gold Certificate	1882-1902	Andrew Jackson
	Gold Certificate	1928-1934	Salmon P. Chase
	United States Note	1878	Andrew Jackson
$100,000	Gold Certificate	1934	Woodrow Wilson

Listed by name

Adams, John Quincy (1767-1848), sixth president of the United States. Born in Quincy, Mass., he served as American minister in the Netherlands, Berlin, St. Petersburg and London, as senator from 1803 to 1808 and was appointed secretary of state in 1817. Elected president in 1824, served until 1829. Elected to the House in 1831 where he served until his death in 1848.
$500 1869 United States (legal tender) note
$2 Southern Bank of Indiana, Terre Haute

Adams, Samuel (1722-1803). Born in Boston, he served as tax collector there from 1756 to 1764. He was elected to the Massachusetts legislature in 1765, serving until 1774. He was a leader in the agitation that led to the Boston Tea Party. Delegate to the first and second Continental Congress, he signed the Declaration of Independence. He was lieutenant governor and then governor (1794-1797) of Massachusetts.
$10 1862 Arkansas Treasury Warrant
Alcorn, J.L., governor of Mississippi.
$1 1870 State of Mississippi, Jackson, Miss.
$2 1870 State of Mississippi, Jackson, Miss.
$3 1870 State of Mississippi, Jackson, Miss.

Baker, E.D. (1811-?). Born in London on Feb. 24, 1811, he came to the U.S. in 1816, studied and practiced law in Springfield, Ill., served as state senator in 1840 and was elected to Congress in 1844. Baker was killed in the early days of the Civil War while commanding a Union brigade.
$5,000 1872 Currency Certificate of Deposit

Beauregard, Gen. P.G.T. (1818-1893). Pierre Gustave Toutant de Beauregard was born near New Orleans, La. Graduated from West Point in 1838, he served through the Mexican War. He was superintendent of West Point at the outbreak of the Civil War; he resigned to enter the Confederate Army. He was in command at the bombardment of Fort Sumter and served at Bull Run, Shiloh and Corinth. He was manager of the Louisiana Lottery and commissioner of public works in New Orleans (1888).
$20 1863 State of Louisiana, Shreveport

Benjamin, Judah Philip (1811-1884). Born in St. Croix, British West Indies (some sources say St. Thomas, Virgin Islands), he entered Yale in 1825. He entered the U.S. Senate in 1852 and withdrew in 1861 to join the Confederacy. He served as attorney general, secretary of war and secretary of state in the Confederacy.
$2 Sept. 2, 1861 Confederate note
$2 June 2, 1862 Confederate note
$2 Dec. 2, 1862 Confederate note
$2 Apr. 6, 1863 Confederate note
$2 Feb. 17, 1864 Confederate note

Bennett, Jonathan M., governor of Virginia.
$5 1862 Virginia Treasury note

Benton, Thomas Hart (1782-1858), served in U.S. Senate (1821-1851) and in the U.S. House of Representatives (1853-1855). He was in favor of Western development and spoke out against slavery.
$100 1863, 1882 gold certificate

Boone, Daniel (1734-1820). Born near Reading, Pa., in 1734, he made trips to Kentucky in 1767, 1769-1770. He guided settlers into Kentucky (1775) and erected a fort on the site of what is now Boonesboro. Served in Virginia legislature. After some years in Virginia he moved into what is now Missouri and secured a land grant.
$3 Clark's Exchange Bank, Springfield, Ill.
$10 Bank of Kentucky, Louisville, Ky.
$10 Bank of Louisville, Kentucky

Boudinot, Elias (1740-1821) born in Philadelphia. Opened law practice in Elizabethtown, N.J. Member and president of the Continental Congress. Member of U.S. Congress (1789-1795). Appointed Director of the Mint in October 1795 by Washington and served until July 1, 1805. Trustee of Princeton (1772-1821). Helped found American Bible Society in 1816 and served as its first president.
$2 1858 Merchants Bank, New Bedford, Mass.
$2 1858 Delaware City Bank, Delaware City, Kan.
$2 1859 Safety Fund Bank, Boston, Mass.
$2 1861 Bank of Penn Township, Philadelphia, Pa.
$2 1861 What Cheer Bank, Providence, R.I.
$5 1863 Belvidere Bank, Belvidere, N.J.
$20 18-- Augusta, Ga., Insurance and Banking Co.
$20 1832 Bank of Darien, Ga.
$20 1857 Augusta, Ga., Insurance and Banking Co.

Brown, Joseph E., governor of Georgia.
$50 1862 The State of Georgia, Milledgeville
$100 1863 The State of Georgia, Milledgeville

Buchanan, James (1791-1868), 15th president of the United States. Born near Mercersburg, Pa., he graduated from Dickinson College in 1809. A volunteer in the War of 1812, member of the House from 1821 to 1831, U.S. minister to Great Britain from 1853-1856, he was elected president in 1856 and served until 1861.
$10 North Western Bank, Ringgold, Ga.
$20 Bank of Pittsylvania, Chatham, Pa.
$3 1856 Fontenelle Bank, Bellevue, Neb.
$5 1852 Omaha, Neb., City Bank and Land Co.
$5 1857 Bank of Tekama, Neb.
$5 1858 Bank of the District of Columbia
$5 1859 Union Bank of Columbia, Washington, D.C.
$5 1861 Monongahela Valley Bank, McKee's Port, Pa.
$5 18-- Bank of Crawford County, Pa.
$10 1857 New England Bank, Fairmount, Maine
$10 1857 Manufacturers Bank, Macon, Ga.

Calhoun, John Caldwell (1782-1850). Born near Calhoun Mills, S.C., he graduated from Yale in 1804. A member of the House from 1811-1817, secretary of war (1817-1825), vice president from 1825 to 1832, senator (1832-1843), secretary of state (1844-1845), he championed slavery and the southern cause in Senate debates.
$2 1860 Eastern Bank of Alabama, Eufala
$2 Bank of the State of S. Carolina, Charleston
$5 Northern Bank of Alabama, Huntsville
$5 Bank of South Carolina
$10 Bank of East Tennessee, Knoxville
$10 Northern Bank of Alabama, Huntsville
$10 Manufacturers Bank, Macon, Ga.
$10 1860 Farmers and Mechanics Bank, Savannah, Ga.
$20 1860 Farmers and Mechanics Bank, Savannah, Ga.
$25 Planters Bank of Fairfield, Tenn.
$100 Confederate note, April 17, 1862
$1,000 Confederate note, Montgomery issue, 1861

Chase, Salmon Portland (1808-1873). Governor of Ohio, Secretary of the Treasury under Lincoln (1861-1864), he originated national banking system. Chief Justice of the Supreme Court (1864-1873).
$1 1862 legal tender

$10 1863, 1864 6 percent compound interest Treasury note

$10 1863 5 percent compound interest Treasury note

$20 1861 6 percent 2-year, interest-bearing Treasury note

$1,000 1861, 1864, 1865 7.3 percent 3-year interest-bearing note

$10,000 1918, 1928, 1934 Federal Reserve note

$10,000 1928, 1934 gold certificate

Clark, Spencer M. (1810-1890), first chief of the National Currency Bureau, predecessor of the Bureau of Engraving and Printing, from 1862 to 1868. This is one of the more curious U.S. paper notes. An order from the Treasury Department directed an issue to honor Lewis and Clark, the famed explorers of the Northwest Territory. Instead, Spencer Clark, a $1,200-a-year chief clerk, interpreted the order to mean his image was to be placed on the note. Congress wanted to fire him, but Salmon P. Chase, the Secretary of the Treasury, intervened and saved his job. As a direct result of this action, Congress enacted a law forbidding the likeness of any living person on any obligation of the U.S.

5¢ fractional currency, third issue

Clark, William (1770-1838), American explorer. The Lewis and Clark Expedition, in 1804, opened up the Louisiana Purchase to settlers.

$10 1901 legal tender (nicknamed "Buffalo") note

Clay, Clement C. (1819-1882). Born in Huntsville, Ala., he graduated from the University of Alabama in 1835, and was admitted to the bar in 1840. He was elected to the Senate in 1853 and reelected in 1861, when he was expelled for "treasonable utterances." He became a member of the Confederate Senate.

$1 1862, 1863, 1864 Confederate note

Clay, Henry (1777-1852). Born in Hanover County, Va., he practiced law in Lexington, Ky., and was elected to the Kentucky legislature in 1803. He acted as counsel for Aaron Burr in 1806. He was elected to the Senate in 1809, and served in the Senate and House until 1821. Reelected to the House in 1823 and serving until 1825, he was secretary of state (1825-1829), senator (1831-1842), Whig candidate for president in 1832 and 1844, again senator (1849-1852).

$50 1869 United States (legal tender) note

$1 Farmers and Millers Bank, Milwaukee, Wis.

$2 American Bank, Baltimore, Md.

$2 Stonington Bank, Stonington, Conn.

$2 Shawnee Bank, Attica, Ind.

$5 Bank of Kentucky, Louisville, Ky.

$5 Farmers and Mechanics Bank, Shippensburg, Pa.

$20 City Bank of New Haven, Conn.

Cleveland, Stephen Grover (1837-1908). Twenty-second (1885-1889) and 24th (1893-1897) president of the United States, the only president to serve two non-consecutive terms. Born in Caldwell, N.J., he was mayor of Buffalo, N.Y. (1881-1882), governor of New York (1883-1885). He was defeated by Benjamin Harrison in his bid for president in 1888.

$20 1915, 1918 Federal Reserve Bank note

$20 1914 Federal Reserve note

$1,000 1928, 1934 Federal Reserve note

$1,000 1928, 1934 gold certificate

Clinton, DeWitt (1769-1828). Born in Little Britain, N.Y., he graduated from Columbia College in 1786. He was elected to the Senate in 1798 and served until 1802, and again from 1806 to 1811. Elected mayor of New York in 1802 and serving three terms as governor of New York, he was the chief sponsor of the Erie Canal.

$1,000 1869, 1878, 1880 United States (legal tender) note

$1 Franklin Bank, Jersey City, N.J.

Conant, Charles Arthur A leading proponent of the Philippine National Bank, Conant is considered to be the "Father" of the United States-Philippine currency system.

1 peso 1918, 1921 & 1924 Philippine national bank circulating notes

Courts, D.W.

$5 1863 State of North Carolina, Raleigh, N.C.

$10 1863 State of North Carolina, Raleigh, N.C.

Crawford, William H. (1772-1834). A senator from Georgia (1807-1813), he also served as secretary of war under President Madison (1815-1816) and Secretary of the Treasury (1815-1825).

50¢ fractional currency, fifth issue

Crittenden, John Jordan (1787-1863). Born near Versailles, Ky., he was a senator (1817-1819, 1835-1841, 1842-1848 and 1850-1853). He also served as attorney general (1841, 1850-1853) and as governor of Kentucky (1848-1850).

$50 Commercial Bank of Kentucky, Paducah, Ky.

Davis, Jefferson (1808-1889). Born in Fairfield, Ky., he was appointed to West Point in 1824 and served in the army until 1835. He was elected to the House in 1845, resigned in 1846 to serve in the Mexican War. He was a senator (1847-1851), secretary of war (1853-1857), and again senator (1857-1861). Chosen president of the Confederacy Feb. 18, 1861, he fled from Richmond in 1865 and was captured and indicted for treason, but the government entered a nolle prosequi in 1868. He retired to his estate near Biloxi, Miss.

50¢ Apr. 6, 1863 Confederate note

50¢ Feb. 17, 1864 Confederate note

$1 1862 State of Missouri, Jefferson City, Mo.

$1, $2, $3, 1862 Arkansas Treasury Warrant

$50 Sept. 2, 1861 Confederate note

$50 Dec. 2, 1862 Confederate note

$50 Apr. 6, 1863 Confederate note

$50 Feb. 17, 1864 Confederate note

$100 Missouri Defense Bond

Decatur, Stephen (1779-1820). Naval officer, hero of the "war" with Tripoli and War of 1812, killed in a duel with James Brown on March 20, 1820.

$20 1878, 1880 silver certificate

Dexter, Samuel (1761-1816), Member of House (1793-1795), Senate (1799-1800), secretary of war (1800), secretary of Treasury (1801).

50¢ fractional currency, fourth issue

Douglas, Stephen A. (1813-1861). Born in Brandon, Vt., he was elected to the House in 1843 and served until 1847. He was a senator (1847-1861), and a nominee for president in 1856.

$10,000 1872, 1875 currency certificate of deposit

$2 Bank of Ottawa, Ill.

$5 State Bank of Illinois, Shawneetown, Ill.

Everett, Edward (1794-1865), Born in Dorchester, Mass., he was appointed professor of Greek at Harvard at age 21. Elected to the House in 1824, he assumed the governorship of Massachusetts in 1835. He was U.S. minister to Great Britain and president of Harvard, and was appointed secretary of state (1852-1853), serving only four months. He was elected to the Senate in 1853 and served until 1854.

$50 1878, 1880, 1891 silver certificate

Farragut, David Glasgow (1801-1870). Born in Tennessee, he was adopted by Commodore Porter in 1808. He served on the Union side during the Civil War and captured New Orleans without bloodshed; his distinguished service during the war earned him the rank of vice-admiral (1864) and admiral (1866), two ranks created specially for him by Congress.
$100 1890, 1891 Treasury note

Fessenden, William Pitt (1806-1869). Born in Boscawen, N.H., he was elected to the House (1841-1843) and Senate (1854-1864), and served as Secretary of the Treasury (1864-1865). He was elected to the Senate again in 1865 and served until 1869.
25¢ fractional currency, third issue
$10 national bank note, Second Charter

Fillmore, Millard (1800-1874), 13th president of the United States. Born at Locke, N.Y., he was a member of the House (1833-1835, 1837-1843), and vice president (1849-1850). He became president upon the death of Zachary Taylor (July 9, 1850), and was a presidential candidate in 1852.
$2 American Bank, Trenton, N.J.
$50 Northern Bank of Alabama, Huntsville, Ala.

Floyd, John B. (1806-1863). Born in Smithfield, Va., he was governor of Virginia (1849-1852), secretary of war (1857-1860). He resigned to enter Confederate services as brigadier of volunteers.
$10 1862 Virginia Treasury note
$1,000 Commonwealth of Virginia bond

Franklin, Benjamin (1706-1790). Born in Boston in 1706, he left there in 1723 for Philadelphia, where he was proprietor of a printing business and publisher of "The Pennsylvania Gazette" (1730-1748) and "Poor Richard's Almanac" (1725-1757). He was the Pennsylvania delegate to the Albany Congress in 1754 and a member of the second Continental Congress in 1775. He was on the committee to draft the Declaration of Independence and one of its signers.
$10 1863, 1864, 1865, 1875 national bank note, all charter periods (vignette: "Franklin Drawing Electricity from the Sky")
$10 1870, 1872, 1873, 1874, 1875 national gold bank note (vignette as above)
$10 1879 refunding certificate
$50 1874, 1875, 1878, 1880 United States (legal tender) notes
$100 1966 and all later series United States (legal tender) notes
$100 1914 and all later series Federal Reserve notes
$100 1929 Federal Reserve Bank note
$100 1929 National Bank note
$100 1928, 1928A gold certificate
$1 Merchants and Planters Bank, Savannah, Ga.
$1 1854 Bank of Anacostia, Washington, D.C.
$3 Bank of Manchester, Mich.
$3 Bank of Augusta, Ga.
$3 1860 Eastern Bank of Alabama, Eufala, Ala.
$3 Columbia Bank, District of Columbia
$5 Mechanics Bank, Memphis
$5 Roxbury Bank, Mass.
$10 Bank of the Republic, District of Columbia
$10 Eagle Bank of New Haven, Conn.
$10 Bank of Augusta, Ga.
$20 South Carolina Bank
$20 Mechanics Bank, Augusta, Ga.
$20 Central Bank of Alabama, Montgomery, Ala.
$1,000 Bank of the U.S., Philadelphia, Pa.

Fulton, Robert (1765-1815). Beginning his career as a painter, he later devoted himself to mechanics and engineering study. He invented the first practical steamboat, the Clermont (1807).
$2 1896 silver certificate (reverse)

Gallatin, Albert (1761-1849). Born in Geneva, Switzerland, he came to America in 1780. He was elected to the Senate in 1793 and served as secretary of the Treasury under Jefferson (1801-1814), and later as U.S. minister to France and Great Britain.
$500 1862, 1863 United States (legal tender) note

Garfield, James A. (1831-1881), 20th president of the United States. Born in Orange, Ohio, he served in the Ohio state senate and later as a Civil War general. He was elected to the House (1863-1880) and was elected president in 1880. He was shot by Charles J. Guiteau in a Washington railroad station July 22, 1881, and died Sept. 19, 1881.
$5 national bank note, Second Charter
$20 1882 gold certificate

Grant, Ulysses S. (1822-1885), 18th president of the United States. Born in Point Pleasant, Ohio, he graduated from West Point in 1843. He served in the Mexican War and was appointed brigadier general in 1861. He was in command at the Battle of Shiloh in the Civil War and received Lee's surrender at Appomattox Court House (April 9, 1865), and was promoted to the rank of general in 1866. He was elected president in 1868 and reelected in 1872.
15¢ fractional currency, fourth issue
$1 1899 silver certificate
$5 1886, 1891 silver certificate
$5 1896 silver certificate (reverse)
$50 1914 and all later issues Federal Reserve notes
$50 1918 Federal Reserve Bank note
$50 1929 national bank note
$50 1928 gold certificate

Hamilton, Alexander (1754-1804), first Secretary of the Treasury. Born on island of Nevis, Leeward Islands, he studied at King's College (now Columbia University). He worked through the Revolution as secretary and aide-de-camp to Washington. A member of the Continental Congress, he was Secretary of the Treasury from 1789 to 1795. He was instrumental in defeating Aaron Burr for the presidency in 1801, later was killed by Burr in a duel. He planned and initiated policies establishing the national fiscal system.
$2 1862 legal tender
$5 1861 demand note
$5 1862, 1863 legal tender
$10 1933 and all later series silver certificates
$10 1929 Federal Reserve Bank notes
$10 1928 and all later series Federal Reserve notes
$10 1929 national bank notes
$10 1928, 1928A gold certificates
$20 1869, 1875, 1878, 1880 legal tender notes
$50 1862 legal tender notes
$50 1863 6 percent compound interest treasury note
$50 5 percent interest-bearing note
$500 1861 7.3 percent three-year interest-bearing note
$1,000 1863, 1870, 1871, 1875, 1882, 1907, 1922 gold certificates
$1,000 1918 Federal Reserve note

Hancock, Gen. Winfield Scott (1824-1886), American Civil War general. He fought in the battles of Chancellorsville, Fredericksburg and Gettysburg and held off Pickett's charge at Gettysburg. He was defeated in his 1880 bid for president by James Garfield.

$2 1886 silver certificate

Harrison, Benjamin (1833-1901), 23rd president of the United States. He was a Civil War general, senator (1881-1887) and served one term as president (1889-1893).

$5 national bank note, Third Charter (all types)

Harrison, William H. (1773-1841), ninth president of the United States. Born in Charles City County, Va., he was secretary of the Northwest Territory in 1798 and governor of the Territory of Indiana (1801-1813). Serving in the House (1816-1819) and Senate (1825-1828), he was elected president in 1840 but died of pneumonia a month after his inauguration.

$1 Southern Bank of Indiana, Terre Haute

Hendricks, Thomas Andrew (1819-1885), vice president of the United States in 1885 under Grover Cleveland, serving for nine months. A member of the House (1851-1855) and Senate (1863-1869), he was elected governor of Indiana in 1872.

$10 1886, 1891, 1908 silver certificates

Henry, Patrick (1736-1799). Born in Hanover County, Va., he served in the Virginia legislature in 1765 and as a member of the Continental Congress. He was twice elected governor of Virginia, 1776-1779 and again 1784-1786.

$10 Bank of Augusta, Ga.

Hillegas, Michael (1729-1804). Born in Philadelphia, Pa., he was first Treasurer of the United States (1775-1789).

$10 1907, 1922 gold certificate

Hunter, R.M.T. (1809-1887). Born in Essex County, Va., he was educated at the University of Virginia. He was elected to the House (1837-1843, 1845-1847), Senate (1847-1861), and was secretary of state of the Confederate States of America. He later served as treasurer of Virginia (1874-1880).

$10 Sept. 2, 1861 Confederate note
$10 Sept. 2, 1862 Confederate note
$10 Dec. 2, 1862 Confederate note
$10 Apr. 6, 1863 Confederate note
$10 Feb. 17, 1864 Confederate note
$20 Sept. 2, 1862 Confederate note

Jackson, Andrew (1767-1845), seventh president of the United States. Born in Waxhaw, S.C., he was a member of the House (1796-1797) and Senate (1797-1798), (1823-1825). He was elected president in 1828 and again in 1832. He refused to renew the charter of the Bank of the United States and withdrew government funds on deposit, ensuring the demise of that institution and opening the way for "wildcat" banking.

$1 Bank of East Tennessee, Knoxville
$1 Mechanics Bank of Memphis, Tenn.
$2 Corn Exchange Bank, Wapun, Wisc.
$3 Mechanics Bank of Memphis, Tenn.
$5 Mechanics Bank of Memphis, Tenn.
$5 Farmers and Merchants Bank, Cecil Co., Md.
$5 Bank of America, Clarksville, Tenn.
$5 Southern Bank of Tennessee, Memphis
$5 1869, 1875, 1878, 1880, 1907 United States (legal tender) note
$10 State of Tennessee, 1875
$10 Bank of Tennessee, Nashville
$10 1923 United States (legal tender) note
$10 1914 Federal Reserve note
$10 1915, 1918 Federal Reserve Bank note
$20 1929 national bank note
$20 1928, 1928A gold certificate
$20 1928 and all later series Federal Reserve notes
$50 6 percent two-year interest-bearing Treasury note

$10,000 1878 United States (legal tender) note
$10,000 1863, 1870, 1871, 1875, 1882, 1888, 1902 gold certificate
$3 Central Bank of Alabama, Montgomery, Ala.
$3 American Bank, Baltimore, Md.
$5 1862 Manufacturers Bank, Macon, Ga.
$5 Mechanics Bank, Concord, N.H.
$10 Mechanics Bank, Concord, N.H.
$1,000 Confederate States of America Montgomery issue, 1861

Jackson, C.F., governor of Missouri who advocated secession immediately prior to the Civil War.

$3 1862 State of Missouri, Jefferson City, Mo.

Jackson, George James.

$20 1836 Bank of Augusta, Ga.

Jackson, Gen. T.J. (1824-1863). Born in Clarksburg, Va., he was admitted to West Point in 1842 and graduated in 1846. He served in the Mexican War under Gen. Winfield Scott, and resigned from the Army in 1852. He entered Confederate service at the outbreak of the Civil War and gained his nickname "Stonewall" from his stand at Bull Run. He was accidentally killed by his own men at the Battle of Chancellorsville in 1863.

$500 Feb. 17, 1864 Confederate note

Jefferson, Thomas (1743-1826), third president of the United States. Born in Goochland, Va., he graduated from the College of William and Mary in 1762 and was admitted to the bar in 1767. A member of the Virginia House of Burgesses (1769-1774) and the Continental Congress (1775, 1776), he was chairman of the committee that prepared the Declaration of Independence. He wrote and presented the first draft of the Declaration to Congress on July 2, 1776. He was governor of Virginia (1779-1781), U.S. minister to France (1785-1789), secretary of state (1790-1793), vice president (1797-1801), and president (1801-1809).

5¢ postage currency, first issue
25¢ postage currency first issue
$2 1869, 1874, 1875, 1878, 1880, 1917 and all later issues of United States (legal tender) notes
$2 1918 Federal Reserve Bank note
$2 1976 Federal Reserve note
$3 Farmers and Mechanics Bank, Milford, Del.
$5 1863 Real Estate Bank, Newport, Del.
$5 Bank of Kentucky, Louisville, Ky.
$20 State of Louisiana, New Orleans, La.
$10 Mechanics Bank, Concord, N.H.
5¢ Jersey City, N.J.
$5 Bank of Charleston, W. Va.
$5 Bank of Chester, Tenn.
$5 Monticello Bank, Va.
$10 Monticello Bank, Va.
$20 Bank of the Commonwealth, Richmond, Va.
$20 Monticello Bank, Va.
$100 Monticello Bank, Va.

Knox, John Jay (1828-1892), comptroller of the currency from 1872 to 1884.

$100 national bank note, Third Charter

Lafayette, Marie Joseph Paul Yves Roch Gilbert du Motier (1757-1834). Entering French military service in 1771, he left to enter American service in the Revolutionary War in 1777 and was made major general in the Continental army. He returned to France in 1781.

$5 Southern Bank of Indiana, Terre Haute, Ind.
$5 Lafayette Bank, Massachusetts
$10 1837 Mississippi and Alabama Railroad Company, Brandon, Miss.

Lamar, Mary.

$2-1/2 1862 The Exchange Bank, Edwards County, Ill.

Letcher, John, governor of Virginia.
$100 1862 Virginia Treasury note
$1 1862 Virginia Treasury note

Lewis, Meriwether (1774-1809). Born in Albermarle County, Va., he was private secretary to President Jefferson (1801-1803) and was named by him to lead an expedition to explore the Louisiana Purchase lands and selected William Clark as his partner. The Lewis and Clark Expedition (1804-1806) went up the Missouri River to its source, crossed the Great Divide and descended the Columbia River to the Pacific Ocean. He was governor of Louisiana from 1807 to 1809.
$10 1901 United States (legal tender) "Buffalo" note

Lincoln, Abraham (1809-1865), 16th president of the United States. Born in Hardin County, Ky., he moved to Indiana (1816) and to Macon County, Ill., in 1830. He studied law in his spare time from 1831 to 1837 and was elected to Illinois legislature (1834-1841). He was a member of the U.S. House of Representatives (1847-1849) and was nominated for vice president in 1856, nominated for Senate in 1858 but lost. Elected president in 1860 and again in 1864. He was shot at Ford's Theatre by John Wilkes Booth on Good Friday, April 14, 1864, and died early the next morning.
50¢ fractional currency, fourth issue
$1 1899 silver certificate
$5 1923 "Porthole" silver certificate
$5 1915, 1918 Federal Reserve Bank note
$5 1914 and all later series Federal Reserve notes
$10 1861 demand note
$10 1862, 1863 legal tender note
$20 1863 6 percent compound interest Treasury note
$20 1863 5 percent interest-bearing note
$100 1869, 1875, 1878, 1880 United States (legal tender) note
$500 1863, 1870, 1871, 1882, 1922 gold certificates
$1 1861 Merchants Bank, Trenton, N.J.
$1 1862 Bank of Commerce, Georgetown, D.C.
$1 1862 Lincoln Bank, Clinton, N.Y.
$2 1862 Lincoln Bank, Clinton, N.Y.

Lind, Jenny, (1820-1887), the "Swedish Nightingale." Appearing first in theater in Die Freischutz (1838), she was a court singer (1840) and studied in Paris under Garcia (1841). She toured Germany and gained popularity in London (1847-1848). She retired from the operatic stage in 1849 and devoted herself to concert singing and oratorio. She was engaged to sing in America by P.T. Barnum (1850-1852) and toured Europe, spending her last years in England and becoming a British subject in 1859.
$1 (var. written dates) Hartford Bank, Conn.
$1 (var. written dates) Stock Security Bank, Danville, Ill.

Longfellow, Alice, Allegra and Edith.
$2 1861 Mechanics Bank, St. Louis, Mo.

Lyon, Pat, an early fire engine builder of considerable fame.
$1 Augusta Insurance and Banking Co., Augusta, Ga.
$3 Bank of Washtenaw, Mich.

Madison, Dolly (1768-1849). Dorthea (nee Payne) Madison was born in Guilford County, N.C., and married James Madison in 1794. She was a famous Washington hostess while her husband was secretary of state (1801-1809) and president (1809-1817).
$10 Pawtucket Bank, Epping, N.H.

Madison, James (1751-1836), fourth president of the

United States. He was born in Port Conway, Va., and graduated from Princeton in 1771. A member of the Continental Congress and Constitutional Convention in 1787 and the House (1789-1797), he was secretary of state under Jefferson (1801-1809) and president (1809-1817).
$5,000 1878 United States (legal tender) note
$5,000 1863, 1870, 1871, 1872, 1882, 1888, 1928 gold certificates
$5,000 1918, 1928, 1934 Federal Reserve note
$5 Bank of Kentucky, Louisville, Ky.

Manning, Daniel (1831-1887), prominent New York banker. He was Secretary of the Treasury under Cleveland (1885-1887).
$20 1886, 1891 silver certificates

Mansfield, Joseph King. Born in New Haven, Conn., in 1803, he graduated from West Point. He was made brigadier general early in the Civil War and was killed at the Battle of Antietam.
$500 1873, 1875, 1878, 1880 United States (legal tender) notes

Marcy, William L. (1786-1857). Born in Southbridge, Mass., he graduated from Brown University. He was comptroller for the state of New York (1823-1829), associate justice of the New York Supreme Court (1829-1831), senator (1831, 1832), governor of New York (1833-1839), secretary of war (1845-1849) and secretary of state under Franklin Pierce (1853-1857).
$1,000 1878, 1880, 1891 silver certificates

Marion, Gen. Francis (1732-1795). Born in Winyah, near Georgetown, S.C., he fought in the Revolutionary War in guerrilla warfare, earning the nickname "the Swamp Fox." Under instructions to get Marion, British General Sir Banastre Tarleton failed to even locate him. Finally Marion invited Gen. Tarleton to dinner at Marion's camp after Tarleton asked for an interview under a truce flag.
$10 Sept. 2, 1861 Confederate note
$5 State of S. Carolina, 1866 and 1872
$10 Bank of Kentucky, Louisville
$20 Bank of Kentucky, Louisville, Ky.
$50 Bank of Kentucky, Louisville, Ky.

Marshall, John (1755-1835). Born in Virginia, he was Chief Justice of the Supreme Court (1801-1835) and established the strength and power of the court.
$20 1890, 1891 Treasury or coin notes
$500 1918 Federal Reserve note
$1 Southern Bank of Indiana, Terre Haute, Ind.
$10 Stafford Bank, Dover, N.H.
$50 Farmers Bank of Schuylkill County, Pa.

Mason, James M., governor of Virginia
$50 1862 Virginia Treasury note
$1,000 Commonwealth of Virginia Bond

McClellan, George B. (1826-1885). Educated at the University of Pennsylvania (1842-1844). Transferred to West Point and graduated 1846, the youngest in his class. Author and railroad executive. Succeeded Winfield Scott as general of the Union Army. Unsuccessful Democratic presidential candidate 1864. Governor of New Jersey 1877-1881.
10¢ 1863 Searsport Bank, Frankfort, Maine
$1 1862 Chicopee Bank, Springfield, Mass.
$2 1861 Merchants Bank, Trenton, N.J.
$20 Rutland County Bank, Vt.

McCullough, Hugh (1808-1895), Secretary of the Treasury under Lincoln (1865-1869) and Arthur (1884-1885).
$20 national bank note, Third Charter (all types)

McKinley, William (1843-1901), 25th president of the United States. Born in Niles, Ohio, he served in the Civil War. He was a member of the House (1877-1883, 1885, 1891), governor of Ohio (1892-1896) and president (1897-1901). He was shot by Leon Czolgosz, an anarchist, in Buffalo, N.Y. Sept. 6, 1901 and died Sept. 14.

$10 national bank note, Third Charter (all types)
$500 1928 and all later series Federal Reserve notes

Meade, George Gordon. Born in 1815, he became a major general in 1864 after serving and being wounded in the Civil War.

$1,000 1890, 1891 Treasury notes

Memminger, Christopher Gustavus (1803-1888). Born in Germany, he came to the U.S. as a child. He was Secretary of the Treasury of the Confederacy (1861-1864).

$5 and $10 Sept. 2, 1861 Confederate note
$5 Dec. 2, 1862 Confederate note
$5 Apr. 6, 1863 Confederate note
$5 Feb. 17, 1864 Confederate note

Meredith, William Morris (1799-1873). Born in Philadelphia, Pa., he was Secretary of the Treasury (1849-1850) and attorney general of Pennsylvania (1861-1867).

10¢ fractional currency, fifth issue

Monroe, James (1758-1831), fifth president of the United States. Born in Westmoreland County, Va., he served in the American Revolution, as a member of the Continental Congress and senator (1790-1794). He was minister to France (1794-1796), governor of Virginia (1799-1802), one of the negotiators of the Louisiana Purchase (1803), minister to England (1803-1807), secretary of state (1811-1817), and secretary of war (1814-1815). He served as president from 1817 to 1825.

$100 1878, 1880, 1881 silver certificate
$4 Bank of Monroe, Monroe, Mich.

Morris, Robert (1734-1806). Born in England, he came to America in 1747 and favored the Colonial cause in the Revolution. He was a member of the Continental Congress and a signer of the Declaration of Independence. He served as superintendent of finance (1781-1784), founded and organized the Bank of North America (1782) and was a delegate to the Constitutional convention in 1787. He served in the Senate from 1789 to 1795.

$10 1878, 1880 silver certificates
$1,000 1862, 1863 United States (legal tender) notes
$1,000 Bank of U.S. note (lower right corner)
$10 Northampton Bank, Pa.

Morse, Samuel Finley Breese (1791-1872). Born in Charleston, Mass., he was a portrait painter in Boston, Charleston and New York. He was founder and first president of the National Academy of Design and was a professor at New York University. He invented Morse code and the magnetic telegraph, sending the first message, "What Hath God Wrought?" on May 24, 1844.

$2 1896 silver certificate (reverse)

Moultrie, Gen. William (1730-1805). Born in Charleston, S.C., he was an American Revolutionary War general. He repulsed the British attack on Sullivan's Island, now Fort Moultrie, in Charleston Harbor in 1776 and served as a brigadier general in the Continental Army in 1776 and defended Charleston in 1779. He was governor of South Carolina (1785-1787, 1794-1796).

$5 1866 and 1872 State of South Carolina

Oglethorpe, James Edward (1696-1785). Born in London, he planned a project for colonizing

unemployed men freed from debtors prison on lands in America. He received a charter in 1732 for Colony of Georgia and accompanied the first band of emigrants there in 1733.

$5 1862 The State of Georgia, Milledgeville, Ga.
$5 Bank of Augusta, Ga.
$10 1836 Bank of Augusta, Ga.

Penn, William (1644-1718). Named trustee to manage the West Jersey Colony in America, he had an important part in framing its charter in 1677. He received a grant of land from Charles II from which he founded Pennsylvania in 1681.

$1 1857 Penn Township Savings Inst., Philadelphia
$2 1856 Bank of Newark, Del.
$5 18-- Erie, Pa., Bank
$5 1820 Stephen Girard, Banker, Philadelphia
$5 1841 Towanda Bank, Pa.
$5 1859 Fort Stanwix Bank, Oneida, N.Y.
$10 1826 Bank of Pennsylvania, Philadelphia
$10 1833 Bank of Pennsylvania, Philadelphia
$20 Piscatqua Exchange Bank, Portsmouth, N.H.
$20 Farmers Bank of Schuylkill County, Pa.

Pettus, J.J., governor of Mississippi.

$100 State of Mississippi
$50 State of Mississippi
$20 State of Mississippi
$10 State of Mississippi

Pewelle, A., a Pennsylvania merchant.

2¢ 1862 note of A. Pewelle, Reading, Pa.
3¢ 1862 note of A. Pewelle, Reading, Pa.

Pickens, Lucy Holcombe, wife of Francis W. Pickens (1805-1869), governor of South Carolina who ordered the bombardment of Fort Sumter, triggering the Civil War.

$1 June 2, 1862 Confederate note
$100 Dec. 2, 1862 Confederate note
$100 Apr. 6, 1863 Confederate note
$100 Feb. 17, 1863 Confederate note

Pierce, Franklin (1804-1869), 14th president of the United States. Born in Hillsboro, N.H., his father, Benjamin Pierce, fought in the Revolution. He served in the New Hampshire House, the House (1833-1837), and the Senate (1837-1843). He served as president from 1853 to 1857.

$10 Amoskeag Bank, Manchester, N.H.

Polk, Gen. Leonidas

$50 1863 State of Louisiana, Shreveport, La.

Raleigh, Sir Walter (1552?-1618). A favorite of Queen Elizabeth, he was granted a patent to send an expedition exploring the American coast from Florida to North Carolina in 1584 and named the coast north of Florida "Virginia." He sent settlers to occupy Roanoke Island, N.C., in 1585, but the colony failed. With the death of Queen Elizabeth in 1603, he fell out of favor with the English court and was eventually beheaded at Whitehall.

$2 original and 1875 "Lazy Deuce" First Charter national bank note (on the reverse), Sir Walter Raleigh in England, 1585, exhibiting corn and smoking tobacco from America)

Randolph, George Wythe (1818-1867). Born March 10, 1818. His father was governor of Virginia (1819-1822). His mother was the daughter of Thomas Jefferson. George W. Randolph entered the U.S. Navy as a midshipman in 1831. Studied law at the University of Virginia. He served as the Confederate States secretary of war from March 1862 to September 1863 when he was appointed envoy to France. He died at Edge Hill, Va., on April 4, 1867.

$100 Dec. 2, 1862 Confederate note
$100 Apr. 6, 1863 Confederate note

$100 Feb. 17, 1864 Confederate note

Rector, H.M., governor of Arkansas.
$5 1862 Arkansas Treasury Warrant

Scott, Gen. Winfield (1786-1866). Born near Petersburg, Va., he was promoted to general-in-chief of the U.S. Army in 1841, and was defeated by Franklin Pierce in his bid for president in 1852.
$100 1865 interest-bearing note
$1 1861 Bank of Otego, Otego County, N.Y.
$1 Farmers and Mechanics Bank, Easton, Pa.
$2 Merchants Bank, Trenton, N.J.
$3 Beverly Bank, Beverly, N.J.
$20 Rutland County, Vt., Bank

Seward, William H. (1801-1872). Governor of New York (1839-1843) senator (1849-1861) and a prominent antislavery advocate, he served as secretary of state (1861-1869) and was responsible for the purchase of Alaska.
$50 1891 Treasury note

Shelby, Isaac (1750-1826). Colonel of militia in Virginia in 1780, he organized a Colonial force after the fall of Charleston and defeated the British at Kings Mountain. He served in the North Carolina legislature in 1781 and 1782 and settled in Kentucky in 1783, where he served as the first governor (1792-1796, 1812-1816). He helped defeat the British at the battle of the Thames on Oct. 5, 1813.
$5 Bank of Kentucky, Louisville, Ky.

Sheridan, Gen. Philip Henry (1831-1888). Born in Albany, N.Y., he graduated from West Point in 1853 and succeeded Sherman as commander in chief of the U.S. Army in 1884. He was promoted to general in 1888.
$5 1896 silver certificate (reverse)
$10 1890, 1891 Treasury or coin notes

Sherman, John (1823-1900). Born in Lancaster, Ohio, he practiced law in Mansfield and Cleveland. He served in the House (1855-1861) and Senate (1861-1877, 1881-1897), as Secretary of the Treasury (1877-1881) and secretary of state (1897-1898).
$50 national bank note, Third Charter (all types)

Sherman, William Tecumseh (1820-1891). Born in Lancaster, Ohio, he was brother of John Sherman and graduated from West Point in 1840. He was made brigadier general of volunteers in the Civil War (1861), served at Bull Run, under Grant at Shiloh and Corinth, and was promoted to major general in 1862. He was promoted to lieutenant general in 1866 and succeeded Grant as general and commander of the Army in 1869.
15¢ fractional currency (proof notes), fourth issue, never circulated

Spinner, Francis Elias (1802-1890). After serving as president of the Mohawk Valley Bank in Herkimer, N.Y., he was elected to the House (1855-1861) and then appointed Treasurer of the United States by Lincoln (1861-1875). Considered the father of fractional currency.
50¢ fractional currency, third issue

Stanton, Edwin McMasters (1814-1869). Born in Steubenville, Ohio, he was attorney general (1860-1861), secretary of war (1862-1868). He refused to support President Johnson's policies after Lincoln's death and was dismissed in 1868. Johnson's impeachment was partially a result of Stanton's dismissal. He was appointed to the Supreme Court in 1869 but died before he could take his seat.
$1 1890, 1891 Treasury or coin notes
50¢ fractional currency, fourth issue

Stephens, Alexander Hamilton (1812-1883). Born near Crawfordville, Ga., he was elected to the Georgia legislature in 1834, the Senate in 1842, and the House (1843-1859). He served as vice president of the Confederacy (1861-1865). After the war he was imprisoned briefly and later elected to the Senate in 1866 but refused to take a seat. He was elected to the House in 1873 and served until 1882, and was elected governor of Georgia in 1883.
$20 1861, 1862, 1863, 1864 Confederate note

Stuyvesant, Petrus (1592-1672). Born in the Netherlands, he served in the Dutch army and in the employ of the Dutch West India Company. He lost his right leg in a campaign against the island of St. Martin in 1644. He was appointed director-general of New Netherlands and adjacent regions in 1646 and arrived in New Amsterdam in 1647. He expelled the Swedes from Delaware in 1655 and surrendered New Netherlands to the English in 1664.
$3 St. Nicholas Bank, New York, N.Y.

Sumner, Charles (1811-1874). Born in Boston and graduated from Harvard Law School, he was elected to the Senate in 1852 and was an opponent of slavery. Serving in the Senate until 1874, he took a prominent part in impeachment proceedings against President Johnson and opposed Grant's re-election in 1872.
$500 1878, 1880 silver certificate

Sumter, Gen. Thomas (1734-1832). Born near Charlottesville, Va., he was a lieutenant-colonel of South Carolina troops during the Revolution. He was elected to the House (1789-1793, 1797-1801) and Senate (1801-1810).
$5 1866 and 1872 State of South Carolina

Taylor, Zachary (1784-1850). 12th president of the United States. Born in Orange County, Va., he entered the U.S. Army as a first lieutenant and spent most of his army life in the West. He defeated Santa Anna at Buena Vista in 1847, ending the war in northern Mexico. He served as president from 1849 to 1850, and died after only a year and four months in office.
$10 Southbridge Bank, Southbridge, Mass.
$20 City Bank of New Haven, Conn.
$20 Bank of Tennessee, Nashville, Tenn.

Thomas, Gen. George Henry (1816-1870). Born in Southampton County, Va., he graduated from West Point in 1840 and remained loyal to the Union during the Civil War. He was made brigadier general in 1861 and major general in 1862. He commanded the Army of the Cumberland in the battle of Chattanooga and in Sherman's Atlanta campaign in 1864. He was promoted to major general in the regular army and commanded the military division of the Pacific in 1869 and 1870.
$5 1890, 1891 Treasury or coin notes

Tucker, J.C.
3¢ July 4, 1864 Townsend Bank, Brookline, N.H.
24¢ July 16, 1862 Tucker and Stiles scrip, Brookline, N.H.

Van Buren, Martin (1782-1862), eighth president of the United States. Born in Kinderhook, N.Y., he was attorney general of New York (1816-1819) and senator from New York (1821-1828), governor of New York (1829), resigning to become secretary of state (1829-1831). He served as vice president (1833-1837) and as president from 1837 to 1841.
$5 Mechanics Bank, Concord, N.H.

Vance, Zebulon, governor of North Carolina.

$20 1863 State of North Carolina, Raleigh, N.C.

Walker, Robert J. (1801-1869). After practicing law in Pittsburgh, Pa., and Natchez, Miss., he served in the Senate (1836-1845) and as secretary of the Treasury (1845-1849). He was the financial agent of the U.S. in Europe (1863-1864) and sold $250 million worth of U.S. bonds and prevented the sale of $75 million worth of Confederate bonds.

25¢ fractional currency, fifth issue

Ward, John E. (1814-1871). Mayor of Savannah, Ga., he was violently opposed to secession and left the South with the outbreak of the Civil War.

$10 1861 Confederate States of America note

Washington, George (1732-1799), first president of the United States. Born in Westmoreland County, Va., he was privately educated and gained experience as a surveyor by assisting in the survey of some Fairfax holdings in Shenandoah Valley. He was county surveyor in Culpeper County, Va. (1749). He was commissioned as district adjutant by Gov. Dinwiddie in 1752, later commissioned lieutenant colonel and sent with 150 men in 1754 to establish an outpost on the site of the present city of Pittsburgh. He served on Gen. Braddock's staff in 1755 and in the British expedition against Fort Duquesne. He was commissioned colonel and commander-in-chief of Virginia troops in 1755. He married Martha Custis in 1759 and joined the Virginia House of Burgesses the same year (1759-1774). He was a member of the first and second Continental Congress and was elected to command all Continental armies in 1775. He resigned his commission in 1783, but was called from retirement to preside at the Federal Convention in Philadelphia in 1787, and was chosen president of the United States under the new Constitution. He took his oath of office in New York City on April 30, 1789, and was unanimously re-elected in 1792. He declined a third term and retired from political life in 1797. He came out of retirement again to accept a commission as lieutenant general and commander-in-chief of the Army in 1798 and retained the commission until his death on Dec. 14, 1799.

3¢ fractional currency, third issue
5¢ fractional currency, second issue
10¢ postage currency, first issue
10¢ fractional currency, second and third issues
25¢ fractional currency, second and fourth issues
50¢ postage currency, first issue
50¢ fractional currency, second issues
$1 1869, 1875, 1878, 1880, 1917 and all later series United States (legal tender) notes
$1 1896, 1923 and all later series silver certificates
$1 1918 Federal Reserve Bank notes
$1 1963 and all later series Federal Reserve notes
$2 1899 silver certificates
$5 national bank notes, Second Charter (dated back and denomination backs, small vignette on reverse)
$20 1901, 1906, 1922 gold certificates
$100 1863 6 percent compound interest Treasury note

$100 1863 5 percent one-year interest-bearing note
$500 1861 7.4 percent three-year interest-bearing note
10-peso 1913 Philippine silver certificates
10-peso 1918, 1924, 1929, 1936, 1941 & Victory Series 66 Philippine Treasury certificates
10 peso 1921 & 1937 Philippine national circulating notes
Many Confederate, obsolete and broken bank notes

Washington, Martha (1732-1802). Wife of George Washington, she was born Martha Dandridge and married Daniel Parke Custis who later died. She married George Washington Jan. 6, 1759.

$1 1886, 1896 silver certificate
$5 Belknap County Bank, N.H.

Watts, Thomas N., governor of Alabama
$50 1864 Alabama State note
$10 1864 Alabama State note

Weaver, John.
$50 Commercial Bank of Alabama, Selma, Ala.

Webster, Daniel (1782-1852). Born in Salisbury, N.H., he graduated from Dartmouth in 1801 and was admitted to the bar in Boston in 1805. He was a member of the House (1813-1817, 1823-1827) and the Senate (1827-1841, 1845-1850). He served as secretary of state from 1841 to 1843 and again from 1850 to 1852. He was an unsuccessful candidate for Whig nomination for the presidency in 1852.

$10 1869, 1875, 1878, 1880 United States (legal tender) "Jackass" note
$10 Thames Bank, Norwich, Conn.
$1 State Bank of Wisconsin, Milwaukee
$2 Bank of Peru, Ill.
$3 DuPage Co. Bank, Naperville, Ill.
$5 Farmers and Traders Bank, Charlestown, Ill.
$5 Shawnee Bank, Attica, Ind.
$20 Bank of Kentucky, Louisville, Ky.

Wilson, Woodrow (1856-1924), 28th president of the United States. Born in Staunton, Va., he graduated from Princeton in 1879 and was admitted to the bar and practiced in Atlanta, Ga., in 1882. After receiving his Ph.D. from Johns Hopkins in 1886, he taught history at Bryn Mawr and Wesleyan and political science at Princeton. He was president of Princeton from 1902 to 1910, and governor of New Jersey (1911-1913). He was elected president in 1912 and served until 1921.

$100,000 1934 gold certificate

Windom, William (1827-1891). Born in Belmont, Ohio, he moved to Minnesota and became the first senator from Minnesota (1870-1881, 1881-1883) after serving in the House (1859-1869). He was Secretary of the Treasury in 1881 and again from 1889 to 1891.

$2 1891 silver certificate

Wright, Silas (1795-1847). After practicing law in Canton, N.Y., he was elected to the House (1827-1829) and served as Comptroller of New York (1829-1833), as senator from New York (1833-1844), and governor of New York (1845-1847).

$50 1882 gold certificate

Military payment certificates

Military payment certificates (MPCs) were used from 1946 to 1973. Prior to that time U.S. military personnel stationed overseas were paid in Allied military currency, produced by the major Allied countries, or in the currency of the country in which they were stationed.

The need for this system arose because

of the necessity to transact business with the locals without risking the loss of large amounts of U.S. currency, which could be used anywhere in the world.

Another reason for the creation of Allied military currency was the possibility that the enemy might flood an occupied territory's economy with currency to induce high inflation, or ordering local banks to burn their money when Allied attack was imminent.

Allied military currency was used in countries being liberated from the Axis powers and the notes were denominated in the liberated country's currency. The local government was required to redeem it at a later date.

Personnel were allowed to convert that foreign currency into U.S. currency as individual needs or wishes required. But it wasn't long before the services accumulated foreign currencies far in excess of pay requirements and the MPC system was developed to protect the services from those surpluses of foreign currencies.

After the MPC system was developed in 1946, all U.S. servicemen, U.S. government civilian employees and U.S. citizens employed by U.S. firms abroad doing business under government contracts were paid in MPCs and were prohibited from holding U.S. currency of any type.

U.S. citizens in the employ of a company of the host country were paid in the local currency. The local population was prohibited from holding any MPCs, which could be used only at U.S. facilities such as post exchanges or ship's stores. The local population was thus effectively restrained from purchasing items at the discounted PX prices, a form of black marketeering control.

If a U.S. serviceman or citizen wanted to buy something in the local civilian market, he was required to convert his MPCs into the local currency. Regulations restricted both the amount and frequency of MPC conversions.

Many of the servicemen supplemented their supply of convertible currency by doing a brisk business in cigarettes, silk or nylon stockings, and candy. It was inevitable that many of the MPCs would then be found in the local economy in spite of strict controls. The usual route was through the black market established both by servicemen and by the local population. Servicemen sold items they had purchased at government-operated stores while local businessmen sold watches and jewelry to servicemen who were returning stateside.

When it was determined that an excessive amount of MPCs were in the local economy via the black market, the old series would be withdrawn and a new series issued. The conversion days (popularly known as "C-days") were unannounced and strictly controlled. All personnel would be restricted to station and only designated persons were allowed to make the exchange of new for old notes.

After C-day the old series was invalid and worthless. The only supply of MPCs available to collectors today are those MPCs that were inadvertently unredeemed by authorized holders, or those illegally held by black marketeers who were unable to convert their holdings.

In the 28-year history of military payment certificates a total of 13 series were used in 21 foreign places in 17 countries. Denominations ranged from five cents to $20. The $20 MPC was issued only in Series 661, 681 and 692.

The first seven series were printed by private contractors in the United States and overprinted by the Bureau of Engraving and Printing. The overprint consisted of adding the series, serial and control numbers to the pre-printed notes. The last six series were completely printed and separated by the BEP.

The first issue, series 461, was released on Sept. 16, 1946. It was followed in order by series 471, 472, 481, 521, 541, 591, 611, 641, 651, 661, 681 and 692. The last issue to circulate, Series 692, was released on Oct. 7, 1970, and was withdrawn from use in South Vietnam on March 15, 1973; and Series 651 in South Korea on Nov. 19, 1973, ending a short but interesting and colorful era in another currency system.

However, two series, 691 and 701, have been printed and are available should an emergency arise.

How to detect counterfeit bills

Know your money by examining and becoming familiar with the bills you receive. Compare a suspected bill with a genuine one of the same denomination. Look at these features:

Portrait

Genuine: Appears lifelike and stands out distinctly from the fine screen-like background. The hairlines are distinct.

Counterfeit: Appears lifeless and the background is usually too dark. Portrait merges into the background. The hairlines are not distinct.

Color seal

Genuine: Saw-toothed points are even, clear and sharp.

Counterfeit: Saw-toothed points on the circumference are usually uneven, blunt and broken off.

Border

Genuine: The fine lines are clear, distinct and unbroken.

Counterfeit: The fine lines that crisscross are not clear or distinct.

Paper

Genuine: Printed on distinctive paper with visible, interspersed red and blue fibers.

Counterfeit: Printed on paper with no colored fibers evident, or with red and blue lines to simulate fibers.

Signatures on U.S. paper money

Hand-written or facsimile signatures lend an aura of authority to paper money. Most U.S. currency bears two signatures and some bears four. Only the postage currency, second issue of fractional currency, and 3-cent third issue fractional currency bear no signatures at all. In the following list, the first name shown is that of the Register of the Treasury, the second is that of the Treasurer of the United States.

National bank notes, in addition to the signatures of the Register and the Treasurer, bear the signatures of the bank president and the bank cashier. Federal Reserve Bank notes also have two additional signatures: those of two Federal Reserve officers.

Realizing that the signing of paper money would be a burdensome task, President Lincoln signed legislation allowing the Secretary of the Treasury to delegate selected personnel to sign the first demand notes for the Treasury officials. Seventy employees were assigned to this task, signing their own names, with a handwritten "For The" before the appropriate title. Within a very short time the words "For The" were engraved into the printing plates.

Starting with the issues of 1863, the signatures of the Treasury officials were engraved directly into the plates and the words "for the" dropped into obscurity. From 1862 to 1925 the signature of the Register of the Treasury appeared on all notes, after 1925 the signature of the Secretary of the Treasury appears with that of the Treasurer of the United States.

The full names of the Treasury officials and their terms in office can be found in the appropriate tables in Chapter 4.

Signatures on large-sized paper money

Legal Tender notes

Series	Denominations	Register of the Treasury	Treasurer
1862	$1, $2, $5, $10, $20, $50, $100, $500	Lucius E. Chittenden	F.E. Spinner
1863	$2, $5, $10, $20, $50, $100, $500	Lucius E. Chittenden	F.E. Spinner
1869	$1, $2, $5, $10, $20, $50, $100, $500	John Allison	F.E. Spinner
1874	$1, $2, $50, $100	John Allison	F.E. Spinner
1875	$1, $2, $5, $10, $20, $500	John Allison	John C. New
1875	$1, $2, $5, $50, $100, $500	John Allison	A.U. Wyman
1875-A	$1, $2, $5, $10, $100	John Allison	John C. New
1875-B	$1, $2, $5	John Allison	John C. New
1875-C	$1	John Allison	John C. New
1875-D	$1	John Allison	John C. New
1875-E	$1	John Allison	John C. New
1878	$1, $2, $5, $10, $20, $50, $100, $500, $1,000	John Allison	James Gilfillan
1878	$2	Glenni W. Scofield	James Gilfillan
1880	$1, $2, $5, $10, $20	William S. Rosecrans	Enos H. Nebecker
1880	$1, $2, $5, $10, $20	Glenni W. Scofield	James Gilfillan
1880	$1, $2, $5, $10, $20, $50, $100	Blanche K. Bruce	James Gilfillan
1880	$1, $2, $5, $10, $20, $50, $100	William S. Rosecrans	J.N. Huston
1880	$1, $2, $5, $10, $20, $50, $100	James F. Tillman	Daniel N. Morgan
1880	$1, $5, $10, $20, $50, $100	Blanche K. Bruce	A.U. Wyman
1880	$5, $10, $20, $50, $100	Blanche K. Bruce	Elias H. Roberts
1880	$5, $10, $20, $50, $100	William S. Rosecrans	James W. Hyatt
1880	$5, $10, $20, $50, $100	William S. Rosecrans	Conrad Jordan
1880	$5, $10, $20, $50, $100, $500	Judson W. Lyons	Elias H. Roberts
1880	$20	William S. Elliott	Frank White
1880	$20	Houston B. Teehee	John Burke
1880	$20	William T. Vernon	Lee McClung
1880	$20	William T. Vernon	Charles H. Treat
1880	$500	John Allison	F.E. Spinner
1901	$10	Judson W. Lyons	Elias H. Roberts
1901	$10	Judson W. Lyons	Charles H. Treat
1901	$10	James C. Napier	Lee McClung
1901	$10	Gabe E. Parker	John Burke
1901	$10	Harley V. Speelman	Frank White
1901	$10	Houston B. Teehee	John Burke
1901	$10	William T. Vernon	Lee McClung
1901	$10	William T. Vernon	Charles H. Treat
1907	$5	William S. Elliott	Frank White
1907	$5	James C. Napier	Lee McClung
1907	$5	James C. Napier	Carmi A. Thompson
1907	$5	Gabe E. Parker	John Burke
1907	$5	Harley V. Speelman	Frank White
1907	$5	Houston B. Teehee	John Burke
1907	$5	William T. Vernon	Charles H. Treat
1907	$5	Walter O. Woods	Frank White
1907	$20	William T. Vernon	Lee McClung
1917	$1, $2	Harley V. Speelman	Frank White
1917	$1, $2	Houston B. Teehee	John Burke
1917	$1, $2, $5	William S. Elliott	John Burke
1923	$10	Harley V. Speelman	Frank White

National Bank notes

Series	Denominations	Register of the Treasury	Treasurer
Original	$1, $2, $5, $10, $20	Noah L. Jeffries	F.E. Spinner
Original	$1, $2, $5, $10, $20, $50, $100	John Allison	F.E. Spinner
Original	$1, $2, $5, $10, $20, $50, $100	S.B. Colby	F.E. Spinner
Original	$5, $10, $20, $50, $100	Lucius E. Chittenden	F.E. Spinner

1875	$1, $2, $5, $10, $20, $50, $100	John Allison	James Gilfillan
1875	$1, $2, $5, $10, $20, $50, $100	John Allison	John C. New
1875	$1, $2, $5, $10, $20, $50, $100	John Allison	A.U. Wyman
1875	$1, $2, $5, $10, $20, $50, $100	Glenni W. Scofield	James Gilfillan
1875	$5	Blanche K. Bruce	Conrad Jordan
1875	$5	William S. Rosecrans	Conrad Jordan
1875	$5, $10, $20, $50, $100	Blanche K. Bruce	James Gilfillan
1875	$5, $10, $20, $50, $100	Blanche K. Bruce	A.U. Wyman
1875	$5, $10, $50, $100	William S. Rosecrans	J.N. Huston
1875	$10, $20, $50, $100	William S. Rosecrans	Enos H. Nebecker
1875	$10, $20, $50, $100	James F. Tillman	Daniel N. Morgan
1882 Brown Back	$5, $10, $20	Judson W. Lyons	Charles H. Treat
1882 Brown Back	$5, $10, $20, $50	William S. Rosecrans	J.N. Huston
1882 Brown Back	$5, $10, $20, $50, $100	Blanche K. Bruce	James Gilfillan
1882 Brown Back	$5, $10, $20, $50, $100	Blanche K. Bruce	Conrad Jordan
1882 Brown Back	$5, $10, $20, $50, $100	Blanche K. Bruce	Elias H. Roberts
1882 Brown Back	$5, $10, $20, $50, $100	Blanche K. Bruce	A.U. Wyman
1882 Brown Back	$5, $10, $20, $50, $100	Judson W. Lyons	Elias H. Roberts
1882 Brown Back	$5, $10, $20, $50, $100	William S. Rosecrans	James W. Hyatt
1882 Brown Back	$5, $10, $20, $50, $100	William S. Rosecrans	Conrad Jordan
1882 Brown Back	$5, $10, $20, $50, $100	William S. Rosecrans	Daniel N. Morgan
1882 Brown Back	$5, $10, $20, $50, $100	William S. Rosecrans	Enos H. Nebecker
1882 Brown Back	$5, $10, $20, $50, $100	James F. Tillman	Daniel N. Morgan
1882 Brown Back	$5, $10, $20, $50, $100	James F. Tillman	Elias H. Roberts
1882 Brown Back	$5, $10, $20, $50, $100	William T. Vernon	Charles H. Treat
1882 Date Back	$5, $10, $20	William S. Rosecrans	Daniel N. Morgan
1882 Date Back	$5, $10, $20	William T. Vernon	Lee McClung
1882 Date Back	$5, $10, $20, $50, $100	Blanche K. Bruce	Elias H. Roberts
1882 Date Back	$5, $10, $20, $50, $100	Judson W. Lyons	Elias H. Roberts
1882 Date Back	$5, $10, $20, $50, $100	James C. Napier	Lee McClung
1882 Date Back	$5, $10, $20, $50, $100	William S. Rosecrans	J.N. Huston
1882 Date Back	$5, $10, $20, $50, $100	William S. Rosecrans	Enos H. Nebecker
1882 Date Back	$5, $10, $20, $50, $100	James F. Tillman	Daniel N. Morgan
1882 Date Back	$5, $10, $20, $50, $100	James F. Tillman	Elias H. Roberts
1882 Date Back	$5, $10, $20, $50, $100	William T. Vernon	Charles H. Treat
1882 Denomination Back	$5, $10, $20	Blanche K. Bruce	Elias H. Roberts
1882 Denomination Back	$5, $10, $20	James C. Napier	Lee McClung
1882 Denomination Back	$5, $10, $20	Houston B. Teehee	John Burke
1882 Denomination Back	$5, $10, $20	James F. Tillman	Daniel N. Morgan
1882 Denomination Back	$5, $10, $20	James F. Tillman	Elias H. Roberts
1882 Denomination Back	$5, $10, $20	William T. Vernon	Charles H. Treat
1882 Denomination Back	$5, $10, $20, $50, $100	Judson W. Lyons	Elias H. Roberts
1882 Denomination Back	$10, $20	Judson W. Lyons	Charles H. Treat
1902 Blue Seal, Date Back	$5, $10, $20, $50, $100	Judson W. Lyons	Elias H. Roberts
1902 Blue Seal, Date Back	$5, $10, $20, $50, $100	Judson W. Lyons	Charles H. Treat
1902 Blue Seal, Date Back	$5, $10, $20, $50, $100	James C. Napier	John Burke
1902 Blue Seal, Date Back	$5, $10, $20, $50, $100	James C. Napier	Lee McClung
1902 Blue Seal, Date Back	$5, $10, $20, $50, $100	James C. Napier	Carmi A. Thompson
1902 Blue Seal, Date Back	$5, $10, $20, $50, $100	Gabe E. Parker	John Burke
1902 Blue Seal, Date Back	$5, $10, $20, $50, $100	Houston B. Teehee	John Burke
1902 Blue Seal, Date Back	$5, $10, $20, $50, $100	William T. Vernon	Lee McClung

1902 Blue Seal, Date Back	$5, $10, $20, $50, $100	William T. Vernon	Charles H. Treat
1902 Blue Seal, No Date Back	$5, $10, $20	Edward E. Jones	Walter O. Woods
1902 Blue Seal, No Date Back	$5, $10, $20	Walter O. Woods	H.T. Tate
1902 Blue Seal, No Date Back	$5, $10, $20, $50	James C. Napier	John Burke
1902 Blue Seal, No Date Back	$5, $10, $20, $50	Walter O. Woods	Frank White
1902 Blue Seal, No Date Back	$5, $10, $20, $50, $100	William S. Elliott	John Burke
1902 Blue Seal, No Date Back	$5, $10, $20, $50, $100	William S. Elliott	Frank White
1902 Blue Seal, No Date Back	$5, $10, $20, $50, $100	Judson W. Lyons	Elias H. Roberts
1902 Blue Seal, No Date Back	$5, $10, $20, $50, $100	Judson W. Lyons	Charles H. Treat
1902 Blue Seal, No Date Back	$5, $10, $20, $50, $100	James C. Napier	Lee McClung
1902 Blue Seal, No Date Back	$5, $10, $20, $50, $100	James C. Napier	Carmi A. Thompson
1902 Blue Seal, No Date Back	$5, $10, $20, $50, $100	Gabe E. Parker	John Burke
1902 Blue Seal, No Date Back	$5, $10, $20, $50, $100	Harley V. Speelman	Frank White
1902 Blue Seal, No Date Back	$5, $10, $20, $50, $100	Houston B. Teehee	John Burke
1902 Blue Seal, No Date Back	$5, $10, $20, $50, $100	William T. Vernon	Lee McClung
1902 Blue Seal, No Date Back	$5, $10, $20, $50, $100	William T. Vernon	Charles H. Treat
1902 Red Seal	$5, $10, $20, $50, $100	Judson W. Lyons	Elias H. Roberts
1902 Red Seal	$5, $10, $20, $50, $100	Judson W. Lyons	Charles H. Treat
1902 Red Seal	$5, $10, $20, $50, $100	William T. Vernon	Charles H. Treat

Silver certificates

Series	Denominations	Register of the Treasury	Treasurer
1878	$10, $20, $50, $100, $500, $1,000	Glenni W. Scofield	James Gilfillan
1880	$10, $20, $50, $100, $1,000	Blanche K. Bruce	A.U. Wyman
1880	$10, $20, $50, $100, $500, $1,000	Blanche K. Bruce	James Gilfillan
1880	$10, $20, $50, $100, $500, $1,000	Glenni W. Scofield	James Gilfillan
1880	$50, $100	William S. Rosecrans	J.N. Huston
1886	$1, $2, $5, $10	William S. Rosecrans	Conrad Jordan
1886	$1, $2, $5, $10, $20	William S. Rosecrans	J.N. Huston
1886	$1, $2, $5, $10, $20	William S. Rosecrans	James W. Hyatt
1886	$1, $5, $10, $20, $50, $100	William S. Rosecrans	Enos H. Nebecker
1891	$1, $2, $5, $10, $20, $50, $100	William S. Rosecrans	Enos H. Nebecker
1891	$1, $2, $5, $10, $20, $50, $100, $1,000	James F. Tillman	Daniel N. Morgan
1891	$10, $20, $50	Blanche K. Bruce	Elias H. Roberts
1891	$10, $20, $50	Judson W. Lyons	Elias H. Roberts
1891	$20	Houston B. Teehee	John Burke
1891	$20, $50	Gabe E. Parker	John Burke
1891	$50	William T. Vernon	Charles H. Treat
1896	$1, $2, $5	Blanche K. Bruce	Elias H. Roberts
1896	$1, $2, $5	James F. Tillman	Daniel N. Morgan
1896	$5	Judson W. Lyons	Elias H. Roberts
1899	$1, $2, $5	William S. Elliott	John Burke
1899	$1, $2, $5	Judson W. Lyons	Elias H. Roberts
1899	$1, $2, $5	Judson W. Lyons	Charles H. Treat
1899	$1, $2, $5	James C. Napier	Lee McClung
1899	$1, $2, $5	James C. Napier	Carmi A. Thompson
1899	$1, $2, $5	Gabe E. Parker	John Burke
1899	$1, $2, $5	Harley V. Speelman	Frank White
1899	$1, $2, $5	Houston B. Teehee	John Burke

1899	$1, $2, $5	William T. Vernon	Lee McClung
1899	$1, $2, $5	William T. Vernon	Charles H. Treat
1899	$1, $5	William S. Elliott	Frank White
1908	$10	Gabe E. Parker	John Burke
1908	$10	William T. Vernon	Lee McClung
1908	$10	William T. Vernon	Charles H. Treat
1923	$1	Walter O. Woods	H.T. Tate
1923	$1	Walter O. Woods	Frank White
1923	$1, $5	Harley V. Speelman	Frank White

Gold certificates

Series	Denominations	Register of the Treasury	Treasurer
1882	$5, $100	James C. Napier	Lee McClung
1882	$20, $50, $100	Blanche K. Bruce	James Gilfillan
1882	$20, $50, $100	Blanche K. Bruce	A.U. Wyman
1882	$20, $50, $100	Judson W. Lyons	Elias H. Roberts
1882	$20, $50, $100	William S. Rosecrans	J.N. Huston
1882	$50, $100	Judson W. Lyons	Charles H. Treat
1882	$50, $100	William S. Rosecrans	James W. Hyatt
1882	$50, $100	William T. Vernon	Lee McClung
1882	$50, $100	William T. Vernon	Charles H. Treat
1882	$100	James C. Napier	John Burke
1882	$100	James C. Napier	Carmi A. Thompson
1882	$100	Gabe E. Parker	John Burke
1882	$100	Houston B. Teehee	John Burke
1905	$20	Judson W. Lyons	Elias H. Roberts
1905	$20	Judson W. Lyons	Charles H. Treat
1906	$20	James C. Napier	Lee McClung
1906	$20	James C. Napier	Carmi A. Thompson
1906	$20	Gabe E. Parker	John Burke
1906	$20	Houston B. Teehee	John Burke
1906	$20	William T. Vernon	Lee McClung
1906	$20	William T. Vernon	Charles H. Treat
1907	$10	James C. Napier	Lee McClung
1907	$10	James C. Napier	Carmi A. Thompson
1907	$10	Gabe E. Parker	John Burke
1907	$10	Houston B. Teehee	John Burke
1907	$10	William T. Vernon	Lee McClung
1907	$10	William T. Vernon	Charles H. Treat
1913	$50	Gabe E. Parker	John Burke
1913	$50	Houston B. Teehee	John Burke
1922	$10, $20, $50, $100	Harley V. Speelman	Frank White

Compound interest Treasury notes

Series	Denominations	Register of the Treasury	Treasurer
All	All	Lucius E. Chittenden	F.E. Spinner
All	All	S.B. Colby	F.E. Spinner

Interest-bearing notes

Series	Denominations	Register of the Treasury	Treasurer
All	All	Lucius E. Chittenden	F.E. Spinner
All	All	S.B. Colby	F.E. Spinner

Treasury (Coin) notes

Series	Denominations	Register of the Treasury	Treasurer
1890	$1, $2, $5, $10, $20, $1,000	William S. Rosecrans	Enos H. Nebecker
1890	$1, $2, $5, $10, $100, $1,000	William S. Rosecrans	J.N. Huston
1891	$1, $2, $5, $10, $20	Blanche K. Bruce	Elias H. Roberts
1891	$1, $2, $5, $10, $20, $1,000	James F. Tillman	Daniel N. Morgan

1891	$1, $2, $5, $10, $50, $100, $1,000	William S. Rosecrans	Enos H. Nebecker
1891	$20	William S. Rosecrans	J.N. Huston
1895	$5	Judson W. Lyons	Elias H. Roberts

Refunding certificate

Series	Denominations	Register of the Treasury	Treasurer
Only	$10	Glenni W. Scofield	James Gilfillan

Fractional currency

Series	Denominations	Register of the Treasury	Treasurer
Third Issue	5¢, 10¢, 15¢, 25¢, 50¢ (Types I, II, III)	S.B. Colby	F.E. Spinner
Third Issue	5¢, 10¢, 15¢, 50¢ (Types I, II)	Noah L. Jeffries	F.E. Spinner
Third Issue	15¢, 50¢ (Type II)	John Allison	F.E. Spinner
Third Issue	50¢ (Type II)	John Allison	John C. New
Fourth Issue	10¢, 15¢, 25¢, 50¢ (Types I, II, III, IV)	John Allison	F.E. Spinner
Fifth Issue	10¢, 25¢	John Allison	F.E. Spinner
Fifth Issue	50¢	John Allison	John C. New

Federal Reserve Bank notes

Series	Denominations	Register of the Treasury	Treasurer
1918	$1, $2, $5, $10, $20	William S. Elliott	John Burke
1918	$1, $2, $5, $10, $20	Houston B. Teehee	John Burke

1914 Federal Reserve notes

Series	Denominations	Secretary	Treasurer
1914 Blue Seal	$5, $10, $20, $50, $100, $500, $1,000, $5,000, $10,000	Carter Glass	John Burke
1914 Blue Seal	$5, $10, $20, $50, $100, $500, $1,000, $5,000, $10,000	David F. Houston	John Burke
1914 Blue Seal	$5, $10, $20, $50, $100, $500, $1,000, $5,000, $10,000	William Gibbs McAdoo	John Burke
1914 Blue Seal	$5, $10, $20, $50, $100, $500, $1,000, $5,000, $10,000	Andrew W. Mellon	Frank White
1914 Red Seal	$5, $10, $20, $50	William Gibbs McAdoo	John Burke

Signatures on small-sized paper money

Federal Reserve Bank notes

Series	Denominations	Register of the Treasury	Treasurer
1929	$5, $10, $20, $50, $100	Edward E. Jones	Walter O. Woods

National Bank notes

Series	Denominations	Register of the Treasury	Treasurer
1929	$5, $10, $20, $50, $100	Edward E. Jones	Walter O. Woods

Gold certificates

Series	Denominations	Treasurer	Secretary
1928	$10, $20, $50, $100, $500, $1,000, $5,000, $10,000	Walter O. Woods	Andrew W. Mellon
1928	$10, $20	Walter O. Woods	Ogden L. Mills
1934	$100, $1,000, $10,000, $100,000	W.A. Julian	Henry Morgenthau Jr.

United States notes

Series	Denominations	Treasurer	Secretary

1928	$1	Walter O. Woods	William H. Woodin
1928	$2	H.T. Tate	Andrew W. Mellon
1928	$5	Walter O. Woods	Andrew W. Mellon
1928-A	$2	Walter O. Woods	Andrew W. Mellon
1928-A	$5	Walter O. Woods	Ogden L. Mills
1928-B	$2	Walter O. Woods	Ogden L. Mills
1928-B	$5	W.A. Julian	Henry Morgenthau Jr.
1928-C	$2, $5	W.A. Julian	Henry Morgenthau Jr.
1928-D	$2	W.A. Julian	Henry Morgenthau Jr.
1928-D	$5	W.A. Julian	Fred M. Vinson
1928-E	$2	W.A. Julian	Fred M. Vinson
1928-E	$5	W.A. Julian	John W. Snyder
1928-F	$2	W.A. Julian	John W. Snyder
1928-F	$5	Georgia Neese Clark	John W. Snyder
1928-G	$2	Georgia Neese Clark	John W. Snyder
1953	$2, $5	Ivy Baker Priest	George M. Humphrey
1953-A	$2, $5	Ivy Baker Priest	Robert B. Anderson
1953-B	$2, $5	Elizabeth Rudel Smith	Douglas Dillon
1953-C	$2, $5	Kathryn O'Hay Granahan	Douglas Dillon
1963	$2, $5	Kathryn O'Hay Granahan	Douglas Dillon
1963-A	$2	Kathryn O'Hay Granahan	Henry H. Fowler
1966	$100	Kathryn O'Hay Granahan	Henry H. Fowler
1966-A	$100	Dorothy Andrews Elston	David M. Kennedy

Silver certificates

Series	Denominations	Treasurer	Secretary
1928	$1	H.T. Tate	Andrew W. Mellon
1928-A	$1	Walter O. Woods	Andrew W. Mellon
1928-B	$1	Walter O. Woods	Ogden L. Mills
1928-C	$1	Walter O. Woods	William H. Woodin
1928-D	$1	W.A. Julian	William H. Woodin
1928-E	$1	W.A. Julian	Henry Morgenthau Jr.
1933	$10	W.A. Julian	William H. Woodin
1934	$1, $5, $10	W.A. Julian	Henry Morgenthau Jr.
1934-A	$5, $10	W.A. Julian	Henry Morgenthau Jr.
1934-B	$5, $10	W.A. Julian	Fred M. Vinson
1934-C	$5, $10	W.A. Julian	John W. Snyder
1934-D	$5, $10	Georgia Neese Clark	John W. Snyder
1935	$1	W.A. Julian	Henry Morgenthau Jr.
1935-A	$1	W.A. Julian	Henry Morgenthau Jr.
1935-B	$1	W.A. Julian	Fred M. Vinson
1935-C	$1	W.A. Julian	John W. Snyder
1935-D	$1	Georgia Neese Clark	John W. Snyder
1935-E	$1	Ivy Baker Priest	George M. Humphrey
1935-F	$1	Ivy Baker Priest	Robert B. Anderson
1935-G	$1	Elizabeth Rudel Smith	Douglas Dillon
1935-H	$1	Kathryn O'Hay Granahan	Douglas Dillon
1953	$5, $10	Ivy Baker Priest	George M. Humphrey
1953-A	$5, $10	Ivy Baker Priest	Robert B. Anderson
1953-B	$5, $10	Elizabeth Rudel Smith	Douglas Dillon
1953-C	$5	Kathryn O'Hay Granahan	Douglas Dillon
1957	$1	Ivy Baker Priest	Robert B. Anderson
1957-A	$1	Elizabeth Rudel Smith	Douglas Dillon
1957-B	$1	Kathryn O'Hay Granahan	Douglas Dillon

Federal Reserve notes

Series	Denominations	Treasurer	Secretary
1928	$5, $10, $20	H.T. Tate	Andrew W. Mellon
1928	$50, $100, $500, $1,000, $5,000, $10,000	Walter O. Woods	Andrew W. Mellon
1928-A	$5, $10, $20, $50, $100	Walter O. Woods	Andrew W. Mellon
1928-B	$5, $10, $20	Walter O. Woods	Andrew W. Mellon
1928-C	$5, $10, $20	Walter O. Woods	Ogden L. Mills

1928-D	$5		Walter O. Woods	William H. Woodin
1934	$5, $10, $20, $50, $100, $500, $1,000, $5,000, $10,000		W.A. Julian	Henry Morgenthau Jr.
1934-A	$5, $10, $20, $50, $100, $500, $1,000		W.A. Julian	Henry Morgenthau Jr.
1934-B	$5, $10, $20, $50, $100		W.A. Julian	Fred M. Vinson
1934-C	$5, $10, $20, $50, $100		W.A. Julian	John W. Snyder
1934-D	$5, $10, $20, $50, $100		Georgia Neese Clark	John W. Snyder
1950	$5, $10, $20, $50, $100		Georgia Neese Clark	John W. Snyder
1950-A	$5, $10, $20, $50, $100		Ivy Baker Priest	George M. Humphrey
1950-B	$5, $10, $20, $50, $100		Ivy Baker Priest	Robert B. Anderson
1950-C	$5, $10, $20, $50, $100		Elizabeth Rudel Smith	Douglas Dillon
1950-D	$5, $10, $20, $50, $100		Kathryn O'Hay Granahan	Douglas Dillon
1950-E	$5, $10, $20, $50, $100		Kathryn O'Hay Granahan	Henry H. Fowler
1963	$1, $5, $10, $20		Kathryn O'Hay Granahan	Douglas Dillon
1963-A	$1, $5, $10, $20, $50, $100		Kathryn O'Hay Granahan	Henry H. Fowler
1963-B	$1		Kathryn O'Hay Granahan	Joseph W. Barr
1969	$1, $5, $10, $20, $50, $100		Dorothy Andrews Elston	David M. Kennedy
1969-A	$1		Dorothy Andrews Kabis	David M. Kennedy
1969-A	$5, $10, $20, $50, $100		Dorothy Andrews Kabis	John B. Connally
1969-B	$1		Dorothy Andrews Kabis	John B. Connally
1969-B	$5, $10, $20, $50		Romana Acosta Banuelos	John B. Connally
1969-C	$1		Romana Acosta Banuelos	John B. Connally
1969-C	$5, $10, $20, $50, $100		Romana Acosta Banuelos	George P. Shultz
1969-D	$1		Romana Acosta Banuelos	George P. Shultz
1974	$1, $5, $10, $20, $50, $100		Francine Irving Neff	William E. Simon
1976	$2		Francine Irving Neff	William E. Simon
1977	$1, $5, $10, $20, $50, $100		Azie Tayor Morton	Blumenthal
1977-A	$1, $5, $10		Azie Tayor Morton	G. William Miller
1981	$1, $5, $10, $20, $50, $100		Angela Buchanan	Donald T. Regan
1981-A	$1, $5, $10, $20, $50, $100		Katherine Davalos Ortega	Donald T. Regan
1985	$1, $5, $10, $20, $50, $100		Katherine Davalos Ortega	James A. Baker III
1988	$1, $5, $10, $20, $50, $100		Katherine Davalos Ortega	Nicholas F. Brady
1988-A	$1, $5, $10, $20, $50, $100 (expected but not all denominations reported at press time)		Catalina Vasquez Villalpando	Nicholas F. Brady

Signers of U.S. paper money, by name

Name	Office	Issue type	Series	Denominations
Allison, John	Register	Legal Tender notes	1869	$1, $2, $5, $10, $20, $50, $100, $500
			1874	$1, $2, $50, $100
			1875	$1, $2, $5, $10, $20, $50, $100, $500
			1875-A	$1, $2, $5, $10, $100
			1875-B	$1, $2, $5
			1875-C	$1
			1875-D	$1
			1875-E	$1
			1878	$1, $2, $5, $10, $20, $50, $100, $500, $1,000
			1880	$500
		National Bank notes	Original	$1, $2, $5, $10, $20, $50, $100
			1875	$1, $2, $5, $10, $20, $50, $100
		Fractional currency	Third Issue	15¢, 50¢ (Type II)
			Fourth Issue	10¢, 15¢, 25¢, 50¢ (Types I, II, III, IV)
			Fifth Issue	10¢, 25¢, 50¢
Anderson, Robert B.	Secretary	United States notes	1953-A	$2, $5
		Silver certificates	1935-F	$1

			1953-A	$5, $10
			1957	$1
		Federal Reserve notes	1950-B	$5, $10, $20, $50, $100
Baker, James A. III	Secretary	Federal Reserve notes	1985	$1, $5, $10, $20, $50, $100
Banuelos, Romana Acosta	Treasurer	Federal Reserve notes	1969-B	$5, $10, $20, $50
			1969-C	$1, $5, $10, $20, $50, $100
			1969-D	$1
Barr, Joseph W.	Secretary	Federal Reserve notes	1963-B	$1
Blumenthal, W. Michael	Secretary	Federal Reserve notes	1977	$1, $5, $10, $20, $50, $100
Brady, Nicholas F.	Secretary	Federal Reserve notes	1988	$1, $5, $10, $20, $50, $100
			1988-A	$1, $5, $10, $20, $50, $100 (expected, but not all denominations reported at press time)
Bruce, Blanche K.	Register	Legal Tender notes	1880	$1, $2, $5, $10, $20, $50, $100
		National Bank notes	1875	$5, $10, $20, $50, $100
			1882 Brown Back	$5, $10, $20, $50, $100
			1882 Date Back	$5, $10, $20, $50, $100
			1882 Denom. Back	$5, $10, $20
		Silver certificates, large-sized	1880	$10, $20, $50, $100, $500, $1,000
			1891	$10, $20, $50
			1896	$1, $2, $5
		Gold certificates	1882	$20, $50, $100
		Treasury (coin) notes	1891	$1, $2, $5, $10, $20
Buchanan, Angela	Treasurer	Federal Reserve notes	1981	$1, $5, $10, $20, $50, $100
Burke, John	Treasurer	Federal Reserve note, large-sized	1914 Blue Seal	$5, $10, $20, $50, $100, $500, $1,000, $5,000, $10,000
			1914 Red Seal	$5, $10, $20, $50
		Legal Tender notes	1880	$20
			1901	$10
			1907	$5
			1917	$1, $2, $5
		National Bank notes	1882 Denom. Back	$5, $10, $20
			1902 Blue Seal, Date Back	$5, $10, $20, $50, $100
			1902 Blue Seal, No Date Back	$5, $10, $20, $50, $100
		Silver certificates, large-sized	1891	$20, $50
			1899	$1, $2, $5
			1908	$10
		Gold certificates	1882	$100
			1906	$20
			1907	$10
			1913	$50
		Federal Reserve Bank notes	1918	$1, $2, $5, $10, $20
Chittenden, Lucius E.	Register	Legal Tender notes	1862	$1, $2, $5, $10, $20, $50, $100, $500
			1863	$2, $5, $10, $20, $50, $100, $500
		National Bank notes	Original	$5, $10, $20, $50, $100
		Compound interest Treasury notes	All	All

		Interest-bearing notes	All	All
Clark, Georgia Neese	Treasurer	United States notes	1928-F	$5
			1928-G	$2
		Silver certificates	1934-D	$5, $10
			1935-D	$1
		Federal Reserve notes	1934-D	$5, $10, $20, $50, $100
			1950	$5, $10, $20, $50, $100
Colby, S.B.	Register	National Bank notes	Original	$1, $2, $5, $10, $20, $50, $100
		Compound interest Treasury notes	All	All
		Interest-bearing notes	All	All
		Fractional currency	Third Issue	5¢, 10¢, 15¢, 25¢, 50¢ (Types I, II, III)
Connally, John B.	Secretary	Federal Reserve notes	1969-A	$5, $10, $20, $50, $100
			1969-B	$1, $5, $10, $20, $50
			1969-C	$1
Dillon, Douglas	Secretary	United States notes	1953-B	$2, $5
			1953-C	$2, $5
			1963	$2, $5
		Silver certificates	1935-G	$1
			1935-H	$1
			1953-B	$5, $10
			1953-C	$5
			1957-A	$1
			1957-B	$1
		Federal Reserve notes	1950-C	$5, $10, $20, $50, $100
			1950-D	$5, $10, $20, $50, $100
			1963	$1, $5, $10, $20
Elliott, William S.	Register	Legal Tender notes	1907	$5
			1917	$1, $2, $5
		National Bank notes	1902 Blue Seal, No Date Back	$5, $10, $20, $50, $100
		Silver certificates, large-sized	1899	$1, $2, $5
		Federal Reserve Bank notes	1918	$1, $2, $5, $10, $20
Elston, Dorothy Andrews (see also Kabis, Dorothy Andrews)	Treasurer	United States notes	1966-A	$100
		Federal Reserve notes	1969	$1, $5, $10, $20, $50, $100
Fowler, Henry H.	Secretary	United States notes	1963-A	$2
			1966	$100
		Federal Reserve notes	1950-E	$5, $10, $20, $50, $100
			1963-A	$1, $5, $10, $20, $50, $100
Gilfillan, James	Treasurer	Legal Tender notes	1878	$1, $2, $5, $10, $20, $50, $100, $500, $1,000
			1880	$1, $2, $5, $10, $20, $50, $100
		National Bank notes	1875	$1, $2, $5, $10, $20, $50, $100
			1882 Brown Back	$5, $10, $20, $50, $100
		Silver certificates, large-sized	1878	$10, $20, $50, $100, $500, $1,000
			1880	$10, $20, $50, $100, $500, $1,000
		Gold certificates	1882	$20, $50, $100
		Refunding certificates	Only	$10
Glass, Carter	Secretary	Federal Reserve note, large-sized	1914 Blue Seal	$5, $10, $20, $50, $100, $500, $1,000, $5,000, $10,000

Granahan, Kathryn O'Hay	Treasurer	United States notes	1953-C	$2, $5
			1963	$2, $5
			1963-A	$2
			1966	$100
		Silver certificates	1935-H	$1
			1953-C	$5
			1957-B	$1
		Federal Reserve notes	1950-D	$5, $10, $20, $50, $100
			1950-E	$5, $10, $20, $50, $100
			1963	$1, $5, $10, $20
			1963-A	$1, $5, $10, $20, $50, $100
			1963-B	$1
Houston, David F.	Secretary	Federal Reserve note, large-sized	1914 Blue Seal	$5, $10, $20, $50, $100, $500, $1,000, $5,000, $10,000
Humphrey, George M.	Secretary	United States notes	1953	$2, $5
		Silver certificates	1935-E	$1
			1953	$5, $10
		Federal Reserve notes	1950-A	$5, $10, $20, $50, $100
Huston, J.N.	Treasurer	Legal Tender notes	1880	$1, $2, $5, $10, $20, $50, $100
		National Bank notes	1875	$5, $10, $50, $100
			1882 Brown Back	$5, $10, $20, $50
			1882 Date Back	$5, $10, $20, $50, $100
		Silver certificates, large-sized	1880	$50, $100
			1886	$1, $2, $5, $10, $20
		Gold certificates	1882	$20, $50, $100
		Treasury (coin) notes	1890	$1, $2, $5, $10, $100, $1,000
			1891	$20
Hyatt, James W.	Treasurer	Legal Tender notes	1880	$5, $10, $20, $50, $100
		National Bank notes	1882 Brown Back	$5, $10, $20, $50, $100
		Silver certificates, large-sized	1886	$1, $2, $5, $10, $20
		Gold certificates	1882	$50, $100
Jeffries, Noah L.	Register	National Bank notes	Original	$1, $2, $5, $10, $20
		Fractional currency	Third Issue	5¢, 10¢, 15¢, 50¢ (Types I, II)
Jones, Edward E.	Register	Federal Reserve Bank notes, small-sized	1929	$5, $10, $20, $50, $100
		National Bank notes, small-sized	1929	$5, $10, $20, $50, $100
		National Bank notes	1902 Blue Seal, No Date Back	$5, $10, $20
Jordan, Conrad	Treasurer	Legal Tender notes	1880	$5, $10, $20, $50, $100
		National Bank notes	1875	$5
			1882 Brown Back	$5, $10, $20, $50, $100
		Silver certificates, large-sized	1886	$1, $2, $5, $10
Julian, W.A.	Treasurer	Gold certificates	1934	$100, $1,000, $10,000, $100,000
		United States notes	1928-B	$5
			1928-C	$2, $5
			1928-D	$2, $5
			1928-E	$2, $5
			1928-F	$2
		Silver certificates	1928-D	$1
			1928-E	$1
			1933	$10
			1934	$1, $5, $10
			1934-A	$5, $10

			1934-B	$5, $10
			1934-C	$5, $10
			1935	$1
			1935-A	$1
			1935-B	$1
			1935-C	$1
		Federal Reserve notes	1934	$5, $10, $20, $50, $100, $500, $1,000, $5,000, $10,000
			1934-A	$5, $10, $20, $50, $100, $500, $1,000
			1934-B	$5, $10, $20, $50, $100
			1934-C	$5, $10, $20, $50, $100
Kabis, Dorothy Andrews (see also Elston, Dorothy Andrews)	Treasurer	Federal Reserve notes	1969-A	$1, $5, $10, $20, $50, $100
			1969-B	$1
Kennedy, David M.	Secretary	United States notes	1966-A	$100
		Federal Reserve notes	1969	$1, $5, $10, $20, $50, $100
			1969-A	$1
Lyons, Judson W.	Register	Legal Tender notes	1880	$5, $10, $20, $50, $100, $500
			1901	$10
		National Bank notes	1882 Brown Back	$5, $10, $20, $50, $100
			1882 Date Back	$5, $10, $20, $50, $100
			1882 Denom. Back	$5, $10, $20, $50, $100
			1902 Blue Seal, Date Back	$5, $10, $20, $50, $100
			1902 Blue Seal, No Date Back	$5, $10, $20, $50, $100
			1902 Red Seal	$5, $10, $20, $50, $100
		Silver certificates, large-sized	1891	$10, $20, $50
			1896	$5
			1899	$1, $2, $5
		Gold certificates	1882	$20, $50, $100
			1905	$20
		Treasury (coin) notes	1895	$5
McAdoo, William Gibbs	Secretary	Federal Reserve note, large-sized	1914 Blue Seal	$5, $10, $20, $50, $100, $500, $1,000, $5,000, $10,000
			1914 Red Seal	$5, $10, $20, $50
McClung, Lee	Treasurer	Legal Tender notes	1880	$20
			1901	$10
			1907	$5, $20
		National Bank notes	1882 Date Back	$5, $10, $20, $50, $100
			1882 Denom. Back	$5, $10, $20
			1902 Blue Seal, Date Back	$5, $10, $20, $50, $100
			1902 Blue Seal, No Date Back	$5, $10, $20, $50, $100
		Silver certificates, large-sized	1899	$1, $2, $5
			1908	$10
		Gold certificates	1882	$5, $50, $100
			1906	$20
			1907	$10
Mellon, Andrew W.	Secretary	Federal Reserve note, large-sized	1914 Blue Seal	$5, $10, $20, $50, $100, $500, $1,000, $5,000, $10,000
		Gold certificates	1928	$10, $20, $50, $100, $500, $1,000, $5,000, $10,000

		United States notes	1928	$2, $5
			1928-A	$2
		Silver certificates	1928	$1
			1928-A	$1
		Federal Reserve notes	1928	$5, $10, $20, $50, $100, $500, $1,000, $5,000, $10,000
			1928-A	$5, $10, $20, $50, $100
			1928-B	$5, $10, $20
Miller, G. William	Secretary	Federal Reserve notes	1977-A	$1, $5, $10
Mills, Ogden L.	Secretary	Gold certificates	1928	$10, $20
		United States notes	1928-A	$5
			1928-B	$2
		Silver certificates	1928-B	$1
		Federal Reserve notes	1928-C	$5, $10, $20
Morgan, Daniel N.	Treasurer	Legal Tender notes	1880	$1, $2, $5, $10, $20, $50, $100
		National Bank notes	1875	$10, $20, $50, $100
			1882 Brown Back	$5, $10, $20, $50, $100
			1882 Date Back	$5, $10, $20, $50, $100
			1882 Denom. Back	$5, $10, $20
		Silver certificates, large-sized	1891	$1, $2, $5, $10, $20, $50, $100, $1,000
			1896	$1, $2, $5
		Treasury (coin) notes	1891	$1, $2, $5, $10, $20, $1,000
Morgenthau, Henry Jr.	Secretary	Gold certificates	1934	$100, $1,000, $10,000, $100,000
		United States notes	1928-B	$5
			1928-C	$2, $5
			1928-D	$2
		Silver certificates	1928-E	$1
			1934	$1, $5, $10
			1934-A	$5, $10
			1935	$1
			1935-A	$1
		Federal Reserve notes	1934	$5, $10, $20, $50, $100, $500, $1,000, $5,000, $10,000
			1934-A	$5, $10, $20, $50, $100, $500, $1,000
Morton, Azie Taylor	Treasurer	Federal Reserve notes	1977	$1, $5, $10, $20, $50, $100
			1977-A	$1, $5, $10
Napier, James C.	Register	Legal Tender notes	1901	$10
			1907	$5
		National Bank notes	1882 Date Back	$5, $10, $20, $50, $100
			1882 Denom. Back	$5, $10, $20
			1902 Blue Seal, Date Back	$5, $10, $20, $50, $100
			1902 Blue Seal, No Date Back	$5, $10, $20, $50, $100
		Silver certificates, large-sized	1899	$1, $2, $5
		Gold certificates	1882	$5, $100
			1906	$20
			1907	$10
Nebecker, Enos H.	Treasurer	Legal Tender notes	1880	$1, $2, $5, $10, $20
		National Bank notes	1875	$10, $20, $50, $100
			1882 Brown Back	$5, $10, $20, $50, $100
			1882 Date Back	$5, $10, $20, $50, $100
		Silver certificates, large-sized	1886	$1, $5, $10, $20, $50, $100

Name	Title	Note type	Series	Denominations
			1891	$1, $2, $5, $10, $20, $50, $100
		Treasury (coin) notes	1890	$1, $2, $5, $10, $20, $1,000
			1891	$1, $2, $5, $10, $50, $100, $1,000
Neff, Francine Irving	Treasurer	Federal Reserve notes	1974	$1, $5, $10, $20, $50, $100
			1976	$2
New, John C.	Treasurer	Legal Tender notes	1875	$1, $2, $5, $10, $20, $500
			1875-A	$1, $2, $5, $10, $100
			1875-B	$1, $2, $5
			1875-C	$1
			1875-D	$1
			1875-E	$1
		National Bank notes	1875	$1, $2, $5, $10, $20, $50, $100
		Fractional currency	Third Issue	50¢ (Type II)
			Fifth Issue	50¢
Ortega, Katherine Davalos	Treasurer	Federal Reserve notes	1981-A	$1, $5, $10, $20, $50, $100
			1985	$1, $5, $10, $20, $50, $100
			1988	$1, $5, $10, $20, $50, $100
Parker, Gabe E.	Register	Legal Tender notes	1901	$10
			1907	$5
		National Bank notes	1902 Blue Seal, Date Back	$5, $10, $20, $50, $100
			1902 Blue Seal, No Date Back	$5, $10, $20, $50, $100
		Silver certificates, large-sized	1891	$20, $50
			1899	$1, $2, $5
			1908	$10
		Gold certificates	1882	$100
			1906	$20
			1907	$10
			1913	$50
Priest, Ivy Baker	Treasurer	United States notes	1953	$2, $5
			1953-A	$2, $5
		Silver certificates	1935-E	$1
			1935-F	$1
			1953	$5, $10
			1953-A	$5, $10
			1957	$1
		Federal Reserve notes	1950-A	$5, $10, $20, $50, $100
			1950-B	$5, $10, $20, $50, $100
Regan, Donald T.	Secretary	Federal Reserve notes	1981	$1, $5, $10, $20, $50, $100
			1981-A	$1, $5, $10, $20, $50, $100
Roberts, Elias H.	Treasurer	Legal Tender notes	1880	$5, $10, $20, $50, $100, $500
			1901	$10
		National Bank notes	1882 Brown Back	$5, $10, $20, $50, $100
			1882 Date Back	$5, $10, $20, $50, $100
			1882 Denom. Back	$5, $10, $20, $50, $100
			1902 Blue Seal, Date Back	$5, $10, $20, $50, $100
			1902 Blue Seal, No Date Back	$5, $10, $20, $50, $100
			1902 Red Seal	$5, $10, $20, $50, $100

		Silver certificates, large-sized	1891	$10, $20, $50
			1896	$1, $2, $5
			1899	$1, $2, $5
		Gold certificates	1882	$20, $50, $100
			1905	$20
		Treasury (coin) notes	1891	$1, $2, $5, $10, $20
			1895	$5
Rosecrans, William S.	Register	Legal Tender notes	1880	$1, $2, $5, $10, $20, $50, $100
		National Bank notes	1875	$5, $10, $20, $50, $100
			1882 Brown Back	$5, $10, $20, $50, $100
			1882 Date Back	$5, $10, $20, $50, $100
		Silver certificates, large-sized	1880	$50, $100
			1886	$1, $2, $5, $10, $20, $50, $100
			1891	$1, $2, $5, $10, $20, $50, $100
		Gold certificates	1882	$20, $50, $100
		Treasury (coin) notes	1890	$1, $2, $5, $10, $20, $100, $1,000
			1891	$1, $2, $5, $10, $20, $50, $100, $1,000
Scofield, Glenni W.	Register	Legal Tender notes	1878	$2
			1880	$1, $2, $5, $10, $20
		National Bank notes	1875	$1, $2, $5, $10, $20, $50, $100
		Silver certificates, large-sized	1878	$10, $20, $50, $100, $500, $1,000
			1880	$10, $20, $50, $100, $500, $1,000
		Refunding certificates	Only	$10
Shultz, George P.	Secretary	Federal Reserve notes	1969-C	$5, $10, $20, $50, $100
			1969-D	$1
Simon, William E.	Secretary	Federal Reserve notes	1974	$1, $5, $10, $20, $50, $100
			1976	$2
Smith, Elizabeth Rudel	Treasurer	United States notes	1953-B	$2, $5
		Silver certificates	1935-G	$1
			1953-B	$5, $10
			1957-A	$1
		Federal Reserve notes	1950-C	$5, $10, $20, $50, $100
Snyder, John W.	Secretary	United States notes	1928-E	$5
			1928-F	$2, $5
			1928-G	$2
		Silver certificates	1934-C	$5, $10
			1934-D	$5, $10
			1935-C	$1
			1935-D	$1
		Federal Reserve notes	1934-C	$5, $10, $20, $50, $100
			1934-D	$5, $10, $20, $50, $100
			1950	$5, $10, $20, $50, $100
Speelman, Harley V.	Register	Legal Tender notes	1901	$10
			1907	$5
			1917	$1, $2
			1923	$10
		National Bank notes	1902 Blue Seal, No Date Back	$5, $10, $20, $50, $100
		Silver certificates, large-sized	1899	$1, $2, $5
			1923	$1, $5
		Gold certificates	1922	$10, $20, $50, $100
Spinner, F.E.	Treasurer	Legal Tender notes	1862	$1, $2, $5, $10, $20, $50, $100, $500

			1863	$2, $5, $10, $20, $50, $100, $500
			1869	$1, $2, $5, $10, $20, $50, $100, $500
			1874	$1, $2, $50, $100
			1880	$500
		National Bank notes	Original	$1, $2, $5, $10, $20, $50, $100
		Compound interest Treasury notes	All	All
		Interest-bearing notes	All	All
		Fractional currency	Third Issue	5¢, 10¢, 15¢, 25¢, 50¢ (Types I, II, III)
			Fourth Issue	10¢, 15¢, 25¢, 50¢ (Types I, II, III, IV)
			Fifth Issue	10¢, 25¢
Tate, H.T.	Treasurer	United States notes	1928	$2
		Silver certificates	1928	$1
		Federal Reserve notes	1928	$5, $10, $20
		National Bank notes	1902 Blue Seal, No Date Back	$5, $10, $20
		Silver certificates, large-sized	1923	$1
Teehee, Houston B.	Register	Legal Tender notes	1880	$20
			1901	$10
			1907	$5
			1917	$1, $2
		National Bank notes	1882 Denom. Back	$5, $10, $20
			1902 Blue Seal, Date Back	$5, $10, $20, $50, $100
			1902 Blue Seal, No Date Back	$5, $10, $20, $50, $100
		Silver certificates, large-sized	1891	$20
			1899	$1, $2, $5
		Gold certificates	1882	$100
			1906	$20
			1907	$10
			1913	$50
		Federal Reserve Bank notes	1918	$1, $2, $5, $10, $20
Thompson, Carmi A.	Treasurer	Legal Tender notes	1907	$5
		National Bank notes	1902 Blue Seal, Date Back	$5, $10, $20, $50, $100
			1902 Blue Seal, No Date Back	$5, $10, $20, $50, $100
		Silver certificates, large-sized	1899	$1, $2, $5
		Gold certificates	1882	$100
			1906	$20
			1907	$10
Tillman, James F.	Register	Legal Tender notes	1880	$1, $2, $5, $10, $20, $50, $100
		National Bank notes	1875	$10, $20, $50, $100
			1882 Brown Back	$5, $10, $20, $50, $100
			1882 Date Back	$5, $10, $20, $50, $100
			1882 Denom. Back	$5, $10, $20
		Silver certificates, large-sized	1891	$1, $2, $5, $10, $20, $50, $100, $1,000
			1896	$1, $2, $5
		Treasury (coin) notes	1891	$1, $2, $5, $10, $20, $1,000
Treat, Charles H.	Treasurer	Legal Tender notes	1880	$20
			1901	$10

			1907	$5
		National Bank notes	1882 Brown Back	$5, $10, $20, $50, $100
			1882 Date Back	$5, $10, $20, $50, $100
			1882 Denom. Back	$5, $10, $20
			1902 Blue Seal, Date Back	$5, $10, $20, $50, $100
			1902 Blue Seal, No Date Back	$5, $10, $20, $50, $100
			1902 Red Seal	$5, $10, $20, $50, $100
		Silver certificates, large-sized	1891	$50
			1899	$1, $2, $5
			1908	$10
		Gold certificates	1882	$50, $100
			1905	$20
			1906	$20
			1907	$10
Vernon, William T.	Register	Legal Tender notes	1880	$20
			1901	$10
			1907	$5, $20
		National Bank notes	1882 Brown Back	$5, $10, $20, $50, $100
			1882 Date Back	$5, $10, $20, $50, $100
			1882 Denom. Back	$5, $10, $20
			1902 Blue Seal, Date Back	$5, $10, $20, $50, $100
			1902 Blue Seal, No Date Back	$5, $10, $20, $50, $100
			1902 Red Seal	$5, $10, $20, $50, $100
		Silver certificates, large-sized	1891	$50
			1899	$1, $2, $5
			1908	$10
		Gold certificates	1882	$50, $100
			1906	$20
			1907	$10
Villalpando, Catalina Vasquez	Treasurer	Federal Reserve notes	1988-A	$1, $5, $10, $20, $50, $100 (expected, but not all denominations reported at press time)
Vinson, Fred M.	Secretary	United States notes	1928-D	$5
			1928-E	$2
		Silver certificates	1934-B	$5, $10
			1935-B	$1
		Federal Reserve notes	1934-B	$5, $10, $20, $50, $100
White, Frank	Treasurer	Federal Reserve note, large-sized	1914 Blue Seal	$5, $10, $20, $50, $100, $500, $1,000, $5,000, $10,000
		Legal Tender notes	1880	$20
			1901	$10
			1907	$5
			1917	$1, $2
			1923	$10
		National Bank notes	1902 Blue Seal, No Date Back	$5, $10, $20, $50, $100
		Silver certificates, large-sized	1899	$1, $2, $5
			1923	$1, $5
		Gold certificates	1922	$10, $20, $50, $100
William S. Elliott	Register	Legal Tender notes	1880	$20
Woodin, William H.	Secretary	United States notes	1928	$1
		Silver certificates	1928-C	$1

			1928-D	$1
			1933	$10
		Federal Reserve notes	1928-D	$5
Woods, Walter O.	Register	Legal Tender notes	1907	$5
		National Bank notes	1902 Blue Seal, No Date Back	$5, $10, $20, $50
		Silver certificates, large-sized	1923	$1
	Treasurer	Gold certificates	1928	$10, $20, $50, $100, $500, $1,000, $5,000, $10,000
		United States notes	1928	$1, $5
			1928-A	$2, $5
			1928-B	$2
		Silver certificates	1928-A	$1
			1928-B	$1
			1928-C	$1
		Federal Reserve notes	1928	$50, $100, $500, $1,000, $5,000, $10,000
			1928-A	$5, $10, $20, $50, $100
			1928-B	$5, $10, $20
			1928-C	$5, $10, $20
			1928-D	$5
		Federal Reserve Bank notes, small-sized	1929	$5, $10, $20, $50, $100
		National Bank notes, small-sized	1929	$5, $10, $20, $50, $100
		National Bank notes	1902 Blue Seal, No Date Back	$5, $10, $20
Wyman, A.U.	Treasurer	Legal Tender notes	1875	$1, $2, $5, $50, $100, $500
			1880	$1, $5, $10, $20, $50, $100
		National Bank notes	1875	$1, $2, $5, $10, $20, $50, $100
			1882 Brown Back	$5, $10, $20, $50, $100
		Silver certificates, large-sized	1880	$10, $20, $50, $100, $1,000
		Gold certificates	1882	$20, $50, $100

U.S. Coins

9

Coins in use in America before 1793

The first coins in circulation in non-Spanish North America were standard French and English issues used in a variety of unsuccessful colonies ranging from the St. Lawrence River to the Caribbean. The colonists were not likely to have too much specie left after they purchased their supplies for the voyage, but what was left most certainly did come along, as the travelers did not dare to leave anything of value in a land to which they were likely never to return.

With the establishment of successful colonies in the early 1600s, the colonists began to trade both with their parent companies and the Spanish colonies of the Caribbean. The trade with England was highly restricted, and most English gold and silver that reached these shores soon returned to Europe in the form of taxes, custom duties, and profit for the companies. The trade with Latin America was much less formal (thanks to smuggling), and provided much of the circulating coinage for the colonies.

Because the Colonies could never acquire enough coinage of the homeland to fulfill their needs, they were eventually forced to produce some themselves. In 1652 the Massachusetts Bay Colony produced silver shillings, sixpence, and threepence, but at a reduced weight so that the coins would not be exported. Various designs were used over a 30-year period, but the date on the coins remained at 1652 as a polite fiction to imply that coins were made at a time when there was no

king, thereby not usurping the king's right to coin money. One die, for an Oak Tree twopence, was inexplicably dated 1662, but it is not known if this was a slip which accidentally revealed the true date of manufacture or a deliberate attempt at testing the British government's willingness to suppress the coinage.

Seeing that there was (supposedly) a market for underweight coins in the Colonies, several speculators began issuing private tokens for export to these markets. Most of these issues were officially sanctioned in some fashion. In effect the speculators were given a license to counterfeit, in exchange for a percentage of the profits. Some of these circulated and some did not, depending upon the greed of the manufacturer and how badly he debased the coins. One of the more candid manufacturers, an American, changed the inscription of his unpopular copper threepence pieces to read VALUE ME AS YOU PLEASE.

Throughout the period of the Revolution and afterward, a large part of the supply of small change was made up of privately issued store card tokens. Most of these were made in England and were of better quality than the majority of the various state issues. Those issued by American merchants were allegedly payable at these stores, but the others were payable only at London or Liverpool or other equally distant places. These tokens circulated for several years after the establishment of the Philadelphia Mint, despite an effort to recoin them into U.S. money.

The Articles of Confederation, adopted in 1778, permitted the states to issue their own coinages, with Congress fixing a uniform "standard of weights and measures." Only three of the 13 states struck coins for circulation under the Articles of Confederation: Connecticut, Massachusetts and New Jersey. Vermont, the 14th state, struck coinage before it entered the union. Most of the state coinages were produced by private manufacturers under contract to the states, although Massachusetts operated its own Mint in 1787 and 1788. Connecticut authorized a Mint, but most of its coinage was struck privately.

The U.S. Constitution, however, brought an end to the state coinage. Article 1, Section 10, Paragraph 1 of the Constitution reads, "No state shall . . . coin money, emit bills of credit, make anything but gold or silver coin a tender in payment of debts." The sole right to coin money was granted to the federal government (although a loophole permitted private coinage until 1864, when the constitutional loophole was closed) by the ratification of the Constitution in 1788.

Federal coinage studies

A federal coinage system had been under study since the early 1780s. Two plans merit attention here. The first was submitted to Congress Jan. 15, 1782, by Superintendent of Finance Robert Morris. The proposal was probably written by Assistant Financier of the Confederation Gouverneur Morris (no relation to Robert Morris). The Morris proposal was a complicated one, substituting the British system of pounds, shillings and pence for a decimal system based on the Spanish milled dollar. The basic unit would be worth 1/1,440 of the Spanish dollar, a sum arrived at by determining the largest common divisor by which state currencies could be divided without a fraction. The denominations would have been copper 5-unit and 8-unit pieces, plus a silver cent worth 100 units, a silver quint worth 500 units and a mark worth 1,000 units. The

cumbersome nature of the Morris system, however, gained little support.

Meanwhile, as Congress debated various monetary plans, it took one concrete step and authorized a copper coin. At this time, 1787, the four states were still producing copper coinage when they were joined by the federal government, still organized under the Articles of Confederation. Members of Congress, meeting in Philadelphia, recognized the need for a standard coinage and on April 21, 1787, ordered that a copper coin be produced by private contract but under federal inspection.

The resulting coins were the Fugio cents, generally acknowledged to be the first coins of the United States government. They are named for the Latin legend FUGIO ("I Fly") that appears on the the coin's obverse. A sundial appears on the obverse, along with the legend MIND YOUR BUSINESS, stressing the importance of time and the need for small business ventures; 13 linked rings on the reverse signify the 13 states, surrounding the legends UNITED STATES and WE ARE ONE. James Jarvis, a Connecticut business, received a contract to strike 300 tons of the copper coins, or about 26,666,666 pieces. Jarvis began coinage of the cents in New Haven, Conn., shortly after approval by Congress, but had struck fewer than 400,000 Fugio cents by June 1, 1787, by which time coinage had ceased. The federal government voided Jarvis' contract for missing the December 1787 delivery date (the coins were not delivered until beginning in May 1788). The Fugio cents proved underweight and were unpopular with the public. Thus the federal government's first experiment in a federal coinage had failed.

The second plan warranting attention was submitted to Congress by Alexander Hamilton, Secretary of the Treasury, on Jan. 21, 1791. In his proposal, Hamilton recommended the basic unit be a dollar. The denominations would have been a gold $10 coin, a gold dollar, a silver dollar, a silver tenth-dollar, a copper coin valued at one hundred to the dollar, and a second copper coin, valued at 200 to the dollar.

The Hamilton proposal was very similar to what Congress would approve in April 1792. Following Hamilton's proposal, Congress passed a resolution March 3, 1791, that a federal Mint be built, and President Washington in his third State of the Union speech agreed. Then, on April 2, 1792, Congress passed a law authorizing both a federal Mint and coinage. Ten denominations of coins, more than recommended by Hamilton, were approved: in gold were a $10 eagle, a $5 half eagle and a $2.50 quarter eagle; in silver were a dollar, half dollar, quarter dollar, disme (the "s" was dropped by 1793, with the 10-cent piece called a dime) and half disme; and in copper, a cent and half cent, neither of which had legal tender status.

History of U.S. Coinage

Denominations

Since coinage began at the Philadelphia Mint in 1793, 21 denominations have appeared on the circulating and commemorative coins of the United States. In gold, there have been the $50 (commemorative and bullion coins only), the $25 (on the American Eagle bullion coins), $20, $10, $5, $3, $2.50 and $1. Among silver coins (many later changed to copper-nickel by the Mint Act of 1965), there have been the silver dollar, the Trade dollar, the 50-cent coin, the quarter dollar, 20-cent coin, dime, half dime and 3-cent coin. There have also been copper-nickel 5-cent, 3-cent and 1-cent coins; a bronze 2-cent coin; cents in six different alloys; and a copper half cent.

Production of U.S. coinage began in earnest in 1793 with the production of copper half cents and cents. The striking of silver coinage began one year after copper coinage production. The Mint began striking silver half dimes, half dollars and dollars in 1794; and silver dimes and quarter dollars in 1796. Gold coinage began in 1795 with the half eagle and the eagle, followed by the quarter eagle in 1796.

During the earlier years of the U.S. Mint, not all denominations were struck in all years. In 1804, coinage of the silver dollar ceased with the striking of 1803-dated coins; dollar coinage was not resumed until 1836. A few gold eagles were struck in 1804, but coinage then ceased until 1838. No quarter eagles were struck from 1809 through 1820. Production of the other denominations was sporadic except for the cent; a fire prevented any 1815-dated cents from being produced, but otherwise the chain has been unbroken since 1793.

Meanwhile, as the country's borders and population grew, the monetary system grew with them. The denominations authorized in 1792 were no longer sufficient to meet the country's monetary needs. New denominations were authorized at the century's midpoint. In 1849, Congress authorized a gold dollar and a gold $20 double eagle (both under the Act of March 3, 1849). In 1851, a silver 3-cent coin was authorized to facilitate the purchase of 3-cent postage stamps (Act of March 3, 1851). A gold $3 coin was introduced in 1854 (Act of Feb. 21, 1853), again to help in the purchase of 3-cent stamps (in sheets of 100). A smaller cent was approved in 1857, replacing the large cent. The half cent was eliminated, also in 1857.

The American Civil War opened in 1861, causing massive hoarding of coinage and the necessity of coinage substitutes like encased postage stamps, privately produced copper-alloy cent-like tokens and finally, the first federal paper money. More changes to U.S. coins began in 1864, when the composition of the cent was changed to 95 percent copper and 5 percent tin and zinc, and when a bronze 2-cent coin was introduced (both under the Act of April 22, 1864). A copper-nickel 3-cent coin was issued beginning in 1865

(Act of March 3, 1865) to replace the silver 3-cent coins (which was struck in decreasing numbers until the last coins were produced in 1873). In 1866, a copper-nickel 5-cent piece was introduced (Act of May 16, 1866); the silver half dime was eliminated after 1873.

The year 1873 brought many changes to the U.S. coinage system, because of a law called by some the "Crime of 1873." The Act of Feb. 12, 1873, is called by numismatic historian Don Taxay "the most exhaustive [coinage act] in our history. Four denominations were abolished by the act: the 2-cent coin, the silver 3-cent coin, the half dime and the silver dollar. A Trade silver dollar was authorized for use by merchants in the Orient; a year later, Congress revoked the coin's legal tender status in the United States. The weights of the silver half dime, dime, quarter dollar and half dollar were increased. In effect, the law demonetized silver and placed the United States on a gold standard, triggering a national debate that would last for the next quarter century.

Another new denomination was authorized under the Act of March 3, 1875 — the silver 20-cent piece. The coin was struck for circulation in 1875-76, setting the record for the shortest-lived silver denomination in U.S. coinage history. Coinage of Proof 20-cent pieces continued in 1877-78, but for collectors only.

Meanwhile, the powerful silver interests in the United States, faced with the demonetization of silver left by the Crime of '73, fought in Congress. The resulting Act of Feb, 28, 1878, reinstituted the standard silver dollar abolished by the Act of Feb. 12, 1873. The specifications were unchanged from the silver dollar of 1837-73: an alloy 90 percent silver and 10 percent copper, weighing 26.73 grams. Obverse and reverse designs created by Mint Engraver George T. Morgan were selected for the dollar, today generally called the Morgan dollar (it was also called the Bland-Allison dollar, after the names of the congressmen responsible for the bill). Coinage of the Morgan dollar continued through 1904.

Coinage denominations in use continued unchanged through 1889, when the gold dollar and gold $3 denominations were struck for the last time.

The silver dollar was resurrected twice for circulation: in 1921, to continue through 1935; and in 1964, although the 1964 Peace silver dollars were all destroyed before entering circulation, after government support for them was withdrawn. The copper-nickel dollar was introduced in 1971, and a smaller dollar was issued briefly from 1979-81.

Since the Mint Act of 1875, only two new denominations have been authorized, neither for circulation. In 1915, a gold $50 coin was approved to commemorate the Panama-Pacific Exposition being held in San Francisco that year. More than 70 years later, in 1986, the $50 denomination was revived for the American Eagle bullion program. That same legislation (Act of Dec. 17, 1986, Public Law 99-185) also approved the United States' first $25 coin, the American Eagle half-ounce coin.

Designs

The story behind the designs of U.S. coinage is one of artistic experimentation and drone-like uniformity; of political necessity and political favoritism; of beauty tempered by the realities of the coining process.

The senators and representatives who approved the U.S. monetary system created design parameters that affect new U.S. coin designs even today, nearly 200 years after that initial legislation. The Mint Act of April 2, 1792, specified that certain design features and legends appear on the coins which were authorized. On one side of all coins was to be an impression symbolic of Liberty, plus the word LIBERTY and the year of coinage. For the silver and gold coins, an eagle and UNITED STATES OF AMERICA were to appear on the reverse. The denomination was to appear on the reverses of the half cents and cents.

For more than 115 years in the history of U.S. coinage, Liberty was portrayed by allegorical female figures, either a bust or a full-length portrait. Liberty's changing face through the years says a lot about the artistic abilities of the craftsmen employed on the Mint staff and the artists hired from outside to design certain coins. Some of the most attractive U.S. coins were designed by non-Mint employees, often in opposition to a jealous Mint engraving staff who seemed more concerned about whether the coin would stack than its physical beauty. Beautiful designs created by Mint staff engravers never went beyond the pattern stage in favor of the period of drone-like uniformity that characterized U.S. designs from the mid-1830s into the early 20th century.

The changing portrait of Liberty also reveals the embodiment of the "ideal woman" by the physical standards set by the American men of the time, and men have always dominated U.S. coinage design. The first coinage portraits of Liberty are "Rubenesque" by modern standards. The most recent allegorical figure of Liberty to appear on U.S. coins is on American Eagle gold bullion coins. They depict a reproduction of an 80-year-old design, "slimmed down" to resemble the trimmer woman championed by American advertising and dietary standards in the 1980s.

The 1793 half cents and cents introduced the allegorical themes used on U.S. coins: The half cent depicts a bust of Liberty with her hair flowing free. A Liberty Cap on a pole, a familiar symbol of Liberty in the American and French revolutions of the latter 18th century, rests on her right shoulder, giving the design its name: the Liberty Cap. On the first cents of 1793, another Flowing Hair Liberty appears. Contemporary reports claim Liberty looks frightened on the cent. The designs are somewhat crude by modern standards. However, the Liberty busts were cut directly into steel by hand. Mint technicians had no access to the modern equipment and techniques available to their counterparts today.

Since the Mint Act of 1792 required only the denomination to appear on the reverses of the copper coins, the Mint engravers had a free rein. The first half cents have a wreath on the reverse, a device used as late as 1958 on the reverse of the Lincoln cent in the form of two ears of wheat. The reverse device on the first cents lasted only months. A 15-link chain meant to represent the unity of the 15 states appears on the first 1793 cents. The chain was believed by the public to be a symbol of enslavement perceived to represent "a bad omen for Liberty." Changes in the design of both sides of the cent came rapidly. The Chain reverse was replaced by a wreath, then the obverse design of the "frightened Liberty" was replaced with a Liberty Cap design similar to that on the half cent. Thus, three distinct cents were struck with the 1793 date: the Flowing Hair Liberty, Chain cent; the Flowing Hair, Wreath cent; and the Liberty Cap, Wreath cent.

Additional design changes were instituted for the cent in 1796, when a Draped Bust design was introduced and used through 1807. Liberty appears without a cap, her hair falling over bare shoulders. Loose drapery covers Liberty's bust. Another Liberty Head design called the Classic Head design was used on the cent from 1808-14. It differs considerably from the earlier allegorical motifs, with Liberty wearing a ribbon inscribed with LIBERTY around her hair.

The Coronet design was introduced in 1816 on the large cent. This design would prove one of the more versatile of the 19th century. A variation of the Coronet design would appear on both copper coins until 1857, and on most of gold denominations from the 1830s to the first decade of the 20th century. The design is similar on all of the coins, depicting Liberty wearing a coronet inscribed with the word LIBERTY.

Designs for the half cent were generally similar to the cent's designs, although the timetable for introduction was often different. The half cent used a Liberty Cap design until 1797, and from 1800-08 a Draped Bust design was used. The Classic Head design was used on the half cent from 1809-36 and the Coronet design was introduced in 1840.

Silver coins

The silver coins of the 18th century feature designs similar to those on the copper coins. The silver coins used a Flowing Hair design in 1794-95, and in 1795-96 a Draped Bust design was introduced on all silver coins. The Capped Bust design was used first for the half dollar in 1807, with the dime following in 1809, the quarter dollar in 1815 and the half dime in 1829. The eagles appearing on the reverse of the silver coins appeared in several forms, first in a Small Eagle design that some critics likened to a pigeon, then a Heraldic Eagle which was used on the dollar beginning in 1798, the half dollar in 1801 and the quarter dollar in 1804.

Allegorical Liberty figures with similar themes but somewhat different details were used on the early gold coins. A Capped Bust, Heraldic Eagle design was used from 1796-1807 for the quarter eagle, then replaced in 1808 with the one-year-only Capped Bust type. The Capped Head quarter eagle was struck between 1821-34. On the half eagle, the Capped Bust design was used from 1796-1807; the Small Eagle reverse was used from 1796-98, and a Heraldic Eagle design was used from 1795-1807, concurrently with the Small Eagle at first. The Capped Draped Bust was used on the half eagle from 1807-12, and the Capped Head, from 1813-29. The Classic Head design was used briefly, from 1834-38. For the $10 eagle, the Capped Bust design was used from 1795 to 1804, when the denomination ceased coinage. On the reverse of the $10 coin, the Small Eagle was used from 1795-97, and the Heraldic Eagle design was used from 1797 to 1804.

Major events

Several things took place in the mid-1830s that were to affect coinage designs for decades. Among them was the Act of Jan. 18, 1837, which eliminated the need for an eagle on the reverses of the half dime and dime. The other event was the resumption of coinage of the silver dollar in 1836, and the adoption of a new design that eventually would appear on six different denominations, on some of them for more than half a century.

Production of the silver dollar resumed in 1836 with the Gobrecht dollar. The obverse depicts a Seated Liberty figure sitting on a rock, her body wrapped in robes. The reverse depicts a Flying Eagle design, first of four coins which would use a similar theme.

With the creation of the Seated Liberty design, a new age of uniformity ensued on U.S. coins. The Seated Liberty obverse design was introduced on the half dime and dime in 1837, the quarter dollar in 1838 and the half dollar in 1839. Wreaths were placed on the half dime and dime in 1837; eagles appeared on the new quarter dollar and half dollar; and the dollar received a new eagle design in 1840, with the Flying Eagle replaced by an eagle similar to those on the quarter and half dollar.

Gold coins, too, entered the uniform age of coin designs when the Coronet (sometimes called Liberty Head on gold coins) design was introduced in 1838 for the eagle, 1839 for the half eagle and 1840 for the quarter eagle. When the gold dollar and double eagle were introduced in 1849, the Coronet design was used for both. Like the silver coins, the gold coins would not break out of uniformity until the early 20th century, except for the dollar.

New theme

A new theme was introduced in 1854 on the gold dollar, replacing the Coronet figure. An Indian Head portrait by James B. Longacre was introduced, the first in a series of medallic tributes to the first native Americans that would last until shortly before the beginning of World War II. Ironically, the Indian was being used as a symbol of Liberty even as the American movement to push the Indians into increasingly smaller portions of the West grew. However, the gold dollar portrait was not a true Indian; Longacre simply placed an Indian headdress on the same

Liberty figure he would use in many different versions. A slightly larger Indian Head was used beginning in 1856 on the gold dollar. The gold $3 coin depicts an Indian Head portrait, and the reverse depicts not an eagle but a wreath.

When the large cent was abandoned in 1857 for a smaller cent (see section titled "specifications"), a Flying Eagle design was placed on the obverse (the 1856 Flying Eagle cents are patterns, struck before Congress authorized a change in composition). This was the first non-human portrayal of Liberty, and the only time an eagle would appear on the cent. The obverse design was changed to an Indian Head design in 1859. Wreaths of various types appear on the two smaller cents.

Several non-allegorical designs began to appear on U.S. coins in the 1850s. On the silver 3-cent piece, a six-point star appears as the central obverse design; the reverse depicts the Roman numeral III inside what resembles a large letter "C." Shields appear on the obverses of the 2-cent piece and the first copper-nickel 5-cent piece. A Liberty Head design replaced the Shield design on the 5-cent coin in 1883. The silver dollar, abandoned in 1873 and reinstated in 1878, depicts a Liberty Head and an eagle (called the Morgan dollar).

The Seated Liberty coinage design was dusted off and placed on the short-lived 20-cent coin of 1875-78. However, the Seated Liberty design, used on most of the silver coins since 1836, was finally abandoned at the end of 1891. By this time, it was in use only on the dime, quarter dollar and half dollar. It was replaced in 1892 with a Liberty Head design by Chief Mint Sculptor-Engraver Charles Barber, who also created a Heraldic Eagle for use on the reverse of the quarter dollar and half dollar; the reverse wreath appearing on the Seated Liberty dime was maintained on the reverse of the "Barber" dime. The Barber designs remained in use through mid-1916.

The first two decades of the 20th century resulted in two major design trends for U.S. coins. One, beginning in 1907, resulted in what can be called the "Golden Age of U.S. Coin Designs." The other, beginning in 1909, was the first step away from the allegorical depictions that had characterized U.S. coins since 1793 in favor of medallic tributes to prominent political figures from American history.

The "golden age" began with the election of Theodore Roosevelt as president of the United States. Roosevelt, best-known among non-numismatists as a vibrant president who built the Panama Canal and advocated the carrying of a "big stick," did more to improve the aesthetics of U.S. coins than any other politician since Washington. He invited Augustus Saint-Gaudens, the premier U.S. sculptor of the day, to create coin designs Roosevelt hoped would relive the beauty of ancient Greece. Saint-Gaudens submitted designs for the cent, $10 eagle and $20 double eagle. Roosevelt choose from the submissions the designs for the two gold coins: The $10 coin depicts an allegorical Liberty Head wearing an Indian headdress on the obverse, and a standing eagle on the reverse; the double eagle depicts a Standing Liberty facing the viewer on the obverse, and a Flying Eagle design for the reverse.

The Mint engraving staff, led by Barber, was not happy with the hiring of outside talent, even though Saint-Gaudens' double eagle design is considered by many collectors to be the finest ever portrayed on a U.S. coin. The first $20 coins struck in 1907 feature high relief features, an artistic creation that created problems in production. The coins required too many strikings of the press for efficient production, so the relief was lowered later in 1907. Saint-Gaudens, who had been in ill-health, was dead by this time and unable to protest the changes in the design.

The "golden age" continued in 1908, with new designs for the $2.50 quarter eagle and $5 eagle: an American Indian on the obverse, and a Standing Eagle on the reverse. These were the first true Indians to appear on U.S. coins. What made the designs so unusual, however, was their placement on the coin. The designs were created in the oxymoronic "incused relief." Often incorrectly referred to as incused, the designs are raised, but sunken into the fields so the highest points are level with the flat fields. This design feature was criticized, with some suggesting that the "incused" portions would permit enough germs to accumulate to prove a health hazard. The experiment also did not please Barber.

In 1913, the designs for the 5-cent coin were changed. An American Indian was placed on the obverse, and an American bison was placed on the reverse. The coin, known variously as the Indian Head, Bison or Buffalo 5-cent coin, is considered the most American of U.S. coin designs because of the two themes portrayed on the coin. The Indian design appearing on the obverse is probably the finest to be placed on a U.S. coin. Three Indians, Iron Tail, Two Moons and Chief John Tree, posed for designer James Fraser, who created a composite portrait.

More design changes were made in 1916, when the Barber designs for the dime, quarter dollar and half dollar were replaced in mid-year (although no 1916 Barber half dollars were struck). The dime features a Winged Liberty Head on the obverse; the design is often called the "Mercury" dime, but Mercury was a Roman male god with wings on his ankles, while the figure on the dime is female and wears a winged cap. The reverse depicts a fasces.

The quarter dollar design introduced in 1916 proved controversial. The Standing Liberty figure had an exposed right breast, an anatomical feature which had also appeared on the allegorical figure of Electricity on the Series 1896 $5 silver certificate until it was replaced in 1899 with a less prurient American Indian vignette. Some citizens of the period deemed the design too revealing on the quarter dollar as well, so in 1917 the offending breast was covered with a coat of mail (both varieties of 1917 design exist). The reverse depicts a Flying Eagle; its position was modified slightly in 1917

when Liberty was given additional clothing. Amusingly, correspondence between Mint officials and designer A.A. Weinman refer to changes in the placement of the eagle but apparently do not mention the unclad Liberty. The coat of mail was added very quietly.

The Walking Liberty half dollar was also introduced in 1916. The obverse depicts a Walking Liberty figure, while the reverse depicts one of the most attractive eagles placed on a regular issue of U.S. coins.

In 1921, the Peace dollar replaced the Morgan, which had been briefly resurrected in 1921 (coinage ceased in 1904). The Peace dollar commemorates the peace which followed the end of World War I. It ceased coinage at the end of 1935 when the dollar denomination was abandoned.

The second coinage trend to begin in the early 20th century occurred in 1909 when Abraham Lincoln replaced the Indian Head on the cent. For the first time, a historical, non-allegorical figure was used on a circulating coin of the United States. Lincoln's 100th birthday was celebrated in 1909. His 150th birthday in 1959 resulted in the Lincoln Memorial replacing the two ears of wheat found on the Lincoln cents of 1909-58.

The trend continued in 1932, when the Standing Liberty quarter dollar was replaced with the Washington design on the bicentennial of Washington's birth. Thomas Jefferson replaced the American Indian in 1938 (the Treasury Department held a design contest), and Franklin Roosevelt was placed on the dime in 1946, a year after his death. Benjamin Franklin was placed on the half dollar in 1948, replacing the Walking Liberty designs. He was replaced in turn in 1964 by John F. Kennedy in a numismatic tribute to the assassinated president.

In 1971, a copper-nickel dollar coin was introduced bearing President Dwight D. Eisenhower's portrait on the obverse and allegorical figure of an eagle landing on Earth's moon, commemorating the Apollo moon landings.

The Bicentennial of the Declaration of Independence in 1976 brought changes to the reverses of the quarter dollar, half dollar and dollar. The reverse of the 1976 quarter dollar depicts a Revolutionary War drummer; the half dollar depicts Independence Hall in Philadelphia; and the dollar depicts the Liberty Bell superimposed over the moon. The designs reverted to their original versions in 1977.

In 1979, a new copper-nickel dollar sized between the quarter dollar and half dollar was introduced, replacing the Eisenhower dollar. The new design depicts feminist Susan B. Anthony and a reduced version of the moon-landing design. Anthony was the first non-allegorical U.S. woman to appear on a circulating coin. The choice was not a popular one, since many collectors had hoped a reincarnation of the Flowing Hair Liberty, designed by Chief Sculptor-Engraver Frank Gasparro especially for the smaller dollar, would appear. Letters from collectors focused on the supposed unattractiveness of Anthony, although those same writers apparently had never criticized the physical attributes of Lincoln (who, after all, was referred to as an ape in the press of his time before his assassination) and Washington. Ironically, a descendant of Anthony was critical of an early version of Gasparro's Anthony portrait as too "pretty" and not at all indicative of the woman's strong character; Gasparro modified the design before it was placed on the coin. However, the coin did not circulate well, mainly because of its similarity in size to the quarter dollar (many found the two denominations too close to each other in diameter). Poor public usage of the smaller dollar resulted in none being struck after 1981 (the 1979-80 coins were struck for circulation, and the 1981 coins were struck for collectors only).

The reintroduction of commemorative coins and the American Eagle bullion coins have brought renewed interest in coinage designs, and renewed controversy. Collectors and others have been critical of some of the designs on the commemorative coins (the two torchbearers on an early version of the 1984 Olympic $10 eagle were lampooned as "Dick and Jane running" by congressional members). Others, most notably the obverse of the 1986-W Statue of Liberty half eagle, designed by Chief Sculptor-Engraver Elizabeth Jones, have been praised. Jones, incidentally, helped to end the male domination of U.S. coinage designs as the first woman to serve as Chief Sculptor-Engraver of the U.S. Mint.

The reintroduction of two older designs on the American Eagle coins has proven controversial. The obverse of the silver dollar depicts the Walking Liberty half dollar obverse, enlarged for placement on the larger coin. A new Heraldic Eagle appears on the reverse.

The designs chosen for the gold bullion coins were even more controversial. Saint-Gaudens' obverse Liberty for the double eagle was chosen, but not until Treasury Secretary James A. Baker III ordered Liberty on a diet. The Mint engraver assigned to the project was ordered to reduce Liberty's apparent weight, by giving her slimmer arms and legs. Members of the Commission of Fine Arts decried the changes to what is considered a classic design. Members were also critical of the reverse, a Family of Eagles design by Dallas sculptor Miley Busiek. The legislation authorizing the gold coins mandated the Busiek design. Busiek had been an untiring champion of her design, which shows two adult eagles and two younger birds. She lobbied in Congress and the Treasury Department for months in a politically successful attempt to have her design placed on the bullion coins. She says the design reflects the values of the American family.

Currently, hobbyists are calling for new designs on circulating coins, which the Treasury Secretary may change without congressional approval after they have been in use 25 years.

The 25-year limitation was placed on the coinage system in the Act of Sept. 26, 1890. Until then, there were no limitations concerning the life of a coin design. This act is now a part of Title 31 of the U.S.

Code.

The Lincoln cent has been in use since 1909 (the reverse, since 1959). The Jefferson 5-cent coin has been around since 1938, and the Roosevelt dime, since 1946. The Kennedy half dollar was introduced in 1964. Mint officials, however, have publicly stated that to change coinage designs would cause hoarding of the old designs, thus generating a coinage shortage.

Specifications

The physical specifications of U.S. coins — metallic content, weights, diameters — have been ever changing. Changes were in response to increases and decreases in the prices of the metals contained in them; public unpopularity of large-diameter coins; and other factors.

Even before the first copper coins were struck in 1793, their weights were reduced under the Act of May 8, 1792. The modified weights are 6.74 grams for the half cent, and 13.48 grams for the cent (weights are given in grams for modern convenience; the early coinage laws specified the weights in grains). Weights for both copper coins were reduced in 1795, to 5.44 grams for the half cent, and to 10.89 grams for the cent.

The 1794-95 silver coinage was struck in a composition of 90 percent silver and 10 percent copper. When additional silver denominations were added in 1796, the composition for all five coins was changed to 892.427 silver and 107.572 copper, until additional change came in 1836-37.

Composition of the first gold coins is 916.667 gold and 83.333 copper and silver.

The only changes made to U.S. coins between the first decade of the 19th century and 1834 were to the designs. Then, on June 28, 1834, the weight of gold coins was reduced and the alloy changed for two years to 899.225 percent gold and 100.775 copper and silver. In 1836, the gold alloy was changed again, to 90 percent gold and 10 percent copper and silver, an alloy unchanged until 1873. Changes were made to silver coins in 1836

as well, when the silver content was changed to 90 percent silver and 10 percent copper, an alloy not abandoned until the mid-1960s.

The rising price of silver resulted in a reduction in weights for the silver coins during 1853 (except for the silver dollar). Arrows were added to both sides of the dates on the reduced weight half dimes, dimes, quarter dollars and dollars, a design feature used for 1853-54. The arrows were removed in 1855 although the weights of the silver coins remained the same.

Major changes to the country's copper coinage were made in 1857. The half cent was eliminated and the large copper cent was replaced during the year with a smaller cent composed of 88 percent copper and 12 percent nickel (Act of Feb. 21, 1857). Diameter of the old cent is approximately 29 millimeters; the new cent has a diameter of 19mm.

The weights of the Seated Liberty silver coinage increased in 1873, and once again arrows were placed at either side of the date for two years to signify the increased weight. At the same time, silver was dropped from the gold-coin alloy; the coins were now composed of 90 percent gold and 10 percent copper.

The next major compositional changes in U.S. coins were made during World War II. At the beginning of the United States' entry into World War II, several metals used in coinage became in critical supply. The first to change was the 5-cent coin, which had nickel removed in mid-1942 after some copper-nickel specimens were struck. The new composition was 56 percent copper, 35 percent silver and 9 percent manganese. The old alloy was resumed in 1946.

Also during the war, the composition of the cent changed. First, tin was removed late in 1942. Then, in 1943, a zinc-plated steel cent was introduced to conserve copper. The brass alloy of 95 percent copper and 5 percent zinc was resumed in 1944 through 1946. The 95 percent copper, 5 percent tin and zinc composition resumed in 1947 and continued until late 1962. Once again, tin was removed from the bronze alloy, turning the alloy into the same brass composition used in 1944-46.

The 175-year-old history of United States coinage was changed with the stroke of a pen on July 23, 1965. On that day President Lyndon Johnson signed into law the Coinage Act of 1965, the most sweeping changes to the U.S. coinage system since the Mint Act of 1873. The 1965 act eliminated silver in dimes and quarter dollars and reduced the silver content of the half dollars to 40 percent.

Special congressional hearings relative to the nationwide coin shortage were first held in 1964. Coin shortages had continually worsened in the decade prior to 1965 as a result of the population growth, expanding vending machine businesses, popularity of Kennedy half dollars and the worldwide silver shortage.

In the face of the worldwide shortage of silver, it was essential that dependence on silver for the production of coins be reduced. Otherwise the country would be faced with a chronic coin shortage.

As a result of studies conducted by both the Treasury and the Battelle Memorial Institute, a clad metal composed of three layers of metal bonded together was selected for the new coinage.

The dimes and quarter dollars were to be composed of two layers of 75 percent copper and 25 percent nickel bonded to a core of pure copper. The half dollars were to be composed of two layers of 80 percent silver and 20 percent copper bonded to a core of approximately 20 percent silver and 80 percent copper, such that the entire coin is composed of 40 percent silver.

The combination of copper-nickel and copper gave the new coins the required electrical conductivity, a necessary property for vending machines. The copper-nickel surfaces also continued the traditional silvery color of the coins. In addition, a clad metal would be much harder to counterfeit.

The legal weights of the coins were affected by the change in alloy. The new clad dime weight is 2.27 grams, the quarter dollar weighs 5.67 grams and the half dollar weighs 11.5 grams. With the elimination of silver from half dollars in 1971 and the introduction of a copper-nickel clad version, the weight was changed to 11.34 grams. The cladding of all coins constitutes approximately 30 percent of the coin by weight.

At first all of the strip was produced at the Olin Brass Division of Olin Mathison Chemical Corp. in East Alton, Ill. From there it was shipped to the U.S. Mints at Philadelphia and Denver and to the San Francisco Assay Office. As time had passed and the Mints built new facilities, more and more of the cladding was produced at the Mints. However, the Mint now buys all strip from outside manufacturers. Mint officials claim it is more efficient and less expensive to do so. In addition, the Mint buys some of its planchets from private contractors, including all of the copper-plated zinc cent planchets and all of the precious metals planchets for special programs like commemorative coins and the American Eagle bullion coins.

In an effort to maximize production of coinage, 1964-dated silver coins were struck into 1965. The Coinage Act of 1965 also made it mandatory that clad coins be dated not earlier than 1965. Therefore, all clad coins actually made in 1965 bear that date. The first clad dimes were struck in late December 1965 and were released March 8, 1966. The first clad quarter dollars were struck Aug. 23, 1965, and released Nov. 1, 1965. The first clad half dollars were released March 8, 1966, but were struck starting Dec. 30, 1965.

The 1965 date was retained until July 31, 1966, when the date was changed to 1966. Normal dating was resumed on Jan. 1, 1967.

The last great compositional change to U.S. circulating coinage came in mid-1982, when the brass cent was replaced with a cent of nearly pure zinc, plated with a thin layer of pure copper to retain its copper appearance. Rising copper prices were the cause. The switchover to the copper-plated zinc cent was made with few non-numismatists noting the difference.

When the American Eagle bullion coins were introduced in 1986, some numismatists were critical of the .9167 gold content, a composition they deemed "non-traditional"; there was some preference for a .900 gold content. However, the chosen composition is virtually identical to the alloy first used for U.S. gold coins, from 1795 to 1834. A new silver composition was introduced with the production of the .999 fine silver American Eagle dollar.

Pioneer gold coins

The pioneer gold issues in the United States are an interesting series of private enterprise and pioneer necessity. Most were produced privately and legally, since the Constitution prohibited the states but not individuals from striking gold coins. However, "pioneer" is a better adjective to describe the gold coins than "private" and "territorial." Some of the coins in California were struck by the U.S. Assayer, and thus are of federal issue and are not true private issues; some of the gold coins were struck in states, not U.S. territories, thus "territorial" is incorrect for many of the issues. "Pioneer" describes the spirit in which the coins were struck: as necessity issues, brought about by the inability of the federal government to provide sufficient quantities of coinage in areas of the country newly opened to settlement.

The pioneer gold coins can best be classified by the region in which they were made, as the years in which they were struck often overlap. These regions are the southern Appalachians, the western Rockies (including Utah, which was much larger then) and Colorado. The scarcity of these coins is primarily due to their often having an intrinsic value less than the face value. The coins were often unaccepted and eventually melted.

The first significant gold mines in the United States were in the mountainous backwoods of North Carolina and Georgia. Transporting the gold overland to the Philadelphia Mint was slow and dangerous, whereas shipping it around Cape Hatteras was fast but expensive and not without risk. As the miners wished to have the convenience of coined gold without the expense of shipping the raw gold to the Philadelphia Mint, two private mints were established in 1830 and 1831.

The first mint was opened by Templeton Reid at Gainesville, Ga. Probably because he had no competition he charged a high fee for processing the bullion into coins. A large quantity of gold was handled during this first and only year, but most of it was eventually melted down as were regular U.S. gold coins, due to the prevailing price ratio of gold to silver. He was forced out of business amid charges that he had debased the coins.

The following year a second mint was opened by the Bechtler family, at Rutherfordton in southwestern North Carolina. For years the company produced coins equal in value to regular U.S. gold, although little of it circulated as the bullion value of the gold was greater than the face value of the coins.

This situation improved after 1834 (ultimately the coinage was accepted), and the new weight coins were temporarily marked with the date Aug. 1, 1834. The founder of the firm died in 1842, and his son and nephew carried on until 1852, but by then their standards of quality had declined and they could no longer compete with the two federal branch Mints in Georgia and North Carolina.

While it was difficult to go from northern Georgia to Philadelphia in 1849, it was virtually impossible to get there from California. The quickest route from San Francisco to Philadelphia or New Orleans was by ship to Mexico or Central America and then overland to a second ship for the voyage north. Although the situation clearly called for a branch Mint in California, one was not officially opened until 1854. In the meantime more than a dozen companies were engaged at various times in the production of gold

coins.

A relic of this shipping route is the S.S. Central America, discovered off the South Carolina coast in 1989. Early in the salvage of the gold treasure carried by the steamship, several discovery pieces of pioneer gold were discovered. As the full cargo is recovered and cataloged, many chapters of this colorful history of American numismatics will have to be rewritten.

The most popular issues were the $5 and $10 denominations, as these were needed for use in daily commerce. Later, $20 coins and $50 slugs were made for use in large business dealings, this being an era when the value of a check was dependent not only upon the solvency of the issuer but of the bank as well.

In addition to the questionable coins from the do-it-yourself mints, there were also in circulation legal tender coins struck by either the U.S. Assayer or the U.S. Assay Office. The first of these were octagonal $50 coins (officially called ingots) struck by the firm of Moffat & Co. but bearing both the legend UNITED STATES OF AMERICA and the name and title of AUGUSTUS HUMBERT, UNITED STATES ASSAYER OF GOLD, CALIFORNIA, 1851 or 1852. Eagles and double eagles were produced in 1852 before the Moffat & Co. firm dissolved.

The government contract was taken over by a new private firm which was called the United States Assay Office of Gold. This semi-official Mint produced eagles, double eagles and $50 "ingots" until December 1853, at which time its facilities were closed for reorganization as the official San Francisco Mint. Because the new official Mint could not at first produce coins as fast as the old semi-official one, several private companies opened to compete with the new federal Mint through 1854 and 1855.

In addition to the shortage of large denomination coins there was always a shortage of small change for use in retail stores. Several small, anonymous

companies therefore produced gold dollars, half dollars, and even quarter dollars using a number of different designs. These fractional coins were struck from 1852 to 1882; federal law in 1864 finally forbid private coinage of any sort. It has been suggested that the later strikes were never intended for circulation but were merely souvenirs of California.

A number of eagles and half eagles were struck in Oregon in 1849, despite the objections of the new territorial governor. Presumably his orders eventually prevailed, as the issue was not repeated.

The Mormon government issued $2.50, $5, $10 and $20 pieces in 1849, as well as half eagles in 1850 and 1860. This last issue was made of Colorado gold from the Pikes Peak area. Most of the early issues of Mormon gold did not receive widespread acceptance, as they were underweight by as much as 15 percent.

The last period of "legal" pioneer gold coins (i.e., issued before 1864), was the Pikes Peak gold rush of 1860-61. Only three major firms produced coins in these two years, although several unverified patterns are known. It is interesting to note that in 1862 the largest of these companies, Clark, Gruber and Co., sold its equipment to the federal government, which intended to open a branch Mint in Denver at this time. The specie hoarding of the Civil War presumably doomed this project, and a Denver Mint did not open until 1906.

Other pioneer gold issues are known for Alaska and the northwestern states, but these were primarily made as souvenirs and did not circulate as coinage.

Just like regular coinage, pioneer gold coins are subject to Gresham's Law. Those which are of full weight and value or better will be hoarded and probably melted, while those that are undervalued are spent as soon as possible so as to avoid getting stuck with the coin.

U.S.-Philippine coinage

By David T. Alexander

David T. Alexander is a frequent contributor to *Coin World*. He is Project Editor of the *Coin World Comprehensive Catalog & Encyclopedia of United States Coins,* and wrote a history of coinage of the Philippines for *World Coins.*

American collectors are often surprised to learn of a series of bronze, copper-nickel and silver coins struck between 1903 and 1945, unknown to them and boldly inscribed UNITED STATES OF AMERICA, bearing the American eagle and shield.

A clue to many collectors' ignorance of this interesting series is the name FILIPINAS also inscribed on the coins, the Spanish name of the vast archipelago of the Philippines, governed by the U.S. from the late 1890s until 1946.

The Philippines became American after Admiral George Dewey's spectacular victory over the enemy fleet at Manila Bay during the Spanish American War. The islands were the United States' largest "colonial" possession and the only one for which the U.S. issued a distinctive coinage.

Unlike Puerto Rico, annexed directly by the U.S., or Cuba, which became an independent republic in 1902, the Philippines formed a unique territory governed by a civil administration appointed from Washington. Uncertain what to do with this vast domain, forced to fight a bloody war to retain it against the army of General Emilio Aquinaldo, the United States finally decided to rule the islands while preparing them for eventual independence.

Civil government was established under Governor General William Howard Taft in 1903 and the Philippine Commission established a new coinage for the islands. In circulation as the American era opened were silver and gold coins of the Spanish rulers.

More plentiful were the popular Mexican silver 8 reales and pesos, preferred trade coins of China and the Far East. Many Filipinos could also recall the countermarked Mexican and Latin American silver coins which circulated under Spanish rules and crude copper coins struck early in the 19th century.

Sent to the islands in 1901 to solve the coinage question was banking expert Charles Arthur Conant. He decided that simply adopting regular American coins would be impractical. U.S. silver coins did not relate to the popular Mexican pesos and their denominations would not fit the low standard of living of many Filipinos.

Monetary system

Created instead was a gold-based Philippine peso divided into 100 centavos. Two of the new pesos would equal one U.S. dollar. No gold coins were struck, but .900 fine silver coins would include a peso weighing 416 grains or 26.9 grams; a 50 centavos weighing 208 grains (13.47 grams); 20 centavos, 83.1 grains (5.26 grams); and 10 centavos, 41.15 grains (2.66 grams). Minor coins would be the copper-nickel 5 centavos, bronze centavo and half centavo.

Designs of the new coins had to express the sovereignty of the U.S. while asserting a distinctive Philippine character. Achieving this synthesis were the designs by the greatest Philippine sculptor-medalist, Melicio Figueroa. A native of Iloilo who had studied art on a royal scholarship in Spain, Figueroa was also a patriot who signed the first Philippine (Malosos) Republic's constitution.

Figueroa's minor coins feature a seated worker at an anvil; silver coins feature a graceful standing lady striking the anvil with a hammer, modeled by the artist's daughter Blanca. In the background is the smoking cone of the Mayon volcano, a unique Philippine touch for the new coins. Denominations appear in English above the figures, the Spanish form of the islands' name FILIPINAS below.

All reverses feature America's stars and stripes shield and spread-winged eagle with legend UNITED STATES OF AMERICA. The date appears below flanked by two dots; coins bearing a Mint mark bear it below the left dot. These designs appeared on the first coins struck in 1903 and continued until the Commonwealth of the Philippines was established in 1935.

Alas for Conant's well-laid plans, world silver values rose just as the new Philippine coins came into circulation. The result was a vast outflow of Mexican silver from the islands. During 1905 the beautiful new Philippine silver coins were worth 13 percent more as silver bullion than their face values. They vanished wholesale despite punitive laws forbidding their export and melting.

Only a drastic reduction of silver content could save the day and in 1907 the U.S. released a second series of silver coins headed by a reduced-size peso struck in .800 silver, weighing 308.64 grains (19.99 grams). The three smaller denominations were reduced to .750 fine, the 50 centavos weighing 154.32 grains (9.99 grams); the 20 centavos 61.72 grains (3.99 grams). This standard lasted until the last U.S.-Philippine coins were struck after World War II.

The Philadelphia Mint struck the bronze centavo and half centavo from 1903 to 1908. After the 500-piece all-Proof coinage of half centavos of 1906 and 1908 this unpopular coin was abolished. From 1908 to 1920 the bronze centavo was struck only at San Francisco bearing the "S" Mint mark.

Philadelphia struck the first large-diameter copper-nickel 5 centavos from 1903 to 1908; the 1916-1919 coins were made in San Francisco. No 1907-dated base metal coins were struck. A major rarity is the 1919-S 5 centavos struck with the reverse die of the silver 20 centavos. Unlike the normal reverse, the mule's

shield fills more of the field and the eagle's wings nearly reach the denticles around its edge.

Silver coins included the 10 centavos of 1903-1908, made at Philadelphia, with San Francisco coins appearing in 1903, 1907, 1908-1019 with the "S" Mint mark. The 20 centavos was also struck at Philadelphia 1903-1908; San Francisco pieces of the dates 1903, 1905 and 1908-1919 followed. The 50 centavos of 1903-1908 again appeared from Philadelphia; San Francisco dates are somewhat scattered: 1903, 1904, 1905, 1907, 1908-1909, 1917-1919.

Silver pesos of 1903-1908 were struck at Philadelphia; San Francisco large-sized pesos bear the dates 1903-1906. Only two Philadelphia small-sized pesos are know dated 1907, and an all-Proof issue of 500 pieces was struck dated 1908.

The peso coinage of 1907 through 1911 and 1921 was struck at San Francisco. Most silver pesos ended up in bank vaults as backing for silver certificates, paper money redeemable in silver similar to that issued in the United States.

Philadelphia struck 2,558 Proof sets of the new Philippine coins dated 1903; 1,355 sets in 1904; only 471 in 1905 and 500 sets in 1906 and 1908. These sets sold poorly at the time and few pristine examples survive today. All are still undervalued in terms of their real scarcity.

Manilla Mint

The American administrators realized that a Mint in the islands would free the Philippines from trans-Pacific shipment of coins. U.S. Mint engineer Clifford Hewitt was sent to Manila and supervised creation of a modern Mint in the old Intendencia Building, inaugurated in July 1920.

Commemorating the opening of the Mint were crown-sized medals portraying President Woodrow Wilson and presenting a modified Assay medal reverse of Columbia instructing a child in modern coining. Five were struck in gold, but only one survives, a satin Proof believed unique. Silver and bronze examples are eagerly collected as So-called Dollars.

The new Manilla Mint went into production with centavo coins of 1920-22, and 1925 through 1936. The 5 centavos was struck at the new Mint from 1920-21, 1925-28. Small-sized 5 centavos were dated 1930-32, 1934-35. The 10 centavos from Manila bore the dates 1920-21, 1929 and 1934.

Twenty-centavo pieces were only struck at Manila in 1929, and only in 1920 did the "M" Mint mark appear on the 50 centavos. Another rare mule exists, combining the Standing Lady of the 20 centavos with a 1928/7 overdate 5 centavos reverse. Here the shield is far smaller than normal. This mule is about five times more common than the very rare 1918-S 5 centavos/20 centavos.

The Commonwealth of the Philippines was established in 1935 in transition to full independence, promised for 1946. The new Commonwealth emblem placed a smaller American eagle atop a tall shield bearing three stars representing the main island groups and the castle and sword-bearing sea lion from the coat of arms of Manila.

Sizes and alloys continued unchanged, the legend UNITED STATES OF AMERICA appeared, and the obverses remained the same as those of earlier issues. All bore the "M" Mint mark until 1941. Centavo coins were struck in 1937 through 1941; 5, 10 and 20 centavos appeared only in 1937-38 and 1941.

The Commonwealth's birth was commemorated by three silver coins designed by Professor Ambrosio Morales of the National University. Silver pesos of two obverse types were struck bearing the bust of Commonwealth President Manuel Quezon y Molina. His portrait was conjoined with the bust of U.S. President Franklin D. Roosevelt on one type, that of Governor General, no High Commissioner Frank Murphy on the other.

Detroit native Murphy faced Quezon on the single type of commemorative 50 centavos. Only 10,000 were struck of each peso and 20,000 of the 50 centavos. Planned to lure profits from the commemorative coin craze then raging in America, these three Philippine commemoratives sold dismally at time of issue, and are very scarce today.

World War II crashed into the Philippines Dec. 8, 1941, as Japanese air attacks on island targets followed their earlier assault on Pearl Harbor. Dangerously unprepared, the Philippines were quickly overwhelmed by invading Japanese forces, despite the heroic resistance of Fil-American forces on the strategic Bataan peninsula and island of Corregidor.

General Douglas MacArthur escaped with President Quezon, but the islands had to endure a savage occupation until MacArthur's return to Leyte in October 1944 and the piecemeal reconquest of the archipelago. The country was devastated, and Manila ranked just behind Warsaw as the most thoroughly destroyed capital city of the war.

Between December 1941 and late 1944, two authorities demanded Filipino loyalty: the exiled Commonwealth of President Quezon; and the agencies set up under the Japanese occupation — the Philippine Executive Commission and post-1943 Republic of the Philippines led by Jose Paciano Laurel.

Laurel's short-lived republic issued three collectible medals but little else of numismatic interest. Issued in the name of the Commonwealth was a flood of Philippine guerrilla currency for the many units that continued battling the Japanese after the surrender of Corregidor.

A major casualty of war was Philippine coinage, much of it confiscated and melted by the Japanese. Plunged in deep water off Corregidor was the Commonwealth silver reserve — hundreds of thousands of pesos preserved from the Japanese, if not from salt-water corrosion.

The returning Commonwealth was led by President Sergio Osmena, since Quezon had died of tuberculosis during 1944. Osmena's task was nearly hopeless, compounded of wartime destruction, shortages of staff, money and equipment. Inflation had ruined the economy, and the president faced the potent hostility of proconsul MacArthur as well as the task of ferreting out alleged collaborators.

Under these circumstances the Mints of Philadelphia, Denver and San Francisco struck vast amounts of pre-war type Commonwealth coins. From the masses of Uncirculated pieces reposing in American coin dealers' junk boxes in the 1950s and 1960s, many of these seemed to have returned to the U.S., possibly as souvenirs with returning soldiers.

San Francisco struck about 52 million 1944-dated bronze centavos; 14 million 1944 and almost 73 million 1945 5 centavos of an alloy that substituted zinc for some of the war-precious nickel. The only regular-design Commonwealth silver 50 centavos ever struck were the 19 million "S" 1944 coins and the 18 million 1945-dated pieces of the same Mint.

Denver's contributions included the 31.5 million 1944 10 centavos of the usual .750 silver and an additional 137 million 1945 pieces. The "D" Mint mark also appeared in 28.5 million 1944 20 centavos and 82.8 million 1945 coins. Most fascinating is the apparently rare "over Mint mark" 1944-D Over S, discovered fairly recently and believed an example of wartime making-do with valuable die steel.

Shattered by war, hampered by internal disorder that would soon include the Communist Hukbalahap insurgency, the Philippines found economic reconstruction frustrated by a miserly U.S. Congress which spent more on defeated enemies than on America's own battered ward.

Independence

Nonetheless, the Philippines became an independent republic on July 4, 1946. Its subsequent political story is one of growing instability and violence, reaching its nadir in the long and phosphorescently corrupt dictatorship of Ferdinand E. Marcos.

Between 1945 and 1958 only two coins appeared: the .750 silver peso and 50 centavos designed by Laura Gardin Fraser and honoring General Douglas MacArthur as Defender and Liberator of the Philippines. Created like the 1935 Commonwealth commemoratives with an eye on U.S. collectors, these low-relief coins were an even greater disappointment on the numismatic market.

Although issued after the U.S. connection officially ended, these two coins are of major U.S. interest. All in all, the U.S. Philippine coinage should exert a strong attraction to American collectors. As a series it is reasonable short, generally low-priced but offers a real challenge for those for whom date and Mint collecting may have grown stale.

Current coins

Lincoln cent

When the Lincoln cent made its initial appearance in 1909, it marked a radical departure from accepted styling, introducing as it did for the first time a portrait coin in the regular series. A strong feeling had prevailed against the use of portraits on the coins of the country but public sentiment stemming from the 100th anniversary celebration of Abraham Lincoln's birthday proved stronger than the long-standing prejudice.

The only person invited to participate in the formulation of the new design was Victor David Brenner. President Theodore Roosevelt was so impressed with the talents of this outstanding sculptor that Brenner was singled out by the president for the commission.

The likeness of Lincoln on the obverse is an adaption of a plaque Brenner executed several years prior which had come to the attention of President Roosevelt. In addition to prescribed elements — LIBERTY and the date — the motto IN GOD WE TRUST appeared for the first time on a U.S. cent. Of interest is that the Congress passed the Act of March 3, 1865, authorizing the use of this expression on U.S. coins during Lincoln's tenure of office.

A study of three models for the reverse resulted in the approval of a very simple design bearing two ears of wheat in memorial style. Between these, in the center of the coin, are the denomination and UNITED STATES OF AMERICA, while curving around the upper border is the national motto, E PLURIBUS UNUM.

Even though no legislation was required for a new design, approval of the Treasury Secretary was necessary. Franklin MacVeagh gave his approval July 14, 1909, and not quite three weeks later, on Aug. 2, the new cent was released to the public.

The original model bore Brenner's name. Prior to issuance, however, the initials VDB were substituted on the lower reverse because Mint officials felt the name was too prominent. After the coin was released, many protested that even the initials were conspicuous and detracted from the design. Because the coin was in great demand, and because making a change in size would have required halting production, the decision was made to eliminate the initials entirely, a simple engraving process. They were restored in 1918, and are to be found in minute form on Lincoln's shoulder.

More cents are produced than any other denomination, which makes the Lincoln cent a familiar item. In its life span this little coin has weathered two world wars, one of which was to change it materially. Metals play a vital part in any war effort. At the time of World War II the cent was composed of 95 percent copper and 5 percent tin and zinc. These metals were denied the Mint for the duration of the emergency, making it necessary to seek a substitute. After much deliberation, even including consideration of plastics, zinc-plated steel was chosen as the best in a limited range of suitable materials.

Production of this wartime cent was provided for in the act approved Dec. 18, 1942, which also set as the expiration date of the authority Dec. 31, 1946. Low-grade carbon steel formed the base, to which a zinc plating .005 inch thick was deposited on each side electrolytically as a rust preventative. The same size was maintained but the weight was reduced from the standard 48 grains to 42 grains, due to the use of a lighter alloy. Operations commenced Feb. 27, 1943, and by Dec. 31 of that year the three Mints then functioning had struck an almost record-breaking number of cents, with the total reaching 1,093,838,670 pieces. The copper released was enough to meet the combined needs of two cruisers, two destroyers, 1,243 B-17 Flying Fortresses, 120 field guns and 120 howitzers; or enough for 1.25 million shells for the U.S. big field guns.

On Jan. 1, 1944, the Mints were able to adopt a modified alloy, the supply being derived from expended shell casings which when melted furnished a composition similar to the original but with only a faint trace of tin; the 6 grains dropped from the total weight were restored. The original alloy was resumed in 1947.

On Feb. 12, 1959, a revised reverse was introduced as a part of the 150th anniversary celebration of the Great Emancipator's birth. No formal competition was held. Frank Gasparro, then Assistant Sculptor-Engraver at the Mint in Philadelphia, prepared the winning entry, selected from a group of 23 models the engraving staff at the Mint had been asked to present for consideration. Again, only the Treasury Secretary's approval was necessary to make the change because the design had been in force for more than the required 25 years.

The imposing marble Lincoln Memorial in Washington, D.C., provides the central motif; the legends E PLURIBUS UNUM and UNITED STATES OF AMERICA form the rest of the design, together with the denomination. Gasparro's initials, FG, appear on the right near the shrubbery.

The composition of the smallest U.S. denomination was changed once more in 1962. Mint officials felt that deletion of the tin content would have no adverse effect upon the wearing qualities of the coin, whereas, the manufacturing advantages to be gained with the alloy stabilized at 95 percent copper and 5 percent zinc would be of much benefit. Congressional authority for this modification is contained in the Act of Sept. 5, 1962.

As the price of copper rose along with the demand for cents, a resolution was introduced Dec. 7, 1973, giving the Treasury Secretary power to change the 1-cent alloy. It appeared the new alloy would be aluminum.

The bill met opposition from the vending machine industry and the medical profession, and when the price of copper took a downhill turn, Mint Director Mary Brooks announced aluminum cents would not be necessary. There was no change in the 1-cent alloy. However, 1,579,324 1974-dated aluminum cents were struck in 1973 as experimental pieces. Most were melted, although a few specimens given to congressional members and staff disappeared. One coin is housed in the National Numismatic Collection of the Smithsonian Institution, where it was given by a congressional staff member.

In a report made public in September 1976, the Research Triangle Institute recommended that cent production be terminated by 1980, due to increasing costs of manufacturing the cent and the poor circulation of the coin. However, in making the study public the Mint said that it did not endorse the recommendations of the report, nor did it plan to adopt the recommendations at that time.

In 1982, feeling the pressure of rising copper prices again, Mint officials decided to switch to a new alloy composed of a core of 99.2 zinc and 0.8 percent copper plated by pure copper (total composition, 97.5 percent zinc, 2.5 percent copper). Both the old alloy and new alloy were produced during the year at all minting facilities striking cents. Copper and brass producers sued the federal government, claiming the Treasury Secretary did not have the authority to alter the composition despite the earlier legislation. A federal judge ruled against the producers,

however, and the cent remains composed of copper-plated zinc.

Jefferson 5 cents

The Thomas Jefferson 5-cent coin was released to the public Nov. 15, 1938, after a national contest for the obverse and reverse designs.

The coin was designed by Felix Schlag of Chicago, Ill. Born in Frankfurt, Germany, in September 1891, Schlag had won numerous prizes in nationwide competitions. He began his art studies in the Munich Academy in Germany and became an American citizen in 1929.

The obverse of the coin carries a profile of Thomas Jefferson. The reverse bears a likeness of Monticello, the president's historic home near Charlottesville, Va.

President Franklin D. Roosevelt was personally interested in the design of the Jefferson 5-cent coin. It was a result of his suggestion that the sculptor altered his original design so as to emphasize certain architectural features, particularly the two wings of the building at Monticello.

Although the law did not then require that the phrase IN GOD WE TRUST appear on the coin, it was placed there at the request of the Director of the Mint. This was the first time this motto had reappeared on the United States 5-cent coin since 1883.

In the years following the release of the coin, there was considerable interest nationally, and particularly on the part of the Michigan congressional delegation, to place on the Jefferson coin the initials of the sculptor, Felix Schlag. (Schlag died in Owosso, Mich., March 9, 1974. He was 82.)

The failure of the sculptor to "sign" his work is said to have been due to the fact that he didn't know he could. All other current issues of United States coins bear the initials of their sculptors.

Placing of the initials on the coin was an administrative decision of the Secretary of the Treasury, at the request of Assistant Secretary Wallace and Mint Director Eva Adams. The initials appear on the 5-cent pieces dated 1966 and subsequent issues.

Roosevelt dime

Almost immediately after President Franklin D. Roosevelt's death in the spring of 1945, letters came to the Treasury Department from all over the country in advocacy of his portrait being placed on a coin of the United States. The dime was most frequently suggested by reason of his having been identified with that coin through the March of Dimes drives for the Infantile Paralysis Fund.

The coinage laws prohibit the changing of a coin design more often than once every 25 years. The same laws empower the Director of the Mint with the approval of the Secretary of the Treasury, to cause new designs to be prepared and adopted at any time after the expiration of said 25-year period. The Winged Liberty Head design having been in use for more than the required time, the Treasury officials acceded to public sentiment and placed the likeness of President Roosevelt on the 10-cent piece. The new Roosevelt dime was released Jan. 30, 1946, the late president's birthday.

The obverse bears a portrait of Roosevelt, facing left and LIBERTY to his left. In the left field is IN GOD WE TRUST and in the lower right field the date.

On the reverse, in the center, is a torch with an olive branch on the left and an oak branch on the right.

Around the border is UNITED STATES OF AMERICA with ONE DIME below and across the lower field is E PLURIBUS UNUM.

The designer was John R. Sinnock, at that time the Mint's Chief Engraver. Known as one of the country's great artists in this highly specialized field, Sinnock produced outstanding medals of the presidential series, various commemorative medals and coins, and designs used on several of the medals for the nation's war heroes, including the Purple Heart.

Washington quarter

The Washington quarter dollar replaced the Standing Liberty quarter dollar in 1932. The Standing Liberty had not been issued for the 25 years required by law, thereby making an act of Congress necessary to issue the Washington quarter. Congress passed the authorization act March 4, 1931, to commemorate the 200th birthday of the first president.

John Flanagan, a noted New York sculptor, designed the coin. His work was chosen from approximately 100 models that were submitted. The Treasury Department worked in close cooperation with the Commission of Fine Arts in selecting the design. However, the commission did not agree with the Treasury Department on the final selection but as law gives the Secretary of the Treasury the right to the final selection, the work of Flanagan was chosen over the commission's objections. The first coins were issued for general circulation Aug. 1, 1932. The designer's initials, J.F., appear on the obverse.

The obverse side shows the head of Washington with LIBERTY around the top of the coin. The date is directly under the head and the motto IN GOD WE TRUST is to the lower left of the head.

The reverse side shows an eagle with wings spread standing on a shaft of arrows. Beneath the eagle are two sprays of olive leaves. Over the top are the words UNITED STATES OF AMERICA and centered directly under these words and above the head of the eagle are the words E PLURIBUS UNUM. The inscription QUARTER DOLLAR is at the bottom under the olive spray.

New plaster models were made for both sides of the quarter in 1977, altering the relief slightly so as to increase die life.

Kennedy half dollar

John Fitzgerald Kennedy was inaugurated president of the United States Jan. 20, 1961, and served not quite three full years of his term of office. His assassination Nov. 22, 1963, resulted in such an outpouring of public sentiment that President Lyndon Johnson, on Dec. 10, 1963, sent to Congress a request for legislation to authorize the Treasury Department to mint new 50-cent pieces bearing the likeness of his predecessor.

Congress gave its overwhelming approval to the president's recommendation and on Dec. 30, 1963, Public Law No. 88-256 was enacted directing the Mint to proceed with the production of the new design. The first of the John F. Kennedy half dollars for general circulation purposes were struck at the Mints in Philadelphia and Denver on Feb. 11, 1964. The half dollar was selected because this would add another presidential portrait to a coin of regular issue.

In the center of the obverse, or face of the coin, is a strong but simple bust of the late president. Above, and around the border is LIBERTY. Just below the bust is IN GOD WE TRUST, which appears on all United States coins of current issue. The date is at the bottom around the border.

The presidential coat of arms forms the motif for the reverse. It is the central part of the presidential seal, the only difference being that the words SEAL OF THE PRESIDENT OF THE UNITED STATES have been removed and in their place are inscriptions required by law to appear on all coins: the words UNITED STATES OF AMERICA, above, around the border, and the denomination, HALF DOLLAR, around the bottom border. Other requirements already incorporated in the coat of arms are the eagle, and E PLURIBUS UNUM, which appears on the ribbon above the eagle's head.

The Kennedy coin had its beginnings when official sculptors were engaged in preparing a new medal for the historic series of presidential pieces manufactured in bronze for sale to the public. Gilroy Roberts, nationally known Chief Sculptor-Engraver of the Mint, and a member of the Philadelphia staff for many years, worked on the likeness of the president, studying first many photographs to capture the character and personality of his subject. He then selected a single portrait and commenced placing his concept in a preliminary model. During the final stages, Roberts called at the White House and studied the president at work, at which time he completed the model.

After the president's death, when the decision was reached to honor him on a United States coin, the Roberts' portrait was adapted from the medal, lowered in relief and simplified for use on a smaller scale necessary for a coin. His initials G.R. appear on the truncated bust.

Frank Gasparro, himself a veteran member of the Philadelphia staff, executed the reverse of the presidential medal. The coat of arms of the president of the United States, an integral part of this design, was chosen as the companion side for the half dollar. Gasparro's initials F.G. appear at the lower right edge of the shield.

The presidential seal originated during the administration of President Rutherford B. Hayes, apparently as a rendering of the Great Seal of the United States. There was no known basis in law for the coat of arms and the seal which had been used by presidents since 1880 and which was reproduced on the presidential flag. President Truman, when he signed the Executive Order of Oct. 25, 1945, containing the official description, established for the first time a legal definition of the president's coat of arms and his seal. According to heraldic custom, the eagle on a coat of arms, unless otherwise specified in the heraldic description, is always made to face to its own right. There is no explanation for the eagle facing to its own left in the case of the president's coat of arms. To conform to heraldic custom, and since there was no authority other than usage for the former coat of arms, President Franklin Roosevelt had asked that it be redesigned. The designs reached Washington after the president's death.

In the new coat of arms, seal and flag, the eagle not only faces to its right — the direction of honor — but also toward the olive branches for peace which it holds in its right talon. Formerly, the eagle faced toward the arrows in its left talon — symbolic of war.

Initial distribution of this newly designed coin took place on March 24, 1964, in the usual manner, when 26 million were released by the Mints directly to the Federal Reserve Banks and Branches for simultaneous distribution through the commercial banking system.

The Research Triangle Institute report of 1976 recommended the elimination of the half dollar from the U.S. coinage system.

Mint officials reported in 1986 that no half dollars would be struck for circulation in 1987; the coin was only to be struck for use in Proof, Uncirculated and Souvenir Mint sets.

Eisenhower dollar

On Dec. 31, 1970, President Nixon signed into law the Bank Holding Company Act. Appended to the legislation were important amendments relating to coinage. Pertinent to this narrative is one which concerns the reissuance of the dollar denomination. Section 203 of the Act reads:

"The dollars initially minted under authority of Section 101 of the Coinage Act of 1965 shall bear the likeness of the late President of the United States Dwight David Eisenhower, and on the other side thereof a design which is emblematic of the symbolic eagle of the Apollo 11 landing on the moon."

The act further provided for the removal of all silver from the dollar denomination and its coinage in the copper-nickel clad composition. The language was qualified, however, to permit the Secretary of the Treasury to mint and issue not more than 150 million dollar pieces composed of 40 percent silver. Of these, 130 million were to be manufactured and sold in Uncirculated condition, and 20 million processed as Proof coins, with the widest possible distribution among citizens interested in acquiring a few each. Production of this denomination for general circulation is in the copper-nickel clad metal.

The coin was designed by the Mint's Chief Sculptor-Engraver, Frank Gasparro, whose initials appear on both sides of the coin. Reverse of the coin shows the bald eagle, symbolic of the [Apollo 11 spacecraft christened Eagle landing on the cratered surface of the moon, clutching an olive branch in both claws. The receding Earth appears above the eagle's head. The 13 stars circling the eagle represent the first states of the Union.

Gasparro began working on the obverse drawing for the coin in spring 1969. He settled on using a profile of the former president and general of the army because of an image Gasparro saw of the supreme commander of the allied armies in Europe as Eisenhower rode through New York City June 20, 1945.

Gasparro made a profile drawing immediately suitable to cut directly in steel and capture the facial features that had impressed him. When he was asked to design the Eisenhower dollar coin, he studied his first drawing of Eisenhower and some 30 other pictures before sketching his design for the obverse of the coin.

He began working on the reverse of the coin in October 1969.

On Nov. 1, 1971, the first Eisenhower dollars were released for circulation.

The Research Triangle Institute report of 1976 recommended a reduction in the size of the dollar coin. Several designs for a smaller coin were tested in 1976, but none was accepted at that time.

Bicentennial dollar varieties

Almost as soon as the first 1776-1976 Bicentennial Eisenhower dollars were struck, Mint officials realized that the design did not lend itself well to high-speed mass production. Minor changes were made on the obverse and major changes on the reverse to facilitate that mode of production. The changes created two varieties of dollars.

Variety 1 dollars have thick, block-style lettering with nearly closed E's and straight tails on the R's. Variety 2 dollars have thinner, more contoured lettering with more open E's and curved tails on the R's.

Two of the reverse details which, if memorized, will enable anyone to tell the variety without having both varieties for comparison are the last S in STATES and the relationship of the first U in UNUM to the first U in PLURIBUS.

On Variety 1 the tail of the last S in STATES is level with the center bar of the E. On Variety 2 the tail of the S barely reaches the top of the bottom bar of the E. On Variety 1 the first U of UNUM is almost directly below the first U of PLURIBUS while on Variety 2 it is between the L and U.

The Denver Mint Variety 1 dollars outnumber the Philadelphia coins by a ratio of approximately six to one.

Anthony dollar

President Carter signed the Susan B. Anthony Dollar Act into law Oct. 10, 1978, but not until after a long fight over the design. A smaller dollar coin, sized between the quarter dollar and the half dollar, was recommended by the Research Triangle Institute report in 1976. The same report recommended that the introduction of a smaller dollar coin coincide with the elimination of the half dollar.

The first design submitted for the dollar was an adaption by Frank Gasparro of the Flowing Hair large cent design, with a Flying Eagle design of Gasparro's creation on the reverse. Collectors almost universally panned the design at first, although supporters welcomed a return to more traditional, non-partisan coinage designs. Meanwhile, in Congress in 1978, a movement toward placing feminist Susan B. Anthony's portrait on the coin was growing (see Chapter 3 for the legislative history of the Anthony dollar) as the legislation for a smaller dollar

advanced through both houses.

Many hobbyists lobbied against the Anthony proposal in favor of a more traditional, allegorical portrait. Ironically, Gasparro's Flowing Hair Liberty design became the darling of the hobby as support for the Anthony design grew in Congress.

The Senate passed the Anthony dollar bill Aug. 22, 1978, without dissent; the House passed the bill Sept. 26 with a vote of 368 to 38. The first coins were struck at the Philadelphia Mint Dec. 13, 1978, with 1979 dates. The Mint mark "P" was used for the first time since the Wartime 5-cent coins of World War II. Denver strikes were produced Jan. 9, 1979, and the San Francisco Assay Office began producing business strikes Feb. 2, 1979.

Despite Treasury hopes to save $30 million a year by reducing demand for the $1 Federal Reserve note, the Anthony dollar never caught on with the public, which claimed the coin was too similar in size to the quarter dollar. The vending industry, which had supported the change in size but fought against a more distinctive multi-sided coin, never fully converted vending machines to accept the new, smaller dollar. The coins were produced for circulation and collectors' sets in 1979 and 1980, and only for collectors in 1981. None have been produced since 1981 although the law authorizing the Anthony dollar is still valid.

In the fall of 1985 the Mint began offering Anthony dollar sets through its catalog of products. The response surprised many, as the Anthony dollars were among the most popular items in the catalog.

History of Mint marks

A Mint mark on U.S. coins is a small letter added to the design of the coin to show which Mint manufactured it. Mint marks on United States coins began with the act of March 3, 1835, establishing the

first branch Mints: in New Orleans, La., Charlotte, N.C., and Dahlonega, Ga. The first Mint marks appeared in 1838.

When other branch Mints were established, coins struck there bore an appropriate Mint mark. The letters used to signify the various Mints are as follows:

"C" for Charlotte, N.C., (gold coins only), 1838-1861

"CC" for Carson City, Nev., 1870-1893

"D" for Dahlonega, Ga. (gold coins only), 1838-1861

"D" for Denver, Colo., 1906-present

"O" for New Orleans, La., 1838-1861; 1879-1909

"P" for Philadelphia, Pa., 1793-present

"S" for San Francisco, Calif., 1854-1955; as an Assay Office, 1968-present

"W" for West Point Mint 1984-present (gold coins only)

With one four-year exception, U.S. coins struck at the Philadelphia Mint bore no Mint marks until 1979. The initial use of the "P" appears on the Jefferson, Wartime 5-cent pieces, struck from 1942 to 1945 in a silver alloy. The "P" Mint mark on these issues was designed to distinguish the silver alloy issues from regular copper-nickel 5-cent pieces; during the war, silver was less important strategically than copper or nickel.

With the passage of the Coinage Act of 1965, which gave the United States copper-nickel clad coinage, Mint marks were removed from coins dated 1965 and from subsequent issues until 1968. The move was designed to help alleviate a coin shortage by removing the distinction between coins struck at branch Mints and those struck in Philadelphia so collectors could not determine which were the more limited strikes.

Since the San Francisco Assay Office opened in 1965 for coinage purposes, after 10 years of inactivity, no coins struck there after 1965 bear Mint marks until 1968, when they were returned to all coinage.

With the announcement Jan. 4, 1968, that Mint marks would return to coinage, Mint Director Eva Adams made several changes in Mint mark application. First, to achieve uniformity, she directed that all Mint marks be placed on the obverse of the coins. The Mint mark, she announced, on the cent, 5-cent piece, dime and quarter dollar would be to the right of the portraits, while on the half dollar it would

appear in the center under the portrait of Kennedy.

Second, she announced Proof coin sets would be manufactured at the San Francisco Assay Office and would bear an "S" Mint mark. Previously, all Proof sets were produced at Philadelphia and so had no Mint mark, except for some 1942 5-cent pieces. Proof sets were discontinued altogether after 1964 because of the coin shortage and revived in 1968.

Mint marks were again omitted from certain U.S. coins when cents were struck at the West Point Bullion Depository in 1974 and later, and when dimes were struck in San Francisco in 1975.

Major changes were made in Mint mark policy beginning in 1978. Mint officials in 1978 announced that the 1979 Susan B. Anthony dollar would bear the "P" Mint mark for Philadelphia business strikes. The list of coins to bear the "P" Mint mark grew in 1980, when all other denominations but the 1-cent piece received the new Mint mark.

A new Mint mark, a "W," the eighth, was added to the U.S. inventory in September 1983, when the West Point Bullion Depository (now the West Point Mint) began striking 1984-dated $10 gold eagles commemorating the Los Angeles Olympic Games. Although other coins were being struck at West Point, the Mint mark was not added to those denominations.

Additional changes were announced in 1984 when it was reported that beginning in 1985, the Mint mark would be placed on the master die instead of the working dies for all Proof coinage. This was to forestall production of errors similar to the Proof 1983 Roosevelt, No S dime and the 1982 Roosevelt, No P dime. Mint officials denied that business strike master dies would be Mint marked as well. But in 1989, Mint officials acknowledged that the procedure would be phased in for circulating coinage, ending a 150-year-old tradition of individually punching Mint marks into each working die.

In 1986, Mint officials decided to add the Mint marks on all commemorative and

Proof coins at the plasticene model stage. Thus, on these special collectors' coins, the Mint mark appears on all stages of models, hubs and dies.

Also in 1986, the S Mint mark of the Proof American Eagle silver dollar was placed on the reverse, to the left of the eagle's tail. Mint officials cited tradition for doing so.

Location of Mint marks

Half cents — All coined at Philadelphia, no Mint mark.

Large cents — All coined at Philadelphia, no Mint mark.

Flying Eagle cents — All coined at Philadelphia, no Mint mark.

Indian cents — 1908 and 1909, under the wreath on reverse side.

Lincoln cents — Under the date.

Two cents, Three cents (copper-nickel) — All coined at Philadelphia, no Mint mark.

Three cents (silver) — All coined at Philadelphia, except 1851 New Orleans Mint — reverse side, at right.

Shield 5-cent pieces — All coined at Philadelphia, no Mint mark.

Liberty 5-cent pieces — All coined at Philadelphia except 1912-S and -D — reverse side to left of word CENTS.

Indian 5-cent pieces — Reverse side under words FIVE CENTS.

Jefferson 5-cent pieces until 1964 — Reverse side at right of the building.

Jefferson 5-cent pieces (1942-1945, silver) — above dome on the reverse side.

Jefferson 5-cent pieces from 1968 to present — on obverse under Jefferson's queue.

Half dimes — Reverse side either within or below the wreath.

Dimes — Old types, reverse side below or within wreath; Winged Liberty Head type (1916-1945) on the reverse to left of base of fasces; Roosevelt type to 1964, left of bottom of torch on reverse; Roosevelt type from 1968 to present, obverse above date.

Twenty cents — Reverse side under the eagle.

Quarter dollars — Old types, on reverse side under eagle; Standing Liberty type, on obverse to left of date; Washington type to 1964, on reverse under eagle; Washington type from 1968 to present, on obverse to right of Washington's queue.

Half dollars — 1838 and 1839 "O" Mint mark above date; other dates to 1915 on reverse under eagle; 1916 on obverse below motto, 1917 on obverse below motto and on reverse. After 1917 on lower left reverse. Franklin type, above bell beam; Kennedy type in 1964, near claw and laurel at left on reverse; Kennedy type from 1968 to present, on obverse under Kennedy portrait.

Dollars — Old types, on reverse under eagle; Peace type, on reverse at lower tip of the eagle's wing; Eisenhower, on obverse above the date. Anthony, on obverse to left of bust.

Trade dollars — On reverse under eagle.

Gold dollars — On reverse under wreath.

Quarter eagles — 1838 and 1839, over the date; other dates prior to 1907, on reverse under the eagle; Indian type (1908-1929), on reverse lower left.

Three dollar pieces — Reverse under the wreath.

Half eagles — Same as quarter eagles.

Eagles — Reverse under eagle; after 1907 at left of value.

Double eagles — Old types on reverse under eagle; Saint-Gaudens (after 1907) above the date.

American Eagle — gold bullion coin, Proof version only, on obverse between second and third rays at right, below date. Silver bullion coin, Proof version only, on reverse to left of eagle's tail.

Dates, edge designs, mottoes, symbols

Dates

The insertion of a chronological mark or word on coins was a practice known to the ancients, but carried out by them on their money in a different method from that pursued by more modern sovereigns.

As for the United States, the original Mint Act of 1792 established the requirement that the date appear on U.S. coins, and this legislation has remained unchanged since that time.

Actually, the date on U.S. coins serves a very useful purpose, in that with it on a coin, counterfeiting is made more difficult and enforcement authorities can isolate specific issues which may have been produced illegally.

Traditionally, all United States coins have been dated the year of their coinage, although this didn't always happen the first few years the Mint was in operation and in recent years. One commemorative coin, the Lafayette-Washington dollar, is considered by Mint officials to be undated. The date 1900 appears on the coin, but that refers to the Paris Exposition; the coin was actually struck in December 1899.

The policy of placing the date in which a coin is struck was interrupted, because of the coin shortage and the speculation in rolls and bags of coins which took place in 1964. As a result, Congress passed legislation so that after the calendar year 1964 coinage was produced, the Mint could still use the 1964 date.

Starting in 1965, therefore, all denominations of United States coinage continued to be struck with the 1964 date.

When the Coinage Act of 1965 was passed, it became mandatory that the Mint continue to use the 1964 date on all 90 percent silver coins (halves, quarters, and dimes). Therefore, all the 90 percent silver coins which were manufactured in 1964, 1965 and 1966 bear the 1964 date.

The last of the 90 percent silver quarters were struck in January 1966, the last of the dimes in February 1966, and the last of the halves in April 1966.

The Coinage Act of 1965 also made it mandatory that the clad coins be dated not earlier than 1965. Therefore, all the clad coins actually made in 1965 bear the 1965 date. All the clad coins made through July 31, 1966, bear the 1965 date.

The first clad dime was struck in December 1965, the first clad quarter dollar in August 1965, and the first clad half dollar in December 1965.

In December 1965, the decision was made to change the 1964 date on the 5-cent pieces and the cents to 1965, as one step in catching up on normal coin dating. From December 1965 through July 31, 1966, all cents and 5-cent pieces struck bear the 1965 date.

Starting on Aug. 1, 1966, and through Dec. 31, 1966, all denominations of United States coins minted during that period carried the 1966 date. Commencing Jan. 1, 1967, the Mints resumed normal dating procedures.

The usual process of dating was interrupted again in December 1974, when Mint Director Mary Brooks announced the date 1974 would continue on dollars, half dollars and quarter dollars produced in the first half of 1975. The date of 1975 appeared, however, on cents, 5-cent and 10-cent coins.

All dollars, half dollars and quarters struck after July 4, 1975, bore the 1776-1976 Bicentennial dates. Normal dating was resumed in 1977.

The Mint Director attributed the date freeze decision to the necessity of building a sufficient coin inventory to conduct business affairs of the nation.

In 1973, the Mint struck 1974-dated aluminum cents in an experiment made necessary because of Mint worries over rising copper prices. When rising copper prices caused Mint officials to finally change the composition of the cent in 1982, the Mint began striking 1982 cents in late 1981 to build up inventories.

Recent special coinage programs have

caused Mint officials to strike coins with dates of following or preceding years. Production of Olympic coinage of 1984 gold eagles and 1984 silver dollars began in 1983 to produce an inventory for collector sales in 1984. Striking of the 1986-dated Statue of Liberty commemorative coins began in late 1985, again to produce an inventory. The production of the Proof 1986-dated American Eagle gold and silver bullion coins, however, did not begin until early 1987 in order to permit the Mint to strike sufficient quantities of the business strike versions.

Edge designs

Edge designs on U.S. coins are one of the more neglected aspects of the field of numismatics. Occasionally differences will be noted in the books, such as the change from lettered edge to reeded edge on 1836 Capped Bust half dollars, some distinctions on early large cents, and, most surprising, Dr. W.Q. Wolfson's discovery of the 1921 Morgan, Infrequently Reeded Edge dollars.

We say "surprising" because collectors generally take reeding for granted. About the only people who examine reeded edges are those trying to compare fakes with genuine coins. Otherwise, almost the only time somebody mentions the edge is when he discovers, accidentally, the words misspelled on early halves.

Mention became even rarer when the lettered edges gave place to reeding. The only published mention of reeding counts we know of was in "Bristles and Barbs" in April 1965, and "Coinology" in June 1969, both in *Coin World*, the first being instigated by Wolfson's aforementioned discovery published in *Coin World's* "Fair to Very Fine" column in December 1964.

"Coinology" for June 11, 1969, reports that the number of reeds on Winged Liberty Head and Roosevelt dimes varies from 104 to 118, an average of 111, so the statement is made that the number of reeds will probably vary also on all other denominations. It also states that "reeding counts are important in the study of any

coinage and should be considered seriously." If the statement that the numbers of reed varies in a series is true, it would make reeding less useful in studying fakes.

Both ornamented and lettered edges on coins to 1836 were made on a Castaing machine, consisting of two edge strips, one moving, the other not. Planchets were rolled between the two strips before going to the coining press. Occasional errors were caused by either the planchets or the movable strip slipping. The strips are known as "edge dies."

The same machine was used to make reeded edges up to 1836, reeds or grooves being used instead of letters. From 1836, a grooved collar was used as it still is, with the edge receiving the reeding at the same instance as the coin is produced. If the grooves were not the same in all collars, then the reeding would vary with the collar used. No detailed study has been made of such variations except for the 1921 Morgan, Infrequently Reeded Edge dollar, and the mention of variations in reedings on dimes. Grooved collars are called "collar dies."

Different strips were used on Castaing machines, also, resulting in differences or varieties of ornamentation, lettering and more. Edge varieties and edge errors are two different things, and always have been true whether the edges contain letters, ornamental devices, reeding or a combination of any two or all of them. We discuss varieties here, caused by changes in Castaing strips or collars as the case may be.

Half cents: Two leaf ornamentation in 1793; one leaf 1794 with both large and small lettering known; 1795, large letters or no letters (plain edges); 1796, plain edges only; 1797, medium and small letters, no leaf, and plain edge varieties, also a "Gripped" variety (rare); 1798 and after, plain edge only.

Large cents: 1793 Vine and bars; two leaves; one leaf pointing down; one leaf pointing up (leaves accompany lettered edges); 1794, one leaf up, one leaf down; 1795, lettered edge, plain edge, reeded edge; 1796 and 1797, plain and partially gripped edges; 1798, plain and reeded edges; 1799 and thereafter, all plain edges.

Five-cent pieces: 1882, normal plain edges, a few patterns known with five raised bars.

Half dimes: reeded from 1794 thereafter.

Dimes: reeded from 1796, with some changes in number of reeds from 1837 and possibly still varying through Winged Liberty Head and Roosevelt.

Quarters: Reeded from 1796 to now with probable variations over the years in number of reeds or spacing; from 1838 normal count is 119, but Walter Breen noted some 1876-CC with 153 reeds.

Half dollars: 1794 to 1806, lettered edge with words separated by stars, squares and circles, occasional lettering errors from slipping edge dies; 1807 to 1813, no star after DOLLAR: 1814-1831, with star; 1830 and 1831, varieties with diagonal reeding between words; 1830 to 1836, star after DOLLAR, varieties with vertical reeding between words; vertical reeding with no letters; 1837 and after, vertical reeding, with four different reeded collars used in 1837, and probably unstudied variations thereafter.

Silver dollars: Lettered edge through 1803 with small designs separating words; 1840-1935, reeded edge with varieties possible. Normal is 188 reeds. Only positively known variety is 1921 Morgan, P-Mint, with 154 reeds, known as 1921 Morgan, Infrequently Reeded Edge, discovered by Wolfson.

Trade dollars: Reeded edges with possibility of variations.

Gold dollars: Reeded edges with apparent variations between Mints and types, but not yet permanently identified.

Quarter eagles: Reeded edges from 1796; 1840 and after differ at branch Mints from P-Mint coins, the former having fewer reeds.

Three dollars: Reeded edges, with possible variations at branch Mints.

Half eagles: Same comment.

Eagles: To 1907, same comment. 1907-1911, 46 stars on edge; 1912-1933, 48 stars on edge (1912 with 46 stars possible but unknown as yet).

Double eagles: To 1907, reeded edge without important variations; 1907 Roman Numerals, large letters on patterns, medium letters on regular issue; 1907 Arabic Numerals, small letters.

American Eagle: gold bullion coins: Reeded edges, no studies done.

Mottoes

In the act establishing the Mint the devices and legends for the new coins were prescribed as follows: "Upon one side of each of the said coins there shall be an impression emblematic of liberty with an inscription of the word LIBERTY and the year of the coinage; and upon the reverse of each of the gold and silver coins there shall be the figure or representation of an eagle, with the inscription, 'United States of America,' and upon the reverse of the copper coins there shall be an inscription which shall express the denomination of the piece."

E PLURIBUS UNUM

Two legends have appeared on many of the coins of the United States, the one from almost the beginning of the national coinage, and the other since the Civil War. Neither, however, has had an uninterrupted history, nor has either been employed on all the denominations of the series.

The motto E PLURIBUS UNUM was first used on U.S. coinage in 1796, when the reverse of the quarter eagle ($2.50 gold piece) presented the main features of the Great Seal, on the scroll of which this inscription belongs. The same device was placed on certain of the silver coins in 1798, and so the motto was soon found on all the coins in the precious metals. In 1834, it was dropped from most of the gold coins to mark the change in the standard fineness of the coins. In 1837 it was dropped from the silver coins, marking the era of the Revised Mint Code. The Act of Feb. 12, 1873, made this inscription a requirement of law upon the coins of the United States. A search will reveal, however, that it does not appear on all coins struck after 1873, and that not until much later were the provisions of this act followed in their entirety. From facts contained in Mint records it would appear that officials did not consider the provisions of the law mandatory, but rather, discretionary. The motto does appear on all coins currently being manufactured.

The motto as it appears on U.S. coins means "One Out of Many," and doubtless has reference to the unity of the early states. It is said that one Colonel Reed of Uxbridge, Mass., was instrumental in having it placed on the coins.

IN GOD WE TRUST

From the records of the Treasury Department it appears that the first suggestion of the recognition of the Deity on the coins of the United States was contained in a letter addressed to the Secretary of the Treasury, by the Rev. M.R. Watkinson, Minister of the Gospel, Ridleyville, Pa., dated Nov. 13, 1861.

This letter states:

"One fact touching our currency has hitherto been seriously overlooked. I mean the recognition of the Almighty God in some form in our coins.

"You are probably a Christian. What if our Republic were now shattered beyond reconstruction? Would not the antiquaries of succeeding centuries rightly reason from our past that we were a heathen nation? What I propose is that instead of the goddess of liberty we shall have next inside the 13 stars a ring inscribed with the words "perpetual union'; within this ring the all-seeing eye, crowned with a halo; beneath this eye the American flag, bearing in its field stars equal to the number of the States united; in the folds of the bars the words 'God, liberty, law.'

"This would make a beautiful coin, to which no possible citizen could object. This would relieve us from the ignominy of heathenism. This would place us openly under the Divine protection we have

personally claimed. From my heart I have felt our national shame in disowning God as not the least of our present national disasters.

"To you first I address a subject that must be agitated."

Under date of Nov. 20, 1861, the Secretary of the Treasury addressed the following letter to the Director of the Mint:

"Dear Sir: No nation can be strong except in the strength of God, or safe except in His defense. The trust of our people in God should be declared on our national coins.

"You will cause a device to be prepared without unnecessary delay with a motto expressing in the fewest and tersest words possible this national recognition."

It was found that the Act of Jan. 18, 1837, prescribed the mottoes and devices that should be placed upon the coins of the United States, so that nothing could be done without legislation.

In December 1863, the Director of the Mint submitted to the Secretary of the Treasury for approval designs for new 1-, 2-, and 3-cent pieces, on which it was proposed that one of the following mottoes should appear: "Our country; our God"; "God, our Trust."

The Secretary of the Treasury, in a letter to the Director of the Mint, dated Dec. 9, 1863, states:

"I approve your mottoes, only suggesting that on that with the Washington obverse the motto should begin with the word 'Our,' so as to read: 'Our God and our country.' And on that with the shield, it should be changed so as to read: 'In God We Trust.'"

An act passed April 22, 1864, changing the composition of the 1-cent piece and authorizing the coinage of the 2-cent piece, the devices of which were to be fixed by the Director of the Mint, with the approval of the Secretary of the Treasury, and it is upon the bronze 2-cent piece that the motto IN GOD WE TRUST first appears.

The Act of March 3, 1865, provided that in addition to the legend and devices on the gold and silver coins of the United States, it should be lawful for the Director of the Mint, with the approval of the Secretary of the Treasury to place the motto IN GOD WE TRUST on such coins as shall admit of the inscription thereon. Under this act, the motto was placed upon the double eagle, eagle and half eagle, and also upon the dollar, half dollar and quarter dollar in 1866.

The Coinage Act of Feb. 12, 1873, provided that the Secretary of the Treasury may cause the motto IN GOD WE TRUST to be inscribed on such coins as shall admit of such motto.

When the double eagle and eagle of new design appeared in 1907, it was soon discovered that the religious motto had been omitted. In response to a general demand, Congress ordered it restored, and the Act of May 18, 1908, made mandatory its appearance on all coins upon which it had heretofore appeared. The motto appears on all gold and silver coins struck since July 1, 1908, with the exception of Barber dimes. It was not mandatory upon the cent and 5-cent coins, but could be placed thereon by the Secretary of the Treasury, or the Director of the Mint with the Secretary's approval.

The issuance of the cent in 1909 honoring the centennial of the birth of Abraham Lincoln brought the motto IN GOD WE TRUST to the smallest denomination U.S. coin. This was an appropriate tribute to Lincoln, one of the most deeply spiritual presidents.

Almost another three decades were to go by before the motto was carried over to the one remaining coin in the U.S. series that did not carry it, the 5-cent piece. In 1938, a design for this coin was chosen as a result of a nationwide competition. The design selected, honoring Thomas Jefferson, was executed by Michigan sculptor Felix Schlag. A feature on the obverse is the motto, IN GOD WE TRUST.

The act approved July 11, 1955, makes appearance of the motto IN GOD WE TRUST mandatory upon all coins of the United States.

Symbols

Eagle

The eagle was a favorite device of the United States' founding fathers before it was placed on U.S. national coinage. It appears on the Great Seal of the United States which was adopted in 1782. At this time the states established their own Mints and Massachusetts saw fit to place on the reverse of its coins a spread eagle with arrows and an olive branch in the claws.

When the Mint was established the devices and legends for the new coins were prescribed. It was ordered that "upon the reverse of each of the gold and silver coins there shall be the figure or representation of an eagle." However, the act of Jan. 18, 1837, removed the legal requirement for the half dime and dime. Subsequent gold and silver coins — the silver 3-cent coin, the gold dollar and the gold $3 coin — were not required to have an eagle on the reverse.

The eagle was added almost as an afterthought on one recent U.S. coin. The eagle on the reverse of the Franklin half dollar, introduced in 1948, is very small. The story that Franklin preferred the wild turkey over the bald eagle as a symbol of American pride is well known among collectors. The Liberty Bell is the most prominent device on the reverse of the Franklin half, with a diminutive eagle to the right of the bell.

Portraits

With the exception of the great statesman, Benjamin Franklin, and the great feminist, Susan B. Anthony, the only individuals whose images appear on regular issue U.S. coins have been U.S. presidents. The Indian used on the 5-cent piece introduced in 1913 is not the image of any individual but is a composite of several Indians studied by the designer (identified as Iron Tail, Two Moons and Chief John Tree). One of the most popular designs has been the Goddess of Liberty who appears on many of U.S. coins.

Use of "V" in Trust

In medieval times the letters "u" and

"v" were used interchangeably. These letters were not given separate alphabetical listings in English dictionaries until about 1800. In recent times many sculptors have used the "V" in place of "U" for artistic reasons, such as, to represent the permanence and long time significance of their work. Artists who design coins may choose to spell "Trust" with a "V." All of the dollars of the Peace dollar design have this characteristic. From 1921 through 1935 the United States Mints made more than 190 million dollars of this type.

It is interesting to note that sometimes the "V" is similarly used in wording on public buildings.

Initials

The custom of placing the signature of the engraver upon a coin die dates from remote antiquity. Many Greek coins, especially in the creations produced by the cities of Sicily and Magna Graecia, are signed with the initials of the artist, and in some cases his full name. The same practice prevailed generally in the European countries. There were no initials on United States coins until the gold dollar appeared in 1849 with the initial of Longacre, L, on the truncation of the bust.

Other symbols

Arrows were sometimes used on U.S. coins to symbolize preparedness. Olive branches or leaves are found often also.

Symbolizing peace, the olive branch is the international emblem of friendship and accord. The fasces on the reverse of the Winged Liberty Head dime has a bundle of rods with protruding ax as the central device. It has been since ancient times a symbol of official authority. Also on this dime, the winged cap on the Roman style Liberty Head symbolizes freedom of thought.

The newer Roosevelt dime bears some representative symbols also. In the center of the reverse is a torch signifying liberty bounded by an olive branch on the left and an oak branch signifying strength and independence on the right.

The Kennedy half dollar contains much symbolism. The presidential coat of arms forms the motif for the reverse. The coat of arms depicts the American eagle holding the olive branch in his right claw and arrows in the left. Symbolism derived from the 13 original states governs the number of olive leaves, berries, arrows, stars and cloud puffs. The upper part of the flag or shield upon the breast of the eagle represents the Congress binding the Colonies into an entity. The vertical stripes complete the motif of the flag of the United States. Each state of the nation is represented in the 50-star amulet which rings the whole.

Issue dates, designers, original engravers, models

Regular issue United States coins

Half cents

Type	Issue dates	Designers[1]	Original Engraver	Model or Source
Liberty Cap Left	1793	Obv: Eckfeldt	Eckfeldt	Dupre's Libertas Americana medal
		Rev: Eckfeldt	Eckfeldt	Original design
Liberty Cap Right (Large Head)	1794	Obv: Scot	Scot	Similar to previous issue, but reversed
		Rev: Scot	Scot	Similar to previous issue
Liberty Cap Right (Small Head)	1795-1797	Obv: Scot-Gardner	Scot	Similar to previous issue
		Rev: Scot-Gardner	Scot	Similar to previous issue
Draped Bust	1800-1808	Obv: Stuart-Scot	Scot	Ann Willing Bingham (?)
		Rev: Scot-Gardner	Scot	Similar to previous issue
Classic Head	1809-1836	Obv: Reich	Reich	Unknown model

		Rev: Reich	Reich	Original design
Coronet Type	1840-1857	Obv: Scot-Gobrecht	Gobrecht	Coronet Type large cent
		Rev: Reich-Gobrecht	Gobrecht	Similar to previous issue

Large cents

Type	Issue dates	Designers[1]	Original Engraver	Model or Source
Flowing Hair, Chain Rev.	1793	Obv: Voigt	Voigt	Unknown model
		Rev: Voigt	Voigt	Fugio cent (?)
Flowing Hair, Wreath Rev.	1793	Obv: Voigt-Eckfeldt	Eckfeldt	Similar to previous issue
		Rev: Eckfeldt	Eckfeldt	Original design
Liberty Cap	1793-1794	Obv: Wright	Wright	Dupre's Libertas Americana medal, reversed
		Rev: Wright	Wright	Similar to previous issue
Liberty Cap (Modified)	1794-1796	Obv: Wright-Gardner	Scot	Similar to previous issue
		Rev: Wright-Gardner	Scot	Similar to previous issue
Draped Bust	1796-1807	Obv: Stuart-Scot	Scot	Ann Willing Bingham (?)
		Rev: Wright-Scot	Scot	Similar to previous issue
Classic Head	1808-1814	Obv: Reich	Reich	Unknown model
		Rev: Reich	Reich	Original design
Coronet	1816-1835	Obv: Scot	Scot	Unknown model
		Rev: Reich	Reich	Same as previous issue
	1835-1839	Obv: Scot-Gobrecht	Gobrecht	Similar to previous issue
		Rev: Reich	Reich	Same as previous issue
	1839-1857	Obv: Scot-Gobrecht	Gobrecht	Similar to previous issue
		Rev: Reich-Gobrecht	Gobrecht	Similar to previous issue

Small cents

Type	Issue dates	Designers[1]	Original Engraver	Model or Source
Flying Eagle	1856-1858	Obv: Gobrecht-Longacre	Longacre	Titian Peale's design for dollar reverse, c. 1836
		Rev: Longacre	Longacre	Reverse of $1 & $3 gold
Indian Head	1859-1909	Obv: Longacre	Longacre	Possibly Longacre's daughter Sarah
		Rev: (Both) Longacre	Longacre	Original designs
Lincoln Head (Wheat Rev.)	1909-1958	Obv: Victor D. Brenner	C. Barber	Brenner's plaque
		Rev: Victor D. Brenner	C. Barber	Original design
Lincoln Head (Memorial Rev.)	1959-	Obv: Brenner	C. Barber	Same as previous issue
		Rev: Gasparro	Roberts	Lincoln Memorial

Two cents

Type	Issue dates	Designers[1]	Original Engraver	Model or Source
Two cents	1864-1873	Obv: Longacre	Longacre	Original design
		Rev: Longacre	Longacre	Original design

Silver 3 cents

Type	Issue dates	Designers[1]	Original Engraver	Model or Source
Silver 3 cents	1851-1873	Obv: Longacre	Longacre	Original design (three varieties)
		Rev: Longacre	Longacre	Original design (two varieties)

Copper-nickel 3 cents

Type	Issue dates	Designers[1]	Original Engraver	Model or Source
Copper-nickel 3 cents	1865-1889	Obv: Longacre	Longacre	Possibly Sarah Longacre
		Rev: Longacre	Longacre	Original design

Half dimes

Type	Issue dates	Designers[1]	Original Engraver	Model or Source
Flowing Hair	1794-1795	Obv: Scot	Scot	Unknown model
		Rev: Scot	Scot	Original design
Draped Bust (Small Eagle)	1796-1797	Obv: Stuart-Scot	Scot	Ann Willing Bingham (?)
		Rev: Scot-Eckstein(?)	Scot	Similar to previous issue
Draped Bust (Heraldic Eagle)	1800-1805	Obv: Stuart-Scot	Scot	Same as previous issue
		Rev: Scot	Scot	Great Seal of the United States
Capped Bust	1829-1837	Obv: Reich-Kneass	Kneass	Unknown model (similar to dime by Reich)
		Rev: Reich-Kneass	Kneass	Original design (similar to dime by Reich)
Seated Liberty (No Drapery)[2]	1837-1840	Obv: Gobrecht	Gobrecht	Drawing by Thomas Sully
		Rev: Gobrecht	Gobrecht	Original design
Seated Liberty (With Drapery)	1840-1859	Obv: Gobrecht-Hughes	Gobrecht	Similar to previous issue
		Rev: Gobrecht	Gobrecht	Same as previous issue
Seated Liberty (Legend Obv.)	1860-1873	Obv: Gobrecht-Hughes-Longacre	Longacre	Similar to previous issue
		Rev: Longacre	Longacre	Original design

Copper-nickel 5 cents

Type	Issue dates	Designers[1]	Original Engraver	Model or Source
Shield	1866-1883	Obv: Longacre	Longacre	Original design
		Rev: Longacre	Longacre	Original design (two varieties)
Liberty Head	1883-1912	Obv: C. Barber	C. Barber	Unknown model
		Rev: C. Barber	C. Barber	Original design (two varieties)
Indian Head	1913-1938	Obv: James E. Fraser	C. Barber	Composite of three Indians
		Rev: James E. Fraser	C. Barber	"Black Diamond," Central Park Zoo
Jefferson Head	1938-	Obv: Felix Schlag	Sinnock	Bust by Houdon, c. 1789
		Rev: Felix Schlag	Sinnock	Monticello

Dimes

Type	Issue dates	Designers[1]	Original Engraver	Model or Source
Draped Bust (Small Eagle)	1796-1797	Obv: Stuart-Scot	Scot	Ann Willing Bingham (?)
		Rev: Scot-Eckstein (?)	Scot	Similar to Scot's 1794 silver reverse
Draped Bust (Heraldic Eagle)	1798-1807	Obv: Stuart-Scot	Scot	Same as previous issue
		Rev: Scot	Scot	Great Seal of the United States
Capped Bust[3]	1809-1837	Obv: Reich	Reich	Unknown model
		Rev: Reich	Reich	Original design
Seated Liberty (No Drapery)[2]	1837-1840	Obv: Gobrecht	Gobrecht	Drawing by Thomas Sully
		Rev: Gobrecht	Gobrecht	Original design
Seated Liberty (With Drapery)	1840-1860	Obv: Gobrecht-Hughes	Gobrecht	Similar to previous issue
		Rev: Gobrecht	Gobrecht	Same as previous issue
Seated Liberty (Legend Obv.)	1860-1891	Obv: Gobrecht-Hughes-Longacre	Longacre	Similar to previous issue
		Rev: Longacre	Longacre	Original design
Barber	1892-1916	Obv: C. Barber	C. Barber	French medal designs
		Rev: Longacre	Longacre	Same as previous issue
Winged Liberty Head	1916-1945	Obv: Adolph A. Weinman	C. Barber	Elsie Kachel Stevens

		Rev: Adolph A. Weinman	C. Barber	Original design
Roosevelt Head	1946-	Obv: Sinnock	Sinnock	Original design
		Rev: Sinnock	Sinnock	Original design

Twenty cents

Type	Issue dates	Designers[1]	Original Engraver	Model or Source
Twenty cents	1875-1878	Obv: Gobrecht-Hughes-W. Barber	W. Barber	Seated Liberty dollar
		Rev: W. Barber	W. Barber	Original design

Quarter dollars

Type	Issue dates	Designers[1]	Original Engraver	Model or Source
Draped Bust (Small Eagle)	1796	Obv: Stuart-Scot	Scot	Ann Willing Bingham (?)
		Rev: Scot-Eckstein (?)	Scot	Similar to Scot's 1794 silver reverse
Draped Bust (Heraldic Eagle)	1804-1807	Obv: Stuart-Scot	Scot	Same as previous issue
		Rev: Scot	Scot	Great Seal of the United States
Capped Bust[4]	1815-1838	Obv: Reich	Reich	Unknown model
		Rev: Reich	Reich	Original design (c. 1807)
Seated Liberty (No Drapery)	1838-1840	Obv: Gobrecht	Gobrecht	Drawing by Thomas Sully
		Rev: Reich-Kneass-Gobrecht	Gobrecht	Similar to previous issue
Seated Liberty (With Drapery)	1840-1891	Obv: Gobrecht-Hughes	Gobrecht	Similar to previous issue
		Rev: Reich-Kneass-Gobrecht	Gobrecht	Same as previous issue
Barber	1892-1916	Obv: C. Barber	C. Barber	French medal designs
		Rev: C. Barber	C. Barber	Great Seal of the United States
Standing Liberty	1916-1930	Obv: Hermon A. MacNeil	C. Barber	Dora Doscher (two varieties)
		Rev: Hermon A. MacNeil	C. Barber	Original design (two varieties)
Washington Head	1932-date	Obv: John Flanagan	Sinnock	Bust by Houdon (1785)
		Rev: John Flanagan	Sinnock	Original design
Bicentennial	1976	Obv: Flanagan	Sinnock	Same as regular issue
		Rev: Jack L. Ahr	Gasparro	Original design

Half dollars

Type	Issue dates	Designers[1]	Original Engraver	Model or Source
Flowing Hair	1794-1795	Obv: Scot	Scot	Unknown model
		Rev: Scot	Scot	Original design
Draped Bust (Small Eagle)	1796-1797	Obv: Stuart-Scot	Scot	Ann Willing Bingham (?)
		Rev: Scot-Eckstein	Scot	Similar to previous issue
Draped Bust (Heraldic Eagle)	1801-1807	Obv: Stuart-Scot	Scot	Same as previous issue
		Rev: Scot	Scot	Great Seal of the United States
Capped Bust[5] (50 C. Rev.)	1807-1836	Obv: Reich	Reich	Unknown model
		Rev: Reich	Reich	Original design
Capped Bust (50 Cents Rev.)	1836-1837	Obv: Reich-Gobrecht	Gobrecht	Similar to previous issue
		Rev: Reich-Gobrecht	Gobrecht	Similar to previous issue
Capped Bust (Half Dol.)	1838-1839	Obv: Reich-Gobrecht	Gobrecht	Same as previous issue
		Rev: Reich-Gobrecht	Gobrecht⁻	Similar to previous issue
Seated Liberty	1839-1891	Obv: Gobrecht	Gobrecht	Drawing by Thomas Sully
		Rev: Reich-Gobrecht	Gobrecht	Similar to previous issue
Barber	1892-1915	Obv: C. Barber	C. Barber	French medal designs
		Rev: C. Barber	C. Barber	Great Seal of the United States
Walking Liberty	1916-1947	Obv: Adolph A. Weinman	C. Barber	Roty's Sower design on French silver

				Rev: Adolph A. Weinman	C. Barber	Original design

Franklin	1948-1963	Obv: Sinnock	Roberts	Bust by Houdon (1778)
		Rev: Sinnock	Roberts	Sesquicentennial half
Kennedy	1964-date	Obv.: Roberts	Roberts	U.S. Mint medal
		Rev: Gasparro	Roberts	Seal of the president of the U.S.
Bicentennial	1976	Obv: Roberts	Roberts	Same as regular issue
		Rev: Seth G. Huntington	Gasparro	Independence Hall

Silver dollars, clad dollars

Type	Issue dates	Designers[1]	Original Engraver	Model or Source
Flowing Hair	1794-1795	Obv: Scot	Scot	Unknown model
		Rev: Scot	Scot	Original design
Draped Bust (Small Eagle)	1795-1798	Obv: Stuart-Scot	Scot	Ann Willing Bingham(?)
		Rev: Scot-Eckstein (?)	Scot	Similar to previous issue
Draped Bust (Heraldic Eagle)	1798-1804	Obv: Stuart-Scot	Scot	Same as previous issue
		Rev: Scot	Scot	Great Seal of the United States
Gobrecht[6]	1836-1839	Obv: Gobrecht	Gobrecht	Drawing by Thomas Sully
		Rev: Gobrecht	Gobrecht	Drawing by Titian Peale
Seated Liberty	1840-1873	Obv: Gobrecht-Hughes	Gobrecht	Similar to pattern issue
		Rev: Reich-Gobrecht	Gobrecht	Reich's 1807 reverse for silver
Morgan's Liberty Head	1878-1921	Obv: Morgan	Morgan	Anna W. Williams
		Rev: Morgan	Morgan	Original design
Peace	1921-1935	Obv: Anthony DeFrancisci	Morgan	Teresa C. DeFrancisci
		Rev: Anthony DeFrancisci	Morgan	Original design
Eisenhower	1971-1978	Obv: Gasparro	Gasparro	Sketch by Gasparro (1945)
		Rev: Gasparro	Gasparro	Apollo 11 emblem
Bicentennial	1976	Obv: Gasparro	Gasparro	Same as regular issue
		Rev: Dennis R. Williams	Gasparro	Original design
Anthony	1979-1981	Obv: Gasparro	Gasparro	Original design
		Rev: Gasparro	Gasparro	Apollo 11 emblem
Trade dollar	1873-1883	Obv: W. Barber	W. Barber	Unknown model
		Rev: W. Barber	W. Barber	Original design

Gold dollars

Type	Issue dates	Designers[1]	Original Engraver	Model or Source
Liberty Head	1849-1854	Obv: Longacre	Longacre	Possibly Sarah Longacre
		Rev: Longacre	Longacre	Original design
Indian Head[7]	1854-1889	Obv: Longacre	Longacre	Possibly Sarah Longacre
		Rev: Longacre	Longacre	Original design

Quarter eagles

Type	Issue dates	Designers[1]	Original Engraver	Model or Source
Capped Bust Right	1796-1807	Obv: Scot	Scot	Martha Washington(?)
		Rev. Scot	Scot	Great Seal of the United States
Capped Bust Left	1808	Obv: Reich	Reich	Unknown model
		Rev: Reich	Reich	1789 Mott token
Capped Head Left[8]	1821-1834	Obv: Reich-Scot	Scot	Similar to previous issue
		Rev: Reich	Reich	Same as previous issue
Classic Head	1834-1839	Obv: Kneass	Kneass	Reich's Classic Head cent
		Rev: Reich-Kneass	Kneass	Similar to previous issue
Coronet	1840-1907	Obv: Gobrecht	Gobrecht	Coronet type large cent
		Rev: Reich-Kneass-Gobrecht	Gobrecht	Similar to previous issue
Indian Head	1908-1929	Obv: Bela Lyon Pratt	C. Barber	Unknown model
		Rev: Bela Lyon Pratt	C. Barber	Original design

Three dollars

Type	Issue dates	Designers[1]	Original Engraver	Model or Source
Three Dollars	1854-1889	Obv: Longacre	Longacre	Possibly Sarah Longacre
		Rev: Longacre	Longacre	Original design

Half eagles

Type	Issue dates	Designers[1]	Original Engraver	Model or Source
Capped Bust Right (Small Eagle)	1795-1798	Obv: Scot	Scot	Martha Washington(?)
		Rev: Scot	Scot	Original design
Capped Bust Right (Heraldic Eagle)	1795-1807	Obv: Scot	Scot	Same as previous issue
		Rev: Scot	Scot	Great Seal of the United States
Capped Bust Left	1807-1812	Obv: Reich	Reich	Unknown model
		Rev: Reich	Reich	1789 Mott token
Capped Head Left[8]	1813-1834	Obv: Reich-Scot	Scot	Similar to previous issue
		Rev: Reich	Reich	Same as previous issue
Classic Head	1834-1838	Obv: Kneass	Kneass	Reich's Classic Head cent
		Rev: Reich-Kneass	Kneass	Similar to previous issue
Coronet Type	1839-1908	Obv: Gobrecht	Gobrecht	Coronet type large cent
		Rev: Reich-Kneass-Gobrecht	Gobrecht	Similar to previous issue
Indian Head	1908-1929	Obv: Bela Lyon Pratt	C. Barber	Unknown model
		Rev. Bela Lyon Pratt	C. Barber	Original design

Eagles

Type	Issue dates	Designers[1]	Original Engraver	Model or Source
Capped Bust Right (Small Eagle)	1795-1797	Obv: Scot	Scot	Possibly Martha Washington
		Rev: Scot	Scot	Original design
Capped Bust Right (Heraldic Eagle)	1797-1804	Obv: Scot	Scot	Same as previous issue
		Rev: Scot	Scot	Great Seal of the United States
Coronet Type	1838-1907	Obv: Gobrecht	Gobrecht	Coronet Type Large Cent
		Rev: Reich-Kneass-Gobrecht	Gobrecht	$2.50, $5 Rev.
Indian Head	1907-1933	Obv: Saint-Gaudens	C. Barber	Unknown model
		Rev: Saint-Gaudens	C. Barber	Original design

Double eagles

Type	Issue dates	Designers[1]	Original Engraver	Model or Source
Liberty Head	1849-1907	Obv: Longacre	Longacre	Possibly Sarah Longacre
		Rev: Longacre	Longacre	Original design
Saint-Gaudens Type	1907-1933	Obv: Saint-Gaudens	C. Barber	Unknown model
		Rev: Saint-Gaudens	C. Barber	Original design

American Eagle bullion coins

Type	Issue dates	Designers[1]	Original Engraver	Model or Source
Silver bullion	1986-date	Obv: Robert A. Weinman	Steever	Walking Liberty half dollar
		Rev: John Mercanti	Mercanti	Great Seal of the United States
Gold bullion	1986-date	Obv: Saint-Gaudens	Peloso	Double eagle design of 1907-33[9]
		Rev: Miley Busiek	Winter	Original design

Notes

1. When two or more names appear hyphenated as the designers, the first person created the design and the others modified it for artistic and/or personal reasons. Modifications of design and/or relief solely for striking purposes are not included.

2. Stars are not on the obverse of 1837 and 1838-O coins.
3. Smaller size (1828-37) engraved by Kneass.
4. Smaller size without E PLURIBUS UNUM (1831-1838) engraved by Kneass.
5. Slight modifications made in 1809 by Reich and in 1834 by Kneass.
6. All coins are patterns but some did circulate.
7. Small Head 1854-56; Large Head 1856-89.
8. Smaller size (1829-34) engraved by Kneass.
9. Saint-Gaudens' Liberty was "slimmed down" to meet modern standards of physical beauty, under the orders of Treasury Secretary James A. Baker III.

How coins are made

United States coins have their beginnings in the private sector, where a number of companies produce some coinage planchets and all coils of strip metal the Mint purchases. The Mint produced its own strip metal as late as fiscal year 1982 at the Philadelphia Mint, but the operations were closed officially in fiscal 1983.

Basically, the coinage metals are assayed, melted and formed into slabs which are then rolled to the proper thickness. For clad coinage, bonding operations are required to bond the two layers of copper-nickel to the core of pure copper. The strip is then coiled and shipped to the Mint for blanking.

Some of the purchased material arrives in planchet form, ready to be coined, including the copper-plated zinc cent planchets used since 1982.

The blanking presses are simply punch presses similar to those found in any machine shop. They have a bank of punches (or rams) which travel downward through the strip and into a steel bedplate which has holes corresponding to the punches. The presses punch out planchets each time the punches make their downward cycle. The planchets made at this stage are slightly larger than the finished coins. Because of the shearing action of the punches, the planchets have rough edges. Most of the rough edges (or burrs) are removed during succeeding operations.

The planchets (also called flans or blanks) are next passed over sorting screens, called riddlers, which are supposed to eliminate all of the defective planchets. Thin and incomplete planchets will fall through the screens. These rejected planchets are remelted.

During the finish rolling and blanking press operations the planchets have again been hardened and must now be softened, or annealed. The planchets are passed through a cylinder which has spiral grooves in its walls. As the cylinder turns, the planchets are forced from one end to the other by the spirals. As they move along the cylinder walls, the planchets are heated to controlled temperatures, approximately 1400 degrees, changing their crystal structure to a softer state. Planchets are "frozen" into that state by a water quench bath. This annealing process prolongs the life of the coining dies by ensuring well-struck coins with lower striking pressures.

Type I planchets

Despite a protective atmosphere, annealing causes some discoloration on the surfaces of the planchets which must be removed. The planchets are tumbled against each other and passed through a chemical bath. Then they are dried by forced hot air. The planchets are now completed Type I planchets and if they happen to bypass the coining presses you will see them as flat disks.

The upsetting mill consists of a rotating wheel with a groove on its edge. The grooved edge of the wheel fits into a curved section (or shoe) which has a corresponding groove. The distance between the wheel and the shoe gets progressively narrower so that, as the planchet is rolled along the groove, a raised rim is formed on both sides of the planchet. This raised rim serves several purposes. It sizes and shapes the planchet for better feed at the press and it work-hardens the edge to prevent escape of metal between the obverse die and the collar.

The planchets are now called Type II planchets and are ready to be struck into coins.

Die preparation

The dies used for striking coins start out as an approved sketch of the coin in the Engraving Department at the Philadelphia Mint. The sculptor-engraver makes a plasticene (modeling wax) model in bas-relief from the sketch. The model will be anywhere from three to 12 times as large as the finished coin. Next, a plaster-of-paris negative is cast from the model. The negative is touched up and details are added. Then a plaster-of-paris positive is made. The positive is used as the model to be approved by the Mint Director and the Secretary of the Treasury. If pictures are required for such approval, they are taken of this positive.

When final approval is received another negative is made and a hard epoxy positive model is prepared. The epoxy model replaces the copper galvano once used by the U.S. Mint.

Epoxy to hub

The completed epoxy is then mounted on a Janvier transfer engraving machine. This machine cuts the design in a soft tool steel blank to the exact size of the coin, following the exact details of the epoxy, producing a positive replica of the model. This positive is called a "hub." The hub is then heat treated to harden it and is used in a hydraulic press to prepare a master die. The original hub is carefully stored in a safe place to ensure against loss of the original reduction.

Working hubs are made from the master die in the hydraulic press, and similarly hardened in the same way.

Working dies are made from the working hub in the same way. Pressing an image into a piece of soft tool steel hardens the metal, so annealing is usually needed to fully form the image. Two to three cycles may be required to properly impress all details into the steel, although the Mint has been working to cut this down to one cycle, to eliminate multiple die image errors.

The working dies for non-Proofs and commemoratives are now complete in every detail except the addition of the Mint mark, although not all dies are Mint marked. Mint marks traditionally had been added by using a handpunch, although some are now Mint marked at the initial modeling stage.

Coinage operations are performed in the coin press room. It is here that the little disks take on their final identity. They go into the presses as blanks and come out bearing the devices and inscriptions which make them coins of the realm.

Coining presses

Coining presses are designed for a fixed class of work, not for a specific denomination of coin. Dies and collars are interchangeable and striking pressures are adjustable for the various denominations and metals. The collar forms the wall of the coining chamber and one die forms the base. The dies impress the various designs and devices on the obverse and reverse for the coin while the collar forms the edge of the coin, square and smooth on cents and 5-cent pieces and reeded on the larger denominations. The collar, which is minutely larger in diameter than the dies, is mounted on springs which allows slight movement.

It is generally assumed that the reverse die is the lower (or anvil) die while the obverse die is the upper (or hammer) die; however, there are exceptions to this general rule. Both dies can be adjusted both horizontally and vertically. Horizontal adjustments center the design of the coin on the planchet. Vertical adjustments determine how well the dies are impressed into the planchet. [In recent years, the Mint has been installing high-speed, single-die Schuler coining presses. These presses differ from the other presses in the Mint in that the striking is horizontal, rather than vertical.]

Planchets are fed by gravity from a basin attached to the press through a cylindrical tube. This tube will stack 20 or so planchets and from this stack the bottom planchet is fed into the press by the feed fingers or a rotating disc with holes to carry the planchets. The dial-feed system can increase the capacity of a press by 20 to 30 percent, according to Mint tests, and older presses are being fitted with the new delivery systems.

Feed fingers are two parallel pieces of metal joined in such a way that they can open and close. On one end of the two pieces is a covered recessed slot and in the center is a hole. Feed fingers shove a finished piece out of the way while depositing a fresh planchet; dial feeders are an "indexed" system, in that the planchet/coin is moved in relative position to others in the machine.

At frequent times, while a press is in operation, the press attendant will pick up a finished coin for inspection. He makes the inspection under a magnifier and it reveals any defects made in the die during operation.

After the coins have been struck they are ready for a final inspection. After passing the inspection, they are counted in automatic machines, weighed and bagged. The bags are sewn shut and are ready for shipment to the Federal Reserve Banks for distribution.

The first coining presses in the Mint were hand operated which severely limited their output. Later presses were powered by steam boilers and capable of 55 strokes per minute. Still later presses, speeded up to 140 strokes per minute, were converted to accept dual dies which doubled the output. And still later some were converted to quadro, four dies, increasing capacity up to 560 per minute. The high-speed Schuler presses can operate at about 600 strikes per minute, but only one coin at a time. Their greatest advantage is in the production of quarter dollars, which require too much pressure for the older presses to produce dual or quad strikes. Cents can be struck four at a time on older presses at about the same coins-per-minute rate as the Schuler.

Not all the old-style coining presses are out of commission, however. The coining press that had its first job striking Carson City silver dollars in 1870 had another assignment over a century later, striking the official Nevada Bicentennial medal.

The old press, rebuilt and moved to the Nevada State Museum, was built in 1869 by the firm of Morgan and Orr of Philadelphia. It struck its first coin, an 1870-CC silver dollar, in the Carson City Mint Feb. 11, 1870.

Another example of the Mint recycling coining presses is the use of 20 dual presses, some retired from the Philadelphia Mint, to strike cents at the West Point Bullion Depository. To help ease the burden of the Bicentennial coins, the Mint received permission to use the West Point facility to manufacture coins. The old presses were moved there in late 1974.

West Point also has struck the 1984-W Olympic gold eagles and the American Arts Gold Medallions, and is now the prime site of producing American Eagle gold bullion coins and other gold coins.

Source: United States Mint

Specifications of U.S. coins

Half cents

COIN/ DATES	GRAMS WGT.	TOL.	GRAINS WGT.	TOL.	DIA. (mm)	COMPOSITION	SPEC. GRAV.
1793-1795	6.739		104.000		23.50*	Pure copper	8.92
1795-1837	5.443		84.000		23.50*	Pure copper	8.92
1837-1857	5.443	0.227	84.000	3.50	23.50*	Pure copper	8.92

Large cents

COIN/	GRAMS	GRAINS	DIA.				SPEC.

DATES	WGT.	TOL.	WGT.	TOL.	(mm)	COMPOSITION	GRAV.
793-1795	13.478		208.000		28.50*	Pure copper	8.92
1795-1837	10.886		168.000		28.50*	Pure copper	8.92
1837-1857	10.886	0.454	168.000	7.00	28.50*	Pure copper	8.92

Small cents

COIN/ DATES	GRAMS WGT.	TOL.	GRAINS WGT.	TOL.	DIA. (mm)	COMPOSITION	SPEC. GRAV.
1856-1864	4.666	0.259	72.000	4.00	19.30*	88 Cu, 12 Ni	8.92
1864-1873	3.110	0.259	48.000	4.00	19.05	95 Cu, 5 Zn & Sn	8.84
1873-1942	3.110	0.130	48.000	2.00	19.05	95 Cu, 5 Zn & Sn	8.84
1943	2.689/ 2.754	0.130	41.500/ 42.500***	2.00	19.05	Zinc-plated steel	7.80
1944-1946	3.110	0.130	48.000	2.00	19.05	95 Cu, 5 Zn	8.83
1947-1962	3.110	0.130	48.000	2.00	19.05	95 Cu, 5 Zn & Sn	8.84
1962-1982	3.110	0.130	48.000	2.00	19.05	95 Cu, 5 Zn	8.83
1982-	2.500	0.100	38.581	1.54	19.05	97.5 Zn,2.5 Cu****	7.17

Two cents

COIN/ DATES	GRAMS WGT.	TOL.	GRAINS WGT.	TOL.	DIA. (mm)	COMPOSITION	SPEC. GRAV.
1864-1873	6.221	0.259	96.000	4.00	23.00*	95 Cu, 5 Zn & Sn	8.84

Copper-nickel 3 cents

COIN/ DATES	GRAMS WGT.	TOL.	GRAINS WGT.	TOL.	DIA. (mm)	COMPOSITION	SPEC. GRAV.
1865-1873	1.944	0.259	30.000	4.00	17.90*	75 Cu, 25 Ni	8.92
1873-1889	1.944	0.130	30.000	2.00	17.90*	75 Cu, 25 Ni	8.92

Copper-nickel 5 cents

COIN/ DATES	GRAMS WGT.	TOL.	GRAINS WGT.	TOL.	DIA. (mm)	COMPOSITION	SPEC. GRAV.
1866-1873	5.000	0.130	77.162	2.00	20.50*	75 Cu, 25 Ni	8.92
1873-1883	5.000	0.194	77.162	3.00	20.50*	75 Cu, 25 Ni	8.92
1883-1942	5.000	0.194	77.162	3.00	21.21	75 Cu, 25 Ni	8.92
1942-1945	5.000	0.194	77.162	3.00	21.21	56 Cu, 35 Ag, 9 Mn	9.25*
1946-	5.000	0.194	77.162	3.00	21.21	75 Cu, 25 Ni	8.92

Silver 3 cents

COIN/ DATES	GRAMS WGT.	TOL.	GRAINS WGT.	TOL.	DIA. (mm)	COMPOSITION	SPEC. GRAV.
1851-1853	0.802	0.032	12.375	0.50	14.00*	750 Ag, 250 Cu	10.11
1854-1873	0.746	0.032	11.520	0.50	14.00*	900 Ag, 100 Cu	10.34

Half dimes

COIN/ DATES	GRAMS WGT.	TOL.	GRAINS WGT.	TOL.	DIA. (mm)	COMPOSITION	SPEC. GRAV.
1794-1795	1.348		20.800		16.50*	900 Ag, 100 Cu	10.34
1795-1805	1.348		20.800		16.50*	892.427 Ag, 107.572 Cu	10.32
1829-1837	1.348		20.800		15.50*	892.427 Ag, 107.572 Cu	10.32
1837-1853	1.336	0.032	20.625	0.50	15.50*	900 Ag, 100 Cu	10.34
1853-1873	1.244	0.032	19.200	0.50	15.50*	900 Ag, 100 Cu	10.34

Dimes

COIN/ DATES	GRAMS WGT.	TOL.	GRAINS WGT.	TOL.	DIA. (mm)	COMPOSITION	SPEC. GRAV.
1796-1828	2.696		41.600		18.80*	892.427 Ag, 107.572 Cu	10.32
1828-187	2.696		41.600		17.90*	892.427 Ag, 107.572 Cu	10.32
1837-1853	2.673	0.032	41.250	0.50	17.90*	900 Ag, 100 Cu	10.34
1853-1873	2.488	0.032	38.400	0.50	17.90*	900 Ag, 100 Cu	10.34
1873-1964	2.500	0.097	38.581	1.50	17.91	900 Ag, 100 Cu	10.34
1965-	2.268	0.091Δ	35.000	1.40Δ	17.91	75 Cu, 25 Ni on pure Cu	8.92

Twenty cents

COIN/ DATES	GRAMS WGT.	TOL.	GRAINS WGT.	TOL.	DIA. (mm)	COMPOSITION	SPEC. GRAV.
1875-1878	5.000	0.097	77.162	1.50	22.50*	900 Ag, 100 Cu	10.34

Quarter dollars

COIN/	GRAMS		GRAINS		DIA.		SPEC.
DATES	WGT.	TOL.	WGT.	TOL.	(mm)	COMPOSITION	GRAV.
1796-1828	6.739		104.000		27.00*	892.427 Ag, 107.572 Cu	10.32
1831-1837	6.739		104.000		24.26*	892.427 Ag, 107.572 Cu	10.32
1837-1853	6.682	0.065	103.125	1.00	24.26*	900 Ag, 100 Cu	10.34
1853-1873	6.221	0.065	96.000	1.00	24.26*	900 Ag, 100 Cu	10.34
1873-1947	6.250	0.097	96.452	1.50	24.26	900 Ag, 100 Cu	10.34
1947-1964	6.250	0.194	96.452	3.00	24.26	900 Ag, 100 Cu	10.34
1965-	5.670	0.227Δ	87.500	3.50Δ	24.26	75 Cu, 25 Ni on pure Cu	8.92
1976	5.750Δ	0.200Δ	88.736Δ	3.09Δ	24.26	40% silver clad**	9.53

Half dollars

COIN/	GRAMS		GRAINS		DIA.		SPEC.
DATES	WGT.	TOL.	WGT.	TOL.	(mm)	COMPOSITION	GRAV.
1794-1795	13.478		208.000		32.50*	900 Ag, 100 Cu	10.34
1796-1836	13.478		208.000		32.50*	892.427 Ag, 107.572 Cu	10.32
1836-1853	13.365	0.097	206.250	1.50	30.61*	900 Ag, 100 Cu	10.34
1853-1873	12.441	0.097	192.000	1.50	30.61*	900 Ag, 100 Cu	10.34
1873-1947	12.500	0.097	192.904	1.50	30.61	900 Ag, 100 Cu	10.34
1947-1964	12.500	0.259	192.904	4.00	30.61	900 Ag, 100 Cu	10.34
1965-1970	11.500	0.400Δ	177.472	6.17Δ	30.61	40% silver clad**	9.53
1971-	11.340	0.454Δ	175.000	7.00Δ	30.61	75 Cu, 25 Ni on pure Cu	8.92
1976	11.500	0.400Δ	177.472	6.17Δ	30.61	40% silver clad**	9.53

Silver dollars, clad dollars

COIN/	GRAMS		GRAINS		DIA.		SPEC.
DATES	WGT.	TOL.	WGT.	TOL.	(mm)	COMPOSITION	GRAV.
1794-1795	26.956		416.000		39.50*	900 Ag, 100 Cu	10.34
1796-1803	26.956		416.000		39.50*	892.427 Ag, 107.572 Cu	10.32
1840-1935	26.730	0.097	412.500	1.50	38.10	900 Ag, 100 Cu	10.34
1971-1978	22.680	0.907Δ	350.000	14.00Δ	38.10	75 Cu, 25 Ni on pure Cu	8.92
1971-1976	24.592	0.984Δ	379.512	15.18Δ	38.10	40% silver clad**	9.53
1979-1981	8.100	0.300Δ	125.000	5.000Δ	26.5	75 Cu, 25 Ni on pure Cu	8.92

Trade dollars

COIN/	GRAMS		GRAINS		DIA.		SPEC.
DATES	WGT.	TOL.	WGT.	TOL.	(mm)	COMPOSITION	GRAV.
1873-1883	27.216	0.097	420.000	1.50	38.10	900 Ag, 100 Cu	10.34

Gold dollars

COIN/	GRAMS		GRAINS		DIA.		SPEC.
DATES	WGT.	TOL.	WGT.	TOL.	(mm)	COMPOSITION	GRAV.
1849-1854	1.672	0.016	25.800	0.25	13.00*	900 Au, 100 Cu & Ag	17.16
1854-1873	1.672	0.016	25.800	0.25	14.86*	900 Au, 100 Cu & Ag	17.16
1873-1889	1.672	0.016	25.800	0.25	14.86*	900 Au, 100 Cu	17.16

Quarter eagles

COIN/	GRAMS		GRAINS		DIA.		SPEC.
DATES	WGT.	TOL.	WGT.	TOL.	(mm)	COMPOSITION	GRAV.
1796-1808	4.374		67.500		20.00*	916.667 Au, 83.333 Cu & Ag	17.45
1821-1827	4.374		67.500		18.50*	916.667 Au, 83.333 Cu & Ag	17.45
1829-1834	4.374		67.500		18.20*	916.667 Au, 83.333 Cu+Ag	17.45
1834-1836	4.180	0.008	64.500	0.13	18.20*	899.225 Au, 100.775 Cu+Ag	17.14
1837-1839	4.180	0.016	64.500	0.25	18.20*	900 Au, 100 Cu+Ag	17.16
1840-1873	4.180	0.016	64.500	0.25	17.78*	900 Au, 100 Cu+Ag	17.16
1873-1929	4.180	0.016	64.500	0.25	17.78*	900 Au, 100 Cu	17.16

Three dollars

COIN/	GRAMS		GRAINS		DIA.		SPEC.
DATES	WGT.	TOL.	WGT.	TOL.	(mm)	COMPOSITION	GRAV.
1854-1873	5.015		77.400		20.63*	900 Au, 100 Cu+Ag	17.16
1873-1889	5.015	0.016	77.400	0.25	20.63*	900 Au, 100 Cu	17.16

Half eagles

COIN/	GRAMS		GRAINS		DIA.		SPEC.
DATES	WGT.	TOL.	WGT.	TOL.	(mm)	COMPOSITION	GRAV.
1795-1829	8.748		135.000		25.00*	916.667 Au, 83.333 Cu+Ag	17.45
1829-1834	8.748		135.000		22.50*	916.667 Au, 83.333 Cu+Ag	17.45

1834-1836	8.359	0.017	129.000	0.26	22.50*	899.225 Au, 100.775 Cu+Ag	17.14
1837-1840	8.359	0.016	129.000	0.25	22.50*	900 Au, 100 Cu+Ag	17.16
1840-1849	8.359	0.016	129.000	0.25	21.54*	900 Au, 100 Cu+Ag	17.16
1849-1873	8.359	0.032	129.000	0.50	21.54*	900 Au, 100 Cu+Ag	17.16
1873-1929	8.359	0.016	129.000	0.25	21.54*	900 Au, 100 Cu	17.16

Eagles

COIN/ DATES	GRAMS WGT.	TOL.	GRAINS WGT.	TOL.	DIA. (mm)	COMPOSITION	SPEC. GRAV.
1795-1804	17.496		270.000		33.00*	916.667 Au, 83.333 Cu+Ag	17.45
1838-1849	16.718	0.016	258.000	0.25	27.00*	900 Au, 100 Cu+Ag	17.16
1849-1873	16.718	0.032	258.000	0.50	27.00*	900 Au, 100 Cu+Ag	17.16
1873-1933	16.718	0.032	258.000	0.50	27.00*	900 Au, 100 Cu	17.16

Double eagles

COIN/ DATES	GRAMS WGT.	TOL.	GRAINS WGT.	TOL.	DIA. (mm)	COMPOSITION	SPEC. GRAV.
1850-1873	33.436	0.032	516.000	0.50	34.29	900 Au, 100 Cu+Ag	17.16
1873-1933	33.436	0.032	516.000	0.50	34.29	900 Au, 100 Cu	17.16

American Eagle bullion coins

DENOM.	GRAMS WGT.	OUNCES WGT.	MM DIA.	COMPOSITION	OUNCE ALLOY WGTS.
$1 one-ounce	31.103	1.000	40.1	.999 Ag	
$5 tenth-ounce	3.393	0.1091	16.5	916.7 Au, 3.0 Ag, 5.33 Cu	1.000 Au
					0.003 Ag
					0.006 Cu
$10 quarter-ounce	8.483	0.2727	22	916.7 Au, 3.0 Ag, 5.33 Cu	0.250 Au
					0.008 Ag
					0.015 Cu
$25 half-ounce	16.966	0.5455	27	916.7 Au, 3.0 Ag, 5.33 Cu	0.500 Au
					0.016 Ag
					0.029 Cu
$50 one-ounce	33.931	1.091	32.7	916.7 Au, 3.0 Ag, 5.33 Cu	1.000 Au
					0.033 Ag
					0.058 Cu

* Unofficial data.
** Consists of layers of 800 Ag, 200 Cu bonded to a core of 215 Ag, 785 Cu.
*** Cents struck on steel planchets produced in 1942 weigh 41.5 grains, while those struck on planchets produced later in 1943 weigh 42.5 grains.
**** Consists of a planchet composed of 99.2 percent zinc and 0.8 copper, the whole plated with pure copper.
Δ Not specified by law, established instead by the Director of the Mint.
Au=Gold; Ag=Silver; Cu=Copper; Mn=Manganese; Ni=Nickel; Sn=Tin; Zn=Zinc.

Proof, Uncirculated production

The following information outlines the differences in production procedures for Proof and Uncirculated coins.

Blanking
Proof: Extra care used in blanking.
Uncirculated: High speed.

Annealing
Proof: Single layer of blanks moved through a special furnace on a slow-moving belt.
Uncirculated: Blanks processed in a high capacity rotary furnace capable of holding 4,000 pounds at a time.

Burnishing blanks
Proof: Burnished to a high luster with shot.
Uncirculated: Self-burnishing only.

Deoxidation treatment, drying
Proof: Use of freon and deoxidation.
Uncirculated: Not treated.

Inspection
Proof: Blanks inspected by hand by pressmen prior to stamping.
Uncirculated: Blanks not inspected by hand.

Coinage dies
Proof: Coinage dies polished to a high luster by hand prior to use and buffed during use to maintain luster.

Uncirculated: Dies not polished.

Press feed
Proof: Press hand fed one at a time and blanks struck twice or more.
Uncirculated: High speed, automatic presses used; coins struck once.

Retrieval from press
Proof: Coins retrieved individually.
Uncirculated: Coins retrieved in bulk.

Handling of struck coin
Proof: Coins specially handled in small boxes.
Uncirculated: Coins handled in bulk.

Visual inspection
Proof: Visual inspection done individually.
Uncirculated: Visual inspection limited.

Precautions in packaging room
Proof: Special lighting, air conditioning, dust control in room; employees wear white gloves.
Uncirculated: Standard accommodations and atmosphere prevail.

Packaging
Proof: Coins individually packaged in sonic sealed cases.
Uncirculated: Sealed in automatic heat sealer.

Regular issue U.S. coins

The following mintage figures are a listing of the number of non-Proof coins struck in each year and each Mint, and which theoretically were released into circulation and thereby made available to collectors. In cases where a certain number of coins in a production run were melted at the Mint, the amount is subtracted from the total and/or footnoted.

In many instances the figures given are reconstructions and may be inaccurate. Prior to about 1950 the generally accepted source of mintage figures was the U.S. Mint Report. Since the Mint Report for many years was simply a bookkeeper's record of how many coins were issued in a particular year, the figures given often had no relation to the actual number of coins struck. In the last two decades much investigation has been done into the actual number of coins struck with each date. The following is a compilation from many sources.

Prior to 1860, production of Proof coins was small and no Proof mintage figures were kept. From 1860 on, Proof figures were kept for gold and silver coins only, as minor coins were considered unimportant. Beginning in 1878 records were kept for the minor coins as well.

Half cents

Year	Mintage
1793	35,334
1794	81,600
1795	139,690
1796	1,390
1797	127,840
1800	202,908
1802	20,266
1803	92,000
1804	1,055,312
1805	814,464
1806	356,000
1807	476,000
1808	400,000
1809	1,154,572
1810	215,000
1811[9]	63,140
1825	63,000
1826	234,000
1828	606,000
1829	487,000

Half cents continued

Year	Mintage
1831[15]	2,200
1832	154,000[16]
1833	120,000[16]
1834	141,000[16]
1835	398,000[16]
1836[21]	0
1840-48 (P)[30]	0
1849 (P)[15]	43,364
1850 (P)	39,812
1851 (P)	147,672
1852(P)[30]	0
1853(P)	129,694
1854 (P)	55,358
1855 (P)	56,500
1856 (P)[15]	40,430
1857 (P)[15]	35,180

Cents

Year	Mintage
1793	110,512[1]
1794	918,521

Cents continued

Year	Mintage
1795	538,500
1796	473,200[3]
1797	897,510
1798	1,841,745
1799	42,540
1800	2,822,175
1801	1,362,837
1802	3,435,100
1803	3,131,691
1804	96,500[9]
1805	941,116
1806	348,000
1807	829,221
1808	1,007,000
1809	222,867
1810	1,458,500
1811	218,025
1812	1,075,500
1813	418,000
1814	357,830
1816	2,820,982
1817	3,948,400
1818	3,167,000

Cents continued

Year	Mintage
1819	2,671,000
1820	4,407,550
1821	389,000
1822	2,072,339
1823[9]	68,061
1824	1,193,939
1825	1,461,100
1826	1,517,425
1827	2,357,732
1828	2,260,624
1829	1,414,500
1830	1,711,500
1831	3,539,260
1832	2,362,000
1833	2,739,000
1834	1,855,100
1835	3,878,400
1836	2,111,000
1837	5,558,300
1838 (P)	6,370,200
1839 (P)	3,128,661
1840 (P)	2,462,700
1841 (P)	1,597,367

Cents continued

1842 (P)	2,383,390
1843 (P)	2,425,342
1844 (P)	2,398,752
1845 (P)	3,894,804
1846 (P)	4,120,800
1847 (P)	6,183,669
1848 (P)	6,415,799
1849 (P)	4,178,500
1850 (P)	4,426,844
1851 (P)	9,889,707
1852 (P)	5,063,094
1853 (P)	6,641,131
1854 (P)	4,236,156
1855 (P)	1,574,829
1856(P)	2,690,463[41]
1857 (P)	17,783,456[42]
1858 (P)	24,600,000
1859 (P)	36,400,000[44]
1860 (P)	20,566,000
1861 (P)	10,100,000
1862 (P)	28,075,000
1863 (P)	49,840,000
1864 (P)	52,973,714[57]
1865 (P)	35,429,286
1866 (P)	9,826,500
1867 (P)	9,821,000
1868 (P)	10,266,500
1869 (P)	6,420,000
1870 (P)	5,275,000
1871 (P)	3,929,500
1872 (P)	4,042,000
1873(P)[68]	11,676,500
1874 (P)	14,187,500
1875 (P)	13,528,000
1876 (P)	7,944,000
1877 (P)	852,500
1878 (P)	5,797,500
1879 (P)	16,228,000
1880 (P)	38,961,000
1881 (P)	39,208,000
1882 (P)	38,578,000
1883 (P)	45,591,500
1884 (P)	23,257,800
1885 (P)	11,761,594
1886 (P)	17,650,000
1887 (P)	45,223,523
1888 (P)	37,489,832
1889 (P)	48,866,025
1892 (P)	37,647,087
1893 (P)	46,640,000
1894 (P)	16,749,500
1895 (P)	38,341,574
1896(P)	39,055,431
1897(P)	50,464,392
1898(P)	49,821,284
1899(P)	53,598,000
1900 (P)	66,821,284
1901(P)	79,609,158
1902(P)	87,374,704
1903(P)	85,092,703
1904 (P)	61,326,198
1905 (P)	80,717,011
1906 (P)	96,020,530
1907 (P)	108,137,143
1908 (P)	32,326,367
1908-S	1,115,000
1909 (P)	115,063,470[89]
1909-S	2,618,00[89]
1910 (P)	146,798,813
1910-S	6,045,000
1911 (P)	101,176,054
1911-D	12,672,000

Cents continued

1911-S	4,026,000
1912 (P)	68,150,915
1912-D	10,411,000
1912-S	4,431,000
1913 (P)	76,529,504
1913-D	15,804,000
1913-S	6,101,000
1914 (P)	75,237,067
1914-D	1,193,000
1914-S	4,137,000
1915 (P)	29,090,970
1915-D	22,050,000
1915-S	4,833,000
1916 (P)	131,832,627
1916-D	35,956,000
1916-S	22,510,000
1917 (P)	196,429,785
1917-D	55,120,000
1917-S	32,620,000
1918 (P)	288,104,634
1918-D	47,830,000
1918-S	34,680,000
1919 (P)	392,021,000
1919-D	57,154,000
1919-S	139,760,000
1920 (P)	310,165,000
1920-D	49,280,000
1920-S	46,220,000
1921 (P)	39,157,000
1921-S	15,274,000
1922-D[97]	7,160,000
1923 (P)	74,723,000
1923-S	8,700,000
1924 (P)	75,178,000
1924-D	2,520,000
1924-S	11,696,000
1925 (P)	139,949,000
1925-D	22,580,000
1925-S	26,380,000
1926 (P)	157,088,000
1926-D	28,020,000
1926-S	4,550,000
1927 (P)	144,440,000
1927-D	27,170,000
1927-S	14,276,000
1928 (P)	134,116,000
1928-D	31,170,000
1928-S	17,266,000
1929 (P)	185,262,000
1929-D	41,730,000
1929-S	50,148,000
1930 (P)	157,415,000
1930-D	40,100,000
1930-S	24,286,000
1931 (P)	19,396,000
1931-D	4,480,000
1931-S	866,000
1932 (P)	9,062,000
1932-D	10,500,000
1933 (P)	14,360,000
1933-D	6,200,000
1934 (P)	219,080,000
1934-D	28,446,000
1935 (P)	245,388,000
1935-D	47,000,000
1935-S	38,702,000
1936 (P)	309,632,000
1936-D	40,620,000
1936-S	29,130,000
1937 (P)	309,170,000
1937-D	50,430,000
1937-S	34,500,000
1938 (P)	156,682,000

Cents continued

1938-D	20,010,000
1938-S	15,180,000
1939 (P)	316,466,000
1939-D	15,160,000
1939-S	52,070,000
1940 (P)	586,810,000
1940-D	81,390,000
1940-S	112,940,000
1941 (P)	887,018,000
1941-D	128,700,000
1941-S	92,360,000
1942 (P)	657,796,000
1942-D	206,698,000
1942-S	85,590,000
1943(P)[102]	684,628,670
1943-D	217,660,000
1943-S	191,550,000
1944 (P)	1,435,400,000
1944-D	430,578,000
1944-S	282,760,000
1945 (P)	1,040,515,000
1945-D	226,268,000
1945-S	181,770,000
1946 (P)	991,655,000
1946-D	315,690,000
1946-S	198,100,000
1947 (P)	190,555,000
1947-D	194,750,000
1947-S	99,000,000
1948 (P)	317,570,000
1948-D	172,637,500
1948-S	81,735,000
1949 (P)	217,775,000
1949-D	153,132,500
1949-S	64,290,000
1950 (P)	272,635,000
1950-D	334,950,000
1950-S	118,505,000
1951 (P)	294,576,000
1951-D	625,355,000
1951-S	136,010,000
1952 (P)	186,765,000
1952-D	746,130,000
1952-S	137,800,004
1953 (P)	256,755,000
1953-D	700,515,000
1953-S	181,835,000
1954 (P)	71,640,050
1954-D	251,552,500
1954-S	96,190,000
1955 (P)	330,580,000
1955-D	563,257,500
1955-S	44,610,000
1956 (P)	420,745,000
1956-D	1,098,210,100
1957 (P)	282,540,000
1957-D	1,051,342,000
1958 (P)	252,525,000
1958-D	800,953,300
1959 (P)	609,715,000
1959-D	1,279,760,000
1960 (P)	586,405,000
1960-D	1,580,884,000
1961 (P)	753,345,000
1961-D	1,753,266,700
1962 (P)	606,045,000
1962-D	1,793,148,400
1963 (P)	754,110,000
1963-D	1,774,020,400
1964(P)[104]	
	2,648,575,000
1964-D	3,799,071,500
1965(P)[104]	301,470,000

Cents continued

1965 (D)	973,364,900
1965 (S)	220,030,000
1966(P)[104]	811,100,000
1966 (D)	991,431,200
1966 (S)	383,355,000
1967(P)[104]	907,575,000
1967 (D)	1,327,377,100
1967 (S)	813,715,000
1968 (P)	1,707,880,970
1968-D	2,886,269,600
1968-S	258,270,001
1969 (P)	1,136,910,000
1969-D	4,002,832,200
1969-S	544,375,000
1970 (P)	1,898,315,000
1970-D	2,891,438,900
1970-S	690,560,004
1971 (P)	1,919,490,000
1971-D	2,911,045,600
1971-S	525,130,054
1972 (P)	2,933,255,000
1972-D	2,655,071,400
1972-S	380,200,104
1973 (P)	3,728,245,000
1973-D	3,549,576,588
1973-S	319,937,634
1974 (P)	4,232,140,523
1974-D	4,235,098,000
1974-S	409,421,878
1975 (P)	3,874,182,000
1975-D	4,505,275,300
1975-S	0(53)
1975 (W)	1,577,294,142
1976 (P)	3,133,580,000
1976-D	4,221,592,455
1976-S	0(53)
1976 (W)	1,540,695,000
1977 (P)	3,074,575,000
1977-D	4,194,062,300
1977-S	0(53)
1977 (W)	1,395,355,000
1978 (P)	3,735,655,000
1978-D	4,280,233,400
1978 (S)	291,700,000
1978 (W)	1,531,250,000
1979 (P)	3,560,940,000
1979-D	4,139,357,254
1979 (S)	751,725,000
1979 (W)	1,705,850,000
1980 (P)	6,230,115,000
1980-D	5,140,098,660
1980 (S)	1,184,590,000
1980 (W)	1,576,200,000
1981 (P)	6,611,305,000
1981-D	5,373,235,677
1981 (S)	880,440,000
1981 (W)	1,882,400,000
1982[114](P)	
	7,135,275,000
1982-D	6,012,979,368
1982 (S)	1,587,245,000
1982 (W)	1,990,005,000
1983 (P)	5,567,190,000
1983-D	6,467,199,428
1983 (S)	180,765,000
1983 (W)	2,004,400,000
1984 (P)	6,114,864,000
1984-D	5,569,238,906
1984 (W)	2,036,215,000
1985 (P)	4,951,904,887
1985-D	5,287,399,926
1985 (W)	696,585,000
1986 (P)	4,490,995,493

Cents continued

Year	Mintage
1986-D	4,442,866,698
1986 (W)	400,000
1987 (P)	4,682,466,931
1987-D	4,879,389,514
1988 (P)	6,092,810,000
1988-D	5,253,740,443
1989 (P)	7,261,535,000
1989-D	5,345,467,711

Two cents

Year	Mintage
1864 (P)[56]	19,847,500
1865 (P)	13,640,000
1866 (P)	3,177,000
1867 (P)	2,938,750
1868 (P)	2,803,750
1869 (P)	1,546,500
1870 (P)	861,250
1871 (P)	721,250
1872 (P)	65,000
1873(P)[68]	0(74)

Three cent
(copper-nickel)

Year	Mintage
1865 (P)	11,382,000
1866 (P)	4,801,000
1867 (P)	3,915,000
1868 (P)	3,252,000
1869 (P)	1,604,000
1870 (P)	1,335,000
1871 (P)	604,000
1872 (P)	862,000
1873 (P)[68]	1,173,000
1874 (P)	790,000
1875 (P)	228,000
1876 (P)	162,000
1877 (P)	0[53]
1878 (P)	0[53]
1879 (P)	38,000
1880 (P)	21,000
1881 (P)	1,077,000
1882 (P)	22,200
1883 (P)	4,000
1884 (P)	1,700
1885 (P)	1,000
1886 (P)	0[53]
1887 (P)	5,001
1888 (P)	36,501
1889 (P)	18,125

Three cent
(silver)

Year	Mintage
1851 (P)	5,447,400
1851-O	720,000
1852 (P)	18,663,500
1853 (P)[34]	11,400,000
1854 (P)	671,000
1855 (P)	139,000
1856 (P)	1,458,000
1857 (P)	1,042,000
1858 (P)	1,604,000
1859 (P)	365,000
1860 (P)	286,000
1861 (P)	497,000
1862 (P)	343,000
1863 (P)	21,000[54]
1864 (P)	12,000[55]
1865 (P)	8,000

Three cents continued

Year	Mintage
1866 (P)	22,000
1867 (P)	4,000
1868 (P)	3,500
1869 (P)	4,500
1870 (P)	3,000
1871 (P)	3,400
1872 (P)	1,000
1873 (P)[68]	0(53)

Five cents

Year	Mintage
1866 (P)	14,742,500
1867 (P)	30,909,500[64]
1868 (P)	28,817,000
1869 (P)	16,395,000
1870 (P)	4,806,000
1871 (P)	561,000
1872 (P)	6,036,000
1873 (P)[68]	4,550,000
1874 (P)	3,538,000
1875 (P)	2,097,000
1876 (P)	2,530,000
1877 (P)	0[53]
1878 (P)	0[53]
1879 (P)	25,900
1880 (P)	16,000
1881 (P)	68,800
1882 (P)	11,473,500
1883 (P)	22,952,000[80]
1884 (P)	11,270,000
1885 (P)	1,472,700
1886 (P)	3,326,000
1887 (P)	15,260,692
1888 (P)	10,715,901
1889 (P)	15,878,025
1890 (P)	16,256,532
1891 (P)	16,832,000
1892 (P)	11,696,897
1893 (P)	13,368,000
1894 (P)	5,410,500
1895 (P)	9,977,822
1896 (P)	8,841,058
1897 (P)	20,426,797
1898 (P)	12,530,292
1899 (P)	26,027,000
1900 (P)	27,253,733
1901 (P)	26,478,228
1902 (P)	31,487,561
1903 (P)	28,004,935
1904 (P)	21,401,350
1905 (P)	29,825,124
1906 (P)	38,612,000
1907 (P)	39,213,325
1908 (P)	22,684,557
1909 (P)	11,585,763
1910 (P)	30,166,948
1911 (P)	39,557,639
1912 (P)	26,234,569
1912-D	8,474,000
1912-S	238,000
1913 (P)[90]	60,849,186[91]
1913-D	9,493,000[91]
1913-S	3,314,000[91]
1914 (P)	20,664,463
1914-D	3,912,000
1914-S	3,470,000
1915 (P)	20,986,220
1915-D	7,569,500
1915-S	1,505,000
1916 (P)	63,497,466
1916-D	13,333,000

Five cents continued

Year	Mintage
1916-S	11,860,000
1917 (P)	51,424,029
1917-D	9,910,800
1917-S	4,193,000
1918 (P)	32,086,314
1918-D	8,362,000
1918-S	4,882,000
1919 (P)	60,868,000
1919-D	8,006,000
1919-S	7,521,000
1920 (P)	63,093,000
1920-D	9,418,000
1920-S	9,689,000
1921 (P)	10,663,000
1921-S	1,557,000
1923 (P)	35,715,000
1923-S	6,142,000
1924 (P)	21,620,000
1924-D	5,258,000
1924-S	1,437,000
1925 (P)	35,565,100
1925-D	4,450,000
1925-S	6,256,000
1926 (P)	44,693,000
1926-D	5,638,000
1926-S	970,000
1927 (P)	37,981,000
1927-D	5,730,000
1927-S	3,430,000
1928 (P)	23,411,000
1928-D	6,436,000
1928-S	6,936,000
1929 (P)	36,446,000
1929-D	8,370,000
1929-S	7,754,000
1930 (P)	22,849,000
1930-S	5,435,000
1931-S	1,200,000
1934 (P)	20,213,003
1934-D	7,480,000
1935 (P)	58,264,000
1935-D	12,092,000
1935-S	10,300,000
1936 (P)	118,997,000
1936-D	24,814,000
1936-S	14,930,000
1937 (P)	79,480,000
1937-D	17,826,000
1937-S	5,635,000
1938 (P)	19,496,000
1938-D	12,396,000[100]
1938-S	4,105,000
1939 (P)	120,615,000
1939-D	3,514,000
1939-S	6,630,000
1940 (P)	176,485,000
1940-D	43,540,000
1940-S	39,690,000
1941 (P)	203,265,000
1941-D	53,432,000
1941-S	43,445,000
1942 (P)P	
	107,662,000[101]
1942-D	13,938,000
1942-S	32,900,000
1943-P	271,165,000
1943-D	15,294,000
1943-S	104,060,000
1944-P[103]	119,150,000
1944-D	32,309,000
1944-S	21,640,000
1945-P	119,408,100
1945-D	37,158,000

Five cents continued

Year	Mintage
1945-S	58,939,000
1946 (P)	161,116,000
1946-D	45,292,200
1946-S	13,560,000
1947 (P)	95,000,000
1947-D	37,822,000
1947-S	24,720,000
1948 (P)	89,348,000
1948-D	44,734,000
1948-S	11,300,000
1949 (P)	60,652,000
1949-D	36,498,000
1949-S	9,716,000
1950 (P)	9,796,000
1950-D	2,630,030
1951 (P)	28,552,000
1951-D	20,460,000
1951-S	7,776,000
1952 (P)	63,988,000
1952-D	30,638,000
1952-S	20,572,000
1953 (P)	46,644,000
1953-D	59,878,600
1953-S	19,210,900
1954 (P)	47,684,050
1954-D	117,136,560
1954-S	29,384,000
1955 (P)	7,888,000
1955-D	74,464,100
1956 (P)	35,216,000
1956-D	67,222,640
1957 (P)	38,408,000
1957-D	136,828,900
1958 (P)	17,088,000
1958-D	168,249,120
1959 (P)	27,248,000
1959-D	160,738,240
1960 (P)	55,416,000
1960-D	192,582,180
1961 (P)	73,640,000
1961-D	229,342,760
1962 (P)	97,384,000
1962-D	280,195,720
1963 (P)	175,776,000
1963-D	276,829,460
1964 (P)[104]	
	1,024,672,000
1964-D	1,787,297,160
1965 (P)[104]	12,440,000
1965 (D)	82,291,380
1965 (S)	39,040,000
1966 (P)[104]	0
1966 (D)	103,546,700
1966 (S)	50,400,000
1967 (P)[104]	0
1967 (D)	75,993,800
1967 (S)	31,332,000
1968 (P)	0
1968-D	91,227,880
1968-S	100,396,004
1969 (P)	0
1969-D	202,807,500
1969-S	120,165,000
1970-D	515,485,380
1970-S	238,832,004
1971 (P)	106,884,000
1971-D	316,144,800
1971-S	0[53]
1972 (P)	202,036,000
1972-D	351,694,600
1972-S	0[53]
1973 (P)	384,396,000

Five cents continued

Year	Mintage
1973-D	261,405,400
1973-S	0[53]
1974 (P)	601,752,000
1974-D	277,373,000
1974-S	0[53]
1975 (P)	181,772,000
1975-D	401,875,300
1976 (P)	367,124,000
1976-D	563,964,147
1976-S	0[53]
1977 (P)	585,376,000
1977-D	297,313,422
1977-S	0[53]
1978 (P)	391,308,000
1978-D	313,092,780
1978-S	0[53]
1979 (P)	463,188,000
1979-D	325,867,672
1979-S	0[53]
1980 -P	593,004,000
1980-D	502,323,448
1980-S	0[53]
1981-P	657,504,000
1981-D	364,801,843
1981-S	0[53]
1982-P	292,355,000
1982-D	373,726,544
1982-S	0[53]
1983-P	561,615,000
1983-D	536,726,276
1983-S	0[53]
1984-P	746,769,000
1984-D	517,675,146
1984-S	0[53]
1985-P	647,114,962
1985-D	459,747,446
1985-S	0[53]
1986-P	536,883,493
1986-D	361,819,144
1986-S	0[53]
1987-P	371,499,481
1987-D	410,590,604
1987-S	0[53]
1988-P	771,360,000
1988-D	663,771,652
1988-S	0[53]
1989-P	898,812,000
1989-D	570,842,474

Half dimes

Year	Mintage
1794	7,756
1795	78,660
1796	10,230
1797	44,527
1800	40,000
1801	33,910
1802	13,010
1803	37,850
1805	15,600
1829	1,230,000
1830	1,240,000
1831	1,242,700
1832	965,000
1833	1,370,000
1834	1,480,000
1835	2,760,000
1836	1,900,000
1837	2,276,000[23]
1838 (P)	2,255,000

Half dimes continued

Year	Mintage
1838-O[26]	115,000
1839 (P)	1,069,150
1839-O	981,550
1840 (P)	1,344,085
1840-O	935,000
1841 (P)	1,150,000
1841-O	815,000
1842 (P)	815,000
1842-O	350,000
1843 (P)	1,165,000
1844 (P)	430,000
1844-O	220,000
1845 (P)	1,564,000
1846 (P)	27,000
1847 (P)	1,274,000
1848 (P)	668,000
1848-O	600,000
1849 (P)	1,309,000
1849-O	140,000
1850 (P)	955,000
1850-O	690,000
1851 (P)	781,000
1851-O	860,000
1852 (P)	1,000,500
1852-O	260,000
1853 (P)[34]	13,345,020[38]
1853-O	2,360,000[38]
1854 (P)	5,740,000
1854-O	1,560,000
1855 (P)	1,750,000
1855-O	600,000
1856 (P)	4,880,000
1856-O	1,100,000
1857 (P)	7,280,000
1857-O	1,380,000
1858 (P)	3,500,000
1858-O	1,660,000
1859 (P)	340,000
1859-O	560,000
1860 (P)[46]	798,000
1860-O	1,060,000
1861 (P)	3,360,000
1862 (P)	1,492,000
1863 (P)	18,000
1863-S	100,000
1864 (P)	48,000[55]
1864-S	90,000
1865 (P)	13,000
1865-S	120,000
1866 (P)	10,000
1866-S	120,000
1867 (P)	8,000
1867-S	120,000
1868 (P)	88,600
1868-S	280,000
1869 (P)	208,000
1869-S	230,000
1870 (P)	535,600
1871 (P)	1,873,000
1871-S	161,000
1872 (P)	2,947,000
1872-S	837,000
1873 (P)[68]	712,000
1873-S[68]	324,000

Dimes

Year	Mintage
1796	22,135
1797	25,261
1798	27,550

Dimes continued

Year	Mintage
1800	21,760
1801	34,640
1802	10,975
1803	33,040
1804	8,265
1805	120,780
1807	165,000
1809	51,065
1811	65,180
1814	421,500
1820	942,587
1821	1,186,512
1822	100,000
1823	440,000
1824	100,000
1825	410,000
1827	1,215,000
1828	125,000
1829	770,000
1830	510,000
1831	771,350
1832	522,500
1833	485,000
1834	635,000
1835	1,410,000
1836	1,190,000
1837	1,042,000[22]
1838 (P)	1,992,500
1838-O[26]	406,034
1839 (P)	1,053,115
1839-O	1,323,000
1840 (P)	1,358,580
1840-O	1,175,000
1841 (P)	1,622,500
1841-O	2,007,500
1842 (P)	1,887,500
1842-O	2,020,000
1843 (P)	1,370,000
1843-O	150,000
1844 (P)	72,500
1845 (P)	1,755,000
1845-O	230,000
1846 (P)	31,300
1847 (P)	245,000
1848 (P)	451,500
1849 (P)	839,000
1849-O	300,000
1850 (P)	1,931,500
1850-O	510,000
1851 (P)	1,026,500
1851-O	400,000
1852 (P)	1,535,500
1852-O	430,000
1853 (P)[34]	12,173,010[37]
1853-O[34]	1,100,000[37]
1854 (P)	4,470,000
1854-O	1,770,000
1855 (P)	2,075,000
1856 (P)	5,780,000
1856-O	1,180,000
1856-S	70,000
1857 (P)	5,580,000
1857-O	1,540,000
1858 (P)	1,540,000
1858-O	290,000
1858-S	60,000
1859 (P)	430,000
1859-O	480,000
1859-S	60,000
1860 (P)[46]	606,000
1860-O	40,000
1860-S	140,000

Dimes continued

Year	Mintage
1861 (P)	1,883,000
1861-S	172,500
1862 (P)	847,000
1862-S	180,750
1863 (P)	14,000
1863-S	157,500
1864 (P)	11,000[55]
1864-S	230,000
1865 (P)	10,000
1865-S	175,000
1866 (P)	8,000
1866-S	135,000
1867 (P)	6,000
1867-S	140,000
1868 (P)	464,000
1868-S	260,000
1869 (P)	256,000
1869-S	450,000
1870 (P)	470,500
1870-S	50,000
1871 (P)	906,750
1871-CC	20,100
1871-S	320,000
1872 (P)	2,395,500
1872-CC	35,480
1872-S	190,000
1873 (P)[68]	3,945,700[73]
1873-CC[68]	31,191[73]
1873-S[68]	455,000[73]
1874 (P)	2,940,000
1874-CC	10,817
1874-S	240,000
1875 (P)	10,350,000
1875-CC	4,645,000
1875-S	9,070,000
1876 (P)	11,460,000
1876-CC	8,270,000
1876-S	10,420,000
1877 (P)	7,310,000
1877-CC	7,700,000
1877-S	2,340,000
1878 (P)	1,678,000
1878-CC	200,000
1879 (P)	14,000
1880 (P)	36,000
1881 (P)	24,000
1882 (P)	3,910,000
1883 (P)	7,674,673
1884 (P)	3,365,505
1884-S	564,969
1885 (P)	2,532,497
1885-S	43,690
1886 (P)	6,376,684
1886-S	206,524
1887 (P)	11,283,229
1887-S	4,454,450
1888 (P)	5,495,655
1888-S	1,720,000
1889 (P)	7,380,000
1889-S	972,678
1890 (P)	9,910,951
1890-S	1,423,076
1891 (P)	15,310,000
1891-O	4,540,000
1891-S	3,196,116
1892 (P)	12,120,000
1892-O	3,841,700
1892-S	990,710
1893 (P)	3,340,000
1893-O	1,760,000
1893-S	2,491,401
1894 (P)	1,330,000
1894-O	720,000

Dimes continued

Year	Mintage
1894-S	0[81]
1895 (P)	690,000
1895-O	440,000
1895-S	1,120,000
1896 (P)	2,000,000
1896-O	610,000
1896-S	575,056
1897 (P)	10,868,533
1897-O	666,000
1897-S	1,342,844
1898 (P)	16,320,000
1898-O	2,130,000
1898-S	1,702,507
1899 (P)	19,580,000
1899-O	2,650,000
1899-S	1,867,493
1900 (P)	17,600,000
1900-O	2,010,000
1900-S	5,168,270
1901 (P)	18,859,665
1901-O	5,620,000
1901-S	593,022
1902 (P)	21,380,000
1902-O	4,500,000
1902-S	2,070,000
1903 (P)	19,500,000
1903-O	8,180,000
1903-S	613,300
1904 (P)	14,600,357
1904-S	800,000
1905 (P)	14,551,623
1905-O	3,400,000
1905-S	6,855,199
1906 (P)	19,957,731
1906-D	4,060,000
1906-O	2,610,000
1906-S	3,136,640
1907 (P)	22,220,000
1907-D	4,080,000
1907-O	5,058,000
1907-S	3,178,470
1908 (P)	10,600,000
1908-D	7,490,000
1908-O	1,789,000
1908-S	3,220,000
1909 (P)	10,240,000
1909-D	954,000
1909-O	2,287,000
1909-S	1,000,000
1910 (P)	11,520,000
1910-D	3,490,000
1910-S	1,240,000
1911 (P)	18,870,000
1911-D	11,209,000
1911-S	3,520,000
1912 (P)	19,350,000
1912-D	11,760,000
1912-S	3,420,000
1913 (P)	19,760,000
1913-S	510,000
1914 (P)	17,360,230
1914-D	11,908,000
1914-S	2,100,000
1915 (P)	5,620,000
1915-S	960,000
1916 (P)	40,670,000[93]
1916-D	264,000[93]
1916-S	16,270,000[93]
1917 (P)	55,230,000
1917-D	9,402,000
1917-S	27,330,000
1918 (P)	26,680,000
1918-D	22,674,800

Dimes continued

Year	Mintage
1918-S	19,300,000
1919 (P)	35,740,000
1919-D	9,939,000
1919-S	8,850,000
1920 (P)	59,030,000
1920-D	19,171,000
1920-S	13,820,000
1921 (P)	1,230,000
1921-D	1,080,000
1923 (P)	50,130,000
1923-S	6,440,000
1924 (P)	24,010,000
1924-D	6,810,000
1924-S	7,120,000
1925 (P)	25,610,000
1925-D	5,117,000
1925-S	5,850,000
1926 (P)	32,160,000
1926-D	6,828,000
1926-S	1,520,000
1927 (P)	28,080,000
1927-D	4,812,000
1927-S	4,770,000
1928 (P)	19,480,000
1928-D	4,161,000
1928-S	7,400,000
1929 (P)	25,970,000
1929-D	5,034,000
1929-S	4,730,000
1930 (P)	6,770,000
1930-S	1,843,000
1931 (P)	3,150,000
1931-D	1,260,000
1931-S	1,800,000
1934 (P)	24,080,000
1934-D	6,772,000
1935 (P)	58,830,000
1935-D	10,477,000
1935-S	15,840,000
1936 (P)	87,500,000
1936-D	16,132,000
1936-S	9,210,000
1937 (P)	56,860,000
1937-D	14,146,000
1937-S	9,740,000
1938 (P)	22,190,000
1938-D	5,537,000
1938-S	8,090,000
1939 (P)	67,740,000
1939-D	24,394,000
1939-S	10,540,000
1940 (P)	65,350,000
1940-D	21,198,000
1940-S	21,560,000
1941 (P)	175,090,000
1941-D	45,634,000
1941-S	43,090,000
1942 (P)	205,410,000
1942-D	60,740,000
1942-S	49,300,000
1943 (P)	191,710,000
1943-D	71,949,000
1943-S	60,400,000
1944 (P)	231,410,000
1944-D	62,224,000
1944-S	49,490,000
1945 (P)	159,130,000
1945-D	40,245,000
1945-S	41,920,000
1946 (P)	255,250,000
1946-D	61,043,500
1946-S	27,900,000
1947 (P)	121,520,000

Dimes continued

Year	Mintage
1947-D	46,835,000
1947-S	34,840,000
1948 (P)	74,950,000
1948-D	52,841,000
1948-S	35,520,000
1949 (P)	30,940,000
1949-D	26,034,000
1949-S	13,510,000
1950 (P)	50,130,114
1950-D	46,803,000
1950-S	20,440,000
1951 (P)	102,880,102
1951-D	56,529,000
1951-S	31,630,000
1952 (P)	99,040,093
1952-D	122,100,000
1952-S	44,419,500
1953 (P)	53,490,120
1953-D	136,433,000
1953-S	39,180,000
1954 (P)	114,010,203
1954-D	106,397,000
1954-S	22,860,000
1955 (P)	12,450,181
1955-D	13,959,000
1955-S	18,510,000
1956 (P)	108,640,000
1956-D	108,015,100
1957 (P)	160,160,000
1957-D	113,354,330
1958 (P)	31,910,000
1958-D	136,564,600
1959 (P)	85,780,000
1959-D	164,919,790
1960 (P)	70,390,000
1960-D	200,160,400
1961 (P)	93,730,000
1961-D	209,146,550
1962 (P)	72,450,000
1962-D	334,948,380
1963 (P)	123,650,000
1963-D	421,476,530
1964 (P)[104]	929,360,000
1964-D	1,357,517,180
1965 (P)[104]	845,130,000
1965 (D)	757,472,820
1965 (S)	47,177,750
1966 (P)[104]	622,550,000
1966 (D)	683,771,010
1966 (S)	74,151,947
1967 (P)[104]	1,030,110,000
1967 (D)	1,156,277,320
1967 (S)	57,620,000
1968 (P)	424,470,400
1968-D	480,748,280
1968-S	0[53]
1969 (P)	145,790,000
1969-D	563,323,870
1969-S	0[53]
1970 (P)	345,570,000
1970-D	754,942,100
1970-S	0[53]
1971 (P)	162,690,000
1971-D	377,914,240
1971-S	0[53]
1972 (P)	431,540,000
1972-D	330,290,000
1972-S	0[53]
1973 (P)	315,670,000

Dimes continued

Year	Mintage
1973-D	455,032,426
1973-S	0[53]
1974 (P)	470,248,000
1974-D	571,083,000
1974-S	0[53]
1975 (P)	513,682,000
1975-D	313,705,300
1975 (S)	71,991,900
1976 (P)	568,760,000
1976-D	695,222,774
1976-S	0[53]
1977 (P)	796,930,000
1977-D	376,607,228
1977-S	0[53]
1978 (P)	663,980,000
1978-D	282,847,540
1978-S	0[53]
1979 (P)	315,440,000
1979-D	390,921,184
1979-S	0[53]
1980 (P)	735,170,000
1980-D	719,354,321
1980-S	0[53]
1981-P	676,650,000
1981-D	712,284,143
1981-S	0[53]
1982-P[115]	519,475,000
1982-D	542,713,584
1982-S	0[53]
1983-P	647,025,000
1983-D	730,129,224
1983-S	0[53]
1984-P	856,669,000
1984-D	704,803,976
1984-S	0[53]
1985-P	705,200,962
1985-D	587,979,970
1985-S	0[53]
1986-P	682,649,693
1986-D	473,326,974
1986-S	0[53]
1987-P	762,709,481
1987-D	653,203,402
1987-S	0[5]
1988-P	1,030,550,000
1988-D	962,385,488
1988-S	0[53]
1989-P	1,298,400,000
1989-D	896,535,597

Twenty cents

Year	Mintage
1875 (P)	38,500
1875-CC	133,290
1875-S	1,155,000
1876 (P)	14,750
1876-CC	10,000[76]
1877 (P)	0[53]
1878 (P)	0[53]

Quarter dollars

Year	Mintage
1796	6,146
1804	6,738
1805	121,394
1806	286,424
1807	140,343

Quarters continued

1815	89,235
1818	361,174
1819	144,000
1820	127,444
1821	216,851
1822	64,080
1823	17,800
1824	24,000
1825	148,000
1827	0[14]
1828	102,000
1831	398,000
1832	320,000
1833	156,000
1834	286,000
1835	1,952,000
1836	472,000
1837	252,400
1838 (P)	832,000[25]
1839 (P)	491,146
1840 (P)	188,127
1840-O	425,200
1841 (P)	120,000
1841-O	452,000
1842 (P)	88,000
1842-O	769,000
1843 (P)	645,600
1843-O	968,000
1844 (P)	421,200
1844-O	740,000
1845 (P)	922,000
1846 (P)	510,000
1847 (P)	734,000
1847-O	368,000
1848 (P)	146,000
1849 (P)	340,000
1849-O	16,000
1850 (P)	190,800
1850-O	396,000
1851 (P)	160,000
1851-O	88,000
1852 (P)	177,060
1852-O	96,000
1853 (P)[34]	15,254,220[36]
1853-O[34]	1,332,000[36]
1854 (P)	12,380,000
1854-O	1,484,000
1855 (P)	2,857,000
1855-O	176,000
1855-S	396,400
1856 (P)	7,264,000
1856-O	968,000
1856-S	286,000
1857 (P)	9,644,000
1857-O	1,180,000
1857-S	82,000
1858 (P)	7,368,000
1858-O	520,000
1858-S	121,000
1859 (P)	1,344,000
1859-O	260,000
1859-S	80,000
1860 (P)	804,400
1860-O	388,000
1860-S	56,000
1861 (P)	4,853,600
1861-S	96,000
1862 (P)	932,000
1862-S	67,000
1863 (P)	191,600
1864 (P)	93,600

Quarters continued

1864-S	20,000
1865 (P)	58,800
1865-S	41,000
1866 (P)	16,800
1866-S	28,000
1867 (P)	20,000
1867-S	48,000
1868 (P)	29,400
1868-S	96,000
1869 (P)	16,000
1869-S	76,000
1870 (P)	86,400
1870-CC	8,340
1871 (P)	118,200
1871-CC	10,890
1871-S	30,900
1872 (P)	182,000
1872-CC	22,850
1872-S	83,000
1873 (P)[68]	1,483,160[72]
1873-CC[68]	16,462[72]
1873-S[68]	156,000[72]
1874 (P)	471,200
1874-S	392,000
1875 (P)	4,292,800
1875-CC	140,000
1875-S	680,000
1876 (P)	17,816,000
1876-CC	4,944,000
1876-S	8,596,000
1877 (P)	10,911,200
1877-CC	4,192,000
1877-S	8,996,000
1878 (P)	2,260,000
1878-CC	996,000
1878-S	140,000
1879 (P)	14,450
1880 (P)	13,600
1881 (P)	12,000
1882 (P)	15,200
1883 (P)	14,400
1884 (P)	8,000
1885 (P)	13,600
1886 (P)	5,000
1887 (P)	10,000
1888 (P)	10,001
1888-S	1,216,000
1889 (P)	12,000
1890 (P)	80,000
1891 (P)	3,920,000
1891-O	68,000
1891-S	2,216,000
1892 (P)	8,236,000
1892-O	2,640,000
1892-S	964,079
1893 (P)	5,444,023
1893-O	3,396,000
1893-S	1,454,535
1894 (P)	3,432,000
1894-O	2,852,000
1894-S	2,648,821
1895 (P)	4,440,000
1895-O	2,816,000
1895-S	1,764,681
1896 (P)	3,874,000
1896-O	1,484,000
1896-S	188,039
1897 (P)	8,140,000
1897-O	1,414,800
1897-S	542,229
1898 (P)	11,100,000
1898-O	1,868,000
1898-S	1,020,592

Quarters continued

1899 (P)	12,624,000
1899-O	2,644,000
1899-S	708,000
1900 (P)	10,016,000
1900-O	3,416,000
1900-S	1,858,585
1901 (P)	8,892,000
1901-O	1,612,000
1901-S	72,664
1902 (P)	12,196,967
1902-O	4,748,000
1902-S	1,524,612
1903 (P)	9,669,309
1903-O	3,500,000
1903-S	1,036,000
1904 (P)	9,588,143
1904-O	2,456,000
1905 (P)	4,967,523
1905-O	1,230,000
1905-S	1,884,000
1906 (P)	3,655,760
1906-D	3,280,000
1906-O	2,056,000
1907 (P)	7,192,000
1907-D	2,484,000
1907-O	4,560,000
1907-S	1,360,000
1908 (P)	4,232,000
1908-D	5,788,000
1908-O	6,244,000
1908-S	784,000
1909 (P)	9,268,000
1909-D	5,114,000
1909-O	712,000
1909-S	1,348,000
1910 (P)	2,244,000
1910-D	1,500,000
1911 (P)	3,720,000
1911-D	933,600
1911-S	988,000
1912 (P)	4,400,000
1912-S	708,000
1913 (P)	484,000
1913-D	1,450,800
1913-S	40,000
1914 (P)	6,244,230
1914-D	3,046,000
1914-S	264,000
1915 (P)	3,480,000
1915-D	3,694,000
1915-S	704,000
1916 (P)	1,840,000[92]
1916-D	6,540,800[92]
1917 (P)	22,620,000[95]
1917-D	7,733,600[95]
1917-S	7,504,000[95]
1918 (P)	14,240,000
1918-D	7,380,000
1918-S	11,072,000
1919 (P)	11,324,000
1919-D	1,944,000
1919-S	1,836,000
1920 (P)	27,860,000
1920-D	3,586,400
1920-S	6,380,000
1921 (P)	1,916,000
1923 (P)	9,716,000
1923-S	1,360,000
1924 (P)	10,920,000
1924-D	3,112,000
1924-S	2,860,000
1925 (P)	12,280,000

Quarters continued

1926 (P)	11,316,000
1926-D	1,716,000
1926-S	2,700,000
1927 (P)	11,912,000
1927-D	976,400
1927-S	396,000
1928 (P)	6,336,000
1928-D	1,627,600
1928-S	2,644,000
1929 (P)	11,140,000
1929-D	1,358,000
1929-S	1,764,000
1930 (P)	5,632,000
1930-S	1,556,000
1932 (P)	5,404,000
1932-D	436,800
1932-S	408,000
1934 (P)	31,912,052
1934-D	3,527,200
1935 (P)	32,484,000
1935-D	5,780,000
1935-S	5,660,000
1936 (P)	41,300,000
1936-D	5,374,000
1936-S	3,828,000
1937 (P)	19,696,000
1937-D	7,189,600
1937-S	1,652,000
1938 (P)	9,472,000
1938-S	2,832,000
1939 (P)	33,540,000
1939-D	7,092,000
1939-S	2,628,000
1940 (P)	35,704,000
1940-D	2,797,600
1940-S	8,244,000
1941 (P)	79,032,000
1941-D	16,714,800
1941-S	16,080,000
1942 (P)	102,096,000
1942-D	17,487,200
1942-S	19,384,000
1943 (P)	99,700,000
1943-D	16,095,600
1943-S	21,700,000
1944 (P)	104,956,000
1944-D	14,600,800
1944-S	12,560,000
1945 (P)	74,372,000
1945-D	12,341,600
1945-S	17,004,001
1946 (P)	53,436,000
1946-D	9,072,800
1946-S	4,204,000
1947 (P)	22,556,000
1947-D	15,338,400
1947-S	5,532,000
1948 (P)	35,196,000
1948-D	16,766,800
1948-S	15,960,000
1949 (P)	9,312,000
1949-D	10,068,400
1950 (P)	24,920,126
1950-D	21,075,600
1950-S	10,284,004
1951 (P)	43,448,102
1951-D	35,354,800
1951-S	9,048,000
1952 (P)	38,780,093
1952-D	49,795,200
1952-S	13,707,800
1953 (P)	18,536,120
1953-D	56,112,400

Quarters continued

Year	Mintage
1953-S	14,016,000
1954 (P)	54,412,203
1954-D	42,305,500
1954-S	11,834,722
1955 (P)	18,180,181
1955-D	3,182,400
1956 (P)	44,144,000
1956-D	32,334,500
1957 (P)	46,532,000
1957-D	77,924,160
1958 (P)	6,360,000
1958-D	78,124,900
1959 (P)	24,384,000
1959-D	62,054,232
1960 (P)	29,164,000
1960-D	63,000,324
1961 (P)	37,036,000
1961-D	83,656,928
1962 (P)	36,156,000
1962-D	127,554,756
1963 (P)	74,316,000
1963-D	135,288,184
1964 (P)[104]	
	560,390,585
1964-D	704,135,528
1965 (P)[104]	
	1,082,216,000
1965 (D)	673,305,540
1965 (S)	61,836,000
1966 (P)[104]	404,416,000
1966 (D)	367,490,400
1966 (S)	46,933,517
1967 (P)[104]	873,524,000
1967 (D)	632,767,848
1967 (S)	17,740,000
1968 (P)	220,731,500
1968-D	101,534,000
1968-S	0[53]
1969 (P)	176,212,000
1969-D	114,372,000
1969-S	0[53]
1970 (P)	136,420,000
1970-D	417,341,364
1970-S	0[53]
1971 (P)	109,284,000
1971-D	258,634,428
1971-S	0[53]
1972 (P)	215,048,000
1972-D	311,067,732
1972-S	0[53]
1973 (P)	346,924,000
1973-D	232,977,400
1973-S	0[53]
1974 (P)[108]	
	801,456,000
1974-D	353,160,300
1974-S	0[53]
1976 (P)[109,110]	
	809,408,016
1976-D	860,118,839
1976-S	0[111]
1976 (W)	376,800
1977 (P)	461,204,000
1977-D	256,524,978
1977-S	0[53]
1977 (W)	7,352,000
1978 (P)	500,652,000
1978-D	287,373,152
1978-S	0[53]
1978 (W)	20,800,000
1979 (P)	493,036,000

Quarters continued

Year	Mintage
1979-D	489,789,780
1979-S	0[53]
1979 (W)	22,672,000
1980-P[112]	635,832,000
1980-D	518,327,487
1980-S	0[53]
1981-P	601,716,000
1981-D	575,722,833
1981-S	0[53]
1982-P	500,931,000
1982-D	480,042,788
1982-S	0[53]
1983-P	673,535,000
1983-D	617,806,446
1983-S	0(53)
1984-P	676,545,000
1984-D	546,483,064
1984-S	0[53]
1985-P	775,818,962
1985-D	519,962,888
1985-S	0[53]
1986-P	551,199,333
1986-D	504,298,660
1986-S	0[53]
1987-P	582,499,481
1987-D	655,595,696
1987-S	0[53]
1988-P	562,052,000
1988-D	596,810,688
1988-S	0[53]
1989-P	512,868,000
1989-D	896,733,858

Half dollars

Year	Mintage
1794	23,464
1795	299,680
1796	934
1797	2,984
1801	30,289
1802	29,890
1803	188,234
1805	211,722
1806	839,576
1807	1,051,576[12]
1808	1,368,600
1809	1,405,810
1810	1,276,276
1811	1,203,644
1812	1,628,059
1813	1,241,903
1814	1,039,075
1815	47,150
1817	1,215,567
1818	1,960,322
1819	2,208,000
1820	751,122
1821	1,305,797
1822	1,559,573
1823	1,694,200
1824	3,504,954
1825	2,943,166
1826	4,004,180
1827	5,493,400
1828	3,075,200
1829	3,712,156
1830	4,764,800
1831	5,873,660
1832	4,797,000
1833	5,206,000
1834	6,412,004

Half dollars continued

Year	Mintage
1835	5,352,006
1836	6,546,200[20]
1837	3,629,820
1838 (P)	3,546,000
1838-O	0[24]
1839 (P)	3,334,560[28]
1839-O	162,976
1840 (P)	1,435,008
1840-O	855,100
1841 (P)	310,000
1841-O	401,000
1842 (P)	2,012,764
1842-O	957,000
1843 (P)	3,844,000
1843-O	2,268,000
1844 (P)	1,766,000
1844-O	2,005,000
1845 (P)	589,000
1845-O	2,094,000
1846 (P)	2,210,000
1846-O	2,304,000
1847 (P)	1,156,000
1847-O	2,584,000
1848 (P)	580,000
1848-O	3,180,000
1849 (P)	1,252,000
1849-O	2,310,000
1850 (P)	227,000
1850-O	2,456,000
1851 (P)	200,750
1851-O	402,000
1852 (P)	77,130
1852-O	144,000
1853 (P)[34]	3,532,708[35]
1853-O	1,328,000[35]
1854 (P)	2,982,000
1854-O	5,240,000
1855 (P)	759,500
1855-O	3,688,000
1855-S	129,950
1856 (P)	938,000
1856-O	2,658,000
1856-S	211,000
1857 (P)	1,988,000
1857-O	818,000
1857-S	158,000
1858 (P)	4,226,000
1858-O	7,294,000
1858-S	476,000
1859 (P)	748,000
1859-O	2,834,000
1859-S	566,000
1860 (P)	302,700
1860-O	1,290,000
1860-S	472,000
1861 (P)	2,887,400
1861-O	2,532,633[52]
1861-S	939,500
1862 (P)	253,000
1862-S	1,352,000
1863 (P)	503,200
1863-S	916,000
1864 (P)	379,100
1864-S	658,000
1865 (P)	511,400
1865-S	675,000
1866 (P)	744,900
1866-S	1,054,000
1867 (P)	449,300
1867-S	1,196,000
1868 (P)	417,600
1868-S	1,160,000

Half dollars continued

Year	Mintage
1869 (P)	795,300
1869-S	656,000
1870 (P)	633,900
1870-CC	54,617
1870-S	1,004,000
1871 (P)	1,203,600
1871-CC	153,950
1871-S	2,178,000
1872 (P)	880,600
1872-CC	257,000
1872-S	580,000
1873 (P)[68]	2,616,350[71]
1873-CC[68]	337,060[71]
1873-S[68]	233,000[71]
1874 (P)	2,359,600
1874-CC	59,000
1874-S	394,000
1875 (P)	6,026,800
1875-CC	1,008,000
1875-S	3,200,000
1876 (P)	8,418,000
1876-CC	1,956,000
1876-S	4,528,000
1877 (P)	8,304,000
1877-CC	1,420,000
1877-S	5,356,000
1878 (P)	1,377,600
1878-CC	62,000
1878-S	12,000
1879 (P)	4,800
1880 (P)	8,400
1881 (P)	10,000
1882 (P)	4,400
1883 (P)	8,000
1884 (P)	4,400
1885 (P)	5,200
1886 (P)	5,000
1887 (P)	5,000
1888 (P)	12,001
1889 (P)	12,000
1890 (P)	12,000
1891 (P)	200,000
1892 (P)	934,245
1892-O	390,000
1892-S	1,029,028
1893 (P)	1,826,000
1893-O	1,389,000
1893-S	740,000
1894 (P)	1,148,000
1894-O	2,138,000
1894-S	4,048,690
1895 (P)	1,834,338
1895-O	1,766,000
1895-S	1,108,086
1896 (P)	950,000
1896-O	924,000
1896-S	1,140,948
1897 (P)	2,480,000
1897-O	632,000
1897-S	933,900
1898 (P)	2,956,000
1898-O	874,000
1898-S	2,358,550
1899 (P)	5,538,000
1899-O	1,724,000
1899-S	1,686,411
1900 (P)	4,762,000
1900-O	2,744,000
1900-S	2,560,322
1901 (P)	4,268,000
1901-O	1,124,000
1901-S	847,044
1902 (P)	4,922,000

Half dollars continued

1902-O	2,526,000
1902-S	1,460,670
1903 (P)	2,278,000
1903-O	2,100,000
1903-S	1,920,772
1904 (P)	2,992,000
1904-O	1,117,600
1904-S	553,038
1905 (P)	662,000
1905-O	505,000
1905-S	2,494,000
1906 (P)	2,638,000
1906-D	4,028,000
1906-O	2,446,000
1906-S	1,740,154
1907 (P)	2,598,000
1907-D	3,856,000
1907-O	3,946,600
1907-S	1,250,000
1908 (P)	1,354,000
1908-D	3,280,000
1908-O	5,360,000
1908-S	1,644,828
1909 (P)	2,368,000
1909-O	925,400
1909-S	1,764,000
1910 (P)	418,000
1910-S	1,948,000
1911 (P)	1,406,000
1911-D	695,080
1911-S	1,272,000
1912 (P)	1,550,000
1912-D	2,300,800
1912-S	1,370,000
1913 (P)	188,000
1913-D	534,000
1913-S	604,000
1914 (P)	124,230
1914-S	992,000
1915 (P)	138,000
1915-D	1,170,400
1915-S	1,604,000
1916 (P)	608,000
1916-D	1,014,400
1916-S	508,000
1917 (P)	12,292,000
1917-D	2,705,400[94]
1917-S	6,506,000[94]
1918 (P)	6,634,000
1918-D	3,853,040
1918-S	10,282,000
1919 (P)	962,000
1919-D	1,165,000
1919-S	1,552,000
1920 (P)	6,372,000
1920-D	1,551,000
1920-S	4,624,000
1921 (P)	246,000
1921-D	208,000
1921-S	548,000
1923-S	2,178,000
1927-S	2,392,000
1928-S	1,940,000
1929-D	1,001,200
1929-S	1,902,000
1933-S	1,786,000
1934 (P)	6,964,000
1934-D	2,361,400
1934-S	3,652,000
1935 (P)	9,162,000
1935-D	3,003,800
1935-S	3,854,000
1936 (P)	12,614,000

Half dollars continued

1936-D	4,252,400
1936-S	3,884,000
1937 (P)	9,522,000
1937-D	1,676,000
1937-S	2,090,000
1938 (P)	4,110,000
1938-D	491,600
1939 (P)	6,812,000
1939-D	4,267,800
1939-S	2,552,000
1940 (P)	9,156,000
1940-S	4,550,000
1941 (P)	24,192,000
1941-D	11,248,400
1941-S	8,098,000
1942 (P)	47,818,000
1942-D	10,973,800
1942-S	12,708,000
1943 (P)	53,190,000
1943-D	11,346,000
1943-S	13,450,000
1944 (P)	28,206,000
1944-D	9,769,000
1944-S	8,904,000
1945 (P)	31,502,000
1945-D	9,996,800
1945-S	10,156,000
1946 (P)	12,118,000
1946-D	2,151,000
1946-S	3,724,000
1947 (P)	4,094,000
1947-D	3,900,600
1948 (P)	3,006,814
1948-D	4,028,600
1949 (P)	5,614,000
1949-D	4,120,600
1949-S	3,744,000
1950 (P)	7,742,123
1950-D	8,031,600
1951 (P)	16,802,102
1951-D	9,475,200
1951-S	13,696,000
1952 (P)	21,192,093
1952-D	25,395,600
1952-S	5,526,000
1953 (P)	2,668,120
1953-D	20,900,400
1953-S	4,148,000
1954 (P)	13,188,203
1954-D	25,445,580
1954-S	4,993,400
1955 (P)	2,498,181
1956 (P)	4,032,000
1957 (P)	5,114,000
1957-D	19,966,850
1958 (P)	4,042,000
1958-D	23,962,412
1959 (P)	6,200,000
1959-D	13,053,750
1960 (P)	6,024,000
1960-D	18,215,812
1961 (P)	8,290,000
1961-D	20,276,442
1962 (P)	9,714,000
1962-D	35,473,281
1963 (P)	22,164,000
1963-D	67,069,292
1964 (P)[104]	273,304,004
1964-D	156,205,446
1965 (P)[104]	0
1965 (D)	63,049,366
1965 (S)	470,000

Half dollars continued

1966 (P)[104]	0
1966 (D)	106,439,312
1966 (S)	284,037
1967 (P)[104]	0
1967 (D)	293,183,634
1967 (S)	0
1968-D	246,951,930
1968-S	0[53]
1969-D	129,881,800
1969-S	0[53]
1970-D	2,150,000[105]
1970-S	0[53]
1971 (P)	155,164,000
1971-D	302,097,424
1971-S	0[53]
1972 (P)	153,180,000
1972-D	141,890,000
1972-S	0[53]
1973 (P)	64,964,000
1973-D	83,171,400
1973-S	0[53]
1974 (P)	201,596,000
1974-D	79,066,300
1974-S	0[53]
1976 (P)[109,11]	234,308,000
1976-D	287,565,248
1976-S[111]	0
1977 (P)	43,598,000
1977-D	31,449,106
1977-S	0[53]
1978 (P)	14,350,000
1978-D	13,765,799
1978-S	0[53]
1979 (P)	68,312,000
1979-D	15,815,422
1979-S	0[53]
1980 (P)	44,134,000[112]
1980-D	33,456,449
1980-S	0[53]
1981-P	29,544,000
1981-D	27,839,533
1981-S	0[53]
1982-P	10,819,000
1982-D	13,140,102
1982-S	0[53]
1983-P	34,139,000
1983-D	32,472,244
1983-S	0[53]
1984-P	26,029,000
1984-D	26,262,158
1984-S	0[53]
1985-P	18,706,962
1985-D	19,814,034
1985-S	0[53]
1986-P	13,107,633
1986-D	15,366,145
1986-S	0[53]
1987-P	0[117]
1987-D	0[117]
1987-S	0[53]
1988-P	13,626,000
1988-D	12,000,096
1988-S	0[53]
1989-P	24,542,000
1989-D	23,000,216

Silver dollars

Year	Mintage
1794	1,758
1795	203,033[2]
1796	72,920
1797	7,776
1798	327,536[6]
1799	423,515
1800	220,920
1801[7]	54,454
1802[7]	41,650
1803[7]	85,634
1804	0[8]
1805	0[10]
1836	1,600[19]
1839 (P)	300[19]
1840 (P)	61,005[29]
1841 (P)	173,000[29]
1842 (P)	184,618[29]
1843 (P)	165,100[29]
1844 (P)	20,000[29]
1845 (P)	24,500[29]
1846 (P)	110,600[29]
1846-O	59,000
1847 (P)	140,750[29]
1848 (P)	15,000[29]
1849 (P)	62,600[29]
1850 (P)	7,500[29]
1850-O	40,000
1851 (P)	1,300[29]
1852 (P)	1,100[29]
1853 (P)	46,110[29]
1854 (P)	33,140
1855 (P)	26,000
1856 (P)	63,500
1857 (P)	94,000
1858 (P)	0[43]
1859 (P)	256,500
1859-O	360,000
1859-S	20,000
1860 (P)	217,600
1860-O	515,000
1861 (P)	77,500
1862 (P)	11,540
1863 (P)	27,200
1864 (P)	30,700
1865 (P)	46,500
1866 (P)	48,900
1867 (P)	46,900
1868 (P)	162,100
1869 (P)	423,700
1870 (P)	415,000
1870-CC	12,462
1870-S	0[67]
1871 (P)	1,073,800
1871-CC	1,376
1872 (P)	1,105,500
1872-CC	3,150
1872-S	9,000
1873 (P)[68]	293,000
1873-CC[53]	2,300
1873-S[68]	700[70]
1878 (P)[79]	10,508,550
1878-CC	2,212,000
1878-S	9,774,000
1879 (P)	14,806,000
1879-CC	756,000
1879-O	2,887,000

Silver dollars continued

1879-S	9,110,000
1880 (P)	12,600,000
1880-CC	591,000
1880-O	5,305,000
1880-S	8,900,000
1881 (P)	9,163,000
1881-CC	296,000
1881-O	5,708,000
1881-S	12,760,000
1882 (P)	11,100,000
1882-CC	1,133,000
1882-O	6,090,000
1882-S	9,250,000
1883 (P)	12,290,000
1883-CC	1,204,000
1883-O	8,725,000
1883-S	6,250,000
1884 (P)	14,070,000
1884-CC	1,136,000
1884-O	9,730,000
1884-S	3,200,000
1885 (P)	17,786,837
1885-CC	228,000
1885-O	9,185,000
1885-S	1,497,000
1886 (P)	19,963,000
1886-O	10,710,000
1886-S	750,000
1887 (P)	20,290,000
1887-O	11,550,000
1887-S	1,771,000
1888 (P)	19,183,000
1888-O	12,150,000
1888-S	657,000
1889 (P)	21,726,000
1889-CC	350,000
1889-O	11,875,000
1889-S	700,000
1890 (P)	16,802,000
1890-CC	2,309,041
1890-O	10,701,000
1890-S	8,230,373
1891 (P)	8,693,556
1891-CC	1,618,000
1891-O	7,954,529
1891-S	5,296,000
1892 (P)	1,036,000
1892-CC	1,352,000
1892-O	2,744,000
1892-S	1,200,000
1893 (P)	389,000
1893-CC	677,000
1893-O	300,000
1893-S	100,000
1894 (P)	110,000
1894-O	1,723,000
1894-S	1,260,000
1895 (P)	12,000[82]
1895-O	450,000
1895-S	400,000
1896 (P)	9,976,000
1896-O	4,900,000
1896-S	5,000,000
1897 (P)	2,822,000
1897-O	4,004,000
1897-S	5,825,000
1898 (P)	5,884,000
1898-O	4,440,000
1898-S	4,102,000
1899 (P)	330,000
1899-O	12,290,000
1899-S	2,562,000
1900 (P)	8,830,000

Silver dollars continued

1900-O	12,590,000
1900-S	3,540,000
1901 (P)	6,962,000
1901-O	13,320,000
1901-S	2,284,000
1902 (P)	7,994,000
1902-O	8,636,000
1902-S	1,530,000
1903 (P)	4,652,000
1903-O	4,450,000
1903-S	1,241,000
1904 (P)	2,788,000
1904-O	3,720,000
1904-S	2,304,000
1921 (P)	45,696,473[96]
1921-D	20,345,000[96]
1921-S	21,695,000[96]
1922 (P)	51,737,000
1922-D	15,063,000
1922-S	17,475,000
1923 (P)	30,800,000
1923-D	6,811,000
1923-S	19,020,000
1924 (P)	11,811,000
1924-S	1,728,000
1925 (P)	10,198,000
1925-S	1,610,000
1926 (P)	1,939,000
1926-D	2,348,700
1926-S	6,980,000
1927 (P)	848,000
1927-D	1,268,900
1927-S	866,000
1928 (P)	360,649
1928-S	1,632,000
1934 (P)	954,057
1934-D	1,569,500
1934-S	1,011,000
1935 (P)	1,576,000
1935-S	1,964,000

Trade dollars

Year	Mintage
1873 (P)[68]	396,635
1873-CC[68]	124,500
1873-S[68]	703,000
1874 (P)	987,100
1874-CC	1,373,200
1874-S	2,549,000
1875 (P)	218,200
1875-CC	1,573,700
1875-S	4,487,000
1876 (P)	455,000
1876-CC	509,000
1876-S	5,227,000
1877 (P)	3,039,200
1877-CC	534,000
1877-S	9,519,000
1878 (P)	0[78]
1878-CC	97,000
1878-S	4,162,000
1879 (P)	0[78]
1880 (P)	0[78]
1881 (P)	0[78]
1882 (P)	0[78]
1883 (P)	0[78]
1884 (P)	0[78]
1885 (P)	0[78]

Clad dollars

Year	Mintage
1971 (P)	47,799,000
1971-D	68,587,424
1971-S[106]	0
1972 (P)	75,890,000
1972-D	92,548,511
1972-S[106]	0
1973 (P)[107]	2,000,056
1973-D	2,000,000
1973-S[106]	0
1974 (P)[108]	27,366,000
1974-D	45,517,000
1974-S[106]	0
1976 (P)[110]	117,337,000
1976-D	103,228,274
1976-S[111]	0
1977 (P)	12,596,000
1977-D	32,983,006
1977-S	0[53]
1978 (P)	25,702,000
1978-D	33,012,890
1978-S	0[53]
1979-P[113]	360,222,000
1979-D	288,015,744
1979-S	109,576,000
1980-P	27,610,000
1980-D	41,628,708
1980-S	20,422,000
1981-P[116]	3,000,000
1981-D	3,250,000
1981-S	3,492,000

Gold dollars

Year	Mintage
1849 (P)	688,567
1849-C	11,634
1849-D	21,588
1849-O	215,000
1850 (P)	481,953
1850-C	6,966
1850-D	8,382
1850-O	14,000
1851 (P)	3,317,671
1851-C	41,267
1851-D	9,882
1851-O	290,000
1852 (P)	2,045,351
1852-C	9,434
1852-D	6,360
1852-O	140,000
1853 (P)	4,076,051
1853-C	11,515
1853-D	6,583
1853-O	290,000
1854 (P)	1,639,445[39]
1854-D	2,935[39]
1854-S	14,632[39]
1855 (P)	758,269
1855-C	9,803
1855-D	1,811
1855-O	55,000
1856 (P)[40]	1,762,936
1856-D[40]	1,460
1856-S[40]	24,600
1857 (P)	774,789
1857-C	13,280
1857-D	3,533

Gold dollars continued

1857-S	10,000
1858 (P)	117,995
1858-D	3,477
1858-S	10,000
1859 (P)	168,244
1859-C	5,235
1859-D	4,952
1859-S	15,000
1860 (P)	36,514
1860-D	1,566
1860-S	13,000
1861 (P)	527,150
1861-D	0[51]
1862 (P)	1,361,365
1863 (P)	6,200
1864 (P)	5,900
1865 (P)	3,700
1866 (P)	7,100
1867 (P)	5,200
1868 (P)	10,500
1869 (P)	5,900
1870 (P)	6,300
1870-S	3,000[66]
1871 (P)	3,900
1872 (P)	3,500
1873 (P)[68]	125,100
1874 (P)	198,800
1875 (P)	400
1876 (P)	3,200
1877 (P)	3,900
1878 (P)	3,000
1879 (P)	3,000
1880 (P)	1,600
1881 (P)	7,620
1882 (P)	5,000
1883 (P)	10,800
1884 (P)	5,230
1885 (P)	11,156
1886 (P)	5,000
1887 (P)	7,500
1888 (P)	15,501
1889 (P)	28,950

Quarter eagles

Year	Mintage
1796	1,395
1797	427
1798	1,094
1802	3,035
1804	3,327
1805	1,781
1806	1,616
1807	6,812
1808	2,710
1821	6,448
1824	2,600
1825	4,434
1826	760
1827	2,800
1829	3,403
1830	4,540
1831	4,520
1832	4,400
1833	4,160
1834	117,370[18]
1835	131,402
1836	547,986
1837	45,080
1838 (P)	47,030
1838-C	7,908
1839 (P)	27,021
1839-C	18,173

$2.50 gold continued

Year	Mintage
1839-D	13,674
1839-O	17,781
1840 (P)	18,859
1840-C	12,838
1840-D	3,532
1840-O	33,580
1841 (P)	0[31]
1841-C	10,297
1841-D	4,164
1842 (P)	2,823
1842-C	6,737
1842-D	4,643
1842-O	19,800
1843 (P)	100,546
1843-C	26,096
1843-D	36,209
1843-O	368,002
1844 (P)	6,784
1844-C	11,622
1844-D	17,332
1845 (P)	91,051
1845-D	19,460
1845-O	4,000
1846 (P)	21,598
1846-C	4,808
1846-D	19,303
1846-O	62,000
1847 (P)	29,814
1847-C	23,226
1847-D	15,784
1847-O	124,000
1848 (P)	8,886[32]
1848-C	16,788
1848-D	13,771
1849 (P)	23,294
1849-C	10,220
1849-D	10,945
1850 (P)	252,923
1850-C	9,148
1850-D	12,148
1850-O	84,000
1851 (P)	1,372,748
1851-C	14,923
1851-D	11,264
1851-O	148,000
1852 (P)	1,159,681
1852-C	9,772
1852-D	4,078
1852-O	140,000
1853 (P)	1,404,668
1853-D	3,178
1854 (P)	596,258
1854-C	7,295
1854-D	1,760
1854-O	153,000
1854-S	246
1855 (P)	235,480
1855-C	3,677
1855-D	1,123
1856 (P)	384,240
1856-C	7,913
1856-D	874
1856-O	21,100
1856-S	71,120
1857 (P)	214,130
1857-D	2,364
1857-O	34,000
1857-S	69,200
1858 (P)	47,377
1858-C	9,056
1859 (P)	39,444
1859-D	2,244
1859-S	15,200

$2.50 gold continued

Year	Mintage
1860 (P)	22,563
1860-C	7,469
1860-S	35,600
1861 (P)	1,272,428
1861-S	24,000
1862 (P)	98,508
1862-S	8,000
1863 (P)	0[53]
1863-S	10,800
1864 (P)	2,824
1865 (P)	1,520
1865-S	23,376
1866 (P)	3,080
1866-S	38,960
1867 (P)	3,200
1867-S	28,000
1868 (P)	3,600
1868-S	34,000
1869 (P)	4,320
1869-S	29,500
1870 (P)	4,520
1870-S	16,000
1871 (P)	5,320
1871-S	22,000
1872 (P)	3,000
1872-S	18,000
1873 (P)[68]	178,000
1873-S[68]	27,000
1874 (P)	3,920
1875 (P)	400
1875-S	11,600
1876 (P)	4,176
1876-S	5,000
1877 (P)	1,632
1877-S	35,400
1878 (P)	286,240
1878-S	178,000
1879 (P)	88,960
1879-S	43,500
1880 (P)	2,960
1881 (P)	640
1882 (P)	4,000
1883 (P)	1,920
1884 (P)	1,950
1885 (P)	800
1886 (P)	4,000
1887 (P)	6,160
1888 (P)	16,006
1889 (P)	17,600
1890 (P)	8,720
1891 (P)	10,960
1892 (P)	2,440
1893 (P)	30,000
1894 (P)	4,000
1895 (P)	6,000
1896 (P)	19,070
1897 (P)	29,768
1898 (P)	24,000
1899 (P)	27,200
1900 (P)	67,000
1901 (P)	91,100
1902 (P)	133,540
1903 (P)	201,060
1904 (P)	160,790
1905 (P)	217,800
1906 (P)	176,330
1907 (P)	336,294
1908 (P)	564,821
1909 (P)	441,760
1910 (P)	492,000
1911 (P)	704,000
1911-D	55,680
1912 (P)	616,000

$2.50 gold continued

Year	Mintage
1913 (P)	722,000
1914 (P)	240,000
1914-D	448,000
1915 (P)	606,000
1925-D	578,000
1926 (P)	446,000
1927 (P)	388,000
1928 (P)	416,000
1929 (P)	532,000

Three dollars

Year	Mintage
1854 (P)	138,618
1854-D	1,120
1854-O	24,000
1855 (P)	50,555
1855-S	6,600
1856 (P)	26,010
1856-S	34,500
1857 (P)	20,891
1857-S	14,000
1858 (P)	2,133
1859 (P)	15,638
1860 (P)	7,036
1860-S	4,408[45]
1861 (P)	5,959
1862 (P)	5,750
1863 (P)	5,000
1864 (P)	2,630
1865 (P)	1,140
1866 (P)	4,000
1867 (P)	2,600
1868 (P)	4,850
1869 (P)	2,500
1870 (P)	3,500
1870-S	0[65]
1871 (P)	1,300
1872 (P)	2,000
1873 (P)[68]	0[69]
1874 (P)	41,800
1875 (P)	0[75]
1876 (P)	0[53]
1877 (P)	1,468
1878 (P)	82,304
1879 (P)	3,000
1880 (P)	1,000
1881 (P)	500
1882 (P)	1,500
1883 (P)	900
1884 (P)	1,000
1885 (P)	800
1886 (P)	1,000
1887 (P)	6,000
1888 (P)	5,000
1889 (P)	2,300

Half eagles

Year	Mintage
1795	8,707
1796	6,196
1797	3,609
1798	24,867[5]
1799	7,451
1800	37,628
1802	53,176
1803	33,506
1804	30,475
1805	33,183
1806	64,093
1807	84,093[11]
1808	55,578

$5 gold continued

Year	Mintage
1809	33,875
1810	100,287
1811	99,581
1812	58,087
1813	95,428
1814	15,454
1815	635
1818	48,588
1819	51,723
1820	263,806
1821	34,641
1822	17,796[13]
1823	14,485
1824	17,340
1825	29,060
1826	18,069
1827	24,913
1828	28,029
1829	57,442
1830	126,351
1831	140,594
1832	157,487
1833	193,630
1834	707,601[17]
1835	371,534
1836	553,147
1837	207,121
1838 (P)	286,588
1838-C	19,145
1838-D	20,583
1839 (P)	118,143
1839-C	17,235
1839-D	18,939
1840 (P)	137,382
1840-C	19,028
1840-D	22,896
1840-O	38,700
1841 (P)	15,833
1841-C	21,511
1841-D	30,495
1841-O	50
1842 (P)	27,578
1842-C	27,480
1842-D	59,608
1842-O	16,400
1843 (P)	611,205
1843-C	44,353
1843-D	98,452
1843-O	101,075
1844 (P)	340,330
1844-C	23,631
1844-D	88,982
1844-O	364,600
1845 (P)	417,099
1845-D	90,629
1845-O	41,000
1846 (P)	395,942
1846-C	12,995
1846-D	80,294
1846-O	58,000
1847 (P)	915,981
1847-C	84,151
1847-D	64,405
1847-O	12,000
1848 (P)	260,775
1848-C	64,472
1848-D	47,465
1849 (P)	133,070
1849-C	64,823
1849-D	39,036
1850 (P)	64,491
1850-C	63,591
1850-D	43,984

$5 gold continued

1851 (P)	377,505
1851-C	49,176
1851-D	62,710
1851-O	41,000
1852 (P)	573,901
1852-C	72,574
1852-D	91,584
1853 (P)	305,770
1853-C	65,571
1853-D	89,678
1854 (P)	160,675
1854-C	39,283
1854-D	56,413
1854-O	46,000
1854-S	268
1855 (P)	117,098
1855-C	39,788
1855-D	22,432
1855-O	11,100
1855-S	61,000
1856 (P)	197,990
1856-C	28,457
1856-D	19,786
1856-O	10,000
1856-S	105,100
1857 (P)	98,188
1857-C	31,360
1857-D	17,046
1857-O	13,000
1857-S	87,000
1858 (P)	15,136
1858-C	38,856
1858-D	15,362
1858-S	18,600
1859 (P)	16,814
1859-C	31,847
1859-D	10,366
1859-S	13,220
1860 (P)	19,763
1860-C	14,813
1860-D	14,635
1860-S	21,200
1861 (P)	688,084
1861-C	6,879[50]
1861-D	1,597
1861-S	18,000
1862 (P)	4,430
1862-S	9,500
1863 (P)	2,442
1863-S	17,000
1864 (P)	4,220
1864-S	3,888
1865 (P)	1,270
1865-S	27,612
1866 (P)	6,700
1866-S	43,920[62]
1867 (P)	6,870
1867-S	29,000
1868 (P)	5,700
1868-S	52,000
1869 (P)	1,760
1869-S	31,000
1870 (P)	4,000
1870-CC	7,675
1870-S	17,000
1871 (P)	3,200
1871-CC	20,770
1871-S	25,000
1872 (P)	1,660
1872-CC	16,980
1872-S	36,400
1873 (P)[68]	112,480
1873-CC[68]	7,416

$5 gold continued

1873-S[68]	31,000
1874 (P)	3,488
1874-CC	21,198
1874-S	16,000
1875 (P)	200
1875-CC	11,828
1875-S	9,000
1876 (P)	1,432
1876-CC	6,887
1876-S	4,000
1877 (P)	1,132
1877-CC	8,680
1877-S	26,700
1878 (P)	131,720
1878-CC	9,054
1878-S	144,700
1879 (P)	301,920
1879-CC	17,281
1879-S	426,200
1880 (P)	3,166,400
1880-CC	51,017
1880-S	1,348,900
1881 (P)	5,708,760
1881-CC	13,886
1881-S	969,000
1882 (P)	2,514,520
1882-CC	82,817
1882-S	969,000
1883 (P)	233,400
1883-CC	12,958
1883-S	83,200
1884 (P)	191,030
1884-CC	16,402
1884-S	177,000
1885 (P)	601,440
1885-S	1,211,500
1886 (P)	388,360
1886-S	3,268,000
1887 (P)	0[53]
1887-S	1,912,000
1888 (P)	18,202
1888-S	293,900
1889 (P)	7,520
1890 (P)	4,240
1890-CC	53,800
1891 (P)	61,360
1891-CC	208,000
1892 (P)	753,480
1892-CC	82,968
1892-O	10,000
1892-S	298,400
1893 (P)	1,528,120
1893-CC	60,000
1893-O	110,000
1893-S	224,000
1894 (P)	957,880
1894-O	16,600
1894-S	55,900
1895 (P)	1,345,855
1895-S	112,000
1896 (P)	58,960
1896-S	155,400
1897 (P)	867,800
1897-S	354,000
1898 (P)	633,420
1898-S	1,397,400
1899 (P)	1,710,630
1899-S	1,545,000
1900 (P)	1,405,500
1900-S	329,000
1901 (P)	615,900
1901-S	3,648,000
1902 (P)	172,400

$5 gold continued

1902-S	939,000
1903 (P)	226,870
1903-S	1,855,000
1904 (P)	392,000
1904-S	97,000
1905 (P)	302,200
1905-S	880,700
1906 (P)	348,735
1906-D[83]	320,000
1906-S	598,000
1907 (P)	626,100
1907-D[83]	888,000
1908 (P)	999,719[88]
1908-D	148,000[88]
1908-S	82,000[88]
1909 (P)	627,060
1909-D	3,423,560
1909-O	34,200
1909-S	297,200
1910 (P)	604,000
1910-D	193,600
1910-S	770,200
1911 (P)	915,000
1911-D	72,500
1911-S	1,416,000
1912 (P)	790,000
1912-S	392,000
1913 (P)	916,000
1913-S	408,000
1914 (P)	247,000
1914-D	247,000
1914-S	263,000
1915 (P)	588,000
1915-S	164,000
1916-S	240,000
1929 (P)	662,000

Eagles

Year	Mintage
1795	5,583
1796	4,146
1797	14,555[4]
1798	1,742
1799	37,449
1800	5,999
1801	44,344
1803	15,017
1804	3,757
1838 (P)	7,200
1839 (P)[27]	38,248
1840 (P)	47,338
1841 (P)	63,131
1841-O	2,500
1842 (P)	81,507
1842-O	27,400
1843 (P)	75,462
1843-O	175,162
1844 (P)	6,361
1844-O	118,700
1845 (P)	26,153
1845-O	47,500
1846 (P)	20,095
1846-O	81,780
1847 (P)	862,258
1847-O	571,500
1848 (P)	145,484
1848-O	35,850
1849 (P)	653,618
1849-O	23,900
1850 (P)	291,451
1850-O	57,500
1851 (P)	176,328

$10 gold continued

1851-O	263,000
1852 (P)	263,106
1852-O	18,000
1853 (P)	201,253
1853-O	51,000
1854 (P)	54,250
1854-O	52,500
1854-S	123,826
1855 (P)	121,701
1855-O	18,000
1855-S	9,000
1856 (P)	60,490
1856-O	14,500
1856-S	68,000
1857 (P)	16,606
1857-O	5,500
1857-S	26,000
1858 (P)	2,521
1858-O	20,000
1858-S	11,800
1859 (P)	16,093
1859-O	2,300
1859-S	7,000
1860 (P)	15,055
1860-O	11,100
1860-S	5,000
1861 (P)	113,164
1861-S	15,500
1862 (P)	10,960
1862-S	12,500
1863 (P)	1,218
1863-S	10,000
1864 (P)	3,530
1864-S	2,500
1865 (P)	3,980
1865-S	16,700
1866 (P)	3,750
1866-S	20,000[61]
1867 (P)	3,090
1867-S	9,000
1868 (P)	10,630
1868-S	13,500
1869 (P)	1,830
1869-S	6,430
1870 (P)	3,990
1870-CC	5,908
1870-S	8,000
1871 (P)	1,790
1871-CC	8,085
1871-S	16,500
1872 (P)	1,620
1872-CC	4,600
1872-S	17,300
1873 (P[68]	800
1873-CC[68]	4,543
1873-S[68]	12,000
1874 (P)	53,140
1874-CC	16,767
1874-S	10,000
1875 (P)	100
1875-CC	7,715
1876 (P)	687
1876-CC	4,696
1876-S	5,000
1877 (P)	797
1877-CC	3,332
1877-S	17,000
1878 (P)	73,780
1878-CC	3,244
1878-S	26,100
1879 (P)	384,740
1879-CC	1,762
1879-O	1,500

$10 gold continued

1879-S	224,000
1880 (P)	1,644,840
1880-CC	11,190
1880-O	9,200
1880-S	506,250
1881 (P)	3,877,220
1881-CC	24,015
1881-O	8,350
1881-S	970,000
1882 (P)	2,324,440
1882-CC	6,764
1882-O	10,820
1882-S	132,000
1883 (P)	208,700
1883-CC	12,000
1883-O	800
1883-S	38,000
1884 (P)	76,890
1884-CC	9,925
1884-S	124,250
1885 (P)	253,462
1885-S	228,000
1886 (P)	236,100
1886-S	826,000
1887 (P)	53,600
1887-S	817,000
1888 (P)	132,924
1888-O	21,335
1888-S	648,700
1889 (P)	4,440
1889-S	425,400
1890 (P)	57,980
1890-CC	17,500
1891 (P)	91,820
1891-CC	103,732
1892 (P)	797,480
1892-CC	40,000
1892-O	28,688
1892-S	115,500
1893 (P)	1,840,840
1893-CC	14,000
1893-O	17,000
1893-S	141,350
1894 (P)	2,470,735
1894-O	107,500
1894-S	25,000
1895 (P)	567,770
1895-O	98,000
1895-S	49,000
1896 (P)	76,270
1896-S	123,750
1897 (P)	1,000,090
1897-O	42,500
1897-S	234,750
1898 (P)	812,130
1898-S	473,600
1899 (P)	1,262,219
1899-O	37,047
1899-S	841,000
1900 (P)	293,840
1900-S	81,000
1901 (P)	1,718,740
1901-O	72,041
1901-S	2,812,750
1902 (P)	82,400
1902-S	469,500
1903 (P)	125,830
1903-O	112,771
1903-S	538,000
1904 (P)	161,930
1904-O	108,950
1905 (P)	200,992
1905-S	369,250

$10 gold continued

1906 (P)	165,420
1906-D	981,000
1906-O	86,895
1906-S	457,000
1907 (P)	1,443,305[85]
1907-D	1,030,000[85]
1907-S	210,500[85]
1908 (P)	374,870[87]
1908-D	1,046,500[87]
1908-S	59,850[87]
1909 (P)	184,789
1909-D	121,540
1909-S	292,350
1910 (P)	318,500
1910-D	2,356,640
1910-S	811,000
1911 (P)	505,500
1911-D	30,100
1911-S	51,000
1912 (P)	405,000
1912-S	300,000
1913 (P)	442,000
1913-S	66,000
1914 (P)	151,000
1914-D	343,500
1914-S	208,000
1915 (P)	351,000
1915-S	59,000
1916-S	138,500
1920-S	126,500
1926 (P)	1,014,000
1930-S	96,000
1932 (P)	4,463,000
1933 (P)[99]	312,500

Double eagles

Year	Mintage
1849 (P)[33]	0
1850 (P)	1,170,261
1850-O	141,000
1851 (P)	2,087,155
1851-O	315,000
1852 (P)	2,053,026
1852-O	190,000
1853 (P)	1,261,326
1853-O	71,000
1854 (P)	757,899
1854-O	3,250
1854-S	141,468
1855 (P)	364,666
1855-O	8,000
1855-S	879,675
1856 (P)	329,878
1856-O	2,250
1856-S	1,189,780
1857 (P)	439,375
1857-O	30,000
1857-S	970,500
1858 (P)	211,714
1858-O	35,250
1858-S	846,710
1859 (P)	43,597
1859-O	9,100
1859-S	636,445
1860 (P)	577,611
1860-O	6,600
1860-S	544,950
1861 (P)[47]	2,976,387
1861-O	17,741[48]
1861-S	768,000[49]
1862 (P)	92,098

$20 gold continued

1862-S	854,173
1863 (P)	142,760
1863-S	966,570
1864 (P)	204,235
1864-S	793,660
1865 (P)	351,175
1865-S	1,042,500
1866 (P)[59]	698,745
1866-S	842,250[60]
1867 (P)	251,015
1867-S	920,750
1868 (P)	98,575
1868-S	837,500
1869 (P)	175,130
1869-S	686,750
1870 (P)	155,150
1870-CC	3,789
1870-S	982,000
1871 (P)	80,120
1871-CC	17,387
1871-S	928,000
1872 (P)	251,850
1872-CC	26,900
1872-S	780,000
1873 (P)[68]	1,709,800
1873-CC[68]	22,410
1873-S[68]	1,040,600
1874 (P)	366,780
1874-CC	115,000
1874-S	1,214,000
1875 (P)	295,720
1875-CC	111,151
1875-S	1,230,000
1876 (P)	583,860
1876-CC	138,441
1876-S	1,597,000
1877 (P)[77]	397,650
1877-CC	42,565
1877-S	1,735,000
1878 (P)	543,625
1878-CC	13,180
1878-S	1,739,000
1879 (P)	207,600
1879-CC	10,708
1879-O	2,325
1879-S	1,223,800
1880 (P)	51,420
1880-S	836,000
1881 (P)	2,220
1881-S	727,000
1882 (P)	590
1882-CC	39,140
1882-S	1,125,000
1883 (P)	0[53]
1883-CC	59,962
1883-S	1,189,000
1884 (P)	0[53]
1884-CC	81,139
1884-S	916,000
1885 (P)	751
1885-CC	9,450
1885-S	683,500
1886 (P)	1,000
1887 (P)	0[53]
1887-S	283,000
1888 (P)	226,164
1888-S	859,600
1889 (P)	44,070
1889-CC	30,945
1889-S	774,700
1890 (P)	75,940
1890-CC	91,209

$20 gold continued

1890-S	802,750
1891 (P)	1,390
1891-CC	5,000
1891-S	1,288,125
1892 (P)	4,430
1892-CC	27,265
1892-S	930,150
1893 (P)	344,280
1893-CC	18,402
1893-S	996,175
1894 (P)	1,368,940
1894-S	1,048,550
1895 (P)	1,114,605
1895-S	1,143,500
1896 (P)	792,535
1896-S	1,403,925
1897 (P)	1,383,175
1897-S	1,470,250
1898 (P)	170,395
1898-S	2,575,175
1899 (P)	1,669,300
1899-S	2,010,300
1900 (P)	1,874,460
1900-S	2,459,500
1901 (P)	111,430
1901-S	1,596,000
1902 (P)	31,140
1902-S	1,753,625
1903 (P)	287,270
1903-S	954,000
1904 (P)	6,256,699
1904-S	5,134,175
1905 (P)	58,919
1905-S	1,813,000
1906 (P)	69,596
1906-D	620,250
1906-S	2,065,750
1907 (P)	1,824,703[84]
1907-D	842,250[84]
1907-S	2,165,800[84]
1908 (P)	4,427,809[86]
1908-D	1,013,250[86]
1908-S	22,000[86]
1909 (P)	161,215
1909-D	52,500
1909-S	2,774,925
1910 (P)	482,000
1910-D	429,000
1910-S	2,128,250
1911 (P)	197,250
1911-D	846,500
1911-S	775,750
1912 (P)	149,750
1913 (P)	168,780
1913-D	393,500
1913-S	34,000
1914 (P)	95,250
1914-D	453,000
1914-S	1,498,000
1915 (P)	152,000
1915-S	567,500
1916-S	796,000
1920 (P)	228,250
1920-S	558,000
1921 (P)	528,500
1922 (P)	1,375,500
1922-S	2,658,000
1923 (P)	566,000
1923-D	1,702,250
1924 (P)	4,323,500
1924-D	3,049,500
1924-S	2,927,500

$20 gold continued	$20 gold continued	$20 gold continued	$20 gold continued
1925 (P)............ 2,831,750	1926-D................ 481,000	1927-S............ 3,107,000	1931 (P)............ 2,938,250
1925-D.............. 2,938,500	1926-S.............. 2,041,500	1928 (P)............ 8,816,000	1931-D................ 106,500
1925-S.............. 3,776,500	1927 (P)............ 2,946,750	1929 (P)............ 1,779,750	1932 (P)............ 1,101,750
1926 (P)............ 816,750	1927-D................ 180,000	1930-S.................. 74,000	1933 (P)[98]........ 445,000

Mintage notes

1. 1793 cent: Flowing Hair obverse, Chain reverse: 36,103; Flowing Hair obverse, Wreath reverse: 63,353; Liberty Cap obverse; Wreath reverse: 11,056.

2. 1795 silver dollar: Flowing Hair type: 160,295; Draped Bust type: 42,738.

3. 1796 cent: Liberty Cap: 109,825; Draped Bust: 363,375.

4. 1797 $10: Mintage includes both reverse types.

5. 1798 $5: Mint Report of 24,867 coins includes Small Eagle reverse coins dated 1798, as well as Heraldic Eagle coins dated 1795, 1797 and 1798. This mixture of mulings is the result of an emergency coinage late in 1798 after the Mint had been closed for a while due to yellow fever. Quantities struck of each are unknown and can only be a guess.

6. 1798 silver dollar: Mintage includes both reverse designs.

7. 1801, 1802, and 1803 silver dollar: All three dates were restruck in Proof in 1858 with a plain edge, using obverse dies made in 1834-5 and the reverse die from the Class I 1804 dollar, which was also made in 1834. Due to the scandal caused by the private issue of 1804 dollars in 1858, these coins were not offered for sale to collectors until 1875, by which time their edges had been lettered.

8. 1804 silver dollar: Although the Mint Report lists 19,570 dollars for this year it is assumed that they were all dated 1803. The 1804 dollars were first struck in 1834-35 for inclusion in diplomatic presentation sets. A few pieces, possibly flawed Proofs or production overruns, reached collectors via trades with the Mint or in circulation and the coin was popularized as a rarity. In 1858 the son of a Mint employee used the obverse die prepared in 1834 and a newly prepared reverse die plus a plain collar to secretly strike 1804 dollars, a few of which were sold to collectors. While the Mint had intended to do exactly the same thing with dollars dated 1801-04, Mint officials were forced to cancel the project due to the public scandal over the privately-issued 1804s. The privately struck coins were recalled, and all but one (which went to the Mint Cabinet collection) were allegedly melted. Instead, they and the plain edged 1801-03s were put in storage and offered for sale in 1875, by which time their edges had been mechanically lettered.

9. 1804, 1823 cent, and 1811 half cent: Counterfeits, called restrikes, exist which were made outside the Mint, using old, genuine but mismatched Mint dies.

10. 1805 silver dollar: The 321 dollars listed in the Mint Report for 1805 were older dollars which were found in deposits of Spanish-American silver and which were re-issued through the Treasury. On the basis of this misinformation a few coins have been altered to this date in the past.

11. 1807 $5: Capped Bust type: 32,488; Capped Draped Bust type: 51,605.

12. 1807 half dollar: Draped Bust type: 301,076; Capped Bust type: 750,500.

13. 1822 $5: Although the Mint Report says 17,796 coins were struck, only three pieces are known and it is likely that most of this mintage was from dies dated 1821.

14. 1827 quarter dollar: Although the Mint Report lists a mintage of 4,000 pieces for this year, it is likely that all of these coins were dated 1825 except for a few Proofs. Later this date was unofficially (but intentionally) restruck at the Mint using an obverse die dated 1827 and a reverse die which had been used in 1819, and which had a Square Base 2 in quarter dollar, rather than the Curled Base 2 of the original 1827.

15. 1831, 1849, 1856 and 1857 half cent: Originally struck in Proof and Uncirculated, the Proofs were restruck for collectors in later years.

16. 1832-35 half cent: The figures shown are listed in the Mint Report for 1833-36 instead, but are assumed to be misplaced.

17. 1834 $5: Total of 732,169 coins struck. This includes 50,141, of the Capped Head design struck and released; 24,568 of the Capped Head struck but melted; and 657,460 of the Classic Head design (and weight), all released.

18. 1834 $2.50: Mintage includes 4,000 of the Capped Head, of which most or all were melted. It may be that all survivors are Proofs and circulated Proofs.

19. 1836, 1838, and 1839 silver dollar: Gobrecht dollars, some patterns and some

intended for circulation, were struck in these years. Also, some varieties were restruck in later years, making mintage figures questionable. Varieties exist with or without stars and/or the designer's name, some of them exceedingly scarce. The 1,600 mintage figure for 1836 represents 1,000 struck for circulation on the 1836 standard of 416 grains, and 600 pieces struck in 1837 (dated 1836) on the new standard of 412.5 grains.

20. 1836 half dollar: Mintage includes 6,545,000 Capped Bust, Lettered Edge coins and 1,200 pieces with a reeded edge and no motto E PLURIBUS UNUM. (The latter was actually a pattern of the design adopted the following year, but much of the mintage was placed into circulation.)

21. 1836 half cent: Originally struck in Proof only, this date was restruck in Proof in later years to provide collectors with specimens of a coin that was listed in the Mint Report but which couldn't be found in circulation. See 16.

22. 1837 dime: Capped Bust type: 359,500; Seated Liberty Without Stars on obverse: 682,500.

23. 1837 half dime: Capped Bust type: 871,000; Seated Liberty, Without Stars on obverse: 1,405,000.

24. 1838-O half dollar: Twenty specimen pieces were struck to celebrate the opening of the New Orleans Mint.

25. 1838 quarter dollar: Capped Bust type: 366,000; Seated Liberty type: 466,000.

26. 1838-O dime and half dime: Both are of Seated Liberty, Without Stars design (type of 1837). 1838 Philadelphia coins have stars, as do all others through 1859.

27. 1839 $10: Includes first design head (type of 1838) and modified head (type of 1840-1907).

28. 1839-(P), O half dollar: Capped Bust type: (P): 1,362,160; O: 178,976. Seated Liberty type: (P): 1,972,400. (Note: Although Christian Gobrecht's half dollar design was slightly modified during 1839 by the addition of a small drapery fold beneath the elbow, the design was never as fully modified as the other Seated Liberty denominations were in 1840. In subsequent years individual dies would occasionally be over-polished, thus removing this small drapery fold. Coins struck from these inferior dies are sometimes referred to as having a "No-Drapery design," when in fact no design change was intended or made.)

29. 1840-53 silver dollar: Proof restrikes exist for all dates.

30. 1840-48 and 1852 half cent: Originally struck in Proof only, all dates were restruck in Proof for sale to collectors.

31. 1841-(P) $2.50: Struck in Proof only, possibly at a later date. Unlisted in Mint Report .

32. 1848-(P) $2.50: Approximately 1,389 coins were counterstamped CAL. above the eagle to show that they were made from California gold. This was done while the coins were resting on an inverted obverse die on a worktable. This virtually eliminated distortion of the obverse, which will probably show on a genuine coin with a fake counterstamp.

33. 1849 $20: One specimen in gold survives of a small number of trial strikes produced in December 1849. The dies were rejected, allegedly because of improper high relief, but in actuality to discredit Longacre in an attempt to force his removal. The attempt failed and Longacre eventually produced a second set of dies, but they were not completed until the following month and so they were dated 1850. The one known gold specimen is in the National Numismatic Collection at the Smithsonian Institution and all others were melted.

34. 1853 silver coinage: In early 1853 the weight of all fractional silver coins was reduced by about 7 percent, to prevent hoarding and melting. To distinguish between the old and new weights, arrows were placed on either side of the date on the half dime through half dollar, and rays were put around the eagle on the quarter and half dollar. The rays were removed after 1853, and the arrows after 1855. Much of the old silver was withdrawn from circulation and melted. The exception to all this was the silver 3-cent piece, which was decreased in weight but increased in fineness, making it intrinsically worth more than before and proportionate with the other fractional silver coins. No coins of the new weight were struck until 1854, at which time an olive branch and a cluster of arrows was added to the reverse.

35. 1853-(P), O half dollar: All 1853-(P) and virtually all 1853-O half dollar are of the new weight. Two or three 1853-O are known without the arrows and rays. Beware of alterations from 1858-O.

36. 1853-(P), O quarter dollar: Without Arrows and Rays: (P): 44,200. With Arrows and Rays: (P): 15,210,020; O: 1,332,000.

37. 1853-(P), O dime: Without Arrows: (P): 95,000. With Arrows: (P): 12,078,010; O:

1,100,000.

38. 1853-(P), O half dime: Without Arrows: (P): 135,000; O: 160,000. With Arrows: (P): 13,210,020; O: 2,200,000.

39. 1854-(P), D, S gold dollar: (P): Coronet 736,709; Indian (small head) 902,736. All 1854-D and S are Coronet design.

40. 1856-(P), D, S gold dollar: All P and D-Mint are Indian (large head); all S-Mint are Indian (small head).

41. 1856 cent: More than 1,000 1856 Flying Eagle cents were struck in Proof and Uncirculated, in this and later years. As they were patterns they are not included in the Mint Report or this figure.

42. 1857 cent: large cents: 333,456; small cents: 17,450,000.

43. 1858 silver dollar: It is estimated that 80 Proofs were struck, some of them possibly at a later date.

44. 1859 cent: This year only comes with a reverse design without a shield. All other Indian cents (1860-1909) have a shield.

45. 1860-S $3: Out of 7,000 coins struck, 2,592 pieces were not released because of short weight. They were melted in 1869 for use in other denominations.

46. 1860-(P), O, S dime and half dime: Beginning in 1860 (with the exception of the 1860-S dime), the half dime and dime were redesigned by eliminating the stars, moving the legend UNITED STATES OF AMERICA to the obverse, and using a larger, more elaborate wreath on the reverse. A number of fabrications with the obverse of 1859 and the reverse of 1860 (thereby omitting the legend UNITED STATES OF AMERICA), were struck by order of the Director of the Mint. These consist of half dimes dated 1859 or 1860, and dimes dated 1859. Although they are considered by some to be patterns, that designation is doubtful as the intentions of the Director were highly questionable.

47. 1861-(P) $20: A few trial pieces are known with a reverse as engraved by Paquet, with taller, thinner letters and a narrow rim. The design was judged unacceptable because the narrow reverse rim would not stack easily. (See 49.)

48. 1861-O $20: Mintage includes 5,000 coins struck by the USA; 9,750 by the State of Louisiana; and 2,991 by the Confederate States of America. It is impossible to prove the issuer of any given coin.

49. 1861-S $20: Mintage includes 19,250 pieces struck with the Paquet reverse and released into circulation. (See 47.) Most of these

were recalled and melted during the next few years, but specie hoarding during the Civil War probably preserved a number of them until later years when the problem was forgotten.

50. 1861-C $5: Mintage includes 5,992 pieces coined by USA and 887 by CSA. It is impossible to prove the issuer.

51. 1861-D gold dollar: A small number were struck by the CSA.

52. 1861-O half dollar: Mintage includes 330,000 struck by the USA; 1,240,000 by the State of Louisiana; and 962,633 by the CSA. It is impossible to tell them apart. One obverse die is identifiable as having been used with the CSA reverse to strike four pattern coins, but there is no way of telling when that die was used with a regular reverse die or who issued the coins struck from it.

53. Struck in Proof only.

54. 1863 silver 3 cents: It is possible that all of these non-Proofs were dated 1862. Proof coins dated 1863/2 were struck in 1864. Obviously these were hard times at the Mint.

55. 1864-(P) dime, half dime and silver 3 cents: These figures, like many others in the years 1861-1871, are highly controversial due to extraordinary bookkeeping methods used in the Mint in this era.

56. 1864 2 cents: Struck with Large and Small Motto IN GOD WE TRUST.

57. 1864 cent: Mintage includes 13,740,000 copper-nickel and 39,233,714 bronze pieces. The bronze coins come with and without the designer's initial L, which appears on all subsequent issues. The 1864 variety With L is the scarcer.

58. 1866 coinage: It was decided to add the motto IN GOD WE TRUST to the reverse of all double eagles, eagles, half eagles, silver dollars, half dollars and quarter dollars beginning in 1866. Early in the year, before the new reverse dies had arrived, the San Francisco Mint produced $20, $10, $5, and half dollar coins without the motto. These are regular issue coins and are not patterns or errors. They are not to be confused with a peculiar set of Philadelphia Mint silver coins without motto, consisting of two dollars, one half dollar and one quarter dollar, which was clandestinely struck inside (but not by) the Mint for sale to a collector. A three-piece set containing the unique quarter dollar and half dollar and one of the two known silver dollars was stolen from the Willis H. DuPont collection

in 1967 and never recovered. Beware of regular coins with motto or Mint mark removed.

59. 1866-(P), S $20: When the reverse of the double eagle was altered to include the motto there were also a few minor changes made in the scrollwork, the most prominent being the change in the shield from flat-sided to curved. Check any alleged 1866-S No Motto $20 for this feature.

60. 1866-S $20: Includes 120,000 No Motto coins.

61. 1866-S $10: Includes 8,500 No Motto coins.

62. 1866-S $5: Includes 9,000 No Motto coins.

63. 1866-S half dollar: Includes 60,000 No Motto coins.

64. 1867 copper-nickel 5 cents: Struck with rays on reverse (type of 1866) and without rays (type of 1868-83).

65. 1870-S $3: Not included in the Mint Report, supposedly one piece was struck for inclusion in the cornerstone of the new San Francisco Mint. One piece is known in a private collection, and the present whereabouts of the cornerstone piece is unknown. It is possible there is only one piece.

66. 1870-S gold dollar: 2,000 coins were struck without a Mint mark. It is unknown if they were melted and recoined or released as is and included in the Mint Report figure of 3,000 coins.

67. 1870-S silver dollar: Not listed in the Mint Report, but a few pieces may have been struck as souvenirs of the opening of the new Mint.

68. 1873 coinage: Early in the year a relatively closed style of 3 was used in the date on all denominations. In response to complaints that the 3 looked like an 8, a new, more open 3 was introduced. Most types were struck with both styles, except for those which were created or discontinued by the Coinage Act of Feb. 12, 1873. This law created the Trade dollar and eliminated the standard silver dollar, the silver 5-cent piece, the 3-cent piece and the 2-cent piece. The weight of the dime, quarter dollar and half dollar were slightly increased, and the heavier coins were marked by arrows for the remainder of 1873 and all of 1874.

69. 1873 $3: Struck in Proof only, later restruck in Proof more than once.

70. 1873-S silver dollar: Presumably all or most were melted at the Mint after production of standard silver dollars was suspended.

71. 1873-(P), CC, S half dollar: Without Arrows: (P): 801,200; CC: 122,500; S:

5,000. With Arrows: (P) 1,815,150; CC: 214,560; S: 228,000. (Note: The 1873-S Seated Liberty, Without Arrows half dollar is unknown in any condition in any collection. Presumably they were all melted with the 1873-S silver dollars. Beware of any regular 1873-S with the arrows removed. The difference in weight between the two issues is insignificant, and use less in checking a suspected altered coin.)

72. 1873-(P), CC, S quarter dollar: Without Arrows: (P): 212,000; CC: 4,000. With Arrows: (P): 1,271,160; CC: 12,462; S: 156,000.

73. 1873-(P), CC, S dime: Without Arrows: (P): 1,568,000; CC: 12,400. With Arrows: (P): 2,377,700; CC: 18,791; S: 455,000. (Note: One 1873-CC Without Arrows known, all others presumably were melted.)

74. 1873 2 cents: Originally struck in Proof only early in 1873 with a Closed 3. Later restruck in Proof with an Open 3.

75. 1875 $3: Struck in Proof only, later restruck in Proof.

76. 1876-CC 20 cents: Virtually all remelted at the Mint. A few escaped, possibly as souvenirs given to visitors. Fewer than 20 are known today.

77. 1877 $20: In this year the master hubs were redesigned slightly, raising the head and changing TWENTY D. to TWENTY DOLLARS.

78. 1878-(P), 1879-85 Trade dollar: The P-Mint Trade dollars from 1878 to 1883 were struck and sold in Proof only. Ten 1884 and five 1885 coins were struck in Proof in the Mint for private distribution, by person or persons unknown. They are not listed in the Mint Report.

79. 1878-(P) silver dollar: Three slightly different designs were used for both the obverse and reverse of this date, including some dies with the second designs impressed over the first. All 1878-CC and 1878-S are from the second designs. Most 1879-1904 dollars are of the third design, except for some second design reverses on 1879-S and 1880-CC coins. New, slightly different master hubs were prepared for 1921.

80. 1883 copper-nickel 5 cents: Shield type: 1,451,500; Liberty Head, No CENTS on reverse: 5,474,300; Liberty Head, With CENTS on reverse: 16,026,200.

81. 1894-S dime: Twenty-four specimen strikings were made for private distribution by the Superintendent of the San Francisco Mint. Twelve can be traced today.

82. 1895 silver dollar: Apparently virtually all business strike coins were never issued and were probably melted in the great silver melt of 1918. One circulated business strike coin has reportedly been authenticated. Beware of altered dates and removed Mint marks.

83. 1906-D and 1907-D $5: These were, of course, struck at the Denver Mint. This is the only design which was struck at both Dahlonega and Denver.

84. 1907-(P), D, S $20: Coronet: 1,451,786 P-Mint and all D and S-Mint coins. Saint-Gaudens type: 11,250 medium-high relief, Roman Numeral date coins and 361,667 lower-relief, Arabic date coins. A few extremely-high relief patterns were also made.

85. 1907-(P), D, S $10: Coronet: 1,203,899 P-Mint and all D and S-Mint coins. Indian Head type: 239,406.

86. 1908-(P), D, S $20: Without motto IN GOD WE TRUST: (type of 1907) (P): 4,271,551; D: 663,750. With motto: (type of 1909-33) (P): 156,258; D: 349,500; S: 22,000.

87. 1908-(P), D, S $10: Without motto IN GOD WE TRUST: (type of 1907) (P): 33,500; D: 210,000. With motto: (type of 1909-33) (P): 341,370; D: 836,500; S: 59,850.

88. 1908-(P), D, S $5: Coronet: 421,874 P-Mint coins. Indian Head: 577,845 P-Mint and all D and S-Mint coins.

89. 1909-(P), S cent: Indian Head : (P): 14,368,470; S: 309,000. Lincoln Head with designer's initials V.D.B.: (P): 27,994,580; S: 484,000. Lincoln Head without V.D.B.: (P): 72,700,420; S: 1,825,000.

90. 1913 Liberty Head copper-nickel 5 cents: Five unauthorized pieces were struck by person or persons unknown, using Mint machinery and dies. All five accounted for by some sources, although numismatic researcher Walter Breen states that one piece is missing. Beware of forgeries. (See also 91.)

91. 1913-(P), D, S Indian Head copper-nickel 5 cents: Variety with the bison standing on a solid mound: (P): 3 0,992,000; D: 5,337,000; S: 2,105,000. Variety with the Bison on Plain, with the base of the mound recessed so as to protect the Mint mark and FIVE CENTS: (P): 29,857,186; D: 4,156,000; S: 1,209,000.

92. 1916-(P), D quarter dollar: Barber Head type: 1,788,000 P-Mint and all D-Mint. Standing Liberty type: 52,000 P-Mint.

93. 1916-(P), D, S dime: Barber Head type: (P); 18,490,000; S: 5,820,000. Winged Liberty Head type: (P): 22,180,080; D: 264,000; S: 10,45 0,000.

94. 1917-D, S half dollar: With Mint mark on obverse (type of 1916): D: 765,400; S: 952,000. On reverse (type of 1918-47): D: 1,940,000; S: 5,554,000.

95. 1917-(P), D, S quarter dollar: Variety 1 (type of 1916, with partially nude figure): (P): 8,740,000; D: 1,509,200; S: 1,952,000. Variety 2 (type of 1918, with fully clothed figure and eagle higher on reverse): (P): 13,880,000; D: 6,224,400; S: 5,552,000.

96. 1921-(P), D, S silver dollar: Morgan type: 44,690,000 P-Mint and all D and S Mints. Peace type: 1,006,473 P-Mint. The 1921 Peace dollars, (and a very few Proof 1922s), are of a higher relief than the 1922-35s.

97. 1922 "Plain" cent: No cents were struck in Philadelphia in 1922. Some 1922-D cents are found with the Mint mark missing due to obstructed dies. Beware of altered coins.

98. 1933 $20: This issue was officially never released, so the coins are considered illegal to own. A few are reported to exist, including one in the National Numismatic Collection at the Smithsonian Institution. Most late-date gold never filtered down through the banks and so it was returned to the Mint for melting.

99. 1933 $10: Very few of these were issued, perhaps several dozens known. Beware of counterfeits.

100. 1938-D copper-nickel 5 cents: Indian Head: 7,020,000. Jefferson: 5,376,000.

101. 1942-1945-(P), P, D, S 5 cents: To conserve nickel during the war, the composition of the 5-cent piece was changed to a 56 percent copper, 35 percent silver, and 9 percent manganese alloy. Coins of this alloy were marked with a large Mint mark over the dome of Monticello, including those from Philadelphia. They consist of some 1942-P, all 1942-S, and all 1943-45 coins. The 1942 Philadelphia coins were made either way, as follows: copper-nickel: 49,789,000; wartime alloy: 57,873,000. Many wartime alloy 5-cent coins have been melted for their silver content.

102. 1943-(P), D, S cent: All 1943 cents were made of zinc-plated steel. A few 1943 bronze and 1944 steel cents were made by accident. Many fakes of these have been produced. Test any suspected off-metal 1943 or 1944 cent with a magnet to see if it has been plated, and check the date for alterations. Cents struck on steel planchets produced in 1942 weigh 41.5 grains, while those struck on planchets produced later in

1943 weigh 42.5 grains.

103. 1944 copper-nickel 5 cents: Coins without a Mint mark are counterfeits made for circulation, as are any 1923-D or 1930-D dimes. Not all counterfeits are of rare dates, meant to sell at high prices. Some were meant to circulate.

104. 1964-67 coinage: All coins dated 1965-67 were made without Mint marks. Many coins dated 1964-66 were struck in later years.

105. 1970-D half dollar: Struck only for inclusion in Mint sets. Not a regular issue coin.

106. S-Mint clad dollars: Struck only for sale to collectors. In 1971-72 struck in 40 percent clad silver in Proof and Uncirculated for individual sale. Beginning in 1973 a copper-nickel clad dollar was added to the Proof sets.

107. 1973-(P), D copper-nickel dollar: Struck only for inclusion in Mint sets. Not a regular issue coin. 1,769,258 Mint sets were sold. 439,899 excess dollars melted, presumably of near-equal distribution. 21,641 coins were kept for possible replacement of defective sets and may have been melted.

108. 1974-dated dollars, half dollars and quarter dollars: Includes coins struck in calendar years 1974 and 1975.

109. 1975-dated dollars, half dollars and quarter dollars: Absolutely none struck. 1975 Proof and Mint sets contain Bicentennial dollars, half dollars and quarters.

110. 1976-dated dollars, half dollars and quarter dollars: Includes coins struck in calendar years 1975 and 1976.

111. 1976-S dollars, half dollars and quarter dollars: Includes copper-nickel clad Proofs sold in 1975 and 1976 in six-piece Proof sets, and 40 percent silver clad Proofs and Uncirculateds of which 15 million pieces of each denomination were struck.

112. P Mint mark: The P Mint mark, placed on the 1979 Anthony dollar, was added to all 1980 denominations from the Philadelphia Mint except for the cent.

113. Anthony dollar: The Anthony design was introduced, replacing the larger Eisenhower dollar. All Philadelphia Mint dollars have a P Mint mark.

114. 1982 cent: The composition of the cent changed from 95 percent copper, 5 percent zinc to 97.5 percent zinc, 2.5 percent copper (composed of a planchet of 99.2 percent zinc, 0.8 percent copper, plated with pure copper). Some 1982 cents were struck in late 1981.

115. 1982 No-P dimes: Some 1982 dimes were released without a Mint mark, although dimes have been Mint marked since 1980. Distribution of the coins, many found in the Sandusky, Ohio, area, indicates they were from the Philadelphia Mint.

116. Anthony dollars: Anthony dollars were sold in three-coin sets only in 1981. None were released into circulation.

117. 1987 half dollar: No 1987 Kennedy half dollars were struck for circulation. The coins were struck for Uncirculated sets, Proof sets and Souvenir Mint sets only.

Annual Proof coinage since 1817

The following series of charts is meant to show the quantities struck of U.S. Proof coins from 1817 to the present. In years prior to 1860, when Proof mintages were small and were not recorded, an asterisk marks those issues that are known or are thought to exist. In many instances from 1860 to 1922 the figures shown are approximate, the result of incomplete records, restrikes and the melting of unsold Proofs.

From 1817 to 1859, Proof coins were made in small batches whenever a number of orders had accumulated. An appropriate pair of dies, sometimes new but often used, was polished and used to strike the required number of coins. This is why many early Proof issues may show many varieties among only a dozen or so coins known. These Proof dies were usually returned to general use, where they would result in prooflike coins until the polished surfaces wore down. Occasionally the die chosen for use was overdated.

During these early years the most popular Proof coins were the half cent and later the silver dollar. It could be that these two coins represented, respectively, the cheapest and the most impressive (from the aspect of size) Proof coins. It could also be that the regular issues of these two coins were small, and collectors thought the Proofs would be good investments. Collecting complete Proof sets was popular from 1840 to 1848, although this fad was not revived until the late 1850s.

Beginning in 1860 the Mint produced Proof coins in quantity in anticipation of selling them, rather than producing them on demand. As a rule, a small but uniform number of gold Proofs and a much larger but also uniform number of silver Proofs were made. As no records were kept of the number of non-silver minor coin Proofs issued before 1878, they are commonly assumed to be equal to the silver Proofs of the same year.

This assumption may be drastically wrong, as it is apparent from the 1878 figures that the minor coins were much more popular. It has been suggested that these Proof minor coins were frequently given as Christmas presents to children. If so, we can probably assume that many of these were spent as soon as possible.

Exceptions to the uniform number plan are many, and can usually be logically explained. Coinage laws usually took effect during the middle of a year, and the new or discontinued issues would be produced for only a part of that year. Issues which were being phased out, such as gold dollars in the 1880s, were popular as investments. Others, such as the Trade dollar, continued on in Proof form after regular coinage had been suspended. In 1883 a large number of each of the three varieties of 5-cent pieces was produced, unlike the 1864 cents where the number of Proof coins struck was proportionate to the varieties of regular coins issued.

Regular production of Proofs was suspended after 1915, with the exceptions of cents and 5-cent pieces in 1916 and a few Proofs of the half dollar and dime in 1916 and of the cent, 5-cent piece and quarter dollar in 1917. A few, perhaps as many as 25, Morgan dollars were struck in Brilliant Proof in 1921. Approximately three of each of the 1921 and 1922 Peace dollars were struck in Matte Proof. The Proof 1922 Peace dollars were of the same high relief as the 1921 Peace dollar and of a slightly different design from the 1922 business-strike Peace dollar. Any alleged 1922 Proof must match the design of a 1921 coin exactly.

The production of Proofs was resumed in 1936, with the total mintage of each coin dependent upon orders. It may be a comment upon the relative popularity of the designs that the Washington quarter dollar was the one usually ordered least. World War II brought about a second suspension of Proof coinage, but not before the wartime metal shortages created a new curiosity, the Proof 1942-P Jefferson 5-cent coin with a "P" Mint mark.

In 1950 the production of Proof coins was again resumed, but now the coins were available only in complete sets. From 1950 to mid-1955 the coins were packaged in individual cellophane envelopes, stapled together across the openings. This arrangement was meant to serve as a shipping device only, but many people left the coins in the package where rust from the staple could damage the coins. Beginning in mid-1955 the coins were sealed in a soft plastic "flat-pack," similar to the packaging currently being used for Uncirculated Mint sets. This series of Proofs continued through 1964.

In 1965, during a coin shortage when the Mint did not have the time to produce Proof sets, the Mint instead made available to collectors "Special Mint sets." These consisted of Uncirculated coins, packaged like the Proofs of previous years. In 1966-67 a long, hard plastic holder was used instead. These three Special Mint sets were sold at $4 per set, an increase over the $2.10 price of a 1950-64 Proof set.

In 1968, when the coin shortage was over and Mint marks were returned to coins, it was decided to strike Proof sets at the San Francisco Assay Office, formerly the San Francisco Mint. Various coins had been struck at this facility since 1964, but without Mint marks to prevent hoarding. These five-coin sets were packaged in a larger, hard plastic case and were issued at $5 per set.

When the Philadelphia and Denver Mints began producing copper-nickel clad Eisenhower dollars for circulation in 1971, the San Francisco Assay Office began striking silver-clad dollars for collectors in Proof and Uncirculated conditions. Beginning with 1973 a copper-nickel clad dollar became part of the regular Proof set. In 1979, the Anthony dollar replaced the Eisenhower dollar; it was removed from sets beginning in 1982. Special Prestige Proof sets containing an Olympic silver dollar were sold in 1983 and 1984 at $59 each. A 1986 Prestige Proof set contains the five regular coins, the Ellis Island dollar and Immigrant half dollar.

With the introduction of the Olympic gold eagle, Mint officials eventually decided to strike Proof eagles at each of the four minting facilities: Philadelphia, Denver, San Francisco and the initial Olympic gold plant, West Point.

Another change for Proofs took place in 1985. Since Mint marks were first used in 1838, the marks have been punched into the individual working dies. However, the inadvertant release of a 1983 Proof dime with no "S" Mint mark prompted Mint officials to place the Mint mark on the master die in an attempt to prevent this type of error from occuring again. In 1986, the Mint mark was included on the plasticene model stage for all Proof coins and commemoratives; thus, the Mint mark appears at every stage of the modeling and die-making process.

The term "Proof" means different things to many collectors, dealers and other hobbyists. Some believe Proof is the top level of preservation, or grade — it is not. Others believe Proof coins are particularly shiny coins destined for collectors rather than circulation — they are only partly correct.

"Proof" in numismatics refers to a special manufacturing process designed to result in coins of the highest quality produced especially for collectors. "Proof" is not a grade, as many beginning collectors think, although there is a growing movement by some dealers and other hobbyists to assign Proof coins a numerical grade such as Proof 63 or Proof 65.

Proof coins result from the same basic processes used in producing the dies and planchets used in producing business strikes for circulation (business strikes refer to the everyday coin, struck for use in circulation). However, Mint employees use special techniques in preparing the surfaces of the dies and planchets intended for Proof coins. Special presses and striking techniques are also used in the production of Proof coins.

The Proof coins sold by the United States Mint today are Frosted Proofs. The flat fields are mirror-like, reflective and shiny. The frosting refers to the white, textured, non-reflective finish found on the raised devices, lettering and other points in relief. Both the frosted and mirror finishes are the results of the special techniques using in preparing the dies.

All dies are produced at the Philadelphia Mint although the surfaces of Proof dies used at the San Francisco Mint are prepared at San Francisco. Remember, a die features a mirror-image, incused version of the finished coin's design. Points that are raised on the coin are incused on the die. Points incused on the coin are in relief on the die.

To prepare a Frosted Proof die, the die is first sandblasted with an aluminum oxide and glass bead compound. This imparts a rough, textured finish to the entire die. After the sandblasting is completed, cellophane tape is placed over the entire surface. The person preparing the die then removes the cellophane tape from around the incused areas in the die; in effect, the fields are uncovered and the incused areas are protected by the cellophane.

The uncovered surfaces are then polished to a high sheen while the textured finish on the incused areas is left intact. Once the polishing is completed, the die receives a light plating of chrome, two- to three-thousandths of an inch thick. The chrome is then buffed. The finished die now has mirror-like fields and textured relief, and will impart the same finishes to the coins it strikes.

The planchets used to strike the Proof coins also receive special treatment. The planchets are run through a burnishing process, by tumbling the planchets in a media of carbon steel balls, water and an alkaline soap. The process cleans and polishes the planchets. The burnished planchets are rinsed in clear water and towel-dried by hand, then go through another cleaning and hand-drying process. Compressed air is used to blow lint and dust from the planchets.

Proof coins are struck on special hand-fed presses which operate at slower speeds than the high-speed presses used for striking business strike coinage. The Proof coining presses tend to impress the design from the dies onto the planchet; the production of a business strike is a much more rapid, violent event. The striking of a Proof coin has been compared more to pressing out a hamburger patty than to cracking a nut. Each Proof coin is struck two or more times, depending on the size of the coin, the design and the composition of the metal. The multiple striking ensures that the detail is brought up fully on each coin. Business strikes are struck only once (although some U.S. business strikes in the past have been struck more than once, most notably the 1907 Saint-Gaudens, High Relief double eagle.

Proof coins are then sealed into plastic capsules or plastic holders to protect their surfaces from potentially damaging environmental factors.

Although most collectors of modern U.S. Proof coins are familiar with the Frosted Proofs in vogue today, there are many other types of Proof finishes. Some no longer used by the U.S. Mint include the Matte Proof, used in the early 20th century. The entire surface of the coin is uniformly dull or granular; the surface results from the struck coin being pickled in acid. A Satin Finish Proof coin has a matte, satiny surface; the finishing process, used in the early 20th century, is currently unknown. A Sandblast Proof is a type of Matte Proof in which the surface of the coin is sandblasted, not pickled in acid. A Roman Finish Proof was used on gold Proofs of 1909-10 and is similar to the Satin Finish Proof. A Brilliant Proof is one in which the entire surface is mirror-like; any frosted devices are accidental, found generally only on the first few strikes of the die. Brilliant Proofs were produced by the U.S. Mint until the late 1970s and early 1980s, when Mint officials began taking care to produce the Frosted Proof.

Miscellaneous notes

Proof $10 eagles dated 1804 are restrikes made in 1834-35, for inclusion in Proof sets meant to be given as diplomatic presents. The 1804 dollar was first struck at this time for this occasion, also in Proof. The 1804 dollar was restruck in Proof in the late 1850s. The Proof dollars of 1801-03 were first struck at this time.

Many different Proof issues before 1880 were restruck in Proof one or more times. In some instances, as with the 1873 $3 gold piece, there are more coins of this date known than were "officially" struck.

Branch Mint Proofs

Until 1968, branch Mint Proofs were rare. From 1968 to 1983, all Proofs were struck in San Francisco. Since 1984, Proofs have been produced in Philadelphia, Denver, San Francisco and West Point for special coin programs.

1838-O half dollar: It is thought that 20 specimens were struck as souvenirs in honor of the opening of the New Orleans Mint. No regular issue coins of this date and Mint were struck, and it is possible that these were struck in 1839.

1839-O half dollar: Three or four known.

1844-O half eagle: One known, reason for issue unknown.

1844-O eagle: One known, reason for issue unknown.

1852-O eagle: Three pieces known, reason for issue unknown.

1853-O eagle: Mintage unknown, reason for issue unknown.

1854-S double eagle: One known, in the Smithsonian Institution. Struck in honor of the opening of the San

Francisco Mint.

1855-S quarter dollar: One known, presumably struck to celebrate the beginning of silver coinage at the San Francisco Mint.

1855-S half dollar: Three known, same occasion as for the quarter dollar.

1856-O half dime: One known, reason for issue unknown.

1860-O half dime: Three known, reason for issue unknown.

1861-O half dollar: Three to six known, probably struck under the authority of either the state of Louisiana or the Confederate States of America.

1870-CC silver dollar: Mintage unknown, possibly struck to mark first Carson City dollar coinage.

1875-S 20 cents: Six to seven known, probably struck to celebrate the first (or last) year of this denomination at this Mint.

1879-O silver dollar: Two now known of 12 struck to celebrate the re-opening of the New Orleans Mint.

1882-CC silver dollar: Mintage unknown, reason for issue unknown.

1883-CC silver dollar: Mintage unknown, reason for issue unknown.

1883-O silver dollar: One now known of 12 struck for presentation to various local dignitaries. Occasion uncertain.

1884-CC silver dollar: One reported, reason for issue unknown.

1891-O quarter dollar: Two known, probably struck to celebrate the resumption of fractional silver coinage at this Mint.

1893-CC silver dollar: 12 struck for presentation to Mint officials to mark the closing of the Carson City Mint.

1894-S dime: Twenty-four struck for private distribution by the Superintendent of the San Francisco Mint. Approximately 12 are currently known, including two circulated pieces.

1895-O half dollar: Issued to mark reopening of New Orleans Mint.

1899-S half eagle: One or two known, reason for issue unknown.

1906-D dime: Struck in honor of the opening of the Denver Mint.

1906-D eagle: Struck in honor of the opening of the Denver Mint.

1906-D double eagle: Two now known of 12 struck in honor of the opening of the Denver Mint.

1907-D double eagle: One known, possibly struck as a specimen of the last year of this design.

Proof coinage to 1942

Half cents

Year	Mintage
1825	•
1826	•
1828	•
1829	•
1831	•1
1832	•
1833	•
1834	•
1835	•
1836	•1
1840	•1
1841	•1
1842	•1
1843	•1
1844	•1
1845	•1
1846	•1
1847	•1
1848	•1
1849	•1
1850	•
1851	•

Half cents continued

1852	•1
1854	•
1855	•
1856	•1
1857	•1

Cents

Year	Mintage
1817	•
1818	•
1819	•
1820	•
1821	•
1822	•
1823	•2
1825	•
1826	•
1827	•
1828	•
1829	•
1830	•
1831	•
1832	•
1833	•
1834	•

Cents continued

1835	•
1836	•
1837	•
1838	•
1839	•
1840	•
1841	•
1842	•
1843	•
1844	•
1845	•
1846	•
1847	•
1848	•
1849	•
1850	•
1852	•
1854	•
1855	•
1856	•3
1857	•4
1858	•
1859	•
1860	1,000
1861	1,000
1862	550

Cents continued

1863	460
1864	4705
1865	500
1866	725
1867	625
1868	600
1869	600
1870	1,000
1871	960
1872	950
1873	1,1006
1874	700
1875	700
1876	1,150
1877	5107
1878	2,350
1879	3,200
1880	3,955
1881	3,575
1882	3,100
1883	6,609
1884	3,942
1885	3,790
1886	4,290
1887	2,960
1888	4,582

Cents continued

Year	Mintage
1889	3,336
1890	2,740
1891	2,350
1892	2,745
1893	2,195
1894	2,632
1895	2,062
1896	1,862
1897	1,938
1898	1,795
1899	2,031
1900	2,262
1901	1,985
1902	2,018
1903	1,790
1904	1,817
1905	2,152
1906	1,725
1907	1,475
1908	1,620
1909	4,793[8]
1910	2,405
1911	1,733
1912	2,145
1913	2,848
1914	1,365
1915	1,150
1916	1,050
1917	*
1936	5,569
1937	9,320
1938	14,734
1939	13,520
1940	15,872
1941	21,100
1942	32,600

Two cents

Year	Mintage
1864	100[9]
1865	500
1866	725
1867	625
1868	600
1869	600
1870	1,000
1871	960
1872	950
1873	1,100[10]

Three cents
(copper-nickel)

Year	Mintage
1865	400
1866	725
1867	625
1868	600
1869	600
1870	1,000
1871	960
1872	950
1873	1,100[6]
1874	700
1875	700
1876	1,150
1877	5107
1878	2,350
1879	3,200
1880	3,955
1881	3,575
1882	3,100

Three cents continued

Year	Mintage
1883	6,609
1884	3,942
1885	3,790
1886	4,290
1887	2,960[11]
1888	4,582
1889	3,436

Three cents
(silver)

Year	Mintage
1851	*
1852	*
1854	*
1855	*
1856	*
1857	*
1858	*
1859	*
1860	1,000
1861	1,000
1862	550
1863	460[12]
1864	470
1865	500
1866	725
1867	625
1868	600
1869	600
1870	1,000
1871	960
1872	950
1873	600[6]

Five cents

Year	Mintage
1866	125
1867	625[13]
1868	600
1869	600
1870	1,000
1871	960
1872	950
1873	1,100[6]
1874	700
1875	700
1876	1,150
1877	510[7]
1878	2,350
1879	3,200
1880	3,955
1881	3,575
1882	3,100
1883	17,421[14]
1884	3,942
1885	3,790
1886	4,290
1887	2,960
1888	4,582
1889	3,336
1890	2,740
1891	2,350
1892	2,745
1893	2,195
1894	2,632
1895	2,062
1896	1,862
1897	1,938
1898	1,795
1899	2,031
1900	2,262

Five cents continued

Year	Mintage
1901	1,985
1902	2,018
1903	1,790
1904	1,817
1905	2,152
1906	1,725
1907	1,475
1908	1,620
1909	4,763
1910	2,405
1911	1,733
1912	2,145
1913	3,034[15]
1914	1,275
1915	1,050
1916	600
1917	*
1936	4,420
1937	5,769
1938	19,365
1939	12,535
1940	14,158
1941	18,720
1942	57,200[16]

Half dimes

Year	Mintage
1829	*
1830	*
1831	*
1832	*
1833	*
1834	*
1835	*
1836	*
1837	*
1838	*
1839	*
1840	*
1841	*
1842	*
1843	*
1844	*
1845	*
1846	*
1847	*
1848	*
1849	*
1850	*
1851	*
1852	*
1853	*17
1854	*
1855	*
1856	*
1857	*
1858	*
1859	*
1860	1,000
1861	1,000
1862	550
1863	460
1864	470
1865	500
1866	725
1867	625
1868	600
1869	600
1870	1,000
1871	960
1872	950
1873	600[6]

Dimes

Year	Mintage
1820	*
1821	*
1822	*
1823	*2
1824	*
1825	*
1827	*
1828	*
1829	*
1830	*
1831	*
1832	*
1833	*
1834	*
1835	*
1836	*
1837	*
1838	*
1839	*
1840	*
1841	*
1842	*
1843	*
1844	*
1845	*
1846	*
1847	*
1848	*
1849	*
1850	*
1851	*
1852	*
1853	*17
1854	*
1855	*
1856	*
1857	*
1858	*
1859	*
1860	1,000
1861	1,000
1862	550
1863	460
1864	470
1865	500
1866	725
1867	625
1868	600
1869	600
1870	1,000
1871	960
1872	950
1873	1,400[18]
1874	700
1875	700
1876	1,150
1877	510
1878	800
1879	1,100
1880	1,355
1881	975
1882	1,100
1883	1,039
1884	875
1885	930
1886	886
1887	710
1888	832
1889	711
1890	590

Dimes continued

Year	Mintage
1891	600
1892	1,245
1893	792
1894	972
1895	880
1896	762
1897	731
1898	735
1899	846
1900	912
1901	813
1902	777
1903	755
1904	670
1905	727
1906	675
1907	575
1908	545
1909	650
1910	551
1911	543
1912	700
1913	622
1914	425
1915	450
1916	*
1936	4,130
1937	5,756
1938	8,728
1939	9,321
1940	11,827
1941	16,557
1942	22,329

Twenty cents

Year	Mintage
1875	1,200
1876	1,150
1877	510
1878	600

Quarter dollars

Year	Mintage
1818	*
1820	*
1821	*
1822	*
1823	*[2]
1824	*
1825	*
1827	*[1]
1828	*
1831	*
1832	*
1833	*
1834	*
1835	*
1836	*
1837	*
1838	*
1839	*
1840	*
1841	*
1842	*
1843	*
1844	*
1845	*
1846	*
1847	*
1848	*

Quarters continued

Year	Mintage
1849	*
1850	*
1851	*
1852	*
1853	*[17]
1854	*
1855	*
1856	*
1857	*
1858	*
1859	*
1860	1,000
1861	1,000
1862	550
1863	460
1864	470
1865	500
1866	725
1867	625
1868	600
1869	600
1870	1,000
1871	960
1872	950
1873	1,140[19]
1874	700
1875	700
1876	1,150
1877	510
1878	800
1879	250[20]
1880	1,355
1881	975
1882	1,100
1883	1,039
1884	875
1885	930
1886	886
1887	710
1888	832
1889	711
1890	590
1891	600
1892	1,245
1893	792
1894	972
1895	880
1896	762
1897	731
1898	735
1899	846
1900	912
1901	813
1902	777
1903	755
1904	670
1905	727
1906	675
1907	575
1908	545
1909	650
1910	551
1911	543
1912	700
1913	613
1914	380
1915	450
1917	*
1936	3,837
1937	5,542
1938	8,045
1939	8,795
1940	11,246

Quarters continued

Year	Mintage
1941	15,287
1942	21,123

Half dollars

Year	Mintage
1817	*[21]
1818	*
1819	*
1820	*
1821	*
1822	*
1823	*
1824	*
1825	*
1826	*
1827	*
1828	*
1829	*
1830	*
1831	*
1832	*
1833	*[1]
1834	*[1]
1835	*[1]
1836	*[22]
1837	*
1838	*
1839	*[23]
1840	*
1841	*
1842	*
1843	*
1844	*
1845	*
1846	*
1847	*
1848	*
1849	*
1850	*
1851	*
1852	*
1853	*[17]
1854	*
1855	*
1856	*
1857	*
1858	*
1859	*
1860	1,000
1861	1,000
1862	550
1863	460
1864	470
1865	500
1866	725
1867	625
1868	600
1869	600
1870	1,000
1871	960
1872	950
1873	1,150[24]
1874	700
1875	700
1876	1,150
1877	510
1878	800
1879	1,100
1880	1,355
1881	975
1882	1,100
1883	1,039

Half dollars continued

Year	Mintage
1884	875
1885	930
1886	886
1887	710
1888	832
1889	711
1890	590
1891	600
1892	1,245
1893	792
1894	972
1895	880
1896	762
1897	731
1898	735
1899	846
1900	912
1901	813
1902	777
1903	755
1904	670
1905	727
1906	675
1907	575
1908	545
1909	650
1910	5 51
1911	543
1912	700
1913	627
1914	380
1915	450
1916	*
1936	3,901
1937	5,728
1938	8,152
1939	8,808
1940	11,279
1941	15,412
1942	21,120

Silver dollars

Year	Mintage
1836	*[25]
1838	*[25]
1839	*[25]
1840	*[1]
1841	*[1]
1842	*[1]
1843	*[1]
1844	*[1]
1845	*[1]
1846	*[1]
1847	*[1]
1848	*[1]
1849	*[1]
1850	*[1]
1851	*[1]
1852	*[1]
1853	*[26]
1854	*
1855	*
1856	*
1857	*
1858	*[27]
1859	*
1860	1,330
1861	1,000
1862	550
1863	460

Silver dollars continued

Year	Mintage
1864	470
1865	500
1866	725
1867	625
1868	600
1869	600
1870	1,000
1871	960
1872	950
1873	600[6]
1878	1,000[28]
1879	1,100
1880	1,355
1881	975
1882	1,100
1883	1,039
1884	875
1885	930
1886	886
1887	710
1888	832
1889	811
1890	590
1891	650
1892	1,245
1893	792
1894	972
1895	880
1896	762
1897	731
1898	735
1899	846
1900	912
1901	813
1902	777
1903	755
1904	650
1921	•
1922	•

Trade dollars

Year	Mintage
1873	865[29]
1874	700
1875	700
1876	1,150
1877	510
1878	900
1879	1,541
1880	1,987
1881	960
1882	1,097
1883	979
1884	10[30]
1885	5[30]

Gold dollars

Year	Mintage
1849	•
1854	•31
1855	•
1856	•
1857	•
1858	•
1859	•
1860	154
1861	349
1862	35
1863	50
1864	50
1865	25

Gold dollars continued

Year	Mintage
1866	30
1867	50
1868	25
1869	25
1870	35
1871	30
1872	30
1873	25[6]
1874	20
1875	20
1876	45
1877	20
1878	20
1879	30
1880	36
1881	87
1882	125
1883	207
1884	1,006
1885	1,105
1886	1,016
1887	1,043
1888	1,079
1889	1,779

Quarter eagles

Year	Mintage
1821	•
1824	•
1825	•
1826	•
1827	•
1829	•
1830	•
1831	•
1832	•
1833	•
1834	•32
1835	•
1836	•
1837	•
1840	•
1841	•33
1842	•
1843	•
1844	•
1845	•
1846	•
1847	•
1848	•
1849	•
1854	•
1855	•
1856	•
1857	•
1858	•
1859	•
1860	112
1861	90
1862	35
1863	30
1864	50
1865	25
1866	30
1867	50
1868	25
1869	25
1870	35
1871	30
1872	30
1873	25[6]
1874	20

$2.50 gold continued

Year	Mintage
1875	20
1876	45
1877	20
1878	20
1879	30
1880	36
1881	51
1882	67
1883	82
1884	73
1885	87
1886	88
1887	122
1888	92
1889	48
1890	93
1891	80
1892	105
1893	106
1894	122
1895	119
1896	132
1897	136
1898	165
1899	150
1900	205
1901	223
1902	193
1903	197
1904	170
1905	144
1906	160
1907	154
1908	236
1909	139
1910	682
1911	191
1912	197
1913	165
1914	117
1915	100

Three dollars

Year	Mintage
1854	•
1855	•
1856	•
1857	•
1858	•
1859	•
1860	119
1861	113
1862	35
1863	39
1864	50
1865	25
1866	30
1867	50
1868	25
1869	25
1870	35
1871	30
1872	30
1873	25[34]
1874	20
1875	20[1]
1876	45
1877	20
1878	20
1879	30
1880	36
1881	54

$3 gold continued

Year	Mintage
1882	76
1883	89
1884	106
1885	110
1886	142
1887	160
1888	291
1889	129

Half eagles

Year	Mintage
1820	•
1821	•
1823	•
1824	•
1825	•35
1826	•
1827	•
1828	•36
1829	•
1830	•
1831	•
1832	•
1833	•
1834	•37
1835	•
1836	•
1837	•
1838	•
1839	•
1840	•
1841	•
1842	•
1843	•
1844	•
1845	•
1846	•
1847	•
1848	•
1855	•
1856	•
1857	•
1858	•
1859	•
1860	62
1861	66
1862	35
1863	30
1864	50
1865	25
1866	30
1867	50
1868	25
1869	25
1870	35
1871	30
1872	30
1873	25[6]
1874	20
1875	20
1876	45
1877	20
1878	20
1879	30
1880	36
1881	42
1882	48
1883	61
1884	48
1885	66
1886	72
1887	87

$5 gold continued	
1888	94
1889	45
1890	88
1891	53
1892	92
1893	77
1894	75
1895	81
1896	103
1897	83
1898	75
1899	99
1900	230
1901	140
1902	162
1903	154
1904	136
1905	108
1906	85
1907	92
1908	167[38]
1909	78
1910	250
1911	139
1912	144
1913	99
1914	125
1915	75

Eagles

Year	Mintage
1838	•
1839	•[39]
1840	•
1841	•
1842	•
1843	•
1844	•
1845	•
1846	•
1847	•
1848	•

$10 gold continued	
1855	•
1856	•
1857	•
1858	•
1859	•
1860	50
1861	69
1862	35
1863	30
1864	50
1865	25
1866	30
1867	50
1868	25
1869	25
1870	35
1871	30
1872	30
1873	25[6]
1874	20
1875	20
1876	45
1877	20
1878	20
1879	30
1880	36
1881	42
1882	44
1883	49
1884	45
1885	67
1886	60
1887	80
1888	72
1889	45
1890	63
1891	48
1892	72
1893	55
1894	43
1895	56
1896	78

$10 gold continued	
1897	69
1898	67
1899	86
1900	120
1901	85
1902	113
1903	96
1904	108
1905	86
1906	77
1907	74[40]
1908	116[41]
1909	74
1910	204
1911	95
1912	83
1913	71
1914	50
1915	75

Double eagles

Year	Mintage
1849	1[42]
1850	•[43]
1856	•
1858	•
1859	•
1860	59
1861	66
1862	35
1863	30
1864	50
1865	25
1866	30
1867	50
1868	25
1869	25
1870	35
1871	30
1872	30
1873	25[6]

$20 gold continued	
1874	20
1875	20
1876	45
1877	20
1878	20
1879	30
1880	36
1881	61
1882	59
1883	92
1884	71
1885	77
1886	106
1887	121
1888	102
1889	41
1890	55
1891	52
1892	93
1893	59
1894	50
1895	51
1896	128
1897	86
1898	75
1899	84
1900	124
1901	96
1902	114
1903	158
1904	98
1905	90
1906	94
1907	78[44]
1908	101[41]
1909	67
1910	167
1911	100
1912	74
1913	58
1914	70
1915	50

Proof set mintages — 1950-1989

Proof coins sold in complete sets only, 1950-1988

Year Minted	Sets Sold	Selling Price	Face Value
1950	51,386	2.10	0.91
1951	57,500	2.10	0.91
1952	81,980	2.10	0.91
1953	128,800	2.10	0.91
1954	233,300	2.10	0.91
1955	378,200	2.10	0.91
1956	669,384	2.10	0.91
1957	1,247,952	2.10	0.91
1958	875,652	2.10	0.91
1959	1,149,291	2.10	0.91
1960	1,691,602	2.10	0.91[45]
1961	3,028,244	2.10	0.91
1962	3,218,019	2.10	0.91
1963	3,075,645	2.10	0.91
1964	3,950,762	2.10	0.91

Production suspended 1965, 1966, 1967

Year Minted	Sets Sold	Selling Price	Face Value
1968	3,041,506	5.00	0.91[46]
1969	2,934,631	5.00	0.91
1970	2,632,810	5.00	0.91[47]
1971	3,220,733	5.00	0.91[48]
1972	3,260,996	5.00	0.91

Year Minted	Sets Sold	Selling Price	Face Value
1973	2,760,339	7.00	1.91
1974	2,612,568	7.00	1.91
1975	2,845,450	7.00	1.91[49]
1976	4,123,056	7.00	1.91[49]
1977	3,236,798	9.00	1.91
1978	3,120,285	9.00	1.91
1979	3,677,175	9.00	1.91[51]
1980	3,554,806	10.00	1.91
1981	4,063,083	11.00	1.91
1982	3,857,479	11.00	0.91[52]
1983	3,138,765	11.00	0.91[53]
1983 Prestige	140,361	59.00	1.91
1984	2,748,430	11.00	0.91
1984 Prestige	316,680	59.00	1.91
1985	3,362,821	11.00	0.91
1986	2,411,180	11.00	0.91
1986 Prestige	599,317	48.50	2.41
1987	3,356,738	11.00	0.91
1987 Prestige	435,495	45.00	1.91
1988	2,368,957	11.00	0.91
1988 Prestige	Pending	45.00	1.91
1989	Pending	11.00	0.91

40% silver clad dollars

Struck in San Francisco

	Uncirculated	Proof
1971	6,868,530	4,265,234
1972	2,193,056	1,811,631
1973	1,883,140	1,013,646
1974	1,900,156	1,306,579

Special Mint Sets

Year Minted	Sets Sold	Selling Price	Face Value
1965	2,360,000	4.00	0.91
1966	2,261,583⁵⁰	4.00	0.91
1967	1,863,344	4.00	0.91

Uncirculated sets

Uncirculated sets contain examples of each business-strike coin struck within a given year. Coins are struck no differently than the circulation strikes.

The United States Mint first offered Uncirculated Mint sets, dated 1947, in 1948. Later, after the 1947 sets sold out, 1948 coinage was offered. Before 1960, the sets were individually packaged in cardboard folders; each set contains two specimens of each coin struck that year.

Beginning in 1959, sets were packaged in polyethylene packets. During the coin shortage of the mid-1960s, Special Mint sets were struck in lieu of Proof sets and Uncirculated sets in 1965, 1966 and 1967. Uncirculated set production resumed in 1968. Philadelphia and Denver Eisenhower dollars were added to the set in 1973, which were replaced in 1979 by three Anthony dollars. No Uncirculated sets were issued in 1982 and 1983 for what Mint officials said were budget-reduction reasons. Congress passed a law in 1983, however, requiring annual sales of Uncirculated sets.

Year Minted	Sets Sold	Selling Price	Face Value	Year Minted	Sets Sold	Selling Price	Face Value
1947	12,600	4.87	4.46	1969	1,817,392	2.50	1.33
1948	17,000	4.92	4.46	1970	2,038,134	2.50	1.33
1949	20,739	5.45	4.96	1971	2,193,396	3.50	1.83
1951	8,654	6.75	5.46	1972	2,750,000	3.50	1.83
1952	11,499	6.14	5.46	1973	1,767,691	6.00	3.83
1953	15,538	6.14	5.46	1974	1,975,981	6.00	3.83
1954	25,599	6.19	5.46	1975	1,921,488	6.00	3.82
1955	49,656	3.57	2.86	1976	1,892,513	6.00	3.82
1956	45,475	3.34	2.64	1977	2,006,869	7.00	3.82
1957	34,324	4.40	3.64	1978	2,162,609	7.00	3.82
1958	50,314	4.43	3.64	1979	2,526,000	8.00	4.82
1959	187,000	2.40	1.82	1980	2,815,066	9.00	4.82
1960	260,485	2.40	1.82	1981	2,908,145	11.00	4.82
1961	223,704	2.40	1.82	1984	1,832,857	7.00	1.82
1962	385,285	2.40	1.82	1985	1,710,571	7.00	1.82
1963	606,612	2.40	1.82	1986	1,153,536	7.00	1.82
1964	1,008,108	2.40	1.82	1987	2,890,758	7.00	1.82
1965	2,360,000	4.00	0.91	1988	1,447,100	7.00	1.82
1966	2,261,583	4.00	0.91	1989	Pending	7.00	1.82
1967	1,863,344	4.00	0.91				
1968	2,105,128	2.50	1.33				

Notes

Proof $10 eagles dated 1804 are restrikes made in 1834-35 for inclusion in Proof sets meant to be given as diplomatic presents. The 1804 dollar was first struck at this time for this occasion, also in Proof. The 1804 dolar was restruck in Proof in the late 1850s. The Proof dollars of 1801-03 were first struck at this time.

Many different Proof issues before 1880 were restruck in Proof one or more times. In some instances, as with the 1873 $3 gold piece, there are more coins of this date known than were "officially" struck.

1. (Various dates): Known to have been restruck at least once.

2. 1823 cent, dime, quarter dollar: Exists with overdate, 1823/2.

3. 1856 cent: Includes several large cents and many hundreds of Flying Eagle cent patterns. The Flying Eagle cent pattern was restruck in later years.

4. 1857 cent: Includes both small and large cents.

5. 1864 cent: Breakdown by varieties; thought to be about 300 to 350 copper-nickel and about 100 to 150 bronze coins without the designer's initial L. Bronze coins with the L are rare in Proof, possibly 20 or less struck.

6. (Most 1873 Proofs): All Proofs are of the relatively Closed 3 variety.

7. 1877 minor coinages: Estimates for this year vary considerably, usually upwards. For lack of any records, the number shown is that of the silver Proofs of this year, conforming with the method used in the preceding years. These figures may be considerably low.

8. 1909 cent: Includes 2,175 Indian Head type; 420 Lincoln Head type with VDB; and 2,198 Lincoln Head without VDB on reverse.

9. 1864 2 cents: Includes Small Motto and Large Motto varieties. The Small Motto in Proof is rare.

10. 1873 2 cents: All originals have the Closed 3. It is estimated that 500 restrikes were made, all of them with an Open 3.

11. 1887 copper-nickel 3 cents: Many struck from an overdated die, 1887/6.

12. 1863 silver 3 cents: Proofs struck from an overdated die, 1863/2, were struck in 1864.

13. 1867 5 cents: Approximately 25 Proofs struck With Rays on reverse (type of 1866), and 600 Without Rays (type of 1868-83).

14. 1883 5 cents: It has been estimated that 5,419 Shield type; 5,219 Liberty Head, No CENTS; and 6,783 Liberty Head, With CENTS were struck. Other estimates exist.

15. 1913 5 cents: Does not include the five privately struck 1913 Liberty Head 5-cent coins. The Indian Head Proofs are thought to be divided into 1,520 Bison on Mound and 1,514 Bison on Plain varieties.

16. 1942 5 cents: Includes 29,600 pre-war alloy, and 27,600 wartime alloy.

17. 1853 half dollar, quarter dollar, dime, half dime. All Proofs are of the new weight, With Arrows (and Rays on the quarter dollar and half dollar).

18. 1873 dime: No Arrows, Closed 3: 600. With Arrows, Open 3: 800.

19. 1873 quarter dollar: No Arrows, Closed 3: 600. With Arrows, Open 3: 540.

20. 1879 quarter dollar: This figure is official, but may be wrong. The true number might be near or equal to 1,100.

21. 1817 half dollar: Only one Proof known, with overdate 1817/3.

22. 1836 half dollar: Includes both Lettered Edge coins and Reeded Edge patterns.

23. 1839 half dollar: Includes all three varieties, Capped Bust and Seated Liberty, With or Without Drapery.

24. 1873 half dollar: No Arrows, Closed 3: 600. With Arrows, Open 3: 550.

25. 1836, 1838, 1839 silver dollar: All are Gobrecht dollars which were struck in Proof in several different varieties, many of which were restruck in later years. Records indicate that 1,900 of the originals were struck for circulation.

26. 1853 silver dollar: All Proofs are restrikes, made 1864-5.

27. 1858 silver dollar: Estimated that 80 pieces were struck, some of them possibly at a later date.

28. 1878 silver dollar: Includes 700 of the 8 Tail Feathers variety and 300 of the 7 Tail Feathers, flat eagle breast variety. Beware of any early strike, prooflike surface Morgan dollar being sold as a Proof.

29. 1873 Trade silver dollar: All Proofs are of the Open 3 variety.

30. 1884-85 Trade dollar: Struck in Proof in the Mint for private distribution by person or persons unknown. Not listed in the Mint Report.

31. 1854 gold dollar: Includes both Coronet and Indian Head.

32. 1834 $2.50: Includes both Capped Head and Classic Head types.

33. 1841 $2.50: Nine known, several of them circulated or otherwise impaired.

34. 1873 $3: All original Proofs are of the more Open 3 variety. There were two restrikes with the Closed 3 and one with the Open 3.

35. 1825 $5: Struck from the regular overdated dies. 1825/4, one known, and 1825/1, two known.

36. 1828 $5: Includes at least one overdate, 1828/7.

37. 1834 $5: Includes both Capped Head and Classic Head types.
38. 1908 $5: All are Indian Head type.
39. 1839 $10: Proofs are of the type of 1838, with large letters and different hair style.
40. 1907 $10: Figure shown is for Coronet coins. An unknown number of Indian Head patterns were also struck in Proof.
41. 1908 $20 and $10: All Proofs have the motto IN GOD WE TRUST on the reverse.
42. 1849 $20: The one known trial strike still surviving is a Proof.
43. 1850 $20: One Proof was once owned by the engraver, James B. Longacre. Whereabouts presently unknown.
44. 1907 $20: Figure shown is for Coronet coins. An unknown number of Saint-Gaudens type coins of pattern or near-pattern status were also struck in Proof.
45. 1960 cent: Includes Large Date and Small Date varieties. As in the regular issues, the Small Date is the scarcer.
46. 1968 dime: Some Proof sets contain dimes which were struck from a Proof die without a Mint mark. This was an engraver's oversight and is not a filled die. It has been unofficially estimated that only 20 specimens from this die are known. Beware of sets opened and reclosed with "processed" P-Mint coins inserted. Check the edge of the case for signs of tampering.
47. 1970 dime: Same engraver's oversight as above. Official estimate is that 2,200 sets were released with this error.
48. 1971 5 cents: Same type of error as above. Official estimate of 1,655 sets released.
49. Including Bicentennial quarters, halves and dollars.
50. 1966 5-cent piece: Two Proof Jefferson 5-cent pieces were struck to mark the addition of designer Felix Schlag's initials, F.S., to the obverse design. At least one coin was presented to Schlag; the other may have been retained by the Mint.
51. 1979 Proof set: The Anthony dollar replaced the Eisenhower dollar. During latter 1979, a new, clearer Mint mark punch was used on the dies. Sets with all six coins bearing the new Mint mark command a premium.
52. 1982 Proof set: A new Mint mark punch with serifs was introduced.
53. 1983 10-cent piece: Some 1983 sets were issued with dimes missing the S Mint mark, similar to errors on 1968, 1970, 1971 and 1975 Proof coins.
54. Contains commemorative 1983-S Olympic silver dollar in addition to the regular Proof coinage.
55. Contains commemorative 1984-S Olympic silver dollar in addition to the regular Proof coinage.
56. Contains commemorative 1986-S Ellis Island dollar and Immigrant half dollar in addition to the regular Proof coinage.
57. Contains commemorative 1987-S Constitution silver dollar in addition to the regular Proof coinage.
58. Contains commemorative 1988-S Olympic silver dollar in addition to the regular Proof coinage.

Bicentennial sets

The 1976 Bicentennial of American Independence was numismatically celebrated with changes in the reverse designs of the Washington quarter dollar, Kennedy half dollar and Eisenhower dollar. Copper-nickel versions of all three were issued for circulation and for the regular Proof set.

Collectors were offered two three-coin sets of the same coins struck in a 40 percent silver composition, in Proof and Uncirculated versions. The silver collectors' coins were first offered Nov. 15, 1974, at prices of $15 for the Proof set and $9 for the Uncirculated set. In the 12 years of sales for the two three-coin sers,

from November 1974 to Dec. 31, 1986, prices for the three-coin sets were changed no fewer than five times due to rising and falling silver prices. Mint officials reduced the prices for the Proof set Jan. 19, 1975, to $12. On Sept. 20, 1979, Mint officials suspended sales of the Bicentennial Uncirculated set because of the rising price of silver; the bullion value of the three coins in the set exceeded the Mint's price of $9. Sales of the Bicentennial Proof set were suspended in December 1979 as silver rose to even greater heights. When sales of the two Bicentennial sets were resumed in Aug. 4, 1980, the prices rose to $15 for the Uncirculated sets and $20 for the Proof sets. Falling silver prices permitted the introduction of lower prices Sept. 1, 1981: $15 for the Proof set, $12 for the Uncirculated set. In September 1982, prices for the coins dropped even lower — to $12 for the Proof set, and $9 for the Uncirculated set.

Prices maintained those levels until sales of the sets ceased: in 1985 for the Proof set, and on Dec. 31, 1986, for the Uncirculated set.

Final mintages are 3,998,621 for the Proof set, and 4,908,319 for the Uncirculated set.

Source: United States Mint

Varieties of Anthony dollars Eisenhower dollars and Kennedy half dollars

Coin World frequently receives letters from its readers asking for a complete listing of Anthony dollars, Eisenhower dollars or the Kennedy half dollars, or all three. These requests are quite understandable, as the three series have been issued in such variety that 62 different Kennedy halves were struck through 1987, 32 different Eisenhower dollars were struck by 1978, and 13 Anthony dollars were issued 1979-81.

The following lists include only those coins which are generally available to collectors. The occasional errors such as the 90 percent silver 1965 halves and the 40 percent silver 1974-D dollars are not included, as these coins were never meant to be struck or released.

Kennedy half dollars

90 Percent Silver
1964.....................................Unc.
1964.....................................Proof
1964-D.................................Unc.

40 Percent Silver Clad
1965.....................................Unc.
1966.....................................Unc.
1967.....................................Unc.
1968-D.................................Unc.
1968-S.................................Proof
1969-D.................................Unc.
1969-S.................................Proof
1970-D (Unc. sets only).........Unc.
1970-S.................................Proof

Copper-Nickel Clad
1971.....................................Unc.
1971-D.................................Unc.
1971-S.................................Proof
1972.....................................Unc.
1972-D.................................Unc.
1972-S.................................Proof
1973.....................................Unc.

1973-D.................................Unc.
1973-S.................................Proof
1974.....................................Unc.
1974-D.................................Unc.
1974-S.................................Proof
1977.....................................Unc.
1977-D.................................Unc.
1977-S.................................Proof
1978.....................................Unc.
1978-D.................................Unc.
1978-S.................................Proof
1979.....................................Unc.
1979-D.................................Unc.
1979-S.................................Proof
1980-P.................................Unc.
1980-D.................................Unc.
1980-S.................................Proof
1981-P.................................Unc.
1981-D.................................Unc.
1981-S.................................Proof
1982-P.................................Unc.
1982-D.................................Unc.
1982-S.................................Proof
1983-P.................................Unc.
1983-D.................................Unc.

1983-S.................................Proof
1984-P.................................Unc.
1984-D.................................Unc.
1984-S.................................Proof
1985-P.................................Unc.
1985-D.................................Unc.
1985-S.................................Proof
1986-P.................................Unc.
1986-D.................................Unc.
1986-S.................................Proof
1987-P (Unc. sets only).........Unc.
1987-D (Unc. sets only).........Unc.
1987-S.................................Proof

Bicentennial Reverse Copper-Nickel Clad
1776-1976.............................Unc.
1776-1976-D.........................Unc.
1776-1976-S.........................Proof

40 Percent Silver Clad
1776-1976-S.........................Unc.
1776-1976-S.........................Proof

Eisenhower dollars

Copper-Nickel Clad
1971.....................................Unc.
1971-D.................................Unc.
1972.....................................Unc.
1972-D.................................Unc.
1973 (Unc. sets only).............Unc.
1973-D (Unc. sets only).........Unc.
1973-S.................................Proof
1974.....................................Unc.
1974-D.................................Unc.
1974-S.................................Proof

1977.....................................Unc.
1977-D.................................Unc.
1977-S.................................Proof
1978.....................................Unc.
1978-D.................................Unc.
1978-S.................................Proof

40 Percent Silver Clad
1971-S.................................Unc.
1971-S.................................Proof
1972-S.................................Unc.
1972-S.................................Proof

1973-S.................................Unc.
1973-S.................................Proof
1974-S.................................Unc.
1974-S.................................Proof

Bicentennial Reverse Copper-Nickel Clad
1776-1976, Var. 1..................Unc.
1776-1976, Var. 2..................Unc.
1776-1976-D, Var. 1..............Unc.
1776-1976-D, Var. 2..............Unc.

1776-1976-S, Var. 1................ Proof
1776-1976-S, Var. 2................ Proof

40 Percent Silver Clad

1776-1976-S, Var. 1 .... Unc.
1776-1976-S, Var. 1 .... Proof

Anthony dollars

Copper-Nickel Clad

1979-P.................................... Unc.
1979-D.................................... Unc.
1979-S.................................... Unc.

1979-S, Filled S........................ Proof
1979-S, Clear S........................ Proof
1980-P .... Unc.
1980-D.................................... Unc.
1980-S .... Unc.

1980-S .... Proof
1981-P.................................... Unc.
1981-D.................................... Unc.
1981-S.................................... Unc.
1981-S .... Proof

Commemoratives 10

Commemorative coins to 1954

Commemorative coins — the most colorful coinage issues struck in the United States — are pure Americana, history of a great nation frozen into metal. Commemorative coins in the United States are historically significant and relatively new. They had their start just before the turn of the 20th century.

It may sound odd that the start of coinage for commemorative purposes in the United States, one of the richest in the world, should stem directly from dire financial straits of an exposition commission. The Columbian Exposition half dollar issued in 1892 and 1893, honoring Christopher Columbus and the 400th anniversary of his first voyage to America, was the first commemorative coin struck in the United States. It was produced to help defray the expenses of the 1892 and 1893 Chicago World's Columbian Exposition. The half dollars struck at the Philadelphia Mint were sold at a cost of $1. The Columbian Exposition was also commemorated with the 1893 Isabella quarter dollar, the United States' only fully commemorative 25-cent coin (however, the 1932 Washington quarter dollar was authorized as a commemorative issue, and some argue that the 1976 Bicentennial quarter dollar also is commemorative in nature).

Between 1899, when the Lafayette-Washington dollar was struck (the 1900 on the coin refers not to the date of issue, but to the year of the Paris Exposition), and 1954, when the first period of commemorative production ceased, more than 150 U.S. commemorative coins were struck. Some commemorative issues were not completely sold and the balance was returned to the Mint and melted down. In the case of the Columbian half, many were just put into circulation by banks, which accounts for the condition in which they are often found. For both reasons, the quantity minted for many commemoratives is larger than the quantity available.

Not all of the issues honor events or persons of national importance. At least one, the 1936 Cincinnati Music Center half dollar, honors a non-existent event — 50 years of Cincinnati as a music center — and depicts an individual, Stephen Foster, who had little connection with the city except for a brief stay there.

Most of the commemorative coins struck by the U.S. Mint were turned over to various celebration committees for face value, with profits going not to the federal government, but to the cause being commemorated on the coin. Committee officials noted that with the production of additional date and Mint mark varieties of a single issue, more sales to collectors could be generated, with additional funds raised.

In 1939, Congress took corrective action when it voted to prohibit the striking of new dates of any pre-1939 commemorative coins. Still, Congress continued to authorize new issues. President Truman approved the Booker T.

Washington and Washington-Carver half dollars, but was the last president to approve a commemorative coinage program for more than 30 years; he joined Presidents Hoover and Franklin Roosevelt in vetoing other commemorative coinage legislation. President Eisenhower, too, exercised his veto powers, killing three commemorative coin bills on Feb. 3, 1954, calling for coins celebrating the tercentennials of New York City and Northampton, Mass., and the 250th anniversary of the Louisiana Purchase.

Eisenhower outlined in a message accompanying his vetoes the same arguments used by Treasury officials for nearly three decades in opposing new legislation: commemorative coins cause confusion among the public and facilitate counterfeiting; public interest in the coins

had been lagging with many coins unsold and consigned to the melting pot; and the authorization of just a few commemoratives results in a "flood" of additional commemorative issues.

Neither the Kennedy half dollar or the Eisenhower dollar are considered commemorative coins by a majority of hobbyists although both coins were issued in the waves of public sentiment that followed the deaths of those two popular presidents.

When the 1976 Bicentennial quarter dollars, half dollars and dollars were issued in 1975-76, Treasury officials carefully avoided any and all use of the word "commemorative," although clearly the coins are commemorative in nature. The official policy remained as stated by Eisenhower in 1954.

Commemoratives since 1982

No commemorative coins were struck from 1954 to 1982. Hundreds of applications for such coins had been made through the years, but government officials were reluctant to issue new coins. Then, in 1981, Congress found a nationally acceptable event that Treasury officials did not object to: the 250th birthday of George Washington in 1982.

Legislation was introduced in the House of Representatives on May 7, 1981 (another bill had been introduced in March and a second in April), authorizing a commemorative half dollar for the Washington birthday celebration, with modifications recommended by Treasury officials (including a 10 million coin limit). A similar bill was introduced in the Senate May 18. Passage came in the House on May 19; in the Senate, the bill was approved Dec. 9. President Reagan signed the bill into law Dec. 13, 1981. The Mint offered the 1982 Washington half dollar in Proof and Uncirculated versions through Dec. 31, 1985.

Even as legislators were arguing the merits of the Washington commemorative coin legislation, others in both houses were preparing legislation for a

commemorative coin series honoring the 1984 Summer Olympic Games in Los Angeles. The first legislation met with strong opposition from the collecting community, Treasury officials and Rep. Frank Annunzio, D-Ill., chairman of the House Banking Subcommittee on Consumer Affairs and Coinage. The original Senate proposal called for 29 different coins (more when counting Proof and Uncirculated versions); it passed the Senate Dec. 9, 1981. Much of the controversy arose from the number of coins and the method in which they would be distributed. The bill called for the coins to be turned over to a private cartel, which would donate some funds to the U.S. Olympic team but keep the profits for themselves. Opponents said this was a return to the system that killed commemorative coin issues in 1938 and 1954.

A legislative compromise was sought. First, a 17-coin proposal was proposed in the House; again, the Senate approved this measure, but not the House. Annunzio introduced a one-coin bill, with the coins to be sold by the U.S. Mint. Annunzio agreed to a compromise, proposing a three-coin program. In a convoluted series of congressional maneuvering, Annunzio's subcommittee approved the three-coin proposal, but the House Banking Committee substituted the 17-coin proposal already approved by the Senate. But Annunzio called for a floor debate and the three-coin proposal was approved by the House May 20, 1982. The Senate agreed to the smaller program July 1, and President Reagan signed the bill into law July 22.

The Annunzio proposal authorized a 1984 gold $10 eagle (first commemorative of that denomination) and 1983 and 1984 silver dollars, each to be offered in Proof and Uncirculated versions. The coins were marketed by the Mint, with surcharges of $10 from the sale of each silver dollar and $50 from the sale of each gold eagle going to United States Olympic Committee, the Los Angeles Olympic Organizing Committee and other athletic organizations. However, the Mint ultimately and legally offered 13 varieties, using Mint marks and different finishes, instead of the six Annunzio wanted, angering the Illinois legislator. The program was deemed successful by most. It raised $73,389,300 for the Olympic teams.

No 1985-dated commemorative coins were authorized. However, the centennial of the dedication of the Statue of Liberty was to take place in 1986. The Statue of Liberty had never appeared on a U.S. coin, although several foreign coins had earlier depicted the symbol of freedom and opportunity in the United States.

Annunzio introduced a bill on Jan. 3, 1985, calling for a 1986 gold $5 half eagle, a 1986 silver dollar and a 1986 copper-nickel half dollar. The Annunzio proposal restricted production of each coin to one Mint. With counting Proof and Uncirculated versions, there was a maximum total of six coins. Surcharges of $35 per gold coin, $7 per silver dollar and $2 per half dollar were earmarked for the restoration of the Statue of Liberty and the immigration facilities on Ellis Island. House approval came quickly, on March 3,

1985, but discussion of a silver bullion coin delayed passage in the Senate. The Senate approved an amended version of Annunzio's bill June 21; it included a silver bullion dollar. The House approved the amended version June 24, and Reagan signed the bill into law July 9. Like the Olympic program, the Statue of Liberty program proved successful as a fund-raising event. U.S. Treasurer Katherine D. Ortega had set a goal of $40 million in surcharges, but the Statue of Liberty program surpassed the Olympic program (in less time, with lower surcharges and fewer varieties of coins available) and raised more than $80 million in surcharges. Total sales were about $300 million.

The Bicentennial of the drafting of the U.S. Constitution was the subject of the 1987 commemorative series. Again, the proposal was introduced by Rep. Annunzio, on Sept. 23, 1985. House approval was delayed until Oct. 1, 1986. The Senate approved the measure Oct. 16, 1986, and President Reagan signed the legislation into law Oct. 29.

A 1987 gold half eagle and a 1987 silver dollar carried surcharges of $35 on each gold coin and $7 on each silver dollar. Rather than being paid to a beneficiary organization, the surcharges were earmarked for retirement of the national debt, a drop-in-the-ocean gesture when one compares the millions of dollars expected to be raised with the multi-trillion dollar spiraling national debt. One estimate calculated that a complete (and unlikely) sell-out of the program, which would raise some $105 million in surcharges, would pay the interest on the national debt for six hours.

In 1988, a gold half eagle and silver dollar were authorized honoring the participation of American athletes during the 1988 Olympic Games. The United States joined the ranks of a bevy of non-host nations who had learned the financial lessons of Olympic commemorative coinage. Controversy erupted over the use of the Olympic rings, a protected symbol of the International Olympic Committee.

Ultimately, the rings appeared on the coins, but the dollar coin was flawed by an incorrect use of the term "Olympiad." The gold coin's obverse design of Nike, goddess of Victory, by Chief Sculptor-Engraver Elizabeth Jones is probably her last on coinage of the United States, as she was about to be replaced in office in mid-1990 as this almanac was going to press..

Flush with at least moderate success, and turning increasingly self-serving, Congress authorized a gold half eagle, silver dollar and copper-nickel half dollar to commemorate the 1989 Bicentennial of Congress (conveniently forgetting that the judicial and administrative branches of federal government also celebrate their bicentennial birthdays in 1989). The Congress Bicentennial coinage offer one piece of interesting numismatic history — first-strike ceremonies were conducted on the U.S. Capitol grounds, a publicity stunt which required legislative approval, and the first time legal tender U.S. coins had been produced outside a U.S. Mint facility.

Turning a deaf ear to President Eisenhower's warning about a commemorative flood, Congress authorized a silver dollar commemorating — ironically — the 100th anniversary in 1990 of the birth of Dwight D. Eisenhower. Despite the fact that Eisenhower's portrait exists on a relatively recent coin, the dollar issued until the Anthony dollar debacle in 1979, Congressional leaders persisted with the plan.

Bills in Congress that have gained at least initial support include those calling for commemoratives for:

• the 200th anniversary of the death of Benjamin Franklin (1990)
• 50th anniversary of Mount Rushmore (1991)
• 38th anniversary of the end of the Korean War (1991)
• 500th anniversary of Christopher Columbus' 1492 voyage to the New World (1992)
• World University Games (1993); and
• the United Services Organization

Have Congress and the Treasury Department avoided the abuses of the earlier commemorative program? The concept of surcharges was conceived in the 1983-84 program, with a fee (not deductible on one's income tax return) added to the price of each coin by the order of Congress; the surcharges went to the United States Olympic Committee, the Los Angeles Olympic Organizing Committee and foreign Olympic committees. Surcharges were also added to the Statue of Liberty coins (to go to the restoration effort on the Statue and the Ellis Island facilities), the Constitution coins (to reduce the national debt), the 1988 Olympic coins (to go to the USOC again) and the 1989 Congress coins (to help restore the Capitol). Already, some members of the numismatic community have voiced their objections to surcharges.

The Columbus anniversary could prove to be an interesting issue, serving the dual purpose of marking the 500th anniversary of the opening of the New World to European settlement, and also marking the centennial of United States commemorative coinage.

However, Columbus is also a leading candidate for being placed on a proposed new, circulating small-sized dollar coin, an idea not without its proponents and controversy. Perhaps, like the Washington quarter, the Lincoln cent, the Peace dollar and the Bicentennial issues, a Columbus coin will be both commemorative and circulating.

Commemorative coins

1892-1990

Commemorative Date	Original Mintage	Melted	Final Mintage	Designer Original Price
Columbian Exposition half dollar			Charles E. Barber and George Morgan	
1892	950,000	None	950,000	$1.00
1893	4,052,105	2,501,700	1,550,405	$1.00
Isabella quarter dollar			Charles E. Barber	
1893	40,023	15,809	24,124	$1.00
Lafayette-Washington silver dollar			Charles E. Barber	
1900	50,026	14,000	36,026	$2.00
Louisiana Purchase Exposition gold dollar			Charles E. Barber	
1903	250,258	215,250	each type 17,375	$3.00
Lewis and Clark Exposition gold dollar			Charles E. Barber	
1904	25,028	15,003	10,025	$2.00
1905	35,041	25,000	10,041	$2.00
Panama-Pacific Exposition half dollar			Charles E. Barber	
1915-S	60,030	32,896	27,134	$1.00
Panama-Pacific Exposition gold dollar			Charles Keck	
1915-S	25,034	10,034	15,000	$2.00
Panama-Pacific Exposition quarter eagle			Charles E. Barber	
1915-S	10,017	3,278	6,749	$4.00
Panama-Pacific Exposition $50			Robert Aitken	
1915-S Round	1,510	1,027	483	$100
1915-S Octag.	1,509	864	645	$100
McKinley Memorial gold dollar			Charles E. Barber and George T. Morgan	
1916	20,026	10,049	9,977	$3.00
1917	10,014	14	10,000	$3.00
Illinois Centennial half dollar			George T. Morgan and John R. Sinnock	
1918	100,058	None	100,058	$1.00
Maine Centennial half dollar			Anthony de Francisci	
1920	50,028	None	50,028	$1.00
Pilgrim Tercentenary half dollar			Cyrus E. Dallin	
1920	200,112	48,000	152,112	$1.00
1921	100,053	80,000	20,053	$1.00
Missouri Centennial half dollar			Robert Aitken	
1921 2H4	5,000	None	5,000	$1.00
1921 No 2H4	45,028	29,600	15,428	$1.00
Alabama Centennial half dollar			Laura Gardin Fraser	
1921 2X2	6,006	None	6,006	$1.00
1921 No 2X2	64,038	5,000	59,038	$1.00
Grant Memorial half dollar			Laura Gardin Fraser	
1922 Star	5,006	750	4,256	$1.00
1922 No Star	95,055	27,650	67,405	$1.00
Grant Memorial gold dollar			Laura Gardin Fraser	
1922 Star	5,016	None	5,016	$3.50
1922 No Star	5,000	None	5,000	$3.00
Monroe Doctrine Centennial half dollar			Chester Beach	
1923-S	274,077	None	274,077	$1.00
Huguenot-Walloon Tercentenary half dollar			George T. Morgan	
1924	142,080	None	142,080	$1.00
Lexington-Concord Sesquicentennial half dollar			Chester Beach	
1925	162,099	86	162,013	$1.00

Commemorative Date	Original Mintage	Melted	Final Mintage	Designer Original Price
Stone Mountain half dollar				Gutzon Borglum
1925	2,314,709	1,000,000	1,314,709	$1.00
California Diamond Jubilee half dollar				Jo Mora
1925-S	150,200	63,606	86,594	$1.00
Fort Vancouver Centennial half dollar				Laura Gardin Fraser
1925	50,028	35,034	14,994	$1.00
American Independence Sesquicentennial half dollar				John R. Sinnock
1926	1,000,528	859,408	141,120	$1.00
American Independence Sesquicentennial quarter eagle				John R. Sinnock
1926	200,226	154,207	46,019	$4.00
Oregon Trail Memorial half dollar				James E. and Laura G. Fraser
1926	48,030	75	47,955	$1.00
1926-S	100,055	17,000	83,055	$1.00
1928	50,028	44,000	6,028	$2.00
1933-D	5,250	242	5,008	$2.00
1934-D	7,006	None	7,006	$2.00
1936	10,006	None	10,006	$1.60
1936-S	5,006	None	5,006	$1.60
1937-D	12,008	None	12,008	$1.60
1938	6,006	None	6,006	$6.25
1938-D	6,005	None	6,005	for
1938-S	6,006	None	6,006	three
1939	3,004	None	3,004	$7.50
1939-D	3,004	None	3,004	for
1939-S	3,005	None	3,005	three
Vermont Sesquicentennial half dollar				Charles Keck
1927	40,034	11,872	28,162	$1.00
Hawaiian Sesquicentennial half dollar				Juliette Mae Fraser and Chester Beach
1928	10,000	None	10,000	$2.00
Maryland Tercentenary half dollar				Hans Schuler
1934	25,015	None	25,015	$1.00
Texas Independence Centennial				Pompeo Coppini
1934	205,113	143,650	61,463	$1.00
1935	10,0078	12	9,996	$1.50
1935-D	10,007	None	10,007	$1.50
1935-S	10,008	None	10,008	$1.50
1936	10,008	1,097	8,911	$1.50
1936-D	10,007	968	9,039	$1.50
1936-S	10,008	943	9,055	$1.50
1937	8,005	1,434	6,571	$1.50
1937-D	8,006	1,401	6,605	$1.50
1937-S	8,007	1,370	6,637	$1.50
1938	5,005	1,225	3,780	$2.00
1938-D	5,005	1,230	3,775	$2.00
1938-S	5,006	1,192	3,814	$2.00
Daniel Boone Bicentennial half dollar				Augustus Lukeman
1934	10,007	None	10,007	$1.60
1935	10,010	None	10,010	$1.10
1935-D	5,005	None	5,005	$1.60
1935-S	5,005	None	5,005	$1.60
1935 W/1934	10,008	None	10,008	$1.10
1935-D W/1934	2,003	None	2,003	$3.70
1935-S W/1934	2,004	None	2,004	for two
1936	12,012	None	12,012	$1.10
1936-D	5,005	None	5,005	$1.60
1936-S	5,006	None	5,006	$1.60
1937	15,010	5,200	9,810	$1.60, $7.25 set
1937-D	7,506	5,000	2,506	$7.25 in set
1937-S	5,006	2,500	2,506	$5.15
1938	5,005	2,905	2,100	$6.50
1938-D	5,005	2,905	2,100	for
1938-S	5,006	2,906	2,100	three

Commemorative Date	Original Mintage	Melted	Final Mintage	Designer Original Price
Connecticut Tercentenary half dollar				Henry G. Kreiss
25,018	None	25,018	$1.00	
Arkansas Centennial half dollar				Edward E. Burr
1935	13,012	None	13,012	$1.00
1935-D	5,005	None	5,005	$1.00
1935-S	5,506	None	5,006	$1.00
1936	10,010	350	9,660	$1.50
1936-D	10,010	350	9,660	$1.50
1936-S	10,012	350	9,662	$1.50
1937	5,505	None	5,505	$8.75
1937-D	5,505	None	5,505	for
1937-S	5,506	None	5,506	three
1938	6,006	2,850	3,156	$8.75
1938-D	6,005	2,850	3,155	for
1938-S	6,006	2,850	3,156	three
1939	2,104	None	2,104	$10
1939-D	2,104	None	2,104	for
1939-S	2,105	None	2,105	three
Arkansas-Robinson half dollar				E.E. Burr and Henry Kreiss
1936	25,265	None	25,265	$1.85
Hudson, N.Y., Sesquicentennial half dollar				Chester Beach
1935	10,008	None	10,008	$1.00
California-Pacific International Expo				Robert Aitken
1935-S	250,132	180,000	70,132	$1.00
1936-D	180,092	150,000	30,092	$1.50
Old Spanish Trail half dollar				L.W. Hoffecker
1935	10,008	None	10,008	$2.00
Providence, R.I., Tercentenary				John H. Benson and Abraham G. Carey
1936	20,013	None	20,013	$1.00
1936-D	15,010	None	15,010	$1.00
1936-S	15,011	None	15,011	$1.00
Cleveland, Great Lakes Exposition half dollar				Brenda Putnam
1936	50,030	None	50,030	$1.50
Wisconsin Territorial Centennial half dollar				David Parsons and Benjamin Hawkins
1936	25,015	None	25,015	$1.50
Cincinnati Music Center half dollar				Constance Ortmayer
1936	5,005	None	5,005	$7.75
1936-D	5,005	None	5,005	for
1936-S	5,006	None	5,006	three
Long Island Tercentenary half dollar				Howard K. Weinmann
1936	100,053	18,227	81,826	$1.00
York County, Maine, Tercentenary half dollar				Walter H. Rich
1936	25,015	None	25,015	$1.50
Bridgeport, Conn., Centennial half dollar				Henry G. Kreiss
1936	25,015	None	25,015	$2.00
Lynchburg, Va., Sesquicentennial half dollar				Charles Keck
1936	20,013	None	20,013	$1.00
Elgin, Ill., Centennial half dollar				Trygve Rovelstad
1936	25,015	5,000	20,015	$1.50
Albany, N.Y., half dollar				Gertrude K. Lathrop
1936	25,013	7,342	17,671	$2.00
San Francisco-Oakland Bay Bridge half dollar				Jacques Schnier
1936-S	100,055	28,631	71,424	$1.50
Columbia, S.C., Sesquicentennial half dollar				A. Wolfe Davidson
1936	9,007	None	9,007	$6.45
1936-D	8,009	None	8,009	for
1936-S	8,007	None	8,007	three

Commemorative Date	Original Mintage	Melted	Final Mintage	Designer Original Price
Delaware Tercentenary half dollar				Carl L. Schmitz
1936	25,015	4,022	20,993	$1.75
Battle of Gettysburg half dollar				Frank Vittor
1936	50,028	23,100	26,928	$1.65
Norfolk, Va., Bicentennial half dollar		William M. Simpson and Marjorie E. Simpson		
1936	25,013	8,077	16,936	$1.50
Roanoke Island, N.C., half dollar				William M. Simpson
1937	50,030	21,000	29,030	$1.65
Battle of Antietam half dollar				William M. Simpson
1937	50,028	32,000	18,028	$1.65
New Rochelle, N.Y., half dollar				Gertrude K. Lathrop
1938	25,015	9,749	15,266	$2.00
Iowa Statehood Centennial half dollar				Adam Pietz
1946	100,057	None	100,057	$2.50/$3.00
Booker T. Washington half dollar				Isaac S. Hathaway
1946	1,000,546	?	?	$1.00
1946-D	200,113	?	?	$1.50
1946-S	500,279	?	?	$1.00
1947	100,017	?	?	$6.00
1947-D	100,017	?	?	for
1947-S	100,017	?	?	three
1948	20,005	12,000	8,005	$7.50
1948-D	20,005	12,000	8,005	for
1948	20,005	12,000	8,005	three
1949	12,004	6,000	6,004	$8.50
1949-D	12,004	6,000	6,004	for
1949-S	12,004	6,000	6,004	three
1950	12,004	6,000	6,004	$8.50
1950-D	12,004	6,000	6,004	for
1950-S	512,091	?	?	three
1951	510,082	?	?	$3 or $10
1951-D	12,004	5,000	7,004	for
1951-S	12,004	5,000	7,004	three
Booker T. Washington/George Washington Carver				Isaac S. Hathaway
1951	?	?	110,018	$10
1951-D	?	?	10,004	for
1951-S	?	?	10,004	three
1952	?	?	2,006,292	$10
1952-D	?	?	8,006	for
1952-S	?	?	8,006	three
1953	?	?	8,003	$10
1953-D	?	?	8,003	for
1953-S	?	?	108,020	three
1954	?	?	12,006	$10
1954-D	?	?	12,006	for
1954-S	?	?	122,024	three
George Washington half dollar				Elizabeth Jones
1982-D			2,210,458	$8.50/$10[1]
1982-S			4,894,044	$10/$12[1]
Los Angeles Olympic Games silver dollar				Elizabeth Jones
1983-P Unc.			294,543	$28 or $89[2]
1983-D Unc.			174,014	for
1983-S Unc.			174,014	three
1983-S Proof			1,577,05	$24.95[2]
Los Angeles Olympic Games silver dollar				Robert Graham
1984-P Unc.			217,954	$28 or $89[2]
1984-D Unc.			116,675	for
1984-S Unc.			116,675	three
1984-S Proof			1,801,210	$32[2]

Commemorative Date	Original Mintage	Melted	Final Mintage	Designer Original Price
Los Angeles Olympic Games gold eagle				James Peed, John Mercanti
1984-P Proof			33,309	$352[2]
1984-D Proof			34,533	$352[2]
1984-S Proof			48,551	$352[2]
1984-W Proof			381,085	$352[2]
1984-W Unc.			75,886	$339[2]
Statue of Liberty, Immigrant half dollar				Edgar Steever, Sherl Winter
1986-D Unc.			928,008	$5/$6[3]
1986-S Proof			6,925,627	$6.50/$7.50[3]
Statue of Liberty, Ellis Island dollar				John Mercanti, Matthew Peleso
1986-P Unc.			723,635	$20.50/$22[3]
1986-S Proof			6,414,638	$22.50/$24[3]
Statue of Liberty half eagle				Elizabeth Jones
1986-W Unc.			95,248	$160/$165[3]
1986-W Proof			404,013	$170/$175[3]
Constitution Bicentennial silver dollar				Patricia L. Veranl
1987-P Unc.			451,629	$22.50/$26[3]
1987-S Proof			2,747,116	$24/$28[3]
Constitution Bicentennial half eagle				Marcel Jovine
1987-W Unc.			214,225	$195/$215[3]
1987-W Proof			651,659	$200/$225[3]
1988 Olympic Games silver dollar				Patricia L. Veranl and Sherl J. Winter
1988-D Unc.			191,368	$22/$27[3]
1988-S Proof			1,359,366	$23/$29[3]
1988 Olympic Games gold half eagle				Elizabeth Jones and Marcel Jovine
1988-W Unc.			62,913	$200/$225[3]
1988-W Proof			281,465	$205/$235[3]
Congress Bicentennial half dollar				Patricia L. Veranl and William Woodward
1989-D Unc.			Pending	$5/$6[3]
1989-S Proof			Pending	$7/$8[3]
Congress Bicentennial silver dollar				William Woodward
1989-D Unc.			Pending	$23/$26[3]
1989-S Proof			Pending	$25/$29[3]
Congress Bicentennial half eagle				John Mercanti
1989-W Unc.			Pending	$185/$200[3]
1989-W Proof			Pending	$195/$215[3]
Eisenhower Birth Centennial silver dollar				John Mercanti and Marcel Jovine
1990-W Unc.			Pending	$23/$26[3]
1990-P Proof			Pending	$25/$29[3]

Notes

1. Prices for 1982 George Washington half dollar is for 1982 and 1983-85.
2. Prices for 1983-84 Olympic coins in some cases are first prices charged and do not reflect higher prices charged later.
3. Prices from 1986-89 are pre-issue/regular issue.

Errors

11

Error coins and paper money

Error coins and paper money are products of the United States Mint and the Bureau of Engraving and Printing that Treasury officials would rather did not exist. An error coin or note deviates from the norm as a result of a mishap in the minting or printing processes; in effect, an error represents a "substandard" product of the agency that produced it. Some collectors prefer these substandard items, however, over normal coins and notes.

Although it sometimes may seem that the Mint and the BEP produce inordinate amounts of error coins and notes, the numbers are generally relatively small when compared to the total numbers of pieces released. Those small numbers in part account for the values some collectors place on error numismatic material. The Mint and BEP are constantly trying to improve quality — and therefore reduce the number of errors. The Mint is installing more precise planchet delivery systems and automated quality checkers on its presses, reducing the potential number of striking errors; placing Mint marks on master dies rather than working dies, to prevent Mint mark errors; and reducing the number of hubbing impressions needed to make a die, reducing doubled-die errors. The BEP will be challenged as the push for ever-more-sophisticated counterfeiting deterrents are phased into production. Security threads embedded in the currency paper and microprinting will introduce new classes of errors for BEP quality control engineers to worry about.

Of course, values for error coins and paper money depend on the same factors affecting normal numismatic merchandise: supply, demand and condition. Obviously, errors are in very short supply when compared to total mintages. However, error collectors represent a fraction of the total number of collectors, so demand is less for most items. Some error coins, such as the 1955 Lincoln, Doubled Die cent, or the 1989 "No Mint mark" Washington quarter dollar because of press publicity and dealer promotion, "cross over" and become popular with general collectors; thus, demand is higher for a fixed supply, and the values are correspondingly higher. Condition is important, although error collectors seem less concerned with "perfection" than other collectors.

Rare does not necessarily mean great value. Many error coins, struck in small quantities, are available for a few dollars. Even errors which are considered unique are often available for only several dollars. Unfortunately, many persons not familiar with errors, including some dealers, place unrealistically high values on error coins and notes.

Any discussion of error coins and notes must include a discussion of varieties. A numismatic variety is defined as the difference between individual dies or hubs of the same basic design or type, or between plates (in the case of paper money). The differences between two varieties of the same type are generally intentional; the 1917 Standing Liberty quarter dollar with Liberty baring her breast is a different variety than the 1917 Standing Liberty quarter with Liberty's breast covered by a coat of chain mail, for example, although both have the same basic design.

Can an error also be a variety? There are some who believe so, especially for certain die errors. Some die error coins have been accepted as varieties and are considered by many as part of the regular series; among these are the 1955 and 1972 Lincoln, Doubled Die cents, the 1937-D Indian Head, Three-Legged 5-cent piece, and others. Others believe that no distinction should be made between varieties or errors; they believe that all errors are varieties.

Error coins and notes can be found in circulation, unlike many other collectors' items. Some collectors go to banks and obtain large quantities of coins or notes to search through; coins and notes not bearing errors are returned to the bank. Many errors, particularly of the minor classification, can be discovered simply by going through pocket change and wallets. All it takes are sharp eyes and a knowledge of what to look for.

Error coins

The minting of a coin is a manufacturing process, and should be fully understood by anyone interested in collecting and studying error coins. Many forms of alteration and damage received outside the Mint resemble certain types of errors, but none precisely duplicate genuine Mint errors. Collectors who understand the minting process should be better able to distinguish between errors and damage and alteration than collectors who have never studied the manufacturing process.

The causes of error coins will be discussed in the section that follows. The section is split into three parts — die errors, planchet errors and striking errors — followed by definitions of common forms of alteration and damage.

Die errors are those produced due to a mishap involving the die or hub. Planchet errors are the result of defective or improper planchets, and striking errors are created during the actual coining.

Die errors

BIE: The term commonly used for minor errors affecting the letters of the word LIBERTY on Lincoln cents. A small break in the die between the letters, especially BE, often resembles the letter I, hence the BIE designation. Such errors are much more common on the coins of the 1950s and early 1960s than more recent issues. Collectors tend to be less interested in such errors in the 1980s than they were 20 years ago.

clashed dies: When during the striking process two dies come together without a planchet between them, the dies clash (come into direct contact). Depending on the force with which the dies come together and the designs, a portion of the obverse design is transferred to the reverse, and a portion of the reverse is transferred to the obverse. Coins struck from the clashed dies will show signs of the transferred designs. Although the cause of this type of error occurs during the striking process, the die is affected; thus it is considered a die error.

cuds: A "cud" is a type of major die break. It occurs when the die breaks at the rim and a piece of the die falls out of the press. The metal of coins struck from that die flows up into the missing area, resulting in a raised blob of metal bearing no image; these are called "cud" errors. The side of the coin opposite the cud is weak and indistinct; this is because metal flows along the path of least resistance, preferring to travel into the broken area and not the recesses of the other die. A retained cud occurs when the die breaks at the rim, but the piece does not fall out. Coins struck from these dies show the break, but also depict the image inside the break.

die breaks, chips, cracks, gouges, scratches: Dies, like any other piece of steel, are subject to all sorts of damage that leave raised areas on coins. Breaks and cracks are similar, appearing on coins as raised lines. A die break affects a larger area than the die crack, and often breaks result in pieces of the die falling out (see "cud"). A die chip occurs when a small portion of the die breaks away, while gouges and scratches generally occur when a foreign object scores the surface of the die.

doubled dies: If during the hubbing and die making process, a misalignment between hub and partially completed die occurs, overlapping, multiple images may appear on the die. Coins struck from that die will show overlapping images as well. Die doubling on coins with raised designs feature a rounded second image; on coins with incused designs, the second image is flat and shelf-like. At the corners of the overlapping images, there are distinct "notches" on coins with raised designs. A tripled die is caused by the same misalignment, but bears a tripled image.

engraving errors: While more common on the dies of the 18th and 19th centuries, engraving errors have been made on modern dies. On the earlier dies, numerals and letters were often recut to strengthen the design, punched in upside down or otherwise out of alignment, and sometimes, wrong letters or numbers were punched into the die. On more modern dies, engraving errors include the use of the wrong size Mint mark by mistake and Mint marks placed too close to design elements or too far from their intended locations. Other engraving errors, discussed in separate sections, included doubled dies, overdates and multiple Mint marks.

filled dies: The Mint is a factory, and like most metal-working factories, has more than its share of dirt, grease and other lubricants, and metal filings. The recessed areas of the dies sometimes fill up with a combination of this foreign material, preventing the metal of the coins from flowing into the incused areas. This results in weak designs or missing design details. Probably the most common type of error. Some 1989 "No Mint mark" Washington quarter dollars missing the P Mint mark gained national publicity, with some pieces trading for exorbitant prices — into the thousands of dollars. The pieces turned out to have been struck from a filled die, and their more reasonable value estimated at $3.

multiple Mint marks: Mint marks have traditionally been punched into each individual working die by hand with mallet and punch. Several blows to the punch are needed to properly sink the Mint mark into the die. If the punch is not properly placed after the first blow, a multiple image may result. These are commonly known as doubled D and doubled S Mint marks, for the Denver and San Francisco Mints. Beginning in 1986 with collector coins and later moving into circulating coinage, the Mint has been adding the Mint mark at the master die stage, and in some cases on the plasticene models themselves.

overdates: When one or more numerals in the date are engraved, sunk or hubbed over a different numeral or numerals, both the original date and the second date can be seen. Examples include the 1943/2-P Jefferson 5-cent piece, the 1942/1 Winged Liberty Head dime and the 1958/7 Lincoln cent. Another overdate occurs when two dies with the same date, but of different varieties, are used. Prime examples of this are the 1960 Lincoln, Large Date Over Small Date cents.

over Mint marks: A form of multiple Mint mark, but when punches of two different Mints are used. Examples include the 1944-D/S Lincoln cent and the 1938-D/S Jefferson 5-cent piece.

polished dies: Mint employees polish dies to extend their working life and to remove such things as clash marks, die scratches, dirt and grease. If the die is polished too much, details may be erased, or small raised lines may appear on the coins. Most over-polished errors have little value, but there are exceptions, including the 1937-D Indian Head, Three-Legged 5-cent piece.

rotated dies: Most U.S. coins have the obverse and reverse sides oriented so each side is upright when rotated vertically. The alignment between the two is 180 degrees. However, if the dies are aligned at anything other than 180 degrees, the dies are considered rotated. Coins rotated 5 degrees or less are considered within tolerance levels by Mint employees.

worn dies: Dies have a set life, based on the hardness of the coinage metal being struck and the striking pressures involved. When a die wears beyond a certain point, details around the rim tend to flow into the rim, while other details weaken. The surface of the die becomes scarred, as though it was very heavily polished. Worn die errors rarely have collector value.

Planchet errors

alloy errors: All U.S. coins are produced from alloyed metals, mixed when molten to strict specifications. If mixed incorrectly, the metals may cool in non-homogeneous form, with streaks of different metals appearing on the surface of the coin.

damaged planchets: Planchets are subject to various sorts of damage, including cracks (not to be confused with die cracks), holes and major breaks.

fragments, scrap struck: Small pieces of coinage metal — fragments and scrap left over from the blanking process — sometimes fall between the dies and are struck. Fragments must be struck on both sides and weigh less than 25 percent of a normal coin's weight to qualify as a struck fragment. Planchet scrap is generally larger than a fragment, and usually has straight or curved edges as a result of the blanking process.

incomplete planchets: Often, though erroneously, called a "clip," an incomplete planchet results from a mishap in the blanking process. If the planchet strip does not advance far enough after a bank of punches rams through the metal, producing planchets, the punches come down and overlap the holes where the planchets were already punched out. Where the overlapping takes place, there is a curved area that appears to be "missing" from the planchet. The word "clip," commonly used, suggests a piece of the planchet was cut off, which is not the cause. "Clip," when properly used, refers to the ancient process of cutting small pieces of metal from the edges of precious metals coins for the bullion; that is why U.S. gold and silver coins have lettered or reeded edges, to make it more difficult to clip a coin.

An "incomplete clip" occurs when the punch does not completely punch a planchet out, but leaves a circular groove. If the strip advances improperly, planchets overlapping the incomplete punch will bear a curved groove; the groove remains visible after the coin is struck.

Most incomplete planchet errors have a "signature" known as the Blakesley effect. The area of the rim 180 degrees opposite the "clip" is weak or non-existent since the rim-making process in the upset mill is negated by the "clip." The lack of pressure in the upset mill at the clip results in improper formation of the rim on the opposite side.

laminations: During the preparation of the planchet strip, foreign materials — grease, dirt, oil, slag or gas — may become trapped just below the surface of the metal. Coins struck from this strip later may begin to flake and peel since adhesion is poor in the location of the trapped material. The Jefferson, Wartime 5-cent pieces are particularly susceptible to lamination, due to the metals used during war metal emergency.

split planchets: Planchets can split due to deep internal laminations, or in the case of clad coinage, because of poor adhesion of the copper-nickel outer layers to the copper core. Planchets may split before or after striking. Those splitting before generally exhibit weak details due to lack of metal to fill the dies, while those split afterwards usually depict full detailing. On non-clad coins, the inner portion of the split shows parallel striations typical of the interior structure of coinage metal.

thick and thin planchets: Planchets of the wrong thickness are produced from strip that was not rolled properly. Too little pressure can result in planchet stock that is too thick; too much can result in a thin planchet. If the rollers are out of alignment on one side, a tapered planchet — one that is thicker on one side than the other — is created.

unplated planchets: New in U.S. coinage, unplated planchets became possible in 1982 with the introduction of the copper-plated zinc cent. The zinc-copper alloy planchets are plated after they are punched from the strip, but some planchets miss the plating process. Coins struck on the unplated planchets are grayish-white in color. Beware of cents which have had their plating removed after leaving the Mint.

wrong metal, planchet, stock: There are several major types of errors in this series. A wrong metal error is a coin struck on a planchet intended for a different denomination of a different composition. This includes 5-cent pieces struck on cent planchets, cents struck on dime planchets, and higher denominations struck on cent and 5-cent planchets.

A second type is the wrong planchet error, defined as a coin struck on a planchet of the correct composition, but the wrong denomination. These include quarter dollars struck on dime planchets, half dollars struck on quarter and dime planchets, and dollars struck on other clad planchets.

A third type is the wrong planchet stock error. It occurs when clad coinage strip rolled to the thickness of one denomination is fed into the blanking press of another denomination; the diameter is correct, but the thickness is greater or less than normal. The most common appears to be quarter dollars struck on planchet stock intended for dimes.

A fourth, rarer form is the double denomination. It occurs when a coin is struck on a previously struck coin, such as a cent struck over a dime. Since the U.S. Mint strikes coins for foreign governments, it is possible to find in circulation U.S. coins struck on planchets intended for foreign coins, as well as coins struck on previously struck foreign coins.

Another rare type of wrong metal error is the transitional error. It occurs as the composition of a coin changes. Some 1965 coins are known struck on silver planchets of 1964 composition, while some 1964 coins were struck on clad planchets (1964 coins were struck through 1965, with planchets for both types of coins available side by side).

One fact true for all errors of this broad category is that the planchets must be of an equal size or smaller than the intended planchet. A 5-cent planchet, for example, would not fit between the dies of the smaller cent.

Striking errors

broadstrikes: If the surrounding collar is pushed below the surface of the lower die during the moment of striking, the metal of the coin being struck is free to expand beyond the confines of the die. The design of the coin is normal at center, but as it nears the periphery, becomes distorted due to the uncontrolled spread of metal.

brockage and capped die strikes: If a newly struck coin sticks to the surface of one of the dies, it acts as a die itself — called a die cap — and produces images on succeeding coins. The image produced by any die is the direct opposite on a coin, and brockages are no different. Since the image is raised on the coin adhering to the die, the image on the brockage is incused and reversed — a true mirror image. The first brockage strikes, perfect mirror images and undistorted, are most prized. As additional coins are struck from the capped die, the die cap begins to spread and thin under the pressures of striking, distorting its image.

At some point, as the die cap becomes more distorted, the coins struck cease to be brockages and are known as capped die strikes. While a brockage image is undistorted or relatively so, images on capped die strikes are increasingly malformed. Although the image is still recognizable, the design expands, producing an image that can be several times the actual size of a normal image. Finally, the die cap breaks off or is pounded so thin it ceases to affect succeeding strikes.

Sometimes, the die caps fall off early and in a relatively undistorted state. Die caps resemble bottle caps, with the metal wrapping around the surface of the die. Die caps are very rare and collectible, much more so than capped die strikes.

double and multiple strikes: Double strikes are coins struck more than once.

If the coin rotates slightly between strikes, but remains inside the collar, two images will appear on both sides of the coin. The first strike will be almost totally obliterated by the second strike, and the first strike will be flattened and have almost no relief. Sometimes, a struck coin will flip — somewhat like a pancake on a hot griddle — and fall upside down onto the surface of the die; thus, the second strike has an obverse image obliterating the original reverse, and a reverse image flattening the first obverse image.

If the coin falls partially outside the dies after the first strike, the second image is only partial. The partial second strike obliterates the original image beneath it, but the rest of the first strike is undistorted, except in the immediate vicinity of the second strike. A saddle strike is generally not a true double strike, but usually the result of having a planchet fall partially between two pairs of dies on a multi-die press. Saddle strikes have two partial images, and an expanse of unstruck planchet between the struck areas.

What happens twice can happen three times or more, though rarely. However, examples of coins struck three or four times are known.

indented errors: An indented error is a coin struck with another coin or planchet lying partially on its surface. The area covered by the planchet does not come into contact with the die, and thus is blank if indented by a planchet, or shows a partial brockage if indented by a struck coin. The most desirable of the indented errors are larger coins with the indentation of a smaller planchet centered on one side.

machine, strike doubling: A form of doubling, this is probably the most common type of Mint error and is considered non-collectible by a majority of hobbyists. Some noted authorities do not consider it an error, but believe it to be a form of Mint-caused damage since it occurs immediately after the strike. The most common cause is a certain looseness of the die or other parts in the press which causes the die to bounce across the surface of the newly struck coin. In bouncing, the die shoves the metal of the raised designs to one side, creating the doubled image. On coins with raised designs, the doubling is flat, like a shelf.

off-center coins: If a planchet lies partially outside of the dies during the striking, it receives an off-center strike. Each coin struck off center is unique, but due to the large numbers available, are very inexpensive in the lower denominations. Off-center coins with dates are more valuable than coins without dates. Generally, on dated coins, the greater the off-center strike, the more it is worth. Some collectors collect off-center coins by their "clock" positions. Hold the coin with portrait upright and look for the direction the strike lies. If it is at 90 degrees, the strike is at 3 o'clock; if it lies at 270 degrees, the strike is at 9 o'clock.

partial collar: Often known as "railroad rim" errors, the edge, not the rim, is the portion of the coin affected. It occurs when the collar is pushed somewhat below the surface of the lower die, so that the upper portion of the coin is free to expand beyond the confines of the collar, while the lower portion is restrained. On coins struck from a reeded collar, partial reeding exists on the area restrained by the collar. The error gets the nickname railroad rim from its appearance — the coin, viewed edge-on, resembles the wheel from a railroad car.

struck-through errors: Filled-die errors and indented coins are related to struck-through errors, which occur when foreign objects fall between die and planchet during striking. In addition to the grease of a filled-die error and the planchet of an indented error, pieces of cloth, metal fragments, wire, slivers of reeding, wire bristles (from wire brushes used to clean dies, resembling staples), die covers and other objects. Sometimes, an incused letter or number of a die will fill up with grease, which solidifies under constant pressure. If the blob of grease — shaped like a letter or number — drops out of the die, it may be struck into the surface of the coin, leaving the impression of the affected letter or number. The most collectible struck-through errors are those with the foreign object still embedded into the surface of the coin.

uniface errors: If two planchets fall between the same dies at the same time, one side of each will be prevented from coming into contact with the dies. One side of each will have a normal image, while the other side — facing the other planchet — will be blank. Uniface errors can also occur on indented coins.

weak strikes: Weak strikes often resemble coins struck from grease-filled dies, but can be identified. They occur either when the press has been turned off — it tends to cycle through several strikings, each with less pressure than the previous — or when the press is being set up by the operators who test the placement of the dies at lower coining pressures. On reeded coins, weak strikes generally have poorly formed reeding (it is strong on filled dies). Depending on the pressure used, the image may be only slightly weak, or practically non-existent, or any stage in between.

Altered and damaged coins

A coin is subjected to a variety of abuses once it leaves the safety of the U.S. Mint. It can receive unintentional damage during normal use that alters the appearance of the coin. Intentional alteration can change the appearance even more drastically, whether the coin was altered by someone just experimenting or by someone who deliberately planned to change the appearance of a coin to deceive a collector or buyer.

To the informed, damaged and altered coins do not resemble Mint errors. The minting process leaves definite signatures on the surfaces of a coin that cannot be duplicated inadvertently in circulation or in the workshop of the coin alterer. The uninformed, however, often mistake damaged or altered coins for Mint errors. Those persons often have mistaken ideas about the values of error coins, believing all errors to worth a great deal. When told that the altered coins are worth face values only, many non-collectors may become discouraged and decide not to continue in the hobby.

Altered and damaged coins have no numismatic value.

A good place to begin to learn about the minting process is to read the section titled "How U.S. coins are made" in the U.S. Coins chapter of the Coin World Almanac. There are also several books about error coins available from coin dealers and book stores. Most have sections about the production of U.S. coins, and how to distinguish between errors and altered or damaged coins. Joining an error coin club is a good idea as well

Education is important. The following descriptions are of damaged and altered coins most likely to cause confusion for the non-specialist in error coins.

acid-treated coins: Coins which have been soaked in an acid solution or have had acid poured over them are thinner than unaltered coins. The thinness of the acid-treated coin depends on the strength of the acid and the duration of the treatment. Some will be so thin the edge will be sharp and knife-like. The acid-treated coin will still have visible design elements, although the designs will be somewhat weakened (the longer the treatment, the weaker the design). Coins which have had acid poured over them may exhibit channels were the acid flowed. If more acid flows over one area, it may be thinner than another area which had less contact with the acid.

added Mint mark: A coin with an added Mint mark is a form of alteration made deliberately to defraud a buyer. The most common form of added Mint mark is one that has been cut from a common coin and added to the Philadelphia version of a rarer coin. Close examination of this kind of added Mint mark will show a sharp line between the field and the Mint mark; metal flow lines found ascending from the field onto the Mint mark on an unaltered coin are not present on this form of alteration.

Another form of added Mint mark was discovered in recent years. The person altering the coin drills a small hole from the edge of a coin to the point where the Mint mark would be found if it had one. Then, a specially made tool with a small, Mint mark-shaped form, is inserted into the hole. Pressure is applied to the Mint mark form from the inside, forcing the surface of the metal to raise in the shape of the Mint mark. Flow lines may be found on this type of alteration. To detect, examine the edge below the Mint mark carefully for any signs of damage left by drilling the hole.

A crude form of added Mint mark is forming by cutting the shape of the Mint mark directly into the surface of the coin. The knife marks are generally clear. Few added Mint marks of this type can pass muster.

glue: The application of a thin layer of transparent glue to the surface of a coin can cause a very deceptive appearance. The design is visible through the glue, and the hardened glue often resembles raised metal. Sometimes, the person altering the coin will press another coin into the wet glue, and let it dry. Once dry, the coins are pried apart and the glue remaining on one coin will have incused, mirror-image details from the other coin. One U.S. cent seen by Coin

World's Collectors' Clearinghouse department personnel had dried glue with the incused image of a Canadian cent embedded on the coin. Most glues can be dissolved with clear acetone, an ingredient used in fingernail polish removers. The acetone can then be rinsed off of the coin. A recent appearance of epoxy glue on coins has been the attempt to mask hairline scratches and other minute defects, giving the coin the appearance of being a higher grade than actual. Grading experts generally spot this quite easily.

hammered edge: Often, coins will be found with a diameter slightly smaller than normal and a high, thick rim. This is done by placing the coin on its edge and hammering away at it. Sometimes, on larger coins, the edge can be hammered flat and the center of the coin cut away, providing the alterer with an inexpensive ring after all the rough edges are polished away. On coins with reeded edges, the reeding is often beaten smooth.

lucky piece coin: Most persons have seen lucky piece coins, generally cents, which are embedded in a surrounding aluminum holder which has advertising or other writing on it. Force is required to squeeze the coin into the hole in the middle of the holder. Generally, the edge is distorted and made somewhat concave; if removed from the holder, the odd appearance of the edge can fool the untrained eye. The legends on the holder are generally stamped into the metal at the same time that the coin is forced into the hole. If the stamping dies overlap the coin, some of the legend can be stamped onto the coin. Again, if removed from the holder, the raised lettering can appear to be an original portion of the design.

1943 bronze cents: America's entry into World War II brought about sacrifice from every quarter, including the United States Mint. Copper became a critical war supply and little could be spared for cent coinage. Extensive testing in 1942 resulted in a zinc-plated steel cent that was used in 1943 only. About a dozen known bronze 1943 cents were struck in error, on planchets remaining from 1942 coinage. Thousands of collectors believe they own one of the dozen pieces, however. Many thousands of steel cents were plated with copper. They can easily be distinguished from genuine 1943 bronze cents by use of a magnet. A magnet will pick up a steel cent, but not a genuine bronze cent. Lack of magnetic properties does not mean the coin is genuine, however. Compare the 3 in the date of a genuine 1943 steel cent to the 3 on a suspected 1943 bronze cent. If the tail of the 3 does not extend the same distance, the coin is probably an altered 1948 cent (the alterer cuts away the left half of the 8). Struck-counterfeit 1943 bronze cents exist as well, so any coins passing all of the above tests should be sent to one of the several authentication services for professional evaluation.

sandwich coin: Two or more coins are placed in a stack between the jaws of a bench vise. Pressure is applied, squeezing the coins together. Design elements will transfer from one coin to the other, creating a false double-struck coin. Unlike a genuine double strike, however, the additional image will be incused and reversed. Most sandwich coins will be distorted as a result of the pressure applied by the vise. Sandwich coins can also be produced by striking the stack of coins with a hammer. (The term sandwich coin was also used in the mid-1960s to describe the then new clad coinage.)

slanted digits: Certain coins, in particular the Lincoln cent, can be damaged by parts in an automatic wrapping machine in such a way that the date resembles an overdate error. Feed fingers in the wrapping machine scrape across the surface of the cent, shoving the metal in the last digit to one side. A slight image of the last digit remains, with the displaced metal sitting above. On some specimens, the displaced metal may resemble the numeral 1 sitting over the ghost of another numeral.

Texas coins: Coins with diameters slightly greater than normal and with proportionally larger designs cannot be struck under the conditions in effect at the U.S. Mint. Nicknamed a Texas coin (for large), the altered pieces are produced by placing the coin between two pieces of leather and striking them with a hammer. The leather somehow causes the entire design to expand, not just the diameter. Some distortion is usually present, although it may be slight.

wood-blocked cent: Coins which have strongly flattened features, plus peripheral lettering and numbers that extend into a flattened rim, have probably been placed between two blocks of wood and struck with a hammer.

Paper money errors

The production processes necessary to produce U.S. paper money, like the minting sequence, are subject to various forms of failure that can lead to error notes. The similarities do not end there. An understanding of the paper money production processes is essential for any serious collector of paper money errors. The ink on U.S. paper money can be altered after the notes enter circulation, both accidently and deliberately; some forms of alteration may resemble errors. Other forms of alteration are possible, too.

The causes of paper money errors will be discussed in the next section, to be followed by a discussion of the most commonly seen forms of altered and damaged notes. The error note section is presented in three sections: first and second printing errors, overprinting errors, and fold and cutting errors.

The basic production sequence is the first, or back printing, followed by the second, or face printing. Initial trimming and cutting comes next, followed by the application of the overprinting and additional trimming steps.

First and second printing errors

blanket impression: Called "offset printing" by hobbyists, and blanket impression by BEP personnel, this is probably the most common type of printing error. A blanket impression is a mirror-image ink impression on the wrong side of the note; a reversed image of the face design will appear on the back, and a reversed image of the back design will appear on the face. Although it may appear that the wayward ink has "bled" through the paper, blanket impressions occur during one of the printing processes. Basically, sheets of currency paper pass between two huge rotating cylinders, one containing inked printing plates and the second a flexible surface that forces the paper into the ink-filled intaglio lines of the plates. If the paper is torn or folded, a portion of the inked printing plates may come into direct contact with the impression cylinder. The impression cylinder picks up ink from the plate cylinder and deposits it on next dozen or so sheets, on the side opposite the side being printed. The image is reversed because the ink lying on the surface of the impression cylinder is normally oriented (the printing plates have a mirror image). Blanket impressions may affect one entire side, or just a small portion of the design. Overprinting blanket impressions are known, but are much rarer than first and second printing blanket impressions. The cause is the same. The use of the term "blanket impression" is technically more accurate than "offset printing"; offset is a printing method, the kind used to produce this edition of the Coin World Almanac, and different from intaglio printing.

board breaks: A board break occurs when a depression is created in the surface of the impression cylinder. The paper opposite the depression is not forced into the ink-filled intaglio lines of the printing plate, and therefore there is an unprinted area on an otherwise normal note. Board breaks generally affect small areas, although larger breaks are known.

double denomination:s Considered the ultimate in error notes, a double denomination note has face and back printings for two different denominations, like a $5 face and a $10 back. The back printing, since it is first, is the correct denomination. The error occurs when the uniface sheet is fed into the wrong press for the face printing, picking up a different denomination than from that of the back. All such notes are rare and are very collectible.

double printings: Double printings can occur if a sheet of currency paper is inadvertently fed through through an intaglio printing press twice. The entire image may be doubled. If the press stops in the middle of a printing pass and the partially printed sheet is deliberately fed into the press again to restart it, a doubled image can also occur. In the case of the latter cause, the note may have one complete printing and a partial second printing. A rarer form is for the second image to be upside down relative to the first image. Both face and back can have a doubled printing. Plate check numbers are rarely the same.

incomplete printing: Any portion or all of the back or face printings may be missing from a note. If two sheets ride through a press stuck together, one sheet does not come into contact with the printing plates. This can occur during the second printing step, which means the note will have a back printing (done first), but no face printing; or, can occur during the back printing, which means the note will have no back image, but will have a face printing. Those with no face printing are visually more spectacular, since the black and green overprinting is applied over a white, blank face. Improperly or incompletely inked plates can also cause an incomplete printing, with only a portion of the design usually missing. Folded or torn sheets, or scrap paper falling between a portion of the sheet and the printing plate can also cause partial or complete failure to print note surfaces. If an uninked plate comes in contact with the paper, an impression of the uninked design can be seen.

ink smears: Called "sly wipes" by BEP personnel, ink smears occur when the surface of the inked printing plate is not properly wiped before printing to remove excess ink from the surface of the plate. Older presses were wiped by an automatically-fed roll of coarse paper, while the modern presses now in use at the Bureau use a "water-wipe" system which sprays a solution of water and caustic soda over the plate to wash away excess ink. On the note, an ink smear is just that — a smear of ink, black (on the face) or green (on the back), obscuring a portion of the design of the note. The smear occurs at the same instant the note is printed, and is not applied afterward. Beware of ink applied to the surface of a note after it reaches circulation.

inverted printings: Occurs when a sheet with a back printing is rotated 180 degrees and fed into a press for the second printing. The face is upside down in relation to the back. Often incorrectly called an "inverted reverse," "inverted face" is the technically-correct term.

off-register printing: Occurs when a currency sheet is fed into the press improperly aligned for one pass. The ink is deposited out of register in relation to the printing on the opposite side. Later, when cut into an individual note, the cuts may be made through the unaligned image so that one side of the note looks off center. Notes with the face off-registered generally have the overprinting in the correct location for the note, but not for the face image.

printed through foreign matter: One of the causes of an incomplete printing, the foreign matter, generally a scrap of paper, sometimes sticks to the surface of the finished note. The note may appear normal to a casual viewer, but the shape of the scrap material should be visible. If the scrap is gently lifted, an unprinted area the same size and shape as the foreign matter will appear on the note. Notes with the foreign matter remaining attached are more collectible than notes on which the scrap is missing, leaving only the incomplete printing.

Overprinting errors

double overprints: These occur much in the same way that a doubled first and second printing error occurs. The half sheet of currency paper is fed through the Currency Overprinting and Processing Equipment twice, picking up one complete overprint and a second partial or complete overprint.

ink smears: The result of excess ink on the overprint wheels or the smudging of fresh overprint ink. Smears can be black or green, depending upon what stage of the overprinting is affected.

inverted overprints: When a half sheet of currency paper is rotated 180 degrees before being fed into the COPE press, the overprint is applied upside down on the face. A major epidemic of inverted overprints occurred in 1976 and 1977, resulting in hundreds of such notes being released. So many were released that it was possible to collect a complete, 12-note Federal Reserve District set of $1 inverts of the same series date.

misaligned overprint: Half sheets must be properly aligned for the overprinting to be perfectly located. If a half sheet is fed into the COPE press off center, the overprint will be misaligned in one or more directions. A small degree of latitude is permitted before a misaligned overprint error becomes collectible; generally, the overprint needs to be touching a portion of the second printing design to be collectible. Not to be confused with off-register notes, which appear similar but are the result of an error during the first or second printing steps.

mismatched serial numbers, letters: Several mishaps can cause the prefix or suffix letters or numbers in the serial numbers on an individual note to be mismatched. The five digits on the far right of the serial number wheels decrease automatically (serial numbers are printed from the highest number to the lowest), but the three digits at the left and the prefix and suffix letters must be changed manually. A digit in the automatically turning wheels can stick in one position, or the person resetting the manual numbers or letters, or the automatic numerals at the beginning of a press run, can make a mistake and set the wrong digit. Any number or letter can be mismatched, and a simple comparison of the left serial number and right serial number will reveal the mismatched digit.

missing and incomplete overprints: Missing and incomplete overprints may occur when scrap falls between the overprint wheels and the currency half sheet, or due to a fold or tear in the paper. Since the green overprint is applied before the black overprint (only seconds apart), one color can be normal and the other missing or incomplete. This can happen if the mishap occurs before the second overprinting step.

overprint on back: If a currency half sheet is turned end over end, so the back faces the overprinting wheels, the overprint is applied on the back. Because the overprint is missing from the face, the blank areas of the face printing remain unprinted.

partially turned digit: If one of the digits in the serial number wheel fails to decrease properly, a partial digit may appear on the overprint. Sometimes, the digit sticks in the partially-turned position and a series of notes are overprinted with the partial digit.

same serial numbers: If all the digits in a serial number wheel fail to decrease, a series of notes bearing the same serial number may be printed. To be collectible, at least two notes with the identical serial numbers must be saved. The notes must be from the same series date, have identical prefix and suffix letters, and must be the same denomination.

scrap through overprint: Like the scrap paper or other foreign matter that remains attached to a note, affecting the first or second printings, notes with the overprint on a piece of scrap that remains attached are more collectible than those where the scrap has fallen off. A unique note of this type had the overprint printed through a Band-Aid brand bandage backing which remained attached to the note.

wrong stock note: If a sheet of currency of one denomination with both first and second printings is mixed in with sheets of another denomination, the overprint for the wrong denomination is applied to the wayward sheet. Since the location of the overprint differs for each denomination, it may appear to be misaligned on the note. Collectible only if the immediately preceding and succeeding notes of the different denomination are saved. Otherwise, the note is visually indistinguishable from a misaligned overprint note in appearance.

Fold and cutting errors

Fold and cutting errors cannot be as neatly categorized as the two other major types of paper money errors, since each fold and cutting error is unique. The large sheets of paper used to print U.S. paper money notes are prone to folding at any time during the production process: first printing, second printing, trimming or overprinting.

Small folds extending vertically from note edge to edge are called gutter folds. They can affect the back, face, or both sides, depending on when the fold took place. Folds at the corners can obscure a portion of the design of either side, or the overprint; when unfolded, a portion of one side may appear on the other side. Major folds can drastically alter the appearance of the note, leaving huge unprinted areas and areas where a portion of one side is printed over the other side, or where a portion of the overprint is placed on the back.

If the fold remains closed during the several cutting and trimming stages, then extraneous paper may exist along one or several edges. Some fold and cutting errors are so large that when unfolded, a portion of another note above, below or beside the main note remains attached.

Values of fold and cutting errors depend on the size of the fold, the complexity of the fold, appearance, and general numismatic factors, including supply and demand, and condition.

Altered and damaged notes

Paper and ink are much more fragile media than brass, copper-nickel and zinc-copper, alloys found in pocket change today, and thus exhibit different types of damage. Notes are also subject to both accidental and deliberate alteration, the latter to either deceive a collector or cashier, or as a lark.

Education about the production processes necessary to make paper money is as important to the paper money collector as knowledge about minting techniques is to the coin collector. There are several general books available about paper money which cover the production of paper money. Membership in syngraphic organizations is encouraged as well.

The following descriptions are of altered and damaged notes most likely to deceive the unknowing person.

added ink smears: Smeared ink other than the black and two greens used on modern U.S. paper money was almost certainly added after the note left the BEP; some green and blacks could also have been added. There is no easy method to distinguish between an ink smear that was placed on the note at the BEP and ink added afterward if there is no obvious color difference. This is where experience and knowledge play a hand.

altered denomination: Persons altering the denomination of a note prey on the public's ignorance about whose portrait appears on paper money, and the fact — shown by government studies — that a majority of persons never examine notes passing through their hands to determine whether they are authentic. The most common method of altering the denomination is to cut several corners bearing the denomination from several notes, and glue four corners to a note of a lower denomination. Some alterers cut the denominational legend from the bottom of a note and glue that in place over the lower denomination. This is not a numismatic type of alteration, but is used to deceive persons handling large quantities of money.

bank teller stamps: Tellers in banks and other persons who handle large sums of money often stamp the band surrounding a stack with an inked seal of some sort. The stamp often has a date or other numbers on it. If the stamp is placed over the edge of the band onto the top note, untrained persons may believe the ink appearing on the note is a part of the original printing.

erased ink: The ink used in printing U.S. paper money is erasable like any other ink on paper. Note alterers can use a soft eraser or an electric eraser to remove any portion of the face or back design, or the overprint. Erasers wielded skillfully can recreate missing overprints, board breaks, notes printed through scrap and related printing errors. However, use of an eraser generally damages the fibers of the paper beneath the erased ink. Close examination, particularly through a magnifying glass or microscope, may reveal the broken fibers.

fake double denomination: The ability to recreate the ultimate in errors offers a note alterer potentially high profits. A Coin World staff member once saw a purported large-sized double denomination error that appeared to have been faked. Someone took two notes and "peeled" away one side of each. The two notes were then joined together to create the double denomination fake. The note was in Poor condition, and the joint between the halves was visible along the edges, which were in a flaked condition.

political messages: Paper money is an excellent medium to spread political messages among the public. The most popular message seems to be a rubber stamp inked onto a note, reading "This note is not legal tender." This stamp is probably used by individuals who believe paper money unbacked by gold or silver is illegal, and who advocate a return to specie currency. Other political messages have been seen as well.

VIP photographs: Novelty notes with the photograph of a Hollywood celebrity, entertainer, politician or other "newsworthy" person pasted over the center vignette are sold by a number of firms. The BEP has never issued a note bearing a portrait of King Kong, or even Elvis Presley.

water-wipe ink fading: The BEP began using water-wipe presses — using a caustic soda solution to clean excess ink from the plates instead of dry paper — in the early 1980s. To do so, the Bureau reformulated the ink to not break down under the solution. The formula was created, but BEP officials found that after the notes reached circulation, the ink on the back faded very quickly, particularly if the note became wet. It was necessary to again reformulate the ink, and the problem appears to have been corrected.

wrong-color backs: The green ink on the back of U.S. paper money is made of blue and yellow pigments. When exposed to an acidic atmosphere the yellow pigment is sometimes destroyed, leaving only the blue. When exposed to an alkali, such as the bleach in detergent when a note is washed, the blue pigment may be destroyed, leaving the yellow pigment. Blue back and yellow back notes deceive many non-collectors who find it difficult to believe that one of the pigments can disappear and leave the design and paper unaffected. The back design remains the same, but is in either blue or yellow ink. The yellow back notes should not be confused with gold certificates, which normally have a yellow-gold back.

Counterfeit coins

Counterfeit coins exist. That simple truth may be as frightening to a professional numismatist as to a neophyte collector, for any counterfeit coin is potentially deceptive. A hobbyist's best defense against counterfeit coins is knowledge — about the coining process and about counterfeits. It helps also to have a dealer who is both trustworthy and knowledgeable about counterfeit coins.

There are two basic types of counterfeit coins. One is produced to deceive the public by passing in circulation as genuine. Counterfeits of this type have plagued coiners since the first coins were produced. The second category of counterfeit is the type meant as a fraudulent numismatic item, designed to deceive the unwary collector, dealer or numismatist for illicit monetary gain.

The best way to learn about counterfeit coins is to examine them and compare the frauds to genuine coins of the same type and date in order to learn about the characteristics of both. Since possession of counterfeit coins is illegal in the United States, few collectors have opportunities to examine the fakes. However, the American Numismatic Association sponsors an annual week-long course in counterfeit detection at its Summer Seminar, held in Colorado Springs, Colo. The ANA Certification Service maintains a counterfeit coin reference collection which federal officials have generally ignored, since the fakes are used as an educational tool. Students attending the course (which is taught in beginning and advance levels) have the opportunity to examine counterfeit coins (and their first cousins, altered coins) through microscopes. Genuine coins are used for comparison purposes. The cost of the course is cheap when compared to the cost of a counterfeit coin. Details about future Summer Seminars are available by writing to the ANA at 818 N. Cascade Ave., Colorado Springs, Colo. 80903. The ANA also sells several books about counterfeit coins, compiled from illustrated articles written by the ANACS staff.

If you are uncertain about the authenticity of any numismatic item, do not buy it. If the dealer refuses to send the coin to an authentication service such as ANACS or the International Numismatic Society Authentication Bureau, be wary of buying the coin. You may, however, have to pay the authentication fee; such an "insurance policy" is well worth the nominal cost, especially for a coin valued at hundreds or even thousands of dollars.

Some counterfeits are very deceptive. During the last 10 years, for example, a fairly rare coin was sold in several auctions by reputable companies and purchased by knowledgeable dealers and collectors. The coin turned out to be a counterfeit of such exceptional quality that many persons were fooled. As is standard in such practices, the money paid for the coin was refunded down the line, with each company and individual returning the money that had been paid for the coin.

The following information focuses on the numismatic counterfeit. No one article can teach everything there is to know about counterfeit coins, especially when unaccompanied by photographs. However, the information in this article provides the collector with some basic knowledge.

Replicas

The replica is a form of counterfeit generally not intentionally deceptive, but potentially so. Most replicas are not illegal, although the passage of the Hobby Protection Act of 1973 regulates modern replicas in the United States.

A replica is generally a cast duplicate of an obsolete coin, token or medal that originally had been produced by private individuals or companies. Replicas are intended as inexpensive souvenirs; rarely is the original intention deceptive in nature. Almost every Colonial and state coin or token illustrated in the front section of *A Guide Book of United States Coins* has been produced in replica form, legally. Some even have the word "COPY" — which is now required by the Hobby Protection Act — "replica" or some abbreviation of either word stamped into or cast onto the coin, often on the edge. The problem arises when "COPY" or "replica" is filed from the surface of a replica.

Some points to look for:

Most replicas are cast, so there is probably a thin line of metal along the center of the edge. The thin line is left by the joint between the two molds in which the molten metal is poured into during the casting process. The joint line, however, can be filed away.

The casting process usually leaves a rough, textured or porous surface.

Cast counterfeits are produced by the same methods and have the same characteristics as cast replicas. However, the cast counterfeits are produced to deceive a buyer into thinking he is purchasing a genuine numismatic item.

Electrotypes

An electrotype is a type of counterfeit so popular in the 19th century that even employees of the United States Mint produced them for sale to willing collectors who knew what they were buying. An electrotype is an inexpensive copy of what is generally a rare, expensive coin unavailable to most collectors.

Electrotypes are two thin shells of metal bearing the image of a particular coin, wrapped around a non-precious metal planchet for inner strength. The shells are made by an electroplating process, in which a wax or plaster cast of the original coin is suspended in a solution of acidic copper sulfate along with a copper anode. A weak electric current is passed through the solution, causing small copper particles from the anode to adhere to the graphite-coated cast until a thin copper shell bearing the cast's image is formed.

An electrotype can be identified fairly easily by examining the edge for signs of where the two shells were joined or by weighing the item.

Electrotypes are considered collectible by many, particularly those produced by the U.S. Mint employees in the mid-19th century. However, production of new electrotypes is frowned upon by modern collectors and dealers.

Die-struck counterfeits

There are a number of advantages to a counterfeiter in employing fake dies. The most obvious, of course, is that counterfeit dies allow an almost exact duplication of Mint production methods, making their detection more difficult.

Also the use of counterfeit dies allows the counterfeiter a much greater latitude in his efforts. Not only can he reproduce a greater number of identical coins, he can also duplicate the rarer coins without actually being in possession of one. He can create mules at will. And error coins such as off-center strikes, rotated reverses, multiple strikes, clipped planchets, thick and thin planchets, railroad rims or partial collars and many others can be created by duplicating the very Mint procedures, or Mint equipment malfunctions, that would cause those errors inside the Mint itself.

Though the physical characteristics, and even the edges, will often faithfully reproduce the characteristics of a genuine coin, the design details and field will often reveal the origin. Logically, then, in order to detect this type of counterfeit, you must know, at the very least, the rudiments of making the fake dies.

Machine-engraved dies are often made by use of machines similar, if not identical, to the Contamin portrait lathes and the Janvier reducing machines used in most Mints.

A tracing tool follows the contours of the coin as the coin rotates about its axis. The tracing tool, through linkages, duplicates the movements of the tracing point with a cutting tool on a soft steel blank. As long as the rotation of the coin and blank remain constant — this being a one-to-one transfer step — the design being reproduced will be identical to the original. However, should the relationship change, the design details will be different. They may be wider or narrower than the original.

After the reproduction is finished the field will consist of circular rings left by the cutting tool. The counterfeiter must polish out those rings, leading to the possibility of also removing parts of the design. On the other hand, if he doesn't do the job well enough, some of those marks may still remain on the die. So, if you spot a coin that has more or less concentric rings on its surface, you would be justified in thinking that it is a product of machine-engraved dies.

Dies can also be made by impacting the coin into a soft steel blank by use of an explosive charge, a heavy press, or any other means that will impart a sudden, tremendous pressure. Impact dies can have many obvious imperfections. Large coins do not impact evenly across their surface. The impact tends to spread the coin, especially silver and copper coins which are relatively soft. This spreading results

in design details that are broader than normal and, quite often, slightly doubled near the edges. Attempts to touch up the dies can be made but careful inspection will usually reveal, not only the remaining defects, but the attempt to correct those defects. Quite often the first clue to an impact die is the fact that the design details are sharper near the center than at the edges.

Students of U.S. coinage have studied the rarer coins extensively. For example, specialists have identified the dies used to strike the 1909-S Lincoln, VDB cent, a classic scarce coin. By carefully examining thousands of coins, specialists know the proper shape of the "S" Mint mark and the letter "B" in the VDB initials. Die gouges and scratches appearing on most examples of certain rare coins have been documented and cataloged. The ANA Summer Seminar courses in counterfeit detection include discussions of these die "signatures" for many rare and scarce numismatic items. One *Coin World* staff member who attended such a course finds his notes invaluable. The ANA, as noted, sells two books which include dozens of articles and hundreds of photographs of die characteristics of genuine and counterfeit coins.

Altered coins

An altered coin is a genuine coin which has had some element changed so that it resembles a rare and thus more expensive variety.

The methods of alteration are many. Thousands of 1943 Lincoln cents, produced on a steel planchet to conserve copper for the war effort, have been plated with copper to resemble the very rare 1943 bronze cent. The third digit on some 1903 Liberty Head 5-cent coins has been changed into a 1 to resemble the 1913 Liberty Head 5-cent coin, a classic rarity. Mint marks have been added to many 1909 Lincoln, VDB cents to resemble the coin's rarer San Francisco counterpart. Mint marks have been removed from many branch Mint 1895 Morgan silver dollars to "create" the scarce Philadelphia Mint version. The list is long.

Some forms of alteration are discussed elsewhere is this chapter.

Like with counterfeit coins, it helps to know about the coin-production process and the characteristics of genuine coins to fight the menace of altered coins. Know what you are buying, or else find a trustworthy and knowledgeable dealer. Otherwise, a "great buy" may turn out to be nothing of the sort.

Collectors' Clearinghouse

One of the longest running regular features of Coin World is its weekly Collectors' Clearinghouse page, devoted mainly to reports of newly discovered error and variety coinage. The Collectors' Clearinghouse department was founded in 1960, shortly after publication of Coin World began. Its first editor, James G. Johnson, served in that capacity for nearly 15 years.

The Collectors' Clearinghouse staff through the years has answered tens of thousands of letters regarding error coins and paper money, varieties, normal coins and notes, and exonumia. Some of the more interesting finds are illustrated and discussed in the weekly full-page column, which, with the letters to the editor column and U.S. coin "Trends," represents one of the most popular features of the newspaper.

Readers may send coins and notes to the Collectors' Clearinghouse for examination and an explanation, whether errors or not. Collectors are asked not to send more than three or four items per letter unless given specific permission to send larger packages of material. If the reader wishes to have his material returned by insured or registered mail, he should send sufficient return postage. Readers not sending material and requesting information only are asked to include a large, self-addressed, stamped envelope. All inquiries should be addressed to Collectors' Clearinghouse, Coin World, P.O. Box 150, Sidney, Ohio 45365.

A Numismatic Chronology

12

A numismatic chronology

The purpose of this chronology is to present in a simple and easy-to-scan form the bare outlines of world numismatics, with special emphasis on the period of history which has seen Christian-dated coins.

Every region of the globe is represented, with a view to presenting those facts that might have seemed noteworthy to the average coin user in a given time and country. The facts presented are of general interest and illustrative of each coin-issuing authority's history.

United States of America

BRITISH COLONIES IN AMERICA

1652 Nominal date on "NE," New England, Willow, Oak and Pine Tree coinage of Massachusetts.

1658 Proprietary coinage of Lord Baltimore in Maryland colony.

1688 Tin 1/24 part real, so-called "Florida token" in the southern colonies.

1722 Rosa Americana copper coinage under George I.

1774 Regal copper half pennies in Virginia, George III.

UNITED STATES

1782 Resolution by Congress that favors establishment of a Mint. Feb. 21, 1782, Committee submits report, "Resolved, that Congress approve of the establishment of a Mint; and, that the superintendent of Finance, be, and hereby is directed to prepare and report to Congress a plan for establishing and conducting the same."

1785 July 6, "Resolved, that the money unit of the United States of America be one dollar. Resolved, that the smallest coin be a copper, of which 200 shall pass for one dollar."

1786 October, "It is hereby ordained by the United States in Congress assembled, that a Mint be established for the coinage of gold, silver and copper money."

1787 Fugio cents struck, first coins authorized by the United States.

1792 Act of Congress to establish Mint, April 2. Same act authorizes eagle, half eagle, quarter eagle, silver dollar, half dollar, quarter dollar, 10 cents, 5 cents, cent, half cent. David Rittenhouse appointed Director of the Mint.

U.S. Mint building erected, first U.S. government structure. Half dimes are first coin struck under Constitution. First metal purchased by Mint for coinage purposes — six pounds of copper.

1793 Cents and half cents struck for first time for general circulation. Albion Cox appointed as first assayer. Joseph Wright named first Mint engraver, Henry Voigt first chief coiner.

1794 Silver dollars, half dollars and half dimes struck for circulation.

1795 Gold half eagles and eagles struck for first time. Mint comes under Department of Treasury instead of Department of State. E PLURIBUS UNUM used on U.S. coins.

1796 Quarter eagles, quarter dollars and dimes struck for first time for circulation.

1804 First U.S. virgin gold received at Mint, valued at $11,000, from Cabarrus County, North Carolina.

1816 Steam engine installed at Philadelphia Mint.

1817 Proof coins struck at U.S. Mint.

1829 July 4, cornerstone laid for Mint at corner of Chestnut and Juniper streets, Philadelphia.

1835 Act of March 3 establishes Mints in New Orleans, La.; Dahlonega, Ga.; and Charlotte, N.C.

1836 Steam coinage presses introduced in U.S. Mint.

1837 Charlotte, N.C., Mint opened, John H. Wheeler superintendent. Seated Liberty dimes and half dimes issued from Philadelphia.

1838 Branch Mints open in New Orleans and Dahlonega, Ga. U.S. Mint establishes "Cabinet of Coins."

1848 Gold discovered in California; California gold deposited at Mint.

1849 First gold dollars for circulation minted. Gold dollar and double eagle authorized by Act of Congress March 3.

1850 Gold double eagle of this year first to bear initials of designer. First double eagles released for circulation.

1851 Silver 3-cent piece released; first coin with limited legal tender value. Three-cent silver coin of this year lowest silver content of U.S. coin to date — .750 fine. Authorized March 3.

1852 Act of Congress, July 3, establishes San Francisco Mint.

1853 Reduced weight silver coins issued. $3 gold coin authorized Feb. 21. Act of Congress authorizes assay office in New York.

1854 First coins issued by San Francisco Mint. First $3 gold coins minted. Three-cent silver coins, .900 fine, issued. New York Assay Office established at 30-32 Wall St.

1857 Flying Eagle cents issued, first of small diameter cents. It was authorized Feb. 21; 12 percent nickel, issued 1857-1858. Foreign coins demonetized.

1858 American Numismatic Society formed. Numismatic and Antiquarian Society of Philadelphia organized. Proof sets offered.

1859 Longacre's Indian Head cent introduced.

1861 Demand notes, authorized July 17 and Aug. 5. Specie payments suspended Dec. 21.

1862 Government issues legal tender notes beginning March 10. Denver Mint established April 21; superintendent appointed; Mint serves as assay office until 1906, when coins first issued. Postage currency commences July 17.

1863 National bank notes authorized; gold certificates first authorized. First deposit of gold at Denver Mint Sept. 24; George W. Lane first assayer-in-charge until July 1, 1867. Fractional currency authorized March 3. Large private outpouring of tokens to relieve coin shortage.

1864 Motto IN GOD WE TRUST appears on coins for first time, on the 2-cent piece authorized April 22. Cent first of that denomination to bear initials of designer. Bronze cents authorized; private tokens banned.

1865 Copper-nickel 3-cent piece authorized April 3.

1866 Motto IN GOD WE TRUST appears on regular silver coin for first time. Abe Curry first superintendent of Carson City Mint. Shield 5-cent pieces first copper-nickel 5-cent coins, struck May 16.

1867 Carson City Mint erected. Sandstone used from Nevada State Prison quarry. Cost, $300,000.

1869 Carson City Mint opens July 1.

1870 Carson City Mint issues coins. Act of Congress establishes Boise City, Idaho, assay office.

1873 Mint made a bureau of Treasury Department. E PLURIBUS UNUM and IN GOD WE TRUST prescribed for coinage by statute. Director of the Mint located in Washington, D.C. James Pollock first Superintendent of the Mint. Trade dollars issued, authorized Feb. 12. Standard silver dollar discontinued, bimetallism effectively ended.

1874 Assay office in Helena, Mont., approved by Congress May 12. Cornerstone laid Oct. 1.

1875 20-cent coins issued. Authorized March 3. Resumption Act of Jan. 14 provides for immediate retirement of fractional currency with subsidiary silver and redemption of greenbacks on and after Jan. 1, 1879.

1878 Large-size silver certificates authorized Feb. 28.

1879 Specie payments resumed Jan. 1; greenbacks and gold at par.

1882 Assay office opens Jan. 3 at St. Louis.

1887 Trade dollar demonetized.

1888 The Numismatist first issued; Dr. George F. Heath editor.

1891 American Numismatic Association organized.

1892 First commemorative coin is Columbian half dollar.

1897 Feb. 19 act provides for assay office in Deadwood, S.D.

1898 April 20: Assay office opened, Deadwood, S.D. Assay Office opened in Seattle, Wash., on July 15; F.A. Wing assayer in charge.

1899 George Washington portrayed for first time on U.S. coin, on Lafayette dollar (with date of 1900). 1900 June 1, enactment of legislation for the mintage of commemorative coins. U.S. goes off bimetallism standard.

1903 Commemorative gold coins, Louisiana Purchase Exposition dollars, struck.

1906 First coins from Denver Mint.

1907 Saint-Gaudens eagles and double eagles first struck.

1908 First minor coinage at a branch Mint.

1909 Portrait of actual person, Lincoln, on first coin for general circulation. First cent to have mottoes IN GOD WE TRUST and E PLURIBUS UNUM.

1912 American Numismatic Association chartered by Congress.

1913 Federal Reserve Act becomes law, authorizes issuance of Federal Reserve notes. Indian Head 5-cent piece minted.

1915 Panama-Pacific coins first commemoratives to carry the mottoes IN GOD WE TRUST and E PLURIBUS UNUM.

1921 Coins and medals under jurisdiction of Commission of Fine Arts. Thomas E. Kilby portrayed on Alabama Centennial half dollar, first living person identified on a coin of the U.S. Peace silver dollar designed by Anthony De Francisci. Coins were first struck in December and released to circulation Jan. 3, 1922.

1924 Julius Guttag starts National Coin Week.

1929 First small-size paper money issued.

1932 George Washington portrayed on U.S. coins of regular issue for first time, quarters.

1933 Act issued prohibiting minting of gold coins; Treasury calls in all gold.

1938 First coin from large-scale design competition, Jefferson 5-cent piece.

1942 Mint mark P designated Philadelphia for first time, 5-cent pieces.

1943 Zinc-coated steel cents issued.

1946 Roosevelt dime issued.

1948 Franklin-Liberty Bell half dollar issued.

1955 IN GOD WE TRUST made mandatory on all U.S. coins and paper money.

1961 Office of Domestic Gold and Silver Operations created; Leland Howard first director.

1962 Tin removed from 1-cent piece.

1963 Kennedy half dollars authorized.

1964 Date 1964 frozen on coinage. Kennedy half dollars struck.

1965 Coinage Act of 1965: copper-nickel cladding on dimes and quarters replaces silver; half dollar clad in reduced silver content alloy. Joint Commission on Coinage established.

1966 Initials of Felix Schlag placed on Jefferson 5-cent piece.

1967 $2 note discontinued by Treasury.

1968 U.S. Proof coins resumed. Silver certificates cease to be redeemed for silver, General Services Administration begins selling silver on the market. Gold backing removed from paper money.

1969 New Philadelphia Mint dedicated. Mary T. Brooks becomes Director of the Mint.

1970 Federal appellate court rules United States is legally warranted to inscribe its coins and currency with IN GOD WE TRUST. GSA conducts silver sale. Eisenhower dollar legislation becomes law.

1971 Mint begins production of silverless Kennedy half dollars, in Denver. First Eisenhower dollar struck March 31. Technicians install new Currency Overprinting and Processing Equipment (COPE) at the Bureau of Engraving and Printing. First dollar devaluation.

1972 President approves transfer of old San Francisco Mint building to Treasury for restoration as Mint working facility and museum. ANA's Certification Service opens in Washington with Charles Hoskins as director.

1973 Second dollar devaluation. President Nixon signs bill providing for Bicentennial coinage, Oct. 31, with manufacture to begin in 1975. Hobby Protection Act becomes law Dec. 12.

1974 President Ford signs bill ending ban on U.S. citizens' ownership of gold, as of Dec. 31, 1974.

1975 First of the nation's Bicentennial coins roll off the presses in the Mints, both copper-nickel clad copper and 40 percent silver, Uncirculated and Proof.

1976 After extended hearings, reports and studies, the $2 bill returns, bearing Trumbull's "Signing of the Declaration of Independence" on the reverse.

1977 Pre-Bicentennial designs resumed. Citizen-members barred from U.S. Assay Commission. Stella Hackel named Director of the Mint.

1979 First Susan B. Anthony dollars issued for circulation.

1980 Mint accepts orders for American Arts Gold Medallions, first gold struck by the Mint in almost half a century.

1981 Section 314-b of the Economic Recovery Act restricts use of collectibles in IRA and Keogh retirement plans.

1982 Mint strikes silver commemorative half dollar marking the 250th anniversary of George Washington's birth, first commemorative coin struck since 1954. Copper-plated zinc cents introduced.

1983 U.S. Mint begins striking 1983 and 1984 Olympic commemorative coinage, and decides to use a W Mint mark on the 1984 gold eagle produced at West Point. Discovery of 1982 No P dime focuses public attention on hobby.

1984 Mint releases 1984 Olympic $10 eagle, first U.S. gold coin struck since 1933. Public attention focuses on hobby as media reports discovery of 1983 Doubled Die cent. U.S. Mint resumes sales of Uncirculated sets.

1985 President Reagan signs an executive order banning the importation of South African Krugerrands effective Oct. 11. A pre-issue discount offering by the U.S. Mint in December results in complete sell-out of the 1986-dated Statue of Liberty gold half eagle commemorative coins. U.S. Mint offers 1986 Ellis Island silver dollar and Immigrant copper-nickel

half dollar at pre-issue discount prices.

1986 American Eagle gold bullion coins, the first non-commemorative gold coins struck for U.S. consumption since 1933, issued in October, followed by the release in November of the American Eagle silver bullion dollar. Sales of Statue of Liberty commemorative coins result in record surcharges being delivered to the Statue of Liberty restoration project. Treasury officials approve the first major changes to U.S. paper money in decades with the decision to incorporate anti-counterfeiting devices on all Federal Reserve notes in early 1987. Fort Worth, Texas, is selected as the site for the Bureau of Engraving and Printing's Western printing plant, which will give the federal government two currency producing plants for the first time in the BEP's 125-year history.

1987 U.S. Mint reports strong sales of Uncirculated souvenir sets in light of plans not to issue the Kennedy half dollar for circulation. Sales of the American Eagle bullion silver dollars more than triple original estimates predicted by U.S. Mint officials during its first year.

1988 The U.S. Department of the Treasury and the Federal Reserve announce plans to upgrade counterfeiting deterrents in United States paper money. Final sales of 1986 Proof sets and Uncirculated Mint sets are the lowest since the advent of copper-nickel clad coinage in 1965. The United States Secret Service investigates the disappearance of 24 obverse dies for the 1988 American Eagle 1-ounce bullion coins.

1989 Three United States Proof error coins to be offered at auction are seized by the United States Mint and turned over to the U.S. Secret Service for an investigation after the Mint technicians determined them to be illegitimate error coins and thus U.S. Mint property. The Secret Service makes its largest seizure of counterfeit United States Federal Reserve notes produced on a color laser photocopier. Coinage production at the San Francisco Mint is halted for more than 24 hours following the Oct. 17 earthquake.

1990 The United States of America formally accepts its satellite Bureau of Engraving and Printing facility in ceremonies at Fort Worth, Texas. A 152-year tradition in die production is coming to an end as the United States Mint plans to eliminate the practice of placing mint marks on each individual working die by hand over the next several years; Mint marks will be added at the master die stage.

(Note: See Chapter 1 for a more detailed chronology of 1987-1990)

Canada

1670 First regal French silver, 5, 15 sols "Gloriam regni tui dicenti" coinage of Louis XIV, copper 2 deniers.

1717 Copper 6, 12 deniers, Louis XV.

1721-22 Copper 9 deniers colonial coinage.

1728 Billon marque, half marque enter circulation.

1813 "Holey dollar," cut and counterstamped Spanish dollars issued by the governor of Prince Edward Island.

1815 Magdalen Island token penny of Sir Isaac

Coffin.

1823 Nova Scotia copper half-penny token introduces types issued through 1840.

1837-52 Bank and bouquet copper token coinages, Upper Canada, Quebec.

1843 New Brunswick tokens.

1856 Arbutus copper Nova Scotia tokens of Victoria.

1858 Silver 5, 10, 20 cents, bronze cent, Canada, young head of Victoria.

1861 Decimal bronze cent, half cent, New Brunswick.

1862 Silver 5, 10, 20 cents, New Brunswick; gold 10, 20 dollars, British Columbia.
1865 Bronze cent, silver 5, 10, 20 cents, gold 2 dollars, Newfoundland.
1870 New Confederation silver coinage of Canada.
1871 Prince Edward Island bronze cent, English inscription obverse.
1876 Large bronze cent introduced of Canadian Confederation type.
1911 Pattern dollar for Canada, George V, "Dei gratia" omitted on first coins of this reign.
1912 Normal inscriptions resumed, new gold 5 and 10 dollar Canadian coins join sovereigns of British type, minted 1908-1919-C.
1920 Small bronze cent replaces older large cent.
1922 Pure nickel round 5 cents replaces small silver 5 cents.
1935 Silver Jubilee of the reign of King George V sees silver dollar finally introduced, and begins ongoing series of commemorative coins for Canada.
1937 New coins of George VI, first wholly redesigned reverses.
1938 Small bronze cent introduced in Newfoundland.
1942 Tombac brass replaces nickel in Canadian 5 cents, coin struck on a 12-sided planchet.
1943 Canada first to issue coinage with international telegraphic code reverse dots and dashes, "We win when we work willingly" around edge of tombac "Victory" 5 cents.
1944 Chrome-plated steel 5 cents, victory reverse.
1946 Nickel 5 cents resumed, 12-sided.
1947 Last Newfoundland coins.
1951 First commemorative in 5-cent denomination marks anniversary of the isolation of nickel as a recognized element.
1967 Centenary of Confederation, completely redesigned coinage, bronze 1 cent through gold 20 dollars.
1968 Pure nickel replaces silver in Canadian coinage, 50 cents and the 1 dollar coins are reduced in size as well.
1971 British Columbia centenary sees re-introduction of large-size silver dollar, along with regular

issue small pure nickel dollar.
1973 Montreal Mayor Drapeau and the Canadian government begin the issue of the first silver $5 and $10 Olympic coins, to be followed by six more four-coin sets for worldwide distribution, to aid in financing the XXI Olympiad held in 1976 in this city.
1976 Joining the 28 silver $5 and $10 Olympic coins are two new gold $100 pieces, struck in .5833 fine for sale as Unc.; .9166 fine in Proof. Measuring 27 and 25 millimeters respectively, the gold coins are offered at a premium over face.
1977 Silver Jubilee silver dollar, gold $100 of Elizabeth II. New, reduced diameter bronze 1-cent piece announced by Royal Canadian Mint. The 16.05mm new cent will be smaller than the existing 10-cent piece.
1979 Smaller bust of Queen Elizabeth II adopted on 1 cent. International trade coin, 31.1 gram, .999 fine gold, 1 ounce Maple Leaf coin issued for first time.
1980 1-cent coin reduced in weight.
1981 Mint begins manufacture of seven-piece Proof sets.
1982 Cent depicts smaller bust and becomes 12-sided coin. 5 cents changed to copper-nickel composition. Paper money adopts raised-print Braille for the blind.
1984 Canadian flax content in paper money replaced with U.S. cotton.
1985 Calgary Winter Olympic coin series unveiled.
1986 Royal Canadian Mint introduces half-ounce Maple Leaf. Maurice Lafontaine succeeds James Corkery as Mint master.
1987 Smaller size dollar coin struck to replace dollar bill. The mysterious disappearance of a pair of master dies for Canada's new smaller Voyageur aureate-nickel dollar forces the Canadian Parliament to approve a new reverse design depicting a common loon
1988 Royal Canadian Mint officials label as counterfeit a 1981 coin struck from the muled dies of a $100 gold coin and 50-cent coins.

Mexico

1521 Following Cortez' capture of Tenochtitlan, now Mexico City, the territory was organized as a Spanish possession. The Aztec Indians were found using cacao bean and beaten copper "hoe money" in daily commerce.
1536 The Mexico City Mint, oldest in the New World, begins coinage of silver in quarter and half reales, 1-, 2-, 3- and 4-real denominations. An issue of copper 2 and 4 maravedis was an unsuccessful experiment, which saw hundreds of the coins thrown in Lake Texcoco.
1556 The reign of King Philip II saw the introduction of the 8-real crown, to be struck in various designs through 1897, becoming a world coin of international circulation and universally admired reliability. The silver coins became known as "cobs," from a Spanish expression "cabo de barra," cut from a bar; their weight was all-important, the actual shape of any one coin a matter of indifference.
1665 Gold coinage began in Mexico during Charles II's reign.
1732 Fully round coins struck within a collar. These are known to Spanish collectors as "dos mundos," or two worlds type from the crowned hemispheres on the reverse; English-speaking

collectors know them as the "Pillar dollar, ancestor of the U.S. dollar.
1772 Portrait 8 reales struck for King Charles III.
1808 Following Ferdinand VII's ouster by Napoleon's brother Joseph, Mexican loyalists, as will be done throughout the Spanish empire, rally to Ferdinand and begin striking coins with his portrait at Mexico and a dozen new Mints.
1811 The revolt of Father Morelos sees a variety of cast and struck crude emergency coins, beginning a complex era of loyalist and revolutionary coinages.
1814 Copper coins in denominations of , quarter and half real struck, to replace private tokens and provide small change.
1822 Following the independence of Mexico under liberator Augustin de Iturbide, imperial coinage began in Augustin's new Mexican empire, bearing the eagle of Aztec legend, seated on a nopal cactus.
1823 Following the overthrow of the empire, a republic was proclaimed, the beginning of a century of turbulence, misrule and civil struggle. A profile hook-necked eagle killing a serpent replaces Iturbide's crowned eagle on the 8-reales piece.

1824-97 Coinage of uniform "Liberty Cap" 8-reales pesos and minor silver.

1829 Copper national coinage in and quarter real denominations. Copper issues of individual states had begun in 1824.

1841 The first pattern decimal 1-centavo piece struck but not adopted.

1863 San Luis Potosi strikes silver decimal 5- and 10-centavo coins.

1864 The Congress of Notables invites Archduke Maximilian of Austria to ascend the throne of a second Mexican empire during the French intervention of Napoleon III. A decimal centavo in copper was issued by the imperial government.

1866-67 Imperial silver coinage of 5, 10 and 50 centavos struck in 1866, the handsome Maximilian peso in 1866 and 1867. The emperor was captured and ordered shot by President Benito Juarez.

1869 A republican copper centavo placed in circulation, although the silver coins were still being struck in real denominations.

1869-73 "Balance type" coin with value expressed as 1 peso; some decimal minor coins as well.

1870 Balance type gold coinage, 1 peso through 20 pesos.

1882 Copper-nickel briefly introduced in 1-, 2- and 5-centavos denominations.

1898 8 reales finally abandoned in favor of a new Liberty Cap peso.

1899 A new small size bronze centavo.

1905 A major monetary reform adopts the gold standard and introduces a new coinage in bronze, silver and gold, bearing a facing eagle and inscription ESTADOS UNIDOS MEXICANOS.

1910 Last of the large size pesos, called the "Caballito" from the equestrian liberty on the obverse introduced.

1918 Size of the peso, weight and fineness reduced. New issue is .800 fine, succeeded by a similar coin of .720 fineness in 1920. This was the start of a gradual disappearance of silver in the coinage in this and other denominations.

1936 Copper-nickel 5 and 10 centavos issued.

1942 Portrait and other scenic views placed on 5 and 20 centavos, beginning a trend toward greater variety of design for all coins.

1947 Morelos peso issued, .500 fine. The succeeding pesos drop to .100 fine by 1957.

1950 A commemorative 5 pesos marking the completion of the southeastern railway continues a modern commemorative series (that began in 1921) which still continues. The sizes of all coins are now reduced, .300 fine 25 and 50 centavos, 1 peso struck.

1954-55 Brass and bronze 5-, 10-, 20- and 50-centavo minor coins join the already brass 1 centavo in circulation; 5 pesos silver coin, .720, and 10 pesos, .900 fine, make their debut.

1964 Copper-nickel, smaller 25 centavos and 50 centavos replace bronze pieces.

1968 A silver 25-pesos introduced, .720 fine.

1970 Bronze coinage reduced further in size; copper-nickel adopted for the 1 peso, with a new copper-nickel 5 pesos planned for 1971. All reverses redesigned to bear an outline-form archaic Aztec treatment of the profile Mexican eagle.

1974 New small-size copper-nickel 20 centavos portrays revolutionary leader Madero, continuing trend toward smaller and smaller coins.

1976 Plans are announced for a .720 fine silver 100 pesos, designed to stimulate the silver mining industry.

1977 Numismatic excitement high as tiny copper-nickel 10 centavos dated 1974, 1975 and 1976 are released; seven-sided copper-nickel 10 pesos appear dated 1974, 1975 and 1976; 1977-dated silver 100 pesos are struck and released.

1980 Design of Aztec dragon adopted for 5-peso coin reverse. Copper-nickel composition commences for 20-peso production.

1981 Gold bullion coins of quarter, half, and 1 ounce pure gold, .900 fine, issued as international trade coins.

1982 Devaluation of peso to 50, then 100 to one U.S. dollar takes place due to high inflation. 50-peso coins issued in copper-nickel.

1983 Design of Almec culture adopted on new bronze 20-centavos coin. Design of Palenque adopted on reverse of new steel 50 centavos.

1984 Libertad of .999 fine silver dated 1982 released, replacing .925 fine silver Onza trade coin.

1985 Mexico Mint becomes an autonomous institution.

1987 500-peso coin replaces note in circulation.

1987 Introduces platinum Onza bullion coins.

1989 Issues inflationary 50,000-peso note.

Central America

BRITISH HONDURAS (Belize)

1864 Decimal system adopted.

1871 Private quarter-real tokens issued by importer John Jex.

1885 Copper cents introduce a new decimal colonial coinage, the first in this hemisphere south of Canada in the British colonial holdings.

1894 Silver coinage, 5 cents to 50 cents begun.

1914 Medium size bronze cent appears.

1946 Last silver coinage of British Honduras.

1954 Cent further reduced, scalloped edge after 1956.

1973 Premier George Price engineers sudden name change of the colony to Belize after the former capital, traditional coin designs modified to reflect the change.

1974 New coinage, first change in designs since 1894 announced, name of the colony, under internal self-government, changed to Belize. Franklin Mint strikes all-new series featuring birds of Belize, denominations expressed in words. Traditional designs with royal portrait continued after loyalist protest over new bird coin designs. One-, 5- and 10-dollar coins in bird series.

1975 Bird series continued with numerical values on reverse, royal types to continue as well.

1978 First 25 dollars of silver and of copper-nickel, and 250-dollar gold produced.

1981 World Food Day coins issued, part of international series.

1990 $1 coin replaces note in circulation.

COSTA RICA

1831 Central American type coins struck, "CR" Mint mark.

1841 Star countermark applied to foreign coins in
circulation.
1845 Woman's head and tree reverse countermarks
on old Spanish 2 reales.
1846 One-real and 2-real dies used to validate
colonial cob coins still in active circulation.
1850 Decimal silver, expressed in fractions to agree
with old real coinage value.
1865 Decimal copper-nickel and silver coins.
1896 New currency unit, the colon of 100 centimos.
1935 Issues of the Banco Internacional in copper-
nickel.
1937 Banco Nacional.
1954 Banco Central stainless steel coinage, first in the
hemisphere.
1974 Gold, silver Conservation coinage released.
1975 Pure nickel 5, 10 and 20 colones, first circulating
commemoratives.
1979 Five centimos changes to brass composition.
1982 Aluminum adopted as new composition for 10
and 25 centimos; stainless steel for the 50
centimos and 1 and 2 colon.

EL SALVADOR

1828 Provisional coins and countermarked issues.
1889 Copper-nickel 1 centavo with Morazon portrait.
1892 Decimal peso-centavo silver coinage.
1909 Short-lived quarter real copper struck and
quickly recalled.
1925 Commemorative silver and gold coins for the
fifth centenary of San Salvador in new unit, the
colon.
1943 Large silver 25 centavos struck during World War
II nickel shortage.
1953 Small size silver, 25 centavos equal a U.S. dime.
1970 Copper-nickel coins replace silver in circulation.
1974 Nickel-brass coinage includes 3-centavo coin
last issued in 1915.
1975 Nickel-clad steel introduced for 5, 10, 25
centavos.
1976 Brass 1 centavo produced.
1977 Copper-nickel 5, 10 and 50 centavos increased
to 2-millimeter coins from 1.65mm thickness.
1984 Copper-nickel 1 colon introduced as regular
issue coin.

GUATEMALA

1824 Guatemala Mint strikes coinage of Central
American Federation.
1829 Provisional coinage of 1 real, federation type
with STATE OF GUATEMALA.
1859 Beginning of President Rafael Carrera's
standardized real-peso coinage.
1869 Attempt at decimal peso of 100 centimos; 25
centimos struck, public reacts negatively.
1870 Decimal peso of 100 centavos decreed,
abandoned the following year.
1881 Another decimalization attempt, four
denominations struck, in copper and silver.
Copper centavo overstruck on the 1871 issue.
1912 Last national coinage in real denominations, a
copper-nickel coin first struck in 1900 as the
economy began floundering.
1915 Copper provisional coinage.
1923 Amid a collapse of the currency, aluminum
bronze 1 and 5 pesos issued.
1926 Thorough overhaul of the Guatemalan finances
sees introduction of the gold and silver quetzal
of 100 centavos.
1943 President Jorge Ubico causes an international

incident by issuing a new 25-centavo piece to
mark inauguration of the national palace, with
a map reverse showing British Honduras as a
part of Guatemala.
1965 Silver coinage replaced with copper-nickel-zinc.

HONDURAS

1823 Coins of Spanish royalist and Mexican imperial
type struck at Tegucigalpa Mint, presumably to
suit all factions.
1832 Provisional Central American type coinage in
base silver and copper.
1871 Republican silver decimal coinage.
1879-1920 Great coinage chaos, old dies of every
type used to strike copper centavo coins.
1931 New coinage of the lempira, equal to 100
centavos.
1967 Copper-nickel coinage replaces silver.

NICARAGUA

1825 Provisional silver of Central American Federation
type.
1878 First regular coinage, copper-nickel centavo.
1880 Silver decimal coins, 1 peso of 100 centavos.
1912 Overhaul of coinage introduces the silver
cordoba of 100 centavos, copper-nickel
coinage replaces silver in 1939.
1943 Brass shell case alloy replaces copper-nickel on
three denominations.
1965 Central Bank becomes bank of issue.
1967 Famed Nicaragua-born Spanish language poet
and writer Ruben Dario honored on gold 50-
cordoba coin.
1974 Aluminum 5 and 10 centavos in Food and
Agriculture Organization (FAO) series join the
range of coins in circulation.
1980 One-year issue of copper-nickel 5 cordobas.
1981 Participates in FAO international issues with 1, 10
and 25 centavos in aluminum.
1982 Nickel-clad steel 50 centavos replaces former
copper-nickel composition.
1990 Issues inflationary 100,000-cordoba note.

PANAMA

1904 First coinage, highlighted by tiny 2-1/2
centesimos and huge half balboa.
1930 Silver coins in U.S. sizes and weights.
1931 First silver balboa issued.
1966 Copper-nickel-clad copper coinage of U.S.
type replaces smaller silver coins in circulation.
1971 A new denomination, 20 balboas, issued in
silver, first as a commemorative for the 150th
anniversary of Central American
independence, then as what the government
of Panama has described as a regular issue.
1975 Franklin Mint strikes all-new portrait coinage
including a 5-balboa piece, 2-1/2 centesimos
"pill" in new designs.
1975 First gold coinage, struck by Franklin Mint.
1976 Franklin Mint produces platinum 150 balboas
with Bolivar head.
1979 Denomination of 200 balboas, 9.5 grams of .980
platinum, begins production.
1981 Denomination of 50 balboas of 5.37 grams of
.500 gold begins production.
1988 Economic crisis and cash shortage forces
circulation of earlier commemorative silver
coins.

South America
(Countries listed alphabetically)

ARGENTINA

1813 United Provinces of Rio de la Plata coinage with radiant sun, reales or soles.

1822 Province of Buenos Aires and other chaotic provincial coinages.

1838 Confederated Argentine Republic coins.

1881 Modern unified bronze, silver and gold coinage of the republic decreed.

1896 Copper-nickel coinage becomes general coin in circulation until 1942.

1952 Copper-nickel-clad steel, first in hemisphere.

1970 New coinage, 100 old pesos equal one new.

1974 Inflation's advance leads to reappearance of small size aluminum-bronze 1 peso.

1983 Aluminum adopted for 10- and 50-centavos coins.

1985 Introduces austral currency in an effort to stop inflation.

1986 Notgeld-type paper "provincial bonds" appear as small change in circulation.

1987 Retires peso bank notes, replaces them with austral denominations.

1989 Strike at Mint causes currency shortage.

1990 Issues inflationary 10,000-austral note.

BOLIVIA

1573 Potosi Mint established on the fabulous "hill of silver."

1841 Republican silver and gold silver soles; gold scudos.

1864 Decimal boliviano of 100 centavos.

1883 First copper-nickel 5, 10 centavos.

1893 Copper-nickel "caduceus" coins, a type in use through the 1940s.

1951 Bronze bolivianos.

1965 Copper and nickel-clad coinage.

1977 A 200 pesos bolivianos of 23.3 grams of .925 silver issued as part of the international issue for the "International Year of the Child."

1984 Inflationary 100,000-peso notes issued.

1987 Strikes first circulating coins since 1980.

BRAZIL

1822 Independent imperial coins of Dom Pedro I.

1831 Dom Pedro II, types of earlier reign.

1853 Modern imperial silver coinage.

1867-68 Portrait silver and copper introduced.

1871 Nickel minor coins introduced.

1889 Republic declared, monetary instability advances.

1900 400th anniversary commemoratives sets a trend. Huge 4,000 reis with the discoverer Pedro Alvares Cabral largest silver coin in hemisphere's history.

1922 First centenary of independence sees beginning of a distinguished series of national commemoratives, continuing through the next decade.

1942 President Getulio Vargas decrees new coinage, the cruzeiro of 100 centavos. Minor coins continue to bear his portrait; 1, 2 and 5 cruzeiros bear a remarkably detailed relief map of Brazil.

1956 Aluminum coins introduced as runaway inflation begins its inroads.

1967 After years of financial chaos, the military

government decrees a coinage reform, introducing the heavy cruzeiro, equal to 1,000 old cruzeiros. New coinage of stainless steel and pure nickel.

1972 Re-introduction of commemoratives in nickel, silver and gold to mark the 150th anniversary of Brazilian independence.

1975 Silver 10 cruzeiros marks anniversary of Central Bank, leads to accusations of favoritism in distribution and Mint director's ouster.

1980 Manufacture begins of stainless steel 5- and 10-cruzeiros coins.

1981 Manufacture begins of stainless steel 20 cruzeiros.

1986 Cruzado currency introduced in an attempt to slow inflation.

1989 Demonetizes cruzado coins and notes due to inflation.

BRITISH GUIANA

1809 Coins of George III, Dutch guilder unit.

1816 More finely struck guilder coinage.

1891 Silver 4 pence struck for "British Guiana - British West Indies"; the English type 4 pence had been in circulation as the equivalent of the quarter guilder during the reign of William IV and Victoria.

1967 Decimal coinage of 1 dollar divided into 100 cents, issued by the new Bank of Guyana."

1970 Copper-nickel dollar portrays slave insurrection leader Cuffy as Guyana joins FAO coin program.

1976 All new coinage portrays historical figures, wildlife of Guyana.

CHILE

1749 Santiago Mint created.

1817 "Chile Independiente" coinage of republic.

1851 Decimal peso of 100 centavos introduced.

1895 Condor standing on mountain peak coinage, designed by French engraver O. Roty; standard design of fluctuating fineness, weight and size through 1941.

1920 Subsidiary coinage in copper-nickel, retaining Roty design.

1942 Bronze peso and minor coins, O'Higgins portrait type.

1954 Aluminum coinage; inflation advances.

1960 New escudo of 100 centesimos, valued at 1,000 old pesos.

1971 Rapid inflation of the escudo after election of Marxist president Allende.

1975 New peso introduced valued at 1,000 escudos.

1978 New 1 peso and 50 centavos issued composed of aluminum-bronze.

COLOMBIA

1627 Santa Fe de Bogota Mint authorized, operated sporadically.

1729 Popayan Mint established, few coins initially struck.

1758 Popayan in regular production.

1811 Cartagena royal coinage.

1815 Independent coinage of Nueva Granada.

1820 Name Colombia on coins, soon replaced by combinations and variations on the old name Nueva Granada.

1862 United States of Colombia decimal coinage, copper, copper-nickel, silver and gold.
1886 Republic of Colombia established as the official title of the country.
1892 Columbus portrait 50 centavos for anniversary of New World's discovery.
1907 Copper-nickel "paper money" 1, 2 and 5 pesos introduced to withdraw depreciated paper currency.
1917 Centavo denominations replace the above coinage.
1930 Last regular gold coinage.
1953 Last regular silver coin, 20 centavos.
1968 First 20th century commemorative marks Eucharistic Congress.
1969 Nickel-clad steel coins introduced.
1978 New denomination, 2 peso, appears. Design changes on 100 and 500 peso oro bank notes.
1979 20-centavo coin the size of 25 centavos of the 1920s is released.
1980 Newly designed 5-, 500- and 750- peso coins are released.
1981 A 30,000-peso coin is issued.
1987 Issues inflationary 5,000-peso note.

DUTCH GUIANA-SURINAME
1762 Copper duit of the Society of Suriname.
1962 Autonomous coinage of Juliana; Suriname now self-governing as a part of the kingdom of the Netherlands.
1976 Gold, silver coins mark Independence anniversary.

ECUADOR
1824 Royalist Cuzco Mint established.
1836 After emergence from union in Great Colombia, republic of Ecuador coins are issued.
1858 Brief experiment with Latin Monetary Union coins, 5 francos struck.
1872 Decimal sucre of 100 centavos adopted.
1927 Small size sucre introduced.
1937 Nickel sucre and minor coins.
1964 Nickel-clad steel coinage.
1980 New 5- and 20-sucre notes are produced.
1988 Releases high-denomination bank notes due to inflation.

FRENCH GUIANA
1780 Billon 2 sous of Louis XVI.
1718 Billon 10 centimes, Louis XVIII.
1846 Billon 10 centimes, Louis-Philippe.

PARAGUAY
1845 First coinage, a copper 1/12 real with lion seated before a pole crowned with a liberty cap.
1870 After devastating wars with her neighbors, Paraguay issued first decimal coins, in copper centesimo denominations of 1, 2 and 4 centesimos.
1889 Only crown-sized silver peso issued.
1925 Copper-nickel small pesos and multiples lead to gradual decay of the coinage.
1944 New aluminum-bronze coins in new currency based on 100 centimos to 1 guarani.
1953 Scalloped-edge aluminum bronze centimo issue.
1968 President Alfredo Stroessner issues commemorative coins for the centenary of the war of the triple alliance against Paraguay, waged by Brazil, Argentina and Uruguay in the 19th century.
1973 Veritable flood of German-struck commemorative "coins" begins in honor of Olympics, popes, world leaders, Indian cultures and other unrelated matters.
1974 Stainless steel regular coinage of 1 through 50 guaranies honors heroes of Paraguayan history.
1977 Bank notes are replaced with stainless steel 1-, 5-, 10- and 50-guarani coins.

PATAGONIA
1874 Fantasy 2-centavos copper coin struck by eccentric Frenchman "Orlie-Antoine I," self-proclaimed "king of Araucania and Patagonia." Silver pesos appear years later, products of a Berlin coin dealer.
1889 The adventurer Julius Popper strikes gold coin-weights in the name of the "Company of the gold-washers of the south."

PERU
1568 Lima Mint first established, coinage sporadic.
1684 More or less regular coinage at Lima Mint.
1822 Republican 8 reales struck at Lima Mint.
1824 The above coin systematically restruck with Spanish crown by Royalists.
1825 Regular republican coinage in real denominations.
1855 Decimal silver sol of 100 centavos introduced.
1880 Brief Latin Monetary Union style coinage of silver pesetas and 5 pesetas at Lima.
1898 The gold libra, or pound, first struck.
1918 A distinctive copper-nickel coinage of 5, 10 and 20 centavos introduced with the obverse date spelled out in words.
1935 Central Reserve Bank of Peru begins coinage emissions in bank note style, ". . . will pay to the bearer one half sol . . .
1942 Brass replaces copper-nickel in minor coins.
1966 New, unified design brass coinage, reduced sizes. Silver commemorative 20 soles for the naval combat with Spain in 1866 begins a continuing commemorative series in various denominations of silver.
1971 Copper-nickel and silver coins for 150th anniversary of Peruvian independence recall earlier struggle of the would-be liberator, the Indian Tupac Amaru.
1975 New, tiny brass sol and half sol mark inflationary trend.
1986 Government purchases precious metals with hard assets to avoid creditor embargos.
1990 Issues inflationary 100,000-inti note.

URUGUAY
1840 Copper decimal coinage in centesimo denominations introduced.
1844 Silver peso fuerte struck during historic siege of Montevideo.
1877-95 Silver peso-centesimo coinage.
1901-51 Radiant sun centesimo coins in copper-nickel and copper.
1930 French-designed coins and notes for the centenary of independence.
1953 Artigas-portrait centesimo coinage begun at the outbreak of a steadily worsening inflationary spiral.
1969 Radiant sun of earliest coinage reappears on aluminum bronze 1-, 5- and 10-peso coins. Spectacularly modernistic 1,000-peso silver crown struck to mark the U.N. Food and Agriculture Organization's world-wide coin

plan.

1975 Monetary reform attempts to halt inflation. New peso introduced, exchanged for 1,000 old pesos. 150th anniversary of the struggle for independence marked by new 5-peso coin.

1981 Coins of 2 new pesos in copper-nickel-zinc, 5 new pesos in copper-nickel-aluminum, and 10 new pesos of copper-nickel released. Largest coin denomination ever issued in the country, a 5,000 new pesos of silver issued as a commemorative.

VENEZUELA

1802 Royal coinage at Caracas.

1817 First coinage by independence forces at the start of a long struggle.

1843 After leaving the union of Great Colombia, the first distinctive Venezuela coinage of copper quarter, half and 1 centavos issued.

1858 Handsome French-designed real coinage struck.

1873 Brief centavo-venezolano coinage.

1879 Latin Monetary Union coinage, 100 centimos to one bolivar, equal to the French franc. Gold and silver coinage with Bolivar head struck.

1965 Last silver bolivar issued, nickel 1 and 2 bolivares and minor pure nickel 25 and 50 centimos introduced.

1973 Large 10 bolivar commemorative issued for centenary of the national coinage with the head of the liberator, Simon Bolivar.

1977 Nickel composition coins depict denominations in larger numerals to stop confusion with silver issues of earlier years.

1990 Issues small-denomination emergency notes.

The Caribbean Islands

(Islands listed alphabetically)

BAHAMAS

1806 Half penny of George III struck for the Bahamas.

1966 New decimal coinage replaces British coins in use; Bahamas dollar of 100 cents, coins in nickel-brass, copper-nickel, pure nickel and silver, from 1 cent to 5 dollars.

1971 New name, Commonwealth of the Bahamas.

1973 Independence greeted by new coin types and a silver 10-dollar piece.

1978 Central bank discontinues acceptance of large quantities of gold coins for redemption.

BARBADOS

1788 Pineapple penny, copper, with Negro crowned with Prince of Wales' plume on obverse.

1792 Similar penny and additional half penny with colony's badge, the British king as Neptune in a marine car drawn by seahorses.

1973 New coinage and notes.

BERMUDA

1616 Sommer Islands "Hogge money" issued for the new colony on Bermuda.

1793 Half penny of George III issued for Bermuda.

1959 Silver 5-shilling crown struck, bearing a map of the island group.

1970 Decimal coinage in bronze and copper-nickel, 100 cents to one dollar.

1984 J. David Gibbons appointed chairman of the Bermuda Monetary Authority.

BRITISH CARIBBEAN TERRITORIES, EASTERN GROUP

1955 Decimal coins in bronze and copper-nickel released for Barbados, British Guiana, Windward Isles, Leeward Isles and Trinidad-Tobago.

BRITISH COLONIES

1820-22 Anchor money, silver fractions of a Spanish dollar in one-sixteenth, used in the West Indian colonies. Many cut and counterstamped coins in this same region.

CUBA

1870 Revolutionary provisional coinage, five centavos to one peso struck, probably at the Potosi, Bolivia, Mint.

1897 "Souvenir" silver peso struck in the U.S. to dramatize Cuban independence aspirations.

1898 Revolutionary committee issues similar coin with denomination ONE PESO.

1915 During the period of peak prosperity and booming economic speculation later recalled as the "dance of the millions" a full range of copper-nickel, silver and gold Cuban coinage is created. Silver 20 and 40 centavos struck to accommodate Spanish peseta denominations of this value still circulating.

1934 Following the overthrow of the first Cuban dictator, General Gerardo Machado, the new silver peso struck is dubbed the "A.B.C." type for the secret society which led in Machado's overthrow.

1951 Melting for the bullion value of millions of A.B.C. pesos held as reserve backing for silver certificates creates a modern rarity.

1952 Silver commemoratives struck for the 50th anniversary of the republic.

1953 Commemorative coinage for the centenary of Jose Marti, Cuba's national hero, includes 25-centavo and 50-centavo coins for the first time.

1962 The Kremnica Mint in Czechoslovakia strikes copper-nickel coins for the new Communist regime of Fidel Castro in 20- and 40-centavo denominations.

1975 Silver 5, 10 pesos announced marking 15th anniversary of the communization of the island's banking system.

CURACAO AND NETHERLANDS ANTILLES

1821 Silver real introduced.

1900 Dutch denominations begin to circulate with a silver quarter guilder.

1944 U.S. Mints strike Dutch denominations with Curacao inscription during World War II for exiled Queen Wilhelmina.

1952 New coinage, still of older Dutch type for self governing Netherlands Antilles, including Curacao, Aruba, Bonaire, Saba and Sankt

Maarten.

1970 Wholly redesigned Netherlands Antilles coinage, pure nickel replacing silver in higher denominations.

DANISH WEST INDIES

1708 Gold ducat of King Frederik IV struck for Danish West India Company.

1740 Copper and silver skilling coinage with royal monogram and ship reverse begin their long circulation.

1816 Small base silver 2-, 10- and 20-skilling coins with royal arms introduced.

1859 Base silver decimal coins of 100 cents to one daler introduced under King Frederik VII.

1904 Multiple good silver, nickel, bronze and gold coinage of Christian IX, based on a 20 cents equals one franc equals 100 bit standard.

1913 Last Danish coin, bronze 1 cent of Christian X. Islands sold to the U.S. in 1917.

DOMINICAN REPUBLIC

1844 Revolt against Haiti sees issue of a brass quarter real.

1877 Brass and small copper-nickel coinage during a period of great unrest.

1891 Latin Monetary Union coinage of the silver franco of 100 centesimos.

1897 Base silver peso of 100 centavos issued.

1937 Restoration of national financial independence after foreign tutelage and U.S. occupation as new bronze, copper-nickel and silver coinage on American standard enters circulation.

1955 The 25th anniversary of the Trujillo dictatorship marked by the first gold coin struck in the hemisphere officially in accord with the U.S. official value of $35 per ounce; face value 30 pesos.

1967 Copper-nickel replaces silver in circulation.

1969 Copper-nickel peso marks 125th anniversary of 1844 revolt against Haitian occupiers.

1972 Silver crown-sized peso returns as commemorative issue, 25th anniversary of Central Bank.

1974 Gold 30 pesos returns for 12th Central American and Caribbean games in greatly reduced size, reflecting rise in gold prices.

1975 Historic 10-reales crown of 16th century recalled on silver 10 pesos marking the first coin struck in Hispaniola.

EAST CARIBBEAN

1970 Copper-nickel and Proof silver specimens of 4-dollar crown-sized coins released to commemorate the inauguration of the Caribbean Development Bank. Antigua, Barbados, St. Kitts, Dominica, Grenada, Montserrat, St. Lucia and St. Vincent, all represented with new coat-of-arms obverses.

1972 Cayman Islands coinage of decimal type.

1989 Antigua issues commemorative legal tender notes made of precious metals.

FRENCH COLONIES

1717 Six- and 12-denier bronze coins of Louis XV designed for colonial commerce.

1721 Bronze 9-denier added.

1740 Billon 12 denier struck.

1767 Same denomination in bronze.

1758 Billon "sou marque" which is to see extended circulation all over the West Indies, where it becomes familiar as the "black dog."

1825 King Charles X strikes yellow bronze 5 and 10 centimes for the colonies.

1839-44 Louis-Philippe continues colonial bronze coinage.

1897 Martinique creates 50-centime and 1 franc copper-nickel coinage, a type secured by precious metal deposited in the colonial treasury. Issued also in 1922.

1903 Similar promissory coinage in copper-nickel for Guadeloupe.

HAITI

1802 Silver escalin denominations struck for the French Republic under the self-governing colony of Governor-General Toussaint l'Ouverture.

1807 President Henry Christophe creates a decimal currency, one gourde equals 100 centimes.

1814 Republic in southern Haiti issues base decimal coinage in denominations interchangeable with the Spanish American real.

1828 Copper coinage of fasces type begun by President J. P. Boyer, ruler of the whole island of Hispaniola.

1850 Imperial coinage of former president Faustin Soulouque, now emperor Faustin I.

1863 Reformed copper coinage of restored republic, President Fabre Geffrard.

1881 Silver gourde coinage of Latin Monetary Union fineness and weight, but not denomination, issued by President Salomon.

1904 President Nord Alexis begins copper-nickel coinage in sizes still current in the coinage of Jean-Claude Duvalier in recent years.

JAMAICA

1869 Copper-nickel farthing, half penny and penny introduced.

1937 Alloy changed to nickel-brass.

1969 Decimal coinage after five years of independence within Commonwealth.

1972 Ten-dollar commemorative of 10 years independence issued in silver.

PUERTO RICO

1895 Silver peso worth five Spanish pesetas introduced by the colonial power.

1896 Silver minor coins introduced.

TRINIDAD AND TOBAGO

1969 Copper-nickel dollar struck for FAO coin plan.

WINDWARD ISLES

1731 Six, 12 sols silver, Louis XV.

Europe
(Countries arranged alphabetically; some grouped by region)

Added Tax in France and Great Britain.

BELGIUM
1790 The historic coinage of the then Austrian Netherlands is interrupted by the rebellion coinage in copper, silver and gold.

1815 Necessity copper coinage in the name of Napoleon, later Louis XVIII, in Anvers, Antwerp.

1831 After a period of unhappy union with the Netherlands, an independent kingdom of Belgium is proclaimed, Leopold of Saxe-Coburg-Gotha becomes "Leopold premier," a double-meaning title. He is both the first Leopold and the first king of the new kingdom.

1832 The first coins are issued, a copper 10 centimes and a silver 5 francs, the latter bearing Leopold's laureate head.

1834 Gold pattern 20 and 40 francs struck.

1848 Beginning of new, bare head coinage in silver, first gold coinage issued.

1860 Copper-nickel 20 centimes struck.

1901 Holed copper-nickel coinage under Leopold II, 5, 10 centimes; 25-centime piece added in 1908.

1915 Zinc coinage issued under the German occupation, 5, 10 and 25 centimes. Necessity coinage, Belgian notgeld of iron with unusual brass plated obverse, copper-plated reverse issued in occupied Ghent.

1918 Zinc 50 centimes struck with central hole.

1922 In the post-war period of financial uncertainty, pure nickel 50 centimes, 1 and 2 franc pieces are struck, still inscribed "good for -" to temporarily replace paper money, as in France, Italy, Luxembourg and Romania in this adjustment period.

1930 In an attempt to replace lower value paper money, a pure nickel coinage of 5, 10 and 20 francs is begun, with a new additional denomination of the belga, equal to 5 francs.

1935 A silver 50 francs is struck to mark the centenary of Belgian railroads, with a regular issue in this denomination appearing in 1939.

1941 Introduction of zinc minor coins under the German occupation, 5, 10, and 25 centimes, 1 and 5 francs eventually struck.

1944 Allied armies entering Belgium issue zinc plated steel 2 francs, the unused planchets of the U.S. zinc-steel Lincoln cent.

1948 Following liberation, a new coinage is begun, highlighted by a 100 francs with the busts of the nation's four kings.

1951 Baudouin I becomes king after a confused era of collaborationist charges against Leopold III. A new and innovative coinage is gradually created, including 50-franc silver commemoratives in 1958 and 1960; and a copper-nickel 10 franc in 1969, uniquely without obverse inscription around the king's head.

1976 Silver commemorative 250 francs in separate French and Flemish types honors 25th anniversary of King Baudouin I.

1979 New coins replace minor denomination circulating notes.

1980 The 25-franc 150th anniversary coin is struck, design determined by competition.

1981 The 25-centime denomination is abolished.

1987 Commemorative ecu coin subject to Value

CENTRAL EUROPE
1828 Coinage of independent Greece resumes, one phoenix equals 100 lepta; coins struck on the island of Aegina, where ancient Greek coinage began about 700 B.C.

1848 Kossuth rebellion sees coins with Hungarian inscriptions.

1857 Austrian empire adopts new florin silver coinage, one florin equals 100 kreuzer.

1867 First coinage of autonomous Romania, in copper.

1867 Prince Michael, Obrenovich III issues Serbian copper coins.

1868 Following the compromise with Austria, Hungary begins distinctive coinage, one forint equals 100 krajczar.

1881 Bulgarian coinage, one lev equals 100 stotinki under Prince Alexander I. Romania becomes a kingdom.

1882 Milan I, King of Serbia, issues first gold coins.

1892 New Austro-Hungarian standard of coinage; 100 heller (Hungarian 100 filler) to one silver corona, (German krone, Hungarian Korona).

1906 Montenegro begins coinage, 100 para to one perper.

1910 Montenegro declared a kingdom, commemorative gold issued.

1917 Iron fenigow coins from embryonic kingdom of Poland, first Polish coinage since the 1850s.

1920 Yugoslavia created, adopts Serbian standard, 100 para equals one dinara.

1921 Czecho-Slovakia begins coinage, 100 haleru equals one koruna.

1922 Estonian mark coins; Latvian coinage of 100 santimu equals one lats begun.

1923 Poland consolidates several monetary systems into 100 groszy equals one zloty system.

1924 After a disastrous inflation, new Austrian coinage of 100 groschen equals one schilling adopted.

1926 Hungary adopts new coinage, 100 filler equals one pengo, "pengo" an adaptation of the term "clinking." Albania commences coinage, 100 qindar ari equals one franka ari.

1939 Independent Slovakia begins coinage, 100 halierov equals one koruna, "Ks."

1941 Independent state of Croatia in former Yugoslavia issues a single zinc 2 kune on standard of 100 banica equals one kuna.

1945-46 Inflation and Communist takeovers in Romania and Hungary begin.

1946 New Hungarian forint currency replaces pengo, which had experienced the worst inflation in history.

1946 Austria resumes schilling coinage interrupted by the Nazi Anschluss.

1947 Zinc first coinage of communist Albania replaces Italian occupation coinage in aluminum-bronze, stainless steel, silver.

1947 Czechoslovakia introduces new reduced size coins of prewar design; royal reform coinage of Romania's Michael I enters circulation.

1948 First communist coins of the Romanian Peoples Republic.

1949 Polish coinage resumed, minus royal crown on the White Eagle, in the name of the Polish

Republic; soviet-style emblem replaces Kossuth arms of Hungary on Peoples Republic issues.
1951 Communist Peoples Republic Bulgarian coinage begins.
1953 New aluminum coins for Peoples Federated Yugoslav Republic; Czechoslovak monetary reform brings new types and designs.
1954 First Greek postwar coinage in aluminum and copper-nickel bears King Paul's likeness.
1955 Start of the long run of Austrian modern commemoratives.
1958 Polish Peoples Republic title appears on coins.
1962 Bulgarian monetary reform.
1963 First new Bulgarian commemoratives, Socialist Federated Yugoslav coinage.
1964 Polish commemorative series begun; new communist Albanian coins in aluminum, a gift of Red China.
1966 Poland begins issue to collectors of limited runs of pattern "Proba" coins, rejected designs for commemoratives; Romania issues new coinage in the name of the Romania Socialist Republic.
1966 Royal Greek coins of Constantine II.
1967 Beginning of present-day system of Hungarian commemoratives.
1970 Czechoslovakia silver commemoratives launch new series.
1971 Greek royal arms of exiled King Constantine II replaced by symbol of ex-colonels' junta.
1973 New republican Greek coins of the junta.
1975 Redesigned Greek coins of post-junta era; Austria fixes upon 100-schilling denomination for silver commemoratives.
1976 Gold 1,000 schilling marks Austria's Millenary; first new gold type in country since 1938.
1979 Yugoslavia ceases legal tender status of 1965-dated 5-, 10- and 50-dinar notes.
1980 Poland begins a "Kings of Poland" coin series.
1981 Austria introduces a gold-colored 20 schilling coin.
1985 Austria bars South African Krugerrand importation.
1986 Bullion non-legal tender Helvetias minted in Switzerland.
1990 Yugoslavia issues inflationary 1 million-dinar notes.
1990 Poland issues note with crowned eagle of the republic.

DENMARK

1537 Crown-sized gulden in silver of King Christian III.
1541 Silver 1 mark.
1563 Klippe emergency coinage of the Seven Years War.
1564 Square gold gulden or krone minted.
1572 Silver speciedaler struck by Frederik II.
1591 Heavy gold Portugaloser struck by Christian IV.
1602 Copper coinage of 2 pennings, Christian IV.
1608 Silver double speciedaler, liondaler and gold sovereign minted.
1644 First coinage with Hebrew inscription and Latin combination, "Jehova the just judge."
1655 Goldkrone struck under Frederik III.
1659 Commemorative double krone issued with hand from clouds hacking a Swedish arm reaching for Denmark's crown.
1670 Silver speciedaler struck to mark the death of Frederik III and the accession of Christian V, beginning a long series of such coinages.
1688 Gold coinage with view of the fortress of Christiansborg in Guinea.
1708 Two ducats struck for the Danish West India Company.

1771 Trade piaster struck in imitation of the Spanish Pillar dollar, with circular Danish and Norwegian arms replacing the two globes.
1808 Serious inflation leads to silver and copper, including the copper roof of the church of Our Lady in Copenhagen, used in dwindling-sized coins.
1813 National Bank tokens struck in copper.
1854 Last speciedaler of Frederik VII, silver rigsdalers form currency.
1873 New Scandinavia coinage of 100 ore to the silver krone, Christian IX.
1888 First commemorative under the new system, the 25th year of the reign.
1920 Copper-nickel 10- and 25-ore pieces replace silver, a consequence of the post-war economic crunch.
1941 Zinc minor coinage under the German occupation, 1, 10 and 25 ore; aluminum 2 and 5 ore.
1960 Copper-nickel replaces aluminum-bronze for the 1-krone piece; a new 5-kroner regular issue is begun in the same metal.
1960 A new bronze 5 ore replaces zinc; a silver 5 kroner marking the silver wedding anniversary of the royal couple begins another series.
1967 Silver 10-kroner commemoratives begin with wedding coins of princess Margrethe and princess Benedikte.
1973 New coinage of Queen Margrethe II includes copper-clad steel 5 ore.
1976 New Mint construction begins.
1980 10-kroner coin and 20-kroner bank note introduced.
1989 Devalues 5- and 10-ore coins.
1990 Circulates 5-krone coin.

ENGLAND

500-575 Beginning of Anglo-Saxon silver sceat coinage.
c. 765 Beginning of silver penny coinage, kingdoms of Kent, Mercia, etc.
c. 786 Pennies of kings of Wessex, later kings of all England.
885 Beginning of Viking coinages in England.
1257 Experimental gold penny of Henry III, worth 20 silver pennies.
1278 Introduction of silver groat, 4 pence; silver half penny and farthing.
1344 Introduction of gold florin, half and quarter florin; noble and parts.
1465 Rose noble introduced in gold, 120 grains valued at 10 shillings. Former gold noble replaced with angel of 80 grains.
1485 Reign of Henry VII, which saw a gold sovereign of 20 shillings and the silver testoon, or shilling.
1543 Start of the systematic debasement of the English coinage by Henry VIII.
1561 First attempt at milled, machine-struck coinage by French engraver Eloye Mestrelle, during reign of Elizabeth I; three-half pence and three-farthing coins introduced.
1601 Silver coinage restored to full fineness, pre-Henry VIII debasement.
1604 Gold unite introduced, lighter weight gold pound.
1613 Harrington farthings, licensed copper coinage, first such in England.
1631 Nicholas Briot actively seeks milled coinage.
1649 Commonwealth coinage, English inscriptions.
1648-72 Seventeenth century token issues, in absence of official copper coins.
1660 Restoration of Charles II, last hammered coinage.

1662 Milled coinage officially adopted.
1695 Great Silver Recoinage begins, removal of worn and clipped coinage from circulation.
1797 Steam machinery produced "cartwheel" twopence and penny.
1804 Bank of England dollar, overstruck on Spanish 8 reales.
1811 Bank of England token 3 shillings, 18 pence, 9 pence.
1816 Complete recoinage, token silver, new gold sovereign, half-sovereign.
1860 Copper penny, half penny and farthing replaced by bronze coinage.
1920 Silver coinage reduced to .500 fine, new quaternary alloy.
1925 End of regular gold coinage.
1937 New 12-sided threepence in nickel-bronze introduced.
1947 Silver replaced by copper-nickel, small threepence discontinued.
1956 Farthing discontinued.
1967 Half penny discontinued.
1968 First decimal denominations introduced alongside pre-decimal coins.
1971 Full decimalization, 100 new pence to one pound.
1972 Crown returns as 25 new pence for anniversary of royal wedding. New coin is twice the size of 50 new pence.
1977 British public, collectors greet Silver Jubilee crowns and medals with record enthusiasm.
1978 Liberalized policy on gold coin importation.
1979 Sir Christopher Wren is portrayed on new 50-pound note. Royal Mint weathers a strike by workers for one week in October.
1980 Sixpence ceases to be legal tender on June 30.
1981 Wedding of Prince Charles and Lady Diana Spencer is marked with commemorative crowns.
1982 Value Added Tax (VAT) is added to all sales of coins more than 100 years old. A new 20-pence coin is introduced.
1984 Half penny production ceases. £1 bank note ceases production and is replaced by £1 coin already in circulation.
1986 £2 coin introduced as a commemorative issue.
1987 Introduces gold bullion Britannia coins.
1987 Introduces security threads into £5 and £10 notes.
1988 Withdraws legal tender status of £1 note.
1990 Begins size reduction of notes and coins.

FINLAND

1860 After groundwork by Minister of Finance J.V. Snellman, the grand duchy of Finland, under the rule of the Russian czar, adopts its own coinage of the Finnish markkaa of 100 pennia.
1917 Following the overthrow of the czar, uncrowned double eagles appear on the Finnish coinage.
1918 A single copper 5 pennia with Communist emblems is uttered by the Red forces during the Civil War. Normalized coinage of the new republic begins.
1926 Only gold coinage of modern Finland, 200, 100 markkaa.
1928 Aluminum-bronze 5, 10 markkaa.
1931 Aluminum-bronze 20 markkaa.
1941 Holed 5, 10 pennia, wartime issue.
1943 Iron war issues, 25, 50 pennia, 1 markkaa.
1951-52 The XV Olympic Games in Helsinki marked by a silver 500 markkaa.
1952 New aluminum-bronze, iron post war coinage.
1960 Silver 1,000 markkaa honors minister Snellman, founder of the coinage.

1963 Coinage reform, one new markkaa equals 100 old.
1967 First silver 10 markkaa honors 50th anniversary of independence. Currency devalued.
1969 Aluminum replaces the bronze 1 penni of the reform currency. Aluminum penni; copper-nickel 1 markkaa.
1972 Aluminum-bronze 5 markkaa.
1977 Aluminum 5 pennia.
1979 Production of penni ceases.
1983 Aluminum 10 pennia.
1984 Braille added to 10-markaa note to aid the blind.
1988 Builds new Mint facility at Vantaa.

FRANCE
(Since accession of Hugues Capet)

956 Hugues Capet, Duke of France, issues silver denier and billon obole, which were to become standard coins in succeeding reigns.
987 Hugues Capet becomes king, continues denier coinage.
1226 Louis IX (St. Louis) strikes gold coins: Ecu d'or (also called denier d'or a l'Ecu), l'agnel d'or and the royal d'or. Silver coinage reform sees introduction of gros tournois, valued at 12 denier old coinage. The once fine silver denier is lapsing into a billon coinage.
1285 Phillip the Fair creates petite royal d'or.
1303 Adds chaise d'or. The term "d'or" indicates gold; first word describes the coin's obverse design, in this case the king on the royal throne, "chaise."
1328 Phillip of Valois adds parisis d'or; pavillon d'or. All of these medieval gold issues are named for their designs.
1350 John the Good introduces the mouton d'or, with the lamb of God.
1360 Adds the franc a cheval, with figure of the king charging on horseback, in silver.
1396 After one of France's first excursions into adventure in Italy, French-style coins in Genoese denominations are struck in the Genoa Mint.
1413 Billon grossus added to French coinage by Charles VI.
1417 Heaume d'or shows king in armor and helmet.
1421 Salut d'or added to gold denominations.
(After 1415, English king Henry V struck French-style coinage during his war in France.)
1436 Charles VII introduces gold ecu de la couronne.
1461 Louis XI, the "Spider king," creates billon douzain and billon liard. The liard, originally valued at three denier, became a familiar copper coin in later years.
1483 Charles VIII introduces the billon hardi.
1494 Further military intervention in Italy sees coins struck in the name of King Charles VII struck in 10 Italian Mint cities, from Pisa to Naples.
1513 Louis XII introduces circulating portrait coins, the silver teston and half teston.
1515 The glittering reign of Francois I sees pattern portrait coin in many denominations, circulating silver testons of several designs, as well as billon hardi "black money" coinage. Much Italian coinage in this reign.
1550 Henri II introduces gold portrait Henri d'or.
1560 Franco-Scots coinage issued during brief reign of Francois II, husband of Mary, Queen of Scots; gros d'argent, silver coin with its half and its quarter.
1968 First decimal denominations introduced alongside decimal coins.

1576 Reign of Henri III, cut short by assassination in France's troubled period, sees portrait silver piefort of the franc.

1594 Henri IV enters Paris after civil strife, sets path for stability and French unity. Earlier coin types become increasingly standardized.

1640 French gold becomes fixed as Louis d'or and multiples under Louis XIII.

1641 Louis d'Argent or Louis blanc, the silver crown of 60 sols known abroad as the ecu is introduced. French coinage is now essentially fixed in general pattern of issue until the great revolution.

1642 French invasion of Spanish Catalonia extends Louis XIII's coin types to the County of Barcelona.

1643 Louis XIV, whose long reign consolidated royal power and fixed the coinage in the general Louis d'or-silver ecu system. French culture, language and influence become all-pervading as a result of Louis' splendor, his military campaigns and the magnificance of his court at Versailles.

1685 The heavy ecu carambole is introduced for use in occupied Flanders; the coin is valued at 80 sols, rather than the 60 or the regular ecu.

1717 Louis XV's reign sees the first coinage for the French colonies in general, the 12 and 9 denier coppers of 1717 and 1721; as well as specialized coin for the Antilles and French India.

1774 Louis XVI, last of the pre-revolutionary rulers of France. First period coinage follows closely that of his predecessors.

1791 Following the revolution, a brief "constitutional period" precedes the reign of terror and the republic. The constitutional coinage began in 1791; the new title "king of the French" and value of six livres are distinguishing marks. Copper and brass coins are struck, partly from looted church bells.

1793 Following execution of Louis XVI, first republican coinage of France is released, followed by a rapid inflation of the increasingly useless assignat paper currency, ostensibly guaranteed by a blanket mortgage of the national domain.

1795 Franc adopted as the chief unit of a decimal coinage, made up of 100 centimes or 10 decimes.

1803 First portrait coins of Napoleon Bonaparte, first consul of the republic. Silver quarter and half franc, franc, 2 and 5 francs silver, 20 and 40 francs gold.

1804 Beginning of imperial coinage of Napoleon I, lasting until the "hundred days" coins of 1815.

1808 Bronze 5 centimes, billon 10 centimes introduced; Napoleon emperor.

1814-15 Restoration of the house of Bourbon, retention of the franc coinage.

1830 Louis Philippe, royal arms replaced by value in wreath. Propaganda coins of pretender Henri V appear, 1831, joined later by Napoleon II, bearing date "1816."

1848 Second republic sees massive issues of medals, jetons and a large pattern coin age before its replacement by the Prince President, Louis-Napoleon as authoritarian ruler in 1851.

1852-70 Second empire of Napoleon III. Copper 1, 2, 5 and 10 centimes join reg ular silver coinage, gold 50 and 100 francs replace the top value 40 francs of earlier issues.

1870-1940 Third republic maintained the Latin Monetary Union standards, established as an international standard by Napoleon III in 1867 until the general collapse of European currencies after World War I.

1903 Nickel 25-centime coinage introduced.

1904 Similar coin prepared with 22 sides in an attempt to reduce danger of confusion with 1-franc piece.

1914 Holed nickel Lindauer type coins be gun, continued in various metal through 1946.

1933 Small Bazor type 5 franc in nickel, quickly withdrawn due to extensive counterfeiting.

1940 French defeat in World War II leads to Parliament calling aged Marshal Philippe Petain, hero of Verdun in the earlier war, to head the new French state.

1941 First coinage of "Vichy" France.

1945 Fourth French republic.

1950 Currency reform, new aluminum bronze and copper-nickel coinage.

1958 Fifth republic of Gen. Charles de Gaulle.

1960 New "heavy franc," equal to 100 old francs, introduced.

1965 Crown-sized coinage resumed with a revival of the Dupre design of Hercules, the republic and justice, first used in 1795.

1970 Silver abandoned in 5-franc coins.

1974 New 50-franc crown to supplant 10- franc silver; new abstract map 10 franc in base metal to be prepared for active circulation.

1979 The 2-franc coin is reinstated.

1982 First commemorative coin issued in nation's history.

1986 Commemoratives honor centennial of the Statue of Liberty in New York Harbor.

1987 Platinum, palladium, silver and silver piefort coins honor LaFayette.

1987 Two-month-old 10-franc coin is withdrawn due to similarity to half franc.

1988 Bimetallic 10-franc coin introduced.

GERMANY

1554 Imperial decree established the fine Cologne mark as coinage measure, a weight of silver weighing 233.855 grams.

1618-23 "Kipper and wipper" period of debasement, inflation and the proliferation of Mints resulting in monetary chaos.

1690 Leipzig Convention established standard of 12 taler to the fine mark.

1747 Austria abandons 1690 standard, adopts a lesser standard of 13-1/3 taler to the fine mark.

1750 Prussia adopts "Graumann standard," 14 taler to the fine mark.

1753 Austria and Bavaria announce "conventionstaler," 10 to the fine mark, a standard adopted by most German states, "ad normam conventionis."

1806 Abolition of Holy Roman Empire and resulting monetary disorganization.

1809 Kronentalers appear in Bavaria, similar to earlier issues in the former Austrian Netherlands, 9.08 to the fine mark.

1837 Bavaria leads south-central German states at the Munich Convention to adopt the gulden as the standard coinage unit, equal to 24-1/2 gulden to the fine mark, or two gulden to one taler. Saxony leads Thuringian states into Dresden Convention, adopting the Graumann standard of 14 taler to the fine mark; the system already in use by Prussia and seven other states.

1838 Dresden and Munich groups agree on an integrated standard of 14 taler equaling one Cologne fine mark equaling 24-1/2 gulden;

two taler equaling 3-1/2 gulden.

1857 Monetary union based on "zollpfund," metric pound of 500 grams or half-kilogram, equal to 30 vereinstaler; gold coinage of one krone and half krone established at 50 kronen to the zollpfund.

1873 Unification of coinage in the new German empire; silver and gold coinage, bronze subsidiary coins on a new one mark to 100 pfennig standard. Surviving vereinstaler to circulate as 3 marks.

1890 First colonial coins, for the German East Africa Company.

1894-95 Bird of Paradise coins of German New Guinea Company.

1904 New German East Africa coinage under Imperial administration.

1908 Beginning of 3-mark coinage, commemorative issues under same decree.

1909 Copper-nickel coins on Mexican peso standard for German treaty port of Kiautschou.

1915 World War I iron minor coinage begins.

1916 Coins struck for emergency use in German East Africa.

1918 State authorized notgeld in Braunschweig begins flood of such necessity coins and notes.

1923 Catastrophic inflation, ending in new rentenmark currency reform.

1924 Adoption of the reichsmark.

1925 Commemorative 3- and 5-mark series begins.

1945 "Denazified" zinc coins under Allied occupation.

1948 Monetary reform in western occupation zones; aluminum coins in east zone.

1949 Bank Deutscher Laender begins issuing coins in west.

1950 Bronze and brass-clad steel coinage of the German Federal Republic, copper-nickel 50 pfennig.

1951 Silver 5 deutsche mark in circulation in Western zones. Copper-nickel 2 marks causes confusion among users, sees one year of striking.

1952 Silver 5 deutsche mark honoring Nuremberg's Germanisches Museum begins long, distinguished series of Federal Republic commemoratives.

1956 First coinage bearing the title of the German Democratic Republic, supplants earlier issues inscribed merely "Germany."

1966 First commemoratives of the German Democratic Republic, or East Germany.

1969 "Magnimat" copper-nickel clad nickel 2 deutsche mark with Adenauer portraits enters circulation in Federal Republic.

1972 Tons of recycled silver used in series of 10 deutsche mark coins honoring the XX Olympiad, first issue with improper legend "In Germany," rather than the Olympic non-national "In Muenchen."

1975 "Magnimat" material introduced for 5 deutsche mark. Only silver coins now are commemoratives in Federal Republic.

1986 Point-of-sale system cashless economy experimented with in Munich and in West Berlin.

1990 Plans for reunification of East and West promise currency compromises. East German currency is withdrawn at midnight June 30 and replaced with West marks.

1989 Austria Mint transfers from government to private ownership.

1989 Austria markets gold bullion Vienna Philharmonic coins.

GREENLAND

1922 Cryolite Mining and Trading Company copper-nickel tokens struck at the Copenhagen, Denmark, Mint.

1926 Royal coinage in copper-nickel and aluminum-bronze.

1944 Brass 5 kroner of 1926 design struck at Philadelphia Mint during the German occupation of Denmark.

1957 Aluminum-bronze 1 kroner struck with crowned polar bear coat-of-arms for the Royal Greenland Company.

1960 Same design struck in copper-nickel.

ICELAND

1926 Bronze, copper-nickel coinage under Iceland's King Christian X; 100 aurar to one krona.

1930 The millenary of Iceland's parliament, the Althing, is marked by commemorative coinage in silver and bronze.

1940 London Mint strikes bronze and copper-nickel of 1926 type without Mint mark during the German occupation of Denmark.

1942 Zinc wartime coinage struck.

1946 First bronze, aluminum-bronze coins of the republic.

1958 Nickel-brass replaces aluminum-bronze.

1961 A gold 500 kronur struck, commemorating Icelandic intellectual leader Jon Sigurdsson.

1967 Copper-nickel 10 kronur introduced.

1968 Copper-nickel 50 kronur marks 50th anniversary of sovereignty.

1969 Nickel-brass 50 aurar, 5 kronur in copper-nickel introduced.

1970 Aluminum 10 aurar, regular issue copper-nickel 50 kronur struck.

1974 Silver and gold coinage commemorates the 1100th anniversary of Iceland's settlement.

1976 The 1 krona is altered to aluminum from nickel-brass.

1981 Marine designs introduced on all circulating coinage.

IRELAND

c. 995 Sihtric, Norse king of Dublin, issues first silver pennies, imitations of Aethelraed II types struck in England.

c. 1185 Anglo-Irish coinage begins in the name of John, Lord of Ireland, son of Henry II of England.

c. 1204 "Triangle coinage" of John as King of England, lord of Ireland.

1461 Silver groat introduced by Edward IV.

1536 The Irish harp first appears on coins of Henry VIII.

1553 Shilling appears under Mary I.

1646 The only two gold coins to be struck in Ireland, a pistole and double pistole, are issued as part of the "Inchiquin money" issue, which began in 1642.

c. 1670 "St. Patrick" copper farthings and half pennies in circulation. Many of these will appear with Mark Newby in Colonial New Jersey in 1681.

1689 Brass emergency "gun money," with some denominations dated by the month as well as the year, issued by exiled King James II, during an attempt to regain the British throne.

1728-36 Widespread issue of private copper tokens.

1760 "Voce populi" tokens appear, privately issued, later transported in some numbers to the American Colonies.

1804 Bank of Ireland tokens begin with 6-shilling crown.

1823 Last Anglo-Irish coinage, George IV penny and half penny.
1928 Percy Metcalfe designs new national coinage, eight new reverses with a uniform Irish Free State obverse featuring the harp. Metcalfe's work was the result of an international artistic competition in which seven artists participated.
1966 First commemorative, silver 10 shillings, marks 50th anniversary of Easter Rising.
1969 First two decimal coins enter circulation.
1970 New seven-sided 50 decimal pence struck with design of former farthing.
1971 Decimalization completed.
1977 First Irish Mint since 1691 opened by Central Bank at Sandyford, Co. Dublin.
1980 Twenty-pound notes are reduced in size by one-third.
1990 £1 coin replaces note.

ITALY

569 Anonymous gold solidi of the dukes of Beneventum.
650 Anonymous one-third solidus of Lucca.
772 Papal coinage begins under Adrian I.
934 Fatimid Arab gold coinage of Palermo, Sicily.
935 Gisnulf I issues Cufic type 1 tari at Salerno.
1042 Amalfi Cufic coinage.
1102 Norman gold tari struck at Messina.
1190 Gold grosso d'oro of emperor Frederick II, St. Vultus, Lucca Mint.
1197 Frederick II strikes gold quarter augustales, in the style of the ancient Roman coinages.
1200 Anonymous cross and castle coinage of the doges of Genoa.
1252 Florence issues the famed florin, which soon becomes a widely imitated world gold trade coin, with its standing Christ and lily reverse.
1266 Coinage of the house of Anjou, Naples Mint.
1280 Doge Giovanni Dandolo issues the first of the famous Venetian gold ducat series, with the figure of the doge kneeling before Christ.
1340 Florins struck by the republic of Siena.
1431 Scudo d'oro struck for Sardinia by Louis I.
1441 Lionel d'Este issues gold ducat.
1445 Mantua coinage of Luigi II Gonzaga.
1495 French coinage in Naples; gold zecchino struck by the republic of Pisa.
1500 Silver testone of Francesco II Gonzaga, Mantua; French coinage in Milan.
1523 Coinage designs by Benevenuto Cellini for Pope Clement VII.
1534 Spanish King Charles V issues coins in Milan as this city continues to play its unhappy role as an international battle ground.
1552 Coinage of the dukes of Modena.
1707 Milanese coinage of Austrian emperor Charles VI.
1726 With the death of Grand Duke Gian Gastone, the long association between the house of Medici and Florence comes to an end.
1749 Charles of Spain produces coinage as King of the Two Sicilies.
1759 Ferdinand IV of Bourbon begins his long years of coinage as King of the Two Sicilies.
1768 Venice strikes new bust type tallero in silver.
1797 Republic of Venice surrendered to Napoleon, soon after seized by Austria.
1798 Napoleon creates Ligurian Republic, coinage of Genoa Mint.
1799 Turin Mint strikes coins for Piedmont Republic after the house of Savoy retreats to Sardinia.
1800 Coinage of the Subalpine Republic, silver 5 francs.
1803 Napoleon's client Louis I of Bourbon begins

coinage for the kingdom of Etruria after deposition of the grand duke of Tuscany.
1804 Coinage of the Italian republic, Bonaparte, president, Milan Mint.
1805 Beginning of the coins of principality of Lucca and Piombino under Napoleon's sister Elisa and her husband Felice.
1807 Napoleonic coinage for the new kingdom of Italy, 100 centesimi to the silver lira, forerunner of later united Italian coinage.
1809 Marshal Murat succeeds Joseph Bonaparte as King of the Two Sicilies; establishes decimal coinage.
1814 Siege silver coinage of Zara on the Adriatic coast.
1815 After Napoleon's overthrow, the duchy of Parma is given to his sometime empress Marie Louise, who issues centesimi-lira coinage.
1816 Papal coinage, interrupted by the Roman Republic of 1798 and by the captivity of the Pope in France, resumes under Pius VII. Victor Emanuel I, restored as king of Sardinia-Piedmont, strikes decimal centesimi-lira coinage.
1835 New decimal coinage of the 100 baiocchi-one scudo type introduced by Pope Gregory XVI.
1848-49 This year of revolutionary upsurge sees new coinages in Venice, Rome and Lombardy, all striving toward a unified Italy.
1859 Italian unification advances as the last coins of Leopold II of Tuscany, Francesco II of the Two Sicilies and Robert of Parma are struck. Victor Emanuel II, "elected king" coinage of Tuscany; Bologna Mint strikes silver 5 lire with head of Victor Emanuel II, king of Italy.
1861 After the Florence Mint has struck a commemorative 5 lire on the occasion of his proclamation as king of Italy, Victor Emanuel II begins the definitive unified Italian coinage, struck at Turin, Naples, and later Milan and Rome.
1870 Last papal coinage at the Rome Mint until 1929; Italian coinage commences at this Mint.
1894 Copper-nickel 20 centesimi introduced as an unsuccessful experiment in small size, non-silver coinage.
1900 Outstanding numismatist Victor Emanuel III becomes king upon the murder of his father Umberto I. Victor Emanuel III is to spend a lifetime in the compilation of the "Corpus Nummorum Italicorum," the exhaustive catalog of all coins ever struck in Italy.
1911 The 50th anniversary of the kingdom of Italy is commemorated by a four-coin set in gold, silver and bronze.
1922 Pure nickel 1- and 2-lire "good for -" token coins issued, joining the 1918 20 centesimi and the 1919 50 centesimi in an increasingly non-precious metal post-war coinage.
1923 The first anniversary of the fascist march on Rome is marked by two gold commemoratives.
1929 Following the Treaty of the Lateran, papal coinage is resumed as the state of the Vatican City is created.
1931 Devaluation of the lire sees new, smaller format coins struck in gold, silver and bronze with the usual classical motifs.
1936 Following the annexation of Ethiopia and the proclamation of the empire, a redesigned imperial coinage in gold, silver, pure nickel and bronze is struck.
1939 Stainless steel, used in coinage for the first time as "acmonital," replaces nickel; aluminum-

bronze replaces bronze in Italian coinage.

1943 After King Victor Emanuel III brings about the overthrow of Mussolini and fascism, the last regularly issued coins of the kingdom of Italy are issued.

1946 Following the artfully manipulated referendum of June, the new Italian republic issues a new aluminum coinage of 1, 2, 5 and 10 lire. Millions are struck; most disappear from circulation immediately, to reappear as the stuffing of Swiss-produced cloth covered buttons.

1951 New small-size aluminum coins are struck as the financial erosion of Italy under the republic continues.

1954 Stainless steel coins are minted again in 50 lire and next year 100-lire denominations.

1957 Aluminum-bronze 20 lire introduced.

1958 Silver returns in the 500-lire coin.

1961 Italian commemoratives begin again with a silver 500 lire for the first centenary of unification under Victor Emanuel II.

1970 A new 1,000-lire denomination celebrates the centenary of Rome as the capital of united Italy.

1972 The tiny republic of San Marino resumes Italian-style coinage in "annual series."

1974 A nationwide coin shortage, caused by unknown factors, sees Italians reduced to using candy, teabags, telephone tokens and even Kleenex as coin substitutes. Import-export limits are established on the lire due to inflation and loss of capital within the country. Stainless steel 100 lire honors radio inventor Marconi, replacing silver 500 lire originally proposed.

1975 Coinage shortages cause the acceptance of plastic tokens in commerce.

1976 Controversy swirls around announced plans to strike and sell at several times face value the 1974 silver Marconi 500 lire; San Marino 500 lire "outside annual series." Emergency 100- and 500-lire notes are declared illegal.

1977 Bronze 200-lire coin commences.

1982 A 500-lire coin is produced of bronze and acmonital composition.

1986 "New lira" denominations introduced, dropping the last three zeros as a reaction to inflation.

LUXEMBOURG

1795 Cast copper siege coins issued by the Austrian defenders against the French invaders.

1854 In personal union with the Netherlands' King Willem III, Grand Duke of Luxembourg, a copper coinage of 2-1/2, 5 and 10 centimes is begun.

1890 Following the death of Willem III, his daughter is prevented from becoming Luxembourg's ruler by the Salic law; the succession goes to the elderly Adolphe of Orange-Nassau, ruling duke of Nassau, Germany, disposed in 1866.

1901 Portrait copper-nickel 5, 10 centimes of Adolphe.

1908 Issue of a slightly larger 5 centimes under William IV.

1915 Zinc coinage under the German occupation, holed types.

1918 Iron occupation coins enter circulation.

1924 Pure nickel "bon pour," good for- coinage of 1, 2 francs.

1939 Moselle-Frankisch name "Letzeburg" appears on the coinage.

1946 After liberation from a second German occupation, a commemorative set of 20, 50 and 100 francs in silver celebrates the 600th anniversary of the medieval warrior-king John

the Blind.

1963 The millenary of Luxembourg sees the striking of a commemorative 250-franc coin in silver; only after striking is it discovered that the coinage laws do not provide for this denomination.

1964 New coinage under grand duke Jean.

1978 The country courts world gold trade by removing 100 percent added gold tax.

1986 Gold bullion Golden Lion 1-ounce legal tender trade coin issued.

THE NETHERLANDS

750 Gold triens of Duurstede, one of the earliest recognizable coinages in what was to become the Netherlands.

1200-1576 Separate provincial coinages of the several provinces which came together to produce the modern Dutch nation. The denominations were to include the gold mouton d'or and the gold florin.

1576 The United Provinces coinage begins, soon to be more or less standardized in the familiar gold ducats, silver ducatoons or rijders, and a number of smaller silver and copper coins, generally bearing a Mint mark or coat-of-arms identifying the provincial Mint at which the coins were struck.

1794 As the traditional world began to come apart under the revolutionary assault of the events in France after 1789, the Low Countries become a battlefield, reflected in such siege coinages as those struck in Maastricht in 1794 and in the city of Luxemburg in 1795.

1795 A triumphant Napoleon sees to the organization of the Batavian Republic, replacing the Stadholders of the house of Orange. Gold, silver and copper coinages continue along familiar lines; only the dates setting the coins of the Batavian Republic aside from those issued earlier.

1806 The emperor Napoleon places his younger brother Louis on the throne of a new kingdom of Holland as Lodewijk Napoleon I.

1808 A regular issue of portrait coins of the new kingdom is begun.

1818 Following the elevation of the last Stadholder as King Willem I of the new kingdom of the Netherlands, a decimal coinage of 100 cents to the gulden is begun; the largest silver piece is the 3 gulden.

1819 Regular gold coinage begins with the 10 gulden.

1840 The crown size 2-1/2 gulden replaces the older 3 gulden as the largest silver coin in circulation.

1848 Gold "Negotiepenning" equal to 20, 10 and 5 gulden struck as trade coins.

1875 Regular gold coinage resumed under Willem III.

1907 Copper-nickel 5 cents introduced.

1933 Last portrait gold coinage.

1941 Zinc minor coins struck by German occupiers.

1948 All new bronze and pure nickel coinage after the liberation.

1954 The silver gulden reappears in smaller size than earlier issues.

1959 The silver "rijksdaalder" or 2-1/2 gulden in silver is reintroduced.

1960 The gold ducat of the old United Provinces is again struck as a trade coin.

1967 Pure nickel 1 and 2-1/2 gulden coins replace silver.

1970 The 25th anniversary of the liberation is marked by a silver 10-gulden commemorative coin, the beginning of a series in this denomination.

1980 First coinage produced for Beatrix as queen.

1982 One-cent coin abolished March 31.
1988 Aureate-nickel 5-guilder coin replaces note.

NORWAY

1546 Silver crown-size gulden of Christian III.
1629 Thick double speciedaler struck by Christian IV.
1660 Gold ducat issued by Frederik III.
1704 First "reisedaler" or travel daler, specially struck to pay expenses of Danish king Frederik IV's trips to his Norwegian domain.
1819 Speciedaler of Carl XIV Johan, the former French Marshal Bernadotte, now king of Sweden and Norway.
1874 Transitional coinage struck for the change-over to the decimal 100 ore equals one krone currency.
1875 First regular issue krone coins struck.
1906 After achieving independence, Norway and her new King Haakon VII mark the occasion with a commemorative 2 kroner.
1910 Only issue of Norwegian gold, 20 and 10 kroner St. Olav coins.
1917 Iron replaces bronze in the 1, 2 and 5 ore coins during World War I.
1920 Copper-nickel minor coinage replaces silver; center holes make their appearance on coins not designed for them.
1925 Copper-nickel holed coins issued, designed around holes.
1941 Zinc and iron coinage of minister-president Vidkun Quisling's regime.
1942 London Mint strikes nickel-brass coinage for the use of the government in exile in the Faroe Islands.
1951 New post-war coins without center holes.
1958 Completely redesigned coinage with bird and animal reverses under new King Olav V.
1964 Silver 10 kroner commemorating the 150th anniversary of the Norwegian constitution.
1970 New 25 kroner marks the 25th anniversary of liberation from the German occupation.
1974 Redesigned coinage of King Olav V.
1981 Ole-Robert Kolberg becomes the new Director of the Mint.
1983 The 5 and 25 ore, and 10-kroner coins are withdrawn from circulation.

PORTUGAL

1641 Coinage of Joao IV, the restorer of Portuguese independence, in silver and copper.
1642 Countermarking of earlier coinages begun.
1656 Gold coinage resumed under Afonso VI.
1683 Finely-styled coinage of Pedro II.
1686 Countermarking of earlier Portuguese coinages.
1722 Portrait coinage introduced by Joao V, gold only. These pieces were a favorite overseas, where they were dubbed "Joes."
1750 Similar portrait gold of Jose I, the real "Joe."
1777 Portrait gold coinage of Maria I and Pedro III.
1786 Widow's veil gold of Maria alone.
1811 Bronze portrait coinage of prince regent Joao.
1826 Brief coinage of Pedro IV, actually in dependent emperor Pedro I of Brazil.
1828 Usurpation of the throne by Dom Miguel, formerly the regent for his absent brother.
1833 Portrait coins of Miguel's niece, Maria da Gloria, as Maria II.
1837 Portrait silver coinage, beginning with the coroa of 1,000 reis.
1847 Countermarked bronze "G.C.P." coin age.
1882 Smaller sized portrait bronze coinage of Luis I, titles in Portuguese.
1898 Commemorative silver 200, 500 and 1,000 reis

mark the fourth centenary of Vasco da Gama's discovery of the sea route to India.
1900 First copper-nickel coinage of 50 and 100 reis.
1908 Following the assassination of Carlos I and crown prince Luis Felipe, Manoel II becomes king; Latin titles resumed on the coinage.
1912 After the coup against king Manoel in 1910, the first republican coin is struck on a new standard of 100 centavos to one escudo.
1914 First crown-sized silver escudo commemorates the revolution of 1910.
1924 Small aluminum-bronze escudo struck.
1927 Nickel-bronze escudo coinage under Dr. Antonio da Oliveira Salazar's New State.
1928 First of many commemoratives of the New State, a silver 10 escudos recalling Portuguese victory over the Moors at Ourique in 1139.
1932 Silver 2-1/2, 5 and 10 escudos introduced.
1942 Small bronze X, XX centavos revive old Roman numeral denominations.
1953 The 25th anniversary of Salazar's financial reforms is marked by a new 20 escudos silver coin.
1963 Copper-nickel replaces silver in 2-1/2-, 5- and 10-escudo denominations.
1968 Fifty-escudo silver commemoratives begin.
1969 Bronze replaces nickel-bronze in quarter escudo coins.
1971 Aluminum appears in the 10-centavo coinage.
1978 The first circulating coin since 1974 military coup, a new denomination 25 escudos, appears.
1981 The government releases 1977 dated copper-nickel coins.
1988 Unveils first platinum and palladium commemorative coins.
1990 Bimetallic 100-escudo coin replaces note.

RUSSIA (Soviet Union)

1704 First modern ruble of Peter the Great replaces archaic issues.
1764 Distinctive Siberian copper coinage, Catherine the Great.
1796 Paul I issues non-portrait coins with penitential inscription "Not unto us but unto thy Name, O Lord."
1834 First modern commemorative coin, ruble with Czar Alexander I memorial.
1828 Beginning of world's first regular platinum coinage, 3, 6 and 12 rubles, ending in 1845.
1902 Experimental international patterns of ruble-franc equivalency.
1917 Last Russian imperial coinage, followed by vast flood of paper civil war necessity currency.
1921 New coinage of the Russian Soviet Federated Socialist Republic, R.S.F.S.R.
1923 Gold chervonetz, 10 rubles, first Soviet gold coin struck.
1924 Coinage begins in the name of the Union of Soviet Socialist Republics.
1961 "New ruble" coinage begun.
1965 First Soviet commemorative, victory in World War II anniversary.
1975 A 10-ruble chervonetz issued, first gold coin since 1923.
1977 An issue of 28 coins commemorating the Moscow Olympics commences in a four-year series.
1980 Last year of 10-ruble chervonetz production.
1988 Issues palladium commemorative coins for Christian millenium.
1989 Introduces palladium bullion Ballerina coins.
1989 Latvian Socialist Republic gains right to issue currency.
1989 Lithuanian Socialist Republic gains right to issue

currency.
1989 Estonian Socialist Republic receives right to issue
its own currency.

SCOTLAND
1124 Silver pennies of King David I.
1249 Silver half penny and farthing introduced by
King Alexander III.
1329 David II introduces silver groat, half-groat.
1460 Billon plack, half-plack of James III, first copper,
"black money."
1513 James V, billon bawbee (sixpence) and
divisions.
1542 Reign of Mary sees many coinage innovations
and types based on the royal marriages both
in Scotland and abroad.
1553 Silver testoon and divisions.
1567 Silver ryal or dollar, and its two-third and one-
third divisions, King James VI.
1555-56 Billon hardhead, quarter pence, billon
penny.
1572 Silver merk, half-merk.
1578 Silver 2 merks, merk.
1581 Silver 2, 4, 8, 16 shillings.
1603 James VI, as James I of Great Britain, France
and Ireland, introduces 60-shilling crown of
English design, first Scots-English
interchangeable coin type.
1706 Ten-shillings and 5-shillings Scots, last of the
distinctively Scottish coins under Queen Anne.
1937 Scottish crest reappears on British coinage as a
tribute to the queen, the former Lady Elizabeth
Bowes-Lyon.
1968 Scots thistle appears on new decimal 5 pence.
1984 Great Britain's 1-pound coin features Scotland.
1990 Two of the three private banks issuing £1 notes
cease their issues.

SPAIN
711 Muslim invasion marked by a gold sol idus dated
93 A.H. begins a long and complex Moorish
coinage in Spain, which continues until the
15th century.
814 Carolingian coinage in Barcelona, silver dinero of
Louis the Pious.
874 Independent coinage of the Counts of
Barcelona begins with a silver dinero of
Wilfredo.
991 Ampurias coinage of Count Hugo I, billon dinero.
Billon becomes a major coinage metal of the
Spanish principalities.
1018 Gold mancuso struck by Berenguer Ramon I,
count of Barcelona.
1035 Kingdom of Leon coinage begins with silver
dinero of Fernando I.
1054 Kingdom of Navarra, billon dineros of Sancho IV.
1063 Kingdom of Aragon's coinage initiated by
Sancho I Ramirez.
1065 Kingdom of Castile coinage begun with dinero
and obolo coins of Alfonso VI.
1157 Gold maravedi with Latin inscriptions of
Fernando II of Leon.
1158 Castilian gold dobla, Moorish inscription and
design with added cross.
1238 Kingdom of Valencia, liberated by El Cid
Campeador, begins coinage of billon dineros
under Jaime I.
1282 Sicilian gold and silver coinage under kings of
Aragon, golden age of Catalan culture and
influence.
1284 Sancho VI of Castile creates the billon cornado.
1297 Sardinia under Aragonese rule, silver real
coinage.

1350 Silver real introduced in Castile by Pedro I, the
Cruel.
1379 The billon "agnus dei" or blanca created by
Juan I of Castile.
1406 Large gold coin of 20 doblas under Juan II of
Castile.
1458 Gold escudo struck by Juan II of Aragon.
1469 Fernando V and Isabel, coinage gradually
stabilizing around copper maravedi, silver real
and gold excelente.
1492 Last Moorish stronghold, Granada, falls to
Fernando and Isabel; gold 20 excelentes
struck, probably to commemorate the final
victory of the reconquest.
1580 Brief royal union with Portugal.
1636 Vast monetary confusion during the reign of
Felipe IV, extensive and repeated revaluation
of copper coinage by countermarking.
1643 During invasion of northern Spain, Louis XIV
strikes coinage as Count of Barcelona.
1705 War of the Spanish Succession sees coins struck
in Barcelona for claimant Carlos III of
Hapsburg; coinage elsewhere for Felipe V of
the new Bourbon dynasty.
1808 Jose Napoleon, brother of the French emperor,
imposed as king of Spain. Coins struck for Jose
Napoleon and Fernando VII, the legitimate
king in guarded exile in France.
1809 French occupation coinage introduces "en
Barcelona" peseta, struck in three silver and
one gold denominations, which provided
important future direction for Spain's monetary
development.
1825 Emancipation of the Spanish colonies in South
and Central America complete as Potosi Mint,
in present day Bolivia, strikes the last Spanish
style silver 8 reales.
1837 First Carlist war produces coins of Don Carlos V,
pretender to the throne.
1864 Coinage reform under Isabel II introduces the
decimal silver escudo, divid ed into 100
centimos. Distinctive Philippine peso-centimo
gold and silver coinage created.
1869 The Provisional Government announces
adoption of the peseta, on the standard of the
Latin Monetary Union, divided into 100
centimos.
1873 Coinage of third Carlist pretender Don Carlos
VII.
1895 Colonial coinage for Puerto Rico, 1 peso equals
5 pesetas.
1933 First coinage of the second Spanish Republic.
1937 Civil War causes a proliferation of local and
regional emergency coinage and notes,
Vienna Mint strikes first coins for Franco's
Nationalist government.
1940 Aluminum minor coinage introduced.
1966 Continued growth and prosperity marked by
issue of silver 100-peseta coin.
1975 Following the death of Generalissimo Francisco
Franco, Council of the Realm drafts legislation
for new portrait coin age of King Juan Carlos I.
1976 Royal portrait appears on Spanish coinage, new
royal arms on 5, 50 pesetas. Copper-nickel 100
pesetas introduced, all coins with star date
1976, authorization date 1975.
1978 The country observes its first National Coin
Week.
1982 A new, crowned M Mint mark is introduced.

SWEDEN
995 Nordic coinage along English and Byzantine lines
at Sweden's Hedeby Mint.
999 First Swedish coinage, King Olof Skotkonung.

c. 1150 "Penningar" bracteate coinage.
1478 First dated Swedish coins, ortug and half ortug.
1521 Reign of Gustaf Vasa, founder of a new dynasty for independent Sweden.
1534 Silver daler issued with standing figure of the king.
1556 Square klippe silver ore coinage.
1568 Gold gulden of Erik XIV, Hebrew name "Jehovah" out of clouds on reverse.
1598 Jehovah-name silver coinage, under regent Karl.
1606 Large silver 20 marks of Karl IX.
1611-32 Reign of Gustaf II Adolf sees Sweden caught up in the Thirty Years War on the continent.
1624 Square klippe emergency copper coinage.
1632 Queen Kristina issues silver riksdaler with standing figure of Christ.
1644 Massive copper "plate money" issues begin, valued in equivalence to the silver coins drained out of the kingdom to redeem fortresses held by the Danes.
1656 Gold ducat coinage under Karl X Gustaf; plate money continues.
1670 Portrait-type 8 marks in silver, similar to English coinage of Charles II, struck by Karl XI.
1661 Large copper circular ore coinage begins.
1697 Beginning of the reign of Karl XII, "Alexander of the North" and the exhausting wars of his reign.
1706 "Alchemy ducat" of gold allegedly produced by "the chemical art."
1715 Beginning of the emergency copper "Goertz dalers" named for the hated finance minister who was assassinated after a period of inflation.
1721 Commemorative riksdaler in silver issued by Fredrik I honoring the Protestant Reformation in Sweden.
1720 Coinage of 1, half ore coppers over old Goertz dalers.
1759 Last copper plate money issued under King Adolf Fredrik.
1810 Beginning of coinage under Karl XIII, Napoleon's candidate who deposed king Gustaf IV Adolf

in 1809. Karl XIII adopts French Marshal Bernadotte as his heir, prince Karl Johan.
1818 Coinage of Bernadotte as Karl XIV Johan.
1821 Another Reformation commemorative riksdaler issued.
1835 Skilling banco token copper coinage.
1856 Decimal half, 1, 2 and 5 ore copper coins of Oscar I.
1861 Decimal silver ore coins of Karl XV in style of Oscar's 1855 coinage, alongside the earlier issue of riksdalers riksmynt, struck until 1873.
1868 International currency gold coinage of Karl XV, one carolin equals 10 francs.
1873 Decimal system of the Scandinavian krona of 100 ore under Oscar II.
1897 Coronation commemorative 2 kronor begins a long series in this denomination.
1906 Following the independence of Norway, the royal motto on the coinage becomes "Sweden's Welfare," rather than "Welfare of the Brother Peoples."
1917 Iron is adopted for World War I 1, 2 and 5 ore.
1920 Copper-nickel replaces silver in 50, 25 and 10 ore.
1935 A commemorative 5 kronor marks the 500th anniversary of Sweden's Riksdag, or Parliament.
1942 New low-silver coinage, iron reappears in the lowest three values.
1952 New ultra-modern designs on the coinage of Gustaf VI Adolf, first modernistic royal portrait in the world.
1959 Smaller 5-kronor commemoratives begin with the 150th anniversary of the constitution.
1962 Copper-nickel replaces silver in the Swedish coinage.
1975 Constitution commemorative introduces silver 50 kroner.
1976 After many delays, new series of minor coins released for King Carl XVI Gustaf, 5 ore through 5 kronor.
1981 The 5 ore issued in brass.

British Colonies

CHANNEL ISLANDS, JERSEY

1834 French currency replaced with British in distinctively Jersey denomination series.
1841 First of the new coins issued, copper 1/13, 1/26, 1/52 shillings.
1866 Bronze coins, smaller sizes, in similar denominations.
1877 Conversion to standard United Kingdom denominations, still uniquely stated as 1/12, 1/24, 1/48 shillings.
1949 The liberation from German occupation in 1945 is commemorated by a bronze 1/12 shilling piece.
1957 A new quarter shilling nickel-brass coin introduced, 3 pence equivalent.
1966 The conquest of England by the duke of Normandy, of which Jersey was a part, is commemorated by three commemoratives, including the first regal 5-shilling copper-nickel crown.
1968 First decimal coins appear.
1971 Decimal range completed, half new penny to 50 new pence.

CYPRUS

1879 Copper piastre coinage of Victoria, first coins for the island since the medieval kingdom under the Lusignan rulers and the Venetians.
1901 Silver coinage begun, with a modified "Jubilee" head of Victoria used only on the Cyprus coinage.
1928 Crown sized 45-piastre coin commemorates 50 years of British rule.
1934 Copper-nickel scalloped 1, half piastre.
1947 Piastre denominations replaced by shilling types in copper-nickel.
1955 Decimalization, 1,000 mils to one Cyprus pound.
1963 Decimal issues by the new Republic of Cyprus.
1970 First crown issued after independence, 500 mils in copper-nickel for the FAO coin program.
1984 Mil coin denominations replaced by nickel-brass 1, 2, 5, 10 and 20 cents, and aluminum half cent.

GIBRALTAR

1802-20 Private copper token coinage in circulation.
1841 Copper 1, 2 quart regal coins of Victoria.
1842 Half-quart completes roster of Gibraltar coinage, which ends in 1861.

1967 Copper-nickel crown issued.
1971 Famed Barbary ape appears on new crown of 25 new pence, start of ongoing crown series.
1975 Issues first gold coin.
1988 Plans circulating domestic legal tender coins.
1990 Reduces diameter of 5 pence coin.

GUERNSEY
1830 Distinctive copper coinage of 1 and 4 doubles, relics of the medieval double tournois, still money of account until 1921.
1834 Eight doubles added to series.
1864 Bronze replaces copper.
1956 Redesigned bronze coins and new scalloped 3 pence.
1966 Round-cornered square copper-nickel 10-shilling Norman Conquest commemorative with portrait of William, Duke of Normandy.
1968 Decimal coinage begins, full range of bronze and copper-nickel complete by 1971.
1977 "New" dropped from pence denomination coins.
1985 First £2 commemorative coin introduced.

IONIAN ISLANDS
1819 Copper obol coinage under British colonial rule.
1834 Silver 30-lepta coinage.

ISLE OF MAN
1709 Cast copper penny, half penny introduced by the Earl of Derby.
1721 Struck coppers of similar type.
1758 Copper penny, half penny of the duke of Atholl.
1786 Regal copper coinage of King George III.
1798 "Cartwheel" type regal coppers.
1811 Silver and copper private bank tokens issued during small change famine caused by the Napoleonic wars.
1839 Manx coinage on sterling system begins under Victoria.
1971 Complete U.K. type decimal coinage, half penny through 50 new pence with designs drawn from Manx history.
1973 Gold coinage, half pound through 5 pounds with Viking king reverse, Pobjoy Mint.
1974 Churchill commemorative crown begins prolific issues struck by Pobjoy Mint.
1976 Redesigned coinage eliminates "new" in new pence.
1983 Plastic notes introduced into circulation.
1984 Enters world bullion market with introduction of gold Angel coin.
1988 Modifies Raphael Maklouf's portrait of the Queen.
1990 Pobjoy Mint introduces "pearl black" coin finish.

LUNDY
1929 Worldwide numismatic stir follows the actions of Martin Coles Harman, Lundy's owner, in issuing his own bronze coins, 1 and half puffin, named for the seabirds which breed on the island. Hauled into the Devonshire court, he was fined £5 for violating the Coinage Act of 1870.

MALTA
1521 Gold coinage of Philippe Villiers, grand master of the Order of St. John of Jerusalem, formerly based in the kingdom of Jerusalem and later on the island of Rhodes.
1553 Copper piccioli coinage under grand master Claude de la Sengle.
1566 The great Grand Master Jean de la Valette begins bronze grano coinage (followed by the tari types in 1567) with reverse inscription "not bronze but faith."
1723 First crown-sized silver coin, the 2 scudi of Antonio Manoel de Vilhena.
1798 Last coinage of the Order under Grand Master Ferdinand Hompesch; Malta conquered by Napoleon's forces, the Order withdraws, eventually relocates in Rome.
1798-1800 Siege of Malta, ingot necessity coinage under French general Vaubois.
1866 The British colonial government issues a distinctive third-farthing to approximate old grani coins, along with earlier British type third-farthings already in circulation.
1902 Edward VII third-farthing.
1913 Last Malta third-farthing under George V.
1961 The Sovereign Military Order of Malta, long domiciled in Rome, resumes a symbolic coinage struck by a small Mint set up in the palace in Rome.
1972 After the attaining of independence from Britain in 1964, a new decimal coinage of 1,000 mils or 100 cents to one Malta pound is begun.

MAURITIUS AND REUNION
1779 Billon coinage of Louis XVI, Isles de France and Bourbon.
1810 Silver 10-livre crown for the Iles de France (Mauritius) and Bonaparte, (earlier Ile de Bourbon, still later the colony of Reunion).
1816 Ile de Bourbon billon 10 centimes of Louis XVIII.
1822 Base silver 50 and 25 sous issued by the Mauritius treasury.
1877 Decimal silver and bronze Victorian coinage, 100 cents to the Mauritius rupee.
1896 French Reunion nickel 1 franc, 50 centimes.
1934 First Mauritius 1 rupee in silver.
1939 Beginning of separate rupee-cent coinage for Seychelles.
1948 Aluminum colonial 1, 2 francs for French Reunion.
1955 Aluminum-bronze higher denominations in Reunion.
1971 Independence coinage of Mauritius, crown-sized 10 rupees bears the extinct dodo bird.
1972 Aluminum FAO minor coins, new copper-nickel seven-sided 5 rupee coins join Seychelles coinage.
1976 Independent coinage of Seychelles portrays President Mancham.

ST. HELENA
1821 Copper half penny struck by the East India Company.
1974 Crown-sized copper-nickel 25 pence marks the anniversary of the E.I.C. royal charter.
1977 Silver Jubilee of Queen Elizabeth II sees crowns for St. Helena and dependency, Tristan da Cunha.

India, Southeast Asia and related areas
(Countries arranged by region)

BURMA

1852 Silver peacock rupee coinage of King Mindon Min.
1865 Peacock copper quarter anna struck.
1866 Gold lion coinage.
1878 Copper quarter anna of the last king, Thibaw.
1949 Copper-nickel and pure nickel rupee standard coinage issued by newly independent Burma.
1952 Decimal rupee of 100 pyas adopted.
1966 Aluminum coinage with portrait of Gen. Aung San, founder of the republic.
1983 Issues 10 pyas bronze FAO coin for international series.
1990 Renamed Myanmar.

CAMBODIA

1846 Gold rooster-obversed fuang struck by King Ong Harizak.
1847 Silver pagoda quarter and 1 tical.
1860 Franc standard coinage of King Norodom I, bronze 5 centimes through 4 francs silver, with a trade dollar or piastre equal to the Mexican peso.
1953 Aluminum three-coin set issued after the restoration of independence, 10, 20 and 50 centimes.
1959 Similar coins issued in denominations of 100 sen to 1 riel.
1975 Controversy is aroused by the release through a numismatic distributor of 50,000-riel gold coins authorized by the now-vanished Lon Nol regime; dispute centered on the terms "legal tender" and "face value," another argument was raised over the "rate of exchange" for the worthless currency of a vanished government.
1981 Moneyless economy experimented with by Kmer Rouge government.

CEYLON, SRI LANKA

1747-93 Silver, tin, lead and copper coinage of the Netherlands East India Company.
1801 First English coinage for Ceylon, crude dump types with Dutch denominations.
1802 Modern, machine-struck copper coinage.
1815 Copper stuiver-denominations and pattern silver rix dollar struck.
1823 Countermarked Arcot rupee and quarter rupee released to circulation.
1830 Reign of William IV sees circulation of British type half farthing and silver quarter pence pieces in Ceylon.
1870 Decimal rupee adopted, 100 cents to one rupee; copper coinage struck.
1892 First silver decimal coinage, 50, 25 and 10 cents.
1909 Square copper-nickel 5-cent coin introduced.
1943 Wartime nickel-brass 50, 25 cents.
1957 First distinctive Ceylon independent coins, Buddhist commemorative issue.
1963 Full range of decimal coins, aluminum, nickel-brass and copper-nickel struck.
1972 First coinage with new national designation, Sri Lanka.

COLONIAL INDOCHINA

1875 Old French 1-centime coins, holed, are released to circulation, valued at 1 sapeque, for the new colony of Cochin China.
1879 Square-holed 2-sapeque coinage in bronze joins a large bronze centime and silver 10, 20 and 50 centimes and a pattern trade dollar, the piastre with inscription "French Cochin China."
1885 Similar coinage is introduced for the whole of French Indochina, which now includes Cambodia, "Annam," Tonkin and Laos.
1896 Smaller, holed 1 centime adopted.
1931 New Liberty Head piastre.
1935 Lindauer-designed bronze half centime introduced.
1938 Holed nickel-bronze 5 centimes issued.
1939 Pure nickel and copper-nickel 10, 20 centimes struck.
1940 Following the collapse of France, locally produced zinc 1 centimes are issued, followed by several aluminum denominations.
1945 Returning over Vietnamese protest, the French issue aluminum and copper-nickel coins of pre-war design.
1947 The last French issue is released, a copper-nickel 1 piastre struck in the name of the still-born Indochinese Federation.

INDIA

1000-1300 Gold coinage of Chola.
1193 Coins of Sultan Muhammad, Delhi.
1302 Royal gold coinage of Bengal.
1495 First Portuguese colonial gold under Manoel I, Goa.
1540 Unusual but distinctive octagonal coinage in Assam.
1556 Innovative coinage of the great Mughal ruler Akbar.
1600 Portcullis silver coinage of Elizabeth I of England enters India to compete with Spanish silver reales.
1605 Portrait coinage of Sultan Jahangir, considered heretical by strict Muslims, who also emphatically disapproved of the appearance of the ruler's wine goblet on the coinage. Famed zodiac gold coinage issued.
1671 Silver 1, 2 speciedalers struck for the Danish East India Company.
1672 First British silver coined at Bombay, a city given by the King of Portugal as a wedding gift to King Charles II.
1677 "The rupee of Bombaim" struck under authority of Charles II.
1700 Beginning of the Muslim type coinage of the Nizams of Hyderabad.
1719 Gold coinage at Diu under Portugal's King Joao V.
1724 Dutch East India Company coinage in Cochin.
1730 Mughal type coinage under the French at Mahe in the name of Sultan Ahmad Shah Bahadur.
1735 British United East India Company, (E.I.C.) silver and lead coinage of Bombay.
1750 Gold mohar coinage in Nepal.
1751 French coinage of the Pondichery Mint in the name of Mughal Sultan Ahmad Shah Bahadur.
1760 Dutch East India Company gold coinage at Negapatam.
1765 E.I.C. coinage begins in Bengal, similarly in Bombay.
1768 Arcot-type French coinage at Mahe.
1791 Modern, machine-struck copper coinage produced by Matthew Boulton for E.I.C. in Bombay.
1794 Machine-struck copper for Calcutta.
1803 Madras struck E.I.C. modern copper.
1807 Silver pagoda coinage with figure of god Vishnu, Madras.
1811 Crown-sized double rupee struck over Spanish 8 reales at Arcot.
1824 Modern copper E.I.C. pice coinage for Bengal.

1833 First all-India coinage by E.I.C., 1/12 anna, half pice, quarter anna, and half anna. These denominations become the standard through decimalization in 1957.

1835 All-India silver portrait coinage, gold mohur coins of "William IIII, king."

1839 Closing of French India Pondichery Mint.

1840 First portrait coinage of Victoria by E.I.C.

1841 State coinage of Kutch bears the name of Victoria.

1846 Last coinage of Danish India, Tranquebar.

1860 Following the great Indian mutiny and demise of the E.I.C., direct rule by Britain sees first all-India "Victoria Queen" silver, copper 1862.

1871 Modern machine-struck Portuguese colonial copper at Goa.

1877 Portrait coins of Victoria as empress of India.

1887 Standardized Victoria empress coins issued by Dewas and Dhar states.

1892 Bikanir state issues standardized portrait rupee; Hyderabad halli sicca coins struck.

1901 Gateway coinage introduced in Hyderabad.

1902 Modern gold in Gwalior, machine-struck silver in Indore.

1903 Bare-head all-India coinage of Edward VII.

1904 Modern copper coinage in Travancore.

1907 Edward VII copper-nickel 1 anna with scalloped edge struck.

1911 Modern silver coinage in Travancore; "pig" rupee of George V recalled.

1917 Modern sharply-struck coins in Kutch, in the name of George V.

1919 An attempt is made to replace smaller silver coinage with copper-nickel 8-, 4-, 2-anna pieces. The 8 anna, or half-rupee, is at once extensively counterfeited.

1942 Nickel-brass 2, 1 and half anna wartime coinage.

1943 Holed bronze 1 pice introduced.

1945 Rajkot state strikes last state gold coin, 1 mohur.

1947 Pure nickel rupee, half and quarter rupee, tiger reverse.

1950 First coinage of independent India.

1957 Decimalization introduces a rupee of 100 naya paisa.

1964 Subsidiary coinage now called simply paisa; first aluminum coin issued, and first commemorative rupee, half rupee honors Jawaharlal Nehru.

1969 Undated Gandhi commemoratives introduce new silver 10 rupees.

1974-75 Trend toward larger commemoratives, 20, 50 rupees; copper-nickel and aluminum small denominations begin to multiply.

1978 High-value notes of 1,000, 5,000 and 10,000 rupees demonetized to curb corruption.

1987 Closes Delhi Mint, opens new Mint at Noida###

LAOS

1952 Holed aluminum set of three coins, 10, 20 and 50 centimes.

1980 Exchange of 100 old kips for one new kip.

PAKISTAN, BANGLADESH

1948 First coinage of the government of Pakistan.

1961 Beginning of decimalization, 100 pice, later paisa to one rupee.

1964 English legends omitted on Pakistani coinage.

1969 Copper-nickel replaces pure nickel in the higher denominations.

1973 Following bloody massacres and civil war, Bangladesh is born. A new coinage begins, based on the taka of 100 poisha.

THAILAND

1767 Silver bullet money introduced by liberator-king Taksin.

1782 Bangkok dynasty introduces bullet coins struck with central ridge from two hammer blow striking.

1860 Modern silver tical coinage of King Phra Chom Klao, Mongkut.

1862 Tin minor coinage.

1865 Cast copper minor coinage.

1874 Royal monogram type struck copper.

1876 Portrait silver coins of King Phra Maha Chulalongkorn, undated.

1887 Portrait type copper struck.

1897 Copper-nickel decimal satang coins struck.

1902 Dates appear on the silver portrait coinage.

1908 Holed bronze 1 satang appears, 100 satangs to one baht.

1939 New national designation, "Muang Thai" or "land of the Thai" officially adopted in place of the former Siam.

1942 Tin replaces silver and bronze in the minor coinage.

1946 Royal portrait coinage resumed in tin.

1950 Aluminum-bronze minor coinage begins under King Pumiphol.

1961 The first Thai commemorative marks the world tour of the royal couple.

1963 The first recent crown-sized silver coin issued to mark the king's 36th birthday, 20 baht.

1970 Large silver 50 baht commemorates the 20th anniversary of the World Buddhist Fellowship.

1972 New polygonal 5-baht copper-nickel coin released.

1976 Silver 100-, 150-baht commemoratives joined by copper-nickel at 1 baht, beginning of a flood of modern commemoratives.

1978 Demonetization of 5-baht coin caused by counterfeiting.

VIETNAM

The early coins of Vietnam resemble those of China, the square holed circular cash coins, which were cast under the Le dynasty until 1789; by the Tayson rebels in southern Vietnam; and by the Nguyen dynasty established by Nguyen Anh in 1802. The ingots and circular Vietnam issues are not considered true coins.

1802 Cast square-holed copper and zinc dong coinage begins under Emperor Gia-Long.

1883 Proclamation of a French protectorate ends independence of Vietnam, which already had lost Cochin-China in 1862-67.

1884 Coinage of the heroic nationalist emperor Ham-Nghi.

1889-1926 Vietnam, its central region of Annam theoretically sovereign under French protection, continues to issue coins through the reign of emperor Bao Dai, 1926-1945.

1945 Following the abdication of the emperor, the Communist-led Viet-Minh follow his earlier declaration of independence from France. The first aluminum 20 xu coin is released.

1946 Aluminum 5 hao and 1 dong, bronze 2-dong coins struck, the latter two with Ho Chi Minh's portrait.

1953 The state of Vietnam, with ex-emperor Bao Dai at its head, issues three aluminum coins, 10, 20 and 50 xu.

1960 After the deposition of Bao Dai, the new republic of Vietnam issues an aluminum 50 su and copper-nickel 1 dong with the portrait of president Ngo Dinh-diem.

1964 Following the murder of Ngo Dinh-diem, republican coins with rice plant obverse are issued in copper-nickel.

1968 Nickel-clad steel coinage released.

1971 An aluminum 1 dong issued in connection with the FAO coin program.

1975 Forcible unification of South and North Vietnam as a newly united Communist state.

1979 North and South Vietnamese notes replaced with new dong notes.

Near East, Africa
(Countries arranged by regions)

ISLAMIC COINAGES, NEAR EAST, NORTH AFRICA, RELATED AREAS

630-720 Anonymous one-third solidus coinages of the Caliphs.

660-750 Gold dinar coinage of the Umayyad caliphs of Damascus.

750-1517 Coinage of the Abbasid caliphs of Baghdad.

969-1173 Coinage of Egypt's Fatimid caliphs.

756-1024 Renewal of Umayyad coin types in Muslim Cordoba, Spain, by a refugee of the Umayyad house.

1040-1308 Seljuk Turkish empire coinage, Asia Minor and neighboring areas.

1056-1147 Coins of Spain's Almoravid Muslim rulers.

1130-1269 Almohad rulers, another splinter group of North African origin in Spain. Saracenic bezant gold coinage of the Crusaders' Latin Kingdom of Jerusalem, types of Muslim derivation.

1192-1300 Coinage of Shahs of Afghanistan.

1259 Last Jerusalem bezants of Latin Kingdom under Conrad and Conradin.

1451 Ottoman gold sequins of Muhammad II.

1502 Gold Ashrafis of Persian shah Ismail I.

1600 Gold of sultans of Morocco.

1773 Last coins of the khanate of Krim, Crimea, in South Russia.

1786 Modern round gold coin struck at Madrid, Spain, Mint for Morocco.

1789 Napoleon's invasion of Egypt sees 1, half and quarter sequin coinage of Turkish type.

1823 Fath Ali Shah in Persia issues gold tomans with equestrian portrait.

1844 Abdul Mejid modernizes Turkish coinage, "Medjidieh dollar" struck.

1855 Distinctive coinage in Tunisia.

1876 Modernization of Persian coinage under Shah Nasr ud-Din.

1882 Round silver machine-struck coins of Morocco's Hasan I.

1885 Sudan coins of the Mahdi, Muhammad Ahmad.

1887 Coins of the khalifa Abdullahi, the mahdi's successor.

1891 Start of modern Afghan coinage under Amir Abd ur-Rahman.

1893 Modern copper coinage in Morocco.

1894 Coppers of Fessul bin Turkee, Imam of Muscat and Oman.

1904 Independent Yemen coinage of imam Yahya bin Muhammad Hamid ad-Din.

1916 First coins of Egypt of sultan Hussein Kamil.

1920 Last coins of Ottoman Turkey under Muhammad VI. Fuad, sultan of Egypt, issues his silver coins.

1921 French mandate issues Bank of Syria coin.

1922 First Turkish republic coinage. Fuad now king in Egypt.

1923 Hejaz coinage in bronze, silver and gold of Hussein ibn Ali.

1924 First coinage of the state of Great Lebanon, French mandate.

1925 Provisional coins of Abdul Aziz ibn as-Saud at occupied Mecca Mint. Reza Shah proclaimed ruler in Persia, solar year adopted.

1927 Distinctive Hebrew, English, Arabic coinage issued in Britain's Palestine Mandate, first coins to bear abbreviated name, "Land of Israel." Gold Pahlavi adopted by Reza Shah in Persia.

1931 First coinage in Iraq under King Faisal I

1934 Latin alphabet, western dates only on Turkish coinage.

1937 First coins of the "Kingdom of Saudi Arabia."

1940 Modern copper-nickel coinage in Muscat and Oman under Sultan Sa'id bin Taimur.

1947 Coinage of the independent Syrian republic.

1949 First coinage of the Hashemite kingdom of the Jordan, "of Jordan," 1955. French-type coinage in Algeria.

1952 Republic of Lebanon independent coinage; also kingdom of Libya.

1954 Egyptian republic coinage.

1956 King Muhammad V strikes Moroccan 500 francs after French protectorate is abolished. New coinage of Independent Sudan.

1958 United Arab Republic established, union of Egypt, (UAR coins 1958) and Syria (separate UAR coins, 1959).

1959 Following the murder of King Faisal II, Republic of Iraq coinage begins. Turkey introduces stainless steel coinage.

1960 Maldive Islands introduce new larin-rupee coinage. First distinctive republican Tunisia coinage in aluminum, aluminum-bronze.

1961 Kuwait strikes first independent coinage.

1962 Following breakup of UAR, Syrian Arab Republic strikes first coinage.

1963 Under Egyptian tutelage, Yemen Arab Republic begins coinage in the territory it is able to hold during continuing war with Imam's government.

1964 First independent coins of Algeria, federation of South Arabia.

1965 Coinage of oil-rich Bahrain, 1,000 fils to one dinar.

1966 Qatar and Dubai coinage issued, 100 dirham to one ryal.

1970 New Oman coinage based on Saudi ryal of 1,000 baizah.

1971 Following bloody revolution, "Democratic Yemen" coinage is struck for the former Federation of South Arabia. UAR (Egypt) adopts name, "Arab Republic of Egypt."

1973 Coinage of United Arab Emirates in Arabian gulf, former Trucial States, including Abu Dhabi, Dubai, Sharjah, Ajman, Umm al-Qaiwain, Fujairah and Ras al-Khaimah. One dirham equals 100 fils; 1,000 fils equals one dinar.

1972 Proclamation of loose union followed by identical eagle on coinage of Egypt, Libya and Syria.

1976 Iran adopts new Imperial calendar, year 2535 on new coins.

1979 Iranian currency no longer depicts monarch after overthrow of the Pahlavi dynasty.
1990 Turkey files suit in United States seeking return of ancient coins allegedly smuggled out of Turkey.

ISRAEL

1948 Israel, only weeks old, strikes provisional aluminum 25 mils.
1949 Israel issues new 1,000 prutah to Israel pound coinage. Tenth anniversary of the independence of Israel sees beginning of commemorative coinage with copper-nickel 1 pound, silver 5 pounds.
1960 New Israeli coinage of 100 agora to one pound.
1985 Devalued Israeli sheqel coins issued in changeover to new sheqel monetary system.
1988 Introduces 20-new sheqalim note.

SUB-SAHARAN AFRICA, ISLANDS

300-850 Coinage of the kingdom of Axum, ancestor of Ethiopia.
1755 Mozambique Portuguese gold coins.
1762 Angola Portuguese silver coins.
1791 Decimal coins for freed slave colony of Sierra Leone, "Lion on Rock" type.
1797 "Free trade to Africa by order of Parliament" coins of the Gold Coast, Ackey denominations.
1815 "Missionary coins" of Griqua Town, South Africa.
1833 American Colonization Society issues 1-cent copper coin for Liberia.
1842 Silver onca ingot-coinage for Maria II, Mozambique.
1847 Copper coins of republic of Liberia.
1874 Thomas Francois Burgers gold "staatspond," first official coin in South Africa, (old South African Republic, the Transvaal).
1881 Sultanate of Zanzibar issues gold, silver and copper riyal coins.
1883 French West African tokens, brass 10, 5, 1 centimes.
1887 Coinage of the Independent State of the Congo under personal rule of the king of the Belgians, Leopold II. Holed copper, unholed silver.
1888 Coins of the Imperial East Africa Company at Mombasa, rupee denominations.
1890 Comoro Islands sultan's coinage, franc standard: first copper of the new German East Africa Company.
1891 First Italian tallero for Eritrea.
1892 Coins for President S.J.P. Kruger in the restored South African Republic, Mints in Berlin, Germany, Pretoria, South Africa.
1893 German East Africa silver coinage, company administration.
1894 Modern Ethiopian coinage in silver and copper under Menelik II.
1896 First regular issue silver coinage in Liberia.
1897 British East Africa pice-rupee standard.
1902 Last independent South African Republic coinage, the "Veld pond" at Pilgrim's Rest, Transvaal.
1904 New German East Africa coinage under the administration of the German Foreign Office.
1906 British East Africa aluminum 1 cent, silver 25, 50 cents. First regular issue aluminum coin in the world.
1907 Aluminum 1/10 penny, British West Africa-Nigeria.
1909 Belgian Congo's first coins under Belgian, rather than personal rule by Leopold II. Italian Somalia

coinage begins on besa-rupia standard.
1913 Silver and copper-nickel coinage for British West Africa-Nigeria.
1916 Emergency coinage in the defense territory of German East Africa under General Paulus von Lettow-Vorbeck. The Tabora Railway shops produce both brass and copper 20- and 5-heller pieces as well as a 15 rupien gold coin.
1918 Italian Eritrea issues a "tallero veneto" in imitation of the standard Maria Theresia taler.
1920 Large franc denominations in copper-nickel in the Belgian Congo.
1921 Following hoarding of silver coins for jewelry purposes, brass coins replace silver in British West Africa.
1923 Pretoria Mint reopens to strike a full range of coins for the Union of South Africa (established 1910).
1924 First French coins for the former German colonies of Togo and Cameroon.
1929 Modern Portuguese coins for Sao Tome e Principe, islands in the gulf of Guinea.
1930 New Portuguese coinage for Cape Verde Islands.
1931 New bronze, nickel coinage of Haile Selassie I of Ethiopia.
1932 New Southern Rhodesia coins.
1933 Modern coinage for Portuguese Guinea.
1935 Portuguese Mozambique introduces new silver standardized coins, adding copper-nickel and bronze in 1936, beginning a long colonial coin standard which was to permeate the rest of Portuguese colonial history.
1942-43 Coinage of the Free French in various African colonies, led by French Equatorial Africa under Governor General Felix Eboue.
1943 Pretoria, South Africa, Mint coinage for Belgian Congo for exile government.
1944 New Ethiopian coinage in bronze and silver under restored emperor.
1946 Portuguese Guinea marks fifth centenary of discovery with standard type commemorative coins.
1948 Standardized Angola Portuguese colonial coinage. French empire begins coinage explosion of standard-obverse Bazor type coins in many African, Indian and Pacific ocean colonies; initial types 1 and 2 francs in aluminum, aluminum-bronze and nickel added in 1960s in surviving colonies such as the Comoro islands.
1949 Cape Verde standardized Portuguese colonial coins.
1950 Italian trusteeship coinage for Somalia, 100 centesimi to one somalo.
1954 Last coins of Southern Rhodesia.
1955 Federation of Rhodesia and Nyasaland coins issued.
1958 Independent Ghana sets type for African coinages with new sterling-type coins portraying the "Osagyefo" Dr. Kwame Nkrumah.
1959 Coinage begins for former French Guinea, Federation of Nigeria. New unified coinage of the Equatorial African States begins.
1960 New coins for independent Cameroon, emission bank of Rwanda and Burundi; long-independent Liberia issues new bronze, copper-nickel and silver sets.
1961 South Africa decimal coins, 100 cents (Afrikaans, sent) to one rand; Katanga, Mali and the unified coinage of the West African States begins.
1964 French colonial coins of the Comoro become

the first to bear a living fossil, the famed coelacanth fish; new independence coins in East Africa, Zambia, Rhodesia, Sierra Leone and Malawi.

1965 Malagasy republic coins in Madagascar introduces stainless steel to Africa; Ghana decimal coins; South Africa, new, smaller bronze, nickel and silver rand-cent/sent coins.

1966 Coins of Gambia, Kenya, Botswana, Tanzania and Uganda.

1967 Somali republic begins coinage; new 100 makuta to one zaire coinage, Congo. South Africa introduces gold Krugerrand coin and enters bullion market.

1968 Zambia, former Northern Rhodesia, begins decimal coinage.

1969 Ill-fated, short lived aluminum coins of republic of Biafra during the epic struggles of the Nigerian assault on the Ibos; new coins of the republic of Equatorial Guinea, formerly Spanish.

1970 Rhodesian decimalization.

1971 After break-up of the Equatorial African States unified currency, the new nickel 100 francs of Gabon, Central African Republic, Popular Republic of the Congo and Chad begins; decimal coins in Malawi, 100 tambala to one kwacha; decimalization in Gambia, 100 bututs to one dalasi; nickel coins introduced in place of silver in Portuguese colonies.

1973 Decimalization in Nigeria, 100 kobo to one naira; new Mauritania coinage of five khoum to one ouguiya.

1974 New decimal coins for Swaziland.

1975 Dissolution of the Portuguese empire leads to new currencies in Guinea-Bissau, Angola, Sao Tome and Mozambique.

1978 Madagascar Democratic Republic issues 10- and 20-ariary coins at five francs to the ariary. Uganda notes drop design depicting Idi Amin.

1979 South African circulating coinage design changes.

1980 Zimbabwe issues six denominations of coins, first issue for country. South Africa issues 1/10, quarter and half Krugerrands.

1981 South Africa introduces metal-plastic threads into paper money.

1985 Many countries ban importation of South African Krugerrand as a protest against racially-segregating apartheid policy.

1989 Zaire coins vanish from circulation due to inflation.

1989 South African Reserve Bank gains control of the Mint.

1989 South Africa releases circulating coinage in three colors.

1990 Angola introduces new bank note designs.

The Orient
(Countries arranged by region)

CHINA

B.C.

c. 1200 First spade coins, bronze "pu" types.

480 "Ming Tao" sword coinage, bronze.

c. 220 "Pan Liang" half-ounce coins, circular with square hole, Ch'in Dynasty.

118 "Wu Ch'u" coinage of Han Dynasty.

A.D.

7 Usurper Wang Mang issues knife type coins, gold-inlaid inscriptions.

618 "Kai Yuan" circular coins with square holes; T'ang dynasty sets pattern for centuries of square-holed coinage which ends only after the new republic is in power, 1911. Similar coins will be in use in Japan, Korea and Vietnam centuries after.

c. 1264 "Wen Sheng," frugal currency bronze tablet coins of Southern Sung dynasty during Mongol invasions.

c. 1280 Paper money issued under Mongol Yuan dynasty, inflation and counterfeiting rampant.

1837 Manchu army issues circular "god of longevity" dollar for Taiwan.

1851 T'ai P'ing rebellion coins of the "Great kingdom of Heavenly Peace" and multiple-cash brass coins of Ch'ing (Manchu) Hsien Feng emperor.

1861 Round silver dollars of Fukien province.

1889 Modernization of Canton Mint. Kwangtung province sees famed "dragon dollars" and subsidiary coinage begin about 1890, soon copied in all China.

1912 First republican coinage, "memento" dollars.

1914 Yuan Shih-kai dollar becomes standard coin.

1915 Announcement of restoration of the empire with President Yuan as the Hung Hsien emperor, effective 1916, sees pattern and commemorative coinage issues.

1928 Kweichow province strikes first coin to show automobile in commemoration of the first motor road in the province.

1931-2 First Communist army coins for territories occupied during the Civil War.

1932 Standard national dollar in silver, famed "birds over junk - rising sun" type modified to show the sailing junk only in the next year.

1936 New, non-silver coinage in bronze and pure nickel.

1937 Japan begins full-scale invasion, Chiang Kai-Shek holds out amid civil war caused by Communists, continuing inflation.

1949 After defeat of Japan, Communist takeover proceeds amid bitter war. U.S. Mint at San Francisco restrikes millions of 1898-dated Mexican pesos for Chiang to pay his troops after inflationary collapse of the national currency.

1949 Nationalist government of Chiang Kai-Shek resumes coinage on Taiwan (Formosa).

1955 First aluminum coinage of the Communist People's Republic of China.

1965 Copper-nickel, silver and gold commemoratives mark centenary of Dr. Sun Yat-Sen's birth in Taiwan coinage, beginning of commemoratives for important anniversaries such as the birthdays of President Chiang Kai-Shek.

1979 Peoples Republic issues its first gold coin.

1980 Peoples Republic introduces copper-zinc coinage.

1982 China Mint issues gold bullion Panda coins.

1987 Bullion gold Panda coins carry Mint mark for first time.

1987 Minster Machine of Ohio supplies Shanghai Mint with new blanking press.

JAPAN

A.D.

708 First coins of native Japanese type cast, "Wado Kaichin" coinage made of copper mined in Musashi province under empress Genmyo. This is the first of 12 early coins called "dynastic sen."

765-950 Rest of dynastic coinage, from "Mannen Tsuho" through "Kengen Saiho" in 958.

1584 "Mumei Obankin" issued under warlord Toyotomi Hideyoshi.

1593 First "Eiraku sen," Japanese copies of China's Ming dynasty "Yung Le" cash coins cast, rapidly take over Japan's internal commerce.

1599 Tokugawa Ieyasu established "Kinza" Mint for gold coins, "Ginza" for silver.

1626-1862 Kanei Tsuho" cash type coinage.

1832 Debased gold and silver coins issued in inflationary period.

1835 Oval cast copper "Tempo Tsuho" coinage begun.

1853 Commodore Perry and his "black ships" begin opening Japan after 200 years of isolation. Japanese gold flows out of country.

1870 Osaka Mint comes into operation, striking modern gold, silver and copper circular coins. New monetary system, one yen equal to 100 sen along American lines.

1889 Copper-nickel introduced for 5-sen coins.

1938 Aluminum war time coinage.

1944 Coinage in tin and porcelain.

1945 Clay "toka" coinage planned, blocked by production bottlenecks, at war's ending.

1946 Coinage reform under Allied occupation, brass 50 sen.

1948 Coin inscriptions now read left to right.

1955 Pure nickel and silver coins introduced.

1964 Olympic Games commemoratives see return of silver crown, 1,000-yen piece; first use of Western dates since pattern yen of 1873.

1976 Copper-nickel 100 yen marks emperor's 50th year, fourth commemorative in this metal and denomination.

1982 500-yen notes replaced with copper-nickel coin.

1984 10,000-yen notes released due to inflation.

1986 Issues commemorative coins sold by lottery system marking 60th year of reign of Emperor Hirohito.

1990 Police investigate a large number of possibly fake gold 100,000-yen coins.

Japanese states in occupied China

1933 First coinage on 100 fen to one yuan coinage in new state of Manchukuo.

1934 Coinage in the name of the Kang Teh emperor, former Hsuan Tung ruler of China until 1911.

1937 Autonomous East Hopei government of Wen Ju-keng issues Chi-tung coins in five fen-yuan denominations.

1938 Autonomous federated government of Inner Mongolia issues coinage.

1941 Federal Reserve Bank of China issues three aluminum coins from Peking.

1945 Red fiber coinage, necessity issue of World War II.

KOREA

996 "Kon Won" cast cash-type coinage of King Song Jong.

1100 Heavy cast cash coin production.

c. 1400 New coinage of Yi dynasty, "Sip Chon" issues begun.

1625 "Cho Son" cast coins.

1633 First stabilized currency "Sang Pyong" coins, often called "Yop Chon," issued well into the 19th century.

1885 Pattern for round, modern coinage of Korea introduced by Paul Georg von Mollendorf, Mint Director from Germany, on a yang-mun standard.

1886 Pattern warn-mun coins in copper, tin and gilt copper.

1892 Actual coinage of modern round pieces on 100 fun-one yang, soon overcome by a flood of officially-struck and counterfeit quarter-yang nickels.

1899 "Russian" 100 chon to one won coinage types prepared, some issued in 1901.

1905 Definitive Phoenix coinage on chon-won standard begun.

1910 Korean coinage ends with annexation to Japan.

1959 Following liberation, Communist invasion and war, coinage resumed on hwan standard.

1966 After overthrow of Syngman Rhee government, new won coinage begins.

1975 The 30th year of the restoration of Korea's sovereignty and independence is marked by a copper-nickel commemorative 100 won of South Korea.

1989 Melts unsold 1988 Olympic commemoratives.

Pacific Region

(Countries arranged alphabetically; some grouped by region)

AUSTRALIA

1813 "Holey dollar," pierced and counterstamped Spanish dollar issued in New South Wales.

1852 Adelaide Assay Office gold pounds, ingots struck.

1853 Fort Philip gold coinage.

1855 Sydney Mint gold coins Victoria 1-, half-pound pieces.

1871 British style gold coins.

1872 Melbourne Mint gold coinage.

1900 Perth Mint regular gold coinage.

1910 First distinctive Australian silver coins of Edward VII.

1911 Bronze penny, half penny issued.

1927 First Australian commemorative coin, Canberra florin.

1937 Complete redesign of the coinage, first crown issued.

1942 Some World War II coins struck in U.S. Mints.

1966 Decimal coinage, 100 cents to the Australian dollar, silver 50 cents.

1969 Polygonal copper-nickel 50 cents joins minor copper-nickel and bronze coins.

1970 First decimal commemorative, Captain Cook's voyages.

1980 Currency futures market opens. Commences coining of $200 gold Koala coin.

1984 Dollar coin replaces dollar bill in circulation.

1986 Issues Proof 1987 Nugget gold bullion coins to

preview gold bullion issue.
1987 Issues Nugget silver and platinum bullion coins.###
1988 Introduces plastic $10 Bicentennial commemorative note.
1989 Introduces Koala platinum bullion coins.

BRITISH MALAYA-EAST INDIES
1783 East India Company coins for Fort Marlbro, Sumatra, during Napoleonic wars.
1787 E.I.C. coins for Pulu Penang, cent-rupee standard.
1811-15 E.I.C. coins for occupied Java.
1841 Sir James Brooke's Sarawak copper kapang.
1845 First coins for the Straits Settlements under E.I.C.; 1862, "India-Straits."
1863 Copper coinage for Raj of Sarawak.
1863 Beginning of British Hong Kong coinage.
1866 Hong Kong Mint dollars.
1882 British North Borneo Company coinage begun.
1892 Sarawak issues world's only holed portrait coin, 1 cent with portrait of Sir Charles Brooke, rajah.
1903 Straits Settlements dollar struck.
1907 Straits dollar reduced size.
1935 Nickel alloys appear in Hong Kong coinage, replacing silver.
1939 New coinage under the Commissioners of Currency, Malaya.
1953 Coinage bears name Malaya and British Borneo.
1960 New copper-nickel Hong Kong dollar issued.
1967 New separate coinages for Malaysia, Brunei and Singapore.
1980 Singapore substitutes pure nickel for silver in $10 coins. Hong Kong Commodities Exchange begins gold futures trading.
1989 Hong Kong demonetizes 5-cent coins.

COOK ISLANDS
1970 Commemorative 1 dollar begins decimal coinage.

FIJI
1934 Sterling-standard coinage of George V, half penny through florin.
1942 Some World War II coinage struck at U.S. Mints.
1969 Decimal coinage, 100 cents to $1.

HAWAII
1847 Copper 1 cent issued by King Kamehameha III.
1883 Silver dime through dollar coinage of King Kalakaua I.

MALAYA-EAST INDIES AREA
896 Hindu coinage in Java.
1297 Gold coins of the sultans of Acheh, Sumatra.
1601 Dordrecht, Netherlands, strikes first trade dollar of 8 reales for the United Amsterdam Company, forerunner of long "VOC" coins soon to follow.
1686 First Batavia gold ducats appear.
1728 Silver ducatoons of the United East India Company.
1786 Silver 3-gulden crowns.
1799 Batavian Republic coinage for the Indies.
1807 Indies coins of Louis Napoleon, King of Holland.
1814 First coins of kingdom of the Netherlands for the Indies.
1913 Copper-nickel 5 cents, first new type in decades.
1936 Holed type 1 cent, bronze.
1943 Aluminum and tin alloy Japanese occupation

coinage.
1945 Last Dutch coinage for the Indies.
1949 Aluminum French colonial coinage for New Caledonia; French Oceania.
1951 First coins of independent Indonesia.
1962 Distinctive Indonesian coins for Riau islands and New Guinea, "West Irian."
1966 Silver 100-franc crown struck by the Paris Mint for New Hebrides, jointly administered with the British.
1967 New pure nickel coinage for New Caledonia, 10, 20, 50 francs; for New Hebrides, 10, 20 francs; 10, 20 and 50 francs for French Polynesia.
1970 Nickel-brass 1, 2 and 5 francs for New Hebrides.
1972-73 First coinage for French islands under Emission.
1972 First of continuing coinage for French-administered islands by Overseas Emission Institute.
1975 Gold-on-silver coin of Solomon Islands repudiated by island government.
1977 Regular minor coinage for Solomons struck by Britain's Royal Mint.
1981 New Hebrides becomes Vanuata; issues new national currency — the vatu.

NEW GUINEA
1894-1895 Coinage of the German New Guinea Company, 100 pfennig to 1 Neu-Guinea Mark.
1929 Pattern coinage for the Territory of New Guinea.
1935 Regular coinage begins on sterling system.
1975 New decimal coinage, 100 toea to 1 kina.
1989 Gold rush stimulates local economy.

NEW ZEALAND
1933 First distinctive New Zealand coins, silver threepence to halfcrown.
1935 Waitangi commemorative crown struck.
1940 Bronze coinage of penny, half penny.
1947 Copper-nickel replaces silver in coinage.
1949 Crown commemorates aborted royal visit.
1967 Decimal coinage, 100 cents to one New Zealand dollar, commemorative dollar series begun.
1982 A new portrait of Queen Elizabeth II is adopted on notes.
1989 Stops production of 1- and 2-cent coins.

PHILIPPINES
1803 Crude copper quarto coinage for Spanish King Charles IV.
1833 Counterstamped pesos of the New World in circulation.
1861 Distinctive centavo-peso coinage of gold, Isabel II.
1864 Silver denominations struck.
1897 Only peso struck for Philippines of Spanish type, Alfonso XIII.
1903 Centavo-peso coins under U.S. sovereignty.
1907 Reduced size silver coinage to halt export and melting of larger coins.
1936 Establishment of the Commonwealth of the Philippines, three commemoratives.
1937 Coinage of the Commonwealth of the Philippines.
1947 Restoration of the Republic commemorated by MacArthur peso, half peso.
1958 First minor coinage of the republic.
1961 Jose Rizal commemoratives begin an ongoing series.
1967 All new coinage with Tagalog or Filipino inscriptions, 100 sentimos to one piso.

1975 Redesign of coinage introduces square sentimo, scalloped 5 sentimos, 5 piso in pure nickel, and silver 25 and 50 piso, the latter in Proof sets. This set was partially struck for the Philippines by four different Mints in the U.S., Canada, Britain and West Germany.

1983 Piso devalued.

1984 1982-dated Reagan-Marcos commemorative appears in numismatic market, unannounced officially as released. Piso devalued by President Marcos due to flight of capital.

1986 Contracts future commemorative coin production with Pobjoy Mint rather than the Franklin Mint.

TONGA

1967 Decimal coinage of 100 seniti to one pa'anga, portrait of late Queen Salote Tupou III.

1967 Coronation coinage of new King Taufa'ahau Tupou IV begins commemorative coin series.

1977 Ingot-shaped coin issued.

TUVALU

1976 Formerly known as the Ellice Islands, Tuvalu opens its coinage history with a seven-coin set in bronze and copper-nickel, 1 cent through $1, featuring wildlife and sealife of this Pacific region.

WESTERN SAMOA

1967 Decimal coins of 100 sene to one tala.

1969 Commemorative tala series begins with Robert Louis Stevenson coin.

1988 American Samoa retracts legal tender status of America's Cup commemorative coins.

World Coins

13

World coin collecting

Many numismatists start their collections with coins, tokens, medals or paper money from their own country. Those items from other countries in the collection are the beginning of a "world collection."

The ancient Greeks collected their own coins, and the Romans collected those of the Greeks. As coin collecting emerged in Europe at the time of the Renaissance the attitude was that current coinage was too barbaric, and that collecting should be limited to that of the ancient world. In 18th and 19th century Europe, it was considered proper that a gentleman should have a cabinet of ancient Roman and Greek coins included somewhere in his study.

Due to lack of published knowledge, these collections tended to have many curious artifacts which were not numismatically related. The pattern for serious collecting, which is beneficial to the collector in any area of numismatics, did not become refined until the late 19th century.

Numismatics can be an adjunct to several disciplines. In many universities, particularly in Europe, courses in numismatics are required of archaeology and history majors. Others finding numismatics of interest are those studying art, economics, religion, languages or metallurgy.

We may want to establish the date the first coin was made. Like the game of chess, coins evolved, and we cannot say

that in accordance with a specific edict of king so-and-so, on a certain date, were coins patented. Gold, silver and other metals represented value, and were bartered in the form of small bars or ingots, or round discs.

Later, someone stamped a weight on these pieces and they passed at fixed values. When the issuing place and king left their marks on these previously blank discs, coins can be considered in use. It is believed that the transition took place in about the seventh century B.C., probably independently in China and Lydia, Asia Minor.

Cultures generally issuing ancient coins which modern collectors study were the Greeks, Celts, Romans, Bactrians and occupants of India and China.

The medieval period begins about A.D. 476, with the fall of the Western Roman Empire. Modern coins generally date from 1500 onward.

Two distinct inventions divide modern coins, and many collectors limit their collections by these boundaries. Movement from hammered coinage to coins struck under pressure in a collar in England in 1662 marks one division, and was a definite step forward in the quality of coins produced.

At the end of the 18th century and the beginning of the 19th century the Industrial Revolution brought along with it steam pressure to operate minting machinery, allowing for more pressure for striking coins, and speedier production.

Famous men who interested themselves in coins, Mint machinery and production methods include Copernicus, Michelangelo and James Watt.

Until the 18th century, the hobby of coin collecting, again like chess, was considered reserved for nobility. Others who held coins were in circumstances where they usually had to spend them.

Hoards of coins which are found around the world today tell archaeologists the nature of the owner. If a hoard of 100 coins represents a time span of five years, with many duplicates, most all from one place and one ruler, it can be assumed the owner was a merchant or banker. On the other hand, if the 100 coins were without duplicates, spanning a couple hundred years, several rulers from many countries, we can speculate that the hoard was part of an early collection.

There have been many coins found in the western Soviet Union, between the Black Sea and the Baltic Sea. Some were Scandinavian coins, others from the Mediterranean area. What would these coins tell us? There was a trade route from the Black Sea, up the Dnieper River, overland about 70 miles to the Duna River and on to the Baltic at Riga. Merchants plying this route might lose or spend some coins, bury them in case of attack, or die with them in their possession — to be found a few centuries later and studied by modern numismatists.

Such hoards of coins would represent varied countries and rulers, spanning many years.

Until recent years, most Mints did not encourage sale of their coins outside of their country, directly from the Mint. Times have changed, and Mints, or central banks or trade agencies of governments, eagerly seek buyers for their coins in the world-wide coin collecting fraternity. Sale of paper money in this manner is just beginning to gain a degree of acceptance by central banks.

How to begin

How does one collect coins of the world?

One way is to acquire a representative coin for each country or place that struck coins; a more ambitious method would be to include a coin of each ruler in each country.

One can limit himself to coins of certain metal, or certain denominations, or size, or certain years. Hence, one collector seeks only coins struck in bronze; or only 20-cent pieces; or only 18 millimeters; or only his birth year.

Topical collecting can lead the numismatist into coin zoos (dogs, birds, fish, elephants) or trees, plants and flowers, bells, folklore, religion, medicine or music. Other subjects could be maps, chess, space (particularly popular on medals), sports, Christmas, ships, aviation, explorers or, in combination with the stamp hobby, seeking coins on stamps.

Doctors who collect coins have diagnosed ailments of rulers appearing on ancient coins.

Some collectors feel they must strive for completeness, and seek all denominations issued by certain countries, or each date and Mint mark of each type. The difficulty in this endeavor is that many scarce coins will be hard to locate, and expensive when found.

Some collectors concentrate only on coins of Proof quality — with polished, mirror-like surfaces. Others want coins that have been circulated.

Emergency coins, paper money and tokens issued by cities, nations or in prisoner of war camps are the goal of other collectors. This can become a highly specialized field, collecting to the exclusion of other numismatic items. History books and catalogs can weave a fascinating story of deprivation caused by war and economic disruption.

Non-circulating coins

Since 1950 the collector of world coins has become the target of opportunists who see the value of catering to collectors. The move started with Mints offering Proof sets at prices above face value plus costs, to add at the beginning what might be anticipated prices in a few years. When collectors began to complain that many coins offered in the early 1960s were not circulating as legal tender in the country whose name appeared on the coins, steps were taken by governments and private firms to see that a decree accompanied contracts for such coins which did not circulate.

Collectors were beset with legal tender coins which, in some instances, would have resulted in the death penalty for a citizen of the country named on the coin should he try to spend it in his local post office. Many of these coins appear separately in some modern catalogs under the heading of "noncirculating legal tender coins."

Today coins and paper money are offered by entities not recognized by the United Nations, often operating on the sovereign territory of another nation or visible as land only at low tide.

Starting in 1968, the Food and Agriculture Organization, a branch of the United Nations, extended a plan they had been fomenting with stamps. Various nations would place a food theme on stamps, coins and paper money and proceeds from the sale of those items would go to the FAO to help needy nations develop agriculture programs. The FAO plan was intended to last three years; in mid-1984 it numbered more than 1 billion coins, issued by more than 94 nations, with no indication of a cutoff date.

Introduced in the summer of 1974 was the Conservation Coinage Collection, intended to highlight endangered animals in numerous nations. Proceeds from sale of coins were to be allocated to those nations taking part in the program to further protection for the endangered animals.

Initially, the program was to include the following countries (followed in parentheses the name of the endangered animal they seek to protect): Mauritius (flycatcher, blue swallowtail butterfly,

kestrel); Indonesia (Komodo dragon, Javan tiger, orangutan); Tanzania (cheetah, southern giraffe, black rhino); Costa Rica (great anteater, green turtle, manatee); Nepal (great Indian rhino, monal pheasant, red panda); and Thailand (white-eyed river martin, Sumatran rhino, brow-antlered deer). At least 24 nations participated in this program to issue uniform size gold and silver coins, three coins per country.

Where may collectors get coins of the world? While other portions of this almanac tell of coin prices nearing $1 million, a satisfying start on world coin collecting can come from coins which may cost less than 25 cents.

One can try writing Mints around the world. If you have the time and patience, the anticipation of waiting for coins in an envelope with colorful stamps from other continents can add to your collecting pleasure.

Do I have to collect coins to build a world numismatic collection? Not by any means, experienced numismatists will tell you. Sought by collectors are military and civilian decorations issued by royalty and military organizations; unit insignia of military and naval organizations; ration tokens and tickets; paper money from around the world, both emergency and regular issue; odd and primitive money; even gas and electric tokens and street car and bus tokens and tickets.

After you have embarked on your collecting plans, join a local club whose members share your interest; join a national organization, such as the American Numismatic Association and numerous specialty groups; display your collection and learn the background information on pieces in your collection. Before long, you will become an expert and others will seek you out for the advice you can offer them.

By all means, subscribe to Coin World. It has a special International section each week.

Canadian numismatics

History of the Royal Canadian Mint

An expanding population, development of new areas and business growth were key factors in Canada's decision to issue its own money in 1858.

A popular early Canadian "money" was the beaver pelt. As the population grew, a mixture of coinage from America, England, France, Spain and other countries came into use. This ultimately proved unsatisfactory, bringing the decision to coin a national Canadian currency.

Canada adopted a decimal system similar to the American system. All Canadian coinage from 1858 to 1907 was struck at the Royal Mint, London, or, under its supervision, by a private concern in Birmingham, England.

In the closing years of the 19th century, the idea of establishing a Mint in Canada was formulated, one of the main reasons being that, at that time, gold production in British Columbia and the Yukon reached unprecedented levels and was being exported to the United States.

Promoters of the plan to establish a Mint believed that this would stabilize the price of gold. Also, government and banking reserves had always been held in gold coins of another country, or in bullion, and it was maintained that a policy of keeping reserves in domestic coinage should be inaugurated.

The subject of Canada having its own Mint was taken up with the British government by W.S. Fielding, then Minister of Finance for the dominion. Canada had never possessed its own gold currency and authorities felt that Canadian gold coins would not be circulated to any extent outside the dominion and that even locally the demand would be limited.

It would therefore be advantageous to the dominion to be able to strike a universally-accepted coin such as the sovereign. Since this could only be done by the Royal Mint or a branch of the Royal Mint, it was agreed that a branch would be established in Ottawa.

On May 2, 1901, Fielding gave notice to the House of Commons of a resolution for the provision of $75,000 as an annuity for the maintenance of a branch of the Royal Mint in Canada. Founded on this resolution, the Ottawa Mint Act was passed and received royal assent on May 23, 1901.

In negotiations with the British government, it was decided that provision be made for a coinage of 20 million pieces a year, and for the refining of gold on a small scale.

In 1905 construction began, and by 1907 the building was completed and machinery installed. The Ottawa Mint Proclamation in 1907, issued under the Imperial Coinage Act of 1870, fixed Jan. 1, 1908, as the formal date for the establishment of the Ottawa branch of the Royal Mint. On Jan. 2, 1908, Governor-General Earl Grey struck the first coin.

An Act of Parliament was passed in 1931 which established the Royal Canadian Mint as a branch of the Department of Finance on Dec. 1 of that year, and the staff of the Mint was transferred from the Imperial service to the Canadian civil service.

A committee was appointed in 1968 to draft the legislation to establish the Mint as a corporate body. Under Part X of the Government Organization Act, 1969, assented to on March 28, 1969, the Mint was established as a Crown corporation on April 1, 1969.

RCM today

The Royal Canadian Mint is recognized as one of the largest and most versatile Mints in the world. It is responsible for the production and supply of circulating Canadian coinage.

The Royal Canadian Mint's activities span many fields, including the design and production of coins, medals, tokens and die production. It has gained recognition throughout the industry for its advanced technology and its standards of quality.

Over the years, the corporation has been awarded significant international contracts and seeks increases in contract volume. In its continuing effort for innovative excellence, the Royal Canadian Mint is actively competing in the international coin market against other national and private mints.

Some recent export customers include the Bahamas, Bangladesh, Barbados, Cayman Islands, Costa Rica, El Salvador, Israel, Nepal, Nicaragua, Panama, Portugal, Trinidad and Tobago and Turks and Caicos Islands.

The Mint refinery's main function is to refine newly-mined gold bullion received from Canadian mines, much of which is made into .9999 fine Maple Leaf gold bullion coins. Subsidiary functions are to refine jewelry, scrap, placer deposits, fused metals and worn coin received from the Bank of Canada, and silver bearing materials received from other government departments and other divisions of the Mint.

Maurice Lafontaine is President and Master of the Royal Canadian Mint.

Facilities

The Royal Canadian Mint maintains its administrative offices at the Ottawa Mint in the capital city of Ottawa. The main production facilites include the Ottawa Mint, on Sussex Drive, which is equipped with furnaces and manufacturing equipment to handle most alloys. Production includes the supply of Canada's precious metal and commemorative coins, as well as medals and numismatic products for Canada and foreign countries. In addition, Ottawa Mint's activities include melting, rolling and refining gold, and the production of planchets and tokens. Its capacity is 300 million coins per year on a one-shift-per-day basis. The facility was shut down for a period to be modernized and was re-opened for production in 1986.

The Winnipeg Mint

The formal inauguration of Canada's new Winnipeg Mint in Manitoba ranked as one of the major numismatic happenings in North America in 1976.

Formally opened by Canada's Minister of Supply and Services, Jean-Pierre Goyer, on April 30, the $20 million facility is capable of producing 2.1 billion coins per year on a three-shift basis.

The Winnipeg Mint produces circulating coinage for Canada and contracted circulating coinage for foreign countries. Numismatic coins are produced at the Ottawa Mint.

Capable of meeting Canada's coinage need far into the future, the Winnipeg Mint's capacity is utilized in the production of foreign coins and blanks. Canadian officials made clear at the Mint opening that Canada, a substantial factor in the world coin market in the past, intends to expand that effort.

Ordering Canadian coins

Orders for Canadian Uncirculated sets are acceptable each year commencing Jan. 1. Included in the set are the dollar, 50-, 25-, 10-, 5- and 1-cent pieces.

Correspondence should be directed to the Royal Canadian Mint, P.O. Box 470, Ottawa, Ontario K1N 8S5, Canada.

All orders must be accompanied by a certified check, post office money order or credit card in United States funds, payable to the Royal Canadian Mint.

The National Collection

The National Collection of coins and paper money is housed at the Bank of Canada, at 234 Wellington Street, Ottawa, Ontario. The emphasis is on Canadian material, but there is a selection of coins of other countries from all periods of numismatic history.

The National Collection of Medals is at the Public Archives of Canada in Ottawa. All types of medals, chiefly Canadian, are kept here, and ocassionally displays on a timely theme are exhibited. The National War Museum in Ottawa has an extensive collection of war medals and decorations.

The first steps toward establishing a national showplace took place in 1880 when the Dominion government purchased a Montreal numismatist's collection.

For many years the Parliamentary Library and the Public Archives of Canada were repositories for numismatic items accumulated from gifts to the Crown and other sources. A full-time curator was appointed in 1963.

Experts say the Bank of Canada now has the largest and most complete collection of Canadian coins, tokens and paper money in existence.

A sizeable addition was the acquisition of the bulk of the collection of Canadian coins, tokens and paper money formed by J. Douglas Ferguson of Rock Island, Quebec, considered the outstanding private collection of Canadian numismatic material in the world.

In late 1989, the RCM in Ottawa opened a display of one of the most complete Canadian coin collections ever compiled, by U.S. collector Jean Bullen.

The Dominion's currency history spans approximately three centuries, broken down by authorities into the French Colonial, the English Colonial, and the post-Confederation periods. Coins and currency from each era are featured in the Bank of Canada's Numismatic Collection.

The first coins were struck for Canada in 1670 and the first paper money issued in 1675. A colorful paper money chapter was written in the late 1600s when playing cards became the first form of paper money in the Western Hemisphere. A shortage of metallic currency for French Canada forced its leaders to make money out of playing cards.

Mexico

Of all the countries in the Western Hemisphere, Mexico can safely boast one of the most colorful numismatic histories, traceable to the pre-coinage era of the Aztec and other native empires of the Americas.

Primitive money was used in exchange by local tribes and most notably by the Aztec Empire. Here copper miniature hoes and spades were used as exchange in much the same way as knife money was used in early China. Other primitive Aztec money included cocoa beans, colored beads, cowry shells, jade figures and quills filled with gold dust.

The Mixtecs used various shaped terracotta beads, often engraved with images. Both the Mixtecs and the Aztecs used miniature bells of copper, both with and without clappers inside.

Organized as a Spanish possession after the successful conquest initiated by Hernan Cortez, Mexico became one of the richest gold, silver and copper mining areas in history, providing a worldwide trade coinage in both gold and silver through three centuries.

The historic Mexico City Mint began production in 1536 with silver quarter and half reales, 1, 2, 3 and 4 reales, issued in the name of Spain's rulers Carlos (later Holy Roman Emperor Charles V) and his mad aunt Juana.

An early copper coinage was unsuccessful, although research seems to indicate that the Indians were content to earn a few coins, drop tools until the coins were used up, stopping produce marketing until the coins were spent. This tendency, rather than any unpopularity of copper, may have led to suspension of the striking of these small denominations.

The silver coin of 8 reales, the famed "piece of eight," saw introduction in 1556 under King Philip II, one of the series of crude, irregularly shaped "cob" coins, struck more as true weights of silver than as fully round, modern coins. This "real de a ocho" became the lineal ancestor of the U.S. silver dollar, remaining legal tender in the U.S. until 1857 as the "Spanish Milled Dollar."

Gold coinage began in 1665 under the last of the Hapsburg kings, Charles II. The next major innovation was the perfecting of fully round "Columnario" or "Dos Mundos" coins, named for their design of two worlds symbolizing the Spanish empire, flanked by the Pillars of Hercules.

These new round coins, beginning with the 1732 date, have been faked extensively, particularly the early dates. This design was superseded by the royal bust type in 1772 under Bourbon King Charles III, which continued under Charles IV and Mexico's last Spanish ruler, Ferdinand VII.

Mexican independence was achieved in 1821. After the revolts of Fathers Hidalgo and Morelos, in this period of uncertainty, revolutionary emergency coinages in copper and silver first appeared.

The first definitive coins of the newly independent nation were the imperial issues of Emperor Augustin I Iturbide. Here appeared the Mexican eagle, crowned, seated upon a nopal cactus, similar to the bird in the Aztec legend of the founding of Mexico City, but without the snake of later designs.

Augustin's gold and silver coins were replaced in 1823 by the first republican coinage, the Hookneck or Profile eagle types which yielded in turn to the facing eagle, used until the 1940s. A number of Mints produced a uniform gold and silver coins, with small denomination copper coins issued by Mexico's states in a wide variety of designs.

The Second Empire of Emperor Maximilian saw new imperial decimal copper, silver and gold, again presenting a crowned eagle, supported by the Hapsburg griffins on the peso and gold 20 pesos. After the overthrow and death of Maximilian, the republic was restored. The decimal 1-peso coin was longed called the 8 reales as a trade coin.

The year 1905 saw the next major overhaul of the coinage, with new sizes and designs for the only remaining Mint, that of Mexico City. The silver types endured with minor changes through four decades. Gold coins first introduced in 1905 are still a regular offering on the bullion coin market, having been struck as late as 1948 for the tiny 2-1/2 pesos; the 5 pesos was last dated 1955, the 10 and 20 pesos, 1959. Bullion quarter-, half- and 1-ounce coins called "onza oro puro" of .900

fine gold were issued in 1981.

Mexico's first commemoratives were struck in 1921 for the first centenary of independence, a silver crown-size 2 pesos with eagle in profile, and a large and heavy 50 pesos which was struck until recently and now is a prime gold bullion coin on world markets, known familiarly as the "Centenario."

Beginning in 1947, silver content in Mexico's coinage began a series of changes, which ended in the adoption of bronze for all minor coins in the mid-1950s, and copper-nickel after 1970. By 1977, copper-nickel 10, 20 and 50 centavos, 1, 5 and 10 pesos were in exclusive use.

Date and design varieties on the most recent Mexican coins provide considerable interest for collectors, as have delays in releasing some denominations, such as the tiny 10 centavos and seven-sided 10 pesos, known to have been struck since 1974 but only appearing years after.

Mexico's commemoratives blossomed in the 1950s, with eight major silver types appearing to honor railway construction, independence struggle heroes, and 19th and 20th century patriots. Most were produced in goodly numbers and are available on the market at reasonable cost.

Mexico's last silver coins were the 1972 25-peso piece with facing bust of President Benito Juarez, the 100 pesos of 1977, struck to encourage the nation's silver mining industry, and the one troy ounce Libertad coins beginning in 1982.

A footnote to Mexican coinage is the 1913-1917 emergency money, struck in a wide range of metals during the revolution which followed the long dictatorship of President Porfirio Diaz.

These crude, locally struck or cast pieces are highlighted by famous coins like the Durango "Muera Huerta," or "Death to Huerta" peso and the massive gold 60 pesos of Oaxaca, today classic rarities of Mexican numismatics.

On Oct. 6, 1983, a new branch Mint was opened in the silver mining town of San Luis Potosi.

The Uncirculated Mint Set Program

began in 1977. The address in Banco National de Mexico, S.A., Division Internacional, I. la Cataolica 44, Mexico 1, D.F.

The Mexico Mint was converted into an autonomus institution having independent status under the law, with its own assets, by a presidential decree dated Dec. 26, 1985.

Under the decree the Mint is still the minting center of coins ordered by the Mexican Congress and authorized by the Bank of Mexico. However, the Mint can now design and produce medals for the Mexican government, commemorative medals for official or private use, bars and plaques of precious metals as authorized by the Secretariat of Finance and the Bank of Mexico, and foreign coinage by order of the Mexican government or directly by the foreign government.

World coinage report, 1988

Total coinages by nation for calendar year 1988. Source is "World Coinage Report 1987-1988" issued by the United States Mint. Countries not listed either did not strike coins in 1988 or did not make information available. For a copy of "World Coinage Report," which details the coinage by denomination in each country, write the Superintendent of Documents, U.S. Government Printing Office, Washington, D.C. 20402.

21	Argentina	260,285,182	57	Kuwait	18,500,000
20	Australia	260,724,547	64	Luxembourg	4,200,000
24	Austria	205,164,200	63	Madagascar	6,000,000
58	Bahamas	12,003,506	30	Malaysia	174,287,480
56	Barbados	19,481,000	59	Malta	11,175,450
36	Belgium	130,620,000	4	Mexico	2,308,000,000
71	Botswana	80,000	49	Nepal	45,581,446
8	Brazil	1,242,247,000	34	Netherlands	134,779,581
9	Canada	854,081,624	45	New Zealand	61,219,500
27	Chile	185,150,000	38	Norway	122,662,700
2	China, People's Rep.	8,487,690,000	67	Oman	2,000,000
19	Colombia	283,900,000	26	Pakistan	189,344,000
55	Cyprus	21,281,000	48	Paraguay	50,000,000
43	Czechoslovakia	76,332,000	35	Peru	131,388,000
33	Denmark	135,134,400	16	Philippines	382,317,000
70	Dominican Republic	165,540	18	Poland	332,188,000
53	Egypt	34,561,018	28	Portugal	180,285,758
46	El Salvador	50,000,000	65	San Marino	3,969,472
68	Fiji	700,000	15	Saudi Arabia	390,000,000
39	Finland	115,367,200	25	Singapore	198,166,500
10	France	750,500,000	11	South Africa	674,059,750
7	Germany, Federal Rep.	1,381,020,000	14	Spain	468,000,000
32	Greece	143,304,422	42	Sri Lanka	80,000,000
41	Guatemala	93,050,000	60	SudanRep. of	9,010,000
62	Guyana	8,080,000	23	Sweden	237,707,204
47	Honduras	50,000,000	37	Switzerland	128,341,000
31	Hong Kong	147,420,000	17	Taiwan	350,096,000
69	Hungary	169,500	52	Tanzania	40,000,000
61	Iceland	8,250,000	13	Thailand	532,343,248
5	India	1,868,052,000	54	Trinidad & Tobago	25,000,000
44	Ireland	70,187,000	40	Turkey	108,191,000
50	Israel	45,419,000	6	United Kingdom	1,444,263,658
22	Italy	253,586,842	1	United States	16,003,243,487
51	Jamaica	43,994,600	29	Venezuela	180,000,000
3	Japan	2,943,716,000	66	Zambia	3,000,000
12	Korea	574,000,000		TOTAL	45,785,037,815

Top 10 in 1988
(account for 81% of total)

1	United States	16,003,243,487	6	United Kingdom	1,444,263,658
2	China, People's Rep.	8,487,690,000	7	GermanyFederal Rep.	1,381,020,000
3	Japan	2,943,716,000	8	Brazil	1,242,247,000
4	Mexico	2,308,000,000	9	Canada	854,081,624
5	India	1,868,052,000	10	France	750,500,000

Coinage Mints active since 1987

(Note: Many official government Mints are becoming private or autonomous institutions; similarly, some nations contract with other government Mints or private facilities for their coinage. The following table shows those Mints — government and private — known to be actively producing legal tender coinage since 1987. The list does not include branch facilities, except where those act autonomously.)

Country	Name of mint	Address
Andorra	Servei Emmissions Vegueria Episcopal	Prat de la Creu 42
Argentina	Central Bank of Argentina	
•Australia	Royal Australian Mint	Denison Street, Deakin, A.C.T. 2600
°Australia	Perth Mint	310 Hay Street, Perth 6000
•Austria	Osterreichisches Hauptmunzamt	Am. Heumarkt I, A-1031 Vienna
•Belgium	Monnaie Royale de Belgique	32 Boulveard Pachéco, B-1000 Bruxelles
•Brazil	Casa da Moeda	Rua René Bitten-Court, 371 Santa Cruz, 23 565 Rio de Janiero
•Canada	Royal Canadian Mint	320 Sussex Drive, Ottawa, Ontario K1A 0G8
Canada	Sherritt Mint	P.O. Box 28, Commerce Court West, Toronto, Ontario M5L 1B1
Chile	Casa de Moneda de Chile	Avada. Portales s. Int. Quinta Normal, Santiago
•China	China Mint	No. 3 Xi Jie, Bai Zhi Fang, Xuan Wu District, Beijing
China	China Gold Coin Inc.	Blg. No. 7, Er Qi Ju Cheng Lu Xi Ji, Xi Cheng Qu, Beijing
•Colombia	Banco de la Republica, Casa de Moneda	Cra 7A No. 14-78, OF 1007 Bogota
°Cuba	Empresa Cubana de Acuñaciones	Calle 18 No 306, e/3ra y 5ta, Miramar, Ciudad de la Habana
Czechoslovakia	State Mint Kremnica	Mennicy, Kremnica
•Denmark	Den Kongelige Mønt	Solmarksvej 5, 2605 Brøndby
Egypt	Mint House	Abbassia, Cairo
•Finland	Mint of Finland	PL13 01671, Vantaa
•France	Administration des Monnaies et Medailles	11, Quai de Conti 75006, Paris
•Germany	Hamburgische Münze	Bei der Neuen, Münze 19, D-2000 Hamburg 73
•Germany	Staatliche Münze Karlsruhe	Stephanienstrasse 28 A, D-7500 Karlsruhe 1
•Germany	Bayerisches Hauptmünzamt	Zamdorfer Strasse 92, D-8000 München 8
•Germany	Staatliche Münze Stuttgart	Reichenhaller Str 58, D-7000 Stuttgart 50
Germany	VDM Nickel-Technologie AG	Plettenberger St. 2, 5980 Werdohl
•Greece	Bank of Greece	341 Messogion Ave., 15231 Halandri, Athens
°Guatemala	Banco de Guatemala	7A Av, 22-01, Zona 1, Guatemala City
Hungary	Hungarian State Mint	H-1450 Budapest
•India	India Government Mint	Shahid Bhagatsingh Road, Bombay 400023
°Indonesia	Indonesian Government Security Printing and Minting	JL, Palatehan No. 4, Kebayoran Baru, Jakarta 12160
Iran	Bank Markazi Iran	Ferdowsi Avenue, Tehran
•Ireland	Central Bank of Ireland	P.O. Box 61, Sandyford, Dublin 16
°Israel	Bank of Israel, Currency Department	POB 780, Jerusalem
¡Israel	Israel Government Coins Corp.	P.O. Box 2270, Jerusalem-91022, Ahad Haam 5
•Italy	La Zecca	Via Principe Umberto 4, 00185 Rome
Italy	Instituto Poligrafico e Zecca Dello Stato	Piazza Giuseppe Verdi, 10, 00100 Rome
°Japan	Mint Bureau, Ministry of Finance	1-1-79 Tenma, Kita-Ku, Osaka 530
•Korea, Republic of	Korea Security Printing and Minting Corp.	90 Kajong-Dong, Taejon 305-350
•Malaysia	Kilang Wang Bank of Negara	P.O. Box 100, 40700 Shah Alam
•Malta	Malta Mint	c/o Central Bank of Malta, Castille Place, Valletta
•Mexico	Casa de Moneda de México	Reforma 295, 5th Floor, Col. Cuauhtémoc — Del. Cuauhtémoc 06500 México DF.
°Morocco	Bank Al-Maghrib	Dar-As-Sikkah, KM8, Route De Sale, A Meknes, BP445-Rabat

°Nepal	Nepal Rastra Bank, Department of Mint	Sundara, Kathmandu
•Netherlands	's Rijks Munt Utrecht	P.O. Box 2407, 3500 GK, Utrecht
•Norway	Den Kongelige Mynt	Hyttegt 1, N-3600 Kongsberg
Pakistan	Pakistan Mint	Baghban Pura, Lahore (Punjab)
Peru	Casa Nacional de Moneda	Jiron Junin 791, Lima 1
°Philippines	Central Bank of Philippines	East Ave., Diliman, Quezon City
•Poland	Polish State Mint	Pereca 21, 00-958 Warsaw
•Portugal	Imprensa Nacional — Casa da Moeda EP	RD Francisco Manuel de Melo 5, 1092 Codex, Lisbon
°Singapore	Singapore Mint	249 Jalan Boon Lay, Jurong 2261
°South Africa, Republic of	South African Mint	Private Bag X66, Pretoria 0001
•Spain	Fabrica Nacional de Moneda y Timbre	Jorge Juan 106, 28009 Madrid
°Sudan	Sudan Mint Co. Ltd.	P.O. Box No. 5043, Khartoum South
•Sweden	AB Tumba Bruk — Royal Mint of Sweden	Box 16283, S-10325, Stockholm
Sweden	The Swedish Mint	Myntverket, S-631 06 Eskilstuna
•Switzerland	Swiss Federal Mint	Federal Administration of Finance, Bernerhof, CH-3003 Berne
Switzerland	Huguenin Medailleurs S.A.	Ru Henry-Grandjean 5, 2400 Le Loche
¡Switzerland	Valcambi SA	Via Passeggiata, 6828-Balerna, Ticino
Taiwan	Central Mint of China	Taoyuan 333, Taiwan
°Thailand	Royal Thai Mint	Treasury Department, Chakrapong Road, Bangkok 10200
•Turkey	Turkish State Mint, Darphane VE	Damga Matbaasi Genel, Müdürlügü, Yildiz 80776 Istanbul
•United Kingdom	Royal Mint	Llantrisant, Pontyclun, Mid-Glamorgan CF7 8YT
¡United Kingdom	The Birmingham Mint Ltd.	Icknield Street, Birmingham B18 6RX
¡United Kingdom	Pobjoy Mint Ltd.	Mint House, Oldfields Road, Sutton, Surrey SM1 2NW
•United States	United States Mint	633 Third St. NW, Washington, D.C. 20220
United States	Franklin Mint	Franklin Center, Pa. 19091
Union of Soviet Socialist Republics	Moscow and Leningrad Mints	9, Puskinskaya Street, Moscow 102009
Yugoslavia	National Bank of Yugoslavia	Bulevar, Revolucije 15, P.O. Box 1010, 11001 Belgrade

• Member, Mint Directors Conference 1990
° Observer, Mint Directors Conference 1990
¡ Industrial Observer, Mint Directors Conference 1990

Foreign coin production in the U.S.

To facilitate collecting of foreign coins struck at the U.S. facilities, this format supplements the United States Mint charts.

Coins struck at United States Mint facilities 1977-87 are listed by country. United States Mint facilities have not struck foreign coins since the 1984-dated coinage for Panama.

DOMINICAN REPUBLIC
1978 50 centavos .... Philadelphia.............. 732,000
1979 50 centavos .... Philadelphia.............. 300,000
1979 50 centavos .... San Francisco 5,015
1980 50 centavos .... Philadelphia.............. 554,000
1981 50 centavos .... Philadelphia............ 1,000,000
1982 50 centavos .... Philadelphia.Mynt ... 1,300,000
1978 25 centavos .... Philadelphia............ 995,000
1979 25 centavos .... Philadelphia............ 1,785,000*
1979 25 centavos .... San Francisco 5,015
1980 25 centavos .... Philadelphia.............. 504,000
1981 25 centavos .... Philadelphia............ 2,600,000
1982 25 centavos .... Philadelphia............ 3,200,000
1978 10 centavos .... Philadelphia............ 6,490,000
1979 10 centavos .... San Francisco 5,015
1980 10 centavos .... Philadelphia.............. 600,000

1981 10 centavos .... Philadelphia 4,400,000
1982 10 centavos .... Philadelphia 6,000,000
1978 5 centavos .... Philadelphia 4,984,000
1979 5 centavos .... San Francisco 5,015
1981 5 centavos .... Philadelphia 5,300,000
1982 5 centavos .... Philadelphia 4,500,000
1978 1 centavo .... Philadelphia 5,980,000
1979 1 centavo .... San Francisco 5,015
1981 1 centavo .... Philadelphia 200,000
1978 1 peso .... Philadelphia 80,000
1979 1 peso .... San Francisco 5,015
1981 1 peso .... Philadelphia 20,000

HAITI
1979 50 centime........ San Francisco 2,000,000

PANAMA
1980 10 balboa .... Philadelphia 5,000,000
1979 half balboa........... Philadelphia 1,000,000

1980 half balboa	Philadelphia	1,000,000
1982 half balboa	Philadelphia	1,500,000
1984 half balboa	Philadelphia	350,000
1979 quarter balboa	Philadelphia	2,000,000
1980 quarter balboa	Philadelphia	2,000,000
1982 quarter balboa	Philadelphia	3,148,000
1984 quarter balboa	Philadelphia	5,000,000
1982 1/10 balboa	Philadelphia	7,740,000
1984 10 centesimo	Philadelphia	7,750,000
1982 5 centesimo	Philadelphia	8,400,000
1983 5 centesimo	Philadelphia	5,500,000
1984 5 centesimo	Philadelphia	2,000,000
1977 1 centesimo	West Point	10,000,000
1978 1 centesimo	West Point	10,000,000
1979 1 centesimo	West Point	10,000,000
1980 1 centesimo	West Point	10,000,000
1981 1 centesimo	West Point	10,000,000
1982 1 centesimo	West Point	2,000,000
1983 1 centesimo	Philadelphia	20,000,000
1984 1 centesimo	Philadelphia	25,000,000

PERU

1977 1 sol	Philadelphia	2,100,000

PHILIPPINES

1977 5 sentimo	Philadelphia	1,088,000

*Struck in 1978, dated 1979.

Summary of foreign coinage by U.S. Mints, by country

Argentina (blanks)	64,058,334
Australia	168,000,000
Belgian Congo	25,000,000
Belgium	25,000,000
Bolivia	30,000,000
Brazil (blanks)	406,249,266
Canada	85,170,000
China	39,720,096
China, Republic of (Taiwan)	428,172,000
Colombia	133,461,872
Costa Rica	131,798,820
Cuba	496,559,888
Curacao	12,000,000
Dominican Republic	105,474,297
Ecuador	214,451,060
El Salvador	226,695,351
Ethiopia	375,433,730
Fiji	4,800,000
France	50,000,000
Greenland	100,000
Guatemala	7,835,000
Haiti	90,324,000
Hawaii*	1,950,000
Honduras	115,929,500
Indochina	135,270,000
Israel	91,000
Korea	295,000,000
Liberia	56,744,679
Mexico	91,076,840
Mexico (blanks)	175,714,411
Nepal	195,608
Netherlands	562,500,000
Neth. E. Indies	1,716,368,000
Nicaragua	26,080,000
Panama (Republic)	268,409,191
Peru	761,067,479
Philippines	3,483,718,169
Poland	6,000,000
Saudi Arabia	124,712,574
Siam (Thailand)	20,000,000
Suriname (Netherlands Guiana)	21,195,000
Syria	7,350,000
Venezuela	306,762,944
Totals (42 countries)	**11,325,756,346**

* Coined prior to Aug. 21, 1959, when Hawaii became the 50th State of the Union.

Foreign coins manufactured by U.S. Mints

Calendar year	Number of pieces produced
July 1, 1875-Dec. 31, 1905	155,896,973
1906	10,204,504
1907	45,253,047
1908	29,645,359
1909	11,298,981
1910	7,153,818
1911	7,794,406
1912	6,244,348
1913	7,309,258
1914	17,335,005
1915	55,485,190
1916	37,441,328
1917	25,208,497
1918	60,102,000
1919	100,269,195
1920	99,002,334
1921	55,094,352
1922	7,863,030
1923	4,369,000
1924	12,663,196
1925	13,461,000
1926	14,987,000
1927	3,650,000
1928	16,701,000
1929	34,980,000
1930	3,300,120
1931	4,498,020
1932	9,756,096
1933	15,240,000
1934	24,280,000
1935	109,600,850
1936	32,350,000
1937	26,800,000
1938	48,579,644
1939	15,725,000
1940	33,170,000
1941	208,603,500
1942	307,737,000
1943	186,682,008
1944	788,498,000
1945	1,802,376,004
1946	504,528,000
1947	277,376,094
1948	21,950,000
1949	156,687,940
1950	2,000,000
1951	25,450,000
1952	45,857,000
1953	193,673,000
1954	19,015,000
1955	67,550,000
1956	38,793,500
1957	59,264,000
1958	152,575,000
1959	129,647,000
1960	238,400,000
1961	148,500,000
1962	256,485,000
1963	293,515,000
1954	—
1965	—
1966	7,440,000
1967	176,196,206

1968	416,088,658
1969	348,653,046
1970	483,988,392
1971	207,959,692
1972	392,723,895
1973	295,408,674
1974	373,293,733
1975	762,126,363
1976	562,372,000
1977	13,188,000
1978	30,846,000
1979	15,530,090
1980	19,658,000
1981	23,520,000
1982	37,788,000
1983	25,500,000
1984	45,600,000
Total	**11,325,756,346**

Source: United States Mint

World monetary units

Country	Basic unit		Divisional (fractional) unit	
	Name	Symbol or abbreviation	Name	Symbol or abbreviation
Afghanistan	afghani	Af.	pul	
Africa, Equatorial States: Cameroon, Central African Republic, Equatorial Guinea, Chad, Congo and Gabon	Communaute Financiere Africaine franc	CFA fr.	centime	
Africa, West (Monetary Union): Benin, Ivory Coast, Mali, Niger, Senegal, Togo, and Burkina Faso	Communaute Financiere Africaine franc	CFA fr.	Centime	
Albania	lek		qindar	
Algeria	dinar	DA	centime	Cme
Andorra	diner		pesetas	
Angola, People's Republic of	kwanza		lwei	
Argentina	austral	$	centavo	ctv.
Australia	dollar	$	cent	c
Austria	schilling	$	groschen	g
Bahamas	dollar	B$	cent	Bc
Bahrain	dinar	BD	fils	
Bangladesh	taka	Tk.	poisha	
Barbados	dollar	BDS$	cent	¢
Belgium	franc	F or BF	centime	C
Belize	dollar	$	cent	
Bermuda	dollar	BD$	cent	¢
Bhutan	ngultrum		chetrum	
Bolivia	peso boliviano	$b	centavos	
Botswana	pula	P	thebe	t
Brazil	new cruzeiro	Cr.$	centavo	
Brunei	dollar		sen	
Bulgaria	leva		stotinki	
Burundi	franc	F	centimes	
Cambodia	riel	£	sen.	
Canada	dollar	$	cent	¢
Cape Verde, Republic of	escudo	Esc. or $	centavo	
Caribbean Territories, Eastern Group: Grenada, Montserrat and Antigua, Dominica, Grenada, St. Kitts, St. Lucia, Montserrat, St. Vincent	East Caribbean dollar	E.C.$	cent	¢
Cayman Islands	dollar	$	cent	¢
Chile	new peso	$	centavo	¢
China, Mainland	yuan	RMB Y	jiao, fen	
Colombia	peso	$ or P	centavo	c., ¢, or Ctv.
Comoros, Republic of	franc	F	centime	
Congo	franc	F	centine	
Cook Islands	dollar	$	cent	c
Costa Rica	colon	C or ¢	centimo	¢
Cuba	peso		centavos	
Cyprus	pound	C£	mil	m
Czechoslovakia	koruna	Kcs	haler	h
Denmark	krone	Kr. of kr.	ore (ore)	(O)
Djibouti, Republic of	franc	F	centime	
Dominica	dollar	E.S.$	cent	c
Dominican Republic	peso	RD $	centavo	ctv or ¢

Country	Basic unit		Divisional (fractional) unit	
	Name	Symbol or abbreviation	Name	Symbol or abbreviation
Ecuador	sucre	S/	centavo	ctv.
Egypt, Arab Republic of	pound	£.E.	piastre, millime	P.T. & Mill.
El Salvador	colon	C or ¢	centavo	¢
Equatorial Guinea	Franc			
Ethiopia	birr	Br. $	cent	ct
Falkland Islands	pound		pence	
Fiji	dollar	$	cent	¢
Finland	markka	mk	penni	p.
France	franc	F	centime	C or Cme.
French Guadeloupe, Guiana, and Martinique	franc	F	centime	
French Polynesia: Austral, Leeward, Marquezas and Windward Isles; and Tuamotu group	Colonies Francaises du Pacifique franc	CFP fr.	centime	
Gambia, The	dalasi	D	butut	b
Germany, Democratic Republic of	mark		pfennig	
Germany, Federal Republic of	deutsche mark	DM	pfennig	Pf.
Ghana	cedi	NC	cesewa	P
Gibraltar	pound		pence	P
Greece	drachma	Dr.	lepton	I
Greenland	krone		ore	
Guatemala	quetzal	Q	centavo	¢
Guernsey	pound		pence	
Guinea, Republic of	franc			
Guinea-Bissau, Republic of	peso		centavo	
Guyana	dollar	G$	cent	¢
Haiti	gourde	G	centime	¢
Honduras	lempira	L.	centavo	¢ or cto.
Hong Kong	dollar	HK$	cent	¢
Hungary	forint	Ft.	filler	Fill.
Iceland	krona	kr. or Kr.	aurar	aur. or au.
India	rupee	Re. (Rs.)	paisa	p.
Indonesia	rupiah	Rp.	sen	
Iran	rial	Rl. (Rls.)	dinar	
Iraq	dinar	ID	fils	
Ireland, Republic of	pound	IR£	penny	P.
Isle of Man	pound		pence	P.
Israel	sheqel	I£	agora	Ag.
Italy	lira	L. or Lit.	centesimo	
Jamaica	dollar	$	cent	¢
Japan	yen	Y	sen	
Jersey	pound		pence	
Jordan	dinar	J.D.	Fils	FLS.
Kenya	shilling	Sh.	Cent	ct.
Kiribati	dollar		Cent	
Korea, Republic of	won	W	Chon	
Kuwait	dinar	KD	fils	
Laos	kip			
Lebanon	livre	L£ or LL	piastre	LP or PL
Lesotho	maloti		sente	
Liberia	dollar	$	cent	
Libya	dinar	L.D.	dirham	
Liechtenstein	Swiss franc		frank	
Luxembourg	franc	fr. or F	centime	Ct.
Macao	pataca	$	avos	
Madagascar, Democratic Republic of	ariary	FMG	franc	Ct.
Malawi	kwacha	K	tambala	T
Malaysia	ringgit	$	sen.	¢
Maldive Republic	rupee		laari	I
Mali	franc	MF		
Malta	pound	£M	cent, mil	
Mauritania, Islamic Republic of	ouguiya		khoum	

Country	Basic unit		Divisional (fractional) unit	
	Name	Symbol or abbreviation	Name	Symbol or abbreviation
Mauritius	rupee	Re	cent	
Mexico	peso	$	centavo	c
Monaco	franc	NF	centime	Cme
Mongolian People's Republic	tukhrik		mongo	
Morocco	dirham	DH	centime	C
Mozambique	metica	Esc. or $	centavo	
Myanmar (formerly Burma)	kyat	K	pya	P
Nepal	rupee	Re.	paisa	P.
Netherlands	guilder	f.	cent	c
Netherlands Antilles (Curacao)	guilder	NAF	cent	ct.
New Caledonia	Colonies Francaises du Pacifique franc	CFP fr.	centime	
New Zealand	dollar	$	cent	c.
Nicaragua	cordoba	C$	centavo	c
Nigeria	naira	N	kobo	K.
Norway	krone	Kr.	ore.	
Oman	rial	ORI	baisa	
Pakistan	rupee	Rs.	paisa	Ps.
Panama, Republic of	balboa	B/.	centesimo	c
Papua New Guinea	kina		toea	
Paraguay	guarani	G	centimo	ctmo.
Peru	sol		centavo	ct.
Philippines	piso	P	sentimo	s.
Poland	zloty	Zl.	grosz	Gr.
Portugal	escudo	Esc. or $	centavo	
Qatar	riyal	QDR	dirham	
Reunion	franc	Fr.	centime	
Romania, Socialist Republic of	leu	n.a.	bani	n.a.
Rwanda, Republic of	franc	FRW.	centime	
Saint-Pierre et Miquelon	Communaute Financiere Africaine franc	CFA fr.	centime	
San Marino	lira	£	centesimi	
Saudi Arabia	riyal	SR	ghirsh, halalah	
Seychelles	rupee	SR.	cent	Cts
Sierra Leone	leone	Le.	cent.	c
Singapore	dollar	S$	cent	c
Solomon Islands	dollar		cent	
Somali Republic	shilin	Sh. So.	senti	
South Africa, Republic of	rand	R	cent	c
Spain	peseta	Pta. (Pts.)	centimo	ctmo.
Sri Lanka	rupee	Rs.	cent	Cts.
St. Thomas & Prince Islands	dobra	Esc.	centimo	
Sudan, Republic of the	pound	£S, LSd, or LS.	piastre, millim	m/m
Suriname	gulden	Sf	cent	ct (cts)
Swaziland	lilangeni		cent	
Sweden	krona	Kr. or kr.	ore	
Switzerland	franc	Fr.	rappen	C.
Syrian Arab Republic	pound	L.S.	iastre	P.S.
Taiwan	new Taiwan dollar	NT $	cent	c
Tanzania, United Republic of	shilingi	sh., shs.	senti	
Thailand	baht	B, b	satang	stg.
Timor	escudo	Esc. or $	centavo	
Tokelau	tala			
Tonga	pa'anga	T$	seniti	
Trinidad and Tobago	dollar	T&T$	cent	c
Tunisia	dinar	DT	millim	M
Turkey	lira	TL.	kurus	Krs.
Turks and Caicos Islands	crown			
Tuvalu	dollar		cent	

Country	Basic unit		Divisional (fractional) unit	
	Name	Symbol or abbreviation	Name	Symbol or abbreviation
Uganda	shilling	Sh.	cent	ct.
Union of Soviet Socialist Republics	ruble		kopek	
United Arab Emirates	dirham		fil	
United Kingdom	pound	£	pence	p.
United States of America	Dollar	$	cent	c
Uruguay	new peso	N$	centesimo	
Vanuata	franc	F	vatu	
Vatican City	Lira	L.	centesimo	
Venezuela	bolivar	B.	centimo	c/or c
Vietnam	dong		hao, xu	
Western Samoa	tala	WS$	sene	
Yemen, Arab Republic	riyal		fil	
Yemen, People's Democratic Republic of	dinar	S.Y.£	fil	
Yugoslavia	new dinar	Din.	para	
Zaire	zaire	Z	makuta	k, s
Zambia	kwacha	K	ngwee	n
Zimbabwe (Rhodesia)	dollar	Rh $	cent	c

Values of foreign monetary units

During the period 1950-1971 the values of most of the "strong" foreign monetary units remained stable in relation to the U.S. dollar, and fluctuated only within 1 percent of the official value, which was defined through the International Monetary Fund. For example, the Belgian franc was set at 2 cents throughout this period. Devaluations and revaluations upwards of the foreign units were declared at infrequent intervals, and still the valuations fluctuated within 1 percent. For example, the British pound was fixed at $4.03 from 1940 to 1949 when it was devalued to $2.80, remaining stable at this rate until 1967 when it was again devalued to $2.40 (or one penny equalled 1 cent on the pre-decimal British system).

Between 1934 and 1971 the U.S. fixed the price of gold at $35 an ounce, and on this basis most countries fixed the value of their monetary units. This system began to disintegrate when the U.S. dollar was divorced from its gold backing, and a free market was established in gold bullion, after which the price of gold began to climb steeply. The start of the present chaos in foreign exchange began in August 1971 when the U.S. dollar began to decline in relation to the stronger foreign currencies, culminating in the first official devaluation of the U.S. dollar in December 1971. During this period, for example, the

normally unstable British pound climbed from $2.40 to $2.60, but fell back to about $2.35 in the middle of the next year when it was allowed to "float" in value on the international exchanges. Another devaluation of the dollar in February 1973 brought about the final collapse of the stable exchange rates experienced during the previous 15 years.

Before 1967, a large number of countries linked their monetary units to the British pound, but when the pound was devalued in 1967, many of them did not devalue, and thus started the disintegration of the former sterling area. Many of these countries did not devalue with the U.S. dollar in 1971 or 1973 either. For example, the Libyan dinar had the same value as the British pound from 1950 to 1967 — $2.80 — but was not devalued with the British pound in 1967, remaining at $2.80 and not devalued to $2.40. However, when the U.S. dollar was devalued in December 1971, the Libyan dinar was not devalued, so its value rose in proportion to the devalued U.S. dollar, to $3.04. In February 1973, the dollar was again devalued, but not the Libyan dinar, which rose from $3.04 to $3.38, and this has remained near this value to the present.

Thus, the Libyan dinar, a stable, oil-backed currency, rose from $2.80 to $3.38 due to the devaluations of the pound and the dollar. The British pound by 1976 only $1.29, or $2.09 less than the Libyan dinar. Before 1967, both had the same value of $2.80.

The devaluations of the dollar were expressed in terms of the official valuation of the troy ounce of pure gold, $35, from 1934 to 1971, $38 from 1971 to 1973, and $42.22 from 1973 to the present. The first devaluation was 7.89 percent and the second one was 10 percent.

The strongest monetary units did not devalue with the U.S. dollar, and additionally revalued their currency units upwards. For example, the West German Deutsch mark was fixed at DM4.20 to the dollar from 1948 to 1961. It was upvalued in 1961 to DM4 to the dollar, or from 23.8 cents to 25 cents. In the late 1960s it had risen to 27 cents. After the two devaluations of the U.S. dollar and further upvaluations of the Deutsch mark, it has risen to its 19907 value of 60 cents.

Four categories

The monetary units of the world can be divided into four categories: the "strong" units which have risen above their pre-1971 values in terms of the U.S. dollar; the units which were devalued with the U.S. dollar either both times or once only, whose units have the same, or nearly the same value in terms of the U.S. dollar of before 1971; the "weak" units which have been devalued further than the two devaluations of the dollar.

The fourth group of currencies are those of the Communist countries, which are not allowed to be exchanged on the international currency markets, and which have artificial values in terms of the U.S.

dollar. Sometimes these countries have an official valuation together with a special, lower valuation for tourists exchanging strong units for the Communist ones.

Thus, the international monetary situation is, at present, an extremely complex problem compared with the pre-1971 period. Some countries have not only one but two or more different values for their monetary units. For example, in India, in December 1971, the rupee was officially valued at 13-2/3 cents, but was exchanged against U.S. dollars locally at 12 cents. However, if one exchanged dollar notes on the streets unofficially, the rupee was worth only 10 cents, and if fairly large amounts were negotiated on the black market, it was worth only 8 cents. This situation is common with most of the very weak currencies.

Before 1971, the monetary units had stable values, fluctuating daily by not more than 1 percent, and often the unit maintained the same value for as long as 20 years. All this is changed now, and values are subject to almost daily changes, some of them violent. The monetary units of different countries must be watched from day to day to verify their current values.

Quotations of currency values may be found in financial publication such as the Wall Street Journal or from foreign exchange specialists such as Manfra, Tordella & Brookes Inc., 30 Rockefeller Plaza, New York, N.Y. 10112. Some currencies are traded in the financial markets, and quotes may be gotten from a number of sources.

A primer of ancient coins

Coinage in any land will tell an observer much about the people who issued and used it. A nation's religious beliefs, politics, artistic sense, sport, wars and above all its basic sense of priorities will emerge in the coinage.

The peoples of the ancient world, of Greek city-states and their colonies, of

Rome with its long-enduring empire, the ancient Jews and the Byzantines, left a numismatic record of their hopes, fears and ambitions that has been unequaled in later ages. They were to create a wealth of design that to this day is considered a model of beauty and excellence.

Coinage had its roots in Asia Minor

during the seventh century, in the bean-shaped blobs of electrum, a natural alloy of gold and silver, issued by Greek settlements along the Aegean coast. These earliest attempts at a metal medium of exchange were crude and simple, marked only by striations or punches.

It was left to the kings of Lydia in southern Asia Minor to refine these beginnings into recognizeable coins. Croesus, whose wealth assured him a permanent place in legend, launched a bimetallic coinage during his reign, 560-546 B.C., by stamping a lion facing a bull on the obverse of the gold staters.

The Mediterranean world, very much of a community in this era, was to accept these new coins, establishing the basic principle that a good coin, of reliable weight and fineness, of easily recognized type, was clearly superior to a commodity offered in barter.

By the early years of the seventh century, the idea of coinage had spread to the Greeks, whose city-states possessed a resilient, dynamic civilization of unequaled artistic consciousness, a consciousness which permeated every aspect of their citizens' daily lives.

Coinage in Europe is believed to have begun with the silver "turtle" staters of Aegina, a small island in the Saronic gulf south of Athens, about the beginning of the seventh century B.C. The Aegina coins set the basic form of ancient Greek coinage, and deserve some examination.

In a world in which many were illiterate, symbols rather than actual inscriptions were of the greatest importance. A simple, clearly recognizable emblem, a bird, animal, god, plant or figure from a shared mythology was of the utmost importance in making coins acceptable in such a world.

Thus, the Aegina turtle, Athenian owl, Corinthian winged horse, Theban shield and the Eretrian gorgon head became metallic purity "trademarks," guaranteeing the recognition and acceptance of the coins upon which they were featured.

Another advantage of such symbolic coinage was that merchants could demand payment in, let us say, Athenian "owls," thus assuring a return of such coins to their city of issue. More than 1,400 Mints were to see operation in ancient Greece, producing a coinage of silver staters, drachms and their many divisions and multiples.

Gold was seldom coined, except in sieges and emergencies. Bronze was not in general circulation, as many carried coins in their mouths, and the development of purses of various sorts was clearly required before copper alloy coinage could gain much popularity. Silver was the only acceptable metal in commerce and trade.

Greek coinage

Greek or Hellenistic coinage was to spread from the coast of Asia Minor to Greece itself, from there to lower Italy, Sicily, what is now the south of France, Spain and North Africa. After Alexander the Great's conquests, Greek-type coinage was to span the known world from what is now Morocco to Bactria in present-day Afghanistan.

Greek coins mirrored the strongly held esthetic ideals of the people they served. Their strong, detailed designs provided an example still pursued in the complex, mechanized world of today.

Numismatists agree that the most beautiful Greek coinages were those of "Magna Graecia," the colonies in southern Italy and Sicily. On the mainland of the "boot" were Mint cities such as Metapontum and Croton, which evolved a beautiful system which saw a simple figure such as the Apollo tripod and ear of barley in relief on one side of the broad, thin coins, with a reiteration of the feature in intaglio on the reverse.

Syracuse in Sicily produced large, heavy 10-drachm coins, decadrachms which set a standard of excellence in design seldom exceeded. Even under siege the designers produced coins of consummate beauty.

Designers such as Euainetos, Kimon, Eumenes and Eucleidas engraved and signed coins that made them immortal in the field of numismatic art. Kimon's commemorative decadrachm marking the naval victory over supposedly invincible Athens carried a head of Arethusa believed by many to be one of the ultimate designs of all time.

The Acragas decadrachm with its two eagles tearing a captured hare; the Mende tetradrachm with the god of wine Bacchus reclining on a donkey; the man-faced bull on the coins of Sicilian city-state of Gela; and the Hercules and lion coins of Tarentum could all be mentioned as outstanding examples of the magnificent numismatic art that attracts collectors to ancient Greek coins today as in centuries past.

Collectors entering the Greek field would do well to arm themselves with a selection of good reference books, a classical atlas and a willingness to study and to learn. It would also be highly advisable to find a knowledgeable and reliable dealer, who can distinguish genuine coins from counterfeits.

The item of expense should also be squarely faced. A Syracusan decadrachm set a record price of $273,000 in a coin auction in Europe during 1974. While most collectors will steer clear of this type of coin, many nice Greek coins in acceptable condition remain at reasonable prices.

Roman coinage

The long and diverse coinage of Rome developed rather late in the history of the Republic, with barter playing a key role until the expansion of the state brought Rome into contact with coin-producing Greek cities in Italy.

The development of Roman coinage mirrored the basic outlook of the Roman mind. While the Greeks sought beauty in all things, the Roman sought practicality, law and power. The first coins of Rome were the cast bronze "aes grave" bearing the image of the double-faced god Janus.

These early coins weighed a pound each and must have been cumbersome in daily use. As time went by, the bronze coinage was gradually reduced to smaller sizes. During the third century B.C., silver didrachms were being struck for Rome by Mint towns in the Campanian plain, and the long career of Roman coinage was under way.

Design features of Roman Republic silver included scenes from the mythical founding of the city, Romulus and Remus suckled by the she-wolf, the rape of the Sabine women, and events of the early wars.

The expanding Roman state was continually at war, making large coin issues a practical necessity to pay soldiers and purchase supplies. As a result Republican silver coins are relatively plentiful and inexpensive, ideal for a collector of moderate means.

Roman coins acted as propaganda for their day. Victories, sporting events, public buildings and political events were all commemorated in a seemingly endless procession of coin types.

The Roman Mint was under the patronage of the goddess Juno Moneta, the personification of money and financial probity. She was one of a number of personified virtues, including hope, security, joy, fertility and abundance, to name only a few of the many that were to adorn the reverses of hundreds of different coins.

Portraits of persons rather than gods were uncommon on Greek coinage until after the time of Alexander the Great; they were unknown on Roman coins until the latest era of the Republic, the Imperatorial period.

In the first century B.C., portraits of living men began to adorn coins, often as a form of personal propaganda for aspiring leaders such as Pompey the Great, Marc Antony and above all Caius Julius Caesar. These imperatorial coins foreshadowed the imperial portrait coins that began with Augustus in the beginning of the Christian era.

Collectors have eagerly sought the coins of this period, largely because of their historic importance. Especially sought have been Caesar's portrait coins and the now rare issues of the several conspirators who assassinated him. A popular piece is the denarius of Brutus, bearing the daggers of the killing and significant inscription, the "Ides of March."

The empire struck coins for four centuries in gold, silver, orichalcum, copper and bronze. Billon, a base silver alloy, was used in provincial Mints in the Near East. Generally, the gold coins, the aureus and solidus, are scarce and high priced. Silver coins are relatively inexpensive, and often are found like the gold in excellent condition.

This is because the precious metal coins tended to be hoarded, leaving the base metal coins, the sestertius, follis and their relations, to bear the brunt of most daily commerce. This has resulted in making bronze coins in the higher categories rather scarce, as they circulated until nearly smooth from handling. Few well-preserved specimens have survived.

The coins of the Roman emperors are masterpieces of portraiture, especially in the early reigns. The engravers plainly sought realistic and sometimes merciless likenesses. It is doubtful that any modern dictator would tolerate the pitiless realism with which Mint engravers highlighted the gross, perverted features of Nero or the vicious vacuousness of Caligula.

One attraction of Roman coins is the historical documentation they represent. The great names of Augustus, Trajan, Hadrian or Marcus Aurelius; the names of tyrants, such as Nero, Caracalla or Heliogabalus; the record of wars, conquests, triumphs and tragedies all are brought to life by these pieces of numismatic history.

As with the Greek series, a collector starting out in the field of Roman coins needs to prepare himself for some study. A knowledge of Latin helps but is really not an absolute necessity. The collector should acquire a small working library of popular-priced books and a historical reference, and go at it; the expense can be kept reasonable, and great satisfaction achieved.

It helps again, to patronize a professional numismatist of integrity and knowledge. In perhaps no other field is it truer that "if you don't know your coins, know your dealer."

There are various ways to go about assembling a representative Roman collection. One of the most logical and popular is to start by seeking one coin of each emperor. With a few exceptions, short-lived or would-be rulers, this goal can be reached at moderate expense.

Collectors can thank the efficiency of the ancient Mint masters for this. They worked fast to introduce new coins for a new ruler. Didius Julianus, for example, bought the throne in A.D. 193 and held it only a few months, but the Mints produced 19 portrait coin types of this emperor, as well as coins portraying his wife and daughter.

Judaic coinage

Another branch of ancient coin collecting which enjoys a great popularity is the historic Judaic coinage. Coinage of Judaea goes back to the fifth century B.C. when Greek type coinage began.

The rule of the Maccabees produced a more national coinage of simple but attractive style, succeeded by the Hellenistic-Roman types of the Herodian client kings.

Perhaps the most beautiful and significant coins before the rebirth of Israel in our time are the bronze and silver coins of the First Revolt, which ended with the Romans' destruction of the Temple in A.D. 70. Their simple and harmonious designs are in strange contrast to the violence and ultimate defeat of the Revolt.

Coins of the first century's Bar-Kochba War evoke a feeling of communion with this last outburst of the Jewish longing for independence and the restoration of Jerusalem and the Temple. The Temple's facade and sacred instruments adorn the coins, many overstruck on contemporary Roman issues.

Byzantine coinage

The basic unit of Byzantine coinage was the gold solidus, or nomisma, the latter often struck in a characteristic cupped shape. There was little silver in circulation; such denominations as the miliaresion and hexagram enjoyed, at best, a limited life.

The emperor Anastasius I decreed a unified bronze coinage in 498, with the actual denomination in multiple nummi expressed on each coin. Byzantine bronze was issued in considerable quantities, and is still available at quite reasonable prices.

Collectors would be well advised to study all Byzantine gold coins with great attention, however, as counterfeits, even in museum collections, are plentiful, as one might expect from a coinage which spanned a large part of the world in its time.

With something to offer to every segment of collecting taste, ancient coins are undoubtedly on the rise. Interest in art, history and even profit spurs activity in the field; and it can safely be said that for expansion of an individual's knowledge, few areas of numismatics can offer as much as the systematic collecting of ancient coins of all types.

Bank notes and other paper money

Not as old as coins but equally fascinating to many are bank notes and other forms of paper money. Checks, stock and bond certificates and even deposit slips and check writing machines are also collected with paper money.

Our purpose here will be to introduce the subject matter on a general basis.

Early notes

Marco Polo brought back to Italy tales of paper money in circulation in China. In 806, 400 years before Marco Polo, Emperor Hien Tsung issued certificates of deposit to merchants, who then had to carry only the paper and not the heavy metal it represented. The earliest notes known to us date from the Ming Dynasty, 1368, when notes made of mulberry bark were issued.

Emergency notes are known to have been issued during the siege of the Alhama in Spain in 1483 and in Granada, Spain, in 1490.

Bank of Stockholm notes in Sweden date from 1661, considered the earliest circulating bank notes in Europe.

Topics

Choices offered in topical collecting are almost as wide in paper money as in coins. There are few genuine, intentional commemorative notes, but they can be found. Some collectors seek bank buildings on notes; others could parallel the coin themes of ships, animals, fruit, trees, women, portraits and even coins and Mints on notes.

Advanced collectors might seek variety of note manufacture methods, including offset, intaglio or engraved notes or lithographic.

The paper money collector has two sources of delight not shared with most coin collectors: serial numbers and signatures. One to four signatures are often found on notes, and as one of the these signatures may change, endless combinations become available to the specialist.

Numbers and letters found on notes can include engraving plate numbers, serial letter combinations, issue-date changes and easiest of all, a serial number. Collectors observe the color of the number; height of the figures; and then may check for palindromes, numbers reading the same both ways, popularly called "radar notes." The more digits in a number, the more difficult this becomes. A number 1441 may be easy to find; more difficult would be 123454321.

Housing

The collector of paper money of the world experiences the same problems of the collector of notes of the United States when he must decide how to store and arrange his collection.

Since notes are not as durable as coins and folding and handling can reduce their desirability, it is important to keep the notes flat and yet in view.

Plastic sheets are made in several sizes, including 8-1/2-by-11-inches, with two, three or four pockets, to hold notes of varying sizes. Also smaller wallet-size holders are made, as well as single plastic pockets slightly larger than the notes to be handled.

Other useful tools for studying your notes are a magnifying glass, a ruler with millimeter readings and a good eye for color shades.

Grading

The grade indicated by many sellers and catalogers of notes is a tool for determining how worn a note is, or how far from being Uncirculated it may be. A crisp note may be worth twice as much as one with a single fold. Once a note has several folds, is dirty, has torn corners and ragged edges, it is probably worth face value only if still circulating, and very little more if obsolete, unless it is extremely rare.

These remarks on condition are not intended to lead the paper money collector to believe that only Uncirculated notes are collectible. Many collectors want a note that has genuinely seen circulation; others will take a worn note, with the expectation of replacing it when a note in better condition becomes available. The collector who turns down notes for the Uncirculated issues may wait a long time; meanwhile, prices may increase for even the worn notes.

Some grade paper money in the same terms by which coins are graded. Others have devised a percentage scale, with a 100 percent note Uncirculated, and the amount of wear indicated by lesser figures; a 90 percent note would be better than a 70 percent note.

Emergency money

Siege notes, issued in times of emergency, have been mentioned already. Collectors of world notes often encounter other emergency notes which should be reviewed.

At least a dozen countries of Europe issued emergency money in the 1914-1923 period of World War I and the aftermath. In France they are called monnaies de necessite and in Germany and Austria, notgeld, emergency money. Many cities issued these; others were issued by the army, the railways or the post offices.

Collectors often separate the emergency issues from inflation issues. The latter appeared first in late 1922, and by 1923 in Germany the issues reached such enormous sums that a single note might represent more than the entire indebtedness of the German people in August 1914. Even more rampant inflation was known in Hungary in 1946.

In some cases, governments have been known to bring out of storage notes not issued for many years and overprint them with new dates and values.

Other specialized forms of emergency money are cited as postage stamp money, encased and unencased; military payment certificates; invasion money; guerrilla issues; prisoner of war camp money; and issues from concentration and displaced persons camps.

Other uses of paper money

Economists can point to the printing press and its unlimited yield of paper money as a major cause of inflation and monetary woes of many a nation. Paper money does not have to reach the point of spiraling inflation.

Paper money can represent 100 percent hard money; that is, $100 worth of gold is on deposit in a bank, with a $100 note issued and the statement that the note is redeemable for $100 in gold.

In practice, the tendency of governments has been that with a gold reserve of $100, notes might be issued in sums of $200 or $500 or $1,000 or more, backed by the same $100 in gold; or eventually, no gold at all.

A study of paper money issues will reveal various names for notes, many based on the type of backing; gold note, silver note, even copper coins depicted on a note, to denote copper coin backing. Other notes found will be treasury note;

certificate of deposit; Federal Reserve note; in France, "billets de confiance," (notes of confidence); gold or silver certificates.

During the French Revolution, and in 1923 in Germany, land was the backing of assignates and rentenmark notes, respectively. Also in 1923 in Germany, there were notes backed by wood, rye, gas, electricity and other tangible commodities.

To readily identify paper money of the United States in circulation in war zones during World War II, United States silver certificates were used to pay troops in the Pacific and North African theaters of operation with distinctive markings.

Had there been a takeover by the enemy, the money could have been immediately disclaimed and redemption refused, if it was believed the enemy would benefit.

These notes included the HAWAII overprint on the reverse of $1, $5, $10 and $20 and the yellow seal silver certificates of $1, $5 and $10, used in North Africa, with a yellow seal on the obverse.

Printers

Some government printing facilities might print bank notes for other governments. Often the name of the printer, government or private, appears on the one side or the other of the note in very small letters.

Private firms which have printed notes around the world include:

American Bank Note Co., New York
British American Bank Note Co., Ottawa, Canada
Barclay and Fry Ltd., England
Blades, East & Blades Bank Note Engravers
Bouligay & Schmidt, Mexico
Bradbury Wilkinson & Co., New Malden, Surrey, England
Calicografia e Cartevalori, Milano, Italy
Canadian Bank Note Co., Ltd., Ottawa, Canada
Charles Skipper & East, England
Chosun Textbook Printing, Co. Ltd., South Korea
Chung Hwa Book Co., China
Commonwealth Banknote Co., Melbourne, Australia
Continental Banknote Co., New York
E.A. Wright, Philadelphia, Pa.
J. Enschede & Son, Haarlem, the Netherlands
Franklin-Lee Bank Note Co.
Forbes Lithograph Manufacturing Co., Boston, Mass.
Homer Lee Bank Note Co., New York
Hong Kong Banknote Co., Hong Kong
Hong Kong Printing Press, Hong Kong
Giesecke & Devrient, Berlin, Leipzig & Munich, Germany
International Bank Note Co., London
Jefferies Bank Note Co., Los Angeles
Nisson & Arnold, London
Orell Fuessli, Zurich
Beijing Bureau of Engraving and Printing, Beijing, China
Perkins, Bacon & Co. Ltd., London
St. Luke's Printing Works, London
Saul Soloman & Co., Cape Town, South Africa
Security Banknote Co., New York
Shanghai Printing Co., Shanghai, China
State of California Bureau of Printing, Sacramento, Calif.
Stecher-Traung Lithograph Corp., San Francisco, Calif.
Thomas de la Rue Ltd., Basingstoke, England
Tokyo Printing Co., Tokyo
Union Printing Co., Shanghai
Union Publishers and Printers Fed. Inc., Shanghai
Waterlow & Sons Ltd., London
Waterlow Bros. & Layton Ltd., London
Watson Printing Co.
Western District Banknote Fed. Inc., Shanghai
William Brown & Co., London
W.W. Sprague & Co., Ltd., England

Precious Metals

14

Gold

Chemical symbol: Au
Atomic number: 79
Atomic weight: 196.967
Density: 18.88 times the weight of an equal volume of water

Gold, the precious and magical yellow metal, has been known and valued by men and women since the dawn of civilization. Egyptian, Etruscan, Assyrian and Minoan cultures all valued gold. Gold coinage began in Lydia (modern-day Turkey) in 700 B.C.

Early gold coinage

The first gold coins were not struck from pure gold, but from a gold and silver alloy called electrum, found in Lydia. In addition to hosting the earliest gold coins made from electrum in 700 B.C., Lydia was also the site of the first pure gold coinage, during the sixth century B.C. Lydia was followed in the same century by gold pieces created by Persian rulers. These were called darics, after King Darius I.

Other rulers of the ancient world, such as Philip and Alexander the Great of Macedon, as well as Lysimachus of Thrace, issued widely circulating gold coins. The Romans issued gold coinage, the so-called aurei, beginning in Caesar's time.

After the fall of Rome, the Byzantine Empire became the important outlet for gold coins. The Byzantines struck their coins in more than 10 Mints throughout the empire.

The early Middle Ages saw the decline of gold coinage in the West. Monetary gold came back into use with the Crusades; the most notable example of the revival is the augustalis, issued during the 13th century by Frederick II of Hohenstaufen. In 1252, Florence issued the gold florin, followed by gold coinage issued in France, Bohemia, Hungary, the Low Countries and Spain. In 1284 Venice issued what became the most popular coin for more than 500 years, the ducat, or zecchino.

In 1343, England issued its first major gold coin, the florin, followed in 1344 by the noble. The English later struck the angel and the crown, in 1663 the guinea, and in 1816 the sovereign. Germany struck the gulden, Spain the excellente and France a variety of gold coins, following England's lead.

The first gold coins in the United States were authorized in 1792 after the Republic was formed.

Sources of gold

The Egyptians obtained gold from the earliest times in Nubia, a region in northeastern Africa, modern-day Sudan and Egypt. The Greeks went as far away as India, the Urals, and the mountains and rivers of Asia Minor to obtain gold. Most of the gold used in the Roman Empire came from Spain, then Hungary and Transylvania, and finally Dalmatia (now Yugoslavia, on the Adriatic coast) and the eastern Alps.

After the fall of the Roman Empire, gold circulation was greatly diminished in the West. From the 10th to the 15th centuries, the gold that was used came from Bohemia (part of modern-day Czechoslovakia), Silesia (part of modern Poland), Transylvania and Hungary. In the 18th century Siberia and the Urals became important gold-producing regions.

The first half of the 19th century was marked by a large production of gold in Russia and by gold discoveries in Georgia, North Carolina, and finally, in 1848, the extensive finds in California. Gold production in Australia began around this time as well, followed in 1885 by finds in South Africa, and in 1897 by production in the Klondike, a gold-rich region in northwestern Canada.

Gold mining and refining

Two techniques are usually used to recover gold from its place in nature — placer mining, used to extract gold from rivers and streams; and lode mining, used to take gold out of hard rock.

Placer mining, named after the alluvial deposits, or "placers" of gold found in the beds of streams, was the most common and productive method of gold mining until the 1920s. The principle is to separate gold from river gravel by washing it with water. The gold, mixed with the river gravel, is washed through a series of sluice boxes, each containing crossbars at the bottom. As the water and gravel pass through the boxes, which are slanted downward to employ the force of gravity, the gold sinks to the bottom and lodges behind the crossbars.

An important derivative of this basic placer mining is dredging. A continuously working chain of buckets brings gravel up from the riverbed onto a ship, where it is broken, screened, and washed through sluices.

Extracting gold from solid rock, or lode mining, uses the same processes common to all underground mining. Entry into the ground is gained by breaking the rock by drilling and blasting; the gold ore is broken away from the surrounding rock in

a transportable size, and hauled out of the mine.

These processes of mining yield an impure gold, containing amounts of silver, copper and other metals. Two methods are most commonly used to extract gold from its metal relatives — a chemical process using chlorine, and the electrolytic process, first used in United States Mints.

In the chlorine process, the impure gold is heated until it becomes molten. Chlorine is bubbled through the molten gold, converting the silver to silver chloride, which can be skimmed off the top of the liquid solution. Unlike the electrolytic process, this chlorine method does not extract platinum from the impure gold.

The electrolytic process involves suspending plates of pure gold alternately with plates of impure gold in a cell containing a solution of gold chloride and hydrochloric acid. The impure gold plates are made the anode, the pure gold plates are the cathode. Through the liquid, a current of electricity is passed from the anode plates to the cathode plates. The gold dissolves from the anodes and is precipitated on the cathodes. The other metals that were combined with the impure gold dissolve in the liquid, except the silver, which is converted into insoluble chloride and falls to the bottom of the cell. The gold which precipitates on the cathode plates is washed and melted into bars. This process yields gold that is more than .999 fine, or 99.9 percent pure.

Measure of worth

Gold is valued not only for its beauty, but for its high resistance to corrosion, malleability and longevity. Gold will not readily combine with other metals. It is one of the greatest conductors of electricity.

A cubic foot of solid gold weighs about 1,200 pounds. The standard gold brick, or bullion bar, contains 1,000 troy ounces, or nearly 68.5 pounds avoirdupois.

The purity of gold is measured in fineness, parts of gold per 1,000. Pure gold is called 24 karat. A small quantity of silver will reduce the yellowish color of gold, and with added quantities it will develop a greenish color. Copper added will deepen the gold color. A pure white alloy is obtained by adding platinum, nickel or zinc; this is called white gold or jeweler's gold, and can also be produced by alloying yellow gold with palladium.

The rise and fall of the gold standard

Because gold is durable and highly malleable, it can be hammered into almost any shape and precisely divided into any size or unit of weight. Since it can be stamped into coins of a precise weight, the values of all other goods could, in the early days of gold coinage, be measured in terms of units of gold. Eventually gold became the absolute standard of value.

Although gold is very dense, its high value compared with its weight and bulk increased the risk of its being stolen. Nevertheless, by the 16th century and even much later, some gold-holding citizens kept their fortunes of gold in their own houses. But most people eventually became accustomed to leaving their gold for safekeeping in the goldsmiths' vaults, where it was well-protected. The goldsmiths would issue a receipt for the gold received.

Before long, gold-holding citizens realized it was much easier, when it came time to make a purchase or pay a debt, to simply issue an order to the goldsmith to pay over the gold to whomever they owed, rather than to transfer the gold itself. The recipient of the order, again, might find it easier to leave the gold he was to receive at the goldsmith's and in turn issue orders to the goldsmith to pay specific amounts of gold to still a third person. Thus, all these monetary transactions took place without the actual gold leaving the goldsmith's vault. This was the origin of bank notes and checks.

As this new paper money began to circulate on its own, goldsmiths discovered they could issue paper promises that exceeded the value of the gold in their vaults. Since this made the medium of exchange more abundant, trade

flourished as the amount of money increased to meet its needs. When paper money became too abundant and exceeded the goods available in the market, it was withdrawn from circulation and exchanged for gold; when paper money became too scarce, gold was returned to the banks and exchanged for its paper representative.

The goldsmiths were gambling that everyone wouldn't demand his gold at once. Since this was a good risk, in nearly every country these new banks went on expanding their credit until the amount of bank note and demand deposit liabilities, that is, the amount of money, was several times the amount of gold held in the banks' vaults.

For centuries this alternating appearance (when paper money was cashed in) and disappearance (when gold was exchanged for paper money) of gold was the only stabilizing factor in a radically fluctuating market. Paper notes were issued freely by goldsmiths, money changers, merchants and bankers. No government could control the system; gold was the only stabilizing influence on the market. As the international monetary system became more complex, more and more governments used this traditional method of balancing and stabilizing international trade and backing up domestic currency with gold.

Gold stands firm

From these origins came the gold standard. First adopted by Great Britain in 1821, it was the system under which governments issued paper money which was backed by, and exchangeable for, gold. The amount of money circulating in a country depended upon the amount of gold it had.

The gold standard had several advantages. Since governments couldn't legally increase the money supply without obtaining more gold, citizens were thought to be protected from politically attractive, printing-press inflation. The threat that people would demand gold for their paper tended to act as a damper on politicians. The gold standard was also supposed to keep a nation's payments to, and receipts from, foreigners automatically in rough balance. Suppose a country bought from foreigners, or imported, more than it exported over a long period. The country would pay out much more gold than it received, which would reduce the amount of money circulating at home. A smaller money supply would, in turn, tend to reduce the prices of things the country produced. Lower prices would make the country's goods and services more attractive to both foreign and domestic buyers. This would encourage purchases by foreigners, or exports, and discourage purchase from them.

Since everyone accepted gold as a medium of exchange, the gold standard also tended to create certainty in international trade by providing a fixed pattern of exchange rates, that is, the rate or price at which the currency of one country is exchanged for currency of another country.

But since the money supply depended on the amount of gold a country had, less money in circulation could mean less domestic business and more unemployment. In other words, the gold standard may not allow enough flexibility in the supply of money. And, since it provided a fixed pattern of exchange rates, the gold standard made it difficult for any nation to isolate its economy from depression or inflation in the rest of the world.

Most major nations of the world had adopted the gold standard by the 1870s. The United States was one of the last, officially adopting it in 1900.

Some countries at this time were using a close relative of the gold standard, the gold exchange standard. In this system, gold was not exported or imported at all. One country would offer to buy and sell the currency of another gold-standard country at a fixed price in the paper currency of the country making the offer. This was much cheaper than the full gold standard since the expense of transporting the gold was eliminated.

1919 and after

World War I spelled an effective end to the gold standard. War-induced inflation caused most nations to change to inconvertible currency or to restrict gold export.

At any other time the gold standard might have supplied its own automatic corrective: inflation at home would have meant that gold, in itself, was a more profitable export than goods, and a partial drain of gold abroad would thus normally have resulted in a contracted volume of money at home, making it necessary to reduce imports until a balance of trade had again been reached by an intensification of cheaper exports.

But the expense of war caused Great Britain and other countries to spend gold profusely to buy arms from the United States.

At the end of World War I, all currencies were inflated, and there was a severe shortage of gold. Most of the world's stock had gone into hiding; half of it was in the United States reserve and the rest was in private hands. Inflation had driven the cost of gold mining up until it approached and sometimes exceeded the official price of gold. Convinced a return to the gold standard would solve the world's monetary ills, the nations of the Atlantic trading community agreed to return to the gold standard in the 1920s.

The stock market crash in 1929 killed this last valiant effort to remain on the gold standard. In 1931, Britain went off the gold standard after using up her gold reserve in an attempt to defend her overvalued pound.

When President Roosevelt signed the Gold Reserve Act of 1934, the United States officially abandoned the gold standard. The dollar was no longer convertible to gold and gold could not be exported. The government prohibited the manufacture of gold coins, the private hoarding of gold and the use of gold as money or in lieu of money.

Gold having a recognized special value to collectors of rare and unusual coins, including gold coins made prior to April 4, 1933, were exempted from delivery to the U.S. Treasury, including U.S. and foreign coins. All other gold coins, gold certificates, and gold bullion were required to be turned in to the Treasury.

At the same time the Secretary of the Treasury issued a public announcement that, beginning Feb. 1, 1934, the Treasury would buy any and all gold delivered to any U.S. Mint, or any Assay office in New York or Seattle, at the rate of $35 per fine troy ounce. An exhausted nation in the depths of a depression jumped at the offer; wedding rings, gold plates and jewelry poured into the Treasury. By the end of 1934 gold was coming into the Philadelphia Mint at the rate of $1.5 million worth a month.

In October 1933 President Roosevelt announced he would establish a government market for gold, and on January 31, 1934, he froze the price at $35 an ounce, thereby devaluing the dollar 40.94 percent. The result was a literal flood of gold pouring into the United States from foreign countries. The onslaught of gold made the government realize it had nowhere to put it, so the gold vaults of Fort Knox, Ky., were built in 1935.

By October 1939, the United States had well over half the world's stock of gold.

Dethroning the king

With the founding of the United Nations after World War II, representatives of 44 nations met in conference at Bretton Woods, N.H., in July 1944, to form the International Monetary Fund. The IMF is a specialized agency affiliated with the UN, designed to stabilize international monetary exchange rates in lieu of the gold standard. It has no power to dictate national monetary policies.

The members of the IMF, it was decided, would all deposit quotas in the fund, only one-quarter of which had to be in gold, and the rest in their own currencies. From this fund members could purchase with their own national currencies the gold or foreign exchange they needed.

The IMF, then, became the world's largest source of quickly available international credit. By June 1972, the 124-nation fund had provided $24.6 billion in short-term financial assistance.

Only the United States decided to keep its currency convertible at all times into gold. The U.S. pledged at Bretton Woods to convert foreign holdings of dollars into gold on demand at the fixed rate of $35 an ounce. The other countries could hold and count dollars as part of their reserves as if dollars were gold. Thus the dollar became the center of the world's monetary system.

Each member of the IMF was required to maintain the dollar or gold parity ($35 an ounce) of its currency by buying its currency when the price fell to 1 percent below parity or selling if the price rose 1 percent above parity.

The London gold market reopened in 1954 after World War II had forced its close in 1939. From 1954 to 1957, the price of gold on the London market fell consistently below $35 an ounce. Private demand for gold was composed almost entirely of industrial-artistic use and hoarding in countries where savings are traditionally held in gold.

Despite the growth in industrial use of gold and that gold, at a fixed price, was cheap in comparison to other commodities, private demand generally did not absorb all newly mined gold and the gold purchased from Communist stocks during this time. Except when the monetary authorities purchased gold to maintain its price at $35 an ounce, most countries bought relatively little gold, and instead built up their dollar holdings.

The gold drain

The system ran into difficulty in 1958 when the United States saw its first significantly large balance of payments deficit. This is a name given to the excess in the amount of dollars going abroad for foreign aid, for investments, for tourist expenditures, for imports, and for other payments, in comparison to the amount of dollars coming in for payments of U.S.

exports to foreign countries. This meant a heavy drain on U.S. gold supply.

The balance of payments deficit persisted into 1960. Rumors began to spread in October that the United States might devalue the dollar (by raising the price of gold) to slow the gold drain. The first sharp gold panic swept the world's monetary trading centers. Under pressure from a sudden and widespread demand for gold, the market price jumped in London from $35 to $42 an ounce.

The crisis was eased temporarily as the U.S. Treasury transferred $135 million in gold to the London market, and as the Bank of England intervened as a substantial seller. This flood of gold forced the price back down to $35 by the spring of 1961.

Relief was short-lived. The supply of new gold coming into the London market began to fall in midsummer of 1961 as the two largest producers of gold, Canada and South Africa, began to add their newly mined gold to their monetary reserves. Demand for gold continued to rise, though, as the U.S. balance of payments deficit continued. The price of gold began to creep upward again.

In the autumn of 1961, the United States proposed that other nations join it to maintain the price of gold at a reasonable level. This was the birth of the London gold pool, a group formed to try to stabilize the gold market and avoid excessive swings in the price of gold that would lead to a loss of confidence in many foreign currencies.

The central banks of eight nations joined the gold pool — Belgium, France, Italy, Switzerland, the Netherlands, West Germany, the United Kingdom and the United States. Each contributed a quota to the pool, with the United States matching their combined payment. The Bank of England acted as agent for the group, given the right to draw on the pool and to sell gold if the price rose too high.

In November 1961, the first sales were made. The price of gold fell and the sales by the pool were recovered in later purchases. By February 1962, all the members of the gold pool had been repaid.

The price was temporarily under control, but the U.S. gold drain continued. To defend the dollar on foreign markets, President Johnson signed legislation in early 1965 to drop the 25 percent requirement for gold backing of commercial banks' deposits at Federal Reserve banks. This bill freed about $5 billion of the country's remaining $15 billion gold stock for additional sale to dollar-holding foreign governments. The requirement that paper currency in circulation be backed 25 percent by gold remained.

Despite United States efforts, in 1966 and 1967 private demand began to exceed the supply of gold available at $35 an ounce. During this time massive losses from official stocks occurred. The rate of expansion of gold production in South Africa, which had been increasing for 15 years, came to a halt in 1966. With rising production costs the outlook for a greatly increased supply of gold didn't look favorable, especially at a fixed price of $35 an ounce. Greatly aggravating this drop in free world gold production in 1966 was the Soviet Union's decision to discontinue its by-then-customary gold sales.

As production of gold decreased, demand climbed, particularly from gold speculators who had entered the market in significant numbers with the gold crisis of 1960. These speculators tried to take advantage of the worsening U.S. balance of payments deficit by purchasing large amounts of gold, which they expected to increase in price.

The two-tier system

In the five months preceeding March 1968, speculation absorbed nearly $3 billion in gold, almost all of which was lost by the gold pool countries, primarily the U.S. Unwilling to suffer such losses in the future, the gold pool members instituted the two-tier system.

The system, outlined in a Washington meeting of the gold pool nations on March 16-17, 1968, set up new guidelines governing the future of gold. On one level, the $35 an ounce price of gold was maintained. At this price, transnational governmental authorities agreed to the unlimited exchange of gold among themselves. On the second level, a free market in gold was established which could fluctuate to reflect whatever the value of gold really was. Three conditions effectively achieved this segregation:

1. An agreement among monetary authorities to trade gold among themselves at an official price of $35 an ounce.

2. Agreement to supply no more gold to private markets from official stocks.

3. Agreement to buy little or no gold from private sellers.

The concept of Special Drawing Rights (SDRs) was introduced at the March meeting and adopted later in 1969 and 1970. SDRs are a form of "paper gold" to be used in the same manner as gold, dollars or other currencies to settle debts between nations. The SDRs were distributed to members of the International Monetary Fund in proportion to their economic importance in the world economy. Designed to protect gold reserves, SDRs could be used to settle international payment deficits that would have otherwise drawn on these reserves. SDRs were given the value in gold of one U.S. dollar, which, at the official price of $35 an ounce, would buy 0.888671 gram of fine gold.

U.S. domestic policy changed to conform to the new system. The Treasury announced it would no longer purchase gold in the private market, nor would it sell gold for industrial, professional or artistic uses. Domestic producers were permitted to sell and export freely to foreign buyers as well as to authorized domestic users. Domestic consumers regularly engaged in an industry, profession or art in which gold is required were permitted to continue to import gold or to purchase gold from domestic producers.

The U.S. government also removed the remaining 25 percent gold backing from paper money in circulation, freeing

another $750 million to stabilize the gold market.

The price of gold on the free-market tier began to rise. On May 17, 1968, it touched $40 an ounce on the London market. In July, however, the price fell again when the French government tried to bolster the franc and rumors spread that South Africa would be selling some of its newly mined gold on the free market. In October, the U.S. and other major nations in the IMF agreed to provide a mechanism for sales of newly mined gold to monetary authorities, but only when the free market price reached or fell below the official price of $35 an ounce.

Dollar devaluation

The economic crisis of the United States worsened as the balance of payments deficit persisted. As a result, on Aug. 16, 1971, President Nixon announced the United States was freeing the dollar for devaluation against other currencies by suspending the full convertibility of foreign-held dollars into gold. This inconvertibility meant no foreign government could convert dollars into Treasury-held gold; thus, the tie between the dollar and gold was severed.

The devaluation of the dollar occurred Dec. 18, 1971, and was accomplished by raising the official price of gold from $35 to $38 an ounce. Other currencies were juggled up or down into a new pattern of exchange rates. Throughout 1972 the price of gold on the free market climbed until it leveled off in December at $61 an ounce.

Economists and monetary authorities almost unanimously regarded the 8.57 percent devaluation of the dollar as inadequate. And since the dollar was no longer exchangeable for gold, it made little difference that the price at which the Treasury did not sell gold was raised from $35 to $38 an ounce.

Another devaluation was forced, then, in February 1973. Treasury Secretary George Shultz announced that the dollar would be devalued 10 percent against Special Drawing Rights (and so against gold) with the official monetary price of gold raised from $38 to $42.22 an ounce.

The price of gold on the London market took a sharp leap upward, breaking through the $100 an ounce barrier on May 14, 1973. Official stocks of gold were virtually frozen because no central bank would give up gold at the official price of $42.22 an ounce when the free market price had climbed so far above it.

The king is dead

Five and a half years after its birth, the two-tier gold system was abandoned by central bank officials Nov. 10, 1973. The system had out-lived its usefulness since it was made when the dollar was still convertible into gold; there was no point in continuing it when the central banks of other nations could not buy gold from the U.S. Treasury with dollars, as the original agreement had allowed for.

By abandoning the system the central bank officials, from Belgium, West Germany, Italy, the Netherlands, Switzerland, Britain and the U.S. relegated gold to the status of commodity, with no special monetary status, opening the way for increased international dependence on Special Drawing Rights.

Two months later the International Monetary Fund met in Rome to finalize the demotion of gold. The IMF's Committee of Twenty decided to adopt a new world currency plan that would end all relationship between Special Drawing Rights and gold. It would be replaced by a "basket" of 14 of the world's strongest paper currencies. The value of SDRs would be based on an average value of a portfolio of these currencies, including the dollar, the British pound, French franc, West German mark, Japanese yen, and a sampling of other currencies. The scheme was approved in June 1974.

The IMF Group of Ten (the U.S., Britain, France, West Germany, Italy, Belgium, the Netherlands, Sweden, Canada and Japan) met in June 1974, and gave gold a new function in the monetary world. Gold stocks stored in the vaults of central banks, it was decided, could be used by economically distressed countries as security for international loans, expanding their borrowing power.

Though this was perfectly legal before, it was economically unfeasible under the two-tier system since no nation was ready to risk its gold as loan collateral at the official price of $42.22 when the market price was four times that. It was agreed the pledged gold could be valued at a price much closer to the free-market quote than to the official level.

President Ford signed a bill Aug. 20, 1974, lifting the 40-year-old restrictions on U.S. citizens' holding of gold. Americans, as of Dec. 31, 1974, would be permitted to buy, hold and sell gold without restriction, as they would deal in any other commodity.

After Ford signed the bill, Treasury Under Secretary Jack F. Bennett commented that the U.S. "might feel free to sell gold from official stocks" directly to domestic buyers. Bennett noted that unless there was such a source of gold inside the country, most of the gold purchased would have to be imported, thus further distorting the U.S. balance of payments deficit.

Gold, once the undisputed king of the international monetary system, was now reduced to the status of another commodity. Still as durable, malleable, and beautiful as it always was, gold's value now rests in the hands of the gold dealers of London, Paris, Zurich and the United States.

In numismatics

Gold coinage, authorized soon after the Republic was formed, had been gradually phased out until the end was spelled out in 1933 when it became illegal to manufacture gold coins or to use gold as money or in lieu of money (See GOLD CHRONOLOGY).

With the gold acts and orders of 1933 and 1934, designed to centralize the gold reserves of the country into the hands of the government, restrictions on collecting gold coins were very stringent. The government wanted to make sure no one was "collecting" gold coins for their gold content rather than for their numismatic value; hence, all gold coins were called in except for those "having a recognized special value to collectors of rare and unusual coin," according to the Treasury.

A determination was made on each individual gold coin presented to the Treasury for a ruling, including gold coins made before and after 1933. The criterion for a pre-1933 coin was whether or not it had "recognized" special collector value on April 4, 1933. That for coins struck after 1933 was whether they had "true numismatic value," based on the number issued, the purpose for which they were issued, the condition of the coin, the Mint mark if any, and all other factors concerning the issue.

Foreign coins struck after 1933 and issued in large quantities or for the purpose of providing a market for gold, or simply as a money-making device, were denied entry.

These strict regulations were relaxed somewhat in 1954 when the Treasury amended the gold regulations. The amendment provided that any gold coin made prior to 1933 would be considered a rare gold coin. Any struck after 1933 would not be considered rare unless a specific determination to the contrary was made by the Treasury Department.

As a numismatic authority, the Treasury called on the Curator of Numismatics of the United States National Museum.

These regulations and the stricter ones made in 1933 still gave the Treasury no control over gold held by U.S. citizens outside the United States. The coin market abroad was flooded with counterfeits and restrikes of coins made before 1933, making it difficult for the Treasury to determine whether the coins held abroad were actually those ruled exempt under Treasury Department rulings.

Restrictions on U.S. citizens holding gold abroad began Jan. 14, 1961, when President Eisenhower issued an executive order prohibiting the holding of gold abroad by any persons subject to the jurisdiction of the United States. An exception was made for gold coins, again,

"of recognized value to collectors of rare and unusual coin."

ODGSO is born

Before October 9, 1961, the function of administering the gold and silver regulations was assigned to the Bureau of the Mint. On that date, a Treasury Department order created the Office of Domestic Gold and Silver Operations (ODGSO) and placed it in the Office of the Undersecretary for Monetary Affairs.

The ODGSO reported directly to the Deputy Undersecretary for Monetary Affairs until April 1, 1969, when it was placed under the new position of Assistant Secretary (Economic Policy).

The primary functions of ODGSO were to:

1. Assist in the formulation of policies regarding the control of gold.

2. Administer the Treasury gold regulations to include the issuance of licenses or other authorizations for the acquisition, possession, ownership, importation, exportation, and uses of gold for industrial, professional and artistic purposes. The office also issued licenses or other authorizations for the importation of gold coins, medals and bars of exceptional numismatic value.

3. Maintain statistical data on the production and uses of gold.

The first director of ODGSO was Leland Howard. He retired Dec. 30, 1966, but remained as an adviser until Thomas Wolfe was named the new director in June 1967.

The new office went to work soon after its creation when President Kennedy, on July 20, 1962, proclaimed that acquiring gold coins abroad was illegal for subjects of the United States. Citizens were ordered to bring home or to dispose of any rare gold coins they held abroad by Jan. 1, 1963.

The proclamation also prohibited the importation of any rare gold coins except under licenses issued by the ODGSO.

Not all pre-1933 gold coins, then, were admissible for import any longer, a partial reinstitution of the 1933 regulations, reflecting the United States gold drain.

The ODGSO also ruled illegal the holding of mutilated gold coins, with any solder on the coin or the drilling of a hole constituting mutilation; and restrikes, which were "subject to forfeiture in the hands of purchasers, no matter how innocent."

The White House commented the action had been taken to prevent large-scale counterfeiting and restriking of rare gold coins in Europe, Argentina and India. Coin dealers reacted with a mixture of suspicion and hostility at the new ruling.

Paper money collectors received a break soon after, however. Another amendment to the gold regulations was issued allowing the holding and importation without license of U.S. gold certificates issued before Jan. 30, 1934. These certificates were issued by the government as a form of paper currency beginning in 1865 and were redeemable on demand in gold. Since it became a crime to hold gold after 1934, the certificates could no longer be cashed in after that date; the certificates themselves, indeed, were supposed to be turned in to the Treasury in 1934.

The government realized that many certificates were still out, in the hands of collectors, since they were no good as currency. The 1964 ruling made their possession legal since they posed no threat to the U.S. gold reserves.

Collectors of gold medals were informed of regulations governing their aspect of numismatics on June 26, 1964. The Treasury issued a release clarifying the acquisition of "fabricated gold":

"'Fabricated gold,'" the Treasury stated, "is gold processed or manufactured gold in any form which: a) has a gold content the value of which does not exceed 90 percent of the total domestic value of such processed or manufactured gold; and b) has in good faith, and not for the purpose of evading or enabling others to evade the provisions of the Acts, the Orders, or the Regulations in this part, been processed or manufactured for some one or more specific and customary industrial, professional or artistic uses. Hence, to

qualify as a fabricated gold object an article must pass all three of the following tests:

"1. The value of the gold content may not exceed 90 percent of the total value.

"2. The article must be manufactured in good faith.

"3. The article must be for specific and customary industrial, professional or artistic uses.

"Award medals which are specially manufactured medals, presented to an individual in recognition of a worthy achievement, may be imported into the United States by the individual receiving the award, that is, the original recipient of the medal."

More regulations governing gold medals were spelled out in an Aug. 21, 1965, Treasury Department order legalizing the possession of rare gold bars:

"The Director, Office of Domestic Gold and Silver Operations, may issue or cause to be issued licenses or other authorizations, permitting the acquisition, holding, transportation and importation of gold bars which the Director is satisfied have been of recognized special value to collectors of numismatic items in all times since prior to April 5, 1933. Gold bars manufactured after Dec. 31, 1900, shall be presumed to not be of such recognized special value to collectors."

The directive continued: "The manufacture of gold medals (other than special award medals) and the plating of coins are not customary industrial, professional or artistic uses of gold within the meaning of the regulations and, accordingly, such uses of gold and the acquisition or possession of any gold medals (other than special award medals) and gold-plated coins are not authorized by the regulations or any licenses issued pursuant thereto. Without limitation the following are not deemed to be of customary industrial, professional or artistic uses of gold:

"1. The plating of any coins.

"2. The manufacture of any gold medals other than special award medals, or,

"3. The acquisition, holding,

transportation, importation or exportation of any gold-plated coins or gold medals other than special award medals."

The ODGSO was called into court early in 1966 to defend its determination of "rare and unusual coin" by Stack's, one of the largest coin dealers in the U.S. The dispute arose when Stack's was denied a license to import a gold coin collection from Amsterdam.

In the extensive and secret hearings, ODGSO disclosed its criterion to determine whether a coin has "exceptional numismatic value" was the ratio between the market value of the coin and its gold bullion content. This was the first public admission by ODGSO of how import licenses were awarded.

Stack's lost the fight Oct. 31, 1966, when the Treasury Deputy Undersecretary for Monetary Affairs upheld the ODGSO position and Stack's was not allowed to import the collection.

The ODGSO did rule, however, on March 21, 1966, that a set of Proof 1965-dated South African gold coins were of exceptional numismatic value and could be licensed for import. In 1968, though, ODGSO ruled against a request for an import license for a set of 1968-dated South African gold coins, taking a turnabout from its former ruling.

Regulations ease

A gradual easing of gold regulations began in 1969, after the U.S. and other International Monetary Fund nations set up the two-tier system for the gold market. On April 26, the Treasury announced that no more licensing would be required for pre-1934 gold coins "of legitimate issue from any nation." The change was made to remove what the Treasury called an "inconsistency" in regulations on imported pre-1934 gold coins, which generally had to have licenses, and those regularly traded within the U.S.

The new ruling freed over 250 additional gold coin issues to come into the U.S. ODGSO Director Thomas Wolfe said the pre-1934 coins constituted 95 percent of all licenses.

The ban continued on importation of all gold coins struck after 1960 except for those already licensed, including: 1961, 500 kronur, Iceland; 1960, 20 pounds, Israel; 1961, 10 scudi, 5 scudi, Malta; 1960, pound and half pound, South Africa; 1961, 1962, 1963, 1964, 1965, rand and two rand, South Africa, all Proof; 1961, 500 piastres, 1962, 250 piastres, Turkey.

The regulations governing coins minted after 1934 remained the same.

Early in 1970 ODGSO granted permission for the importation of one complete six-coin set of Yemen 1969 gold coins and allowed two Israel 1969 gold 100-pound "Shalom" coins to come into the country.

Regulations on gold medals were eased in April 1971. Licenses would be issued for the acquisition, holding, transportation and exportation of gold-plated coins or gold medals which were either antique or for public display by an institution serving the public.

The amendment also authorized the ODGSO to license foreign subsidiaries of U.S. corporations to manufacture gold medals for sale to persons not subject to the jurisdiction of the United States.

Mexican gold coins caused difficulty for the ODGSO after the office allowed importation of coins struck between 1934 and 1959. The flood of restrikes coming from Mexico caused the office to reverse its ruling three months after it was made, and place a ban on importation of all gold coins of Mexico dated since 1933.

The ruling did not stand for long. On Dec. 17, 1973, ODGSO ruled "any gold coin legally issued, dated between 1934 and 1959, may now enter the United States without the formality of applying for a license." The ruling liberated many gold coins of Mexico, Iran, 100 franc pieces of Switzerland dated 1934 and 1939, a four-coin Coronation set of the United Kingdom dated 1937 and gold sovereigns of earlier years restruck in this period, as long as they were dated 1959 or earlier.

But at the same time all coins struck since 1960 were barred, including some for which licenses previously had been granted. So some gold coins that had been legal were now illegal for import. Counterfeit coins and gold bullion or bars continued to be denied passage into the United States.

With President Ford's signature on the bill allowing U.S. citizens to buy, hold and sell gold without restriction ended the back and forth battle between the ODGSO and coin collectors and dealers. All gold coins, as of Dec. 31, 1974, are legal for American citizens to hold. The confusion of regulations raging since 1934 has been cleared and closed. Treasury Secretary William E. Simon announced the abolition of the ODGSO in August 1975. The remaining gold responsibilities of the agency were transferred to the Treasury's Assistant Secretary for International Affairs.

"Gold rush"

European gold dealers, anticipating a "gold rush" by Americans after it became legal once again for them to own gold, were dismayed when this failed to come about. Indeed, the price of gold, which reached $195.25 on Dec. 27, 1974, actually slipped to 186.75 on Dec. 31, and continued to tumble to $175.25 on Jan. 2, 1975.

Free to buy and own gold after a hiatus of more than 40 years, Americans found themselves unfamiliar with the precious metal as an investment medium. They were further aswailed with the prevailing official concept that gold was a "barbarous" medium, reflecting the Keynsian philosophy that remained heavily entrenched in government circles.

The government's role in thwarting citizens' speculating in gold became apparent when Sen. William Proxmire, D-Wis., chairman of the powerful Senate Banking Committee, announced that he would introduce legislation for the sale of 25 million ounces of gold from the government stockpile in 1975.

When a previously authorized 2 million ounces of 400-ounce gold bars were offered at auction on Jan. 6, however, the market showed little interest. Only one-third of the gold offered was taken. The sale had the effect of depressing the London price of gold from $173.50 to $169.50; however, two days later in jumped back to $180.25, registering the sharpest one-day price rise on record.

General Services Administration and International Monetary Fund auctions, together with the importation of tons of gold by refugees following the fall of South Vietnam and Cambodia had a bearish effect on the market throughout 1975 and most of 1976. On July 20, the price plunged to a 31-month low of $107.75, following a second IMF auction.

Inflation heats up

The Carter election victory and the OPEC energy crunch resulted in a turn-around in the gold price and the gold market, so that by Jan. 4, 1978, the gold price registered a 2-1/2-year high of $172.50 at the morning fix in London.

In April Sens. Jesse Helms, R-N.C., and Barry Goldwater, R-Ariz., introduced the American Arts Gold Medallion Act of 1978 as an alternative to the mostly unsuccessful GSA auctions. Meantime, the InternationalGold Corp. (Intergold), the marketing arm of the South African gold mining industry, was aggressively marketing the Krugerrand 1-ounce bullion coin throughout the world.

Higher inflation, increasing U.S. trade deficits and a weakening dollar drove the London morning fix for gold to $223.50 by Oct. 3, 1978. Nine months later, on July 18, 1979, it was fixed at $303.85. The gold price continued to escalate through the year, reaching the all-time record high of $850 on Jan. 21, 1980.

Gold chronology

1782

Thomas Jefferson reports finding a lump of gold ore on the north side of the Rappahannock River in Virginia.

1792

April 2 — Authorizing act issued to strike U.S. gold eagle ($10, standard weight 270 grains, .91666 fineness), half eagle ($5, standard weight 135 grains, .91666 fineness), and quarter eagle ($2.50, standard weight 67.5 grains, .91666 fineness). Dollar defined as a unit containing 24.75 grains of fine gold or 371.25 grains of fine silver (exchange rate between the two metals set at 15 to one.)

1799
Gold discovered in Cabarrus County, North Carolina.

1802
Gold discovered in South Carolina.

1821
Britain adopts the gold standard.

1827
Indians recovering gold near Coker Creek, Tennessee.

1833
Samples of gold found near Georgetown, Texas.

1834
June 28 — Authorizing act issued to change the standard weight of the eagle to 258 grains, .899225 fineness; the half eagle to 129 grains, .899225 fineness; and the Quarter Eagle to 64.5 grains, .899225 fineness.
Standard definition of dollar changed; redefined as unit containing 23.2 grains of fine gold (changed from 24.75 grains). Silver definition unchanged, remains at 371.25 grains of fine silver in one dollar. Exchange rate becomes 16 to one.
Gold mining town of Dahlonega, Ga., built.

1837
Jan. 18 — Authorizing act issued to change fineness of eagle, half eagle, and quarter eagle to .900. Exchange rate becomes 15.988 to one.

1848
Jan. 24 — Gold discovered by James W. Marshall, who was erecting a sawmill in partnership with Captain John A. Sutter on American River, a branch of the Sacramento, near Coloma, Calif.

1849
March 3 — Authorizing act issued to strike U.S. gold double eagle ($20, standard weight 516 grains, .900 fineness), and $1 gold coin (25.8 grains, .900 fineness).

1853
Feb. 21 — Authorizing act issued to strike $3 gold coin (77.4 grains, .900 fineness).

1863
March 3 — Authorizing act issued to produce gold certificates.

1865
November 13 — First U.S. gold certificates issued.

1867
International monetary conference in Paris. Delegates vote to adopt the gold standard.

1869
Sept. 24 — Financial "Black Friday" in New York, caused by an attempt by Jay Gould, financier and speculator, and James Fisk, Erie railroad magnate, to corner the gold market. Gold touched $163.50 per ounce. To bring the price down and foil the financiers' scheme, the Secretary of the Treasury ordered the sale of $4 million in government gold, forcing the price down to $133 and causing a panic in the securities market.

1873
U.S. drops silver dollar from the list of coins to be struck at the Mint; effectively ends bimetallism.

1890
Sept. 26 — $1, $3 gold coins ordered discontinued.

1896
July 8 — William Jennings Bryan, Democratic candidate for president, delivers his impassioned "Cross of Gold" speech at the Democratic National Convention in Chicago, calling for restoration of the bimetallic (silver and gold) standard.

1900
Bimetallism legislation repealed; Gold Standard act passed, officially placing the United States on the gold standard. Gold dollar of 25.8 grains, .900 fine becomes the unit of value; all other forms of currency maintained at parity with the gold dollar.

1902
June 28 — Authorizing act issued to strike $1 gold commemorative coins (25.8 grains, .900 fineness) for the Louisiana Purchase Exposition.

1904
April 13 — Authorizing act issued to strike $1 gold commemorative coins (25.8 grains, .900 fineness) for the Lewis and Clark Exposition.

1915
Jan. 16 — Authorizing act issued to strike $50 (1,290 grains, .900 fineness), $1 (25.8 grains, .900 fineness) and quarter eagle (64.5 grains, .900 fineness) commemorative gold coins for the Panama-Pacific International Exposition.

1916
Feb. 23 — Authorizing act issued to strike $1 gold commemorative coins (25.8 grains, .900 fineness) in honor of President William McKinley.

1925
March 3 — Authorizing act issued to strike quarter eagle gold commemorative coins (64.5 grains, .900 fineness) for the Sesquicentennial Exhibition.
Nations of the Atlantic trading community agree to return to the gold standard after inflated post-World War I currency had caused its demise; Britain returns to the gold standard.

1929
Oct. 29 — Stock market crash marks the end of post-

World War I prosperity. Depression begins.

1931
Britain goes off the gold standard.

1933
June 5 — The United States goes off the gold standard.
April 5 — (Executive Order 6102), August 28 (Executive Order 6260), December 28 (Order of the Secretary of the Treasury) — Government prohibits the manufacture of gold coins, private hoarding of gold and the use of gold as money or in lieu of money. Gold coins having a recognized special value to collectors of rare and unusual coin, including gold coins made prior to April 5, 1933, are exempted from delivery to the U.S. Treasury, including U.S. and foreign coins. All other gold coins, gold certificates and gold bullion are required to be turned in to the Treasury.

1934
Jan. 31 — Executive Order freezes the price of gold at $35 an ounce, up from its former $20.67 an ounce, thereby devaluing the dollar 40.94 percent.

1942
President Roosevelt issues an Executive Order closing all gold mines in the United States.

1944
July — Articles and agreements of the International Monetary Fund, a specialized agency affiliated with the United Nations, signed at Bretton Woods, New Hampshire.

1945
Federal Reserve requirement to hold title to gold in an amount greater than or equal to 40 percent of outstanding Federal Reserve notes plus 35 percent of commercial bank deposits with Federal Reserve banks revised; requirement lowered to 25 percent of the total combined sum of Federal Reserve liabilities.

1946
Ban against gold mining lifted.

1954
London gold market reopens after 15 years of inactivity.
Amendment to gold regulations issued; gold coins made prior to April 5, 1933, both foreign and domestic, declared to be of special value to collectors of rare and unusual coins. Gold coins made after 1933 are presumed not to be rare unless determined otherwise by the Treasury Department.

1958
United States runs a significantly large balance of payments deficit; currency of 14 nations becomes convertible for non-residents.

1960
October — Gold panic sweeps world's monetary trading centers. Free market price of gold jumps from $29.67 to $35 an ounce in London. As a result, eight-nation Gold Pool formed.

1961
Jan. 14 — President Eisenhower issues an Executive Order prohibiting U.S. citizens from purchasing or holding gold abroad in any form except numismatic gold coins. Gold owned by U.S. citizens, residents and corporations abroad must be sold before June 1, 1961.

1962
July 20 — President Kennedy proclaims no person subject to the jurisdiction of the U.S. can acquire gold coins abroad except under Treasury Department license, and no gold coins can be imported without a license. Prohibits ownership abroad of any kind of gold coins. Citizens ordered to bring back to the U.S. or to dispose of any rare gold coins held abroad by Jan. 1, 1963.
September — Treasury Department, for the first time in 17 years, moves a large amount of gold from Fort Knox to the Treasury's Assay Office in New York City to meet foreign demand for U.S. gold bullion.

1963
Jan. 3 — Treasury Secretary Dillon clarifies phrase "customary industrial, professional or artistic use" in Part 54, Title 31; adds definition reading: "Customary industrial professional or artistic use means the use of gold in industry, profession or art, in a manner, for a purpose, in a form, and in quantities in which gold is customarily used in industry, profession or art."
June 26 — Treasury Department clarifies rules on fabricated gold.
Aug. 13 — Customs agents confiscate 21 gold coins from the Witte Museum's $50,000 Albert Hirschfeld collection in San Antonio, Texas, saying the coins were illegally imported.

1964
April 24 — Treasury Department removes all restrictions on the acquisition or holding of gold certificates issued by the U.S. prior to Jan. 30, 1934.
Nov. 30 — Monetary gold reserves drop $75 million for the week ended Nov. 25.

1965
Jan. 7 — France announces its government will convert $150 million of its currency reserves into gold by buying the gold in the United States.
Jan. 13 — U.S. monetary gold reserves drop $200 million in the week ended Jan. 13.
February 19 — Senate passes legislation to repeal requirement for 25 percent gold backing of commerical banks' deposits at Federal Reserve banks. Bill would free about $5 billion of the country's $15 billion gold stock for additional sale to dollar-holding foreign governments and for future growth of the domestic money supply.
March 4 — President Johnson approves and signs legislation freeing $5 billion in U.S. gold in an effort to maintain the stability of the dollar in the world market. Leaves in effect the required 25 percent gold backing of the paper currency in circulation.
Aug. 21 — Treasury Department order issued, allowing the importation, transporting, holding and exportation of numismatically valued gold bars, with license. Also clarifies rules regarding

gold medals and gold-plated coins.

1966

April 27 — Chancellor of the Exchequer announces in Parliament that Great Britain will forbid the use of gold in the making of medallions, plaques, medals and other articles. The new order also bars United Kingdom residents from holding more than four gold coins minted after 1837, except with official permission.

1967

March — Treasury reports gold stock at lowest level since 1938.

March — French government lifts restrictions on the import and export of gold, ending restrictions in effect since September 1939.

March 23 — South African 1966 Proof gold coins are not admissible into the U.S. as collectors' items, the ODGSO rules.

June — Thomas W. Wolfe appointed acting director of ODGSO.

Aug. 2 — Gold reserves reach 29-year low as gold goes into the Treasury's stabilization fund, which handles sales of U.S. gold to foreign nations.

Nov. 18 — Britian devalues the pound, from $2.80 to $2.40

Nov. 27 — Dollar remains strong; Gold Pool members pledge support of the $35 an ounce gold price.

December — U.S. moves almost $1 billion in gold bullion, half going to London to prevent price rise on gold.

1968

Feb. 7 — Treasury reports reserves of gold have dropped to the lowest level since 1937.

Feb. 9 — House Banking and Currency Committee recommends passage of administration bill to remove the 25 percent gold cover from U.S. paper money.

March 17 — Treasury amends gold regulations; Treasury will no longer purchase gold in the private market, nor will it sell gold for industrial, professional or artistic uses. Domestic producers are permitted to sell and export freely to foreign buyers as well as to authorized domestic users. The amendment authorizes domestic users regularly engaged in an industry, profession or art in which gold is required may continue to import gold or to purchase gold from domestic producers within the limits of their licenses or authorization in the gold regulations.

March 17 — Central Banks announce the formation of a two-tier price system for gold. Under the new plan, the price of gold would remain at $35 an ounce in transactions between cooperating governments, while it will be permitted to seek its own price in the private market.

March 20 — With President Johnson's signature on the bill removing gold backing from U.S. paper money, the Treasury transfers $750 million to the Exchange Stabilization Fund. Gold prices fall on European markets.

April 7 — Gold remains stable at about $37-$38 an ounce in London.

April 16 — Treasury issues new gold regulations, noting the ODGSO will accept applications for licenses submitted by persons wishing to buy and sell gold for authorized industrial, professional and artistic uses; that persons, including banks, may, without a license, buy gold for the account of persons licensed and offer storage and safekeeping services for licensed persons; and

that persons holding licenses may continue to acquire newly mined gold or to import gold for authorized uses. All transactions in gold with foreign monetary authorities are prohibited.

April 19 — ODGSO grants temporary permission to import a 1967 Canadian $20 gold coin so it can be displayed at the Northwest Central States Numismatic Association show.

May 2 — Gold reaches a record high of $39.35 an ounce in London.

May 17 — Gold tops $40 an ounce in London; pound falls to its lowest point since 1967, $2.3853.

May 30 — Treasury reports gold stockpile lowest since 1936, at $10.547 billion.

July 9 — Attempts by the French government to bolster the franc and rumors that South Africa would be selling some of its newly mined gold on the free market brings gold prices below $40 in London.

July — ODGSO denies a license for the importation of gold coins of South Africa dated 1968.

October — U.S. and other leading industrial nations in the International Monetary Fund reach an accord providing a mechanism for limited sales of newly minted gold to monetary authorities, but only when the free market price is at or below the official price of $35 an ounce.

1969

Feb. 24 — Sensitive world gold market reacts to President Nixon's visit to Europe and drives the price of gold up to $46.33 in Paris.

March 5 — Devaluation-jittery Frenchmen drive gold up to $47 an ounce in Paris.

April 25 — ODGSO allows import of gold coins made before 1934 without a license.

June 5 — ODGSO revises medal regulations; permits licenses to be issued for the acquisition, holding, transportation and exportation of gold-plated coins or gold medals which are either antique or are for public display by an institution serving the public.

July 30 — Swiss bankers confirm that South Africa is unloading sizable quantities of gold on the bullion market in Zurich.

Nov. 6 — Free market gold drops to $39 an ounce in London.

Nov. 24 — Gold drops to $37.90; attributed to general world monetary stability partly caused by the revaluation of the German mark.

Nov. 28 — Treasury rules after December 31 it will no longer be possible to deposit gold for exchange into gold bars at U.S. Mints and Assay Offices.

Dec. 2 — Gold drops five cents below the International Monetary Fund ceiling of $35.35.

1970

January 8 — Gold reaches a 12-year low of $34.95 in London.

April 8 — ODGSO grants permission for the import of one complete six-coin set of Yemen 1969 gold coins, to be donated to and become part of the permanent collection of the Smithsonian Institution.

December — Gold price up to $41.90 in New York.

1971

April 1 — United Kingdom lifts all gold coin and medal restrictions; gold coin can again be freely bought, sold and held.

April 19 — Treasury amends gold regulations, authorizing the Director of ODGSO to license foreign subsidiaries of U.S. corporations to manufacture gold medals for sale to persons not subject to the jurisdiction of the U.S. Also removes restrictions on the gold plating of any coins and the acquisition, holding, transportation, importation, or exportation of any gold-plated coins.

July 12 — Thomas Wolfe, director of the ODGSO, determines Mexican gold coins struck between 1934 and 1959 are eligible for import into the U.S., with license.

July 22 — Gold regulations amended, prohibiting the trading of gold in any form on commodity exchanges, and the acquisition of American or foreign gold coins of any description for speculative purposes. Reaffirms existing regulations.

Aug. 15 — President Nixon frees the dollar for devaluation against other currencies by cutting its tie with gold and halts the conversion of foreign-held dollars into gold.

Oct. 21 — Treasury Department places a ban on importation of all gold coins of Mexico dated since 1933. Designed to prevent the importation of restrikes.

Dec. 18 — President Nixon announces an 8.57 percent devaluation of the U.S. dollar. The devaluation would be accomplished by a $3 increase in the price of gold, from $35 to $38 an ounce.

1972

March 13 — House postpones for a week the bill to devalue the dollar.

March 21 — Dollar devaluation bill passes the House without proposed amendment to permit U.S. citizens to own gold.

March 22 — Sen. Peter Dominick (R-Colo.) introduces a Senate bill to allow private ownership of gold.

April 3 — President Nixon signs bill to devalue the dollar.

May 8 — Treasury Department formally adopts the $3 increase in the price of monetary gold to $38 an ounce.

May 17 — Gold climbs to $57.75 on the London exchange.

May 29 — Gold closes at $58.55 in London. Common date gold coins advancing on the average of $5 in value in two weeks.

June 6 — Gold goes through $60 mark.

July — Dealer reports common date Double Eagles up from $80 to $95 over a five week period.

Aug. 2 — Gold at $70 an ounce in London.

Aug. 22 — Private ownership of gold endorsed by the Republican National Convention meeting in Miami, Fla.

Oct. 12 — Industrial demand for gold softens, speculative pressure subsides, South Africa announces increased gold reserves; price of gold in London falls.

November — Treasury announces U.S. firms will be permitted to trade in gold futures on the new Winnipeg Commodity Exchange when it opens in mid-November, but "only to an extent consistent with their licenses."

Nov. 15 — Winnipeg Commodity Exchange opens, world's first commodities market in gold futures.

Nov. 20 — Gold levels off at $61 in London.

1973

January — ODGSO clarifies regulations on gold coin jewelry.

Feb. 12 — Treasury Secretary George Shultz announces the dollar is devalued 10 percent;

official price of gold raised to $42.22 an ounce.

Feb. 23 — Gold at $95 an ounce in London, up $10 overnight.

April 1 — Japanese government allows its citizens to buy, sell, hoard and own gold.

April 4 — Senate OKs legislation ending ban on private ownership of gold, an amendment to President Nixon's 10 percent devaluation of the dollar (Par Value Modification Act).

May 14 — Gold breaks through $100 barrier, closing at $102.50 an ounce in London.

May 29 — Gold-holding amendment to Par Value Modification Act fails in the House.

June 1 — Gold at $119 an ounce in London.

July 12 — Senate approves free ownership of gold, an amendment to the Bicentennial coinage bill.

Aug. 14 — Gold drops to $95.50 in London.

Nov. 10 — Central Banks end two-tier gold system following a Berne, Switzerland, meeting. Price of gold drops to $90.

Nov. 28 — Gold rallies, up to $97.25 in London.

Dec. 17 — ODGSO rules any gold coin legally issued, dated between 1934 and 1959, may now enter the United States without the formality of applying for a license. Gold coins issued after 1959 assumed not to be rare.

1974

January 3 — Gold jumps, at $121.25 an ounce in London.

January 8 — Continues rise, at $126.50.

January 18 — More than 750 attend a two-day symposium in New Orleans sponsored by the National Committee to Legalize Gold.

January 21 — Gold reaches $161.31 in the Paris Bourse. Double eagles priced at $238.

January 30 — Gold drops to $135 in London.

Feb. 5 — G. Drake Jacobs of Aspen, Colo., files suit challenging the constitutionality of the U.S. Gold Regulations and the Trading with the Enemy Act under which the regulations were promulgated.

Feb. 10 — Gold closes at $146 an ounce in London.

Feb. 21 — Gold, silver, platinum and copper break all world records. Gold at $160 in London, a new world record fixing for that market.

Feb. 26 — Gold crests at $188 in Paris.

March 27 — Gold searches for a new floor price, settles at $174.

April 3 — Gold leaps to $197 in Paris, fixed at London at a record $179.50.

May 3 — Gold steady at $169 in London.

May 29 — Senate approves an amendment allowing citizen ownership of gold as of Sept. 1, 1974. Tacked on to a bill authorizing $1.5 billion in funds to the International Development Association.

May 30 — Gold jumps to $161 in London.

June 11 — Treasury Secretary William E. Simon says he believes President Nixon will probably end restrictions on U.S. gold ownership by the end of the year.

June 11 — Finance leaders in the Group of Ten industrial nations meet; decide to use gold stocks as security for international loans by economically distressed countries; agree that the pledge metal could be valued at a price much closer to the free-market quote than to the official level, the price determined as a result of agreement between the borrower and the lender.

June 11 — Committee of Twenty of the International Monetary Fund meets, approves new scheme for valuing the Standard Drawing Rights in terms of a "basket" of currencies, including the U.S. dollar, British pound, French franc, West German mark,

Japanese yen and a sampling of other currencies on international monetary markets.

June 18 — House Banking and Currency Committee votes to amend the International Development Association bill with a measure to permit U.S. citizens to own gold after Dec. 31, 1974.

July 2 — House passes International Development Association bill, with gold ownership amendment.

July 4 — Gold prices slump to $129 an ounce in London.

July 31 — House passes IDA bill with gold ownership amendment; goes to President Nixon for his signature.

Aug. 1 — Gold price at $159.40 in London.

Aug. 14 — President Ford signs legislation lifting 40-year ban on U.S. citizens' holding of gold. The law will take effect at the end of December, unless the President decides to speed up the process by declaring an earlier date.

Aug. 20 — ODGSO director Thomas Wolfe says gold coins may be ordered by American citizens if coin firms are willing to place names on mailing lists in anticipation of coming legalization of holding gold by U.S. citizens.

Aug. 27 — Treasury Department invites congressmen to Fort Knox Sept. 23.

Sept. 11 — Rep. Philip M. Crane (R-Ill.) introduces a bill prohibiting authorization by the Secretary of the Treasury or the president to sell gold from the American stockpile.

Sept. 23 — A seven-man congressional inspection team and nearly 100 reporters inspect the Fort Knox Bullion Depository.

October 10 — Several major U.S. brokerage houses announce plans to enter gold trading market at the end of 1974.

October 17 — ODGSO denies rumor that the Treasury is considering a Bicentennial gold coin, claiming such a coin would be illegal under current laws.

October 24 — Gold prices rise past $160 per ounce level, amid rumors of Middle Eastern dollar manipulations.

October 24 — California legislature prepares bill regulating gold dealings in post-ban days. Several coin dealers object to restrictions.

November 8 — Gold price hits $183 per ounce in London, leading to speculation of $200 gold by the end of the year.

November 8 — Federal Trade Commission orders jewelry replicas of pioneer gold coins marked with COPY in incuse lettering.

November 8 — New York Stock Exchange contemplates establishment of a gold trading center after the end of the gold ban.

November 11 — Gold climbs to $188.25 per ounce. Treasury Secretary denies there will be a delay in the legalization of gold.

November 20 — Last minute opposition to the freeing of gold sees the introduction into Congress of bills delaying gold ban lifting.

November 20 — Great Britain resumes striking of sovereigns for release through Bank of England.

Dec. 3 — U.S. Treasury announces plans for sale of 2 million ounces of gold bullion on Jan. 6, 1975. Sale intended to ease the balance of payments deficit which would result from U.S. citizens buying gold from overseas.

Dec. 5 — Federal Reserve Board Chairman Arthur Burns urges delay in lifting of gold ban, fearing that Americans will withdraw savings to buy gold.

Dec. 19 — Proposal for Canadian gold Olympic coin receives unexpected endorsement from postmaster-general, minister responsible for Olympic coin program.

Dec. 27 — Gold reaches $195.25 per ounce in London, expected to reach $200 by the end of the year.

Dec. 27 — France to revalue its gold reserves to near-market level shortly after the first of the year.

Dec. 27 — Philippines reported to be considering a legal tender gold coin for 1975.

Dec. 31 — Striking of Panamanian 100-balboa gold coin at Franklin Mint marks end of U.S. gold ban.

Dec. 31 — President Ford inaugural medal struck in gold for public sale, first such medal since 1933.

Dec. 31 — Gold prices drop sharply in first day of legalized gold in America.

1975

Jan. 2 — Gold drops to $175.25 per ounce from Dec. 31 close of $186.75, confusing metal market experts. Profit-taking blamed.

Jan. 6 — U.S. Treasury opens bids on 2 million ounces of gold in 400-ounce bars. Demand so small that only 753,600 ounces sold, at an average price of $165.67 per ounce. Lowest bid accepted is $153 per ounce. Treasury Secretary delighted at the "failure" of the sale.

Jan. 8 — London gold market jumps from $169.50 to $180 per ounce, despite the lack of interest shown in the U.S. Treasury gold sale. Gold experts unable to explain trend.

Jan. 15 — Gold prices settle down near $175 per ounce level, stay there for several weeks.

Jan. 19 — U.S. hobby leaders meet at American Numismatic Association round table; Mint Director says that the rumors of the death of the Bicentennial gold coin are greatly exaggerated.

January — Gold imports for the month of January more than double those for December. Most of increase thought to be for industrial purposes, rather than speculative.

Jan. 31 — Gold closes at $176.05 per ounce.

Feb. 10 — GAO audit verifies U.S. gold supplies. U.S. Mint controls called "adequate."

Feb. 19 — Gold prices spurt upwards to $184.50 per ounce, highest price since Jan. 2. Rumors of changes in European central bank operations blamed.

Feb. 28 — Gold closes at $182 per ounce.

March — Twelve rare Adelaide Assay Office gold pounds found to be missing from the Library of New South Wales, Sydney, Australia. The genuine coins had been replaced by worthless modern replicas.

March 31 — Gold closes at $176 per ounce.

April 15 — United Kingdom bans sale of newly minted sovereigns to U.K. residents, making them available only to overseas buyers.

April 15 — U.S. Treasury announces updated gold regulations in wake of legalization.

April 15 — Gold drops to $164 per ounce, several dollars below the official figure used to value French gold reserves. Speculators disappointed when France does not step in to buy gold at the unofficial "floor" price.

April 30 — Gold closes at $167 per ounce.

May — Several bills introduced into U.S. House and Senate calling for a Bicentennial gold coin. Legislation receives ANA support.

May 30 — U.S. Treasury announces upcoming sale of an additional half million ounces of gold on June 30.

May 30 — Gold closes at $167.20 per ounce.

May — Following the fall of South Vietnam and Cambodia, tons of gold come to light as refugees leave Southeast Asia.

June 2 — The Treasury Department announces it will sell about a half million of its 276 million ounces of gold on hand, in bars of 250 ounces each. Gold prices on world markets fall.

June 30 — The General Services Administration opens bids for the Treasury gold auction; in contrast with the Jan. 6 sale, Treasury calls interest in the June sale "substantial," with 41 sucessful bidders for 499,500 ounces of gold at $165.05 per ounce. Largest successful bidder is Swiss Bank Corporation of Zurich (140,000 ounces).

Aug. 11 — Gold lists two-month low in London, $161.90 per ounce.

Aug. 27 — Office of Domestic Gold and Silver Operations abolished; functions remaining after the lift of the gold ban are transferred to the Treasury's Assistant Secretary for International Affairs. J. H. Nisenson named Deputy Director of Gold Market Activities.

Aug. 29 — The International Monetary Fund announces it will sell about $1.1 billion of its gold for the benefit of poor nations, permitting central banks to buy 25 million ounces at market-related prices. Markets begin decline.

Sept. 19 — Gold plunges to year's low of $135.00.

Nov. 28 — Charles Heim, publisher of Heim's Investment Letter, says outlook for gold is "negative." Price stands at $138.15 in London.

Dec. 19 — The IMF Group of Ten meets in Paris, discusses possibility of reducing amount of gold to be auctioned from 25 million ounces to 17.5 million.

Dec. 31 — Thomas Wolfe, former Director of the Office of Domestic Gold and Silver Operations, begins a government-sponsored study of world gold and silver markets.

1976

Jan. 8 — Franklin Mint strikes first gold coin of the Netherlands Antilles.

Jan. 30 — Gold continues to slide, closing month of January at $128.40 per ounce in New York.

Feb. 27 — Gold steady for February, closing at monthly average of $130.81 per ounce in New York.

March 31 — Stack's sells five gold coins from the Garrett collection for $408,000; total sale brings more than $2.3 million.

April 21 — Jesse Owens receives first $100 gold Canadian Olympic gold coin presented to an American.

April 28 — International Monetary Fund anticipates beginning its gold sales in May, planning to auction off 25 million ounces over the next four years.

May 19 — Australians gain the right to own, buy and sell gold.

June 2 — IMF auctions 780,000 ounces of gold at a common price of $126 per ounce. The "Dutch auction" system adopted, permitting all successful bidders to receive gold at the same price. Next auction set for July 14.

July 7 — Internal Revenue Service rules that trades of investment coins qualify as "like kind" exchanges and thus are not taxable transactions. The ruling involved a trade of five lots of Mexican 50-peso gold coins for six and a half lots of Austrian 100-corona coins. Since both lots were restrikes, their value depended on their gold content; thus, though the pieces differed in size and gold content, their nature was the same.

July 20 — Gold plunges to 31-month low on London gold exchange, with a closing fix of $107.75, following second IMF auction.

Sept. 15 — IMF sells 780,000 ounces of gold at $109.40 per ounce; market responds by moving up $2.75 to $114 per ounce.

Sept. 29 — American Stock Exchange proposes to set up affiliate to trade in gold bullion options.

Oct. 27 — Thomas Wolfe, former ODGSO chief, believes gold price has bottomed out and should move up in years ahead, based on increased industrial demand and other factors.

Nov. 15 — Gold climbs to $139.20 on London exchange, in wake of Carter election victory; boom replaces gloom among speculators.

Oct. 1 — President Ford signs Gold Labeling Act into law. The bill reduces tolerances permitted in gold products.

1977

Feb. 9 — American Stock Exchange continues to promote its gold and silver commodity options program while awaiting Commodity Futures Trading Commission approval. Also plans a spot market in gold and silver.

March 15 — London gold market appears to level at $140 to $150 per ounce during first weeks of March.

March 30 — Gold reaches high of $153.55 per troy ounce; slips to $149.95 five days later.

April 6 — Bidders pay an average of $149.18 per troy ounce in IMF gold sale. Rep. Henry S. Reuss, D-Wis., urges Treasury to release U.S. gold for auction to "cool" price.

April 13 — South Africa revalues gold from "official" $42.40-per-ounce price to market-related price. The move benefits the nation's gold mines by eliminating the time they must wait between receiving the "official" price and getting the difference between it and the actual selling price from the government.

April 23 — Historic Reed Mine in Cabarrus County, N.C., the first gold mine in the U.S., is opened to the public. Restoration includes 300 feet of original shafts.

May 11 — Gold futures trading on New York's COMEX and Chicago's IMM triple in volume from the previous year, with 171,849 contracts traded in March.

June 1 — Canada announces plans to strike 300,000 $100 22-karat gold coins for the Silver Jubilee of Queen Elizabeth II. IMF sells 525,000 ounces of gold at $143.32.

June 15 — International Precious Metals Institute holds its first international conference at New York's World Trade Center.

June 29 — North Carolina's gold rush days are recalled in three dioramas depicting the minting of gold coins at the Charlotte Mint Museum.

Oct. 10 — London price of gold reaches two-year high of $157.15 per troy ounce.

Oct. 30 — President Carter signs "gold clause" bill, permitting U.S. citizens to enter into contracts specifying payment in gold, or in dollars based on the value of gold.

1978

Jan. 4 — Gold opens at 2/4-year high of $172.50 at the morning fix in the London gold market.

March 28 — Weak dollar combined with energy crunch drive London gold price upward to $183.20 per troy ounce.

April 20 — Treasury announces plans to sell 1.8 million troy ounces of stockpiled gold to prop up the U.S. dollar; gold responds with a price drop of more than $10.

April 20 — Sen. Jesse Helms, R-N.C., and Barry Goldwater, R-Ariz., co-sponsor Gold Medallion Act of 1978 as an alternative to stockpile auctions.

Aug. 1 — London's major gold merchants set the morning fix at $207.50 per troy ounce.

Oct. 4 — U.S. gold coin imports averaged 236,000 ounces during the first seven months of 1978, 76 percent ahead of the previous year's imports of these items.

Oct. 3 — Gold breaks upward to $223.50 in London, as U.S. trade deficits continue to take their toll on the dollar.

1979

July 18 — London gold prices shatter $300 barrier as price is fixed at $303.85.

Sept. 29 — Gold sells for $400.20 in Hong Kong as world paper currencies register distress.

Sept. 29 — Appropriations legislation for funding American Arts Gold Medallion program is signed by President Carter.

Dec. 12 — Price of gold continues climb to $462.50 per troy ounce.

1980

Jan. 3 — Gold price continues upward to $634 per troy ounce.

Jan. 21 — All-time record price of $850 reached in gold trading; Comex silver trades for $50.35 per troy ounce.

April 15 — Gold price slips below $500, to $495.50 per ounce.

June 16 and July 1 are the opening dates for ordering half-ounce American Arts Gold Medallions honoring Marian Anderson and the 1-ounce pieces commemorating artist Grant Wood.

July 7 — Price of gold drops to $397.75, lowest price since Nov. 27, 1978. Prime interest rate climbs to 20.5 percent.

1981

Feb. 11 — Gold price continues slippage to $490 per troy ounce.

June 24 — London price of gold drops off plateau, to $460 level.

July 8 — Gold price falls through $400 as it is fixed·in London at $397.75, the lowest price since Nov. 27, 1979; prime interest rate climbs to 20.5 percent.

Sept. 16 — The U.S. Gold Commission meets to consider returning to the gold standard, and other questions relating to the yellow metal. Rep. Ron Paul, R-Texas, and Lewis Lehrman of New York are the only members of the 16-person commission known to favor this move.

1982

Feb. 17 — Study by the Aden sisters predicts return to $850 gold by 1984; $3,600-to-$4,500 gold by 1986.

March 12 — Gold price falls to $322 under pressure of high interest rates.

March 24 — Reduction in prime rate bounces the gold price upward to $411.50 for the first time since Jan. 8.

1983

Jan. 18 — Gold tops $500 for the first time in 22 months, as it trades at $502.50 on the New York Commodity Exchange.

Feb. 22 — Gold price tumbles from $503.50 to $485.50

in a single day's trading on the Comex.

Feb. 29 — J. Aron & Co. wins marketing contract for American Arts Gold Medallions; accents bullion nature of pieces by renaming them "U.S. Gold."

April 2 — Designs approved for 1983 U.S. Gold, commemorating poet Robert Frost and artist Alexander Calder.

May 25 — Rep. Ron Paul introduces legislation which proposes that the International Monetary Fund sell gold at the spot price to the United States, rather than increasing the U.S. contribution to the fund.

May 31 — The price of gold drops $23.90, to $412 per troy ounce on the Comex; price future is "confused" as a bill to ban Krugerrand sales is introduced in Congress.

Aug. 17 - J. Aron & Co. vice president Arnold Reishman reports satisfaction with share U.S. Gold has carved in slow gold bullion market.

Sept. 13 — The United States Mint strikes the first Olympic gold eagle at West Point, N.Y. This is the first gold coin struck by the U.S. Mint in 50 years, and is the first to bear the "W" Mint mark.

1984

Jan. 9 — Price of gold drops to $365.90 on the Comex in New York as the U.S. dollar gains strength against world currencies.

June 20 — The U.S. Treasury terminates its U.S. Gold distribution contract with J. Aron & Co. The Treasury absorbs $2 million advertising costs, while J. Aron will reimburse $1.3 million for material on hand.

July 25 — Gold plunges to an almost-two-year low of $333.50 on the Comex; experts anticipate lower price levels.

Oct. 17 — A U.S. Senate and House committee drops a bill which would prohibit the importation of Krugerrands and Soviet Union gold coins.

Oct. 17 — A bill introduced in the final days of the 98th Congress to continue the American Arts Gold Medallion program is modified to make the issue legal tender $20 one-ounce gold coins showing the Statue of Liberty on one side and a family of eagles on the other.

Dec. 12 — U.S. Mint officials, after five weeks of telemarketing, report a "planned, smooth rise in sales of American Arts gold medallions.

1985

Jan. 16 — Chairman Frank Annunzio of the House Consumer Affairs and Coinage subcommittee introduces legislation authorizing the sale of gold and silver coins to commemorate the Centennial of the Statue of Liberty.

Feb. 27 — Jammed telephone lines for ordering American Arts Gold Medallions (U.S. Gold) result in an extension of the ordering date beyond Jan. 31.

June 19 — House passes legislation that would impose immediate sanctions against South Africa, including the importation of Krugerrands.

July 3 — Senate passes Statue of Liberty commemorative coin bill with an amendment calling for a 1-ounce silver bullion coin to follow the Statue program.

July 17 — Bullion dealers report the Canadian Maple Leaf is overtaking the Krugerrand in the bullion market.

July 24 -- The Senate passes its version of the anti-apartheid act containing a U.S. bullion coin amendment.

Aug. 14 — South Africa halts release of its worldwide

sales figures for Krugerrands.

Sept. 25 — President Reagan issues executive order for economic sanctions against the government of South Africa and requests the Treasury Department to report on the feasibility of minting U.S. gold bullion coins.

Oct. 11 — President Reagan signs executive order banning importation of the Krugerrand.

Dec. 4 — Passage by the House of gold bullion coinage legislation is blocked at the Treasury Department's request, to provide an opportunity to amend the bill to conform with Treasury recommendations

Dec. 18 — House passes gold bullion coin legislation already approved by the Senate on Dec. 2.

Dec. 17 — President Reagan signs legislation authorizing the minting of four gold bullion coins — one-ounce $50, half-ounce $25, quarter-ounce $10 and tenth-ounce $5 face values — to be struck from newly mined domestic gold.

1986

March 12 — Mint Director Donna Pope predicts sales of 2.2 million ounces of gold bullion coins and 4 million ounces of silver bullion coins in first year at House Appropriations subcommittee hearing.

June 11 — U.S. Mint Director Donna Pope reveals all four gold bullion coins will carry a revised Augustus Saint-Gaudens double eagle design, with Texas sculptor Miley Biesek's "Family of Eagles" design for the reverse.

July 23 — The Royal Canadian Mint reports 8 million ounces of Maple Leaf gold bullion coins have been sold since their introduction in 1979, through the end of 1985 — 1985 sales increased 87.4 percent over 1984.

Aug. 13 — U.S. Mint defines criteria for gold bullion coin wholesalers, who must have a net worth in excess of $50 million and liquid assets of $10 million. Minimum purchases of 5,000 ounces of gold, 50 million ounces of silver will be required.

Sept. 8 — Though the Mint schedules its ceremonial striking of the new bullion coins for Sept. 8, sales are being delayed until Oct. 20 to permit an inventory buildup.

Sept. 9 — The ban against importation of the South African Krugerrand, due to expire, is extended by President Reagan.

October — Twenty-five U.S. and foreign firms are selected by the Treasury Department to make the market for the American Eagle gold bullion coins.

Nov. 5 — American Eagle gold bullion coin orders empty Mint vaults, with 558,000 ounces moving out in two days.

November — Three-week sales total for American Eagle gold coins climbs to 820,500 ounces, or 1,253,000 coins.

Nov. 26 — "Eaglemania" continues: Retail premiums range from 6.7 to 16.9 percent for one-ounce coins; 49.2 to 81.8 percent for half-ounce coins; 57.6 to 82.5 percent for the quarter ounce; and 69.9 to 84.7 percent for the tenth-ounce.

Dec. 3 — Sales of American Eagle gold coin year-end production goals set at 1.4 million 1-ounce, 50,000 half-ounce, 600,000 quarter-ounce and 650,000 tenth-ounce pieces.

November — U.S. Mint reports that for the first time in seven weeks, demand for 1-ounce gold bullion coins fell below supply on Dec. 1. Total sales of all four coins climbs to 1,278,750 ounces or 1,932,000 coins.

Dec. 24 — 1986 Proof American Eagle gold coin sales exceed $187 million; Proofs to be offered in some

denominations in 1987.

1987

Jan. 7 — Supply of all four denominations of American Eagle gold coins exceeded demand on Dec. 23 for the second week in a row. Total produced amounts to 1,607,250 ounces, or 2,675,000 coins.

Jan. 14 — Mint reaches gold bullion production goals; sells 1,312,500 1-ounce coins, 486,500 half-ounce coins, 587,000 quarter-ounce coins and 825,000 tenth-ounce coins, for a total of 1,787,750 ounces.

Jan. 14 — The governor of South Dakota unveils the state's new gold South Dakota Centennial Medallion.

Jan. 21 — Coinage subcommittee hears Jan.5 that eight U.S. distributors bought 34 percent of gold bullion coins; the balance were sold to 17 foreign dealers.

Feb. 6 — The Nevada State Ways and Means Committee introduces a bill proposing a $16.50 fee on each ounce of gold produced by Nevada mines.

Feb. — Belgium announces it will mint and sell gold and silver coins denominated in European Currency Units to commemorate the 30th anniversary of the European Community's founding treaty.

March — The United Kingdom announces intentions of entering the gold bullion coin market by the fall of 1987.

March 25 — Great Britain announces it will enter the gold bullion coin market in 1987, with a gold "Britannia" to be issued in 1-ounce and three fractional-ounce sizes, joining similar programs operated by South Africa, Canada, the United States, Australia, the Isle of Man and China.

April 20 — Worldwide sales of the Australian Nugget gold bullion coins begins.

April — Korea begins minting gold and silver coins to commemorate the 1988 Olympics.

April 30 — By a vote of 5-2, Nevada's Senate Taxation Committee kills legislation for a tax on gold mined in Nevada.

May — The New York Commodities Exchange temporarily shortens trading hours to catch up on a backlog of orders for silver and gold futures.

June 16 — Chicago Mercantile Exchange resumes trading gold futures after a 2-year hiatus.

July 1 — U.S. Mint begins production of gold and silver Bicentennial of the Constitution commemorative coins.

August 9 — More than 200,000 mine workers in South Africa strike for higher wages and improved benefits; during the 3-week strike, some 320,000 ounces of gold production is lost, and more than 40,000 miners are fired.

Oct. 13 — Britain unveils the new Britannia gold bullion coin.

Oct. 19 — Dramatic crash of world stock markets sends many investors scurrying for cover in precious metals.

Dec. 14 — Daily prioce of gold briefly exceeds $500 per ounce for the first time since February 1983.

1988

March — South Dakota exempts the state's gold and silver Bison bullion pieces from state sales taxes.

April — The Chicago Board of Trade receives Commodity Futures Trading Commission approval to begin trading 100-ounce gold futures.

July 1 — Taiwan Parliament approves a proposal to eliminate the 5 percent sales tax on gold trading.

Oct. 19 — Tokyo Commodity Exchange for Industry begins spot gold trading.

1989

March — The official China Daily newspaper reports government intentions of raising the state purchasing price of gold by almost 50 percent in an attempt to curb widespread smuggling.

April 1 — Japan's 3 percent consumption tax takes effect, lowering tax on precious metal coins from 15 percent, but taking gold bullion, which was previously untaxed.

April — Turkey opens official gold market to halt gold smuggling and raise trading standards.

June 9 — Governor of Texas signs bill removing 4.12 percent sales tax on gold bullion, bars, ingots and coins in transactions greater than $1,000.

June 14 — U.S. Mint begins production of gold and silver coins commemorating the Bicentennial of the U.S. Congress.

September — Newmont Gold Co. announces the production of its 1 millionth ounce of gold in 1989, reportedly the first time a gold company has produced 1 million troy ounces of gold within a single year in North America.

Sept. 1 — A New York law exempting the transactions exceeding $1,000 of precious metal bars and bullion coins from a 4 percent state sales tax becomes effective; coins produced by South Africa and coins and bars not produced for investment purposes are not eligible for the exemption.

September — Canada announces plans for series of gold, platinum and silver coins to commemorate the 10th anniversary of the Maple Leaf; Soviet Union announces platinum, palladium, gold and silver commemorative coins depicting events in Russian history; Pobjoy Mint in the U.K. issues gold and silver cat coins.

Nov. 6 — Pakistan lifts 30-year ban on private imports of gold to discourage smuggling.

1990

February — Svzal, a Soviet-Alaskan joint venture, is established to develop minreal deposits and market mining technology in the Soviet Union and North America.

Top 10 users of pure gold in coinage 1988
(troy ounces)

Canada	1,231,325	Turkey	246,602
United States	970,732	Great Britain	188,543
South Africa	647,568	Belgium	156,925
Mexico	377,650	Korea	150,200
China	292,130	All other countries	358,648
Australia	283,713	**TOTAL**	**4,904,036**

Top 10 users of pure gold in coinage 1979-1988
(millions of troy ounces)

Country	1979	1980	1981	1982	1983	1984	1985	1986	1987	1988	Total
South Africa	4.7	3.5	3.5	3.3	3.5	2.4	1.1	—	0.1	0.6	22.7
Canada	1.1	1.3	0.9	1.0	0.9	1.2	1.9	1.5	1.5	1.2	12.5
Japan	—	—	—	—	—	—	—	6.4	0.6	—	7.0
Mexico	1.5	0.7	1.6	0.2	—	0.3	0.3	0.6	0.3	0.4	5.9
United States	—	—	—	—	—	0.3	—	1.8	1.7	1.0	4.8
Great Britain	1.8	0.1	1.2	1.0	—	—	—	—	0.3	0.2	4.6
Iran	—	—	—	—	—	—	0.5	0.7	0.1	0.1	1.4
Turkey	—	—	—	—	0.3	—	—	0.3	0.4	0.2	1.2
China	0.2	—	—	—	—	—	0.1	0.3	0.3	0.3	1.2
Australia	—	—	—	—	—	—	—	—	0.5	0.3	0.8
All others	0.6	0.5	0.7	0.4	0.3	0.2	0.3	0.3	1.1	0.6	5.0
TOTAL	9.9	6.1	7.9	5.9	5.0	4.4	4.2	11.9	6.9	4.9	67.1

Source: The Gold Institute

Monthly gold prices
(Dollars per troy ounce)

	Low/Date	Engelhard Industries High/Date	Average	Handy and Harman Average	London final Average
1987					
January	400.48/5	423.83/19	409.81	408.26	408.26
February	391.51/18	408.29/2	402.85	401.32	401.12
March	405.34/3	425.58/30	410.46	408.91	408.91
April	420.07/7	476.44/27	440.35	438.72	438.35
May	452.64/29	476.95/20	461.73	460.12	460.23
June	439.61/22	458.66/11	451.23	449.59	449.59
July	446.13/7	464.17/31	452.45	450.81	450.52
August	454.95/17	475.09/4	462.58	460.88	461.15
September	455.40/1	466.42/4	461.78	460.20	460.35
October	455.77/2	482.47/19	466.80	465.36	465.36
November	458.98/5	493.99/30	467.91	466.47	467.57
December	478.96/17	501.25/14	487.68	486.30	486.24
1988					
January	459.43/29	485.37/8,11	478.04	476.58	476.58
February	427.52/29	457.33/2	443.30	441.90	442.07
March	430.28/2	458.38/31	445.01	443.61	443.61
April	448.41/26	459.43/18	453.26	451.83	451.55
May	444.20/6	459.33/19	452.18	450.84	451.07
June	434.94/29	466.14/3	452.75	451.33	451.33
July	432.58/26	446.21/20	439.03	437.63	437.63
August	427.17/9	435.99/1	432.66	431.31	431.28
September	396.62/26	431.78/1	414.14	412.79	413.46
October	396.77/5	414.35/17	408.12	406.78	406.78
November	412.25/1	425.62/28	421.35	420.07	420.17
December	411.60/29	430.38/5	419.84	418.49	419.05
1989					
January	395.32/30,31	412.95/3	405.35	404.01	404.01
February	381.70/17	395.12/9	389.08	387.78	387.51
March	384.25/29	396.82/20	391.46	390.14	390.15
April	378.84/28	391.56/13	385.70	384.40	384.40
May	361.01/22	379.89/3	372.61	371.32	371.06
June	359.96/13	377.59/29	368.90	367.60	367.60
July	369.58/31	386.81/6	376.29	374.98	375.04
August	361.06/29,31	371.78/4	366.19	364.93	365.14
September	357.00/15	370.28/27	363.16	361.89	361.75
October	362.31/11	376.59/31	368.16	366.84	366.88
November	374.33/1	415.10/27	393.64	392.32	394.26
December	399.93/28	416.86/11,12	410.44	409.15	409.39
1990					
January	396.32/3	422.12/24	411.46	410.11	410.11
February	408.89/27	425.12/7	418.20	416.83	416.81
March	369.28/27	498.58/13	394.38	393.06	393.06

Source: Bureau of Mines

Silver

Chemical symbol: Ag
Atomic number: 47
Atomic weight: 107.88
Density: 10.49 times the weight of an equal volume of water

Silver, the brilliant white metal, is second only to its sister gold in malleability. It is harder than gold, has a high resistance to corrosion, and is an excellent conductor of heat and electricity.

Silver was used for decorative purposes as far back as 4000 B.C., as a standard of value by 3500 B.C., and was widely used in coinage by 450 B.C.

The leading world producer of silver has been Mexico since 1900. Mexico, the United States, Canada and Peru produce more than two-thirds of the world's total of silver. The world's largest silver mine is the Real de Monte y Pachuca, in Hidalgo, Mexico.

In the United States, Idaho is the leading producer of silver; in Canada the topmost producers are Ontario, British Columbia and the Yukon territory.

Silver mining and refining

Most of the silver presently mined occurs in the native condition, that is, as an alloy of silver and some other metals. Most of this native silver is finely dispersed throughout other metals. Traditional mining techniques, then, are used to bring silver out of the ground.

Silver can be extracted from its ores using a variety of methods. The amalgamation process involves treating ores with water and mercury; the cyanidation process uses pulverized ore that is treated with sodium cyanide. Crude silver can be smelted, yielding a gold-silver alloy called dore.

Since gold and silver often occur together, as in forming dore, several methods are employed to separate and purify them. Electrolysis is one (see GOLD), the parting method is another. In the latter, the dore or very high-purity gold and silver bullion is bathed with hot concentrated sulfuric or strong nitric acid and the silver dissolves. Once the gold is removed, the silver is precipitated using ferrous sulfate, copper or iron.

The crime of silver

The following appeared in large part in a Federal Reserve Bank of San Francisco Monthly Review supplement, reprinted in Coin World, in 1969. It has been updated to include significant events of the 1970s and '80s.

By William Burke and Yvonne Levy

Populist orators, finding no rational explanation for the grinding deflation that racked the nation's economy before the turn of the century, argued that hard times were the result of a monstrous conspiracy organized by London bankers and their Wall Street minions. When asked for evidence, these orators automatically cited the "Crime of 1873" — the (temporary) demonetization of silver.

"A crime, because it has brought tears to strong men's eyes and hunger and pinching want to widows and orphans. A crime because it is destroying the honest yeomanry of the land, the bulwark of the nation. A crime because it has brought this once great republic to the verge of ruin, where it is now in imminent danger of tottering to its fall." (Coin's Financial School)

The Populists denounced this "crime" so fervently because they equated the dethronement of silver with a deliberate policy of deflation. In their eyes, the "crime" was compounded in 1900 with the formal adoption of the gold standard, and it was only partly assuaged in the 1930s with the discarding of gold as a domestic means of payment and the adoption of a silver-purchase program.

Yet in the late 1960s when the Treasury ceased redeeming silver certificates in silver and began to mint quarters and dimes out of baser metals, few observers if any suggested that the republic was on the verge of ruin. Aside from a few nostalgic editorials, the news of this final dethronement of monetary silver was confined to the financial pages.

The nation easily survived this latest episode in silver's checkered career, in large part because the turn-of-the-century monetary battles had eventually led to the enactment of the Federal Reserve Act, and thus to the institution of flexible methods of monetary control. But more to the point, this time it was silver's rebirth as an industrial and artistic material that contributed to its problems as a monetary metal.

Silver today

Speculative excesses undoubtedly have helped drive silver prices upward in the last few decades but a more basic reason for this upsurge is the deficit in the major sources of supply — Western mines and Treasury stockpiles — in relation to the significant increase in the worldwide demand for silver. Because of its varied characteristics — silver is foremost in electrical and thermal conductivity, highest in optical reflectivity, and second only to gold in ductility — the white metal has gained new luster among dentists as well as debutantes, and among spacemen as well as shutterbugs.

This latest episode has been closely involved with the metal's dazzling price performance during the decade of the 1960s. The major episodes in silver's earlier monetary history, by way of contrast, were products of prolonged price declines for silver, and for everything else, in the Great Depression of the 1890s and the even greater catastrophe of the 1930s. So, just as the "Crime of '73" epitomized the earlier time of monetary troubles, the virtual repetition of that act may well typify silver's new-found period of prosperity.

Yesterday's silver

Since a major chapter in silver's long emotion-drenched monetary history came to a close in the 1960s, some perspective may be gained from a review of the legislative highlights. The record dates back to 1792 when the new nation set up two units of value: a gold dollar containing 24.75 grains of pure gold and a silver dollar containing 371.25 grains of pure silver.

Silver's monetary value of $1.2929 per ounce, although not defined in such terms in the law, could be derived by dividing the number of grains in an ounce (480) by the number of grains of pure silver in the silver dollar (371.25). Silver's monetary value was still measured in the same way in the 1960s but that apparently was the only sign of stability that could be found in the metal's volatile behavior.

The Founding Fathers — specifically Alexander Hamilton — had opted for a bimetallic standard, with the unit of account and all types of money kept at a constant value in terms of gold and also in terms of silver. Practically, however, an alternating standard developed because of the implacable workings of Gresham's Law, the principle that bad money drives good money out of circulation. Although the relative values of the two metals at the Mint were constant by legal definition, the relative values in commodity markets fluctuated continuously, producing "bargain" prices at the Mint now for one metal and again for the other; the metal that was overvalued at the Mint consistently drove out of monetary use the metal that was undervalued for such purposes.

The original 15-1 Mint ratio of silver to gold (by weight of equivalent value) was below the market ratio existing at that time and the consequent gold outflow tended to make silver the nation's standard money until the 1830s. Gold was then revalued, however, and the resultant 16-1 Mint ratio caused a reversal of the situation and led to a disappearance of silver.

Debts and debtors

Then came the Civil War — and then came the losing 30-year battle on the part of debtor groups to maintain prices at the high wartime levels at which they had contracted their debts. The postwar price decline had developed partly because of the cessation of the war-induced demand for commodities and partly because of the sudden build-up in farm surpluses resulting from the rapid expansion of the trans-Mississippi West — but also because of a shift in monetary policy toward contraction of the paper currency and resumption of specie payment.

The struggle of Populist farmers and other debtors to restore wartime price levels through currency inflation was led initially by the Greenbackers. That doughty group, which demanded the redemption of war bonds in paper and not in gold, suffered a crucial defeat when the administration resumed specie payments in 1879. But even before that event the inflationists had arrived at the view that they could attain their ends by injecting silver into the monetary system at an inflated ratio.

In accordance with Gresham's Law, silver at the 16-1 Mint ratio had been undervalued and had long since disappeared from circulation. In fact, such a long time had elapsed since any silver had been presented to the Mints for coinage that Congress in 1873 stopped the further minting of the standard silver dollar and thereby effectively demonetized silver. Whether deliberately or through oversight, Congress simply failed to include in a long, very detailed and technical revision of the coinage laws any provision for the continuing coinage of the standard (371.25-grain) silver dollar. Thus was the "Crime of '73" perpetrated.

No cries of outrage greeted the event at the time it occurred, since every ounce of silver was then worth $1.30. But within three years the situation altered drastically. The price of silver dropped to $1.16 and below, on the heels of a glut occasioned by the opening of new mines in Nevada and the closing of silver markets in the new gold-standard countries of western and southern Europe.

The Populists cried conspiracy, for if silver could have been coined freely at the old 16-1 ratio the debtors could have paid their debts with the easier-to-earn white metal. In order to repair the ravages of the crime, therefore, these inflationists demanded that Congress restore the free and unlimited coinage of silver at the old 16-1 ratio.

The best they could obtain, however, was the passage of the Bland-Allison Act of 1878, which required the Treasury to buy not less than $2 million of silver every month for coinage or for backing of silver certificates. But the net increase in currency, which amounted to $253 million in the 1879-90 period, failed to match the hopes of the backers of this legislation; the new silver certificates simply took the place of national bank notes which were being retired in connection with the reduction of the national debt.

The price of silver dropped to $0.94 within the following decade, so the inflationists demanded that more be done. This time the best they could accomplish was the passage of the Sherman Silver Purchase Act of 1890, in a trade whereby Westerners voted for a tariff bill which they disliked while Easterners voted for a silver bill which they feared.

The Sherman Act directed the Secretary of the Treasury to buy 4.5 million ounces of silver bullion — almost the entire domestic production — every month. The bullion was to be paid for through the issue of new legal-tender Treasury notes, which were to be redeemable in either gold or silver — a provision which permitted an "endless chain" of gold withdrawals in the panic of 1893.

Despite these efforts, the Sherman Act did not succeed in its purpose. It failed to raise the price of silver, and moreover it failed to increase the amount of money in circulation and to reverse the steady decline in farm prices. (Sen. Sherman's influence was far more lasting in the antitrust field.)

President Cleveland and other gold supporters wanted to abandon silver to its fate and to adhere formally to the gold standard. The silverites, on the other hand, continued to favor the unlimited coinage of silver and the pegging of the silver price at the traditional 16-1 ratio. For a while, Cleveland had his way; faced with the panic of 1893 and with a substantial gold outflow which reduced the gold reserve below the tacitly recognized floor of $100 million, he forced through Congress the repeal of the Silver Purchase Act. Yet this led to his repudiation by his own party and to the mighty Populist upsurge which in 1896 brought William Jennings Bryan to the verge of the presidency.

Gold on the throne

Nonetheless, within four years the money question was no longer at the center of public controversy — in fact, was hardly in the public eye at all. Early in 1900 the victorious "goldbugs" secured the passage of an act providing that the gold dollar of 25.8 grains nine-tenths fine should be the unit of value and that all other forms of currency should be maintained at parity with this dollar. (Parity was to be maintained through a $150-million gold reserve which the Treasury would hold available for the redemption of paper money.) Then, later in 1900, Bryan's second defeat sealed the doom of silver as a dominant political issue.

The issue died out simply because of the long-awaited reversal of the downward trend in prices. Between 1896 (the low point) and 1914, the general price level increased 40 percent. But inflation and farm prosperity were achieved not through the Populists' chosen instrument, silver, but rather through several unexpected developments — developments related to the metal which they detested (gold) and to the center of the gold "conspiracy" which they despised (the city).

New gold discoveries in South Africa and North America, along with the development of new processes for extracting the precious metal from the ore, flooded the world with gold during these critical years. Over two decades, the amount of gold coinage increased by half, and thereby permitted a corresponding expansion of the currency supply. After 1896, therefore, the gold inflation helped bring about the happy situation which the farmers for so long had tried to win with silver. The evidence was apparent on every hand — wheat rising from 72 cents a bushel in 1896 to 98 cents a bushel in 1909, corn rising from 21 cents to 57 cents, and so on throughout list.

But the American city itself, and not simply the gold inflation, saved the American farmer. Throughout that golden age, the foreign market for many of his products sharply declined. Yet his income situation sharply improved, because of the very thing that was cited as evidence of his political submergence — the great increase of the urban population. In 1890, 4.6 million American farms supplied a domestic urban population of 22 million; in 1910, 6.4 million farms supplied 42 million city-dwellers. The larger, more efficient, and more mechanized farms which developed over those two decades produced an increasing part of their total produce for the home market (and less for the foreign market), under far stabler and more advantageous conditions of transportation and finance than had prevailed in the past. And yet this favorable trend — labeled "From Pathos to Parity" by one historian — was achieved without any aid from the Populists' favorite weapon, silver inflation.

Silver in the '30s

The second major development in silver's dramatic history occurred in another major period of deflation — the 1930s. Once again a movement arose to halt a prolonged deflationary spiral by restoring currency values to the level at which wartime and postwar debts had been contracted. And once again a remedy was proposed, in the Thomas Amendment to the Agricultural Adjustment Act of 1933, that envisioned both the printing of more paper money and unlimited coinage of silver. The Amendment, in addition, authorized increased open-market purchases of government securities and a reduction in the gold content of the dollar.

The last-named of these alternatives received the most emphasis in the early New Deal days. Under the authority of the Gold Reserve Act of 1934, the value of the dollar was fixed at 59.08 percent of its formerly established (1900) value in terms of gold.

But much to the surprise of the theorists who influenced the administration's decision — theorists who posited a close relationship between the price level of commodities and the gold content of the monetary medium — the price level did not automatically respond. True enough, the wholesale price index increased somewhat in line with the general expansion of demand following the Depression low, but the increase was only about half of what the inflationists expected in view of the 41 percent reduction in the gold content of the dollar. Silver inflation, therefore, was brought forward as a supplement to the incomplete gold inflation — and as an answer to the perennial legislative demand to "do something for silver."

Since 1873, the downward trend in the price of silver had been interrupted only twice, during the silver-purchase period around 1890 and again during World War I. After the turn of the century, in fact, the market price rarely exceeded one-half the nominal Mint value.

Silver had remained in a monetary limbo with respect to new acquisitions; some was used for subsidiary coins, some circulated in the West in the form of standard silver dollars, and a roughly fixed stock of silver certificates remained as a relic of the 1890s. Thus, by the 1930s, only about 650 million ounces were in use as coin or as currency backing at the Treasury.

Government purchase

At the end of 1933, with the market price of silver standing at about 44 cents an ounce — 75 percent above the Depression low — unlimited purchase of newly minted silver was initiated at $0.6464 an ounce under the authority granted by the Thomas Amendment. But inflationist pressure then brought about even further action, in the form of the Silver Purchase Act of 1934. Under its terms, the Secretary of the Treasury was directed to purchase silver at home and abroad until the market price reached the traditional Mint price of $1.2929 an ounce, or until the monetary value of the Treasury's silver stock reached one-third of the monetary value of its gold stock. The support price at which purchases were made was changed on several different occasions during the ensuing dozen years; originally $0.6464, it was eventually set at $0.9050 in 1946.

Under the authority of the silver-purchase legislation of the 1930s and subsequent Presidential proclamations the Treasury acquired some 3,200 million ounces of silver — about half of it in the four-year period 1934-37, and the remaining half of it in the subsequent quarter-century. A minor part (about 110 million ounces) consisted of silver that was "nationalized" in mid-1934, when the administration required nonmonetary silver to be turned in at $0.5001 per fine ounce, so as to capture the profits expected to be realized from the increased government purchase price. About 2,210 million ounces consisted of metal purchased abroad at prevailing market prices, and the remaining 830 million ounces consisted of newly minted domestic silver.

Until 1955, the Treasury support price for newly mined domestic silver was higher than the market price, so the U.S. government purchased domestic metal at the higher price while U.S. silver-using industries purchased low-priced foreign metal. But from 1955 to late 1961, the market price approximated the support price, and silver users then began to purchase some supplies from the Treasury as well as from foreign and domestic mines.

In little more than a quarter-century, the Treasury purchased $2 billion in silver and sextupled the physical quantity used as currency or held in stockpiles. Nevertheless, the silver program during that period failed to achieve either of the objectives specified in the 1934 Silver Purchase Act: a market price equal to the monetary value of $1.2929, or a one-to-three ratio of the monetary stocks of silver and gold.

Prior to the 1960s and to the upsurge of world demand, market pressures failed to push prices above the $0.5001 floor. Meanwhile, the ratio of monetary silver to monetary gold stocks — both at their nominal monetary values — failed to reach the one-to-three target figure. (The ratio ranged around one-to-five in the pre-war period, then rose to one-to-seven as a consequence of the early postwar gold inflow, and finally dropped to one-to-four during the following decade as gold began to flow out instead of in.) Then, when silver's supporters achieved the price upsurge they wanted, it turned out to be a mixed blessing indeed.

On its way up

Eventually, the market accomplished what a century's legislation could not do for the cause of silver price support. In the late 1950s, world consumption of silver increased about 4 percent annually, while world production rose only about 1.5 percent annually. Sales from Treasury stockpiles filled the gap — and held the price line — for almost a decade, but the depletion of stocks finally brought the process to a halt.

The first scene in a long drawn-out final act occurred in late 1961. By that time, the worldwide industrial and coinage demand for silver approximated 300 million ounces annually, about half of which was American demand, whereas worldwide production approximated 235 million ounces annually, about one-sixth of which was from American mines. The gap had to be filled by sales from the Treasury's "free silver" stocks — that is, stocks that were not earmarked for currency backing or coinage.

The Treasury's supply of free silver had reached its peak in early 1959 at 222 million ounces. But by the end of 1960, half that supply was gone and by late 1961, only 22 million ounces were left. There remained, however, nearly 1,700 million ounces in a bullion reserve held against the issuance of part of the nation's

paper currency. About one-fourth was held against $5 and $10 silver certificates, and the remainder was used to support $1 and $2 silver certificates. The larger denominations could have been issued in the form of Federal Reserve notes, but then-existing legislation authorized only silver certificates for the smaller denominations.

The legislative stage was thus set for the beginning of the final act. In November 1961, President Kennedy wrote Treasury Secretary Dillon, "I have reached the decision that silver metal should gradually be withdrawn from our monetary reserves" — and with that, he instructed the Secretary to suspend further sales of the Treasury's free silver, to suspend the use of free silver for coinage, and to obtain the silver required for coinage needs through the retirement from circulation of $5 and $10 silver certificates. By this measure, some 400 million ounces of the total reserve of 1,700 million ounces were released for coinage purposes. (Interpreting the President's statement as a Treasury withdrawal from the supply side of the market, the market responded with a 10 percent jump in price the very next day, and with a further 30 percent rise the following year.)

The next scene occurred with the passage of Public Law 88-36 (June 1963). The Act repealed the Silver Purchase Act of 1934 and subsequent silver legislation, repealed the tax on transfers of interest in silver bullion, and confirmed the redeemability of silver certificates for silver dollars or bullion at the monetary value of $1.2929 an ounce. But in particular, it authorized the issuance of Federal Reserve notes in the smaller denominations, thereby providing for the eventual elimination of silver as backing for $1 and $2 bills. The new policy, in effect, "provided for the eventual demonetization of silver except for its use in subsidiary coinage."

In congressional hearings which preceded the passage of this new law, Secretary Dillon argued that the new legislation would not mean the disappearance of the silver dollar, since the Treasury had ample supplies of "cartwheels" and other traditional coins. But the market felt otherwise, and soon thereafter staged the dramatic epilogue to the Act of 1963 — the great silver rush of '64.

Part of the explanation was the inability of the Philadelphia and Denver Mints to keep up with the public's burgeoning demand for coin. The amount of circulating coin, which had increased roughly 50 percent in the first postwar decade, more than doubled in the following decade because of the heavy toll levied by vending machines, sales taxes, school lunches, parking meters and coin telephones — and because of the insatiable demands of the growing band of coin collectors and speculators.

The Mints, intent on supplying the public demand for minor coin, had not minted standard silver dollars during the entire post-war periods; in fact, the last of these "cartwheels" came out in 1935. Yet, for some time, there appeared to be no problem. Out of a total supply of 485 million silver dollars, about one-third were circulating in 1950, and about two-thirds in 1960. But then the outflow increased sharply, and accelerated even more in the months following the enactment of the new silver legislation.

Only 28 million "cartwheels" were left in Treasury hands at the beginning of 1964. Many of them went into circulation by early March, and then, when the House Appropriations Committee rejected a Treasury request for authorization to begin minting these pieces again, the rush was on. In two weeks' time the Treasury shipped out more than 11 million pieces to the tradition-loving Western states — and meanwhile distributed more than three million pieces to a jostling, haggling crowd which besieged the Treasury building in search of choice "Morgan" dollars of turn-of-the-century vintage.

Out of the temple

Only 2.9 million "cartwheels" were left when, in the *Wall Street Journal's*

description, "Secretary Dillon drove the money changers out of his temple." Exercising the option open to him under the terms of the 1963 legislation, the Secretary decreed that silver certificates thenceforth would be redeemable only in silver bullion at the monetary value of $1.2929 per ounce. Holders of silver certificates could continue to exercise their legal right to demand an amount of silver precisely equal to the silver content of a standard silver dollar, but they would be assured of getting only several slivers of metal in an envelope instead of a coin of considerable numismatic value.

Still, most observers continued to feel that silver dollars represented only a special case, and that a silver shortage was practically out of the question in the foreseeable future. In his 1963 congressional testimony, Secretary Dillon argued that, with the passage of the proposed legislation, the government's silver reserves would "assure an adequate supply of silver to meet our coinage requirements for the next 10 to 20 years." But over the next two years alone, consumption of silver came to exceed all earlier expectations, and it became readily apparent that even the Act of 1963 had failed to provide a lasting solution to the Treasury's problems.

Production of silver in this country had fallen short of U.S. consumption consistently throughout the postwar period, but the gap began to widen appreciably after 1958. In fact, domestic production actually declined slightly from 1958 to 1963, while domestic consumption for coinage and industrial use rose sharply, from 124 to 222 million ounces. As a result, the annual deficits increased from a sizeable 100 million ounces or so in the 1950-58 period to an even more substantial 187 million ounces in 1963. But then, in 1964 the deficit jumped to 289 million ounces, as production remained level in the face of a soaring demand of 326 million ounces.

Moreover, the same type of situation existed elsewhere, as total world consumption (outside the Soviet Bloc) grew to more than two and one-half times total new production. With total metal usage at 556 million ounces, the world supply deficit in 1964 amounted to 338 million ounces.

Foreign sources came to fill less and less of the U.S. deficit over the 1958-63 period, because of the expanding needs for the metal abroad. At the same time, returns of lend-lease silver which had been shipped out during World War II dropped steadily, from a peak of 103 million ounces in 1958 to zero in 1963. In making up the growing deficiency, Treasury stocks receded by 523 million ounces in the five-year period, to 1,583 million ounces in 1963.

In 1964, moreover, foreign demand actually comprised a drain on Treasury stocks, and this country became a net exporter of silver for the first time since the lend-lease shipments of World War II. Total exports during the year amounted to 110 million ounces, more than triple the 1963 figure, while imports declined from 64 to 55 million ounces. In meeting both this new export demand and the soaring domestic demand, Treasury stocks of the metal dropped 23 percent in 1964 alone, to 1,214 million ounces.

Hungry industries

An increase in industrial consumption of silver — mainly for use in photographic film, electronic components, and storage batteries — helped to intensify the growing shortage. Industrial consumption in this country, which had dropped from an annual average of 100 million ounces in the early 1950s to 86 million ounces in 1958, rose by more than 5 percent annually over the next five years, and then jumped 11 percent more in 1964, to 123 million ounces.

Overseas, the expansion in industrial consumption had been even more impressive, particularly in West Germany and Japan. Between 1950 and 1958, foreign industrial consumption doubled and by 1964 it increased again by half to 163 million ounces. Thus a shortage existed from industrial demands alone,

since world industrial consumption exceeded total mine production by 71 million ounces in 1964.

The sharp upsurge in silver usage took place even in the face of a 40 percent increase in silver prices between November 1961 and June 1963. The demand for silver evidently was quite inelastic — unresponsive to an increase in price — because no known alternative equaled its high electrical and heat conductivity, resistance to corrosion and sensitivity to light.

Consumption of silver for photographic film, plates and sensitized paper — the largest single market in this country for the metal — increased at an annual rate of about 2 percent between 1959 and 1963, and then jumped 20 percent, to 40.3 million ounces, in 1964 alone. The photographic industry's consumption would have increased even more rapidly had it not learned to economize on its supplies. By extracting silver from photographic solutions used in developing film, for example, it was able to reclaim as much as 10 million ounces in 1964.

Under the stimulus of the sharp run-up in silver prices, the photographic industry also accelerated its research aimed at the development of substitutes. In many of silver's most important applications, however, no other material could be found with silver's unique ability to record an image when exposed to light. (The only major alternative was the use of electrostatic copying methods in office equipment.) Because silver was all but indispensable to the photographic process, its use in this field tended to increase with the continued growth of the industry.

The electrical-equipment and electronics industry represented another rapidly growing outlet. Consumption of silver in these fields rose almost 50 percent between 1959 and 1964, from 20.5 to 30.3 million ounces, and, as a result, the electrical industry surpassed silverware and jewelry to become silver's second market.

Unequalled as an electrical conductor, silver's use as an electrical contact had expanded until it could be found in practically every on-off switch and electrical appliance. Silver-wire contact relays also were at the heart of most computers and almost every piece of telephone and aviation equipment. Besides, suitable substitutes were not available for applications accounting for perhaps three-fourths of the entire market — primarily voltage connections for space vehicle guidance systems, military electronic systems and the like.

Consumption in brazing alloys and solders, another rapidly growing field, expanded from 10.5 million ounces in 1959 to 15.8 ounces in 1964. During World War II the use of silver alloys as industrial joining metal gained impetus in the manufacture of shells, gun parts and ordnance. After the war, silver brazing alloys became important in air-conditioning and refrigeration equipment, electrical appliances, and automobile parts — in fact, in virtually every end-product where joining or bonding was involved. An entirely new application also arose: silver-infiltrated tungsten for rocket fuels, as well as silver brazing alloys capable of withstanding heat and pressures generated at supersonic speeds. For these applications, which require high temperature soldering, substitution of other materials was completely impractical.

Consumption of silver in storage batteries, a relatively new use, almost tripled between 1959 and 1964, reaching nine million ounces. Batteries utilizing silver (in association with zinc or cadmium) can be recharged, and they are very useful for applications requiring high output in relation to weight, for example in spacecraft and portable tools and appliances. Because these batteries rely on the chemical reactivity of silver, the substitution of other materials again was impractical.

For all these reasons, the industrial demand for silver expanded inexorably in the early '60s, even in the face of stable or declining demand for the metal in its more traditional uses. (Silver consumption for silverware and jewelry had actually declined, as a result of the rising price of sterling silver and the increasing acceptance of modern design.) But industry had to meet much of its rapidly increasing needs through the redemption of silver certificates. With each dollar exchangeable for .7734 ounces of silver, the availability of Treasury supplies held the market price at $1.2929, the level first reached in September 1963. But because of this drain and additional withdrawals for speculative holdings and inventories, redemptions totaled 141 million ounces in 1964.

Coinage pull

Nevertheless, by far the largest drain on Treasury stocks resulted from the tremendous expansion in silver usage for coinage. The actual silver crisis might have been delayed for years had not a terrific coin shortage developed. Consumption of silver for U.S. coinage began to rise sharply in 1961, and doubled over the next two years, reaching 112 million ounces in 1963. Even with this, the demand could not be met, and the coin shortage turned critical around mid-1964.

At one time limited to relatively few geographical areas to particular coins, and to particular seasons of the year, the shortage eventually became a general problem affecting the entire economy. Merchants found it difficult, and in some instances impossible, to make change. Banks, unable to satisfy their customers' requests for coin, found it necessary to ration their supplies. In fact, coin rationing was instituted down the line — from the Mints, to the Federal Reserve, to the commercial banks, to the public.

A new type of entrepreneur, "the money merchant," appeared on the scene, acquiring coins by the bagful and selling them to the highest bidder. The American Bankers Association staged a "Calling All Coins" campaign, in an attempt to bring to market the large supply of coins stored in the nation's piggy banks. And one chain of food stores conceived of the idea of issuing scrip, in denominations of 1, 5, and

10 cents, redeemable at the company's stores. (The chain dropped the plan when it found that it might be violating federal law.)

Some observers blamed the shortage on the growing use of some 12 million automatic coin-operated vending and service machines — ranging from parking meters and telephone pay stations to machines that dispense hot and cold drinks, sandwiches, candy, cigarettes, music and laundry and drycleaning services — and upon the growing coin requirements of toll roads, sales taxes and school lunches. Other observers simply traced the shortage to the burgeoning demands of a rapidly growing population and a rapidly expanding economy.

According to Treasury officials, the expansion in coin production should have been more than adequate to compensate for all these developments. From fiscal 1959 through fiscal 1964, the Mint had nearly tripled the production of coins, from 1.6 to 4.3 billion pieces — yet during that same period, population had increased only 8 percent, gross national product 28 percent and vending machine sales by 47 percent. Furthermore, the 48 billion coins available for circulation provided an average of 240 coins for every man, woman and child in the entire country.

The Committee on Government Operations, investigating the coin shortage, drew attention to the problem of availability as opposed to the actual supply of coins. Large amounts had been placed in circulation, but large amounts had been withdrawn, by businessmen anxious to assure themselves of an adequate supply for the needs of trade, by the nation's 8-to-10 million coin collectors — and by speculators, who bought up new coin by the roll, by the bag and even by the ton in the hope of profiting from a possible increase in the price of silver or coin. Incidentally, vending industry spokesmen argued in their own defense that only about $22 million remained in their machines at any one time, even though the machines swallowed some $3,500 million in coins every year.

As commercial banks found themselves with less and less coin, the "flowback" of coin returned to the Federal Reserve Banks had dropped sharply, from 11.4 billion coins in fiscal 1962 to only 6.7 million pieces in fiscal 1964. Deliveries of new coin from the Mint had risen, but the added supply had been more than offset by the drying up of return flows from circulation.

Coin shortage

By mid-1964, the return flow had shrunk to the point where it was less than the amount of new coin received from the Mint, whereas in more normal times the return flow was nine times as great as Mint deliveries. Consequently, the Reserve Banks were unable to deliver coin on request and had to ration the limited supply.

The rise in the price of silver to $1.2929 an ounce — that is, the development of a situation where the silver dollar was worth a dollar of silver — had encouraged the run on the Treasury's depleted stock of silver dollars, as described above. Thus, broad new public interest in coins was stimulated when the Treasury found itself with less than 3 million "cartwheels" and, amidst great publicity, was forced to restrict redemption of silver certificates to bullion.

Whatever the reasons for the coin shortage, Treasury officials decided that it could be overcome only by a rapid and substantial increase in production. By flooding the economy with coins, they hoped to convince those who held them for speculative reasons that the market would soon be saturated.

The Treasury previously had planned to boost production at the existing Mint facilities gradually over time, while waiting for the completion of the new Philadelphia Mint authorized by Congress in 1963. This new Mint was designed to have as much production capacity as the Denver and old Philadelphia Mints combined.

Events, however, forced the adoption of another approach. In mid-1964, the

Treasury placed its two operating Mints on a round-the-clock seven-day-a-week intensified "crash program" in an attempt to double the annual production of coins from 4 to 8 billion in a year's time. It pushed into production all possible equipment and facilities — including the San Francisco Assay Office, which was assigned to produce annealed planchets for 5-cent coins and cents — and also purchased metal strip for coinage from private industry. Moreover, it obtained congressional authorization to continue the 1964 date on new coins indefinitely, so that it could flood the market with 1964 coins and thus destroy the incentive for dealers and hoarders to divert such coins from normal commercial uses.

As 1964 drew to a close, the Treasury was well along in its crash program. During that calendar year the Mint produced 5.5 billion coins, compared with 3.4 billion the year before — and in the second half of the year, it produced as many coins as in all of 1962. But about 203 million ounces of silver were consumed during 1964's rapid upsurge of Mint production. In fact, about 73 million ounces alone went into the production of some 200 million Kennedy half dollars, which collectors, hoarders and souvenir hunters snapped up as soon as they went into circulation.

By early 1965, the Director of the Mint was able to report a definite improvement in the coin situation. Businessmen were able to get through 1964, including a busy Christmas, without an actual crisis, even though consumer spending was up $26 billion (7 percent) for the year. The shortage of cents, which at one point had been critical, was completely relieved, while the shortage of nickels was almost over. Nonetheless, shortages continued in the minor silver coins, and the half dollar was not circulating at all.

At the same time, the problem of silver supplies had grown more acute. By June 1965, consumption for coinage purposes was running at a 300-million-ounce annual rate, and the Treasury's supply was down to 1,000 million ounces.

The Treasury thus faced the prospect of total depletion of its stocks within a relatively short period of time. In that event, the Mints would have had to stop coining dimes, quarters and halves of the kind then in use. The Treasury would no longer be able to offer silver to all comers at $1.2929 an ounce. The price of the metal could rise beyond $1.3824 — the point at which the silver content of these minor coins would be equal to their face value — and coins would begin to disappear from circulation. Obviously, drastic new action was required.

Demonetization of silver

The soaring industrial and coinage demand for silver and the rapid depletion of the government's silver stock forced the Treasury in May 1965, to make a momentous decision: "The world and the U.S. silver supply and production situation and outlook do not warrant continuation of the large-scale use of silver in the U.S. coinage," (*Staff Study of Silver and Coinage*).

Moreover, the Treasury argued for a once-and-for-all change; otherwise, subsidiary silver coinage undoubtedly could suffer from difficult transitional problems and from the fear in future changes in silver content.

On the basis of technical studies, the Treasury recommended copper-nickel clad on a copper core as the best metal for a new and permanent subsidiary coinage. This material had several desirable characteristics — ability to provide uninterrupted service as a medium of exchange; acceptability to the public in terms of weight, color, wearing qualities and operation in vending machines; ease and certainty of production; cost and availability; and compatibility with present coinage.

Copper-nickel was already the most widely used coinage material in the world. It was familiar as the basis for the American 5-cent piece, and it had circulated side by side with silver coinage in high-denomination coins in the United Kingdom. Coins of copper-nickel clad on a copper core could operate readily in vending machines without the difficulty, expense and inconvenience of modifying existing rejectors. Furthermore, the Mint had made sizeable production runs using the copper-nickel material and had not encountered any serious difficulties.

According to the Treasury, the cost of the alloy — 45 cents a pound, based on 33-cent copper and 79-cent nickel — would be much less than silver at $18.81 a pound. Coinage at the projected fiscal 1965 rate would require approximately 5,355 short tons of copper and 1,785 short tons of nickel annually. In both cases, the tonnages would represent a small fractional part of total domestic consumption and could be drawn from surpluses in the strategic stockpile.

Many of these Treasury recommendations were contained in the legislation which President Johnson submitted to Congress in June 1965, and which was passed soon thereafter as Public Law 89-91, the Coinage Act of 1965. In the president's words, the legislation was designed to "insure a stable and dignified coinage, fully adequate in quantity and in its specially designed technical characteristics to the needs of our 20th century life."

The need for this legislation was evident: "There is no dependable or likely prospect that new, economically workable sources of silver may be found that could appreciably narrow the gap between silver supply and demand. ... The one part of the demand for silver that can be reduced is governmental demand for use in coinage."

Under the Coinage Act, some 90 percent of the silver formerly used for coinage would be made available for other purposes. The new half dollar was a composite — an outside layer (80 percent silver, 20 percent copper) clad on an alloy core (21 percent silver, 79 percent copper). To the naked eye the coin would be almost indistinguishable from the old half dollar, but it would be 40 percent instead of 90 percent silver.

The new dimes and quarter dollars, although identical in size and design to the former 90 percent silver coins, were made silverless. Each of these also was a composite — an outer layer (75 percent copper, 25 percent nickel) clad on a core of pure copper. The legislation did not call for any change in the silver dollar, but it specified that none be minted for five years.

The government's readiness to sell silver bullion from its stocks at $1.2929 an ounce had previously provided protection against the melting of silver coins, since it effectively prevented the price of silver from rising above the face value of the coins. Now, since the Treasury intended the silver coins to circulate alongside the new coins, the Act provided further protection for the silver coinage by authorizing the Secretary of the Treasury to prohibit the melting, treating or export of any U.S. coin. Again, to discourage hoarding it stipulated that any .900-fine coins minted after the law's enactment would be inscribed with the date 1964.

Finally, the legislation authorized the President to establish a Joint Commission on the Coinage, a 24-man body representing the legislative and executive branches as well as the general public. The commission, when convened, would be expected to make recommendations on such matters as the economy's need for coins, technological developments in metallurgy and coin-selector devices, the supply of the various metals, the future of the silver dollar, and the government's future role in maintaining the price of silver.

Public opinion — as expressed in the congressional hearings which preceded the passage of the Coinage Act — was virtually unanimous in regard to the need for reducing the silver content of the nation's subsidiary coinage. Emotions ran high, however, on the question of "how much," as would be expected from the diversity of interests with a stake in silver's future.

Users and producers

Silver users, anxious to have ample supplies of the metal available at stable or declining prices, wanted silver to be completely eliminated from the coinage. They pointed out that total world production could fall 100 million ounces below annual industrial demand alone, so that even under the most favorable circumstances, Treasury stocks could disappear within a half-decade.

In their analysis, silver-consuming industries projected a sharp reduction world-wide in silver usage for coinage. In this country, Mint requirements could drop perhaps 90 percent from the 1965 peak to about 30 million ounces; in other countries coinage requirements could drop 50 percent, also to about 30 million ounces. (Most countries throughout the world had already eliminated or drastically reduced the use of silver for coinage.) However, consumers projected an increase in world-wide industrial consumption to 360 million ounces by 1970, even assuming a reduced growth rate in that segment of the market. The resultant world-wide demand, 420 million ounces annually, would substantially exceed the projected supply, which (optimistically) could be estimated at about 340 million ounces from mine production and secondary sources.

Silver producers took a somewhat different view of the future. Fearing that a sharp swing away from silver might trigger a price break, they argued for the retention of silver in the coinage to the maximum extent feasible. They claimed that the supply deficit had been abnormally inflated in 1964 by the hoarding of well more than 100 million ounces in the form of Kennedy halves and speculative stocks; furthermore, they claimed on the basis of current exploration that world mine production could increase by one-fourth or more within several years' time. (They were right on the first count, but wrong on the second.) Thus, they argued that increased mine production along with the gradual recovery of the 1,800 million ounces of silver outstanding in coins would permit the retention of some silver in both the half dollar and the smaller denominations.

Western legislators argued that Treasury stocks would soon be depleted unless the government permitted the price of silver to rise in a free market. Moreover, they felt that the Treasury approach failed to attract increased production and thereby in effect aggravated the coin shortage. Thus, the Western governors conference in 1965 resolved "that Congress provide for retention of silver in reduced amounts in all coins now silver, that an affirmative program be adopted to increase exploration for and development of domestic silver supplies, and that silver be permitted to seek its own price in the market place."

The vending industry, with its $3.5-billion annual take in coins, wanted coins that would be "compatible" with the nation's 12 million coin-operated merchandising devices. About half of these machines tended to reject coins that lacked the correct electrical properties, and major changes in them could require several years' time and could cost perhaps $100 million. Furthermore, the industry wanted coins that would pose no inconvenience to the consuming public, which plunked 30 billion pieces into these machines annually for more than 12 billion cups of coffee, milk and soft drinks, about 4.5 billion candy bars, and numerous other goods and services.

Finally, almost every company with a material in any way suitable for coinage — from aluminum to zirconium — pressed its claim for inclusion in the new coinage.

Actually, the Coinage Act, like the new coinage, was a composite containing something for nearly everyone. For Western silver producers, silver kept at least a stake in the coinage, with the new half dollars requiring at least 15 million ounces per year. Producers were also assured a minimum of $1.25 per ounce for their silver supplies.

Silver users did not get an entirely silverless coinage, but they did get silverless dimes and quarters. In addition, the continued redemption of silver certificates by the Treasury provided an effective ceiling on the price — at least for awhile. The vending industry also was well enough satisfied, because the copper-nickel and copper coins had the same electrical properties as the silver coins and worked in existing machines.

To the marketplace

Considering the persistence of the coin shortage, the release of the new coins apparently did not come a moment too soon. Despite the continued expansion in production of silver coins under the "crash program," Federal Reserve inventories of quarters had shrunk to only 15 million pieces for the entire nation prior to the 1965 Christmas season.

But with the help of the new Coinage Act — which authorized the reactivation of coin production at the San Francisco Assay Office, the construction of new facilities, and the acquisition of necessary metallic strip, equipment and supplies — the Mint was able to achieve an unprecedented production rate. In November 1965, the Mint released more than 230 million new clad quarters, and scheduled the release of that many more pieces every single month — four times the highest production rate ever previously attained. These new coins carried the economy safely through the Christmas season without a crisis.

In early 1966, when almost 700 million new quarters already were in circulation and the first new dimes and half dollars were about to be released, Assistant Treasury Secretary Wallace told a Senate subcommittee that "the supply of our most vital coins is in better shape now than in any comparable period during the last 10 years. ... There is no shortage of those coins most vital to the transaction of business." Flow-back and inventories at the Federal Reserve banks had increased in all denominations except the half dollar. But relatively few of the latter were in circulation, despite the production of 480 million Franklin halves in the 1948-63 period and of almost that many Kennedy halves in the following several years.

The Treasury scheduled total production for the fiscal 1965-67 period at 34 billion coins — enough to provide every person in the country with 180 additional pieces. Its objective was to manufacture enough of the new clad coins to replace over a relatively brief period all of the 13 billion old dimes and quarters then in circulation.

The steps taken under the new Coinage Act were successful in overcoming the nationwide coin shortage, but failed to halt the drain on the Treasury's silver supplies.

As 1966 advanced, in fact, the feeling grew that the Treasury might not be able to hold the line until the completion of the transition to the new coinage. The Treasury used only 54 million ounces for coinage in 1966, as against the 1965 peak of 320 million ounces, but its stocks continued to decline as both domestic and foreign industrial users increased their demands. So Treasury stocks dropped, and then dropped some more — from 1,218 million ounces in December 1964 to 804 million ounces in December 1965, and then to 594 million ounces in December 1966.

Moreover, an ominous threat existed in the form of the silver certificates that had not yet been turned in for redemption. At the end of 1966, all but 154 million of the 594 million ounces in the Treasury's holdings were earmarked for redemption of certificates.

The Administration acted to meet this situation by introducing a new piece of silver legislation in March 1967. (As P.L. 90-29, it became law on June 24.) The law authorized the Treasury to write off $200 million in certificates — on the assumption that at least that amount had been lost, destroyed or held in collections, and thus would not be turned in for redemption. In addition, it limited the time for the redemption of certificates to one year after the passage of the legislation. Any stocks then remaining, aside from 165 million ounces earmarked for the strategic stockpile, could be sold at not less than $1.2929.

The crisis would not wait, however, as the Treasury was hit by an unprecedented flood of orders for silver bullion during the spring. (During the first half of May alone,

33 million ounces flowed out — much of it out of the country.) Thereupon, the Treasury turned for advice to the Joint Commission on the Coinage. That 24-man commission — composed of 12 members of Congress concerned with silver policies, along with four members from the executive branch and eight public members appointed by the president — had been organized under the terms of the 1965 legislation to formulate long-range coinage plans for the post-silver era. Its first meeting was held in May 1967 when it was hastily convened to make recommendations dealing with the Treasury's current dilemma.

Immediately following the commission's May 18 meeting, the Treasury moved to assure the continued availability of silver to the U.S. market by discontinuing silver sales to other than "legitimate domestic concerns" and by invoking its statutory authority to prohibit the melting or export of coins. The result was the creation of a dual market. While the dealer price in New York remained at $1.30 an ounce, silver prices on the dealer and exchange markets abroad rose sharply.

Then, as soon as the President signed the new law on June 24, the Treasury wrote off $150 million of certificates, thereby freeing 116 million ounces of previously earmarked silver stocks and raising its free stocks to 135 million ounces. But the spread between the unrestricted price on world markets and the Treasury price proved to be too wide to be long maintained. With the London price fluctuating around the $1.70-level in early July producers quite naturally sold their supplies in the premium markets while industrial users turned increasingly to the Treasury for their purchases.

By mid-July, the Mint had produced 8/2 billion new dimes and quarters — virtually duplicating the entire old stock of circulating silver dimes and quarters — and it was minting more of these clad coins at a 3.1-billion annual rate. Thus the problem of transition appeared solved: even if all other silver coins followed the silver dollars out of circulation, enough clad coins would be available in circulation and in inventory to meet the foreseeable needs of a growing economy.

At that point, following the Commission's second meeting on July 14, the Treasury halted all sales of silver at the old monetary value of $1.2929, and announced that it would sell thereafter only two million ounces a week, with the General Services Administration handling the sales at the metal's going market price. This reduction in Treasury offerings by itself would have pushed prices upward. But by an unfortunate coincidence, the very next day the copper strike shut down nearly all nonferrous-metals refineries, and thereby pulled off the market, for almost nine months' time, a large part of the normal refinery supply of silver.

Prices surge

These two developments in combination created an explosive price situation. The New York price immediately jumped from the old $1.29 ceiling to $1.87 an ounce, and after a brief period of stability, it surged upward again during the international financial crises of late 1967 and 1968. In June 1968, the New York price reached a whopping $2.565 an ounce.

These rousing price developments, along with the Treasury's June 24 deadline for redemption of silver certificates, set the stage for one final silver rush. In the Wall Street Journal's description, "Newcomers needn't pack picks, shovels, and Klondike maps, but just have wads of paper money (silver certificates, to be specific), a future contract, and taxi fare to the nearest Federal Reserve bank." In May and June especially, when half of the final year's redemptions occurred, long lines of people formed early each morning at the New York and San Francisco Assay Offices to make the guaranteed .77-ounce-per-dollar exchange. (Those with $1,300 or more first had to exchange their certificates for a receipt at the Federal Reserve Bank.)

Altogether, 77 million ounces left the Treasury's coffers during this final silver rush — roughly three times more than had been expected on the basis of the earlier pace of redemptions. But with that transfer out of the way — and with allowances made for certain supplies earmarked either for the strategic stockpile or for the last small remnant of the silver-coinage system, part-silver Kennedy halves — the Treasury by late 1968 had about 250 million ounces left in bullion and coins.

The Treasury's one remaining commitment, then, was to help make up the deficiency in the nation's industrial consumption of silver — the difference between total annual consumption of roughly 50 million ounces. The deficiency was covered by the continuation of weekly GSA sales in the amount of two million ounces, the purpose being to maintain sales at a level that will have a neutral effect on prices.

In March 1970, the GSA reduced the number of ounces of silver at its sales to 1.5 million ounces a week. The sales were halted November 10, 1970.

In any event, demonetization was in effect completed on June 24, 1968, when the right to redeem silver certificates for silver was finally terminated. The transition of the last several years has brought about a slight change in the composition and appearance of the nation's coins and currency, but it in no way affects their value as a means of payment. Silver meanwhile remains a commodity, but it is no longer money.

Silver in the West

As a major mining center, the West has always had a vital interest in the fortunes of silver. And on frequent occasions since the opening of the Comstock Lode, the white metal has dominated the regional as well as the national stage. The voice of silver has been heard in the halls of Congress; and the economy, the society and the politics of the West have harkened to its voice.

Prosperity has been only a fitful visitor to silver mining camps, however. Prices have fluctuated violently over the years, while the long-term trend of output and employment has been downward. But, as

of today, the versatile metal can bask in the upsurge of industrial demand which — along with the speculation which accompanied depletion of Treasury stocks — has caused prices to triple within the past several decades. In the context of this new situation, the silver camps of the West are bustling with new life.

The birth of the nation's silver industry occurred in the Washoe Hills of Nevada in 1858, as thousands of miners rushed across the Sierra from the already failing placers of California's Mother Lode to stake a claim in the fabulously rich Comstock Lode. Over the next twenty years, the Comstock bonanza helped finance the Civil War, provided the foundation for a transcontinental railroad, and established San Francisco as a glittering and opulent metropolis. By the time the lode played out at the end of the century, the bonanza had yielded over $200 million worth of silver and almost as much in gold.

But Comstock was only one of a series of rich silver finds. In the late 1860s, there was Black Hawk Canyon (Colorado), Cottonwood Canyon (Utah), Butte (Montana), and Owyhee County (Idaho). The 1870s and 1880s saw the development of the great silver deposits at Leadville, Colo., as well as the mines in the Calico District of California.

From this series of beginnings, the Western states, as the center of U.S. mining activity, soon made this country the world's leading silver producer. (After 1900, however, Mexico took first place.) Colorado and Montana, topping the roster of producing states in 1900, accounted at that time for 60 percent of the domestic total of about 58 million fine ounces. Utah, Idaho, and Arizona were next — and then came Nevada, despite the virtual exhaustion of the Comstock.

Western states have dominated the industry during this century; in 1966 they supplied almost 80 percent of the 44 million ounces produced domestically. Idaho's share began to rise dramatically in the late 1930s, and in recent years has produced almost half of the United States' silver; in 1986, it produced about 47.8 percent of the new silver mined in the United States. Most of it emanates from the rich silver-base deposits of the Coeur d'Alene District in northern Idaho, the home of the nation's three largest silver mines.

In 1986, the second largest producer of U.S.-mined silver was Nevada, with about 12.5 percent of the total. Arizona was a close third, about 12.4 percent. Montana produced about 10 percent of the total ounces of new silver mined in the United States in 1986.

Silver since 1970

Silver market manipulations in the 1970s by the heirs of oil magnate H. Lamarr Hunt once again spotlighted the white metal and resulted in a financial crisis in January 1980.

Traders on the Commodity Exchange in New York became aware in late 1973 of an anonymous source that had been taking delivery on silver contracts bought on the Comex.

An estimated 30 million ounces had been taken out of the market by mid-February of the following year, when the source of this activity was identified as Texas millionaire Nelson Bunker Hunt.

The 20 million ounces he accepted in December 1973 was the equivalent of about one year's production at Idaho's Coeur d'Alene mining district, and one source estimated the paper profits from his "squeeze" operation at $200 million in the U.S. market and $78 million in London.

Commodity brokers already expressed concern over Hunt's activities. Trusting that delivery will be taken on a relatively small number of contracts at any given time, they normally maintain only a small percentage of bullion to cover these contracts.

Faced with a large demand for delivery of contracts, they were forced to go into the market and buy silver at the rapidly escalating market price, which had moved from $2.80 an ounce in October 1973 to $5.70 early in the second week of February 1974.

Silver traders sought congressional aid to stabilize the market, without avail, estimating that the silver holdings accumulated by Hunt and his brother, Herbert, amounted to 50 million ounces, close to half the 117 million ounces held by the U.S. Treasury at the time.

The Hunt brothers' efforts to corner the silver market continued until January 1980, when the price on the Comex in New York closed at just under $50. The price of silver nosedived to $10.80 on March 27, 1980, and Hunt's broker, the New York based Bache Group, issued a call to the brothers for $100 million margin, which they failed to meet.

Bache Vice President Elliot J. Smith revealed that the firm met the margin call by selling the silver, and that the Hunt family still owed an unspecified amount of money to the brokerage firm.

At the order of the Securities and Exchange Commission, however, trading in Bache stock was suspended in the midafternoon of Thursday, March 27.

The Commodities Futures Trading Commission rejected a request by Bache that silver trading be closed and an administrative price be arranged for settling contracts.

CFTC Chairman James M. Stone commented that the commission"s primary job is "to protect small customers and commercial users. We are not here to protect large speculators," he said.

The only grounds for suspending silver trading, according to Stone, would be if it appeared supply and demand were not the chief regulators of the marketplace. "And that has not happened," he said. He also noted that permanent position limits, which would curb the speculation in which the Hunts participated, were being investigated.

Stone said CFTC investigators currently were looking into several troubled brokerages — including Bache — to be sure they don't dip into other investors' funds to cover their possible losses.

A later recapitulation indicated that Hunt lost an estimated $1 billion in paper profits after the price of silver plummeted to $10.30 in four days. The squeeze left him $33 million in debt to the Bache Group; $10 million to Paine Webber, another brokerage firm; and $4 million to St. Louis broker A.G. Edwards.

His biggest debt, however, was to Engelhard Mineral & Chemical Co., with whom he had a contract to buy 19 million ounces of silver at $35 an ounce, paying $665 million for metal which was worth only $270 million following the price drop.

Hunt escaped from this commitment by giving Engelhard 8.5 million ounces of silver worth $121 million, together with oil and drilling rights in Canada's Beauford Sea, which had a value of $350 to $700 million.

It was also learned as a result of the debacle, that Hunt was a 6.5 percent owner of the Bache Group, which sustained losses of $50 million, and faced an SEC investigation to determine whether the firm acted in the interest of all of its stockholders when it became involved in Hunt's silver deals.

Silver Thursday

As the full skein of financial embarrassments resulting from "Silver Thursday" was unravelled, it became apparent that ACLI Commodity Services and ContiCommodites Corp. were among those also affected by the credit they had given to the Hunts, as well as 10 banks and many other firms.

In an unprecedented move for a commodity exchange, Comex put together a revealing "Chronology of Activities of the Silver Market from September 1979 to March 1980," which detailed the extent of both individual and brokerage firm holdings in silver during this period, as well as the action taken by the exchange to increase minimum margins and limit the number of positions held by individuals, in an attempt to avoid a "squeeze" on the market.

Federal Reserve Board Chairman Paul A. Volcker subsequently encountered strong hostility when he appeared before a House committee to justify the authorization by the Fed of $1 billion in Fed loans to cover their losses from the collapse of the silver market.

At one time, Volcker revealed, the Texas brothers controlled two-thirds of the 170 million ounces of silver in circulation throughout the world.

A forced sale of these holdings, he argued, would not be in the interest of the brothers' creditors, and would shake the entire U.S. economy.

A wide-ranging two-year investigation of the Hunt brothers by the SEC concluded in July 1982 with a citation for a minor disclosure violation.

The SEC accused Nelson Bunker and Herbert L. Hunt of failing to file reports disclosing that they had acquired more than 5 percent of the stock of Bache Group Inc.

The Hunts agreed to a consent judgment in which they promised not to violate SEC regulations in the future, but neither admitted nor denied that they had done so in the past.

The Hunts dropped a multimillion-dollar lawsuit they had filed against the SEC, which accused government investigators of violating federal privacy laws during their probe.

The chief victim of the silver market "squeeze" was, of course, the white metal itself, which never has experienced substantial price recovery, and still lies like an albatross in the Hunts' portfolio.

Silver chronology

1792

April 2 — Authorizing act issued to strike U.S. silver dollar (standard weight 416 grains, .89224 fine), half dollar (standard weight 208 grains, .89244 fine), quarter dollar (standard weight 104 grains, .89244 fine), dime (standard weight 41.6 grains, .89244 fine) and half dime (standard weight 20.8 grains, .89244 fine). Dollar defined as a unit containing 24.75 grains of fine gold or 371.25 grains of fine silver (exchange rate between the two metals set at 15 to 1).

1834

Standard definition of gold dollar changed to unit containing 23.2 grains of fine gold; silver unchanged at 371.25 grains. Silver-gold ratio becomes 16 to 1.

1837

Jan. 18 — Authorizing act issued to change silver dollar standard weight to 412.50 grains, .900 fine; half dollar standard weight changed to 206.25 grains, .900 fine; quarter dollar changed to 103.125 grains, .900 fine; dime changed to 41.25 grains, .900 fine; half dime to 20.625 grains, .900 fine. Exchange rate becomes 15.988 to one.

1851

March 3 — Authorizing act issued to strike silver 3-cent piece, standard weight 12.375 grains, .750 fine.

1853

Feb. 21 — Half dollar standard weight changed to 192 grains, quarter dollar to 96 grains, dime to 38.4 grains, half dime to 19.2 grains. All remain .900 fine.

1854

Three-cent piece changed to 11.52 grains, .900 fine.

1859

Silver discovered in Comstock Lode in Nevada.

1860

Decade sees silver finds in Black Hawk Canyon, Colo.; Cottonwood Canyon, Utah; Butte, Mont.; and Owyhee County, Idaho.

1873

Feb. 12 — Authorizing act issued to strike silver Trade dollar, 420 grains, .900 fine. Half dollar changed to 192.9 grains, .900 fine; quarter dollar changed to 96.45 grains, .900 fine; dime changed to 38.58 grains, .900 fine. Half dime and 3-cent piece discontinued.
Standard silver dollar discontinued; bi-metallism effectively ended.

1875

March 3 — Authorizing act issued to strike 20-cent piece, 77.16 grains, .900 fine.

1878

May 2 — Twenty-cent piece discontinued.
Bland-Allison Act passed, requiring Treasury to buy not less than $2 million in silver every month for coinage or for backing silver certificates.

1887

March 3 — Trade dollar officially discontinued.

1890

Sherman Silver Purchase Act passed, directing the Secretary of the Treasury to buy 4.5 million ounces of silver bullion every month.

1896

July 8 — William Jennings Bryan delivers "Cross of Gold" speech calling for a restoration of the bimetallic (silver and gold) standard.

1900

Bimetallism legislation repealed, Gold Standard Act passed, officially placing the U.S. on the gold standard. Gold dollar of 25.8 grains, .900 fine becomes the unit of value; all other forms of currency maintained at parity with the gold dollar.

1920

Jan. 10 — Silver reaches an all-time high of $1.37 an ounce, caused by speculation and worldwide monetary devaluation.

1923

Silver reaches an all-time low of 24 cents an ounce.

1933

June 5 — U.S. goes off the gold standard.
Thomas Amendment to Agricultural Adjustment Act passed, authorizing unlimited coinage of silver.

1934

Silver Purchase Act passed, directing the Secretary of the Treasury to purchase silver at home and abroad until the market price reaches the Mint price of $1.2929 an ounce, or until the monetary value of Treasury silver stock reaches one-third of the monetary value of its gold stock.

1935

Minting of silver dollars halted.

1961

November — President Kennedy orders Secretary of the Treasury to suspend further sales of Treasury's free silver, to suspend the use of free silver for coinage, and to obtain coinage silver through the retirement from circulation of $5 and $10 silver certificates. Silver begins upward price climb.

1962

Oct. 20 — Silver hits 42-year high in New York, $1.22 per ounce.

1963

March 13 — Silver stands at $1.28; when it reaches $1.2929 it becomes profitable to turn in silver certificates in exchange for silver bullion.
June 4 — Silver Purchase Act repealed; tax on transfers of interest in silver bullion repealed, $1 and $2 silver certificates to be gradually retired. Treasury is authorized to issue Federal Reserve notes in smaller denominations and is required to hold an amount of silver equal in monetary value (at $1.2929 an ounce) to the face value of all silver certificates outstanding.
July 8 — Silver reaches $1.29 in New York, the "numismatic melting point" at which speculators could profit by converting silver certificates to silver and then selling the silver.
Dec. 30 — Authorizing act issued to strike Kennedy half dollars, 90 percent silver, 10 percent copper.

1964

Jan. 29 — Treasury announces silver dollars depleted from the Treasury at the rate of 700,000 per week as citizens cash in silver certificates in exchange for silver dollars.
Feb. 11 — First Kennedy half dollars struck.
March 20 — House Appropriations Committee refuses to give Treasury funds to strike more silver dollars.
March 23 — Less than three million silver dollars left in the Treasury; long lines form outside the Treasury

building as people wait to buy silver dollars.

March 24 — First Kennedy half dollars issued.

March 26 — Treasury Secretary Douglas Dillon issues an order saying citizens who want to exchange $1 silver certificates for a dollar's worth of silver will have to go to New York or San Francisco, and that the Treasury will redeem the certificates in silver bullion rather than in silver dollars.

April — Mints go on stepped-up schedule in an attempt to double the annual production of coins to ease the coin shortage. Treasury obtains permission to continue the 1964 dates on new coins indefinitely to stop hoarding.

June 17 — Senate Appropriations Committee approves striking of 45 million silver dollars.

Aug. 3 — President Johnson signs a bill authorizing to provide for the striking of the first silver dollars since 1935. Peace dollar design to be used.

Sept. 3 — President Johnson signs a bill authorizing the Secretary of the Treasury to continue using the date 1964 on all coins minted from this time on until he decides the coin shortage is over.

November — Government announces no more Proof or Mint sets will be made after 1964 until the coin shortage is over.

Dec. 28 — Mint Director Eva Adams says silver dollars will not be considered for striking until after the coin shortage is over.

1965

May 15 — President Johnson directs the Bureau of the Mint to strike 45 million silver dollars before June 30.

May 25 — Treasury announces it has decided against minting any new silver dollars at this time, after a conference with the White House.

June 3 — President Johnson sends proposal to Congress calling for the elimination of silver from dimes and quarters and a reduction of silver in the Kennedy half dollars; asks Congress to reopen the San Francisco Mint for all coin processes; and for authorization to prohibit exportation, melting or treating U.S. coins.

June 24 — New coinage bill passes the Senate without change.

July 14 — House passes coinage bill with amendments: no Mint marks to be used on the new coins, and no Mint marks for five years; there will be no silver dollars for five years; the coins are to be dated with the year of issuance or coinage unless the Treasury Secretary decides this will contribute to a coin shortage; the President may enlarge the membership of the proposed Joint Commission on the Coinage to 24; and the Secretary of the Treasury has standby authority to prohibit the use of coins as security on loans.

July 23 — President Johnson signs the Coinage Act of 1965, providing for new dimes and quarters to be three-layered "sandwich" coins with faces of the same copper-nickel alloy now used in 5-cent coins, 75 percent copper, 25 percent nickel, and bonded to a core of pure copper; and for the silver content of the Kennedy half to be reduced from 90 to 40 percent. Bill includes House amendments as well as Senate provisions.

Aug. 23 — First clad coins, 25-cent pieces, struck at the Philadelphia Mint; these are also the first coins to bear the 1965 date.

Nov. 1 — Treasury releases first clad quarters to Federal Reserve banks for circulation.

1966

March 8 — Bureau of the Mint releases clad dimes

and 40 percent silver half dollars for circulation.

June — Treasury Secretary Henry Fowler announces "the coin shortage is over."

July 7 — Treasury Department says all U.S. coins manufactured after Aug. 1, 1966, will be dated 1966, and on Jan. 1, 1967, current annual dating of coins will be resumed.

July 12 — Treasury Department announces new regulations: mutilated silver coins will be purchased at the Philadelphia and Denver Mints at approximately the going price of silver bullion.

July 26 — Hearings begin on a proposal to sell the three million silver dollars in the Treasury Department's vaults at face value to the American Cancer Society and the American Heart Fund for resale to coin collectors at a profit. The Treasury Department voices its opposition to the bill.

Aug. 27 — Royal Canadian Mintmaster predicts silver will disappear from Canadian coins within two years.

November — *American Metal Market* newspaper predicts silver prices will rise to between $1.50 and $1.80 an ounce in 1967.

Nov. 2 — Treasury reports the silver stockpile continues to diminish, dropping by almost three million ounces during the five-day period from Oct. 28 to Nov. 2.

Nov. 17 — Treasury reports silver stockpile down to 608.5 million ounces.

Dec. 1 — Stockpile down to 601.3 million ounces.

Dec. 24 — Canadian Finance Minister announces Canada will drop silver from most of its coinage, changing to nickel, in 1968. Silver is to be retained in the dollar.

1967

Jan. 3 — Treasury announces its stockpile is at 591.9 million ounces.

March 1 — Treasury reports its stockpile dropped 45 million ounces in the first two months of 1967.

March 17 — Treasury Secretary Fowler asks Congress for the power to free the remaining silver held by the Treasury as backing for silver certificates.

April 10 — Treasury stock of silver down to 524.9 million ounces.

May 18 — Treasury Department discontinues immediately sales of silver to any buyers other than legitimate domestic concerns which use silver in their businesses. The Treasury also invokes its power to prohibit the melting, treatment and export of silver coins. The announcement creates a two-price system for silver; silver jumps to $1.60 an ounce in London markets.

June 2 — Canada announces it is changing to the manufacture of nickel 10- and 25-cent pieces.

June 5 — Senate passes a measure allowing the Treasury to write off lost or destroyed silver certificates and to free for other use the silver now held against the certificates, and to allow the Bureau of the Mint to return Mint marks to U.S. coins.

June 24 — President Johnson signs bill authorizing the eventual end of the redemption of silver certificates with silver bullion, and authorizing the Mint to restore Mint marks to U.S. coinage. The Treasury Department will stop redeeming silver certificates with bullion in a year. The Treasury also now has permission to begin the write-off of an obligation to hold 116 million ounces of silver against $200 million worth of silver certificates believed lost, destroyed or held by collectors.

July 14 — Treasury announces it will no longer keep the price of silver at $1.2929, saying it believes there are enough new clad coins in circulation to serve the nation's commerce even if all of the silver coins drop out of circulation. Silver sales from the Treasury stockpiles will now be handled by the General Services Administration (GSA) and will be limited to two million ounces a week at the going market prices (over $1.71 an ounce in London).

July 18 — New York silver quotations reach $1.87 an ounce. Coin dealers who are buying silver certificates for redemption in silver report a booming business.

Aug. 4 — GSA begins selling silver on a competitive bid basis.

Aug. 21 — Silver dollars in Uncirculated and circulated bags of $1,000 offered on the New York Mercantile Exchange.

Aug. 30 — New York Mercantile Exchange reports silver dollar market is brisk, with Uncirculated bags opening at $2,160 and circulated at $1,895 for $1,000 face. GSA reports about 10 million ounces of silver have been sold at its weekly sales since they began.

Oct. 12 — Treasury Department announces beginning Nov. 1 silver bars issued in exchange for silver certificates will be of fineness of .996 and .998 rather than the .999 fine bars presently issued.

Oct. 13 — GSA reports a sharp rise in silver prices, at $1.7715 an ounce for silver stores at West Point Bullion Depository.

Oct. 24 — New record set for silver price in New York markets as a dealer pays $20,000 for a contract of 10,000 ounces on the Commodity Exchange.

Nov. 8 — London reports an all-time high for silver, $1.951 per ounce.

Nov. 18 — Britain devalues the pound, from $2.80 to $2.40, causing increased silver speculation and a rise in early December prices to $2.17 an ounce in New York.

Nov. 22 — Treasury says it has enough silver to redeem all the silver certificates presented to them before the June 24, 1968, cut-off date for redemption.

Dec. 11 — U.S. to resume selling .999 fine silver to industrial consumers.

1968

Jan. 4 — First coins struck with Mint marks since those dated 1964.

Jan. 19 — Silver steady in New York at $2.07 an ounce.

Handy & Harman Review of the Silver Market terms 1967 market "confused, unpredictable."

Feb. 2 — Treasury reports it redeemed only $8 million worth of silver certificates during the first seven weeks of 1968.

March 1 — Joint Commission on the Coinage recommends governmental melting of silver dimes and quarters. Process in full swing soon after in the Philadelphia and Denver Mints and the San Francisco Assay Office.

March 25 — GSA announces prices ranging from $2.03 to $2.13 an ounce in its sales.

April 3 — Treasury reports the government has melted enough silver coins to produce 403,726.2 ounces of silver.

April 29 — Coin silver derived from melted coins will be sold to industrial users, the Treasury says. Sale of .999 fine silver is suspended; the GSA will sell a million ounces of .996 fine silver to .998 fine silver each week, beginning May 3, in addition to a million ounces of .897 to .900 fine coinage silver.

June 24 — Deadline for redeeming silver certificates

for silver bullion. Silver certificates remain legal tender.

June 25 — Total Treasury silver estimated at 482 million ounces.

July 15 — Joint Commission on the Coinage meets to work out a plan for the disposition of the 2.9 million rare silver dollars still held in the Treasury vaults.

Sept. 10 — GSA announces the sale of 452,000 ounces of silver to 12 firms in category B, the portion set aside for small business concerns. Handy & Harman price per ounce stands at $2.220.

Oct. 16 — Silver continues month-long retreat; stands at $1.92 per ounce in London.

Oct. 31 — Silver prices show inclination to firm up; New York spot price at $1.933.

Dec. 5 — Joint Commission on the Coinage meets to consider a new non-silver dollar; recommends the 2.9 million silver dollars now held by the Treasury be sold on a bid sale basis at minimum fixed prices.

Dec. 20 — Treasury Secretary Fowler says the Joint Commission on Coinage has recommended minting non-silver clad half dollars to replace the existing 40 percent silver half dollar, and to make the current ban on melting silver coins permanent.

1969

Feb. 13 — Silver hits a 15-month low of $1.76 per ounce on the New York and Chicago exchanges.

March 14 — Spot silver at $1.79 in Chicago.

May 12 — Treasury Department lifts ban on melting and exporting silver coins following a meeting of the Joint Commission on the Coinage. The Commission also recommended minting a non-silver half dollar and a non-silver dollar, as well as selling the 2.9 million silver dollars remaining in the Treasury. Treasury also to reduce the amount of silver offered at its weekly auction from two million ounces to 1/4 million.

June 17 — Silver slides to $1.59 an ounce in London, the lowest price since the British devalued the pound in 1967.

July 10 — Rep. James A. McClure and 146 other representatives propose the Treasury resume minting a 40 percent silver dollar with the likeness of Dwight D. Eisenhower on it. Sen. Peter Dominick introduces a similar measure in the Senate, joined by 20 other senators.

August — Members of the Chicago Board of Trade approve the establishment of a futures market in silver, calling for trading in units of 5,000 troy ounces at not less than .999 fineness.

Sept. 9 — GSA auction sets a new sales record, selling more than 14 million ounces of silver.

Sept. 22 — Silver advances, spot price in New York at $1.82 an ounce, with the one-year future price moving to $2.038.

Oct. 6 — Bill calling for a silverless Eisenhower dollar, a silverless half dollar and machinery for the sale of the 2.9 million silver dollars held in the Treasury fails to pass the House.

Oct. 7 — Senate joint resolution introduced to mint copper-nickel dollar Eisenhower coins.

Oct. 15 — Treasury reports its stock of coinage silver dropped by almost four million ounces during the week of Oct. 8 to 15.

Nov. 10 — Wright Patman, chairman of the House Banking and Currency Committee, confirms he opposes any silver in the Eisenhower dollars.

Nov. 17 — Office of Domestic Gold and Silver

Operations chief Thomas Wolfe indicates GSA silver sales will probably be halted in a year.

Dec. 2 — Silver prices rise in GSA sale; prices at $1.9121.

1970

March 4 — Senate and House leaders reach a compromise agreement on a plan to mint 150 million 40 percent silver dollars and an undetermined number of copper-nickel dollar coins, all with the likeness of President Dwight D. Eisenhower. The conferees also agree that the Treasury will continue through Nov. 10 sales of silver at the rate of 1/4 million ounces a week, and that the Office of Emergency Planning will transfer to the Mint 25.5 million ounces of surplus silver no longer needed in the nation's stockpile to be used for coinage.

March 19 — Senate passes Eisenhower dollar bill; House Banking and Currency Committee chairman Wright Patman maintains his opposition to striking silver dollar coins.

April 9 — Silver prices continue to falter, closing at season's low of $1.85 an ounce.

April 29 — Silver continues to slide, closing at $1.663 an ounce in New York.

May 13 — Joint Commission on the Coinage votes in favor of a silver Eisenhower dollar. Patman says he will use his influence to block House passage of the legislation for the remainder of the year.

June 4 — Federal Reserve Board proposes that banks stop counting silver coins they hold in their vaults as part of their reserve requirements.

June 17 — Senate approves a bill to authorize further adjustments in the amount of silver certificates outstanding, and to include Federal Reserve Bank notes and national bank notes in the estimates of notes that are irretrievable as a result of being lost or in collections.

September — Senate approves the Bank Holding bill, onto which is tacked authorization to strike 150 million Eisenhower 40 percent silver dollars.

Oct. 9 — Federal Register notes that effective Nov. 10 the U.S. Mints and Assay Offices will no longer accept deposits of silver for exchange into bars.

Nov. 10 — GSA silver auctions end with the Franklin Mint buying the last silver sold by the Treasury, marking the end of the government's 194-year role in the silver market.

Nov. 24 — Both the Senate and the House make concessions; passage of the Eisenhower dollar bill, tied onto revisions in the Banking Holding Company bill, draws nearer.

Dec. 8 — Senate-House conferees reach agreement on the Eisenhower dollar bill; approve coinage amendments authorizing the Mint to produce Eisenhower dollar coins in silver and copper-nickel, and half dollars in copper-nickel. Bill now goes before the Senate and House.

Dec. 18 — Senate unanimously passes Eisenhower dollar bill, following House passage the previous day.

Dec. 31 — President Nixon signs Eisenhower dollar bill, marking the first dollar coin issued since 1935. The Mint is to produce over a four or five year period 150 million 40 percent silver coins for sale at premium prices and an undetermined number of copper-nickel clad dollars for general circulation. The bill also eliminates the 40 percent silver content from the half dollar and authorizes minting copper-nickel clad coins in an effort to achieve general circulation of the half dollar; and authorizes the GSA to sell the 2.9 million silver dollars now in the vaults of the Treasury, on a bid basis. Most of the dollars to be offered for sale are Carson City specimens, 90 percent silver, minted between 1878 and 1891.

1971

Jan. 25 — First trial strikes for new Eisenhower dollar performed at the Philadelphia Mint.

Jan. 29 — Treasury announces Eisenhower dollars of 40 percent silver will sell for $10 per coin in Proof and $3 per coin in Uncirculated. Orders will be accepted beginning July 1.

Feb. 1 — Handy & Harman releases annual Review of the Silver Market, noting that the world silver markets were still dominated by speculators in 1970 for the fourth year in a row. The report also comments that with the end of GSA silver sales the price of silver dropped rather than climbed, contrary to expectations.

Feb. 3 — Denver Mint begins producing copper-nickel half dollars.

March 31 — First silver Eisenhower dollars struck at the San Francisco Assay Office.

April 1 — The Royal Canadian Mint begins accepting orders for its British Columbia Commemorative silver dollar.

April 1 — Trading in silver coin futures begins on the New York Mercantile Exchange, with the contract covering U.S. dimes, quarters and half dollars minted in 1964 or before.

May 17 — West Coast Commodity Exchange begins listing U.S. silver coins as a new commodity futures contract.

May 28 — New York Mercantile Exchange reflects softening silver prices; closing price slips to $1,205 for July delivery of a $1,000 face silver coin contract.

June 6 — A GSA spokesman says he expects as many as 15 million bids on the silver dollars being held in the Treasury.

June 29 — Prices drop on the New York Mercantile Exchange; $1,155 per bag of $1,000 face U.S. silver coins on July contracts.

July 2 — Prices bounce back; $1,175 per bag of $1,000 face U.S. silver coins on July contracts.

Oct. 5 — Silver slips to a four and a half year low, closing at $1.331 an ounce in New York.

Oct. 27 — Silver closes at below $1.30 an ounce in New York.

Nov. 1 — First Eisenhower dollars released for circulation.

Nov. 3 — Downward trend continues; silver at $1.27 an ounce for November futures.

Dec. 6 — The Treasury's 2.9 million Carson City silver dollars are transferred to the U.S. bullion depository in West Point, N.Y., as a major step toward public sale of the coins in about a year.

1972

Feb. 16 — San Francisco Federal Reserve bank official William Burke notes in a Coin World article that many traders are now referring to silver ironically as a "semi-precious metal." He notes that from a quotation of $1.80 an ounce at the time of the last Treasury sale in November 1970, the price went down instead of up, as many had expected, reaching $1.31 an ounce in October 1971.

March 27 — Trade begins on silver coin contracts in the Chicago Open Board of Trade.

April 12 — Sustained price advance peaks; reaches $1.65 an ounce in New York.

May 19 — Senator Jacob K. Javits presents testimony on a bill he sponsored to authorize the Secretary of the Treasury to make grants to Eisenhower College, Seneca Falls, N.Y., out of proceeds from the sale of Proof Eisenhower dollars sold by the Mint.

June 8 — Senate passes bill to supply 10 percent of the proceeds from the sale of Proof Eisenhower dollars to the Eisenhower College.

July 17 — Silver reaches a two-year high of $1.80 in New York.

Sept. 5 — Silver prices slide to $1.772 in New York.

Sept. 25 — The Silver Institute, Inc., sponsors an exhibition of the silver coins issued by over 30 nations in the past 10 years for those attending the International Monetary Fund meeting in Washington, D.C.

Oct. 31 — Bids open for Carson City silver dollar sale; public may submit bids for the 1882, 1883, and 1884 coins produced at the now obsolete Carson City Mint. Minimum acceptable bid placed at $30 for each coin, with bids limited to one coin of each year.

Nov. 3 — Coin firm Stack's of New York calls for a Securities and Exchange Commission investigation of the GSA and its use of the terms investment and investments in its Carson City silver dollar sale brochure. SEC later declares the GSA claims are beyond the jurisdiction of the SEC.

1973

Jan. 3 — GSA announces inspection of Carson City dollars complete, meeting standards set for Uncirculated coins.

Jan. 17 — Federal Trade Commission refuses to intervene at the request of Professional Numismatists Guild in the fight against advertising use of the term "silver dollar" for silverless coins.

Feb. 2 — A total of 700,000 Carson City dollars sold for $30 each.

Feb. 27 — Silver continues to rise; at $2.381 in London.

March 15 — Senator Jacob Javits introduces another bill to provide money from the sale of Eisenhower Proof dollars for the Eisenhower College, Seneca Falls, N.Y. Similar legislation introduced in 1972 died in the 92nd Congress.

April 17 — Senate Banking, Housing and Urban Affairs committee approves bill providing $1 from the sale of each Proof Eisenhower dollar to the Eisenhower College.

April 19 — Wright Patman introduces Eisenhower College bill in the House.

April 30 — GSA sells 70,000 more Carson City dollars, at $30 each.

May 2 — Senate approves bill allocating $1 from the sale of each Proof Eisenhower silver dollar to Eisenhower College.

June 8 — GSA announces it will auction off 2 million ounces of reclaimed silver obtained from Defense Department projects, not part of the national stockpile. Silver coin futures drop by as much as $50 a bag.

June 20 — GSA sells first of 2 million ounces of silver on a competitive bid basis, selling a total of 1,240,000 ounces.

Aug. 1 — Mint Director Mary Brooks announces there will be no 1973-dated copper-nickel Eisenhower dollars for general circulation.

Aug. 3 — Rep. Chalmer P. Wylie introduces bill to make an outright grant of $6 million to both the Eisenhower College and the Rayburn Library.

Oct. 31 — GSA closes bids on sales of Carson City dollars dated 1880, 1881, and 1885; bids total $14,071,958.

Dec. 10 — Royal Canadian Mint unveils first four silver

coins in the Montreal Olympic commemorative series.

1974

Jan. 8 — Spot silver prices reach $3.40 in New York.

Jan. 21 — Silver soars to $3.97 in London.

Feb. 10 — Silver futures stand at $4.815 in London.

Feb. 14 — Silver at $4.427 an ounce in London.

Feb. 21 — Silver breaks world price record at $5.965 in London.

April 1 — GSA opens bidding for what is expected to be its last Carson City dollar sale.

April 11 — Silver drops; closes at $4.27 in New York.

April 17 — Silver bounces back, at $4.828 in New York for May futures.

May 3 — Silver shows new strength; at $5.501 an ounce in London.

June 5 — Silver Institute releases figures showing the rising price of silver in April drove 1,480,053 ounces of pre-1965 U.S. silver coins into the melting pot.

July 16 — Mint Director Mary Brooks announces the Park Hill section of Denver will be the site of the new Denver Mint.

July 22 — Rep. Wright Patman again introduces a bill authorizing grants from the sale of Eisenhower Proof dollars to the Eisenhower College in Seneca Falls, N.Y. The bill also gives power to the Bureau of the Mint to change the alloy and weight of the 1-cent piece. Patman's last Eisenhower College bill met defeat under a House rule technicality Aug. 3, 1973.

Aug. 3 — Eisenhower College bill wins House Banking and Currency committee OK.

Aug. 21 — The Pacific Commodities Exchange in San Francisco launches trading in silver futures with a new "mini-contract" for delivery of 1,000 troy ounces of silver.

Aug. 21 — The GSA says there are no plans for the present about disposing of the remaining one million Carson City silver dollars held by the Treasury.

Sept. 11 — Silver slips to $3.89 an ounce in New York. Mining stocks in both gold and silver drop.

Sept. 18 — Silver falls back to $3.87 an ounce. The Silver Institute reports substantial melting of silver coins by U.S. refiners during August.

Sept. 25 — House passes bill including a provision for $9 million grant to the Eisenhower College at Seneca Falls, N.Y., tapped from the proceeds of the sale of 40 percent silver Proof Eisenhower dollars.

Sept. 26 — Eisenhower College bill passes Senate, goes to president for signature.

Oct. 10 — Las Vegas blackjack dealer brings 1974-D Eisenhower dollar struck on 40 percent silver planchet to Coin World offices. U.S. Mint confirms that a quantity of copper-nickel clad dollar planchets unfit for striking into Proofs had been shipped from San Francisco to Denver, accidentally including an unknown number of 40 percent silver planchets intended for Proof or Uncirculated collector coins.

Oct. 10 — U.S. Bicentennial 40 percent silver coins to go on sale Nov. 15 through Jan. 31, 1975. Price of three-piece Proof sets $15, Uncirculated set $9, limit of five sets of each per customer.

Nov. 13 — Presentation set of 40 percent silver Bicentennial coins presented to President Ford at White House ceremonies.

Nov. 20 — Senate passes appropriations bill releasing Eisenhower dollar funds for Eisenhower College and Sam Rayburn Library.

1975

Jan. 10 — Royal Canadian Mint employees strike for higher wages, delaying production of third series of silver Olympic coins.

Jan. 19 — U.S. Mint reduces price of three-piece, 40 percent silver Bicentennial Proof set from $15 to $12 per set. Quantity limit removed and ordering deadline extended to July 4, 1976, for Proof and Uncirculated Bicentennial sets.

Feb. 19 — GSA considering new plans for the disposal of approximately one million Carson City silver dollars left unsold in earlier sales. Coins may be put in storage for future sale.

February — Handy & Harman, precious metal dealer, releases annual review of the previous year's metal markets. Refers to 1974 as "the most chaotic period in the history of the world's silver markets."

March 2 — Royal Canadian Mint strike ends. Production of silver Olympic coins to resume.

April 23 — U.S. Mint begins striking 40 percent silver Bicentennial coins for release on July 4, 1975.

June 24 — The newly organized Commodity Futures Trading Commission imposes new stringent regulations to protect public against fraud in transactions involving gold and silver bullion and bulk silver and gold coins. Exchange members must now file reports on silver market activities.

July 16 — Silver Institute credits the 1974 increase in use of silver for coinage to the Olympic Coin Program, which put Canada in first place as a user of silver for coins.

Oct. 1 — Bureau of Mines reports domestic industrial silver consumption increased seven million ounces above the first quarter of 1975; new mine production remains unchanged.

Oct. 31 — Bureau of the Mint taps over one million ounces of its silver stocks between Aug. 1 and Oct. 31 to produce 40 percent silver Bicentennial coins, Bureau of Mines reports.

Dec. 17 — Japanese exports of silver bullion at 219.7 metric tons during the first nine months of 1975.

1976

Feb. 11 — A-Mark Coin Co., Beverly Hills, Calif., spends $7.3 million to acquire the dollar hoard of LaVere Redfield.

April 1 — Indian government announces exporters of silver will be required to have a license, to be granted on a quota system. Before, India had permitted unlicensed export of silver. Prices rise in New York in response to the news.

April 12 — Wall Street Journal reports silver experts show optimism about an increase in use of silver as the economy improves.

Aug. 26 — Indian government decrees that all exports of silver be channeled through the State Trading Corporation.

Sept. 8 — The House Armed Services Committee votes to reinstate the bill permitting the sale of 118 million ounces of silver from the national stockpile after silver has been eliminated from an earlier stockpile sale bill.

Oct. 2 — The 94th Congress adjourns without having taken action on pending legislation authorizing disposal of silver deemed in excess of stockpile objectives.

Dec. 31 — Handy & Harman estimates industrial consumption of silver increased about 6 percent during 1976 to an estimated 167.5 million ounces compared to a revised figure of 157.7 million ounces in 1975.

World consumption for industrial and coinage uses combined, excluding Communist-dominated areas, amounted to about 442 million ounces about 7 percent ahead of Handy & Harman's revised 1975 figure.

Industrial consumption rose about 8 percent over the previous year, to some 395 million ounces; consumption for coinage decreased by the same percentage to 27 million ounces, from 29.2 million ounces in 1975.

An unexpected boost was given to silver supplies in 1976 as a result of the demonetizing and melting of 28,000,000 ounces of German coins.

1977

Jan. 12 — The Silver Institute reports coins supplied the ingredients for 4,579,119 ounces of silver refined in the U.S. during November 1976, the second month in a row that substantial quantities of coins were supplied to refiners of .999 fine silver.

Feb. 23 — Handy & Harman's 61st annual report on the silver market anticipates little change in conditions in 1977, with a somewhat higher price for the year.

March 9 — Rep. Silvio Conte, R-Mass., introduces a bill to release 118 million troy ounces of silver from the national stockpile. Experts have little expectation the bill will pass in 1977.

March 28 — Silver price marches to $4.983 per troy ounce in a bid to break the $5 barrier; yields to profit-taking in the next few days.

April 27 — Hecla Mines' Philip Lindstrom sees silver demand growing in 1977, and higher prices in the long term.

May 1 — J. Aron Commodities Corp. researchers believe inflation could carry silver to as high as $5.50 per ounce during 1977; they believe a price well above $5 will be required to free a substantial amount of silver coins for the refiners.

July 20 — Coinage consumed 10 percent of the silver mined in 1976, with 180 types issued by 72 countries, according to the Silver Institute. Canada, France, Austria, the German Federal Republic and Belgium were the major producers, with the United States sixth.

July 20 — Sen. James McClure, R-Idaho, introduces a bill which would set strategic stockpile objectives based on average annual import deficits. This would require a one- or two-year supply of silver for emergencies.

1978

March 8 — The price of silver on the Commodity Exchange in New York gains 35 cents since March 6, to clear the $5 price barrier.

June 7 — Sen. Gary Hart, D-Colo., proposes a silver stockpile sales target of 15 million ounces as a compromise between the Carter administration's request to sell 62.5 million ounces and other Western senators' opposition to any sale.

Oct. 17 — Silver price climbs to $5.945 on the Comex; warehouse stocks are down by nearly 10 million ounces.

1979

Jan. 3 — Silver consumption for the third quarter of 1978 (37.3 million ounces) was 5.9 million ounces, or 13.6 percent, lower than the second quarter.

Feb. 20 — The price of silver climbs to a record $7.94 on the Comex, in response to political and military tensions.

May 2 - Mint Director Stella Hackel says she would

consider striking a silver commemorative coin for the Olympics in 1984.

July 25 — Rep. Larry McDonald, D-Ga., introduces bill that would authorize the purchase of 140 million ounces of silver over the next six years, calling silver "the first of the strategic metals the world will run out of."

Aug. 8 — The House is considering three silver bills: An administration request for the sale of 15 million ounces; a bill introduced by Rep. Silvio Conte, R-Mass., to sell all 139.5 million ounces in the stockpile; and the bill by Larry McDonald, to increase the stockpile by 240 million ounces.

Sept. 4 — Silver climbs to a record $11.02 on the Comex in New York.

Dec. 12 — Silver price on the Comex crosses $20, as it is traded for $20.08.

1980

Jan. 2 — House votes to keep silver stockpile intact.

Jan. 18 — Silver price soars to an all-time record of $50.35 in trading on Comex.

Jan. 28 — The Chicago Board of Trade joins Comex in halting silver trading for a three-month period to stabilize prices at $33-$36.50 level.

April 9 — Silver prices tumble below $20; Hunts fail to meet $100 million margin call.

May 7 — Commodity Futures Trading Commission probes the Hunt family's role in the "Great Silver Runup."

May 21 — The Federal Reserve approves more than $800 million in bailout loans to the Hunt family.

July 9 — The Silver Institute reports the Soviet Union was the world's major silver producer in 1979, mining 49.8 million tons, 400,000 tons more than Mexico produced.

Nov. 26 — The General Services Administration is accepting bids for 140,173.29 ounces of silver reclaimed by the Veterans Administration and refined by the New York Assay Office.

1981

April 1 — The Reagan administration announces plans to sell 139.5 million ounces of stockpiled silver.

May 27 — The Commodity Futures Trading Commission fails to pin a market manipulation "rap" on the Hunt brothers.

June 24 — House subcommittee on Seapower and Strategic and Critical Materials seeks to block Reagan administration's proposal to sell stockpiled silver.

July 8 — Sen. James McClure, R-Idaho, voices opposition to the sale of silver in the strategic stockpile.

Oct. 14 — First General Serices Administration sale of stockpiled silver draws few successful bidders.

Nov. 11 — Interior Secretary James Watt joins Republican Senators McClure and Symms and Reps. Craig and Hansen of Idaho in opposition to the silver stockpile sell-off.

Nov. 25 — Idaho Senators James McClure and Steven Symms introduce legislation to halt weekly silver stockpile sales and turn any excess silver into commemorative coins.

Dec. 9 — GSA suspends Nov. 25 auction after not accepting any bids at the two previous weekly auctions.

Dec. 30 — President signs Defense Appropriations Act with amendment that halts the sale of strategic silver for six months to permit a study of GSA sales and alternate disposal methods.

1982

Feb. 10 — General Accounting Office calls silver bullion coin sales a viable alternative to stockpile auctions.

March 8 — Spot price of silver drops to $6.85 on the Comex in New York.

May 19 — Seventy-seven nations issued 180 different silver coin types during 1981, including 14 that did not issue any the previous year.

July 7 — The U.S. Mint begins accepting orders for Washington commemorative silver half dollars.

July 7 — The use of silver for coins and medals in the first quarter of 1982 was down 100,000 ounces from the same quarter in 1981; but the 900,000 ounces consumed was 50 percent greater than that used in the fourth quarter of the previous year.

Sept. 15 — The price of silver reaches $8.465 per ounce, high for the year on the Comex on Aug. 26.

Oct. 14 — The Treasury Department announces plans to strike 1983 and 1984 .900 fine silver dollar Proof coins together with a 1984 Proof gold coin, to commemorate the 1984 Summer Olympic Games in Los Angeles. The silver coins will be struck at the San Francisco Assay Office and will bear an "S" Mint mark.

1983

Jan. 19 — Washington commemorative half dollar sales exceed 5 million.

Feb. 16 — Bureau of the Mint announces availability for future purchase of P, D and S Uncirculated 1983 and 1984 silver Olympic commemorative dollars.

Feb. 23 — Secretary Watt tells silver miners that the silver stockpile disposal is still "under review" by the Interior Department.

May 18 — Mint officials announce the availability of Prestige Proof sets in 1983 and 1984, each of which will contain specimens of the 1983-S and 1984-S Proof Olympic commemorative dollars.

June 29 — The Ad Hoc Committee for American Silver recommends that the 137.5 million ounces of silver in the stockpile be reduced to zero through the sale of silver bullion coins.

Oct. 5 — A joint survey by the Ad Hoc Committee for American Silver and the Silver Institute shows strong public interest in silver bullion coins struck from stockpiled silver.

Nov. 2 — Domestic silver usage during the first half of 1983, at 59 million ounces, was down 8 percent from the same period in 1982.

Dec. 14 — The Treasury launches a feasibility study for marketing bullion coins struck from stockpiled silver; no action is likely before 1985.

1984

Jan. 9 — Silver plummets to $7.79 as the U.S. dollar overwhelms foreign currencies.

Jan. 11 — The Mint ceases Washington commemorative half dollar production.

May 16 — Silver dollar specialist Wayne Miller sells his virtually complete set of Morgan and Peace dollars to professional numismatist David Hall, for a reported sum in excess of $1 million.

May 23 — The House Armed Services Committee recommends the sale of 10 million ounces of stockpiled silver, leaving open the possibility of minting coins from the silver.

May 30 — The 1982 United States George Washington commemorative silver half dollar wins "Coin of the Year" honors in a competition sponsored by Krause Publications.

June 13 — Two separate measures introduced in Congress could pave the way for Americans to buy newly-minted Morgan dollars this year.

July 18 — Industrial consumption of silver for the first quarter of 1984 was 30.7 million ounces, up 5 percent from a year ago, according to the Bureau of Mines.

July 25 — World Mints in 1983 used nearly 500,000 more ounces of silver for coinage than in 1982, with 77 countries issuing 264 coin types, according to the Silver Institute.

Aug. 22 — The doubling found on numerous 1984 Olympic silver dollars is positively identified as an unusual form of strike doubling and is not the result of doubled dies, according to U.S. Mint and hobby experts.

Sept. 26 — An 1804 silver dollar and 1894-S dime are among the silver rarities included in millionaire Dr. Jerry Buss' collection, to be sold soon at public auction.

Dec. 5 — Mexico's new silver bullion coin, the Libertad, is selling beyond expectations, with the 1983 version released Nov. 1 and a new method of pricing due to be introduced with the release of the 1985 coin.

1985

Jan. 30 — Canada plans 10 silver $20 gold coins and one $100 gold coin to commemorate the 1988 Olympics in Calgary.

Feb. 20 — the 1984-S Proof silver dollar seems destined to be the most-purchased U.S. Olympic coin, according to Treasury Department figures.

March 13 — The Centennial of Canada's National Park system is the theme of the 1985 Canadian silver dollar and $100 gold commemorative coins.

March 27 — A Montreal firm purchased the only privately-held specimen of the 1911 Canadian silver dollar for an undisclosed amount.

June 21 — The Senate passes the Statue of Liberty coin program with an amendment calling for a 1-ounce silver bullion coin to follow the Statue program.

July 9 — President Reagan signs bill authorizing the striking of a 1-ounce silver bullion coin and four gold bullion coins.

Oct. 16 — The Republic of Korea plans a 28-coin Olympic coin program for the 1988 Summer Games in Seoul.

Oct. 30 — International Numismatic Society Authentication Bureau reports receiving excellent counterfeits of the 1917-S Obverse Mint mark Walking Liberty half dollar in recent weeks.

Dec. 25 — Final sales figures for Los Angeles Olympics commemorative coins show Proof 1983-S and 1984-S silver dollars to be the big sellers.

1986

Jan. 29 — Silver Users Association executive calls the failure of silver prices to move up as interest rates and the dollar weakened the "biggest surprise" of 1985.

Feb. 12 — The Wayne Miller collection of Morgan and Peace dollars, sold at auction by Superior Galleries, realizes $1,109,375.

March 12 — Mint Director Donna Pope predicts 4 million ounces of silver bullion coins will be sold during their first year of production to a House Appropriations subcommittee.

May 23 — Clayton silver mine in Idaho's Coeur d'Alene district joins Hecla's Lucky Friday and Sunshine mines in closing down because of unprofitable silver prices.

June 18 — Mexico releases 1986 Libertad silver coin; mintage of the 1985 date was 2,015,000 pieces. Mintages were limited to 1 million for 1982, 1983 and 1984.

June 25 — Silver bullion coin features A.A. Weinman's Walking Liberty design on the obverse; a new Heraldic Eagle design by John Mercanti on the reverse.

Aug. 20 — Mint announces plans to strike Proof specimens of its 1986 silver bullion coins, with Mint marks. Uncirculated strikes will carry no Mint mark.

Sept. 3 — Ceremonial striking of the first silver bullion coin is tentatively set for Oct. 29 at the San Francisco Assay Office.

Oct. 29 — Congress approves legislation for a .900 fine silver coin with a face value of $1 and a gold coin containing about one-quarter ounce, to be struck to mark the Bicentennial of the U.S. Constitution.

Nov. 24 — The Mint releases American Eagle silver bullion coins to 27 authorized bulk dealers and marketmakers.

Dec. 3 — Mint expands production of silver bullion coins from the San Francisco Assay Office to the Denver Mint, with an end-of-the-year goal of 5 million pieces.

Dec. 3 — Preliminary orders for Proof 1986 silver bullion coins climb to 624,743.

Dec. 3 — Sales of Proof gold bullion coins amount to $168,117,400; Proof silver, $18,962,055, for a total of $187,079,055.

Dec. 14 — Gold and silver Proof coin sales pass $200 million mark.

1987

Jan. 14 — 1986 silver bullion coin production exceeds 5 million-coin goal by 96,000 pieces.

Jan. — Banco de Mexico officially releases a Proof issue of the Libertad silver bullion coin, the first attempt by the Baco de Mexico to market a Proof coin.

Feb. — Belgium announces it will mint and sell gold and silver coins denominated in European Currency Units to commemorate the 30th anniversary of the European Community's founding treaty.

March 11 — The Mint reports the sale of 7,286,000 silver bullion coins since the program began Oct. 29; projects a need for 18-24 million ounces of silver in 1987.

April — Korea begins minting gold and silver coins to commemorate the 1988 Olympics.

April — Germany approves plans to mint silver-copper coin to commemorate 30th anniversary of the founding of the European Community.

May — The New York Commodities Exchange temporarily shortens trading hours to catch up on a backlog of orders for silver and gold futures.

July 1 — U.S. Mint begins production of gold and silver Bicentennial of the Constitution commemorative coins.

September — Mexico issues 40,000 bonds — Certificados de Plata — each backed by 100 ounces of newly mined Mexican silver.

Oct. 19 — Dramatic crash of world stock markets sends many investors scurrying for cover in precious metals.

1988

March — South Dakota exempts the state's gold and silver Bison bullion pieces from state sales taxes.

April — The Chicago Board of Trade receives Commodity Futures Trading Commission approval to begin trading 5,000-ounce silver futures.

June — Chicago Mercantile Exchange receives Commodity Futures Trading Commission approval to begin trading 5,000-ounce silver futures, but delays start of silver futures trading indefinitely.

July — Canada's Royal Canadian Mint announces plans to begin production of silver and platinum bullion coins.

October — U.S. Treasury's Fiscal Year 1989 appropriations bill contains provisions for selling 2.5 million ounces of its more than 400 million ounces of stockpile silver in each of the next three years.

1989

June 14 — U.S. Mint begins production of gold and silver coins commemorating the Bicentennial of the U.S. Congress.

July 18 — The Defense Logistics Agency sale of surplus Treasury silver brings accepted bids ranging from $5.01 to $5.08 per ounce.

August — Japan announces intentions of issuing up to 10 million silver coins to commemorate the International Garden and Greenery Exposition in 1990.

September — Canada announces plans for series of gold, platinum and silver coins to commemorate the 10th anniversary of the Maple Leaf; Soviet Union announces platinum, palladium, gold and silver commemorative coins depicting events in Russian history; Pobjoy Mint in the U.K. issues gold and silver cat coins.

1990

June — The coin and antiquities collections of the Hunt brothers are sold at auction, in part to settle debts arising from their failed attempt to corner the silver market.

Monthly silver prices
(Dollars per troy ounce)

	Handy and Harman, New York			London spot		
	Low/Date	High/Date	Average	Low/Date	High/Date	Average
1987						
January	5.36/7	5.68/27	5.53	5.36/7	5.73/28	5.52
February	5.39/18	5.57/2,9	5.49	5.39/18	5.56/6	5.48
March	5.45/2,3	6.31/31	5.68	5.43/2	6.31/31	5.56
April	6.28/1	10.20/27	7.43	6.62/1	10.93/27	7.47
May	7.41/26	9.73/18	8.44	7.30/27	9.44/18	8.47
June	6.84/25	7.86/11	7.41	6.76/23	7.93/10	7.43
July	7.24/1	8.26/31	7.68	7.20/6	8.32/31	7.64
August	7.39/28	8.80/4	7.85	7.53/17	8.73/4	7.87
September	7.28/1	7.72/4	7.59	7.36/21	7.82/11	7.60
October	6.91/29	8.20/19	7.56	6.88/30	8.31/16,19	7.63
November	6.36/5,10	7.07/30	6.66	6.29/5	7.25/30	6.72
December	6.60/4	7.00/14	6.79	6.67/7	7.04/14	6.81
1988						
January	6.50/29	7.00/6	6.73	6.50/5	7.00/7	6.73
February	6.12/29	6.58/2	6.32	6.14/2	6.62/2	6.34
March	6.16/3	6.73/29	6.41	6.20/3	6.75/31	6.41
April	6.37/26	6.83/4	6.48	6.36/14	6.73/5	6.45
May	6.34/4	6.76/23	6.54	6.32/4	6.76/23	6.54
June	6.63/29	7.37/7	7.04	6.65/30	7.28/7	7.02
July	6.76/6	7.99/21	7.15	6.69/1	7.82/20	7.10
August	6.52/30,31	6.91/5	6.71	6.45/31	6.86/1	6.71
September	6.11/30	6.62/1	6.36	6.10/26	6.63/9	6.37
October	6.16/5	6.40/17	6.28	6.12/3	6.41/18	6.28
November	6.01/21	6.47/10	6.29	6.07/22,30	6.52/10	6.29
December	6.01/29	6.21/7	6.11	6.05/30	6.19/5	6.12
1989						
January	5.82/31	6.17/23	5.97	5.84/31	6.21/24	5.99
February	5.80/13	6.00/23	5.89	5.79/13	5.97/23	5.88
March	5.76/30	6.14/14,21	5.93	5.76/2	6.15/20	5.95
April	5.65/28	5.88/12,13	5.79	5.64/28	5.88/13	5.79
May	5.20/30	5.66/1,2	5.45	5.22/30	5.67/10	5.44
June	5.15/30	5.44/8	5.28	5.16/1	5.42/8	5.28
July	5.13/31	5.38/6	5.24	5.15/31	5.36/6	5.23
August	5.07/31	5.24/2,22	5.18	5.07/31	5.29/4	5.19
September	5.02/15	5.29/26	5.13	5.05/1	5.32/25	5.13
October	5.06/10	5.25/4	5.13	5.05/11	5.25/5,30	5.14
November	5.17/1	5.84/22	5.47	5.16/2	5.89/24	5.48
December	5.14/29	5.71/12	5.53	5.21/29	5.70/11	5.57

1990

January	5.19/3	5.34/12	5.24	5.16/3	5.33/12	5.25
February	5.10/27	5.39/7	5.28	5.12/28	5.36/20	5.29
March	4.91/28	5.14/1,8	5.06	4.96/27	5.14/8	5.08

Source: Bureau of Mines

Top 10 users of pure silver in coinage 1988
(millions of troy ounces)

United States	9.2	The Netherlands	0.7
Federal Republic of Germany	5.2	Austria	0.6
France	2.2	Poland	0.5
Canada	2.0	Isle of Man	0.5
Mexico	1.3	All other countries	2.4
Korea	1.1	TOTAL	25.7

Top 10 users of pure silver in coinage 1979-1988
(millions of troy ounces)

Country	1979	1980	1981	1982	1983	1984	1985	1986	1987	1988	Total
United States	0.2	0.1	0.1	1.8	2.0	2.0	0.8	10.3	12.2	9.2	38.7
France	7.6	0.1	—	1.3	2.2	3.9	2.2	2.4	2.3	2.2	24.2
Austria	3.9	2.1	2.2	1.5	1.8	1.7	4.9	1.2	0.6	0.6	20.5
Mexico	0.5	5.1	—	—	—	2.5	3.5	2.0	2.3	1.3	17.2
Germany, W.	3.7	—	—	—	—	—	—	—	5.2	5.2	14.1
Canada	0.3	0.2	0.3	0.3	0.3	0.3	0.5	1.3	1.2	2.0	6.7
Japan	—	—	—	—	—	—	—	6.4	—	—	6.4
Korea	—	—	—	0.2	—	—	—	0.6	2.1	1.1	4.0
USSR	1.7	2.2	—	—	—	—	—	—	—	0.1	4.0
Isle of Man	0.2	0.2	0.3	0.2	0.4	0.2	—	0.5	0.2	0.5	2.7
All others	6.3	3.8	3.0	4.6	3.2	2.4	1.5	2.1	3.9	3.5	34.3
TOTAL	24.4	13.8	5.9	9.9	9.9	13.0	13.4	26.8	30.0	25.7	172.8

Source: The Silver Institute

Summary of silver and gold coinages 1988

	SILVER		GOLD	
Area of origin	Issues	Troy ounces	Issues	Troy ounces
Afghanistan	2	4,497	—	—
Albania	1	10,027	2	174
Andorra	3	29,577	2	1,478
Antigua & Barbuda	4	12,323	—	—
Australia	7	301,064	9	2,83,713
Austria	3	642,420	—	—
Bahamas	3	7,337	4	630
Barbados	1	139	—	—
Belgium	1	49,311	1	1,56,925
Belize	2	2,729	—	—
Bermuda	3	9,302	—	—
Botswana	6	7,960	1	70
Brunei	8	5,580	1	1,473
Cambodia	4	5,664	—	—
Canada	13	1,997,723	7	1,231,325
Cayman Islands	4	27,716	2	446
China	16	227,550	20	292,130
Cook Islands	5	19,717	—	—
Cuba	22	63,241	11	652
Cyprus	2	5,046	—	—
Czechoslovakia	5	107,192	—	—
Dominica	1	11,563	—	—
Dominican Republic	3	33,469	6	5,894
Ecuador	2	3,573	—	—
Egypt	5	46,082	1	3,722
France	19	2,225,818	9	15,875
Germany, Federal Rep.	2	5,202,050	—	—
Gibraltar	2	5,130	2	891
Great Britain	3	23,118	20	188,543
Grenada	1	11,563	—	—
Guernsey	1	2,103	—	—
Hungary	3	60,765	—	—
India	2	4,806	—	—

Area of origin	SILVER		GOLD	
	Issues	Troy ounces	Issues	Troy ounces
Iran	—	—	3	129,764
Isle of Man	25	474,336	43	79,651
Israel	6	25,063	2	3,749
Italy	7	107,222	—	—
Jamaica	7	16,642	—	—
Jersey	2	1,738	2	290
Korea	8	1,079,920	4	150,200
Laos	3	6,045	—	—
Lesotho	1	12,615	—	—
Liberia	4	99,986	2	4,996
Liechtenstein	1	30,384	1	10,129
Macau	4	19,245	4	5,058
Madagascar	1	14,453	1	1,474
Malta	3	3,813	—	—
Mauritius	—	—	4	6,274
Mexico	8	1,281,065	7	377,650
Morocco	1	1,671	2	132
Mozambique	1	2,944	—	—
Nepal	1	4,995	—	—
The Netherlands	1	735,322	1	5,246
New Zealand	1	14,974	—	—
Niue	8	127,216	4	5,892
Oman	1	841	5	853
Paraguay	1	841	1	666
Philippines	1	2,498	—	—
Pitcairn Islands	1	49,961	1	1,177
Poland	6	483,327	5	6,439
Portugal	5	135,820	4	15,141
St. Christopher-Nevis	1	11,563	—	—
St. Lucia	1	11,563	—	—
St. Vincent & The Grenadines	1	11,563	—	—
San Marino	3	42,860	3	4,300
Seychelles	1	2,891	2	2,604
Singapore	8	40,178	1	1,999
Solomon Islands	1	128	—	—
South Africa	4	20,572	10	647,568
Spain	2	130,096	—	—
Sudan	1	116	—	—
Suriname	—	—	2	1,177
Sweden	1	71,370	1	1,678
Thailand	9	28,731	7	8,432
Tokelau	1	8,837	—	—
Tonga	8	56,097	7	15,115
Turkey	6	11,031	8	246,602
USSR	2	70,000	2	13,250
United States	3	9,203,410	6	970,732
Uruguay	1	145	1	37
Vatican City	1	31,360	—	—
Vietnam	2	3,469	—	—
Western Samoa	2	9,489	1	1,105
Yemen	3	4,368	1	715
81 silver, 49 gold	329 issues	2,566,8929 troy ounces	246 issues	4,904,036 troy ounces

Source: The Gold and Silver Institutes

Platinum and palladium

Platinum is one of the rarest and most precious of metals. Each year, from 70 to 80 tons of platinum reach the free world market, compared to 10,000 tons of silver and 1,000 tons of gold. Ninety-five percent of the world's supply of platinum is mined in only two countries — South Africa and the Soviet Union — and it requires eight tons of ore to yield a single ounce of platinum.

Platinum's great strength, high melting point and unique catalytic properties have made it vital to industry, and its rarity and purity have created a demand for it in the jewelry industry as well.

Much stronger than gold, 1 troy ounce of platinum can be spun into a wire two miles long. It is all but impervious to acids; it does not tarnish; and will not melt, except at extraordinary temperatures. Moreover, as a catalyst, platinum is one of those rare elements capable of triggering a chemical reaction in another substance, while remaining unchanged in the process. And, since it doesn't oxidize, platinum has been used by the National Bureau of Standards to make weights that will remain accurate forever.

Until the late 18th century, platinum was considered a nuisance. Though traces of it have been found in ancient Egyptian inlays, artisans of the time probably believed it was some form of silver. Pre-Columbian Indians forged jewelry from copper alloys, but it was the Spanish who officially reported its "discovery" in the 16th century. They found it mixed with gold and called it "platina" — little silver. Most of the time, they threw the heavy metal back into the river, to permit it to "ripen" into gold.

The only "commercial" use made of platinum at this time was in the creation of counterfeit gold pieces, which were actually platinum coated with gold. When discovered by authorities, these imitation coins were thrown into the sea.

In the early 1700s, European metallurgists began to experiment with platinum for use in industry, but the metal's high melting point — 3,216 degrees Fahrenheit — proved frustrating to them. It wasn't until 1782, when scientists developed new techniques for melting platinum, that the metal became a useful material for artisans. People became interested in platinum because it has the sheen of silver, does not tarnish, and its metallic bonding makes it stronger than gold. Scientists continued to experiment with the metal, and in the early 1800s they discovered that platinum had five related metals in its group — palladium, rhodium, iridium, osmium and ruthenium. These were sometimes known as the "exotic" metals, because of their super-rarity. Today, many of these related metals are mixed with platinum to create special alloys that resist melting in the 3,000-4,000 degree Fahrenheit temperature range.

As a jewelry metal, the platinum vogue reached its peak in the United States in the jazz age of the 1920s, the era of Jean Harlow and platinum blondes. The icy-white metal was favored for its durability and nobility. Far harder than gold, it resists the nicks and scratches of daily wear; and, unlike silver, it never has to be polished to retain its lustrous sheen.

Platinum is much stronger than gold or silver, and so it is the preferred metal for holding fine stones and weaving delicate designs. It is also heavier, and is the purest of the precious jewelry metals. Most platinum is 95 percent pure, while sterling silver is 92.5 percent, and 18-karat gold is only 75 percent.

Ironically, it was platinum's very unique physical and chemical properties that brought about its eclipse as the country's premier jewelry metal in the 1940s. When World War II began, platinum was declared a strategic metal of critical importance to the national defense, and its sale as a jewelry metal was critically limited. Because the sources of platinum are limited to only a few countries, and it would be difficult to obtain in the event of a protracted war or other national emergency, the United States maintains 453,000 ounces of it in the National Defense Stockpile, and has a current goal of increasing this amount to 1,310,000 ounces.

While the vogue for platinum jewelry in America disappeared almost half a century ago, its popularity in Japan continues to rival or exceed that of gold to this day.

Ninety percent of platinum's use is as an industrial and decorative metal. Experts say that today platinum is used in one out of five products. In catalytic converters, the platinum catalyst changes noxious auto fumes into carbon dioxide and water vapor. In 1983, platinum use in this area in the United States alone accounted for 32 percent of total worldwide fabrication demand.

Outside the United States, the British are moving toward banning leaded gasoline, and Germany and other countries are setting new air quality standard laws. In both cases, their next step is the installation of catalytic converters in automobiles, thereby opening a large market for platinum abroad.

Platinum also is essential in the manufacture of fertilizer, pacemakers, cancer-combating drugs, industrial rubies (used in lasers), high-grade optical glass, fiberglass and razorblades.

One of the most promising new areas for platinum is its use as a catalytic electrode coating in fuel cells, which are electrochemical devices that generate electricity. Fuel cells today are used in space shuttles and some military applications. Experiments with these cells are now being conducted by public utilities in New York City and Tokyo, to supply electricity to their city power grids.

Ninety-five percent of today's platinum is mined in South Africa and the Soviet Arctic, with Canada and Colombia producing most of the balance. Another potential source of the metal will be "recycled" platinum taken from catalytic converters in junked cars. The converters are removed by the wrecker and sent to a plant where the platinum is stripped off chemically. This process, which yields only a small amount of platinum per converter, promises to be an important resource for the future, because of the sheer volume of converters available for recycling.

Platinum — and its cousin palladium — have been gaining a reputation for coinage, especially as "numismatic bullion," limited mintage pieces aimed at investors. Its use in commemorative coins is also gaining.

Canada now has a series of platinum Maple Leaf coins, Australia issues its Koala platinum coins, and the Isle of Man continues to produce the Noble in a variety of weights. Mexico has issued an "unzo platino." Industry standard for platinum bullion pieces is .9995 fine, as compared to .9999 fine for gold or silver.

Bullion Coins

15

Bullion coins

Bullion coins are a popular investment — and to a growing extent, collectible — medium. But just what is a bullion coin? How is it different from any other precious metal coin?

The dictionary definition of "bullion" is "uncoined precious metal of precious metal fineness," so at first glance, the term "bullion coin" seems to be self-contradictory. For our purposes, bullion coin can be defined as a non-circulating legal tender coin intended for sale for its precious metal content rather than for face value or at a collector's premium.

However, this brings us to the even murkier world of the "Proof bullion coin," which is a collectible version of the "Uncirculated" bullion coin. Proof bullion coins are generally issued in limited mintages and at significant premiums above the precious metal value.

From the earliest days of coinage to well into the 20th century, coinage was tied to the value of the metal in which it was struck. In theory, a silver or gold coin's face value (denomination) was representative of its weight.

Since the time of the death of the Austrian empress Maria Theresia in 1780, restrikes of a 42.5 millimeter, .8333 fine silver taler dated 1780 depicting her portrait have been minted by at least 15 Mints, most of them outside Austria.

Prior to the mid 1970s legalization of gold ownership by U.S. citizens, this coin was accepted internationally, not only in Europe, but in areas of the world where a firm local coinage did not or does not now exist. In particular, these included southeastern Africa and the countries around and including Saudi Arabia.

The Maria Theresia taler, as it is called, can be found with many types of chop marks and other banker test marks, indicative of a coin which was being accepted in international trade. It was not the only coin which enjoyed this wide acceptance. However, it is by far the best known. An estimated 800 million of the coins have been struck to date.

The U.S. silver Trade dollar struck from 1873 to 1885, widely considered a bullion coin, was another example of a silver bullion coin used throughout the world for trade. The coin was intended for use in the Orient.

As recently as the mid-1960s in the United States, 90 percent silver coinage was issued for circulation; gold coinage stopped in 1933. Today, no nation on Earth issues a circulating silver or gold coin.

With a worldwide market in silver and gold where prices change daily, money can be made (and lost) in speculation. The stage was now set for government-issued bullion coins.

The Republic of South Africa in 1967 struck 50,065 pieces of a coin called the "Krugerrand." Like the 1-rand and 2-rand pieces still being struck by South Africa, the Krugerrand is composed of .917 fine gold. The gold rand had a gross weight of 3.99 grams; the Krugerrand 33.9 grams.

The Krugerrand contains a full ounce of gold where the rand contained about an eighth ounce and the 2-rand about a quarter ounce.

(As a footnote, South Africa was at the time withdrawing from circulation silver coins minted from 1923-1964 and replacing them with pure nickel coinage. An .800 fine silver 1-rand coin was being struck concurrently with the gold rand.)

Through 1969, Krugerrand annual mintages held below 50,000 pieces. In 1970, the mintage jumped to 242,000, including for the first time 10,000 Proof versions. From 1971-73, Krugerrand mintages hovered around half a million pieces, with fewer than 10,000 Proofs.

In 1974, the mintage jumped to 3,180,075 pieces. This jump, which was to be sustained for the next decade, is attributable in large part to a single act — the Aug. 14, 1974, signing by President Gerald Ford of legislation lifting a 40-year ban on the ownership of gold by United States citizens.

Intergold

Today, the gold bullion coin industry is a multi-billion-dollar-a-year business. Credit can largely be given to one organization — the International Gold Corp.

Intergold, as the International Gold Corp. was known in the marketplace until its reorganization in 1986 into the Gold Information Center, was the marketing arm of the South African Chamber of Mines, the semi-official consortium responsible for distribution of the Krugerrand.

Intergold established offices worldwide with the goal of educating the investing public about gold in general, bullion coins especially and Krugerrands specifically. The measure of Intergold's success can be seen in that during the early 1980s, the Krugerrand commanded as much as 80 percent of the world's gold bullion coin market.

But two factors in 1984-85 beyond Intergold's influence combined to bring down the Krugerrand as the undisputed

king of bullion coins. First, the price of gold stayed relatively flat and many investors shied away from tangibles. Second, and perhaps most devastatingly, the Krugerrand became identified as a symbol of South Africa's apartheid policy of racial discrimination.

Paul Kruger, for whom the Krugerrand is named and whose effigy appears on the coins' obverse, laid the foundation of apartheid government. South Africa was much in the news and the idea of political and economic sanctions to persuade South Africa to change its policy took hold popularly and in Congress.

It was perhaps inevitable that, when no fewer than 10 pieces of legislation introduced in Congress in 1985 called for some restriction on the importation of Krugerrands into the United States, the Reagan administration which had staunchly defended against sanctions finally acceded. Reagan on Oct. 1, 1985, signed an executive order banning the importation of the Krugerrand effective Oct. 11. No restrictions were placed on Krugerrands already trading within the United States.

However, the death knell had sounded. By late 1985 and early 1986, nearly every major market for the Krugerrand had been affected by government bans or banking agreements. Krugerrands are still traded by bullion coin investors, but the net effect of the prolonged debate about the morality of South Africa's policies and the destabilizing effect of months of doubt severely dulled the coin's sheen. The Royal Canadian Mint, which had introduced its .9999 fine Maple Leaf in 1979, was ready to grab the throne.

In 1984, despite growing pressures against South Africa, the Krugerrand still held about two thirds of the gold bullion coin market worldwide. By early 1986, that distinction belonged to the Maple Leaf.

The market

The bullion coin market is different from the numismatic market to which many collectors are accustomed. The bullion coin market operates in a tier system structured something like a ziggurat, with the issuing authority at the top. The issuing government produces and then distributes the coins in large quantity through a narrow system of large distributors. Distributors in turn sell to wholesalers, who sell to a network of retailers, who then sell to the public. There is, of course, nothing to prevent a distributor or wholesaler from also being a retailer.

At each step down on the ziggurat, the field widens. Let's say a government sells to 10 distributors (these numbers are simply to show how the marketing system works). Each distributor sells to 10 wholesalers, for a total of 100 wholesalers. Each wholesaler then sells to 10 retailers, for a total of 1,000 retailers.

The tiered distribution system (ziggurat) is often referred to as the "pipeline." It is the supply system to the consumer — the bullion coin investor. During a program start-up, such as with the Maple Leaf in 1979 and to a more dramatic extent the American Eagle in 1986, the period spanning the first release of the coins to the time when the pipeline is filled can often be rather turbulent.

Supply limitations can cause high premiums for a short time, but barring any sustained artificial restrictions on supply, the "open valve" effect subsides in a matter of a few months.

The ziggurat's most important function is in providing a buy-back market. Bullion coins are investments; investments must have a degree of liquidity. Governments will sell coins into the pipeline but will not buy them back.

It is the ziggurat structure which enables a ready two-way market in bullion coins. Large distributors absorb buy-backs while at the same time hedging their positions in the marketplace and hold the coins until the market turns favorable. A small dealer, such as a coin shop or local bank, would place a serious strain on its liquidity if it were compelled to buy and hold coins from an investor taking a profit. And investors would not likely purchase coins for investment that could not be resold for profit.

Legal tender

No aspect of bullion coins is quite so important nor quite so difficult to explain as legal tender status. Just what, in fact, constitutes a legal tender bullion coin is the matter of no little debate, and seems to change from nation to nation.

Legal tender status for a bullion coin distiguishes it, at least in the mind of the collector or investor, from the many privately-issued bullion pieces on the market. It is a badge of honor and legitimacy.

As an example, the American Arts Gold Medallion series of 1980-84, although issued by the United States Mint under congressional mandate, was not afforded legal tender status. The distinction between "official," which they are, and "legal tender," which they are not, may seem trivial to the point of an argument of semantics. However, the investors who were expected to purchase a minimum of a million ounces of the medallions every year stayed away in droves. The program is today largely seen as a failure.

The American Arts Gold Medallions were designed with the investor in mind, the larger piece containing 1.00 ounce of fine gold and the smaller 0.50 ounce. However, the pieces of 1980-81 have a "medal-like" appearance. Obverses are portraits of the artist with the name above the bust. Reverses show a scene reminiscent of the artist with the legend A M E R I C A N   A R T S COMMEMORATIVE SERIES and the date of issue around. The edges are plain.

In 1982 the pieces were altered to give them a more "coin-like" appearance. Reeded edges and rim beading were added. Dates were moved into the field. The legend UNITED STATES OF AMERICA was added to the obverse and ONE OUNCE GOLD or ONE HALF OUNCE GOLD was added to the reverse.

In comparison to the Krugerrand, the later American Arts Gold Medallions certainly looked like bullion coins. The

Krugerrand has a reeded edge and beading. The obverse has a portrait of Paul Kruger and SUID-AFRIKA • SOUTH AFRICA; the reverse the date, and the legends KRUGERRAND and FYN GOUD 1 OUNCE FINE GOLD around a springbok design.

Marketing attempts for the sale of the American Arts Gold Medallions included the name U.S. Gold, which was given the program by J. Aron & Co., the firm that contracted in 1983 to be the prime distributor of the U.S. Mint-produced gold medallions. The public did not respond to this marketing attempt. The Mint set up a telephone ordering system which was also unsuccessful.

Maple Leaf

The Canadians did not overlook the success of the South African Krugerrand or the failure of the American Arts Gold Medallions program. The Canadians studied the U.S. experiment and did extensive market research in the U.S. — their largest single market potential at start-up. The study showed that a legal tender status coin with reeded edges was what the public wanted.

The Royal Canadian Mint introduced its .9999 fine gold Maple Leaf in 1979 in 1-ounce, quarter-ounce and tenth-ounce sizes. The Maple Leaf is the purest gold bullion coin in the world with a fineness of .9999 gold.

Production of the Maple Leaf gold bullion coins has at times consumed over half of all the gold produced by Canadian gold mines.

In 1985 sales of the Maple Leaf reached 1.878 million ounces, an 87.4 percent increase over 1984. This amounted to a 65 percent share of the worldwide market for gold bullion investment coins in 1985. Bans on importation of the Krugerrand and other government and private sector sanctions against South Africa played a major role in driving the gold-buying public to the Maple Leaf.

In June 1986 the half-ounce Maple Leaf gold bullion coin was introduced. Denominations assigned to the coins are $50 for the 1-ounce piece, $20 for the half-ounce piece, $10 for the quarter-ounce piece and $5 for the tenth-ounce piece.

The distribution system used for the sale of the Canadian Maple Leaf gold bullion coins involves approximately 25 primary distributors selected and recognized as being actual coin marketers, those who could make a two-way market and give the coin liquidity.

To try to capture some of the silver bullion coin market dominated by the United States' American Eagle silver dollar, Canada began issuing a silver Maple Leaf, and upped the ante to include a platinum series.

American Eagle

The United States gold and silver bullion coin program began with the release of the American Eagle gold bullion coins on Oct. 20, 1986.

The gold coins are being produced in sizes and denominations of 1-ounce $50, half-ounce $25, quarter-ounce $10 and tenth-ounce $5.

The gold bullion coins consist of .917 fine gold. The 1-ounce pieces are produced with guaranteed weight planchets, each containing a full ounce of .999 fine gold. The fractional pieces are produced with average weight planchets.

Designs on the gold bullion coins include a modified Saint-Gaudens Liberty design on the obverse and the "Family of Eagles" design by Dallas sculptor Miley Busiek on the reverse.

In addition to the Uncirculated gold bullion coins, a Proof 1-ounce version was issued during a one-month sales period ending Dec. 1, 1986. The Proof coin was priced at $550.

The 1-ounce, $1 silver American Eagle bullion coin was issued with first-strike ceremonies Oct. 29, 1986. The silver coins contain 1 troy ounce of .999 fine silver. The design includes A.A. Weinman's Walking Liberty design on the obverse and the Heraldic Eagle design of John Mercanti on the reverse.

A Proof version of the silver bullion coin was offered along with the offer for the gold bullion coin at $21 each. The "S" Mint mark appears on the reverse of the Proof silver bullion coin.

In the six months after the issue of the gold bullion coins, more than 2.3 million ounces had been sold. Silver bullion coin sales topped 9 million in just six months after issue.

Bulk distributors of the gold bullion coins include 26 distributors who purchase the bullion coins from the United States Mint at a percentage over the spot price of gold. Silver bullion coin distributors number approximately 30.

The American Eagle silver bullion coins are made from silver in the National Strategic Stockpile. Authorizing legislation specified that gold for the bullion coins must come from newly mined U.S. gold, unless it is not available. The Treasury Department used gold reserves for the program start-up and purchased on the open market when available in the U.S. and from countries which are signatories to the General Agreement on Tariffs and Trade (GATT).

Other countries

Bullion coin programs exist in a number of other countries. China's gold Panda bullion coins are issued in sizes of 1-ounce, half-ounce, quarter-ounce, tenth-ounce and twentieth-ounce. The coins were first issued in 1982 with panda designs that change with each new issue. The China Pandas consist of .999 fine gold and are produced at the Shanghai and Shengyang Mints by the China Mint Company. While ostensibly bullion issues, the China Panda gold coins carry a numismatic premium due to low mintages. The coins are legal tender and carry nominal face values.

Mexican bullion coins include the .999 silver 1-ounce Libertads issued each year since 1982 (the first, dated and struck in 1982, were not released until 1984). The coins are legal tender.

The Australian gold bullion program began in 1986 with the issue of Proof Australian Nugget .9999 fine gold bullion coins in 1-ounce, half-ounce, quarter-ounce and tenth-ounce sizes. Each coin carries a depiction of a different Australian gold nugget. The 1986 coins were the first in the world to be produced in Proof .9999 fine gold. The regular issue gold bullion coins were issued in 1987. A platinum and silver series followed, called the Koala and Kookaburra, respectively.

Britain's gold bullion program was initiated in 1987 with the issue of the 1-ounce legal tender Britannia .9166 fine gold coin. Fractional issues in sizes half-ounce, quarter-ounce and tenth-ounce were scheduled to be issued later in 1987.

The Isle of Man bullion program was launched in 1983 with the issue of the 1-ounce platinum Noble. A tenth-ounce piece was issued in 1984.

The Soviet Union has even gotten into the act, launching in 1990 the palladium Ballerina ounce and half-ounce coins.

Private bullion pieces

A variety of gold and silver bullion pieces are produced by private firms. The majority of these pieces are 1-ounce .999 fine silver round or rectangular bars, often called "art bars." Some private mints produce rounds with reeded edges which have the appearance of bullion coins issued by governments. Pieces in different sizes and shapes exist, as well as similar products produced in gold. Many of these products depict artistic renderings of past coinage designs, and should not be confused with actual coinage. These pieces are neither official government bullion issues nor legal tender, and should not be confused with government bullion coin programs.

Official state bullion issues exist. California, South Dakota and Texas have issued a variety of silver and gold bullion pieces. Many of these bullion pieces are exempt from state sales taxes. The state receives a profit from the sale of these official bullion pieces.

Gold and silver bullion coins

By Michael Brown

The Gold and Silver Institutes

Suite 101, 1026 16th Street, N.W., Washington, D.C. 20036

Precious metals have been used in coinage since antiquity. Their durability, rarity and beauty have made silver and gold the most treasured of coinage metals.

Gold and silver's use in modern coinage is primarily in commemorative and bullion coins issued by many of the world's leading governments. From 1979 to 1988, more than 67 million troy ounces of gold was used to produce modern gold coinage issued by 49 nations. In the same period, more than 172 million ounces of silver was used to produce coinage from 81 nations.

Since no government today issues gold coinage for everyday circulation, gold coinage is either commemorative or bullion. Gold bullion coins — first introduced by the government of South Africa in the form of the Krugerrand — are the preferred means of holding gold for millions of investors. The price of gold bullion coins varies with the daily price of gold and they can be bought and sold around the world through organized financial markets. Unlike commemorative coins, which are marketed on the basis of the potential rarity or collector appeal, gold bullion coins are intended for consumers interested only in the intrinsic value of the gold.

Gold bullion coins are now issued by the governments of Australia, Austria, Belgium, Canada, China, Great Britain, Mexico, South Africa and the United States. The coins are issued in a variety of affordable weights (1 troy ounce and its fractions) and their purity is guaranteed by the issuing government. Unlike gold bars, gold bullion coins do not require an assay when they are bought and sold. Traditionally, a gold bullion coin is minted in quantities to meet demand and the design remains consistent from year to year.

During the 1980s the demand for gold bullion coins was influenced by the world economy and political conditions. In the period of 1979-80, the demand for gold bullion coins was high as gold prices rose due to high inflation and political turmoil. At that time, only the governments of South Africa, Mexico and Canada offered bullion coins, and their sales boomed. By the mid-1980s, other nations were eager to tap into this expanding market. American Eagle gold bullion coins were introduced in 1986 (while the importation into the United States of the Krugerrand, then the world's leading gold bullion coin, was banned for political reasons) and quickly became the world's leading gold coin. The British Britannia, Australian Nugget and other coins soon followed. Some analysts predicted a 10-million-ounce-per-year market for gold bullion coins. However, they neglected to consider other changes in the financial markets.

By the end of the 1980s, the Canadian Maple Leaf had regained market dominance from the American Eagle, in large part because of demand for the pure gold Maple Leaf in the markets of Hong Kong and Japan. There the price of gold was low because of the extraordinary strength of the local currencies. But at the same time, North American and European demand for gold bullion coins declined because of the lack of inflation in the U.S. economy and the higher returns available from equity investments. As a result, overall sales of gold bullion coins in the latter part of the 1980s declined.

Market-makers responded to this decline by repositioning bullion coins as both a bullion coin and a numismatic coin. In 1990, the Australian Nugget was reintroduced as the Kangaroo Nugget and its mintage was limited. The Chinese Panda is marketed in a similar fashion.

Canada and the United States both began to rely on their Proof issues to supplement their regular marketing programs. Many in the industry now believe that the definition of the bullion coin, as first established by the Krugerrand, is changing. In the future, gold bullion coins will most likely offer the intrinsic appeal of gold combined with a potential for collectibility.

Silver bullion coins enjoy continued success. The American Eagle silver bullion coin, a 1-ounce pure silver dollar, is the world's most popular silver coin. Similar coins are issued by the governments of Australia, Canada and Mexico. Demand for these affordable coins continues unabated. Less expensive than gold, silver bullion coins allow investors to "buy more metal for their money." Silver investment demand is centered in North America and because of the coins' low cost, there is a large gift market.

Both silver and gold coins have well-defined niches in the investment market as demonstrated by the rush to precious metals following the stock market crash of 1987. The repositioning of the coins as "numismatic bullion" and the strength of the worldwide distribution system ensures the continued presence of these two precious metals in coinage.

Specifications of select bullion coins

Australia

Nugget (Kangaroo) gold

Denomination	Fineness	Gold weight	Total weight	Diameter	Edge
$100	.9999	1.00	1.00	32.1mm	Reeded
$50	.9999	0.50	0.50	25.1mm	Reeded
$25	.9999	0.25	0.25	20.1mm	Reeded
$15	.9999	0.10	0.10	16.1mm	Reeded
$5	.9999	0.05	0.05	NA	Reeded

Koala platinum

Denomination	Fineness	Platinum weight	Total weight	Diameter	Edge
$100	.9995	1.00	1.00	32.1mm	Serrated
$50	.9995	0.50	0.50	25.1mm	Serrated
$25	.9995	0.25	0.25	20.1mm	Serrated
$15	.9995	0.10	0.10	16.1mm	Serrated

Kookaburra silver

Denomination	Fineness	Silver weight	Total weight	Diameter	Edge
$5	.999	1.00	1.00	NA	NA

Canada

Maple Leaf gold

Denomination	Fineness	Gold weight	Total weight	Diameter	Edge
$50	.9999	1.00	1.00	30.0mm	Reeded
$20	.9999	0.50	0.50	25.0mm	Reeded
$10	.9999	0.25	0.25	20.0mm	Reeded
$5	.9999	0.10	0.10	16.0mm	Reeded

Maple Leaf platinum

Denomination	Fineness	Platinum weight	Total weight	Diameter	Edge
$50	.9995	1.00	1.00	30.0mm	Reeded
$20	.9995	0.50	0.50	25.0mm	Reeded
$10	.9995	0.25	0.25	20.0mm	Reeded
$5	.9995	0.10	0.10	16.0mm	Reeded

Maple Leaf silver

Denomination	Fineness	Silver weight	Total weight	Diameter	Edge
$5	.9999	1.00	1.00	38.0mm	Reeded

China

Panda gold

Denomination	Fineness	Gold weight	Total weight	Diameter	Edge
100 yuan	.9999	1.00	1.00	32.05mm	Reeded
50 yuan	.9999	0.50	0.50	27.00mm	Reeded

25 yuan	.9999	0.25	0.25	21.95mm	Reeded
10 yuan	.9999	0.10	0.10	17.95mm	Reeded
5 yuan	.9999	0.05	0.05	13.92mm	Reeded

Great Britain

Britannia gold

Denomination	Fineness	Gold weight	Total weight	Diameter	Edge
£100	.9167	1.00	1.094	34.050mm	Reeded
£50	.9167	0.50	0.547	17.025mm	Reeded
£25	.9167	0.25	0.274	8.513mm	Reeded
£10	.9167	0.10	0.1096	3.412mm	Reeded

Isle of Man

Angel gold

Denomination	Fineness	Gold weight	Total weight	Diameter	Edge
£50	.9167	10.00	10.90	63.00mm	Reeded
£25	.9167	5.00	5.45	50.00mm	Reeded
£5	.9167	1.00	1.09	32.76mm	Reeded
£2.50	.9167	0.50	0.54	27.0mm	Reeded

Angel gold continued

Denomination	Fineness	Gold weight	Total weight	Diameter	Edge
£1.25	.9167	0.25	0.27	22.0mm	Reeded
50 pence	.9167	0.10	0.109	16.5mm	Reeded
25 pence	.9167	0.05	0.054	15.0mm	Reeded

South Africa

Krugerrand gold

Denomination	Fineness	Gold weight	Total weight	Diameter	Edge
Krugerrand	.9167	1.00	1.091	32.7mm	Reeded
Half Krugerrand	.9167	0.50	0.545	27.0mm	Reeded
Quarter Krugerrand	.9167	0.25	0.273	22.0mm	Reeded
Tenth Krugerrand	.9167	0.10	0.109	16.5mm	Reeded

Soviet Union

Ballerina palladium

Denomination	Fineness	Palladium weight	Total weight	Diameter	Edge
25 rubles	.999	1.00	1.00	37.0mm	NA
10 rubles	.999	0.50	0.50	NA	NA

United States

American Eagle gold

Denomination	Fineness	Gold weight	Total weight	Diameter	Edge
$50	.9167	1.00	1.091	32.7mm	Reeded
$25	.9167	0.50	0.545	27.0mm	Reeded
$10	.9167	0.25	0.273	22.0mm	Reeded
$5	.9167	0.10	0.109	16.5mm	Reeded

American Eagle silver

Denomination	Fineness	Silver weight	Total weight	Diameter	Edge
$1	.9999	1.00	1.00	40.6mm	Reeded

American Arts Gold Medallions

Year	Size	Portrait	Struck	Sold	Melted
1980	1-ounce	Grant Wood	500,000	312,709	187,291
	half-ounce	Marian Anderson	1,000,000	281,624	718,376
1981	1-ounce	Mark Twain	141,000	116,371	24,629
	half-ounce	Willa Cather	200,000	97,331	102,669
1982	1-ounce	Louis Armstrong	420,000	409,098	10,902
	half-ounce	Frank Lloyd Wright	360,000	348,305	11,695
1983	1-ounce	Robert Frost	500,000	390,669	109,331
	half-ounce	Alexander Calder	410,000	74,571	335,429
1984	1-ounce	Helen Hayes	**35,000	33,546	**1,454
	half-ounce	John Steinbeck	**35,000	32,572	**2,428

* The number melted is the number sold subtracted from the number struck. Number sold is in effect the final net mintage. Audited figures supplied by the United States Mint.

** The 1984 issues began with a striking of 20,000 pieces in each weight and to demand from then on, accounting for the relatively low melt figures.

Grading

16

Grading coins and paper money

Probably no other subject has been more hotly debated in American numismatists by collectors, and investors as grading. Since the dealer first charged more for one specimen of a coin than for another of the same type, date and Mint mark simply because the second had less wear than the other, there has been controversy.

What is grading and why the controversy?

The grade of a coin (note, medal or token) represents what professional numismatist and researcher Dr. Richard Bagg aptly called its "level of preservation" in a 1977 collection of readings about grading that he co-edited. The grading controversy arises both from disagreements over the grade of a coin and the often enormous differences in price between two specimens of the same type and date of a U.S. coin, even when the only difference lies in the placement of one or two marks or surface abrasions from contact with other coins, commonly referred to as "bag marks."

The grade measures the amount of wear, natural mishaps and other surface degradation a coin has received after leaving the coining press. The more wear and surface marks a coin has received, the less it is worth compared to other specimens of the same coin with less surface degradation.

However, not all coins have received circulation wear since they were struck. These coins are called Uncirculated or Mint State, and rather than being easier to grade because there are no points of wear

to determine, the coin becomes much harder to grade if it has received no wear.

A non-collector unexposed to the intricacies of grading might be expected to show surprise at this last statement. After all, he might think, it seems logicial that a coin which has received less wear is worth more than one which has received more wear. But if a coin hasn't received any wear, how can it be different from other unworn specimens of the same coin? Suffice to say, there are graduated levels of Mint State, as many as 11 (from Mint State 60 to Mint State 70), determined by such factors as contact marks, luster and depending on the grading standard being used, the strength of the strike and toning. Therein lies the heart of the controversy.

This chapter discusses the grading of U.S. coins in three parts: a background section about grading, a history of grading and written descriptions of grading levels. The chapter also discusses the grading of paper money and foreign coins, in lesser detail since there is less controversy in those areas.

Grading: What's involved?

Richard Bagg, in Grading Coins: A Collection of Readings which he co-edited in 1977 with James J. Jelinski, described the grade of a coin as its "level of preservation." It is not entirely accurate to call grading the charting of wear on a coin, since the very definition of an Uncirculated coin (also called Mint State) is "a coin which has seen no circulation" (in Official American Numismatic

Association Grading Standards for United States Coins) and a coin with "no wear" (in New Photograde: A Photographic Grading Guide for United States Coins). However, Uncirculated coins are subject to other forms of surface degradation other than circulation wear.

A coin becomes subject to external factors affecting its surface from the moment it leaves the press. The moment a coin is struck, it is pushed from the surface of the lower die. (Prior to 1836, the coin was removed manually by a nimble-fingered press operator; after the widescale mechanization of the Mint, mechanical devices have shoved or slid the newly struck coin from the die.) The coin then falls into a bin of other coins. When the coin hits the previously struck coins lying in the bin, the portion of its surface coming into contact with the other coins will probably be marred. Then, as the coins are bundled into bags for shipment to banks, the coins will scrape, scratch and bump each other.

Contact marks

The collisions between coins create a variety of surface marks called "contact marks" or "bag marks," the first factor concerning grading to be discussed. A contact mark may range in severity from a light, minor disruption of the coin's surface, to a large, heavy scrape. Generally, the bigger and heavier the coin, the larger and more unsightly the contact marks, due to the heavier weight of the coins.

The placement of contact marks plays a major role in determining at what level of Mint State a coin may be categorized. For example, marks that are clearly visible in the field of a coin, or on the cheeks, chin or forehead of a Liberty Head device, are more distracting than marks of equal severity hidden in curls of Liberty's hair or the wing feathers of the eagle found on the reverse of many U.S. coins.

The size of contact marks also plays a role in determining the proper Mint State level. Larger marks, of course, are more distracting than smaller marks. Remember,

however, that a contact mark 1 millimeter long is less distracting on a large coin such as a silver dollar (diameter of 38.1mm) than it is on a smaller coin such as a silver half dime (diameter of 15.5mm).

The number of contact marks also play a significant role in determining the proper level of a Mint State coin. A coin with numerous contact marks is less appealing to the eye than a coin with one or two distracting marks. The diameter of the coin plays a role here too. A silver dollar with five contact marks scattered across its surfaces may be judged appealing; a much smaller half dime with five contact marks may be judged less appealing, since the half dime has a smaller surface area in which the marks may lay.

Luster

Another factor involved in determining the level of Mint State and high-level circulated grades is luster. "Luster is simply the way light reflects from the microscopic flow lines of a coin," according to ANA grader/authenticator Michael Fahey in "Basic Grading," a reprint from his series of articles in the American Numismatic Association's The Numismatist. James L. Halperin, in his NCI Grading Guide, defines luster as, "The brightness of a coin which results from the way in which it reflects light."

Luster is imparted to the surfaces of a coin at the moment of striking. The immense pressures used in the coining process create flow lines, the microscopic lines that trace the paths the metal took while filling the crevices of the die that compose the designs.

A coin with full luster is generally one which has a bright, shiny surface (although toning, to be discussed later, may obscure full luster), caused by the light reflecting off the surface of the coin. If the luster has been disturbed, the light reflects from the surface of the coin differently; the coin may appear dull.

Circulation wear erases the microscopic flow lines which cause the luster. Heavy cleaning, or cleaning with a substance that removes a microscopic layer of the surface metal, will also damage the flow lines and disrupt or eliminate the luster of a coin.

A Mint State coin cannot be lackluster. At best, an Uncirculated coin without full luster can be no higher than Mint State 63 under the American Numismatic Association grading standards. However, high-level circulated coins may show small patches of luster in protected areas.

Wear vs. friction

Once a coin enters the channels of commerce, it begins to receive wear. A man reaches into his pocket to pull out some change and his fingers rub across the surfaces of the coin, creating wear. A coin is thrown into a cash register drawer where it bumps against other coins, creating more wear. A dime is used as an inpromptu screwdriver, damaging the edge and creating more wear.

The amount of wear a coin receives determines its grade among the circulated grade levels. The high points of a design are usually the first to depict wear, since they are the most exposed. Then the raised inscriptions and date depict wear, and finally, the flat fields.

Circulation wear erases design details, ultimately to the point where only the slightest design features are visible to the naked eye. The separate curls of hair tend to merge, the eagle's feathers are rubbed out and the inscriptions begin to disappear into the fields.

Coins with only the slightest hint of wear are called About Uncirculated, a term which, if studied closely, defies logic (a coin is either Uncirculated or it is not). Then, in descending order, are Extremely Fine, Very Fine, Fine, Very Good, Good, About Good, Fair (and many years ago, Poor). Some of the higher circulated grades are broken into several levels to denote, for example, an Extremely Fine coin of higher quality than another legitimate Extremely Fine coin.

Many hobbyists differentiate between circulation wear and another form of wear labeled "friction." According to Halperin in NCI Grading Guide, friction is "A disturbance which appears either on the high points of a coin or in the fields, as a result of that coin rubbing against other projections." It is often referred to as cabinet friction, a term applied to the minute wear a coin received when sliding back and forth in the drawer of a cabinet used for storage by earlier numismatists.

Friction does disturb the luster of the coin, but it should not disturb the metal underneath. If it does, the disturbance falls into the category of wear. It may be difficult for a novice to distinguish between the two. However, a close examination of the suspected friction should reveal whether the metal itself has been disturbed, and not just the surface luster.

Some grading standards permit coins with friction to be Mint State. For example, the ANA distinguishes between a coin with circulation wear and one with friction wear, permitting Mint State coins to possess small amounts of friction.

Strike

Strike is "The sharpness of detail which the coin had when it was Mint State," according to Halperin; Fahey defines it as "the evenness and fullness of metal-flow into all the crevices of a die."

The amount of pressure used to strike a coin controls the sharpness of a strike. Design elements may also affect the strike; if two large design features are centered on both sides of the same coin, there may not be enough metal to flow into every little crevice of the design, thus leaving some details weak and ill-defined

A coin with a sharp strike has sharp design details. For example, the curls of hair on Liberty's head are strong and distinct. The feathers on the eagle's wings and breast are clearly visible. All of the other design details, legends and other elements are sharp and well defined.

A coin with a weak strike has weak and ill-defined design details. It may look worn, since design details are missing from the high points of a coin. However, luster is unimpaired. Lower striking pressures may not force the metal into the deepest crevices of the die (the highest point on the coin), thus the weaker design details.

The American Numismatic Association does not take strike into consideration when determining the grade of a coin. The ANA uses a technical grading system, which considers only those factors taking place after the strike.

However, most dealers consider strike an important part of a coin's grade. An Uncirculated coin relatively free of marks and with full luster may still be placed at the lower end of the Mint State scale if it has a weak strike.

Strike does affect the value of a coin. A coin with a sharp strike will generally have a higher value than a coin with a weak strike, all other factors being equal. ANA graders acknowledge that while strike does not affect the grade under the ANA standards, it does affect the value.

Toning and color

As coins age, the original color changes in reaction to the environment. The original red of copper coins becomes brown (or green; witness the copper of the Statue of Liberty, which once had a deep copper color). Silver coins may tone into any color of the rainbow, depending on enviromental factors. Gold is a more stable metal and even when immersed in seawater for centuries, generally shows little change in tone and color.

Many years ago, toned coins, particularly silver coins, were judged unattractive. Silver coins were "dipped," placed into a chemical solution that removed the toning and restored the shiny surface by stripping away the outer surface of the silver or the dirt.

However, in the last decade in the United States, attractively toned coins are more appreciated from an aesthetic viewpoint. A silver dollar with rainbow toning may bring a considerable premium because of the its coloration. Still, coins which exhibit unattractive tarnish (a form of toning) are still considered to be lesser specimens.

Because attractively toned coins bring higher prices, some unscrupulous

individuals have devised ways of artificially toning coins. Some use the bluing materials used by gunsmiths. Others bake their coins in ovens using various substances to impart different colors.

Novices will find it difficult to judge between natural toning and artificial toning. Experience is important here. An individual who has looked at a large number of coins will find that he can determine at a glance whether the toning is natural or whether it looks "odd."

Other factors

There are other factors involved in grading that under some grading standards, do not affect the grade but may affect the value. Under such standards, those same factors affect both the grade and the value of the coin.

Among these factors are die scratches, not to be confused with "hairline" scratches. Die scratches are thin raised lines on a coin, resulting from minute scratches in the surface of the die. A hairline is a thin scratch into the surface of a coin.

A close examination of a coin's surface through a magnifying glass should indicate whether a line on a coin is raised, and thus a die scratch, or incused, making it a hairline scratch.

Hairlines tend to affect the value more than die scratches. The ANA will not lower the grade of a coin for die scratches, since the scratches took place before the striking. Other grading standards, however, will lower the grade of a coin for more extensive, distracting die scratches.

Adjustment marks are often found on older U.S. silver and gold coins. Planchets (unstruck coins) were individually weighed before striking. If found to be a little overweight, the excess gold or silver was filed away.

The striking pressures often did not obliterate the adjustment marks, which may resemble a series of parallel grooves. Under ANA standards, adjustment marks do not affect the grade, although they may affect value. Under other standards, adjustment marks may affect both the grade and the value.

Grading history

As any regular reader of letters to the editor of any numismatic publication can tell you, grading is one of the most frequent and most hotly debated issues of all. One series of letters appearing in a monthly magazine, the American Journal of Numismatics, concerning a major auction, pits the dealer, the consignor of the coins and a bidder against each other in a grading dispute. However, the series of letters did not run in a recent issue of Coin World, but in two issues of the magazine dated November and December 1868. Nothing is new under the sun.

The grading of Edward Cogan, the first full-time coin dealer in the United States, has been described by modern numismatist John W. Adams as on the "conservative end of the spectrum." Therefore, his letter to the editor of the American Journal of Numismatics published in the November 1868 issue is enlightening. Cogan had attended the Oct. 28-29, 1868, auction of the collection of J. Colvin Randall, conducted in Philadelphia by Mason & Co. It was, incidentally, Ebenezer Locke Mason's first public auction.

Cogan's first letter was critical of the grading in the auction. Among the quarter dollars, he noted that "five or six of them [were] described as Proofs, without stating that they were considerably injured by circulation." Three dimes, dated 1796, 1798 and 1800, "were much over-described," Cogan said. "In regard to the Cents, I regret to say that many of them were ridiculously over-described — in the earlier dates especially," he added.

Mason was angered by Cogan's comments, and penned a letter in response that appeared in the December AJN. He wrote that Cogan's comments were "very vague and indefinite," basically complaining that Cogan had failed to note that some coins were described accurately. Mason notes that in regards to one 1793 Flowing Hair, Chain, AMERI. cent mentioned by Cogan as bringing the low price of $1.25, the coin was cataloged as "Poor." Mason asks, "Is that coin over-described?"

Cogan, responding in a second letter, also appearing in the December issue, records a conversation he had with the consignor, J. Colvin Randall, whom he told that a 1793 cent described as Uncirculated was a "long way" from being Uncirculated. Randall replied, according to Cogan, "Why, it is Uncirculated for a 1793 cent."

Rarity and wear

What this dispute shows is that even 119 years ago, grading was a subject taken very seriously by collectors and dealers. The letters indicate that there was even less standardization concerning grading terms than there is today. There were, however, fewer grades.

A perusal of several issues of the American Journal of Numismatics in 1866-67 reveals about a half dozen grading terms in use: Good, Very Good, Fine, Very Fine, Uncirculated; in addition, Proof and nearly Proof appear.

As Cogan noted in his two letters, some catalogers in the 1860s graded not only by the amount of wear on a coin, but by its rarity. Mason even admitted that "a spot so indistinct that a microscope would scarcely make the defect observable, [on] such excessively rare coins, in this condition, were usually described as uncirculated." Mason noted that the practice of omitting mention of such wear "had been customary with all persons catalogueing collections . . . on coins very nearly unique."

The practice of grading by a combination of wear and rarity was still in force at the end of the 1870s, some 11 years after the Cogan-Mason letters. In W. Elliot Woodward's Oct. 15-16, 1879, auction, for example, a 1796 Draped Bust quarter dollar is described as "Fair for this date." In the same auction, the cataloger says a 1799 Draped Bust cent "may be fairly called very fine for date; extremely rare."

Woodward was also using a greater

number of grading terms in his auction catalogs of 1879-82: Good, Very Good, Fine, Very Fine, Nearly Uncirculated, Almost Uncirculated, Uncirculated and Brilliant Uncirculated, among others.

Beginnings of codification

It wasn't until a decade later, in the 1890s, that U.S. numismatists began to seriously consider codification of standard grading terms. Richard Bagg and James J. Jelinski cover this issue in quite some detail in their Grading Coins: A Collection of Readings. The 1977 book compiles articles from various numismatic publications, beginning with The Numismatist in February 1892.

A February 1892 article by J. Hopper is perhaps one of the earliest in a national publication concerning grading. In it, Hopper lists 12 grade levels, describing three of them: Mint Brilliant Proof, Mint Proof, Uncirculated, Extremely Fine, Very Fine, Fine, Very Good, Good, Very Fair, Fair, Poor and Very Poor.

He defines both levels of Proof as conditions; today, most numismatists consider Proof to represent a method of manufacture and not a grade, although most will recognize that not all Proofs are equal in quality. The other level he identifies are Uncirculated ("showing no abrasion or wearing . . . yet not [necessarily having] the sharp impression of the first strikes as the dies tire").

Of the lower grades, he notes that from Good and lower "are often disappointing, the terms applied misleading, until being understood, being used by dealers to describe a certain state of preservation."

In February 1913, some members of the American Numismatic Association began pressing for the ANA "to take some stand with reference to issuing some kind of statement classifying coins so that all dealers that catalogue and sell coins at auction must use the same classification."

The editor of The Numismatist, in the February 1913 issue, reprints a 1910 statement by ANA Secretary H.O. Granberg. The statement might have been written today except for the lack of any grades between Very Fine and Uncirculated. It is a concise and serious attempt to persuade dealers to ethically describe coins they are selling so that the buyer knows about any problems the coins may have. Granberg describes in detail eight levels of preservation: Proof, Uncirculated, Very Fine, Fine, Very Good, Good, Fair and Poor. Granberg recommends coins that have been cleaned should be noted as such, and suggests split grading for obverse and reverse where necessary.

In a departure from the catalogs of the latter half of the 19th century, Granberg recommends against grading a piece by its rarity. "Terms, such as "good for piece' should never be used unless the reason why is stated as well," he writes.

A decade and a half later, ANA members were still calling for standardized grades. One writer in November 1927 calls for standard classifications and notes that when he was younger, he had been cheated by a dealer who sent him an 1866 Shield 5-cent coin graded Fine but advertised as Uncirculated. ". . . I concluded this sort of establishment was too big for my schoolboy orders of three or four dollars." This statement might have been written today by a young collector.

Adding more grades

During this period, a new-old grade between Very Fine and Uncirculated was being used more often — Extremely Fine. The grade had been used before, but apparently not by everyone. The lists of grades published in the ANA's journal in the first two decades of the 20th century left a huge gap between Very Fine and Uncirculated. In 1928, a writer in The Numismatist defined Extremely Fine: "A coin which is perfect in all details of design, except that its luster is gone or else the signs of wear show on the more exposed parts. Otherwise, the coin must show details as strong as when first struck."

However, Extremely Fine did not catch on quickly. In late 1930s the first edition of Wayte Raymond's The Standard Catalogue of United States Coins and Tokens was published. The hard-cover book was the "Red Book" of its day. A writer in the November 1939 issue of The Numismatist recommends that the Standard Catalogue "be the accepted authority on the classification of coins as to their condition." The Standard Catalogue recognized seven conditions: Proof, Uncirculated, Very Fine, Fine, Very Good, Good and Fair. Very Fine is described as "From circulation, but no signs of wear," and Fine is described as "Slightest sign of wear, but still an attractive piece."

It was not until the 17th edition, published in 1954 and dated 1954-55, that the Raymond book listed Extremely Fine as a grade. It is described as "A new coin displaying only the lightest rubbing or friction on the highest parts." Very Fine is now described as "Showing only slight evidence of circulation," and the definition for Fine is basically unchanged in meaning.

By now Raymond's book had some serious competition, R.S. Yeoman's "Red Book," formally called A Guide Book of United States Coins. The 1954-55 Guide Book lists six levels of condition: Proof, Uncirculated, Very Fine, Fine, Very Good and Good. The text notes, however, that grades such as Extremely Fine and About Uncirculated "are terms frequently used to describe the degree of wear between Very Fine and Uncirculated."

Sheldon system

The greatest innovation in the grading of U.S. coins in the post-war period came, however, not in the Standard Catalogue or Guide Book, but in a book about the large cents of 1793-1814 first published in 1949. The title of that first edition is Early American Cents and its author was Dr. William H. Sheldon. Dr. Sheldon was already nationally famous, though not for his numismatic contributions. He devised a method of physically classifying three main types of human physiology: ectomorph, endomorph and mesomorph.

He is best known to numismatists, however, as the creator of the numerical system of grading, what some now call the Mint State system. In his 1949 Early American Cents (called Penny Whimsy in subsequent editions), Sheldon devised a numerical grading scale of 1-70, with 70 representing the perfect coin and 1 representing a coin in the poorest possible condition. Sheldon devised 10 basic levels of condition, several of which were broken into various sublevels; from poorest to best, Sheldon's grades were: Basal State, Fair, Very Fair, Good, Very Good, Fine, Very Fine, Extremely Fine, About Uncirculated and Mint State.

The system was designed specifically for large cents. When Sheldon first devised the system, which he called "quantitative grading of condition," an MS-70 cent was worth 70 times the value of the same variety in Basal State 1 condition. Sheldon wrote that "For at least three grades of condition, . . . there appears to be some relationship between value and conventional descriptions of condition." These levels were Fair, Good and Fine. According to Sheldon, a coin in Fair 2 condition was worth about twice a coin in Basal State 1 condition. A Good 4 coin was worth twice a Fair 2 coin. A Fine 12 coin was worth about three times a Good 4 coin.

Sheldon listed three levels of Mint State or Uncirculated: MS-60, MS-65 and MS-70.

Sheldon's system was innovative at the time, but intended strictly for the early large cents. Not long after the book was first published, changing prices made his theory of the relationship between numerical grade and value obsolete.

During the late 1950s the grade About Uncirculated began to receive greater recognition and use. However, The Standard Catalogue, which ceased publication in the 1950s, never used the AU grade. Yeoman's Guide Book did not recognize About Uncirculated until the 1978 edition, published in 1977.

In an article appearing in the May 1956 issue of The Numismatist, Loyd B. Gettys and Edward M. Catich attempted to define the line drawn between Uncirculated coins and those those which are not. In "'AU' or 'BU'" the two illustrate with photographs the high points of wear for each U.S. coin type. In a later article, the same is done for commemorative coins.

Brown and Dunn

Another major event took place in 1958 — the publishing of the first grading guide in book form. Martin R. Brown and John W. Dunn published A Guide to the Grading of United States Coins, a book known today as "Brown and Dunn." The first edition had no illustrations; in 1961, a revised edition was published containing a single photograph for each major coin type.

Brown and Dunn recognized seven grades of U.S. coins in their early editions: Good, Very Good, Fine, Very Fine, Extremely Fine, About Uncirculated and Uncirculated. The authors note that for Uncirculated coins, "there are grades." Like Sheldon who recognized three levels of Mint State, the authors recognize that not all Uncirculated coins are equal in condition. Coins which are free of marks and defects, they say, "are more desirable." The Brown and Dunn book was eventually recognized as the official grading guide of the ANA.

In the fourth edition, published in 1964, Brown and Dunn included line illustrations for each grade in each major coin type, a feature all subsequent editions have maintained.

Meanwhile, dealers began to use Sheldon's numerical system of 1-70 for other series of coins other than early large cents. Paramount International Coin Co., then with its headquarters in Ohio, is generally credited with introducing the Mint State system to Morgan silver dollars, in the late 1960s and early 1970s. Later, Paramount began "using the quantitative grading method of describing most of the lots in this sale" (May 10, 1971, mail-bid sale).

Another major movement in U.S. coin grading came in 1970 with the publication of James F. Ruddy's Photograde. Unlike the Brown and Dunn book, Ruddy used photographs instead of line illustrations. The book contains black-and-white photographs of every major coin type in each of seven circulated grade levels: About Good, Good, Very Good, Fine, Very Fine, Extremely Fine and About Uncirculated. No photographs were used for Uncirculated coins.

Ruddy's Photograde was designated in 1972 as the official grading guide of the American Numismatic Association. It would be designated as such until 1977, when the ANA took a giant step forward and published its own grading guide.

ANA grading guide

As noted, members of the ANA had been calling for an official ANA grading standards almost since it was founded in 1892. The adoption of the Brown and Dunn and Photograde volumes as official ANA grading guides proved to be temporary measures. In 1973, ANA President Virginia Culver asked dealer Abe Kosoff to attempt to standardize grading. "Our goal was to standardize grading by defining significant degrees of wear and establishing guide lines so that the various grades may be easily identified," Kosoff wrote in the introduction. "Now, after four years of effort on the part of many, there is an easy-to-use and officially approved set of standards which everyone can apply to the grading of United States coins. Now the confusion in grading caused by multiple systems and biased private opinions should be eliminated."

The 1977 edition of The Official ANA Grading Standards for United States Coins, visually, appears to be a combination of Brown and Dunn, using line illustrations, and the Sheldon system, using a 1-70 numerical system. The first edition recognized three levels of Mint State (MS-60, MS-65 and MS-70). The circulated levels recognized were Choice About Uncirculated 55, AU-50, Choice Extremely Fine 45, EF-40, Choice Very Fine 30, VF-20, Fine 12, Very Good 8,

Good 4 and About Good 3.

Two second editions were published, both with line illustrations. The first, published in hard-cover in 1981, recognized two additional levels of Mint State: MS-67 and MS-63. A revised second edition, was published in soft-cover in 1984.

A new, third edition of the ANA grading guide was published in April 1987. The new ANA guide eliminates the line illustrations and substitutes black-and-white photographs. It also recognizes changes made by the ANA Board of Governors in June 1986.

During the mid- to late-1970s, numismatic organizations began grading coins for a fee, providing a certificate. The International Numismatic Society Authentication Bureau began grading coins in December 1976, several months after it began authenticating coins. The INS is based in Washington, D.C.

Probably what is the major step taken by the ANA concerning grading began March 1, 1979, when the ANA Certification Service began grading coins for a fee and providing third-party certificates noting a grading opinion. ANACS was founded June 22, 1972, to provide third-party opinions concerning the authenticity of a coin. Staff members would examine coins to determine whether they were genuine, counterfeit or altered.

The decision to begin grading coins for a fee was a revolution for ANA, and a controversial revolution at that. Many collectors welcomed what they called independent, non-biased grading opinions. Others, including dealers, questioned the grading ability and experience of the ANACS personnel doing the grading.

As ANACS began grading more and more coins, it soon became a profit center for the association. Some dealers began trading exclusively in ANACS-graded materials. The ANA Board of Governors expanded the number of Uncirculated grades from the three found in the first edition of the ANA grading guide to five, recognizing the intermediate grades of MS-67 and MS-63.

ANACS began receiving competition from other third-party graders. Private grading companies were formed, although ANACS continued to lead the pack of third-party grading services. Until early 1986, that is.

In February 1986, a group of dealers formed the Professional Coin Grading Service. Like ANACS, the PCGS used a modified version of William Sheldon's 1-70 scale, with a major change. Now, instead of three or five levels of Mint State, PCGS used 11 levels: MS-60, -61, -62, -63, -64, -65, -66, -67, -68, -69 and -70. Many collectors, and some dealers, were outraged. No one, they claimed, could consistently and accurately distinguish between single levels of Mint State. No matter. PCGS rapidly overtook ANACS to become the largest (by volume) third-party grading service.

In June 1986, the ANA Board of Governors, faced with a loss of revenue by the channeling of coins to PCGS that once would have been sent to ANACS, recognized all 11 levels of Mint State, plus About Uncirculated 58, and authorized their use by ANACS. The ANA Board of Governors stipulated, however, that ANA authenticator-graders, could not use the intermediate levels of MS-61, -62, -64, -66, -68 and -69 until a specimen of a specific coin in that grade was purchased and placed into the ANACS reference grading set. That decision was modified in February 1987 when the ANA Board voted to permit the use of representative grading sets based on general design types, not specific design types. A portrait coin in a specific grade, for example, may now be used to grade various portrait coins. For example, a Seated Liberty half dollar might be used to grade all denominations of Seated Liberty coinage once a specimen is located.

Encapsulated coins

Perhaps even more far-reaching — and controversial — than defining grading standards was the introduction of the encapsulated coin, or "slab." An encapsulated coin is one that, after having been graded, is encased in a permanently-sealed rigid plastic holder, together with documentation of grade and authenticity. These holders are generally rectangular, hence "slab."

The implication is that encapsulating a coin "freezes" its condition at the time of its being graded. This, in turn, raises the confidence of the buyer, since he can be assured that the coin inside the slab is as it is described in the documentation.

More than any other single factor, the slab allows non-experts to buy investment-type coins with a higher degree of confidence than ever before. Slabbed coins are aimed directly at these non-expert investors. Many dealers profess to trading these coins "sight-unseen," that is, they will quote a price based on the description assigned by the grading service, rather than on a first-hand examination of the actual specimen.

The Professional Coin Grading Service introduced encapsulation in February 1986 as a "solution" to the grading controversy. Following suit in short order were the commercial grading services Numismatic Guaranty Corporation of America and Numismatic Certification Institute. INSAB and ANACS followed in 1989 and 1990.

What PCGS first touted as a "solution" has brought with it its own set of problems. The controversy over standards and consistency remains. The slab of one service is not necessarily equal to that from another. Certain services maintain a premium over others based on reputation of strictness or consistency. On some coin show bourses, it is possible to hear the distinctive crack of plastic slabs being broken open so that the coins inside can be resubmitted in hopes of getting a more favorable grade.

Computer grading

Consistency of grading is the next battleground, and it promises to be a high-tech one. As personal computers become increasingly sophisticated — packing the power of a room-sized mainframe into a box that can sit on a desk — it has been touted as the new "solution" to the grading

problem.

Marrying the computer with high-resolution video imaging systems, artificial intelligence "expert" software, and a database of codified grading standards, the race is on to establish the new definitive grading service.

At the Long Beach Numismatic, Philatelic and Baseball Card Exposition in California May 31-June 3, 1990, PCGS demonstrated its "ExpΣrt" grading system. The system quantifies surface marks, strike, luster, eye appeal, toning and color, mirror finish and other conditions, according to PCGS officials. At the time of the demonstration, the system could analyze only Morgan dollars. At the demonstration, one coin was graded twice, and each time earned the grade of Mint State 63.46. PCGS officials say that the final grade will be rounded to a whole number.

At about the same time, CompuGrade, a New Orleans numismatic research and development company, announced its computerized system, which was hoped to be on-line either by CompuGrade or by licensing to other gfrading services, by late in the year.

Amos Press Inc., Sidney, Ohio, has been developing with Battelle Memorial Institute in Columbus, Ohio, a computerized coin analysis system.

As this book was going to press in June 1990, the American Numismatic Association had just acted to enter an agreement to sell ANACS to Amos Press, parent company of Coin World. ANA officials stated at the time that they were increasingly facing a dilemma of running a non-profit organization that relied so heavily on a profit-making division. It is the ANA's intention to focus on education and consumer protection, while retaining the right to authenticate — but not grade — coins. Part of the concern of the ANA was the expense involved in developing a computerized grading system to compete with the orther services.

Amos Press had been developing a computerized coin analysis system before the purchase of ANACS. Articles published in Coin World indicating that ANA officials had been exploring the option of selling the grading service led Amos Press officials to inquire about the service, and the transaction happened very quickly. Amos Press officials said that the grading service would be operated as a wholly-owned subsidiary of Amos Press, and that it would not be connected to Coin World.

Grading U.S. coins

The following guides are not presented as grading systems, but as introductions to the terminology of grading and its usage.

A few words regarding grading usage. When two grades are linked together by a virgule — as in Mint State 65/63 — it means that the coin has two grades; the first grade represents the obverse and the second, the reverse. When two grades are linked by a hyphen — as in Mint State 65-63 — it means that the grade for both sides is indeterminate and lies somewhere between the two grades given. Sometimes, a combination of both usages will appear, as in MS-60/60-63, meaning the obverse grades MS-60 and the reverse somewhere between MS-60 and -63.

Plus signs are used by many to indicate a coin slightly better than the numerical graded indicated, but not as good as the next numerical grade. A coin graded MS-60+ is better than an MS-60 coin, but not as good as an MS-63 coin.

Many dealers and collectors use adjectives instead of numerals, or combine adjectives and numerals when speaking about Mint State coins. A superb or superb gem coin is generally MS-67, and a gem coin is usually MS-65. Some dealers use choice to describe an MS-63 coin, and others use choice for an MS-65 coin. Mint State 60 coins are generally refered to as Uncirculated or Brilliant Uncirculated; sometimes an MS-60 coin is called typical Uncirculated. Collectors should determine what adjectival "system" the dealer uses when no numerals are present because of the disagreement over what the adjectives represent numerically.

Buyers should remember that different dealers use different systems.

Grading guide

Proof: Many persons in the hobby maintain that Proof represents a method of manufacture only, and not a grade; this is the traditional belief, held by most. However, others believe that since numerals are often assigned to Proof coins, there are different qualities of Proof coins; in effect, different grades. A circulated Proof is often called an "impaired Proof." Proof is rarely abbreviated, and never in Coin World articles.

Brilliant Proof coins are struck on highly--polished planchets, using slower, high-pressure presses; coins are struck two or more times to bring up greater detail in the design.

Mint State and Uncirculated: The two terms are used interchangably to describe a coin which has no wear. Mint State is most often used with numerals.

The numerical Mint State system so widely used in the current rare coin market is based on a system created by Dr. William H. Sheldon for the U.S. large cents of 1793-1814. When the numerical system began to spread to other series, three levels of Mint State were used: Mint State 60, for an Uncirculated coin of average luster, strike and marks; MS-65, an Uncirculated coin of above average quality; and MS-70, a perfect coin as regards luster, strike and marks.

As prices of rare coins began to rise in the later years of the 1970s, dealers began paying more for certain Mint State coins than for others; the price range between an MS-60 coin and an MS-65 coin grew. To account for the rising prices, two additional levels of

Mint State were created: MS-63, for a coin located between MS-60 and MS-65; and MS-67, for a coin better than MS-65, but not perfect.

In the mid-1980s, the price gap between MS-63 and MS-65 grew. Coins that were superior MS-63 specimens were bringing better prices than an "average" MS-63 coin, but still less than an MS-65 coin. Thus was born the MS-64 grade, first used for Morgan and Peace silver dollars. An earlier supporter of MS-64 was the National Silver Dollar Roundtable, an organization of dealers specializing in silver dollars.

In February 1986, the Professional Coin Grading Service, a private grading service comprising rare coin dealers, began operations. The company adopted an 11-point Mint State grading system for all series of U.S. coins: MS-60, -61, -62, -63, -64, -65, -66, -67, -68, -69 and -70. Within a few months, the private firm became the largest coin grading service in the United States. The American Numismatic Association, which had previously been the largest grading service, became second by volume of coins submitted for grading.

The ANA Board of Governors recognized all 11 levels of Mint State in June 1986, but stipulated that ANACS could not use the new intermediate grade levels until reference grading sets containing the coins were built. The ANA did not codify the 11 levels until the April 1987 publication of the third edition of its Official ANA Grading Standards for United States Coins.

The descriptions were written by Kenneth E. Bressett, director of education for the ANA. The following descriptions reprinted here are published with the permission of the ANA:

MS-70: The perfect coin. Has very attractive full original luster of the highest quality for the date and Mint. No contact marks are visible under magnification. There are absolutely no hairlines or scuff marks. Attractive and outstanding eye appeal. Copper coins must be bright with full original color and blazing luster.

MS-69: Must have very attractive full original luster for the date and Mint, with no more than two small non-detracting contact marks. Absolutely no hairlines or scuff marks can be seen. Attractive with exceptional eye appeal. Copper coins must be bright with full original color and blazing luster.

MS-68: Attractive full original luster for date and Mint, with no more than four light scattered contact marks. No hairlines or scuff marks show. Exceptional eye appeal. Copper coins must have lusterous original color.

MS-67: Has full original luster for date and Mint. May have three or four very small contact marks and one more noticeable but not detracting mark. On comparable coins, one or two small single hairlines may show under magnification or one or two partially hidden scuff marks may be present. Eye appeal is exceptional. Copper coins have lusterous original color.

MS-66: Must have above average quality full original Mint luster, with no more than two or three noticeable contact marks. A few very light scuffmarks showing on frosted surfaces or in the field. The eye appeal must be above average for the date and Mint. Copper coins display full original color and tone.

MS-65: Shows attractive average quality of luster for the type. A few small scattered contact marks or two larger marks may be present, and one or two small patches of hairlines may show under magnification. Noticeable scuff marks may show on the high points of the design. Overall quality is above average and overall eye appeal is very pleasing. Copper coins must have full original color and tone.

MS-64: Full average luster for the type is necessary. Several small contact marks in groups, as well as one or two heavy marks may be present. One or two small patches of hairlines may show under low magnification. Noticeable scuff marks might be seen throughout the design or in the field. Average overall quality with a pleasing eye appeal. Copper coins may be slightly dull but show original color.

MS-63: Mint luster may be slighly impaired. Numerous small contact marks, and a few scattered heavy marks may be seen. Small hairlines are visible without magnification. Several detracting scuff marks may be present throughout the design or in the fields. The general quality is slightly below average, but overall the coin is rather attractive. Copper pieces will retain parts of the original color.

MS-62: An impaired or dull luster may be evident. Clusters of small marks are seen throughout with a few large marks or nicks in the prime focal areas. Hairlines may be very noticeable. Large unattractive scuff marks might be seen on major features, and the quality may be noticeably below average. Overall eye appeal is generally acceptable. Copper coins will show a diminished color and tone.

MS-61: Mint luster may be diminished or noticeably impaired, and the surface has clusters of large and small contact marks throughout. Hairlines could be very noticeable. Scuff marks may show as unattractive patches on large areas or major features. Small rim nicks may show, and the quality may be noticeably poor. Eye appeal is quite unattractive. Copper pieces will be generally dark and possibly spotted.

MS-60: Unattractive, dull or washed-out Mint luster may mark this coin. There may be many ugly or large contact marks, or damage spots, but absolutely no trace of wear. There could be heavy concentrations of hairlines, or unattractive large areas of scuff marks. Rim nicks may be present, and eye appeal is very poor. Copper coins may be dark, dull and spotted.

Uncirculated is usually abbreviated as Unc.; it often appears as Brilliant Uncirculated, abbreviated as BU. Sometimes used with numerals, generally as Unc. 60, and so on. Some dealers use a plus sign to indicate a coin better than one level of Mint State, but not as good as the next level.

About Uncirculated: This is a coin with only the barest traces of wear on the high points of the design. It is abbreviated AU and often appears with numerals as AU-50, AU-55 and AU-58. The term has gained acceptance despite seeming inconsistency. Some people in the hobby still say that no coin can be About Uncirculated — it is either Uncirculated or it's not. Some use Almost Uncirculated, although all three U.S. grading guides use About.

The AU-58 grade has been described as an MS-63 coin with just the slightest hint of wear. It should have fewer contact marks than lower level Mint State coins: MS-60, MS-61 and MS-62.

Extremely Fine: Light overall wear on highest points, but with all design elements sharp and clear distinguishes this grade. It is abbreviated by most hobbyists as EF, although a few use XF. It appears with numerals as EF-40 and EF-45.

Very Fine: The coin has light to moderate even wear on surface and high points of design. Abbreviated VF, it appears with numerals as VF-20 and VF-30. Infrequently used are VF-25 and VF-35.

Fine: The wear is considerable although the entire design is still strong and visible. It is not abbreviated unless with numeral as in F-12.

Very Good: The design and surface are well worn, main features are clear but flat. Abbreviated as VG, it is used with numeral as VG-8. Infrequently used is VG-10.

Good: Design and surface are heavily worn, with some details weak and many details flat. It is abbreviated only when used with numeral, G-4; infrequently used is G-6. Ironically, a coin in Good condition is not a "good" coin to collect; a Good coin is generally the lowest collectible grade.

About Good: The design is heavily worn with surface fading into rim, many details weak or missing. Abbreviated as AG, it is used with a numeral as AG-3. Few coins are collectible in About Good condition. Dealers also use the terms Fair and Fair 3 to describe a coin in this state of preservation.

Grading ancient and foreign coins

The grading of foreign and ancient coins is described differently from those of the United States, as is paper money. The terms are similar to those used with coins of the United States; however, the Sheldon system is not to be considered as a single standard for universal numismatic usage. It does find wide use with Canadian coins, however.

Ancient coins

Ancient coins are graded in a different set of terminology from modern foreign coins. The grading which is outlined in David Sear's books Greek Coins and Their Values, Roman Coins and Their Values and Byzantine Coins and their Values is generally accepted as the guideline for this field by collectors, dealers and numismatists in countries all over the world.

It should be kept in mind by readers that the opinion and interpretation of these grades may vary from dealer to dealer.

Fleur-de-Coin: It is considered to be synonymous with the U.S. coin term "Mint State." The coin is as it was struck, without wear. This does not mean that a weakly struck coin does not fall into this catagory. Such a piece is still "as struck." A coin is not considered to be FDC if it has surface problems such as corrosion, pitting or scratches. Patina is not considered a reason to treat an ancient coin as less than FDC. Original Mint luster on ancient coins is quite rare and not necessarily expected on coins in this grade.

Superb: This grade has caused much confusion in recent years due to its use by various auction houses to mean either of two things. Sear originally identified it as the French word which translated to mean Extremely Fine. Many of the most important auction houses in both the United States and abroad have been utilizing it separately from EF within their catalogs, as a grade where a coin does not exhibit wear, but is less than perfect "as struck." When used separately from EF, Superb is better than EF, but less than a perfect FDC.

Extremely Fine: In ancient coins, the EF designation is given to coins which have only very minor wear, and only on the high points of detail. All original detail is still sharp and clear beyond these high points. If these were modern U.S. coins, they would grade About Uncirculated.

Very Fine: This designates a coin where design is still in sharp relief; however, more progressive wear has begun. If a portrait is depicted, fillets between individual hairs begin to disappear. This is still a coin with great detail, which a collector would be proud to possess.

Fine: Advancing wear, particularly in the raised areas of design and loss of much detail, are present in the Fine grade. The coin must still have significant detail on surfaces, and not be worn smooth, leaving, as an example, only the profile of a personification's bust. Edges of designs are still sharp and all coin inscriptions are completely legible to the degree which they existed when struck.

Fair: Heavy wear may now leave only the outline of former designs. All details have been worn to blend into the remaining design. Flattening along the edges has taken portions of border lettering. Other surface problems may exist.

Mediocre: The coin is able to be identified, with some of the design still recognizable. Inscriptions may no longer be readable in their entirety.

Poor: The coin may appear to be as if dredged from a river bed, or have heavy corrosion from perhaps burial. It may or may not have enough detail to be identified.

World coins

Grading standards for modern world coins lack any definitive studies which are accepted to be the guide to the terms to be used. This dilemma surfaces especially within auctions and fixed-price sales of foreign coins within the United States, where dealers who attempt to adopt standards used on U.S. coins find themselves grading drastically more liberally than for the same coins when offered by their foreign counterparts.

Some have attempted to define grading terms for foreign coins in such texts as World Coin Catalogue by Simon and Schuster and Standard Catalog of World Coins by Krause Publications. On the other hand such popular books as Fell's International Coin Book and Current Coins of the World by Richard Yeoman avoid the subject entirely.

The most satisfactory way to approach the terminology is to examine how coins are described when sold by coin dealers in the countries from which they originate.

The following list of terms was compiled based on terms accepted by the well-known firms of: B.A. Seaby Ltd., London; Spink & Son Ltd., London; Schweizerischer Bankverein, Basel, Switzerland; Bank Leu, Zurich, Switzerland; Munzen und Medaillen A.G., Basel, Switzerland; Dr. Busso Peus Nachf. Munzhandlung, Frankfurt-am-Main, West Germany; Emporium Hamburg, Hamburg, West Germany; and Jacques Schulman B.V., Amsterdam, the Netherlands.

Proof: Proof coins are struck on highly-polished planchets, using slower, high-pressure presses. The coins are struck more than once to bring up greater detail on the coin.

Proof-like: Not to be confused with the U.S. term prooflike, this is a quality of choice Uncirculated coins, not business strikes, whose surfaces are not as bright as those of Proofs. These are struck using selected dies and planchets and on slower moving presses than for circulation strikes. These are not highly polished.

Fleur-de-Coin and Uncirculated: Two terms used interchangably to describe a coin which is "as struck" — without wear. Further adjectives may be used to note contact marks and other problems.

Extremely Fine: Commonly misunderstood by U.S. coin dealers, this grade describes a coin with only the highest points showing wear. The grade About Uncirculated is only used on U.S. and on Canadian coins. A foreign EF coin equates to an AU coin, as described generally for U.S. coins.

Very Fine: Light to moderate wear appears on the surfaces of the coin. All design elements are still visible, yet beyond the point of EF wear.

Fine: The wear becomes more considerable, with high points of the coin possibly gone. Still quite attractive, with the entire design strong and visible.

Very Good: Design and surface show much wear; however, the coin is quite identifiable and all legends are readable. Denticles, if present, and the rim are becoming flat.

Good: Heavy wear may leave just the outline of the designs. Legends must still be readable; however, denticles will be flat.

Grading U.S. paper money

A formal, hobby-wide grading system for U.S. paper money is non-existent. Two individuals attempted to establish a set of "guidelines" for the grading of U.S. paper money during the 1960s, and Guy A. Cruse created a system in 1970. Herbert J. Kwart published a 44-page pamphlet, United States Paper Money Grading Standard, in June 1984, using a numerical system. The earlier systems apparently never achieved widespread acceptance, and Kwart's system has not caught on.

Paper money grading standards in print before Kwart's had basically consisted of those used in three catalogs. Gene Hessler's The Comprehensive Catalog of U.S. Paper Money lists notes in three conditions — New, Extra Fine and Fine — and describes six, including Very Fine, Very Good and Good in addition. Paper Money of the United States, by Robert Friedberg, lists three grades — New or Uncirculated, Very Fine and Very Good — plus describes Fine. Krause Publications' Standard Catalog of United States Paper Money lists three grades — Crisp Uncirculated, Extremely Fine and Fine — but does not define them.

Minor differences in opinion among the authors of the books are apparent. Hessler writes that notes in Very Good condition "are usually not desirable unless the notes are very rare or extremely scarce," but Friedberg prices most large-sized notes in Very Good. The Krause catalog assumes that readers know what the three grades it uses represent, for it does not describe them.

The following guide is an introduction to the grading of paper money, but is not meant to serve as a grading system.

New and Uncirculated: Both terms are interchangable, and often preceded by Crisp. A New note cannot show any folds, creases or tears, but may show bank teller handling, including pinholes. Notes that have the image well-centered on each side and even margins bring a premium over more typical notes. A Crisp Uncirculated note is abbreviated CU.

Extremely Fine: A note in this condition must retain crispness, but may have a light center fold or light corner fold. Tears and major stains are not permitted. Abbreviated as EF, or sometimes as XF.

Very Fine: Some crispness must remain, but a note in Very Fine condition is permitted two to four folds and corner creases. A Very Fine note has seen moderate circulation, but is still attractive to the eye and touch. Several small stains or one larger stain are permitted, but should not detract from the general appearance of the note. No tears are permitted.

Fine: Horizontal and vertical folds and creases are well defined. Most of the crispness is gone from a Fine note, and some limpness may be noticeable. A Fine note has seen considerable circulation and may have a minor tear or two. It may have some larger, more noticeable stains detracting from the note's general appearance.

Very Good: Well worn, with considerable folding and limpness. Note may be dirty, but not filthy. The print may have worn away along the heavy creases.

Good: Note is ragged and dirty, and may have holes, large tears, missing corners and considerable wear and damage.

Coins as Investments
17

Coins as investments

Previous editions of the *Coin World Alamanc* have used this chapter to offer Trends of United States coins and sometimes of other countries. However, developments since the last edition have caused the editors to rethink this use of these pages. One factor is that the market tends to move quite quickly, and the shelf life of this *Almanac* quickly outstrips any meaningful representation of values contained herein.

Trends is a regular feature of *Coin World*, the newslweekly for the entire numismatic field. Additionally, values of U.S. coins can be found in *The Coin World Guide to U.S. Coins, Prices & Value Trends*, an annual publication, and in the *Coin World Comprehensive Catalog & Encyclopedia of United States Coins*, and in other publications. Trends of Canada and other nations are published in *Coin World* periodically, and in other publications with varying degrees of regularity.

Therefore, the editors have chosen to offer the advice and experience of two numismatic investment experts: Q. David Bowers and Scott A. Travers. Both are award-winning authors in the field of coins as investments, and each can offer his unique perspective into this complex, potentially risky but potentially profitable arena. The opinions expressed in the following two essays are the authors' own; neither *Coin World* as an entity nor its employees will advise anyone on the profitability of coin investment. The following essays are intended as lessons for familiarization of the coin investment marketplace; the realities of market variables preclude any valid, specific investment direction in this format.

One other note — both authors discuss the American Numismatic Association Certification Service (ANACS). Just as this Almanac was going to press, ANA officials announced the sale of the service to Amos Press Inc. in Sidney, Ohio.

——*Editor*

By Q. David Bowers

Q. David Bowers, a regular columnist for *Coin World*, is an owner of Bowers and Merena Galleries, Wolfeboro, N.H. He has written extensively about the subject of coin investment, with his book *High Profits From Rare Coin Investment* being the most popular reference ever published on the subject. A numismatist since 1953, the author served as president of the Professional Numismatists Guild from 1977-79 and of the American Numismatic Association from 1983-85.

"The more things change, the more they are the same" — an old saying. And, perhaps this is nowhere truer than with the subject of rare coin investment. It was my privilege to write about coin investment for previous editions of the *Coin World Almanac*. Re-reading these recently, I could not help but note a comment made nine years ago:

"At any given time — including right now — it is difficult to survey the current coin market and have confidence that there are indeed many excellent values remaining — purchases with ample room for future price appreciation from an investment viewpoint."

History shows that a given $1,000 invested in choice Uncirculated United States coins in 1978 would have doubled or tripled by 1980, two years later! However, in subsequent years some prices rolled back, and today there are certain pieces which cost little more than they did back in 1980. On the other hand, many issues are worth substantially more now.

The coin hobby, of which investment plays an important part, has been likened by some to an industry. Like a chameleon, the field of coins and coin investment is always changing. Collecting rare coins is different now from what it was 10 years ago, much different from what it was 20 years earlier, and bears only a slight resemblance to the field a decade more distant. Undoubtedly, 10 years from now we'll see changes which would amaze us if we could only know of them in advance!

Having been involved in numismatics since 1953 I have had a front-row seat during the changing panorama of persons, places, things and events. And, I must say, it has been a lot of fun! I was one of the first to emphasize the investment aspect of rare coins. Indeed, a monthly investment program instituted by my firm in 1958 was the first in the coin field.

Back in 1953, or in 1963, or in any other point in time I can remember, the future was not certain. This situation is not unique to the coin market. Look at today's newspaper and survey the stock prices. Are there any good buys? On one hand you can reason that all the good buys have already been bought by people who know more than you do — and that everything is priced "just right." The more you study the situation, the more apt you are to become confused! And yet, you know that three years from now if you could look at today's paper you would find items which did very, very well in the stock market and, of course, items which did poorly.

In the meantime, millions of dollars are spent annually by people seeking advice in the stock market. This is the stuff that keeps investment newsletters in business. So it is with coins. It seems people are always willing to pay for predictions of the future. Never mind that the predictions may not turn out as hoped. Undoubtedly there was "an unforeseen reason" that a prediction did not materialize, but, of course, the person doing the predicting is not responsible.

Are there any bargains left in the coin market? After all, coin prices have risen quite sharply in recent decades. What $3,000 buys in coins this year might have cost only $500 15 years ago. So, 15 years ago there were many investment opportunities, and those fortunate enough to buy coins back then did well. But what about right now?

At any given time we have to deal with today — not yesterday. While "the good old days" are fun to think about, and while it certainly is nostalgic to look through old issues of *Coin World* to see all of the "bargains," the fact is that we now have to deal with the present — right now. I personally believe that the present offers the investor many opportunities. Indeed, the opportunities today are in my mind much better than they were in 1979-1980, a peak in the market cycle for many popular coins. This peak will be discussed later.

Future unknown

In my book *High Profits From Rare Coin Investment* I raised the question: "How high is high? How far can coin prices go?"

My answer is that the future is unknown and that no one can predict it with accuracy. As stated, millions of dollars are spent in the quest for future knowledge, but even the United States government, with enormous resources at its disposal, cannot figure out what the interest rate, employment rate or inflation rate will be even six months from now, let alone five or 10 years from now! Similarly, one cannot predict coin prices with accuracy. However, on a comparative basis it can be said with certainty that coin prices have a long, long way to go in relation to prices of rarities in other fields.

Right now many classic American rarities can be purchased for $50,000 to $100,000. During the decade of the 1980s such pieces as examples of the 1894-S dime, 1876-CC 20-cent piece, 1838-O half dollar, $4 Stellas of 1880, original 1915-S Panama-Pacific sets and other legendary properties have sold for less than $100,000. It may be significant to note that *Irises,* a painting by Van Gogh, sold for $53 million during the same decade. This is more than the total realized by the two most valuable rare coin collections ever sold, the $25 million Garrett Collection and the $20 million Norweb Collection! *Juliet's Nurse,* a painting by Turner, sold at auction for close to the figure realized for the entire Eliasberg Collection of United States gold coins ($12.4 million was realized for this collection when it was auctioned in 1982), a collection which contained one of every date and Mint mark of United States gold issue from the dollar through the double eagle!

Examples of the 1918 24-cent airmail stamp with inverted plane have sold well over $100,000, and yet 100 examples of this stamp were distributed to collectors. By contrast, there are many famous coins of which approximately 100 are in collector's hands which sell for $1,000 to $10,000 each! This is not to say that the aforementioned paintings or the famous stamp are overpriced. Rather, it merely reflects that classic numismatic items may have quite a way to go.

For the price of $5,544,000 paid a few years ago for a rather obscure painting, *Portrait of Juan de Pareja,* by artist Velasquez, one could spend a lifetime collecting United States colonial and early American coins, half cents, large cents, small cents and all issues from 2-cent pieces through silver dollars, acquire a complete or nearly complete collection, and have lots of money left over! Such an exhibition would fill a large volume of description. Are coins overpriced? You can judge for yourself.

Actually, the answer is not as simple as that. Within any given market, there are some pieces which are probably overpriced and others which are probably bargains. The object of the present article is to make you aware of how such can be identified — not to identify them specifically, but to point out such elements as coin cycles, market changes, popularity and the like. Then you can think for yourself. In any investment market — coins included — the buyer who is knowledgeable makes the greatest profits. My aim is to set you on the road to knowledge.

Days gone by

It always takes a measure of courage to buy at the current market price. It is easy to look back at catalogs published in 1953, 1958, 1962, 1974 or some other early year and determine by hindsight that the right thing to have done would have been to mortgage your house, borrow on your life insurance, and do everything else you could to put every last penny into the rare coin market. And, if you did, your stake would have multiplied many times in the years since.

Looking over a catalog I issued in 1956, I see many bargains which seem to be unbelievable: Uncirculated Indian cents of the early 1900s priced at $1.25 each (about 1/100th of today's price!), a 1931-S Uncirculated cent at $2 (described as a "fast climbing item" — climb fast it did, and now it is worth approximately 100 times that price!), Proof copper-nickel 3-cent pieces in the 1880s at $5.50 to $6.50 each (less than 1/25th of today's price!), and so on. If you had invested, say, $1,000 in such items back in 1956, today you would have approximately $100,000 in replacement value.

(Note: In this edition of the *Coin World Almanac* I use numerical grading, the ANA official grading standards scale. For now, in the 1990s, its use is widespread. In earlier editions of this work, and also earlier editions of published reference works such as *A Guide Book of United States Coins,* grading was adjectival. Because of this change, certain price comparisons may be approximate rather than precise. Further, today, in the 1990s, the Uncirculated and Proof grade categories are split into various numerical subdivisions, whereas years ago the catalogs simply listed coins as "Uncirculated" or "Proof" without any distinction being made for exceptional or inferior coins with those categories.)

Uncirculated Liberty Head 5-cent pieces at $5 were plentiful in my 1956 catalog. In 1978, when I wrote an article for an earlier edition of the *Coin World Almanac,* I noted that "the same coins are worth in the $100 range." Now that same Liberty Head 5-cent piece, if gem Uncirculated, or MS-65, would cost you the best part of $1,000!

A Proof 1880 Trade dollar at $34 was available from me in 1956. By 1978 the price had climbed to $1,500, leading me to state that "whoever purchased it in 1956 can be happy now!" Today he or she can be even happier, for the same choice Proof-65 1880 Trade dollar sells in the $12,000 to $15,000 range! Indeed, certain of the 1978 prices are now appearing to be great bargains, but to readers of *The Coin World Almanac* in 1978 all these were "fully priced." Similarly, in another early edition of this almanac, prepared in 1984, I noted that a Proof 1880 Trade dollar was then selling in the $4,000 range — but now, in 1990, the price has more than tripled!

Back in 1956 when I issued my "bargain" catalog, the coins were not bargains then. The telephone did not ring off the hook, and the mailman did not have to make five trips to my door each day. Rather, sales came in at a normal rate. No one said, "Send me 10 1880 Trade dollars at $34 each." Indeed, it was hard enough to sell even one piece to a customer! From the viewpoint of a dealer, these coins required the same effort to sell then that they do now. Each piece had to be graded, properly described and priced to be competitive.

The reason I mention this is that I do not want to imply that the days of 1956 (or any other earlier year) were times in which coins were parceled out to just a favored few, and that such "bargains" were not really available. They were available, and if you had the inclination you could have bought virtually all the coins you wanted. We are dealing with reality, not theory. Back in 1956 it would have been appropriate for me to have written an article asking, "Are prices too high?" After all, $34 was a lot of money for a Proof 1880 Trade dollar at the time, and there were probably individuals among my clients who remembered when they were available for just $5 each! I did not have the faintest dream, not the foggiest notion, that such a piece would ever sell for more than $12,000! Nor did I know that the price I was charging for an 1879 gold $4 Stella, $995, would be just 1/50th of the price it would sell for nearly 40 years later!

All of this emphasizes the fact that we must now think of the present and what opportunities it offers. The past is interesting to contemplate, but it is gone. I posit that the present offers many opportunities. While I do not expect that a Proof-65 1880 Trade dollar purchased at, say, $12,000 will be worth 100 times more 30 years from now — this would price the piece at close to $1 million — I do feel that there is ample room left for price movements among certain issues.

Price cycles

When analyzing coin investment it is important to realize that all series run in cycles. In the 1976 issue of the *Coin World Almanac* I said: "Right now gold coins are 'hot' and sell very well. At the same time, Indian cents are 'quiet' and there is no rush to buy them."

In the 1977 issue, I reported that: "Gold coins are now 'quiet' and Indian cents are more active! Perhaps in 1980 the situation will reverse itself again."

In the 1978 edition, I wrote: "Gold coins have indeed picked up in activity, particularly scarcer issues. Indian cents remain active as well. Perhaps a few years from now gold coins will become intensely active and Indian cents will become quiet once more."

In mid-1984, when I wrote my comments for the 25th anniversary edition of the *Coin World Almanac,* I noted that "gold coins are 'quiet,' with very little activity among common or bullion-type issues, especially in comparison with the activity of the recent past. Indian cents are neither active nor dormant but, rather, are somewhere in between. Moving to other series, I note that Colonial coins are very quiet. Large cents and half cents, never the scene of frenzied activity, are moderately active in keeping with interest by collectors. The same goes for Indian and Lincoln cents. United States 'type' coins are fairly quiet but seem to be stirring. These were the heroes of the 1979-1980 boom market. Commemoratives are fairly active at levels less than they were several years ago. Silver dollars are very active, 'down' from 'extremely active' a few years ago, but still a lot of buying and selling is going on. Silver dollars form a special category, for they, more than any other series, are an investment medium."

In 1987, for the last edition of the *Almanac,* I wrote: "Gold coins are very active, with great interest for common and rare coins alike. Bullion-type issues are especially popular, with interest focused on the gold American Eagles issued by the United States Mint for the first time in the autumn of 1986. Half cents and large cents are extremely active, and my own recent auctions, together with the Robinson S. Brown Jr. collection sold by Superior Galleries in 1986, have seen numerous price estimates shattered. Indian cents and Lincoln cents remain quiescent as do colonial coins, although I notice some interesting stirrings in the latter series. United States 'type' coins are very active and are a centerpiece in the market. Likewise, commemoratives are among the hottest series, in sharp contrast with the situation three years ago. Silver dollars remain active, but the market is more selective. Highly publicized issues such as an 1881-S Morgan dollar in Mint State 65 grade are down sharply from what they were as recently as a year ago, but truly scarce issues — 1879-CC, 1893-CC, 1895 Proof, 1895-S, 1896-S, being examples — are in extremely strong demand."

Today in 1990, American Eagle gold coins are no longer on the "most active" list. Commemorative coins, Morgan silver dollars, and "type" coins, especially in MS-65 or Proof-65 grades, are front row, center in investment interest. Recently in his *Coin World* "Trends" column, Keith Zaner noted that MS-65 coins have risen sharply during the past five years, while circulated coins, such as Very Fine, Extremely Fine, AU, etc. pieces, are priced for just slightly more than they were half a decade earlier.

Now in 1990 there is a great, almost overwhelming, demand for coins encapsulated ("slabbed") by PCGS, NGC, Hallmark, and ANA Cache, to mention several of the more popular services. The typical slab gives the numerical grade of a coin, such as MS-63, MS-64, or MS-65. Many investors eagerly buy coins based solely upon the numbers printed on the slabs, without regard to brilliance or toning, sharpness of strike, or aesthetic appeal. It remains to be seen whether or not premium quality coins in slabs will sell for higher prices than regular coins within the same grade categories. I will answer this in the *next* issue of the *Almanac!*

Over the years coin cycles have occurred in every series. I have seen them again and again and again — and I'll see them more in the future.

While the long-term trend of rare numismatic coins has been upward, on a short-term basis (less than five to 10 years) market activities are often subject to cycles. Prior to a study I published in February 1964, to my knowledge no one had ever written about the subject of coin cycles before. Since then numerous references have appeared in the numismatic press.

While cycles need not be of primary concern to the long-term investor who diversifies his holdings across many areas, they are nevertheless worthy of study and give the explanation of why a coin can sometimes be worth less this year than it was last year. This can be a sharp advantage so far as buying is concerned. Unquestionably, it is more advisable to buy at a low or valley in the cycle than it is at the top of a peak.

In the field of coin collecting and investing nearly every series has had its turn in the limelight. Commemorative half dollars have gone through a number of well-marked cycles over the years. United States gold coins have waxed and waned in popularity — with a huge increase in interest in value taking place during the years 1973-74, followed by a slump in 1975-76, a gathering of interest in 1977 and 1978, and new high prices in 1979-1980. I noted in 1984 that commemoratives were "fairly active at levels less than they were several years ago," but now, in 1991, the levels of years earlier have been surpassed, and commemoratives once again are breaking into new pricing ground.

During the 1940s, 1950s, 1960s rolls and Proof sets underwent many cycles. Certain type coins (different major designs of United States coinage) have faded and sharpened in interest from time to time. Early Proof sets from 1858 through 1916 have been immensely popular in one market and then have had few buyers in another. Each in its day has been the "hottest" series.

Each has had short-term cyclical characteristics in addition to long-term price growth. A typical short-term cycle in coin investment has a number of characteristics. If you check through old coin magazines and fixed-price lists you will see that certain things repeat themselves. Most coin prices can be plotted easily using standard methods of business statistics and economics.

The anatomy of a coin cycle

The performance of coin "X" is typical. It may be a roll, it may be a commemorative, it may be a type coin, it may be a foreign Proof set, it may be one of many different coins or sets which have commanded the attention of investors during the past few decades. The time span of each "stage" varies. Due to the availability of monthly publications, cycles prior to 1960 used to take longer than they do now. Beginning in 1960 *Coin World* was published on a weekly basis, a few years later *Numismatic News* and the *Coin Dealer Newsletter* joined the same publishing frequency. Still later, the *Certified Coin Dealer Newsletter* began to be published weekly. During the 1960s teletypewriter services, something formerly reserved for newspaper offices and stock brokers, became a familiar sight in many coin dealerships. In the 1980s the American Numismatic Exchange (abbreviated as ANE and familiarly known as "Annie") and other services posted bid and ask prices for certified coins via electronic transmission, and display on a computer screen. The long distance telephone has also contributed to the speed at which a cycle takes place. In today's market a cycle may occur in a matter of months or even weeks.

Stage I. The market for coin X is not particularly active. Some dealers price X for $120 each; some for $110. One dealer offers a group of 10 X for $995. At a convention, a sharp buyer who knows that a dealer has had trouble selling his large holding of X succeeds in buying 375 pieces of X for only $85 each. In various numismatic publications there are few, if any, dealers stating realistic buying prices for X. In other words, there just isn't much life to X at all.

Popular psychology being what it is, there isn't much support for X on the behalf of anyone. A dealer is apt to say "X is dead, so I am not even interested in discussing buying any for stock." A collector might say: "Why should I bother collecting items like X, there doesn't seem to be much interest in them and apparently they would be a poor investment — I don't see any buy ads and the last dealer I talked to said he couldn't care less about X."

Stage II. Some alert persons note that X is selling for $100 and $120 and has been selling at that price for quite some time, without any extensive market activity and without any increase in price. In fact, as time wears on the price weakens as dealers give discounts and special deals to move unwanted X items out of stock.

In the meantime item "Y," which is not as scarce as X but which is in a currently popular field, sells for $250. Dealers are publishing many ads offering to buy Y, and many are offering close to the $250 retail price. Item Y is hard to buy in quantities as most people owning Y are busy watching the price go up! Other investors have been watching X stagnate price-wise, decide that X is underpriced and start buying. Dealers are contacted by telephone, by letter, by personal contact in shops and at conventions, and by any other feasible means. The formerly unwanted large supply of X is now dried up!

Stage III. Having bought all of the X available at $100 and $120, collectors and investors are now willing to pay $140 or $150 and say so in print and in voice. Dealers run "wanted to buy" ads and post electronic bids for X offering $135 for all specimens submitted, knowing that a dollar or two profit awaits them for each X acquired. These "buy" notices prompt thousands of collectors and dealers and other investors to start thinking about X. After all, why is X selling for a super-bargain $150 when Y, which is not as scarce, finds a ready market at a new high price of $300.

Stage IV. X becomes a hot item! Everyone is talking about X. Everyone wants to buy X. There are not enough X to go around. The price of X rises to $200, and then to $250, and then to $300. Meanwhile, many sell their supply of Y to raise money to buy X. Y drops in value to $180.

Stage V. Those who bought X at prices from $85 to $120 each find the $300 price very attractive. Some sell. Others hold out for a higher price. The great activity in X has lessened somewhat as investors turn to other things. X advances to $305 and then to $310. Noting that the market is not rising as sharply as before, thousands of X

are now sold by many different investors and speculators. The first ones to sell realize $300 to $310 each. Some of the later ones have to be satisfied with $270, and a few are only able to get $250. At this $250 point, the supply curve intersects with the demand curve and the price stabilizes — for a while.

Stage VI. At the new $250 price very few people want to invest in X. It takes fortitude to buy on a falling market, and they have just seen the price fall from $310 down to $250. Other investors, who missed the higher profit, now sell additional X for less than $250. The market is sluggish. X is now available in quantity for $220 each. If you are in the market for a large quantity, you may be able to drive a hard bargain and buy some X for $195. A story is told of a large metropolitan convention in which the investor helped a dealer unload 243 pieces of X by offering him $185 each — an unheard of low price in the recent market. In other words, stage VI brings us back to stage I. The cycle is complete!

The preceding illustration is remarkably typical of many, many past coin price movements, particularly those of the past two or three decades. Each cycle seems to take place at a succeedingly higher plateau. In the next cycle, X will start out at $195 and may rise to a new high of $500 before settling back at, say $350.

While knowledge of earlier cycles is not particularly critical to the long-term investor (except that a knowledge of cycles will permit buying "dead" series at favorable prices and perhaps passing by "hot" coins until they settle in price somewhat), it is of vital importance to the short-term buyer. Any purchaser who keeps in mind the fact that coins are subject to cyclical variations will have little cause to worry. Anyone who takes the time to research the investment market of recent years will notice various definite cycles and will gain a valuable insight into coin price behavior. This work will pay off in being able to recognize cycles that are yet to come. There is no short-cut to this research. You will not be able to calculate cycles by reading today's advertisements, as very few advertisements mention price drops.

The cycle theory fits neatly many price movements over the years — but not all. Do you know, for example, that there was a series that was extremely "hot" over 110 years ago in the 1860s and which hasn't been on the "most active" list since then? Skeptical? Don't be. I'm speaking of medals honoring George Washington — the hottest item in the numismatic market of the 1860s.

Today in the 1980s Washington medals are the domain of the specialized collector of colonial and early American coins and are hardly in the mainstream of numismatics. Anyone buying certain expensive Washington medals in the 19th century to hold them for price increases in certain instances might still be waiting!

In 1978 in the *Coin World Almanac* I noted: "It would be difficult to foresee a boom in common day gold coins which would equal the 1973-1974 activity. The explanation for that activity was a special circumstance — tremendous interest on behalf of the public, fueled by heavy advertising from bullion firms and others not previously in professional numismatics. It is doubtful if a situation like this will recur."

Little did I know back in 1978 that a situation like that indeed would recur, except that the names of the players would be different and the circumstances contributing to the situation would involve other factors. But, the net result was that prices of gold coins far outstripped the almost unbelievable 1973-74 activity of just a few years earlier.

In 1975 and 1976 there was a general market slump. In 1977 interest gathered momentum, in 1978 it increased further, and by 1979 there was a full-scale rush toward rare coins, a frenetic activity which culminated in 1980 when coin prices reached a peak.

Coming together all at once in 1979-1980 were many factors. The price of gold bullion rose to brush the $900 per ounce mark, a historic high, providing much glittering excitement. Silver touched $50 at one point, creating so much interest that many dealers were faced with long lines of people selling the precious metal. In the process, numerous dealers made hundreds of thousands or millions of dollars' worth of profits. The logical place to spend these profits was to make a "splash" in the rare coin market — by buying scarce and rare pieces, thus driving the prices upward.

Back in 1979-1980 the stability of American dollar was called into question, especially when Arab oil interests demanded payment in gold. During the administration of President Jimmy Carter we had the reality of double-digit inflation. The oil crisis and the Organization of Petroleum Exporting Countries caused additional concern. "Tangible assets" became a new and popular investment medium, and many banks, pension funds, financial advisers and others in the world of finance became attracted to the field.

The success of coin investment became publicized. Previously, coin investment was primarily the domain of numismatists — knowledgeable collectors. During the 1979-80 period we had a great outreach to the public though advertisements in popular magazines, television programs, seminars and other ways — which brought many new investors into the fold. As the supply of scarce coins remained the same, there was no alternative but a rise in price as more and more people scrambled to spend money.

In 1984 I wrote that coin prices had drifted lower, and many issues were selling half or a third of what they brought in the top of the market. Now, in 1991, the market has strengthened immensely, and most coins, especially in higher grade levels such as MS-65 and Proof-65, are bringing more than they did during the earlier market peak. The advent of certified coins (initiated by David Hall, who founded PCGS in 1986) has brought many new investors, and "Wall Street money," into the market and has forced prices upward in many series.

The investment market today

Driven to the sidelines by the dominance of the investor in the 1980s, and by controversies concerning grading interpretations and market prices during the 1980s, the typical collector almost faded from the scene. Now, the collector, representing the true ultimate "consumer" of a coin, is coming back, especially in specialized series such as large cents, Liberty Seated coinage, patterns, etc. Except for high-grade coins, the market for which is driven by investors, I and numerous other professionals look for a healthy collector-oriented market in many series in the years to come.

What about the market for certified coins in MS-65 and other high grades. It is very active now. Price levels for many issues are such that *collectors* find better values in lower-level, lower-priced issues such as MS-60 to MS-63. Whether the prices of certified MS-65 and related coins will continue to rise is dependent upon the growth of rare coins as an investment medium, and whether or not coins continue to appeal to "Wall Street money." Beginning in 1989, several coin funds and limited partnerships were set up by Kidder Peabody & Co., Merrill Lynch, and other securities firms. If these funds and partnerships do well and reward their investors, then "you ain't seen nothin' yet." If the funds perform poorly, the edge will probably go off of high-grade certified coins and they will drop in value to a point at which collectors, rather than investors, will buy them.

Market cycles are not unique to the coin market. Earlier I observed that uncertainty is part of the game of stock investment. The stock market runs in cycles, and an entire library could be filled with studies in the subject, none of which particularly points the way clearly as to what one should do next month! The field of rare books, rare prints, art, commemorative plates and other fields of collectibles likewise show cyclical tendencies. In general, the more investors there are in a field, the sharper the cycles tend to be.

When a field is composed of pure collectors, with investment considerations nowhere to be seen, then cyclical considerations are either absent or consist only of changes, usually slight within a given short-term period, in the numbers of collectors attracted to the area.

The knowledge of coin cycles is valuable in that it helps explain certain price movements. However, cycles don't tell everything. As noted, anyone buying certain expensive Washington medals in the 19th century would have long since died of old age waiting for the next cycle peak! And, sometimes cyclical effects can be observed but not acted on. Take my example of the 1973-74 market which I viewed as a temporary phenomenon — never dreaming that the prices of a later era, 1979-80, would make certain earlier prices appear to be bargains!

Cycles can be an aid to buying and selling. If an area seems to be more popular than it should be and if prices have risen at an unnatural rate, then stop to think about it. Was the run-up in price caused by an increased number of collectors (for the collector is the ultimate "consumer" of a coin), or was it caused by investors selling to other investors, accompanied by lots of advertising promotion? If the answer is that there are more collectors, then "not to worry," as they say. However, if the price increase was fueled by promotional or strictly investment considerations with very little in the way of numismatic or collector activity, then watch out! It might indeed be the time to sell.

Conversely, a person seeking to buy will do best when the market is quiet. This was noted in my earlier illustration of a coin cycle. Now, in the early 1990s, it is a truly wonderful time to buy colonial and early American coins. Lincoln cents and Indian cents are likewise inexpensive. Scarce dates and mintmark varieties of Seated Liberty silver coins, while not inexpensive and while subject to a fair amount of interest, still are far from being "hot." It is a low or nearly low point in the cycle for such pieces, and activity seems to be at a small percentage of its potential. And yet, the rarity, numismatic considerations, romance and appeal of the coins remain. Sooner or later the activity will again build, prices will rise and anyone buying now will be in the driver's seat. In the field of paper money, the market is likewise quiet today, as it is in California fractional gold pieces and a number of other disciplines. It takes a strong-willed individual to buy against the tide, to make an investment in a market when a given series is quiet, but the historical record vividly demonstrates that such times are far and away the most profitable acquisition opportunities.

Similarly, the prices of numerous rarities, "type" coins, patterns, large-size United States paper money, and certain other series in circulated grades and in the lower ranges of Mint State grades (below MS-64) are are in many instances priced no more than they were five or more years ago. This situation may be temporary.

With whom you do business

Most of the problems I have observed in the coin investment field today have had to do with buyers who invested only for the sake of investment and who completely ignored the collecting aspect. In 1984, news accounts told of certain rare Canadian coins advertised for close to $100 each in daily newspapers, while at the same time such pieces were commonly available for about $15 in coin shops. When I was president of the American Numismatic Association (1983-85), I saw many letters from coin buyers who bought, for example, "rare" Morgan silver dollars from promotional outfits at prices many multiples of what they would have paid had they purchased from an established professional numismatist. Often such promotional offerings are overpriced or sharply overgraded, or worse, even counterfeit.

In recent times there have been many abuses in the field of financial planning. An investigation conducted by the Federal Trade Commission in 1986 revealed, for example, that naive investors were being sold Walking Liberty half dollars billed as "MS-65" for hundreds of dollars each, whereas in reality the coins were not even Mint State (Uncirculated) and were worth $10 to $15 each.

The same investigation showed, as one of many examples, a group of coins sold for $10,000 which had a true numismatic retail value of perhaps $2,000. The coins were overpriced and overgraded. In other instances, coins are properly graded and are given good numismatic descriptions, but the prices charged are significantly more than what the buyer would have paid had the sale been arranged through an established professional numismatic firm.

I recall one instance in which an investor paid $15,000 for a scarce Trade dollar, a coin that an investment adviser had purchased a few weeks earlier for $4,000. In another instance, a 1652 Massachusetts Oak Tree shilling was called "Uncirculated" and bought by an investor for $8,000. When the investor tried to sell it shortly thereafter, it realized just $2,000.

Among other writers, Kenneth E. Bressett has pinpointed many such abuses in his column published in *The Numismatist,* and Scott Travers has written books on the subject.

To avoid abuses it is always advisable in my opinion to buy from a dealer with established numismatic credentials. The fact that you are reading the *Coin World Almanac* probably means that you are somewhat familiar with coins, or have an interest in becoming so. As a start, when you pick one or more dealers be sure they are in good standing with the American Numismatic Association. If a firm is a very large one, then membership in the Professional Numismatists Guild or the International Association of Professional Numismatists indicates that the dealer has pledged not to sell counterfeit coins, has pledged to grade properly, and has subscribed to a rigid code of ethics. Also there is the protection that in the event of a dispute the organization will take fast and effective action on your behalf.

Of course, there are thousands of

smaller dealers who, because of capital requirements or length of time they may have been in business, have not been able to meet the membership requirements of the PNG or IAPN but who may be equally fine to deal with. Perhaps the best way to learn about which dealers are good and which ones are not is to join a local coin club and ask others in the hobby, particularly the old-timers. There is usually a feeling of sentiment one way or the other toward professionals in the business — and a little conversation on this point may pay you great rewards.

Quality, not quantity

For investment purposes, in my opinion, quality is preferable to quantity. I consider it better, for example, to have 10 $50 coins (representing a total investment of $500) than 50 $10 coins or 500 $1 coins. One reason for this is that the dealer's margin of profit is usually less on a more expensive coin for there is less handling. For a $50 coin a dealer will often pay $35 to $40 or so — say 70 to 80% of the purchase price. However, for a $1 coin the dealer might want to pay just 30 cents to 50 cents, because there is so much handling involved. Obviously, when time comes for you to sell your investment it is better to own a piece in which the dealer's margin of profit is less.

Another precept is to invest with the long term in view. If you buy coins today and sell them just three months from now or a year from now you are making money just for the dealer — which is fine for the dealer, but which isn't fine for you! Considering that most dealers and major auction houses operate on a margin of 20% to 25%, it is only rarely that you can buy and resell at a profit within a space of a year or so. However, if you hold coins for five to 10 years, then the dealer's margin of profit becomes less significant, and most of the profit goes into your own pocket.

Grading is another important — actually vital — consideration. When you purchase coins for investment you are faced with the uncertainty of what they will do in the

future. Will they go up in value or won't they? Of course, we both hope that they will. Why add to this the uncertainty of whether or not your coins are in the correct condition? Instead, be very sure you are buying the grade value you expect, the grade you are paying for. If you are new to numismatics, then buying coins certified by PCGS, NGC, Hallmark or ANA Cache can be an important protection, and one worth investigating.

In recent years many coins have been "treated" and "processed." Lower grade coins have been given the false appearance of "Uncirculated" or "Proof." There is a lot of money to be made by selling processed, treated and over-graded coins. Such operations prey on the bargain seeker.

An Extremely Fine 1853 Coronet cent, a coin worth, say, in the $40-50 range, if "processed" and wrongly sold as "Uncirculated" for $100 (just a fraction of the going price for true Uncirculated), is no bargain at $100. In fact, you would be overpaying by a factor of two or three! And yet it is continually amazing to see how many collectors, particularly new ones, fall into such a trap. While dealers are sometimes reluctant to discuss "processed" coins, if you want a discussion concerning this subject you can talk with the representatives of numismatic publications. Grading is a big problem. I might mention that ethical dealers do not "process" coins. Your best protection is to buy from an ethical dealer or, as noted, to investigate certified coins. Warning: There numerous certification services, some of which overgrade or practice deception; investigate the credentials and reputation of any grading service before you invest in their certified coins.

In summary, it costs no more, in fact it is infinitely cheaper in the long run (when the time comes to sell your coins) to buy properly graded coins. Otherwise you are just kidding yourself and are impairing the chances for the success of your investment. I don't mean to be negative in a discussion which perhaps should be 100% positive, but I do want to clarify this situation and make you aware of it. In many years of buying millions of dollars worth of collections I have seen large sums of money lost by collectors who are hoodwinked in this regard. "There is no Santa Claus in numismatics," Lee Hewitt (founder of the *Numismatic Scrapbook Magazine*) once wrote. This is one of my favorite quotations.

If you are uncertain about coin grading, do some "comparison shopping." The same coin advertised as "Uncirculated" at $100 and $150 can be a better buy at $150 than $100 if, for instance, the $150 coin is really Uncirculated and the $100 coin is really Extremely Fine.

Certification

In the mid-1980s, a market developed for certified coins. Some of these pieces were accompanied by fancy certificates issued by the American Numismatic Association Certification Service or by more than a dozen individual private grading services. Some were given "guaranteed grades." While the intention of the coin graders was good, the prospective buyer must remember that grading is only part of a coin's value.

Indeed, in an informational pamphlet the ANA itself noted, for example, that certain coins graded as MS-63 might have a market value of About Uncirculated 55 or less, while others graded MS-63 might be worth as much as MS-65 coins. This is because other factors intervene, such as the quality of striking, presence or absence of toning, quality of the planchet, centering and overall aesthetic appeal. Time and time again I have seen two coins, each "certified" as MS-65, bring vastly different values. In a letter to Coin World, one West Coast appraiser told of evaluating a group of MS-65 Morgan silver dollars, all of which had the correct MS-65 "technical" grade, but yet the market values ranged from $400 all the way up to $1,200.

Further, grading interpretations have changed over a period of years. In February 1986, the Board of Governors of the ANA issued an official announcement stating that numerous coins certified as MS-65 by the ANA Grading Service several years earlier were, upon recertification at the changed grading interpretations of 1986, only MS-60 to MS-63. Thus, depending on the date of an ANA certificate, one certificate may be more "valuable" or accurate than another.

In 1986 David Hall launched the Professional Coin Grading Service (PCGS). Coins encapsulated in plastic ("slabs") by this service were guaranteed to have a marketability in the grade assigned, or PCGS would refund the difference. Later, the Numismatic Guaranty Corporation of America (NGC), and Hallmark offered slabs with similar guarantees. In 1989 the ANA devised a new service, ANA Cache, a special slab. PCGS, NGC, Hallmark, and "new" ANA Cache slabs have an excellent reputation for quality. Even so, you should not buy blindly.

There have been problems with encapsulated coins. At a convention in 1987, I saw a 1910-D Indian Head gold $10 eagle which had a "guaranteed grade" of MS-63 on it. Once the coin was on the market, a "recall notice" was issued, stating that it was a typographical error, and that the coin was just barely MS-60. Similarly, around the same time it was announced that tens of thousands of dollars' worth of coins had been given erroneous grades, and that when the attention of a particular service was called to these, it was generously buying them back. The only fly in the ointment — and this situation was pointed out by Martin Paul in an advertisement in *Coin World* — is that those people buying certified coins might not know whether they have one of the "mistakes" or whether they have a properly graded one. In other instances, slabs have been counterfeited or have had lower-grade coins substituted and then resealed.

While certified and encapsulated coins issued by PCGS, NGC, Hallmark, and ANA Cache are a boon to the investor, grading is still a matter of opinion, experts can and do differ, and even when experts agree on the grade of a coin, the market value may vary because of such other aspects as toning, striking, aesthetic appeal and so on. So, don't be a slave to someone else's formulas or guarantees. As noted, think for yourself, do some comparison shopping, and be sure that what you want is in the grade you want and is priced as you want it to be.

Holistic relationship

I encourage you to have a holistic relationship with numismatics. By this I mean that the whole is worth more than the sum of the parts. A modest amount of time spent by you reading and studying coins, plus some intelligent buying, will not only reward you with a nice coin collection but should over a period of time give you much collecting enjoyment and the possibility for really super investment. Along the way, build a numismatic library. In fact, don't wait until you have bought a lot of coins. Start on your library first! If you contemplate spending $5,000 for coins, then spend at least $500 for a basic library. There is no substitute for knowledge, and a library can literally be worth its weight in gold. There are more excellent numismatic references available now than at any other time in the history of our hobby.

When contemplating an investment, consider its past price movement. This can be done by referring to old issues of *A Guide Book of United States Coins, The Coin Dealer Newsletter* and other data. If the prices seem to be unnaturally high, then beware. On the other hand, if prices are attractively low in comparison to other years, now may be a good time to buy.

Learn about grading. *Photograde* and the *Official ANA Grading Standards for United States Coins* are essential in this regard. There are probably more abuses and complaints in the field of grading than in any other in the numismatic hobby. Grading is not only important, it is absolutely essential. Don't rely upon others to do grading for you. Learn about it yourself! The examination of slabbed

coins can be very educational and will be particularly instructive in the differentiation of such finely-divided grades as MS-63, MS-64, MS-65, etc.

Learn about different dealers, their techniques and how they compare with each other. Consult with other numismatists. When buying, do comparison shopping. If you consider coins to be strictly an investment you probably will do well providing you buy the coins from an established numismatic source and differentiate between speculative coins and numismatic coins. If you consider coins to be an investment and collection combined you will do even better!

Your knowledge gained in being a collector will enable you to be more careful and more intelligent with your coin purchases. This will result in a better performance of what you buy. It might seem strange for you to read this, but the best investment performances I've ever seen in the field of numismatics have been turned in by collectors, not by investors! There may be a few exceptions, but such exceptions are occasional.

Further, the coins themselves will provide countless hours of enjoyment. Actually, with coin collecting and investment combined you can literally have your cake and eat it too. Your favorite hobby can also be your best investment!

Ten years from now, hopefully I will be writing about coin investment and will be discussing a future market. At that time we can look back on 1990 and see what happened. Between now and then there will be fortunes made in coin collecting, and there will be money lost as well. Just as in any field, some will prosper and some will not. The difference between the haves and the have-nots is summarized by one word: knowledge. In addition, right now you have the advantage of a low point in the market cycle for many series. Investigate it!

Coins as investments

By Scott A. Travers

Scott Travers is president of Scott Travers Rare Coin Galleries Inc., 599 Lexington Ave., Suite 2300, New York, N.Y. 10022. He is the author of *The Coin Collector's Survival Manual*, *Travers' Rare Coin Investment Strategy*, and *The Investor's Guide to Coin Trading*.

Over the last two decades, the rare coin marketplace has evolved from a cottage industry into a multibillion-dollar investment mecca.

Not so many years ago, an individual would walk into his or her local coin shop, plunk down a few thousand dollars and tell the proprietor: "Buy me something attractive. I don't know anything about coins." Many of those proprietors — in fact, the vast majority — were honest and conscientious and tried to help such investors acquire material tailored to the buyers' financial needs. But some would take advantage of people. To some extent, this may have been inadvertent: Through ignorance of grading standards or marketplace conditions, for example, a dealer might not have given certain investors optimum value.

For whatever reason, a troubling number of buyers *didn't* get optimum value when purchasing coins. As a consequence, the Federal Trade Commission (FTC) stepped in and charged some "boiler-room operations" — high-pressure, high-profit telephone sales centers — with false, deceptive and misleading practices in trade and in commerce. This, in turn, jarred many dealers into cleaning up their acts. In the mid-1980s, the marketplace as a whole began taking steps to put its house in order by setting up a system which would serve as an example of self-regulation at its best.

The self-regulatory process and the magic of the marketplace manifested themselves in 1986 with the establishment of the Professional Coin Grading Service (PCGS). This Irvine, California company offered a much needed service: It would certify and grade coins that were submitted for review and encapsulate them in sonically sealed, tamper-resistant hard plastic holders. Under the direction of its founder-owner, coin dealer David Hall, PCGS achieved a remarkable degree of success and revolutionized the marketplace almost overnight. The expert graders at PCGS provided investors with unprecedented reassurance regarding the grade — the level of preservation — of coins they were buying. Since grade determines price to a great extent, investors buying coins for appreciation were now better able than ever before to make educated decisions about which coins to purchase.

The introduction of PCGS certification transformed and uplifted the rare coin marketplace. It has commoditized and securitized the marketplace, and allowed the casual investor to become involved with coins as never before.

Because of the grading revolution, rare coins in a sense have been rediscovered as an investment vehicle. For all practical purposes, they've become a new investment. The real and potential abuses that plagued the market just a few years ago have abated tremendously, and when buying coins today the investor can be reasonably certain — as long as they have been independently certified by a credible, respected third-party grading service — that they are indeed of the grade represented. That, in turn, makes it easy to determine their market value.

In the 1950s and 1960s, the rare coin marketplace didn't have — and perhaps didn't need — the kind of sophistication provided today by PCGS and other top coin-grading services. Coins were either new or used. With the coin roll boom of the 1960s and the subsequent evolution of the rare coin investment marketplace in the 1970s, the need became apparent for consumer protection safeguards such as reliable third-party certification. Today, that kind of safeguard is in place, and it's giving consumers confidence they never had before.

Despite the absence of safeguards, many of the coins purchased years ago turned out to be outstanding investments. We've all heard examples of such success stories — stories of coins acquired in the 1940s, 1950s and 1960s which were sold at tremendous profits in the 1970s and 1980s. In fact, it was these successes — achieved by the knowledgeable collectors of the 1940s, 1950s and 1960s — that drew outside investors to the coin market in the first place and thus gave rise to the need for independent grading.

Consider the case of New York City lawyer Harold Bareford. Bareford began buying coins about 1940. He almost never paid more than a few hundred dollars for any coin, but he bought with great discrimination; at a time when most collectors were satisfied with less, he insisted on the very best in quality. Bareford spent a total of $40,000 putting together sets of U.S. coins. Following his death in 1978, these coins were sold at auction for a total of $3.1 million. That's 77.5 times more than he had paid for them just a generation earlier. While that's a phenomenal average, certain coins in the collection did far better than that. One of these was a specimen-quality 1827 dime: Bareford bought this coin in 1947 for $20 — and just a little over 30 years later, it sold for a spectacular $29,000.

Harold Bareford might have amassed an even more valuable collection if he hadn't decided to stop buying U.S. coins in 1955. Prices were still extremely low by present-day standards, but Bareford felt the coins were getting too expensive. That, in itself, should serve as a lesson to rare coin investors of the Nineties and beyond: Everything is relative — and while the past is prologue, no one really knows how far or in what direction the rare coin

marketplace may expand.

Harold Bareford's story, while certainly dramatic, is hardly just an isolated episode. Other outstanding coin collections — formed in years gone by at very modest cost — have also come up for auction during the last dozen years, and all have achieved vast profits for their owners.

• The Garrett Collection, sold at a series of four public auctions from 1979 to 1981, realized a total of more than $25 million. It included many coins acquired at face value from the United States Mint during the late 1800s and early 1900s, as well as great rarities purchased during that time for well under $1,000 apiece.

• The Norweb Collection, lovingly assembled by Cleveland philanthropist Emery May Norweb and her diplomat husband, Ambassador R. Henry Norweb, came up for sale in the late 1980s, a few years after these famous collectors died. At a series of three auctions in 1987 and 1988, the U.S. coins from the Norweb Collection brought a total of nearly $20 million — far in excess of what the Norwebs paid for the coins or probably ever dreamed they might be worth.

• The Eliasberg Collection of U.S. coins, largely put together during the 1940s by Baltimore numismatist Louis Eliasberg, gained nationwide publicity because of its unparalleled completeness. In 1982, the gold coins from this collection were sold at a single record-breaking auction for $12.4 million. And the sale occurred at a time when the coin market as a whole was deeply depressed!

Prologue to the grading revolution

The idiosyncrasies of today's rare coin marketplace — including the strengths and weaknesses of the various grading services — are chronicled in detail in my book *The Investor's Guide to Coin Trading*. As I demonstrate there, the marketplace was ripe for self-regulation by the mid-1980s. This became apparent to me in 1984, when my first book, *The Coin Collector's Survival Manual*, was released. Although it received high praise from critics for its consumer advocacy stance and candid revelations about the marketplace, that book was greeted less than enthusiastically by many coin dealers. They took issue with my exposure of abuses in the marketplace, and also with the fact that I set forth these abuses in a way that was understandable to consumers. To many dealers in 1984, this appeared to pose a serious threat.

To understand the climate in which those abuses arose, we have to examine the marketplace of the early 1980s. As the decade of the Eighties got under way, the rare coin market was experiencing a boom like nothing ever seen before or since. Coin dealers caught up in the precious metals frenzy of the time had bid up the prices of coins to levels that were previously unimagined. Few safeguards were in place for consumers, and an eager investment public threw money at coin "investments" that never even returned their initial outlay.

The only safeguards available to consumers of the time were those in place regarding authentication and grading by the American Numismatic Association Certification Service (ANACS), based in Colorado Springs, Colorado, and the International Numismatic Society Authentication Bureau (INSAB), based in Washington, D.C. ANACS, originally intended to provide opinions as to coins' authenticity, had started to grade coins, as well, in 1979.

Demand for ANACS grading was immediate and intense. Coins accompanied by authoritative-looking photo certificates from ANACS became almost a craze. But, before long, the bottom fell out on both ANACS and the coin market as a whole.

The greatest coin boom of our time ended abruptly on April 15, 1980, at the annual convention of the Central States Numismatic Society. Prices plummeted and soon the big boom was replaced by a prolonged market slump. As the marketplace languished, grading standards tightened — or rather, the interpretation of those grading standards tightened. By 1985, many coins with ANACS grades of Mint State-65 — grades that had been

assigned in 1980 and 1981 — no longer met the marketplace criteria for that grade. By 1985 standards, these were only Mint State-64, or possibly even Mint State-63.

In part, this reflected the coin market's response to low levels of buying activity; the fewer buyers around had become more finicky and dealers were accommodating them by providing higher quality within each grade. To a great extent, too, it represented progress in making coin grading more precise: The industry had grown more sophisticated and more conscious of the complexities and idiosyncracies of various coin series and date and mint-mark varieties, and all this translated into more accurate — and often stricter — grading.

Unfortunately, the change created a nightmare for owners of the coins that ANACS had graded years before. Under the new, stricter interpretation, these were overgraded and as a result their value was discounted in the marketplace.

The difficulty arose because ANACS, then the only major certifier of coins, had not formed a grading set of representative coins to serve as a fixed standard. PCGS did not repeat that mistake.

More protection

The Professional Coin Grading Service led the way in the grading revolution, but it's no longer all alone in the vanguard. In 1987, one of the founders of PCGS, veteran coin dealer John Albanese, organized the Numismatic Guaranty Corporation of America (NGC). This new service quickly established itself as a leader in independent certification and encapsulation of coins. NGC encapsulates coins in sonically sealed, tamper-resistant hard plastic holders with distinctive white inserts. Like PCGS-graded coins, those in NGC holders are traded extensively on a sight-unseen basis at established market levels. Also like PCGS, NGC maintains a grading set to guide its expert graders in ensuring that their standards remain consistent.

Demand for certification

Demand for ANACS grading was exceptionally feverish in the early 1980s, just as demand for PCGS and NGC grading is feverish today. This serves to underscore just how badly needed this type of service was — and still is. Once coin prices reached substantial levels, increasing numbers of buyers — and even many sellers — felt a growing need for professional, arm's-length review of their coins by an independent third-party entity which then could render an informed, widely accepted opinion as to their level of preservation. Indeed, it is surprising, given this demand, that PCGS or NGC or some similar entity hadn't been established years earlier.

The coin industry is an easy-entry, easy-exit field where dealers come and go at will. That's all the more reason for buyers to seek and get reassurance from an uninvolved third party — the kind of reassurance provided to them today by PCGS and NGC.

Even as far back as the 1950s, the difference in price between "new" and "used" coins was often substantial, and even back then the potential existed for abuse. Nor was overgrading the only kind of dubious business practice seen in the "good old days."

One such practice — a practice also curbed to a great extent today by certification — was that of bad-mouthing coins that were bought from a competitor. The scenario went something like this:

A collector would purchase a coin, take it to another dealer's shop and say, "Hey, is this worth anything? I just bought it at the coin shop down the street." Because the competing dealer had a vested interest in the outcome of the transaction, he wasn't going to say, "Yes, you should buy all your coins from that dealer; you got a wonderful deal." That dealer, seeing a potential new client, would say: "Oh, you got a terrible deal. This coin is terrible; that scratch can be measured with a ruler. Don't buy any more coins from that dealer; buy your coins from me."

That kind of vignette undoubtedly occurs less frequently today, thanks to certified coins. With NGC and PCGS grading enjoying such wide acceptance, there's little or no dispute about the grade or value of coins in these services' holders.

Investors have always been encouraged to buy coins in the very highest levels of preservation — the highest grades. Today, that means just one thing: certified coins from one of the leading services. With every passing day, the desire and demand for such coins — coins that have been independently certified — grow greater and greater. We've reached the point, in fact, where potential buyers want *every* coin certified. The King of Siam Proof set, a numismatic treasure with a long and famous pedigree — a set that really didn't *need* to be certified — *was* certified because of this obsessive market attitude.

The abuses that took place in years gone by were so commonplace, and so pervasive, that we're seeing an exaggerated response — and in some cases a kind of paranoia — on the part of investors and even some collectors. They're insisting on independent grading.

While NGC and PCGS are the two most reliable and most widely respected coin grading services today, others may well join them in the forefront of the field. The initial market acceptance has been positive, for example, for the Hallmark Grading Service Inc., based in Woburn, Massachusetts. Evidence to date suggests that its grading is reliable, consistent and conservative. And ANACS, with its encapsulated "Cache," is quickly becoming a major market force in terms of the number of coins it has certified and "slabbed." In fact, at this writing, the day is fast approaching when ANACS coins will be traded on a sight-unseen basis just like NGC and PCGS coins.

Coins and personal wealth

The coin market's performance has been tied, to a great extent, to fluctuating levels of personal wealth. When people feel good about their income — when they're making a lot of money from stocks and other investments and personal wealth is high, they tend to invest substantial sums of that money in rare coins. But when people feel buffeted financially, even if their setbacks are only paper losses, they're far less likely to invest in rare coins.

Electronic trading

The development of certified grading and coin encapsulation has transformed rare coins into virtual commodities. They're very much akin to stocks, bonds and similar securities in that they can now be traded sight-unseen at levels that are accepted throughout the marketplace.

To facilitate such trading, industry leaders established an electronic trading system called the American Numismatic Exchange (ANE, or "Annie," for short). ANE is an Atlanta-based network through which dealer members post bid and ask prices on a broad spectrum of certified coins. Sight-unseen trading is permitted on certified ("slabbed") coins from any grading service that has encapsulated more than 100,000 coins. At present, that includes just two services: PCGS and NGC. Soon, however, those two are likely to be joined by ANACS. Rebounding from its setback of the mid-1980s, ANACS began encapsulating coins in 1988 and by mid-1990 it was nearing the point where it would encapsulate its 100,000th coin. At that point, coins graded by ANACS could also be traded on ANE.

Coin-price cycles

In the first edition of my book *Rare Coin Investment Strategy*, published in 1986, I wrote that a typical coin-price cycle took about four years to complete. I explained that this cycle was basically a four-year, four-phase process. The cycle still has four phases; that's as true today as it was back in 1986. But the process no longer takes four years: Today, a typical cycle takes just 10 months — and if present trends continue, it could be compressed someday to only two or three months.

Phase 1, as explained in my book, is the acquisition phase. During this phase, the secret is to buy high-quality coins and stick with coins that seem depressed the most. Even though certain coins may be going down in price, as evidenced by minus signs in price guides, you shouldn't be afraid to buy them — as long as the prices you pay are far enough below the indicated levels in the price guides.

Phase 2 is characterized by electrifying price performance. Coins are rising in value almost continually; the market seems to have a life of its own and momentum is building. During this phase, skeptics will seek to discourage you. However, you shouldn't listen to them. You should buy high-quality coins of proven rarity and stay away from peripheral areas and off-quality coins that are often promoted as being the next to increase.

In **Phase 3**, the skeptics have turned to believers and the continuing increase in coin prices has convinced even the most pessimistic observers that the boom is real and the coin market is headed for ever-higher levels. In this phase, you should buy high-quality coins of proven rarity only in inactive areas that have performed well in the past or have solid investor bases. Phase Three is the time to sell.

In **Phase 4**, we see the market collapse. The market is overheating and experiencing burnout. This is *not* the time to sell; it's a time to take advantage of the excellent buying opportunities by purchasing high-quality coins.

One way to anticipate possible buying opportunities is to monitor the offerings of direct-mail promotion houses. These companies, which issue sales brochures at the rate of five, six, seven hundred thousand or a million pieces a month, frequently promote generic coins such as Walking Liberty half dollars, Saint-Gaudens double eagles and Morgan silver dollars in grades of Mint State-65, 64 and 63. And they make a habit of regularly promoting certain coins. I would recommend that you get on the mailing lists of several of these large retailers and find out what they're promoting. If they're promoting Mint State-63 Morgan dollars today and Mint State-63 Morgan dollars have increased in value 100 percent, common sense will tell you that the next item promoted will be something else. You might reason, "Well, they haven't promoted Saint-Gaudens double eagles in Mint State-63 for a while; I think that's the next thing to increase in value. I may want to be a trader and buy some of those." At the same time, you should check the current performance of coins you're thinking of buying. In this illustration, for example, you could review the Coin World Trends listings from recent weeks and see how well Saint-Gaudens double eagles have performed.

Each coin has a turn in the market-cycle process. Collectors and investors should never get depressed to the point where they believe that a coin, or group of coins, is a lost cause. An item will always decrease only to a point — and once it stops decreasing, it starts to increase. That's what market cycles are all about. Never say "never." Never tell yourself, "These coins are all through; they'll never come back." They *always* come back. The marketplace is like a pillow: No matter how much you punch it, it always comes back; it's just a matter of how long you need to wait.

Of course, you may conclude that a given coin investment isn't worth the wait. You may decide it would be more cost-effective to take a loss on that item, sell it and buy something else.

Market volatility

Coin certification and sight-unseen trading have given rare coins unprecedented liquidity. However, they have also given rise to much greater volatility in the marketplace — greater volatility than we've ever seen before. In part, this is because the sight-unseen network makes it easier to detect the cash-flow problems and market manipulations to which the coin industry is inherently prone.

The rare coin industry is a sensitive, delicate marketplace made up, for the most part, of thinly capitalized entrepreneurs. For this reason, marketplace movements tend to elicit exaggerated responses. If we see slight buyer resistance to certain coins, the market's extreme sensitivity often magnifies this softness and drives price levels sharply lower. Suppose, for example, that Proof Liberty Seated quarters graded Proof-65 by PCGS are trading at $6,000 apiece on the sight-unseen system and a dealer drops his bid to $5,800. Other dealers may panic and bids could soon drop to $5,000. If, on the other hand, a dealer increases his bid on a $5,000 coin to $5,200, we might see 10 or 15 dealers jump on the sight-unseen system and increase their bids within five minutes to $6,000 or $6,500.

Movements both up and down are exaggerated today by these entrepreneurs, and the coin market has been forever changed because of the sight-unseen system and this new way of doing business.

Enter Wall Street

As a direct result of independent certification and the rediscovery of coins as an investment, a number of major institutional players have become involved in rare coins in a very big way.

The Wall Street firm of Kidder, Peabody, for example, boasts that during 1989 it spent $42 million on rare coins through its private-placement American Rare Coin Fund limited partnership, managed by coin dealer Hugh J. Sconyers. The fund announced that during calendar year 1990, it planned to purchase an additional $100 million in high-quality United States coins. Another big Wall Street company, Shearson Lehman Hutton, has been buying coins on a sight-unseen basis at the wholesale level through the American Numismatic Exchange. Merrill Lynch Pierce Fenner & Smith declared its intention to sponsor a limited partnership that would invest $50 million to $75 million in rare U.S. and foreign coins. And smaller investment groups were entering the field, or poised to enter, as well. The Continental Investment Group, for example, said it would invest $40 million to $50 million in high-quality U.S. coins through limited partnerships.

If these funds really do invest such large sums in rare coins, and if this investment takes place over an extended period of time, the impact on the market will be tremendous. This influx of money will override other factors that normally play key roles in determining price levels in the coin market — factors such as inflation and bullion prices. If Merrill Lynch enters the marketplace with $75 million and Kidder, Peabody comes in with $100 million, it really doesn't matter if inflation is rampant — traditionally an important barometer of coin-market performance — or if gold and silver prices go up by 2 percent or down by 3 percent. These millions of dollars from limited partnerships and institutional investors represent enormous sums of money and their impact is likely to be immense.

Clearly, there is no guarantee as to what's going to happen in the future. These funds could become disenchanted; our marketplace, after all, is a subjective one and we certainly have a lot of idiosyncratic qualities. This is fresh money and it's really an experiment. These funds could pull out of this industry just as quickly as they've come in. With this in mind, it's important for someone investing in coins to commit just a very small portion of his or her total net worth. In fact, even with the protection of independent certification, I still recommend that anyone planning to purchase rare coins become a collector first and an investor second.

We're seeing a new breed of collector in the rare coin field — a healthy, vibrant breed. This breed is the collector/investor — the baby boomer grown up. It's made up of individuals who have educated themselves to the ways of the marketplace. And this new-style collector/investor isn't necessarily cut from the same mold as Harold Bareford or Emery May Norweb or Louis Eliasberg.

In many cases, these new-breed individuals collected coins as youngsters, when they were 14 or 15 or 16 years old, and built a solid foundation in the hobby. Then they took a hiatus from the field to pursue other interests — normal preoccupations such as college, courtship and careers. Now, they've returned to coins — often with a vengeance — with their Harvard and Chicago MBA's and very deep pockets. These baby-boomers grown up are consuming 25-and 50-thousand-dollar coins almost in the way that you and I would consume kernels of popcorn in a movie theater.

This new breed is knowledgeble, informed and extremely savvy. And its attitude toward the market differs in crucial ways from that of the traditional collector. If an old-style collector purchases a coin for $500 and it goes up in value to $1,000, chances are he isn't going to sell it; he bought it, first and foremost, for its history, artistry and cultural significance. Today's collector/investor shares this appreciation of rare coins' intangible values. But if he sees his $500 coin increase in value to $1,000, he'll take the profit.

The emergence of collector/investors has strengthed the marketplace substantially, but the increased tendency toward profit-taking has added to the market's volatility. When coins go up in value today, greater numbers of people sell off — and since rare coin economics is simple supply and demand, the price will drop, sometimes very quickly, when supply comes up to meet demand.

Today's collector/investors are attending coin conventions, reading coin books and periodicals and buying coins certified by the leading services. They know all about such tools as the population and census reports issued by PCGS and NGC, respectively, which indicate how many coins have been graded by each of those services.

As we move through the 1990s, these collector/investors will become an ever more dominant force in the coin market. They will play a pivotal role in determining market prices, since they know what they are doing and won't let anyone take advantage of them. This will force dealers to keep their profit margins at the slimmest possible levels.

"Supergrade coins"

Through most of the late 1980s, special emphasis was placed on coins in the highest levels of preservation — those which graded 66 or above on the 1 through 70 scale. Through the years, these meticulously preserved coins have always appreciated monetarily at the fastest possible rates. Coins such as those graded Proof-66 and Proof-67, or Mint State-66 and Mint State-67, by leading independent grading services have been in the greatest demand and have increased in value most rapidly and dramatically.

Respected newsletter writer Maurice H. Rosen, writing in the *Rosen Numismatic Advisory* (Plainview, New York) coined the term "supergrade coin." Shortly after Rosen spotlighted the concept of investing in the highest-grade and lowest-population coins, such as U.S. type coins graded 66 and above, those coins increased by close to 40 percent in 1988.

This area remains an extremely popular one for collectors and investors alike. Historically, collectors have demanded the very best — not necessarily because such coins have increased in value the most (for them, that's a peripheral consideration), but because these coins are really and truly the most beautiful. A Proof-68 Barber quarter with lovely concentric-circle toning — ocean green, fading into sky blue, fading into a sunset golden center — is a breathtaking sight to behold. It's a thrilling, awe-inspiring specimen which, if placed at public auction, might well command a premium in the stratosphere. A Proof-66 Trade dollar whose devices (the parts which stand out from the coin) are frosted and white — and whose fields (the background areas of the coin) are mirror-like and reflective — is a sensational, phenomenal coin, one truly worthy of a connoisseur's collection and worthy of an eye-popping premium based upon its beauty, rarity, quality and overall appreciation potential.

Rare coins as a whole have enjoyed good appreciation in recent years and exceptional coins have achieved spectacular prices. In 1989, for example, an Augustus Humbert $20 gold piece reportedly changed hands privately for $1.3 million and an 1804 silver dollar was sold at public auction for $990,000. But, while these prices are impressive, what they really demonstrate is not so much the *strength* of rare coins, but rather their great *potential*. Bugatti cars, which are manufactured items, sometimes sell for 15 or 20 million dollars apiece. Paintings sell for tens of millions of dollars. Chairs sell for millions of dollars. But, when it comes to rare coins, the greatest of the great sell for only a million dollars, more or less.

There is, of course, no ironclad guarantee that supergrade coins — or any other coins — will rise in value. But in view of their potential, and the gap between their prices and those of other collectibles, institutional investors feel confident in purchasing 25-and 50-thousand-dollar coins. And marketplace analysts have no reservations in predicting that many 5-or 10-thousand-dollar coins will also rise in value geometrically.

One leading investment banker I know insists that $25,000 coins are innately $150,000 and $200,000 coins. Again, there's no guarantee of any profits; this is strictly his personal opinion. But I greatly admire his enthusiasm, and I think it reflects the thinking of a whole new generation of coin buyers. These buyers are comfortable with today's coin market and confident that it's safe to go into the water again. The market is no longer an ocean of hungry sharks, as I wrote it to be in 1984 in *The Coin Collector's Survival Manual*. On the contrary, I have heard coin buying today, in the certified coin market, described as being no more dangerous than taking a swim in the deep end of your swimming pool without a lifeguard. There's a risk, but it's not like swimming with sharks.

Supergrade glamour coins

Coins which are Mint State-66 or above

and are also classic rarities, such as Flowing Hair dimes and Flowing Hair dollars, are especially popular with collector/investors from the baby-boom generation, and many observers believe that these coins — now selling for $70,000 and $80,000 — could be our next $500,000 to $750,000 rarities.

Generic coins

With the advent of independent grading, common-date coins such as 1881-S Morgan dollars and 1942 Walking Liberty half dollars and Mint State-64 and Mint State-63 Saint-Gaudens double eagles have become the most commoditized of all coins. These coins are said to be "fungible" — that is, they are interchangeable with other common-date coins of the same kind and grade. All trade within the same price range, so it really doesn't matter from the standpoint of investment which specific date-and-mint variety you obtain. And as far as investors are concerned, dates and mint marks matter little anyway; their concern is really profit and loss.

Generic, commoditized coins tend to move up or down in value within specific ranges. As this is written, the trading range for common-date S-mint Morgan dollars graded Mint State-65 runs from a low of $200 to a high of $500. Many investors have done quite well by buying at $275 or $300 and selling at $450. But the trick is not to get greedy when trading such coins: Don't wait for the absolute top of the range; if you're in a profit position, cash your chips.

The commoditization of the marketplace has allowed for coins to be traded with greater ease than at any time before. We're almost like a commodities market today: The grading services crank out thousands of newly certified S-mint dollars in 65 slabs every month and people keep selling them back and forth. The question is, can new money be found to readily absorb this constantly growing supply of newly certified coins. Even if it does, you can be sure that as soon as prices rise to any respectable level — if they go up from

$300 to $400, for example, someone will turn up with a hoard of several thousand certified coins of the same type, date and grade and sell them into the marketplace, and prices will fall just as quickly as they rose.

Generic and fungible coins are popular with Wall Street investors. These people relate to such coins because they're very much like shares of stock. To a very great extent, these coins simply duplicate each other. It's interesting to note that very few collectors have a need for 1881-S Morgan dollars in Mint State-65. The typical collector may have *one* — just to complete a type set — but that's all.

Copper coins

Many copper coins are extremely inexpensive. But this doesn't mean they're likely to rise in value anytime soon — for while they're highly popular with collectors, their level of acceptance is relatively low with investors.

In coin economics, value is determined by three basic factors: the level of preservation of a coin, the number of pieces extant and the size of the collector base. Copper coins enjoy the biggest collector base of any U.S. coins; a great many collectors are putting together sets of half cents, large cents, Flying Eagle cents, Indian Head cents and Lincoln cents. But investors have traditionally avoided copper coins because these coins pose a storage nightmare.

Copper coins must be stored in a very dry environment. In Florida, where the atmosphere is humid, collectors run the risk of losing their investment unless they store copper coins with the utmost care. A coin made of an unstable metal — one that is prone to deterioration — can be just as bad an investment as a coin that was overpriced significantly in the first place. The Numismatic Guaranty Corporation provides a guarantee for coins that it grades, but the guarantee doesn't cover copper coins; these have been known to deteriorate even while encased in inert plastic.

I recommend strongly that buyers of

copper coins obtain and use a product called Metal SAFE corrosion inhibitor. This is a vapor-phase inhibitor which changes the molecular composition of the air to prevent deterioration of coins that are stored in that environment. I also would urge those with copper coins to neutralize them, before storing them, in a substance called trichlorotrifluoroethane. This is a highly evaporative type of freon; it will remove airborne particulate matter and contaminants from the surfaces of the coins.

Ironically, copper coins which are bright command the highest premiums — yet, these are the ones most susceptible to rapid deterioration. Copper coins with a very light patina are naturally protected for future generations. In bygone years, New England merchants would store large cents in jugs — glass jars — and bury them in soil in their back yards. Many of these coins developed protective patinas on the highest points — and when they were found, 50, 75 and 100 years later, they would have no corrosion and would seem to have been meticulously preserved, with glossy brown patinas.

Indian cents represent very good values in the high grades. Colonial coins and half cents are also very good values. But don't forget that even though something may be a sleeper, there may be no *reason* for it to wake up. Something can be scarce and underrated for years, decades and even generations and not increase in value. There has to be a stimulus to cause its value to rise. Still, having said all this, I believe that given the increased interest in all areas of U.S. coins, there is every reason for copper coins to wake up and be among the best performers of all U.S. coins during the near future. Incidentally, the same caveats which apply to copper coins also pertain to nickel coins. Despite their name, U.S. nickel coins are actually made up of 75 percent copper and just 25 percent nickel.

Silver coins
Silver coins are excellent investments. Nicely "toned" silver coins — coins with attractively oxidized surfaces — are particularly popular with a certain group of buyers. Keep in mind, however, that any coin with toning is in an intermediate state between being totally brilliant and turning completely black. It's the goal of every collector to keep that coin in a state of suspended animation.

Among the best-performing silver coins are dimes, quarters, half dollars and dollars of the Seated Liberty type. These coins enjoy a large and devoted following in both proof and business-strike versions. Even in circulated conditions, these coins are very acceptable to many buyers — and putting together a set of such coins can be very rewarding. They're quite inexpensive, and assembling them into sets can be profitable monetarily as well as in terms of psychic income.

Barber dimes, quarters and half dollars and Gobrecht dollars are also highly popular silver coins, and those who have acquired them with care and discrimination have found them to be wise investments. Trade dollars are underrated and rare in the highest grades. Even Proof-64 Trade dollars represent excellent values.

Gold coins
Proof gold coins are tremendously underpriced — and these coins have everything going for them. Proof gold coins from the 19th century have very low mintages, the population reports indicate that they're almost nonexistent — and these coins are a sight to behold!

A proof $20 gold piece — say, a Proof Liberty double eagle graded Proof-64 with golden pond-like reflective fields and frosty golden devices — is perhaps the most spectacular of all American coins. And at just a bit more than $40,000, it may actually prove to be among the finest investments. If the marketplace continues to see rapid expansion and large sums of fresh money, some observers believe that coins such as this could increase in value 15 or 20 percent a year — and maybe even more.

All Proof gold coins have potential —

even those in Proof-63. But when you buy proof gold, be certain that the coins aren't cloudy; make sure they're brilliant. Proof gold, by the way, is one of the few areas where even the very small coins have great potential. The population reports show that in certain areas, only 12 to 15 specimens may exist in certain high grades within an entire gold type. But the baby-boom generation has dozens of buyers, hundreds of buyers, out there looking for these coins. What's more, there are many collectors who really love these coins and have formed a tremendous emotional attachment to them.

Generic gold coins may not be that great an investment. But Saint-Gaudens double eagles graded Mint State-62 and Mint State-63 have very low premiums above their intrinsic value — that is to say, their metal value. This may make them a very good investment for the astute collector who wants to assemble a set. The risk, after all, is minimal — and this is an important consideration. When investing in coins, as in anything else, there's always a risk involved. But you want to take that risk only when the odds are clearly in your favor. If a gold coin contains $350 worth of gold and the coin costs only $425 in a slab, the odds are clearly in the buyer's favor and there's not much downside risk.

Commemoratives

Commemorative coins are a very volatile area. It's especially important when buying very high-quality commemoratives — those graded Mint State-66 or Mint State-67 — that you study the population reports and buy only those coins which have very high populations in these grades, or which are known in great quantities. Commemoratives in 66 and 67 which are almost unknown in those grades have been subject to heavy manipulation. Let's say you buy a commemorative graded Mint State-67 from an individual who owns the entire population known to have been certified in that grade. Chances are, he could be the sight-unseen bidder for that coin on the American Numismatic Exchange. His sight-unseen bid could be $5,000, and once he sells his coins to various retail customers he could withdraw his bid from ANE, at which point its price might drop from $5,000 to $1,500. If that happens, you've lost $3,500. This is a very risky area, and you really should stick with specialists when dealing in commemorative coins.

Abuses aside, many commemorative coins represent great investments. Commemoratives are scarce, they're attractive, they're originally toned and they're beaming with historical significance as well as original Mint luster.

Choosing the right dealer

Choosing the right dealer is just as important as choosing the right coin. You can teach yourself the basics of coin grading by reading such books as *The Coin Collector's Survival Manual, Travers' Rare Coin Investment Strategy* (which contains a full-color grading guide of coins selected from more than 4,000 color transparencies), *The Investor's Guide to Coin Trading, Photograde* and *The Official ANA Grading Standards for United States Coins*. However, knowledge of grading is a combination of book knowledge and practical experience, and unless you're a coin trader and you've handled many millions of dollars worth of coins, your knowledge is not going to be nearly as sophisticated as that of expert traders. John Albanese, founder, president and chief grader of NGC, told me that it took him five years to tell the difference consistently between the grades of 64 and 65 — and during those five years he traded many millions of dollars worth of coins. He learned by doing.

You need to place great confidence and trust in your dealer. And the dealer himself shoulders a tremendous amount of responsibility in regard to disclosure of the standards he is using and of the innate value of the coins.

A number of organizations can be helpful in selecting dealers. These include the American Numismatic Association, the

Professional Numismatists Guild Inc. (PNG) and the Industry Council for Tangible Assets (ICTA). One organization which has come under close — and favorable — scrutiny is the Coin and Bullion Dealer Accreditation Program, a division of ICTA. CABDAP has established a voluntary accreditation and compliance program that refuses to admit any dealer who has a lawsuit — even a single frivolous lawsuit — pending against him at the time of application. CABDAP members must undergo strict personal and financial background checks by an investigative agency. Furthermore, CABDAP members (and PNG members, as well) must submit to legally binding arbitration at the request of any customer for any reason whatsoever. Ethically, CABDAP is the strongest and best of the dealer organizations. As of this writing, however, there are 4,000 coin dealers in the United States and only 96 CABDAP dealer members.

In addition to seeking out dealers who are CABDAP-accredited, I recommend that you contact the U.S. Postal Service and the Federal Trade Commission before doing business with a dealer you're not familiar with. Find out whether that dealer has been charged with false, deceptive or misleading practices in trade and in commerce. Your state attorney general's office or local department of consumer affairs can assist you in this regard.

The coin business is a totally unregulated field in which the expression "Caveat emptor" (Let the buyer beware) is an understatement. But the coin market is also the ultimate example of the magic of freedom of the marketplace. If you use this magic to your advantage, you will find coin collecting and investing a highly rewarding experience — both financially and aesthetically — and find the rare coin market a place of exceptional opportunities.

Rarities

18

How a coin becomes rare

There are many factors which can make a particular issue coin rare. These include total mintage, the normal attrition of circulation, official and private meltings, and the level of collector interest at the time of issue.

The most important factor is total mintage. This figure sets the upper limit of potential collectible specimens. The actual number of specimens extant might sink to zero, but it will never rise above the total mintage figure (except for counterfeits and several issues of the 19th century which were restruck so flagrantly that even today more specimens are known than were "officially" minted).

In many instances the actual total mintage of an issue will never be definitely known, and not because of any illicit practices. For many years the United States Mint's bookkeeping consisted solely of recording the number of coins turned over to the Treasury during a calendar year, regardless of the actual year in which the coins were struck or of the date on the dies used to strike them.

Once the coins of a particular issue are released they begin to disappear. Coins are engraved, burnt, swallowed, buried by misers, placed in cornerstones and under masts, nailed to the aforesaid masts (a la Moby Dick), drilled for use as washers, made into rings and bracelets, and thrown into wishing wells. Although these deletions should normally occur in equal proportion to the number of coins in circulation, this is not always the case.

Many relatively common coins, such as 1889 dollars and 1916 dimes, have been altered in an attempt to disguise them as their more valuable counterparts that came from the branch Mints. Manufacturers of coin jewelry often prefer 1964 Kennedy halves over the later years because of the higher silver content.

Even pattern coins were subject to this selective destruction, as a large number of $4 gold Stellas were holed and made into earrings for presentation to the wives of congressmen, in an attempt to influence the husbands into approving the design.

Melting

In addition to the occasional random destruction of coins by accident or carelessness, coins have often been intentionally melted in wholesale lots for their bullion. The most zealous smelter of U.S. coins has always been the U.S. government, although private enterprise has contributed greatly to the death and dearth of coinage. During the great increases in bullion values during 1979-1980, millions of coins were melted privately as their intrinsic value increased dramatically in the space of several months. Occasionally the government's reasons have been aesthetic rather than intrinsic, as in the practice of recoining worn or multilated coins.

Early U.S. silver coins, especially dollars, were often exchanged for worn Spanish colonial coins and the heavier dollars were then exported and melted. In

1834 the standard weight of each U.S. gold denomination was reduced, which resulted in most of the older coins being melted.

By 1853 the price of silver had risen to the point that all silver coins (except for the 3-cent piece) were worth more than their face value and were being privately melted. To combat this problem the government reduced the weight of the half dime through the half dollar by about 7 percent, except the dollar, which represented a hypothetical standard and was minted in only token quantities during this era. The new weight coins were marked with arrows at the date through 1855, not to inform the public of the change in weight, but to assist the Treasury in withdrawing the heavier coins for melting at a profit to the government.

In 1873, an otherwise insignificant increase was made in the weight of the dime, quarter dollar and half dollar. Once again arrows were placed at the date of the new weight coins, even though no withdrawal of the old coins was necessary. Nevertheless, many coins already struck at the branch Mints in the old weights were melted, resulting in several unknown or unique issues. Other denominations were discontinued after only six weeks production; in some cases only Proofs had yet been struck.

The Morgan silver dollar was never a necessary or popular coin, and much of the mintage was shipped directly into storage in the original Mint-sewn bags. More than 270 million of these surplus coins were melted after World War I, at which time presumably all 1895 non-Proof dollars were melted. One circulated non-Proof has been reported, possibly a souvenir presented to a visitor at the Mint.

Although large quantities of unwanted and unnecessary silver dollars had been melted in 1918, the silver interests in the United States were powerful enough to see to it that all of these coins were replaced through the striking of new coins. The result was the production of tens of millions of equally unwanted and unnecessary Morgan and Peace dollars in 1921 and subsequent years. Virtually all of these coins ended up in the Treasury's vaults, and for years these "common date" coins filled the limited demand for gifts and for circulation in the Western states.

This supply of coins might have lasted forever, at least until the price of silver rose above $1.29 per ounce, had it not been noticed that the Treasury was occasionally giving out older coins as well as the common dates of the 1920s. When it was discovered that a few bags of Seated Liberty dollars had been released at face value, thousands of collectors and speculators rushed to the Treasury to see what they might find. Within months the stock of silver dollars fell from hundreds of millions to less than 3 million, and several formerly scarce coins suddenly became common.

Virtually all of the nearly 3 million dollars retained by the Treasury were Uncirculated coins struck at the Carson City Mint. Most of these pieces were struck in the years 1882-1884, making these three dates uncommon, when compared to certain other Morgan dollars. After seven successive sales by the General Services Administration begining in October 1972, all of the coins were sold.

In many instances the heavy production of one denomination, such as silver dollars, was made at the expense of other denominations. See the mintage figures for dimes through halves of 1878-90 and for cents through halves of 1921-28 in the chapter about U.S. coins. The production of fractional silver increased after 1890 because of the Sherman Silver Purchase Act, not because of a decrease in the production of dollars. The production of dollars declined from 1893 to 1895 because of opposition to them from President Cleveland, who blamed them for the business panic of 1893.

Collector conservation

Once a coin has been struck, its best chance for survival is to be acquired by a collector who knows how to care for it. Prior to the 1820s there were very few collectors in the United States. Most of the

Uncirculated coins from before this decade have come from the collections of Europeans who visited the United States Mint.

Once collecting became popular the collectors became aware of condition and wanted the best coins available. If the number of Proof coins of an earlier year was insufficient to meet the current demand, the Mint could often be induced to create a few more. In a few instances these semi-official restrikes were augmented with counterfeits produced outside the Mint from old dies, such as the 1804 "restrike" cent.

Throughout the remainder of the 19th century the several hundred collectors in the United States mainly concentrated on obtaining one specimen of each date for whatever denominations in which they were interested. Since this was often taken care of with a Proof, the Uncirculated coins were usually ignored. This was especially so for the branch Mints, as many dates from San Francisco and Carson City are unknown in Uncirculated condition. Non-silver minor coins are the easiest to collect, because they were all made in Philadelphia at a time when most collectors lived between Boston and Washington, D.C.

The national economy also has a great deal to do with the number of coins preserved from a particular era. During times of recession or depression, few coins are produced and few people have surplus cash to invest in BU rolls. Examples are the Great Depression of 1929-39 and the recessions of 1949 and 1958.

There are always exceptions to this rule, such as the 1931-S cents and 5-cent pieces which are more common in BU than one would expect, considering their low mintages. Either business was so bad that the coin never filtered down through the banks into circulation, or else some individual hoarded a great many of them. Other seemingly scarce issues, such as the 1950-D 5-cent piece and the 1955 half dollar, are common in BU because of speculators who were able to obtain the coins in bag quantities.

The number of collectors is never static, and an increased collector base places greater demand on supply. Generally, prices increase as the number of collectors grows, and drop if fewer persons are searching for the same coins.

Rarities can be caused by a whim of nature, an act of God, or the greed of man. Mintages have risen and fallen with the price of gold and the price of wheat. The lowly mosquito and the mighty politician have each been able to restrict production, in direct proportion to the venom of their sting. As long as coins are being struck there will always be an occasional rarity. They are, like gold, where you find them.

Famous collections

John Andrew Beck

John A. Beck was born in Chestnut Ridge, Pa., Jan. 5, 1859. After attending St. Vincent's College, he and his brothers went into their father's salt-producing business, drilling for salt on the Ohio River.

When salt was more profitably produced by mining in the West, he sold out his salt and chemical interests and prospected for oil. He continued in this business until his death Jan. 27, 1924.

Beck began collecting coins when he was 10 years old. Major coins in his collection were acquired with the help of a prominent Philadelphia coin dealer, Henry Chapman.

The Beck collection contains an outstanding array of United States gold coins and other U.S. rarities. He considered his pioneer gold coins his most highly prized acquisitions.

Pioneer gold, a complete set of eagles, 1795-1804, commemorative gold, the 1861-D gold dollar, $4 Stellas and the rare 1900 Indian Head cent struck in gold comprise only part of this all-encompassing collection. He also possessed 531 1856 Flying Eagle cents.

Beck's collection remained intact until January 27, 1975, when the first portion of it was offered at public auction by the Trust Division, Pittsburgh National Bank, Pittsburgh, executors of the Beck estate. Three such sales were conducted by Abner Kreisberg Corp., in Beverly Hills, Calif., realizing $3,232,169. These sales were held Jan. 27-29, 1975 ($1,837,021); Feb. 12-13, 1976 ($741,816); and Feb. 14, 1977 ($653,332).

Virgil M. Brand

Virgil Michael Brand, born in Blue Island, Ill., in 1862, heir to one of the largest brewing businesses in Chicago, began collecting coins in 1889 when about 23 years old. His initial recorded purchases were of California gold issues, and by the time of his death in 1926, Brand had purchased more than 350,000 pieces. Some consider his collection to be among the greatest ever formed.

Brand purchased everything, refusing to specialize. He bought coins in all areas, from nearly every major dealer in the late 19th and early 20th centuries. He did so quietly, preferring to remain an unknown, unlike many prominent collectors of his era.

Following his death, Brand's two brothers, Horace and Armin, fought over the collection after failing to sell it intact. Dealers Henry Chapman and Burdette G. Johnson were hired in 1932 and 1933 to appraise the collection, and parts were sold through consignments and direct sales.

Many coins were given to Armin Brand's daughter, Jane, who kept them in her estate until her death. Bowers and Merena Galleries was selected to sell the Jane Brand Allen estate collection, doing so in two sales. The first, of American gold and copper coins, plus several foreign pieces, was held Nov. 7-8, 1983, realizing $1.9 million; the second, offering American coins and exonumia, sold June 18-19, 1984, for $1,417,977.

Sotheby Parke Bernet & Co. auctioned the bulk of Brand's estate of ancient and foreign coinage. Coins from the Soviet Union, Poland, Germany, Switzerland, France, Austria, Italy, England, Sweden, Finland and Portugal are just some of the countries represented taking place from July 1982 through October 1985 in 10 European sales totaling £4,514,334. The Brand auctions took place in New York, London, Amsterdam and Zurich. Also of note, Brand's numismatic book and literature auction realized $20,500 when it was auctioned by George Frederick Kolbe Aug. 13, 1983, in Los Angeles.

Robinson S. Brown Jr.

Robinson S. Brown Jr. from Louisville, Ky., began his hobby interests with stamps before moving on to coins.

He was fascinated with completing a set of U.S. large cents by die varieties.

Determination played an important role in the success of his nearly-complete collection which is the second finest and most complete collection in the world, according to Brown. The collection assembled by Brown consisted of 1457 lots by Sheldon and Newcomb varieties of cents from 1793 through 1857. The collection of cents from 1816-1839 was complete while the collection by Newcomb variety from 1840-1857 is nearly complete.

The collection was sold at auction Sept.30-Oct.1, 1986, in West Hollywood, Calif., by Superior Galleries and realized a hammer price of $1,273,215. The catalog for the auction is destined to become the standard catalog of large cents.

Since the auction, Brown has begun to put together another large cent collection along with collecting other numismatic coins and tokens.

Amon G. Carter Jr.

Paper money collectors invariably think of Amon G. Carter Jr. when they think of great collections. His collection of Texas notes, including national bank notes, was undoubtedly the greatest in the world. Major U.S. rarities owned by Carter included a Series 1863 $1,000 legal tender note, an 1863 $100 legal tender note, an 1891 $100 "Open Back" Treasury note, and an 1874 $500 legal tender. Among the rarer nationals in the collection was an 1875 $100 note from the Deseret National Bank of Salt Lake City, Utah Territory, possibly the only First Charter $100 territorial national in existence.

Carter's coin collection contained such rarities as the Adams specimen 1804 silver dollar, a Very Fine 1870-S Seated Liberty silver dollar, the 1801, 1802, 1803 dollar restrikes and 1884 and 1885 Trade dollars, and many other rare pieces.

The coins were sold Jan. 18-21, 1984, by Stack's of New York, where the 1,798 lots brought more than $8 million including a 10 percent buyer's fee. His paper money collection is being sold at fixed prices by various dealers.

Carter, publisher of the Fort Worth Star-Telegram, which his father founded, died July 24, 1982, at the age of 62.

William Forrester Dunham

William Forrester Dunham was born Oct. 3, 1857, at Barnard, Vt., and died Oct. 12, 1936, at the age of 79.

In early life Dunham was a school teacher, and later a wholesale and retail grocer. He studied pharmacy and became one of the leading druggists in Chicago. He retired from active business in 1916. He was a graduate of Tabor College, Iowa, and the University of Illinois.

Dunham was an ardent numismatist, beginning his collection early in life. He took an active interest in the affairs of the ANA and attended its conventions regularly. He served as a member of the ANA board of governors as well as chairman of the board. He was a charter member of the Chicago Coin Club.

Some of the items in his collection included:

1804 silver dollar, 1822 half eagle, 1852 half cent, 1802 half dime, Proof set of the gold coins of 1875, complete set of quarter eagles, complete set of $3 gold, largest collection of encased postage stamps ever formed, extensive collection of Hard Times tokens, Canada coins and medals, 2,500 varieties of Confederate paper currency, world gold, silver and platinum coins.

The collection was sold by B. Max Mehl June 3, 1941, with a total of 4,169 lots bringing $83,364.08.

Louis Eliasberg

On April 21, 1976, the Louis Eliasberg memorial exhibition, a complete date and Mint collection of United States coins, plus pattern coins, paper money, world coins and primitive means of exchange, opened as a Bicentennial feature at the Philadelphia Mint.

It was designated as a memorial exhibit in honor of its late owner who died Feb. 20, 1976. His sons, Louis Eliasberg Jr. and Richard Eliasberg, and his widow, Mrs. Lucille Eliasberg, officiated at the opening of the exhibit with Acting Mint Director Frank H. MacDonald.

The collection remained on display throughout the entire Bicentennial year and into America's third century.

Louis Eliasberg was life member 169 of the American Numismatic Association and a member of the Baltimore Coin Club.

In 1942 he startled the numismatic world by acquiring the famous collection formed by John H. Clapp. It cost more than $100,000 and at that time was the all-time high single cash transaction in the history of numismatics.

Eliasberg had a very nearly complete collection of regular-issue United States coins including a 1913 Liberty Head 5-cent piece and an 1804 silver dollar. The only pieces he was known to be missing were the 1841-O and 1797 16 Star obverse, Large Eagle reverse half eagles.

The Eliasberg gold coin collection was sold Oct. 27-29, 1982, by Bowers and Ruddy Galleries Inc., under the sobriquet "The United States Gold Collection" at the request of the family. However, it was widely known throughout the hobby that the coins being sold were from the Eliasberg collection and the news was eventually published in the numismatic press. The 1,074 lots brought more than $11.4 million, including two coins which each brought record prices of $652,000 — the unique 1870-S $3 gold piece and the 1822 half eagle.

King Farouk

King Farouk was born in 1919. At the age of 17 he succeeded his father, King Fuad, as king of Egypt. He ruled Egypt from 1936 to 1952 when he was deposed and forced into exile.

King Farouk assembled one of the largest coin collections in the world. After he was deposed in 1952, his collection was seized by the Egyptian government and sold at public auction by Sotheby's of London, England.

An accumulator rather than a student of numismatics, Farouk's collection represented one of the finest ever assembled. There were about 8,500 coins and medals in gold and 164 in platinum. In addition, of course, were many copper and silver coins.

Among the pre-19th century items was a group of 19 Brazilian gold bars dating back to 1767. Also included were a few ancients of the Ptolemys of Egypt, some Roman aureii and some Roman gold bars of the fourth century A.D. Also represented were extensive selections from Europe, the Far East and an important selection of U.S. gold and patterns. The collection included a 1933 Saint-Gaudens double eagle, never officially released and considered illegal to own. U.S. authorities requested the coin be removed from the London auction, which it was, but it was not turned over and its location is unknown.

Many of the most famous U.S. and foreign rarities are still referred to as "ex Farouk" — from the Farouk collection.

Garrett family collection

T. Harrison Garrett was a student at Princeton in the mid-1860s when he began collecting coins, beginning what was to become one of the major collections of U.S. coins and exonumia. Upon his death in 1888, he left the collection to his son Robert, who loaned it to Princeton University where it was on display for nearly 20 years.

Robert Garrett added to the collection until 1919 when he traded it to a brother,

John Work Garrett, for art objects. J.W. Garrett was able to buy the pick of the Col. James W. Ellsworth Collection when it was sold in March 1923, including many 1792 patterns. Garrett died in 1942, and he continued his numismatic activity until shortly before then.

The Garrett collection was given to Johns Hopkins University in Baltimore, which sold duplicates in March 1976 in a Stack's auction, and consigned the bulk to Bowers and Ruddy Galleries which held a series of four auctions from 1979 to 1981. The coins sold by Bowers and Ruddy included two Brasher doubloons, many rare Colonial pieces, Washington medals, one of the greatest collections of 1792 pattern coinage assembled, a Proof 1795 silver dollar, an 1804 silver dollar and rare gold coins.

The four sales were held Nov. 28-29, 1979; March 26-27, 1980; Oct. 1-2, 1980; and March 25-26, 1981. Total prices realized was $25,235,360.

Col. E.H.R. Green

"Texas Colonel" Green was born Aug. 22, 1868, and died June 8, 1936. Before he reached the age of 20, his right leg was amputated 7 inches above the knee. Even so, he stood 6 feet, 4 inches, and weighed 300 pounds.

Green was the eccentric playboy son of the equally eccentric, but miserly, Hetty Green, the famous Wall Street financier and manipulator, known as the "Witch of Wall Street." She died July 3, 1916, and left her entire estate to her son and to a frightened, eremitic daughter, Sylvia Wilks.

Green reputedly spent $3 million a year on yachts, coins, stamps, pornography, orchid culture and Texas politics.

At the time of his death, Green's collection contained some of the finest and rarest numismatic pieces ever assembled by one person, including all five known 1913 Liberty Head 5-cent pieces plus a specimen of the 1913 Buffalo 5-cent piece in copper.

Herman Halpern

Herman Halpern was a collector who kept his focus on maintaining quality and rarity. His main interest was large cents. The completeness of his collection was enhanced by rich pedigrees including the names of Harold Bareford, Denis W. Loring and Del Bland.

Stack's auctioned Halpern's collection of large cents March 16-17, 1988. An amazing hammer price of $1.8 million was paid for 774 lots of cents, face value of $7.74.

Jimmy Hayes

The Jimmy Hayes Collection of United States Silver Coins demonstrates the ability of one collector to assemble a type collection consisting of the first year of issue of virtually every type of U.S. silver coins from silver 3 cents to silver dollars and commemoratives. The extreme high quality throughout sets this collection apart from others of its type.

The 128 coins of the Hayes auction Oct. 22, 1988, brought nearly $1.2 million, an average of almost $10,000 per lot.

Jascha Heifetz

The Jascha Heifetz collection of United States coins and patterns was sold by Superior Galleries Oct. 1-4, 1989, together with the Albert Hanten collection of U.S. paper money and the Paul Munson collection of Bust half dollars. The 6,200 lots in nine session brought a total hammer of more than $16 million.

Among the record-breaking highlights were a 1907 Saint-Gaudens, High Relief Roman Numerals double eagle that brought $200,000 and a Proof 65 Flowing Hair $4 Stella pattern at $270,000.

Nelson Bunker Hunt and William Herbert Hunt

The collection of ancient coins of Nelson Bunker Hunt may represent a breakthrough in numismatic auction prices. For the first time, coins were sold as art, attracting the heady prices often attributed to other areas of the fine arts but rarely seen in the coin field.

A June 19, 1990, Sotheby's session in New York offering just 110 coins of Greek and Roman coins brought a total hammer price of $8.6 million. More of the collection of the fabled Hunt brothers were to go to auction in four sessions June 21-22, and again Dec. 4-7.

The highest price paid at the session, and for any non-U.S. coin at auction, was $520,000 for a silver decadrachm of Agrigentum, Sicily. Nelson Hunt had purchased the coin from Bruce McNall of Numismatic Fine Arts in a 1980 private transaction for $1 million.

Arnold H. Kagan

Known both in Israel and the United States as builder, publisher, collector and numismatist, A.H. Kagan has many outstanding accomplishments to his credit. Where Rome's legions failed to ascend, Kagan built the cable railway linking historic Masada to the Judaean desert.

In less than 10 years, Kagan assembled the most complete collection of Israel's coins, medals and paper money in history, arranging them in 86 plastic panels which duplicate with actual coins and medals the pages of his standard reference, Israel's Money and Medals.

The 160-foot long exhibit, known as the Kagan-Maremba Collection, has been placed at the disposal of the Israel Government Coins and Medals Corp., and the American Israel Numismatic Association by Kagan, a long-time member of the American Numismatic Association.

Included are such rarities as the Utrecht die 100 prutot of 1954; various SPECIMEN pieces of the prutot series; three types of the 1960 eight grains one agora; commemorative rarities in all metals; and the rarest state, commissioned and presentation medals of the State of Israel. Since 1984, five rare medals have been added to the collection along with some Palestine Mandate pieces. The total value of the collection as of June 1987 exceeds $1.3 million.

The collection has been in the process of being refurbished. Plastic panels are being prepared to house the collection for display. Future plans include exhibit at various museums. When the refurbishing is completed, the weight of the collection is expected to approach 2,000 pounds.

Both in assembling the Kagan-Maremba Collection and in generously making it available to the world, Arnold H. Kagan has assured a prominent place for himself and his family in the numismatic history of the 20th century.

Josiah Kirby Lilly

The Josiah K. Lilly Collection specializing in United States and foreign gold coins was passed to the Smithsonian Institution after an act of Congress in 1968 gave the Lilly estate a tax credit of $5.5 million.

Included in the collection of 6,125 gold coins are 1,227 United States gold coins, among them an 1822 half eagle (three known) and a 1797 half eagle with 16 star obverse; 1,236 Latin American coins; 3,227 European coins; and 243 Africa, Asia and Far East coins, all of which are in gold.

The only United States gold coin Lilly did not possess was the 1870-S $3 piece, which was owned by Louis Eliasberg.

Lilly also possessed an extensive collection of stamps which was sold for a total value of $3,123,127.

Wayne Miller

Wayne Miller, a Helena, Mont., coin dealer and collector, during a span of 16 years starting in the late 1960s acquired a complete set of Morgan and Peace silver dollars.

The characteristic that set his complete collection aside from others who have complete sets was the quality. The set included many of the finest known specimens, Proof Morgan dollars and several branch Mint Proof coins rarely seen were among the 160 pieces which made up the collection.

Miller had sold the collection in April 1984 to dealer David Hall, who was serving as a broker for an unnamed collector on the West Coast for a price believed to be in excess of $1 million.

The coin collection was subsequently sold at public auction by Superior Galleries, Jan.27-28, 1986 in Beverly Hills, Calif. and realized a hammer price of $1,109,375.

Miguel Muñoz

When one thinks of a numismatist who is dedicated not only to his hobby but to sharing his knowledge of rare coins with others, the name Miguel Muñoz comes quickly to mind. Muñoz became interested in rare coins at an early age and his interest never waned.

The Muñoz collection was strong in Mexican coinage, United States coinage, ancient coins and world gold coins.

The first two parts of his collection were auctioned in the 1970s. The final two sections in 1981 and 1982 brought more than $2.5 million.

Emery May and R. Henry Norweb

Emery May Holden became interested in coins when she was about 9 years old in 1905 when she was given a half cent piece. R. Henry Norweb began collecting during his long diplomatic career in U.S. diplomatic service. Norweb died Oct. 1, 1983, and Mrs. Norweb died March 27, 1984.

Mrs. Norweb's collection of English gold coins is believed to be the greatest in the United States, and her collections of American Colonial, United States and Latin American coins were extensive as well.

The Norwebs were philanthropic in nature, and donated many rarities to museums. Among them were a 1913 Liberty 5-cent piece, given to the Smithsonian Institution in 1978, and a Brasher doubloon, given to the American Numismatic Society in 1969. A 52-piece collection of Colonial rarities was donated to the Smithsonian in 1982.

The legendary American portion of the Norweb collection was sold in three parts by Bowers & Merena in 1987 and 1988. The three sessions brought a total prices realized of $18,103,365.

Richard Picker

Richard Picker was an individual interested in collecting, researching and dealing in United States Colonial coins and paper money. He built an outstanding collection of state coinage which was sold in 326 lots by Stack's Oct. 24, 1984, for $404,470

John L. Roper 2nd

Born Sept. 18, 1902, John L. Roper 2nd was an heir to a shipbuilding firm in Norfolk, Va., that gave him the money to build one of the major collections of Colonial and early American coinage of the 20th century. Roper died in April 1983.

The Dec. 8-9, 1983, auction of Roper's collection by Stack's included a half dozen Sommer Islands pieces, two New England silver pieces, 34 Massachusetts silver tree coins, plus copper and silver coins of most American Colonies and the early Confederation and federal issues. Fifteen Fugio coppers, five 1792 patterns and three Chain cents were also in the collection.

A second Roper sale, held March 20, 1984, offered paper money, Hard Times tokens and other items of numismatic Americana.

Matthew Adams Stickney

Matthew Adams Stickney was born Sept. 23, 1805, at Rowley, Mass., and died Aug. 11, 1894, in Salem, Mass.

He began collecting coins in 1823 and was probably the first person in America to form a systematic collection of the various dates in several series.

He assisted Sylvester S. Crosby in preparing his monumental work on U.S. Colonial, state and Washington coins in 1873-1875. Many of the Stickney coins were used to illustrate the Crosby book.

Some of the more famous coins in his collection included:

1787 New York Brasher doubloon, 1815 half eagle, 1804 silver dollar, 1776 cent of New Hampshire, the unique 1776 "Janus head" halfpenny, cent series of Massachusetts, Vermont, Connecticut, New York, New Jersey, many pattern pieces, world coins, Canada coins and medals, private and pioneer gold coins, plus numerous others.

The entire Stickney collection was sold by Henry Chapman June 25-29, 1907, with a total of 3,026 lots bringing $37,859.21.

Pedigrees

Following are pedigrees — or records of owners — of three of the rarest coins in United States numismatics. Curiously, none of the three are considered true issues, but are official restrikes or fantasy pieces. However, their histories are legendary, and their values are inestimable.

Because many collectors (or investors) are reluctant to have their identities known, largely for reasons of security, there may be holes in some of the pedigrees, but every effort has been made to see that they are complete. And in recent years, investment groups working through multiple agents have begun purchasing and reselling rarities such as these. It may be that pedigrees for some of these rarities may be lost in quick-profit transactions involving faceless "fund-managers." However, the romance (and somewhat notorious origins) of the great rarities will always intrigue collectors. Additions or changes may be sent to Coin World, P.O. Box 150, Sidney, Ohio 45365.

1913 Liberty 5-cent piece

Apparently struck by or for Samuel W. Brown, one-time clerk and storekeeper of the Philadelphia Mint. Heavily publicized by B. Max Mehl. Specimen 2 brought $385,000 at auction in 1985.

Specimen 1		Specimen 4	
	Samuel W. Brown		Samuel W. Brown
	August Wagner		August Wagner
	Col. E.H.R. Green		Col. E.H.R. Green
	Burdette G. Johnson		Burdette G. Johnson
	James F. Kelly		Eric P. Newman
	Dr. C.A. Bolt		Abe Kosoff
	George Walton		Louis Elisaberg
	R.J. Reynolds family		Eliasberg Family
Specimen 2		**Specimen 5**	
	Samuel W. Brown		Samuel W. Brown
	August Wagner		August Wagner
	Col. E.H.R. Green		Col. E.H.R. Green
	Burdette G. Johnson		Burdette G. Johnson
	James F. Kelly		F.C.C. Boyd
	Fred Olsen		Abe Kosoff
	B. Max Mehl		King Farouk
	King Farouk		Sol Kaplan
	Edwin Hydeman		Abe Kosoff
	Abe Kosoff		R. Henry and Mrs. Norweb
	World-Wide Coin Corp.		Smithsonian
	Bowers & Ruddy Galleries		
	A-Mark Coin Co.		
	Robert L. Hughes Ent.		
	Superior Stamp & Coin Co.		
	Dr. Jerry Buss		
	Reed Hawn		
Specimen 3			
	Samuel W. Brown		
	August Wagner		
	Col. E.H.R. Green		
	Burdette G. Johnson		
	James F. Kelly		
	James V. McDermott		
	James F. Kelly		
	Aubrey Bebee		
	American Numismatic Association		

1894-S Barber dime

Privately struck for friends of Mint Superintendent J. Daggett. A famous story is how Daggett's daughter Hallie spent one for ice cream. James A. Stack Sale in 1990 saw a bid of $250,000 for Specimen 3.

Specimen 1		Specimen 2	
	Waldo Newcomer		John H. Clapp
	F.C.C. Boyd		Stack's
	Abe Kosoff		Louis Eliasberg
	Will W. Niel		Eliasberg Family
	B. Max Mehl	**Specimen 3**	
	Edwin Hydeman		John H. Clapp
	Abe Kosoff		Louis Elisaberg
	Empire Coin Co.		H.R. Lee
	Hazen Hinman		Stack's
	James Kelly, Paramount		James A. Stack Sr.
	Leo A. Young		Unidentified collector
	Rarcoa		Group of five investors
	Ronald J. Gillio	**Specimen 4**	
	Unidentified collector		Stack's
			James A. Stack Estate

Specimen 5	J. Daggett
	Hallie Daggett
	Earl Parker
	Dan Brown
	Stack's
	Chicago collector
Specimen 6	J. Daggett
	Hallie Daggett
	Earl Parker
	W.R. Johnson
	Abner Kriesberg
	World-Wide Coin
	Investment
	Bowers & Ruddy Galleries
	Inc.
	Midwest collector
Specimen 7	C.A. Cass
	Stack's
	James Ruddy
	Q. David Bowers
	Mr. & Mrs. R. Henry Norweb
	Unidentified collector
Specimen 8	(not verified)
	J.C. Mitchelson
	Connecticut State Library
Specimen 9	Rappaport
	Kagin's
	Reuter
	Abner Kriesberg
	Bowers & Ruddy Galleries
	Inc.
	Eastern collector

Specimen 10	(not verified)
	California collector
	Kagin's
	Private collector
	Kagin's
	National Coin Co.
	Superior Stamp & Coin Co.
	Dr. Jerry Buss
	Michelle Johnson
Specimen 11	(circulation)
	Friedberg/Gimbels
	Kagin's
	New Netherlands Coin Co.
	Kagin's
	Harmer-Rooke
	James G. Johnson
	Old Roman Coin Co.
	Robert L. Hughes
Specimen 12	(circulation)
	Romito-Montesano
	Robert Hughes

1804 silver dollar

No 1804 dollars bearing that date were actually struck that year. In 1834, the State Department requested Proof sets for diplomatic gifts. Mint Director Samuel Moore interpreted the order to mean 1804-dated dollars should be struck. Sets were presented to the Sultan of Muscat and the King of Siam (specimens 7 and 8). Other coins were kept by the Mint. These are referred to as Class I.

By the 1850s, the 1804 dollar was recognized as a rarity, and the Mint prepared to strike more, using a new reverse die because the original was missing. However, night watchman Theodore Eckfeldt, son of the chief coiner, surreptitiously struck several pieces and sold them to Phildaelphia area coin dealers. Eckfeldt lacked the skill to letter the edges, and the plain-edged coins aroused suspicions in the Mint.

Mint officials, to conceal their own plans to restrike the coins, quietly repurchased all the plain edge pieces and reported them destroyed. In fact, the coins went into a Mint vault for 20 years, after lettering was added to their edges. All but one piece — it having been struck over a cut-down 1857 Swiss shooting taler. It was left undistrubed and exists as the sole surviving Class II 1804 dollar in the Smithsonian Institution.

The pieces with edge lettering added are referred to as Class III 1804 dollars.

The definitive history of the 1804 dollar is *The Fantastic 1804 Dollar* by Eric P. Newman and Kenneth E. Bressett. It was updated in 1987 in the American Numismatic Society's *American Silver Coinage, 1794-1891.*

The Dexter specimen (specimen 6) brought a hammer price of $900,000 at auction in 1989, still a record for a single coin at auction.

CLASS I	
Specimen 1	Smithsonian

Specimen 2 **"Stickney** **specimen"**	United States Mint Matthew A. Stickney Stickney Estate Col. James W. Ellsworth Wayte Raymond William C. Atwater Louis Eliasberg Eliasberg Family
Specimen 3	Edward Cohen Collection Col. M.I. Cohen H.S. Adams Lorin G. Parmelee H.G. Sampson William B. Wetmore S.H. & H. Chapman James H. Manning Elmer S. Sears Lammot du Pont Lammot du Pont Family Willis du Pont (stolen 1967)
Specimen 4 **"Mickley** **specimen"**	Henry C. Young Joseph J. Mickley W.A. Lilliendahl Edward Cogan William S. Appleton Massachusetts Historical Society Chicago collector Reed Hawn Stack's
Specimen 5 **"Parmelee** **specimen"**	Unknown woman E.H. Sanford Lorin G. Parmelee Byron Reed City of Omaha, Neb.

Specimen 6
"Dexter
specimen"
	Adolph Weyl
	S.H. & H. Chapman
	J.W. Scott
	James V. Dexter
	Dexter Estate
	H.G. Brown
	William F. Dunham
	C.H. Williams
	Harold Bareford
	Rarcoa
	Leon Hendrickson and
	  George Weingart
	Blanchard & Co. and
	  Kidder Peabody

Specimen 7 **"Watters** **specimen"**	Sultan of Muscat C.A. Watters Henry Chapman Virgil Brand Virgil M. Brand Estate Armin W. Brand C.F. Childs Childs Family
Specimen 8 **(part of the** **King of Siam** **Proof set of** **1834)**	King of Siam David Spink Family Elvin I Unterman Family Continental Rare Coin Fund Terry Brand and Iraj Sayah
CLASS II	

Specimen #9	Smithsonian
Class III	
Specimen 10 **"Berg** **specimen"**	Koch & Co. O.H. Berg T.H. Garrett T.H. Garrett Estate Johns Hopkins University Larry Hanks Sam Colavita Texas collector Martin Paul American Coin Portofilios Inc. for "Mrs. Sommer"
Specimen 11 **"Adams** **specimen" or** **"Adams-** **French** **specimen"**	John Haseltine Phineas Adams Henry Ahlborn John P. Lyman Waldo Newcomer Col. E.H.R. Green A.J. Allen F.C.C. Boyd Percy A. Smith Amon Carter Sr. Amon Carter Jr. Stack's Martin Paul National Gold Exchange Heritage Rare Coin Galleries Unidentified collector
Specimen 12 **"Davis** **specimen"**	J.W. Haseltine R. Couton Davis J.W. Haseltine George M. Klein R. Coulton Davis John N. Hale Hale Family H.P. Graves H.P. Graves Estate Fairbanks, Alaska, Collection Samuel W. Wolfson Norton Simon James H.T. McConnell Jr.
Specimen 13 **"Linderman** **specimen" or** **"Ten Eyck** **specimen"**	Henry R. Linderman James Ten Eyck James Ten Eyck Estate Lammot du Pont Lammot du Pont Family Willis du Pont (stolen 1967) (recovered 1982) American Numismatic Association, loan
Specimen 14 **"Rosenthal** **specimen"**	W. Julius Driefus Isaac Rosenthal James Ellsworth Wayte Raymond Farran Zerbe Chase Manhattan Bank American Numismatic Society

Specimen 15	William Idler
"Idler	H.O. Granberg
specimen"	William C. Atwater
	William C. Atwater Family
	Will W. Niel
	Abe Kosoff
	Edwin Hydeman
	World-Wide Coin Co.
	Bowers & Ruddy Galleries
	Mark Blackburn
	Continental Coin Galleries
	Superior Stamp & Coin Co.
	Dr. Jerry Buss
	Aubrey Bebee

High prices of rare coins

The numismatic market underwent a major transformation in the mid-1970s — the five-figure bid at auction became commonplace, and several times a year exceptional coins traded at $100,000 or more. A sellers' market was born in 1978, when in August two major collections were placed on the auction block, the N.M. Kaufman Collection, sold by the Rare Coin Company of America, and the Richard Branigan sale, auctioned by Bowers and Ruddy Galleries during the American Numismatic Association convention.

High prices were not unknown before 1978; there are nearly 225 prices $21,000 or higher listed in the 1978 edition of the Coin World Almanac, including 16 reaching $100,000 or more. The record-holder at that time was a 2,300-year-old coin, a silver decadrachm of Athens, Greece, which sold in 1974 for approximately $272,240 (U.S. figure computed from foreign funds). However, five-figure prices were still relatively uncommon; no Brasher doubloon had been sold at auction since 1907, when it brought $6,200; and the top price for a U.S. coin was the $225,000 paid in 1974 for the Idler specimen of the 1804 dollar restrike.

The U.S. sections following were compoiled by P. Scott Rubin. Only single-coin lots sold at auction are included in the list, and this necessitates excluding many record prices. Private transactions often excede prices realized at auction, but their reporting is haphazard. Multiple-coin lots

and sets are difficult to compare. A complete type set may contain hundreds of quality coins, while the King of Siam Proof set, for instance, which contains just nine coins (albeit one being an 1804 dollar) itself brought $2.9 million in a 1990 auction.

It is also important to point out that some prioces reported include a buyer's fee in addition to the hammer price. Buyer's fees may vary, but usually are 10 percent of the final, winning bid. The argument against reporting a price with buyer's fee is that it represents additional charges, not a true hammer price; it is Coin World's general preference to report just the hammer price. The argument for including the buyer's fee is that the buyer knows it will be added to the winning bid and adjusts his bid accordingly.

The records listed below are as reported in the official auction prices realized by the individual firms. Later auctions almost certainly include the 10 percent buyer's fee; earlier sales may not. To find the hammer price of a lot reported with a 10 percent buyer's fee, divide the price by 1.1. Thus, the $990,000 reported for the Dexter specimen 1804 dollar is actually $900,000 hammer price plus $90,000 buyer's fee.

Prices are not always obviously inclusive of a buyer's fee. Auctions tend to progress by round figures. Thus, a price of $16,500 looks like a $15,000 bid plus $1,500 fee; however, it is difficult to determine whether a price of $11,000 is actually a $10,000 bid plus $1,000 fee, or merely a hammer price of $11,000. Refer to individual firm's catalogs for their practices.

The foreign and ancient section is compiled by Coin World from auction reports received. Auctions conducted overseas in foreign currencies have been translated to dollars on an exchange rate at the time of the auction. A nice, round bid of 1 million francs may translate into a rather odd number in U.S. dollars.

The listing is as complete as possible, but the sheer volume of coin sales ensures that some sales may be missing. Additions are welcome. Write to Coin World, P.O. Box 150, Sidney, Ohio 45365 or P. Scott Rubin at P.O. Box 6885, Lawrenceville, N.J. 08648.

Abbreviations used for space economy in the U.S. section include: B&R, Bowers & Ruddy; B&M, Bowers & Merena. A-'[89] is Auction '[89]. EAC is Early American Coppers; VF, Very Fine; EF, Extremely Fine; AU, About Uncirculated. Grades or statements of condition are as cataloged.

Half Cents

1	63,250	1797 1 Over 1	Unc.-63+ Faded Mint Red	1989 Stack's 11/29, #33
2	63,250	1831 2nd Restrike, G-3	Proof-63+ Red	1989 Stack's 11/29, #65
3	55,000	1836 2nd Restrike, G-3	Proof-65 Red	1989 Stack's 11/29, #70
4	52,500	1796 With Pole	Unc. Red-Brown	1980 Stack's A-'80, # 1005
5	48,400	1796 With Pole	Unc.-63 Red-Brown	1986 Stack's Carter II, #790
6	42,000	1793	Unc.-Red-Brown	1980 Rarcoa's A-'80, #1512
7	41,800	1831 2nd Restrike	Proof-60-63 Brown	1987 B&M's Norweb I, #81
8	39,600	1852 Large Berries	Proof-63 Red	1987 B&M's Norweb I, #128
9	34,000	1796 No Pole	Unc. Brown	1975 Stack's Spence, #823
10	33,000	1836 2nd Restrike	Proof Red	1989 Stack's A-'89, #1513
11	30,800	1811 Presentation Specimen	Prooflike -60	1987 B&M's Norweb I, #67
12	30,000	1796 With Pole	Unc. Red-Brown	1973 Kagin's MANA, #980
13	30,000	1796 With Pole	AU-55 Brown	1980 New England's Metropolitan N.Y., #900
14	30,000	1795 C-1	Unc.-65 Brown	1979 B&R's Garrett I, #3
15	29,000	1796 No Pole	VF-35 Brown	1982 Stack's Robison, #313
16	28,600	1793	Unc.-60 Brown	1986 Superior's 9/29, #3007
17	28,600	1802 Reverse of 1800	Fine-15-VF-20	1987 B&M's Norweb I, #32
18	27,500	1831 1st Restrike G-2	Proof-65 Red	1989 Stack's 11/29, #64
19	27,500	1793	Unc.-63 Red-Brown	1986 Stack's Carter II, #784
20	25,300	1796 With Pole	Virtually Unc.-60 Brown	1987 Superior's A-'87, #1629
21	25,300	1796 No Pole	Fine-15-VF-20	1987 B&M's Norweb I, #22
22	25,300	1796 With Pole	Unc.-60 Brown	1987 B&M's Norweb I, #23
23	25,300	1852 Large Berries	Proof-67 Brown	1983 William Doyle Galleries' Lauder, #316

Large Cents

1	120,000	1793 Chain S-3	Unc.-65	1980 Paramount's A- '80, #554
2	115,000	1793 Chain S-3	Unc.-60+ Red-Brown	1979 B&R's Garrett I, #53
3	88,000	1793 Chain S-2	Unc.-63 Red-Brown	1989 Akers' A- '89, #1003
4	82,500	1793 Chain S-2	Unc.-60 Brown	1988 Stack's Halpern, #2
5	71,500	1793 Chain S-1	Unc.-60 Red-Brown	1988 Stack's Halpern, #1
6	63,800	1795 Reeded Edge	Good-6	1989 Superior's Robinson, #147
7	51,700	1793 Strawberry Leaf	Very Fair-3	1984 Stack's Starr, #7
8	50,600	1793 Strawberry Leaf	Basal State-1	1984 Stack's Starr, #6
9	50,600	1793 Chain S-2	Unc.-60+ Red-Brown	1989 Superior's Shore , #50
10	49,500	1793 Chain S-1	AU-50	1987 Stack's Romano, #144
11	49,500	1793 Wreath S-10	Unc.-65 Red-Brown	1989 Stack's 10/18, #655
12	46,750	1793 Wreath S-6	Unc.-65+ Red-Brown	1988 Stack's Halpern, #6
13	46,200	1793 Chain S-2	AU-55	1984 Stack's Starr, #2
14	44,000	1793 Wreath S-8	Unc.-63 Red-Brown	1989 EAC , #16
15	38,500	1794 S-50	AU-50 Brown	1990 Superior's Chalkley, #210
16	38,000	1793 Wreath S-9	Unc. Red-Brown	1982 Rarcoa's A- '82, #510
17	37,400	1794 S-37	VF-25	1989 Superior's Robinson, #61

18	37,000	1794 S-69	Unc.-67 Red-Brown	1980 Ivy's A.N.A., #942
19	36,000	1793 Liberty Cap S-13	AU-50 Red-Brown	1979 B&R's Garrett I, #55
20	36,000	1793 Liberty Cap S-14	EF-45	1989 EAC, #18
21	36,000	1794 Head '93 S-18b	Unc.-60 Red-Brown	1989 EAC, #20
22	35,200	1793 Wreath S-8	Unc.-65 Brown	1984 Stack's Starr, #13
23	35,200	1794 S-53	EF-40	1989 Superior's Robinson, #93
24	35,200	1834 N-7	Proof-65 Red	1988 B&M's Norweb III, #2919
25	35,000	1794 Starred Rev. S-48	VF-20	1989 Superior's Robinson, #84
26	35,000	1793 S-12	VF-20	1990 EAC, #17

Small Cents, Two Cents, Three Cents

1	47,300	1864 bronze cent "L"	Proof-64 Red	1987 B&M's Norweb I, #156
2	33,000	1864 bronze cent "L"	Proof	1988 Superior's 6/5, #4077
3	33,000	1901 cent	Proof-69 Red	1990 Superior's 1/28, #2119
4	32,500	1851 3-cent silver	Proof	1980 B&R's Garrett III, #1549
5	18,700	1856 Flying Eagle cent		1987 B&M's A.N.A., #69
6	18,000	1854 3-cent silver	Proof	1980 B&R's Garrett III, #1551
7	16,500	1864 bronze cent "No L"	Proof-65 Red	1987 B&M's Norweb I, #155
8	16,500	1864 bronze cent "L"	Proof-60 Red	1988 Superior's A-'88, #24
9	16,500	1864 Small Motto 2-cent	Proof-64-65 Red	1987 B&M's Norweb I, #233
10	15,675	1854 3-cent silver	Unc.	1989 Stack's 11/29, #235
11	15,400	1864 bronze cent "L"	Proof	1987 Stack's 10/20, #1139
12	15,000	1922 Plain cent	Unc.-65 Red	1980 Paramount's A-'80, #561
13	14,850	1864 bronze cent "L"	Proof	1987 Stack's 9/9, #532
14	14,850	1864 Small Motto 2-cent	Proof	1987 Stack's 10/20, #1140
15	14,500	1943-S bronze cent	EF-45	1989 Heritage's 3/30, #56
16	14,000	1943 bronze cent	AU-55	1986 Mid-American 1/3, #475
17	13,200	1856 Flying Eagle cent		1989 B&M 11/16, #25
18	13,200	1857 3-cent silver	Proof-65	1989 Superior's A-'89, #513
19	12,100	1856 Flying Eagle cent	Proof-65	1989 Akers' A-'89, #1009
20	11,500	1922 Plain cent	Unc. Red	1984 Rarcoa's A-'84, #1518
21	11,000	1864 Small Motto 2-cent	Prf-64 Red-Brown	1988 Superior's A-'88, #29
22	10,000	1943 bronze cent	EF	1981 B&R's A.N.A., #414

Five Cents

1	385,000	1913 Liberty Head		1985 Superior's Buss, #366
2	• 50,000	1913 Liberty Head		1961 Kosoff's Hydeman, #280
3	46,000	1913 Liberty Head	Unc.	1967 Paramount's A.N.A., #2241
4	44,000	1937	Proof-69	1990 Superior's 1/28, #2338
5	35,200	1925-S	Unc.	1989 Stack's 5/3, #890
6	25,850	1918 Over 7-D	Unc.	1985 Bellini, #121
7	23,100	1867 With Rays	Proof	1990 Stack's 1/16, #620
8	19,800	1926-S	Unc.-65	1990 Superior's 1/28, #2326
9	16,500	1918 Over 7-D	Unc.	1987 B&M's A.N.A., #214
10	15,400	1923-S	Unc.-67	1988 Akers' A-'88, #807
11	14,300	1923-S	Unc.-66	1989 Superior's Heifetz, #3514
12	14,300	1936	Proof-65+	1986 Paramount's A-'86, #1581
13	13,500	1918 Over 7-D	Unc.	1979 B&R's Helwig, #1856
14	13,200	1918 Over 7-D	Unc.	1986 B&M's 9/8, #1746
15	11,825	1918 Over 7-D	AU	1988 B&M 9/13, #118
16	11,550	1867 With Rays	Proof	1988 B&M's Norweb II, #1415
17	11,500	1866 With Rays	Proof-65	1980 Superior's A-'80, #56
18	11,000	1917	Proof-67	1988 Akers' A-'88, #799
19	10,450	1867 With Rays	Proof-64	1989 Superior's Heifetz, #1097
20	10,450	1916 Double Die		1989 A-'89, #1607
21	10,450	1937-D 3 Legged	Unc.-67	1988 Akers' Auciton '88, #813
22	10,175	1918 Over 7-D	Unc.	1983 Rarcoa's A-'83, #1047
23	10,175	1918 Over 7-D	Unc.-63	1983 Superior's A-'83, #1612
24	9,900	1918 Over 7-D	Unc.-66	1989 Superior's Heifetz, #3513
25	9,500	1918 Over 7-D	Unc.-63	1985 Heritage's A.N.A., #626

•Price is from prices realized list; may not have sold

Half Dimes

1	253,000	1870-S	Unc.-60	1986 Superior's A-'86, #1053

2	176,000	1870-S		1985 B&M's 9/9, #174
3	71,500	1801 V-1-B	Unc.	1989 Stack's 11/29, #366
4	70,400	1800 V-1	Unc.	1987 B&M's Norweb I, #308
5	60,000	1796 Over 5	Unc.	1979 B&R's Garrett I, #229
6	55,000	1802	EF	1984 Mid-American's 9/28, #276
7	50,600	1794 V-2 Presentation Piece		1989 Stack's 10/18, #670
8	50,600	1796 Over 5	Unc.	1985 Stack's Hayes, #5
9	48,400	1800 V-2 LIKERTY	Unc.-65	1988 Akers' A- '88, #526
10	45,000	1802	EF	1979 B&R's Garrett I, #234
11	44,000	1800 V-2 LIKERTY	Unc.	1987 B&M's Norweb I, #310
12	41,250	1802	EF-40	1986 Superior's A- '86, #1041
13	40,700	1802	EF	1986 Stack's A- '86, #78
14	40,000	1794	Unc.	1980 Stack's A- '80, #1118
15	39,600	1802	EF	1988 Superior's Lee, #2411
16	37,400	1800 V-2 LIKERTY	Unc.	1987 B&M's Norweb I, #309
17	35,200	1802	EF	1989 Stack's 11/29, #368
18	33,000	1794	Unc.	1985 Stack's Hayes, #4
19	32,000	1796 LIKERTY	Unc.	1980 Stack's 6/19, #287
20	31,000	1797 16 Stars V-4	Unc.-65	1989 Heritage's 6/15, #150
21	28,600	1795 V-4	Unc.	1989 Stack's 11/29, #356
22	28,600	1800 V-2 LIKERTY	Unc.	1989 Stack's 10/18, #671
23	26,400	1797 V-2	Unc.	1987 B&M's A.N.A., #227
24	26,400	1800 V-1a	Unc.	1985 Stack's 10/22, #6
25	25,300	1794	Unc.	1987 Stack's Romano, #269
26	25,300	1802	VF	1987 Superior's Ebsen, #459

Dimes

1	275,000	1894-S	Unc.	1990 Stack's 1/16, #206
2	148,500	1797 JR-1	Unc.	1990 Stack's 1/16, #3
3	148,500	1805 JR-2	Unc.-67	1989 Superior's A- '89, #535
4	145,000	1894-S	Proof	1980 Rarcoa's A- '80, #1578
5	88,000	1831	Proof-67	1989 Akers' A- '89, #1047
6	83,000	1894-S	Proof	1986 Pacific Coast's 9/25, #110
7	77,000	1835 JR-4	Proof	1990 Stack's 1/16, #50
8	77,000	1894-S	Proof	1987 B&M's Norweb I, #584
9	70,400	1894-S	Proof	1988 Superior's 6/5, #4516
10	61,600	1873-CC With Arrows	Unc.	1987 B&M's Norweb I, #537
11	60,500	1822 JR-1	Proof	1990 Stack's 1/16, #28
12	57,750	1807	Unc.-65	1989 Rarcoa's A- '89, #93
13	57,200	1820 JR-7	Proof	1990 Stack's 1/16, #23
14	55,000	1873-CC With Arrows	Unc.	1990 Stack's 1/16, #153
15	52,250	1796	Unc.	1990 Stack's 1/16, #2
16	52,000	1894-S	Proof	1973 Kagin's MANA, #1114
17	50,600	1827 JR-10	Proof-65	1989 Superior's A- '89, #540
18	50,600	1871-CC	Unc.	1990 Stack's 1/16, #146
19	50,600	1894-S	Proof	1985 Superior's Buss, #617
20	44,000	1796	Proof	1985 Stack's Hayes, #16
21	41,250	1796	Unc.-65+	1983 Superior's A- '83, #1635
22	41,250	1823 Over 2	Unc.-66	1989 Akers' A- '89, #1046
23	39,600	1796	Unc.	1987 Stack's Romano, #333
24	38,000	1796	Unc.	1980 B&R's Garrett III, #1568
25	37,400	1796	Unc.-67	1984 Paramount's A- '84, #612

#6 same coin as #4.

Twenty Cents

1	85,250	1876-CC	Unc.-65	1988 Superior's A- '88, #108
2	85,000	1876-CC	AU-55	1980 Superior's A- '80, #110
3	69,300	1876-CC	Unc.	1987 B&M's Norweb I, #691
4	66,000	1876-CC	Unc.	1983 Stack's A-'83, #625
5	66,000	1876-CC	Unc.	1984 Emery, #492
6	63,500	1876-CC	Unc.	1976 Carlson, #369
7	63,250	1876-CC	Unc.	1988 Stack's 1/13, #1405
8	57,750	1876-CC	Unc.	1983 Kagin's A.N.A., #2229
9	57,750	1876-CC	Unc.	1985 Stack's A-'85, #1653

10	48,400	1876	Proof-67	1989 Superior's A-'89, #564
11	45,000	1876-CC	Unc.	1975 Superior's A.N.A., #349
12	44,000	1876-CC	Unc.	1984 B&R's Arnold, #2211
13	39,500	1876-CC	Unc.	1978 Hughes' Henderson, #439
14	35,500	1876-CC	Unc.-60+	1978 Hughes' Pacific, #659
15	29,700	1876-CC	VF-20	1989 Superior's A-'89, #565
16	25,000	1876-CC	EF	1982 Rarcoa's A-'82, #707
17	19,800	1876-CC	VF	1989 Stack's 1/18, #423
18	17,600	1877	Proof	1990 Stack's 1/16, #711
19	16,000	1876-CC	Unc.	1972 B&R's Champa, #791
20	16,000	1876-CC	EF	1976 B&R's Willing, #72
21	13,750	1875-CC	Unc.	1989 Stack's 5/3, #903
22	13,200	1875-S	Unc.	1990 B&M's 3/28, #2305
23	12,750	1876-CC	Unc.	1966 Kreisberg & Schulman, #1166

Quarter Dollars

1	205,000	1873-CC No Arrows	Unc.-65	1980 New England's Met. N.Y., #519
2	190,000	1827 Original	Proof	1980 B&R's Garrett II, #641
3	187,000	1838 No Drapery	Unc.-68	1989 Superior's A-'89, #572
4	88,000	1873-CC No Arrows	Unc.	1988 B&M's Norweb II, #1647
5	87,500	1823 Over 2	Proof	1980 Stack's A-'80, #1176
6	85,000	1901-S	Unc.	1980 Stack's A-'80, #1217
7	80,000	1804	AU	1980 B&R's Garrett II, #623
8	80,000	1873-CC No Arrows	Unc.	1975 Stack's James A. Stack, #136
9	79,750	1827 Original	Proof-64	1989 Superior's A-'89, #570
10	75,000	1835 B-7	Proof	1980 B&R's Garrett II, #649
11	70,400	1833 B-1	Proof-65	1990 Superior's 1/28, #2568
12	70,000	1804	Unc.	1980 Stack's A-'80, #1173
13	70,000	1827 Original	Proof	1980 Stack's A-'80, #1177
14	68,750	1891-O	Specimen Unc.-65	1989 Superior's Heifetz, #3652
15	67,000	1823 Over 2	Prooflike	1973 Kagin's MANA, #1140
16	66,000	1820 B-1	Proof-64	1989 Superior's A-'89, #566
17	64,900	1827 Original	Proof	1983 Brown, #2981
18	61,600	1827 Original	Proof	1988 B&M's Norweb II, #1542
19	60,000	1822 25 Over 50C.	Proof	1980 B&R's Garrett II, #636
20	60,000	1828 B-4	Unc.	1980 B&R's Garrett II, #642
21	57,750	1804 B-1	Unc.	1985 Stack's 10/22, #34
22	55,000	1827 Original	Proof	1984 Dodson, #3975
23	55,000	1864	Unc.-68	1990 Superior's 1/28, #2584
24	51,000	1901-S	Unc.	1981 Superior's Turkus, #596
25	50,000	1827 Original	Proof	1975 Stack's James A. Stack, #29
26	50,000	1842 Small Date	Proof	1974 Stack's Steckler, #39

Half Dollars

1	220,000	1797	Unc.	1988 B&M's Norweb III, #3027
2	137,500	1794 O-101	Unc.	1989 Stack's 10/18, #693
3	99,000	1796 15 Stars	Unc.	1988 B&M's Norweb III, #5024
4	99,000	1797	Unc.	1989 B&M's A.N.A., #273
5	99,000	1807 Draped Bust O-105	Unc.-65	1990 Superior's 1/28, #3436
6	93,500	1838-O	Proof	1988 B&M's Norweb III, #3119
7	83,600	1796 15 Stars	Unc.	1990 B&M's 1/24, #256
8	79,750	1796 15 Stars	Unc.	1989 Superior's 1/29, #4417
9	75,000	1796 15 Stars	Unc.	1980 Rarcoa's A-'80, #1594
10	74,800	1796 15 Stars	AU	1989 B&M 3/27, #1990
11	70,000	1838-O	Proof	1982 Stack's Robison, #1605
12	68,750	1917-S on Obverse	Unc.-67	1989 Superior's A-'89, #651
13	66,550	1797	Unc.	1989 B&M's 3/27, #288
14	66,000	1839-O	Unc.-66	1989 Rarcoa's A-'89, #205
15	64,900	1797	Unc.	1988 Superior's Shore, #1732
16	62,000	1838-O	Proof-60	1979 Superior's A-'79, #1569
17	60,500	1794 O-101	Unc.	1985 Stack's 10/22, #50
18	57,750	1866 Motto	Unc.	1989 Stack's 10/18, #704
19	55,000	1838-O	Proof	1984 Rarcoa's A-'84, #1666
20	54,000	1797	Unc.	1981 Rarcoa's A-'81, #132

| 21 | 50,600 | 1822 O-103 | Proof | 1988 B&M's Norweb III, #3077 |
| 22 | 50,000 | 1838-O | Proof | 1975 Stack's James A. Stack, #415 |

Silver Dollars

1	990,000	1804 Original	Proof	1989 Rarcoa's A-'89, #247
2	400,000	1804 Restrike	EF	1980 B&R's Garrett II, #698
3	357,500	1893-S	Unc.	1988 B&M's Norweb III, #3887
4	308,000	1804 Restrike	Unc.	1985 Superior's Buss, #1337
5	280,000	1804 Original	Proof	1981 Stack's Bareford, #424
6	264,000	1794	Unc.	1984 Stack's Carter, #207
7	242,000	1794	Unc.	1988 B&M's Norweb III, #3741
8	242,000	1804 Restrike	EF	1989 Stack's L.R. French, #15
9	231,000	1795 Draped Bust B-14	Unc.-66	1989 Superior's Heifetz, #3816
10	220,000	1794	Unc.	1985 Stack's Hayes, #72
11	209,000	1794	Unc.	1986 Superior's 1/27, #1173
12	198,000	1799 B-12b	Unc.-67	1989 Superior's Heifetz, #3817
13	198,000	1804 Restrike	EF	1984 Stack's Carter, #241
14	190,000	1804 Restrike	EF-40	1982 Pullen & Hanks 2/5, #1076
15	187,000	1804 Restrike	EF	1986 B&M's Einstein, #1736
16	170,000	1795 Draped Bust B-14	Proof	1980 B&R's Garrett II, #680
17	165,000	1803 Restrike	Proof-65	1989 Superior's A-'89, #666
18	154,000	1794	Unc.	1989 Stack's L.R. French, #2
19	143,000	1795 Flowing Hair B-2	Unc.-65	1989 Superior's Heifetz, #3815
20	143,000	1795 Draped Bust B-14	Proof	1985 Stack's 10/22, #73
21	126,500	1870-S	AU	1988 B&M's Norweb III, #3825
22	110,000	1794	Unc.	1973 Superior's Gilhousen, #1209
23	110,000	1794	Unc.-63	1983 Ivy's 8/11, #3769
24	93,500	1794	Unc.-60+	1984 Paramount's A-'84, #725
25	90,750	1802 Restrike	Proof	1989 B&M's 3/27, #1981

#2 same coin as #14, #1 same coin as #5

Trade Dollars

1	121,000	1885	Proof	1988 B&M's Norweb II, #1848
2	110,000	1885	Proof	1980 Rarcoa's A-'80, #1626
3	110,000	1885	Proof	1984 Stack's Carter, #441
4	104,500	1885	Proof	1989 Stack's L.R. French, #202
5	96,250	1885	Proof	1984 Rarcoa's A-'84, #1810
6	96,250	1885	Proof	1987 Superior's 2/8, #1446B
7	90,750	1885	Proof-63	1984 Superior's A-'84, #192
8	77,000	1884	Proof-63	1989 Rarcoa's A-'89, #327
9	72,600	1884	Proof	1989 Stack's L.R. French, #201
10	61,600	1884	Proof	1988 Stack's 6/21, #196
11	57,200	1884	Proof	1988 B&M's Norweb II, #1847
12	45,100	1884	Proof	1984 Stack's Carter, #440
13	44,000	1879	Proof-67	1989 Heritage's 10/5, #1026
14	40,000	1878-S	Unc.	1980 B&R's Garrett II, #731
15	39,000	1884	Proof	1975 New England's 11/7, #639
16	37,400	1884	Proof	1984 B&R's Arnold, #2342
17	30,000	1884	Proof	1974 B&R's Herstal, #734
18	30,000	1884	Proof-60	1980 Ivy's A.N.A., #2643
19	27,500	1878	Proof	1990 Stack's 1/16, #723
20	27,500	1878-CC	Unc.-65+	1988 Superior's A-'88, #231
21	27,500	1884	Proof	1984 Rarcoa's A-'84, #1809
22	26,400	1884	Proof	1987 Superior's 2/8, #1446A
23	22,000	1883	Proof	1990 Stack's 1/16, #763

#2 same coin as #5, #3 same coin as #7

Gold Dollars

1	90,000	1849-C Open Wreath		1979 A-'79, #749
2	90,000	1854 Type II	Proof	1979 B&R's Garrett I, #403
3	88,000	1854 Type II	Unc.-67	1989 Akers' A-'89, #1341
4	68,750	1854 Type I	Proof	1985 Stack's A-'85, #1874
5	55,000	1884	Proof-67	1990 Superior's 1/28, #4323
6	52,000	1861-D	Unc.	1987 FUN, #1810

7	50,000	1849-C Open Wreath		1982 FUN, #1350
8	46,000	1855	Proof	1978 Stack's Bareford, #29
9	44,000	1850	Proof-67	1989 Superior's 1/31, #5
10	44,000	1861-D	Unc.	1984 Stack's A-'84, #1307
11	42,900	1854	Unc.-65	1989 Superior's 1/31, #12
12	42,900	1854 Type 2	Unc.-65	1990 Superior's 1/28, #4281
13	42,000	1861-D	Unc.	1981 Vincennes, #375
14	41,800	1849 Small Head No L	Proof-65	1989 Superior's 1/31, #239
15	41,800	1857	Unc.-68	1989 Superior's 1/31, #15
16	41,000	1884	Proof-67	1989 Heritage's 3/30, #566
17	39,600	1857	Unc.-68	1989 Superior's A-'89, #823
18	37,400	1875	Proof	1986 Stack's Carter, #70
19	37,400	1881	Unc.-68	1990 Superior's 1/28, #4314
20	35,200	1861-D	Unc.-64	1989 Superior's 1/31, #273
21	35,200	1875	Proof-65	1989 Akers' A-'89, #1351
22	35,000	1849-C Open Wreath		1974 Pine Tree's GENA, #1952
23	33,000	1855	Unc.	1988 Stack's A-'88, #1335
24	31,900	1861-D	Unc.	1990 Stack's 1/16, #1594

#15 same coin as #17

Quarter Eagles

1	231,000	1808	Unc.-64	1989 Akers' A-'89, #1361
2	231,000	1831	Proof-66	1989 Akers' A-'89, #1365
3	176,000	1796 With Stars	Unc.-63+	1989 Akers' A-'89, #1356
4	154,000	1821	Unc.-65	1989 Akers' A-'89, #1362
5	137,500	1825	Unc.-66	1988 Rarcoa's A-'88, #1872
6	135,000	1834 No Motto	Proof	1980 B&R's Garrett II, #754
7	132,000	1825	Unc.-65	1989 Akers' A-'89, #1363
8	125,000	1796 No Stars	AU	1980 B&R's Garrett II, #732
9	120,000	1821	Proof	1980 B&R's Garrett II, #743
10	105,000	1831	Unc.	1980 B&R's Garrett II, #750
11	104,500	1850	Proof	1988 Rarcoa's A-'88, #1876
12	104,500	1824 Over 1	Unc.	1985 Rarcoa's A-'85, #357
13	99,000	1808	Unc.	1984 Stack's A-'84, #1372
14	93,500	1848 CAL.	Unc.-67	1989 Superior's 1/31, #305
15	82,500	1841	Proof-63	1982 B&R's U.S.G.C., #117
16	75,000	1826	Unc.	1980 B&R's Garrett II, #746
17	74,250	1796 With Stars	Unc.	1984 Stack's A-'84, #1365
18	71,500	1821	Proof	1984 Stack's A-'84, #1373
19	70,000	1848 CAL.	Unc.	1980 B&R's Garrett II, #762
20	68,750	1856	Proof	1989 Superior's 5/30, #5557
21	63,250	1848 CAL.	Unc.-63	1990 Superior's 1/28, #4376
22	61,600	1857	Proof	1987 B&M's Norweb II, #2035
23	61,600	1908	Proof-67	1990 Superior's 1/28, #4469
24	60,500	1834 No Motto	Proof	1984 Rarcoa's A-'84, #1887
25	60,500	1827	Unc.-64	1989 Akers' A-'89, #1364
26	60,500	1863	Proof	1989 B&M's 9/11, #477

Three Dollar Gold

1	687,500	1870-S	EF-40	1982 B&R's U.S.G.C., #296
2	150,000	1875	Proof	1974 Stack's Ullmer, #421
3	132,000	1854	Unc.-67	1990 Superior's 1/28, #4520
4	125,000	1875	Proof	1981 Rarcoa's A-'81, #418
5	121,000	1875	Proof	1984 Stack's Carter, #610
6	120,000	1875	Proof	1975 Stack's Clarke, #22
7	110,000	1875	Proof-65	1982 B&R's U.S.G.C., #301
8	110,000	1875	Proof	1987 B&M's Norweb I, #721
9	110,000	1875	Proof-63+	1988 Akers' A-'88, #880
10	99,000	1875	Proof-65	1985 Superior's A-'85, #936
11	99,000	1875	Proof	1987 Superior's Ebsen, #2419
12	96,250	1875	Proof	1986 Stack's Carter, #134
13	91,000	1875	Proof	1976 Stack's Garrett, #455
14	90,750	1875	Proof	1988 Stack's & Superior's Kramer, #269
15	82,500	1863	Unc.-67	1988 Akers' A-'88, #844

16	77,000	1875	Proof	1986 Stack's 10/22, #911
17	72,500	1854-D	Unc.	1981 Rarcoa's A-'81, #386
18	70,000	1875	Proof	1977 Rarcoa's Central States, #399
19	65,000	1875	Proof	1977 Davenport, #1373
20	62,500	1875	Proof	1981 Stack's 12/12, #1121
21	60,500	1863	Unc.-66	1990 Superior's 1/28, #4530
22	60,500	1877	Proof-65	1989 Superior's 1/31, #114
23	55,000	1854-D		1987 FUN, #1814
24	55,000	1878	Unc.-66	1989 Superior's Heifetz, #4271
25	53,000	1875	Proof	1980 Kreisberg & Cohen's Gainsborough, #1256

Half Eagles

1	687,500	1822	VF-30-EF-40	1982 B&R's U.S.G.C., #378
2	352,000	1829 Small Date	Proof-64-65	1987 B&M's Norweb I, #779
3	220,000	1825 Over 4	Proof-60	B&R's 1982 U.S.G.C., #381
4	198,000	1821	Proof-63-64	1987 B&M's Norweb I, #773
5	187,000	1854-S	AU-55	1982 B&R's U.S.G.C., #471
6	165,000	1829 Large Date	Unc.	1979 B&R's Garrett I, #471
7	150,000	1815	AU-55	1979 B&R's Garrett I, #460
8	148,500	1825 Over 4	EF-AU	1989 B&M's 3/27, #617
9	140,000	1825 Over 4	VF	1978 Rarcoa's Kaufman, #809
10	132,000	1825 Over 4	VF	1988 Kagin's 246th, #1080
11	115,500	1894-S	Unc.-69	1988 Akers' A-'88, #845
12	115,500	1829 Large Date	Unc.	1989 B&M's A.N.A., #548
13	110,000	1798 Small Eagle	EF-40	1979 B&R's Garrett I, #437
14	110,000	1828	Unc.	1979 A-'79, #819
15	110,000	1864-S	Unc.-64	1987 B&M's Norweb I, #875
16	104,500	1829 Large Date	Unc.-65	1985 Superior's A-'85, #941
17	100,000	1829 Small Date	Unc.	1974 Kagin's MANA, #1618
18	93,500	1875	Proof-64	1989 Akers' A-'89, #1394
19	92,500	1828	Unc.	1975 Paramount's 2/14, #561
20	88,000	1829 Large Date	Prf-67 Obv.,-Unc.-67 Rev.	1983 B&M's Brand I, #280
21	85,000	1819	Unc.-65	1979 B&R's Garrett I, #462
22	82,500	1815	AU-55	1987 B&M's Norweb I, #767
23	82,500	1829 Large Date	Unc.-65-67	1982 B&R's U.S.G.C., #387
24	82,500	1829 Small Date	Unc.	1990 B&M 1/24, #570
25	81,000	1875	Proof	1976 Stack's Garrett I, #454

#8 same coin as #9 and #10

Eagles

1	308,000	1795	Unc.-63	1989 Superior's A-'89, #908
2	214,500	1908-S	Unc.-68	1989 Superior's 1/31, #142
3	198,000	1913-S	Unc.-65	1989 Superior's 1/31, #146
4	198,000	1915-S	Unc.-65	1989 Superior's 1/31, #148
5	159,500	1899	Proof-67	1990 Superior's 1/28, #4840
6	154,000	1858	Unc.-64	1989 Superior's A-'89, #916
7	148,500	1907 Rolled Rim, Periods	Unc.-67	1989 Superior's 10/1, #4937
8	137,500	1795	Unc.-60	1989 Superior's 10/1, #4621
9	132,000	1860	Proof	1989 Superior's 5/30, #3627
10	132,000	1911-D	Unc.-65	1988 B&M's Norweb II, #2313
11	130,000	1795	Unc.	1980 B&R's Garrett III, #1655
12	121,000	1858	Proof	1984 Stack's Carter, #759
13	121,000	1907 Rolled Rim Periods	Unc.-66	1989 Akers' A-'89, #1426
14	121,000	1907 Rolled Rim Periods	Unc.-65	1990 Superior 1/28, #4874
15	120,000	1798 Over 7, 7 Stars Left	AU	1980 B&R's Garrett II, #1660
16	115,000	1858	Unc.-67	1980 Paramount's A-'80, #954
17	110,000	1933	Unc.-64	1989 Akers' A-'89, #1440
18	105,000	1838	Proof	1975 Paramount's 2/14, #612
19	104,500	1875	Proof-65	1982 B&R's U.S.G.C., #748
20	104,500	1904-O	Unc.-68	1989 Akers' A-'89, #1422
21	97,500	1933	Unc.	1980 Stack's Kahn, #793
22	95,700	1933	Unc.-64	1988 B&M's Norweb II, #2329
23	93,500	1933	Unc.-65	1982 B&R's U.S.G.C., #873

24	93,500	1933	Unc.-63	1989 Superior's 10/1, #5015
25	92,500	1933	Unc.	1978 Stack's Bareford, #225

#6 is same coin as #16

Double Eagles

1	660,000	1861 Paquet Reverse	Unc.-67	1988 B&M's Norweb III, #3984
2	286,000	1907 Ex. High Relief	Proof-65+	1985 Superior's A-'85, #983
3	275,000	1927-D	Unc.	1985 Stack's 10/22, #868
4	264,000	1907 Ex. High Relief	Proof	1985 B&M's Kosoff, #848
5	242,000	1907 Ex. High Relief	Proof-67	1982 B&R's U.S.G.S., #1021
6	242,000	1927-D	Unc.	1987 B&M's King of Siam, #2201
7	230,000	1907 Ex. High Relief	Proof-69	1980 Paramount's A-'80 , #977
8	225,000	1907 Ex. High Relief	Proof	1979 Stack's 6/21, #781
9	220,000	1907 Ex. High Relief	Proof	1985 Stack's 10/22, #822
10	220,000	1907 High Relief	Unc.-67	1989 Superor's Heifetz, #5200
11	220,000	1927-D	Unc.	1981 Stack's 12/12, #1252
12	200,000	1907 Ex. High Relief	Proof	1974 Stack's Ullmer, #546
13	198,000	1927-D	Unc.-65	1984 Paramount's A-'84, #999
14	187,000	1927-D	Unc.	1988 Stack's & Superior's Kramer, #913
15	181,500	1861	Unc.-67	1989 Superior's Heifetz, #5039
16	176,000	1927-D	Unc.-65	1982 B&R's U.S.G.C., #1067
17	121,000	1907 High Relief Flat Rim	Unc.-67	1989 Akers' A-'89, #1456
18	110,000	1884	Proof	1974 Stack's Ullmer, #528
19	93,500	1926-D	Unc.-65+	1989 Akers' A-'89, #1473
20	92,500	1883	Proof	1979 Stack's 6/21, #694
21	90,000	1891	Proof	1980 B&R's Garrett II, #798
22	90,000	1910	Proof	1980 B&R's Garrett II, #807
23	88,000	1883	Proof-67	1982 B&R's U.S.G.C., #962
24	88,000	1907 High Relief	Unc.	1987 Superior's 9/22, #5903
25	88,000	1883	Proof-65	1988 B&M's Norweb III, #4028

Silver Commemoratives

1	35,750	1922 Grant With Star	Unc.-65	1988 Superior's Lee, #1117
2	35,750	1926 Oregon	Proof-67	1989 Akers' A-'89, #1203
3	35,200	1921 Missouri	Unc.-66	1988 Superior's Lee, #1133
4	27,000	1900 Lafayette dollar		1980 B&R's Garrett II , #863
5	26,400	1928 Hawaiian	Unc.-66	1990 Superior's 1/28, #4022
6	25,300	1900 Lafayette dollar	Unc.-65	1988 Superior's Lee, #1056
7	20,900	1921 Alabama 2X2	Unc.-66	1990 Superior's 1/28, #3919
8	20,900	1893 Isabella quarter	Unc.-67	1990 B&M's 3/28 , #2556
9	19,800	1915-S Pan-Pacific	Unc.-67	1989 Superior's Heifetz, #2204
10	19,800	1900 Lafayette dollar	Unc.-65	1990 B&M's 3/28, #2558
11	18,700	1946 Iowa	Proof-66	1989 Akers' A-'89, #1198
12	18,700	1900 Lafayette dollar	Unc.-65	1990 B&M's 3/28, #2559
13	15,400	1921 Missouri 2X4	Unc.-65	1988 Superior's Lee, #1132
14	14,300	1921 Alabama 2X2	Unc.-67	1988 Akers' A-'88, #689
15	14,300	1921 Alabama 2X2	Unc.-65	1990 Superior's 1/28, #3920
16	13,450	1915-S Pan-Pacific	Unc.-65	1988 Superior's Lee, #1153
17	12,500	1900 Lafayette dollar	Unc.-65+	1980 Superior's A-'80 , #283
18	12,250	1924 Huguenot-Walloon	Unc.-67	1988 Mid-American's 5/27, #1615
19	12,000	1915-S Pan-Pacific	Unc.	1980 B&R's Garrett II, #816
20	11,550	1928 Hawaii	Proof-67-65	1986 Paramount's A-'86, #1769
21	11,550	1921 Missouri 2X4	Unc.-65	1990 B&M's 3/28, #2581
22	11,000	1928 Hawaiian	Unc.-65	1990 Superior's 1/28, #4023
23	10,450	1921 Missouri 2X4	Unc.-65+	1988 Akers' A-'88, #703
24	10,450	1915-S Pan-Pacific	Unc.-67	1988 Akers' A-'88, #718
25	10,450	1893 Isabella quarter	Unc.-66	1988 Superior's Lee, #1055

Gold Commemoratives

1	126,500	1915-S Pan-Pacific Round $50	Unc.	1989 Superior's Heifetz, #5474
2	100,000	1915-S Pan-Pacific Octagon $50	Unc.	1980 B&R's Garrett II, #876
3	95,000	1915-S Pan-Pacific Round $50	Unc.	1980 B&R's Garrett II, #873
4	71,500	1915-S Pan-Pacific Octagon $50	Unc.-64	1990 Superior's 1/28, #5205
5	68,750	1915-S Pan-Pacific Round $50	Unc.-64	1990 Superior's 1/28, #5202

6	68,750	1915-S Pan-Pacific Octagon $50	Unc.-64	1990 Superior's 1/28, #5204
7	68,200	1915-S Pan-Pacific Round $50	Unc.-64	1990 Superior's 1/28, #5203
8	60,500	1915-S Pan-Pacific Round $50	Unc.-64	1989 Akers' A-'89, #1214
9	56,100	1915-S Pan-Pacific Round $50	Unc.	1989 Stack's A-'89, #1877
10	52,250	1915-S Pan-Pacific Round $50	Unc.-65	1989 Akers' A-'89, #1213
11	50,600	1915-S Pan-Pacific Round $50	Unc.	1987 B&M's A.N.A., #756
12	49,000	1915-S Pan-Pacific Round $50	Unc.	1980 Stack's Kahn, #84
13	45,100	1915-S Pan-Pacific Round $50	Unc.	1987 Stack's A-'87, #978
14	44,000	1915-S Pan-Pacific Round $50	Unc.	1980 Stack's Kahn, #639
15	44,000	1915-S Pan-Pacific Round $50	Unc.	1986 Kagin's A.N.A., #2177
16	44,000	1915-S Pan-Pacific Round $50	Unc.-65	1989 Superior's 1/31, #541
17	42,000	1915-S Pan-Pacific Octagon $50	Unc.	1980 Stack's Kahn, #640
18	39,600	1915-S Pan-Pacific Round $50	Unc.	1988 Stack's A-'88, #1478
19	38,500	1915-S Pan-Pacific Octagon $50	Unc.	1989 Superior's 5/28, #2341
20	38,500	1915-S Pan-Pacific Round $50	Unc.	1984 Stack's Carter, #1118
21	37,400	1915-S Pan-Pacific Octagon $50	Unc.	1987 B&M's A.N.A., #755
22	37,400	1915-S Pan-Pacific Octagon $50	Unc.	1987 Stack's A-'87, #977
23	37,400	1915-S Pan-Pacific Round $50	Unc.-63	1988 Akers' A-'88, #728
24	37,400	1915-S Pan-Pacific Octagon $50	Unc.	1988 Rarcoa's A-'88, #1824
25	34,500	1915-S Pan-Pacific Round $50	Unc.	1981 B&R's A.N.A., #1736

Four Dollar Gold Patterns

1	297,000	1880 Flowing Hair	Proof	1989 Superior's 10/1, #4297
2	175,000	1879 Coiled Hair	Proof-65	1980 Superior's A-'80, #385
3	165,000	1879 Coiled Hair	Proof	1987 Superior's Ebsen, #2444
4	135,000	1880 Coiled Hair	Proof	1981 Stack's 12/12, #1139
5	115,000	1879 Coiled Hair	Proof	1979 B&R's Garrett I, #431
6	105,000	1879 Coiled Hair	Proof	1974 Superior's Rio Rancho, #133
7	105,000	1880 Flowing Hair	Proof-65	1980 Superior's A-'80, #386
8	104,500	1879 Coiled Hair	Proof	1985 Superior's Buss, #1766
9	102,300	1880 Coiled Hair	Proof	1982 Sotheby's DuPont, #252
10	101,750	1879 Coiled Hair	Proof-67	1982 B&R's U.S.G.C., #317
11	99,000	1880 Coiled Hair	Proof-65	1982 B&R's U.S.G.C., #319
12	90,000	1879 Coiled Hair	Proof	1978 Stack's Lighthouse, #828
13	88,000	1879 Coiled Hair	Proof	1984 Stack's Carter, #632
14	88,000	1879 Flowing Hair	Proof	1989 Superior's 10/1, #4295
15	84,750	1880 Flowing Hair	Proof	1988 Superior's 6/5, #6731
16	80,000	1879 Coiled Hair	Proof	1981 Stack's 12/12, #1137
17	79,200	1879 Flowing Hair	Proof	1988 Stack's & Superior's Kramer, #284
18	74,800	1879 Coiled Hair	Proof	1983 Stack's Coles, #57
19	74,250	1880 Coiled Hair	Proof	1984 Stack's Carter, #634
20	72,600	1880 Flowing Hair	Proof	1988 Stack's & Superior's Kramer, #285
21	72,600	1880 Flowing Hair	Proof	1989 Stack's A-'89, #1930
22	68,750	1880 Flowing Hair	Proof	1984 Stack's Carter, #633
23	67,500	1880 Coiled Hair	Proof	1975 Paramount's 2/14, #547
24	65,000	1880 Flowing Hair	Proof	1979 B&R's Garrett I, #432
25	65,000	1880 Flowing Hair	Proof	1980 Stack's A-'80, #1451

Patterns

1	475,000	1907 $20 J-1776	Proof	1981 B&R's A.N.A., #2434
2	467,500	1907 $20 J-1776	Proof-67	1984 Paramount's A-'84, #542
3	200,000	1792 Birch cent J-4	Unc.	1981 B&R's Garrett IV, #2349
4	170,000	1879 $20 J-1643	Proof	1989 Superior's Moreira, #402
5	143,000	1792 Silver Center cent J-1	Unc.-60	1988 B&M's Norweb III, #3392
6	137,500	1792 half disme J-7	Unc.-65	1990 Superior's 1/28, #2354
7	105,000	1792 Silver Center cent J-1		1974 Pine Tree's 9/18, #1272a
8	105,000	1879 silver dollar J-1608		1980 B&R's Garrett II, #1056
9	100,000	1792 half disme J-7	Unc.-65	1988 Pacific Coast's 6/1, #25
10	99,000	1876 $20 J-1490	Proof-65	1986 Superior's A-'86, #1451
11	95,000	1792 Silver Center cent J-1	Unc.	1981 B&R's Garrett IV, #2347
12	93,500	1879 $20 J-1643	Proof	1984 Stack's Carter, #635
13	90,000	1792 Birch cent J-6	Unc.	1981 B&R's Garrett IV, #2350
14	90,000	1874 $10 J-1373		1981 B&R's A.N.A., #2433
15	90,000	1879 $20 J-1643		1980 B&R's Garrett II, #1097

16	82,500	1874 Eagle J-1373	Proof-67	1985 Paramount's A- '85, #1306
17	68,750	1792 Silver Center cent J-1	EF-40	1987 Stack's Romano, #143
18	68,750	1792 half disme J-7	Unc.	1988 Stack's 10/18, #536
19	66,000	1915 Pan-Pac 50¢ J-1793	Unc.-60	1988 B&M's Norweb III, #3307
20	60,500	1879 half dollar J-1601	Proof-67	1989 Superior's Heifetz, #3281
21	60,000	1792 half disme J-7	Unc.-65	1987 Mid-American's 5/22, #721
22	59,400	1792 Birch cent J-5	EF-40	1988 B&M's Norweb III, #3395
23	57,750	1792 half disme J-7	Unc.-67	1985 Stack's 10/22, #3
24	57,750	1863 $10 J-349		1980 B&R's Garrett II, #1088
25	55,000	1877 $50 J-1547		1980 B&R's Garrett II , #3281

#1 same coin as #2

Colonials

1	725,000	1787 Brasher doubloon	Unc.-63	1979 B&R's Garrett I, #607
2	625,000	1787 Brasher doubloon "EB" on Breast	VF	1981 B&R's Garrett IV, #2340
3	430,000	1787 Brasher doubloon	AU	1979 Rarcoa's A- '79 , #1433
4	190,000	1783 Nova Constellatio mark	Unc.-60	1979 B&R's Garrett I, #622
5	165,000	1783 Nova Constellatio quint Type I	Unc.-65	1979 B&R's Garrett I, #620
6	99,000	1776 silver Continental dollar N-1-C	VF	1987 Stack's Romano, #24
7	97,500	1783 Nova Constellatio bit	Unc.-65	1979 B&R's Garrett I, #619
8	95,000	1776 silver Continental dollar N-1-C		1980 B&R's Garrett III, #1491
9	80,000	1742-dated Brasher Lima style doubloon	EF	1981 B&R's Garrett IV, #2341
10	75,000	(1652) N.E. sixpence	VF	1980 B&R's Garrett III, #1201
11	75,000	(1737) Higley Copper "The Wheele Goes Round"		1980 B&R's Garrett III, #1306
12	75,000	1783 Chalmers shilling, Rings on Reverse	EF	1980 B&R's Garrett III, #1313
13	70,400	1616 Sommer Islands threepence	VF-20	1987 B&M's Norweb I, #1141
14	65,000	1795 Washington oval engraved Peace medal		1981 B&R's Garrett II, #1914
15	63,800	1787 American Congress Fugio cent N.1-CC	AU-50	1988 B&M's Norweb III, #3516
16	60,500	(1737) Higley copper "The Wheele Goes Round"	Fine	1983 Stack's Roper, #154
17	56,100	(1652) N.E. Sixpence	EF	1983 Stack's Roper, #8
18	55,000	1783 Nova Constellatio quint Type II	AU-55,	1979 B&R's Garrett I, #621
19	55,000	1786 New Jersey copper M-10-h	AU-50	1987 B&M's Norweb I, #1310
20	52,800	1652 Willow Tree shilling N-II-A	VF-20	1987 B&M' s Norweb I, #1154
21	52,000	1786 New Jersey copper M-8-F	EF	1980 B&R's Garrett III, #1393
22	50,600	1776 Continental dollar N-5-D	AU-50	1988 B&M's Norweb I, #2458
23	50,000	(1786) New Jersey copper/Gen. Washington M-4-C	EF	1980 B&R's Garrett III, #1390

Pioneer Gold

1	500,000	1851 Humbert Octagon $50	Proof	1980 B&R's Garrett II, #897
2	325,000	1852 Over 1 Aug. Humbert $20	Proof	1980 B&R's Garrett II, #890
3	300,000	1855 Kellogg & Co. $50	Proof	1980 B&R'Garrett II, #910
4	275,000	1855 Wass, Molitor $50	Unc.	1980 B&R's Garrett II, #947
5	270,000	1849 Cincinnati Mining $10	EF	1980 B&R's Garrett II, #885
6	230,000	1854 Kellogg & Co. $20	Proof	1980 B&R's Garrett II, #908
7	200,000	1830 Templeton Reid $5	EF-40	1979 B&R's Garrett I, #505
8	200,000	1850 F.D. Kohler $50 ingot	EF	1980 B&R's Garrett II, #911
9	200,000	1855 Kellogg & Co. $50	Proof	1984 Rarcoa's A- '84, #2000
10	180,000	1849 Pacific Co. $5	VF	1980 B&R's Garrett II, #935
11	154,000	1855 Kellogg & Co. $50	Proof	1984 Stack's Carter, #1149
12	140,000	1855 Kellogg & Co. $50	Proof	1979 A- '79, #996
13	137,500	(1849) J.S. Ormsby $5	VF	1989 Superior's A- '89, #997
14	135,000	(1849) Miners' Bank $10	Unc.	1980 B&R's Garrett II, #916
15	132,000	1849 Pacific Co. $10	AU	1984 B&M's Brand II, #1544
16	132,000	1849 Mormon $10	AU	1984 Stack's Carter, #1163
17	130,000	1855 Kellogg & Co. $50	Proof-63	1980 Paramount's A- '80, #982
18	110,000	1851 Baldwin & Co. $20	VF	1980 B&R's Garrett II, #881
19	108,350	1855 Kellogg & Co. $50	Proof	1987 Superior's Ebsen , #3140
20	104,500	1849 Cincinnati Mining $10	EF-40	1984 B&M's Brand II, #1539
21	100,000	(1849) J.S. Ormsby $10	Fine	1980 B&R's Garrett II, #933
22	100,000	(1861) John Parsons $5	VF-20	1979 B&R's Garrett I, #549

23	100,000	(1861) J.J. Conway $50	EF-45	1979 B&R's Garrett I, #550
24	90,750	1830 Templeton Reid $10	EF	1984 B&M's Brand II, #1537
25	88,000	1855 Kellogg & Co. $50	Proof-55	1988 Superior's A- '88, #491

Fractional Gold

1	44,000	1854 25¢ Round BG-220	Unc.	1988 Superior's Lee, #29
2	35,200	1853 $1 Round BG-604	Unc.	1987 Superior's 9/20, #4487
3	16,000	1854 $1 Round D-505A	EF	1980 Ivy's A.N.A., #556
4	13,200	1854 50¢ Round BG-424	Unc.	1988 Lee, #73
5	13,200	1854 $1 Round BG-601	Fine	1988 Lee, #111
6	13,000	1874 $1 Octagon D-432	AU	1980 A.N.A., #553
7	12,100	No Date 25¢ Round BG-221	Unc.	1987 Superior's 9/20, #4396
8	12,100	1853 50¢ Round BG-402	Unc.-60	1987 B&M's Norweb I, #1027
9	12,100	1853 25¢ Round BG-218	AU	1989 Superior's Heifetz, #8
10	11,550	1853 50¢ Round BG-410	Unc.	1988 Superior's Lee, #60
11	10,500	1853 50¢ Round L-10	Unc.	1980 Rarcoa's A- '80, #1887
12	10,450	1853 50¢ Round BG-412	Unc.	1988 Superior's Lee, #61
13	10,450	1853 50¢ Round BG-412	Unc.	1989 Superior's Heifetz, #54
14	9,900	1854 50¢ Round BG-424	Unc.	1989 Superior's Heifetz, #68
15	8,500	1872 $1 Round L-8B	EF	1980 Rarcoa's A- '80, #1895
16	7,150	1853 50¢ Round BG-435	Unc.-63	1983 B&M's Brand I, #815
17	7,150	1854 25¢ Octagon BG-103	Unc.	1988 Superior's Lee, #3
18	6,050	1853 50¢ Round BG-435	Unc.	1984 B&M's Brand II, #1578
19	5,720	No Date 25¢ Round -Unlisted		1990 B&M's 3/28, #1701
20	5,400	1853 50¢ Octagon L-38	AU	1981 B&R's Garrett IV, #2168
21	5,280	1856 $1 Octagon BG-512	Unc.	1988 Superior's Lee, #95
22	5,200	1853 50¢ Round L-9B	EF	1981 B&R's Garrett IV, #2184
23	5,000	1870-G $1 Round D-507	Unc.-60	Ivy's 1980 A.N.A., #557
24	5,000	No Date $1 Octagon L-1A	EF	1980 Rarcoa's A- '80, #1891

Ancients

$520,000	Agrigentum	silver decadrachm, fast quadriga left, eagles perched on hare	ca 410 B.C.	EF, flan crack	Sotheby's June 19, 1990
$480,000	Athens	silver decadrachm, Athena right, owl in square	ca 465 B.C.	EF	Sotheby's June 19, 1990
$340,000	Catana	silver tetradrachm, laureate Apollo, fast quadriga left	ca 405 B.C.	EF	Sotheby's June 19, 1990
$301,704	Islamic, post Reform Umayyad	gold dinar	A.H. 77, A.D. 697		Spink & Son June 20, 1989
$280,000	Western Asia Minor	electrum stater, griffin head right, incuse square	ca. 575 B.C.	EF	Sotheby's June 19, 1990
$272,240	Athens, Attica	decadrachm	470 B.C.	EF, finest style.	Bank Leu-Munzen & Medaillen May 28, 1974
$272,240	Athens, Attica	decadrachm	470 B.C.	EF, finest style.	Bank Leu-Munzen & Medaillen May 28, 1974
$270,000	Rome, Ticinum Mint	gold medallion of 5 aurei, head of Maximian right, nude Hercules standing right	A.D. 293	EF	Sotheby's June 19, 1990
$270,000	Syracuse	silver decadrachm by Cimon, fast quadriga left, head of Arethusa	ca. 405-400 B.C.	EF	Sotheby's June 19, 1990
$252,525	Islamic, Post Reform Umayyad	gold dinar	A.H. 77, 697 A.D.		Sotheby's Sept. 29-30, 1988
$210,000	Roman, Carthage Mint	gold solidus, Alexander, Carthage standing left	A.D. 310-311	Mint State	NFA June 1, 1989
$210,000	Roman Republic	gold aureus, Brutus, military and naval trophy	42 B.C.	EF	NFA June 1, 1989
$210,000	Rome, Trevari Mint	gold medallion of 9 solidi, bust of Constantine right, emperor standing right	A.D. 310	Good VF	Sotheby's June 19, 1990

$195,000	Rome Mint	orichalcum sestertius, draped bust of Hadrian right, Pax standing left	A.D. 135	Good EF	Sotheby's June 19, 1990
$195,000	Rome Mint	gold aureus, head of Clodius Albinus right, African god standing left	A.D. 194	As struck	Sotheby's June 19, 1990
$190,000	Rome, Antioch Mint	gold medallion of 4-1/2 solidi, bust of Constantinius Gallus left, Constantinopolis seated left	ca. A.D. 351	EF	Sotheby's June 19, 1990
$190,000	Sicilian Naxos	silver tetradrachm, head of Dionysus right, ithyphallic silenus seated	ca 460 B.C.	EF	Sotheby's June 19, 1990
$185,000	Agrigentum	silver tetradrachm, fast quadriga right, two eagles perched on hare	ca. 410 B.C.	EF, scuffed	Sotheby's June 19, 1990
$185,000	Metapontum	silver stater, head of Dionysus left, barley	ca 340 B.C.	EF	Sotheby's June 19, 1990
$184,000	Islamic, Post Reform Umayyad	gold dinar	AH. 77, 697 A.D.		Munzen & Medaillen Oct. 9, 1982
$171,100	Rome, Maxentius	aureus , Rev: winged Victory offers orb to emperor	310-311 A.D.	FDC.	Bank Leu May 8-9, 1979
$170,000	Judea, First Revolt	silver shekel, Omer cup, branch wioth three pomegranates	Year 5, A.D. 70	VF	Sotheby's June 19, 1990
$168,600	Amphipoli Macedona	silver tetradrachm	355 B.C.	EF	Bank Leu May 26, 1988
$168,200	Rome, Quintillus	aureus , Rev: Concordia standing left, holds cornucopia and standards	269-270 A.D.	EF.	Schweizerischer Bankverein Apr. 19, 1980
$165,000	Roman Empire, London Mint	gold aureus, Carausius, Jupiter standing	A.D. 292-293	Superb	NFA June 1, 1989
$160,000	Rome, mint moving with Marcus Junius Brutus	gold aureus, head of Brutus right, military trophy	43-42 B.C.	EF	Sotheby's June 19, 1990
$155,000	Naxos, Sicily	tetradrachm , Obv: Bearded Head of Dionysus. , Rev: Seated Silenus with shallow bowl.	460 B.C.	Superb	Numismatic Fine Arts Sept. 17-18, 1981
$154,550	Panticapaion Black Sea (Kertsh on Crimea)	gold stater	350 B.C.	EF	Bank Leu May 26, 1988
$150,000	Amphipolis, Macedon	silver tetradrachm, Apollo right, square frame	356/5 B.C.	EF	NFA June 1, 1989
$147,500	Rome, Allectus, London Mint	aureus , Rev: Pax standing left	286-293 A.D.	EF	Bank Leu May 8-9, 1979
$145,000	Rome, Alexandria Mint	gold aureus, bust of Pecennius Niger right, Roma seated left on shield	A.D. 193	EF	Sotheby's June 19, 1990
$140,000	Roman Republic	gold aureus, Ahenobarbus, tetrastyle temple	41 B.C.	EF	NFA June 1, 1989
$140,000	Seleucid, Syria, Antiochus III, Antioch Mint	gold octadrachm	circa 208-200 B.C.	Superb.	Numismatic Fine Arts March 31, 1987
$140,000	Syracuse	silver tetradrachm, fast quadriga left, head of Athena	ca. 410 B.C.	VF/EF	Sotheby's June 19, 1990
$137,500	Syracuse, Sicily	decadrachm, signed by Kimon		Superb	Bank Leu May 3-4, 1983
$132,000	Rome, Galerius Maximian, Arras hoard	5 aureii , Rev: Mars advancing right.		EF	Sotheby's July 1, 1982
$130,000	Rome, Greek states	gold stater, head of Flaminius right, Nike standing left	ca. 196 B.C.	EF	Sotheby's June 19, 1990

$130,000	Seleucid, Syria, Pergamum Mint	silver tetradrachm , Obv: Horned horse head right. Rev: Elephant right	281-280 B.C.	EF	Numismatic Fine Arts March 31, 1987
$126,506	Syracuse, Sicily	decadrachm signed by Kimon	405-400 B.C.	Superb	Bank Leu-Munzen & Medaillen May 28, 1974
$125,000	Camarina	silver didrachm, Hipparis left, nymph Camarina on swan	ca. 410 B.C.	About EF	Sotheby's June 19, 1990
$120,000	Rome, Valentinian I, Valens and Gratian.	gold bar			NFA Nov. 29, 1986.
$115,000	Western Asia Minor	electrum stater, lioness walking right, two incuse squares	ca. 575 B.C.	EF	Sotheby's June 19, 1990
$110,140	Syracuse, Sicily	tetradrachm , signed by Eucleidis. , Obv: Fast quadriga gallops left, crowned by winged Nike. , Rev: Head of Athena, plumed helmet	410 B.C..		Bank Leu May 13-14, 1986
$105,000	Roman Republic, Sicilian Mint	gold aureus, Sextus Pompey, Pompey the Great and Cn. Pompey Jr.	42-40 B.C.	EF	NFA June 1, 1989
$104,633	Amphipoli, Macedon	tetradrachm , Obv: Facing Apollo, curly locks. , Rev: Hand held candle within square	420 B.C.	Superb	Bank Leu May 13-14, 1986
$100,300	Rome, Julia Titi, Rome Mint	aureus Rev: peacock	90 A.D.	EF	Bank Leu May 8-9, 1979
$100,300	Rome, Vespasian and Domitilla	aureus, Rev: Bust of empress	A.D. 81-84	EF	Bank Leu May 8-9, 1979
$98, 350	Calymna, Caria	silver didrachm	530 B.C.	EF	Bank Leu May 26, 1988
$95,000	Rome, mint moving with Marcus Antonius	gold aureus, head of Antony right, head of Marc Antony Jr. right	34 B.C.	Good EF	Sotheby's June 19, 1990
$95,000	Seleucid, Syria, Antiochus III, .Seleucia on the Tigris Mint	gold octadrachm	circa 210 B.C.	Mint State	Numismatic Fine Arts March 31, 1987
$95,000	Seleucid, Syria, Sardes Mint.	silver tetradrachm	220-213 B.C.	EF	Numismatic Fine Arts March 31, 1987
$94,400	Rome , Probus	unique gold medal , Rev: Three standing figures	277 A.D.	EF	Bank Leu May 8-9, 1979
$92,800	Rome, Claudius Gothicus	eight aureii	268-270 A.D.		Schweizerischer Bankverein Apr. 19, 1980
$90,000	Rome, mint moving with Marcus Junius Brutus	silver denarius, head of Brutus right, Pileus between daggers ("Ides of March")	43-42 B.C.	Good VF	Sotheby's June 19, 1990
$90,000	Syracuse, Pyrrhus of Epirus	gold stater, head of Athena right, Nike walking left	ca. 278 B.C.	EF	Sotheby's June 19, 1990
$90,000	Syracuse, Sicily	silver decadrachm, slow quadriga right, four dolphins around head of Arethusa	ca. 465 B.C.	VF	Sotheby's June 19, 1990
$88,500	Rome, Didia Clara	aureus, Rev: Hilaritas standing left		EF	Bank Leu May 8-9, 1979
$87,500	Syracuse	silver decadrachm by Cimon, fast quadriga left, head of Arethusa	ca. 405 B.C.	Good VF	Sotheby's June 19, 1990

$85,000	Naxos, Sicily	silver tetradrachm , Obv: Head of Dionysus right , Rev: Nude Ithyphallic Silenus squatting	460 B.C.	EF	Numismatic Fine Arts March 31, 1987
$84,300	Naxos, Sicily	silver tetradrachm	460 B.C.	EF	Bank Leu May 26, 1988
$82,831	Syracuse, Sicily	decadrachm signed by Kimon	400 B.C.	EF	Bank Leu-Munzen & Medaillen May 28, 1974
$82,500	Rome Mint	gold aureus, bust of Diadumenian right, Spes walking left	A.D. 218	Good EF	Sotheby's June 19, 1990
$82,000	Pontus, King Pharnaces I	gold stater	185-160 B.C.	FDC.	Numismatic Fine Arts Mar. 25-26, 1976
$81,250	Egypt, Cleopatra VII	silver tetradrachm , Obv: Draped bust facing right.	38 B.C.		Christie's-London Oct. 9, 1984
$80,787	Leontini, Sicily	silver tetradrachm	470 B.C.	Unc.	Bank Leu May 26, 1988
$80,000	Catana	silver tetradrachm, fast quadriga left, laureate Apollo left	ca. 410 B.C.	EF	Sotheby's June 19, 1990
$80,000	Rome, Plotina and Matilda	aureus			Numismatic Fine Arts March 9-10, 1988
$80,000	Syracuse	silver tetradrachm, head of Arethusa, fast quadriga left	ca. 406 B.C.	About EF	Sotheby's June 19, 1990 .
$79,650	Pontus, King Pharnakes I	gold stater	185-170 B.C.	Superb	Bank Leu May 8-9, 1979
$78,313	Seleucid, Syria, Seleucus I, Pergamon Mint	tetradrachm	about 280 B.C.	EF	Bank Leu May 28, 1974
$78,313	Syracuse, Sicily	tetradrachm , Obv: Facing helmeted Athena	410 B.C.	EF	Bank Leu May 28, 1974
$76,700	Rome, Brutus, an Asia Minor Mint	aureus	43-42 B.C.	EF	Bank Leu May 8-9, 1979
$76,250	Syracuse, Sicily	decadrachm quadriga and olive-crowned female, Demareteion, signed by Evrakoeio	480-479 B.C.	VF	Schweizerischer Bank Oct. 16, 1979
$75,301	Naxos, Sicily	silver tetradrachm , Obv: Head of Bacchus right. , Rev: Seated Silenus with shallow bowl	460-B.C.	EF	Bank Leu May 28, 1974
$75,000	Carthage, Zeutania	gold hexadrachm, Tanit left, palm tree	264 B.C.	EF	NFA June 1, 1989
$75,000	Rome, Carthage Mint	silver denarius, head of Clodius Macer right, galley sailing right	A.D. 68	EF toned	Sotheby's June 19, 1990
$75,000	Rome, Constantius I, Chlorus, Trier Mint	5 aureii gold medallion , Rev: Mars advancing right	A.D. 293-305	About EF	NFA-Bank Leu May 16-18, 1984.
$75,000	Rome, Gallienus	gold medallion of 12 aureii , Obv: Half-length bust of Gallienus			Spink-London Oct. 9, 1984
$75,000	Rome, Mint uncertain	gold aureus, head of Octavian, crocodile right	27 B.C.	About EF	Sotheby's June 19, 1990

Medieval, Modern World

$190,000	Spain	100 pesetas	1870	Proof	Stack's Sept. 15-16, 1982
$160,000	Canada	silver dollar pattern	1911	MS65+	Auction '79-Paramount July 26-27, 1979
$145,000	Austria, Archduke Sigismund	seven-ducat	1486	FDC.	Swiss Bank Corp. Jan. 26-27, 1983

$125,000	Austria, Maximilian I, struck at Modena.	double ducat	1513-1514	EF	Swiss Bank Corp. Jan. 26-27, 1983
$122,500	Russian, Constantine I	pattern ruble, smooth edge	1825		ANA-NERCA July 29-Aug. 1, 1979
$120,000	Poland, King Sigismund III	100 gold ducats	1621	EF	Stack's Sept. 18, 1980
$115,000	Spain, J. Madrid.	gold 8 escudos	1710		Stack's March 4-5, 1988
$113,814	Spanish colonial America, Philip II, Lima Mint	8 reales	n.d.		Swiss Bank Corp. Sept. 14-15, 1988
$100,000	Canada	50 cents	1921	Unc.	Bowers & Merena and Bank Leu Sept. 11-13, 1989
$96,050	Australia	half sovereign pattern of Queen Victoria	1855	FDC	Spink's-Australia Nov. 19-20, 1979
$87,500	Salzburg, Austria	gold 25 ducaton	1594	EF	Spink's-Zurich 1981.
$85,280	Spain, Philip III, Segovia Mint	gold 50 reales or cincuenton	1613		Glendinings May 27, 1987
$83,233	England, Henry III	gold penny of 20 pence , Obv: Bearded figure of king holding orb and sceptre	1216-1272		Spink June 13, 1985
$82,280	Spain, Philip III, Segovia Mint	50 reales	1613		Glendining's May 27, 1987
$81,900	Australia, Adelaide Govt. Assay Office	£1	1852	Superb	Spink's-Australia Nov. 19, 1980
$79,200	Scotland, James VI	gold £20	1575	VF	Paramount July 29-30, 1983
$75,000	Milan, Italy, Philip IV	20 zecchini	1643	EF	Bowers & Merena March 23-24, 1988

Potpourri

19

Ordering coins

Ordering coins from dealers is a simple matter. We assume the dealer has advertised or issued a price list. The buyer picks out the coin or coins he wants, and then reads the instructions at the beginning of the price list or the end of the advertisement.

If there is a minimum order the dealer will accept, the buyer must reach it or not buy from that dealer. If the dealer requires an added amount for postage, insurance and handling, the order must include it.

The instructions may say that a postal money order is required, or a bank certified check, or that a delay will be made to allow a personal check to clear the banks. The buyer will take note of all this, and do as instructed and be prepared to wait for his order, from two to four weeks, depending on distance from the dealer and how payment is made.

Half that time will be credited to the check clearing, and the other half to the time it takes for the mail to get the shipment through. This can be up to three weeks or so from coast to coast, after the check clears if that is the method of payment.

Wait at least three weeks before sending a query to the dealer, but it is justified after that time. However, it should be a tactful one and include a return envelope or government postcard for reply. There is no reason why a buyer can't write and ask for the date of mailing, so he can check with his local post office. No dealer would get mad at that.

Buying by mail is a two-way proposition, of course. The dealer should hold up his end. One of the biggest "blow-ups" on record was caused when a dealer didn't.

A California collector ordered a good-sized package of rolls from an Eastern dealer. The latter duly sent them by express, but didn't notify the buyer. The buyer didn't receive the coins, and wrote the dealer. The latter assumed the shipment would have arrived by that time, and did not answer the letter. The buyer got madder and madder, and complained to *Coin World*.

Final investigation disclosed that the shipment arrived at the nearest express office the day the agent went on vacation. He didn't notify the addressee, and his substitute thought he had. The vacation lasted a month, and there sat the coins, with nobody aware of it, and the buyer ready to sue everybody he could think of.

One little postcard from the dealer at shipment, or one polite query from the buyer asking when the coins were shipped and how, with a postcard for reply, would have avoided the whole mess.

Finally, to the buyer, do not forget to include your name and full address including zip code when sending the order, both inside and outside the envelope, preferably printed or typed. More disputes have been caused by the buyer's failure to include a legible or any return address than all other causes put together. And, strange as it may seem, some buyers have been known to forget to sign their check.

Just a few more tips to ensure that transactions go smoothly. If the seller says returns will be allowed for three, five or seven days or any other period, for unsatisfactory merchandise, he means it. If the buyer needs more time to get a coin authenticated or graded elsewhere, he should ask for it. He would also be wise to ask for a written guarantee of authenticity with the coin, if it's worth more than a few dollars.

Incidentally, the *Coin World* advertising department has a policy that time limits are invalid if a coin should turn out to be counterfeit. But the buyer has to prove he didn't switch, if there is any question.

If an advertisement contains the phrase "prices subject to change without notice," in a period of fast-rising markets, the buyer should be prepared to get his check returned. If the coin is one-of-a-kind, he should also be prepared for a "sold-out" answer to his order.

Finally, in some cases it is wise for the buyer to phone the dealer for a confirmation of an order at a given price. The buyer should get the name of the person confirming the order at that price, and how many days he will be allowed to get the payment in.

Most transactions are simple, and most dealers and buyers are well-meaning and honest. There are a few exceptions on both sides. If either buyer or dealer should get "taken" once, they will be suspicious from then on, and that will make things harder for everybody thereafter. If both dealer and buyer stick to the "Golden Rule" the hobby and business of numismatics would be much more pleasant for everyone.

Whether buying or selling coins should be any different from buying and selling neckties or shoes is an interesting question. However, that there is a difference is one of the facts of life, and collectors would be advised to keep that in mind. It is true for all hobbies, and dealers who cater to hobbyists are likely to be different from those who sell the necessities of life.

Mailing coins

The Postal Service is usually blamed for lost coins. Most of the time the blame should be placed on the sender.

Mail, on its long and often arduous journey from sender to addressee, is subjected to much handling, by many people.

In most cases, it is recommended you write or call the person you are sending coins before doing so. Postal law permits individuals to keep unsolicited material, including coins, although that has never been a major problem in the hobby. Dealers, authenticators and other professional hobbyists expect to receive coins, but a letter asking permission to send coins is a courtesy and a form of protection. Coin World advertisers are required to accept mailings and to return them if not purchased.

The sender should provide as much protection as possible for his letters and packages. Enclose the coin in the readily available 2X2 coin envelopes or holders. Tape or staple the holders between cardboard. "Jiffy" bags are no longer acceptable by the post office for registered mail.

Include a letter identifying the coin(s) and stating the reason they are being sent. The person who is to examine the coins should not have to waste time trying to figure out why the coins were sent.

Your letter of transmittal should also include instructions for the return of the coins and sufficient return postage to provide whatever level of protection you wish.

Registered mail provides signature protection for the contents. That means that anyone handling the package en route must sign for it. Registered mail also provides for a declared value up to the amount specified by the sender upon payment of the proper fee.

Insured mail can go via first class, third

class or fourth class mail, although the sender must request first class mail if he prefers faster service. It provides indemnity for declared value but only up to $200. Contrary to popular belief, insuring a package does not guarantee delivery. It guarantees only that the sender will be reimbursed for loss in transit. Further, the sender is not guaranteed to recover the amount declared.

The Postal Service will often attempt to establish a value for the lost coins based on findings of a disinterested authority. This is one of the ways by which the Postal Service attempts to protect itself against fraud.

If the coin has no intrinsic value, it can be sent via certified mail. A receipt is issued to the sender and, for an additional fee, a return receipt can be obtained showing when, where and to whom the mail was delivered.

Both registered and certified mail are traceable from initial mailing to ultimate delivery.

Express mail ensures the fastest possible delivery, often overnight between larger communities. The initial cost is $10.75 for up to two pounds; rates increase with greater weight. Express mail is insured up to $50,000.

Whatever means of mailing is selected, be certain that the package is securely sealed. An authenticator's nightmare begins with the receipt of a package that is empty because the sender neglected to seal it properly.

Unless special arrangements have been made, limit the number of coins sent at any one time to three or four. The person to whom you are sending them will also be receiving coins from many others. He would be forced to ignore your large number of coins in order to satisfy a greater number of people who have complied with this basic tenet of courtesy. His only alternative to ignoring your coins would be to ignore all his other correspondents. So, no matter which avenue he chooses, he is automatically guilty of slighting someone.

Auctions—How to Participate

by Raymond N. Merena

The following section was prepared by Raymond N. Merena, with his associate, Q. David Bowers. Merena is president of Auctions by Bowers and Merena Inc., which with its predecessor firm, Bowers and Ruddy Galleries, is the holder of many of the world's numismatic auction records.

Auctions: A Key to the Market

Auctions may well be the truest test of coin values. A rare coin auction, nationally advertised and presented in an authoritative catalog, sets the stage for bidding competition. Ultimately, a coin (or any other object) is worth what someone will pay for it. Asking prices, as reflected in dealers' price lists, may represent wishful thinking, where an actual auction transaction generally represents true value.

As such, the reader seeking what a coin is worth would do well to study auction prices realized. While one can point to all sorts of price lists, guides, market indexes, and the like, a list of auction prices realized is usually much more realistic. The situation, however, is not as simple as it sounds. When analyzing an auction list of prices it is important to know how the dealer graded his coins. In instances in which coins have been independently graded by a recognized certification service, comparisons are easier, but even coins graded by these services are apt to vary widely in aesthetic appeal and other considerations, and, consequently, price. And, as noted, it is important that the sale be widely advertised and made known to specialists in a given area. It is important to know whether or not reserves are disclosed. If a piece sold for, say, $10,000, but went back to the original owner, this is not as meaningful as knowing that it sold for $10,000 to an outside collector or dealer.

The usefulness of auction records is echoed by Walter Breen, who in his *Encyclopedia of United States Half Cents,* notes: "What of prices? I have no better answer at the moment than to list the top coins of each variety known to me, together with their auction records. In a market that is far more unstable than it was in previous decades, this seems to be the only sensible procedure. . . . Values will be established by subsequent auction results. Fixed-price lists too often represent dealers' dreams; they may or may not change hands at the stated values, or in trade, or in negotiated agreement at lower (or sometimes higher!) figures. . . ."

If you are a coin buyer you may wish to consider the advantages of auction. If you are a coin seller, some of what I have to say may be valuable to you. In the following paragraphs are some of my personal observations based upon cataloging and selling some of the most important collections ever to cross the auction block. First, let me discuss different types of "auctions," some of which are not auctions in true sense.

Mail-Bid and Telephone Sales

Mail-bid sales have a rich numismatic tradition. B. Max Mehl, the famous Fort Worth, Texas, dealer, conducted many auctions during his long career, but as no participation by floor bidders was involved, and as all participation was by mail, the term "mail-bid sale" would be more appropriate today—even for such landmark events as his Dunham Collection which in 1941 stood as one the greatest cabinets of American coins ever dispersed. Although it was not announced at the time and, in fact, was kept a secret until Q. David Bowers unearthed information concerning it in the files of John Work Garrett (presently in Johns Hopkins University), Mehl bought the collection outright, so when it was "auctioned" he was simply soliciting bids on his own material, which points out another feature

of certain auctions that will be discussed later.

The traditional mail-bid sale has been joined in recent years by sales in which bidding is accomplished by pushing buttons on a telephone, by faxing bids, or by other electronic means. Many mail-bid and electronic sales are featured in the pages of *Coin World* and other numismatic periodicals, and consist of listings of coins or other numismatic items for sale. Usually such descriptions are brief and consist of little more than the date, mintmark (if any), and grade. Some electronic sales specialize only in coins certified by the Professional Coin Grading Service (PCGS), the Numismatic Guaranty Corporation of America (NGC), Hallmark, ANA Cache, or other authority. Prospective buyers are invited to submit bids. Sometimes estimates are provided.

As is true of any auction sale, it is important to read the terms of sale stated by the seller. There are no standard rules in this regard, although some (*Coin World* for one) have suggested guidelines. Determine the following things:

What is my return privilege? If I disagree with the grade of a coin can I return it? If so, what is the time period involved? Do I have to pay for the lots immediately, or are credit terms given? Can I bid on several lots but limit my total purchases to a stated amount? What is the reputation of the auctioneer or seller? Are there any extra charges such as postage, handling, or a buyer's fee? If my bid is far higher than other bids received, will a reduction be made? What are the other policies of the seller?

Before submitting offers in a mail-bid or electronic sale, you must determine the total cost to you. If there is a buyer's fee of 10% added, and if you bid $100 on a coin, then your bill, before sales taxes and postage, will be $110. If you have in mind bidding a total of $100 (excluding taxes and handling), you would be better bidding somewhere around $90, for this will be closer to $100 when the 10% is added.

The terms for a mail-bid or electronic

sale may include payment of state or local sales tax, postage and handling charges, some or all of these. These costs, too, must be factored into the total amount you wish to pay for a given item. In particular, sales taxes can be costly.

The bidding procedure is often outlined in the terms of sale. In some auctions the highest bid received takes the lot for the total amount of the bid, without regard to what the underbid might be. For example, if you bid $100 on a lot and the next highest bid is $50, you are charged the full $100 price. Other sellers may adopt some percentage increment over the next highest bid, whereby you pay an advance of 5% to 10% over the lower figure. In this example, you would pay, say, 10% over the next highest $50 bid, or a total of $55. This gives you the advantage of buying the piece at the lowest possible prices, almost as if it were a public sale and you were bidding in person.

Return privileges are an important consideration. While most auctions with floor bidding permit no returns by floor bidders, mail and telephone bids are often different. Read carefully to determine exactly what your rights and privileges are. For example, if you do not agree with the grade of a coin, can you return it within a certain period?

Some people conducting mail-bid sales permit telephone bids. In this way you can call the seller and determine what the bid level is at a given time and then submit your offers accordingly. Other mail-bid sales are strictly that, sales by mail with no telephone calls allowed. Some sales are strictly electronic and are conducted by receiving bids punched into a keyboard and transmitted on telephone lines.

Assuming that the pieces are properly graded—and proper grading must always be an important factor—bidding in a mail-bid or electronic sale can be a very enjoyable and profitable way to add to your collections. You are buying the coins you want at the prices you want to pay, an ideal situation.

Public Auctions

Many large auctions, especially those featuring old-time collections, are of the public variety with in-person attendance by bidders in addition to bids by mail. An important difference between public auctions and mail-bid sales is that, with few exceptions, public coin sale auctioneers do not permit items to be returned. An exception might be in the case of authenticity, but not grading. Other auctioneers may have slightly more lenient rules for mail bidders but with the proviso that all sales to floor bidders are final without any possibility of return (except for reasons of authenticity). So, before bidding in a public auction, check the terms of sale carefully. If you are not familiar with the auctioneer or his grading standards, it may pay you to examine the coins in advance or give your bids to a dealer or fellow collector who will be attending the sale in person and who can view the lots beforehand.

It is the custom of American auction houses to charge a buyer's fee, often 10%, in addition to the "hammer price." By this method, a coin which has a hammer price of $1,000 and which is sold for $1,000 at the sale has 10% added so that the invoice totals $1,100. This arrangement took root when auction houses decided to split the selling costs between seller and buyer. As the auctioneer will announce only the hammer price at the sale, be sure to do your calculations in advance so that you do not pay more than you want to once the buyer's fee is added.

Advance preparation on all fronts is suggested for participation in a public auction if you plan to attend in person. All auctions have a lot viewing period in which time the individual coins, paper money, and other items can be examined in detail. Take your auction catalog with you and make appropriate notes. If you agree with the grading and description, then a simple check mark can indicate this. On the other hand, if you feel that the coin is undergraded or overgraded, this can be noted as well. Sometimes two coins can be in an identical grade or be certified the same, but one will be more appealing due to the presence of attractive toning, the sharpness of strike, or some other consideration. Any extra factors that influence positively or negatively the value of a coin should be likewise noted.

Once you have completed lot viewing, then determine the price you want to bid on each lot. "Auction fever" is well known, and many are the bidders who later say they were carried away during the heat of a sale. While saving your bidding calculations until the sale takes place may have the advantage that you can gauge the market at the sale itself, a more leisurely view can be obtained if you do your calculations prior to the auction.

A simple way is to enter the maximum hammer price you want to pay into your catalog. As other people may see your catalog during the sale, you may wish to do this in code. There are several ways of doing this. One way is to put an irrelevant figure before and after the price you want to pay. In such an example, the number 75003 would indicate that you want to bid $500 (ignore the first and last numbers of the code). Or, you can use a letter substitution code whereby a word with 10 non-repetitive letters is used. As an example, the term HARDMONEYS (H=1, A=2, etc.) would be used whereby the notation "MSS" in your auction catalog would indicate that you want to pay a maximum of $500 for the lot. Other 10 letter designations I have seen used include CHARLESTON, TRADEQUICK, INDUSTRYCO and BRICKMASON.

When the sale time arrives, be there early. By this time you will have viewed the lots, done your homework so far as prices are concerned, and will have established credit with the auctioneer. Arrive early at the sale, sign a registration card, and determine where you want to sit in the audience.

Over the years, I have heard many ideas concerning the best place to be when a sale takes place. Ask a dozen veteran sale-attenders and you are apt to get a dozen different answers! One leading Maryland dealer invariably sits in the front row near the aisle. He figures that the auctioneer will see him first, will recognize his signals without mistake, and may give him precedence in case of a tie bid. Further, by sitting in the front row his hand movements, if done in front of his chest, cannot be observed by anyone in the rows behind, thus his bids are more confidential than would otherwise be the case.

A New York City dealer I know always sits in the front row, but slightly to the side so that he can watch other people in the front row. Still another dealer, this one from New Jersey, likes nothing better than to sit even with the first row but far off to the right, so he can watch the front row, watch the audience, but not have his own actions easily observed.

A leading California bidder, a gentleman who has attended many of our sales over the years, usually sits three or four rows back from the front. In this way, he can see the bidding action in the front rows and get a general idea of what's going on, but still his movements cannot be seen by many in the audience. Several other acquaintances like nothing better than to sit against the back wall so that they have a view of the audience in front of them. Who is bidding seems to be more important than the price paid, it would seem!

So, study the possibilities and the room layout, pick a place where the auctioneer can see you and where you will not be distracted by nearby doors or openings, and settle down for some serious bidding.

How to bid once you have found your seat is another area that is far from standard. Chances are that you will be provided with a card or a paddle with a number on it, such number representing that given to you when you registered at the door. The typical bidder will hold his paddle in the air until his maximum bid has been reached, at which time he will take it down, either owning the coin or not owning it as competition dictates. However, I have seen people stand up straight as an arrow, bidder paddle aloft toward the ceiling, looking like the Statue of Liberty. Other bidders will wildly wave the paddle high in the air to the left and to the right as if they were flagging down a runaway express train! Still others may keep the paddle in front of them for identification but indicate bids by a nod of the head, the lifting of a pencil, or a slight hand movement.

Don't get too complicated. There is nothing at all wrong with being discreet. If you want to create the least amount of attention, sit near the front where the auctioneer can see you and make slight movements while bidding. If the auctioneer fails to notice your bid, you can always call out, but if the auctioneer knows your specialty is in a particular area, chances are he will look directly at you when coins of your specialty come up. One of the functions of a commercial auctioneer is to know the audience.

Still other bidders will call out a price in an effort to frighten off competition. Time and time again in our sales, I have seen a coin open at, say, $2,000, go to $2,200, $2,400, $2,600, then to be interrupted by a shout, "four thousand dollars!" Of course, the person bidding $4,000 hopes that he will have frightened away all competition, which indeed may be the case. On the other hand, perhaps if he had bid in a more leisurely manner he would have obtained the coin for less. The theory is that another bidder, hearing the shout, would think that the bidder was prepared to go much higher, even if he might not be. It's like a game of poker!

In a large auction there may be many dozens of bidders in attendance. The auctioneer only has one pair of eyes, and with talking among the audience, sharp eyes and careful ears might not be able to detect all bids. So, if your bid is missed, be sure to call out at the time of sale. The auctioneer will usually reopen the lot and recognize your bid. If you wait until several lots have passed, however, the auctioneer may not do this. Or, if the auctioneer simply thinks you are daydreaming and should have been paying attention, he may elect not to reopen the lot. So, when bidding, be alert!

Mail Bidding in Public Sales

Public auctions usually encourage participation by mail as well. My own firm, for one, encourages bidding by mail and devotes a special section of each catalog to instructions in this regard. If you bid by mail, be sure to read the terms of sale carefully, for mail bidding in an auction is different from ordering coins on approval or even from a fixed price list. In general, coins are to be paid for as soon as your invoice is received. One of the terms of sale in my own catalog is especially important—and this particular sale point is found in one form of wording or another in most other sale catalogs as well:

Any claims involving errors in the catalog must be made within three days of receipt of the coins. Grading is a subjective description that represents the opinion of the cataloger as to the state of preservation of a particular coin or lot. "Proof" is used to describe a method of manufacturing and it not a grade or condition. All such terms, including adjectival and numerical descriptions of coins and other numismatic items, are the opinion of the cataloger and are not an attribution. No warranty, whether expressed or implied, is made with repect to such adjectival or numerical descriptions, which can and do vary among experts. Coins graded by PCGS, NGC, Hallmark, or the ANA may be offered on the basis that no further grading guarantee is given; check the terms of sale to determine the seller's policy.

In other words, if you are not certain about grading, then do not bid until you determine that the grade is what you want. The reason for this is that the sale will have floor competition as well, and the floor bidders will have examined the coins in person and will be bidding without a return privilege. If an auctioneer were to accept a mail bid of, say, $2,000 for a coin which is graded Mint State 65, but then after the sale took place the buyer wanted to return it, the auctioneer would not have any possibility to sell it elsewhere, for all the floor bidders would have long since gone home. There would be no alternative except to return the coin to the consignor as an unsold item. It would be far better to have not entered the mail bid at all, but, rather, let the coin sell in a floor competition where chances are good that it would have brought the same price or more.

Some auction houses offer special services for mail bidders. One of these is a "maximum expenditure" service. Under this procedure you can mark at the top of your bid sheet the total amount you wish to spend. You can then submit bids for amounts up to several times that of the maximum expenditure. A customer representative will personally attend to your bid sheet by bidding from the auction floor, or this may be handled by a computer (which keeps a running track of the sale as it progresses). In this way, you can bid on, say, $5,000 worth of coins and be assured of winning no more than $1,000 worth. This sharply increases your chances for success.

Another service is that called "one lot only" whereby if you wish to purchase only one example of a coin of which several examples appear in a sale, you can mark these on a list, and your bid will be entered progressively as the different lots appear in the catalog. Then when (and if) one lot is bought, your bidding will stop there. I remember one sale in which we had several dozen beautiful Uncirculated examples of the 1925 Vancouver commemorative half dollar. By bids such as this, clients could buy just one coin but could spread their chances of success by competing on many different lots until one was finally obtained.

When you bid by mail, be sure to do some homework before sending your bid sheet. Just as the floor bidder has to do, carefully calculate the most you want to pay. If the sale has many different items offered, you may wish to make up a "work sheet." In this way you can adjust and readjust your prices and the coins you bid on until you have it in final form. Then enter your bids on the bid sheet provided with the catalog.

I have found that it is best to write your bids in ink (not pencil, for pencil tends to blur), or type them, being sure there is no confusion among similar numbers such as 9 and 4 or 1 and 7. After you have filled out your bid sheet, then carefully recheck each and every bid. Remember, if you bid $500 on a lot by mistake, you may wind up owning it! The bid sheet is a legal contract, and when you sign your bid and send it in, you are bound to abide by the terms.

If you are new to an auction firm, a deposit and reference may be required. These deposits are refundable if your bids are not successful.

Be sure to send in your bid sheet as early as possible, this is for two reasons: First, this will help avoid any delays in the mail. Second, in the event of a tie bid, your bid will win if received first. As a further consideration, if the auctioneer has any questions when your bid sheet is received, he has time to contact you. It is always a good idea to put your telephone number on the bid sheet to aid in the event of such a possibility.

Floor-Bid Only Auctions

Another type of auction, and one not frequently encountered, is that in which floor bids are accepted but for which no catalog is issued and there are no mail bids. Auctions conducted by the United States Customs Service, unclaimed packages at the post office, sheriffs' sales, and the like are examples. Sometimes some valuable coins can be acquired in this way. In such auctions, everything is usually sold "as is" without any recourse at all, even if a coin proves to be counterfeit. So, before bidding, be sure you know what you are doing when it comes to the matter of authenticity, for if there is a problem later you will be out of luck. Still, this should not deter you from bidding, and if you do not know about authenticity yourself, then it may pay to enlist the aid of an expert.

Such sales are usually not advertised in coin periodicals, so the best way to find out about them is in local newspapers or in government publications. Your bank or attorney may be able to tell you of such events. They are few and far between, but occasionally nice pieces can be found.

Another type of floor-bid only sale is the country auction. Often an estate, a group of antiques, or the like will include some old coins, again usually offered on an "as is" basis. Such sales may be fun to attend, and you may walk away with some nice furniture or paintings, but probably the chance of finding a true bargain among coins is relatively slight, especially if you consider the time and expense involved in attending the sale.

Somewhat related are coin sales held by art auction houses. In this instance, read the terms of sale very carefully, for I have seen art auction house sale catalogs which give the bidder no recourse in the event a coin proves counterfeit, unless the bidder is alert enough to detect the counterfeit coin relatively quickly. Many such sales are sold "as is." As a result, most serious coin collectors do not consign coins to other than numismatic auction specialists, but occasionally art auction houses or antique auction houses will acquire coins as part of an estate or as a result of their reputation in the art or antique field. Such sales can offer excellent values, for often the catalogs are poorly distributed and are not widely advertised. However, grading is apt to be very erratic and, as noted, coins may be sold "as is."

Summary

Over the years, most large collections of United States coins, world coins, and paper money have been formed, at least in part, by bidding at auction. As noted earlier in the present text, auctions give you the ideal possibility of buying the pieces you want at the price you want to pay—not at the price someone else says you should pay. And, auctions represent the true value of a coin. While there may be occasional instances of unknowledgeable bidders bidding against other unknowledgeable bidders, by and large those attending numismatic auctions know what they are doing, and if you pay

$2,000 for a coin, you have a reasonable assurance that the price represents the current market value at the time and place of sale.

Bidding in auctions requires some homework, and to be successful, you should be familiar with grading procedures and the grading practices of the dealer conducting the sale. You should read the terms of sale carefully and be prepared to abide by them, and you should spend time studying the pieces you want and formulating in advance the price you wish to pay.

B. Max Mehl, the famous Texas dealer, used to stress the OPPORTUNITIES that his sales presented. It is indeed the case that many extremely rare and one-of-a-kind pieces are available only at auction, and if you do not participate in the sale in which they are offered, you may do without them for a long time, if not forever. My recommendation is to become acquainted with different auction houses. Most offer their catalogs on a subscription basis. The price paid for the catalog includes a key to the prices realized which will be sent to you after the sale. Thus, not only do you have the chance to bid in an auction, but the prices realized list will give you a good view of market values (providing there are not undisclosed reserves or other situations not readily apparent).

For the collector interested in research, I highly recommend seeking out back issues of auction catalogs. How many times has an Uncirculated 1921-S half dollar appeared at auction? From the standpoint of auction appearances, what are the scarcest Seated Liberty silver dollars of the 1840s? According to auction prices, what is the current value of an Uncirculated 1915-S Panama-Pacific commemorative half dollar? A perusal of auction catalogs and prices-realized lists will provide such information and much other data as well. Dealers, who make their living by buying and selling coins, consider auction catalogs to be among their most valuable sources of information. You should do likewise.

Selling at auction

Sooner or later the time will come to sell your coins. There are several ways to sell them, and it would be to your advantage to check out the features of each. However, the frequency with which large collections cross the auction block indicates that those who have some of the most valuable numismatic property consider the auction route the best way to go. There must be reason for this, and some of the reasons are given herewith.

By offering your coins at auction, you expose your coins to thousands of potential bidders. The firm conducting the sale typically will send out news releases and place advertisements, with the result that if you have a rare 1876-CC 20-cent piece, some German multiple talers, a pattern 1831 crown of King William IV, a Proof 1877 Indian cent, a set of $1, $2, $5 "Educational" notes of 1896, or other rare items, readers of numismatic and other periodicals will be aware that they will be crossing the auction block. They are invited to send for a catalog which contains descriptions of these and other pieces. In addition to prospective bidders attracted by advertisements and publicity, a typical auction house has its own mailing list of thousands of proven buyers.

With such an array of potential buyers to choose from, chances are excellent that your coins will bring current market value. On the other hand, if you were to sell by fixed price, you probably could not expose your coins to more than a few dozen bidders if you spent all year doing so, and these bidders, if they are dealers, would want to buy the coins wholesale anyway. Then there are such considerations as security and safety involved in showing coins personally to many different buyers, not to overlook the value of your time. The auction route is simplicity itself. You ship the coins to the auctioneer, or if the coins are very valuable, the auctioneer may send a representative to call for them. Receipts are exchanged, then the next thing you do is to wait for your check to arrive in the mail.

Not all auction houses are the same. Before selecting a firm to sell your coins, do some investigating. If I were selling coins, here are some of the questions I might ask:

What is the commission rate? The typical commission rate charged by a large auction house may be 10% to the seller (plus a fee of 10% to the buyer). Other firms will advertise a lower commission. For items which are bulky or which involve fairly low value in relation to the catalog space occupied—numismatic books, certain tokens and medals and the like being examples—a higher fee may be charged.

The commission rate should be studied, but more important is the question: What do I get for the commission paid? It may be false economy to pick a lower commission rate if the firm does not do a good job for you. For example, if firm "A" sells a coin for $10,000 and charges you a 10% fee, this might be a better deal than firm "B" who charges you a 5% fee but the coin realizes just $7,000, or firm "C" which charges no fee at all but sells the coin for $6,000. It is the bottom line, the net results, that should interest you most. So, once you have established the fee, there are more questions to ask:

What type of advertising does the firm do? Does the firm acquire consignments and then forget about them, or does the firm pursue with great energy an advertising campaign offering your pieces? In my opinion, it is important that a sale be advertised so that prospective bidders have a chance to know about this. Such advertising is quite expensive, and not all firms do it effectively.

Can I be sure my coins are being kept properly? Insist upon insurance coverage for your coins from the moment the auction firm takes possession of them. If your consignment is particularly large, you may wish to request an insurance certificate outlining the coverage. What type of security precautions will be taken? Will the firm be casual with your coins or careful with them?

What is the financial reputation of the

firm? Is the company known for its financial strength? When settlement time comes (usually 45 days after the sale) will I be assured of receiving my check promptly? Does the firm have good financial and numismatic references?

What is the quantity and quality of the mailing list? How many catalogs will be distributed? And will they go to knowledgeable buyers? For example, 4,000 catalogs distributed to proven auction buyers will probably be more effective than 20,000 catalogs distributed to casual collectors, most of whom have never bid in an auction. Carefully ask about the quality and quantity of the mailing list.

When and where will the auction be held? Will it be held in a major metropolitan center or will it be held in a smaller community? Experience shows that a large city will usually yield better results than a smaller town, unless a major convention is being held in an out-of-the-way location. My own preference is to conduct auctions in New York or Los Angeles, for these seem to attract the most buyers, although sales in such places as Houston, Dearborn, Mich., and New Orleans have also done quite well, especially in conjunction with leading conventions.

Who will be cataloging the coins? Does the auction firm have leading numismatists who are prepared to attribute the coins, grade them properly, and write interesting and appealing descriptions concerning them? How have the past catalogs been received by the collecting fraternity? Ask to see some issues of older catalogs and carefully study them for style and content. Review the prices realized of former sales. "Nothing succeeds like success," it has been said, and chances are that the firm with the most successful track record in the past will be the most successful for you.

What outstanding coins and collections has the firm handled, and what prices have they brought? Again, check into the past and determine the track record of the firm in years gone by. If your collection will fit in nicely with those offered in the past, you know that the firm has bidders on its mailing list who want your type of material and who are prepared to pay good prices for it. You do not want to have an auction firm experiment or gain knowledge at your expense!

In any field, it pays to see a specialist, and when time comes to sell your coins, I personally recommend that you have an auction specialist handle them.

As is true of any method of selling, there are advantages and disadvantages to selling by auction. The disadvantage is that you do not know precisely what your coins will bring until they sell. Further, it is usually several months or so until you receive your funds (although cash advances are often available).

Some prospective consignors have hesitated to auction their coins, fearing tax consequences. In my opinion, the present tax rates in the United States are sufficiently low that this should not be a factor in anyone's mind. It would be far better, in my opinion, to sell your coins and receive money that you can put into interest-bearing financial assets, if you choose.

There are many positive aspects of selling by auction. If you pay a 10% commission to the seller, and if the buyer pays a 10% fee, then if a coin brings $1,100 you net $900, or approximately 80% of the price. Dealers buying directly usually cannot operate on such a small margin of profit except, perhaps, for bullion-type coins and certain closely-traded items. If you have particularly scarce or rare pieces, it is often the situation that there will be a "fight" on the auction floor and new records will be set. Time and time again, I have seen pieces expected to bring $1,000 soar to $1,500, $2,000 or even more! As noted, when you sell your coins at auction, thousands of potential bidders have a chance to review your coins and consider bidding on them.

Auction! An effective way to buy or sell coins. It will pay you to learn as much as possible about this important aspect of the rare coin market.

Coin World's basic advertising policy

Coin World, Amos Press Inc.
P.O. Box 150, Sidney, Ohio 45365

The publisher offers advertising space for the purpose of bringing buyer and seller together for their mutual benefit. Years of publishing experience indicate the reader must be able to expect satisfactory service from the advertiser in order to respond to future advertisements. It is by giving such satisfactory service that advertisers can expect to continue productive advertising. Readers are reminded that all transactions are "two-way streets," and equity must exist for both parties for a satisfactory transaction.

Advertisements submitted which are not in the best interest of the advertiser specifically and of the trade generally, in the opinion of the publisher, or which may mislead readers, will be rejected. Customer checks of advertisers are periodically made by the publisher in a practical effort to assure accuracy and reliability of all advertisements. However, it is impossible to guarantee the reader's satisfaction with the advertiser's manner of doing business, and the reader is therefore reminded to exercise common sense in responding to any advertisement. The reader is also urged to exercise patience in awaiting response from an advertiser by making allowances for mail transit time.

Coin World assumes no responsibility for representations made in advertisements.

Inspection and return period

All individual coins are to be shipped in holders which permit thorough inspection of the coin. Any coin removed from holder is not returnable. Coins or numismatic material which the buyer finds to be unsatisfactory may be returned to the seller for full refund or replacement. Returns must be made within five days of receipt by the buyer, unless other return periods are specified in the advertisement. Refund or replacement will be made by the seller within seven days upon receipt of the returned item. Maximum return period allowed by advertisers is 30 days. The buyer MUST verify any extension of return period if coins are to be shipped to a grading service for verification.

Return postage on buy and trade ads

All advertisers who do not state "Write First" in their ads are expected to return merchandise postpaid. Refusal of packages at the post office may be grounds for suspension unless the ad indicates that confirmation is needed before shipping. If overgraded coins are to be returned at seller's or trader's expense, advertisement must so state.

Telephone transactions

In the case of telephone transactions when a confirmation number has been issued, both buyer and seller are expected to adhere to the telephonic agreement. Telephone and mail order transactions are subject to the same standards.

Complaints

All advertisers will be notified of complaints received in writing from the readers and prompt adjustment by the advertiser, if warranted, and notification to the publisher will be expected as a condition of continued acceptance of advertising. Failure of any advertiser to correct the cause of a complaint, or satisfactorily explain the same, may result in suspension of advertising privileges at the discretion of Coin World.

Verification, inspection, financial statement

Acceptance of advertising for any item or service is subject to investigation and verification of the product or service, and of the claims made for it, in the advertisement submitted for publication.

Coin World will utilize its Customer Checking Service to verify the accuracy of the specified grade of advertised numismatic items. Collectors living throughout the United States, upon instruction from the publishers, place orders for merchandise advertised. The parcels are forwarded unopened to the publisher for examination of the contents.

Verification by the Customer Checking Service of an advertiser shipping overgraded coin(s) may result in suspension of advertising privileges at the discretion of Coin World.

The publisher reserves the right to require a current financial statement from any advertiser at any time.

Copy regulations

All advertisements submitted are subject to copy regulations contained in the rate card. By submitting advertising, the advertiser acknowledges that he is familiar with the advertising contract and copy regulations then in effect. Additional copies will be furnished upon request.

Layaway sales

Advertisers must write for complete policy requirements prior to offering layaways in ads.

Sold out

In the event an item is sold out, remittance will be returned within 48 hours. The advertiser will not hold the remittance pending arrival of a new supply without obtaining permission of the buyer.

Reserve right to reject advertising

All advertising submitted is subject to publisher's approval. The publisher reserves the right to reject advertising, or suspend advertising privileges at the publisher's discretion.

Liability for contents of ads

Advertiser assumes liability for all contents (including text representation and illustrations) of advertisement printed, and also assumes responsibility for any claims therefrom.

Use of post office box

California law requires complete legal company name and full street address from which the business is actually being conducted. A post office box or phone number is not considered sufficient.

Coin World urges that complete information be included in all ads to promote uniformity and fairness between advertiser and reader.

Advance orders or futures

Advertisements offering coins or paper money which are not physically delivered into the hands of dealers at the time of placing the advertisement will not be accepted. EXCEPTION: Advertisements will be accepted from governments or their officially appointed agents or distributors when such is the only source from which anyone may order the items. Dealers serving as official agents or distributors in the advance sale of such items are required to supply documentation of such appointment.

Fake, counterfeit or altered coins and paper money

Only genuine numismatic items may be offered for sale. Coins which have been buffed, whizzed, polished, plugged or chemically treated to appear other than their original state must be accurately described as such in Coin World.

Altered or counterfeit coins and paper money and gold plated coins or bars are not acceptable for advertising in Coin World.

Any buyer of a fake or spurious item shall be entitled to full refund, and the normal return period shall be nullified.

The word "coin" may be used only when referring to legal tender.

Coin restrikes

Restrikes are numismatic items reproduced from the original dies or plates, but at a later date than appears on the item: the item must be restruck or reissued by the original issuing government authority, or authorized by decree or proclamation of the issuing government authority.

1. STRUCK FROM U.S. MINT DIES, whether inside or outside the Mint. Strictly speaking, these seem to be illegal, but they have a long history of collectibility, and many are listed in standard catalogs. They may be advertised in Coin World, always at the dealer's risk of the illegality.

2. COINS STRUCK FROM

ORIGINAL DIES other than U.S. Mint dies, but for items which either circulated or were intended to circulate making them coins rather than tokens, and with denominations usually on them: these include pioneer issues, the Confederate half dollar and cent, etc. These are acceptable for advertising, provided they are accurately described and identified as restrikes. Second or later restrikes must be distinguished from earlier restrikes in a permanent manner, such as metal used or appreciable difference in thickness, to be acceptable.

Any numismatic item created, designed or originally manufactured on or after March 1, 1963, which the owner wishes to advertise in Coin World as a restrike, must use the original dies on both obverse and reverse and make the impression transferral directly from die to planchet without otherwise making transferrals to any intermediate materials, dies, hubs, etc. Each piece must be indelibly labeled as a restrike.

It will be incumbent upon the advertiser to verify all facts concerning method and date of production.

Copies

Ads offering reproductions, imitations, replicas or copies of coins or other numismatic items are acceptable for advertising under the following conditions:

1. That such items are in compliance with the Hobby Protection Act and the U.S. Treasury's policy regarding coin replicas.

2. That the advertising copy or offer NOT contain false or misleading statements of the legal tender status of such items.

3. That the items be fully described in ads and samples of such items be submitted to Coin World with the initial ad.

4. That all items falling into this category must be clearly marked "COPY."

Cleaned coins

Cleaned coins are those from which something has been removed, such as tarnish, dirt, grit, carbon, etc., but not including any of the metal which would fall into the whizzed category. Cleaned coins can be advertised but it must be clearly stated that the coin is cleaned.

Applying a new surface to a coin to change its appearance is the same as replating and not acceptable for advertising in Coin World. Applying lacquer or similar protective coating to prevent tarnish is traditionally permissible, if neither the appearance nor the grade of the coin is changed.

Coin grading and descriptions

Coins and numismatic material offered for sale shall be accurately described. Coin World recognizes The American Numismatic Association Grading Standards for United States Coins, Photograde, The Numismatic Certification Institute Grading Guide and A Guide to the Grading of United States Coins by Brown and Dunn as the accepted standard methods of grading U.S. coins. Advertisers who do not use any of these standard grading methods must describe, in each ad, accurately and in detail the method of grading used. Advertisers using any one of the standard methods need to make reference to the grading method(s) used in the ads. Coin World reserves the right to reject any ad using methods other than the four standard methods listed.

Coin World has adopted the following minimum standards for grading terms used in Coin World advertisements in order that buyer and seller can better communicate. Borderline Uncirculated must be minimum of About Uncirculated 55. Uncirculated, Brilliant Uncirculated and Select Uncirculated must be minimum of Mint State 60. Choice Uncirculated or Choice Brilliant Uncirculated must be a minimum of Mint State 63. Gem Uncirculated or Gem Brilliant Uncirculated must be a minimum of Mint State 65. Superb Brilliant Uncirculated must be a minimum of Mint State 67. Split grades such as MS-63/65 must fall back into the lowest adjective level. MS-63/65 may be described as Choice Brilliant Uncirculated or Choice Uncirculated.

Any advertiser placing an advertisement in Coin World agrees to adhere to these minimum standards. Advertisers found in violation may have their advertising privileges suspended or revoked at the discretion of Coin World.

Exonumia

By Col. Bill Murray, NLG
San Antonio, Texas

Col. Bill Murray is a COIN WORLD columnist whose column, the "Newmismatist," covers a wide variety of subjects of interest to the beginning collector. He is a member of the Numismatic Literary Guild and numerous other numismatic organizations. Murray has a special interest in exonumia.

Among the first usages of the word exonumia was in correspondence between Russell Rulau and James Curto in the 1960s, but the subject matter included in the topic, according to some scholars, harks back to Roman medallions of the second century. Today's definition of exonumia is "numismatic items (as tokens, medals or scrip) other than coins or paper money."

Tokens, medals and scrip are given as examples of items an exonumist might study or collect, but the field of exonumia includes a myriad of subjects. Some are inclusive within the three subjects enumerated, but additional areas of interest do exist. The colletion of exonumia lends itself to topical collecting, and it is doubtful if any area of human endeavor is not represented by examples of exonumia. Such diverse fields as photography, politics and popes; lunches, lumber and liquor; sex, slavery and science; buses, bakers and boats; and coal, circuses and calendars have intrigued collectors over the years.

In this brief review of exonumia, tokens, medals and scrip will be examined, but no attempt at an exhaustive dissertation is intended. Also, only exonumic items of the United States will be included.

Tokens

A token is usually a piece of durable material appropriately marked and unofficially issued for monetary, advertising, services or other purposes.

Early tokens in the United States emanated from England as a principal source but also were occasionally made locally or in other countries. Almost from the outset of colonization they were to be found in America. Sylvester S. Crosby in his book, The Early Coins of America, says, ". . . my intention has been to give . . . [information about] . . . those coins or tokens which were intended to serve as coins . . . in those parts of America which now constitute the United States."

These early tokens were needed because of a shortage of coinage. The tokens looked like and passed for money.

The Coin World Comprehensive Catalog and Encyclopedia of United States Coins is another useful reference for Colonial tokens, as is Walter Breen's Complete Encyclopedia of U.S. and Colonial Coins.

Store cards

One favorite type of token with collectors, the store card, is a token bearing a business name or address, and often intended as a local or ad-hoc medium of exchange as well as an advertisement for the issuer.

Generally accepted as the first store card in the United States is the Mott token, according to Rulau in his book, Early American Tokens. The token was issued by William and John Mott, who ". . . were importers, dealers and manufacturers of gold and silver wares, jewelry, watches and clocks. . . ."

Store cards have been popular with U.S. merchants ever since. Current store cards are being issued today. Rarely have they passed as money in recent years. However, both in the past and presently, they may be pure advertising pieces, or sometimes, called "good fors." They are redeemable and may be exchanged by the issuer for merchandise or a service. "Good fors" bear messages such as "Good for 5 cents in trade," "Good for one drink," "Good for a cup of coffee" or "Good for $10 on purchase of a piano."

Tokens designed to pass locally as currency, as previously indicated, have a tendency to appear during times when money is hard to come by. It is no surprise that such tokens were found in the Colonies, because of the economic policies of the mother country. Money was short.

Hard Times tokens came a bit later, during the period 1832-1844. They are normally of copper and about the size of the United States large cent. Rulau, in his definitive reference about the subject, Hard Times Tokens, says tokens were issued ". . . in a time when, to use of the phrases of the day, "money was a cash article,' hard to get for daily needs."

He identifies five categories of Hard Times tokens. His categories are: 1. pieces referring to the Bank of the United States and the controversy surrounding it; 2. those with inscriptions relating to political and satirical situations of the era; 3. tokens with inscriptions and designs closely resembling the regular cent coinage, but with some differences in order to evade the counterfeiting laws; 4. store cards; and 5. die mulings — combinations with obverses and reverses of any of the preceding.

No organization dedicated to collectors of these early tokens exists, but an organization devoted primarily to the United States large cents and half cents, the Early American Coppers club, caters to collectors of early American tokens.

Civil War tokens issued during the Civil War when small change became scarce also was money of necessity. Civil War tokens, though often referred to as copperheads, were struck not only in copper but in brass and other alloys as well. Many of the off-metal varities were struck specifically for collectors and in small numbers.

The production and use of Civil War tokens was limited primarily to the Eastern and Midwestern states, but they were produced in prodigious numbers and are readily available to collectors today. Rare pieces, of course, demand premium prices.

Two general categories of Civil War tokens are identified — patriotics and store cards. Though thousands of varities exist, they are well cataloged and recent, updated catalogs have been published by the Civil War Token Society. The books are U.S. Civil War Store Cards and Patriotic Civil War Tokens, by George and Melvin Fuld.

A popular and generally more modern token is the transportation token. Transportation tokens — or vectures, as they are sometimes called — include items such as bus and street car tokens and tokens for toll roads and bridges and ferries. Tokens for a ride in a carriage, on a carousel, other amusement rides and in horsecars and taxis also exist.

The American Vecturist Association is an active organization. The monthly periodical, "The Fare Box," regularly updates listings for The Atwood-Coffee Catalogue of United States and Canadian Transportation Tokens, an important reference for transportation collectors. In addition to transportation tokens, the AVA monitors activities for collectors of parking tokens and car wash tokens.

Wooden money

Many collectors who specialize in wooden money can also be added to the list of exonumists. The science of wooden money collecting is called lignadenarics. Most people, however, still use the phrase "wooden money." While most of the pieces found in such a person's collection are round, and many are labeled "nickel," many more are rectangular. Any may be identified with different monetary denominations, such as 50 cents, $1, $10 and even more.

The first known use of wooden tokens in the United States was in Tenino, Wash., in 1931. The Tenino bank had failed, and

Don Major, a local publisher, suggested the idea of issuing the wooden money for local use as an emergency measure.

Wooden pieces may be used for any of the purposes of other, non-wooden, tokens already discussed. Also we find some which are commemorative in nature, and frequently they are used in promotion of an event or person. Politicians often distribute them to promote their cause. For collectors they are inexpensive and are popular with many who have tight budgets. Two national wooden money organizations offer services to the collector: Dedicated Wooden Money Collectors and International Organization of Wooden Money Collectors.

During World War II, rationing was a way of life. Practically all commodities were rationed. The Office of Price Administration was responsible for the program and issued ration stamps and coupons, usually in booklet form. The coupons for meat and processed food were issued in denominations of five points, 10 points and 20 points.

In 1944 tokens good for one point were issued to be used in making change for the meat and processed food coupons. These tokens were red or blue and were made of a tough fibrous material. They are 16 millimeters in diameter. Each has an outlined number 1 stamped in the center with two small letters on either side of the 1. The letters are found in various unexplained combinations such as MV, HH, UX, CH and HH. Perhaps this was an attempt to foil counterfeiters. A complete set requires 30 red tokens and 24 blue tokens. Only the red MV token can be considered scarce or costly. Most OPA token collectors also collect other ration material, but ration token collectors, per se, have their own national organization, the Society of Ration Token Collectors.

Medals

Medals, as collector's items, frequently seem to be the province of experienced collectors with a long background in coin collecting. The term medal is defined as "usually a piece of metal marked with a design or inscription made to honor a person, place or event, and is not intended to pass as money."

A medal may be a piece of metal hanging at the end of a ribbon, as commonly thought and given as a prize or award for some personal action such as winning a contest or for an act of heroism. The term medal encompasses much more than this type of award. Collectors of medals often collect them as art objects, and the art medal, so called, undoubtedly represents the zenith of numismatic art. Well-known American sculptors such as Augustus Saint-Gaudens, James Earle Fraser, Victor D. Brenner and Karen Worth are recognized for their work as medallic artists.

Probably the earliest definitive work concerning medals in the United States is C. Wyllys Betts' American Colonial History Illustrated by Contemporary Medals. His volume covers the period 1556-1786 and still is the basic reference for the era.

When discussing medals, one must reflect on the generalization of the definition and realize that not all medals will be paragons of the medalist's art. Many "lesser" medals exist which, because of their contribution to the recording of historial, parochial or topical subjects, are desired by collectors.

In his prize-winning book, Medals of the United States Mint, The First Century, 1792-1892, R.W. Julian lists, describes, discusses and illustrates United States medals under the following categories: Assay Commission, Indian peace, presidential, military, naval, Mint and Treasury, personal, commemorative, school, agricultural, mechanical, scientific and professional, life saving, marksmanship, religious and fraternal and unclassified. The U.S. Mint is still producing medals today and will send a list of available medals for sale on request.

Not included in Julian's catalog, it may come as a surprise, are medals issued by the various military departments. Though authorized by the federal government or one of its executive branches, they were not designed nor struck at the Mint.

These last mentioned items are properly categorized under the general heading of medals but usually are listed in the sub-categories of decorations or awards. The study of medals includes consideration of at least the following: medalets, medallions, plaques, plaquettes, badges, decorations, awards and orders.

Scrip

Scrip is the last example included in the definition of exonumia. A good definition for scrip is: "tokens and paper currency, often in denominations of less than $1, issued as substitutes for currency to private persons or organizations."

Someone has devised the mnemonic "Substitute Currency Received in Payment" — SCRIP, probably because one often encounters the incorrect spelling as "script." There is no terminal "T" on the word scrip.

Coal companies, sutlers, lumber companies, prisons and an agency of the United States government (the Alaskan Rural Rehabilitation Corp.) are examples of issuing agencies. Paper scrip was used but often was replaced by metallic scrip which better withstood the damaging effects of hard, daily usage. Denominations issued may usually have less than $1, but $5 and $10 pieces are not uncommon. The U.S. government, or its agencies, have issued scrip. Most notable are military payment certificates provided for the armed forces in certain overseas locations.

One organization (National Scrip Collectors Association) is dedicated to scrip collecting with emphasis primarily on metallic coal and lumber scrip.

Altered coins

Three exonomic categories, properly included in a complete discussion of exonumia, depend on alteration of coins after they have left the Mint — love tokens, elongated coins and counterstamped coins. Two of these have sufficient following to have their own national organizations. The Love Token

Society and The Elongated Collectors are the organizations involved.

Counterstamped coins

Counterstamped coins are the simplest alteration, and the title clearly indicates what you might expect — the use of punches to make marks on the coins. United States collectors of counterstamps often direct their efforts towards coins where the counterstamp alters the coin into a presentation piece, a store card or some other use of the piece as a token. Large cents were often used in this fashion.

Love tokens

Love tokens may "mutilate" the coin as a piece of money, but most collectors collect love tokens because of their intrinsic beauty. A love token is a coin which has been altered by smoothing one or both surfaces and engraving initials, scenes, messages and so on thereon. The engraved coins were often given to an individual's loved one, hence the name given them.

Love tokens were especially popular in the 19th century, a time when the engraver's art was pervasive in the United States. Many of the names, monograms or scenes depicted are beautifully done. Often the engraving appears on the side opposite from the date because the date may have had significance to the originator.

Elongated coins

An elongated coin is an oval medalet produced by a roller die using a coin, token or medal as a planchet — usually a cent.

Lee Martin and Dottie Dow in their book, Yesterday's Elongateds, discuss the techniques of elongated "rolling." Elongated coins are dated from the World's Columbian Expositon in Chaicago during 1892-93. However, many people think the technique may have been developed before then, but to date, elongates from that exposition are the earliest that have been identified.

The typical elongated coin has been rolled with a die which impresses one side of the coin. The die has been engraved with a design, often commemorative, or a message. Subject matter, as Martin and Dow aver, "It's as wide-ranging as the imagination."

As can be inferred from previous discussion, exonumia lends itself to topical collecting. Geography frequently dictates the direction of a collection — a certain state, county or town of interest to the collector. Many individuals relate their collections to personal interests: business, hobby, a sport or other. Just a few examples will suffice: photography, good-luck pieces, insurance, boats, animals, religion, automobiles, flowers, dairies, banks and the United States Bicentennial.

Two organizations devoted to exonumia not specifically aligned with any of the special areas of exonumia previously discussed are the Token and Medal Society and the Active Token Collectors Organization. Both are important organizations serving the exonumist.

TAMS is the one organization catering to all aspects of exonumia. The TAMS Journal is professional in aspect and content. In addition to the regular issues of the journal, TAMS publishes supplementary issues which are catalogs of special topics of exonumia and most useful to the collector. Also, TAMS has published several quality books about various facets of the subject. R.W. Julian's book about the U.S. Mint medals is just one example.

ATCO is composed of several hundred members who are collectors of many types of tokens. Its publication affords a primary outlet for collectors to buy, sell or trade. Among serious token collectors, trading is a way of life.

The magnitude and complexity of the study of exonumia eliminates the possibility of a single book covering the subject adequately. As a consequence, many books of specialized interest exist. Books and catalogs in profusion, devoted to special, individual aspects of exonumia are available.

Several of the organizations dedicated to exonumia maintain libraries related to the subject. In addition, the American Numismatic Association has many volumes about exonumia. Books can be borrowed by collector members of these organizations usually at the cost of postage and insurance.

Hard Times tokens

The period between the end of the Revolutionary War and the beginning of the Civil War was marked by times of economic upheavals which were separated by periods of monetary stability. The infant government was attempting to cope with the westward expansion of the country, with animosity directed toward the United States by foreign powers, and the slow process of learning self-government.

The first United States Mint had been established in Philadelphia in 1792 but crude equipment and limited experience curtailed production. At the same time an ever-increasing population required more and more coins. During periods of economic stability coin production was able to keep up with use, but during periods of economic upheaval, hard money was taken out of circulation and hoarded.

By the early 1830s the lack of available coinage had almost reached the critical stage. Though tokens had been issued even before the Revolutionary War, mainly of an advertising nature, they had never been used in commerce to any great degree.

The extreme shortage of small change caused more and more merchants to use tokens in lieu of cents in ever greater numbers in their day-to-day business transactions. Privately issued token coinage was a preferable alternative to the barter system.

The Hard Times tokens consist of two main types: merchant's advertising tokens and political tokens.

The advertising tokens carry information about the location and type of business the merchant was engaged in. Most of them are of copper, bronze or brass but some were issued in other metals, such as Feuchtwanger's "American Silver" composition.

An interesting view of the practice of issuing token coinage is given in a paper read by Thomas Elder to the New York Numismatic Club on Jan. 8, 1915: "It is of interest to read that H.M. & E.I. Richards, of Attleboro, Mass., sold their tokens by the keg-full to their customers for from 60 to 75 cents per hundred."

Elder's statement helps make the practice understandable. Not only was the merchant able to make change for his customers, he bought the tokens at less than 1 cent each and knew that many would be lost or otherwise unredeemed, reducing his cost per token even more.

The tokens are generally about the size of the large cents of that period in which they were issued. For that reason they were accepted in commerce.

As the economy demanded small change which couldn't be provided in quantity by the Mints and was thus provided by merchants, so too did political actions result in another type of token coinage.

Champions of political causes and detractors of those same causes often issued tokens hoping thereby to advance their particular aims. Many of the political tokens centered around the refusal of President Jackson to renew the charter of the Bank of the United States.

Whatever the reason for issuing Hard Times tokens may have been, they do form an interesting and historical segment of numismatics.

Civil War tokens

The Civil War gave rise to numerous forms of emergency money, the variety and ingenuity of which have never been equaled. Early in 1862 all metallic currency was gradually withdrawn from circulation. During the war people feared the total devaluation of currency and started to hoard gold and silver. Finally even copper currency disappeared from circulation. The result was chaos for those conducting day-to-day business — there was simply no way to make change.

The first attempt was the use of ordinary U.S. postage stamps. But, because of their flimsy nature, stamps had a very short circulating lifespan. Next, the merchants issued small envelopes, generally with some advertising on the back, so the postage stamps would be afforded some degree of protection.

In 1862, John Gault patented a novel brass encasement for the stamps, with a mica cover, so the stamps were easily visible. These encased stamps, made by the Scoville Manufacturing Co. in Waterbury, Conn., with the merchant's advertising on one side, circulated widely. Their one disadvantage was that they cost more than face value to issue because the cost of manufacture of the case had to be added to the face value of the stamp.

Various forms of fractional, privately issued, paper money then appeared but, because it had no intrinsic value (and doubtful backing in many cases) it did not meet with wide acceptance. Cardboard scrip met with the same fate.

Finally the most popular and realistic form of emergency money, in the form of small copper tokens, began circulating extensively throughout the Northeast and Midwest in late 1862. These small coins, generally the size and weight of small bronze cents, met with immediate acceptance. The use soon spread to other states and cities.

Two general types of tokens were issued — the so-called "patriotic" tokens and the "tradesmen's" tokens. The patriotic series, mainly issued in and around New York, have patriotic slogans on the tokens but bear no merchant's advertising. Many of the pieces are in general imitation of the Indian cent. The tradesmen's (or merchant's) store cards were widely issued and usually bear the merchant's advertisement on one side and some patriotic symbol on the other.

The issue of Civil War tokens exceeded 25 million pieces, which amply filled the needs of the merchants. And the merchants were happy with the arrangement since the tokens not only advertised their business but also cost only 23/100ths of a cent to produce.

The tokens were undoubtedly a source of great relief and convenience, but their irresponsible character soon attracted the attentions of the federal government, because some of the merchants refused to redeem the tokens they had issued. Government attempts at issuing bronze coins and fractional currency were not sufficient to suppress the Civil War tokens then current. Finally, in 1864, an act of Congress forbid the practice of issuing money in any form. Thus ended another era.

The authoritative book about the subject of Civil War Tokens had long been Hetrich and Guttag's epic work Civil War Tokens and Tradesmen's Cards, published in 1924. They listed some 7,000 varieties but, at the present time, more than 11,000 different specimens (different die-metal varieties) are known to exist.

At present the most comprehensive works on the subject are the two books, Patriotic Civil War Tokens and U.S. Civil War Store Card Tokens by George and Melvin Fuld.

Storage and preservation

Coins and paper money change over time, and not for the better.

This simple maxim is too often neglected by collectors, dealers and investors, and received little coverage in the numismatic press until the late 1970s, when it was learned that most of the coin storage methods then in use tended to cause coins and notes to deteriorate instead of protecting the materials being stored. Deterioration is at odds with the long-accepted belief that the better the condition of a numismatic collectible, the more it is worth.

The greater awareness of coin storage and preservation has resulted in safer storage materials being offered. However, most coins sold, bought and stored are probably being held in a holder that does not offer much protection, or may even harm the coin.

In general, storage materials that are safe for coins are also safe for paper money, but common sense must be applied.

The following observations are based on a series of Collectors' Clearinghouse articles by Bernard Nagengast, a Sidney, Ohio, specialist in coin storage and preservation and a dealer in materials he says are safe for storage and handling.

Metal

Metals vary in their resistance to corrosion; however, all coinage metals can be affected. Gold is probably the most resistant coinage metal, being unaffected by most corrosive agents. A problem arises with some gold coins because they usually contain copper, and a poor mix can result in areas of high concentration of copper which can corrode, causing streaks, spotting and other surface blemishes.

Fortunately, this does not often occur. Gold coins are remarkably resistant to storage in dangerous coin holders, polluted atmospheres, and under other adverse conditions. Be careful with gold coins if you smoke, however. Tobacco will stain gold. Avoid handling gold coins with tobacco contaminated fingers, or blowing smoke on the coins, which can condense on the surface.

Silver is also quite resistant, but subject to tarnish, especially in the presence of sulfur compounds and nitrates. Since sulfur and nitrate compounds are frequent components of air pollution, modern times are especially hard on silver coins.

As with gold, silver U.S. coins contain copper. Since the percentage is about 10 percent, it is possible to oxidize copper at the coin's surface, resulting in green to blue corrosion. Attractive, irridescent patina is considered desirable on silver coins by some collectors. This patina results from complex chemical processes over a long period of time, thus the rainbow hues seen on some 19th century silver coins.

There have been modern day attempts to duplicate natural toning when it was discovered that such coins sometimes bring premium prices. By experimenting with various chemicals, some found that they could produce instant toning, and there are "midnight labs" in various parts of the country turning out these coins. Beware when toning is used to cover up rubbing on an Uncirculated coin or hairlines on a Proof coin.

Copper-nickel alloy is even more susceptible to chemical attack because of the 75 percent copper present. Not only is it affected by atmospheric contaminants, but it is also more subject to electrochemical action (battery action) than silver and gold. Small black spots, called "carbon spots," are sometimes seen. These are the result of oxygen cells, discussed later, or the result of a contaminant imbedded in the coin's surface, which later corrodes or oxidizes, or causes the surrounding metal to corrode or oxidize.

Copper is possibly the most fragile commonly used U.S. coinage material. Upon oxidation, it forms green to blue copper oxide. Copper alloy coins are very susceptible to carbon spots.

The atmosphere

This was touched on in the topic above, and it should be obvious by now that airborne gases can adversely affect a coin. Normal pollutants found in the air can cause long-term problems. They can combine with oxygen at the coin's surface. Artificial gases produced while a coin is in a plastic holder, coming from the plastic itself, can also have an adverse effect.

The atmosphere also contains moisture and dust, both dangerous to a coin's surface. Both are carriers of oxygen and other compounds, bringing them into intimate contact with the coin's surface. Since we don't have much direct control over the air around us, the only way to protect a coin from the atmospheric pollutants is to isolate it in a container that is airtight and inert, so the container itself won't contaminate the coin.

Contaminants

Coins are dirty, even when coming off the coinage press! Since the metal is rolled, punched, annealed, struck by dies and handled by various mechanical devices, even a Mint State or Proof coin will be contaminated with metallic particles, oil and grease, rag dust, bag dust, and other foreign material. Contaminants may even be imbedded in the surface from the rollers, dies and other mechanical devices.

Once the coins leave the Mint, they are further contaminated by counting machines, rolling machine, and handling by the collector himself. Collectors can contaminate a coin when they handle it — grease on fingers, dust particles in the air, dandruff or the surface the coin is laid on.

Coin holders themselves can contaminate the coin. They may contain dust particles picked up by static electricity from the air on surfaces. Many also contain paper or cardboard dust, highly dangerous to pristine coins. As discussed above, some plastic holders give off dangerous gases due to their volatility. Some release acetic, hydrochloric and other acids. Some "sweat" and the liquid coming out of the plastic is deposited on the coin.

Dust particles on the coins are dangerous not only because they themselves may be corrosive, but also because they can form oxygen cells. When a particle rests on a coin, it causes an oxygen deficiency at that point and this sets up an electrochemical reaction resulting in precipitation of corrosive compounds around the particle. A spot forms as a result, and the surface of the coin pits directly under the dust particle. Experience indicates that paper and cardboard dust particles are especially prone to forming oxygen cells.

Handling

Improper handling causes abrasion, decreasing the value of the coin itself and also exposes fresh metal which can oxidize and corrode. Although every collector should be aware of these facts, some can be seen carelessly handling coins. Don't allow coins to come in contact with each other if you value their long-term life.

Vibration from street traffic, footsteps and other sources can cause them to rub imperceptibly, and over a long period of time, rub marks may develop on the high spots. When you lay a coin down, be aware of the surface. Is it clean? If not, the coin may pick up contaminants. Coins stored in slide-type albums may develop "slide mark" abrasion on the high points from sliding the windows past the coins.

Storage materials

The factors described above will have an adverse effect on coins over time, but can be reduced and perhaps eliminated by careful selection of materials for storage or display. Length of time for storage needs consideration. A certain material may not harm the coin on a short-term level, but could be highly dangerous in the long term.

Common sense would dictate that it is unnecessary to spend a lot of time and money on a container if the coin is only being temporarily stored. Once the coin is in the hands of the collector who plans on keeping it for a long time, it is foolish not to take the steps necessary to protect the coin.

One interesting fact about collecting is that people will often spend a fortune on a coin without a second thought about properly preserving it, risking the possibility of large financial losses if the coin deteriorates while they own it. Consider then that selection of a good holder is the coin owner's responsibility, simply because the previous owner or dealer probably didn't give it a thought.

The following statement may shock you, but it is a fact: many of the coin holders on the market are not suitable for long-term storage. The following discusses the most common coin holders and their suitability.

Coin albums: One expert on coin storage has said he has yet to see an album he would call satisfactory. The cardboard ones with plastic slides are bad because of the cardboard and paper, the abrasion possible with the plastic slides, and the fact that a large number of coins are exposed at the same time when the slides are pulled.

These albums also don't protect against the atmosphere or moisture since the cardboard is porous. Some newer albums are made of plastic, and although they eliminate the slides, they are also not suitable because the plastic itself is not inert. Some of them "sweat" over a period of time, causing tarnished or green corrosion. Coin boards without any covering should obviously never be used for high-grade coins.

Two-by-twos: Probably the most common coin holder is the cardboard 2-by-2-inch or 1.5-by-1.5-inch square container. They come as one piece usually, with a plastic window and are stapled or glued together with the coin in between. This holder is one of the most dangerous holders around. Many of the plastics used are dangerous, the holder is not airtight, and worst of all, many are badly contaminated with paper and cardboard dust on the surface of the plastic.

Even when wiped off, the holder still has microscopic dust particles which fly to the coin's surface when it is inserted. You would be amazed how big a spot a dust particle invisible to the naked eye can cause. Certainly these holders can be used for short-term transactions, but should never be used to store a collection for an extended period of time.

Flips: This is the name given to the 2-by-2-inch solid plastic holder. There are usually two sections hinged at the top, and one section contains a paper insert for labeling. Most are made of vinyl, a dangerous plastic because it can combine with oxygen to form compounds which will attack the coin.

Some are Mylar, a polyethylene derivative, and these are basically inert, but are moisture permeable. The mylars are reasonably safe for short-term storage though. There is a possibility of contaminating the interiors of the flips with paper dust from the inserts. Also, the flips do not seal at the top, thus the coins are exposed to the atmosphere.

Plexiglass: Three-layer plexiglass holders are available for single coins or sets. They are much better than most holders, but have the disadvantage of high cost. Plexiglass contains polymethacrylic acid, which can attack the coin's surface. The coins usually are loose in the holes and can rattle around, abrading the plastic and picking up dust from the plastic, thus the acid can come in contact with the coin. Plexiglass can also absorb moisture.

Polystyrene holders: Single coin or Proof and Mint holders, as well as roll tubes, are available. Made of clear brittle plastic, the holders usually snap together. Polystyrene is one of the few inert plastics and therefore can be considered safe. The edges of these holders, however, frequently do not seal airtight.

Preparation for storage

There is no point in storing a coin in a safe holder if the coin itself is contaminated with materials which can cause corrosion. All coins contain varying amounts of Mint oil and grease, counting machine grease, bag dust, and the dust particles from the air and from previous storage methods. This contamination should be removed before the coin is put into its final storage holder.

The coin should be dipped into a good solvent which will dissolve grease and oil and carry away dust. It is advisable to swish the coin in the solvent, and may be necessary to take a cotton swab to remove heavy accumulations of grease. Two dips should be used, an initial one of any good solvent (alcohol, trichloroethane) to remove most of the contamination, and a final rinse to neutralize the solvent and carry away final traces of contamination.

There are only two safe solvents which can be used for neutralizing. Both will evaporate readily and leave no residue on the coin. One is pure medical Benzene, available at a drug store. The other is Trichlorotrifluoroethane, which is not easily available, but has the advantage of being non-toxic, and completely non-flammable.

Benzene should be used with adequate ventilation since it is considered toxic and cancer-causing as well as being highly flammable. The solvents should be free of any water or contaminants.

After dipping the coin, let the solvent evaporate in the air and immediately insert it into the holder. It is best not to allow the coin to come in contact with anything other than the inside of the holder to prevent re-contamination with dust.

Once the coin is placed in an airtight, safe holder, it is irrelevant where the coin is stored, since atmosphere won't affect the coin itself. However, heat should be avoided, as well as sunlight.

Following these suggestions will not guarantee that a coin will not deteriorate, but they do suggest the best methods known to ensure that coins which are the pride and joy of a collector will survive for the lifetime of this and future generations of collectors.

Coin weights and measures

Weights and measures pertaining to coins are almost as numerous as coin types issued over the centuries. It is only natural that a nation would issue coins based on the weight system recognized by that government.

Ancient weights in many cases have been adapted to coin denominations. The shekel, a weight mentioned in the Old Testament, became a coin of the ancient Jews.

The British pound and Mexican peso are other examples of denominations named for weights.

The grains-ounces-pounds system of Great Britain was adapted for use by the American Colonies and the United States. The metric system was adopted later by the French and then almost all other countries of the world.

In Europe in the 16th, 17th and 18th centuries, as trade between nations brought coins of many denominations and metals from other countries into a merchant's counting room, special scales were developed to weigh each coin. Instead of a weight representing so many drachma, pennyweights or grams, the weight represented a gold French louis d'or, Spanish pistole or British sovereign. The boxes holding the scales and weights were often inlaid, quite ornate, and are collector's items today.

In Great Britain, three 1-penny coins equaled 1 ounce. Struck to such a fine tolerance were British halfpenny and penny coins that bank clerks counted coins by weighing them. Two hundred and forty 1-penny coins (£1) weighed 80 ounces, and triangular-shaped packages were prepared for sale to the public on the basis of weight, not counting machines.

An early system used to measure coins in England was to assign a number for each 16th of an inch of a coin; a coin measuring 1 inch in diameter was considered size 16; 1/4-inches, size 24; 2 inches, size 32; and so on. U.S. numismatists adopted this system too, although it is no longer used.

Before the metric system, a Frenchman named Mionnet devised a series of concentric lines emanating from a common plane; whichever number line the coin met, when placed on the plane, such was the size of the coin.

The U.S. Mint Reports list coin diameters in both inches and millimeters, and coin weights in grains and grams.

Weights and measures

Following is a chart of coin weight and measure conversions. Included are conversion values for grams, grains, millimeters, centimeters and inches.

Gold, silver and platinum coins are usually weighed in grams or grains.

One gram equals:
.001 kilogram
15.43235639 grains
.002204622 pound, avoirdupois
.03527396 ounce, avoirdupois

.002679229 pound, troy
.03215075 ounce, troy
One grain equals:
.00006479 kilogram
.0647989 gram
.000142857 pound, avoirdupois
.002285 ounce, avoirdupois
.000173611 pound, troy
.002083 ounce, troy
One millimeter equals:
.03937 inch
One centimeter equals:
.3937 inch
One inch equals:
25.4 millimeters
2.54 centimeters
.0254 meter

Metric conversion

mm	inches	mm	inches	mm	inches
10	.39	27	1.06	44	1.73
11	.43	28	1.10	45	1.77
12	.47	29	1.14	46	1.81
13	.51	30	1.18	47	1.85
14	.55	31	1.22	48	1.89
15	.59	32	1.26	49	1.93
16	.63	33	1.30	50	1.97
17	.67	34	1.34	51	2.01
18	.71	35	1.38	52	2.05
19	.75	36	1.42	53	2.09
20	.79	37	1.46	54	2.13
21	.83	38	1.50	55	2.17
22	.87	39	1.54	56	2.21
23	.91	40	1.58	57	2.24
24	.95	41	1.61	58	2.28
25	.98	42	1.65	59	2.32
26	1.02	43	1.69	60	2.36

Specific gravity of common elements

Element	Sym.	Sp. Grav.
Aluminum	Al	2.6989
Antimony	Sb	6.691
Beryllium	Be	1.848
Bismuth	Bi	9.747
Cadmium	Cd	8.650
Carbon	C	2.250[1]
Chromium	Cr	7.19[2]
Copper	Cu	8.96
Gold	Au	18.88[3]
Iron	Fe	7.874
Lead	Pb	11.35

Magnesium	Mg	1.738
Manganese	Mn	7.3[4]
Molybdenum	Mo	10.22
Nickel	Ni	8.902
Palladium	Pd	12.02
Platinum	Pt	21.45
Ruthenium	Ru	12.41
Silicon	Si	2.33
Silver	Ag	10.50
Tantalum	Ta	16.654
Tin	Sn	7.298[5]
Titanium	Ti	4.54
Tungsten	W	19.3
Vanadium	V	6.11
Zinc	Zn	7.133

[1] Carbon has three distinct ranges of specific gravity, depending upon its form. Amorphous carbon ranges from 1.8 to 2.1; diamonds have the highest, at 3.15 to 3.53.

[2] Average in the range of 7.18 to 7.20.

[3] Value for elemental gold. See "Specific gravity of gold and copper" below.

[4] Average in the range of 7.21 to 7.44.

[5] Gray tin has a specific gravity of 5.75; white tin has a specific gravity of 7.31. Value given is approximate value of combined white and gray in normally occuring proportions.

Gold and copper

Gold is the one metal which does not lend itself to this method of specific gravity determination. When gold is alloyed with copper there is an molecular interaction with the result that the specific gravity of the two metals in alloy is smaller than the specific gravity of the individual parts that were used to make up the alloy. The following is a table of the specific gravity figures of the most common gold-copper alloys.

Au %	Cu %	Sp. Gr.
99	01	19.099
98	02	18.883
97	03	18.672
96	04	18.465
95	05	18.264
94	06	18.066
93	07	17.873
92	08	17.684
91	09	17.499
90	10	17.317
89	11	17.140
88	12	16.966
87	13	16.795
86	14	16.628
85	15	16.464
84	16	16.303
83	17	16.146
82	18	15.991
81	19	15.840
80	20	15.691

Karat to fineness conversion

Karat is a unit of measure of fineness of gold, a measure of 24 parts. To find any fineness from karats, divide the karat measure by 24. (Pure gold is always reported as ".9999 fine" to allow for minute impurities; no more than 1 part in 10,000 is not gold.)

24 karat	=	.9999 fine
22 karat	=	.9167 fine
18 karat	=	.7500 fine
14 karat	=	.5833 fine
12 karat	=	.5000 fine
10 karat	=	.4167 fine

Therefore, if a piece contains 1 ounce of 18 karat gold, multiply 1 by .7500 to find that the piece contains .75 ounce of pure gold.

Getting a copyright

The United States joined the Berne Union March 1, 1989. by entering into an international treaty called the Berne Convention, or the Berne Convention for the Protection of Literary and Artistic Works. In order to comply with the standards under the Berne Union, the United States copyright law was amended.

The changes took effect March 1, 1989, and affect only works published after March 1, 1989. Works published prior to that date are still regulated under the previous law.

Protection under the Berne Union gurantees minimum rights. Works first published in the United States are minimally guaranteed all rights effective in the U.S. for all nations in the Berne Union (about 80). Conversely, works first published in another Berne Union nation are guaranteed at least that nation's rights, or more.

Important changes

A full explanation of the new copyright laws can be obtained from the Copyright Office, Library of Congress, Washington, D.C. 20559.

Among the highlights of the new copyright regulations:

• Mandatory notice of copyright has been abolished for works published for the first time on or after March 1, 1989. Failure to place a notice of copyright on copies or phono-records of such works can no longer result in the loss of copyright. (Please note, however, that voluntary use of notice is encouraged. One of the benefits of placing a notice such as © 1990 by John Doe is that an infringer will not be able to claim that he "innocently infringed" a work, thereby reducing

damages.

• Copyright owners must deposit in the Copyright Office two complete copies of the best edition of all works subject to copyright that are publicly distributed in the United States . . . (For more information, request Circular 7d.)

• Works first copyrighted before 1978 must still be renewed in the 28th year in order to receive the second term of 47 years. If such a work is not timely renewed, it will fall into the public domain in the United States at the end of the 28th year.

A copyright owner has the right to:
• Sell or distribute the work.
• Transform or revise the work.
• Record the work.
• Perform the work publicly.
• Print, reprint and copy the work.

Please be aware that the owner of a copyright is not necessarily the author. Generally, works created under a work-for-hire agreement are owned by the employer. Similarly, selling publication rights to a publisher, either in book form or as an article for a periodical, may entail relinquishing all rights to the work to the publisher.

An author who sells the rights to an article to newspaper A, then sells the article again to newspaper B, is very likely infringing upon newspaper A's copyright, even though the article was originally the author's work.

Submitting articles to Coin World

Coin World is a newsweekly covering most aspects of the numismatic hobby. Articles range from breaking news to analysis to feature material and columns.

Free-lance writers are encouraged to consider Coin World as an evenue for publication, but there are some guidelines that should be followed.

First, write an inquiry to the editor. Briefly summarize the article idea or give a brief outline and estimated length. Say whether you can supply photographs or other illustrations. It is not recommended

that you send a finished manuscript as first contact. Often, the editors will have special needs, and could work with you to meet those needs. Also, there is the simple matter of time. A backlog of unread manuscripts leads to frustrations for writers and editors alike.

Second, consider your topic carefully. It should be something that can be addressed fully in about 500 to 1,000 words. If it is taking appreciably longer, or you find you are skimming to make this length, perhaps your topic is too broad.

First priority is given to original numismatic research or presentation of popular topics in new and interesting ways.

Broader or deeper topics that may require serialization should be pre-arranged with the editors. Serialized articles work best when each segment can stand on its own merits. Remember, not everyone who reads the second installment will have seen the first.

If you are encouraged to the point of actually finishing a manuscript, take some care with its physical appearance. Typed is a necessity. Double-spaced is strongly encouraged. If you use a computer or word-processor, your print-out should be double-spaced and dark enough to be easily readable. Also, you may want to inquire about the possibility of electronic transmission.

Finally, if your idea or manuscript is rejected, don't be discouraged. It may be that that particular publication has had a number of similar manuscripts recently, or any of a number of good reasons why good articles are turned down. Try somewhere else, and try again with a new idea.

Inquiries about articles for Coin World should be addressed to Beth Deisher, Editor, Coin World, 911 Vandemark Road, Sidney, Ohio 45365. Inquiries about books or other non-newspaper projects should be addressed to P. Bradley Reed, Ancillary Products Manager at the same address.

Museums

20

History of the national collection

The national numismatic collection, now housed in the Smithsonian Institution, had its beginnings soon after the United States was formed.

The history begins around 1818, when the Columbian Institute for the Promotion of Arts and Sciences was granted a charter from Congress. Located in Washington, D.C., the Institute had a small numismatic collection kept in the Institute's cabinets, not available to the public.

When the charter for the Columbian Institute expired in 1838, associates became members of the National Institution, and deposited their effects, books and papers in its cabinet.

The National Institution for the Promotion of Science, or the National Institute as it was later called, was organized on May 15, 1840, under the leadership of Joel Roberts Poinsett. Its purpose was to establish a national museum.

John Varden, however, must be given credit as the first to offer public exhibits featuring numismatic objects. He was an enterprising private citizen of Washington, D.C., who opened a small museum adjoining his home in 1836, with displays consisting of some 500 curiosities.

In 1840 Varden sold his collection to the National Institute for $1,500. The curator of the National Institute, Dr. Henry King, had the entire inventory of Varden's museum installed in the National Gallery Hall at the United States Patent Office. Varden accompanied the collection as an assistant.

For four years following its organization in 1840, the National Institute was exceedingly active and prosperous. In rooms made available at the Patent Office Building it gathered, under the name of the "National Cabinet of Curiosities."

Smithson fortune

In 1846 James Smithson, an English scientist, bequeathed his fortune, including many numismatic items, to the United States for the "increase and diffusion of knowledge." On Aug. 10, 1846, an act of Congress was signed by President Polk establishing the Smithsonian Institution and on May 1, 1847, the cornerstone of its first building was laid on the Mall.

During this time the National Institute failed to secure public recognition and in 1858 the transfer of its collection to the Smithsonian began, but was not completed until 1883.

When the centennial exposition of 1876 was held in Philadelphia, the Institution found that it had such an enormous quantity of material in its custody that it became necessary to move to a new building, the United States National Museum, now the Arts and Industries Building. George Brown Goode was appointed assistant secretary in charge of the museum.

In 1893 the entire numismatic collection was withdrawn from display and stored, after being crowded out by expanding natural history collections. During this time an attempt was made to assemble a general collection of currencies of the world and numismatic acquisitions were both numerous and varied.

One of the most outstanding groups of coins received was a collection of 28 Japanese gold and silver pieces, which came to the Museum in 1886 together with other relics once owned by Ulysses S. Grant.

Another major accession was a collection of 2,025 Far Eastern coins bequeathed to the Smithsonian by George Bunker Glover in 1897.

Theodore Belote was appointed assistant curator in 1909. This provided a fresh opportunity for the development of numismatic collections in the Smithsonian, for Belote had a particular interest in this subject. Also, in the years from 1910 to 1914, with the addition of a new museum building for natural history, space was gradually relinquished for the numismatic exhibits. By 1914 Belote had finished selecting, classifying, cleaning and labeling coins and medals for the display.

During World War I and the early postwar years, the numismatic acquisitions were heavily weighted toward medals and decorations, including 1,200 Lincoln items covering nearly every phase of his life, assembled by Robert Hewitt.

Mint collection

The most important event of this period was the transfer of the Mint collection in Philadelphia to the Smithsonian. When Dr. T. Louis Comparette, curator, died suddenly in 1922 the Mint collection was closed to the public. At that time it was suggested that it be moved to Washington.

Formal acceptance by the Secretary of the Smithsonian Institution followed on Feb. 19, 1923. A total of 18,291 specimens was included in the transfer, increasing the holdings of the national numismatic collection from 21,523 to 39,814 items. In addition to the numismatic items, the Mint transferred 814 books selected by Belote from the specialized library at the Philadelphia Mint in 1924.

The history of the Mint collection

officially started in June 1838, but its actual history goes back to the beginning of the Mint in 1792-1793. The Chief Coiner, Adam Eckfeldt, connected with the Mint since its inception, "led as well by his own taste as by the expectation that a conservatory would some day be established, took pains to preserve master-coins of the different annual issues of the Mint, and to retain some of the finest foreign specimens, as they appeared in deposit for recoinage."

Among the coins deposited by Adam Eckfeldt was, for instance, the Brasher doubloon. When a special annual appropriation was instituted for this purpose by Congress in 1838, the collection took permanent form and grew continuously.

The eagerness of the Mint assayers William E. Du Bois and Jacob R. Eckfeldt to complete the Mint collection contributed to its continued growth. Du Bois in his Pledges of History (1846) mentions that after the collection was officially established in June 1838, it "has gone on in a continual augmentation . . . specimens of new coinage, domestic or foreign, must be added as they appear."

In the same volume Du Bois also describes the early Mint exhibit, located at that time at 17th and Spring Garden streets in Philadelphia.

Data about the growth of the Philadelphia Mint collection may be gleaned from Mint records preserved in the National Archives as well as from occasional published notes and reports. Some early illustrations of coins from the cabinet are contained in Jacob R. Eckfeldt and William E. Du Bois' A Manual of Gold and Silver Coins of All Nations, Struck Within the Past Century (1842).

The first full catalog of the collection appeared in 1860 under the direction of James Ross Snowden. Titled A Description of Ancient and Modern-Coins, in the Cabinet Collection at the Mint of the United States (1860), it was prepared by George Bull, in charge of the cabinet, with the advice and assistance of Du Bois, at that time assistant assayer and curator of the cabinet.

In 1861 Snowden published The Medallic Memorials of Washington in the Mint of the United States. He was very much interested in this particular section of the cabinet and made every effort to enlarge it.

Notes about additions to the collections were published by W.E. Du Bois in The United States Mint Cabinet, where he mentions that "the whole number of coins and medals at this time [1874] is 6,484," and in Recent Additions to the Mint Cabinet.

In 1891, R.A. McClure, curator of the Mint collection, prepared An Index to the Coins and Medals of the Cabinet of the Mint of the United States at Philadelphia, published by the Superintendent of the Mint, O.C. Bosbyshell; and in 1894 the Philadelphia Telegraph reported on "Late Additions" to the Mint cabinet: "8,000 coins were on display, the case of current coins stands to the left of the museum door, opposite the curator's desk."

With the completion of a new Mint in Philadelphia in 1902, described as "the finest building ever constructed for coinage purposes in the world," the cabinet was moved to the new location. It was reinstalled there in sumptuous surroundings and in new, rather ponderous exhibit cases.

The first and only formally recognized curator of the Mint collection was Dr. Thomas Louis Comparette, appointed to the post in 1905. (Various other people had been delegated to take care of the cabinet but without the curator title.) Comparette immediately made plans for expansion and improvement of the Mint collection.

"The most pressing needs appear to be a new catalog and a rearrangement of the coins in the cases," according to his comprehensive report about the numismatic collection.

In the same report he mentions, referring to the past, "An apparent tendency to give undue preference to rather expensive rarities for exhibitions as "show pieces' has resulted in restricting the numerical development of the collection, in the increase of certain series at the expense of others, and especially in the neglect of the coins of lower denomination, which are much less attractive to the average visitor but necessary in order to gain a proper idea of the complete coinage of a given country or period and highly valued by the better informed.

"The more serious purpose better harmonizes with what is felt to be the worthier function of the collection, for the attitude of the cabinet has been from the first that of an educational institution," he recorded.

The preparation of the catalog took Comparette about seven years; it appeared in 1912 comprising 634 pages and 15 plates. In 1914 a so-called "third edition" followed with the same number of plates but expanded through additions to 694 pages. A most useful 106-page Guide to the Numismatic Collection of the Mint of The United States at Philadelphia, Pa. was published in 1913. In addition to the catalog Dr. Comparette published various papers, particularly in the field of ancient numismatics.

While in charge of the Mint cabinet Comparette expended considerable time and effort to mobilize support for the improvement of the collection. He attempted to obtain the support of President Theodore Roosevelt to secure for the cabinet the H.C. Hoskier collection of Greek and Roman coins when the owners who lived in South Orange, N.J., offered it for sale.

Comparette succeeded in obtaining the support of the Assay Commission of 1909; its committee on resolutions passed a motion recommending that the coin collection be improved and suggested the striking of artistic medals with the understanding that the profits from their sale should benefit the Mint collection. Similar resolutions were passed by the annual Assay Commissions meeting in subsequent years.

Reports about the growth of the collection were incorporated in the

Director's Annual Report from 1910 through 1921 under the title "The State of the Numismatic Collection" (after 1917, "The Progress of the Numismatic Collection"). All these activities ended with Dr. Comparette's sudden death on July 3, 1922.

Transferring the collection

The idea of the transfer of the collection to Washington had been proposed as early as 1916 by Dr. George F. Kunz of New York, president of the American Scenic and Historic Preservation Society and one of the most active members of the American Numismatic Society. He discussed the idea with Dr. Charles D. Walcott, secretary of the Smithsonian, and with Director of the Mint Robert W. Wooley on April 4, 1916.

The lack of a curator after the death of Dr. Comparette and the closing of the Mint to the public because of a robbery at the Denver Mint (committed after thieves obtained information through a previous visit) were among the factors that persuaded Secretary of the Treasury Andrew W. Mellon to decide to transfer the collection to the National Museum in Washington, and he so notified Secretary Walcott in February 1923.

The secretary of the Smithsonian acknowledged Andrew Mellon's letter on Feb. 12 and delegated W. de C. Ravenel, director of the museum, and T.T. Belote, curator of history, to discuss the necessary arrangements for the transfer.

Formal acceptance of the collection by the secretary of the Smithsonian Institution followed on Feb. 19.

On Feb. 28, Theodore T. Belote was authorized to inspect the numismatic collection at the Mint in order to plan for its packing and transportation to the National Museum. He spent March 6 and 7 there and reported on March 8 to Miss M.M. O'Reilly, Acting Director of the Mint, his findings and recommendations.

Pressure, however, built up in Philadelphia against the proposed transfer. The Philadelphia Ledger of March 31 expressed great concern "that the Philadelphia Mint's invaluable collections of coins, medals and tokens is being boxed, ready for shipment to the National Museum in Washington. The collection which was begun with the inception of the Philadelphia Mint in 1792, is believed to be one of the finest in the world." Another editorial on the same subject appeared in the Ledger on April 1.

Various local organizations, and through them congressmen from the area, were mobilized in an intensive but futile action to reverse the Treasury Department's decision.

On a national level, however, the American Numismatic Association immediately supported the transfer. In an editorial comment which appeared in the May 1923 issue of The Numismatist, this position was made very clear:

"Taking a broad view of the matter, the National Museum in Washington is the logical place for the coin collection. It has been termed the Mint collection, though, strictly speaking, it is the national collection. The National Museum already has a collection of medals, and the merging of the two collections will be advantageous.

"The construction of the Mint Cabinet is such that it would be impossible to enlarge the space for the collection without remodeling the entire rotunda. This fact would prevent the material growth of the collection. . . . In the national Museum more space will probably be available, and perhaps more money for the purchase of additional specimens can be obtained.

"Washington is the home of our other national collections. . . . The Capital City is a Mecca for sightseers and visitors, and the other collections will help to attract a larger number of visitors than a collection of coins alone could command.

"There is one phase of the matter that is worthy of reflection, but which may not have received consideration by the Treasury officials in reaching their decision. The late Dr. Comparette . . . is said to have been greatly concerned . . . about the apparent deterioration of the condition of the coins in the collection. The cause of this . . . was believed to be due to an atmospheric condition . . . on The Mall in Washington, all such conditions will be removed."

The editorial concludes that the closing of the Mints to visitors "is to be regretted more than the transfer of the collection from one city to another."

Concerned about the protests from Philadelphia, which multiplied during the month of April, Belote tried to obtain the active support of the national numismatic organizations.

He visited New York where he had a series of meetings on May 7 and 8 with Edward T. Newell, president of the American Numismatic Society, Moritz Wormser, president of the American Numismatic Association, and Howland Wood, curator of the American Numismatic Society's collections.

He obtained assurances that efforts would be made to have resolutions passed by the executive bodies of the two societies for presentation to the Secretary of the Treasury recommending the proposed transfer without delay.

As a result of these conferences, the Council of the American Numismatic Society passed a resolution favoring the transfer of the Mint collection to the Smithsonian, and on May 15 a letter to that effect was sent to the Secretary of the Treasury.

Howland Wood reported to Belote that: "Our Council passed a Resolution to write to Secretary Mellon favoring the transfer of the Mint collection to Washington, and a letter was sent to that effect on Saturday last. Also, the N.Y. Numismatic Club on Friday evening passed a similar Resolution. It looks now fairly favorable for the National Museum's getting it."

Similar action was taken by the New York Numismatic Club upon motion brought by Moritz Wormser at its May meeting. After obtaining the unanimous support of the board of governors of the American Numismatic Association as well, Wormser notified Andrew Mellon of this support.

In short sequence, Secretary Walcott informed Mellon on May 16 that "the

National Museum has entirely perfected its plans for the acceptance and appropriate installation of the numismatic collection from the United States Mint" and asked whether the Secretary of the Treasury could advise him "of the exact time when transfer . . . will be completed."

Actually, all arrangements for the transportation of the collection were completed without further delay. The shipment went forward by registered mail, insured and accompanied by Secret Service men. It arrived at the Smithsonian the next morning. It was formally "accessioned" as a transfer on June 13, 1923.

In 1931, the Smithsonian Institution numismatic collection was moved from poorly lighted quarters to a smaller, but much brighter area of the Arts and Industries building where it remained until its transfer to the Museum of History and Technology.

Theodore Belote, curator of the Division of History, remained in charge of the collections until 1948, and by this time the collection had increased to 54,175 pieces.

In 1948, Stuart Mosher was appointed acting curator of the division. He held this position until his death in February 1956. At the time of his death, the collection had a total of 64,522 pieces. This growth included the contribution of Paul Straub consisting of 1,860 gold and 3,886 silver coins.

From February through September 1956, Mendel Peterson served as acting curator of the division until Dr. Vladimir Clain-Stefanelli was appointed curator in October 1956, and Elvira Clain-Stefanelli was appointed as assistant curator in 1957 and associate curator in 1959. She now serves as executive director, a position to which she was named after the death of her husband in 1982.

In October 1964, the Hall of Monetary History and Medallic Art, in the newly built Museum of American History, became the home of the Smithsonian Institution collection.

In 1966, the Smithsonian started acquiring from the Bureau of Engraving and Printing, 306,275 "certified proofs" of just about everything the BEP has printed. The certified proofs of paper money, government documents and other inked impressions from new printing plates submitted to BEP officials for approval before the plates went into regular use were transferred to the Smithsonian when the BEP ran out of room to store a century's worth of printing treasures. This acquisition was completed in July 1984.

In 1968, after governmental maneuvering and eventual sanction, the Smithsonian acquired the Josiah K. Lilly collection of gold coins in exchange for a $5.5 million tax write-off for the Lilly estate. The collection contains 6,125 gold coins and is considered one of the finest gold coin collections in the world. The collection arrived at the Smithsonian June 13, 1968.

New exhibit

The Smithsonian opened a new exhibit, "The History of Money and Medals," July 12, 1972, showing the history of mankind as it is mirrored in coinage.

The exhibit was compiled in slightly more than six months. Containing more than 10,000 numismatic specimens arranged in 130 units, the display has something for everyone from the most knowledgeable scholars to children (coins for touching have been provided for the latter).

Vladimir and Elvira Clain-Stefanelli, co-curators of the Division of Numismatics for more than two decades, used for the central theme of the main display the evolution of the money economy as an integral aspect of the cultural, economic and social development of human society.

Significant contributions to the exhibit were made by private collectors and corporations as well as by government agencies such as the Library of Congress, the Secret Service and the Mints of the United States, Britain and France.

Early in 1974 the Smithsonian and the American Bankers Association announced plans to mount a major Bicentennial exhibit concerning commercial banking in the Smithsonian's National Museum of History and Technology.

The exhibit opened to the public Sept. 18, 1975. It told the story of America's involvement in banking, from Colonial barter systems, when prices were expressed in beaver skins, to the sophisticated electronic techniques of today.

The exhibit was supplemented by an illustrated essay, "Two Centuries of American Banking," written by Mrs. Clain-Stefanelli and her husband.

The exhibit remained in place through the American Bicentennial celebration of 1976.

Important acquisitions

The year 1978 proved one of important acquisitions for the Smithsonian. Formal papers for the transfer of the Chase Manhattan Bank money collection, one of the most famous in the history of the United States, were signed on Jan. 16 by S. Dillon Ripley, secretary of the Smithsonian Institution, and David Rockefeller, chairman of the Chase Manhattan Bank.

The massive collection of coins, tokens, medals and paper money was formed by the American numismatic immortal, Farran Zerbe, who became the Chase Manhattan Museum's first curator.

On May 17, 1978, in a historic ceremony, the Treasury Department turned over to the Smithsonian a collection of 800 pieces of U.S. paper money with a numismatic value of more than $1 million. The collection, with a face value of $578,365.79, includes nearly one note for every issue of U.S. currency between the Civil War period and the early 1960s.

Three months later, in August, Mr. and Mrs. R. Henry Norweb donated a Proof specimen of the 1913 Liberty Head 5-cent piece — one of only five such pieces known — to the Smithsonian.

Death ends tenure

On Oct. 19, 1982, Dr. Vladimir Clain-Stefanelli, chairman of the Department of

Applied Arts of the Smithsonian Institution and senior historian and curator of the National Numismatic Collection, died at Georgetown University Hospital in Washington, D.C.

During the quarter of a century he was associated with the Smithsonian, Dr. Clain-Stefanelli's acumen and diplomacy were successful in increasing the size of the National Numismatic Collection more than tenfold, building it from a relatively insignificant collection of about 64,000 to one of the most outstanding in the world numbering close to 900,000 pieces.

On Dec. 28, 1982, Emery May Norweb donated a 52-piece collection of U.S. Colonial coins in memory of Dr. Vladimir Clain-Stefanelli.

In September 1983, Mrs. Elvira Clain-Stefanelli, who had served with her husband as co-curator and carried on the curatorial work they had shared prior to his death, was named to the new title of executive director of the National Numismatic Collection.

At the same time, Cory Gillilland was named curator for the Division of Numismatics, leaving her position as chief of the Bureau of the Mint's consumer affairs staff to assume her new post. She was associated with the Smithsonian's Division of Numismatics earlier, from 1965 to 1975. Her areas of responsibility include American and foreign medals.

In July 1984, the United States Mint transferred 114 Olympic coins, American Arts Gold Medallions, bronze and pewter national medals to the national collection. This was the largest transaction of its kind since 1923. Participating were Mint Director Donna Pope, Mrs. Clain-Stefanelli and Smithsonian officials Roger G. Kennedy and John Jameson.

On April 21, 1986, Dr. Richard G. Doty became the curator of Western Hemisphere Numismatics for the National Numismatic Collection. His responsibilities at the Smithsonian include the vast collections of U.S. paper money, foreign currency and financial documents. He also oversees the world token collection and the collections of medieval and Roman coinages. Prior to this position, Doty was curator of modern coins and paper money at the American Numismatic Society in New York.

The Smithsonian Institution's National Numismatic Collection is displayed in segments, often with themes or focusing upon current events or persons. The Museum of American History, which houses the collection, is located on Constitution Avenue at 14th Street Northwest on the Mall. It is open to the public from 10 a.m. to 5:30 p.m. every day and is closed Christmas Day. There is no admission charge.

American Numismatic Society

The American Numismatic Society Museum, Broadway between 155th and 156th streets in New York, is unique in being the first museum in the world devoted entirely to numismatics.

In honor of the society's 125th anniversary celebration in 1983, a new exhibition, "The World of Coins," was mounted with a wholly new approach to the story of money. It shows the use, value and design of money in a cross-cultural story, shedding light on such humanistic issues as economic development, trade patterns, social and political symbolism and the relationship of religion and public life.

The first annual exhibition of medallic and bas-relief works sponsored by the American Medallic Sculpture Association was held in the east hall in 1983, co-sponsored by the AMSA and the society. The east hall was re-structured in 1984 and re-carpeted to provide for temporary displays, including those placed each fall since December 1984, in conjunction with the annual Coinage of the Americas Conference.

The society has pioneered in the use of

the computer, integrating the computer facility into the exhibition experience in the refurbished west hall. The society's extensive holdings are in the process of being computerized with all of the relevant information available being included for the benefit of the researcher.

The ANS collection is large and representative. All fields are covered, but particularly important are the coins of ancient Greece and Rome, the Far Eastern series, and the Islamic issues. The medieval, modern and American groups are also distinguished.

By far the greater portion of the collection has been received through bequests and gifts both of collections and of single specimens. A relatively small proportion has been acquired by purchase.

As American tax law continues to change, ANS officials report a decline in bequests as tax breaks to donors are lessened. However, historically important donations continue to be received at an impressive rate. In late 1987, the ANS received Victor David Brenner's personal collection of medals; in early 1988, a bequest of Herbert Oechsner turned over a rare 1776 New Hampshire copper to the society; and later that year R. Henry Norweb Jr. mdonated a rare gold St. Patrick's guinea.

The collection's great strength in the ancient Greek, Roman and Byzantine periods lies in the great collection bequeathed by Edward T. Newell, the society's president from 1916 until his death in 1941. Newell's collection, long known throughout the numismatic world for its quality, is especially rich in those series to which his scholarly publications were devoted — the coinages of Alexander the Great and his successors. Altogether his collection numbers more than 87,000 pieces.

The collection of ancient coins has been enriched also by the F. Munroe Endicott collection of Greek and Roman coins, the Richard Hoe Lawrence collection of Roman coins, the W. Gedney Beatty collection of Greek coins, the Harold W. Bell collection of Byzantine coins, the

Gautier collection of Greek coins presented by an anonymous donor, the Abraham A. Rosen gift of Greek fractional silver and bronze coins and by many other gifts of whole groups or single coins.

A monumental bequest, with an estimated value of $500,000, was received from the estate of the late Robert F. Kelley, a former head of the U.S. State Department's East European Division. Amassed largely through $8 to $10 purchases from Turkish bazaars, Kelley's collection included 1,155 ancient Greek and Byzantine coins. Among the 855 Greek pieces were coins minted from the seventh to the first centuries B.C. The 300 Byzantine coins span the fourth century B.C. through the late 12th century A.D. All coins are of gold, silver or electrum.

In 1980 the society received the Arthur J. Fecht collection, 3,310 pieces of world gold coins, United States and modern foreign.

Coinage of the Far East is likewise well represented in the society's cabinets. The Chinese coins alone number more than 18,000 and constitute one of the largest collections of its kind in the world. The Far Eastern section derives its great strength from a large private collection, that of John Reilly Jr., one-time treasurer of ANS, which was presented to the society by his daughter. The collections of two famous numismatists, Henry A. Ramsden and Neil Gordon Munro, form important sections of the Reilly collection.

In the field of Islamic numismatics, the collection ranks among the leading in the world. Its growth from small beginnings began in 1917 with the gift by Edward T. Newell of both his own collection of more than 5,000 Islamic coins and that of Howland Wood of 6,000 odd specimens. The Durkee, A.F.R. Hoernle, W.H. Valentine, Longworth Dames, among other collections, have provided additions especially in the series for India.

An important adjunct to this section is a remarkable collection of Arabic glass weights built on a nucleus bequeathed the society by James B. Nies and expanded by gifts from Edward T. Newell and Louis H.

Schroeder. With its extensive coverage of the entire Near and Middle Eastern world, this section of the society's cabinet contains much material for study and publication. Among the coins of the many dynasties in its trays there are some whose inscriptions add to historical record the name of a Mint or ruler otherwise unknown.

Coinages of the lands of America's forefathers have representative selections, strong in some sections, weaker in others. Thanks to gifts from J. Sanford Saltus and the bequest of Herbert E. Ives, there are important pieces in the English series. The medieval and later periods of Italy are well represented through the Herbert Scoville collection of more than 3,600 coins and collection of Florentine florins and Venetian ducats bequeathed by Herbert E. Ives. Poland and its history are well illustrated by the Alexandre Orlowski collection of more than 2,000 specimens.

Early Latin American coinages from Mexico and Peru are strong through gifts from Wayte Raymond, as are the cut and counter-stamped pieces of the West Indies from the Julius Guttag collection.

Coinage struck in the 19th and 20th centuries is well represented through the gift of Wayte Raymond of the specimens gathered in preparation of his Standard Catalogues of contemporary coins.

The coinage of the United States naturally forms an important section of the society's cabinet. Notable sections have come from the J. Pierpont Morgan, William B. Osgood Field, and Elliott Smith collections. The society possesses such treasures as one of the four known specimens of the original Confederate half dollar, a gift of J. Sanford Saltus, and the press used by Augustus Bechtler in striking private gold coins in North Carolina, given by Julius Guttag.

One of the richest series is that of the United States copper cents struck between 1793 and 1857, the collection gathered by George H. Clapp and given by him to the society. The Colonial issues of Massachusetts are present with specimens from the Field collection, and the state

coinages before the adoption of the Constitution are well represented.

Tokens, helpmates to coinages in times of stress, offer interesting sidelights to the history of periods of monetary crisis. The richest series of tokens in the collection are those of the "Hard Times" period in the United States, 1837-41, and the merchants' tokens of the Civil War period of the 1860s, including the Edward Groh collection of 5,286 specimens donated in 1900.

Although weak in medals of the Renaissance, the age in which medallic art was born, the collection has strength in later periods of its development. English medals from the period of Elizabeth from the Daniel Parish Jr. collection, Indian Peace medals from the Stephen H.P. Pell collection, Adm. Vernon medals from the L. McCormick-Goodhart collection, along with a good selection of medals designed by contemporary American and European sculptors, provide a record of the progress of medallic art. Of special interest as a development in modern medallic art is the complete series of porcelain medals made at the Meissen Porcelain Works since World War I, a gift from Louis H. Schroeder.

In 1978, Ira, Mark and Lawrence Goldberg gave 1,000 medals, trial strikes, models and dies of Karl Goetz.

Decorations of orders of knighthood and of governments for military or civil merit form a special section of the collection. It is one of the most comprehensive of such collections in the world. It was built on a nucleus given by J. Sanford Saltus and expanded by gifts from Harold E. Gillingham and others.

Paper money, which in the present century is more and more encroaching on coins as a medium of currency, is also present in the collection. The obsolete bank notes of the "wildcat" bank era of the United States, Continental notes of Revolutionary times, are supplemented with selections of foreign paper currencies and special series as prisoner of war money, occupational currency, and more. As have other fields, this section has benefited from donations, such as the 4,431 specimens of paper currency donated by Archer M. Huntington in 1914.

American Numismatic Association

The American Numismatic Association continually expands its collection of all numismatic items in the museum located at its Colorado Springs, Colo., headquarters. Presently, it holds an estimated 300,000 specimens.

The museum's holdings have been increased greatly of late, largely through the generosity of Aubrey and Adeline Bebee. The Bebee's donated a landmark $2 million collection of United States paper money to the ANA in 1987, then followed with coin donations including a 1913 Liberty Head 5-cent piece, a $20 pionner gold piece, Swedish plate money and Yap Island stone money.

The ANA was the recipient in 1990 of the Combined Organizations of Numismatic Error Collectors of America assets of The Error Coin Museum, one of the most comprehensive collections of examples of Mint errors.

Displays are mounted in the museum's entrance rotunda and eight galleries, all of which are open to the public free of charge. The entrance rotunda features the "Hall of Nations," a touching gallery for the visually-impaired. Here, coin models contributed by Mints throughout the world are mounted.

A separate gallery houses the ANA Numismatic Hall of Fame, while other permanent exhibits are mounted in the Americana I and Americana II galleries. Americana I houses displays of tokens, paper money and coins used by the Colonies and United States prior to the establishment of the U.S. Mint.

Coinage and paper money of the United States, including regular issue and commemorative coins and medals, are on permanent display in the Americana II gallery, where visitors also will find displays of Hard Times tokens, Civil War tokens and private issue gold coins.

Dedication of the Arthur Braddan Coole Oriental library in July 1983, prompted an exhibit of Far Eastern Numismatic material in the upper level of the west gallery of the ANA museum. Later in the year the American Medallic Sculpture Association's exhibition traveled from New York to ANA through a grant from the Lewis M. Reagan Memorial Foundation Inc. The exhibit was installed in the museum's hall of modern medallic art.

These were part of the program of temporary exhibitions which the ANA continues to install in its galleries. It has an ongoing program of improving collection storage facilities, expanding service through lectures and tours, and publicizing its collections.

Highlighting the Los Angeles Olympic Games was an exhibit in the ANA museum galleries, "The Olympic Games: A Numismatic Celebration." This was co-sponsored by the United States Olympic Committee and utilized the Stack's galleries, the museum's primary changing exhibits area. It opened in connection with the USOC's National Sports festival in Colorado Springs in June 1983.

Three special exhibits mounted include the Hall of Presidents, in which the famed Elliott Markoff collection of coins and presidential memorabilia can be found; the Colorado gallery, with displays that relate to the state's role in numismatics; and the Hall of Modern Medallic Art, a gift of the Franklin Mint.

A major exhibit of medallic art was mounted when the ANA played host to the Fédération Internationale de la Médaille Congress in 1987.

Also integral to the ANA Museum is the Amos Memorial Theater, donated by the publishers of Coin World, in which educational talks, slide programs and films are presented, as well as other educational programs.

United States museums

California

BERKELEY. Judah L. Magnes Museum, 2911 Russell St., 94705. Jewish American Hall of Fame medal series, modern foreign coins and ancients. Open 10 a.m. to 4 p.m. Sunday through Thursday.

LOS ANGELES. Hebrew Union College Skirball Museum, 3077 University Mall, 90007. Ancient Jewish coins, medals, tokens and numismatic literature. Open only to scholars by appointment.

SAN FRANCISCO. Bank of California Money Museum, 400 California St., 94104. Gold rush period coins and ingots. Open 10 a.m. to 3:30 p.m. Monday through Thursday, 10 a.m. to 5 p.m. Friday, closed weekends and national holidays.

SAN FRANCISCO. Old Mint Museum, 5th and Mission Sts., 94103. Million dollars in gold bullion, United States coins, medals and paper money. Open 10 a.m. to 4 p.m. Monday through Friday; closed legal holidays. Free

SAN FRANCISCO. Wells Fargo Bank History Museum, 420 Montgomery St., 94104. Wells Fargo and Company history from 1852 to present. U.S. coins, paper money and modern foreign coins. Open 9 a.m. to 5 p.m. Monday through Friday, closed weekends and national holidays.

Colorado

COLORADO SPRINGS. American Numismatic Association, 818 N. Cascade Ave., 80903. U.S. and foreign coins, medals, tokens, paper money, medieval, ancients and a numismatic library. Open 8:30 a.m. to 4 p.m. Tuesday through Saturday, closed some national holidays. Tours by arrangement (719) 632-2646. Free.

COLORADO SPRINGS. Pioneers' Museum, 215 S. Tejon St., 80903. U.S. paper money and medals. Open 10 a.m. to 5 p.m. Monday through Saturday and 1 p.m. to 5 p.m. Sunday, closed national holidays. Free.

DENVER. Denver Museum of Natural History, City Park, 80205. Houses the gold boulder of Summitville. Open 9 a.m. to 5 p.m. daily. Closed Christmas.

DENVER. United States Mint, 320 West Colfax Ave., 80204. Million dollar gold display, coin production history, U.S. coins and paper money. Open 8 a.m. to 3:30 p.m. daily except Wednesday 9 a.m. to 3:30 p.m. Closed holidays. Free.

FORT COLLINS. Fort Collins Museum, 200 Mathews St., 80524. Coins, medals, tokens and paper money. Open 10 a.m. to 5 p.m. Tuesday through Saturday and noon to 5 p.m. on Sunday. Free.

Connecticut

HARTFORD. Raymond E. Baldwin Museum of Connecticut History, Connecticut State Library, 231 Capitol Ave., 06106. Joseph C. Mitchelson collection, U.S. coins and medals. Open 9 a.m. to 4:45 p.m. Monday through Friday, 9 a.m. to 1 p.m. Saturday. Closed state holidays. Free.

MYSTIC. Mystic Seaport, Inc., P.O. Box 6000, 06355. U.S. and foreign coins, medals and paper money. Available to scholars upon written request. Open 9 a.m. to 5 p.m. Monday through Friday. Closed holidays.

Delaware

DOVER. Delaware State Museum, 316 S. Governors Ave., 19901. U.S. coins, medals, tokens and paper money. Open 10 a.m. to 4:30 p.m. Tuesday through Saturday and 1 p.m. to 4:30 p.m. Sunday, closed national holidays. Free.

District of Columbia

WASHINGTON. B'nai B'rith Museum, 1640 Rhode Island St. N.W., 20036. Ancients. Open 10 a.m. to 5 p.m. Sunday through Friday, closed national and Jewish holidays. Free.

WASHINGTON. Smithsonian Institution, National Museum of American History,

Constitution Ave. between 12th and 14th Sts., N.W., 20560. Oriental, Islamic, U.S. and foreign tokens, orders and decorations, U.S. and foreign coins, paper money, medals, medieval and ancients, on display in the Hall of Monetary History and Medallic Art, third floor. Open 10 a.m. to 5:30 p.m. daily during the winter and 10 a.m. to 7:30 p.m. daily from April to first week of September. Closed Christmas Day. (202) 357-1798. Free.

WASHINGTON. National Archives and Records Administration Exhibition Hall, 8th St. and Constitution Ave. N.W., 20408, where the Declaration of Independence, Constitution and Bill of Rights are permanently displayed. U.S. presidents and constitution medals. Exhibition Hall open daily 10 a.m. to 9 p.m. April 1 through Labor Day and 10 a.m. to 5:30 p.m. Labor Day through March 31, except Christmas.

Florida

KEY WEST. Mel Fisher Maritime Heritage Society Museum, 200 Greene St. Contains the treasures removed from the sunken Spanish treasure ship *Nuestra Senora de Atocha*, including gold and silver bars, ship's artifacts, jewels, etc. Open 10 a.m. to 5:30 p.m., seven days a week. Admission $5 for adults, $1 for children. Senior Citizens' discounts available.

PENSACOLA. T. T. Wentworth Jr. Museum, 8382 Palafax, 32594. U.S. coins, medals, paper money, foreign coins, paper money, medieval and ancients. Open 2 p.m. to 6 p.m. Saturday and Sunday. Free.

TALLAHASSEE. Museum of Florida History, R.A. Gray Bldg., 32399. 18th century Spanish coins from new world Mints, U.S. and foreign coins and paper money. Open 9 a.m. to 4:30 p.m. Monday through Friday, 10 a.m. to 4:30 p.m. Saturday and 1 p.m. to 4:30 p.m. Sunday. Closed Christmas. Free.

Georgia

DAHLONEGA. Dahlonega Courthouse Gold Museum, 1-A Public Square, 30533. Georgia's gold mining history, U.S. coins. Open 9 a.m. to 5 p.m. Tuesday through Saturday, 2 p.m. to 5:30 p.m. Sunday. Closed Mondays, Christmas and Thanksgiving. $1 adults, 50¢ for children under 12. Groups rates available.

DAHLONEGA. North Georgia College, 30597. A complete set of gold coins minted at the Dahlonega branch Mint. Open 8 a.m. to 5 p.m. Monday through Friday, closed Thanksgiving, July 4 and Christmas. Free.

FORT BENNING. National Infantry Museum, U.S. Army Infantry Center, 31905. U.S. and world service medals. Open Tuesday through Friday 10 a.m. to 4:30 p.m. and Saturday-Sunday 12:30 p.m. to 4:30 p.m.. Closed New Year's Day, Thanksgiving and Christmas. Free.

ROYSTON. Northeast Georgia Bank, 30662. J.H. Beasley collection of gold and silver coins from 1799 and paper money from 1861 to present. Open 9 a.m. to 1 p.m. and 3 p.m. to 5 p.m. Monday, Tuesday, Thursday and Friday; 9 a.m. to noon Saturday. Closed Wednesday, Sunday and holidays. Free.

Idaho

COEUR D'ALENE. Museum of North Idaho, P.O. Box 812, 83814. Idaho medals and tokens. Open 11 a.m. to 5 p.m. Tuesday through Saturday from April 1 to Oct. 31 and by appointment only during the winter. Closed on holidays. Donation admission.

Illinois

CHICAGO. Balzekas Museum of Lithuanian Culture, 6500 S. Pulaski Road, 60629. Lithuanian medals, medieval, ancients and numismatic literature. Closed Christmas and New Year's Day. Adults $2, children and senior citizens $1.

CHICAGO. Field Museum of Natural History, Roosevelt Road at Lake Shore Drive, 60605. 80 different varieties of money displayed. Open 9 a.m. to 5 p.m. daily. Closed Thanksgiving, Christmas and New Year's Day.

WATSEKA. Iroquois County Historical Society, Old Court House, 103 W. Cherry, 60970. Coins, medals, tokens and paper money. Open 10:30 a.m. to 4:30 p.m. Monday through Friday; 1 p.m. to 4:30 p.m. Saturday and Sunday April-Dec. Closed Christmas and weekends Jan.-March. Donation admission.

Indiana

BLOOMINGTON. Indiana University Art Museum, 47405. Ancient and Byzantine coins. Open Wednesday, Friday and Saturday 9 a.m. to 5 p.m.; Thursday 10 a.m. to 8 p.m. and Sunday 1 p.m. to 5 p.m. Closed major holidays. Free.

INDIANAPOLIS. U.S. Army Finance Corps Museum, Building 1, Fort Harrison, 46249. Military currency, U.S. and foreign paper money. Open 8 a.m. to 4:30 p.m. Monday through Friday; closed national holidays. Free.

Iowa

LAKE OKOBOJI. Higgins Paper Money Museum, Airport Rd., 51355. Iowa National Bank notes and U.S. paper money. Open Memorial Day through Labor Day, Tuesday through Sunday 11 a.m. to 5:30 p.m. Closed Monday.

MAXWELL. Community Historical Museum, 50161. U.S. and foreign coins and paper money. Open 2 p.m. to 5 p.m. Sundays only from May 30 to October. Closed during the winter. Free

Kansas

BALDWIN. Old Castle Museum, Baker University, 515 Fifth St., 66006. U.S. and foreign coins and U.S. paper money including Confederate notes and notes of Louisiana banks. Open 2 p.m. to 5 p.m. daily except Monday, closed Christmas and New Year's Day. Free.

LOGAN. Dane G. Hansen Memorial Museum, 67646. Medals, tokens, paper money and other related items. Open 9 a.m. to noon and 1 p.m. to 4 p.m. Monday through Friday, 9 a.m. to noon and 1 p.m. to 5 p.m. Saturday and 1 p.m. to 5 p.m. Sunday and holidays. Closed Christmas. Free.

LYONS. Coronado Quivira Museum, 105 W. Lyon, 67554. First medal of the Catholic missionary. Open Tuesday through Saturday 10 a.m. to noon and 1 p.m. to 5 p.m. and Sunday 2 p.m. to 5 p.m. Closed Monday, Thanksgiving, Christmas and New Year's Day. Free.

Kentucky

OWENSBORO. Owensboro Area Museum, 2829 S. Griffith Ave., 42301. Coins, tokens, paper money, Colonial currency, Confederate and obsolete bank notes. Open 8 a.m. to 4 p.m. weekdays, 1 p.m. to 4 p.m. Saturday and Sunday. Closed national holidays. Free.

Louisiana

SHREVEPORT. The R.W. Norton Art Gallery, 4700 block of Creswell Ave., 71106. U.S. coins, medals, paper money and foreign coins. Open 1 p.m. to 5 p.m. daily except Mondays, closed national holidays. Free.

Maine

BRUNSWICK. Bowdoin College Museum of Art, Walker Art Museum, 04011. World medals and ancients. Open July-Labor Day Tuesday through Saturday 10 a.m. to 8 p.m. Sunday 2 p.m. to 5 p.m. September-June Tuesday through Friday 10 a.m. to 4 p.m.; Saturday 10 a.m. to 5 p.m.; Sunday 2 p.m. to 5 p.m. Closed national holidays. Free.

Maryland

ANNAPOLIS. U.S. Naval Academy Museum, 21402. U.S. and world naval medals. Open 9 a.m. to 4:50 p.m. Monday through Saturday; 11 a.m. to 4:50 p.m. Sunday. Closed New Year's Day, Thanksgiving and Christmas. Free.

BALTIMORE. Baltimore Museum of Art, Art Museum Drive, 21218. U.S. medals.

Massachusetts

BOSTON. Museum of Fine Arts, Huntington Ave., 02115. Ancients and medals. Open Tuesday 10 a.m. to 5 p.m., Wednesday 10 a.m. to 10 p.m., Thursday through Sunday 10 a.m. to 5 p.m. Closed

Mondays and holidays. Adults $5, senior citizens $4 and free to all on Saturdays from 10 a.m. to noon, children 16 and under free.

LYNN. Lynn Historical Society, 125 Green St., 01902. U.S. coins, medals, tokens and paper money shown by appointment. Open to scholars only 9 a.m. to 4 p.m. Monday through Friday and 1 p.m. to 4 p.m. Saturday. Closed national holidays.

SALEM. Peabody Museum of Salem, East India Square, 01970. Coins, medals, tokens and paper money. Stored items open to scholars only. Open to public 10 a.m. to 5 p.m. Monday through Friday, 1 p.m. to 5 p.m. Sunday. Closed Thanksgiving, Christmas and New Year's Day. $3 for adults, $1.50 children.

WORCESTER. American Antiquarian Society, Salisbury St. and Park Ave., 01609. U.S. paper money, medals and numismatic literature. Open to scholars only. Library open 9 a.m. to 5 p.m. Monday through Friday, closed legal holidays. Free.

Michigan

DETROIT. Detroit Historical Museum, 5401 Woodward Ave., 48202. Detroit and Michigan scrip and coins, U.S. coins, medals and paper money. Available to scholars only. Open 9:30 a.m. to 5:30 p.m. Wednesday through Sunday, closed Monday and Tuesday. Free.

Mississippi

STATE COLLEGE. Cobb Institute of Archeology, Mississippi State University, 39762. Ancient Greek, Roman and Jewish coins, especially those relating to the Bible, medals and numismatic literature. Open Monday through Friday with certain restrictions. Closed regular holidays. Free.

Missouri

COLUMBIA. Museum of Art and Archeology, University of Missouri-Columbia, 1 Pickard Hall, 65211. Permanent exhibit of Ancient coins.

Extensive collection of numismatic literature. Open 8 a.m. to 5 p.m. Tuesday through Friday, noon to 5 p.m. Saturday and Sunday. Closed some holidays. Free.

INDEPENDENCE. Truman Library, 64050. U.S. coins and medals on display; U.S. and foreign paper money in study collections only. Open to public 9 a.m. to 5 p.m. daily, closed Christmas, Thanksgiving and New Year's Day. $1.50 admission.

ST. LOUIS. Concordia Historical Institute, 801 De Mun Ave., 63105. Lutheran anniversary medals, foreign coins, medals, paper money and medieval. Shown by appointment. Open 8:30 a.m. to 4:30 p.m. Monday through Friday. Free.

ST. LOUIS. Mercantile-Newman Money Museum, Mercantile Tower, 7th and Washington Streets, 63101. Eric Newman collection of coins and currency, numismatic literature, U.S. coins, U.S. and foreign paper money and money changers. Open 9 a.m. to 4 p.m. Monday through Friday except holidays. Free.

ST. LOUIS. Washington University Gallery of Art, Forsyth and Skinker Campus, 63130. More than 1,000 Greek and Roman coins shown by appointment to scholars.

Nebraska

BOYS TOWN. Philamatic Center, P.O. Box 1, 68010. U.S. and foreign coins, paper money, medals and ancients. Open 8 a.m. to 4:30 p.m. Monday through Saturday, 9 a.m. to 4:30 p.m. Sunday, closed Thanksgiving, Christmas and New Year's Day. Free admission.

HASTINGS. Hastings Museum, 1330 N. Burlington, 68901. U.S. coins, medals, paper money, medieval and ancients. Open 9 a.m. to 5 p.m. Monday through Saturday, 1 p.m. to 5 p.m. Sunday. Closed Thanksgiving, Christmas and New Year's Day. $3 for adults; $1 ages 7-15.

OMAHA. Omaha Public Library, 215 S. 15th St., 68102. Ancients, medieval, foreign and U.S. coins, paper money and medals. Open 9 a.m. to 8:30 p.m. Monday through Friday, 9 a.m. to 5:30 p.m. Saturday, closed national holidays. Free.

OMAHA. Western Heritage Museum, 801 S. Tenth St. Featuring the Byron Reed collection, which includes the Parmelee specimen of the 1804 dollar. Tuesday through Sunday. Admission $2 adults, $1 children under 12.

Nevada

CARSON CITY. Nevada State Museum, 600 North Carson St., 89710. Exhibit of Carson City Mint mark coins and coin press. Open daily 8:30 a.m. to 4:30 p.m. Closed Thanksgiving, Christmas and New Year's Day. Admission 50¢ adults, children free.

New Hampshire

HANOVER. Hood Museum of Art, Dartmouth College, 03755. U.S. coins, paper money, medals, ancients and foreign coins. Open 9 a.m. to 5 p.m. Monday through Saturday; 2 p.m. to 5 p.m. Sunday. Numismatic collection shown by appointment only.

MANCHESTER. The Manchester Historic Association, 129 Amherst St., 03104. U.S. coins, paper money, medals and world medals. Open 9 a.m. to 4 p.m. Tuesday through Friday, 10 a.m. to 4 p.m. Saturday, closed national holidays. Free.

New Jersey

NEWARK. The Newark Museum, 49 Washington St., 07101. Extensive collection of coins, medals, tokens, paper money and numismatic literature. Open noon to 5 p.m. Tuesday through Sunday. Closed New Year's Day, July 4, Thanksgiving and Christmas. Free.

New York

BUFFALO. Buffalo and Erie County Historical Society, 25 Nottingham Court. Collections relate primarily to Buffalo, Erie County and Western New York. U.S. coins, paper money, medals, tokens and foreign paper money. Research by appointment.

NEW YORK. The American Numismatic Society, Broadway between 155th and 156th Sts., 10032. World's most comprehensive numismatic library and extensive numismatic collection in the United States, including over a million items; U.S. and foreign coins, medals, decorations, paper money, numismatic literature, medieval and ancients. "'The World of Coins'' art exhibition on the history of money. Open 9 a.m. to 4:30 p.m. Tuesday through Saturday and 1 p.m. to 4 p.m. Sunday. Closed national holidays. Free.

NEW YORK. The Jewish Museum, 92nd St. and Fifth Ave., 11028. Jewish/Israel coins, medals and ancients. Open noon to 5 p.m. Monday through Thursday, until 8 p.m. Tuesday evenings and 11 a.m. to 6 p.m. Sunday. Closed Jewish holidays. Admission charged.

POUGHKEEPSIE. The Elongated Coin Museum, 228 Vassar Road, 12603. 10,000 elongated coins with machines and data, still banks and numismatic literature. Open to collectors only, appointments two weeks in advance. Free.

North Carolina

CHARLOTTE. Mint Museum of Art, 2730 Randolph Road, 28207. Charlotte and Bechtler gold coins, Confederate, North Carolina and state bank notes and bonds. Open Wednesday through Saturday 10 a.m. to 5 p.m., Sunday 1 p.m. to 6 p.m. and Tuesday 10 a.m. to 10 p.m. Admission $2 adults, $1 senior citizens and students and childred 12 and under free.

RALEIGH. North Carolina Museum of History, 109 E. Jones St., 27611. Bechtler gold, ancient and mixed coins, military medals, paper money. Open to scholars only, 9 a.m. to 5 p.m. Tuesday through Saturday; 2 p.m. to 5 p.m. Sunday. Closed Christmas and New Year's Day. Free.

SHELBY. Cleveland County Historical Museum, Courtsquare, P.O. Box 1335, 28150. U.S. coins, paper money, medals, Civil War tokens and world medals.

Open Monday through Friday 9 a.m. to 4 p.m. and Sunday 2 p.m. to 5 p.m. Closed holidays. Free.

Ohio

CLEVELAND. Cleveland Museum of Art, 11150 East Blvd., 44106. Ancients, modern coins, Renaissance medallions and the R. Henry Norweb British gold coin collection. Open 10 a.m. to 6 p.m. Tuesday, Thursday, Friday, 10 a.m. to 10 p.m. Wednesday, 9 a.m. to 5 p.m. Saturday and 1 p.m. to 6 p.m. Sunday. Closed New Year's Day, July 4, Thanksgiving, Christmas. Free.

CLEVELAND. Howard Dittrick Museum of Historical Medicine, 11000 Euclid Ave., 44106. Medical medals. Open 10 a.m. to 5 p.m. Monday through Friday and noon to 5 p.m. Saturday. Closed national holidays and Friday after Thanksgiving. Free.

DAYTON. Air Force Museum, Wright-Patterson Air Force Base, 45433. U.S. and world Air Force aircraft insignia, decorations, medals and commemorative coins. Open 9 a.m. to 5 p.m. weekdays, 10 a.m. to 6 p.m. weekends, closed Christmas. Free.

MARIETTA. Campus Maritus Museum, 45750. Coins, medals, paper money. Some items in storage available by appointment.

MILAN. Milan Historical Museum, 10 Edison Drive, 44846. U.S. coins, medals, tokens and paper money. Open 1 p.m. to 5 p.m. daily except Monday, closed Oct. 1 to April 1. Free.

OXFORD. Miami University Art Museum, Patterson Ave., 45056. Greek and Roman ancients in storage, available for research on request. Open 11 a.m. to 5 p.m. Tuesday through Sunday. Closed national and university holidays. Free.

PIQUA. Johnston Farm, 9845 N. Hardin Road, 45356. Indian peace medals. Open Memorial Day to Labor Day 9:30 a.m. to 5 p.m. Wednesday through Saturday, noon to 5 p.m. Sunday and holidays; open Saturdays and Sundays in September and October only; closed from November through March.

Admission $3 for adults and free to children 12 and under.

WAPAKONETA. Neil Armstrong Museum, 45895. U.S. and world air and space medals. Open March through November 9:30 a.m. to 5 p.m. Monday through Saturday, noon to 5 p.m. Sunday and holidays. Admission $2 adults and children 6-12 $1. Group rates available.

Oregon

JACKSONVILLE. Jacksonville Museum, Southern Oregon Historical Society, P.O. Box 480, 206 N. 5th St., 97530. U.S. coins, foreign coins and paper money. Open 10 a.m. to 5 p.m. daily Memorial Day to Labor Day. Closed Mondays, Labor Day to Memorial Day. Free.

Pennsylvania

FRANKLIN CENTER. The Franklin Mint Museum, 19091. Modern foreign coins, medieval and ancients. Open 9:30 a.m. to 4:30 p.m. Tuesday through Saturday, 1 p.m. to 4:30 p.m. Sunday, closed Mondays and major holidays. Free.

PHILADELPHIA. Atwater Kent Museum, History Museum of Philadelphia, 15 S. 7th St., 19106. Collection of U.S. coins, medals, tokens and paper money. Exhibition galleries open to general public, storage collections can be seen by appointment with the curators in advance. Open 9:30 a.m. to 4:45 p.m. Tuesday through Satuday. Closed Sunday, Monday and city holidays. Free.

PHILADELPHIA. Philadelphia Civic Center, Civic Center Blvd. at 34th Street, 19104. Medals won by the Philadelphia Commercial Museum in national and international expositions and American Negro Commemorative Society medals.

PHILADELPHIA. Presbyterian Historical Society, 425 Lombard St., 19147. 6,000 communion tokens shown by appointment. Open Monday through Friday. Closed regular holidays. Free.

PITTSBURGH. Carnegie Museum of Natural History, 4400 Forbes Ave., 15213. U.S. coins, medals and ancients.

Puerto Rico

SAN JUAN. Banco Popular de Puerto

Rico Numismatic Collection. Rafael Carion Pacheco Exhibition Hall, Old San Juan Branch. Exhibits illustrating the economic, political and banking development of Puerto Rico.

Rhode Island

PROVIDENCE. Museum of Art, R.I. School of Design, 224 Benefit St., 02903. Ancient Greek coins, U.S. and world medals. Open during the winter: Tuesday, Wednesday, Friday and Saturday 10:30 a.m. to 5 p.m., Sunday and holidays 2 p.m. to 5 p.m., Thursdays 1 p.m. to 7 p.m. Summer: Tuesday-Saturday 11 a.m. to 4 p.m. Adults $1, Children 5-18 25¢. Closed some holidays.

South Carolina

COLUMBIA. South Carolina Confederate Relic Room and Museum, World War Memorial Building, Sumter St. at Pendleton, 29201. Confederate bonds, U.S. coins, paper money, medals, foreign paper money and medals. Open 9 a.m. to 5 p.m. Monday through Friday, closed national and state holidays. Free.

South Dakota

PIERRE. Robinson Museum, Memorial Building, 500 E. Capitol Ave., 57501. South Dakota trade tokens, U.S. medals, foreign paper money and coins. Most open to scholars only. Open 8 a.m. to 5 p.m. Monday through Friday, 10 a.m. to 5 p.m. Saturday and 1 p.m. to 5 p.m. Sunday. Closed national holidays. Free.

Tennessee

HARROGATE. Abraham Lincoln Library and Museum, Lincoln Memorial University, 37752. Coins, medals, tokens, paper money and historical artifacts of the Lincoln Civil War Period. Open 9 a.m. to 4 p.m. Monday through Friday, 11 a.m. to 4 p.m. Saturday and 1 p.m. to 4 p.m. Sunday. Closed academic holidays. Research collection open for study by appointment only. Admission charge.

KNOXVILLE. Students' Museum, 516 Beaman, Chilhowee Park, 37914. U.S. coins and paper money, foreign paper money, ancients, slides and tapes on coinage history, story of money and silver dollars and a Mint errors exhibit. Open 9 a.m. to 5 p.m. Monday through Friday, 1 a.m. to 5 p.m. Saturday and 2 p.m. to 5 p.m. Sunday. Admission $1.75 adults, $1.25 children; group rates.

Texas

AUSTIN. Texas Memorial Museum, 2400 Trinity St., 78705. Swenson collection of coins and medallions. U.S. coins, paper money and medals, foreign paper money and medals, medieval and ancients. Open 9 a.m. to 5 p.m. Monday through Friday and 1 p.m. to 5 p.m. Saturday and Sunday

GARLAND. Garrett Electronics Treasures Found Museum, Garrett Electronics Plant, 2814 National Drive, 75041. U.S. coins and medals. Open Monday through Friday from 8:30 a.m. to 4:30 p.m.. Free.

NACOGDOCHES. Stone Fort Museum, Stephen F. Austin University, 75962. Confederate money, U.S. coins, paper money and medals, foreign paper money and medals. Numismatic material available for reseach by appointment only. Open 9 a.m. to 5 p.m. Monday through Saturday, 1 p.m. to 5 p.m. Sunday. Closed Christmas and New Year's Day. Free.

WACO. Strecker Museum, Baylor University, 76798. Large collection of German notgeld, Chinese coins previous to 1850, U.S. and foreign medals, thousands of notes and coins from many countries. All collections available for examination upon appointment. Open 9 a.m. to 4 p.m. weekdays, 10 a.m. to 1 p.m. Saturdays; 2 p.m. to 5 p.m. Sundays and closed university holidays.

Vermont

BENNINGTON. Bennington Museum, Inc., West Main St., 05201. Coins and paper money of Vermont. Open 9 a.m. to 5 p.m. March 1-Nov. 30. Closed Thanksgiving Day. Admission charged.[]

Virginia

PETERSBURG. Farmers Bank Museum,

19 Bollingbrook St., 23803. Confederate money and documents. Open daily 9 a.m. to 5 p.m.

RICHMOND. Money Museum, Federal Reserve Bank of Richmond, 701 E. Byrd St., 23219. History of U.S. coins and paper money, money-related artifacts, primitive, ancients and precious metals. Open 9:30 a.m. to 3:30 p.m. Monday through Friday.

RICHMOND. Virginia Museum, Boulevard and Grove Ave., 23221. Ancient Greek and Roman coins. Open 11 a.m. to 5 p.m. Tuesday through Saturday, until 10 p.m. Thursday evenings, 1 p.m. to 5 p.m. Sunday, closed major holidays. No admission fee for members, senior citizens and children under 16. Non-members $2. Part of Greco-Roman collection on permanent view; remainder by appointment.

Washington
GOLDENDALE. Maryhill Museum of Art, 55 Maryhill Museum Drive, 98620. U.S. coins, ancients and U.S. and world medals. Open March 15-Nov. 15 daily 9 a.m. to 5 p.m.. Adults $3, senior citizens $2 and students 6-16 $1.50.

West Virginia
CHARLESTON. West Virginia State Museum, The Cultural Center, Capitol Complex, 25305. U.S. coins, paper money and medals, foreign coins, paper money and medals. Open 9 a.m. to 9 p.m. Monday through Friday and 1 p.m. to 9 p.m. Saturday and Sunday. Closed Christmas.

Wisconsin
MADISON. State Historical Society of Wisconsin, 816 State St., 53706. U.S. coins, paper money and medals. Open 8 a.m. to 5 p.m. Monday-Friday to scholars only. Closed Wisconsin state holidays. Free.

STURGEON BAY. Door County Historical Museum, 18-4th and Michigan, 54235. U.S. coins, paper money and medals. Open 10 a.m. to 5 p.m. daily from May 1-Oct. 30.

World museums

Australia
HOBART. Tasmanian Museum and Art Gallery, 40 Macquarie St., Hobart. Tasmanian tokens and promissory notes, U.S. coins, paper money, ancients, medieval coins, world coins and medals. Open daily 10 a.m. to 5 p.m. Admission free.

Austria
ENNS. Museum Lauriacum Enns, Hauptplatz 19, Enns. Modern and Roman coins. April 1 to October 31 — daily: 10 a.m. to 12, 2 p.m. to 4 p.m.; closed Monday. November 1 to March 31 — Sundays: 10 a.m. to 12 a.m., 2 p.m. to 4 p.m. Admission ÖS20.-.

GRAZ. Landesmuseum Joanneum, Schloss Eggenberg, Graz, A-8020. World coins, medals and paper money, medieval and ancient coins. Open daily 9 a.m. to 5 p.m., closed Dec. and Jan. Admission ÖS25.-.

INNSBRUCK. Tiroler Landesmuseum Ferdinandeum, Museumstrasse 15, Innsbruck, A-6020. Historical collection, art from Romanesque to modern, coins, medallions. Open October to April, Tuesday to Saturday 10 a.m. to 12 noon, 2 p.m. to 5 p.m., Sunday 9 a.m. to 12 noon. CLosed Monday.

KLAGENFURT. Landesmuseum fur Karnten, Museumgasse 2, Klagenfurt, A-9021. Ancient and medieval coins. Tuesday-Saturday 9 a.m. to 4 p.m. Sunday 10 a.m. to 1 p.m. Admission ÖS15.-.

Belgium
BRUSSELS. Koninklike Bibliotheek Albert I, Penningkabinet, Keizerslaan 4, Brussels. Coins, medals, scales & weights, orders & decorations, books. Open Monday through Wednesday 9 a.m. to 12 a.m. and 2 p.m. to 5 p.m. Admission free (research unit, not a

museum, no exhibition).

Bermuda

HAMILTON. Bermuda Monetary Authority Numismatic Bureau Museum, 4th Floor, Govt. Adm. Bldg., Parliament St., Hamilton, HM12. Bermuda coins and paper money. Open Monday through Friday 8:45 a.m. to 5 p.m.

Canada

CALGARY. University of Calgary Nickle Arts Museum, 2500 University Drive N.W., Calgary, Alberta T2N 1N4. Ancient: Greek, Roman and Byzantine. Small collections of medallions and U.S. paper money. Tuesday - Friday 10-5; Saturday and Sunday 1-5. Closed Monday. Admission Adult $2, Child, Student and Senior Citizen $1. Children under 6 free.

HALIFAX. Public Archives of Nova Scotia, 6016 University Avenue, Halifax, Nova Scotia B3H 1W4. Coins, tokens and paper money. Open 8:30 a.m. to 10 p.m. Monday through Friday, 9 a.m. to 6 p.m. Saturday and 1 p.m. to 10 p.m. Sunday, closed national holidays. Admission free.

KAMLOOPS. Kamloops Museum and Archives, 207 Seymour Street, Kamloops, B.C. V2C 2E7. Foreign coins, medals, tokens and paper money. Open 10 a.m. to 5 p.m. Mon. through Sat., 1 p.m. to 5 p.m. Sunday. Admission free.

KELOWNA. Kelowna Museum and National Exhibit Centre, 470 Queensway Avenue, Kelowna, B.C. V1Y 6S7. Foreign coins, paper money, medals and tokens. Open 10 a.m. to 5 p.m. Tuesday through Saturday. Admission free.

MONTREAL. Musee du Seminaire de Quebec, 9 rue de l'Universite, CP 460, Hauteville, Montreal, Quebec. Ancient and Old World coins, medals, tokens and paper money. Specializing in Canadian paper money, tokens and coins. Open to public June through Oct. 10:30 a.m. to 5:30 p.m.. October through June 11 a.m. to 5 p.m. Admission: $2 adults, $1 students and senior citizens, $5 families.

Group rates available.

OTTAWA. Bank of Canada Currency Museum, 245 Sparks St., Ottawa, Ontario K1A 0G9. National Currency Collection of Canada. U.S. coins and paper money, foreign coins and paper money, medieval, ancients and primitives. Open Tuesday through Saturday 10:30 a.m. to 5 p.m. and Sunday 1 p.m. to 5 p.m. Closed Monday and most statutory holidays except during the summer months.

OTTAWA. Canadian War Museum, 330 Sussex Drive, Ottawa, Ontario K1A 0M8. Canadian, U.S. and foreign military medals, orders, badges, insignia and scrip. Material on display and in reference collections. Research scholars may have access to reference materials subject to request to curator in chief. Open daily 9:30 a.m. to 5 p.m. Closed Christmas Day. Admission: adults $2, seniors and students $1; Canadian Veterans, friends of the CWM, school groups and children under 6 free; Thursdays free.

OTTAWA. National Archives of Canada, 395 Wellington Street, Ottawa, Ontario K1A 0N3. Medal Collection. 12,000 Canadian, British, French, U.S. and other medals. Open 8:30 a.m. to 4:30 p.m. Monday through Friday, research by appointment. Closed statutory holidays. Admission free.

OTTAWA. Royal Canadian Mint, 320 Sussex Drive, Ottawa, Ontario K1N 8V5. Viewing of striking of gold and silver coins, audio and visual presentation on coin production and displays of coins, medals and other products of the RCM, with an emphasis on current issues. Open Monday through Friday 8:30 a.m. to 11 a.m. and 12:30 p.m. to 2:30 p.m. Admission is free, tours are guided and reservations are required. (613) 992-2348.

PRINCE RUPERT. Museum of Northern British Columbia, Box 669, Prince Rupert, B.C. V8J 3S1. Ancients, U.S. and foreign coins, medals and paper money. Open 10 a.m. to 5 p.m. Monday through Saturday during the winter, 9 a.m. to 9 p.m. Monday through Saturday and 9 a.m. to 5 p.m. Sunday during the summer. Closed Christmas, New Year's, Easter and Remembrance Day. Donations accepted at door.

TORONTO. Royal Ontario Museum, Toronto, Canada, 100 Queen's Park, Toronto, Ontario M5S 2C6. Ancient Greek, Roman, Celtic and medieval coins; foreign and Canadian coins and medals. Main building: 10 a.m. to 6 p.m. daily, to 8 p.m. Tuesday and Thursday. Canadian Decorative Arts, Sigmund Samuel Building: Monday to Saturday 10 a.m. to 5 p.m.; Sunday 1 p.m. to 5 p.m. Admission — Main Building: Adults $5; seniors, children, students $3; families $12. Seniors admitted free on Tuesdays. Admission free for everyone after 4:30 p.m. Thursdays. Sigmund Samuel Building admission free.

Denmark

COPENHAGEN. Copenhagen Museum, Vesterbrogade 59, Copenhagen, DK-1620. History and life of Copenhagen for 800 years. Open Oct. through April 1 p.m. to 4 p.m., closed Monday. Open May through Sept. 10 a.m. to 4 p.m., closed Monday. Admission free.

COPENHAGEN. National Museum, Royal Collection of Coins and Medals, Frederiksholms Kanal 12, Copenhagen, KD-1220. The exhibition is under reconstruction. The medals will be reopened in April 1990; the rest, we hope, in the latter half of 1990. OPen June 16 to Sept. 15 daily 10 a.m. to 4 p.m.; Sept. 16 to June 15, 11 a.m. to 3 p.m.; Sunday 12 a.m. to 4 p.m., Closed Monday. Admission free.

Finland

HELSINKI. National Museum Kansallismuseo, Mannerheimintie 34, PO Box 913, Helsinki, 00101. Finnish, Swedish and Russian coins, bank notes and medals. Ancient and medieval coins, world coins, medals and paper money. Open May through Sept. daily 11 a.m. to 4 p.m.; Oct. through April 11 a.m. to 3 p.m.; Saturday and Sunday 11 a.m. to 4 p.m., Tuesday 6 p.m. to 9 p.m. Admission Admission FIM5, children FIM2.50.

France

PARIS. Cabinet des Médailles, Bibliotheque Nationale, 58 Rue de Richelieu, Paris, F-75084. Coins, medals and antiques. Open weekdays 1 p.m. to 5 p.m. Sundays 12 to 6 p.m. Admission 20 francs.

PARIS. Paris Mint Museum, 11, Quai de Conti, Paris, F-75270. Ancient and medieval coins, world coins, medals and paper money; French medals and jetons. Minting material since 17th century, documents. Open Tuesday through Sunday 1 p.m. to 6 p.m., Wednesday until 9 p.m. Admission free for children under 16, teachers and school groups.

Germany

BERLIN. Staatliche Museen zu Berlin, Münzkabinett, Bodemuseum, Bodestrasse 1-3, DDR-1020. Ancient and medieval coins, world coins, medals and paper money. Jetons, seals, shares and bonds. Wednesday through Friday 10 a.m. to 4 p.m.

BRAUNFELS. Furstliches Familien-Museum, Schloss, Braunfels, D-6333. Medieval, Roman and German coins from 1871-1918. Coins and dies of Solms dynasty. Open daily 8 a.m. to 5 p.m. April through Sept. and daily 9 a.m. to 4 p.m. Oct. through March. Admission DM2.

COLOGNE. Kolnisches Stadtmuseum, Zeughausstrasse 1-3, Cologne, D-5000. Coins of the Bishops of Cologne and city of Cologne.

DRESDEN. Staatliche Kunstsammlungen Dresden, Münzkabinett, State and public holdings. Monday, Wednesday, Friday, Saturday, Sunday 9 a.m. to 5 p.m.; Tuesday 9 a.m. to 6 p.m.; closed Thursday. Admission adults DM5, senior citizens and students DM2,50; Tuesday 2 p.m. to 6 p.m. free.

FRANKFURT/MAIN. Degussa Munzkabinett, Postfach 110533, Frankfurt/Main, D-6000. German coinages since 1871. Not open to public.

FRANKFURT/MAIN. Deutsche Bundesbank, Money Museum, Central Bank of the Federal Republic of Germany, Postfach 100602, Frankfurt/Main, D-6000. More than 230,000 bank notes and 80,000 coins.

HAMBURG. Museum für Hamburgische Geschichte, Munzkabinett, Holstenwall 24, Hamburg, D-2000. Modern world coins and coins from Hamburg. Exhibition under preparation 4/90.

KARLSRUHE. Badisches Landesmuseum, Schloss, Karlsruhe, D-7500. World coins, medals and paper money. Ancients and coins of South Germany. Open Tuesday to Sunday 10 a.m. to 5:30 p.m. Admission free.

LUBECK. Archiv der Hansestadt Lubeck, Muhlendamm 1-3, Lubeck, D-2400. Coins of Lubeck. Only on special announcement: Phone 0451/1224152.

MAINZ. Landesmuseum Mainz, Grosse Bleiche 49-51, Mainz, D-6500. Ancient, medieval, baroque and world coins. Open Tuesday to Thursday 10 a.m. to 5 p.m., Friday to 4 p.m., closed Monday.

MAINZ. Römish-Germanische Zentralmuseum Mainz Forschungsinstitut für Vor- und Frühgeschichte, Ernst-Ludwig-Platz 2, Mainz, D-6500. Celtic and Roman republic and imperial coins. Coins of the early middle ages. Open by appointment.

MÜNSTER, D-4400. Westfalisches Landesmuseum für Kunst u. Kulturgeschichte, Domplatz 10, Münster, D-4400. World coins, medals and paper money. Germany paper money, coins and medals of the region of Westphalia. Open Tuesday to Sunday 10 a.m. to 6 p.m.

NUERNBERG. Germanic National Museum, Kartausergasse 1, Nuernberg, D-8500. Coins and medals from German-speaking countries. Open Tuesday to Friday 9 a.m. to 5 p.m., Thursday also 8 p.m. to 9:30 p.m., Saturday and Sunday 10 a.m. to 5 p.m. Admission DM4, groups (per person) DM2.50.

SPEYER. Historiches Museum der Pfalz, Grosse Pfaffengasse 7, Speyer, D-6720. Ancient, medieval and modern material. (Scheduled to reopen mid-1990.)

TRIER. Rheinisches Landesmuseum Trier, Ostallee 44, Trier, D-5500. Ancient and medieval coins of Trier. Open daily 10 a.m. to 4 p.m.

Greece

ATHENS. Athens Numismatic Museum, Tossitsa 1 GR, Athens, 10682. Greek, Roman, Byzantine, Medieval, modern coins and medals, Greek and Byzantine weights, Byzantine seals and gems. Open summer and winter 8:30 a.m. to 3:00 p.m. Tuesday through Saturday. Closed Monday. Admission free.

Israel

HAIFA. National Maritime Museum, 198 Allenby Road, Haifa, 44855. Large collection of coins and medals pertaining to the sea. Extensive collection of Hebrew and Mediterranean maritime history and archaeology. Open Sunday through Thursday 10 a.m. to 4 p.m.; closed Friday. Saturday and holidays 10 a.m. to 1 p.m. Admission adults IS6.-; children IS2.50; groups (20 and more) IS4.80.

JERUSALEM. Israel Museum, Kiryat Ben-Gurion, Jerusalem. Bronfman Biblical and Archaeological Museum, contains collection of ancient Jewish, Greek, Roman Provincial, Islamic and Crusader coins. Open Sunday, Monday, Wednesday and Thursday 10 a.m. to 5 p.m.; Tuesday 4 p.m. to 10 p.m. and Friday and Saturday 10 a.m. to 2 p.m. Admission adult IS9, children IS4.

Italy

NAPLES. Museo Archeologico Nazionale di Napoli, Piazza Museo, 19, Napoli 80135. Greek, Roman and modern coins and medals. Viewing by appointment only.

Luxembourg

LUXEMBOURG. Musée National D'Histoire et D'art, Marche-aux-Poissons, Luxembourg, 2345. More than 80,000 numismatic items from Celtic to modern times. Open Tuesday through Friday 10 a.m. to 12 p.m. and 1 p.m. to 5 p.m.; Saturday 2 p.m. to 6 p.m.; Sunday 10 a.m. to 12 p.m. and 2 p.m. to 6 p.m. Closed Monday. Admission free.

Malaysia

KUALA LUMPUR. Bank Negara Money Museum, Peti Surat 109 22, Jalan Dato'Onn, Kuala Lumpur, 50566. Coins bank notes and other monetary exhibits with particular emphasis on Malaysian numismatics. Monday to Friday 9 a.m. to 4:30 p.m. Saturday 9 a.m. to 5 p.m. CLosed Sunday. Admission free.

KUALA LUMPUR. Muzium Numismatik Maybank, Kuala Lumpur. Coins from Melaka Kingdom to present day coins and bank notes including King Farouk's gold and silver Straits Settlement coins (believed to be the only set in the world). Open daily (including Sunday 10 a.m. to 6 p.m. excluding public holidays. Admission free.

KUALA LUMPUR. National Museum of Malaysia (Muzium Negara), Kuala Lumpur, 50566. Malaysian and world coins and paper money. 9 a.m. - 6 p.m. (everyday). Admission free.

Netherlands

LEIDEN. State Museum of Coins and Medals., Rapenburg 28, Leiden, 2301 EA. The national collection of coins, paper money, medals, engraved gems and seals. By way of thematic exhibitions every six months different segments of the large collection are shown to the public. Open Tuesday through Saturday 10 a.m. to 5 p.m.; Sunday 12 p.m. to 5 p.m. Admission Fl. 3,50.

UTRECHT, 3500 GK. Museum van 's Rijks Munt, Leidseweg 90, Utrecht, 3500 GK. Dutch coins from 7th Century to present times, medals, decorations, minting equipment. Open: working days only 10 a.m. to 4 p.m. Admission free, visitors can strike their own token on an authentic press.

Philippines

MANILA. Central Bank of the Philippines, Money Museum, Manila, 2801. Philippine coins, bank notes, medals; world coins, bank notes and medals; gold artifacts and potteries. Open Tuesday through Sunday 9:00 a.m. to 4:30 p.m. Admission free.

Poland

WARSAW. The Royal Castle, Plac Zamkowy 4, 00277. Polish coins and medals, medieval coins, modern world coins and paper money. Open daily 10 a.m. to 3 p.m.

Spain

MADRID. Lazaro Galdiano Museum, Calle Serrano 122, Madrid, 28006. Medal collection. Open daily 10 a.m. to 2 p.m. Closed Monday. Admission 300 pesetas.

MADRID. Museo del Ejercito, c/o Mendez Nunez, No. 1, Madrid, 28014. Medals and decorations. Open daily 10 a.m. to 2 p.m. Closed Monday. Admission 100 pesetas.

MADRID. Palacio Real (Royal Palace), Plaza de Oriente, Madrid. Arts collection, some medals and decorations. Open April to September, weekdays 9 a.m. to 6:15 p.m., weekends 9 a.m. to 3:15 p.m.; October to March, weekdays 9:30 a.m. to 5:15 p.m., weekends 9 a.m. to 2:15 p.m. Closed holidays.

SEGOVIA. Cathedral de Segovia Museum, Segovia. Coins minted from all Spanish periods, in copper, silver and gold. Open daily April to October 9:15 a.m. to 6:45 p.m.; October to April 9:15 a.m. to 1 p.m.; from 3 p.m. p.m. to 6 p.m.

Sweden

MALMO. Malmo Museums, Malmohusvagen, Box 406, Malmo, 20124. Ancient, medieval and Scandinavian coins. Open daily 12 a.m. to 4 p.m. Admission adults 20 kronor; children under 7 free.

STOCKHOLM. Ostasiatiska Museet (Museum of Far Eastern Antiquities), Skeppsholmen, Stockholm, S-103 27. Chinese coins, spade and knife money. Coins are not on permanent display. Open daily 11 a.m. to 4 p.m. Tuesday until 9 p.m. Closed Monday. Admission adults 20 crowns, students 10 crowns and youths under 16 free.

Switzerland

GENEVA. Museum of Art and History, 2 rue Charles Galland, Geneva, CH-1211. Ancient, medieval and world coins, and coins of Geneva. Open Tuesday through Sunday 10 a.m. to 5 p.m. Closed Monday. Admission free.

LAUSANNE. Cabinet des Medailles du Canton de Vaud, Palais de Rumine, Lausanne, CH-1005. Ancient, medieval and world coins, medals and paper money. Library: Monday-Friday 10 a.m.-12 noon, Tuesday: 10 a.m.-12 noon and 2 p.m.-5 p.m.

LUCERNE. Historisches Museum Luzern, Pfistergasse 24, Postfach 164, Lucerne, CH-6000. Coins and medals of Lucerne, ancient, medieval and modern world coins. Open Tuesday through Friday 10 a.m. to 12 a.m. and 2 p.m. to 5 p.m.; Saturday and Sunday 10 a.m. to 5 p.m.

WINTERTHUR. Munzkabinett der Stadt Winterthur, Villa Buhler, Lindstrasse 8, Winterthur, CH-8401. Ancient Greek and Roman coins. Tuesday, Wednesday, Saturday, Sunday from 2 to 5 p.m. Admission free.

WINTERTHUR. Munzkabinett der Stadt Winterthur, Winterthur. Ancient Greek and Roman coins. Tuesday, Wednesday, Saturday, Sunday from 2 to 5 p.m. Admission free.

ZURICH. Swiss National Museum, Museumstrasse 2, Zurich, CH-8023. Swiss coins and medals, world coins, medals and paper money. A small but representative selection is permanently on view. Open Tuesday to Sunday from 10 a.m. to 5 p.m. Closed Mondays. Admission free.

United Kingdom

BELFAST. Ulster Museum, Botanic Gardens, Belfast, BT9 5AB. 50,000 coins, tokens and medals from ancients to modern, plus Irish bank notes. Open Monday through Friday 10 a.m. to 5 p.m.; Saturday and Sunday 2 p.m. to 5 p.m. Admission free.

BIRMINGHAM. Birmingham Assay Office, P.O. Box 151, Newhall St., Birmingham, B3 1SB. Coins, medals and tokens of Birmingham. Private museum with viewing by appointment only. Admission free.

BIRMINGHAM. City Museum and Art Gallery, Reception No. 021-235 2834, Chamberlain Square, Birmingham, B3 3DH. Ancient and medieval coins. Products of the Soho and Birmingham Mints. Mon.-Sat. 9:30 a.m.-5 p.m.; Sun. 2 p.m.-5 p.m. Admission free.

BRISTOL, BS8 1RL. City of Bristol Museum and Art Gallery, Queens Road, Bristol, BS8 1RL. Local Iron Age; Roman; Bristol Mint, local hoards; trade tokens. Open Monday through Sunday, 10 a.m. to 5 p.m. Reserve collections by appointment only. Admission free.

CAMBRIDGE. Fitzwilliam Museum, Department of Coins and Medals, Cambridge, CB2 1RB. Collection comprises some 100,000 specimens, of Ancient, British Isles, European medieval and Indian coins. Open Monday through Friday 10 a.m. to 1 p.m. and 2 p.m. to 5 p.m. A collection of art medals is on permanent display in the main museum galleries: Tuesday through Saturday 10 a.m. to 5 p.m.; Sunday 2:15 p.m. to 5 p.m. Admission free.

EDINBURGH. Royal Museum of Scotland (National Museum of Scotland), Chambers Street, Edinburgh EH1 1JF. Classical, European and Oriental items, modern world coins. Open Monday through Saturday 10 a.m. to 5 p.m., Sunday 2 p.m. to 5 p.m. Admission free.

LONDON. Bank of England Museum, London. Bank notes, token money, regal coinage, silver, documents, books, photographs relating to social life and economic history of the bank. 10-5 p.m. Monday-Friday. Admission free.

LONDON. British Museum, Great Russell Street, London, WC1B 3DG. 600,000 numismatic items (including paper money). Monday-Friday 2 p.m.-4:30 p.m. (Students Room) Saturday 10 a.m.-

12:30 p.m. Admission free.

OXFORD. Ashmolean Museum, Heberden Coin Room, Beaumont Street, Oxford, OX1 2PH. Coins of all periods and areas. Open Tuesday through Saturday 10 a.m. to 4 p.m.; Sunday 2 p.m. to 4 p.m. Admission free.

Organizations

21

American Numismatic Society

Broadway Between 155th and 156th streets
New York, N.Y. 10032

Officials		
Harry W. Fowler .... President		
R. Henry Norweb Jr. .... **First Vice President**		
Roger A. Hornsby .... **Second Vice President**		
Leslie A. Elam........................ **Director and Secretary**		
John D. Leggett Jr. .... Treasurer		
Richard A. Phillips...................... Assistant Treasurer		

Executive Committee	Harry W. Bass Jr.	John D. Leggett, Jr.	R. Henry Norweb Jr
	Harry W. Fowler	Glen W. Bowersock	Mrs. Marion Russell
	Roger A. Hornsby		

Finance Committee	Landon Thomas	Harry W. Fowler	R. Henry Norweb Jr.
	Alan B. Coleman	John D. Leggett Jr.	

Council (Term ending in January of year)	Roger A. Hornsby.......... 1994	Glen W. Bowersock...... 1992
	R. Henry Norweb Jr....... 1994	Mrs. Marion Russell..... 1992
	John J. Slocum............... 1994	Harry W. Fowler 1991
	Fred S. Kleiner............... 1994	John H. Kroll................. 1991
	Arthur A. Houghton....... 1993	John D. Leggett Jr......... 1991
	Eric P. Newman.............. 1993	Alan B. Coleman........... 1990
	Allen F. Lovejoy........... 1993	Landon Thomas............ 1990
	Harry W. Bass Jr............. 1992	Speros Vyronis Jr......... 1990

Museum staff	
Leslie A. Elam... Director	
William E. Metcalf .... Chief Curator	

Curatorial staff	Roman & Byzantine Coins
Alan M. Stahl .... Medieval Coins, Medals	
Carmen F. Arnold-Biucchi ....Greek Coins	
Michael L. Bates... Islamic Coins	
Johanna Bergmann ....Curatorial Assistant	
Francis D. Campbell Jr.. Librarian	
Kay M. Brooks...................................... Assistant Librarian	
Marie H. Martin.. Editor	
Frank Deak .... Photographer	

About the ANS

The American Numismatic Society was founded by a group of 12 New Yorkers April 6, 1858. Its objective was "the collection and preservation of coins and medals, with an investigation into their history, and other subjects connected therewith." The group was incorporated in 1864.

Coins, medals and books were collected from the Society's early days. As the collections grew, it became necessary to find quarters to house them. A succession of rented rooms served as meeting-places and headquarters during the first 50 years.

Through contributions by interested officers and members, the Society was able to erect its own building in 1907. Since then, its collections and activities have grown progressively.

The ANS Museum houses one of the finest collections of numismatics in the United States. Located in uptown Manhattan, New York City, in the same building which houses its offices, collections and libraries, the museum includes coins of all periods from their inception to modern times, and medals and decorations.

Selections from the museum cabinets are on display in an exhibition.

The ANS Library is the most comprehensive numismatic library in the world, consisting of some 100,000 items. In addition to its excellent book collection, which includes virtually all of the standard references on numismatics, the library holds rare manuscripts, all of the major numismatic periodicals, a special collection of some 8,000 auction catalogs and six distinct topical pamphlet files.

In all, the ANS houses over a million numismatic items. Located on Broadway between 155th and 156th Streets, the exhibit halls are open from 9 to 5 Tuesday through Saturday, 1 to 4 Sunday, and are closed national holidays. No admission is charged.

The ANS has been active in publishing since its founding. Today it publishes the Numismatic Notes and Monographs, separately issued publications, each on a single topic. The *American Journal of Numismatics* (formerly *Museum Notes*), is the official journal of the Society which appears annually. *Numismatic Literature,* published twice a year, listing current numismatic publications with abstracts of their content; *Ancient Coins in North*

American Collections and Numismatic Studies, a series accommodating works in a larger format.

The Society is governed and managed by a council of 15 members from which a president and two vice presidents are elected. The other officers are appointed by the council.

There are four classes of members: Fellows, Honorary Fellows, Associate Members, and Corresponding Members. The Fellows are limited in number to 200; persons or organizations who have rendered special service to the Society or to numismatics may be elected Honorary Fellows. Only Fellows and Honorary Fellows may vote at the meetings of the Society, and it is from their number the council is selected.

Persons or organizations not residing in the U.S. may be elected Corresponding Members. Associate membership, which is unlimited in number, is open to all with an interest in numismatics.

A summer seminar in numismatics has been held by the Society since 1952. Grants-in-aid are offered to university graduate students in humanistic fields such as classics, archaeology, Oriental languages, history, economics, and art history. The aim of the seminar is to provide the students with an understanding of the contribution numismatics has to make in their own fields of study and to provide them with sufficient training in numismatic techniques to be of use to them in their future careers.

The ANS has offered, since 1958, Graduate Fellowships to qualified university students in the fields of the humanities or the social sciences. Applications are accepted annually from students who have completed the general examinations (or the equivalent) for the doctorate, who will be writing dissertations on topics in which the use of numismatics plays a significant part, and who will have attended one of the Society's summer seminars.

Other activities of the Society include a photographic service, specially equipped for the photography of numismatic objects; and two awards, the Archer M. Huntington Medal, awarded for outstanding scholarly contributions to numismatics, and the J. Sanford Saltus Medal, honoring sculptors who have achieved merit in the art of the medal.

In early 1990, the Coin Rooms and the East Exhibition Hall were closed for renovation. The East Hall renovation is to provide a multi-purpose area, specifically for display of short-term exhibits on topical themes. New security and proximity to coin rooms will permit "hands-on" workshops.

For more information about the American Numismatic Society, write: Secretary of the Society, The American Numismatic Society, Broadway Between 155th and 156th Sts., New York, N.Y. 10032.

Coinage of the Americas Conferences topics and papers

America's Copper Coinage, 1783-1857
Nov. 30-Dec. 2, 1984

John Adams	Benjamin Collins. A Brief Essay on the People and Traditions of Large Cent Collecting
Walter Breen	Robert Scot's Earliest Device Punches
Elvira Clain-Stefanelli	Copper Coinage and the Monetary Economy of the Early United States
David H. Cohen	The Randall Hoard
Roger S. Cohen Jr.	Original and Restrike Half Cents
George E. Ewing Jr.	Origins of Edge Lettering on Early American Copper Coinage
Cory Gillilland	Early American Copper Coinage in Relation to the Art and Taste of the Period
Ronald J. Guth	The Copper Coinage of Vermont
Denis W. Loring	Emission Sequences of Early Cents
Eric P. Newman	Circulation of Pre-U.S. Mint Copper Coins in Nineteenth Century America
Donald G. Patrick	The Mysterious 1784 "Washington the Great" Coinage
Jules Reiver	Attributing the Late Date Large Cents
P. Scott Rubin	Auction Appearances and Pedigrees of the 1792 Silver Center Cent
Peter Smith	United States Turban Cents, 1808-1814
R. Tettenhorst	Overstrikes and Other Anomalies on Early Half Cents

America's Currency, 1789-1866
Oct. 31-Nov. 2, 1985

Douglas B. Ball	The Confederate Currency Reform of 1862
Carl W.A. Carlson	The CSA Banking Convention of 1861 and its Delegates
Elvira Clain-Stefanelli	An Historian's View of the State Bank Notes: A Mirror of Life in the Early Republic
Grover C. Criswell	Collecting Trends in Obsolete American Currency
Cory Gillilland	The Financial Concerns of a Government Employee in the 1840s
Gene Hessler	The History and Development of "America" as Symbolized by an American Indian Female
Glenn E. Jackson	The Smillie Family: Banknote Artists
Eric P. Newman	New York City Small Change Bills of 1814-1816
Robert Vlack	Currency in Crisis: America's Money, 1840-1845
Raymond H. Williamson	Lynchburg (Va.) City Paper Money of 1862

America's Silver Coinage
Nov. 1-2, 1986

Harry X Boosel	The Silver Coinage of 1873, and the So-Called Crime of 1873
David H. Cohen	The Industrial Revolution Overtakes the Production of Dies
David Davis	New Varieties of Early Half Dimes

Robert P. Hilt II	The "Group Strength" of Dies for Early Half Dollars
Ivan Leaman and Donald Gunnet	Edges and Die Sequences on Early Half Dollars
Russell Logan	The Third Die: A Different Look
Allen F. Lovejoy and William L. Subjack	Early Dimes, 1796-1837
John W. McCloskey	"Unheralded" Hub Changes in the Gobrecht Series
Eric P. Newman and Kenneth E. Bressett	*The Fantastic 1804 Dollar:* 25th Anniversary Follow-up
Robert Stark	The Dollars of 1794-1803
Randall E. Wiley and William Bugert	Liberty Seated Half Dollars

The Medal in America

Sept. 26-27, 1987

Ebenezer Nii Quarcoopome	The Indian Peace Medal of King George I
George J. Fuld and Barry D. Tayman	The Montreal and Happy While United Indian Peace Medals
Javier Gimeno	The Spanish Medal in America
Yvonne Korshack	The Winds of Libertas: Augustin Dupre's *Libertas Americana*
Cornelius Vermeule	Medallic and Marble Memorials: Mint to Mausoleum in Victorian America
Dorothy Budd Bartle	John Cotton Dana and the Ideal Museum Collection of Medals
Donna J. Hassler	The Medals of John Flanagan
Michael Richman	The Medals of Daniel Chester French
Cynthia (Pratt) Kennedy Sam	Bela Lyon Pratt (1867-1917): Medals, Medallions and Coins
August L. Freundlich	The Coins and Medals of James Earle Fraser
Elaine J. Leotti	The American Woman Medalist, A Critical Survey
Joseph Veach Noble	The Society of Medalists

The Coinage of El Perú

Oct. 29-30, 1988

Freeman Craig Jr.	Coinage of the Viceroyalty of El Perú — an Overview
Adon A. and Jeanne P. Gordus	Identification of Potosí Silver Usage in Sixteenth-Seventeenth Century European Coinage through Gold-Impurity Content of Coins
Eduardo Dargent Chamot	The Early Lima Mint (1568-1572
Arnaldo J. Cunietti-Ferrando	Documentary Evidence Regarding the La Plata Mint and the First Issues of Potosí
K.A. Dym	The First Assayers at Potosí
Frank Sedwick	The Gold Cobs of Peru, 1696-1750
Barry W. Stallard	The Enigmatic Sixteenth-Century AP Coins: Issues of a Peruvian Mint in Alto Peru?
Joseph R. Lasser	The Silver Cobs of Colombia, 1622-1748
Glenn S. Murray	Mechanization of the Peruvian Mints: Problems of Implementation
Robert D. Leonard Jr.	The "Large Crown" Counterstamp on Peruvian 2 Reales: A Guatemalan Issue of 1663
William B. Christiansen	The Pattern Coinage of Independent Peru
H.P. Flatt	Moneda Feble in Peru, 1830-1867
Richard G. Doty	Nationhood through Numismatics: Latin American Proclamation Pieces
George Lill III	A Preliminary Study of the Possible Production Outside the Potosí Mint of Bolivian Mules, Pieforts, and Uniface Examples of the "Monedas Especiales" Series

America's Gold Coinage
Nov. 4-5, 1989

John W. McCloskey	A Study of Classic Half Eagles, 1834-1838
Cory Gillilland	U.S. Gold Bullion Coins: A Nineteenth-Century Proposal
Walter H. Breen	Metallic Panaceas: Gold Bugs, Silver Crusaders, and the Wizard of Oz
Charles R. Hoskins	In Search of the Imperfect Coin: A Cautionary Tale
Richard G. Doty	"an onerous and delicate task": Franklin Peale's Mission South, 1837
Q. David Bowers	Collecting United States Gold Coins: A Numismatic History
James A. Hayes	The Politics of Coinage as Illustrated by Recent Commemorative Issues
Elizabeth Jones	Reflections on the Gold Coinage of the Twentieth Century
Harry W. Bass Jr.	The Harry W. Bass Jr. Reference Collection of U.S. Federal Gold Coins

America's Pre-federal Coins and Currency
May 1991

Archer M. Huntington Medal award

The Archer M. Huntington Medal award is given by the American Numismatic Society for outstanding numismatic scholarship. It is the highest award the society bestows.

Winner	Year	Winner	Year
Edward T. Newell	1918	George C. Miles	1949
Agnes Baldwin Brett	1919	C.H.V. Sutherland	1950
Howland Wood	1920	Henri Seyrig	1952
Jean N. Svoronos	1921	Walter Havernick	1953
Ernest Babelon	1922	Charles T. Seltman	1954
George F. Hill	1923	John Walker	1955
Albert R. Frey	1924	Jocelyn M.C. Toynbee	1956
George Macdonald	1925	Arthur Suhle	1957
Jose Toribio Medina	1926	Robert I. Nesmith	1958
Robert James Eidlitz	1927	Oscar Ulrich-Bansa	1959
Edouard von Zambaur	1928	Humberto F. Burzio	1960
Kurt Regling	1929	Margaret Thompson	1961
Baumann L. Belden	1930	Philip Grierson	1962
Harold E. Gillingham	1931	Jean Mazard	1963
Adolph Dieudonne	1932	Michael Grant	1964
Wilhelm Kubitschek	1933	Andrew Alfoldi	1965
Adrien Blanchet	1934	Georg Galster	1966
E. Stanley G. Robinson	1935	Willy Schwabacher	1967
John Allan	1936	George LeRider	1968
Sydney P. Noe	1937	Emanuela Nohejlova-Pratova	1969
Harold Mattingly	1938	Anne S. Robertson	1970
Sir Arthur J. Evans	1940	Paul Balog	1971
Albert Gallatin	1941	H. Enno van Gelder	1972
Alfred Bellinger	1943	Christopher Blunt	1973
J. Grafton Milne	1944	Jean LaFaurie	1974
Alabert F. Pradeau	1945	Pierre Bastien	1975
Max Bernhart	1946	G. Kenneth Jenkins	1976
Richard Bertram Whitehead	1947	R.A.G. Carson	1977
J.W.E. Pearce	1948	Eric P. Newman	1978

Felipe Mateu y Llopis	1979	Leo Mildenberg	1985
Colin Kraay	1980	Paul Naster	1986
Otto Morkholm	1981	Parmeshwari Lal Gupta	1987
Michael Dolley	1982	Brita Malmer	1988
Herbert Cahn	1983	Patrick Magnus Bruun	1989
Peter Berghaus	1984		

J. Sanford Saltus Medal award

The J. Sanford Saltus Medal award is given by ANS for distinguished achievement in the field of the art of the medal.

Winner	Year	Winner	Year
James E. Fraser	1919	Thomas G. Lo Medico	1956
Adolph A. Weinman	1920	Abram Belskie	1959
John Flanagan	1921	Bruno Mankowski	1960
Victor D. Brenner	1922	Robert A. Weinman	1964
Hermon A. MacNeil	1923	Albino Manca	1966
Paul Manship	1925	Donald DeLue	1967
Laura G. Fraser	1926	Michael Lantz	1968
Anthony DeFrancisci	1927	Stanley F. Martineau	1969
Edward W. Sawyer	1931	Joseph Kiselewski	1970
Lee Lawrie	1937	Granville W. Carter	1975
Chester Beach	1946	Karen Worth	1979
Henry Kreis	1948	Agop Agopoff	1980
C.P. Jennewein	1949	Guido Veroi	1983
Gertrude K. Lathrop	1950	Marcel Jovine	1984
Albert Laessle	1951	Edward R. Grove	1985
Bruce Moore	1952	Kauko Rasanen	1986
Walker Hancock	1953	John Cook	1987
Sidney Waugh	1954	Jirí Harcuba	1988
Theodore Spicer-Simson	1955	Keiichi Uryu	1990

American Numismatic Association

818 N. Cascade Ave., Colorado Springs, Colo. 80903-3279; (719) 632-2646ßß

Officials

Robert J. Leuver	Executive Director
George D. Hatie	General Counsel
Adna G. Wilde	Treasurer
John J. Gabarron	Sergeant-At-Arms
Carl W.A. Carlson	Historian
David L. Ganz	Legislative Counsel
Ruthann Brettell	Convention Director
Aimee Tihonovich	Controller
James Taylor	Educational Services Director
Robin Mathias	Membership Director
Richard Conway	Development Director
Stephen Bobbitt	Public Relations Officer
Nancy W. Green	Librarian
Barbara J. Gregory	Publisher
Robert W. Hoge	Museum Curator

| Board of Governors | Kenneth L. Hallenbeck.................................... President |
| | Edward C. Rochette............................... Vice President |

Governors	Kenneth E. Bressett	John Jay Pittman
	David L. Ganz	Florence M. Schook
	James L. Halperin	Nancy Wilson
	Donn Pearlman	

The beginning

George F. Heath, M.D., of Monroe, Michigan, a physician of the "old school," gained a knowledge of world history through the study of his collection of coins. Seeking to expand his contact with other collectors and to sell duplicates from his collection, Heath in 1888 published a leaflet titled *The American Numismatist.* After the first issue the periodical was retitled as *The Numismatist,* a name unchanged to the present day.

The little publication found many friends among collectors of the era, especially those in rural areas away from numismatic clubs and societies. As Heath's subscription list increased, it became evident that there was a growing need for a society similar to those in the cities, but one which would reach the more isolated, and serve the less advanced and the beginner: a national organization of numismatists.

The February 1891 issue of *The Numismatist* printed a question, "What is the matter with having an American Numismatic Association?" Wisely, Heath added, "There is nothing like the alliance of kindred pursuits to stimulate growth and interest." Aided by Charles T. Tatman, the editor of the coin column in a leading hobby magazine, *Plain Talk,* a campaign was begun to organize such an association. Numismatists from across the United States reacted favorably when they were urged to band together in order to derive greater benefits and pleasure from their avocation.

Founding

On Oct. 7-8, 1891, five men, Heath, William G. Jerrems, David Harlow, J.A. Heckelman, and John Brydon, holding 26 proxies, met in Chicago and with 61 charter members, founded the American Numismatic Association. Tatman was unable to attend. Dr. Heath declined the presidency in favor of his good friend, Jerrems, a collector of ancient coins. He did, however, accept the honor of having No. 1 on the membership roll. At first, the coin column in *Plain Talk* was selected as the official ANA publication, but soon *The Numismatist* became the official voice of the organization.

Since that meeting in October 1891 the American Numismatic Association, a non-profit educational association, has grown to become the largest numismatic organization of its kind in the world.

The ANA was progressing smoothly when an unfavorable national economic climate, plus apathy on the part of ANA officers, caused the Association to become moribund. Many months passed without the officers submitting reports. Heath withdrew *The Numismatist* from the ANA, and it seemd that the organization would disband. In 1898 the ANA awoke, and, due primarily to the efforts of Heath, the ANA experienced growth and expansion.

ANA conventions were held in various cities from 1891 to 1895, in 1901, and in 1904. The 1907 meeting, well publicized, was an oustanding success. It was decided to hold annual meetings, henceforth. This procedure has been followed, with the exception of 1918, when a nationwide influenza epidemic forced the cancellation of public meetings, and 1945, when wartime conditions intervened.

On June 16, 1908, the beloved Dr. Heath suddenly died. Farran Zerbe, then president, assumed the task of editing and publishing *The Numismatist,* and soon purchased the publication from Heath's heirs in a private deal, a transaction which was fraught with controversy, as many ANA members felt that the ANA, not Zerbe, should have been the buyer. By 1911 Zerbe, realizing that he could not turn a profit, decided to sell *The Numismatist*. A Canadian ANA member, W.W.C. Wilson, provided the money to give Zerbe what was described as "a long price," and to present the magazine to the ANA.

Over the years copies of *The Numismatist* have become collectors' items in their own right. Today it is believed that only about a dozen complete sets, from 1888 to date, exist. Particularly rare are issues of the 1888-1893 span.

Federal charter

On May 9, 1912, through the efforts of Rep. William A. Ashbrook of Ohio, an ANA member, the Association was granted a federal charter, signed by President Taft. Fifty years later in 1962 Congress granted permanent status to the ANA Charter.

From the early years onward, the ANA was managed by various officials, including, for a long span of years, General Secretary Lewis M. Reagan. Offices were maintained in cities in which officials lived, including Wichita, Baltimore, and Phoenix. An ANA national home and headquarters building fund was established in 1961, and by 1966 the ANA Headquarters, in Colorado Springs, Colorado, became a reality. Officially opened on June 10, 1967, the Headquarters building contained business offices, a library, a museum, and other facilities. In 1981 construction began on an addition to the facility, to accommodate the growth in staff size from about a dozen to 50. The ANA Museum was expanded to include seven galleries.

ANA services and programs

One of the first services, established in the early years for the benefit of its members, was a numismatic library. This library remained small and unpretentious for years, but gained in size with the growth of the membership. Today, housed at ANA Headquarters, it is the largest circulating numismatic library in the world, and comprises more than 10,000 hard-cover reference books and other library items which are loaned to members without charge, other than postage. In 1977 an entirely new sectionalized library catalog was published for members.

The Association, through a fund established by Robert P. King in 1927, deposited in the Smithsonian Institution in Washington, D.C., a collection of coins and medals. In the 1960s this collection, augmented by donations over the years, was moved to ANA Headquarters. Many gifts have been donated by members to the ANA Museum, representing collections consisting of coins, paper money and medallic art. Notable among the benefactors are Aubrey and Adeline Bebee, who donated a superb collection of paper money and a 1913 Liberty Head 5-cent piece, valued in the aggregate at over $2 million. Among the related facilities in the Headquarters building is the Amos Memorial Theater.

Coin Week, begun in the 1920s, is an annual event sponsored by the ANA, by which private collectors, clubs, and others mount public displays to promote coin collecting. From its beginning in 1950 the Edward T. Newell Visual Educational Program has grown to include nearly 80 illustrated programs, complete with narrative material.

Awards, prizes and medals

Numismatic displays have been outstanding attractions at ANA conventions since 1904. Thousands of numismatists, as well as curious non-collectors, have viewed these exhibits featuring famous collections and highly publicized rarities. Prizes for exhibits were inaugurated in the early 1940s. Competition for awards is spirited. First-place winners and runners-up in all classifications are presented with memorial award plaques or medals.

Numismatic literary awards were initiated in 1924. Articles published in *The Numismatist* are judged on their merits by an impartial committee. In 1949 the established award was renamed the "Heath Literary Award" through a suggestion by John Jay Pittman. Silver and bronze medals, along with cash awards, were presented from 1945 through 1954, with honorable mention certificates commencing in 1947. Cash awards were discontinued in 1955, but were resumed in 1973. Since their inception, more than 250 writers have received gold or bronze medals and/or cash awards for their superior efforts. Another literary honor, the annual Wayte and Olga Raymond Award, funded by John J. Ford, Jr., provides a cash stipend to the authors of outstanding research articles.

Two membership awards were established during the 1947 convention. A gold medal is presented to 50-year members of the association, and a silver medal is given to members who have completed 25 consecutive years of membership. Clubs that have completed 25 or 50 years of corporate membership in the ANA receive gold or silver certificates.

The beautiful silver Medal of Merit was first awarded in 1948 to members rendering outstanding service to the ANA and the science of numismatics. In 1950 the annual Farran Zerbe Award was instituted and first sponsored by Louis S. Werner. The award, the highest honor bestowed by the Association, is presented to a member for distinguished service to the ANA. The traditional plaque was replaced in 1984 with a two-inch 10-karat gold medallion.

In 1966 the ANA, in conjunction with the Franklin Mint, brought into existence the ANA Numismatic Art Award to pay tribute to talented sculptors.

The ANA Numismatic Hall of Fame was established Aug. 18, 1964, enshrines the names of famous numismatists. Portraits of Hall of Fame members are on view in a special display at ANA Headquarters.

Over a period of years many commemorative medals, membership medals, convention badges, and other medallic items have been issued by the ANA for distribution and sale to its members.

Education, achievements, and policies

The annual Educational Forums were formulated in 1946, moving the ANA closer to adequately fulfilling its credo as stated in the federal charter and constitution, "that the objectives of said corporation shall be to advance the knowledge of numismatics along educational, historical and scientific lines in all its various branches." Since then the Educational Forum has become increasingly important to the membership. Today it is a convention highlight showcasing the knowledge of many of the most accomplished numismatists of the United States and other countries.

A new official ANA movement began in 1965 with the establishment of the Young Numismatists Committee. Since its inception, the committee has worked hard to bring the junior movement into its own by sponsoring literary awards, service awards, exhibit awards and other beneficial achievement tributes to those who will, one day, carry on the hobby. In 1965 the ANA lowered the minimum membership age from 17 to 11 and the junior movement really sprang to life! The youth movement, championed by many adult members acting as advisers, now has developed a well-rounded program for the Young Numismatist at the annual convention and by publications distributed by mail.

By board action in 1965, the ANA Code of Ethics was established, and outlined principles of moral conduct that collectors and dealers are required to follow. Any breach of the code is considered cause for disciplinary action by the board.

The District Representatives Committee was established in 1967, through which appointed ANA representatives served the United States, Canada and Mexico through 18 districts. Today, there are 55 districts with one or more representatives (depending on the size of the area involved) for each of the 50 states, Canada, Mexico and certain foreign countries. Representatives promote good will for ANA, assist in resolving complaints and misunderstandings, visit ANA members at club meetings and conventions, provide information regarding all ANA services and, generally, act as a liaison between the membership and the ANA board.

In 1969, the ANA initiated the first Summer Seminar, since retitled the ANA Summer Conferences, now an annual numismatic educational opportunity conducted at Colorado Springs and elsewhere. The program provides instruction on various numismatic subjects and offers tours, food and lodging at a very nominal cost to students.

The ANA announced in February 1970 an all-risk coin insurance plan. The low-cost plan offers the member a broad coverage of theft and fire insurance for his collection.

ANACS

The inauguration, on June 22, 1972, of the ANA Certification Service, popularly known as ANACS, in Washington, D.C. launched one of the Association's most popular services. In 1977 ANACS was transferred to the Headquarters in Colorado Springs. ANACS became the world's first service designed specifically to give an authoritative answer as to the authenticity of numismatic material submitted by anyone, from any place in the world. Numismatic material is photographed and, if genuine, a certificate is issued to verify same. On March 1, 1979 ANACS began grading coins for a fee and issuing ANACS certificates stating opinion as to grade. Since its inception, the grading service has generated controversy. Some collectors and dealers defended the service as an impartial answer to sometimes erroneous grading in the marketplace. Others claimed ANACS grading was inconsistent. In the meantime, A. Kosoff, Kenneth E. Bressett, and Q. David Bowers wrote *Official ANA Grading Standards for United States Coins,* which utilized the numerical grading system and went on to be published in three editions.

[As this Almanac was going to press, the American Numismatic Association had arrange to sell the grading service to Amos Press Inc., Sidney, Ohio, for $1.5 million plus royalties. Under terms of the agreement, the ANA retains the right to authenticate coins, and retains copyright to the *Official ANA Grading Standards for United States Coins.* The grading service was to be relocated out of ANA headquarters by July 31, 1990.

It was the Board's decision that a non-profit organization could not reasonable operate a profit-making enterprise such as ANACS. The decision was made, therefore, to sell the service and concentrate on education and consumer protection.]

Membership information

The ANA and its home and headquarters have other services available to the membership, such as free certificate awards for speakers and exhibitors at functions of member clubs, and ribbons for coin show awards; the latter services provided at approximate cost.

ANA's doors have opened to such a roster of famed people that it would be impossible to name all of them. Wealthy numismatic scholars and collectors, millionaire industrialists, government officials, famous numismatists, stars of the entertainment and music world, philanthropists and kings have graced its membership roll. Authors, painters, sculptors, composers, doctors, clergymen, people from the four corners of the world, rich and poor, young and old, through their interest and devotion to its cause, brought ANA thus far, and made it the largest numismatic organization on earth. Its span of life is short in the march of time, but filled with many accomplishments.

The ANA will accept for membership all worthy persons who have an interest in the collecting and study of coins, paper money, tokens, medals or related items. With each membership comes a subscription to *The Numismatist,* published monthly.

For more information, including current

fees, write: American Numismatic Association, 818 N. Cascade Ave., Colorado Springs, Colo. 80903.

Centennial celebration

As 1991, the centennial year of the American Numismatic Association, approached, plans were made for a gala convention to be held in August 1991 in Chicago, the city in which the ANA held its first organizational meeting a century earlier. The 1991 Club, whose membership is open to all interested ANA members, has planned over a dozen different events, and the ANA itself has promised the largest, most memorable convention ever.

In connection with the celebration, two reference books will be published: *The ANA Centennial History*, by Q. David Bowers, will be approximately 1,000 pages in size and will tell of the growth of the ANA and of the numismatic hobby; and *The ANA Anthology*, edited by ANA Historian Carl W. Carlson, will feature research articles contributed by over two dozen prominent numismatic historians. Special badges and medals will also be issued.

As the ANA looks toward its second century, Executive Director Robert Leuver, the Board of Governors, and all associated with the ANA envision a new era of membership growth, expanded services, and numismatic prominence for an organization which now numbers over 30,000 individual members worldwide.

ANA presidents, 1891-1985

William G. Jerrems	1891	Martin F. Kortjohn	1943
George F. Heath	1892	V. Leon Belt	1945
A.G. Heaton	1894	Loyd B. Gettys	1947
Joseph Hooper	1898	M. Vernon Sheldon	1949
B.P. Wright	1901	Joseph Moss	1951
Albert .R. Frey	1904	J. Hewitt Judd	1953
Farran Zerbe	1907	Leonel C. Panosh	1955
J.M. Henderson	1909	Oscar H. Dodson	1957
Judson Brenner	1911	C.C. Shroyer	1961
Frank G. Duffield	1913	P.K. Anderson	1963
H.O. Granberg	1915	Matt Rothert	1965
Carl Wurtzbach	1917	Arthur Sipe	1967
Waldo C. Moore	1919	Herbert M. Bergen	1969
Moritz Wormser	1921	John J. Pittman	1971
Harry H. Yawger	1926	Virginia Culver	1973
Charles Markus	1927	Virgil Hancock	1975
George J. Bauer	1930	Grover C. Criswell	1977
Alden Scott Boyer	1932	George D. Hatie	1979
Nelson T. Thorson	1933	Adna G. Wilde	1981
T. James Clarke	1935	Q. David Bowers	1983
J. Henri Ripstra	1937	Florence M. Schook	1985
L.W. Hoffecker	1939	Stephen R. Taylor	1987
J. Douglas Ferguson	1941	Kenneth L. Hallenbeck	1989

ANA board chairmen
(Office discontinued in 1937)

B.P. Wright	1907	Carl Wurtzbach	1916
Howland Wood	1908	Waldo Moore	1917-18
William F. Dunham	1909	Moritz Wormser	1919-20
H.O. Granberg	1910-1914	H.H. Yawger	1921-1925
Judson Brenner	1915	Charles Markus	1926

Harry W. Rapp	1927	Harley L. Freeman	1933-34
Farran Zerbe	1928	Henry Hunt	1935
Nelson Thorson	1929-1932	T. James Clarke	1936

Editors of *The Numismatist*

The Numismatist is the official publication of the American Numismatic Association. It was first published in September, 1888.

George F. Heath	1888-1908	Elston G. Bradfield	1954-1966
Farran Zerbe	1909-1910	Glenn B. Smedley	1966-1967
Albert Frey	1911-1912	Edward Rochette	1967-1972
Edgar H. Adams	1912-1915	Thomas Marshall	1972-1973
Frank G. Duffield	1915-1942	Edward Rochette	1973-1974
Lee F. Hewitt	1942-1943	N. Neil Harris	1974-1988
Burton H. Saxton	1943-1944	Barbara Gregory	1988-
Stuart Mosher	1945-1954		

National Coin Week

To the Editor of The Numismatist:

It is my opinion that it would be a very good plan to have a "Coin Week" each year. My idea is to have, say, the first week in February set aside as "Coin Week," and I think the dealers throughout the country should form an association, which could obtain funds to carry on an extensive, nationwide advertising campaign in magazines, newspapers, etc., during that week. Dealers and collectors alike would be stimulated, and instead of interesting and starting one collector here and there we would find new collectors by the hundred. In fact, I think such a "drive" would mean a new era for numismatics.

—— Julius Guttag
The Numismatist, November 1923

National Coin Week has been sponsored by the American Numismatic Association since 1924. Its purpose is to bring numismatics to the attention of the general public and to win new coin collecting devotees.

National Coin Week aims to advance the cultural and artistic aspects of coin collecting, to advance the enjoyment of the hobby through proper education and to advance interest in coin collecting as a science. In 1974 it was acclaimed by Presidential proclamation.

Julius Guttag founded the annual effort in 1924 and served as the first chairman. Other National Coin Week chairmen include:

Date	Theme	Chairman
Feb. 9-16, 1924	Coin Week	Julius Guttag
Feb. 15-21, 1925	Coin Week	Moritz Wormser
Feb. 14-21, 1926	Coin Week	H.H. Yawger
Feb. 14-21, 1927	Coin Week	H.H. Yawger
1928-38	Not held	—
March 25-31, 1939	Make America Coin Conscious	Ted Hammer
March 30-April 6, 1940	National Coin Week	David N. Bullowa
March 23-29, 1941	National Coin Week	Various regional chairmen
April 19-25, 1942	National Coin Week	Ted Hammer
April 11-17, 1943	National Coin Week	Lewis M. Reagan
April 16-22, 1944	Sesquicentennial of the Silver Dollar	Charles P. Knoth
April 21-29, 1945	Sesquicentennial of the Eagle & Half Eagle, Our First Gold Coins	Richard S. Yeoman
April 7-13, 1946	National Coin Week	Lillard W. Culver

Date	Theme	Chairperson
March 23-29, 1947	Colonial Currency & Postage Currency Including Encased Postage Stamps	Henry Schuhmacher
April 11-17, 1948	National Coin Week	Charles Wormser
April 22-28, 1949	National Coin Week	Abe Kosoff
April 14-21, 1950	U.S. Dollars	Harry X Boosel
April 20-26, 1951	Numismatics of American History	James W. Curtis
April 18-24, 1952	Coins, Tokens & Currency of the Colonies	F. Stevens Epps
April 17-23, 1953	Coins of Historical Significance	E. Ward Russell
April 26-May 2, 1954	Universal Numismatics With Particular Emphasis On the Coins, Currency and Medals of the UN	Don Sherer
April 23-29, 1955	Coins of the Americas	I.T. Kopicki
April 16-22, 1956	Pennies of the World	Peter B. Payne
May 6-12, 1957	Collecting Coins For Fun & Profit	Gene N. Nichols
April 21-27, 1958	Around the World With Coins	Leo G. Terry
April 12-18, 1959	Portrayal of Lincoln Through Numismatics, 1809-1959	Wilma Dean Roethke
April 24-30, 1960	Why It Pays to Be a Numismatist	E.I. "Jack" Rand
April 23-30, 1961	Coins & Currency of Yesteryears	Dolly-Maude Harris
April 28-May 6, 1962	Coinage of Nations	Dolly-Maude Harris
April 27-May 4, 1963	Education Through Numismatics	Jack R. Koch
April 18-26, 1964	Art On Coins	Jack R. Koch
April 24-May 1, 1965	Good Will Through Numismatics	Lois R. Otis
April 16-23, 1966	Friendships Flower Through Numismatics	Lois R. Otis
April 22-29, 1967	Numismatics, Portrait of History	Rick and Virginia Bronson
April 21-27, 1968	History Under Glass	Clark A. Yowell
April 20-26, 1969	Coins — Links In a Chain of Peace	Edward C. Rochette
April 19-25, 1970	Coins — Heralds of a Great Nation	Edward C. Rochette
April 19-24, 1971	Numismatics — The Hobby of All Ages	Lee Martin
April 16-22, 1972	Coins Are Forever	Edward C. Rochette
April 14-21, 1973	Money Talks	John Watson
April 21-27, 1974	History In Your Hands	Maurice M. Gould
April 20-26, 1975	Monuments In Miniature	Maurice M. Gould
April 18-24, 1976	In the Spirit of '76	F. Morton Reed
April 17-23, 1977	Coins Are History	F. Morton Reed
April 16-22, 1978	Happiness Is ... Coin Collecting	F. Morton Reed
April 15-21, 1979	Numismatics — A Study of Man's Roots	ANA staff
April 13-19, 1980	Numismatics — More Than A Lot of Bullion	ANA staff
April 19-25, 1981	An Enduring Reflection of Man	Gary Lewis
April 18-24, 1982	Numismatics — A High Road to Adventure	Leslie A. Winners
April 17-23, 1983	Exploring Our Proud Heritage	Leslie A. Winners
April 15-21, 1984	Numismatics: A Foundation For Friendship	Nancy W. Green
April 21-27, 1985	Numismatics: Open the Door With Books	Nancy W. Green
April 20-26, 1986	Coin Collecting — Family Fun	Nancy W. Green
April 19-25, 1987	Currency Worth Noting	Nancy W. Green
April 17-23, 1988	Windows On the World	Nancy W. Green
April 16-22, 1989	Money Matters	Nancy W. Green
April 15-21, 1990	Cointinuum	— —
April 21-27, 1991		

* Beginning in 1939 called National Coin Week
Special thanks to Nancy Green, ANA Librarian, for her assistance

ANA convention sites

Location	Date Held
Chicago, Ill.	Oct. 7, 1891
Pittsburgh, Pa.	Oct. 1, 1892
Douglas Hall, Chicago, Ill.	Aug. 21, 1893
Detroit Museum of Art	
Detroit, Mich.	Aug. 23-24, 1894
Art Parlors of B. H. Collins	
Washington, D.C.	Sept. 19-20, 1895
Office of Dr. B. P. Wright	
Buffalo, N.Y.	Aug. 22, 1901
Congress Hall, World's Fair Grounds	
St. Louis, Mo.	Oct. 15, 1904
Neil House,	
Columbus, Ohio	Sept. 2-4, 1907
Hotel Stenton	
Philadelphia, Pa.	Sept. 28-Oct. 2, 1908
St. Lawrence Hall Hotel	
Montreal, Canada	Aug. 9-14, 1909
American Numismatic Society Bldg.	
New York, N.Y.	Sept. 6-10, 1910
Art Institute	
Chicago, Ill.	Aug. 28-31, 1911
Hotel Rochester	
Rochester, N.Y.	Aug. 26-28, 1912
Detroit Museum of Art	
Detroit, Mich.	Aug. 23-27, 1913
Springfield Group Auditorium	
Springfield, Mass.	Aug. 22-26, 1914
Hotel Stewart	
San Francisco	Aug. 30-Sept. 1, 1915
Peabody Institute	
Baltimore, Md.	Sept. 23-27, 1916
Memorial Art Gallery	
Rochester, N.Y.	Aug. 25-29, 1917
Academy of Fine Arts	
Philadelphia, Pa.	Oct. 4-8, 1919
Art Institute	
Chicago, Ill.	Aug. 23-26, 1920
Boston Public Library	
Boston, Mass.	Aug. 20-25, 1921
American Fine Arts Society Bldg.	
New York, N.Y.	Aug. 26-31, 1922
Chateau de Ramezay	
Montreal, Quebec	Aug. 25-30, 1923
Hollenden Hotel	
Cleveland, Ohio	Aug. 23-28, 1924
Hotel Statler	
Detroit, Mich.	Aug. 21-27, 1925
Hotel Washington	
Washington, D.C.	Aug. 21-26, 1926
Supreme Court, State Library Bldg.	
Hartford, Conn.	Aug. 20-25, 1927
Hotel Seneca	
Rochester, N.Y.	Aug. 18-23, 1928
Congress Hotel	
Chicago, Ill.	Aug. 24-29, 1929
Hotel Statler	
Buffalo, N.Y.	Aug. 23-28, 1930
Netherland Plaza Hotel	
Cincinnati, Ohio	Aug. 29-Sept. 3, 1931
Hotel Biltmore	
Los Angeles, Calif.	Aug. 20-26, 1932
Congress Hotel	
Chicago, Ill.	Aug. 26-31, 1933
Carter Hotel	
Cleveland, Ohio	Aug. 18-23, 1934
Carnegie Institute	
Pittsburgh, Pa.	Aug. 24-29, 1935
Nicollet Hotel	
Minneapolis, Minn.	Aug. 22-27, 1936
Hotel Washington	
Washington, D.C.	Aug. 21-26, 1937
Neil House	
Columbus, Ohio	Aug. 13-18, 1938
Hotel Pennsylvania	
New York, N.Y.	Sept. 31-Oct. 5, 1939
Detroit-Leland Hotel	
Detroit, Mich.	Aug. 24-29, 1940
Benjamin Franklin Hotel	
Philadelphia, Pa.	Aug. 18-21, 1941
Netherland Plaza Hotel	
Cincinnati, Ohio	Aug. 24-26, 1942
LaSalle Hotel	
Chicago, Ill.	Sept. 11-13, 1943
LaSalle Hotel	
Chicago, Ill.	Aug. 27-28, 1944
Blackhawk Hotel	
Davenport, Iowa	Aug. 17-21, 1946
Statler Hotel	
Buffalo, N.Y.	Aug. 23-27, 1947
Copley-Plaza Hotel	
Boston, Mass.	Aug. 21-25, 1948
Palace Hotel	
San Francisco, Calif.	Aug. 23-27, 1949
Schroeder Hotel	
Milwaukee, Wis.	Aug. 25-29, 1950
Westward Ho Hotel	
Phoenix, Ariz.	Aug. 25-28, 1951
Hotel Statler	
New York, N.Y.	Aug. 16-20, 1952

Baker Hotel
Dallas, Texas .... Aug. 22-26, 1953
Carter Hotel
Cleveland, Ohio .... Aug. 17-21, 1954
Hotel Fontenelle
Omaha, Neb................ Aug. 24-27, 1955
Congress Hotel
Chicago, Ill. .... Aug. 22-25, 1956
Sheraton Hotel
Philadelphia, Pa. .... Aug. 21-24, 1957
Statler-Hilton Hotel
Los Angeles, Calif. ...... Aug. 13-16, 1958
Multnomah Hotel
Portland, Ore................ Aug. 26-29, 1959
Statler-Hilton Hotel
Boston, Mass. ....Aug. 24-27, 1960
Atlanta-Biltmore Hotel
Atlanta, Ga.................. Aug. 16-19, 1961
Sheraton-Cadillac Hotel
Detroit, Mich. ....Aug. 15-18, 1962
Hilton Hotel
Denver, Colo................. Aug. 7-10, 1963
Sheraton Hotel
Cleveland, Ohio .... Aug. 19-22, 1964
Shamrock-Hilton Hotel
Houston, Texas............. Aug. 25-28, 1965
Pick-Congress Hotel
Chicago, Ill. .... Aug. 16-20, 1966
Americana Hotel
Miami Beach, Fla. .... Aug. 8-12, 1967
El Cortez Hotel
San Diego, Calif. ....Aug. 20-25, 1968
Sheraton Hotel
Philadelphia, Pa. .... Aug. 12-16, 1969
Chase Park Plaza Hotel
St. Louis, Mo. .... Aug. 18-22, 1970
Statler-Hilton Hotel
Washington, D.C. .... Aug. 10-14, 1971
Jung Hotel
New Orleans, La...........Aug. 15-19, 1972
Sheraton-Boston Hotel
Boston, Mass. ....Aug. 23-27, 1973
Americana Hotel

Miami Beach, Fla. .... Aug. 13-18, 1974
Marriott Hotel
Los Angeles, Calif. ...... Aug. 19-24, 1975
Americana Hotel
New York, N.Y. .... Aug. 24-29, 1976
Atlanta Marriott Hotel
Atlanta, Ga. .... Aug. 23-28, 1977
Astro-World Hotels
Houston, Texas.............Aug. 22-27, 1978
Chase Park-Plaza Hotel
St. Louis, Mo............... Aug. 14-19, 1979
Stouffer's Cincinnati Towers
Cincinnati, Ohio .... Aug. 19-24, 1980
Hilton Hotel
New Orleans, La.....July 28-Aug. 2, 1981
Sheraton-Boston Hotel
Boston, Mass................Aug. 16-21, 1982
Town & Country Hotel
San Diego, Calif. ....Aug. 15-20, 1983
Westin Hotel/Cobo Hall Convention
Center
Detroit, Mich. .... July 28-Aug. 1, 1984
Baltimore Convention Center
Baltimore, Md. ....Aug. 20-25, 1985
Milwaukee Exposition & Convention
Center & Arena
Milwaukee, Wis. .... Aug. 6-10, 1986
Georgia World Congress Center
Atlanta, Ga. .... Aug. 26-30, 1987
Convention Center
Cincinnati, Ohio .... July 20-24, 1988
Pittsburgh, Pa. .... Aug. 5-9, 1989
Seattle, Wash................ Aug. 22-26, 1990
Chicago, Ill. .... Aug. 13-18, 1991
Orlando, Fla................. Aug. 12-16, 1992
Baltimore, Md. ....July 28-Aug. 1, 1993
Detroit, Mich.................July 27-31, 1994
Anaheim, Calif. .... July 26-30, 1995
Denver, Colo. .... Aug. 14-18, 1996
New York, N.Y. .... July 23-27, 1997
TBA.. 1998
Chicago, Ill. .... Aug. 11-15, 1999

ANA Midwinter convention sites

Broadmoor Hotel
Colorado Springs, Colo. Feb. 15-18, 1978
Albuquerque Inn
Albuquerque, N.M. .... Feb. 15-17, 1980
Hilton Hawaiian Village
Honolulu, Hawaii .... Feb. 5-8, 1981
Broadmoor Hotel

Colorado Springs, Colo. Feb. 18-21, 1982
Marriott Hotel
Tucson, Ariz..................Feb. 24-27, 1983
Broadmoor Hotel
Colorado Springs, Colo. Feb. 22-26, 1984
Marriott Hotel,
San Antonio, Texas ....Feb. 21-24, 1985

Salt Palace Convention Center
Salt Lake City, Utah..... Feb. 20-22, 1986
Charlotte Convention Center
Charlotte, N.C. ....Feb. 27-March 1, 1987
Statehouse Convention Center
Little Rock, Ark. .... March 11-13, 1988

Broadmoor Hotel
Colorado Springs, Colo. March 3-5, 1989
Town and Country Inn
San Diego, Calif. .... March 2-4, 1990
Dallas, Texas................. March 1-3, 1991
Dallas, Texas .... March 6-8, 1992

The Farran Zerbe Award

The Farran Zerbe Memorial Award, highest American Numismatic Association honor, was established by Louis S. Werner of New York, a close friend of Zerbe. Zerbe was at one time the owner and editor of The Numismatist; he was often referred to as the dean of American numismatics. Zerbe served two terms as president of the American Numismatic Association. He died Dec. 25, 1949, at the age of 78.

The recipient of the Zerbe award each year is selected by the awards committee and approved by the board of governors of the ANA as one considered to have rendered the association distinguished service and to be worthy of the highest honor it can bestow. The traditional plaque was replaced in 1984 by a 2-inch, 10-karat gold medal.

M. Vernon Sheldon	1951	Abe Kosoff	1972
June T. Pond	1952	Matt Rothert	1973
Joseph Moss	1953	Herbert M. Bergen	1974
Lewis M. Reagan	1954	Margo Russell	1975
J. Hewitt Judd	1955	Maurice M. Gould (posthumous)	1976
Richard S. Yeoman	1956	Fred Bowman	1976
Burton H. Saxton	1958	Chester Krause	1977
Louis S. Werner	1959	William Henderson	1978
Glenn B. Smedley	1960	John J. Gabarron	1979
John F. Lhotka Jr.	1961	John J. Pittman	1980
Lee F. Hewitt	1962	Virgil Hancock	1981
Elston G. Bradfield	1963	George D. Hatie	1982
Jack W. Ogilvie	1964	Clyde Hubbard	1983
Leonel C. Panosh	1965	Clifford Mishler	1984
J. Douglas Ferguson	1966	Adna G. Wilde Jr.	1985
John S. Davenport	1967	Charles H. Wolfe	1986
Oscar H. Dodson	1968	Edward C. Rochette	1987
Eric P. Newman	1969	Virginia Culver (psthumous)	1987
Charles M. Johnson	1970	Aubrey and Adeline Bebee	1988
Don Sherer	1971	Harry X Boosel	1989

Heath Literary Awards

Heath Literary Awards were established in 1945 while V. Leon Belt was president of the American Numismatic Association. Each year, all papers published in The Numismatist are judged on their merits by an impartial committee. First, second and third place medals are presented with as many as five honorable mention awards possible. Winners of the silver medals since 1945:

Philip H. Chase	1945	Lt. Sheridan L. McGarry	1950
James J. Curto	1946	Wm. A. Philpott, Jr.	1951
Philip H. Chase	1947	Stanley J. Schillinger	1952
William H. Dillistin	1948	Richard T. Hoober	1953
H.A. Seaby	1949	Col. Phares O. Sigler	1954

Dr. John F. Lhotka........................ 1955
Loyd B. Gettys and E.M. Catich...... 1956
Melvin and George Fuld......... 1957-1958
Eric P. Newman............................ 1959
Helen Woodburn.......................... 1960
Philip Chase................................ 1961
Ted Weissbuch............................ 1961
James Risk.................................. 1962
David F. Spink............................. 1962
Alan B. Shaw...............................'1963
Ernest Weidhaas.......................... 1963
Eric P. Newman............................ 1964
George Fuld................................. 1964
John F. Lhotka Jr.......................... 1965
Eric P. Newman.................... 1965-1966
Miguel L. Munoz.......................... 1966
Thomas Becker............................. 1967
Philip Chase................................ 1968
Randolph Zander........................... 1968
John D. Wright.............................. 1969
John S. Davenport......................... 1969
Ray Byrne................................... 1970
Miguel L. Munoz.......................... 1970

Phares Sigler............................... 1971
Walter J. Zimmerman...................... 1972
Ray Byrne................................... 1973
David R. Cervin............................ 1974
Thomas P. Rockwell....................... 1975
William G. Anderson...................... 1976
Miguel Munoz 1977-1978
Eric P. Newman............................ 1979
Peter Gaspar................................ 1979
David McBride.............................. 1980
Eric Newman................................ 1980
John Isted................................... 1980
Tom DeLorey................................ 1981
Thomas Schweich........................... 1982
R.W. Julian................................. 1983
Carl W.A. Carlson.......................... 1983
David & Charlotte Gale................... 1984
Henry Schab................................. 1985
David & Charlotte Gale................... 1986
N. Neil Harris............................. 1987
George E. Ewing Jr........................ 1988
Douglas B. MacDonald 1989

Wayte and Olga Raymond Literary Awards

The Wayte and Olga Raymond Literary award is for distinguished numismatic achievement in the field of United States numismatics.

Gerome Walton 1978
Adna G. Wilde Jr........................... 1979
Eric P. Newman............................. 1979
David P. McBride........................... 1980
Thomas K. DeLorey........................ 1981
Thomas Schweich........................... 1982
Kirk Hillman............................... 1982
Anthony Swiatek........................... 1982
Jeanne Madeline Weinmann............. 1982
Ronald J. Guth.............................. 1983

Eric P. Newman............................. 1984
Glenn B. Smedley........................... 1984
Henry Schab................................. 1985
David & Charlotte Gale................... 1985
William D. Hyder & R.W. Colbert. 1986
Thomas K. DeLorey........................ 1986
Herbert P. Hicks........................... 1987
R.W. Julian................................. 1988
William S. Dewey & O.L. Wallis.... 1989

Winners of ANA Medal of Merit

The ANA Medal of Merit is one of the highest awards of the ANA, and is reserved for "those who have shown outstanding devotion to numismatics, the organization and its goals." The medals are given each year in ceremonies at the ANA Convention.

Medals of Merit are always accompanied by special citations which describe in detail the contributions made by the recipient to the American Numismatic Association.

The Grecian-styled medal, approximately two and one-eighths inches in diameter, bears a Greek warrior on the obverse, and on the reverse, a goddess-driven biga ascending a panel on which the recipient's name is engraved.

J. Douglas Ferguson 1947
Martin Kortjohn............................ 1947

Joseph Moss................................. 1947
Max M. Schwartz 1947

Louis S. Werner	1948	Arthur Sipe	1962
Damon G. Douglas	1949	George M. Todd	1962
C.H. Ryan	1949	Dolly-Maude Harris	1962
M. Vernon Sheldon	1949	John J. Pittman	1962
J. Hewitt Judd	1949	Robert G. McArthur	1962
Lewis M. Reagan	1949	Sol Kaplan	1962
Julius Windner	1949	Melvin Fuld	1962
George H. Blake	1950	S.W. Freeman	1963
Floyd B. Newell	1950	John W. Dunn	1964
Lee F. Hewitt	1950	Richard T. Hoober	1964
Ted R. Hammer	1950	Ralph C. Mitchell	1964
Oscar H. Dodson	1950	Eric P. Newman	1964
Burton H. Saxton	1950	William A. Philpott	1965
T.O. Mabbott	1950	Dan Brown	1965
Charles L. Ruby	1950	Doris Martin	1966
Charles F. Nettleship	1950	Michael M. Dolnick	1966
Lawrence Lee Howe	1950	Julian Blancherd	1966
Loyd B. Gettys	1951	Chester Krause	1967
Vernon L. Brown	1951	Al Overton	1967
V. Leon Belt	1952	Margo Russell	1967
Marcella L. Sheldon	1952	Lois Otis	1968
William Sheldon	1952	Charles R. Hoskins	1968
Richard Yeoman	1952	Harley Freeman	1968
Stuart Mosher	1953	Aubrey Bebee	1968
Jack W. Ogilvie	1953	Byrnadette Gabarron	1969
Glenn B. Smedley	1953	Jake B. Sureck	1969
Marjorie L. Williams	1953	Albert F. Pradeau	1969
Ernst Kraus	1954	Henry Grunthal	1970
Harold R. Klein	1954	Maurice M. Gould	1970
John S. Davenport	1955	Ray Byrne	1971
Edward Fogler	1955	Sheldon S. Carroll	1971
Leonel C. Panosh	1955	William C. Henderson	1971
Michael A. Powills	1955	Vir Den Mayo	1971
Earl C. Brown	1956	Edward C. Rochette	1972
James W. Curtis	1956	Herbert M. Bergen	1972
John J. Gabarron	1956	Herbert W. Price	1972
Elston G. Bradfield	1957	Charles M. Johnson	1973
August F. Hausske	1957	Geneva Karlson	1973
D. Dee DeNise	1957	Evie Kelley	1973
James J. Curto	1958	Genevieve Herdegen	1974
P.K. Anderson	1958	Ellis Edlow	1974
Abe Kosoff	1958	Joseph M. Segel	1974
A.H. Leatherman	1958	Valentine Pasvolsky	1975
John F. Lhotka	1959	Pat Suthers, posthumously	1975
C.C. Shroyer	1959	Clyde Hubbard	1976
P.O. Sigler	1959	Florence Schook	1976
Leo G. Terry	1960	Robert E. Medlar	1977
Don Sherer	1960	Rev. Arthur Braddan Coole	1977
Matt Rothert	1960	Frank & Laurese Katen	1978
George T. Fuld	1961	Ruthann Brettell	1978
William N. Worth	1961	Paul Whitnah	1978
Earl C. Schill	1961	Kenneth Bressett	1978

Miguel Munoz	1979	Eva B. Adams	1984
Col. Robert Kriz	1979	Frank Annunzio	1985
James Miller	1979	Cheryl & Robert Maisch	1985
Eldridge Jones	1980	Roy Pennell	1985
Henry Spangenberger	1980	Harry X Boosel	1986
N. Neil Harris	1980	Robert & Marjorie Hendershott	1986
Ralph Cleaver	1981	John A. Muscalus	1986
Virginia Culver	1981	Joseph & Mae Clarke	1987
Charles Wolfe	1981	Opal & John Morris	1987
Margaret Lloyd	1982	Purnie Moore	1987
Betty Higby	1982	Q. David Bowers	1987
John Smies	1982	Dorothy & Albert Baber	1988
Ben Stack	1982	Elizabeth & William Wisslead	1988
Harvey Stack	1982	Mary Brooks	1988
Norman Stack	1982	Morris Bram	1988
Gene Hynds	1983	Royal Canadian Mint	1989
Clifford Mishler	1983	Harry Bass	1989
Austin M. Sheehen Jr	1983	Julius Reiver	1989
Arthur M. Kagin	1983	Paul Koppenhaver	1989
David R. Cervin	1984	Bill Fivaz	1989
Bill Fivaz	1984		

Howland Wood Award winners

The Howland Wood Grand Award for "The Best in Show" is presented at the annual convention of the ANA. A proposal and resolution for the exhibit medal award program was introduced at the 1949 convention in San Francisco. It was continued at the 1950 Milwaukee gathering and established at the 1951 Phoenix convention.

Richard S. Yeoman	1951	Margaret Frantz	1970
Dr. J. Hewitt Judd	1952	David R. Cervin	1971
William A. Philpott Jr	1953	Lt. Col. Frank O'Sullivan	1972
New York Orders & Medals Soc.	1954	Ray Byrne	1973
Burton H. Saxton	1955	Emil Voigt	1974
R.F. Schermerhorn	1956	Peter E. Brander	1975
Amon G. Carter Jr	1957	Dr. C. Radford Stearns	1976
August F. Hausske	1958	Maurice M. Burgett	1977
C.L. Liss	1959	Stephen Taylor	1978 & 1979
Mrs. James Nestor	1960	Jean Bullen	1980
R.E. Cox Jr	1961	Jack Huggins	1981
Gaston Di Bello	1962	Denis Loring	1982
Julius Turoff	1963	F.M. Rose	1983
Fred R. Marckhoff	1964	Nancy Wilson	1984
Robert E. Medlar	1965	Robert F. Kriz	1985
George L. Podlusky	1966	Jean Bullen	1986
Julio M. Ruiz	1967	R.W. Colbert	1987
Opal H. Morris	1968	William Spengler	1988
Lelan G. Rogers	1969	John Page	1989

ANA Numismatic Art Award for Excellence in Medallic Sculpture

The ANA Numismatic Art Award for Excellence in Medallic Sculpture, popularly known as the Outstanding Sculptor of the Year Award, was brought into existence in 1966 by the ANA, in conjunction with the Franklin Mint. The large gold medal award is presented annually to pay tribute to talented sculptors.

Paul Vincze	1966	Miko Kaufman	1978
Gilroy Roberts	1967	Donald De Lue	1979
Frank Gasparro	1968	Bruno Mankowski	1980
Edward R. Grove	1969	Joseph Kiselewski	1981
C. Paul Jennewein	1970	Adlai S. Hardin	1982
Ralph Menconi	1971	Not Awarded	1983
Elizabeth Jones	1972	Anthony Jones	1984
Gertrude Lathrop	1973	Phillip Nathan	1985
Abram Belskie	1974	Not Awarded	1986
Robert Weinman	1975	Marcel Jovine	1987
Adolph Block	1976	John Cook	1988
Karen Worth	1977	Marika Somogyi	1989

Members of ANA Hall of Fame

The ANA Hall of Fame is open to "persons whose contributions to the field of numismatics have been of the highest excellence and most outstanding." Nominations are accepted between October and December of the year preceding the year of award, and may be made by any ANA member except junior members. Members and the year in which they were inducted:

Edgar H. Adams	1969	B. Max Mehl	1974
George J. Bauer	1969	Howard Rounds Newcomb	1974
Frank G. Duffield	1969	William A. Philpott, Jr.	1974
George F. Heath	1969	Dr. Benjamin P. Wright	1974
Edward T. Newell	1969	Frederick Boyd	1978
Wayte Raymond	1969	Victor Brenner	1978
David C. Wismer	1969	Lee Hewitt	1978
Howland Wood	1969	J. Ripstra	1978
Farran Zerbe	1969	David Bullowa	1978
George H. Blake	1970	Richard Yeoman	1978
Henry Chapman	1970	Herbert Bergen	1982
Sylvester S. Crosby	1970	Abe Kosoff	1982
Lewis M. Reagan	1970	Glenn B. Smedley	1982
Moritz Wormser	1970	Elston G. Bradfield	1982
Olie P. Eklund	1972	J. Douglas Ferguson	1982
Albert Frey	1972	Robert Wallace McLachlan	1982
Barclay P. Head	1972	Louis S. Werner	1982
John M. Henderson	1972	Sheldon S. Carroll	1984
Lyman H. Low	1972	William T.R. Marvin	1984
Waldo C. Moore	1972	Leonel Panosh	1984
Stuart Mosher	1972	Norman Schultz	1984
Burton H. Saxton	1972	Eva B. Adams	1986
Agnes Baldwin Brett	1974	S.W. Freeman	1986
Capt. John W. Haseltine	1974	Robert Friedberg	1986
Joseph Hooper	1974	Eric P. Newman	1986

Margo Russell...................................... 1986   Maurice M. Gould........................... 1988
John S. Davenport............................. 1988   M. Vernon Sheldon 1988

Young Numismatist awards

Thirteen awards in connection with the Young Numismatist program are offered yearly. These awards are given by the Association, other organizations and individuals interested in encouraging the participation of young collectors in the hobby. The 13 awards are designated as follows:

(1) The Abe Kosoff Memorial Literary Award
(2) The Gould Memorial Literary Award
(3) The Ray Byrne Memorial Literary Award
(4) The Florence Schook Outstanding Young Numismatist Award
(5) The Outstanding Adult Leader or Advisor Award — anonymous
(6) The Charles H. Wolfe Class C (YN) Convention Exhibit Award
(7) The Gordon Z. Greene Memorial U.S. Exhibit Award
(8) The James L. Betton Foreign Exhibit Award
(9) The Kurt Krueger Paper Money Exhibit Award
(10) The Melissa Van Grover Israel or Judiac Exhibit Award
(11) The Arlie Slabaugh Medals and Tokens Exhibit Award
(12) The Charles E. Wolfe Medieval and Ancient Exhibit Award
(13) The Alan Herbert Error/Variety Exhibit Award.

Fédération Internationale de la Médaille

Lars O. Lagerqvist.. President
Mariangela Johnson Pasqualetti... General Secretary

History and functions

The International Medal Federation (Fédération Internationale de la Médaille or FIDEM) was founded in the 1930s as an organization representing the major producers of commemorative medals. In the succeeding decades, the scope has been enlarged to emphasize the activity of sculptors and collectors, and the main focus is on the art of the medal.

The principal activity of FIDEM is the organization of an international congress and exhibition, usually every two years. At the congress, lectures and workshops explore the aesthetic, production and history of the medal. The exhibitions feature thousands of medals by artists from dozens of member countries; each country's exhibition is selected by its own delegation.

The membership of FIDEM is organized by participating countries, with each country having an official delegate, which may be an individual or group, responsible for organizing the participation of that country in the congresses and exhibitions.

The central government of FIDEM comprises a president, two vice presidents and several additional members as well as the secretary-general and treasurer, who are the principal executive officers. All officers are elected in the General Assemblies held at the congresses.

FIDEM publishes a journal, *Médailles*, which publishes the texts of presentations at the congresses, and supports and distributes the magazine *The Medal*, published four times a year. Membership in FIDEM is open to individual artists, collectors, scholars and producers, as well as institutions and firms.

For convenience in currency transactions, membership fees for Americans and Canadians are collected in U.S. dollars by the American Medallic Sculpture Association.

For more information about FIDEM membership, contact the United States delegate to FIDEM, Dr. Alan M. Stahl, The American Numismatic Society,

Broadway and 155th Street, New York,   N.Y. 10032; telephone (212) 234-3130.

FIDEM Congress sites

1937	Paris	1969	Prague
1939	Liége	1971	Cologne
1949	Paris	1973	Helsinki
1951	Madrid	1975	Crakow
1953	Rome	1977	Budapest
1955	Stockholm	1979	Lisbon
1957	Paris	1983	Florence
1959	Vienna	1985	Stockholm
1961	Rome	1987	Colorado Springs
1963	The Hague	1990	Helsinki
1966	Athens	1992	London
1967	Paris		

Professional Numismatists Guild
P.O. Box 430, Van Nuys, Calif. 91408; Phone (818) 781-1764

Officers

Harvey G. Stack	President
Ronald J. Gillio	Vice president
Richard J. Schwary	Treasurer
Ira M. Goldberg	Secretary
Leon Hendrickson	Director
Everett W. Hull	Director
Randall L. Pollock	Director
Fred C. Weinberg	Director
Harlan White	Director
Paul L. Koppenhaver	Executive Director
David L. Ganz	Legal Counsel

Professional Numismatists Guild Inc. is a non-profit membership corporation founded in the mid-1950s by the late Abe Kosoff with 33 members represented. The group was incorporated in 1955.

Requirements for membership
• A minimum of 21 years of age and 5 years as a full-time professional numismatist.
• A minimum of $100,000 in numismatic assets.
• Agreement to the PNG's strict Code of Ethics.
• Screening by the PNG's Board of Directors.
• Financial and character scrutiny by an outside firm.
• Acceptance by ballot of the entire PNG membership.
• Agreement to submit to legally binding arbitration to settle any dispute between a buyer and the PNG member-dealer.

Requirements for associate membership
• A minimum of 21 years of age and 2 years as a full-time professional numismatist.
• A minimum of $25,000 in numismatic assets.
• Agreement to the PNG's strict Code of Ethics.
• Screening by the PNG's Board of Directors.
• Financial and character scrutiny by an outside firm.

• Agreement to submit to legally binding arbitration to settle any dispute between a buyer and the PNG member-dealer.

Requirements for affiliate membership

This class is open to any individual who is not a professional numismatist, but is associated with the numismatic community and supports the principles of the PNG.

Aims and purposes of PNG

"We seek the establishment and the maintenance of an harmonious atmosphere in which all who participate as amateur or professional numismatists will derive the pleasure and profit they seek, giving an equal measure of satisfaction in the process.

"First, we must make the organization available to any professional numismatists of good moral character who meet reasonable simple qualifications.

"We must recognize that, as simple as these requirements may be, some may not qualify and yet be worthy of collectors' confidence.

"We must insist that our members live up to our code of ethics, and that those who are found to be in violation be appropriately penalized.

"We must contribute leadership in the field of numismatic education by preparing papers, giving talks, supplying information and contributing to organizations which can assist in this endeavor.

"We must lend our talents to collector organizations in any manner possible.

"We must help provide authentication programs to create the confidence of the collector and to discourage the traffic in spurious coins.

"We must try to prevent the theft of coin collections and assist in the apprehension of any guilty persons. Let us continue to do these things and we will indeed create the atmosphere which will give all who participate, be it as a hobby or as a profession, the ultimate in satisfaction."

Among the awards presented by the PNG are the Abe Kosoff Founders Award for significant contributions to the PNG or to numismatics in general; the Sol Kaplan Award for assistance in bringing to justice perpetrators of fraud or thievery; and the Robert Friedberg Award for literary achievement. The Kaplan and Friedberg awards are presented through the auspices of the Lewis M. Reagan Memorial Foundation Inc.

To obtain a membership application or information or for a PNG Membership Directory, write: Paul L. Koppenhaver, P.O. Box 430, Van Nuys, Calif. 91408.

PNG code of ethics

As a coin dealer, I recognize my obligations towards the public and towards my fellow members and Associate Members of the Professional Numismatists Guild, Inc. It is my intention to be worthy of the confidence and respect of those with whom I come in contact in the numismatic trade. For this purpose I have pledged myself as follows:

A. In my relation with the public:

1. To furnish my clientele advice on numismatic matters to the best of my ability.

2. To sell at prices commensurate with a reasonable return of my investment and the then-prevailing market conditions.

3. To purchase coins from the public at reasonable prices, with due allowance for buyers' risks and prevailing market conditions.

4. To neither broadcast, publish nor advertise in any manner any representation or any implication with intent to create a false or incorrect conclusion with regard to my own goods, prices or services or those of a competitor or to make false claims to a policy or to make any flase representation as to my prices or those of my competitors.

5. To assist recognized governmental authorities in the prosecution of violators of the law in numismatic matters.

6. To refrain from knowingly dealing in stolen coins, medals or other numismatic material or publications offering counterfeits as genuine coins; and when knowingly selling coins that have been altered or are contemporary counterfeits or altered specimens that are legal to own, to furnish the buyer with an invoice showing in detail the nature of such coins sold; and when selling a processed coin or treated coin, where known, to furnish the buyer with an invoice showing in detail the nature of such coins sold.

7. To accurately grade merchandise, giving cognizance to the fact that grading is inherently subjective and a matter of personal opinion.

8. Each member of the PNG shall notify his employer in writing of the provisions of the By-laws and furnish a copy of such notice to the Executive Director. The employer must accept the provisions in writing to utilize the PNG member's benefits.

B. In my relations with my fellow members of this association, I have pledged to:

1. Refrain from the voluntary public expressions of adverse criticism of other members or their merchandise.

2. To recognize and respect my own contracts and undertakings and those of fellow members.

3. To freely exchange information with other members when requested.

4. To avoid making false statements or representations in my relations with my competitors and to cooperate generally towards the betterment of our industry and the hobby in relations with fellow members.

5. To obey this Code of Ethics and the terms and conditions of these By-laws and membership in the Guild.

Founding President

Abe Kosoff..............................1954-1955

Past Presidents

Sol Kaplan	1955-1960	Jess Peters	1971-1973
Arthur Cohn	1960-1961	Douglas Weaver	1973-1975
Max Kaplan	1961-1962	Robert Johnson	1975-1977
Tom Wass	1962-1963	Q. David Bowers	1977-1979
Arthur Kagin	1963-1964	Joe Flynn	1979-1981
Abe Kosoff	1964-1965	Gary Sturtridge	1981-1983
Leo Young	1965-1967	Ed Milas	1983-1985
Dan Brown	1967-1969	Leon Hendrickson	1985-1989
David Shapiro	1969-1971		

Abe Kosoff Founders Award

John J. Ford	1973	Jess Peters	1982
Q. David Bowers	1974	Paul L. Koppenhaver	1983
John J. Smies	1975	No recipient	1984
Abe Kosoff	1976	Robert E. Medlar	1985
M. Kliman	1977	No recipient	1986
Peter Seaby	1978	No recipient	1987
Dan Brown	1979	No recipient	1987
David Akers	1980	Charles H. Wolfe	1989
Douglas W. Weaver	1981		

The Sol Kaplan Award

Fred Weinberg	1975	Dennis Forgue	1979
Michael L. Pittman	1976	No recipient	1980
Donn Pearlman	1977	Albert Levy	1981
David Sanderman	1978	Mitch Utz	1982

No recipient	1983	Jan Olav Aamlid & Gunnar Thesen	1987
Edward Kuzsmar	1984	Doug Davis	1988
Martin E. Anderson	1985	Eugene Mushinski	1988
No recipient	1986	Julian M. Liedman	1989

The Robert Friedberg Award

Jack Friedberg	1963	Chuck O'Donnell	1977
Matt H. Rothert	1964	Milton Friedberg	1978
William P. Donlon	1965	David W. Akers	1979
William Philpott	1966	Q. David Bowers	1980
No recipient	1967	Chet Krause	1981
Theodore Kemm	1968	Don C. Kelly	1982
William P. Donlon	1969	Dean Oakes & John Hickman	1983
No recipient	1970	Q. David Bowers	1984
No recipient	1971	Michael F. Hendy	1985
Burton Hobson	1972	Q. David Bowers	1986
No recipient	1973	Harlan J. Berk	1987
Nathan Goldstein II	1974	Walter Breen	1988
Gene Hessler	1975	James A. Haxby	1989
Louis W. Van Belkum	1976		

Numismatic Literary Guild

P.O. Box 6909, San Diego, Calif. 92106

Officials

David T. Alexander	Executive director
Kay E. Lenker	Treasurer
Robin Ellis	Newsletter editor
Thomas K. DeLorey	Director
Anthony Swiatek	Director
David C. Harper	Director
R.W. Julian	Director
Jim Miller	Director

History and function

The Numismatic Literary Guild was founded in August 1969 during the 77th anniversary convention of the American Numismatic Association in San Diego, Calif.

Membership is open to publications numismatic full-time staff members of publication, researchers, museum workers, free-lance writers, editors, and publishers in the field of numismatics, as well as full-time numismatic staff members of publications. New members must be sponsored by one NLG member in good standing; dues are $10 per year.

The purposes of NLG are to encourage numismatic writing, provide a central forum for both full-time and part-time writers, and to share conviviality and fellowship at ANA conventions.

NLG recognizes excellence by a series of annual awards for writers and columnists, as well as offering the "Clemy" award and the Maurice M. Gould award for outstanding literary contributions to numismatics.

Members receive a regular newsletter, keeping them informed of the activities of fellow writers everywhere, and featuring original articles and observations of the members.

New NLG members accepted by the membership committee pay an initial fee of $25, besides the first year's dues.

Clemy winners

Clement F. Bailey	1968	Abe Kosoff	1979
Edward C. Rochette	1969	Glenn B. Smedley	1980
Lee Martin	1970	Arlie Slabaugh	1981
Margo Russell	1971	Eric P. Newman	1982
Virginia Culver	1972	Kenneth E. Bressett	1983
Maurice M. Gould	1973	Donn Pearlman	1984
Eva Adams	1974	Walter Breen	1985
Ray Byrne	1975	Ed Reiter	1986
Chester Krause	1976	David T. Alexander	1987
Richard S. Yeoman	1977	Jim Miller	1988
Lee F. Hewitt	1978	Q. David Bowers	1989

Industry Council for Tangible Assets

25 E Street, NW, 8th Floor, Washington, D.C. 20001; (202) 783-3500

The Industry Council for Tangible Assets is a trade association of more than 600 members representing the interests of dealers in tangible assets, including bullion and coins. The members are interested in upholding ethical standards in the industry and working to create a favorable regulatory climate in the states and federal government for manufacture, distribution and sale of tangible assets. ICTA conducts lobbying in Congress and monitors and advises state organizations regarding the application of state sales taxes on coin and bullion transactions.

Members must uphold a code of ethics and be dealers. The dues vary depending on the size of the company. ICTA was formed in 1983.

Officers

Mike Clark	Chairman
Tom Noe	Vice-chairman
Jim Hildebrandt	Treasurer
John Muery	Secretary

Staff

Luis Vigdor	Chief executive officer
Howard Segermark	President
Paul Mousseau	Director of state affairs
Diane Piret	Membership director
William Olson	Legal counsel
Michael Murray	Legislative counsel

Board of directors

Dan Avena	Robert Harwell	
Clark Allyn Aylsworth	Michael Haynes	Executive committee
Joe Battaglia	Jim Hildebrandt	Executive committee
James U. Blanchard	Harry Ireland	
Louis Carabini	Al Johnbrier	
Mike Clark	Executive committee	Bruce Kaplan	Executive committee
chairman	Mike Kelsey	
Nelson Colton	Bret Leifer	
Joe de Marinis	Steven Mayer	
Sondra Fell	Mark Mendelson	Executive committee
Ned Fenton	John Muery	Executive committee
David Ganz	Edward Mote	
Paul Grozs	Tom Noe	Executive committee
George Hallock	John Norris	Executive committee
Larry Hanks	Executive committee	Paul Nugget	
Terry Hanlon	Craig Rhyne	Executive committee

Gary Rossman
Otto Ruesch
Iraj Sayah
Barry Stuppler........ Executive committee
Susan Sweeney...... Executive committee

Hannes Tulving
Darren Schulman

Advisory council
Steve Gotwald

Coin and Bullion Dealer Accreditation Program

25 E Street, NW, 8th Floor, Washington, D.C. 20001; (201) 783-0300

The Coin and Bullion Dealer Accreditation Program is a distinct division of the Industry Council for Tangible Assets. It is an accreditation service rather than a membership organization. It operates with its own funding and staff, and is not involved in ICTA's lobbying efforts.

CABDAP program summary

The Coin and Bullion Dealer Accreditation Program is an independent, voluntary and industry-wide program of self-regulation.

CABDAP promotes sound business practices among rare coin dealers and precious metals dealers and provides notice to the public of the program, its features and its accredited dealers. Under CABDAP:

• Membership in ICTA or any other organization is not required

• The program has been designed and is governed by rare coin and precious metals dealers

• The program is self-contained and utilizes no ICTA funds

• A portion of annual enrollment fees will be devoted to industry promotion and consumer awareness initiatives

• Numismatic testing is not required for accredititation

The program consists of four parts. These four parts are (I) Personal and Business Credentials Accreditation; (II) Discipline: review of Credentials for Cause; (III) Risk Disclosure Information and Code of Ethics; (IV) Consumer and Accredited Dealer Arbitration Program.

Part I: Personal and Business Credentials Accreditation

The first procedure for dealers and dealer firms to become accredited involves completetion of a detailed questionnaire and reference review. The questionnaire and CABDAP accreditation standards were develped to elicit and consider pertinent information bearing on reliable rare coin and precious metals dealings.

Part II: Discipline: Review of Credentials for Cause

Accreditation of all CABDAP dealers is governed by standards. Violation of those standards may lead to sanctions including suspension or revocation. The program will be administered by a Commission of accredited dealers elected by other accredited dealers. The Commission will determine, after giving a dealer notice and opportunity to respond, whether alleged infractions have occurred and what discipline is warranted. Due process is provided to dealers throughout all CABDAP activities.

Part III: Risk Disclosure Information and Code of Ethics

CABDAP dealers are required to conform to minumum risk disclosure information to be provided to consumers prior to rare coin and precious metals transactions. To encourage sound business and marketing practices, CABDAP provids dealers with a Code of Ethics.

Part IV: Consumer and CABDAP Dealer Arbitration Program

An arbitration program for all CABDAP accredited dealers provides a means of prompt recourse in the event of any unresolved consumer or accredited dealer complaint. The consumer will be able to choose arbitration if desired; the accredited dealer will be required to arbitrate when a consumer or any other CABDAP dealer initiates the process (providing the transaction in question took place after the dealer was accredited.)

CABDAP eligibility summary

To be eligible for accreditation, a dealer must:

1. Truthfully complete and sign an application (with fee attached) in the form provided by CABDAP and must provide additional explanatory information as requested.

2. Not have been convicted of, entered a plea of guilty or plea of nolo contendere to a felony or misdemeanor relating to performance as a numismatic, bullion, or precious metals dealer moral turpitude or improper business practice. This includes but is not limited to crimes involving: embezzlement, theft, larceny, extortion, fraud, fraudulent concealment, conversion, missaparopriation of funds, securities or property, forgery, counterfeiting, false pretenses, bribery, concealment of assets, making of false oaths or claims, mail fraud, false statements, perjury, racketeering, distribution or possession with intent to distribute a controlled substance, robbery, deceit or breach of trust.

3. Not be under any indictment or charge pending before any court, or administrative agency, directly relating to numismatic, bullion or precious metals dealing, integrity or improper business practice.

4. Be actively engaged in numismatic, bullion or precious metals dealing for a minimum of three (3) consecutive years prior to making application for CABDAP accreditation.

5. Otherwise be in compliance and agree to comply with all CABDAP rules.

Grounds for review of accredited status or denial of applicant shall include:

1. Obtaining or attempting to obtain accreditation or re-accreditation by a false or misleading statement, fraud or deceit in an application, re-application or any other communication to CABDAP, including but not limited to (i) misstatement of a material fact; and (ii) failure to make a statement of material fact.

2. Misrepresentation of CABDAP accredititation or accreditation status.

3. False, misleading, unfair, deceptive or fraudulent statements, acts or practices.

4. The conviction of, plea of guilty or plea of nolo contendere to a misdemeanor or felony which is related to performance as a numismatic, bullion, or precious metals dealer, moral turpitude or improper business practice. (definition in #2 provided above.)

5. Failure to provide CABDAP risk disclosure information as required.

6. Failure to participate in any CABDAP arbitration or to honor a CABDAP arbitration order or award.

7. Unauthorized use of the certificates, cards, logos, emblems or marketing materials of CABDAP.

8. Suspension or other limitation by the Commoditiy Futures Trading Commission, the Securities Exchange Commission, The National Association of Securities Dealers or other regularoty board, exchange or association.

9. Adjudged by administrative or judicial order to have violated the Federal Trade Commission Act.

10. Failure to provide timely update information to CABDAP or other violation of a CABDAP rule.

National, regional coin associations

Following is a list of national and regional coin associations.

Active Token Collectors Organization
Box 1573
Sioux Falls, S.D. 57101

American Coin Society
P.O. Box 983
Valley Stream, N.Y. 11582

American Medallic Sculpture Association
431 Buena Vista Road
New City, N.Y. 10956

American Numismatic Association
818 N. Cascade Ave.
Colorado Springs, Colo. 80903

American Numismatic Society
Broadway at 155th St.
New York, N.Y. 10032

American Political Items Collectors
P.O. Box 340339
San Antonio, Texas 78234

American Tax Token Society
7512 N.E. Bothell Way
Bothell, Wash. 98011

American Vecturist Association
46 Fenwood Drive
Old Saybrook, Conn. 06475

Amusement Token Collectors Association
328 Avenue F
Redondo Beach, Calif. 90277

Bank Token Society
P.O. Box 383
Newtonville, Mass. 02160

Barber Coin Collectors Society
P.O. Box 5353
Akron, Ohio 44313

Blue Ridge Numismatic Association
1501 Akins Drive
Chattanooga, Tenn. 37411

Bust Half Nut Club
P.O. Box 4875
Margate, Fla. 33063

Central States Numismatic Society
58 Devonwood Ave SW
Cedar Rapids, Iowa 52404

Civil War Token Society
P.O. Box 951988
Lake Mary, Fla. 32795-1988

Colorado-Wyoming Numismatic Association
519 W. Mountain Ave.
Fort Collins, Colo. 80521

Colonial Coin Club
P.O. Box 884
Annapolis, Md. 21401

Combined Organizations of Numismatic Error Collectors of America
Box 195
Palo Alto, Calif. 94302

Credit Card Collector
150 Hohldale
Houston, Texas 77022

Dedicated Wooden Money Collectors
P.O. Box 90156
Houston, Texas 77290

Early American Coppers Inc.
Box 15782
Concinnati, Ohio 45215

The Elongated Collectors
5700 Flagler St.
Metairie, La. 70003

Essay Proof Society
Route 4, Colonial Drive
Katonah, N.Y. 10536

Great Eastern Numismatic Association
490 Green Hill
Berwyn, Pa. 19312

Indiana-Kentucky-Ohio Token & Medal Society
P.O. Box 192
Dayton, Ohio 45449

International Association of Silver Art Collectors
Box 28415
Seattle, Wash. 98118

International Organization of Wooden Money Collectors
413 Delaware Ave.
Elkton, Md. 21921

Liberty Seated Collectors Club
Box 1062
Midland, Mich. 48641

Love Token Society
3575 Sipler Lane
Huntingdon Valley, Pa. 19006

Middle Atlantic Numismatic
Association
James K. Brandt
P.O. Box 787
Pearl River, N.Y. 10965

Midwest Numismatic Association
9723 Marsh
Kansas City, Mo. 64134

National Silver Dollar Roundtable
P.O. Box 913
Bowie, Md. 20715

New England Numismatic Association
P.O. Box 383
Newtonville, Mass. 02160

Numismania Society of America
8033 Sunset Blvd.
Los Angeles, Calif. 90046

Numismatic Bibliomania Society
4223 Iroquois Ave.
Lakewood Calif. 90713

Old Timer Assay Commission Society
3070 S. Franklin
Denver, Colo. 80210

Pacific Coast Numismatic Society
610 Arlington Ave.
Berkeley, Calif. 94707

Pacific Northwest Numismatic
Association
20121 1st Ave. S.

Seattle, Wash. 98198

PAK Jefferson Full Step Nickel Club
P.O. Box 1205
Montclair, N.J. 07042

Penn-Ohio Coin Clubs
612 White St.
Toledo, Ohio 43605

John Reich Collectors Society
Box 205
Ypsilanti, Mich. 48197

Society for U.S. Commemorative Coins
P.O. Box 302
Huntington Beach, Calif. 92648

Society of Lincoln Cent Collectors
P.O. Box 5465
N. Hollywood, Calif. 91616

Society of Philatelists and Numismatists
1929 Millis St.
Montebello, Calif. 90640

Society of Private and Pioneer
Numismatics
P.O. Box 4423
Davis, Calif. 95617

Society of Ration Token Collectors
44 Kendall Pond Road, Apt. E
Londonderry, N.H. 03053

Society of Silver Dollar Collectors
P.O. Box 2123
Sepulveda, Calif. 91393

Token and Medal Society
P.O. Box 951988
Lake Mary, Fla. 32795-1988

World's Fair Collectors Society
P.O. Box 20806
Sarasota, Fla. 34238-3806

State numismatic associations

Alabama Numismatic Society
P.O. Box 3601
West End Station
Birmingham, Ala. 35211

Arkansas Numismatic Society
6600 Baseline Road
Little Rock, Ark. 72209

California Association of Token
Collectors
Box 66331

Los Angeles, Calif. 90066

California Exonumist Society
P.O. Box 6909
San Diego, Calif. 92109

California State Numismatic
Association
611 Oakwood Way
El Cajon, Calif. 92021

Northern California Numismatic
Association
P.O. Box 4104
Vallejo, Calif. 94590

Numismatic Association of Southern
California
Box 1028
Colton, Calif. 92324

Metropolitan Washington Numismatic
Association
P.O. Box 9413
Washington, D.C. 20016

Washington Numismatic Society
P.O. Box 4047
Silver Spring, Md. 20904

Florida Token Society
Box 1091
Lake Alfred, Fla. 33850

Florida United Numismatists
P.O. Box 349
Gainesville, Fla. 32609

Georgia Numismatic Association
P.O. Box 611
Lilburn, Ga. 30247

Georgia State Token- Exonumia
Association
P.O. Box 951988
Lake Mary, Fla. 32795-1988

Hawaii State Numismatic Association
P.O. Box 477
Honolulu, Hawaii 96809

Illinois Numismatic Association
175 W. Wood St.
New Lenox, Ill. 60451

Club of Illinois Numismatists
P.O. Box 171
Markham, Ill. 60426

Indiana State Numismatic Association
1147 S. White River Parkway
Indianapolis, Ind. 46225

Iowa Numismatic Association
Box 65356
West Des Moines, Iowa 50265

Kansas Numismatic Association
Route #3, P.O. Box 5
Chanute, Kan. 66720

Kentucky State Numismatic Association
1318 E. Breckenridge
Louisville, Ky. 40204

Louisiana Numismatic Society
73191 Military Road
Covington, La. 70433

Maryland State Numismatic Association
P.O. Box 6533
Sparrows Point, Md. 21219

Maryland Token & Medal Society
P.O. Box 3273
Baltimore, Md. 21228

Michigan State Numismatic Society
P.O. Box 2575
Kalamazoo, Mich. 49003

Minnesota Organization of
Numismatists
P.O. Box 565
Rochester, Minn. 55903

Mississippi Numismatic Association
6813 Oahu Court
Bay St. Louis, Miss. 38520

Missouri Numismatic Society
5005 S. Grand Ave.
St. Louis, Mo. 63111

National Utah Token Society
1123 E. 2100 S.
Salt Lake City, Utah 84106

Nebraska Numismatic Association
P.O. Box 683
Sutherland, Neb. 69165

New Hampshire Numismatic
Association
Box 1655
Dover, N.H. 03820

New Jersey Exonumia Society
P.O. Box 363
Cranford, N.J. 07016

New Jersey Numismatic Society
41 Bassett Ave.
Dover, N.J. 07801

Garden State Numismatic Association
P.O. Box 74
Lincoln Park, N.J. 07035

New York State Wooden Money Society
25 N. Wayne Ave.
West Haverstraw, N.Y. 10993

Empire State Numismatic Association
8026 Trina Circle W.
Clay, N.Y. 13041

North Carolina Numismatic Association
P.O. Box 20653
Greensboro, N.C. 27420

Oklahoma Numismatic Association
P.O. Box 18753
Oklahoma City, Okla. 73154

Oregon Numismatic Society
214 Medical Dental Building
Portland, Ore. 97201

Pennsylvania Association of
Numismatists
P.O. Box 144
Pittsburgh, Pa. 15230

Coin Club of Rhode Island
P.O. Box 8495
Warwick, R.I. 02888

South Carolina Numismatic Association
P.O. Box 12163

Columbia, S.C. 29211

South Dakota Coin & Stamp
Association
106 W. 5th
Pierre, S.D. 57501

Tennessee State Numismatic Society
P.O. Box 80052
Chattanooga, Tenn. 37411

Texas Numismatic Association
2155 S. First St.
Abilene, Texas 79605

Utah Numismatic Society
P.O. Box 15054
Salt Lake City, Utah 84115

Virginia Numismatic Association
712 Westover Road
Richmond, Va. 23220

Numismatists of Wisconsin
Box 155
Mazomanie, Wis. 53560

Syngraphic organizations

American Society of Check Collectors
2145 Roman Court
Warren, Mich. 48092

Currency Club of Chester County, Pa.
420 Owen Road
West Chester, Pa. 19380

Currency Club of New England
P.O. Box 512
North Andover, Mass. 01845

International Bank Note Society
Box 1642
Racine, Wis. 53401

Latin American Paper Money Society
3304 Milford Mill Road
Baltimore, Md. 21207

National Scrip Collectors Association
P.O. Box 29

Fayetteville, W.Va. 25840

Paper Money Collectors of Michigan
Box 163
Victor, N.Y. 14564-0163

Society of Paper Money Collectors
P.O. Box 1985
Florissant, Mo. 63031

Souvenir Card Collectors Society
P.O. Box 4155
Tulsa, Okla. 74159

World Paper Currency Club
P.O. Box 23384
San Jose, Calif. 95133

World Paper Currency Collectors
Box 1586
Morgan Hill, Calif. 95038

Treasure hunting clubs

Black Diamond Treasure Hunters Club
106 Lines Lane
Mountaintop, Pa. 18707

Central Pennsylvania Treasure Seekers
328 Sawmill Road
Newville, Pa. 17241

First State Treasure Hunters Club
3502 Caley Road
Newtown Square, Pa. 19073

Hawkeye State Coinshooters
P.O. Box 251
Waverly, Iowa 50677

Keystone Searchers
Kim Krajnak
Box 143, Hill Street
Yukon, Pa. 15698

Massachusetts Treasure Hunting
Association
P.O. Box 185
Fayville, Mass. 01745

Midwest Historical Research Society
5311 N. Austin Ave.
Chicago, Ill. 60630

Mt. Diablo Metal Detectors Club
P.O. Box 5492
Concord, Calif. 94524

New England Treasure Finders Assoc.
P.O. Box 490
Agawam, Mass. 01001

New York Treasure Hunters League
9203 Flatlands Ave.
Brooklyn, N.Y. 11236

Niagara Frontier Relic Hunters Assoc.
P.O. Box 493
Buffalo, N.Y. 14215

North American Treasure Hunters
P.O. Box 204
Lancaster, N.Y. 14086

Northwest Treasure Hunters Club
11404 E. Broadway
Spokane, Wash. 99206

Pilchuck Treasure Hunting Club
3096 125th N.E.
Bellevue, Wash. 98005

Puget Sound Treasure Hunters Club
P.O. Box 98206
Tacoma, Wash. 98499

Rubber City Treasure Hunters Club
1225 S. Diamond St.
Ravenna, Ohio 44266

Stone Mountain Treasure Hunters
1354 Bramble
Atlanta, Ga. 30329

Treasure Coast Coin Club
Box 3373
Ft. Pierce, Fla. 34948

Yankee Territory Coinshooters
1242 South St.
Suffield, Conn. 06078

American Israel Numismatic Association
P.O. Box 277
Rockaway Park, N.Y. 11694

Organized in 1967, the American Israel Numismatic Association serves a specialty collecting interest: The coins, medals, tokens and bank notes of Israel and the Holy Land; numismatic Judaica, including the ancient coins of Israel; and all forms of later medals, tokens and scrip.

AINA publishes *The Shekel*, a journal of Judaic numismatics, participates in major coin conventions, issues an annual membership medal and others on important occasions, and sponsors annual study tours to Israel.

In addition, there are many affiliated state and local INS clubs. Write for addresses of active clubs in your area.

American-based world numismatic organizations

American British Numismatic
Association
P.O. Box 652

Saugus, Calif. 91350

American Israel Numismatic
Association
P.O. Box 277
Rockaway Park, N.Y. 11694

American Society for Portuguese
Numismatics
3491 Clearview Ave.
Columbus, Ohio 43220

Armenian Numis. Society
8511 Beverly Park Place
Pico Rivera, Calif. 90660

Atlanta Society for the Study of Money
other than American
P.O. Box 8303
Atlanta, Ga. 30306

International Numismatic Society
P.O. Box 66555
Washington, D.C. 20035

International Numismatic Society
P.O. Box 6909
San Diego, Calif. 92106

International Primitive Money Society
P.O. Box 1510
Redlands, Calif. 92373

International Society of Jeton Collectors
Box 235
Greenbelt, Md. 20770

Lithuanian Numis. Assoc.
P.O. Box 612
Columbia, Md. 21045

Minnesota International Numismatists
5315 Hodgson Road
St. Paul, Minn. 55126

Numismatics International
P.O. Box 670013
Dallas, Texas 75367

Oriental Numis. Society
P.O. Box 356

New Hope, Pa. 18938

Original Globe Coin Traders Club
3941 Pacific Blvd.
San Mateo, Calif. 94403

Philippine Collectors Society
P.O. Box 267
Biloxi, Mich. 39533

Polish-American Numismatic
Association
4201 N. Paulina, Apt. A2
Chicago, Ill. 60613

Russian Numismatic Society
P.O. Box 3013
Alexandria, Va. 22302

Societe Americaine Pour l'Etude de la
Numismatique Francaise
204 Rose Lane S.W.
North Canton, Ohio 44720

Society for Ancient Numismatics
3125 Washington Blvd., D
Marina Del Rey, Calif. 90292

Society for International Numismatics
P.O. Box 533
Santa Monica, Calif. 90406

Society for Medieval Numismatics
10 Manning Road
Glen Cove, N.Y. 11542

World Coin Club
P.O. Box 908
Goshen, Ind. 46526

World Coin Club of Missouri
1591 Eastham Drive
St. Louis, Mo. 63141

World Proof Numis. Assoc.
P.O. Box 4094
Pittsburgh, Pa. 15201

Canadian Numismatic Association

The Canadian Numismatic Association was established in 1950 and incorporated in 1963. Application for membership in the CNA may be made by any reputable person upon payment to: Executive Secretary, P.O. Box 226, Barrie, Ont., Canada L4M 4T2.

The CNA publishes *The Canadian Numismatic Journal* monthly, distributed free to members.

Officers

Executive Committee:
Al Bliman.................................. President

L.H. Lewry....... Immediate past president
Earl Salterio.............. First vice-president
Second Vice-President .... Marvin Kay
Bernard G. Kline........................ Director
Brian L. MacKenzie .... Director
Barry Uman............................... Director
Yvon Marquis............................ Director
Allan Davies.............................. Director
Tom Kennedy .... Director
James E. Bailie .... Director
Dean Neald .... Director
Al Munro .... Director
Raymond R. Mah........................ Director
J. Richard Becker....................... Director
George Beach............................. Director
Charles D. Moore....................... Director

Appointed Officers:
Kenneth B. Prophet.. Executive Secretary
Robert C. Willey............................ Editor
Carol Gregory .... Librarian

Honorary President
Sheldon S. Carroll

Honorary Past President
L.J.P. Brunet (1950-1953)
J. Douglas Ferguson (1953-1981)

Past Presidents

Sheldon S. Carroll 1950-1953
L. J. P. Brunet......................... 1953-1955
G. R. L. Potter........................ 1955-1956
Vincent G. Greene 1956-1959
C. C. Tannahill 1959-1961
Dr. John S. Wilkinson............. 1961-1963
Edwin Echenberg..................... 1963-1965
A. Mitchell MacDonald.......... 1965-1967
E. Victor Snell 1967-1969
John Jay Pittman..................... 1969-1971
Norman W. Williams.............. 1971-1973
Mrs. Louise Graham............... 1973-1975
A. L. Munro............................ 1975-1977
James E. Charlton................... 1977-1979
Jack Veffer............................. 1979-1981
John Regitko........................... 1981-1983
Geoffrey G. Bell..................... 1983-1985
Stan Clute 1985-1987
L.H. Scoop Lewry 1987-1989

Conventions 1954 to 1989
Location   **Date**
Host Club

Toronto, Ontario   Aug. 23-34, 1954
King Edward Hotel
Toronto Coin Club

Ottawa, Ontario   Sept. 7-8, 1955
Chateau Laurier
C.N.A. Ottawa Chapter No. 1

London, Ontario   Sept. 21-22, 1956
Hotel London
London Numis. Society

Hamilton, Ontario   Aug. 30-31, 1957
Wentworth Arms
Hamilton Coin Club

Ottawa, Ontario   Sept. 4-6, 1958
Chateau Laurier
C.N.A. Ottawa Chapter No. 1

Regina, Saskatchewan   Sept. 2-4, 1959
The Saskatchewan Hotel
Regina Coin Club

Sherbrooke, Quebec   Aug. 18-20, 1960
Hotel Sherbrooke
Sherbrooke Coin Club

Hamilton, Ont. Aug. 31, Sept. 1-2, 1961
Sheraton-Connaught Hotel
Hamilton Coin Club

Detroit, Mich.   Aug. 15-18, 1962
Sheraton Cadillac
American & Canadian Numismatic Assoc.

Vancouver, B.C.   Aug. 15-17, 1963
Hotel Vancouver
Vancouver Numismatic Society

Halifax, Nova Scotia Aug. 27-29, 1964
Nova Scotian
Halifax Coin Club

Montreal, Quebec   Aug. 12-14, 1965
Sheraton Mount Royal
Montreal Numismatic Society

Winnipeg, Manitoba Aug. 25-27, 1966
New Marlborough
Manitoba Coin Club

Ottawa, Ont.   Aug. 31, Sept. 1-2, 1967
Chateau Laurier
Ottawa Coin Club & Capital City Coin Club

Calgary, Alberta   July 15-17, 1968
Palliser Hotel
Calgary Coin Assoc.

Toronto, Ontario Aug. 28-30, 1969 Royal York Toronto Coin Club	**Montreal, Quebec** July 23-27, 1980 Mount Royal Hotel Assoc. des Numismates et Philatelistes de Boucherville, Inc.

Toronto, Ontario Aug. 28-30, 1969
Royal York
Toronto Coin Club

Halifax, Nova Scotia Aug. 5-8, 1970
Nova Scotian
Halifax Coin Club

Vancouver, B.C. Aug. 26-28, 1971
Hotel Vancouver
Vancouver Numismatic Society

Toronto, Ontario Aug. 2-5, 1972
Holiday Inn
Canadian Numis. Assoc. & Canadian
Paper Money Society

Saskatoon, Sask. July 19-21, 1973
Sheraton-Cavalier
Saskatoon Coin Club

Hamilton, Ontario Aug. 21-24, 1974
Royal Connaught
Hamilton Coin Club

Calgary, Alberta July 11-15, 1975
Palliser Hotel
Calgary Numis. Society

Ottawa, Ontario July 7-10, 1976
Chateau Laurier
City of Ottawa Coin Club

Vancouver, B.C. Aug. 1-7, 1977
Holiday Inn
Vancouver Numis. Society

London, Ontario July 27-30, 1978
Holiday Inn
London Numis. Society

Edmonton, Alberta July 19-21, 1979
Chateau Locombe
Edmonton Coin Club

Montreal, Quebec July 23-27, 1980
Mount Royal Hotel
Assoc. des Numismates et Philatelistes de
Boucherville, Inc.

Winnipeg, Manitoba July 15-18, 1981
Holiday Inn Downtown
Manitoba Coin Club

Toronto, Ontario July 23-26, 1982
Royal York Hotel
Toronto Coin Club

Moncton, NB July 20-23, 1983
Keddy's Brunswick Hotel
Moncton Coin Club

Hamilton, Ontario July 18-22, 1984
Royal Connaught Hotel
Canadian Numismatic Assoc.

Regina, Saskatchewan July 17-21, 1985
Regina Inn
Regina Coin Club

Toronto, Ontario July 24-26, 1986
Westbury Hotel
North York Coin Club

Calgary, Alberta July 16-18, 1987
Westin Hotel
Calgary Numismatic Society

Charlottetown, P.E.I. July 21-23, 1988
CP Prince Edward Hotel & Conv. Centre
Prince Edward Island Numismatic Assoc.

Quebec City, Quebec July 26-30, 1989
Quebec Convention Center
La Societe Numismatique de Quebec

Vancouver, B.C. Aug. 16-19, 1990
Hyatt Regency Hotel
North Shore Numismatic Society

Canadian coin associations

Following is a list of Canadian coin associations that operate on a national or regional scale.

**Assoc. des Numismates Francophones
du Canada**
P.O. Box 1000
Daveluyvill, Quebec G0Z 1C0

**Atlantic Provinces Numismatic
Association**
R.R. 1
College Bridge

New Brunswick E0A 1L0

**British Columbia Numismatic
Association**
P.O. Box 4311
Vancouver, B.C. V6B 3Z7

Calgary Numismatic Society
P.O. Box 633
Calgary, Alberta T2P 2J3

Canadian Association of Numismatic Dealers
P.O. Box 37, Station A
Toronto, Ont. M5W 1A2

Canadian Association of Token Collectors
10 Wesanford Place
Hamilton, Ont. L8P 1N6

Canadian Association of Wooden Money Collectors
P.O. Box 48, Station M
Calgary, Alberta T2P 2G9

Canadian Cents Club
L.H. Lewry
1161 3rd Ave. N.W.
Moose Jaw, Saskatchewan S6H 3V1

Canadian Numismatic Association
Kenneth Prophet
P.O. Box 226
Barrie, Ont. L4M 4T2

Canadian Numismatic Research Society
Ronald Greene
P.O. Box 1351
Victoria, B.C. V8W 2W7

Canadian Paper Money Society
Box 465
West Hill, Ontario M1E 2P0
Cape Breton Coin Club
P.O. Box 12
Sydney, Nova Scotia B1N 3B1

Edmonton Coin Club
P.O. Box 4111
Edmonton, Alberta T6E 4S8

Nova Scotia Museum
1747 Summer St.
Halifax, N.S. B3H 3A6

Kamloops Numismatic Society
P.O. Box 585
Kamloops, B.C. V2C 5L7

London Numismatic Society
P.O. Box 6221, Station D
London, Ontario N5W 5S1

Manitoba Coin Club
P.O. Box 321
Winnipeg, Manitoba R3C 2H6

Montreal Numismatic Society
MacDonald Stewart Foundation
1195 Sherbrooke St. W.

Montreal, Quebec H3A 1H9

Ontario Numis. Assoc.
P.O. Box 33
Waterloo, Ontario N2J 3Z6

Prince Edward Island Numismatic Association
P.O. 2921
Charlottetown, P.E.I. C1A 8C5

Prince George Numismatic Society
Northland Coin & Stamp
201-1253 5th Ave.
Prince George, B.C.

Regina Coin Club
Box 174
Regina, Sask. S4P 2Z6

Saskatoon Coin Club
Box 7514
Saskatoon, Sask. S7K 4L4

La Societe Numismatique de Quebec
C.P. 281
Sillery, Quebec G1T 2R1

Toronto Coin Club
P.O. Box 865
Adelaide St.
Toronto, Ont. M5C 2K1

Vancouver Numismatic Society
P.O. Box 67737
Station O
Vancouver, B.C. V5W 3V2

Victoria Numis. Society
P.O. Box 1601
Victoria, B.C. V8W 2X7

Windsor Coin Club
1165 Lincoln Road
Winsdor, Ont. N8Y 2H6

World coin organizations

ARGENTINA

Circulo Numismatico De Rosario
Laprida 1145
Rosario, Argentina

AUSTRALIA

Adelaide Coin Club
Box 329 G.P.O.
Adelaide 5001
South Australia

Australian Numis. Society
Brisbane Branch
The Secretary
P.O. Box 78
Fortitude Valley,
Queensland
4006 Australia

Australian Numis. Society
The Secretary
P.O. R4, Royal Exchange
Sydney, N.S.W.
2000 Australia

Bathurst Stamp & Coin Club
The Secretary
P.O. Box 63
Bathurst, N.S.W.
2795 Australia

Bendigo & District Coin Club
The Secretary
P.O. Box 589
Bendigo, Victoria
3550 Australia

Broken Hill Stamp & Coin Club
The Secretary
P.O. Box 852
Broken Hill, N.S.W.
2880 Australia

Cairns Coin Club
Bradfords Coins and Stamps
Shop 5, 51 Sheridan St.,
Cairns, N.Q., 4870 Australia

Canberra Coin Club
P.O. Box 1063
Woden, A.C.T.
2606 Australia

Capricorn Coin Club
The Secretary
433 Homer Street
Earlwood, N.S.W.
2206 Australia

Central Gold Coast Stamp & Coin Club
P.O. Box 86
Miami, Queensland
4220 Australia

Crookwell Stamp & Coin Club
The Secretary
Grabben Gullen, via Crookwell, N.S.W.
2625 Australia

Griffith Stamp & Coin Club
Post Office
Griffith, N.S.W.
2680 Australia

Gympie & District Coin Club
P.O. Box 111
Gympie, Queensland
4570 Australia

International Bank Note Society
Sydney Chapter
c/o Spink & Son (Australia Pty. Ltd.)
53 Martin Place
Sydney, N.S.W.
2000 Australia

Mackay & District Coin Club
The Secretary
27 Hoey Street
Mackay, Queensland
4740 Australia

Maitland & District Coin Club
P.O. Box 185
East Maitland, N.S.W.
2323 Australia

Melbourne Numis. Society
The Secretary
Box 312
Box Hill, Victoria
3128 Australia

Metropolitan Coin Club of Sydney
P.O. Box 137
Strathfield, N.S.W
2135 Australia

Morwell Numis. Society
The Secretary
P.O. Box 432
Moe, Victoria
3825 Australia

Newcastle Numis. Society
The Secretary
P.O. Box 5237D
Newcastle West, N.S.W.
2302 Australia

Numismatic Association of Victoria
Box 615D
G.P.O. Melbourne, Victoria
3001 Australia

Numismatic Society of South Australia
Box 80B, G.P.O.
Adelaide, 5001

South Australia Orana Numis. Society
P.O. Box 1456
Dubbo, N.S.W.
2830 Australia

Orange & District Coin & Stamp Club
P.O. Box 324
Orange, N.S.W,
2800 Australia

Perth Numis. Society
G.P.O. Box 259
Fremantle 6160 Australia

Queensland Numis. Society
P.O. Box 399
North Quay, Queensland
4000 Australia

Rockhampton Coin Club
P.O. Box 490
Rockhampton, Queensland
4700 Australia

Tamworth and District Coin Club
P.O. Box 123
West Tamworth, N.S.W
2340 Australia

Tasmanian Numis. Society
G.P.O. Box 884J
Hobart, Tasmania
7001 Australia

Wollongong Coin Club
The Secretary
P.O. Box 118
Thirroul, N.S.W.

2515 Australia

AUSTRIA

Grazer Num. Vereinigung
Stainzerhofgasse 1,
Graz 1, Austria

Oesterreichische Num. Gesellschaft
Burgring 5
A-1010 Vienna, Austria

Vorarlberger Coin Friends
Frz. Michel Felderstrasse 4,
A-6850 Dornbirn, Austria

BELGIUM

Alliance Numismatique Europeene
Maurice Colaert,
20 Rue de L'Anemone,
B-1180 Brussels
Belgium

Cercle d' Etudes Numismatiques
Boulevard de l'Empereur 4,
B-1000 Brussels
Belgium

BRAZIL

Brazilian Numis. Society
Caixa Postal 3660
Sao Paulo, Brazil

BULGARIA

Bulgarian Numismatic Society
P.O. Box 1122
Sofia, Bulgaria

CHINA, P.R.C

Chinese Numis. Society
c/o China Mint Co
Jia-1, Xin an Nan Li,
You An Men Nie,
Beijing, People's Republic of China

COLOMBIA

Numismaticos Colombianos
Dr. Hernando Albornoz
Plata, Sec.,
Apartado Aereo 5630
Bogota, D.E., Colombia

CUBA

Federation of Numismatists of Cuba
Apartado No. 736

La Habana, Cuba
Cuban Numis. Assoc.
456 Aguiar St.
Havana, Cuba

CYPRUS

Cyprus Numismatic Society
27A Makarios Avenue
Larnaca, Cyprus

CZECHOSLOVAKIA

Numismaticka Spolecnost
Ceskoslovenska
Brezinova 5
Prague 8, CSSR

DENMARK

Aabybro Montklub
Peter Madsen
Mortensgade 25
DK-9440 Aabybro,
Denmark

Amagerlands Numismatiske Association
Skottegaardssden
Saltvaerksvej 65
Kastrup, Denmark

Dansk Montsamler Union
Erik Storgaard
Hestehavvej 4
DK-5492 Vissenbjerg, Denmark

European Token Society
Jorgen Thingvad
Lapmejsevej 9
DK-6500 Vojens, Denmark

Fyns Numismatiske Forening
Jorgen Larsen
Staugstedlund 71
DK-5600 Faborg, Denmark

Holstebro Og Omegns Montklub
K. E. Halgaard
Nygade 11
DK-7570 Vemb, Denmark

Montklubben for Udenlandsk Mont
Norrevold 19
Krudttarnsvej 117
Copenhagen, Denmark

ENGLAND

Bampton & District Numis. Society
Barry Allan

76 Meadow Close
Farmoor, Oxford
OX2 9NZ England

Banbury & District Numis. Society
A. Bedford
12 Grosvenor Road
Banbury, Oxford
OX16 8HN England

Barrow Numis. Society
H. Walker
18 Brighton St.
Barrow-in-Furness
Lancashire, England

Bath & Bristol Numis. Society
M.C.J. Manning
c/ 75 North Street
Berdminster, Bristol
BS3 1ES England

Bedford Numis. Society
G.W. Dawson
51 Northampton Road
Lavendon, Bucks
MK46 4EY England

Bexley Coin Club
A.J. Gilbert
76 Merlin Road
Welling, Kent
DA16 2JR England

Birmingham Numis. Society
Philip J. Leighton
17 Roughley Dr.
Four Oakes,
Sutton Coldfield
West Midlands
B75 6PW England

Bradford & District Numis. Society
A.J. Ferguson
58 Spennithane Avenue
Leeds LS16 6JA England

Brighton & Hove Coin Club
L.R. Keen
74 Hangleton Road
Hove, East Sussex
BN3 7GF England

British Cheque Collectors Society
John Purser
71 Mile Lane, Cheylesmore
Coventry, W. Midlands
CO3 4GB England

British Numis. Association
David Fletcher
P.O. Box 82
Coventry CV5 6RS England

British Numis. Society
W. Slayter
63 West Way
Edgeware, Middlesex
HA8 9LA England

British Society for Young Numismatists
A.N. Wilkinson
7 Carnoustie Dr.
Eaglescliffe
Stockton-on-Tees,
Cleveland, England

Buckinghamshire Numis. Society
J.A. Wilson
21 Finmere Crescent
Aylesbury, Bucks
HP27 7DQ England

Cambridgeshire Numis. Society
M.A. Marsh
Northgate
63 St. Neots Rd.
Hardwick, Cambridgeshire
CB3 7QH England

Cheltenham Numis. Society
B.M. Greenaway
Lordswood
The Butts
Lydiard Millicent, Swindon
Wilts SN5 9LR, England

Cleveland Coin Club
L. Whitehouse
85 Hambledon Road
Middlesborough, Cleveland England

Crawley Coin Club
M.F. Dixon
78 St. Marys Drive
Crawley, West Sussex
RH10 6NW England

Crewe & District Coin & Medal Society
Brian Edge
48 Woodside Ave.
Crewe, Cheshire, England

Darlington & District Numis. Society
Mrs. P. Laycock
48 Langholm Crescent
Darlington, Durham

DL1 5DX England

Derbyshire Numis. Society
E.W. Danson
63 Ferrers Way
Darley Abbey, Derby
DE3 2BB England

Devon & Exeter Numis. Society
Norman Shiel
4 St. Leonards Road
Exeter, Devon
EX2 4LA England

Dewsbury & District Coin Club
D. Firby
13 Glendale Estate
Morley, Leeds,
W. Yorkshire
LS27 9HL England

Durham Numis. Society
J.J.A. Morris
High Farm, Elwick,
Hartlepool, Cleveland
TS27 3HD England

Edward VIII Coin Collectors Club
D.J. Shepherd
18 Wide Lane, Swaything,
Southampton, Hampshire
SO2 2HH England

Enfield & District Numis. Society
R.B. Burnett
14 Gerrards Close
Southgate, London
N14 4RH England

Essex Numis. Society
R.I. Thomas
The Mowles
Courtlands, London Rd.
Billericay, Essex
CM7 7LU England

Harrow & Northwest Middlesex Numis. Society
G.H. Hickman
49 Grafton Rd.
Harrow, Middlesex
HA1 4QS England

Havering Numis. Society
F. Bonner
80 Painesbrook Way
Harold Hill, Romford,
Essex RM3 9JS England

Hayes & District Coin Club
C.D. Haselden
83 Parkfield Crescent,
Biuslip, Middlesex
HA4 ORD England

Horncastle & District Coin Club
W.A. Mant
6 Linden Drive
Burgh-Le-Marsh
Skegness, Lincs.
PE24 5BP England

Hull & District Num. Society
G. Percival
86A Victoria Ave.
Hull, England

International Bank Note Society
S.K. Gupta
11 Middle Row
Kensington, London
W10 5AT England

Ipswich Numis. Society
S.E. Sewell
103 Penzance Road
Ipswich, Suffolk
1PS 7LEl England

Kent & Medway Towns Num. Society
E.H. Redfern
Perrydene,
Pear Tree Lounge
Shorne, Gravesend, Kent
DA12 3JS England

Kingston Numis. Society
R.N. Clarkson
62 Cheshire Gardens
Chessington, Surrey
KT9 2PS England

Lancashire & Cheshire Numis. Society
Dr. M. Robinson
c/o Friends Meeting House
6 Mount St.
Manchester 2, England

Leicester & District Num. Society
E.H. Papworth
98 Leire St.
Leicester, England

Lincolnshire Numis. Society
D. Goodey
13 Hunsley Cres.
Grimsby, South Humberside

DN32 8PU England

London Numismatic Club
S.J. Mansfield
P.E.B.M. Rueff
2 Kings Bench Walk
Temple, London
EC4 7DY England

Loughborough Coin & Search Society
G.C. Fowler
155 Parklands Dr.
Loughborough, Leicestershire, England

Merseyside Num. Society
W.H.R. Cook
c/o E.C. Southworth
Merseyside County Museum
William Brown St.
Liverpool LS 8EN England

Mid Northamptonshire Coin & Medal Society
F.H. Harris
7 Dene Close
Kettering, Northampton
NN16 9HH England

Morecambe & Lancaster Numis. Society
K.F. Brook
55 Yorkshire St.
Morecambe, Lancs, England

Newbury Coin & Medal Club
J.W. Child
97 Enborne Road
Newbury, Berkshire
RG14 6AR England

Norfolk & Norwich Numis. Society
A.W. Gidney
10 Rocelin Close
Norwich, Norfolk
NR3 4DQ England

Northhampton Numis. Society
P. Waddell
69 Marlon Road
Towcester, Northampton
NN12 7QR England

Numismatic Society of Nottinghamshire
Grenville Chamberlain
32 Park St.
Beeston, Nottingham
NG9 1DF England

Orders & Medals Research Society
N.G. Gooding
123 Turnpike Link
Croydon, Surrey CR0 5NU England

Oriental Numis. Society
K.N. Wiggins
9 Cold Harbour Close
Cronsborough, East Sussex
TN6 1EU England

**Ormskirk & West Lancashire Numis.
Society**
D.M. Regan
62 Thirlmere Drive
Ainsdale, Southport,
Merseyside
PR8 3TY England

Paignton & District Coin Club
D.B. Cox
22 Shirburn Rd.
Torquay, Devon
TQ1 3JL England

Peterborough & District Numis. Society
R. Heford
105 Welland Rd.
Peterborough, Cambs
PE1 3SJ, England

Plymouth Coin & Medal Club
James Cavanaugh
27 Sutherland Rd.
Plymouth, Devon
PL5 2EG England

Preston & District Numis. Society
William G. Kay
1 Reigate
Great Knowley, Chorley
Lancs PR6 8UJ England

Reading Coin Club
Secretary
c/o The Numismery
1898 Oxford Rd.
Reading, Berkshire
RG1 7UZ England

Rochford Hundred Numis. Society
J. Bispham
103 Ferry Road
Hullbridge, Essex, England

Romsey Numis. Society
R. Chuter
5 Peverells Wood Ave.

Chandlers Ford, Hamps.
SO5 2AX England

Royal Numismatic Society
J.E. Cribb
Dept. of Coins & Medals
British Museum
London WC1B 3DG, England

Rye Coin Club
C.W. Banks
9 Conqueror Rd.
St. Leonards on Sea
East Sussex TN38 8DD England

**St. Albans & Hertfordshire Numis.
Society**
Gerald G. Sommerville
19 The Lawns, Mount
Pleasant
St. Albans, Herts.
AL3 4TB England

St. Helens Coin & Medals Society
W.S. Pennington
53 Hold Lane
Rainhill, Merseyside
L35 8NA, England

Scunthorpe & District Numis. Society
E.S. Smith
11 Morley St.
Gainsborough, Lincs.
DN21 2NF England

Sheffield & District Numis. Society
A.J. Miller
22 Spooner Road, Sheffield
S10 5BN England

Southampton & District Numis. Society
H.J.M. Good
7 Wood Rd.
Ashurst, Nr. Southampton
SO4 2BD England

Swindon & District Numis. Society
Princess Hotel
Beatrice Street, Swindon,
Wilts, England

The North Devon Numis. Society
F. Metherell
16 Fort Street
Barnstaple
Devon EX32 8BJ, England

Thurrock Numis. Society
R.H. Clark

152 Hamlet Court Road
Westcliff-on-Sea
Essex SSO 7LL England

Torbay & District Numis. Society
D.B.W. Cox
22 Shirbyron Road
Torquay, Devon
TQ12 4DN England

Tyneside Numis. Society
J.H. Corbitt
11 Ashfield Grove
Whitley Bay, Tyne & Wear
NE26 1QT England

Uxbridge Coin Club
C.E. Watkins
35 Sherborne Way
Croxley Green
Rickmansworth, Harts.
WO3 3PE England

Wessex Numis. Society
D.W. Sadler
Oakdene, 30 Oak Ave.
Christchurch, Dorset
BH23 2QE England

Wickford Numis. Society
J. Bispham
103 Ferry Rd.
Hullbridge, Essex, England

Wiltshire Numis. Society
M.J. Butt
1 Court Orchard, Bratton
Westbury, Wilts.
BA13 4RY England

Worksop & District Numis. Society
W.E. Gray
12 Hamilton Park Rd.
Cusworth, Doncaster
South Yorkshire
DN5 8TX England

Worthing & District Numis. Society
J.A. Warner
6 Wallace Ave.
Worthing, West Sussex,
BN11 5RA England

Yorkshire Numis. Society
Cyril Peel
162 Acreshall Ave.
Pudsey, West Yorkshire
LS28 9EQ England

York Numis. Society
W. Moore
66 Sutherland St.
York, North Yorkshire
YO2 1NQ England

FINLAND

Helsinki Numismatic Association
Erik Johanson
Louhentie 1B5
02130 Tapiola 3, Finland

FRANCE

Association Numismatique Armoricaine
M.E. Grall, Sec.
32 Avenue de Brequigny
F-35100 Rennes, France

Cercle Numismatique Clermontois
Maurice Muszynski
Apt. 132
ILM Lavoisier
Rue de Nohanent
F-6300 Clermont-Ferrano
France

Club Francaise de la Medaille
11 Quai de Conti
Paris F-75006
France

Groupe Numismatique de Provence
Harry Lips
24 Bd Chancel "Le Gallia"
F-06600 Antibes
France

Societe Numismatique de Paris
Bernard Favier
4 av. des Marronniers
F-94350 Villiers sur Marne
France

GREECE

Hellenic Numis. Society
P.O. Box 736
Athens, Greece

HAITI

Societe Numismatique d'Haiti
Post Office Box 63
Port-au-Prince, Haiti

HONG KONG

Hong Kong Numismatic Society
Cheng Po-hung
G.P.O. Box 8977
Hong Kong

HUNGARY

Hungarian Numismatic Society
Csepreghy u.4 II. 15
H-1085 Budapest, Hungary

ICELAND

Icelandic Numis. Society
P.O. Box 5024
Reykjavik, Iceland

INDIA

**Gujrat Coin and Stamp Collectors
Society**
Ghanshyam V. Thacker
Vokla-Falia
Bhuj-Kutch (Gujrat), India

Numismatic Society of India
Prof. A.K. Narain, Secy.
P. O. Hindu University
Varanasi 5, India

INDONESIA

Indonesian Numis. Society
H. Natasuwarna
J.l. Syryalaya Tengah
7 Buah Batu
Bandung, Indonesia

IRAQ

Iraqi Club for Stamps and Coins
P.O. Box 2294
Alwiya, Iraq

Iraqi Philatelic Society
P.O. Box 344
Baghdad, Iraq

IRELAND, NORTHERN

**Northern Branch of Numismatic Society
of Ireland**
S.G. Rowe, Hon. Secy.
"Langdale,"
Kensington Ave.
Banbridge, Co. Down
N. Ireland

Numismatic Correspondents of Ireland
Munster, Portora
Enniskillen
N. Ireland

IRELAND, REPUBLIC

Numismatic Society of Ireland
Francis Heaney
St. Heliers
Stillorgan Park
Blackrock, Co. Dublin
Irish Republic

Royal Dublin Society
Ballsbridge
Dublin
Irish Republic

ISRAEL

Haifa Numismatic Society
Mike Fox
38 Pinsker Street
Neve Shaanan
Haifa 31060 Israel

Israel Numismatic Society
Dr. E. Klimowsky
43 Yehuda Halevi St.
Tel Aviv, Israel

ITALY

**Associazione Filatelica Numismatica
Modenese**
Casella Postal 224
I-41100 Modenese, Italy

Associazione Medaglistica Esaltazioni
Storiche (A.M.E.S.)
Via Poggi D'oro 35
I-00179 Rome, Italy

Assonummus
Via Santa Maria
Fulcorina 17
I-20123 Milano, Italy

Circolo Filatelica Numis.
Piazza Cavour-4
I-47037 Rimini, Italy

Circolo Filatelico Numis.
"G. Piani" Imola
Galleria Risorgimento 1
I-40026 Imola, Italy

Circolo Filatelico Numis.
Mantovano
Casella Postale 229
I-46100 Mantova, Italy

Circolo Filatelico Numis. Reggiano
Casella Postale 102
I-42100 Reggio Emilia, Italy

Circolo Numismatico
"Alfa Cure"
Via Firenzuola 7/9R
I-50133 Firenze, Italy

KOREA

Korea Coin Club
United States Forces
Stephen W. Gaunt
Yongsan District
Seventh Region, USA CIDC
APO San Francisco 96301

MALAYSIA

Malaysian Numis. Society
Secretary
P.O. Box 2367
Kuala Lumpur
01-02 Malaysia

MEXICO

Sociedad Numismatica de Mexico
Eugenia No. 13-301
Apartado Postal 60-589
Mexico 18, D.F., Mexico

Sociedad Numismatica de Monterrey, A.C.
P.O. Box 422
Monterrey, N.L.-Mexico

Sociedad Numismatica de Morelos A.C.
Calle 8 No. 4 Condominio
Bugambilias
Cuernavaca, Morelos,
Mexico

MOROCCO

American Coin and Stamp Club of Morocco
USNCS
P.O. Box 303
FPO New York 09544

NEW ZEALAND

Auckland Coin Club
Box 1440, G.P.O.
Auckland 1, New Zealand

Numismatic Society of Auckland
Box 818
Auckland C.1, New Zealand

Royal Numismatic Society of New Zealand
G.P.O. Box 2023
Wellington, New Zealand

Tauranga Numis. Society
P.O. Box 202
Tauranga, New Zealand

Wellington Coin Club
P.O. Box 3705
Wellington, New Zealand

NORWAY

Norsk Numismatisk Forening
Box 180
Oslo, Norway

PANAMA

Crossroads Coin Club
(Club Cruce de Camino)
P.O. Box 1833
Balboa, Rep. of Panama

PERU

Sociedad Numismatica del Peru
P.O. Box 4345
Lima 1, Peru

PHILIPPINES

Bank Note Society of the Philippines
P.O. Box 1960 MCC
Makati, Philippines

Philippine Numismatic and Antiquarian Society
P.O. Box 1955
Manila, Philippines

POLAND

Polskie Towarzystwo Archeologiczne
Polish Arch. Society
Numismatic Section
ul. Jezuicka 6
00281 Warsaw, Poland

PORTUGAL

Associacao Recreativa Aurora de Liberdade
Numismatic Section
Matosinhos, Leca
Portugal

Clube Numismatico de Portugal
Nestor Vital
Casa do Minho
Lisbon, Portugal

PUERTO RICO

Sociedad Numismatica de Puerto Rico
P.O. Box 178
San Juan, Puerto Rico 00902

SCOTLAND

Aberdeen Coin Club
N. Thomson
54 Richmondhill Place
Aberdeen AB2 4EP Scotland

Glasgow & West of Scotland Numismatic Society
N.G. Brodie
Cruachan, Dullatur
Glasgow G68 OAW Scotland

Mid-Lanark Coin Circle
J.W. Wright
Milton View, Waygateshaw
Carluke ML8 5PX Scotland

SINGAPORE

Singapore Numismatic Association
GPO 2594
Singapore 2, Republic of Singapore

SOUTH AFRICA

Johannesburg Numismatic Society
75A Troye St.
Johannesburg, South Africa

Natal Numismatic Society
7 Hansworth-on-the-Hill
169 Jan Smuts Highway
Westridge
Durban, South Africa

South African Numismatic Society
P.O. Box 1689
Cape Town 8000
South Africa

Transvaal Numismatic Society
P.O. Box 2594
Pretoria, Transvaal
South Africa

SPAIN

Associacion Numismatica Espanola
Gran Via de les Cortes
Catalanes 627,
Barcelona 10, Spain

SWEDEN

Svenska Numismatiska Foreningen
Ostermalmsgatan 81
S-114 50 Stockholm, Sweden

SWITZERLAND

Numimatischer Verein Bern
Postfach 1995
S-3001 Bern, Switzerland

THAILAND

Thai Numismatic Society
P.O. Box 189
Bangkok, Thailand

VENEZUELA

Associacion Venezolana de Numismaticos
Apartado Los Ruices
170165
Caracas, Venezuela

WALES

South Wales & Mon- mouthshire Numis. Society
A.G. Cox
9 Maynard Court
Fairwater Road
Cardiff, South Glamorgan
CF5 2LS Wales

WEST GERMANY

Augsburger Munzfreunde
Ernst Stempfle
Am Zehntstadel 18
D-8900 Augsburg W. Germany

Bayerische Numismatische Gesellschaft e.V.
Residenzstr. 1
D-8000 Munich, W. Germany

Bremer Numis. Gesellschaft
K. H. Buhse
Blumenkamp 6
D-2820 Bremen-St. Magnus
W. Germany

Bremerhavener Munzfreunde
Heinrich Walker
Max-Eyth-Platz 2
D-2850 Bremerhaven-Mitte
W. Germany

Eifeler Munzfreunde
Otto Kersting
1M Wiesengrundig 19
D-5332 Schleiden W. Germany

Frankfurter Numismatische
Gesellschaft
Frau Dr. Gisela Forschner
Historisches Museum, Munzkabinett
Saalgasse 19
D-6000 Frankfurt/Main W. Germany

Giessener Numismatische Gesellschaft
e.V.
Dr. H.D. Kahl
Otto Behagel Str. 10
D-6300 Giessen W. Germany

Heidelberg Coin & Stamp Club
Harley G. Miller
im Kreuz 18
D-6927 Wollenberg W. Germany

Munzfreunde Fulda
Gunther Auth

Bachstrasse 22
D-6418 Hunfeld W. Germany

Numismatische Gesellschaft Mainz
Dr. Rudolph Walther
Nikolaus Beckerstrasse 8
D-6500 Mainz, W. Germany

Numismatische Gesellschaft Speyer
E.V.
Helfried Ehrend
Laharstrasse 17
D-6720 Speyer, W. Germany

Oberhausener Munzfreunde
Hans-Gunter Beck
Laubstrasse 39
D-4200 Oberhausen 11 W. Germany

Wuppertaler Munz- freunde
Horst Kimpel
Reichstrasse 12
D-5600 Wuppertal 2 W. Germany

Wurttembergischer Verein fur
Munzkunde e.V.
Dr. Ulrich Klein
Wurttemburg Landes- museum
Schillerplatz 6
D-7000 Stuttgart 1 W. Germany

ZIMBABWE

Zimbabwe Numis. Society
Glyn Tunley
P.O. Box 2356
Salisbury 705701, Zimbabwe

World coin dealer organizations

Canadian Assoc. of Numismatic Dealers
P.O. Box 3145, Station D, Willowdale,
Ontario M2R 3G5 Canada

British Numismatic Trade Association
of the United Kingdom, The Secretary
3c Earlsdon St., Coventry CV5 6EP
England

Syndicat National des Experts
Numismates et Numismatique
Professionnels
38 rue de Richelieu, F-75001 Paris, France

Verband der Deutsche Munzenhandler
e.V.
Anders Ringberg

Achenbachstrasse 3 D-4000 Dusseldorf 1,
W. Germany

Verband der Deutschen Munzenhandler
e.V.
Mittelweg 54, D-6000 Frankfurt 1, W.
Germany

Verband der Munzhandler im APHV
Klettenberggurtel 60, D-5000 Koln-
Klettenberg, W. Germany

Japan Coin Dealers Association
3-9-9 Kyobashi, Chuo-ku, Tokyo 104,
Japan

**Verband Schweizerischer
Munzenhandler**
Erwin Dietrich

Postfach 73 84, CH-8023 Zurich,
Switzerland

International Association of Professional Numismatists

The object of the IAPN is, according to its charter, "the coordination of all efforts and ideas of the development of the numismatic trade, the encouragement of scientific research and the propagation of numismatics, and the creation of lasting and friendly relations among professional numismatists throughout the world.

"The members of the Association guarantee the authenticity of all coins and medals which they sell."

The IAPN was founded in Geneva, Switzerland, on May 12, 1951. The registered office of the Association is in Switzerland.

To be eligible to join the IAPN, a candidate must:

1. Have been established as a professional numismatist as his or her principal activity for at least four years, and to have carried on a numismatic business honorably for at least the same period.

2. Have given proof of his or her numismatic knowledge by submitting his or her commercial publications, catalogues, price lists, books, articles, or the text of lectures.

3. Be proposed to the Association by three members:

For information on the IAPN, write Jean-Paul Divo, Secretary, I.A.P.N., Lowenstrasse 65, CH-8001 Zurich, Switzerland.

IAPN Executive Committee

President	Robert Schulman
First vice president	Michel Kampmann
Second vice president	William Christensen
Secretary	Jean-Paul Divo
Treasurer	Wilfried Albrecht
Committee	Jan Olav Aamlid
	Wilfried Albrecht

Giulio Bernardi
Francisca Bernheimer
Sabine Bourgey
Ferran Calico
William Christensen
Alberto De Falco
Jean-Paul Divo
Silvia Hurter
Michel Kampmann
B.H. Lim
Edward Milas
Anders Ringberg
Jon Subak
Hans Voegtli

IAPN General Assemblies

Location	Date
Florence	May-June 1952
Paris	July 1953
Oxford	June 1954
Munich	May 1955
Amsterdam	May 1956
Barcelona	June 1957
Vienna	May 1958
Copenhagen	May 1959
Lausanne	June 1960
Rome	Sept. 1961
Igls (Austria)	May 1962
Monte Carlo	May-June 1963
London	May 1964
Paris	June 1965
New York	May 1966
Stockholm	May 1967
Naples	May 1968
Palma	May 1969
Scheveningen	May 1970
Estoril	May 1971
Athens	May 1972
Washington	Sept. 1973
Brussels	June 1974
Edinburgh	May 1975
Corsica	June 1976
Wiesbaden	May 1977
Malta	May 1978

Interlaken	Sept. 1979	Oslo	May 1985
Los Angeles	June 1980	Kent	Sept. 1986
Marbella	June 1981	Haifa & Jerusalem	June 1987
Salzburg	May 1982	Trieste	May 1988
Singapore	May 1983	Monaco	June 1989
Greek Islands	June 1984		

Books and Periodicals

22

First the book

An oft-repeated adage by longtime numismatists is "First the book and then the coin." We at *Coin World* believe that to be an important philosophy that every collector, especially the beginner, should adopt.

Books are an open door to knowledge, and knowledge is power. Knowledge is also history, art, politics and science — subjects which numismatics has to offer in large quantities. Knowledge is never dull, and is invaluable in the hobby.

Books, when used properly, arm the potential buyer with the knowledge to buy numismatic material intelligently, and the seller to sell wisely. Investors will find advice from market analysts to consider when investing in the market.

The editors of this almanac believe every collector and investor should have his own library, whether it is just a few books or a multi-volume library that gives its owner hours of enjoyment. A good numismatic library is essential for full enjoyment of the hobby, and we have found that most collectors will turn from their collections to their library as their thirst for knowledge grows.

Where does one buy numismatic books? A good, economical place to start is category 181 of *Coin World* classified advertisements, "coin books." Dealers advertising in this section offer the latest in numismatic books, as well as the useful volumes published earlier, often at competitive prices. Purchasing numismatic books through advertisements introduces buyers to numismatic book specialists. They often conduct mail-bid sales and auctions of out-of-print books, many of which bring high prices, but also others which are within the budgets of most collectors.

Other sources of books include local coin dealers, newsstands and book stores. Both businesses should be able to order books not in their stocks from wholesalers or directly from the publisher. Coin dealers often bring books with them to coin shows and conventions. Larger conventions often have dealers who deal exclusively in numismatic books.

Major libraries have selections of numismatic books. Librarians are always willing to consider requests and recommendations about books they might want to buy for the library. Collectors should consider a visit to the local library, armed with a list of books they would like to see on its shelves. Some coin clubs purchase and deposit books in their local library to serve the general public.

Many small coin clubs have libraries, usually maintained by an officer, and the books are available for members to borrow.

Membership in the American Numismatic Association offers two special advantages: The world's largest free, circulating numismatic library, and a numismatic book club that offers newly published books at substantial discounts from the retail price. The ANA library has 35,000 circulating volumes, most available only for a few dollars each to cover postage and insurance both ways.

Volumes available in the ANA library cover all aspects of U.S. and world numismatics: coins, paper money, tokens, medals, orders and decorations, and stocks and bonds. In addition to books, the library has one of the finest selections of auction catalogs in the world plus a wide range of numismatic periodicals, including more than 30 years of *Coin World* on microfilm.

The following books are recommended by Coin World staff members because these are the books they turn to most often when researching, answering a letter from a reader, or writing an article for publication. *Coin World* has a working reference library. The lists are not meant to be complete, and in fact many good, useful specialized books do not appear on these lists. For a complete listing and scope of numismatic literature, the ANA Library catalog has no equal.

Books listed here should be available in the United States, although many in the sections concerning world material and ancients are published in other countries. Some of the books are out of print, though available through some numismatic book dealers. Other older volumes have been reprinted in modern editions. For the ordinary collector, these inexpensive reprints are recommended over the expensive original editions, some centuries old and collector's items themselves.

An introduction to books in these listings should inspire readers to explore the entire numismatic publishing field for more scope. These just touch the surface.

U.S. coins

General works

Annual Report of the Director of the Mint. United States Mint, Department of the Treasury, issued annually. An invaluable source for numismatists with mintage figures, photographs of new coins and medals, reports about new coinage programs, reports about technology changes at the Mint, charts about gold and silver deposits to Mint and more. May be ordered from the United States Mint, Treasury Department, Washington, D.C. 20220.

The Coin World Comprehensive Catalog & Encyclopedia of United States Coins. Alexander, David T., project editor. Amos Press Inc., Sidney, Ohio, 1990. Catalog-style compendium detailing Colonial and early states coins and tokens, federal issues, patterns, Confederate coinage, and pioneer gold.

The Coin World Guide to U.S. Coins, Prices & Value Trends. Coin World. Amos Press Inc., Sidney, Ohio. Published annually since 1989. Price guide plus basic collector and investor information.

The Basics of Collecting Money. Staff of Coin World. Amos Press Inc., Sidney, Ohio, 1989. This soft-cover work offers information for the beginning collector and investor, both youths and adults.

Coin World Almanac. Staff of Coin World. Amos Press Inc., Sidney, Ohio. Earlier editions dated 1976, 1977, 1978, 1984, 1987.

A Guide Book of United States Coins. Yeoman, R.S. Western Publishing Co., Racine, Wis., annually since 1947. A basic catalog listing of U.S. Colonial, state, Mint and commemorative coins, plus pioneer gold; the "Red Book."

A Handbook of United States Coins. Yeoman, R.S. Western Publishing Co., Racine, Wis., annually. Formerly hard-cover, now soft-cover, this guide is for the beginning collector of U.S. coins; the "Blue Book."

Walter Breen's Complete Encyclopedia of U.S. and Colonial Coins. Doubleday, New York, 1988. Massive volume covering the full range of United States and related coinage.

The History of United States Coinage as Illustrated by the Garrett Collection. Bowers, Q. David. Bowers and Ruddy

Galleries Inc., Los Angeles, Calif., 1979. Covers the history of U.S. coins and collecting, with numerous letters and other documents quoted extensively.

The Macmillan Encyclopedic Dictionary of Numismatics. Doty, Richard G. Macmillan Publishing Co., New York, 1982. Illustrated dictionary, plus bibliography.

Numismatic Art in America. Vermeule, Cornelius. Belknap Press of Harvard University Press, Cambridge, Mass., 1971. Examines the aesthetics of U.S. coinage, and traces development of engraving skills of U.S. engravers.

Official American Numismatic Association Grading Standards for United States Coins. ANA and Western Publishing Co. Racine, Wis., 1987. Black-and-white photos of all regular issues in most conditions from Mint State 70 to About Good 3, plus section about commems. (Earlier editions have line illustrations.)

U.S. Mint and Coinage. Taxay, Don. Durst Numismatic Publications, New York, 1983 (reprint of 1966 book). Early history of U.S. Mint and minting processes in detail, plus history from mid-19th century to current coinage.

Special series

California Pioneer Fractional Gold. Breen, Walter, and Gillio, Ronald J. Pacific Coast Auctions Galleries Inc., Santa Barbara, Calif. 1983. Catalog listing of varieties of California fractional gold, including black and white photos of most coins.

The Early Coins of America. Crosby, Sylvester S. Quarterman Publications Inc., New York, 1983 (facsimile reprint of 1875 book). Covers all Colonial, Confederation and state issues, with extracts from authorizing legislation, plus plates.

Encyclopedia of United States and Colonial Proof Coins 1722-1977. Breen, Walter. FCI Press Inc., Albertson, N.Y., 1977. Historical information and pedigrees about U.S.

Proofs, with sections covering branch Mint Proofs and fantasy and restrike pieces.

The Encyclopedia of United States Silver & Gold Commemorative Coins, 1892-1989. Breen, Walter, and Swiatek, Anthony; updates by Walter Breen. Bowers and Merena Galleries, Inc., Wolfeboro, N.H., 1990. Historical and investment information about all U.S. commemorative coinage through 1989.

Private Gold Coins and Patterns of the United States. Kagin, Donald H. Arco Publishing Inc., 1981, History and catalog of pioneer gold, excluding fractional parts of a dollar.

United States Pattern, Experimental and Trial Pieces Judd, J. Hewitt, and Kosoff, A. Western Publishing Co. Inc., 1982. Covers all non-issued U.S. coin designs in catalog form, with illustrations, pedigrees, rarity ratings and recut prices.

U.S. copper coins

American Half Cents. Cohen, Roger S. Wigglesworth & Ghatt Co., Arlington, Va., 1982. Catalog listing of all known half cent varieties, with photos accompanying listings.

America's Copper Coinage 1783-1857. American Numismatic Society, 1985. Features articles about state and federal copper coinage through the demise of the large cent. Reprints of papers presented at the ANS's 1984 Coinage of the Americas Conference.

Encyclopedia of United States Half Cents 1793-1857. Breen, Walter. American Institute of Numismatic Research, South Gate, Calif., 1984. Historical information and pedigrees, plus catalog listing of all known half cent varieties, with photos accompanying the listings.

The Fugio Cents. Kessler, Alan. Colony Coin Co., Newtonville, Mass., 1976. A catalog listing of varieties of the United States' first coinage, with historical information.

Penny Whimsy. Sheldon, William H. Quarterman Publications Inc., Lawrence, Mass., 1983 (reprint of 1958 edition, 1976 copyright). Catalog listing of known varieties of large cents from 1793 to 1814, with plates in back.

The Two-Cent Piece and Varieties. Kliman, Myron M. Sanford J. Durst Numismatic Publications, New York, 1983. Catalog listing of known varieties, with no photos.

United States Copper Cents 1816-1857. Newcomb, Howard R. Quarterman Publications Inc., Lawrence, Mass., 1981 (facsimile reprint of 1944 book). Catalog listing of known varieties of later large cents, with plates in back.

United States Copper Coins — An Action Guide for the Collector and Investor. Bowers, Q. David. Bowers and Merena Inc., Wolfeboro, N.H., 1984. Covers half cents, large cents, small cents and 2-cent pieces with historical information and investment advice.

U.S. silver dollars

The Comprehensive Catalogue and Encyclopedia of U.S. Morgan and Peace Silver Dollars. Van Allen, Leroy C., and Mallis, A. George. Arco Publishing Co., New York, 1976. Historical information and catalog listing of all known varieties.

The Fantastic 1804 Dollar. Bressett, Kenneth E., and Newman, Eric. P. Whitman Publishing Co., Racine, Wis., 1962. A wonderful numismatic mystery is solved in this in-depth study of the 1804 dollar, one of the United States' greatest rarities. Updated at the ANS Coinage of the Americas Conference, 1986.

The Morgan and Peace Dollar Textbook. Miller, Wayne. Adam Smith Publishing Co., Metairie, La., 1982.

The United States Early Silver Dollars from 1794 to 1803. Bolender, M.H. Krause Publications, Iola, Wis., 1988 (fifth edition revised by Julius Reiver). Catalog listing of dollar varieties, with plates in back.

The United States Trade Dollar. Willem, John M. Sanford J. Durst Numismatic Publications, New York, 1983 (reprint of 1959 edition). Historical treatment of the Trade dollar, with mintages by month, varieties and rarity levels.

U.S. silver half dollars

Early Half Dollar Varieties. Overton, Al C. Colorado Springs, Colo., 1970. Catalog listing of all known varieties, with photos accompanying listings. Supplement published in 1987 by the Bust Half Nut Club.

The Walking Liberty Half Dollar. Swiatek, Anthony. Sanford J. Durst Numismatic Publications, New York, 1983. Catalog listing, with emphasis on distinguishing between strong strikes and weak strikes.

U.S. silver quarter dollars

The Early Quarter Dollars of the United States. Browning, A.W. Sanford J. Durst Numismatic Publications, New York, 1977 (reprint of 1925 book). Catalog listing of known varieties, with plates at back.

Standing Liberty Quarters. Cline, J.H. Cline's Rare Coins, Palm Harbor, Fla., 1988. Historical information, including correspondence between designer and Treasury officials, plus catalog listing and investment advice.

U.S. silver dimes

Encyclopedia of United States Liberty Seated Dimes. Ahwash, Kamal M. Kamal Press, 1977. Catalog listings of known varieties, with over-sized photos accompanying listings.

Early United States Dimes: 1796-1837. Davis, David J.; Logan, Russell J.; Lovejoy, Allen F.; McCloskey, John W.; Subjack, William L. John Reich Collectors Society, 1984. Catalog of known varieties for Draped Bust and Capped Bust dimes, with over-sized photos accompanying listings.

U.S. silver half dimes

The United States Half Dimes. Valentine, Daniel W. Quarterman Publications Inc., Lawrence, Mass., 1975 (reprint of 1931 book). Valentine catalog listing, plus updated information by other individuals.

U.S. gold coins

United States Gold Coins, an Illustrated History. Bowers, Q. David. Bowers & Ruddy Galleries, Los Angeles, 1982. The history of U.S. gold coins.

U.S. Gold Dollars through U.S. Double Eagles. Akers, David W. Paramount Publications, Englewood, Ohio, 1975-1982. A series of six books covering gold dollars, quarter eagles, $3 and $4 gold pieces, half eagles, eagles, and double eagles; basically it records auction appearances by denomination, date and Mint mark.

United States Gold Patterns. Akers, David W. Paramount International Coin Corp., Englewood, Ohio, 1975. Subtitled "A photographic study of the gold patterns struck at the United States Mint from 1836 to 1907."

U.S. exonumia

The Atwood-Coffee Catalogue of United States and Canadian Transportation Tokens. Coffee Jr., John M., and Ford, Harold V. The American Vecturist Association, Boston, 1987. The book catalogs mass transportation tokens and similar items, based on earlier Atwood system and catalog. Other volumes catalog minor die varieties and record the history of the transportation token.

Early American Tokens, Hard Times Tokens, U.S. Merchant Tokens 1845-1860, United States Trade Tokens 1866-1889, Tokens of the Gay Nineties 1890-1900. Rulau, Russell. Krause Publication, Iola, Wis., 1981-1983. Five volumes in a planned series listing of all U.S. merchant tokens (except Civil War pieces) and related pieces in a soft-cover catalog format.

Medals of the United States Mint — The First Century 1792-1892. Julian, Robert W. Token and Medal Society Inc., 1977. Massive historical work covering all medallic works produced by the Mint during its first 100 years.

Medals of the United States Mint Issued for Sale. Department of the Treasury, 1972. Lists medals struck by the Mint of which it sells duplicates; does not list the many medals it struck and does not sell.

Patriotic Civil War Tokens. Fuld, George, and Fuld, Melvin. Civil War Token Society, 1982 (released 1984). Catalog lists all Civil War patriotic tokens, with historical information and chapters on related topics.

So-Called Dollars. Hibler, Harold E., and Kappen, Charles V. The Coin and Currency Institute, New York, 1963. Covers commemorative and exposition medals of near-dollar size in catalog format, listing metal varieties and historical information.

U.S. Civil War Store Cards. Fuld, George, and Fuld, Melvin. Quarterman Publications, Lawrence, Mass., 1975. Catalogs all Civil War store cards by city and state, with historical information.

Video Arcade, Pinball, Slot Machine, and Other Amusement Tokens of North America. Alpert, Stephen A., and Smith, Kenneth E. Amusement Token Collectors Association, Redondo Beach, Calif., 1984. It catalogs all known amusement tokens by state, province and miscellaneous categories.

Counterfeit detection

Counterfeit Detection. Staff of the American Numismatic Association Certification Service. American Numismatic Association, Colorado Springs, Colo., two volumes, 1983 and 1987. Reprints ANACS's columns appearing in The Numismatist, discussing and illustrating counterfeits and genuine specimens of dozens of U.S. coins, plus information about collectible varieties and ANACS procedures.

Counterfeits of U.S. States Coins. Spanbauer, Larry. Service Litho-Print Inc., Oshkosh, Wis., 1975. Illustrates many Colonial, private Mint and modern counterfeits and replicas.

Detecting Counterfeit Coins, Book 1. Devine, "Lonesome" John. Heigh Ho Printing Co., Newbury Park, Calif.,

1975. Illustrates and describes many counterfeit U.S. minor and silver coins.
Detecting Counterfeit Gold Coins, Book 2. Devine, "Lonesome" John. Heigh Ho Printing Co., Newbury Park, Calif., 1977. Illustrates and describes many counterfeit gold coins.

Grading

The Accugrade System. Hager, Alan. Silver Dollars Unlimited Inc., Bedford, N.Y., 1984, Accugrade Inc., Greenwich, Conn. 1986. A three-volume guide to grading Uncirculated, Proof and prooflike Morgan, Peace and Eisenhower dollars.
Grading Coins: A Collection of Readings. Edited by Bagg, Richard, and Jelinski, James J. Essex Publications, Portsmouth, N.H., 1977. Collection of articles about grading from The Numismatist, Whitman Numismatic Journal and Numismatic Scrapbook Magazine from 1892 to 1976. Takes a historical approach.
A Guide to the Grading of United States Coins. Brown, Martin R. and Dunn, John W. General Distributors Inc., Denison, Texas, 1980. Uses line illustrations for U.S. coins in all denominations from half cent to double eagle in all grades.
NCI Grading Guide. Halperin, James L. Ivy Press, 1986, Dallas, Texas. Written by a principle grader of the Numismatic Certification Institute. Provides a step-by-step approach to the grading of Uncirculated and Proof coins. Does not cover circulated grades.
New Photograde. Ruddy, James F. Revised and expanded by Bowers, Q. David. Bowers and Merena Galleries Inc., Wolfeboro, N.H., 1988. Photographic guide to the grading of U.S. coins in all denominations from half cent to double eagle.
Official American Numismatic Association Grading Standards for United States Coins. Bressett, Kenneth, and Kosoff,

A. Whitman Numismatic Products, Western Publishing, Racine, Wis., 1987. Official ANA guide to grading U.S. coins; third edition (1987) uses black-and-white photographs; first two editions use line illustrations. Includes non-illustrated guide to grading U.S. commemorative coins.

Errors

The Classification and Value of Errors on the Lincoln Cent. Cohen, Jean. Bonita Springs, Fla., 1969. Out of print. Illustrates through line drawings minor errors on Lincoln cents, and lists their (outdated) values.
The Design Cud. Marvin, Paul, and Margolis, Arnold. Heigh Ho Printing Co., Newbury Park, Calif., 1979. In-depth explanation and photographs of how major die breaks, cuds, occur.
The Encyclopedia of Doubled Dies, Vol. 1 and 2. Wexler, John A. Robert C. Wilharm News Printing Co. Inc., Fort Worth, Texas, 1978 and 1981. Illustrates and describes doubled dies on U.S. coins, and how they occur.
How Error Coins are Made at the U.S. Mints. Margolis, Arnold. Heigh Ho Printing Co., Newbury Park, Calif., 1981. Describes and illustrates how coins are minted and how error coins occur.
Modern Mint Mistakes. Steiner, Phillip, and Zimpfer, Michael. Whispering Pines Printing, Indiana, 1975-1976. Provides general information and a price guide to error coins.
Official Price Guide to Mint Errors and Varieties. Herbert, Alan. House of Collectibles Inc., Orlando, Fla., 1981. Offers a general, overall look at error coins.
The RPM Book. Wexler, John A., and Miller, Tom. Lonesome John Publishing Co., Newbury Park, Calif., 1983. Describes and illustrates repunched and over Mint marks, with price information.

U.S. paper money

U.S. government issues

Bureau of Engraving and Printing — The First Hundred Years 1862-1962. Sanford J. Durst Numismatic Publications, New York, 1978 (reprint of 1962 book published by the Treasury Department). Government history tracing history of BEP and government-issued paper money, postage stamps and revenue items.

The Comprehensive Catalog of U.S. Paper Money. Hessler, Gene. BNR Press, Port Clinton, Ohio, 1983. Catalog listings of government issues, with historical information.

The Encyclopedia of United States Fractional & Postal Currency. Friedberg, Milton. Numismatic and Antiquarian Service Corporation of America, Long Island, N.Y., 1978. Historical information and catalog of federal fractional notes of Civil War and Reconstruction.

Military Payment Certificates. Schwan, Fred. BNR Press, Port Clinton, Ohio, 1981. Covers notes issued for use by U.S. military personnel stationed overseas from 1946 to 1973.

Paper Money of the United States. Friedberg, Robert. Krause Publications, Iola, Wis., 1986. Catalog listings, with numbering system that is used hobby-wide.

Standard Catalog of National Bank Notes. Hickman, John, and Oakes, Dean. Krause Publications, Iola, Wis., 1982. Lists 117,007 different national bank notes in catalog fashion, plus historical information.

Standard Catalog of United States Paper Money. Krause, Chester L. and Lemke, Robert F. Krause Publications, Iola, Wis. 1989.

Standard Handbook of Modern United States Paper Money. O'Donnell, Chuck. Krause Publications, Iola, Wis., 1982. For collectors of small-sized notes, with complete listings of all blocks and star blocks issued, varieties and quantities produced.

Non-federal issues

Confederate and Southern States Currency. Criswell, Grover C. Criswell's Publications, Florida, 1976. Covers all CSA issues, plus states issues of the Civil War.

The Early Paper Money of America. Newman, Eric P. Western Publishing Co., Racine, Wis., 1976. Covers all paper money issued by the Continental Congress, 13 original Colonies.

Society of Paper Money Collectors Wismer update series. The SPMC has published a series of catalogs of obsolete notes by state and territory. Books available from the SPMC (see numismatic organizations chapter) include Rhode Island, Florida, Mississippi, Texas, Iowa, Minnesota, Alabama, Maine, Indiana, New Jersey, Vermont, Arkansas, Pennsylvania and a volume covering the Indian Territory, Oklahoma and Kansas.

Standard Catalog of United States Obsolete Bank Notes 1782-1866. Haxby, James A. Krause Publications, Iola, Wis., 1988. Four volumes.

Modern world coins

General works

World Coin Catalogue, Twentieth Century. Schon, Gunter. Amos Press Inc., Sidney, Ohio, 1988. Catalog form with listings by country.

A Catalog of Modern World Coins, 1850-1964. Yeoman, Richard S. The Coin and Currency Institute, Fort Lee, N.J. 13th edition. Catalog form.

Coin Atlas. Cribb, Joe; Cook, Barrie; and Carradice, Ian. Facts on File, New

York, 1990. Geographical listing, color photography throughout.

Current Coins of the World. Yeoman, Richard S. Coin & Currency Institute Inc., Clifton, N.J., 1988. Eighth edition revised by Arthur and Ira Friedberg. Catalog form.

Standard Price Guide to World Crowns & Talers, 1484-1968. Draskovic, Frank & Rubenfeld, Stuart. Krause Publ., Iola, Wis. 1984. Catalog form.

Standard Catalog of World Coins. Krause, Chester L. & Mishler, Clifford. Krause Publ., Iola, Wis., 1990. Catalog form.

Gold Coins of the World. Friedberg, Robert, Coin and Currency Institute Inc., New York, N.Y., 1980. Catalog format.

The Beauty & Lore of Coins, Currency & Medals. Clain-Stefanelli, E. & V. Riverwood Publ., Croton-on-Hudson, N.Y., 1974.

The Art of Coins & Their Photography. Hoberman, Gerald. Spink & Son Ltd., London, 1981.

Numismatic Bilbliography. Clain-Stefanelli, Elvira Eliza. Battenberg, Munich, West Germany, 1985. A comprehensive listing by subject of numismatic books.

Dictionary of Numismatic Names with Addenda. Frey, Albert R. Spink's, London, 1973. A comprehensive dictionary of numismatic terms, which includes a glossary of equivalent terms in English, French, German, Italian and Swedish.

Coins of the World. Carson, R.A.G. Harper & Brothers, New York, 1962. A brief numismatic history of virtually every country which has issued coins from ancient times to modern.

Biographical Dictionary of Medallists. Forrer, L. A.H. Baldwin & Sons, London. 8 volumes. A comprehensive encyclopedia listing coin and medal engravers and their works from ancient times to modern.

Africa, general works

The Silver Dollars of Africa. Davenport, John S. Whitman Publ. Co., Racine, Wis., 1959. Catalog format with photographs.

Australia

Renniks Australian Coin and Banknote Guide. Skinner, Dion H. Skinner & Warnes, Salisbury Heights, South Australia, 1976. Catalog form with illustrations, later editions exist.

Coins & Tokens of Tasmania. McNeice, Roger V. Platypus Publ., Hobart, Australia, 1969. Text with some photographs.

Coinage and Currency in New South Wales, 1788-1829. Mira, W.J.D. Wentwork Press, New South Wales, Australia, 1981. Text and almanac form with some photographs.

Austria

Osterreichische Munzpragungen von 1657-1969 (Austrian Money from 1657-1969). Herinek, Ludwig. Herinek, Munzhandlung, Vienna, 1970. Two volumes. Catalog with illustrations of Austrian coins.

Bolivia

The Coins of Bolivia. Seppa, Dale. Almanzar's, San Antonio, Texas, 1970.

Canada

The Charlton Standard Catalogue of Canadian Coins. Charlton, James. The Charlton Press, Toronto, Canada, 1990. Catalog form with prices.

The Charlton Standard Catalogue of Canadian Colonial Tokens. Charlton, James. The Charlton Press, Toronto, Canada, 1990. Catalog form with prices.

Standard Grading Guide to Canadian Decimal Coins. Charlton, James E. & Willey, Robert C. Whitman Publ. Co., Racine Wis., 1965. Line drawing guide to grading Canadian coins.

Striking Impressions: The Royal Canadian Mint and Canadian Coinage. Haxby, James A. Royal Canadian Mint, Ottawa, 1984. A history of the Royal Canadian Mint and its coinage.

Coins of Canada. Haxby, J.A. and Wiley, R.C. Unitrade Press, Toronto, Ontario,

Canada, 1983. Catalog form with prices.

China

The Currencies of China. Kann, Eduard. Kelly & Walsh Ltd., Shanghai, China, 1926 (1978 reprint of 1926 work by Sanford J. Durst, New York, N.Y.). Discussion of the currencies and their effects.

Colombia

Coins of Colombia. Seppa, Dale, and Almanzar, Alcedo. Almanzar's Coins of the World, San Antonio, Texas, 1973.

Cuba

The Coinage of Cuba, 1870 to date. Lismore, Thomas. Roy Renderer, Miami, Fla., 1966.

Czechoslovakia

Czechoslovak Coins. Davis, Dolores H. Numismatics International, Dallas, Texas, 1972. Catalog form with some illustrations.

Dominican Republic

Monedas Dominicanas, (Dominican Money). Gomez, Miguel E. Sociedad Dominicana de Biblofilos, Santo Domingo, Dominican Republic, 1979. Text in Spanish.

El Salvador

The Coins and Paper Money of El Salvador. Almanzar, Alcedo F. & Stickney. Brian R.

Ethiopia

Ethiopia, Treasure House of Africa. Kohl, Melvin J. The Society for International Numismatics, Santa Monica, Calif., 1969. Text with photographs.

Finland

Suomi, Rahat Ja Setelit (Finland, Coins and Bank Notes 1811-1981). von Schantz, C. Holmasto Coins & Medals Co. Helsinki, Finland, 1982. Catalog form in Finnish and English language.

France

Monnaies Francaises. Gadoury, Victor, Franz W. Wesel Druckerie und Verlag, Baden, West Germany, 1977. Catalog form, text in French.

Repertoire de la Numismatique Francaise Contemporaine, 1793 a nos jours (Numismatics of Contemporary France from 1793). De Mey, Jean & Poindessault, Bernard, Imprimerie Cultura, Brussels, Belgium, 1976. Catalog form, text in French.

Les Monnaies Royales Francaises de Hugues Capet a Louis XVI (French Royal Money from Hugh Capet to Louis XVI). Ciani, Louis, Paris, 1926. (Reprinted by A.G. Van der Dussen in Maastricht, Netherlands.) Comprehensive catalog of early-modern French coins.

Catalogue General Illustre des Editions de la Monnaie de Paris (General Illustrated Catalog of Issues of the Paris Mint). Monnaie de Paris, Paris, Four volumes. Illustrated catalog of the medals of the French Mint.

The Talers or Ecus of Alsace-Lorraine. Davenport, John S. American Numismatic Association.

Germany

Germanic Coinage (Charlemagne through Wilhelm II). Craig, William D. Mountain View, 1954. Invaluable reference for identifying and dating rulers of German city-states.

German Talers 1500-1600. Davenport, John S. Schulten, P.N., Frankfurt, 1979. Illustrated catalog of taler-size silver coins from 1500-1600.

German Secular Talers, 1600-1700. Davenport, John S. Schulten, P.N., Frankfurt, 1976. Illustrated catalog of talers from 1600-1700.

German Church and City Talers, 1600-1700. Davenport, John S. Galesburg, 1975. Illustrated catalog of talers, 1600-1700.

German Talers, 1700-1800. Davenport, John S. Spink & Son, London, 1979. Illustrated catalog of talers issued from

1700-1800.

Silver Gulden, 1559-1763. Davenport, John S. Schulten, P.N., Frankfurt, 1982. An illustrated catalog of gulden, a denomination of silver coin smaller than the taler.

Great Britain

Standard Catalogue of British Coins: England. Seaby, Peter. Seaby Publications, London, England. Catalog with illustrations, published annually.

Sylloge of Coins of the British Isles. Various authors, British Academy & Carlberg Foundation, London, England, 1970. Comprehensive catalog in 23 volumes. Contains 1. Fitzwilliam Museum, Cambridge Part, 2. Hunterian & Coats collections, Univ. of Glasgow, Part I, 3. Coins of the Coritani, 4. Royal collection of coins & medals, Nat. Museum, Copenhagen, Part I 5. Grosvenor Museum, Chester Part I, 6. Nat. Museum of Antiquities of Scotland, Edinburgh, Part I, 7. The Royal Danish Collection, Copenhagen, Part II, 8. The Hiberian-Norse coins in the British Museum, 9. Ashmolean Museum, Oxford, Part 1, 10. Ulster Museum, Belfast, 11. Reading University, 12. Ashmolean Museum, Oxford, Part II 13-15. The Royal Danish Collection Copenhagen, Part III, 16. Mrs. Emery May Norweb, Part I, 17. Ancient British, Anglo-Saxon & Norman coins in Midlands Museums, 18. The Royal Danish Collection, Copenhagen, Part IV, 19. Ancient British coins and coins of the Bristol & Gloucestershire Mints, 20. n/a, 21. n/a, 22. The Royal Danish Collection, Copenhagen Part V, 23. Ashmolean Museum, Oxford, Part III.

Standard Catalogue of British Coins: Coins of Scotland, Ireland and the Islands. Seaby, Peter, and Purvey, P. Frank. Seaby, London, 1987. Basic price catalog of coins of Scotland, Ireland and the islands of Jersey, Guernsey, Man and Lundy.

English Coins. Brooke, George C.

Methuen, London, 1966. History of the coinage of Great Britain.

British Tokens and Their Values. Seaby, Peter, Bussell, Monica Seaby, London, 1984. Priced catalog of British tokens, 17th through 19th century.

Coins of England and the United Kingdom. Seaby, London, England, 1985.

Guatemala

Historia Numismatica de Guatemala (Numismatic History of Guatemala). Prober, Kurt. Bank of Guatemala, 1973. Text and catalog in Spanish language.

Haiti

Coins of Haiti, 1803-1970. Arroyo, Carmen. Almanzar's Coins of the World, San Antonio, Texas 1970.

Hungary

Munzkatalog Ungarn von 1000 bis Heute (Catalog of Hungarian Coins from 1000 Forward). Huszar, Lajos. Battenberg, Munich, West Germany, 1979. Catalog form with illustrations, in German language.

India

Coins. Gupta, Parmeshwari Lal. Natl. Book Trust, New Delhi, India, 1969. Catalog form, text in English.

Studies in Indian Coins. Sircar, D.C. Motilal Banarsidas, Delhi, India, 1968. Catalog form, text in Indian language.

Iran

Modern Coinage of Iran, 1876-1974. Clarke, Robert L. & Mohabat-Ayin, A. Numismatics International, Dallas, Texas, 1974. Catalog form with some illustrations.

Israel

The History of Modern Israel's Money, 1917-1970. Haffner, Sylvia. Philip J. Matthew, Tarzana, Calif., 1970.

Israel's Money & Medals, 1948-1973. Kagan, A.H. Valley Stream, N.Y., 1974. Later editions may exist.

AINA Guide Book of Israel Coins & Medals. Schuman, Edward. American

Israel Numismatic Assn, Tamarac, Fla., 1980.

Israel Coins and Medals. Shoham, David. Ben Zvi Printing Enterprises Ltd., Jerusalem, Israel, 1982.

Israel's 20-year Catalog of Coins and Currency. Bertram, Fred & Weber, Robert. Louis Denberg Foundation Inc., N.Y., 1968.

Numismatics of the Holocaust, The Shekel. American Israel Numismatic Assn., Tamarac, Fla., Sept.-Oct., 1982 and March-April, 1983, combined reprint.

Italy

Super Collezionista di Monete Decimali Italiane, (Comprehensive Manual of Collecting the Decimal Money of Italy). Cesare Bobba, Torino, Italy, 1977. Catalog form with text in Italian. Later editions exist.

Jamaica

The Coinage of Jamaica. Byrne, Ray & Remick, Jerome H.

Japan

Japanese Coin Catalogue 1985. Oka, M. An illustrated, 1985 catalog in the Japanese language of coins and paper money.

Modern Japanese Coinage. Cummings, Michael L. Far East Journal, Tokyo, Japan, 1978. Catalog form with illustrations, later editions may exist.

Japanese Coinage. Jacobs, Norman & Vermeule, Cornelius C. Numismatic Revue, New York, N.Y. 1972. Text and illustrated catalog.

Lithuania

Senoves Lietuviu Pinigai (Ancient Lithuanian Currencies). Karys, Jonas K. Immaculata Press, Putnam, Conn. 1959. Identifies and explains coinage, text in English and Lithuanian.

Mexico

A Guidebook of Mexican Coins, 1822 to Date, fourth edition. Buttrey, T.V. & Hubbard, Clyde. Krause Publications, Iola, Wis. 1986. Catalog with prices.

Coins of Mexico. Grove, Frank W. Quarterman Publ. Inc., Lawrence, Mass., 1981. Catalog format.

Standard Catalogue of Mexican Coins, Paper Money, Stock, Bonds and Medals. Bruce, Colin R. II. Krause Publ., Racine, Wis., 1981. Catalog form with text of history, illustrated.

Numismatic History of Mexico. Pradeau, Alberto Francisco, Durst, Sanford J. New York. 1978 (reprint of 1938 edition). A numismatic history of Mexico.

Coins of Mexico, 1905-1971. Utberg, Neil S. Colonial Publ. Co., Houston, Texas, 1971.

Morocco

Mondeas de Marruecos, (Moroccan Coins, 1879-1971). Sanchez-Giron, J.M. publ. by author, Ceuta, Spain, 1972. Catalog format, in Spanish and English languages.

Mozambique

Catalogo das Moedas de Mocambique (Catalog of Money of Mozambique). Azevedo, Vasco, Livraria Fernando Machado, Porto, 1969. Catalog with each coin photographed, text in Portuguese.

Netherlands

Nederlandse Munten van 1795-1961 (Dutch Money from 1795-1961). Schulman, Jacques, Jacques Schulman N.V., Amsterdam, Netherlands, 1962. Catalog form, well illustrated. Text in Dutch language.

Norway

Norges Mynter, (Coinage of Norway). Ahlstrom, Bjarne, Brekke, Bernhard F. & Hemmingsson, Bengt, Numismatiska Bokforlaget AB, Stockholm, Sweden, 1976. Catalog form in Swedish and English language.

Oriental, general works

The Standard Guide to South Asian Coins & Paper Money Since 1556 AD. Bruce, Colin R. II, Deyell, John S. Rhodes, Nicholas, & Spengler, William F.

Krause Publ., Iola, Wis., 1981. General catalog of non-Japanese & non-Chinese oriental coins.

Numismata Orientalia Illustrata, (Oriental Numismatics Illustrated). Album, Stephen. Attic Books Ltd., New York, N.Y., 1977. Catalog form with some charts.

Panama
Coins & Currency of Panama. Grigore, Julius Jr. Krause Publ., Iola, Wis., 1972. Illustrated text in English language.

Paraguay
The Coins of Paraguay. Seppa, Dale & Almanzar, Alcedo, Almanzar's Coins of the World, San Antonio, Texas, 1971.

Poland
Hanbuch der Polnischen Numismatik (Handbook of Polish Numismatics). Gumowski, Marian, Akademische Druck-U, Graz, Austria, 1960. Identifies and explains coinage in German language.

Rhodesia-Zimbabwe
Keogh On Coins of Rhodesia-Zimbabwe. Keogh, John, Keogh Coins, Durban North, South Africa, 1980. Catalog form.

Russia
A Guidebook of Russian Coins, 1725-1982. Harris, Robert P. Mevius Numisbooks Int. B.V., Vriezenveen, Netherlands, 1983. Catalog form with many illustrations.

Scandinavia, general works
Sieg Montkatalog 1978 (Sieg's Catalog of Money). Sieg, Frovin. Ulbjerg gl. Skole, Skals, Denmark, 1977. Catalog form in Danish language with English summary. Covers all of Scandinavia, revised annually.

South Africa
The Coins of South Africa. Kaplan, Alec. Alec Kaplan & Son Pty. Ltd., Germiston, South Africa, 1984.

Catalog form.
Coins of South Africa. Jacobs, Ken Publ. by author. Boksburg North, South Africa, 1983. Catalog form of type coins, in full color.
Studies in Indian Coins. Sircar, D.C. Motilal Banarsidas, Delhi, India, 1968. Catalog form, text in Indian language.

Spain
Las Monedas Espanolas Desde D. Pelaya 718 a Juan Carlos I 1980, (The Money of Spain from D. Pelayo in 718 to Juan Carlos I 1980). Castan, Carlos & Cayon, Juan R. Artegraf, IGSA, Madrid, Spain, 1979. Catalog form with illustrations, text in Spanish.

Sweden
Sveriges Mynt 1521-1977 (Coinage of Sweden). Ahlstrom, Bjarne. Almer, Yngve & Hemmingsson, Bengt, Numismatiska Bokforlaget AB, Stockholm, 1976. Catalog form in Swedish and English language.

Switzerland
Die Munzen der Schweiz (The Money of Switzerland). Divo, Jean-Paul & Tobler, Edwin. Bank Leu, Zurich, Switzerland, 1974. Catalog form in German language. Possible later editions exist.

Uruguay
The Coins of Uruguay, 1840-1971. Seppa, Dale & Almanzar, Alcedo F. Almanzar's Coins of the World, San Antonio, Texas, 1971.

Coinage of the Americas
America's Foreign Coins; An Illustrated Standard Catalogue with Valuations of Foreign Coins with Legal Tender Status in the U.S., 1793-1857. Schilke, O.G. Coin & Currency Institute, N.Y., 1964. (Reprint of 1964 edition.)
Coinage of the Americas. Buttrey, Theodore V. Jr. American Numismatic Society, New York, N.Y. 1973. Discussions of coinage of both continents.
The Coins of Central America, Silver &

Copper, 1824-1940. Raymond, Wayte. New York, 1941.

The Coins of South America, Silver & Copper, Raymond, Wayte. New York, 1942.

The Coins of the West Indies, Silver & Copper, Including the Cut & Counterstamped Pieces. Raymond, Wayte. New York, 1942.

Copper Coins of Central & South America. Eklund, O.P. from The Numismatist, Colorado Springs, Colo., 1962.

The Gold Coins of North & South America, An Illustrated Catalogue of All the Types with an Indication of Their Retail Value. Raymond, Wayte. New York, 1937.

Gold Coins of the Americas with Values. Harris, Robert P. Anco, Florence, Ala., 1971. Catalog form with some illustrations.

The Julius Guttag Collection of Latin American Coins. Adams, Edgar H. Quarterman Publ., Lawrence, Mass., 1974.

Sammlung Uberseeischer Munzen und Medaillen, (Oversees Money and Medals). Weyl, Adolph, J.A. Stargardt, Berlin, Germany, 1878 (1970 reprint of 1878 work by Organization of International Numismatists, Sepulveda, Calif.). Catalog form with some line drawings and text in German language.

The Silver Dollars of North & South America; An Illustrated Catalogue of All the Types & an Indication of Their Retail Value. Raymond, Wayte. New York, 1964.

The Silver & Minor Coins of North & South America Exclusive of the United States, Raymond, Wayte. New York, N.Y.

Spanish American Gold Coins; Being a Detailed List of the Gold Coins Struck by the Spanish Kings in America at the Mints of Mexico, Guadalxara, Lima, Potosi, Bogota, Popayan, Guatemala, Santiago. Raymond, Wayte. New York, 1936.

Odd & curious

Odd and Curious Money: Descriptions and Values. Opitz, Charles J. First Impressions Printing, Ocala, Fla., 1986. Encyclopedic listing of odd and curious moneys.

A Survey of Primitive Money. Quiggin, A. Higston. Methuen & Co. Ltd., Strand, Great Britain, 1963 (Reprint of the 1963 edition by Sanford J. Durst, New York, N.Y.). Text with line drawings and photographs.

Primitive Money in its Ethnological, Historical and Economic Aspects. Einzig, Paul. Eyre & Spottswood, London, England, 1948 (1982 reprint of the 1948 edition by Sanford J. Durst, New York, N.Y.). Text with photographs.

Odd and Curious. Reed, Mort. Fisher Printing Co., 1963 (1980 reprint of the 1963 edition by Sanford J. Durst, New York, N.Y.). Text and line drawings.

Ancient coins

Ancient Greece

Greek Coins & Their Values. Sear, David R. Seaby Publications Ltd., London, England, 1978. Two volumes; Europe, and Asia and Africa in catalog form.

An Outline of Ancient Greek Coins. Klawans, Zander H. Western Publishing Co. Inc., Racine, Wis. (1982 reprint by Sanford J. Durst, New York, N.Y.). Identified and explains Greek coinage in general form.

Historia Numorum. Head, Barclay V. Oxford, England, 1911 (1983 reprint of 1911 work by Sanford J. Durst, New York, N.Y.). Comprehensive catalog of ancient Greek city-state coinage.

Greek Coins. Seltman, Charles, Spink & Son, London, 1977. A history of metallic currency and coinage down to the fall of the Hellenistic kingdoms.

Greek Coin Types and Their Identification.

Plant, Richard. Seaby, London, 1979. Line drawings help to identify Greek coins.

Dictionary of Greek Coin Inscriptions. Icard, Severin, Sanford Durst, New York, 1979. This is a comprehensive reference for translating Greek coin inscriptions.

Ancient Greek & Roman Coins: A Handbook. Hill, Sir George F. Argonaut, Chicago, 1964.

Greek Imperial Coins and Their Values. Sear, David R. Seaby Publications Ltd., London, England, 1982. General catalog of the subject; illustrated.

Roman Republic

The Coinage of the Roman Republic. Sydenham, Edward A. Spink & Son, Ltd., London, England. 1952 (1982 reprint of 1952 work by Sanford, J. Durst, New York, N.Y.). Catalog with historical entries on the field in general.

Descripcion General de las Monedas de la Republica Romana (General Description of the Money of the Roman Republic). Cohen, Por H. Chez M. Curt, London & Paris, 1857 (1976 reprint of 1857 work by Juan R. Cayon, Madrid, Spain). Catalog with historical entries on the field in general.

Roman Republic Coinage. Crawford, Michael H. Cambridge University Press, London, 1974. Two volumes. A comprehensive catalog of Roman Republican coins.

Roman Silver Coins. Seaby, H.A. Seaby, London. Four volumes. A catalog of Roman silver coins.

Roman Empire

Roman Coins and Their Values. Sear, David R. Seaby Publications Ltd., London, England, 1981. Catalog form of the field in general.

Roman Imperial Coins. Klawans, Zander H. Western Publishing Co. Inc., Racine, Wis., 1977 (1982 reprint of 1977 work by Sanford J. Durst, New York, N.Y.). Identifies and explains Imperial Roman coins in general form.

The Roman Imperial Coinage. Mattingly, Harold, edited by Edward A. Sydenham, Spink & Son. Ltd., London, England, 1968 (1968 reprint of the 1884 work). Catalog form, eight volumes, contents: 1. Augustus to Vitellius, 2. Vespasian to Hadrian, 3. Antoninus Pius to Commodus, 4. Pertinax to Geta & Macrinus to Pupienus & Gordian III to Urania Antoninus, 5. Valerian I to Florian, Probus to Amandus, 6. Diocletian's reform to death of Maximinus, 7. Constantine & Licinius, 8. Valentinian I to Theodosius I.

Reading and Dating Roman Imperial Coins. Klawans, Zander H. Sanford Durst, New York, 1982. Simple guide for identifying and attributing Roman coins.

Judaea

Handy Guide to Jewish Coins. Rogers, Edgar, Spink & Son Ltd., London, England, 1914 (1982 reprint of 1914 work by Sanford J. Durst, New York, N.Y.). Catalog form on the field in general.

Sylloge Nummorum Graecorum, (Sylloge of Greek Money). American Numismatic Society, New York, N.Y. 1981. Part six Palestine-South Arabia volume only. Comprehensive catalog form of the field from the ANS collection.

Moneys of the Bible: An Illustrated Digest of the Coinage of Biblical Times with Scriptural References. Yeoman, R.S. Whitman, Racine, Wis., 1961.

Ancient Jewish Coinage. Meshorer Ya'akov, Amphora Books, N.Y., 1982. Two volumes in catalog form covering 1) Persian period-Hasmonaeons, and 2) Herod the Great-Bar Cochba.

Catalog of Judaea Capta Coinage. Brin, Howard B. Minnesota, 1986. Complete listing of Judaea Capta coins; illustrated.

The Coinage of the Bar Kokhba War. Mildenberg, Leo. Verlag Sauerlander. Frankfurt am Main, West Germany, 1984. Examines coinage of Jews in Judaea about A.D. 132-135.

Other ancient empires

An Introduction to the Coinage of Parthia.
Sellwood, David, Spink & Son Ltd.,
London, England, 1971. Catalog form
of the field in general.

Chinese Currency. Schjoth, Fr. Andrew
Publ. Co., London, England, 1929
(1976 reprint of 1929 work by W & J
Mackay Ltd., Chatham, England).
Catalog format with line drawings.

Coins in China's History. Coole, Arthur
Braddan, Inter-Collegiate Press, 1965.
Comprehensive, historical overview of
Chinese numismatics including a time
line relating events in China with
events in the Western world.

Imperial Persian Coinage. Hill, George F.
Obol International, Oak Park, Ill.,
1968. Catalog form of the field of the
Persian Empire.

Sasandische Numismatik, (Sassanian
Numismatics). Gobl, Robert,
Klinkhardt & Biermann,
Braunschweig, West Germany, 1968.
Catalog form of the field of Sassanian
coinage.

Medieval

General Medieval works

The Coinage of the European Continent.
Hazlitt, W. Carew, Swan Sonnenschein
& Co., London, England, 1893 (1974
reprint of the 1893 work by Ares Publ.
Enc., Chicago, Ill.). General text with
data on the subject.

*Medieval European Coinage with a
Catalogue of the Coins in the
Fitzwilliam Museum.* Grierson, Philip,
and Blackburn, Mark. Cambridge
University Press, England, 1986. First
in a series about medieval coinage.

Reading Medieval European Coins.
Walker, Ralph S. Attic Books Ltd.,
New York, N.Y. 1979. Basic book on
how to decipher inscriptions on
medieval coins.

*The Dated European Coinage Prior to
1501.* Frey, Albert R. American Journal
of Numismatics, New York, N.Y.,
1915 (1978 reprint of the 1915 work by
Sanford J. Durst, New York, N.Y.).
Catalog of all Christian dated coins
before 1501.

*Die Ritter von Schulthess-Rechberg'sche
Munz-u. Medaillen-Sammlung* (The
Knights of Schulthess-Rechberg,
Money and Medals). Erbstein, Julius
and Albert. Quarterman, Boston, 1974
(reprint of 1869 edition). Invaluable in
identifying coins not cataloged
elsewhere.

*Beschreibung der Bekanntesten
Kupfermunzen* (Description of Copper
Money). Neumann, Josef. Johnson
Reprint Corp., New York, 1965 (reprint
of 1858 edition). Seven volumes.
Useful for identifying copper coins of
Europe.

Austria

*The Coinage of Medieval Austria, 1156-
1521.* Szego, Alfred, A. Szego Publ.,
West Sayville, N.Y. 1970. A basic
outline on the subject.

*Corpus Nummorum: Moser/Tursky, Die
Munzen Kaiser Rudolfs II aus der
Munzstatte Hall in Tirol 1602-1612.*
Lanz, Dr. Herbert. Numismatik,
Munich, West Germany, 1987.
Comprehensive syllogue about the
subject; illustrated.

Byzantine

Byzantine Coins and their Values. Sear,
David R. Seaby Publishing Ltd.,
London, England, 1974. General
catalog on the subject, illustrated.

Byzantine Coins. Grierson, Philip,
University of California Press,
Berkeley & Los Angeles, Calif., 1982.
Text with charts and tables on the
subject, very detailed.

*Imperial Byzantine Coins in the British
Museum.* Wroth, Warwick. Argonaut
Inc., Chicago, Ill., 1966. Detailed
catalog format with photographic plates
and charts.

Moneta Imperii Byzantini. Hahn,

Wolfgang. Vienna, Austria, 1981. Three-volume illustrated set covering subject from 491-720. Volume I: Anastasius I to Justinian I; Volume II: Justin II to Phocas; Volume III: Heraclius to Leo II.

England

England Hammered Coinage. North, J.J. Spink & Son Ltd., London, England, 1960. Two volumes in catalog form, illustrated.

Coins of England and the United Kingdom. Seaby, Peter. Seaby Publications, London, England, 1984. Catalog of ancient, medieval and modern coins of the realm. A new edition is printed annually.

France

Carolingian Coinage of France. Morrison, Karl F. Karl F. Morrison & Henry Grunthal, New York, N.Y., 1967. Maps, notes and monograms; part of the ANS series.

The Barbaric Tremissis in Spain & Southern France. American Numismatic Society, New York, N.Y. 1964. Notes and monograms; part of the ANS series.

Catalogue General Illustre et a Prix Marques en Francs or de Monnaies Francaises Provinciales (General Illustrated Catalog of the Money of France and the Provinces). Boudeau, E. Nouvelle ed., Maastricht, Netherlands, 1970. Catalog format with illustrations and maps, text in French language.

Germany

Germanic Coinages, Charlemagne Through Wilhelm II. Craig, William D. Wm. D. Craig, Mountain View, Calif., 1954. General work with illustrations on the subject.

Altdeutschland 768-1806 (Old Germany). Ernst Battenberg, Munich, West Germany, ca. 1975 (1982 reprint of 1975 work by Sanford Durst, New York, N.Y.). Catalog format of general work in German language.

The Coinage of South Germany in the Thirteen Century. Metcalf, David M. Spink & Son Ltd., London England, 1961. Catalog format on the subject.

Islamic countries

Oriental Coins and Their Values, The World of Islam. Mitchiner, Michael, Hawkins Publications, London, England, 1977. Catalog form with photographs and some historical facts.

A Catalogue of the Muhammadan Coins in the British Museum. Walker, John, British Museum, London, England, 1956. Two volumes: 1) Arab-Sassanian coins, 2) Arab-Byzantine & post-reform Umaiyad coins.

Oriental Coins and Their Values, the Ancient & Classical World 600 B.C.-A.D. 650. Mitchiner, Michael. Hawkins Publications, London, 1978. Contains much information on ancient coins from this area not found elsewhere.

Italy

The Venetian Tornesello: A Medieval Colonial Coinage. Stahl, Alan. American Numismatic Society, New York, 1985.

World paper money

General works

A Collector's Guide to Paper Money. Beresiner, Yasha. Stein & Day Publ., New York, N.Y., 1977. Text with some photographs.

Banknotes & Banking in The Isle of Man, 1788-1970. Quarmby, Ernest. Spink & Son Ltd., London, England, 1971. Text with photographs.

The Charlton Standard Catalogue of Canadian Paper Money. Charlton Press, Toronto, 1980. Priced and illustrated guide to Canadian paper money.

English Paper Money. Duggleby, Vincent. Stanley Gibbons Publ. Ltd., London, England, 1980. Catalog form.

Scottish Banknotes. Douglas, James. Stanley Gibbons Publ. Ltd., London, England, 1975. Catalog form, later editions may exist.

Standard Catalog of World Paper Money. Pick, Albert, Krause Publ., Iola, Wis. 1990. Catalog form in two volumes: 1. general issues, 2. specialized issues.

World War II Military Currency. Schwan, C. Frederick & Boling, Joseph E. BNR Press, Portage, Ohio, 1978. Catalog form.

Notgeld

Das Deutsche Notgeld, (The German Notgeld). Keller, Arnold, Battenberg, Verlag, Munich, West Germany, 1976. Catalog in German language in 11 volumes: 1. 1914, 2. Germany, Austria, Hungary 1914-1918, 3. large paper money 1918-1921, 4. small paper money 1916-1922, etc.

Das Lagergeld der Konzentrations — und DR — Lager, 1933-1945, (The Money of the Concentration Camps and Displaced Persons Camps, 1933-1945). Oick, Albert, and Siemsen, Carl. Battenberg, Verlag, Munich, West Germany, 1976. Catalog in German language.

Guide and Checklist of World Notgeld 1914-1947. Coffing, Courtney L. Krause Publications, Iola, Wis., 1988.

Investing

Past performance of coins as an investment is not necessarily an indication of the future. It is important to remember that the future is unknown.

There are hundreds of books on investing in rare coins. The following titles are provided as a sampling of those published within recent years. They do not reflect the personal recommendations of any Coin World staff member or an endorsement by the publication. The listing is alphabetical and in no way reflects importance or selectivity.

Opinions and advice contained in these and other investment books are those of the authors.

The Big Silver Melt. Merton, Henry A.; Macmillan Publishing Co. Inc., New York. 1983.

The Investor's Guide to Coin Trading. Travers, Scott A. John Wiley & Sons, New York, 1989.

The Coin Collector's Survival Manual. Travers, Scott A. Arco Publishing Inc., New York City, 1988 (second edition)

Travers' Rare Coin Investment Strategy. Travers, Scott A. Prentice Hall Press, 1989 (second edition).

Donald Kagin's Personal Guide to Rare Coin Investments. Kagin, Donald; Kagin's Investment Corp., Des Moines, Iowa. 1984.

Heads You Win, Tails You Win. Prichard, Jeffrey J.; Reston Publishing Company Inc., Reston, Va. 1983.

High Profits From Rare Coin Investment. Bowers, Q. David; Bowers and Merena Galleries Inc., Wolfeboro, N.H. 1989 (12th edition.)

Investing in Rare Coins. Steinmetz, Dennis; Steinmetz Coins and Currency, Lancaster, Pa. 1981.

The Investor's Guide to United States Coins. Berman, Neil S., and Schulman, Hans M.F. Coin & Currency Institute Inc., New York City, 1986.

Investor's Yearbook - 1984. Owen, Al; Newsletter Digest, Huntsville, Ala. 1984.

A Mercenary's Guide to the Rare Coin Market. Hall, David. 1987.

Survive and Win in the Inflationary '80s. Ruff, Howard J.; Warner Books, New York. 1982.

The World of Coins and Coin Collecting. Ganz, David L.; Charles Scribner's Sons, New York. 1980.

Common book references

Most definitive reference catalogs assign numbers to the coins, bank notes or whatever listed in them, as a convenience to the collectors of that series. This also allows advertisers of this material to list a particular item for sale with only the briefest description of the piece, where otherwise several paragraphs might be necessary to describe the type or variety.

To help the beginning collector identify a reference he might not be familiar with, we include here a listing of the references most likely to be encountered in an advertisement or an auction catalog. The title of the book is given first, followed by the name of the author and the style in which one might find a catalog listing.

Colonial and state coinage:

The Early Coins of America	Sylvester S. Crosby	Crosby 2-A
The Coins of New Jersey	Dr. Edward Maris	Maris 1-A
The State Coinage of Connecticut	Henry C. Miller	Miller 2-B
The Silver Coinage of Massachusetts	Hillyer Ryder	Ryder 2
The Colonial Coins of Vermont	Hillyer Ryder	Ryder 2
"The Copper Coins of Vermont," 1947 The Numismatist reprint	John M. Richardson	Ryder-Richardson 7

Copper coins:

The Fugio Cents	Alan Kessler	
"Varieties of the Fugio Cent," The Coin Collectors Journal July-August 1952	Eric P. Newman	Newman
Walter Breen's Encyclopedia of United States Half Cents 1793-1857	Walter Breen	Breen 3c, Breen 9
American Half Cents: The "Little Half Sisters"	Roger S. Cohen Jr.	Cohen 1-A
United States Half Cents	Ebenezer Gilbert	Gilbert 1
Penny Whimsy	William H. heldon	Sheldon 101, S-101
United States Copper Cents: 1816-1857	Howard R. Newcomb	Newcomb 1, N-1

Silver coins:

The United States Half Dimes	Daniel W. Valentine	Valentine 1a, V-1a
Early United States Dimes	David J. Davis, Russell J. Logan, Allen F. Lovejoy, John W. McCloskey, William L. Subjack	Variety 13
Encyclopedia of United States Liberty Seated Dimes	Kamal M. Ahwash	Ahwash 1
The Early Quarter Dollars of the United States	A.W. Browning	Browning 1
Half Dollar Die Varieties	M.L. Beistle	Beistle 11-L
Early Half Dollar Varieties: 1794-1836	Al C. Overton	Overton 110, O-110
The United States Early Silver Dollars from 1794-1803	M.H. Bolender	Bolender B-14a
The Comprehensive Catalogue and Encyclopedia of U.S. Morgan and Peace Silver Dollars	Leroy C. Van Allen and A. George Mallis	Van Allen-Mallis 1, VAM-1
Variety Identification for United States Coins 1796-1837	Jules Reiver	Reiver 1a

Special Series:

California Pioneer Fractional Gold	Walter Breen and Ronald J. Gillio	Breen-Gillio 753

Private Gold Coins and Patterns of the United States	Donald H. Kagin	Kagin 20, Kagin 20a
United States Pattern, Experimental and Trial Pieces	J. Hewitt Judd and Abe Kosoff	Judd 1294

Exonumia:

Hard Times Tokens	Lyman H. Low	Low 151
Patriotic Civil War Tokens	George and Melvin Fuld	Fuld 120/256
U.S. Civil War Store Cards	George and Melvin Fuld	Fuld NY10H
So-Called Dollars	Harold E. Hibler and Charles V. Kappen	Hibler and Kappen 11a, HK-11a

Paper Money:

Paper Money of the United States	Robert Friedberg	Friedberg 12, F-12
The Encyclopedia of United States Fractional & Postal Currency	Milton Friedberg	Milton 3R25.2c

World coins

Coins of the World	William D. Craig.	Craig 13, C-13
Standard Price Guide to World Crowns & Talers	Frank Draskovic and Stuart Rubenfeld	Davenport 143, Dav-143.
A Catalog of Modern World Coins: 1850-1950	R.S. Yeoman	Yeoman 1, Y-1
Current Coins of the World	R.S. Yeoman	Yeoman 1, Y-1

Commercial numismatic publications

Following is a list of United States commercial numismatic publications and their addresses.

Bank Note Reporter
Krause Publications Inc.
Iola, Wis. 54945

Coin Prices
Krause Publications Inc.
Iola, Wis. 54945

Coin World
Box 150
Sidney, Ohio 45365

COINage
Miller Magazines Inc.
2660 E. Main St.
Ventura, Calif. 93003

Coins Magazine
Krause Publications Inc.

Iola, Wis. 54945

Error Trends Coin Magazine
P.O. Box 158
Oceanside, N.Y. 11572

Error-Variety News/The Numismistake
3475 Old Conejo Road, C6
Newbury Park, Calif. 91320

Numismatic News
Krause Publications Inc.
Iola, Wis. 54945

World Coin News
Krause Publications Inc.
Iola, Wis. 54945

Numismatic Terms

23

Those basic numismatic terms likely to cause the most difficulty for both the novice and the advanced collector are included in this guide. Experts in the science of numismatics differ in their interpretation of a number of terms, and reference to a standard dictionary often fails to settle disputes. Terms relating to grading and error coins and notes are more comprehensively defined in their respective chapters.

- A -

accolated, conjoined, jugate — Design with two heads facing the same direction and overlapping.

accumulation — Coins, tokens, etc., unsorted, unclassified, and unattributed; not a collection.

adjustment — Filing down the face of an overweight planchet. Such filing marks often survive the coining process. This is common on 18th century coins.

aes grave — Cast bronze issue of the Roman republic; literally "heavy bronze."

aes rude — Large cast rectangular bronze coin, one of the earliest Roman coins.

alloy — Mixture of more than one metal.

altered — A coin or other numismatic item that has been deliberately changed, usually to make it resemble a rare or more valuable piece.

American Arts Gold Medallions — A series of 1-ounce and half-ounce gold bullion medals issued by the U.S. Mint from 1980-84. Medals depict great American artists, writers and actors.

American Eagle — Bullion coins released by the U.S. Mint beginning in October 1986. Five coins are available: a 1-ounce, .999 fine silver coin with $1 face value; a 1-ounce, .9167 fine gold coin with $50 face value; a half-ounce, .9167 fine gold coin with $25 face value; a quarter-ounce, .9167 fine gold coin with $10 face value; and a tenth-ounce, .9167 fine gold coin with $5 face value. Coins are sold at prices based on current metal prices plus a markup.

ancient coin — Generally any coin issued before A.D. 500.

anneal — To soften dies, planchets or metal by heat treatment.

ant nose — Primitive copper money of China ca. 600 B.C.

as — (Plural: asses) Bronze or orichalcum coins of the Roman republic.

assay — Analytic test or trial to ascertain the fineness, weight and consistency of precious or other metal in coin or bullion. An assay piece is one that has been assayed.

attribution — The identification of a numismatic item by characteristics such as issuing authority, date or period, Mint, denomination, metal in which

struck, and by a standard reference.

auction — Method of selling by which items are presented for sale to the highest bidder.

authentication — Authoritative determination of the genuineness of a numismatic item.

-B -

back — The paper money side opposite the "face"; analogous to the reverse of a coin.

bag marks — See contact marks.

bank note — A promissory note issued by a bank in useful denominations, payable to bearer and intended to circulate as money. Should not be used as a generic term for all forms of paper money.

bas-relief — Sculpture style featuring slight differences between the raised design and the field and in which no part of the design is undercut; used to execute models for coins and medals.

base metal — Non-precious metal; e.g., copper.

Bicentennial coins — The special quarter dollar, half dollar and dollar struck from mid-1975 to the end of 1976 in honor of the 200th anniversary of American Independence. Coins feature the dual date 1776-1976 and special reverses emblematic of the celebration. Issued in copper-nickel clad versions for circulation. Special 40 percent silver clad versions were sold to collectors.

bid sheet — A form used by a buyer in an auction or mail-bid sale, on which the buyer lists the item being bid on by the number it is assigned and the price he is willing to pay.

bid-buy sale — A combination form of fixed-price list and mail-bid sale. Rules may vary from dealer to dealer. However, customers usually may either buy a lot outright at the fixed price or place a bid (higher or lower). It permits buyers to purchase a lot at less than fixed price (in some cases), or by paying more, ensures a greater chance of obtaining the lot.

billon — A low-grade alloy used for some minor coin issues consisting usually of a mixture of silver and copper, and sometimes coated with a silver wash.

bison — Species considered typically North American, used on coinage and paper money of the United States; bison is a better term than buffalo, which is a more general term referring to a number of related but different species outside North America.

bit — A popular term for the Spanish-American 1-real piece (also Danish West Indies and other neighboring islands) which formerly circulated in the United States. More often used in the plural, as two bits (25 cents) or four bits (50 cents). A bit is 12-1/2 cents.

blank — (See planchet.)

block — In paper money collecting, a series of related notes indicated by the same prefix and suffix letters in the serial number. When the suffix letter changes, a new block is created. The suffix currently changes when the serial number reaches 99 920 000.

"Blue Book" — Nickname given to Handbook of United States Coins, an annual price guide for collectors. The book has a blue cover, hence the nickname. Gives wholesale prices, or what dealers might pay for U.S. coins.

bourse — Rhymes with "horse," the area at a coin show or convention where dealers set up tables of collectibles for sale.

brass — Coinage metal alloy containing chiefly copper and zinc.

Britannia — Gold bullion coin and its fractionals to be issued by Great Britain beginning in 1987; also, the allegorical figure representing Britain.

broadstrike — Coin struck outside a restraining collar.

broken bank note — Paper money of a defunct bank or a bank which has failed (broken), but often applied to any obsolete bank note.

bronze — Coinage metal alloy containing chiefly copper and tin.

Brown Back — A Brown Back note is a Second Charter, First Issue national bank note. Has brown ink on the back.

Buffalo nickel — More properly: Indian Head 5-cent piece.

buffalo — (See bison.)

bullion coin — A precious metal coin traded at the current bullion price.

bullion — Uncoined precious metal in the form of bars, plates, ingots, and other items.

buyer's fee — Winning bidders in a public auction in the United States are usually charged a buyer's fee based on a certain percentage of the winning bid. Most U.S. auction houses charge a 10 percent buyer's fee; a buyer placing a $110 hammer bid on a coin would pay an additional $11 buyer's fee, or $121.

-C-

cabinet friction — Slight surface wear on a coin, token or medal caused by friction between it and the tray or envelope in which it is contained.

check number — On modern paper money, used as a cross reference to the plate number -which appears on the margin of a currency sheet and which is trimmed from the note before it enters circulation -to identify the printing plate from which the note came. On the obverse, the check number is a letter and number combination appearing in lower right corner; on the reverse, it is a number only appearing at the lower right. Often incorrectly called the plate number.

chop mark (shroff mark) — A small punched impression applied by Chinese (chop) or Indian (shroff) banks or change offices to attest to the full weight and metallic content of a coin.

Civil War tokens — Privately-issued emergency coin-like tokens, the approximate size of current U.S.

cents, which circulated during the Civil War because of a scarcity of small change. Two major types were issued: patriotic tokens, with patriotic themes; and store cards, advertising pieces often carrying the issuer's name, address and type of business or services.

clad — Composite coinage metal strip composed of a core, usually of a base metal such as copper, and surface layers of more valuable metal, silver (or sometimes copper-nickel). Cladding is a cost-saving measure, making coins cheaper to produce while maintaining a desired appearance.

clip — Sometimes used to denote an incomplete planchet coin; in earlier days, clipping was a process of shaving edges of coins to remove small amounts of metal for illegal gain (which gave rise to lettered or reeded edges).

Coin note — See Treasury note.

coin — Usually a piece of metal, marked with a device, issued by a governing authority and intended to be used as money.

collar — A retaining ring die within which the coin dies operate; the collar forms the edge design of the piece such as reeding or lettering.

Colonial — Refers to coins or paper money issued by the Colonial governments of the 13 British Colonies that became the United States. See "state coinages."

commemorative — A piece issued to mark, honor or observe an anniversary, other event, place or person, or to preserve its memory.

compound-interest Treasury note — A type of U.S. paper money authorized in 1863 and 1864; they brought 6 percent interest, and were to be redeemed three years after issue.

condition census — Term introduced by Dr. William H. Sheldon to denote the finest specimen and average condition of next five finest known of a given variety of large cents. Catalogers are gradually extending the use of the term to other series.

conjoined — (See: accolated.)

contact marks — Minor abrasions on an otherwise Uncirculated coin, caused by handling in Mint-sewn bags and contact with other surfaces. Sometimes called bag marks.

Continental currency — Paper money issued by the authority of the Continental Congress during the Revolutionary War.

Continental dollar — A dollar-sized pattern struck in 1776 as a proposed coinage.

COPE, COPE PAK — Acronyms used at Bureau of Engraving and Printing for Currency Overprinting and Processing Equipment and Currency Overprinting and Processing Equipment, Packaging. Machines used to apply overprinting of seals, serial numbers and Federal Reserve index numbers to 16-note half sheets of paper money; then the COPE cuts the half sheets into single notes, bundles them into 100-note packages with a paper band, and into larger plastic-wrapped packages.

copper-nickel — Coinage alloy composed of copper and nickel in varying amounts.

copy — A reproduction or imitation of an original.

Coronet — Style of Liberty Head used on U.S. copper and gold coins for much of the 19th century. Liberty wears a coronet (most depicting the world LIBERTY).

counterfeit — An object made to imitate a genuine numismatic piece with intent to deceive or defraud, irrespective of whether the intended fraud is primarily monetary or numismatic.

crown — A general term embracing most silver coins from about 20 to 30 grams in weight and from about 33 to 42 millimeters in size. The term has become applicable also to most nickel-alloy coins of the same range of size and weight. Coins of 43 or more millimeters in diameter are said to be multiple crowns.

cud — A form of die break that leaves a shapeless lump of metal on part of a coin.

cupro-nickel — Copper-nickel; term often employed by the government.

currency — Applies to both coins and paper money. Many use the word currency for paper money only. Currency is legal tender.

current — Coins and paper money in circulation.

- D -

Date Back — A Date Back note is a Second Charter, Second Issue national bank note. Refers to the dates 1902-1908 found on the back.

debase — To become less valuable.

Demand note — Demand notes, authorized in 1861, were the first paper money issued by the United States federal government for circulation. Nicknamed the "greenback" because of the green ink used on the reverse.

denarius — (Plural: denarii) Roman silver coin, later debased, roughly equal to a Greek drachm. Initiated in 268 B.C., it equaled 16 asses; 25 denarii equals 1 gold aureus.

denomination — The face value of a coin or paper note; the amount of money it is worth.

denticles — Ornamental device used on rims of coins, often resembling teeth, hence the name; also "beading."

device — The principal element, such as a portrait, shield or heraldic emblem, of the design on the obverse and reverse of a coin, token or medal.

Devil's Face note — On some of Bank of Canada notes, First Issue of 1954, Queen Elizabeth II's hair has a coincidental combination of shading and light that looks like a "devil's" face. Shading was quickly changed under public pressure to remove the "face."

die scratch — Raised line on the surface of a coin, caused by a scratch in the coinage die.

die — A hardened metal punch, the face of which carries an intaglio or incuse mirror-image to be impressed on one side of a planchet.

disme — Spelling of the word "dime" on U.S. 1792 pattern pieces and name given the 10-cent coin authorized in the Mint Act of April 2, 1792. Probably pronounced like "steam" or "time." The "s" is silent.

double eagle — A gold $20 coin of the United States.

doubled die — A die which has a multiple image created during the die-making process. Coins struck from a doubled die show a doubled image. There are many different causes of doubled dies, and many doubled die coins. Sometimes mistakenly called double die.

doubloon — Popular slang name given to Spanish gold 8-escudo pieces of the Conquistador era, often associated with pirate treasure; also, a medal in special circumstances -Mardi Gras doubloon.

drachm — (Pronounced "dram") An ancient Greek silver coin, plural drachms. Drachma (pronounced "DRAHK-muh") is the modern Greek denomination, plural drachmas.

ducat — (Pronounced "DUCK-et") Medieval gold coin; also any of a number of modern issues of the Dutch Mint. Modern slang has spread its use to mean "ticket."

- E -

eagle — A gold $10 coin of the United States.

edge — Often termed the third side of a coin, it is the surface perpendicular to the obverse and reverse. Not to be confused with rim. Edges can be plain, lettered or milled (reeded or with some other repetitious device). Edges became particularly important with the advent of machine-struck coinage.

Educational notes — The Series 1896 $1, $2 and $5 silver certificates are called Educational notes because of the allegorical and educational themes of the vignettes. Replaced in 1899 with a new series.

electrotype — A copy or reproduction of a coin, token or medal made by the electroplating process.

electrum — Naturally-occurring alloy of gold and silver used for early coins of the Mediterranean region.

elongated coin — An oval medalet produced by a roller die using a coin, token or medal as a planchet -usually a cent.

encapsulated coin — One which has been sealed in a plastic holder, especially by a third-party grading service.

encased postage stamp — A postage stamp unofficially encased in a metal, plastic or cardboard frame and intended to be used as small change.

error — A coin, token, medal or paper money item evidencing a mistake made in its manufacture.

essai; essay — In paper money, a print made to test a design; analogous to a trial strike in coinage. (See also: proof)

exergue — (Pronounced "EX-surge") Area on a coin generally below the main design area, often site of date.

exonumia — A broad category of non-money, non-legal-tender numismatic items, including tokens, medals and badges. An exonumist is a specialist in exonumia.

experimental pieces — Struck from any convenient dies to test a new metal, new alloy or new denomination; those testing a new shape; those testing a standard metal for a new denomination; and those representing changes in planchets for the purposes of combating counterfeiting.

eye appeal — The quality of a coin's attractiveness, distinct from any quantifiable measure of condition.

- F -

face value — Refers to the value of a piece of currency; the denomination multiple that appears on the note or coin.

face — The front of a currency note, generally the side with signatures; analogous to the obverse of a coin.

fantasy — An object having the physical characteristics of a coin, issued by an agency other than a governing authority yet purporting to be issued by a real or imaginary governing authority as a coin.

Federal Reserve Bank note — A form of U.S. paper money authorized by the Federal Reserve Acts of Dec. 23, 1913, and April 23, 1918, and by the Act of March 9, 1933. The obligation to pay was by the individual issuing bank, not the federal government or other Federal Reserve Banks. The 1933 notes were an emergency issue to alleviate a shortage of paper money. Not to be confused with Federal Reserve notes.

Federal Reserve note — A form of U.S. paper money authorized by the Federal Reserve Act of February 1913. The obligation to pay is on the United States government and not the issuing banks. This is the only form of paper money currently being printed in the United States.

fiat money — "Unbacked" currency, that which cannot be converted into coin or specie of equal value.

field — The flat part of a surface of a coin surrounding and between the head, legend or other designs.

fineness — Represents the purity of precious metal, either in monetary or bullion form. Most forms of precious metal require an additional metal to provide a durable alloy. Often stated in terms of purity per 1,000 parts: A .925 fine silver coin has 92.5 percent silver and 7.5 percent other metal.

fixed-price list — A price list or catalog of coins, exonumia, paper money or other numismatic items offered at set prices.

flan — Planchet.

flip — A coin holder, usually plastic, that has two pouches, one to hold a coin and the other to hold identification. It is folded over, or "flipped," to close.

flow lines — Microscopic striations in a coin's surface caused by the movement of metal under striking pressures.

follis — A Roman and Byzantine coin denomination; plural is folli.

fractional currency — Usually refers to the United States paper money issued from 1862 to 1876 in denominations from 3 to 50 cents.

fractional — Referring to bullion coin, those of less that 1 ounce.

frost — Effect caused by striking coin with sandblasted dies, often used in reference to Proof coins.

- G -

German silver — An alloy of copper, nickel and zinc but no silver. Also called American silver, Feuchtwanger's composition, nickel silver.

gold certificate — A form of U.S. paper money once redeemable in gold coin. Temporarily made illegal for most to hold between 1933 and 1964.

goldine — A gold-colored finish often used for medals or tokens.

grading — The process of determining a coin's condition

- H -

hairlines — Fine scratches in the surface of the coin. Not to be confused with die scratches.

half dime, half disme — A silver 5-cent coin of the United States. The Mint Act of April 2, 1792, authorizes "half dismes."

half eagle — A gold $5 coin of the United States.

hammer die — See anvil die; the die that performs the striking action.

hammer price — In an auction, the price the auctioneer calls the winning bid, excluding any additional fees the buyer may have to pay for the lot.

Hard Times token — An unofficial large cent-sized copper token struck in a wide variety of types during 1833-1843, serving as de facto currency, and bearing a politically inspired legend; or issued with advertising as a store card.

Helvetia — Gold bullion coins issued by Switzerland; also, the allegorical figure representing Switzerland. From the name given to the area by the Romans.

hoard — Usually a deposit of coins, secreted at some time in the past, discovered accidentally.

hobo nickel — An Indian Head 5-cent coin with Indian bust engraved to resemble "hobo" or other individual. Engraving may also alter the bison on the reverse.

hologram — A three-dimensional image on a flat surface, gaining experimental use as a security device on credit cards and printed currency.

hub — A right-reading, positive punch used to impress wrong-reading working dies.

- I -

inaugural medal — A medal issued by the official inaugural committee commemorating the inauguration of a U.S. president.

incuse — The opposite of bas-relief; design is recessed rather than raised. Used when referring to coins, medals, tokens and other metallic items.

Indian Head — The preferred name for the 5-cent coin often called "Buffalo nickel." Indian Head cents, gold dollars, gold $3 coins, $5 half eagles, $10 eagles and $20 double eagles exist.

Indian peace medal — A medal issued by a government agency to an Indian in an attempt to earn goodwill. The U.S. government issued Indian peace medals from the administration of George Washington through the administration of Andrew Johnson.

intaglio — A method of printing using engraved plates. Paper is forced into the ink-filled lines of the plate, leaving a raised line of ink on the paper. All U.S. paper money is printed by the intaglio method.

intrinsic — As applied to value, the net metallic value as distinguished from face and numismatic value.

irradiated dime — Collectible made by exposing Roosevelt dimes to cesium or other radioactive substance and then placing in a special package; harmless, as any "acquired radioactivity" has dissipated by the time it reaches collectors' hands.

- J -

jugate — Accolated, conjoined.

- K -

Krugerrand — A gold bullion coin of South Africa. It is composed of .9167 fine gold. Exists in 1-ounce, half-ounce, quarter-ounce and tenth-ounce sizes.

- L -

lamination — Coinage defect consisting of a portion of the metal separating from the rest due to impurities or internal stresses; common with clad or plated coinage.

large cent — Refers to the U.S. cents of 1793 to 1857, with diameters between 26-29 millimeters, depending on the year it was struck.

large date — A variety of coin on which the date is physically larger than other varieties of the same year.

legal tender bullion coin — Government-issued precious metal coins produced for investors, they have legal tender status, and usually a nominal face value, even though they are not intended to circulate as currency.

legal tender — Currency explicitly determined by a government to be acceptable in the discharge of debts.

legend — The inscription on a numismatic item.

lepton — Denomination of various values and weights used throughout the ancient Greek world and in modern Greece, generally a small copper or bronze coin.

lettered edge — An incused or raised inscription on the edge of a coin.

Libertad — A silver bullion coin of Mexico, containing 1 ounce of .999 fine gold.

lignadenarist — A collector of wooden nickels and similar items.

love token — A coin which has been altered by smoothing one or both surfaces and engraving initials, scenes, messages, etc., thereon.

luster — Surface quality of a coin, result of light reflected from the microscopic flow lines.

- M -

mail-bid sale — Similar to an auction, but all bids and transactions are completed through the mail or by telephone; no bidding is conducted "in person."

Maple Leaf — A gold bullion coin of Canada. It is composed of .9999 fine gold. Produced in four sizes: 1-ounce with a $50 face value; half-ounce, $25; quarter-ounce, $10; and tenth-ounce, $5. Plural, Maple Leafs.

Maria Theresia taler — An Austrian silver trade coin dated 1780, but struck repeatedly since then with the one date.

master die — A metal punch used to produce "working hubs," which are then used to produce "working dies."

master hub — A metal punch used to produce "master dies."

Matte Proof — Especially U.S. gold coins of 1908-1916, coins produced from dies entirely sandblasted with no mirror surfaces. (See frost)

maverick — An unidentifiable specimen, generally referring to a token.

medal — Usually a piece of metal, marked with a design or inscription, made to honor a person, place or event; not intended to pass as money.

medalet — Depending on sources, a small medal no larger than 1 inch in diameter or a medal 35 millimeters in diameter or less.

medallion — A large Roman presentation piece of the fifth century. Sometimes used for a large medal, usually 3 or more inches in diameter.

medieval coin — A coin struck from about A.D. 500 to 1500.

"Mercury" — The unofficial nickname given to the Winged Liberty Head dime of 1916-45. The designer never intended the coin to depict Mercury, a male Greek god with wings on his ankles. The bust on the dime is an allegorical female Liberty Head figure with a winged cap. Also, some coins have been plated outside the Mint with mercury to give them a "Prooflike" appearance; mercury metal is highly toxic and these coins should be destroyed.

microprinting — Extremely small lettering difficult to discern with the naked eye, used as an anti-counterfeiting device on paper money.

milling; milled coin — Milling refers to the devices on the edge of a coin; a milled coin is one struck by machine. They are related due to the rise of the importance of the collar with machine-produced coinage.

minor coin — A silver coin of less than crown weight, or any coin struck in base metal.

Mint luster — The sheen or bloom on the surface of an Uncirculated numismatic object resulting from the centrifugal flow of metal caused by striking with dies. Mint luster or bloom is somewhat frosty in appearance as opposed to the mirror-like smoothness of the field of a Proof.

Mint mark — A letter or other symbol, sometimes of a privy nature, indicating the Mint of origin.

Mint set — Common term for an Uncirculated Mint set, an official set containing one of each coin struck during a given year.

mirror — Highly reflective surface or field of a coin; usually mirror field with frosted relief.

model — A clay or plaster three-dimensional design for a coin or medal.

modern coin — A coin struck after about A.D. 1500.

money — A medium of exchange.

mule — A coin, token or medal whose obverse die is not matched with its official or regular reverse die.

- N -

national bank note — Paper money issued in United States by national banks from 1863 through 1929 and secured by government bonds or other collateral. Also called national currency.

National Coin Week — An annual observance sponsored by American Numismatic Association to acquaint the public with the hobby and science of numismatics.

national gold bank note — National bank notes payable in gold coin by some California banks and one Boston bank pursuant to authorization by Act of July 12, 1870.

nickel — A silver-white metal widely used for coinage, usually alloyed with copper. Do not use for the copper-nickel 5-cent coin. In the mid-19th century, copper-nickel cents and 3-cent coins were also nicknamed "nickel," like the 5-cent coin.

numismatics — The science, study or collecting of coins, tokens, medals, orders and decorations, paper money and similar objects.

numismatist — A person knowledgeable in numismatics, with greater knowledge than a collector.

- O -

obol — Greek denomination equal to one-sixth drachma.

obsolete bank note — Note of an American bank of issue prior to 1865; a more accurate term than "broken" bank note, since many note-issuing banks converted into national banks or liquidated without failing.

obverse — The side of a numismatic item which bears the principal design or device, often as prescribed by the issuing authority. In paper money, this is called the face.

offset — Printing method in which a metallic plate places an ink impression on an elastic blanket and is then transferred to the paper. Also, a term sometimes used to describe a blanket impression paper money error.

OPA token — A cardboard fiber token issued in the United States by the Office of Price Administration in 1944 during World War II. They were used to make change for meat and processed food coupons (to keep track of ration points awarded each family during periods of rationing). They were issued in red and blue versions. Both sides of the OPA token depicts a numeral 1 flanked by two small initials.

overdate — The date made by a Mint engraver superimposing one or more numbers over the date on a previously dated die.

- P -

paper money — Printed monetary instruments. Modern collectors may be challenged for a new term as nations experiment with plastics and other materials for their printed currency.

patina — The surface quality that a coin acquires over time as the metal reacts with the environment.

pattern — Coin-like pieces designed to test proposed coin designs, mottoes or denominations proposed for adoption as a regular issue, struck in the metal to be issued for circulation and which were not adopted, at least in year of pattern issue. Do not use as a generic term describing experimental pieces and trial pieces.

pieces of eight — Popular term for silver Spanish 8-real pieces; often associated with pirate treasure.

piefort — A piece struck on a planchet twice or more the normal thickness. The French spelling used in Europe is piedfort.

pioneer gold — Gold coins, often privately produced, struck in areas of the United States to meet the needs of a coin shortage, generally in traditional U.S. denominations. The U.S. Assay Office coins of California -official coinage struck before the establishment of the San Francisco Mint -are part of the series. Also known as private gold and territorial gold.

planchet — The disc of metal or other material on which the dies of the coin, token or medal are impressed; also called blank, disc, flan. In paper money, a small colored disc embedded in the paper used as an anti-counterfeiting device.

plaster — See model.

plasticene — Synthetic modelling clay.

PNC — Abbreviation of philatelic-numismatic combination (or cover). A combination of a coin, medal, token or other numismatic item inserted into an envelope that is postmarked on a special occasion, such as the release of a new postage stamp. The numismatic item (or numis) is generally visible through a window in the envelope.

postage note — The First Issue fractional note series.

postal note — Forerunner of the postal money order, issued by the U.S. Post Office.

Prestige Proof set — A special U.S. Proof set, commemorating regular Proof coins plus commemorative coins of that year. Offered first in 1983 with 1983-S Olympic silver dollar; also offered in 1984 (with 1984-S Olympic dollar) and 1986 (with 1986-S Immigrant half dollar and 1986-S Ellis Island dollar).

privy mark — Small device used on coinage often commemorative in nature, similar to Mint mark in placement, but not indicative of Mint of origin.

Proof — A coin struck on specially-prepared planchets on special presses to receive the highest quality strike possible, especially for collectors. For paper money, a print made to test the plate, analogous to a die trial strike in coinage.

Proof set — A set of one Proof coin of each current denomination issued by a recognized Mint for a specific year. See "Prestige Proof set."

prooflike — An Uncirculated coin having received special minting treatment and a mirror surface for the benefit of collectors, with minor imperfections due to the minting process permissible.

- Q -

quarter eagle — A gold $2.50 coin of the United States.

- R -

rare — A comparative term denoting a high degree of scarcity. Often modified adverbially, e.g., very rare or extremely rare; or modified by the use of figures, e.g., R-4 or R-7. There is no universally accepted scale of rarity.

"Red Book" — Nickname given to A Guide Book of United States Coins, an annually published price guide. The cover is red, hence the nickname. Gives retail prices, or what dealers might charge for U.S. coins.

reeded edge — The result of a minting process which creates vertical serrations on the edge of a coin.

relief — Raised. In coinage and medallic numismatic items, a relief design is raised above the surface of the field. Sometimes called bas-relief. Opposite of incuse and intaglio.

replica — A copy of the original, a facsimile. A reproduction.

restrike — A numismatic item produced from original dies at a later date; in the case of a coin usually not with a view to meeting monetary requirements but to fill a demand for a numismatic rarity.

reverse — The side opposite to that on which the head or principal figure is impressed. The side opposite from the obverse. On paper money this is called the back.

rim — Raised border around the circumference of a coin, not to be confused with the edge.

- S -

scarce — Not common, but not as uncommon as rare.

screw press — early hand-operated machine for striking coins.

scrip — Paper currency usually of denominations less than $1 issued as substitutes for currency to private persons or organizations. Tokens issued by coal mines and sutlers also are called scrip.

scripophily — The study and science of collecting financial documents, including stock certificates, shares, government and private bonds, and checks. A student of scripophily is a scripophilist.

seal — A device placed on paper money indicating authority of issue. Modern Federal Reserve notes have two seals — a green Department of Treasury seal and a black Fed seal.

seigniorage — The profits resulting from the difference between the cost to make a coin and its face value, or its worth as money and legal tender. Most coins cost less to make than their face value; when it becomes too expensive to make a certain coin, size, weight and composition are often changed.

serial number — Number used chiefly on paper money and sometimes on limited-issue medals to indicate order of production.

series — Related coinage of the same denomination, design and type, including modifications, or varieties, of design. The Lincoln/Wheat Ears cents of 1909 to 1958 represent a complete series.

sestertius — An ancient Roman coin; plural, sestertii.

shekel, sheqel — Shekel is a silver coin of ancient Judea of various weights; sheqel is modern Israeli denomination, plural "sheqalim."

silver certificate — Authorized by the Acts of Feb. 28, 1878, and Aug. 4, 1886. Were redeemable in silver coin, and in early to mid-1960s, silver bullion. No longer produced, but all specimens remain legal tender although the notes can no longer be redeemed in silver.

slab — Popular nickname for certain kinds of coin encapsulation methods, especially those that are permanently sealed and rectangular.

slug — A term applied to the $50 gold coin issued by various private Mints in California from 1851 to 1855 occurring in both round and octagonal shapes, or to tokens manufactured expressly for use in certain coin-operated machines.

small date — A variety of coin on which the date is physically smaller than other varieties of the same year. Similar varieties include medium date and large date.

so-called dollar — A silver dollar-sized medal commemorating a special event. Cataloged in So-Called Dollars (see Chapter 22 books).

souvenir card — Popular collectible item, usually well-printed on heavy paper using an engraving used on paper money. They also contain information of a historical or commemorative nature.

Souvenir Mint sets — An issue of the U.S. Mint, containing the coinage of one Mint. It is generally sold only at the Mint represented by the coins.

Special Mint sets (SMS) — Coins produced under special conditions by the United States Mint at San Francisco during the years 1965, 1966 and 1967. Coins have no Mint marks.

specie — In the form of coin, especially precious metal coin; paper money redeemable in coin. From Latin meaning "in kind"; see also fiat money.

star notes — Mainly intended as replacements for notes that were damaged or produced with errors or mistakes at the Bureau of Engraving and Printing. On modern Federal Reserve notes, a solid star appears at the end of the serial number; on earlier notes, the star appears at the beginning of the number. Until the 1980s, star notes were also used to represent the 100 millionth note since the serial numbering machinery has only eight digits.

state coinages or notes — Refers to coins issued by one of four state governments (Connecticut, Massachusetts, New Jersey and Vermont) between the Declaration of Independence and the ratification of the U.S. Constitution when the states' rights to issue coins were suspended. Among paper money, refers to notes issued between Declaration of Independence and Civil War by state governments. See "Colonials."

stater — Greek coin equal to two drachms or didrachm, or 12 obols.

Stella — A gold $4 pattern never issued for circulation. Also struck in other metals.

sterling silver — Silver that is .925 fine; in Israel, .935 fine silver. From the British standard "pound sterling."

store card — A token bearing a business name and/or address, and often intended as a local or ad-hoc medium of exchange as well as an advertisement for the issuer.

strike — The act of impressing the image of a die into a planchet, making a coin. The quality of strike is important when determing the amount of wear on a coin.

strip — Rolls of coinage metal to be punched into planchets.

surcharge — An extra charge placed on an item, the revenue of which is usually earmarked for a specific fund. It has been the recent practice of the Uniuted States Congress to place a surcharge on commemorative coins, sometimes to benefit a worthy organization.

syngraphics — The study of printed currency and reated items; from "syngraph," a writing signed by all parties to a contract or bond.

- T -

token — Usually a piece of durable material appropriately marked and unofficially issued for monetary, advertising, services or other purposes.

Trade dollar — A silver dollar coin produced for overseas markets. The United States issued a Trade dollar between 1873-85 for use in the Orient. Great Britain also issued a trade dollar. Also used incorrectly to refer to Canadian trade tokens of $1 nominal value.

Treasury note — Sometimes called a coin note. Issued under the Act of July 14, 1890. Redeemable in silver and gold coins.

tree coinage — Silver coins issued by the Massachusetts Colony in three forms: Willow Tree, Oak Tree and Pine Tree. Issued between 1652-82 although all but one are dated 1652.

Trends — A market value guide based on averages derived from auction results, dealer advertisements, price lists and other sources. Represents a guide, not firm buying or selling prices.

tribute penny — A silver denarius of the Roman emperor Tiberius.

trime — Unofficial nickname given to the silver 3-cent coin. Formed by combining "tri" and the last two letters of "dime."

type set — A collection composed of one of each coin of a given series or period.

- U -

U.S. Gold — Marketing name for American Arts Gold Medallions.

Uncirculated set — Set of coins issued by the U.S. Mint, consisting of one of each coin issued for circulated. Also called Uncirculated Mint set, or unofficially, a Mint set.

uncut sheet — Refers to the 32-note (or 32-subject) sheets of Federal Reserve notes being sold by the Bureau of Engraving and Printing. The 16-note and four-note sheets being sold are cut partial sheets, although they are often referred to as uncut sheets. Earlier sheets of U.S. paper money came with different numbers of notes.

uniface — Having a design on one side only.

unique — Extant in only one known specimen. Very often misused, as in "semi-unique."

United States note — A specific type of note first authorized in 1862 and called legal tender notes; name officially changed to United States notes in July 1873. By law, $346,681,016 in United States notes must be kept in circulation. The term United States note is not a generic term for all forms of U.S. paper money.

upsetting mill — A machine that sqeezes planchets so that they have a raised rim, in preparation for striking.

- V -

vectures — Transportation tokens.

vecturist — A collector who specializes in transportation tokens.

vignette — A pictorial element of a bank note design that shades off gradually into the surrounding unprinted paper or background rather than having sharp outlines or a frame.

- W -

want list — A list given by a collector to a dealer listing items the collector needs for a collection.

The dealer keeps the want list and attempts to purchase items listed on it for the collector.

watermark — Design formed by differing thickness of paper during production; often used as security device in paper money.

whizzing — The severe polishing of a coin in an attempt to improve its appearance and salability to the uninformed. A form of alteration regarded as misleading by the numismatic community, and which actually lowers the value of the coin.

widow's mite — An ancient Jewish lepton denomination coin of the time of Christ.

wire rim — Slight flange on coins or medals caused by heavy striking pressure, often characteristic on Proof coins. The metal is squeezed up the side of the die faces by the collar die. Sometimes incorrectly called wire edge.

wooden nickels — Originally, substitute for coins first used in the 1931-35 depression, having originated in Tenino, Wash. Issued in round or rectangular form and in many denominations. Currently used for advertising and souvenir purposes.

working die — A metal punch that is used to impress images into coins; wrong-reading.

working hub — A metal punch used to produce "working dies"; right-reading.

- Y -

year set — A set of coins for any given year, generally containing one specimen of each coin from each Mint issued for circulation, and packaged privately, not by the government.

Index

$ sign 271
1099 tax form 64
1776 New Hampshire copper *12,*
622
1794 Flowing Hair half dollar *12*
1804 dollar *7, 22,* 553, 629
pedigrees of 569
1812 interest-bearing notes 249
1852/1 Augustus Humbert $20
pioneer gold piece *23*
1861 Coronet, Paquet Reverse
double eagle *18, 24, 25*
1872 Liberty Head U.S. gold
pattern set *8, 26*
1879 Morgan dollar *9*
1894-S Barber dime *26, 27*
pedigrees of 568
1901-S Barber quarter dollar *27*
1911 pattern silver dollar *13*
1913 Liberty Head 5-cent piece
620, 624, *646*
pedigrees of 568
1943 bronze cents 393
1955 Lincoln, Doubled Die cent
385
1964 date freeze 326
extract of law 144
legislative history 145
1964 Peace silver dollars 304
1988 Olympic Games gold half
eagle 383
1988 Olympic Games silver dollar
383
1989 "No Mint Mark" Washington
quarter dollar 22, 385, 387
altered *23*
1991 Club 649
8 reales 438

— A —

A Description of Ancient and
Modern-Coins, in the Cabinet
Collection at the Mint of the
United States 616
A Manual of Gold and Silver Coins
of All Nations, Struck Within the
Past Century 616
A-Mark Precious Metals Inc. *1, 17*
A.B.C. pesos 411
Aamlid, Jan Olav 663, 687
Abdul Aziz ibn as-Saud 426
Abdul Mejid 426
Abdullahi 426
Abe Kosoff Founders Award 662
Abe Kosoff Memorial Literary
Award 659
About Good **530**
About Uncirculated **529**
Abrahamson, Joan 46
Abu Dhabi 426

accolated 709
accreditation 665
accumulation 709
acid-treated coins 392
Act of April 2, 1792 179
Active Token Collectors
Organization 605, 667
Adams, Edgar H. 650, 658
Adams, Eva B. 197, 210, 319, 324,
657, 658, 664
Adams, Jewett W. 199
Adams, John 217, 641
Adams, John Quincy 274
Adams, John W. 521
Adams, Samuel 274
added Mint mark 392
adjustment 709
adjustment marks 520
Adolf Fredrik 422
Adolphe of Orange-Nassau 419
Adriente, Vincent 183
advertising policy, Coin World
598-601
Advisory Committee on Coinage,
Medal and Currency Design
163
advisory policies, Treasury, Secret
Service 157
Aegina 413, 449
Aegina turtle 449
aes grave 709
aes rude 709
Aethelraed II 417
afghani 444
Afghanistan 426, 444, 504
Afonso VI 420
Africa
chronology 426
Agopoff, Agop 644
agora 445
agricultural financing 237
Ahmad Shah Bahadur 424
Aitken, Robert 379, 381
Ajman 426
Akbar 424
Akers, David W. 662, 663
Alabama Centennial half dollar
379
Alabama Numismatic Society 668
Alan Herbert Error/Variety Exhibit
Award 659
Albanese, John 548, 556
Albania 413, 414, 444, 504
Albany, N.Y., half dollar 381
Albrecht, Leonard *28*
Albrecht, Wilfried 687
Alchemy ducat 422
Alcorn, J.L. 274
Alcott, Walter *30*
Aldrich, Nelson W. 237
Alexander I 413, 420

Alexander III 421
Alexander of the North 422
Alexander the Great 449, 455, 622
Alexander, David T. *5, 14, 17,* 314,
663, 664
Alexander, H.A. 192
Alexander, William Julius 199
Alexis, Nord 412
Alfoldi, Andrew 643
Alfonso VI 421
Alfonso XIII 430
Algeria 426, 444
Alhama 452
Allan, John 643
Allende 409
Allied military currency 282
Allied occupation 417, 429
Allison, John 290
alloy 709
alloy errors 388
Alpuente, John H. 200
altered 709
altered and damaged coins 391
altered and damaged notes 397
aluminum 489
aluminum cents 319
Alvarez Cabral, Pedro 409
America in Space medals *18*
America's Cup 431
American Arts Gold Medallions
405, 511, 709
mintages 516
American Bank Note Co. *9,* 225,
255
American Bankers Association
485, 620
American British Numismatic
Association 671
American Coin Society 667
American Coins and Currency
program *21*
American Colonization Society
427
American Eagle *1, 2, 3, 4, 7, 8, 9,
11, 13, 14, 15, 18, 20, 28,* 41, 305,
312, 405, **512,** 709
authority for 52
designers, engravers of 336
edge designs of 328
gold
text of law 132
legislative history 111
Mint marks on 325
silver
text of law 135
specifications 516
specifications of 342
American Express Co. *4*
American Independence
Sesquicentennial half dollar 380

American Independence
Sesquicentennial quarter eagle
380
American Israel Numismatic
Association 671, 672
American Journal of Numismatics
640
American Medallic Sculpture
Association 18, 621, 624, 659,
667
American Numismatic Association
2, 3, 4, 6, 16, 19, 27, 29, 399, 556,
605, 644, 667
    ANACS Cache 19
    awards (See also individual
      award names) 646
    Board chairmen of 649
    centennial celebration 649
    Certification Service 2, 11, 17,
      525, 648
       reference grading set
        525
       sale of 29, 526
    convention sites 652
    editors of The Numismatist 650
    federal charter 646
    lending library 689
    museum 624
    presidents of 649
American Numismatic Association
Certification Service 3, 5, 16, 28,
533, 544, 548
American Numismatic Association
Money Museum 25
American Numismatic Exchange
12, 16, 25, 538, 550
American Numismatic Society 1,
8, 10, 12, 16, 17, 19, 21, 618, 639-
644, 667
    Graduate Fellowship 640
    library 640
    museum 621-624, 640
American Numismatist, The 645
American Political Items
Collectors 667
American Rare Coin Fund 551
American Samoa 431
American Scenic and Historic
Preservation Society 618
American Silver 605
American Society for Portuguese
Numismatics 672
American Society of Check
Collectors 670
American Tax Token Society 667
American Train in Japan 15
American Vecturist Association
602, 667
American-based world
numismatic organizations 671-
672
Amin, Idi 428
Amir Abd ur-Rahman 426
Amos Memorial Theater 624, 646
Amos Press Inc. 29, 526, 533, 648
amulet 331
Amusement Token Collectors
Association 667
an Francisco Old Mint Museum 16
ANA Cache 590
ANA Centennial History 649
ANA grading guide 524

ANACS (See American
Numismatic Association
Certification Service)
ancient bronze artifacts 26
ancient coin 709
ancient coins 26, 448-452
    auction records 582
    grading 530
Anderson, Bette B. 189
Anderson, Martin E. 663
Anderson, P.K. 649, 656
Anderson, Robert B. 171, 290
Anderson, William G. 655
Andorra 441, 444, 504
Andrew, A. Piatt 197
Angel 423
    specifications 516
Angell, Wayne D. 247
Anglo-Saxon 414
Angola 427, 428, 444
animals, endangered 435
Annam 424, 425
Anne, Queen 421
anneal 709
annealing 337
Annear, Thomas 198
Annual Report of the Director of
the Mint 44, 180
Annual Report of the Director of
the Mint for Fiscal Year 1987 22
Annuit coeptis 271
Annunzio, Rep. Frank 2, 6, 12, 13,
16, 22, 106, 376, 657
Anschluss 413
ant nose 709
anthonize 6
Anthony dollar 5, 373
    history of 323
    legislative history 108
Anthony, Susan B. 323, 330
anti-counterfeiting devices 5
anti-counterfeiting security
features 24
Antigua 412, 444, 504
Antilles 416
anvil die 338
apartheid 60, 428, 510
Apollo 11
Apollo 11 322
Appalachian gold rush 191
Aquinaldo, Emilio 314
Aragon 421
Araucania 410
Arcana Foundation 19
Archer M. Huntington Medal
Award 10, 19, 28, 643
Archive Series 9
Ardrey, W.E. 199
Arethusa 450
Argentina 409, 440, 441, 443, 444
ariary 445
Arkansas Centennial half dollar
381
Arkansas Numismatic Society 668
Arkansas-Robinson half dollar 381
Arlie Slabaugh Medals and Tokens
Exhibit Award 659
Armenian Numis. Society 672
Armstrong, Rep. William 184
Arnold-Biucchi, Carmen F. 639
arrows on coins 331
art bars 513
Articles of Confederation 3, 215,
302

artificial intelligence 526
Aruba 411
as 709
Ashbrook, Rep. William A. 646
Asia Minor 426, 433, 448
Asian Development Bank 167, 268
Assam 424
assay 709
Assay Commission 92, 617
    history of 223-224
Assay offices, former 196
Assoc. des Numismates
Francophones du Canada 674
Athenian decadrachm 9
Athenian owl 449
Atherton, Charles H. 46
Atholl 423
Atlanta Society for the Study of
Money other than American
672
Atlantic Provinces Numismatic
Association 674
attribution 709
auction 709
Auction '89 22
auction records 571
    ancients 582
    Colonials 581
    dimes 574
    double eagles 579
    eagles 578
    five cents 573
    four dollar patterns 580
    fractional gold 582
    gold commemoratives 579
    gold dollars 576
    half cents 572
    half dimes 573
    half dollars 575
    half eagles 578
    large cents 572
    medieval and modern world
      585
    patterns 580
    pioneer gold 581
    quarter dollars 575
    quarter eagles 577
    silver commemoratives 579
    silver dollars 576
    small cents 573
    three cents 573
    three dollars 577
    Trade dollars 576
    twenty cents 574
    two cents 573
    world coins 585
Auctions by Bowers and Merena
Inc. 16, 20
auctions, how to participate 589-
597
Augustin I Iturbide 439
Aung San 424
aurar 445
Austin, Richard G. 41
austral 444
Austral Islands 445
Australia 429, 440, 441, 443, 444,
475, 504
    bullion coins 513
Australian Nugget 5
Austria 413, 414, 416, 418, 440, 441,
444, 504
Austria Mint 417
Austrian Netherlands 413, 416

authentication 709
automobile 428
Avena, Dan 664
avos 445
Axum 427
Ayers, Gilvin "Corky" *31*
Aylsworth, Clark Allyn 664
Azcuenaga, Mary 36
Aztec 438
Aztec Indians 406

— B —

Babelon, Ernest 643
Baber, Dorothy and Albert 657
Bacchus 450
back 709
Bactria 449
bag marks 517, **518**, 709
Bagg, Richard 517
Bahamas 411, 437, 440, 444, 504
Bahrain 426, 444
baht 446
Bailey, Clement F. *29*, 664
Bailey, Don 9
Bailie, James E. 673
baisa 446
Baker, Cynthia Grassby *8, 10, 11,*
185, 198
Baker, E.D. 274
Baker, James A. III *5, 15, 16, 171,*
291
Baker, Raymond T. 197
balboa 446
Ball, Douglas B. 641
Ballerina 420, 513
specifications 516
Balog, Paul 643
Band-Aid 397
Bangladesh 425, 437, 444
bani 446
Bank Holding Company Act 322
Bank Holding Company Act
amendments 139
bank note 709
Bank Note Reporter 707
Bank of Canada 438
Bank of Korea 23
Bank of the United States 606
bank teller stamps 398
Bank Token Society 667
Banking Act of 1935 239
banking crisis 239
Banuelos, Romana Acosta 172,
291
Bao Dai 425
Bar-Kochba War 451
Barbados 411, 412, 437, 440, 444,
504
Barbary ape 423
Barber Coin Collectors Society
667
Barber, Charles E. 203, 307, 379
Barber, Clifford M. 180, 199
Barber, William **203**
Barbuda 504
Barcelona 421
Bareford, Harold 547
Barnum, P.T. 278
Barr notes **268**
Barr, Joseph W. 171, 268, 291
barter 449
barter exchange 65
Bartle, Dorothy Budd 642
bas-relief 709

base metal 709
Bass, Harry W. Jr. 639, 643, 657
Bastien, Pierre 643
Bataan peninsula 316
Batavia 430
Batavian Republic 419
Bates, Michael L. 639
Battaglia, Joe 664
Battelle Memorial Institute 6, 311,
526
batteries 485
Battle of Antietam half dollar 382
Battle of Gettysburg half dollar
382
Battle of Saratoga 5
Baudouin I 413
Bauer, George J. 649, 658
Bavaria 416
Beach, Chester 379, 380, 381, 644
Beach, George 673
beads 438
Beasely, J.H. 626
Beatrix 419
Beatty, W. Gedney 622
Beauregard, Gen. P.G.T. 274
beaver pelt 436
Bebee, Aubrey 656
Bebee, Aubrey and Adeline *10,*
15, 624, 646, 654
Bechtler Mint 192
Bechtler, Augustus 623
Bechtler, Christian 191
Beck, John A.
collection 561
Becker, J. Richard 673
Becker, Thomas 655
Belden, Baumann L. 643
Belgian Congo 427, 443
Belgium 413, 440, 441, 443, 444,
475, 504
Belize 407, 444, 504
Bell, Geoffrey G. 673
Bell, Harold W. 622
Bell, R.C. *18*
Bellinger, Alfred 643
Belote, Theodore T. 616, 618
Belskie, Abram *31*, 644, 658
Belt, V. Leon 649, 654, 656
Benedikte 414
Benfield, James C. *18*
Bengal 424
Benin 444
Benjamin, Judah Philip 274
Bennet, Jack F. 462
Bennett, Jonathan M. 274
Benson, John H. 381
Benton, Thomas Hart 274
Berenguer Ramon I 421
Beresiner, Yasha 8
Bergen, Herbert M. *31*, 649, 654,
656, 658
Berghaus, Peter 644
Bergmann, Johanna 639
Berk, Harlan J. 663
Berman, Neil S. *1*
Bermuda 411, 444, 504
Bermuda Monetary Authority 411
Bernadotte, Marshal 420, 422
Bernardi, Giulio 687
Berne Convention for the
Protection of Literary and
Artistic Works 612
Berne Union 612
Bernhart, Max 643

Bernheimer, Francisca 687
Berry, Seymour 235
Bertschy, Adelbert P. "Del" *30*
Betts, Wyllys 603
Bey, Shallie M. Jr. 197
Bhutan 444
Biafra 428
Bibb, George M. 169
Bible, Alan H. *30*
Bicentennial $2 notes **267**
Bicentennial coinage 405
Bicentennial coins 709
Bicentennial dates 326
Bicentennial dollar 322
Bicentennial of Congress *13*, 378
Bicentennial of the Treasury *23*
Bicentennial of the U.S. Congress
9
Bicentennial of the U.S. Mint *25*
Bicentennial of the United States
Mint *28*
Bicentennial sets 371
bid sheet 709
bid-buy sale 709
BIE 386
Bienvenu, Charles 200
Biester, Rae V. 197
Bill of Rights *3, 6,* **42**
Billon 451, 709
bimetallism 404
Bingham, Ann Willing 331
Birdsall, L.A. 198
Birmingham Mint 442
birr 445
bison 308, 709
bit 710
Black Diamond 333
Black Diamond Treasure Hunters
Club 670
black dog 412
Black Sea hoard *20*
Blackmer, L. Paul Jr. 234
Blake & Co. *26*
Blake, George H. 656, 658
Blakesley effect 388
Blanchard and Company *17*
Blanchard, James U. 664
Blancherd, Julian 656
Blanchet, Adrien 643
Bland, Rep. Richard 204
Bland-Allison Act 204
Bland-Allison dollar 304
blank 337, 710
blanket impression 394
Blashfield, Edwin Howland 183
Bleck, Kim 172
Blevins Estate *14*
Bliman, Al 672
block 710
Block, Adolph 658
Blue Book 710
Blue Ridge Numismatic
Association 667
Blumenthal, W. Michael 171, 189,
291
Blunt, Christopher *30*, 643
board breaks 395
Bobbitt, Stephen 644
Bodway collection *14*
Boggs, Rep. Lindy *19*
boiler-room operations 546
Boling, Joseph E. *15*
bolivar 447
Bolivar, Simon 411

Bolivia 409, 443, 444
Bolton, John Roger 172
Bonaire 411
Bonaparte, Joseph 418
Bonzano, M.F. 194, 200
Booker T. Washington/George
  Washington Carver 382
books
  ancient coins 701-703
  common catalog references
    706
  counterfeit detection 693
  error coins 694
  grading 694
  investing 705
  medieval coins 703-704
  modern world coins 695-701
  odd & curious 701
  U.S. coins 690-693
  U.S. exonumia 693
  U.S. paper money 695
  where to buy 689
  world paper money 704
Boone, Daniel 274
Boosel, Harry X 23, 641, 651, 654,
  657
Boothby, Charles W. 200
Borglum, Gutzon 380
Bosbyshell, O.C. 197, 617
Botswana 428, 440, 444, 504
Boudinot, Elias 196, 274
Bourgey, Sabine 8, 687
bourse 710
Boutwell, George S. 170
Bowers and Merena Inc. 14
Bowers, Q. David 533, 590, 643,
  648, 649, 657, 662, 663, 664
Bowersock, Glen W. 639
Bowman, Fred 654
Boyd, Frederick 658
Boyer, Alden Scott 649
Boyer, Henry 197
Boyer, J.P. 412
Boys Town 28
Bradfield, Elston G. 650, 654, 656,
  658
Bradford, David 200
Brady, Nicholas F. 18, 25, 171, 172,
  291
Braille 406, 415
Bram, Lena 31
Bram, Morris 29, 657
Branch Mint Proofs 363
Brand, Terry 29
Brand, Virgil M.
  collection 562
Brander, Peter E. 657
Brasher doubloon 3, 616
brass 710
Brazil 409, 440, 441, 443, 444
Breaden, Richard P. 31
Breen, Walter 14, 590, 641, 643,
  663, 664
Brekle, John F. 198
Brenner, Judson 649
Brenner, Victor D. 8, 317, 603, 622,
  644, 658
Bressett, Kenneth E. 528, 542, 642,
  645, 648, 656, 664
Brett, Agnes Baldwin 643, 658
Brett, William H. 31, 197
Brettell, Ruthann 3, 11, 644, 656
Bretton Woods 459

Bridgeport, Conn., Centennial half
  dollar 381
Brilliant Proofs 363
Briot, Nicholas 414
Bristow, Benjamin H. 170
Britannia 3, 6, 8, 9, 415, 513, 710
  specifications 516
British Borneo 430
British Caribbean Territories,
  Eastern Group 411
British Colonies
  Caribbean 411
  chronology 422
British Columbia 406
British Columbia Numismatic
  Association 674
British Guiana 409, 411
British Honduras 407
British Malaya 430
British North Borneo Company 430
British Royal Mint 7, 8, 9
British United East India Company
  424
British West Africa 427
Broadfield, Helen 16
broadstrike 710
broadstrikes 390
brockage 390
Brockenborough, Bland T. 198
broken bank note 710
broken-bank notes (See Obsolete
  notes)
broker reporting 64
Bromberg, Nathan 32
Bronson, Rick and Virginia 651
bronze 710
Brooke, Sir James 430
Brooks, Kay M. 639
Brooks, Mary 184, 187, 189, 197,
  224, 326, 404, 657
Brown and Dunn 524
Brown Back 710
Brown, Dan 656, 662
Brown, Earl C. 656
Brown, J. Carter 46
Brown, Joseph E., 274
Brown, Martin R. 32, 524
Brown, Michael 19, 514
Brown, Robinson S. Jr. 537
  collection 562
Brown, Vernon L. 656
Bruce, Blanche K. 291
Brunei 430, 444, 504
Brunet, L.J.P. 673
Bruun, Patrick Magnus 27, 644
Bryan, William Jennings 467, 480
Brydon, John 645
Buchanan, Angela 172, 291
Buchanan, James 274
Buell, R.P. 198
Buffalo 308, 710
Buffalo nickel 710
Bugatti cars 553
Bugert, William 642
Bulgaria 413, 414, 444
Bull, George 616
Bullen, Jean 25, 438, 657
bullion 710
bullion coin 710
bullion coins 509
  sales tax on 151
  specifications 515
Bullowa, David N. 650, 658
Burchard, Horatio C. 197

Bureau of Consumer Protection 36
Bureau of Engraving and Printing
  2, 3, 4, 6, 12, 16, 24, 25, 27, 28,
  175, 405
  Directors 235
  first engraver 227
  Fort Worth facility 228
  history of 225-229
  officials 234
  operating budget 59
  operations 228-233
  products 233
  tours 233
Burgers, Thomas Francois 427
Burgett, Maurice M. 657
Burke, John 171, 291
Burkina Faso 444
Burma 424, 446
Burr, Edward E. 381
Burrill, Truman N. 235
Burt, Charles 227
Burt, E.F. 198
Burundi 427, 444
Burzio, Humberto F. 643
Bush, George 21, 26, 27
Busiek, Miley 309, 336, 512
Bust Half Nut Club 667
butut 445
Butzky, Leon 180
Buy American 6, 9
buyer's fee 571, 591, 710
Byrne, Ray 655, 656, 657, 664
Byzantine coinage 26, 451

— C —

Caballito 407
Cabarrus County, North Carolina
  467
Cabarrus County, North Carolina.
  403
CABDAP (See Coin and Bullion
  Dealer Accreditation Program)
cabinet friction 519, 710
Cade, Overton 200
Cahill, Daniel P. 2
Cahn, Herbert 644
Caldwell, Greene Washington 199
Calgary Numismatic Society 674
Calhoun, John Caldwell 274
Calico, Ferran 687
California Association of Token
  Collectors 668
California Diamond Jubilee half
  dollar 380
California Exonumist Society 668
California Registered Historical
  Landmark No. 875 188
California State Numismatic
  Association 668
California-Pacific International
  Expo 381
Caligula 451
Callaghan, N.H. 198
Calling All Coins 485
Calvani, Terry 36
Cambodia 424, 444, 504
Cameroon 427, 444
Campbell, Francis D. Jr. 639
Campbell, George W. 169
Campbell, John 171
Canada 436-438, 440, 441, 443,
  444, 475, 504
  bullion coins 512
  chronology 405-406

first coins 438
first paper money 438
national coin collection 437
ordering coins of 437
Canadian Association of
Numismatic Dealers 675
Canadian Association of Token
Collectors 675
Canadian Association of Wooden
Money Collectors 675
Canadian Broadcasting
Corporation 24
Canadian Cents Club 675
Canadian coin associations 674
Canadian coins 22
Canadian Numismatic
Association 672, 675
convention sites 673
past presidents 673
Canadian Numismatic Journal,
The 672
Canadian Numismatic Research
Society 675
Canadian Paper Money Society
675
Canadian prairies 26
Cape Verde 427, 444
Cape Verde Islands 427
Capet, Hugues 415
Capitol 166
Capitol Building 19
Capitol Hill 21
capped die strikes 390
Carabini, Louis 664
Carey, Abraham G. 381
Caribbean Development Bank
412
Caribbean Islands
chronology 411-412
Caribbean Territories 444
Carl XIV Johan 420
Carl XVI Gustaf 422
Carlisle, John G. 170
Carlos I 420
Carlos III of Hapsburg 421
Carlson, Carl W.A. 641, 644, 649,
655
Carmichael, A.C. 198
Carnegie Museum of Natural
History 23
Carr, J.R. 198
Carrera, Rafael 408
Carrol, Sheldon S. 673
Carroll, Sheldon S. 656, 658, 673
Carson City Mint
history of 193-194
Superintendents 199
Carson, R.A.G. 643
Carter Administration 224
Carter, Amon G. Jr. 657
collection 562
Carter, Christiane K. 234
Carter, Granville W. 644
Carter, Jimmy 323
cartwheel 415
Casey, Samuel 171
Cash Room 166
cash transactions, reporting 83
Casilear, George W. 227
Cass, Lewis 216
cast counterfeits 400
Castaing machine 327
Castile 421
Castro, Fidel 411

Cataloging sources
Colonial and state coinage
706
Copper coinage 706
Exonumia 707
Paper money 707
Silver coinage 706
Special series 706
catalytic converters 507
Catherine the Great 420
Catich, Edward M. 524, 655
Caveat emptor 557
Cayman Islands 412, 437, 444, 504
cedi 445
Cellini, Benevenuto 418
cent 24, 25, 444, 445, 446, 447
composition change
text of law 145
discontinuing 29, 319
cent, discontinuing 185
centavo 444, 445, 446
centavos 444
centennial exposition of 1876 615
centesimi 446
centesimo 445, 446, 447
centime 444, 445, 446
centimes 444
centimo 444, 446, 447
centine 444
Central African Republic 428, 444
Central America
chronology 407-408
Central American Federation 408
Central Europe
chronology 413-414
Central Park Zoo 333
Central Pennsylvania Treasure
Seekers 670
Central States Numismatic Society
548, 667
cents
export prohibited, historical 75
mintages
Proofs 364
cents, large
auction records 572
cents, small
auction records 573
Certified Coin Dealer Newsletter
538
certified mail 589
certified proofs 620
Cervin, David R. 5, 655, 657
cesewa 445
Ceylon 424
Ch'in Dynasty 428
Chad 428, 444
Chairs 553
Challenger space shuttle 11
Chamot, Eduardo Dargent 642
Channel Islands 422
Chapin medal, legislative history
113
Chapin, Harry 113
Chapman, Henry 658
Charles E. Wolfe Medieval and
Ancient Exhibit Award 659
Charles H. Wolfe Class C (YN)
Convention Exhibit Award 659
Charles II 406, 414, 424, 438
Charles III 406, 439
Charles IV 430, 439
Charles of Spain 418
Charles V 418, 438

Charles VI 415, 418
Charles VII 222, 415
Charles VIII 415
Charles X 412
Charles, Prince of Wales 415
Charley, Alfred 30
Charlotte Mint
history of 191-192
Superintendents 199
Charlton, James E. 11, 673
Chase Manhattan Bank money
collection 620
Chase, Philip H. 654, 655
Chase, Salmon P. 170, 194, 201,
225, 255, 274
Chatfield-Taylor, Adele 46
check number 710
Cherokee nation 192
chetrum 444
Chiang Kai-Shek 428
Chicago Federal Reserve 19
Chicken McNuggets Fiesta 15
Chief Engravers 201-212
Chief John Tree 308
Chief Sculptor—Engraver 201
Chile 203, 409, 440, 441, 444
China 414, 428, 433, 440, 441, 443,
444, 475, 504
bullion coins 513
Chinese Panda 22, 23
Chittenden, Lucius E. 291
Chola 424
Chon 445
chop mark 710
Christensen, William 687
Christian III 414, 420
Christian IV 414, 420
Christian IX 412, 414
Christian V 414
Christian X 412, 417
Christiansen, William B. 642
Christiansen, William B. 642
Christopher Columbus 22
Church, Murray 5
Cincinnati Music Center half
dollar 375, 381
Civil War 165, 191, 192, 225, 250,
252, 255, 303, 605, 606
Civil War Token Society 602, 667
Civil War tokens 602, 606-607, 710
clad 710
clad dollars
mintages
business strikes 351
specifications of 341
Clain-Stefanelli, Dr. Valdimir 620
Clain-Stefanelli, Dr. Vladimir 619
Clain-Stefanelli, Elvira 212, 619,
621, 641
Clanton, W.S. 199
Clapp, George H. 23, 623
Clapp, John H.
collection 563
Clark, Donald S. 36
Clark, Georgia Neese 171, 292
Clark, Gruber and Co. 182, 313
Clark, Mike 664
Clark, Robert L. 172
Clark, Spencer M. 225, 235, 255,
275
Clark, William 171, 216, 275
Clark, Yancey 180
Clarke, Joseph A. 32
Clarke, Joseph and Mae 657
Clarke, T. James 649, 650

clashed dies 386
Clay, Clement C. 275
Clay, Henry 275
Clayton Act 37
Cleaver, Ralph 657
Clement VII 418
Clements, Harry R. 235
Clemy winners 664
Cleveland, Great Lakes Exposition
    half dollar 381
Cleveland, Stephen Grover 275
Clifford-Kagin Pioneer Gold
    Collection 16, 21, 188
Clinton, DeWitt 275
clip 388, 710
Club of Illinois Numismatists 669
Clute, Stan 673
cob 438
Cobb, Howell 170
cobs 406
Cochin 424
Cochin China 424
cocoa beans 438
Coffin, Sir Isaac 405
Cogan, Edward 521
Cohen, David H. 641
Cohen, Roger S. Jr. 32, 641
Cohn, Arthur 662
coin 710
Coin albums 609
Coin and Bullion Dealer
    Accreditation Program 12, 13,
    27, 557, 665
Coin Club of Rhode Island 670
coin collections
    famous 561
Coin Dealer Newsletter 538
coin designs
    authority to change 52
    history of U.S. 304-310
    judging quality of 163
coin designs, changing 3, 4, 6, 8,
    9, 12, 13, 14, 15, 16, 19, 22, 23,
    24, 28, 310
Coin Fraud Prevention Act 14
coin jewelry 157
Coin note 710
coin notes 255
Coin Prices 707
coin shortage 311, 486
coin substitutes 419
Coin Week (See National Coin
    Week)
    proclamation 92
Coin World 10, 435, 533, 707
    Collectors' Clearinghouse 402
    submitting articles to 613
Coin World Almanac, previous
    editions 47, 533
Coin World Comprehensive
    Catalog & Encyclopedia of
    United States Coins 28, 533
Coin World Guide to U.S. Coins,
    Prices & Value Trends 18, 533
Coin World Index charts 1
Coin World Trends 6
COINage 707
Coinage Act of 1873 48, 179
Coinage Act of 1965 223, 243,
    311, 324, 326, 488
    extract of text 141
    legislative history 144
coinage laws, American 103
coinage metal fund 51

Coinage of the Americas
    Conference 16, 25, 621, 641
coinage profit fund 51
Coinage Redesign Act 19
coinage strip 337
coinage, earliest 433, 448
coinage, U.S.
    authority 51
Coinology 327
Coins and Medals — Twenty
    Centuries of French Art 8
Coins Magazine 707
coins, Colonial 301
coins, missing 19
coins, struck outside a U.S. Mint
    facility 21
Colbert, R.W. 655, 657
Colburn, Charles 193
Colby, S.B. 292
Colcord, Roswell K. 199
Cole, Anthony F. 35
Coleman, Alan B. 639
collar 710
collar dies 327
collectibles in retirement
    accounts 61
collecting, origins 433
Collectors' Clearinghouse 402
Colombia 409, 440, 441, 443, 444
colon 444, 445
Colonial 710
Colonial Coin Club 667
Colonial coins
    auction records 581
Colonial currency 249
Colonies Francaises du Pacifique
    franc 445, 446
color 520
color laser photocopier 22, 405
Colorado-Wyoming Numismatic
    Association 667
Colton, Nelson 664
Columbia, S.C., Sesquicentennial
    half dollar 381
Columbian Exposition half dollar
    203, 379
Columbian Institute for the
    Promotion of Arts and Sciences
    615
Columbus, Christopher 203, 375,
    378, 410
Combined Organizations of
    Numismatic Error Collectors of
    America 22, 624, 667
commemorative 710
commemorative coin legislation,
    vetoed 376
commemorative coins 3
    government marketing of 146
    investing in 556
commemorative coins, U.S.
    history of 375
commemoratives
    gold
        auction records 579
    silver
        auction records 579
Commission of Fine Arts 3, 11, 12,
    24, 46, 92, 163, 309, 320
Commission on the Bicentennial
    of the United States Constitution
    4, 6
commission rate 596

Commodities Futures Trading
    Commission 2
Communaute Financiere
    Africaine franc 444, 446
Communist takeovers 413
Comoro 427
Comoro Islands 427
Comoros 444
Comparette, Dr. T. Louis 616, 617
composition
    authority to change 52
compound interest Treasury notes
    252
compound-interest Treasury note
    710
Comptroller of the Currency 173
CompuGrade 29, 526
computer grading 526
Comstock Lode 492
Conant, Charles Arthur 275, 314
concentration camp money 453
condition census 710
Confederate half dollar 623
Confederate Mint 191
Confederate States of America
    192, 194, 200
Congo 427, 428, 444
Congress Bicentennial coinage
    378
    first-strike ceremony
        text of law 125
    half dollar 383
    half eagle 383
    legislative history 113
    silver dollar 383
    text of law 127
Congress of Notables 407
conjoined 709, 710
Conlon, James A. 235
Connally, John B. 171, 292
Connecticut Tercentenary half
    dollar 381
connecting parts of different
    notes 99
Conrad 426
Conradin 426
Conservation Coinage Collection
    435
consigning coins to auction 596
Constantine II 414
Constitution 42
Constitution Bicentennial 5
    coin design competition 2
    coin designs 3
    first strike 5
Constitution Bicentennial coinage
    5
    half eagle 383
    legislative history 111, 112
    silver dollar 383
    text of law 131
Constitutional Congress 165
consumer alert 11
Consumer Alert on Investing in
    Rare Coins 12
contact marks 518, 710
Contamin portrait lathes 401
Contaminants 608
Continental Bank Note Co. 255
Continental Congress 165, 172
Continental Currency 249, 710
Continental dollar 710
Continental Investment Group 26,
    551

Conway, Richard 644
Cook Islands 430, 444, 504
Cook, Captain James 429
Cook, John 10, 644, 658
Cooksey, Emily Ford 25
Coole, Arthur Bradden 624, 656
Coolidge, Calvin 204
Cooper, James F. 199
COPE 710
COPE Pak 230, 710
Copernicus 434
Copland medal, legislative history 112
Copland, Aaron 112
copper coins
    investing in 554
copper-nickel 710
copper-nickel clad 487
copperheads 602
Coppini, Pompeo 380
COPY 17, 710
copyright, obtaining 612
Corcoran, William W. 228
cordoba 446
Corkery, James 406
Comeby, Bert W. 199
Coronet 306, 710
Corpus Nummorum Italicorum 418
Corregidor 316
corrosion 607
Cortelyou, George B. 170
Cortez, Hernan 438
Corwin, Thomas 170
Cosgarea, Andrew Jr. 180
Costa Rica 407, 435, 437, 443, 444
counterfeit 710
counterfeit detection 399
counterfeit paper money,
    detecting 283
counterfeit U.S. paper money 28
counterfeit United States Federal
    Reserve notes 22, 405
counterfeiting 464
    penalties for 97
counterfeiting deterrents 10, 230,
    251, 385, 405
counterfeits 399, 452
    recovering gold from 80
    Treasury disposition of 79
counterstamped coins 604
Courts, D.W. 275
Cowles, Calvin Josiah 199
cowry shells 438
Cox, Albion 403
Cox, R.E. Jr. 657
Craig, Freeman 30, 642
Cramer, Stuart Warren 199
Crane Paper Co. 228
Crane, Rep. Philip M. 189
Crawford, James 199
Crawford, William H. 169, 275
Credit Card Collector 667
Crime of 1873 304, 477
Crimea 426
Crisp 532
Cristophe, Henry 412
Criswell, Grover C. 641, 649
Crittenden, John Jordan 275
Croatia 413
Croesus 449
Crosby, Sylvester S. 601, 658
Cross of Gold speech 467
Croton 449
crown 446, 711

Crusades 455
Cruse, Guy A. 532
Cryolite Mining and Trading
    Company 417
Cuba 411, 441, 443, 444, 504
cud 711
cuds 386
Cuffy 409
Cullinane, Kevin B. 180
Culver, Lillard W. 650
Culver, Virginia 7, 524, 649, 654,
    657, 664
Cumberland Sound 1
Cunietti-Ferrando, Arnaldo J. 642
cupro-nickel 711
Curacao 411, 443, 446
currency 711
    issuance of by Federal
        Reserve 245
    penalties for mutilating 96
    relative values 447
currency certificates of deposit
    252
Currency Club of Chester County,
    Pa. 670
Currency Club of New England
    670
Currency Overprinting and
    Processing Equipment 396, 405
Currency Overprinting, Processing
    and Packaging Equipment 230
currency paper
    codified 81
    possession of 82
currency units 444
currency, exchange of 76
current 711
Current Coins of the World 531
Curry, Abe 193, 199, 404
Curtis, James 180, 189
Curtis, James W. 651, 656
Curto, James 601
Curto, James J. 654, 656
Customer Service Center 180
Customs Service 174
Cutler, Barry J. 36
Cyprus 422, 440, 444, 504
Czechoslovakia 413, 440, 441, 444,
    504

— D —

D'Allesandro, Carl V. 234
d'Este, Lionel 418
da Oliveira Salazar, Dr. Antonio
    420
Daddio, William F. 180
Daggett, J. 198
Dahlonega Mint
    Assayers 200
    Coiners 200
    history of 192-193
    Superintendents 199
dalasi 445
Dali, Salvador 31
Dallas, Alexander J. 169
Dallin, Cyrus E. 379
Daly, Peter H. 16, 172, 234, 235
damaged planchets 388
Dames, Longworth 622
Dandolo, Doge Giovanni 418
Daniel Boone Bicentennial half
    dollar 380
Danish East India Company 424
Danish India 425

Danish West India Company 414
Danish West Indies 412
Dario, Ruben 408
Darius I 455
Date Back 711
date freeze, 1964 311
dates on U.S. coins 326
Davenport, John S. 654, 655, 656,
    659
David I 421
David II 421
Davidson, A. Wolfe 381
Davidson, Evelyn 198
Davies, Allan 673
Davis Strait 1
Davis, David 641
Davis, Doug 663
Davis, Jefferson 275
Davis, John 1
Davis, Martin V. 200
De Falco, Alberto 687
de Francisci, Anthony 379, 404
de Gaulle, Charles 416
de la Sengle, Claude 423
de la Valette, Jean 423
De Lue, Donald 658
de Marinis, Joe 664
de Saussure, Henry William 196
Deak, Frank 639
dealer accreditation 27
dealer, first in U.S. 521
debase 711
decadrachm hoard 14, 26
Decatur, Stephen 275
decimal system 436
Declaration of Independence 3,
    42
Dedicated Wooden Money
    Collectors 603, 667
DeFrancisci, Anthony 335, 644
DeFrancisci, Teresa C. 335
Deisher, Beth 614
DeLaRue Giori 231
Delaware Tercentenary half dollar
    382
DeLeo, Francis R. 180
Delnoce, Louis 227
DeLorey, Thomas K. 655, 663
DeLue, Donald 30, 644
Demand note 711
demand notes 225, 250
Den Mayo, Vir 656
denarius 711
DeNise, D. Dee 656
Denmark 414, 440, 441, 444
denomination 711
denominations
    authority for 52
    history of U.S. 303-304
denticles 711
Denver Mint 4, 8, 10, 11, 13, 20,
    180
    history of 182-185
    Superintendents 198
    tours 213
Department of Defense, Defense
    Logistics Agency 28
design elements
    codified 52
designs 304
deutsche mark 445
device 711
Devil's Face note 711
Dewey, George 314

Dewey, William S. 655
Dexter, Samuel 169, 275
Di Bello, Gaston 657
dial-feed system 339
Diamond, W.H. 198
Diaz, Porfirio 439
die 711
die breaks 387
die cap 390
die chips 387
die cracks 387
die errors 386
die gouges 387
die scratch 711
die scratches 387, 520
die-struck counterfeits 400
dies, missing 7, 14, 405, 406
dies, preparing 338
Dieudonne, Adolph 643
Dillistin, William H. 654
Dillon, Douglas 171, 292
dimes
   auction records 574
   designers, engravers of 333
   edge designs of 328
   Mint marks on 325
   mintages
      business strikes 346
      Proofs 365
   specifications of 340
dinar 444, 445, 446, 447
diner 444
dirham 445, 446, 447
discovery piece 26
disme 711
Disney Dollars 4, 13, 18, 24
Disneyland 18, 24
distinctive paper 228
   possession of 82
distribution system 511
Divo, Jean-Paul 687
Dix, John A. 170
Djibouti 444
dobra 446
Dodge, H.L. 198
Dodson, Oscar H. 649, 654, 656
dollar 302, 444, 445, 446, 447
   devaluation of 461
Dollar Coalition 18
dollar coin 7, 8, 9, 14, 15, 18, 20,
   24, 28, 378
dollar sign, origin 271
dollars
   designers, engravers of 335
   edge designs of 328
   gold
      auction records 576
   Mint marks on 325
   silver
      auction records 576
Dolley, Michael 644
Dolnick, Michael M. 656
Dom Pedro I 409
Dom Pedro II 409
Dominica 412, 444, 504
Dominican Republic 412, 440, 442,
   443, 444, 504
Don Carlos V 421
Don Carlos VII 421
Donato, Guiseppe 208
Donelson, Mary Emily 168
dong 447
Donlon, William P. 663
dos mundos 406, 438

Doscher, Dora 334
Doty, Richard G. 4, 621, 642, 643
double denomination 389, 395
double eagle 711
double eagles
   auction records 579
   designers, engravers of 336
   edge designs of 328
   Mint marks on 325
   mintages
      business strikes 354
      Proofs 368
   specifications of 342
double overprints 396
double printings 395
doubled die 711
doubled dies 387
doubloon 711
Douglas, Damon G. 656
Douglas, Stephen A. 275
Dow, Dottie 604
Downer, Frank M. 198
drachm 711
drachma 445
Drane, Frank Parker 199
Dresden Convention 416
Dressel, Edward H. 197
Du Bois, William E. 616
Duane, William J. 169
Dubai 426
ducat 711
Duffield, Frank G. 649, 650, 658
Dunham, William Forrester 649
   collection 563
Dunn, John W. 524, 656
Dutch East India Company 424
Dutch Guiana 410
Duthie, James 226
Duvalier, Jean-Claude 412
Dyer, Graham 16
Dym, K.A. 642

— E —
E PLURIBUS UNUM 328
eagle 711
eagle on U.S. coins 330
eagles
   auction records 578
   designers, engravers of 336
   edge designs of 328
   Mint marks on 325
   mintages
      business strikes 353
      Proofs 368
   specifications of 342
Earl of Derby 423
Early American Cents 523
Early American Coppers 602, 667
Earth 322
earthquake 24, 186, 405
East Caribbean 412
East Caribbean dollar 444
East India Company 423, 430
East Indies 430
Eboue, Felix 427
Echenberg, Edwin 673
Eckert, George N. 196
Eckfeldt, Adam 202, 616
Eckfeldt, Jacob R. 616
Economic Recovery Act of 1981
   61
Ecuador 410, 443, 445, 504
edge 711
edge designs on U.S. coins 327

edge dies 327
Edlow, Ellis 656
Edmonton Coin Club 675
Educational notes 711
Edward IV 417
Edward VII 423, 425, 429
Edwards, Edwin W. 195
Egypt 426, 440, 441, 445, 504
Eidlitz, Robert James 643
Eisenhower Birth Centennial silver
   dollar 383
Eisenhower commemorative 9
   legislative history 113
   text of law 126
Eisenhower dollar 25
   history of 322-323
Eisenhower dollars 372
Eisenhower silver dollar 14
Eisenhower, Dwight D. 9, 16, 17,
   24, 271, 322
   vetoes of commemorative
      coin legislation 376
Eklund, Olie P. 658
El Cid Campeador 421
El Salvador 408, 437, 440, 443, 445
Elam, Leslie A. 639
Elder, Thomas 606
electronic public auction 7
electrotype 400, 711
electrum 449, 455, 711
Elgin, Ill., Centennial half dollar
   381
Eliasberg Collection 535, 547
Eliasberg, Louis 547
   collection 563
eligible paper 232, 239
Elizabeth I 414, 424
Elizabeth II 22, 406, 423, 430
Ellice Islands 431
Elliott, William S. 292
Ellis, Robin 663
Ellis, Salathiel 218
Ellsworth, Col. James
   collection 564
Elmali Hoard 26
Elmore, William A. 200
elongated coin 711
elongated coins 604
Elongated Collectors, The 604, 667
Elston, Dorothy Andrews 172, 292
Elvis 398
EMAC Trading Ltd. 12
Emergency Banking Act of 1933
   239
emergency money 453
emergency notes 453
Empire State Numismatic
   Association 670
encapsulated coin 525, 711
encapsulated coins 544
encased postage 262, 303
encased postage stamp 711
encased postage stamps 606
Endicott, F. Munroe 622
England, chronology 414
engraved printings 234
engraving errors 387
epoxy 338, 393
Epps, F. Stevens 651
Equatorial African States 427, 428
Equatorial Guinea 428, 444, 445
erased ink 398
Erik XIV 422
Eritrea 427

Erlanger, Herbert J. *30*
error 711
Error Coin Museum, The 624
Error Trends Coin Magazine 707
Error-Variety News/The
   Numismistake 707
errors 385-402
   coins 386-391
   paper money 394
escudo 444, 446
essai 711
essay 711
Essay Proof Society 667
Essner, Eugene *11*, 180
Estonia 413, 421
Ethiopia 418, 427, 443, 445
Etruria 418
Euainetos 449
Eucharistic Congress 410
Eucleidas 449
Eumenes 449
Europe
   chronology 413-422
Evans, Sir Arthur J. 643
Everett, Edward 275
Everson and Faught collection *14*
Ewing, George E. Jr. 641, 655
Ewing, Thomas 169
exchange of currency 76
exchange rates of currency 448
executive orders 91
exergue 711
exonumia 601-607, 711
experimental pieces 711
Express mail 589
Exp∑rt 526
Extremely Fine **529**, 530, 531, 532
eye 271
eye appeal 711

— F —

fabricated gold 464
face 711
face value 711
facsimile signatures 225
Fahey, Michael 518
Fair **530**
Fairchild, Charles S. 170
Faisal I 426
Faisal II 426
Falkland Islands 445
Family of Eagles 309
famous coin collections 561
fantasy 711
FAO (See Food and Agriculture
   Organization)
Farnum, Joseph W. 200
Faroe Islands 420
Farouk, King
   collection 564
Farragut, David Glasgow 276
Farran Zerbe Memorial Award *7,
   15, 23*, **654**
fasces 331
fascism 419
Fath Ali Shah 426
Fatimid 418
Faustin I 412
Fawcett, John T. 43
Fecht, Arthur J. 622
Federal Art Administration 208
Federal Bureau of Investigation **38**
federal coinage system 302

Federal Deposit Insurance
   Corporation 2
Federal Property and
   Administrative Services Act of
   1949 42
Federal Register 162
Federal Reserve 10, 55, 405
   banks and branches 246
   governors 247
Federal Reserve Bank note 711
Federal Reserve Bank notes
   large-sized **261**
   small-sized **266**
Federal Reserve note 712
Federal Reserve notes 25, 26, **266**
Federal Reserve symbols 270
Federal Reserve System 232
   Board of Governors 244
   function of 244-246
   history of 237-243
Federal Trade Commission 4, 11,
   12, 14, 17, 22, 27, **36**, 103, 160,
   174, 542, 546, 557
   Regional Offices 37
   regulatory activity 160
Federal Trade Commission Act of
   1914 37
Federation Internationale de la
   Medaille *5, 7*
feed fingers 339
Felipe IV 421
Felipe V 421
Fell's International Coin Book 531
Fell, Sondra 664
fen 444
Fenton, Ned 664
Ferdinand IV 418
Ferdinand VII 406, 439
Ferguson, J. Douglas 438, 649, 654,
   655, 658, 673
Ferguson, Thomas 234
Fernando I 421
Fernando II of Leon 421
Fernando V 421
Fernando VII 421
Fessenden, William Pitt 170, 276
Fessul bin Turkee 426
Fédéderation Internationale de la
   Médaille (See FIDEM)
fiat money 712
FIDEM 624, 659
   congress sites 660
field 712
Field, John D. Jr. 200
Fielding, W.S. 436
Figueroa, Melicio 314
Fiji 430, 440, 443, 445
fil 447
Filed, William B. Osgood 623
FILIPINAS 315
filled dies 387
filler 445
Fillmore, Millard 185, 276
fils 444, 445
financial markets 448
Financing Freedom for 200 Years
   23
Fine **529**, 530, 531, 532
fineness 712
Finland 415, 440, 441, 445
First Baptist Church of Washington,
   D.C. 168
first coins 433

First State Treasure Hunters Club
   671
Fiscal Service 175
Fisher, Samuel *31*
Fitzgerald, Thomas F. *8*
Fivaz, Bill 657
five cents
   auction records 573
   designers, engravers of 333
   edge designs of 328
   mintages
      business strikes 345
      Proofs 365
   specifications of 340
fixed-price list 712
flaking 26
flan 337, 712
Flanagan, John 320, 644
Flanders 416
Flatt, H.P. 642
Fleur-de-Coin 530, 531
flip 712
Flips 609
Florence Schook Outstanding
   Young Numismatist Award 659
Florida token 403
Florida Token Society 669
Florida United Numismatists 669
florin 418, 455
flow lines 712
Floyd, John B. 276
Flying Eagle cent 203
Flying Eagle cents
   Mint marks on 325
Flynn, Joe 662
Fogler, Edward 656
FOIA 115
fold and cutting errors 397
Folger, Charles J. 170
follis 451, 712
Food and Agriculture
   Organization 408, 410, 412, 422,
   423, 424, 426, 435
Foote, Henry S. 200
Ford, Gerald 169, 462, 510
Ford, John J. Jr. 647, 662
forgery, penalties for 97
Forgue, Dennis 662
forint 445
Form 8300 86
Formosa 428
Forrer, Leonard 201
Fort Knox **180**
Fort Knox Gold Bullion Depository
   188
Fort St. Charles 194
Fort Vancouver Centennial half
   dollar 380
Fort Worth printing plant 228
Fort Worth, Texas 4, 27, 405
Forward, Walter 169
Foster, Charles 170
Foster, Stephen 375
four dollar patterns
   auction records 580
Fowler, Harry W. 639
Fowler, Henry H. 171, 292
Fox, Daniel M. 197
fractional 712
fractional currency 227, 262, 404,
   607, 712
fractional gold
   auction records 582
fragments 388

franc 444, 445, 446, 447
France 413, 415, 440, 441, 443, 445, 504
Francesco II 418
Francesco II Gonzaga 418
Franco, Francisco 421
Francois I 415
Francois II 415
frank 445
Franklin Mint 207, 407, 408, 431, 442, 624, 647, 658
Franklin, Benjamin 276, 330, 378
Frantz, Margaret 657
Fraser, James E. 46, 308, 380, 603, 644
Fraser, Juliette May 380
Fraser, Laura G. 317, 379, 380, 644
Frederick II 418
Frederik II 414
Frederik III 414, 420
Frederik IV 412, 420
Frederik VII 412, 414
Fredrik I 422
Freedom of Information Act 115
Freeman, Harley 650, 656
Freeman, S.W. 656, 658
French Cochin China 424
French Colonies 412
French Equatorial Africa 427
French Guadeloupe 445
French Guiana 410
French Guinea 427
French India 416
French Indochina 424
French Oceania 430
French Polynesia 430, 445
French Reunion 423
French Revolution 454
French West Africa 427
Frere, Francis B. 180
Freundlich, August L. 642
Frey, Albert 643, 649, 650, 658
friction **519**
Friedberg, Jack 663
Friedberg, Milton 663
Friedberg, Robert 658
Friedberg, Robert, Award (See Robert Friedberg Award)
frost 712
Frosted Proofs 362
FTC v Security Rare Coin 160
Fuad, King of Egypt 426
Fugio cents **302**
Fujairah 426
Fuld, George 655, 656
Fuld, George and Melvin 602, 607
Fuld, George J. 642
Fuld, Melvin 656
Fuld, Melvin and George 655
Fulton, Robert 276
fungible 554
Furst, Moritz 218
FW 27

— G —

Gabarron, Byrnadette 656
Gabarron, John J. 644, 654, 656
Gabon 428, 444
Gage, Lyman J. 170
Gaither, Burgess Sidney 199
Gale, David and Charlotte 655
Gallatin, Albert 166, 169, 276, 643
Galster, Georg 643
galvano 338

Gambia 428, 445
Gandhi 425
Gans, Edward 7
Ganz & Sivin P.A. 47
Ganz, David L. 2, 47, 644, 645, 660, 664
Ganz, Hollinger & Towe, P.C., 47
Garden State Numismatic Association 669
Garfield, James A. 276
Garn, Sen. Jake 35
Garrard, William 199
Garrett Collection 535, 547
Garrett family collection 564
Garrett, John Work 590 collection 564
Garrett, Robert collection 564
Garrett, T. Harrison collection 564
Gaspar, Peter 655
Gasparro, Frank **208**, 318, 321, 658
Gastone, Gian 418
Gault, John 262, 606
Gaver, Esther Lasure 29
Geffrard, Fabre 412
General Accounting Office 23, 24, 28, 29, 185, 189
General Agreement on Tariffs and Trade 60, 513
General Numismatics Corp. 207
General Services Administration 41, 187, 404, 466, 560
Generic coins 554
Genmyo 429
George I 403
George III 249, 403, 409, 411, 423
George IV 418
George V 406, 423, 425, 430
George VI 406
George Washington half dollar 382
Georgia Numismatic Association 669
Georgia State Token- Exonumia Association 669
German Democratic Republic 417
German East Africa 417
German East Africa Company 417, 427
German Federal Republic 417
German New Guinea Company 417, 430
German reunification 417
German silver 712
Germany 416, 440, 441, 445, 454, 504
Gettys, Loyd B. 523, 649, 655, 656
Ghana 427, 445
ghirsh 446
Gia-Long 425
Gibbon, J.H. 199
Gibbons, J. David 411
Gibraltar 422, 445, 504
Gibson, John 183
Giddeon, Kenneth W. 172
Giedroyc, Richard 3, 11, 13
Gilberg, David L. 162
Gilfillan, James 171, 292
Gilliland, Cory 6, 621, 641, 643
Gillin, G.B. 198
Gillingham, Harold E. 623, 643
Gillio, Ronald J. 660

Gimeno, Javier 642
Gisnulf I 418
Glaeser, Ludwig 212
Glass, Carter 170, 292
Glass-Steagall Act 239
glasnost 61
Glauber, Robert R. 172
Glendining's 9
Gloriam regni 405
Glover, George Bunker 616
glue 392
Gobrecht dollar 306
Gobrecht, Christian **202**
Goertz dalers 422
Goetz, Karl 623
gold
    chronology 466-475
    commodity status 462
    history of 455-466
    measure of worth 456
    mining and refining 456
    monthly prices 476
    numismatic issues 462
    ownership banned 458
    payments required in 55
    recalled in U.S. 458
    record price 473
    sale of government stockpile 466
    seizure of 91
    source of 455
    use in coinage 475
Gold and Silver Institutes 19, 514
gold ban lifted 462
gold certificate 712
gold certificates 55, **259**
gold clause 55
Gold Coast 427
gold coin turn-in order 93
gold coins
    investing in 555
gold dollars
    auction records 576
    designers, engravers of 335
    edge designs of 328
    Mint marks on 325
    mintages
        business strikes 351
        Proofs 367
    specifications of 341
Gold Institute 4
gold ownership ban lifted 510
gold ownership, restrictions on 92
Gold Reserve Act of 1934 458
Gold Rush of '49 182, 185, 261
gold standard 457
    Great Britain adopts 457
    United States adopts 458
Gold Standard Corp. 14
GOLD STANDARD® certificates 14
gold-plated coins 158
Goldberg, Elliott L. 30
Goldberg, Fred T. Jr. 172
Goldberg, Ira M. 660
Goldberg, Ira, Mark and Lawrence 623
Golden Age of U.S. Coin Designs 307
Golden Lion 419
Golden Rule 588
goldine 712
Goldstein, Nathan II 663
Gonzalez, Rep. Henry B. 18, 19, 35
Good **529**, 531, 532

Good fors 602
Goode, George Brown 615
Gordon Z. Greene Memorial U.S. Exhibit Award 659
Gordus, Adon A. and Jeanne P. 642
Gottlieb, Kevin C. 35
Gotwald, Steve 665
Gould Memorial Literary Award 659
Gould, Maurice M. 651, 654, 656, 659, 664
Gould, Maurice M., Award (See Maurice M. Gould Award
gourde 445
government agencies, regulations 153
Government Printing Office **44**
  bookstores 45
Goyer, Jean-Pierre 437
grading 3, 4, 11, 517-532, 712
  adjectival 536
  ancient coins 530
  by computer 28, 526
  computer 6
  establishing standards 160
  history of 521-527
  standards codified 522
  terms
      adjectives 527
      numerical 527
      U.S. coins **527**
  U.S. paper money 532
  world coins 5, 531
  world paper money 453
grading, computer 28, 29
Grafly, Charles 208
Graham, Louise 673
Graham, Robert 382
Granada 421
Granahan, Kathryn O'Hay 172, 293
Granberg, H.O. 522, 649
Grand Masonic Lodge of Nevada 193
Granite Lady 187
Grant Memorial gold dollar 379
Grant Memorial half dollar 379
Grant, Michael 643
Grant, Robert J. 197, 198
Grant, Ulysses S. 167, 276, 616
Graves, Edward O. 235
Grazs, Paul 664
Great Britain 3, 475, 504
  bullion coins 513
Great Depression 208, 238, 561
Great Eastern Numismatic Association 667
Great Seal of the United States 183, **271**, 321, 330
Great Silver Recoinage 415
Greece 413, 414, 440, 441, 445
Greek coinage, ancient 449-450
Greek vases 26
Green, Col. E.H.R. collection 564
Green, Hetty 564
Green, Nancy W. 644, 651
greenbacks 250, 255
Greene, Vincent G. 673
Greenland 417, 443, 445
Greenspan, Alan 247
Gregg, Richard L. 172
Gregory XVI 418

Gregory, Barbara J. 644, 650
Gregory, Carol 673
Grenada 412, 444, 504
Grenadines 505
Gresham's Law 313
Gresham, Walter Q. 170
Grey, Cecil 200
Grey, Earl 436
Grierson, Philip 643
Groh, Edward 623
groschen 444
Grossman, Leon "Lee" 30
grosz 446
Grove, Edward R. 644, 658
Grunthal, Henry 656
Guadeloupe 412
guarani 446
Guatemala 408, 440, 441, 443, 445
Gubin, Kenneth B. 180
Guernsey 423, 445, 504
guerrilla currency 316
guerrilla issues 453
Gugler Lithographic Co. 227
Gugler, Henry 227
Guiana 445
Guide Book of United States Coins 523
Guide to the Numismatic Collection of the Mint of The United States at Philadelphia, Pa. 617
guilder 446
Guinea 445
Guinea-Bissau 428, 445
gulden 446
gun money 417
Gunnet, Donald 642
Gupta, Parmeshwari Lal 10, 644
Gustaf II Adolf 422
Gustaf IV Adolf 422
Gustaf Vasa 422
Gustaf VI Adolf 422
Guth, Ronald J. 641, 655
Guthrie, James 170
Guttag, Julius 404, 623, 650
Guyana 440, 445

— H —

Haakon VII 420
Habsburg, Feldman S.A. 9
Hackel, Stella 405
Haggerty, P.J. 198
Hahn, Michael 200
Haile Selassie I 427
hairline 520
hairlines 712
Haiti 412, 442, 443, 445
halalah 446
haler 444
half cents
  auction records 572
  designers, engravers of 331
  edge designs of 327
  Mint marks on 325
  mintages
      business strikes 343
      Proofs 364
  specifications of 339
half dime 712
half dimes
  auction records 573
  designers, engravers of 333
  edge designs of 328
  Mint marks on 325

mintages
      business strikes 346
      Proofs 365
  specifications of 340
half disme 712
half dollar
  discontinuing 29, 322
half dollars
  auction records 575
  designers, engravers of 334
  edge designs of 328
  Mint marks on 325
  mintages
      business strikes 349
      Proofs 366
  specifications of 341
half eagle 712
half eagles
  auction records 578
  designers, engravers of 336
  edge designs of 328
  Mint marks on 325
  mintages
      business strikes 352
      Proofs 367
  specifications of 341
Hall of Fame **658**
Hall of Monetary History and Medallic Art 619
Hall, Alvin W. 235
Hall, David 544, 546
Hallenbeck, Kenneth L. 27, 645, 649
Hallmark 544, 590
Hallmark Grading Service 549
Hallock, George 664
Halperin, James L. 518, 645
Halpern, Herman collection 565
Ham-Nghi 425
Hamilton, Alexander 166, 169, 222, 276, 302
hammer and sickle 206
hammer die 338, 712
hammer price 571, 591, 712
Hammer, Ted 650, 656
hammered coinage 433
hammered edge 393
Han Dynasty 428
Hancock, Gen. Winfield Scott 276
Hancock, Virgil 29, 649, 654
Hancock, Walker 208, 644
Handling 608
Hanks, Larry 664
Hanlon, Terry 664
hao 447
Harcuba, Jiří 19, 644
Hard Times token 712
Hard Times tokens 602, 605-606
Hardin, Adlai S. 658
Harlow, Bryce L. 172
Harlow, David 645
Harlow, Jean 506
Harman, Martin Coles 423
harp 417
Harper, David C. 9, 663
Harris, Dolly-Maude 651, 656
Harris, N. Neil 650, 655, 657
Harrison, Benjamin 277
Harrison, William H. 277
Hartman, George 46
Harwell, Robert 664
Hasan I 426
Haseltine, Capt. John W. 658

Hassler, Donna J. 642
Hathaway, Isaac S. 382
Hatie, George D. 644, 649, 654
Hausske, August F. 656, 657
Havernick, Walter 643
Hawaii 443
HAWAII overprint 454
Hawaii State Numismatic
    Association 669
Hawaii, pre-U.S. 430
Hawaiian Sesquicentennial half
    dollar 380
Hawkeye State Coinshooters 671
Hawkins, Benjamin 381
Haxby, James A. 663
Hayes, James A. 643
Hayes, Jimmy
    collection 565
Hayes, Rep. James A. 25
Hayes, Rutherford B. 321
Haynes, Michael 664
Head, Barclay P. 658
Heath Literary Awards 654
Heath, George F. 645, 649, 650,
    658
Heaton, A.G. 649
Hebert, George 13
Heckelman, J.A. 645
Heifetz, Jascha
    collection 565
Heisei era 20
Hellenistic coinage 449
Helvetia 712
Hempstead, C.H. 198
Hendershott, Robert and Marjorie
    657
Henderson, J.M. 649
Henderson, John M. 658
Henderson, William C. 31, 654, 656
Hendricks, Thomas Andrew 277
Hendrickson, Leon 22, 660, 662
Hendy, Michael F. 663
Henri II 415
Henri III 416
Henri IV 416
Henri V 416
Henry III 414
Henry V 415
Henry VII 414
Henry VIII 414, 417
Henry, Patrick 277
heraldic custom 321
Heraldic Eagle 306
Hercules 416, 450
Herdegen, Genevieve 656
Heritage Capital Corp. 3
Heritage Numismatic Auctions
    Inc. 2
Hessler, Gene 532, 641, 663
Hetrich, Frank D. 199
Hewitt, Clifford 315
Hewitt, Lee F. 29, 544, 650, 654,
    656, 658, 664
Hewitt, Robert 616
Hickman, John 663
Hicks, Herbert P. 655
Hidalgo, Father 439
Hien Tsung 452
Higby, Betty 198, 657
Higgins, Stephen E. 172
high-denomination notes,
    destruction of 233
Hildebrandt, Jim 664
Hiler, Rep. John P. 4, 35

Hill, George F. 643
Hill, James G. 228
Hill, Louis A. 235
Hill, Michael F. 234
Hillegas, Michael 171, 277
Hillman, Kirk 655
Hilt, Robert P. II 642
Hirohito 429
Hispaniola 412
Ho Chi Minh 425
hoard 712
hoards 434
Hoback, Joseph N. 180
Hobart, Elisha 227
Hobby Protection Act 17, 37, 162,
    400, 405
hobo nickel 712
Hobson, Burton 663
hoe money 406
Hoernle, A.F.R. 622
Hofer, Theodore R. 199
Hoffecker, L.W. 381, 649
Hoge, Robert W. 644
Hogge money 411
holey dollar
    Australia 429
    Canadian 405
Holiday, Edith E. 172
hologram 712
Holtzclaw, Henry J. 235
Holy Roman Empire 416
Hompesch, Ferdinand 423
Honduras 408, 440, 443, 445
Hong Kong 430, 440, 445
Hong Kong Commodities
    Exchange 430
Hoober, Richard T. 654, 656
Hooper, Joseph 649, 658
Hoover, Herbert 376
Hopper, J. 522
Hornsby, Roger A. 639
horse blankets 250
Hoskier, H.C. 617
Hoskins, Charles 19, 405, 643, 656
Houghton, Arthur A. 639
House Banking Subcommittee on
    Consumer Affairs and Coinage
    3, 4, 6, 13, 18, 19, 22, 24, 25, 27,
    106
House Banking, Housing and
    Urban Affairs Committee 18
House Committee on Banking,
    Finance and Urban Affairs 35
House of Representatives, United
    States 34
House Subcommittee on
    Consumer Affairs and Coinage
    24
Houston, David F. 293
Houston, David M. 170
Howard, Leland 404, 463
Howe, Lawrence Lee 656
Howland Wood Award 657
hub 338, 712
Hubbard, Clyde 654, 656
Hudson, N.Y., Sesquicentennial
    half dollar 381
Huggins, Jack 657
Hugo I 421
Huguenot-Walloon Tercentenary
    half dollar 379
Hukbalahap insurgency 317
Hull, Everett W. 660
human physiology, classifying 523

Humbert $20 gold piece 553
Humphrey, George M. 170, 293
Humphris, John G. 2
Hungary 413, 414, 440, 441, 445,
    504
Hunt, H. Lamarr 493
Hunt, Henry 650
Hunt, Nelson Bunker 26, 493
    collection 565
Hunt, William Herbert 26
    collection 565
Hunter, George E. 180
Hunter, R.M.T. 277
Huntington, Archer M. 624
Huntington, Archer M. Award (See
    Archer M. Huntington Medal
    award)
Huot, Robert 12
Hurter, Silvia 687
Hussein ibn Ali 426
Hussein Kamil 426
Hussey, Nora 4, 8, 198
Huston, J.N. 171, 293
Hyatt, James W. 171, 293
Hyde, Barbara 31
Hyder, William D. 655
Hyderabad 425
Hynds, Gene 657

— I —

Ibos 428
Iceland 417, 440, 445
ICTA (See Industry Council for
    Tangible Assets)
Ides of March 451
Ile de Bourbon 423
illicit PCGS-graded coins 15
Illinois Centennial half dollar 379
Illinois Numismatic Association 669
illustrating currency, restrictions on
    102
imitation numismatic items 162
impact die 401
impaired Proof 527
Imperial East Africa Company 427
import ban 28
In God We Trust 271, 329
    first appearance 329
    text of law 145
inaugural medal 712
incomplete planchets 388
incomplete printing 395
incuse 712
incused relief 308
indented errors 390
India 424, 440, 441, 445, 504
India-Straits 430
Indian 5 cents
    Mint marks on 325
Indian Department 216
Indian Head 306, 307, 712
Indian Head cents
    Mint marks on 325
Indian peace medal 712
Indian peace medals 215
Indiana State Numismatic
    Association 669
Indiana-Kentucky-Ohio Token &
    Medal Society 667
Individual Retirement Accounts 14
Indochina 443
Indochina, Colonial 424
Indochinese Federation 424
Indonesia 430, 435, 441, 445

Industrial Revolution 433
Industry Council for Tangible
   Assets *3, 4, 5, 6, 12, 14, 28,* 64,
   152, 557, 664
Infantile Paralysis Fund 320
inflation 237, 243, 453, 552
Ingham, Samuel D. 169
initials on U.S. coins 331
ink smears 395
Inner Mongolia 429
insured mail 588
intaglio **229,** 712
intaglio printing 394
Inter-American Development
   Bank 167
Inter-American Development
   Fund 268
interest-bearing notes **252**
interest-bearing Treasury notes
   250
Intergold 466, 510
Internal Revenue Service 83
Internal Revenue Service
   reporting regulations *28*
International Association of
   Professional Numismatists 542,
   687
      general assemblies 687
International Association of Silver
   Art Collectors 667
International Bank for
   Reconstruction and
   Development 167, 268
International Bank Note Society
   670
International Banking Act of 1978
   243
International Council on
   Monuments and Sites *21*
International Emergency
   Economic Powers Act 60
International Medal Federation
   (See FIDEM)
International Monetary Fund *8,* 60,
   167, 268, 447, 459
International Numismatic Society
   672
International Numismatic Society
   Authentication Bureau *19,* 399,
   525, 548
International Numismatic Trade
   Organization *5, 11*
International Olympic Committee
   12
International Organization of
   Wooden Money Collectors 603,
   667
International Primitive Money
   Society 672
International Society of Jeton
   Collectors 672
International Year of the Child 409
intrinsic 712
Inuktitut language *27*
invasion money 453
inverted Jenny stamp 535
inverted overprints 396
inverted printings 395
Investor's Guide to United States
   Coins *1*
investors 526
Ionian Islands 423
Iowa Numismatic Association 669

Iowa Statehood Centennial half
   dollar 382
Iran 426, 441, 445, 475, 505
Iraq 426, 445
IRAs 61
Ireland 417, 440, 441, 445
Ireland, Harry 664
Irish Free State 418
Irish, O.H. 235
Iron Tail 308
irradiated dime 712
Irwin, Louis *31*
Isabel 421
Isabel II 421, 430
Isabella quarter dollar 375, 379
Islamic coinages 426
Isle of Man 423, 445, 504, 505
      bullion coins 513
Isles de France 423
Ismail I 426
Israel 427, 437, 440, 441, 443, 445,
   505
Isted, John 655
Italian Eritrea 427
Italy 413, 418, 440, 441, 445, 505
Iturbide 406
Ives, Herbert E. 623
Ivory Coast 444
Ivy, Steve *3*

— J —

J. Aron & Co. 512
J. Sanford Saltus Medal Award *10,*
   19, 27, 644
Jackson, Andrew 165, 277, 606
Jackson, C.F. 277
Jackson, Gen. T.J. 277
Jackson, George James 277
Jackson, Glenn E. *31,* 641
Jahangir 424
Jaime I 421
Jamaica 412, 440, 445, 505
James I of Great Britain, France
   and Ireland 421
James II 417
James III 421
James L. Betton Foreign Exhibit
   Award 659
James V 421
James VI 421
Jameson, John 621
Janus 450
Janus Gallery *18*
Janvier reducing machines 338,
   401
Japan 428, 429, 440, 441, 445, 475,
   504
Japanese states in occupied
   China 429
Jarvis, James 302
Java 430
Jean, Grand Duke of Luxembourg
   419
Jefferson 5 cents
      history of 319
      Mint marks on 325
Jefferson, Thomas 201, 215, 217,
   277, 319, 466
Jeffries, Noah L. 293
Jehovah 422
Jelinski, James J. 517
Jenifer, Joseph E. 44
Jenkins, G. Kenneth 643
Jennewein, C. Paul 644, 658

Jerrems, William G. 645, 649
Jersey 422, 445, 505
Jerusalem 426
Jewell, Henry C. 235
Jewish American Hall of Fame *17,*
   625
Jex, John 407
jiao 444
Joao IV 420
Joao V 420, 424
John Reich Collectors Society 668
John the Blind 419
John the Good 415
John, Lord of Ireland 417
Johnbrier, Al 664
Johns Hopkins University 590
Johnson, Byron F. *30*
Johnson, Charles M. 654, 656
Johnson, Claude M. 235
Johnson, James G. 402
Johnson, Lyndon B. 187, 208, 311,
   320
Johnson, Manuel H. 247
Johnson, Robert 662
Jones, Anthony 658
Jones, Edward E. 293
Jones, Eldridge *31,* 657
Jones, Elizabeth *14, 19, 23,* **209,**
   378, 382, 383, 643, 658
Jones, Isaac W. 199
Jones, Sidney 172
Jordan 426, 445
Jordan, Conrad 171, 293
Jose I 420
Jovine, Marcel *1, 20, 29,* 383, 644,
   658
Joyce, Adam M. 197
Juan Carlos I 421
Juan I of Castile 421
Juan II of Aragon 421
Juan II of Castile 421
Juarez, Benito 407, 439
Judaea 451
Judaic coinage 451
Judd, J. Hewitt *29,* 649, 654, 656,
   657
jugate 709, 712
Julian, R.W. 603, 655, 663
Julian, Robert W. *12*
Julian, W.A. 171, 293
Juliet's Nurse 535
Julius Caesar 450

— K —

Kabis, Dorothy Andrews (See also
   Elston, Dorothy Andrews), 294
Kagan, Arnold H.
      collection 565
Kagan-Maremba Collection 565
Kagin's Numismatic Investment
   Corp. *13, 16*
Kagin, Arthur M. 657, 662
Kagin, Henrietta Spitz *31*
Kalakaua I 430
Kamehameha III 430
Kamloops Numismatic Society 675
Kampmann, Michel 687
Kangaroo Nugget 514
Kansas Numismatic Association
   669
Kaplan, Bruce 664
Kaplan, Max 662
Kaplan, Sol 656, 662

Kaplan, Sol, Award (See Sol Kaplan Award)
Kaptur, Rep. Marcy 27
karat equivalents 612
Karl IX 422
Karl X Gustaf 422
Karl XI 422
Karl XII 422
Karl XIII 422
Karl XIV Johan 422
Karl XV 422
Karlson, Geneva 656
Karmol, David L. 180
Katanga 427
Katen, Frank and Laurese 656
Kaufman, Mico 7, 658
Kay, Marvin 673
Keck, Charles 379, 380, 381
Keith, Alexandra B. 172
Kelley, Edward W. Jr. 247
Kelley, Evie 656
Kelley, Robert F. 622
Kellogg, George 200
Kelly, Don C. 663
Kelly, M.J. 198
Kelsey, Henry 26
Kelsey, Mike 664
Kemm, Theodore 663
Kennedy half dollar 17
    history of 320-322
        legislative history 145
        text of law 145
Kennedy half dollars 11, 372
Kennedy, David M. 171, 294
Kennedy, John F. 17, 320
Kennedy, Joseph M. 200
Kennedy, Roger G. 621
Kennedy, Tom 673
Kent 414
Kentucky State Numismatic Association 669
Kenya 428, 445
Keogh Plan 62
Keystone Searchers 671
khoum 445
Kilby, Thomas E. 404
Kimball, James P. 197
Kimbler, Eugene 189
Kimon 449
kina 446
King Kong 398
King of Siam Proof set 7, 22, 23, 26, 29, 549, 570, 571
King of the Two Sicilies 418
King, Dr. Henry 615
King, Robert P. 646
kip 445
Kirby, Wallace W. 235
Kiribati 445
Kiselewski, Joseph 644, 658
Klein, Harold R. 656
Kleiner, Fred S. 639
Kliman, M. 662
Kline, Bernard G. 673
Kmer Rouge 424
Kneass, William 201
Knoth, Charles P. 650
Knox, Henry 215
Knox, John Jay 195, 277
Koala 429, 430, 513
    specifications 515
kobo 446
Koch, Jack R. 651
Kolberg, Ole-Robert 420

Kookaburra 513
    specifications 515
Kopecki, I.T. 651
kopek 447
Koppenhaver, Paul 657, 660, 661, 662
Korea 428, 440, 441, 443, 445, 475, 504, 505
Korean War 378
Korshack, Yvonne 642
Kortjohn, Martin 649, 655
koruna 444
Kosoff, Abe 524, 648, 651, 654, 656, 658, 660, 662, 664
Kosoff, Abe, Founders Award (See Abe Kosoff Founders Award)
Kossuth rebellion 413
Kraay, Colin 644
Kraus, Ernst 656
Krause Publications 707
Krause, Chester 654, 656, 663, 664
Kreiss, Henry G. 381
Kretz, Maj. Herman 197
Kries, Henry 644
Kristina 422
Kriz, Col. Robert 657
Kriz, Robert F. 657
Kroll, John H. 639
krona 445, 446
krone 444, 445, 446
Kruger, Paul 510
Kruger, S.J.P. 427
Krugerrand 414, 428, 466, 509, 514, 712
    executive order banning 60
    specifications 516
Krugerrand jewelry 61
Krugerrands 405
Krugerrands, fractional 428
Kubitschek, Wilhelm 643
Kuntz, Dr. George F. 618
Kurt Krueger Paper Money Exhibit Award 659
kurus 446
Kutch 425
Kuwait 426, 440, 445
Kuzsmar, Edward 663
kwacha 445, 447
kwanza 444
Kwart, Herbert J. 532
kyat 446

— L —

l'Ouverture, General Toussaint 412
La Grange, A.H. 198
La Societe Numismatique de Quebec 675
laari 445
Laessle, Albert 208, 644
LaFaurie, Jean 643
Lafayette, Marie Joseph Paul Yves Roch Gilbert du Motier 277
Lafayette-Washington silver dollar 379
Lafontaine, Maurice 406, 437
Lagerqvist, Lars O. 659
Lake Texcoco 406
Lamar, Mary 277
lamination 712
laminations 388
Landis, John H. 197
Lane, George W. 404
Lantz, Michael 644
Laos 424, 425, 505

large cent 712
large cents
    designers, engravers of 332
    edge designs of 327
    Mint marks on 325
    mintages
        business strikes 343
    specifications of 339
large date 712
Lasker medal, legislative history 112
Lasker, Mary 112
Lasser, Joseph R. 642
Lathrop, Gertrude 658
Lathrop, Gertrude K. 381, 382, 644
Latin 451
Latin American coins 15
Latin American Paper Money Society 670
Latin Monetary Union 410, 411, 412, 416, 421
Latvia 413, 420
Laurel, Jose Paciano 316
LaWare, John P. 247
Lawrence, Richard Hoe 622
Lawrie, Lee 644
laws, texts of 125
Lawton, I. 198
Lazard, Calme L. 31
Leach, F.A. 198
Leach, Frank A. 186, 197, 198
Leaman, Ivan 642
Leatherman, A.H. 656
Lebanon 426, 445
Lee, Richard Henry 172
Leech, Edward O. 197
Leeward Isles 411, 445
legal tender 712
    Title 31 50
legal tender bullion coin 511, 712
legal tender notes 250
legal tender notes, precious metal 412
legal tender status 511
legend 713
legends on U.S. coins 328
Leggett, John D. Jr. 639
Legislative update 9
Lehman, Rep. Richard 19, 24, 35, 106
Leifer, Bret 664
Leipzig Convention 416
lek 444
lempira 445
Lenker, Kay 663
Leonard, Robert D. Jr. 10, 642
leone 446
Leopold II 413, 418, 427
Leopold III 413
Leopold of Saxe-Coburg-Gotha 413
Leotto, Elaine J. 642
lepton 445, 713
LeRider, George 643
Lesotho 445, 505
Letcher, John 278
lettered edge 713
lettered edges 327
Letzeburg 419
leu 446
Leuver, Robert J. 6, 12, 27, 235, 644, 649
leva 444
Levy, Albert 662

Levy, Commodore Uriah Phillips *17*
Lewis and Clark Exposition gold dollar 379
Lewis M. Reagan Memorial Foundation Inc. 624, 661
Lewis, Gary 651
Lewis, Meriwether 278
Lewry, L.H. "Scoop" 673
Lexington-Concord Sesquicentennial half dollar 379
Lhotka, Dr. John F. 655
Lhotka, John F. 656
Lhotka, John F. Jr. 654, 655
Liberia 427, 443, 445, 505
Libertad 407, 439, 713
Libertas Americana medal 331
Liberty 304, 328
Liberty 5 cents
  Mint marks on 325
Liberty Bell 330
Liberty Cap 305
Liberty Cap cent 201
Liberty Coin Act 135
Liberty Seated (See Seated Liberty)
Liberty Seated Collectors Club 668
Libya 426, 445
Lieberman, Marvin 36
Liechtenstein 445, 505
Liedman, Julian M. 663
lignadenarics 602
lignadenarist 713
Ligurian Republic 418
lilangeni 446
Lill, George III 642
Lilly, Josiah K. 620
  collection 566
Lim, B.H. 687
Lima Mint 410
limited partnerships 552
Lincoln cent
  history of 317-319
Lincoln cents
  Mint marks on 325
Lincoln Memorial 318
Lincoln, Abraham 168, 225, 278, 317
Lind, Jenny 278
Linderman, Henry Richard 196
lira 445, 446, 447
Liss, C.L. 657
list medals 213
lithographed printings 234
Lithuania 420
Lithuanian Numis. Assoc. 672
livre 445
Lloyd, Margaret 657
Lo Medico, Thomas G. 644
Lodewijk Napoleon I 419
Logan, Russell 642
Lombardy 418
London Numismatic Society 675
Long Beach Numismatic, Philatelic and Baseball Card Exposition 526
Long Island Tercentenary half dollar 381
Longacre, James B. *202*, 306
Longacre, Sarah 332
Longfellow, Alice, Allegra and Edith 278
loon *1*, 406
loon dollar *4, 5*

Lord Baltimore 403
Loring, Denis 657
Loring, Denis W. 641
Los Angeles Olympic Games gold eagle 383
Los Angeles Olympic Games silver dollar 382
Los Angeles Olympics 376
Lott, P.G. 198
Louganis, Greg *17*
Louis I 418
Louis IX 415
Louis Napoleon 430
Louis Philippe 416
Louis the Pious 421
Louis XI 415
Louis XII 415
Louis XIII 416
Louis XIV 416, 421
Louis XV 412, 416
Louis XVI 410, 416, 423
Louis XVIII 410, 413, 423
Louis-Napoleon 416
Louis-Philippe 410, 412
Louisiana Numismatic Society 669
Louisiana Purchase 168
Louisiana Purchase Exposition gold dollar 379
Louisiana State Museum. *21*
love token 713
Love Token Society 604, 668
love tokens 604
Lovejoy, Allen F. 639, 642
Low Countries 419
Low, Lyman H. 658
lucky piece coin 393
Luigi II Gonzaga 418
Luis Felipe 420
Luis I 420
Lukeman, Augustus 380
Lundy 423
luster *518*, 713
Luxembourg 413, 419, 440, 445
lwei 444
Lydia 433, 449, 455
Lynch, William M. 200
Lynchburg, Va., Sesquicentennial half dollar 381
Lyon, Pat 278
Lyons, Judson W. 294
Lysimachus of Thrace 455

— M —

Mabbot, T.O. 656
Macao 445
MacArthur, Douglas 316, 430
Macau 505
MacDonald, A. Mitchell 673
Macdonald, David 184
MacDonald, Douglas B. 655
MacDonald, Frank H. 184
Macdonald, George 643
Machado, Gerardo 411
machine doubling 390
machined coins 433
MacKay-Coghill, Don *5*
MacKenzie, Brian L. 673
MacNeil, Hermon A. 334, 644
MacVeagh, Franklin 170, 318
Madagascar 428, 440, 445, 505
Madagascar Democratic Republic 428
Madison, Dolly 278
Madison, James 217, 278

Magdalen Island 405
Magna Carta *3*, 249
Magna Graecia 449
Magruder, Leonard 200
Mah, Raymond R. 673
Mahdi, Muhammad Ahmad 426
mail-bid sale 713
mail-order firms *21*
Mailing coins 588
Maine Centennial half dollar 379
Maisch, Cheryl and Robert 657
Major, Don 603
Maklouf, Raphael 423
makuta 447
Malagasy 428
Malawi 428, 445
Malaya 430
Malaya-East Indies 430
Malaysia 430, 440, 441, 445
Maldive Islands 426
Maldive Republic 445
Mali 427, 444, 445
Malmer, Brita *19*, 644
maloti 445
Malta 423, 440, 441, 445, 505
Manca, Albino 644
Manfra, Tordella & Brookes Inc. 448
Manila Mint, history of 315
Manitoba Coin Club 675
Mankowski, Bruno 644, 658
Mann, Philip M. Jr. *15*
Manoel de Vilhena, Antonio 423
Manoel I, Goa 424
Manoel II 420
Mansfield, Joseph King 278
Manship, Paul 644
Manx 423
Maple Leaf *26*, 406, 437, 510, *512*, 713
  specifications 515
March of Dimes 320
Marckhoff, Fred R. 657
Marco Polo 452
Marconi 419
Marcos, Ferdinand 317, 431
Marcy, William L. 278
Margaret Thompson Chair in Greek Numismatics *19*
Margrethe 414
Margrethe II 414
Maria I 420
Maria II 420, 427
Maria Theresia 509
Maria Theresia taler 427, 509, 713
Marie Louise 418
Marion, Gen. Francis 278
mark 302, 445
markka 445
Markoff, Elliott 624
Markus, Charles 649
Marquezas 445
Marquis, Yvon 673
Marshall, Carol Mayer 180, 198
Marshall, John 185, 278
Marshall, Thomas 650
Marti, Jose 411
Martin, Doris 656
Martin, Janice *31*
Martin, Lee 604, 651, 664
Martin, Marie H. 639
Martineau, Stanley F. 644
Martinique 412, 445

Martino, John T. 180, 198
Martoche, Salvatore R. 172
Marvin, Paul 30
Marvin, William T.R. 658
Mary I 417
Mary, Queen of Scots 415, 421
Maryland State Numismatic
   Association 669
Maryland Tercentenary half dollar
   380
Maryland Token & Medal Society
   669
Mason & Co. 521
Mason, David H. 200
Mason, Ebenezer Locke 521
Mason, James M. 278
Mason, John 217
Massachusetts Bay Colony 249,
   301
Massachusetts Treasure Hunting
   Association 671
master die 27, 338, 405, 713
master hub 713
Mateu y Llopis, Felipe 644
Mathias, Robin 644
Matte Proof 363, 713
Mattingly, Harold 643
Mauritania 428, 445
Mauritius 423, 435, 446, 505
maverick 713
Maximilian 439
Maximilian, Archduke of Austria
   407
May, Edmund Ware 30
Mayer, Marian 107
Mayer, Steven 664
Mayon volcano 314
Mazard, Jean 643
McAdoo, William Gibbs 170, 294
McAlpine, Robert M. 200
McArthur, Robert G. 656
McBride, David 655
McBride, David P. 655
McCambridge, Mercedes 187
McCartee, George B. 235
McClellan, George B. 278
McCloskey, John W. 642, 643
McClung, Lee 171, 294
McClure, R.A. 617
McCormick-Goodhart, L. 623
McCulloch, Hugh 170, 193
McCullough, Hugh 278
McDonald's 15
McEnery, J.P. 198
McGarry, Lt. Sheridan L. 654
McKenney, Thomas L. 216
McKinley Memorial gold dollar
   379
McKinley, William 279
McLachian, Robert Wallace 658
McLane, Louis 169
McLees, Archibald 227
McNall, Bruce 565
McNight, Logan 200
McPherson, Edward 235
McTurk, Barbara 180, 198
Meade, George Gordon 279
Mecca 426
medal 713
Medal of Merit 655
Medal, The 659
medalet 713

Medallic Memorials of
   Washington in the Mint of the
   United States 617
medallion 713
medals 603
   current House requirements
      for consideration 106
medals produced by U.S. Mint 213
Medici 418
medieval coin 713
medieval coins
   auction records 585
medieval period, defined 433
Mediocre 531
Medlar, Robert E. 656, 657, 662
Medlar, Robert Eugene "Gene"
   Jr. 32
Meek, Kelsay R. 35
Megna, Rebecca 47
Mehl, B. Max 590, 595, 658
Meissen Porcelain Works 623
Meister, Edward M. 31
Melissa Van Grover Israel or
   Judiac Exhibit Award 659
Mellon, Andrew W. 170, 294, 618
melting coins 559
Memminger, Christopher
   Gustavus 279
Menconi, Ralph 658
Mendelson, Mark 664
Menelik II 427
Mercanti, John 21, 23, 336, 383
Merchant Marine medal,
   legislative history 113
merchant's advertising tokens 605
Mercia 414
Mercury 308, 713
Meredith, Samuel 171
Meredith, William M. 170, 235
Meredith, William Morris 235, 279
Merena, Raymond N. 589
Merrill Lynch Pierce Fenner &
   Smith 551
Merrill Lynch, Pierce Fenner &
   Smith 26
Merton, Henry 11
Mestrelle, Eloye 414
Metal SAFE 555
metallic content 310
metals, resistance to corrosion 607
Metapontum 449
Metcalf, William E. 639
Metcalfe, Percy 418
metica 446
metric system 611
Metropolitan Washington
   Numismatic Association 669
Mexico 438-440, 441, 443, 446,
   475, 504, 505
   chronology 406-407
   gold coins from 465
Mexico City Mint 406, 438
Médailles 659
Michael I 413
Michael, Obrenovich III 413
Michelangelo 434
Michigan State Numismatic
   Society 669
microprinting 5, 230, 385, 713
Middle Ages 222
Middle Atlantic Numismatic
   Association 668
Midwest Historical Research
   Society 671

Midwest Numismatic Association
   668
Midwinter Convention 10
Miguel, Dom 420
mil 444, 445
Milan I 413
Milas, Ed 662, 687
Mildenberg, Leo 644
Miles, George C. 643
Military payment certificates 281,
   453
milled coin 713
milled coinage 414
Miller Magazines Inc. 707
Miller, Charles M. 200
Miller, Fern V. 198
Miller, G. William 171, 295
Miller, James 657
Miller, Jim 663, 664
Miller, Thomas H. 180, 198
Miller, Wayne
   collection 566
millim 446
millime 445
milling 713
Mills, John 193
Mills, Ogden L. 170, 295
Millspaugh, Howard 200
Millward, William 196
Milne, J. Grafton 643
Mindon Min 424
Ming Dynasty 452
Minnesota International
   Numismatists 672
Minnesota Organization of
   Numismatists 669
Minnie Mouse 24
minor coin 713
Minster Machine 428
Mint Act of 1792 326
Mint collection 616
Mint Directors Conference 442
Mint Directors' Conference 13, 29
   funds appropriated to host 58
Mint luster 713
Mint mark 713
Mint marks 27, 405
   first U.S. 323
   history of U.S. 323-325
   location on U.S. coins 325
   placement on master die 324
Mint set 713
Mint State 527
Mint State system, origins of 523
Mint State, distinguishing 11 levels
   525
Mint status for San Francisco
   Assay Office and West Point
   Bullion Depository 12
Mint, U.S. (See United States Mint)
mintages
   40% silver clad dollars 369
   business strikes 343
   Proof sets 368
   Proofs 364
   Special Mint Sets 369
   Uncirculated sets 369
mints, active world 441-442
Mionnet 611
mirror 713
misaligned overprint 396
Mishler, Clifford 654, 662
mismatched serial numbers,
   letters 396

missing and incomplete overprints 396
Mississippi Numismatic Association 669
Missouri Centennial half dollar 379
Missouri Numismatic Society 669
Mitchell, Ralph C. 656
Mitchelson, Joseph C. 625
Mixtecs 438
model 713
modern coin 713
modern coins, defined 433
Moffat & Co. 313
Mogul India 9
mohar coinage 424
Monaco 446
monetary system 237
monetary system, U.S. codified 50
monetary units values of 447
monetary units, world 444
money 713
Moneyless economy 424
mongo 446
Mongol invasion 428
Mongolia 446
Monroe Doctrine Centennial half dollar 379
Monroe, James 279
Montegut, Gabriel 200
Montenegro 413
Montevideo, siege of 410
Montgomery, Rick 7
Monticello 319
Montreal Numismatic Society 675
Montserrat 412, 444
moon 322
Moore, Bruce 644
Moore, Charles D. 673
Moore, Purnie 657
Moore, Robert H. 200
Moore, Samuel 196
Moore, Waldo C. 649, 658
Moorish coinage in Spain 421
Mora, Jo 380
Morales, Ambrosio 316
Morelock, Gladys P. 198
Morelos, Father 406, 439
Morgan dollar 307
Morgan, Daniel N. 171, 295
Morgan, George T. 204, 304, 379
Morgan, J. Pierpont 623
Morgenthau, Henry Jr. 92, 170, 295
Morkholm, Otto 644
Mormon gold 313
Morocco 426, 441, 446, 505
Morrill, Lot M. 170
Morris, Gouverneur 172, 302
Morris, Opal and John 657
Morris, Opal H. 657
Morris, Robert 279, 302
Morse, Phoebe 27
Morse, Samuel Finley Breese 279
Morton, Azie Taylor 172, 295
Mosher, Stuart 619, 650, 656, 658
Moss, Joseph 649, 654, 655
Mote, Edward 664
Mott token 335, 601
Mott, William and John 601
mottoes on U.S. coins 328
Moultrie, Gen. William 279
Mount Rushmore 28, 378

Mount Rushmore National Memorial 14, 24, 25
Mount Rushmore National Park 19
Mousseau, Paul 664
mouth, coins carried in 449
Mozambique 427, 428, 446, 505
Mt. Diablo Metal Detectors Club 671
MTB Banking Corp. 13, 18
Muang Thai 425
Muery, John 664
Muhammad II 426
Muhammad V 426
Muhammad VI 426
mule 713
mules 400
Mulford, David C. 172
Mullins, David W. 172, 247
multiple Mint marks 387
multiple strikes 390
Munich Convention 416
Munro, Al 673
Munroe, Neil Gordon 622
Muñoz, Miguel L. 7, 18, 31, 655, 657
    collection 566
Murat, Marshal 418
Murphy, Frank 316
Murphy, Gerald 172
Murray, Anthony J. Jr. 198
Murray, Col. Bill 601
Murray, Draper, Fairman and Co. 202
Murray, George 202
Murray, Glenn S. 13, 642
Murray, Michael 664
Muscalus, John A. 657
Muscat 426
Musee de la Monnaie 17
Museum Notes 640
Museum of American History 619
museums
    United States 625-632
    world 632-638
Mushinski, Eugene 663
Mussolini 419
mutilated currency 176
    exchange of 77, 232
Myanmar 446
Myanmar 424

— N —

Nagengast, Bernard 607
naira 446
Napier, James C. 295
Napoleon 413, 418, 419
Napoleon Bonaparte 416
Napoleon I 416
Napoleon II 416
Napoleon III 407, 416
Napoleon, Jose 421
Nasr ud-Din 426
Naster, Paul 1, 644
Nathan, Phillip 658
National Silver Dollar Roundtable 668
National Archives and Records Administration 42
National Audiovisual Center 44
national bank note 713
National Bank Note Co. 225, 255
national bank notes 255
National Banking Act of June 3, 1864 255

National Bureau of Standards 223
National Cabinet of Curiosities 615
National Coin Week 2, 26, 91, 650, 713
    proclamations 114
National Crime Information Center 38
National Currency 261
National Currency Act of Feb. 25, 1863 255
national debt 377
National Defense Stockpile 506
National Defense Strategic and Critical Materials Stockpile 41
National Endowment for the Humanities 10
national gold bank note 713
national gold bank notes 261
National Institute (See National Institute for the Promotion of Science
National Institute of Standards and Technology 50
National Institution for the Promotion of Science 615
National Monetary Conference 237
National Numismatic Collection 13, 25, 319
    history of 615
National Numismatic Collection, history of 621
National Scrip Collectors Association 604, 670
National Silver Dollar Roundtable 528
National Stolen Coin File 38
National Strategic Stockpile 513
National Utah Token Society 669
National, regional coin associations 667-668
Navarra 421
Nazi 413
NE coinage 403
Neald, Dean 673
Near East
    chronology 426
Nebecker, Enos H. 171, 295
Nebraska Numismatic Association 669
necessity money 453
Neff, Francine Irving 169, 172, 296
Negapatam 424
Nehru, Jawaharlal 425
Nepal 424, 435, 437, 440, 442, 443, 446, 505
Neptune 411
Nero 181
Nesmith, Robert 643
Nestor, Mrs. James 657
Netherlands 419, 440, 442, 443, 446, 504, 505
Netherlands Antilles 411, 446
Netherlands East India Company 424
Netherlands East Indies 443
Netherlands Guiana 443
Nettleship, Charles F. 656
Neuce, Edwin O. 30
Nevada Bicentennial medal 339
Nevada State Prison quarry 404
New 532
New Brunswick 405
New Caledonia 430, 446

new cruzeiro 444
New Deal 480
new dinar 447
New England Numismatic Association 668
New England Rare Coin Galleries 2
New England Treasure Finders Assoc. 671
New Guinea 430
New Hampshire Numismatic Association 669
New Hebrides 430
New Jersey Exonumia Society 669
New Jersey Numismatic Society 28, 669
New Orleans Mint 21
  history of 194-196
  Superintendents 200
new peso 444, 447
New Rochelle, N.Y., half dollar 382
New South Wales 429
new Taiwan dollar 446
New York Assay Office
  transfer of gold from 190
New York Numismatic Club 606
New York Orders & Medals Soc. 657
New York State Wooden Money Society 669
New York Treasure Hunters League 671
New Zealand 430, 440, 446, 505
New, John C. 171, 296
Newby, Mark 417
Newcomb, Howard R. 658
Newell, Edward T. 619, 622, 643, 658
Newell, Floyd B. 656
Newfoundland 406
Newman, Eric P. 628, 639, 641, 642, 643, 654, 655, 656, 658, 664
Ngo Dinh-diem 426
ngultrum 444
ngwee 447
Niagara Frontier Relic Hunters Assoc. 671
Nicaragua 408, 437, 443, 446
Nichols, Gene N. 651
nickel 713
Nies, James B. 622
Niger 444
Nigeria 427, 428, 446
Nike 378
Nishioki, Scott H. 35
Niue 505
Nixon, Richard M. 187, 322
Nizams of Hyderabad 424
Nkrumah, Kwame 427
NLG (See Numismatic Literary Guild)
Noble 513
Noble, Joseph Veach 642
Noe, Sydney P. 643
Noe, Tom 664
Nohejlova-Pratova, Emanuela 643
noncirculating legal tender coins 435
Norfolk, Va., Bicentennial half dollar 382
Noriega, Manuel 12
Norman Conquest 423
Norodom I 424
Norris, John 664

North Africa 426
North American Treasure Hunters 671
North Carolina 2
North Carolina Numismatic Association 670
North Georgia College 192
Northern California Numismatic Association 669
Northwest Treasure Hunters Club 671
Norway 420, 440, 442, 446
Norweb collection 2, 8, 16, 18, 535, 547
Norweb, Emery May 547, 621
Norweb, Mr. and Mrs. R. Henry 620
  collection 547
Norweb, R. Henry 547
Norweb, R. Henry Jr. 622, 639
notgeld 453
Nova Scotia 405
Nova Scotia Museum 675
Novus Ordo Seclorum 271
Nueva Granada 409
Nugget 429, 513
  specifications 515
Nugget, Paul 664
numerota 231
Numismania Society of America 668
Numismatic Art Award for Excellence in Medallic Sculpture 658
Numismatic Association of Southern California 669
Numismatic Bibliomania Society 668
numismatic bullion 507, 515
Numismatic Certification Institute 526
Numismatic Fine Arts Inc. 9
Numismatic Guaranty Corporation of America 12, 14, 23, 25, 26, 526, 544, 548, 590
Numismatic Hall of Fame 624, 647
numismatic items
  legal definition of 53
Numismatic Literary Guild 663
  awards (See also individual award names) 663
Numismatic Literature 640
Numismatic News 9, 538, 707
numismatic publications 707
Numismatic Quote System 25
Numismatic Scrapbook Magazine 544
numismatic terms 709
numismatics 713
  related disciplines 433
Numismatics International 672
numismatist 713
Numismatist, The 645
Numismatists of Wisconsin 670
nummi 452
Nummy, David M. 172
Nyasaland 427

— O —
O'Donnell, Chuck 663
O'Higgins 409
O'Reilly, M.M. 618
O'Sullivan, Lt. Col. Frank 657
oak branch 331
Oakes, Dean 663

obol 713
obsolete bank note 713
Obsolete notes 249
obverse 713
Odesser, Benjamin 32
ODGSO 463
Oechsner, Herbert M. 12, 622
off-center coins 391
off-register printing 395
Office of Domestic Gold and Silver Operations 70, 463
Office of Indian Affairs 216
Office of Price Administration 603
Official ANA Grading Standards for United States Coins 4, 524, 556, 648
offset 713
offset printing 394
Ogilvie, Jack W. 654, 656
Oglethorpe, James Edward 279
Oklahoma Numismatic Association 670
Olav V 420
Olcer, Cüneyt 32
Old Mint 180, 187
  tours 213
Old Spanish Trail half dollar 381
Old Testament 610
Old Timer Assay Commission Society 668
olive branch 321, 331
Olof Skotkonung 421
Olsen, William 664
Olympiad 378
Olympic coinage
  1988 5, 6, 9
    legislative history 112
    text of law 129
  1992 29
  Calgary 406
  Helsinki 415
  Los Angeles
    legislative history 109
    text of law 136
  Montreal 406
  Moscow 420
  Munich 417
  Seoul 429
  Tokyo 429
Olympic rings 11, 12
Oman 426, 440, 446, 505
Omnibus Drug Act 24
Ong Harizak 424
Ontario Numis. Assoc. 675
Onza 407
OPA token 713
OPA tokens 603
Open Market Committee 241
optical scanning device 24
Order of St. John of Jerusalem 423
ordering coins 587-589
ore 444, 445, 446
Oregon Numismatic Society 670
Oregon Trail Memorial half dollar 380
Orient
  chronology 428
Oriental Numis. Society 672
Original Globe Coin Traders Club 672
Orleans Token and Medal Society 195
Orlie-Antoine I 410
Orlowski, Alexandre 623

Ortega, Katherine D. *10, 18, 22,* 83, 172, 377
Ortega, Katherine Davalos 296
Ortmayer, Constance 381
Osaka Mint *20*
Osborne, James Walker 199
Oscar I 422
Oscar II 422
Osmena, Sergio 316
Otis, Lois 656
Otis, Lois R. 651
Ottawa Mint 437
Ottoman 426
ouguiya 445
Ourdan, Joseph P. 227
Outstanding Adult Leader or Advisor Award 659
Outstanding Sculptor of the Year Award (See Numismatic Art Award for Excellence in Medallic Sculpture)
over Mint marks 387
Overcash, Leonard *31*
overdate 713
overdates 387
overprinting errors 396
Overseas Emission Institute 430
Overton, Al C. 656
Owen, Deborah K. 36
Owens medal, legislative history 113
Owens, Jesse *15, 27,* 113
Owens, Ruth *27*

— P —

P Mint mark 323
pa'anga 446
Pacific Coast Numismatic Society 668
Pacific Northwest Numismatic Association 668
Pacific Region chronology 429
Page, John 657
Pahlavi dynasty 427
Paintings 553
paisa 445, 446
PAK Jefferson Full Step Nickel Club 668
Pakistan 425, 440, 442, 446
Palestine Mandate 426
palladium *22,* 420, 505, 513
palladium coins *14, 25*
palladium commemorative coin *15*
Panama *12,* 408, 437, 442, 443, 446
Panama-Pacific Exposition $50 379
Panama-Pacific Exposition gold dollar 379
Panama-Pacific Exposition half dollar 379
Panama-Pacific Exposition quarter eagle 379
Panda 428, 513 specifications 515
Panosh, Leonel 656, 658
Panosh, Leonel C. 649, 654
Papa, John J. 180
papal coinage 418
paper money *10, 21, 24, 25,* 405, 714 distribution of 232-233

earliest 452
errors 394
features of 269-271
grading 532
large-sized U.S. 250-262
life of 232
manufacturing 229-232
portraits on 54
by name 274-281
denominational 272-273
pre-federal 249-250
security threads 428
signatures on 283-300
history of 225
signers of 290-300
small-sized 264-269
test sheets *24*
world 452-454
printers of 454
Paper Money Collectors of Michigan 670
Papua New Guinea 446
Paquet, Anthony 219
para 447
Paraguay 410, 440, 446, 505
Paramount International Coin Co. 524
Paris Exposition 375
Paris Mint *17*
Parish, Daniel Jr. 623
Parker, Gabe E. 296
Parrotto, Barbara 47
Parsons, David 381
partial collar 391
partially turned digit 396
Pasqualetti, Mariangela Johnson 659
Pasvolsky, Valentine 656
pataca 445
Patagonia 410
patina 714
Patrick, Donald G. 641
pattern 714
patterns auction records 580
Patterson, Robert M. 196, 202, 218
Patton, Julius M. 200
Paul I 420
Paul, Martin 544
Payne, Peter B. 651
Peace dollar 308
Peale, Franklin 218
Peale, Titian 332
Pearce, J.W. 643
pearl black 423
Pearlman, Donn 645, 662, 664
Pearson, William S. 199
Peck, Robert 46
pedigrees of rare coins 567-571
1804 dollar 569
1894-S Barber dime 568
1913 Liberty 5-cent piece 568
Pedro I 420
Pedro I, the Cruel 421
Pedro II 420
Pedro III 420
Pedro IV 420
Peed, James 383
Pell, Stephen H.P. 623
Peloso, Matthew 383
pence 445, 447
Penn, William 279
Penn-Ohio Coin Clubs 668

Pennell, Roy 657
penni 445
Pennsylvania Association of Numismatists 670
penny 445
Penny Whimsy 523
pennyweights 611
People's Republic of China 428
Perestroika *18*
Perry, Commodore Matthew 429
Perschke, Walter *3*
Persia 426
Person, Joseph F. *32*
Peru 440, 442, 443, 446
Peru Mint 410
peseta 446
pesetas 444
peso 444, 445, 446, 610
peso boliviano 444
peso, Philippine 314
Petain, Philippe 416
Peter the Great 420
Peters, Jess 662
Peterson, Mendel 619
petition drive *4*
Pettit, Thomas M. 196
Pettus, J.J. 279
Pewelle, A. 279
pfennig 445
Philadelphia Academy of the Fine Arts 204
Philadelphia Mint *180* history of 181-182 Superintendents 197 tours 213
Philadelphia Sketch Club 204, 206
Philip II 438
Philippine Collectors Society 672
Philippine Executive Commission 316
Philippines 430, 440, 442, 443, 446, 505 as U.S. possession 314 Commonwealth of 315 Republic of 316
Philippines, as U.S. possession 317
Phillip of Valois 415
Phillip the Fair 415
Phillips, Richard A. 639
Philpott, William 663
Philpott, William A. 656
Philpott, William A. Jr. 657, 658
Philpott, Wm. A. Jr. 654
Photograde 524, 556
photographic industry 484
photography at U.S. Mint facilities 74
Phra Chom Klao, Mongkut 425
Phra Maha Chulalongkorn 425
piastre 445, 446
Pickens, David 180
Pickens, Lucy Holcombe 279
Picker, Richard collection 567
piece of eight 438
pieces of eight 714
Piedmont Republic 418
piefort 714
Pierce, Franklin 279
Pietz, Adam 382
Pikes Peak *19*
Pilchuck Treasure Hunting Club 671

Pilgrim Tercentenary half dollar 379
Pillar dollar 406
Pillars of Hercules 439
pinholes 532
pioneer gold 13, 23, 312-313, 714
    auction records 581
pipeline 511
Piret, Diane 664
piso 446
Pitcairn Islands 505
Pittman, John Jay 645, 646, 649, 654, 656, 673
Pittman, Michael L. 662
Pius VII 418
Plain Talk 645
planchet 337, 714
planchet errors 388
plaster 714
plastic note 430
plasticene 714
plate money 422
plate position numbers 269
plate serial numbers 269
platina 506
platinum
    history of 505-507
playing card money 438
Pledges of History 616
PNC 714
PNG (See Professional Numismatists Guild)
Pobjoy Mint 423, 431, 442
Podlusky, George L. 657
Poinsett, Joel Roberts 615
poisha 444
Poland 413, 414, 440, 442, 443, 446, 504, 505
Polikoff, Ira 234
Polish-American Numismatic Association 672
polished dies 388
political tokens 605
Polk, Gen. Leonidas 279
Polk, James K. 615
Pollock, James 196, 197, 404
Pollock, Randall L. 660
Pond, June T. 654
Poor 531
Pope, D. Kirby 199
Pope, Donna 4, 8, 13, 19, 20, 27, 28, 172, 180, 185, 189, 197, 621
Popper, Julius 410
Popular Republic of the Congo 428
Porterfield, Neil 46
Portrait of Juan de Pareja 535
portraits on U.S. coins 330
Portugal 420, 421, 437, 440, 442, 446, 505
Portuguese Guinea 427
postage currency 262
postage note 714
postage stamp money 453
postage stamps 606
postal note 714
Postal Service 557
postally canceled note 267
Potosi Mint 409, 421
Potter, G.R.L. 673
pound 444, 445, 446, 447, 610
Powills, Michael A. 656
Pradeau, Alabert F. 643
Pradeau, Albert F. 656

presidential coat of arms 321, 331
Presidential libraries 43
Presidential medal series
    descriptions 219-221
    history of 215-219
presidential seal 321
    authority for 96
Presley, Elvis 398
Pressler, Sen. Larry 14
Prestige Proof set 714
Preston, Robert E. 197
price performance graphs 18
Price Rounding Act of 1989 25
Price, George 407
Price, Herbert W. 656
Price, William C. 171
Priest, Ivy Baker 171, 296
Primitive money 438
Prince Edward Island 405
Prince Edward Island Numismatic Association 675
Prince George Numismatic Society 675
Prins, Curtis 13, 18
prisoner of war camp money 453
private bullion pieces 513
private gold (See pioneer gold)
privy mark 714
procurement of coinage materials 51
Professional Coin Grading Service 2, 8, 11, 12, 15, 16, 21, 24, 26, 28, 525, 526, 528, 544, 546, 590
Professional Membership 7
Professional Numismatists Guild 16, 27, 533, 542, 557, 660
    awards (See also individual award names) 661
    code of ethics 661
    past presidents 662
Project Golden Steeple 193
Project Segovia '92 21
Proof 527, 531, 714
Proof bullion coin 509
Proof coins, production methods 342
Proof error coins 20, 405
Proof set 714
Proof set mintages 368
Proof sets
    legal requirements 58
Proof Trade dollar patterns 28
Proof-like 531
prooflike 714
Prophet, Kenneth B. 673
Providence, R.I., Tercentenary 381
Proxmire, Sen. William 15, 185, 466
Prud'homme, John F.E. 227
Public Enterprise Fund 20, 23
publications, numismatic 707
Puerto Rico 412, 421
Puget Sound Treasure Hunters Club 671
pul 444
pula 444
Pulu Penang 430
Pumiphol 425
Purple Heart 205
Putnam, Brenda 381
pya 446
pyramid 271

— Q —
Qatar 426, 446

qindar 444
Quarcoopome, Ebenezer Nii 642
quarter dollars
    auction records 575
    designers, engravers of 334
    edge designs of 328
    Mint marks on 325
    mintages
        business strikes 347
        Proofs 366
    specifications of 341
quarter eagle 714
quarter eagles
    auction records 577
    designers, engravers of 335
    edge designs of 328
    Mint marks on 325
    mintages
        business strikes 351
        Proofs 367
    specifications of 341
Quebec 405
quetzal 445
Quezon y Molina, Manuel 316
Quillian, Lewis W. 200
quills 438
quint 302
Quisling, Vidkun 420

— R —
radar notes 452
Raff, A. Raymond 197
railroad rim 391
Raj of Sarawak 430
Raleigh, Sir Walter 279
Ralph, Joseph E. 235
Ramsden, Henry A. 622
rand 446
Rand, E.I. "Jack" 651
Randall, J. Colvin 521
Randolph, George Wythe 279
Rangel, Rep. Charles B. 19
Rapp, Harry W. 650
Rappahannock River 466
rappen 446
rare 714
Rare Coin Galleries of America Inc. 4
rarity, affecting grade 521
rarity, factors affecting 559
Ras al-Khaimah 426
Rasanen, Kauko 1, 644
Ravenel, W. de C. 618
Rawlson, Jon B. 180
Ray Byrne Memorial Literary Award 659
Raymond, Wayte 523, 623, 658
Raymond, Wayte and Olga Literary Award (See Wayte and Olga Raymond Literary Awards)
Reagan, Lewis M. 646, 650, 654, 656, 658
Reagan, Ronald 8, 12, 17, 18, 176, 210
Reagan-Marcos commemorative 431
Rector, H.M. 280
Red Book 523, 714
Red Jacket 217
Redding, Anderson W. 200
Redfield Hoard 17
Reed, Byron 629
    collection 17, 19
Reed, Colonel 329

Reed, F. Morton 30, 651
Reed, P. Bradley 614
reeded edge 714
reeding 327
reference grading set 525
refunding certificates 254
Regan v. Time Inc. 103
Regan, Donald T. 171, 211, 296
Regina Coin Club 675
Registered mail 588
Regitko, John 673
Regling, Kurt 643
regulations by government
    agencies 153
Reid, Templeton 312
Reilly, John Jr. 622
Reiter, Ed 664
Reiver, Julius "Jules" 641, 657
relief 714
Remy, Paul 206
replica 714
replicas 158, 400
representative grading sets 525
reproductions of paper money
    158
Research Triangle Institute 319,
    322, 323
restrike 714
restrikes, official 561
retirement accounts
    bullion coins in 62
    collectibles in 61
    state coins in 62
Reunion 423, 446
reverse 714
Revolutionary War 605
Revolutionary War state issues 249
Reza Shah 426
Rhee, Syngman 429
Rhodes 423
Rhodesia 427, 428, 447
Rhyne, Craig 664
rial 445, 446
Riau islands 430
Rice, F. 193
Rice, Foster Wild 201
Rice, H.F. 199
Rich, Walter H. 381
Richards, H.M. and E.I. 606
Richardson, William A. 170
Richman, Michael 642
riddlers 337
Riegle Sen. Donald W. 35
riel 444
rim 714
Ringberg, Anders 687
ringgit 445
Ripley, S. Dillon 620
Rippeto, Hugh T. 200
Ripstra, J. Henri 649, 658
Risk, James 655
Rittenhouse, David 196, 201, 403
riyal 446, 447
Rizal, Jose 430
Roanoke Island, N.C., half dollar
    382
Robert Friedberg Award 663
Robert of Parma 418
Roberts, Elias H. 296
Roberts, Ellis H. 171
Roberts, George E. 197
Roberts, Gilroy 206, 321, 658
Robertson, Anne S. 643
Robinson, E. Stanley G. 643

Robinson, Jack 7
Robson, John E. 172
Rochette, Edward C. 7, 645, 650,
    651, 654, 656, 664
Rockefeller, David 620
Rockwell, Thomas P. 655
Rodin 208
Roethke, Wilma Dean 651
Rogers, John F.W. 10
Rogers, Lelan G. 657
Roman coinage, ancient 450-451
Roman Finish Proof 363
Romania 413, 414, 446
Rome at War as Seen Through
    Coins 17
Rome, ancient 450
Rome, Bernard 2
Roosevelt dime
    history of 320
Roosevelt, Franklin D. 93, 189, 316,
    319, 320, 376, 458
Roosevelt, Theodore 307, 317, 617
Roper, John L. 2nd
    collection 567
Rosa Americana 403
Rose, F.M. 657
Rosecrans, William S. 297
Rosen Numismatic Advisory 553
Rosen, Abraham A. 622
Rosen, Maurice H. 553
Ross, Nellie Tayloe 197
Rossignol, Paul 199
Rossman, Gary 665
Rossmiller, Marian N. 198
rotated dies 388
Rothert, Matthew H. 32, 271, 649,
    654, 656, 663
Roty 409
Rovelstad, Trygve 381
Royal Canadian Mint 1, 5, 12, 16,
    22, 24, 25, 26, 406, 657
    facilities 437
    history 436
Royal Canadian Mounted Police
    16
Royal Greenland Company 417
Rubber City Treasure Hunters Club
    671
Rubin, P. Scott 571, 641
ruble 447
Ruby, Charles L. 656
Ruddy, James F. 524
Ruesch, Otto 665
Ruiz, Julio M. 657
Rulau, Russell 601, 602
Running Antelope 254
rupee 445, 446
rupiah 445
Rush, Richard 169
Russell, E. Ward 651
Russell, Margo 639, 654, 656, 659,
    664
Russell, Mrs. Marion (See Russell,
    Margo)
Russia 420
Russian Numismatic Society 672
Russian Soviet Federated Socialist
    Republic 420
Rwanda 427, 446
Ryan, C.H. 656
Ryder, David J. 25

— S —

S.S. Central America 313

Sa'id bin Taimur 426
Saba 411
saddle blankets 250
saddle strike 390
Saint Maurice Ironworks 10
Saint-Gaudens, Augustus 307, 336,
    603
Saint-Pierre et Miquelon 446
sales tax 151
Salomon Brothers survey 1, 5, 14,
    22, 29, 61
Salote Tupou III 431
Saltus, J. Sanford 623
Saltus, J. Sanford Medal award
    (See J. Sanford Saltus Medal
    award)
Sam, Cynthia (Pratt) Kennedy 642
San Francisco Assay Office 5, 11,
    12, (See San Francisco Mint)
    Officers in Charge 198
San Francisco Mint 24, 180, 405,
    428
    history of 185-188
    Superintendents 198
San Francisco Old Mint 13, 21
San Francisco-Oakland Bay
    Bridge half dollar 381
San Marino 419, 440, 446, 505
Sancho I Ramirez 421
Sancho IV 421
Sancho VI 421
Sandblast Proof 363
Sanderman, David 662
sandwich coin 393
Sankt Maarten 411
Santa Claus in numismatics 544
Santa Fe de Bogota Mint 409
Sao Tome 428
Sao Tome e Principe 427
Sarawak 430
Sardinia 421
Saskatoon Coin Club 675
satang 446
satellite facility, Bureau of
    Engraving and Printing 27, 405
Saudi Arabia 426, 440, 443, 446
Sawyer, Edward W. 644
Saxton, Burton H. 650, 654, 656,
    657, 658
Sayah, Iraj 29, 665
scarce 714
Schab, Henry 655
Schermerhorn, R.F. 657
Schill, Earl C. 656
schilling 444
Schillinger Stanley J. 654
Schlag, Felix 319, 404
Schmitz, Carl L. 382
Schneebeli, Jean 172
Schneider, Alma K. 198
Schneider, John 16
Schnier, Jacques 381
Schook, Florence M. 2, 645, 649,
    656
School of the Medal Art 19
Schroeder, Louis H. 622, 623
Schroeder, Rep. Pat 185
Schuhmacher, Henry 651
Schuler coining presses 338
Schuler, Hans 380
Schulman, Darren 665
Schulman, Hans M.F. 1, 32
Schulman, Robert 687
Schultz, James Norman 30

Schultz, Norman 658
Schuylerville, N.Y. 5
Schwabacher, Willy 643
Schwartz, Max M. 655
Schwary, Richard J. 660
Schweich, Thomas 655
Scobey, F.E. 197
Scofield, Glenni W. 297
Sconyers, Hugh J. 551
Scot, Robert 201
Scotland 421
Scott, Gen. Winfield 280
Scoville Manufacturing Co. 606
Scoville, Herbert 623
screw press 714
scrip 160, 262, 485, 604, 714
    issuing 101
scripophily 714
SDRs 461
Seaby, H.A. 654
Seaby, Peter 662
seal 714
Sealey, Alfred 227
seals 7
    presidential 96
    Treasury 225
    vice presidential 96
Sear, David R. 530
Seated Liberty 307
Secret Service 9, 14, 20, 22, 166, 175, 405
    advisory policies 157
Secretaries of the Treasury 169
Securities and Exchange Commission 26
Securities Exchange Act 241
security thread 5, 230
security threads in paper money 385
Sedwick, Frank 642
Seeney, Susan 665
Segel, Joseph M. 656
Seger, Martha R. 247
Segermark, Howard 664
Segovia Mint 13, 21
Seidel, Milton J. 234
seigniorage 221-223, 714
Selden, William 171
self-regulation 2, 3, 13, 546, 665
Selling at auction 596
Seltman, Charlie T. 643
sen 444, 445
Senate Appropriations Subcommittee on Treasury, Postal Service and General Government 20
Senate Committee on Banking, Housing and Urban Affairs 9, 12, 13, 34
Senate Foreign Relations Committee 22
Senate, United States 33
sene 447
Senegal 444
seniti 446
sente 445
senti 446
sentimo 446
Serbia 413
serial number 714
serial numbers 270, 397
series 714
series date 269
Serrano, Joseph Hugo 30

Sessions, William S. 38
sestertius 451, 714
Seven Years War 414
Seward, William H. 280
Seychelles 423, 446, 505
Seyrig, Henri 643
Shanahan, T.W. 198
Shapiro, David 662
Sharjah 426
Shaw, Alan B. 655
Shaw, L.M. 170
Shcharansky medal, legislative history 112
Shcharansky, Anatoly (Natan) & Avital 112
Shearson Lehman Hutton 21, 551
Sheehen, Austin M. Jr. 657
shekel 610, 714
Shekel, The 671
Shelby, Isaac 280
Sheldon, M. Vernon 649, 654, 656, 659
Sheldon, Marcella L. 656
Sheldon, William H. 523, 527, 656
Shepard, Frank E. 198
sheqel 445, 714
Sherer, Don 651, 654, 656
Sheridan, Gen. Philip Henry 280
Sherman, John 170, 280
Sherman, William Tecumseh 280
Shield 5 cents
    Mint marks on 325
shilin 446
shilingi 446
shilling 445, 447
shortage of small change 605
shroff mark 710
Shroyer, C.C. 649, 656
Shultz, George 461
Shultz, George P. 171, 297
Siam 425, 443
Sicily 449
Siege notes 453
Sierra Leone 427, 428, 446
sight-unseen trading 526
Sigler, Col. Phares O. 654, 655
Sigler, P.O. 656
signatures on paper money
    by name 290
    fractional currency 288
    large-sized 284-288
        1914 Federal Reserve notes 288
        compound interest Treasury notes 287
        Federal Reserve Bank notes 288
        gold certificates 287
        interest-bearing notes 287
        Legal Tender notes 284
        National Bank notes 284
        refunding certificate 288
        silver certificates 286
        Treasury (coin) notes 287
    small-sized 288-290
        Federal Reserve Bank notes 288
        Federal Reserve notes 289
        gold certificates 288

        National Bank notes 288
        silver certificates 289
        United States notes 288
Sigurdsson, Jon 417
Sihtric, Norse king of Dublin 417
silver
    chronology 494-503
    demonetized 477
    government sales of 70
    history of 477-494
    industrial demand for 484
    mining and refining 477
    monthly prices 503
    record price 473, 493, 501
    sources of 477
    use in coinage 504
silver certificate 714
silver certificates
    large-sized 253
    small-sized 264
    text of law affecting 140
silver coins
    investing in 555
silver dollar, ancestor of 438
silver dollars
    auction records 576
    mintages
        business strikes 350
        Proofs 366
    specifications of 341
Silver Jubilee 415
silver mine, largest 477
silver Proof set 19, 20, 22, 24
Silver Purchase Act 560
Silver Purchase Act of 1934 481
silver rush of '64 483
silver rushes 264
Simon, William 267, 466
Simon, William E. 169, 171, 189, 297
Simpson, John R. 172
Simpson, Marjorie E. 382
Simpson, William M. 382
Sims, Stella Hackel 197
Singapore 430, 440, 442, 446, 505
Singleton, Joseph J. 199
Sinnock, John R. 204, 320, 379, 380
Sipe, Arthur 29, 649, 656
Sithon, Hugh S. 200
Skinner, Mark A. 198
slab 525, 715
Slabaugh, Arlie 664
slanted digits 393
Slaterio, Earl 673
Sloan, John 171
Slocum, John J. 639
Sloss, James O. 30
Slovakia 413
slug 715
slugs 313
sly wipes 395
Small Business Investment Act 242
small cents
    designers, engravers of 332
    mintages
        business strikes 344
    specifications of 340
small date 715
small-sized dollar coin 5
Smedley, Glenn 30
Smedley, Glenn B. 15, 650, 654, 655, 656, 658, 664
Smies, John 657
Smies, John J. 662

Smillie, George F.C. 254
Smith, Elizabeth Rudel 172, 297
Smith, Elliot J. 493
Smith, Elliott J. 623
Smith, Ingrid 7
Smith, Moses E. 198
Smith, Peter 641
Smith, W. Lamar 35
Smithson, James 615
Smithsonian Institution 12, 13, 17, 25, 319, 615
Smithsonian National Associates Lecture and Seminar Program 21
smuggling 301
Smyth, A.W. 200
Snedaker, Paul 31
Snell, E. Victor 673
Snellman, J.V. 415
Snowden, Col. A. Louden 197
Snowden, James Ross 196, 616
Snyder, John W. 170, 189, 297
Snyder, William S. 2, 8, 13
so-called dollar 715
Societe Americaine Pour l'Etude de la Numismatique Francaise 672
Society for Ancient Numismatics 672
Society for International Numismatics 672
Society for Medieval Numismatics 672
Society for U.S. Commemorative Coins 672
Society of Lincoln Cent Collectors 668
Society of Paper Money Collectors 670
Society of Philatelists and Numismatists 668
Society of Private and Pioneer Numismatics 668
Society of Ration Token Collectors 603, 668
Society of Silver Dollar Collectors 668
sol 446
Sol Kaplan Award 662
Solomon Islands 430, 446, 505
Somali 428
Somali Republic 446
Somalia 427
Sommer Islands 411
Somogyi, Marika 658
Song Jong 429
Sotheby's 26
sou marque 412
Soulouque, Faustin 412
South Africa 23, 60, 427, 428, 440, 442, 446, 475, 505, 514
South African Chamber of Mines 510
South America
  chronology 409-411
South Arabi 426
South Carolina 23
South Carolina Numismatic Association 670
South Dakota Coin & Stamp Association 670
Southeast Asia
  chronology 423
Southern Rhodesia 427

souvenir card 715
Souvenir Card Collectors Society 670
souvenir cards 234
Souvenir Mint sets 715
sovereign 19
Sovereign Military Order of Malta 423
Soviet gold coins 26, 28
Soviet Union 12, 18, 28, 420, 504, 505
  executive order banning gold coins 61
Space exploration 15
spade coins 428
Spain 421, 440, 442, 446, 505
Spangenberger, Henry 657
Spanish American War 314
Spanish Catalonia 416
Spanish Civil War 421
Spanish Milled Dollar 438
Spears, James 36
Special Drawing Rights 232, 461
Special Mint Sets 369, 715
specie 715
specific gravity 611, 612
  gold and copper 612
specifications of coins
  history of U.S. 310-312
Speelman, Harley V. 297
Spencer, John C. 169
Spencer, Lady Diana 415
Spengler, William 657
Spicer-Simson, Theodore 644
Spider king 415
spider press plate prints 234
Spink & Son Numismatics Ltd. 22
Spink, David F. 655
Spinner, F.E. 171, 280, 297
split grades 527
split planchets 389
Sri Lanka 424, 440, 446
SS Central America 24, 25, 26
St. Christopher-Nevis 505
St. Helena 423
St. Kitts 412, 444
St. Lucia 412, 444, 505
St. Thomas & Prince Islands 446
St. Vincent 412, 444, 505
Stabler, Edward 172
Stack's 22, 23, 26
  denied gold import permit 465
Stack, Benjamin 657
Stack, Harvey G. 12, 657, 660
Stack, James A. Sr. 27
Stack, Norman 12, 657
Stahl, Alan M. 8, 639, 659
Stalin, Joseph 205
Stallard, Barry W. 642
stamps, monetized 262
Standard Catalog of World Coins 531
Standard Catalogue of United States Coins and Tokens 523
Stanton, Edwin McMasters 280
star notes 231, 715
Stark, Robert 642
state bullion issues 513
state coinage 302
state coinages 715
State numismatic associations 668-670
statehood centennial 22

Statehood Centennial Commemorative Coin Act of 1989 25
stater 715
Statue of Freedom 22
Statue of Liberty 377, 416
Statue of Liberty coinage 1
  half dollar 383
  half eagle 383
  legislative history 110
  text of law 133
Statue of Liberty coinage, dollar 383
Statue of Liberty/Ellis Island commemorative coins 4
Statutes at Large 125
Stearns, C. Radford 657
steel cent 310, 393
Steever, Edgar 383
Stefanelli (See Clain-Stefanelli)
Steiger, Janet D. 36
Stella 203, 715
Stellas
  auction records 580
Stephens, Alexander Hamilton 280
Stephenson, M.F. 200
sterling silver 715
Stevens, Elsie Kachel 333
Stevens, R.J. 198
Stevenson, Robert Louis 431
Stewart, Frank 201
Stickney, Matthew
  collection 567
stock market crash 458
stock market crash of 1989 9
Stolen Coin File 19
Stone Mountain half dollar 380
Stone Mountain Treasure Hunters 671
Stone, James M. 493
storage and preservation 607, 610
Storage materials 609
store card 715
Store cards 601
stotinki 444
Straits Settlements 430
Strategic and Critical Materials Stock Piling Act 54
Strategic and Critical Minerals Stockpile 28
Straub, Paul 619
Strayer, Harry 32
Street Cents 24
Strenio, Andrew J. Jr. 36
Strickland, William 194
strike 519, 715
strike doubling 390
striking errors 390
strip 715
Stroessner, Alfredo 410
struck-through errors 391
Stuppler, Barry 665
Sturtridge, Gary 662
Stuyvesant, Petrus 280
Styer, Freas 197
Sub-Saharan Africa 427
Subak, Jon 687
Subalpine Republic 418
Subjack, William L. 642
sucre 445
Sudan 426, 440, 442, 446, 505
Suhle, Arthur 643
Sullivan, Leonor K. 30
Sullivan, Thomas J. 235

Sully, Thomas 210, 333
Sumatra 430
Sumner, Charles 280
Sumter, Gen. Thomas 280
Sun Yat-Sen 428
Superb 530
Superior Galleries *14, 26, 28, 29,*
537
Superior Stamp and Coin Co. *9*
Supreme Court 102
Sura, Michael H. 197
surcharge 715
Surcharges *1,* 377
Sureck, Jake B. 656
Suriname 410, 443, 446, 505
Suros, Juan *21*
Surplus silver, sale of 41
Sutherland, C.H.V. 643
Suthers, Pat 656
Sutter's Mill 185
Svoronos, Jean N. 643
Swagler, William F. *32*
Swain, R.B. 198
Swaziland 428, 446
Sweden 420, 421, 440, 442, 446,
505
Swedish Nightingale 278
Sweeney, E. 198
Swiatek, Anthony 655, 663
swimming with sharks 553
Swiss franc 445
Switzerland 414, 440, 442, 446
symbols on U.S. coins 330
Symms, Sen. Steve *26*
syngraphics 715
Syria 426, 443, 446

— T —

T'ang dynasty 428
Taft, William Howard 314, 646
Tagalog 430
Taiwan 428, 440, 442, 443, 446
taka 444
Taksin 425
tala 446, 447
tambala 445
Taney, Roger B. 169
Tangible Investments of America
Inc. *16*
Tannahill, C.C. 673
Tanzania 428, 435, 440, 446
Tate, H.T. 171, 298
Tatman, Charles T. 645
Taufa'ahau Tupou IV 431
Tax Act changes of 1986 146
Taxay, Don 304
taxes, collecting state and local
21
Taylor, James 644
Taylor, Stephen R. *15,* 649, 657
Taylor, Zachary 280
Tayman, Barry D. 642
Teehee, Houston B. 298
televised rare coin auction *2*
Tenino, Wash. 602, 716
Tennessee State Numismatic
Society 670
Tenochtitlan 406
territorial gold (See pioneer gold)
Terry, Leo G. 651, 656
Tettenhorst, R. 641
Texas coins 394
Texas Independence Centennial
380

Texas Numismatic Association 670
Thailand 425, 435, 440, 442, 443,
446, 505
thebe 444
Theodore, Nicholas G. 197
Thesen, Gunnar 663
thick and thin planchets 389
Thirty Years War 422
Thomas Inflation Amendment 239
Thomas, Gen. George Henry 280
Thomas, Landon 639
Thomas, Philip 170
Thompson, Carmi A. 171, 298
Thompson, Margaret 643
Thorson, Nelson T. 649, 650
three cents
auction records 573
Three cents, copper-nickel
designers, engravers of 332
Mint marks on 325
mintages
business strikes 345
Proofs 365
specifications of 340
three cents, silver
designers, engravers of 332
Mint marks on 325
mintages
business strikes 345
Proofs 365
specifications of 340
three dollars
auction records 577
designers, engravers of 336
edge designs of 328
Mint marks on 325
mintages
business strikes 352
Proofs 367
specifications of 341
Thrift Institutions Advisory Council
244
Tihonovich, Aimee 644
Tillman, James F. 298
Time Capsule 169
Time Inc. 103
Timor 446
Titanic *8*
Title 18, United States Code 95
Title 31, United States Code 49
Todd, George M. 656
Todd, Isaac L. 200
toea 446
Togo 427, 444
Tokelau 446, 505
token 715
Token and Medal Society 605, 668
tokens 601
issuing 101
restrictions on 82
Treasury use of 82
tokens, Revolutionary period 301
Tombac brass 406
tone 520
Tonga 431, 446, 505
toning, artificial 520
Tonkin 424
Topical collecting 434, 452
torch 331
Toribio Medina, Jose 643
Toronto Coin Club 675
Townsend, Eugene 197
Townsend, W. Laird *30*

Toynbee, Jocelyn M.C. 643
Toyotomi Hideyoshi 429
Trade dollar 203, 509, 715
legal tender status revoked
304
Trade dollars
auction records 576
edge designs of 328
Mint marks on 325
mintages
business strikes 351
Proofs 367
specifications of 341
Tranquebar 425
transitional error 389
Transportation tokens 602
Transvaal 427
Travers, Scott A. 533, 542, 546
Treasure Coast Coin Club 671
Treasure hunting clubs 670
treasure salvage 313
Treasurers of the United States 171
Treasury
advisory policies 157
bicentennial of 167
functions 173
history of 165-168
officials 172
Treasury Building
architectural features of 167
Treasury Building, public tours of
167
Treasury Historical Association 168
Treasury note 715
Treasury Notes 249, **255**
Treasury seal 172
Treasury Security Force 166
Treasury silver reserves *17*
Treat, Charles H. 171, 298
Treaty of the Lateran 418
Tree coinage 403, 715
Trends 533, 551, 715
Trends Index *10*
Trends of Canada 533
tribute penny 715
trichlorotrifluoroethane 555
trime 715
Trinidad & Tobago 440
Trinidad and Tobago 437, 446
Trinidad-Tobago 411, 412
Tristan da Cunha 423
Trucial States 426
Trujillo dictatorship 412
Truman, Harry S. 206, 321, 375
Tuamotu group 445
Tucker, J.C. 280
Tucker, Thomas T. 171
tukhrik 446
Tulving, Hannes 665
Tunisia 426, 446
Tupac Amaru 410
Turkey *26,* 330, 426, 427, 440, 442,
446, 475, 505
Turks and Caicos Islands 437, 446
Turoff, Julius 657
Tuvalu 431, 446
twenty cents
auction records 574
designers, engravers of 334
Mint marks on 325
mintages
business strikes 347
Proofs 366
specifications of 340

two cents
    auction records 573
    designers, engravers of 332
    Mint marks on 325
    mintages
        business strikes 345
        Proofs 365
    specifications of 340
Two Moons 308
two-headed "Morgan dollar" 9
Type I 337
Type II planchets 338
type set 715

— U —

U.S. Assay Commission (See Assay
    Commission)
U.S. Assay Office 313
U.S. Capitol 22
U.S. coinage
    history of 303-312
U.S. coins
    bullion 512
    commemoratives 375-383
    counterfeit 399
    current types 317-323
    damaged, exchange of 78
    dates on 326
    design elements of 326-331
    designers of 331
    edge designs 327
    engravers of 331
    first 302
    initials on 331
    laws affecting 103, 120
    manufacturing 337-339
    Mint marks on 323
    mintages
        business strikes 343-360
        Proofs 360-368
    mottoes and legends on 328
    specifications codified 52
    specifications of 339-342
    struck outside Mint 378
    symbols on 330
    uncurrent, exchange of 78
U.S. Constitution Council of the
    Thirteen Original States Inc. 4
U.S. Gold 512, 715
U.S. paper money 9
Ubico, Jorge 408
Uganda 428, 447
Ulrich-Bansa, Oscar 643
Uman, Barry 673
Umayyad Islamic gold dinar 22
Umberto I 418
Umm al-Qaiwain 426
Uncirculated 527, 531, 532
Uncirculated set 715
Uncirculated sets 369
    legal requirements 58
uncut sheet 715
uncut sheets 233
undated U.S. coin 326
unfit currency, destruction of 232
uniface 715
uniface errors 391
Union of Soviet Socialist Republics
    420, 442, 447
Union Pacific Railroad 182
unique 715
United Amsterdam Company 430
United Arab Emirates 426, 447
United Arab Republic 426

United East India Company 430
United Kingdom 440, 442, 447
United Nations 435
United Nations Security Council 60
United Services Organization 27,
    28, 378
United States 440, 442, 447, 475,
    504, 505
    chronology 403-405
United States Air Corps 167
United States Bullion Depository
    180
United States Capitol Historical
    Society 1, 13, 20, 29
United States code, numismatic
    sections 147
United States Code, Title 18 95
United States Code, Title 31 48
    excerpts from 49
United States coins
    models for designs 331
United States Merchant Marine
    113
United States Mint 1, 2, 3, 174, 179
    assay standards, historical 70
    Chief Engravers 201-212
    creation of 179
    Customer Service Center 213,
        214
    Directors 196
    facilities 180
    foreign coin production at
        442
    former institutions 191-196
    medals 213
    Office of Marketing 2
    officials 180
    regulations of 70
    sales centers, over-the-
        counter 214
    services offered by 213
    Superintendents 197-201
    tours 213
United States Mint Cabinet 617
United States National Museum
    615
United States note 715
United States notes 264
United States of America 328
United States Olympic Committee
    12, 624
United States Paper Money
    Grading Standard 532
United States Patent Office 615
units of currency 444
University of California, Berkeley 7
unplated planchets 389
unzo platino 507
upsetting mill 337, 715
Uruguay 410, 447, 505
Uryu, Keiichi 27, 644
Utah Numismatic Society 670
Utz, Mitch 662

— V —

Vagi, David 16
Valencia 421
Valentine, W.H. 622
Value Added Tax 413, 415
Van Belkum, Louis W. 663
Van Buren, Martin 280
van Gelder, H. Enno 643
Vance, Zebulon 280

Vancouver Numismatic Society
    675
Vanuata 430, 447
Varden, John 615
Vargas, Getulio 409
Vasco da Gama 420
Vatican City 418, 447, 505
vatu 447
Vaughan, John 217
VDB 318
vectures 602, 715
vecturist 715
Veffer, Jack 673
Vend-A-Coin 16
vending machines 16, 488
Venezuela 411, 440, 443, 447
Verani, Patricia L. 383
verifiers 16
Vermeule, Cornelius 642
Vermont Sesquicentennial half
    dollar 380
Vernon, William T. 299
Veroi, Guido 644
Very Fine 529, 530, 531, 532
Very Good 529, 531, 532
Viceroyalty of El Peru 16, 17
Vichy France 416
Victor Emanuel I 418
Victor Emanuel II 418, 419
Victor Emanuel III 418
Victoria 409, 422, 423, 425
Victoria Numis. Society 675
Vietnam 424, 425, 428, 447, 505
Vigdor, Luis 664
vignette 715
Viking coinages in England 414
Villalpando, Catalina V. 172
Villalpando, Catalina Vasquez 21,
    25, 172, 299
Villiers, Philippe 423
Vincze, Paul 658
Vinson, Fred M. 170, 299
Virginia and Truckee Railroad 194
Virginia Numismatic Association
    670
Vishnu 424
Vittor, Frank 382
Vlack, Robert 641
Voce populi 417
Voegtli, Hans 687
Vogel, Leo 11
Voigt, Emil 657
Voigt, Henry (See Voight, Henry,
    201, 403
Volcker, Paul A. 494
von Engelken, F.J.H. 197
von Lettow-Vorbeck, Paulus 427
von Mollendorf, Paul Georg 429
von Zambir, Edouard 643
Voyageur 1, 406
Vyronis, Speros 639

— W —

Waggoner, Nancy M. 31
Wagner, Judith L. 180
Waitangi crown 430
Walcott, Dr. Charles D. 618
Walker, John 643
Walker, Robert J. 170, 281
Walking Liberty 308
Wall Street 26, 551
Wall Street Journal 448
Wallis, O.L. 655
Walsh, Paul 47

Walt Disney Co. 4
Walt Disney World 18, 24
Walter Breen's Complete
  Encyclopedia of U.S. and
  Colonial Coins 14
Walton, Gerome 655
Walton, Robert S. III 36
Wang Mang 428
want list 715
War of 1812 249
War of the Spanish Succession 421
Ward, John E. 281
Waring, Robert P. 199
Warneke, Heinz 206
Warns, Melvin Owen 31
Wartime 5-cent coins 323
wartime cent 318
Washington half dollar
  commemorative history 109
Washington medals 216, 540
Washington Numismatic Society
  669
Washington quarter
  history of 320
Washington Tourist Information
  Center 167
Washington, Booker T. 375
Washington, George 168, 179,
  201, 281, 303, 320, 376, 404
Washington, Martha 281, 335
Wass, Tom 662
watermark 716
Watkinson, Rev. M.R. 329
Watson, John 651
Watt, James 434
Watts, Thomas N. 281
Waugh, Sidney 644
Wayte and Olga Raymond
  Literary Awards 655
weak strikes 391
wear 519
Weaver, Douglas 662
Weaver, John 281
web intaglio press 25
web press, prototype BEP 231
Webster, Daniel 281
Weeks, Thomas 271
Weidhass, Ernest 655
weights and measures 610-611
Weiher, Claudine J. 42
Weinberg, Fred C. 660, 662
Weinman, Adolph A. 46, 333, 644
Weinman, Robert A. 336, 644, 658
Weinmann, Howard K. 381
Weinmann, Jeanne Madeline 655
Weis, Eugene 206
Weissbuch, Ted 655
Wells Fargo and Company 625
Werner, Louis S. 647, 654, 656, 658
Wessex 414
West Indian colonies 411
West Irian 430
West Point 3
West Point Bullion Depository 7, 12,
  (See West Point Mint)
West Point Mint 180
  history of 189
  Superintendents 199
western currency-production
  facility 4
Western Heritage Museum 17
Western Samoa 431, 447, 505
wheat ears 318
Wheeler, John H. 199, 403

White House 166
White, Frank 171, 299
White, Harlan 660
Whitehead, Richard Bertram 643
Whitnah, Paul 656
whizzing 716
widow's mite 716
Wilde, Adna G. 644, 649, 654, 655
Wiley, Randall E. 642
Wilfredo 421
Wilhelmina 411
Wilkinson, John S. 673
Willem I 419
Willem III 419
Willey, Robert C. 673
William IV 409, 419, 424
William S. Elliott 299
William, Duke of Normandy 423
Williams, Anna W. 335
Williams, Dennis R. 335
Williams, Marjorie L. 656
Williams, Norman W. 673
Williamson, Raymond H. 641
Willson, Joseph 218
Wilmeth, James L. 235
Wilson, Don W. 42
Wilson, Nancy 645, 657
Wilson, Robert L. 30
Wilson, W.W.C. 646
Wilson, Woodrow 237, 281, 315
Windner, Julius 656
Windom, William 170, 281
Windsor Coin Club 675
Windward Isles 411, 412, 445
Wing, F.A. 404
Winged Liberty Head 308
Winners, Leslie A. 651
Winnipeg 4, 22
Winnipeg Mint 437
Winter, Sheri 383
wire rim 716
Wisconsin Territorial Centennial
  half dollar 381
Wismer, David C. 658
Wisslead, Elizabeth and William
  657
Witch of Wall Street 564
Witherspoon, John 172
Wogoman, C.P. 30
Wolcott, Oliver 169
Wolf, Diane 3, 6, 46, 106
Wolfe, Charles 657
Wolfe, Charles E. 662
Wolfe, Charles H. 654
Wolfe, Thomas 463
Wolfson, W.Q. 327
won 445
Wood, Howland 619, 622, 643,
  649, 658
Wood, Howland Award (See
  Howland Wood Award)
wood-blocked cent 394
Woodburn, Helen 655
Woodbury, Levi 169
Wooden money 602
wooden nickels 716
Woodin, William H. 170, 299
Woods, Walter O. 171, 300
Woodward, W. Elliot 521
Woodward, William 383
Wooley, Robert W. 197, 618
working die 27, 405, 716
working hub 338, 716
Works Progress Administration 208

World Buddhist Fellowship 425
World Coin Catalogue 531
World Coin Club 672
World Coin Club of Missouri 672
World Coin News 707
World coin organizations 676-687
World coinage report, 1988 440
World Coins 2
  auction records 585
  grading 531
world coins, collecting 433-435
World Food Day 407
World Paper Currency Club 670
World Paper Currency Collectors
  670
World Proof Numis. Assoc. 672
World University Games 378
World War I 237, 308, 416, 417,
  420, 422, 453, 458
World War II 27, 167, 186, 306, 310,
  316, 318, 393, 416, 420, 429, 430,
  454, 459, 506, 603
World's Fair Collectors Society 668
World's Columbian Exposition 375
World's Columbian Expositon 604
Wormser, Charles 32, 651
Wormser, Moritz 619, 649, 650, 658
worn dies 388
Worth, Karen 603, 644, 658
Worth, William N. 656
Wren, Sir Christopher 415
Wright, B.P. 649
Wright, Benjamin P. 649, 658
Wright, John D. 655
Wright, Joseph 201, 403
Wright, Samuel Coleman 199
Wright, Silas 281
wrong metal, planchet, stock 389
wrong stock note 397
wrong-color backs 399
Wurtzbach, Carl 649
Wyeth medal, legislative history
  113
Wyeth, Andrew 113
Wylie, Rep. Chalmers P. 35
Wyman, A.U. 171, 300

— X —

XF 529, 532
xu 447

— Y —

Yahya bin Muhammad Hamid
  ad-Din 426
Yankee Territory Coinshooters 671
Yawger, H.H. 649, 650
Yawger, Harry H. 649
year set 716
Yellin, Jerome A. 180
Yemen 426, 447, 505
Yemen Arab Republic 426
yen 445
Yeoman, Richard S. 31, 531, 650,
  654, 656, 657, 658, 664
York County, Maine, Tercentenary
  half dollar 381
Yosemite National Park 28
Young Astronaut Council 15, 18,
  21
Young Astronauts medals
  legislative history 111
Young Numismatist awards 659
Young, Leo 662

Yowell, Clark A. 651
yuan 444
Yugoslavia 413, 414, 442, 447
Yukon 436

— Z —

Zaire 428, 447
Zambia 428, 440, 447

Zander, Randolph 655
Zaner, Keith M. 537
Zanzibar 427
Zerbe, Farran 620, 645, 649, 650, 658
Zerbe, Farran Memorial Award (See Farran Zerbe Memorial Award)

Zerder, Morton J. *30*
Zimbabwe 428, 447
Zimmerman, Walter J. 655
zinc cent 311, 319
zirconium 489
zloty 446